Socio-Economic Developme

Why are poor countries poor and rich countries rich? How are wealth and poverty related to changes in health, life expectancy, education, population growth and politics? This non-technical introduction to development studies explores the dynamics of socio-economic development and stagnation in developing countries. Thoroughly updated and revised, this second edition includes new material on the effects of the 2008 financial crisis, the emergence of the BRICS economies, the role of institutions in development and the accelerated growth of economies in Africa and Asia. Taking a comparative approach, Szirmai places contemporary debates within their broader contexts and combines insights and theories from economics, economic history, political science, anthropology and sociology. Each chapter includes comparative statistics and time series for thirty-one developing countries. Assuming no prior knowledge of economics, this book is well suited for students in interdisciplinary development studies and development economics, for policy makers and for practitioners pursuing careers in developing countries.

Adam Szirmai is Professorial Fellow at the United Nations University Maastricht Economic and Social Research Institute on Innovation and Technology (UNU-MERIT) and Professor of Development Economics at Maastricht University. His research focuses on the determinants of long-run growth, catch-up and stagnation in the developing world, with particular emphasis on the role of the manufacturing sector. A second focus of his research concerns the relationships between innovation, technological change and economic growth.

Socio-Economic Development

Second edition

ADAM SZIRMAI
Maastricht University/UNU-MERIT

CAMBRIDGE
UNIVERSITY PRESS

University Printing House, Cambridge CB2 8BS, United Kingdom

Cambridge University Press is part of the University of Cambridge.

It furthers the University's mission by disseminating knowledge in the pursuit of education, learning and research at the highest international levels of excellence.

www.cambridge.org
Information on this title: www.cambridge.org/9781107624498

First published 2005
Second edition 2015
Reprinted 2016

Printed in the United Kingdom by Clays, St Ives plc

A catalogue record for this publication is available from the British Library

ISBN 978-1-107-04595-8 Hardback
ISBN 978-1-107-62449-8 Paperback

Additional resources for this publication at www.cambridge.org/szirmai2.

CONTENTS

10 Agricultural development and rural development   382

11 State formation and political aspects of development   451

TABLES

FIGURES

BOXES

PREFACE

The aim of this book is to provide a general introduction to the dynamics of socio-economic development and to the study of the problems of developing countries. The book was written for students of universities and other institutions of higher education from a variety of disciplines, who encounter the problems of developing countries in their studies and who are in need of a general introduction to this field. It is also intended for people pursuing a professional career in developing countries and international organisations, for policy makers and for readers with a general interest in development. The text can be read as an introduction by students with no prior knowledge of development. It also can be used at an advanced level as a handbook of development, providing a comprehensive overview of past and present theoretical and empirical debates and controversies in the field of development studies. The book provides non-economists with a non-technical introduction to economic perspectives on development, while introducing economists to a broader socio-economic view of development.

The central issue in development, as approached in this book, lies in low levels of per capita income and low standards of living among the mass of the population in the so-called developing countries. The key elements in the book are trends in productive capacity, per capita income, changes in standards of living and poverty, and the factors that affect economic development or economic stagnation in the long term. The core of development is thus defined in economic terms. However, the explanatory factors are not limited to economic ones. Historical, institutional, cultural, demographic, political, social and eco-logical factors are all of great importance for the analysis of economic development. They will receive ample attention in the book.

It needs to be emphasised that the concept of development is much broader than that of economic development alone. Development involves changes in a wide range of social outcomes, such as poverty, health, education, life expectancy, human rights or political participation, which are directly or indirectly linked to economic changes but which need to be studied in their own right. This is reflected in the title of the book, which refers to socio-economic development.

The structure of the book takes the key proximate factors distinguished in economic theories of growth – labour, capital and land and technological change – as its point of departure. However, in line with the interdisciplinary nature of the book, these factors are interpreted in a broad fashion. Technological change lies at the heart of growth and economic development. Two main issues discussed in Chapter 4 are the role of techno-logical change in development, and the consequences of accelerating technological change for developing countries. The treatment of the primary production factor 'labour' is couched in terms of a more general discussion of demographic and human factors in development. These include population growth and the interrelationships between population growth and economic development (Chapter 5), topics such as health, disease, mortality and life expectancy (Chapter 6) and education, human capital and literacy (Chapter 7). I argue that

Socio-Economic Development: An Introduction. In the ten years since the appearance of the previous edition, there have been major changes in the global economy. Former developing countries such as Korea and Taiwan have become high-income advanced economies. The giants China and India have become middle-income economies. China has become the manufacturing workplace of the world. The increasing importance of the BRICS (Brazil, Russia, India, China and South Africa), as well as other large emerging economies such as Malaysia, Indonesia and Turkey, has changed the nature of the international order and the international balance of power. Many emerging economies now engage in outward-bound FDI, a substantial part of which flows to developing countries (South–South investment). The deep financial crisis of 2007–8 and beyond has exposed weaknesses in advanced country financial institutions. The crisis has affected the advanced economies much more than developing countries. Not only have there been major changes in the global economy and developing countries, the literature on development has experienced an explosive growth. The present revision tries to take into account the changes in the world and the advances in research and in the literature. Though the structure of the book remains unchanged, all chapters have been revised very substantially. In particular, Chapter 12 has been revamped to include the large new literature on the role of institutions. The chapter on the international order (Chapter 13) has been extensively rewritten to reflect the changes in the international economic order. The chapters on structural change and industrialisation (Chapters 8 and 9) have tried to incorporate new thinking on these topics. One of the important new elements of the revised text is the development of a systematic framework of proximate, intermediate and ultimate causality in Chapters 1 and 3. This framework is applied in all subsequent chapters, so that the reader is better able to understand how a given chapter fits into the large framework.

The fact that the book has a twenty-year history provides both risks and opportunities. The danger of a book conceived long ago is that parts of the discussion become dated. The challenge is to show how some of the older debates and concepts remain relevant in the present. Too often, lessons learned from older debates are forgotten or neglected, to our detriment. We should learn the lessons from recent developments without forgetting the lessons derived from older experiences. I have tried to strike a balance between the newest theories and approaches and important older intellectual contributions and debates. In doing so, the book also provides something of an intellectual history of development debates.

Adam Szirmai
Maastricht

ACKNOWLEDGEMENTS

I could not have written this book without the support of numerous colleagues and ex-colleagues. They generously let me profit from their knowledge of and insights into the various aspects of development. I have made extensive use of their advice, their publications, and their empirical research. I have enjoyed years of fruitful and intensive discussions with them. I would like to thank the following persons for their advice on substantive or statistical issues and their stimulating comments on previous editions of the book and drafts of the present version: Bart van Ark, Anne van den Ban, Richard Bluhm, Tobias Broich, Michael Bruneforth, Carlo Cafiero, Carolina Castaldi, Luciana Cingolani, Samuel Cohn, Geske Dijkstra, Peter Druijven, Pierre van der Eng, Jacob de Haan, Gerhard Heilig, Hal Hill, Niels Hermes, Karel van Hoestenberghe, Jojo Jacob, René Kemp, Hans-Paul Klijnsma, Jos Koetsier, Remco Kouwenhoven, Lutz Krebs, Paul Lapperre, Alejandro Lavopa, Robert Lensink, Kees van der Meer, Nicolas Meisel, Nanno Mulder, Wim Naudé, Chris de Neubourg, Alessandro Nuvolari, Jacques Ould-Aoudia, Howard Pack, Dirk Pilat, Neville Postlethwaite, Gé Prince, Baseer Qazi, Shyama Ramani, Henny Romijn, Johan Schot, Jan Stel, Ida Terluin, Marcel Timmer, Kaj Thomsson, Peter de Valk, Harry van Vianen, Geert Verbong, Bart Verspagen, Daniel Vertesy and Ton Zwaan. I would like to acknowledge a special intellectual debt to Angus Maddison. Long ago, he encouraged me to write a first version of this book. He has always been a major source of intellectual stimulation. It is more important than ever to emphasise that the responsibility for the book and for its shortcomings rests entirely with the author.

Since, 2007, the United Nations University – Maastricht Economic and Social Research Institute on Innovation and Technology (UNU-MERIT) – has provided me with a creative environment for the study of development. I am thankful to the past and present directors Luc Soete and Bart Verspagen for creating this environment and making me part of it. My colleagues at UNU-MERIT have created an open and supportive intellectual atmosphere, which deserves to be nurtured. I have particularly enjoyed intensive inter-actions and debates with PhD students from more than forty countries across the globe, most of them from developing countries. The full list of people that should be thanked is too long to specify. I would like to single out Eveline in de Braek, who provided enthusiastic and efficient support for this book, and for many other activities I was engaged in, while at UNU-MERIT. Ad Notten was an exemplary librarian, in full command of the intricacies of modern digital search techniques, while providing a level of personal support and help that can only be described as old fashioned. Herman Pijpers and Mourik-Jan Heupink have provided invaluable IT support. Tobias Broich provided statistical assistance in updating several of the tables. Finally, I am also very thankful for the generous backing provided by Chris Harrison and his colleagues at Cambridge University Press. I thank them for their encouragement as well as for their patience. This book is dedicated to my wife Veronika in gratitude for our shared life, her unflagging support and her forbearance.

ACRONYMS AND ABBREVIATIONS

ACER	age specific enrolment rate
ACP	Asian, Caribbean and Pacific Countries
ADB	Asian Development Bank
ADER	average dietary energy requirements
ADLI	Agricultural Development Led Industrialisation (Ethiopia)
AFD	Agence Française de Développement
AfDB	African Development Bank
ASEAN	Association of Southeast Asian Nations
BMI	body mass index
BMR	basal metabolism rate
BRICS	Brazil, Russia, India, China and South Africa
CEE	Central and Eastern Europe
CFC	chlorofluorcarbon
CGIAR	Consultative Group on International Agricultural Research (now CGIAR Consortium)
CIMMYT	Centro Internacional de Mejoramienta de Maiz y Trigo (International Maize and Wheat Improvement Centre)
CIS	Community Innovation Surveys
CMEA	Council for Mutual Economic Assistance
CPI	Corruption Perceptions Index
CPIA	Country Policy and Institutional Assessment
CVD	cardiovascular diseases
DAC	Development Assistance Committee (OECD)
DALY	disability adjusted life years lost
DGBAS	Directorate General of Budget Accounting and Statistics (Taiwan)
DRS	debt reporting system (World Bank)
EC	European Community
ECLAC	United Nations Economic Commission for Latin America
ECOSOC	Economic and Social Council (United Nations)
EDF	European Development Fund
EEC	European Economic Community
EPA	Economic Partner Agreement (EU)
ESAF	Enhanced Structural Fund Facility (IMF)
ESCAP	United Nations Economic and Social Commission for Asia and the Pacific
EU	European Union
EWLP	Experimental World Literacy Program
FAO	United Nations Food and Agriculture Organisation
FCCC	Framework Convention on Climate Change (United Nations)

FDI	foreign direct investment
FYR	Former Republic of Yugoslavia
GATT	General Agreement on Tariffs and Trade
GDFF	Geographical Distribution of Financial Flows to Developing Countries
GDI	gross domestic income
GDP	gross domestic product
GER	gross enrolment ratio
GERD	gross domestic expenditure on R&D
GGDC	Groningen Growth and Development Centre
GHG	greenhouse gas
GMO	genetically modified organism
GNERD	gross national expenditure on R&D
GNI	gross national income
GNP	gross national product
GPI	Gender Parity Index
GSP	generalised system of preferences
HALE	health life expectancy
HDI	Human Development Index
HDR	Human Development Report
HIC	high-income country
HIE	high-income economy
HIPC	heavily indebted poor country
IBPGR	International Board for Plant Genetic Resources
IBRD	International Bank for Reconstruction and Development (World Bank)
ICARDA	International Center for Agricultural Research in the Dry Areas
ICC	International Criminal Court
ICJ	International Court of Justice
ICRISAT	International Crops Research Institute for the Semi-Arid Tropics
ICT	information and communication technologies
IDA	International Development Association
IDB	Interamerican Development Bank
IFAD	International Fund for Agricultural Development
IFC	International Finance Corporation
IFI	international financial institution
IGO	intergovernmental organisation
ILO	International Labour Organization
IMF	International Monetary Fund
IPCC	Intergovernmental Panel on Climate Change
IPR	intellectual property rights
IRRI	International Rice Research Institute
ISI	import substituting industrialisation
ISIC	International Standard Industrial Classification
IT	information technology
ITO	International Trade Organisation
LAFTA	Latin American Free Trade Association
LAO	limited access order

LDC	less developed country
LEISA	low external input and sustainable agriculture
LIC	low-income country
LMIC	lower-middle-income country
MDER	minimum dietary energy requirement
MDG	Millennium Development Goal
MDRI	Multilateral Debt Relief Initiative
MFA	Multi Fibre Arrangement
MFN	most favoured nation
MICS	middle-income country
MITI	Ministry of International Trade and Industry (Japan)
MNC	multinational corporation
MNE	multinational enterprise
MPS	material product system
NAFTA	North American Free Trade Association
NATO	North Atlantic Treaty Organisation
NER	net enrolment ratio
NGO	non-governmental organisation
NIC	newly industrialised country
NIE	newly industrialising economy
NIEO	new international economic order
NNI	net national income
NTB	non-tariff barrier
NTRF	net total resource flows
OA	other assistance
OAO	open access order
OAS	Organisation of American States
OAU	Organisation of African Unity
OBM	own brand manufacturing
ODA	official development assistance
ODM	own design manufacturing
OECD	Organisation for Economic Cooperation and Development
OEM	original equipment manufacturing
OFID	OPEC Fund for International Development
OOF	other official flows
OPEC	Organisation of Petroleum Exporting Countries
PAL	physical activity level
PISA	Programme for International Student Assessment
PPP	purchasing power parity
PRIO	Peace Research Institute Oslo
PRS	poverty reduction strategy
PRSP	Poverty Reduction Strategy Paper
PWT	Penn World Tables
QALY	quality adjusted life year
R&D	research and development
RAUI	risk aversion causes under investment (hypothesis)

RCT	randomised controlled trial
SAF	Structural Adjustment Facility (IMF)
SAL	Structural Adjustment Loan (World Bank)
SAP	Structural Adjustment Programme (IMF)
SECAL	Sectoral Adjustment Loan (World Bank)
SIC	semi-industrialised country
SME	small and medium-sized enterprise
SNA	System of National Accounts
SSA	Sub-Saharan Africa
STABEX	Système de Stabilisation des Recettes d'Exportation (System for Stabilisation of Export Earnings)
SWAp	sectorwide approach (in aid debate)
SYSMIN	system of stabilisation of export earnings from mining products
TBC	tuberculosis
TF	total factor
TFP	total factor productivity
TIMMS	Trends in International Mathematics and Sciences Studies
TNC	transnational corporation
TRIPS	Agreement on Trade-Related Aspects of Intellectual Property Rights
TVE	township and village enterprise
UCDP	Uppsala Conflict Data Programme
UIA	Union of International Organisations
UMIC	upper-middle-income country
UN	United Nations
UNCED	United Nations Conference on Environment and Development
UNCTAD	United Nations Conference on Trade and Development
UNDP	United Nations Development Programme
UNEP	United Nations Environmental Programme
UNEPTA	United Nations Expanded Program of Technical Assistance
UNESCO	United Nations Educational, Scientific and Cultural Organisation
UNHCR	United Nations High Commissioner for Refugees
UNICEF	United Nations Childrens' Fund
UNIDO	United Nations Industrial Development Organisation
UNITAR	United Nations Institute for Training and Research
UNPD	United Nations Population Division
UNPF	United Nations Population Fund
UNRWA	United Nations Relief and Works Agency
UNSO	United Nations Statistical Organisation
USAID	United States Agency for International Development
USSR	Union of Soviet Socialist Republics
WB	World Bank (*see* IBRD)
WDI	World Development Indicators (World Bank)
WDR	World Development Report (World Bank)
WDT	World Debt Tables (World Bank)
WFP	World Food Program
WGI	World Governance Indicators (World Bank)

technocratic approach, focusing on policies, instruments or projects, others choose a more radical–political approach. The latter believe that political mobilisation and political action are needed to achieve rapid changes in the existing order.

A potential drawback of strong involvement is a certain trendiness in thinking about development. One can point to the endless succession of ideas and slogans that have played a role in post-war discussions of development: the idea that large-scale injections of capital are the key to development ('Big Push'); the 'small is beautiful' movement; human capital as the missing link in development; the green revolution as a technological fix for agricultural development; community development; appropriate technologies; basic needs; integrated rural development; self-reliance; the New International Economic Order (NIEO); the Washington consensus; promotion of the informal sector; structural adjustment policies (SAPs); sustainable development, micro-finance or the present focus on the Millennium Development Goals (MDGs).

A common characteristic of these recipes for development is their short-term perspective. Time and again, proposals have been put forward in order to achieve certain goals, preferably within a decade or two (see, for example, Brandt et al., 1980, 1983; Brundtland et al., 1987; Sachs, 2005; the Millennium Declaration of 2000; UNDP, 2003). These fashions often evoke a brief surge of enthusiasm in the world of politics, policy and the development sciences. But when the immediate results are slow in materialising, disenchantment sets in again. The issue disappears from the public eye, and new and more appealing solutions and catch phrases emerge. The greater the involvement, the harder it is to distinguish between desirability and reality, and the greater the disappointment that follows when the real world proved less manageable than one had hoped (see Elias, 1970). Some of the major mistakes in development policies are a direct consequence of erroneous advice from development advisors and experts. An example is the neglect of the agricultural sector in the drive for industrialisation at all cost in the 1950s.

The long-term approach to development is more detached. One tries to comprehend why, in the long term, such great differences in development have occurred in the different parts of the world (Szirmai et al., 1993; Szirmai, 2013). One tries to identify the factors that may help to explain different patterns of development, such as the accumulation of production factors, the efficiency with which these factors of production are being used, technological changes, external political and economic influences, historical factors, institutions and cultural differences. Economic and social policies figure among these factors, but considering policy as only one of many relevant factors may help to deflate the immoderate pretensions and hopes of policy makers, politicians and scientific advisors.

The long-term approach emphasises that economic growth in its modern form is intimately associated with the economic development of the Western countries since the mid eighteenth century (Landes, 1998; Maddison, 2001). Therefore, the history of the economic development of prosperous European and North American countries will often serve as a point of reference in our comparative discussions of the experiences of developing countries. This is not simply to advocate the copying of Western solutions by developing countries. Rather we hope to gain an insight into the similarities and differences in development processes.

The history of modern economic growth is also associated with industrialisation and a process that Higgins and Higgins (1979: 3) have ironically described as 'getting rid of farmers'. Again, this historical relationship between industrialisation and economic growth cannot be applied indiscriminately to developing countries. It does, however, serve as another point of reference. Furthermore, comparisons of the historical development of economically advanced countries and developing countries may teach us a lot about the role of institutions in advancing or impeding economic development (North, 1990, North *et al.*, 2009). In this context one can think of land tenure institutions, property rights, patent institutions and intellectual property rights (IPRs), processes of state formation, the quality of governance or the emergence of financial institutions.

Finally, the historical study of processes of economic growth reveals the importance of processes of saving and investment in the accumulation of factors of production. Such a study leaves us under no illusion with regard to the human costs of economic growth. In the past, economic growth has always been coupled with an enormous increase in the capital–labour ratio. In order to invest in capital goods a considerable portion of the national income has to be saved. In poor countries, saving means that people living at subsistence levels have to postpone present consumption for the sake of investment in future production. This is not easy. In Western countries such savings have been realised through the ruthless workings of the market mechanism of nineteenth-century capitalism, which kept wages low. In the centrally planned economies of the twentieth century exploitation of people by people through the market was replaced by direct coercion by the state. Both mechanisms have resulted in the transfer of income from consumers to social groups (capitalists, entrepreneurs, government officials) that were both able and willing to save and invest. It is unlikely that such tough choices can be avoided in the future.

An objection to the long-term approach is that it seldom offers neat solutions to the kind of practical problems and choices that policy makers, politicians, entrepreneurs or aid workers are inevitably faced with on a day-to-day basis. On the other hand, it is exactly this kind of distance to policy that enables one to analyse problems and developments in a more independent and critical manner. The emphasis on long-term trends can help make us more immune to the fashions and fads of the day and may dramatically alter our perceptions of development.

The choice between the two approaches is not a matter of all or nothing. Both are important. It is perfectly legitimate for politicians, policy makers, engineers, entrepreneurs or aid workers to ask for support and advice from scientific researchers and development experts. Also, passionate involvement in the plight of people in poor developing countries does not preclude independent judgement or critical analysis. On the other hand, a long-term approach offers a starting point for a realistic assessment of the effects of national and international development strategies and policies. It provides us with greater insight into the significance and scope of socio-economic policies amid the many factors that impinge on processes of development.

Central questions that will be tackled in each chapter are: How do the factors discussed influence the growth of productive capacity, the development of per capita income, the standard of living and the conditions of life in poor countries? Which are the factors that contribute to socio-economic development? Which are the factors that hamper development? What are the explanations for the observed developments and trends?

How can the differences between regions and between historical periods be interpreted and explained?

1.2 The development debate

There are no final answers to the questions mentioned at the end of the previous section. There is no such thing as scientific certainty, especially not in a field as controversial as that of economic and social development. Although the author's views will undoubtedly leave their imprint on this book, it is primarily intended as an introduction to the *debates on issues of development*. These debates are characterised by numerous clashing perspectives and theories and deep differences of opinion. The results of empirical studies are often contradictory or ambiguous. At times it even seems that empirical research leads to more rather than less uncertainty. This book tries to represent different views and perspectives of development in a balanced fashion, providing the reader with suggestions for further reading. Further, the book provides an overview of trends in thinking about development issues since the end of the Second World War.

This approach should definitely not result in a non-committal enumeration of points of view, perspectives and approaches, between which no choices need to be made. Though differences of opinion may exist, this does not mean that 'everything goes'. It is of great importance for students of development to learn to evaluate statements on development critically and to ascertain to what extent they are consistent with or are contradicted by the best empirical evidence available to us at present. Therefore, the exposition is illustrated as much as possible with statistics on development in several countries and regions. The purpose of this material is to introduce readers to international statistics and to stimulate them to distinguish between sense and nonsense in development studies and to find their own way in empirically grounded discussions of the issues of development. Background material to these statistics is presented in a separate website accompanying this book: http://www.dynamicsofdevelopment.com.

1.3 Growth and development

In the preceding sections, the term 'development' has figured prominently. In common parlance the term is used both frequently and rather casually: development studies, problems of development, developing countries, less developed countries, development cooperation, underdevelopment, development aid, development strategies, development policy and so forth. So what do we mean by 'development'?

Rich countries and poor countries: development as economic growth

Implicit in almost every use of the term 'development' is the notion that some countries and regions of the world are extremely poor, whereas other countries, representing a relatively small fraction of world population, are very prosperous. The discussion of development is always tied up with basic questions like: Why are poor countries poor and rich countries rich? Why do poor countries lag behind rich countries in the development of their standards of living? How can poor countries become more prosperous? How can poor countries catch-up with rich countries? In this sense an important dimension of the concept of 'development' refers to economic growth – or, more precisely, growth of national income per capita.

Development as structural change

Development conceived of as economic growth is a quantitative concept and basically means 'more of the same'. Yet, even if we limit ourselves to the economic sphere, it is clear that economic development is more than economic growth alone. Economic development refers to growth accompanied by qualitative changes in the structure of production and employment, generally referred to as *structural change* (Kuznets, 1966). Of particular importance for developing economies are increases in the share of the dynamic sectors such as manufacturing and decreases of the share of agriculture in national output and employment. More recently dynamic sectors include ICT production or software services. This implies that economic growth could take place without any economic development. An example is provided by those oil-exporting countries which experienced sharp increases in national income but saw hardly any changes in their economic structure. Another important qualitative change is *technological change*: the ongoing process of change in process and product technologies, resulting in radically new modes of production and new product ranges (Abramovitz, 1989b).

[handwritten margin note: Mexico 1976–1982]

Development as poverty reduction

In the 1960s the identification of development with economic growth came under increasing criticism. Authors such as Dudley Seers, Gunnar Myrdal, Paul Streeten, Hollis Chenery, Mahbub ul Haq and institutions like the International Labour Organization (ILO) pointed out that developing countries did not experience much change in the living conditions of the masses of the poor in spite of the impressive growth figures in the post-Second World War period (Chenery *et al.*, 1974; ILO, 1976; Myrdal, 1971; Seers, 1979; Streeten, 1972; Ul Haq, 1976). They came to the conclusion that development involves more than economic growth and changes in economic structures. Seers formulated three additional requirements for the use of the term 'development', namely that there should be a decrease in poverty and malnutrition, that income inequality should decline, and that the employment situation should improve (Seers, 1979). In modern development thinking, poverty reduction has become a key aspect of the development concept. In order to contribute to development, growth should be 'pro-poor' (see Kakwani, Khandker and Son, 2004).

The position taken in this book is that without rapid and sustained growth large-scale poverty reduction is not possible. If such growth is not achieved, there will be no major reduction in the poverty. But there is considerable scope for economic and social policies which allow the poor to participate more in the benefits of growth.

Development as social welfare

Other critics went even further and challenged the too narrow focus on the economic dimensions of development alone. A country can grow rapidly, but can still do badly in terms of literacy, health, life expectancy and nutrition (Sen, 1999). Economic growth does not necessarily make people more happy or satisfied (Easterlin, 1972). Criticism of growth fetishism led to the emergence of so-called 'social indicators': life expectancy, literacy, levels of education, infant mortality, availability of telephones, computer connections, hospital beds, licensed doctors, availability of calories and so forth. Some authors even went so far as to posit an opposition between growth and development. Cuba, Sri Lanka or the Indian state of Kerala, where growth was not very rapid but where welfare facilities and the level of education were improving, were compared with countries like Brazil, where extremely rapid growth had hardly affected poverty levels. Still, most authors reached the conclusion that, especially in the poorest countries, growth of productive capacity is a prerequisite for development, while development involves more than just growth.

Development as modernisation

Social scientists have stated that development should not be viewed in terms of economics only. One should also pay attention to changes in family structures, attitudes and mentalities, cultural changes, demographic developments, political changes and nation building, the transformation of rural societies and processes of urbanisation.

The Swedish Nobel Prize winner Gunnar Myrdal has argued that discussions of development have implicitly been based on a series of modernisation ideals or values. The concept of development is inevitably value laden. Opinions may differ on the way in which these ideals should be pursued. Nevertheless, according to Myrdal, there was a widespread consensus on the ultimate objectives of development among the members of political elites in developing countries involved in developmental policy (Myrdal, 1968, pp. 57–69). The broad concept of development therefore involves a change of the entire society in the direction of the modernisation ideals. The modernisation ideals are reproduced in Box 1.1.

Development as freedom

Compared to the 1960s, the climate of opinion has changed. Some political leaders in developing countries would now hesitate to use the term 'modernisation'. But the list of modernisation ideals compiled by Myrdal still seems highly relevant. Amartya Sen (1999) has argued for an even broader concept of development focusing on the concept of freedom. He sees development as an integrated process of expansion of substantive freedoms. Economic growth, technological advance and political change are all to be judged in the light of their contributions to the expansion of human freedoms. Among the most important of these freedoms are freedom from famine and malnutrition, freedom from poverty, access to healthcare and freedom from premature mortality. In a telling empirical example, Sen shows that urban African Americans have lower life expectancies than the average Chinese person or inhabitants of the Indian state of Kerala, in spite of much higher average per capita incomes in the USA.

According to Sen, freedoms are both ends and means. Thus, markets can be an engine for economic growth (means), but – what is sometimes forgotten – they constitute important freedoms in themselves, namely freedoms to exchange or transact. One important area where freedoms have frequently been restricted is the labour market, where slavery, serfdom or other institutional arrangements can restrict the free movement of labour. Political freedoms can contribute to economic dynamism, but are also goals in themselves. Sen argues somewhat optimistically that all freedoms are strongly interconnected and reinforce each other. He also tends to underemphasise clashes between

BOX 1.1   Modernisation ideals

- **Rationality**: in policy, in the application of technological knowledge, in structuring social relations, in thinking about objectives and means.
- **Planning for development**: searching for a coherent system of policy measures in order to change situations that are considered undesirable.
- **Increases in production per capita and production per worker**: primarily through industrialisation and increased capital intensity of production.
- **Improvements in the standard of living**.
- **Declines in social and economic inequality**: development ought to be for the benefit of the people, the masses.
- **More efficient institutions and attitudes**: those conducive to an increase in productivity and to development in general (for example, institutions that allow for mobility, initiative, entrepreneurship, effective competition and equal opportunities; attitudes like efficiency, diligence, orderliness, punctuality, economy, honesty, rationality, openness to change, solidarity and future-orientedness).
- **Consolidation of the national state and national integration**.
- **National independence**.
- **Political democratisation**: the concept of democratisation can be interpreted in various ways, of which parliamentary democracy is but one. Democratisation always implies some notion of involving the masses of the population in political decision making.
- **Increased social discipline**: developmental goals cannot be attained if governments cannot impose obligations on their citizens.

Source: Myrdal (1968).

freedoms of different groups of people and the value choices that still need to be made. There is no objective definition of development and there may be basic differences of opinion about the goals of development, even including that of the very goal of freedom, which may not be the ultimate goal from a variety of religious perspectives. Nevertheless, Sen's use of the concept of freedom as a normative yardstick for development is insightful. In his perspective economic growth remains important, but not as goal in itself. It is important in its potential contribution to a wide range of freedoms. It is not enough in itself. Sometimes changes in other spheres, such as education and health, can be at least as important in the expansion of freedoms.

Development as sustainability

Since the mid 1980s, disturbing reports of global warming, man-made climate change, the disappearance of rain forests, declining biodiversity and pollution of air and water have revived the discussion concerning the 'environmental constraints to growth'. Critics of economic growth have argued that the environmental costs of growth and development

pollution, global warming and climate change are good examples of this way of thinking (Lindahl-Kiessling and Landberg, 1994; IPCC, 2001; World Bank-WDR, 2003; World Bank-WDR, 2010).

Other authors see 'development' as a euphemism for Western penetration and domination of the world, involving great misery and exploitation both in past and present (Frank, 1969). An eloquent example of this viewpoint is Stanley Diamond's frontal attack (Diamond, 1974) on a concept associated with development and progress, namely 'civilisation'. Diamond argues that processes of civilisation have always involved conquest, violence, coercion and oppression with respect to so-called less civilised peoples. For instance, the Indians have been victims of Western penetration into North America, the African slaves have been victims of Western penetration into Africa, and the Eskimos have been victims of the spread of Western culture to Alaska. Yet, Diamond does not restrict himself to the results of Western expansion in the world. Wherever people try to spread their civilisation the fire and the sword are always involved, whether it concerns the expansion of the Greek, the Roman, the Egyptian, the Chinese or the Islamic civilisations.

Such criticism is valuable though at times one-sided. First, it creates an awareness of the costs involved in development. Secondly – and perhaps most important – it brings to our attention the relation between the 'concept of development' and international power relationships. What one understands under 'development' in a particular historical period is strongly influenced by dominant cultures and powers of that period.

On the other hand, it is no coincidence that fiercest criticisms of growth and development are often formulated by members of the elites in the richest countries in the world. When members of traditional tribal societies come in contact with modern consumer goods, their needs turn out to be far from limited. The possession of new goods will be sought for eagerly and widely. If one were to ask poor peasants or residents of urban slums in Africa or Asia whether they would prefer improvement in their productivity and standards of living, an overwhelming majority would respond positively. Only people who have been raised in very affluent societies can afford to have their doubts about the merits of economic growth and material progress.

Criticism of economic growth and development is sometimes inspired by a romantic idealisation of a harmonious and balanced society that may never have existed. And even if isolated and socially and ecologically balanced societies did exist in days gone by, they no longer exist today. The problems developing countries are facing today have much to do with the fact that these countries have already been 'opened up' to trade, investment, colonial domination and partial penetration by the money economy many years ago (Myint, 1980). If there ever was a choice in whether or not to strive for development, this 'choice' has already been made. Traditional self-sufficient societies have been disrupted. Modern technologies have contributed to a rapid growth of population, the needs of which cannot be met by traditional technologies and methods of production. Contact with the outside world has led to the emergence of modern preferences and needs. Present-day societies have no choice but to strive for socio-economic development. Given the rapid rates of population growth the alternative would be to sink ever deeper into a situation of poverty, misery and starvation. Although not all developmental ideals are supported by all inhabitants of developing countries, almost everybody longs for the socio-economic side of development (see Lewis, 1950, Appendix 1; North and Thomas, 1973: 1–2; Jones, 1988). In turn, socio-economic development is impossible without extensive social modernisation and institutional changes.

The ambivalence with regard to development is very obvious in the continuing attempts to develop hybrids of the ideals of sustained growth of welfare and productivity and modernisation of social institutions, on the one hand, and preservation of valued elements of cultural traditions, on the other. Examples are African socialism as advocated in the 1960s by political leaders such as Nyerere and Senghor, Indian socialism advocated by Gandhi and Nehru, and the present-day search for an Islamic development model.

1.5   Development and Westernisation

Apart from such elements as economic growth and productivity, it is difficult to define the concept of development in an objective, abstract and ahistorical manner. The substance and meaning of words like 'development' and 'modernisation' are strongly determined by the international political and economic balance of power. The countries that are economically and technologically advanced and politically and culturally dominant become the models for development in the eyes of their own citizens as well as in the eyes of the peoples trying to break away from their dominance. In the last 400 years the 'West' has emerged as the economic and political centre of the world (Findlay and O'Rourke, 2007; Jones, 1988; Landes, 1998; Maddison, 2007). Western countries have become the models for 'modern' societies. This means that present-day 'development' – which has been described above as a change in society in the direction of specific modernisation or developmental ideals – and 'Westernisation' are inevitably entwined. As is illustrated by Myrdal's modernisation ideals, notions of development have been derived from the historical development experiences of the present prosperous Western countries.[2]

This conclusion may shock those who criticise a Western ethnocentric view on issues of development. They may consider it another attempt to project the blueprint of Western development on non-Western societies. This is by no means our intention. First, there is no question of Western society being considered 'superior' to other societies. We simply want to note that the explicit or implicit ideals and objectives of development are modelled on the powers that dominate the world economy.

Secondly, the interweaving of development and Westernisation does not imply that all countries or societies should or can adopt one and the same development path. Initial conditions and circumstances are so different for each country, region and historical period, that previous developmental experiences cannot be blindly copied. Besides, at every stage there are alternative paths and options. Furthermore, we do not say that countries or societies will converge to a common standard. We only note that the measures for 'developed' or 'less developed' have been highly coloured by the developmental experiences of Western countries.

Thirdly, we nowhere state that the relationship between developmental values and Westernisation is a lasting one. As the centre of gravity of economic and political power relationships shifts towards Asia, our understanding of the terms 'modern' and 'less modern', 'developed' and 'less developed' will gradually change. At one time British society was the model of a 'developed' and 'modern' society. In the twentieth century this

---

[2] Sen (1999) argues that so-called Western notions such as tolerance or human rights are also prominent in ancient Asian traditions, for instance dating back to the third century BC during the reign of King Ashoka in India. But the spread of these ideas in their modern form remains inextricably linked to the Western expansion.

role has been taken over by the USA. During the 1980s attention started to shift towards Japan as an example of a modern and successful economy that might be imitated. Japanese concepts of quality control, flexible production and management were held up as examples for Western production organisations. In the course of the twenty-first century an emerging China may well become the new model of modernity.

1.6 Indicators of growth and development

Given the centrality of economic growth in the development process, the summary indicator most often used to indicate the degree of 'development' of a country is still national income per capita. National income can be calculated in three different ways (for example, see Allen, 1980):

1. As the sum of all incomes – wages, profits, interest, dividend, and rent – that have been earned by workers, owners of capital and owners of land in a country during the period of one year (the income approach, national income).
2. As the sum of all value added in an economy in a given year (national product).
3. As the sum of all expenditures in a country (consumer spending (C) + investment (I) + government expenditures (G) + the value of exports (X) – expenditures on imports (I)) in a given year (national expenditure).

In theory, national income, national product and national expenditure should be equal. In practice, there are statistical discrepancies. An important conceptual distinction is that between gross national product (GNP) and gross domestic product (GDP). The difference between GNP and GDP lies in the net balance of foreign income accruing to nationals of a country, deriving from factors of production abroad and payments to other countries for factors of production within the country, owned by nationals of other countries. This distinction is very important for developing countries. Since a significant part of investment in developing countries is foreign investment, there is a net annual outflow of dividends and profits. Therefore, GNP (or gross national income (GNI) or gross national expenditure) will be less than GDP (or gross domestic income or gross domestic expenditure).

There are two kinds of debates on growth indicators such as per capita GNP or per capita GDP. First, there are all sorts of technical objections to the use of per capita GNP as an adequate indicator of the level of economic development of a country. Secondly, there are substantive objections to the use of per capita GNP as an indicator of development. After all, as mentioned in section 1.3, development involves much more than economic growth alone.

The technical objections to the use of per capita GNP as an indicator of economic development are summarised in Box 1.3 (Bauer, 1976, pp. 55–66; Myint, 1980, pp. 8–10; Stiglitz *et al.*, 2009).

International comparisons based on purchasing power parities

These technical criticisms have given rise various improvements in the measurement of economic growth. Modern national accounts make a variety of adjustments for informal sector production or parts of non-market production, such as food produced for own consumption. Poverty lines take the differences in local conditions and differences in purchasing power parities (PPPs) into account (Milanović, 2005). The newly revised system

BOX 1.3 ## Technical problems in the measurement of economic growth

- In principle, GNP refers to that part of the national income that is traded via the market for money. In developing countries, however, there is widespread subsistence production. If there is a shift from subsistence production to production for the market in the process of economic development, it seems as if national income is increasing, whereas in reality there is no increase in production.
- GNP does not adequately account for the output of the informal or non-registered sector of the economy.
- GNP does not allow for differences in climate and conditions of life that require different types of clothing, food, transportation and housing.
- Economic growth and industrialisation involve substantial costs that do not occur in pre-industrial societies: the costs of transporting goods and people, the costs of the disposal of waste and the costs of urban living.
- The costs of environmental pollution, global warming and depletion of natural resources are not adequately accounted for in the measurement of national income (Hueting *et al.*, 1992; Mishan,1967; SNA, 2009; Stiglitz *et al.*, 2009).
- Dollar incomes of developing countries calculated with exchange rates do not provide us with realistic estimates of standards of living in these countries. Relative levels of prosperity in developing countries are higher than suggested by official international statistics on national incomes in dollars. One of the reasons for this is that many services and domestically traded goods in developing countries are much cheaper than in prosperous countries (see Kravis, Heston and Summers, 1982).

of national accounts (SNA, 2009) includes 'satellite accounts' to account for the environmental effects of economic growth.

From an international comparative perspective, one of the important advances in the measurement of national income is the development of PPPs. Exchange rates do not provide adequate measures of the purchasing power of currencies because they are based on internationally traded goods only, because they are distorted by policy interventions and influenced by global capital flows. For many years, researchers have been trying to overcome the disadvantages of the use of exchange rates in international comparisons, by calculating measures that explicitly take into account the relative purchasing power of the currencies of the countries being compared (see Kravis, Heston and Summers, 1982; Summers and Heston, 1991). These PPPs are based on price comparisons of a standardised basket of goods and services collected in over 130 countries. By now PPP-based estimates of national income have become available for many countries, though it should be stressed that the quality and reliability of these estimates still varies substantially. In Table 1.1, both exchange rate and PPP-based estimates are presented.

The use of PPPs has several important effects. In the first place, the dollar incomes of the poorest countries tend to be two to three times higher, than their dollar incomes calculated with exchange rates. PPP-based comparisons provide a more realistic picture of poverty, because they take into account the relative cheapness of services and basic necessities in developing countries. A second effect of the use of PPPs is that the income ranking of countries can change quite substantially, also among developing countries themselves.

In Table 1.1 a difference in ranking of seven points or more occurs for 26 of the 145 countries for which we have PPP estimates as well as exchange rate comparisons. Finally, the inequality of average per capita incomes in the world economy is diminished, as incomes in the poorest countries tend to be higher, while incomes in the richest countries tend to be lower than estimates based on exchange rates.

Of course, the use of PPPs changes nothing in the underlying reality of poverty and destitution in large parts of the world. It does, however, result in more adequate descriptions and measurements of poverty (and affluence). Therefore, PPPs are used ever more frequently.

Social indicators

Substantive objections to the use of GNP as an indicator of development are all based on the fact that development involves a lot more than economic growth only. Even from an economic point of view, GNP does not provide us with a good picture of the changes in the life circumstances of the poor masses. Per capita GNP is an average figure. It does not account for the distribution of income and consumption, which is often very unequal. Furthermore, the level of the national income is not directly related to the standard of living. When a considerable part of a country's national income is invested or used for military spending, the consumption expenditure of the inhabitants of this country may for many years lag far behind the growth of the national income.

Despite increases in national income, living conditions of the very poorest groups in a society may thus deteriorate. In other countries, their situation may improve in spite of a stagnation or slow growth of GNP. From this perspective, it is argued that various other economic and social indicators should be used along with GNP. This point has been re-emphasised in a critical report on national income measures by Stiglitz, Sen and Fitoussi (2009). Such economic and social indicators give a more straightforward picture of developments in a country: the number of people below poverty thresholds, data on malnutrition, employment figures, life expectancy at birth, infant mortality, numbers of doctors, nurses and hospital beds for every thousand inhabitants, energy consumption, the degree of illiteracy, years of education, data on income distribution, miles of roads and railways, access to clean water, equal opportunities for both men and women, human rights and so forth.

Since 1990 the United Nations Development Programme (UNDP) has published the *Human Development Report (HDR)*, which reports on many of these indicators annually. This report has introduced a measure called the Human Development Index (HDI). The HDI is a non-weighted average of three variables: an index of per capita gross domestic investment, life expectancy at birth, and the level of education. In the income index the income categories above the poverty threshold are given progressively lower weights in order to represent the declining marginal utility of higher incomes. The education index is a weighted average of literacy (two-thirds) and the average number of years of schooling (one-third) (see UNDP, 1991: 88–91). A country's ranking on the HDI may differ substantially from its ranking in terms of per capita income. For example, in 1999, 30 countries had a HDI ranking that differed more than 20 points from their ranking according to their per capita income in PPP US dollars (UNDP, 2001: 141).

These indicators are a valuable addition to the national income data. Still, in practice, they have not yet superseded per capita GNP as a summary indicator of the level of development. First, the quality of many social indicators is often still inadequate for international comparisons of levels and trends between many countries. In contrast, work on standard-isation of concepts and measurement techniques with regard to national income has already been continuing for many decades (see SNA, 2009; UNSO, 1968). Secondly, the weighting of social indicators is arbitrary. For instance, if higher incomes get lower weights, one automatically gets a different ranking. Thirdly, in the longer run many social indicators appear to be closely connected with per capita national income trends (Beckerman, 1974, 1993). At any given moment, large discrepancies can be found between the rank order based on income and the rank order based on social indicators for health or life expectancy. These discrepancies provide an interesting indication of policy priorities and institutional influ-ences. However, if per capita national income in a country stagnates over time, this will sooner or later be reflected in a deterioration of social indicators, while income growth is reflected in improvements in such indicators.

The development of GDP provides an indication of the development of a country's productive potential. How this capacity will be used cannot be known in advance. For example, it may be used for fulfilment of basic needs, healthcare, education or for military hardware, foreign payments, or conspicuous consumption by the elites. This depends very much on the social policies pursued in a country. In any event it is a well-established fact that there can be no long-term improvement of the living conditions of the masses of the population without a corresponding growth of productive capacity. As has been shown in section 1.3, an increase in per capita income is one of the important elements in most definitions of the development concept. This view is also endorsed in the *HDR* (UNDP, 1991: 1). The chapters in this book on demography, healthcare, education and state forma-tion (Chapters 5–7, 11) will pay explicit attention to the interplay of economic growth and social indicators. Long-run trends in a variety of social indicators will be presented separately. No attempt will be made to calculate a single composite index.

1.7   Does the 'Third World' exist?

After the Second World War the term 'Third World' came into vogue as a designation for developing countries (Worsley, 1964). This Third World was contrasted with the First World of the advanced capitalist countries and the Second World of the industrialised socialist countries in Eastern Europe. The use of this term implies that all Third World countries have common characteristics and interests, and that a wide and growing gap separates them from the affluent industrialised countries. The same is implied by terms such as 'North' versus 'South'. With regard to these terms, the similarities and differences in circumstances in developing countries will be discussed. In this section the emphasis will be on the diversity of circumstances; similarities will be discussed in section 1.8.

Table 1.1, derived from the *World Development Indicators Online* (World Bank-WDI, 2014), shows a highly diversified world economy in 2012 with enormous differences in per capita incomes, and great inequality both between rich and poor countries and among poor countries themselves. In Table 1.1 countries have primarily been ranked by income per capita. Countries have been divided into three categories: low-income countries (LICs, sometimes called least developed countries or LDCs), middle-income countries and high-income countries. The middle-income countries (MICs) are subdivided into lower-middle-income countries (LMICs) and upper-middle-income countries (UMICs).

Table 1.1:   Population, GNI per capita and growth in the world economy

		Population	GNP per capita		Average annual growth of GDP/cap (%)
		2012 (million[a])	2012 (US$)	2012 (PPP $)	2000–12
	Low-income countries (LICs) (GNI per capita< 1,035 US$)	846.5	588	1375	3.2
1	Congo, Dem. Rep.	65.7	230	390	2.4
2	Burundi	9.8	240	550	0.2
3	Malawi	15.9	320	730	−0.1
4	Liberia	4.2	370	580	4.3
5	Ethiopia	91.7	380	1110	5.4
6	Niger	17.2	390	760	1.1
7	Madagascar	22.3	430	930	−0.4
8	Guinea	11.5	440	970	0.5
9	Uganda	36.3	440	1120	3.5
10	Eritrea	6.1	450	550	−1.7
11	Togo	6.6	500	900	0.0
12	Central African Rep.	4.5	510	1080	2.8
13	Gambia, The	1.8	510	1830	0.1
14	Guinea-Bissau	1.7	510	1100	−0.4
15	Mozambique	25.2	510	1000	4.9
16	Tanzania	47.8	570	1560	3.9
17	Sierra Leone	6.0	580	1340	3.9
18	Rwanda	11.5	600	1320	5.3
19	Zimbabwe	13.7	650		−3.7
20	Mali	14.9	660	1140	1.9
21	Burkina Faso	16.5	670	1490	3.1
22	Afghanistan	29.8	680	1560	6.0[i]
23	Nepal	27.5	700	1470	2.5
24	Benin	10.1	750	1550	0.9
25	Haiti	10.2	760	1220	−0.7
26	Chad	12.4	770	1620	6.0
27	South Sudan	10.8	790		−16.4[j]
28	Bangladesh	154.7	840	2030	4.6
29	Kenya	43.2	860	1730	1.4
30	Tajikistan	8.0	860	2180	5.8
31	Cambodia	14.9	880	2330	6.1
32	Kyrgyz Rep.	5.6	990	2230	2.7
33	Senegal	13.7	1030	1880	1.1
34	Korea, Dem. Rep.	24.8			
35	Myanmar	52.8			11.9[f]
36	Somalia	10.2			

Table 1.1:   *(cont.)*

		Population	GNP per capita		Average annual growth of GDP/cap (%)
		2012 (million[a])	2012 (US$)	2012 (PPP $)	2000–12
	Middle-income countries (MICs)	4897.8	4383	7172	4.7
	Lower-middle-income countries (LMICs)	2507.0	1913	3923	4.3
	(GNI per capita between 1,036 and 4,085 US$)				
37	Mauritania	3.8	1110	2480	2.2
38	Cameroon	21.7	1170	2270	0.9
39	Côte d'Ivoire	19.8	1220	1920	−0.5
40	Pakistan	179.2	1260	2880	2.2
41	Lao PDR	6.6	1270	2690	5.4
42	Yemen, Rep.	23.9	1270	2310	0.0
43	West Bank and Gaza	4.0	1340[b]		
44	Zambia	14.1	1350	1590	3.0
45	Lesotho	2.1	1380	2170	3.2
46	Nigeria	168.8	1440	2450	5.7
47	Sudan	37.2	1500	2070	3.3
48	Ghana	25.4	1550	1910	4.1
49	Vietnam	88.8	1550	3620	5.3
50	India	1236.7	1580	3910	5.6
51	Nicaragua	6.0	1650	3890	2.0
52	Uzbekistan	29.8	1720	3670	5.5
53	Papua New Guinea	7.2	1790	2740	2.1
54	Moldova	3.6	2070	3630	4.9
55	Honduras	7.9	2120	3880	2.0
56	Bolivia	10.5	2220	4880	2.2
57	Philippines	96.7	2500	4380	2.9
58	Congo, Rep.	4.3	2550	3450	1.7
59	Syrian Arab Rep.	22.4	2610[d]	5120	2.1
60	Swaziland	1.2	2860	4760	0.6
61	Sri Lanka	20.3	2920	6030	5.0
62	Morocco	32.5	2960	5060	3.8
63	Egypt, Arab Rep.	80.7	2980	6450	2.6
64	Guatemala	15.1	3120	4880	0.9
65	Mongolia	2.8	3160	5020	6.5
66	Georgia	4.5	3270	5770	6.1
67	Paraguay	6.7	3400	5720	1.2
68	Indonesia	246.9	3420	4730	4.0
69	Ukraine	45.6	3500	7180	4.7

Table 1.1: *(cont.)*

		Population	GNP per capita		Average annual growth of GDP/cap (%)
		2012 (million[a])	2012 (US$)	2012 (PPP $)	2000–12
70	El Salvador	6.3	3590	6720	1.4
71	Kosovo	1.8	3600		5.4
72	Timor-Leste	1.2	3620	6230	2.7
73	Armenia	3.0	3720	8820	10.2
74	Albania	3.2	4030	9280	5.1
	Upper-middle-income countries (UMICs) (GNP per capita between 4,086 and 12,615 US$)	2390.8	6977	10584	5.1
75	Tunisia	10.8	4150	9210	2.8
76	Iran	76.4	4290[c]	10250[c]	3.8[g]
77	Angola	20.8	4580	5400	6.7
78	Macedonia, FYR	2.1	4620	11540	2.1
79	Jordan	6.3	4670	5980	3.3
80	Bosnia and Herzegovina	3.8	4750	9650	3.4
81	Algeria	38.5	5020	8360	2.2
82	Jamaica	2.7	5120		0.3
83	Ecuador	15.5	5170	9490	2.6
84	Thailand	66.8	5210	9280	3.6
85	Serbia	7.2	5280	11430	3.4
86	Turkmenistan	5.2	5410	9070	7.3
87	Dominican Rep.	10.3	5470	9660	3.6
88	Namibia	2.3	5610	7240	3.2
89	China	1350.7	5720	9040	9.5
90	Iraq	32.6	4291	4230	−2.1
91	Cuba	11.3	5890[e]		
92	Peru	30.0	6060	10090	4.6
93	Azerbaijan	9.3	6220	9310	11.2
94	Belarus	9.5	6530	14960	7.2
95	Bulgaria	7.3	6840	15450	4.6
96	Colombia	47.7	7020	9990	2.8
97	South Africa	51.2	7610	11010	2.1
98	Botswana	2.0	7650	16060	2.9
99	Panama	3.8	8510	15150	5.1
100	Mauritius	1.3	8570	15060	3.0
101	Costa Rica	4.8	8820	12500	2.7
102	Romania	21.3	8820	16860	4.4
103	Lebanon	4.4	9190	14160	2.0
104	Mexico	120.8	9640	16450	0.8

Table 1.1:   *(cont.)*

		Population	GNP per capita		Average annual growth of GDP/cap (%)
		2012 (million[a])	2012 (US$)	2012 (PPP $)	2000–12
105	Kazakhstan	16.8	9780	11780	6.9
106	Malaysia	29.2	9820	16270	2.8
107	Gabon	1.6	10040	14090	0.3
108	Turkey	74.0	10830	18190	2.8
109	Argentina	41.1	11330		2.6[k]
110	Brazil	198.7	11630	11530	2.2
111	Hungary	9.9	12380	20710	1.8
112	Venezuela, RB	30.0	12460	12920	1.7
	Low- and middle-income countries (LMICs) of which	5744.3	3825.2	6314.9	4.5
	Sub-Saharan Africa	910.4	1351	2233	2.3
	East Asia and the Pacific	1991.6	4884	7758	8.0
	South Asia	1649.2	1463	3565	5.1
	Europe and Central Asia	272.1	6691	11854	3.8
	Middle East and North Africa	339.6	3439[c]	6827[c]	2.5
	Latin America and the Caribbean	581.4	8981	11859	1.9
	Heavily indebted poor countries (HIPCs)	656.0	722	1390	2.1
	High-income countries (HICs) (GNP per capita>12,616 US$)	1302.1	38182	38325	1.1
113	Poland	38.5	12660	21170	3.8
114	Russian Federation	143.5	12700	22720	4.8
115	Libya	6.2	12930[c]	17430[c]	2.6[g]
116	Croatia	4.3	13490	20200	2.2
117	Uruguay	3.4	13580	15310	3.1
118	Lithuania	3.0	13830	23560	5.8
119	Latvia	2.0	14120	21920	5.3
120	Chile	17.5	14310	21310	3.1
121	Trinidad and Tobago	1.3	14710	22860	4.2
122	Bahrain	1.3	14820[d]	18910[d]	−0.4
123	Estonia	1.3	16150	22500	4.2
124	Slovak Rep.	5.4	17180	24770	4.3
125	Puerto Rico	3.7	18000		0.3
126	Czech Republic	10.5	18120	24720	2.7
127	Oman	3.3	19110[d]	25320[d]	1.5[i]
128	Portugal	10.5	20620	24770	0.0
129	Saudi Arabia	28.3	21210[e]	30160[e]	2.7

Socio-Economic Development

Table 1.1: *(cont.)*

		Population	GNP per capita		Average annual growth of GDP/cap (%)
		2012 (million[a])	2012 (US$)	2012 (PPP $)	2000–12
130	Korea, Rep.	50.0	22670	30970	3.4
131	Slovenia	2.1	22800	27240	1.8
132	Greece	11.3	23260	25460	0.2
133	Cyprus	1.1	26110	29840	0.3
134	Israel	7.9	28380[e]	28070[e]	1.4
135	Spain	46.2	29620	31670	0.4
136	New Zealand	4.4	30640[e]	30030[e]	1.1
137	Italy	60.9	33860	32920	−0.4
138	United Arab Emirates	9.2	35770[e]	41550[e]	−5.2
139	Hong Kong, China	7.2	36560	52190	3.3
140	United Kingdom	63.2	38670	37340	0.9
141	Ireland	4.6	39110	35670	0.8
142	France	65.7	41750	36720	0.5
143	Kuwait	3.3	44100[d]	47770[d]	0.2[h]
144	Germany	81.9	44260	42230	1.2
145	Belgium	11.1	44660	39860	0.6
146	Finland	5.4	46490	38220	1.2
147	Singapore	5.3	47210	60110	2.8
148	Austria	8.5	47660	43390	1.1
149	Japan	127.6	47880	36300	0.7
150	Netherlands	16.8	47970	43510	0.7
151	Canada	34.9	50970	42530	0.9
152	USA	313.9	52340	52610	0.8
153	Sweden	9.5	55970	43980	1.5
154	Australia	22.7	59360	43300	1.6
155	Denmark	5.6	59850	43430	0.2
156	Qatar	2.1	76010[e]	80470[e]	0.9
157	Switzerland	8.0	80970	55090	0.8
158	Norway	5.0	98860	66960	0.7
	World	7046.4	10138	12186	1.3

Notes:

[a] Countries with more than1 million inhabitants; aggregates include countries with less than 1 million inhabitants; income levels based on World Bank (2014) classification.

[b] 2005. [c] 2009. [d] 2010. [e] 2011. [f] 2000–4. [g] 2000–9. [h] 2000–11. [i] 2002–12. [j] 2008–12.

[k] GNI per capita calculated not using the Atlas Method but simply dividing GNI by population.

Source:

World Bank, *World Development Indicators Online*, downloaded March 2014.

Low-income countries

The category of *LICs* consists of thirty-six countries with a per capita GNI of less than 1036 dollars in 2012. Countries in this category are eligible for aid and loans on more favourable terms than richer developing countries. Within the LICs, the LDCs are singled out for special attention. These are defined in terms of low income, weak human resource base (education, health, nutrition, literacy) and high economic vulnerability.

The total population of the countries in the low-income category is 847 million people, with an average per capita income of 588 dollars in 2012. In this category, we primarily find 27 African countries and another eight countries in South, Central and Southeast Asia. There is only one Latin American country here, Haiti.

Natural circumstances in Africa (climate, rainfall, quality of the soil, tropical diseases, landlocked location) are relatively unfavourable in comparison with other parts of the world (World Bank, 1989). Mineral wealth is abundant in many African countries. However, up until now these potentialities have not been exploited to the full. Among other things, this is due to poorly developed physical infrastructure (roads, transport, communication). An inadequate infrastructure is a barrier to economic development in this region in other respects as well. Also, many poor resource rich countries suffered from the 'resource curse', where an abundance of natural resources promoted widespread corruption, rent seeking and economic mismanagement (Collier, 2007).

In contrast with Asia, which has experienced rapid growth since 1973, there was stagnation rather than growth in the poor Sub-Saharan African countries until 2000. In no less than ten countries per capita income was lower in 1980 than in 1965 (see World Bank, 1989; World Bank-WDR, 1989). Between 1980 and 2000, per capita income decreased in twenty-one of the thirty-seven Sub-Saharan African countries, for which data are included in the World Bank database (World Bank, 2002). However, after 2000, growth in Africa picked up due to the increasing demand for primary commodities. As indicated in Table 1.1 several African countries registered positive rates of growth, sometimes even fairly rapid rates of growth as in the case of Mozambique, Ethiopia, Rwanda, Sierra Leone and Tanzania. Other countries, such as Eritrea, Zimbabwe and the new state of South Sudan continued to contract. They are often characterised by civil strife and bad governance. Excluding South Sudan, GDP per capita in the low-income Sub-Saharan African countries grew at 1.7 per cent per year.

Lower-middle-income countries

Developing countries that are less poor are described as the *middle-income countries*. In this rather heterogeneous category it is customary to distinguish between the '*lower-middle-income countries'(LMICs)* with an annual per capita income of 1,036–4,085 dollars and the '*upper-middle-income countries'* *(UMICs)* with an annual per capita income of 4,086–12,615 dollars in 2012.

The distinction between the LMICs and the LICs is somewhat arbitrary. The LMIC category includes several poor countries that are hardly distinguishable from the LICs. As in the LIC category, we find many African countries in the LMIC category, such as for instance Côte d'Ivoire, Cameroun, Ghana, Nigeria, Sudan and Zambia. The LMIC category includes several smaller poor countries from Central and South America (Bolivia, El Salvador, Guatemala, Honduras, Nicaragua, Paraguay). In this category we also find five North African and Middle Eastern countries: Egypt, Morocco, Syria, Yemen and the West

Bank and Gaza. Finally, this category also includes some of the less successful transition countries such as Armenia, Georgia, Moldova, Mongolia, Uzbekistan and Ukraine.

The LMIC category includes several Asian countries with large populations such as India (1.4 billion), Indonesia (247 million), Pakistan (179 million), the Philippines (97 million) and Vietnam (89 million). Until fairly recently, most of these countries were classified as LICs, but unlike most African LICs, the poor Asian countries have experienced very rapid growth in the past thirty years. This lifted hundreds of millions of people out of poverty and allowed them to graduate into the LMIC category. China has experienced spectacular growth rates of 9 per cent or more since its economic reforms of 1978 and has now even graduated from the LIC to the UMIC category. In India, growth accelerated after its liberalisation of the economy in 1991. Between 1966 and the Asian crisis of 1967, Indonesia grew at 5.6 per cent per annum under the New Order of Suharto. It was hard hit by the Asian crisis of 1997 and was thrown back into the LIC category. After ten years of struggle, it has now rejoined the emerging dynamic Asian economies. The Asian exception is the Philippines which has continued to grow at a sluggish rate compared to the Asian tigers (Balisacan and Hill, 2003).

One institutional difference between Africa and Asia is worth noting here. Many of the poor Asian countries which have experienced rapid growth are characterised by ancient urban civilisations and age-old experience of centralised political rule and unity. In contrast, most states in Sub-Saharan African countries are new. There have been some tendencies towards larger political entities in African history, but in comparison with Asian countries political centralisation and urban traditions did not develop very much during the precolonial age.

The average annual per capita income in the LMIC category is 1913 dollars; the total population of these countries is 2.5 billion. In the past ten years, the average growth rate of the LMIC countries was 4.3 per cent per annum.

Upper-middle-income countries

The category of *upper-middle-income countries (UMICs)* consists of thirty-eight countries with a total of 2.4 billion inhabitants (of which China accounts for 1.4 billion) and an annual per capita income between 4,086 and 12,615 dollars. The average annual income is 6,977 dollars. In this category one will find six large Latin American countries: Argentina, Brazil, Columbia, Mexico, Peru and Venezuela and six smaller ones: Chile, Costa Rica, Cuba, Dominican Republic, Ecuador, Jamaica and Panama. It is striking that Latin American countries are among the more prosperous of developing countries, in spite of their long history of colonial and neocolonial exploitation. The large Latin American countries are characterised by relatively favourable natural circumstances, great natural wealth and a relatively low population density. Often, comparisons are drawn between these Latin American countries and the North American continent; it is an interesting question why Latin America has experienced a less favourable economic development since the nineteenth century in comparison with not dissimilar ex-colonies like the USA and Canada.

In the period 1950–80, many Latin American countries experienced rapid economic growth. Compared with Asian countries these countries are characterised by an extremely unequal income distribution, as a result of which the poor masses have benefited little from average increases in welfare. A country like Brazil was often mentioned as an illustration of the fact that large-scale poverty can coexist together with rapid economic growth and a high average income per capita.

In the 1980s growth in Latin America stagnated. Most countries were hit by the debt crisis, which negatively affected both their growth performance and their economic prospects. Moreover, countries like Argentina, Brazil and Mexico experienced extremely high inflation. The situation stabilised somewhat in the 1990s, though the Latin American economies remained vulnerable to shocks and crises. Growth resumed in the years after 2000.

Several countries in the UMIC category – Algeria, Angola, Iran, Iraq, Libya, Mexico and Venezuela – are important oil- and gas-exporting countries (as are the Russian Federation, Saudi Arabia and Quatar in the high-income category). It is interesting to note that in Asia, China, Malaysia and Thailand are now ranked as UMICs, due to their dynamic economic performance over recent decades. The African continent is represented by Algeria, Angola, Botswana, Gabon, Mauritius, Namibia and South Africa. Botswana and Mauritius are often seen as Africa's star performers (Habiyaremre, 2009; Rodrik, 2003). Like Brazil, South Africa is a comparatively rich country plagued by excessive inequality – the legacy of *apartheid* – and high levels of domestic violence. It has continued to show a modest degree of positive growth, but large segments of the population remain excluded from formal employment.

High-income countries

The category of *high-income countries (HICs)* consists of forty-six countries with a per capita income of over 12,616 dollars and a total population of 1.3 billion. From 1989, the World Bank no longer distinguished a separate category of industrialised market economies (the rich Western countries and Japan). The HIC category now includes the most successful of the former communist countries such as the Czech Republic, Estonia, Hungary, Croatia, Latvia, Lithuania, Poland, Slovenia and the Slovak Republic. It includes two successful Asian city states Singapore and Hong Kong (now a separate entity within China), as well as Israel. South Korea and Taiwan have graduated from the MIC to the HIC category, showing that a developing country can move from the bottom to the top of the income scale in two-and-a-half generations. Finally, the HIC category also includes the richest of the Arab oil exporters such as Kuwait, Oman, Quatar, Saudi Arabia and the United Arab Republic. It is worth noting that the average growth rate of the richest countries (1.1 per cent) is much lower than that of the LMICs (4.5 per cent).

The impact of the 2008 global financial crisis

At the time of writing, the world is still suffering from the aftermath of the global financial crisis of 2008. It seems clear that the USA, the countries of the European Union and Japan have suffered far more from the crisis than the emerging economies in Asia and Latin America such as India, Brazil, Indonesia and China (e.g. Asian Development Bank, 2010). The effects of the crisis on other developing countries have been mixed. Countries whose economies are closely tied to the Western countries through finance and tourism are experiencing serious slowdowns, but other countries such as China, India, Brazil and Indonesia are bearing up quite well. Growth in primary exporting countries slowed down in 2008, but has picked up due to increasing demand from China and other emerging economies.

Oil-exporting developing countries

The *oil-exporting developing countries* form a separate category. This category cuts across the income classification. Several of these countries belong to the UMIC category (Algeria, Angola, Iraq, Iran, Mexico and Venezuela), sometimes in spite of political upheavals and civil strife. Countries like Kuwait, Libya, Oman, the Russian Federation, Saudi Arabia and the United Arab Emirates are HICs. Nevertheless, many of them are still considered to be developing countries, since their economic structure is extremely one-sided, depending on a single export product: oil/gas. The oil exporters also include LMICs such as Indonesia and Nigeria.

The central challenge for oil-exporting economies is how to realise a *structural transformation* into a more diversified economic structure. Indonesia is the one oil exporter which has been relatively successful in doing this. The problems involved in structural transformation are not only economic but social as well. Attempts to transform and modernise an economy using oil wealth may evoke great social stress and give rise to social protest movements.

Newly industrialising countries

Several developing countries – including Brazil, Hong Kong, India, Israel, Mexico, Singapore, South Africa, South Korea and Taiwan – have experienced impressive industrial growth since the Second World War. They are called the *newly industrialising countries (NICs)*. These countries have succeeded in building up a modern industrial structure in a short period of time. They are a striking illustration of the thesis that developing countries are not condemned to primary production and that industrialisation is a realistic option for developing countries. Some of these countries have built up capital goods industries and have become exporters of capital goods and technology to other developing countries.

Until recently, all of these countries were classified as MICs. Since 1989 Singapore, Hong Kong – reunited with mainland China in 1996 – and Israel have joined the HIC category; South Korea and Taiwan have recently reached this income level, and Japan had already succeeded in doing so earlier.

Other countries that have realised a considerable growth of their industrial sector since the Second World War are Colombia, Egypt, Greece, the Philippines, Portugal, Spain and Turkey. These countries are sometimes referred to as the *semi-industrialised countries (SICs, see OECD, 1979)*. In the last quarter of the twentieth century, the so-called second-tier NICs – China, Indonesia, Malaysia, Sri Lanka, and Thailand – experienced rapid growth of industrial production and industrial exports. There was a rude interruption with the Asian crisis of 1997, which temporarily halted growth in Indonesia, Thailand, Malaysia, South Korea and the Philippines. But with the exception of Indonesia, growth resumed very quickly a year later.

Countries in transition

Until 1988, socialist countries in Central and Eastern Europe (CEE) were considered a separate category in the consecutive editions of the World Bank's *World Development Report (WDR)*. However, very few comparable statistics on these countries were available. It was hard to judge their relative standing. The same applied to centrally planned economies in other parts of the world.

Since 1989, the socialist countries are no longer regarded as a separate category. In 1989 the Berlin Wall collapsed and in 1991 the Soviet Union disintegrated. Since then the former Eastern European countries, the former Yugoslav republics and the former Soviet republics are referred to as *transition economies*. Somewhat to our surprise, many of the former Soviet republics in Asia turned out to have much in common with poor developing countries in other parts of the world. In 2000, no less than eighteen former socialist CEE countries and former Soviet republics were categorised as LICs or LMICs.

Yet, the historical path of development of both the former Eastern European socialist economies and the former Soviet republics has been very different from that of other developing countries. They started out with rather high levels of income, human skills, health, infrastructure, technological capabilities and industrial production. After 1989, per capita incomes in most former Soviet States and Eastern European satellites plummeted. By 2000, only six countries had regained their pre-1989 income levels, namely the Czech Republic, Hungary, Poland, Slovakia and Slovenia. Per capita income in Georgia, Tajikistan and Moldova stood at less than a third of pre-transition levels. There were also massive declines in life expectancy, health and human capital.

Since then, some of the transition economies have experienced substantial economic recovery. Azerbaijan, Kazakhstan, Bulgaria, Hungary, Romania and Turkmenistan are now UMICs. The Russian Federation, Poland, the Czech Rublic the Slovak Republic and the Baltic states Estonia, Latvia and Lithuania have even joined the high-income club. Other post-communist economies fared less well. The central Asian countries of Kyrgistan and Tajikistan are LICs. Albania, Armenia, Georgia, Mongolia, Moldova, the Ukraine and Uzbekistan are LMICs.

Regional differences in poverty, welfare and growth dynamics

Table 1.5 (p. 34) also offers some first insights into the regional distribution of wealth and poverty. Poverty is primarily concentrated in Sub-Saharan Africa and Asia, though Asia with its large and dense populations shows much more economic dynamism than sparsely populated Africa, which has been characterised by long periods of stagnation. Economic stagnation in Africa is compounded by wars, civil wars and political instability, which have much to do with the relatively recent emergence of modern states on the continent (see the discussion in Chapter 11).

The implication is that our intuitive association between the problems of development and the African continent results in too gloomy a picture of the achievements of developing countries as a whole. It is understandable that the media often concentrate on hunger in Africa. But the greatest numbers of poor people actually live in East and South Asia (see Table 1.5, p. 34, on world poverty). In terms of changes in the life situation of the very poor, one should factor in the dynamic developments in the populous Asian countries.

The large Latin American countries are much more affluent and come closer to the levels of prosperity of rich Western countries than most other developing countries. To some extent the Latin America development problem can be characterised as a distributive problem: how can the masses share in the increased average welfare, achieved in the course of the twentieth century? This applies less to poor African and Asian countries where there is not much to distribute in the first place. In the 1980s economic growth in Latin America faltered. At the same time many Asian countries experienced continued growth. Differences in economic policy are among the causes of this contrast in development (see Chapter 13). Rapid growth in Asia was interrupted by the unexpected financial crisis of 1997. Since then, rapid growth has resumed in most some Asian economies. Large countries such as India and China were less affected by the crisis and continued to grow rapidly.

Dimensions of difference

The discussion above highlights the diversity of developmental experiences. This will be elaborated further in Chapter 2, which discusses historical patterns and paths of development. Important dimensions of variation are summarised in Box 1.4.

BOX 1.4 : Differences between developing countries

- **Levels of per capita income**. There are great differences in levels of prosperity among developing countries, both between and within income categories (LDCs, LMICs, UMICs).
- **Demographic characteristics**. Developing countries differ in terms of population size, population density and population growth rates.
- **Natural resources and geography**. Developing countries differ in climate, geography, soil quality and natural resources. One of the important distinctions is that between oil-exporting developing countries and oil-importing developing countries. Another distinction is between landlocked and non-landlocked economies.
- **Structure of production**. Developing countries have different structures of production. Some developing countries are still predominantly agricultural. Others have developed large industrial sectors. These are referred to as the NICs.
- **Economic regime** Developing countries show great variation in their economic regimes and their paths of economic development. One can distinguish inward-looking regimes from outward-looking regimes and centrally planned regimes from market economies. Market economies differ greatly in their degrees of intervention. Many former socialist countries are in transition from centrally planned regimes to more market-oriented regimes. These are referred to as economies in transition.
- **Differences in colonial experiences**. Some developing countries were colonised at a very early stage, others at a later stage. Some areas have never been colonised at all. There have been great variations in the nature and the intensity of the colonial relationships (see further Chapters 2 and 11).
- **Differences in precolonial history**. For a full understanding of present-day developments, one has to take into account the precolonial history and the cultural and religious development of the different societies. Of particular importance are the age-old traditions of political centralisation and urbanisation in countries on the Asian continent.
- **Economic dynamism**. Developing countries are characterised by pronounced differences in economic dynamism, with long periods of growth in some regions and long periods of stagnation in others.
- **Regional characteristics**. Developmental experiences differ by region. It is useful to distinguish the regional experiences of Sub-Saharan Africa, South Asia, East Asia, North Africa, the Middle East and Latin America.

We conclude that terms such as *Third World or the South* are unacceptable simplifications. They do not do justice to the diversity of circumstances and developmental experiences in different parts of the world. The preferred term in this book is the plural 'developing countries', which emphasises the diversity of development experiences and the dynamic nature of development processes.[3]

1.8   The gap between rich and poor countries

One of the connotations of the term 'Third World' is that of a wide and insurmountable divide between two distinct entities: the developed First World and the poor Third World. Let us approach this issue in two ways, first by looking at the degree of income inequality in the world economy, second by looking at the immutability of international income rankings. Next, we enquire whether individual developing countries can catch-up and bridge the gap separating them from rich countries.

1.   *How unequal is the world economy?*
The degree of inequality in the world economy is very great. Table 1.1 shows that – using PPPs as converters – the average per capita income of the forty-six high-income countries is 27.8 times as high as that of the thirty-six poorest countries for which PPP income estimates are available.[4] The ratio between the richest country in PPP terms in 2012, Norway, and the poorest country, the Democratic Republic of Congo, is a breathtaking 172 to 1. The gap between rich and poor countries has been increasing dramatically over time. Around 1820, the ratio of per capita incomes of Western countries versus countries in Latin America, Asia and Africa was in the order of 2 to 1 (PPP-based estimates of Maddison, 2001: Table 1–9b).

The distribution of world income over households is even more unequal than the distribution of the world income over countries, since incomes within countries are also distributed unequally. Furthermore, income inequality in developing countries is considerably greater than in affluent countries. This is illustrated in Table 1.2, which provides data on within-country inequality for thirty developing countries in 2005. The shares of the bottom 10 per cent of the population in income are lower than in the advanced economies, while the shares of the top 10 per cent are much higher. Asian countries are more egalitarian than countries on other continents. Latin American countries are most inegalitarian.[5]

Berry, Bourguignon and Morrisson (1983) have estimated the distribution of the world income in 124 countries in 1970. They estimate the share of the bottom 50 per cent of the world population at 8.4 per cent of world income, whereas the share of the top 10 per cent is no less than 49.4 per cent of world income. Research by Milanović (1999) for ninety-one countries based on household survey data presents a rather similar pattern for the years 1988 and 1993. Milanović (2005) has updated these results until 1998. The results are reproduced in Table 1.3. In this table, the bottom 50 per cent of households receives less

---

[3]   A potential drawback of the term 'developing countries' is that it might suggest that all countries are developing in a 'positive' direction. This is not necessarily the case.

[4]   Using exchange rates, the ratio of HICs to LICs is 65 to 1. This illustrates the importance of the choice of converter.

[5]   Comparisons of inequality are fraught with difficulties. Some studies focus on disposable income, others on expenditure or consumption. Some studies use households as units, other individuals. For a discussion of these technicalities see the UN-WIDER, *World Income Inequality Database* (2010) and Milanović (2005).

Table 1.2: Income inequality within countries, 2005

	Share of income (%)[a]					
	Bottom 10	Bottom 20	Bottom 60	Bottom 80	Top 20	Top 10
Bangladesh	3.8	8.8	36.5	57.5	42.5	28.0
China	1.6	4.3	26.4	48.1	51.9	34.9
India	3.6	8.1	34.3	54.7	45.3	31.1
Indonesia	3.0	7.1	32.3	52.7	47.3	32.3
Iran	2.5	6.5	32.8	54.9	45.1	29.6
Malaysia	1.7	4.4	25.4	45.7	54.3	38.4
Pakistan	3.9	9.1	38.1	59.2	40.8	26.5
Philippines	2.2	5.4	28.1	49.4	50.6	34.2
South Korea	2.9	7.9	39.5	62.5	37.5	22.5
Sri Lanka	3.0	7.0	31.6	52.0	48.0	28.0
Taiwan	3.3	6.7	36.0	59.2	40.9	26.0
Thailand	2.3	5.7	28.8	51.1	48.9	32.5
Turkey	2.3	6.1	31.6	53.3	46.7	30.7
Vietnam	4.2	9.0	35.2	55.7	44.3	28.8
Argentina	1.2	3.7	25.6	47.4	52.6	35.7
Brazil	1.0	3.0	20.6	39.1	60.9	60.9
Chile	1.4	3.9	22.3	40.1	59.9	59.9
Colombia	0.8	2.9	20.9	39.3	60.7	60.7
Mexico	1.2	3.8	24.5	44.1	55.9	55.9
Peru	1.6	4.3	26.1	47.1	52.9	52.9
Venezuela	1.0	3.7	26.5	48.1	51.9	14.0
Congo, Dem. Rep.						
Côte d'Ivoire	2.0	5.2	28.0	49.3	50.7	34.0
Egypt	3.8	8.9	37.7	58.5	41.5	27.6
Ghana	2.1	5.6	30.6	53.4	46.6	30.0
Kenya	0.8	2.5	20.7	79.9	20.1	59.2
Morocco	2.6	6.5	31.9	53.4	46.6	30.9
Nigeria	1.9	5.0	29.1	50.8	49.2	33.2
South Africa	1.4	3.5	19.8	37.8	62.2	44.7
Tanzania	2.8	6.9	33.9	55.8	44.2	30.1
Zambia	1.2	3.6	24.1	44.9	55.1	38.8
Average Asian countries[b]	2.9	6.8	31.8	52.9	47.1	31.3
Average Latin American countries	1.2	3.6	23.8	43.6	56.4	48.6
Average African countries	2.1	5.3	28.4	53.8	46.2	36.5
Average developing countries[b]	2.2	5.5	28.7	50.8	49.2	37.3
Average 16 advanced economies[c]	3.2	8.3	35.5	61.4	38.6	24.1

Notes:

[a] Unless otherwise indicated, most recent year in period 2000–5; Switzerland, 1992; Japan, 1993; Malaysia, 1997; Korea, 1998; Ghana, Kenya, Morocco, 1999.

[b] Excl. South Korea and Taiwan, which are no longer classifed as developing countries.

[c] Australia, Austria, Belgium, Canada, Denmark, Finland, France, Germany, Italy, Japan, Netherlands, Norway, Sweden, Switzerland, UK, USA.

Source:

UNU-WIDER, *World Income Inequality Database* V2.0c May 2008, downloaded January 2010.

Table 1.3: Inequality in the world economy

Cumulative % of world population	Cumulative % of world income		
	1988	1993	1998
Bottom 10%	0.9	0.8	0.8
Bottom 20%	2.3	2.0	2.1
Bottom 50%	9.6	8.5	9.2
Bottom 75%	25.9	22.3	24.7
Bottom 85%	41.0	37.1	37.9
Top 10%	46.9	50.8	50.7
Top 5%	31.2	33.7	33.7
Top 1%	9.3	9.5	9.5
Gini	61.9	65.2	64.2

Sources:
1988 and 1993: Milanović (1999); Gini coefficients and 1998: Milanović (2005).

then 10 per cent of world income and the world income distribution has become more unequal in the ten years between 1988 and 1998, though the distribution in 1998 is less unequal than that of 1993. Such estimates are subject to many uncertainties and comparisons across time are not easy. However, they do provide us with a striking illustration of the profoundly skewed distribution of world incomes. In the following chapters, data will also be presented on inequalities in the social indicators.

2. *Can the gap be bridged?*
In spite of the huge differences in per capita income, it is not correct to speak of an

insurmountable gap between rich and poor countries. The discussion of Table 1.1 shows that the transition from developing countries to affluent countries is a gradual one, rather than a sharp divide. Some countries designated as developing are more affluent than the poorer Western countries or the former socialist countries in Eastern Europe. Countries like Japan, Korea, Singapore or Taiwan, which once used to be considered as developing countries, are now seen as advanced economies. China has graduated from the LIC to the UMIC category; Malaysia has entered the UMIC category.

The paradox of increasing inequality and increasing mobility

Also, as world income differentials widen, the speed with which some countries engage in catch-up has accelerated. For instance, growth rates in Asian economies such as China, South Korea or Singapore have been far higher than the historical growth rates of the presently affluent countries. The jump from a very poor country to an upper-middle-income country can be realised in the course of one or two generations. The speed of catch-up in successful countries in the twentieth century is twice as high as it was in the nineteenth century (Szirmai, 2013). This is the paradox of increasing unequality combined with increasing mobility. The acceleration of the rate of catch-up is illustrated in Table 1.4, which compares rates of catch-up in the nineteenth century with the rates after 1950.

Table 1.4: Catch-up episodes

Country	Period[a]	Growth of GDP	Growth of GDP per capita	Rate of Catch-up[b]
	1820–1913			
USA	1820–1905	4.1	1.5	1.3
Germany	1880–1913	3.1	1.9	1.8
Russia	1900–1913	3.2	1.4	2.0
Japan	1870–1913	2.5	1.5	1.5
UK	1820–1913	2.0	1.1	
World average	1820–1913	1.5	0.9	
	1950–2006			
China	1978–2006	8.1	6.9	3.6
West Germany	1950–1973	6.0	5.0	2.7
India	1994–2006	6.7	5.1	2.4
Indonesia	1967–1997	6.8	4.8	2.4
Ireland	1995–2006	6.2	6.2	2.8
Japan	1946–1973	9.3	8.0	3.6
Korea	1952–1997	8.2	6.3	3.0
Malaysia	1968–1997	7.5	5.1	2.6
Russia	1998–2005	7.2	7.2	3.9
Singapore	1960–1973	10.0	7.6	2.5
Taiwan	1962–1973	11.4	8.7	2.8
Thailand	1973–1996	7.6	5.8	3.2
Vietnam	1992–2005	7.6	6.1	2.9
World average	1950–1973	4.9	2.9	
World average	1973–1997	3.1	1.4	
World average	1997–2003	3.5	2.3	

Notes:

[a] The periods have been chosen so as to maximise sustained high growth rates over an extended period.

[b] Ratio of growth of GDP per capita compared to growth in lead economy in corresponding period. Prior to 1913, the comparison is with the UK, after 1950 with the USA.

Sources:

Country data 1990 and before, plus figures for world total from: Maddison, *Historical Statistics, World Population, GDP and per capita GDP, 1–2003 AD* (update: August 2007)www.ggdc.net/maddison/.Country data 1991–2006 and West Germany from: The Conference Board and Groningen Growth and Development Centre, *Total Economy Database*, November 2007, www.conference–board.org/economics.West Germany from: Conference Board/ GGDC.

In the nineteenth century, GDP per capita in the catch-up countries of Germany, Russia and Japan was growing at between 1.4 and 1.9 per cent per year. After 1950, we see growth rates of between 5 and 9 per cent per year. Prior to 1913, the ratio of per capita GDP growth in catch-up episodes, relative to the growth of the technological leader the UK, was between 1.3 and 2. After 1950, the catch-up countries – most of them located in Asia – were growing on average three times as fast as the world leader, the USA. The acceleration of catch-up is related to globalisation and greater possibilities for international technology diffusion.

While some countries move upwards, others experience decline and comparative stagnation. Before the Second World War, Argentina was considered to be a reasonably developed country on the verge of breakthrough to affluence. It is now unmistakably seen as a developing country. The Russian Federation experienced dramatic declines in its per capita income after 1990, accompanied by declines in its social indicators and only regained its 1990 income level by 2006. The same is true of many of the former Soviet republics. The conclusion is that there is a constant process of change in the ranking of countries rather than a fixed order and an unbridgeable and immutable gap between rich and poor countries (see Reynolds, 1986).

As a counterbalance to unwarranted optimism, Paul Collier calls special attention to the plight of fifty-seven of the poorest developing countries, accounting for about one billion of global population. In his exciting book *The Bottom Billion* (Collier, 2007), he argues that these countries are mired in stagnation and are diverging from the rest of developing countries. He agrees with the view expounded above that many developing countries are dynamic and that the world income distribution is fluid. But some countries in Africa and Latin America seem trapped at the bottom of the global hierarchy, facing obstacles which make it very difficult to embark on growth and development. These obstacles or traps include political conflict, the natural resource trap, bad governance and landlocked economies with lack of access to transport. The central characteristic of the 'bottom billion' countries is that they have not been growing, in contrast to the majority of developing countries (see also Milanović, 2005, Chapter 7).

1.9   What do developing countries have in common?

If the Third World does not exist, the question arises whether there is a future for development studies. After the Second World War, development studies and development economics emerged as specific scientific subdisciplines and specialisations (Meier and Stiglitz, 2000). It was felt that the specific economic and social conditions in poor developing countries, with institutions that differed greatly from the so-called 'advanced' Western nations, called for specific scientific theories and approaches which could take these circumstances into account. The standard theories and propositions of economics, sociology and the other social sciences would not apply in these very different circumstances. All over the world specialisations emerged in development studies, development economics, development sociology and so forth.

From the 1980s onwards, there was a counter tendency to reintegrate development studies into mainstream theorising and research. Though different conditions still had to be taken into account, the theories and approaches were not seen as fundamentally different from those of the mainstream disciplines. Thus, the introduction to the well-known six-volume *Handbook of Development Economics* (Chenery and Srinivasan, 1988) sees development economics as an integral part of the wider discipline of economics. Some authors went even further and called for the abolition of development studies (Lal, 2000).

The position taken in this book is that the reintegration of development studies into the more general disciplines of economics, history, demography or sociology provides a creative and stimulating impulse to the study of developing countries. The focus of development studies on the dynamics of socio-economic development also provides a stimulus to the mainstream disciplines themselves. Nevertheless, there continues to be a need for scientific specialisations focusing on the problems of development, based on intimate knowledge of conditions in developing countries. The specialisation of development studies also has a function in integrating or combining the insights from a wide range of disciplines, which would be lost if too strong a disciplinary focus were taken.

In spite of the diversity of circumstances and developmental experiences discussed in section 1.7, developing countries do have a number of important characteristics and problems in common, which justify a specialised professional focus on development. If we were not able to identify such characteristics, there would not be much sense in writing a book about developing countries. Important common characteristics of developing countries are summarised in Box 1.5.

BOX 1.5 : Common characteristics of developing countries

1. Widespread poverty and malnutrition.
2. A relatively large share of agriculture in output and employment.
3. Pronounced dualism in economic structure.
4. Very rapid growth of population.
5. Explosive urbanisation.
6. Large-scale underutilisation of labour.
7. Political instability.
8. Weak governance, pervasive corruption.
9. Environmental degradation.
10. Low levels of technological capabilities.

Poverty and malnutrition

As can be calculated from Table 1.1, in 2012 over 2.7 billion persons lived in countries with a average per capita income of 1,210 dollars per year.[6] Even this low average income does not offer a correct impression of the incomes of the very poor since the income distribution in most developing countries is heavily skewed. At the beginning of the twenty-first century, the share of the total income or total consumer spending of the bottom 20 per cent of the households in the LICs ranged from 2.5 to 9.1 per cent (see Table 1.2). The average share was 5.5 per cent. The average share of the bottom 10 per cent of the population was only 2.2

---

[6] Average of countries in Table 1.1 with per capita incomes of less than 1,650 US dollars in 2012. The population of countries strictly in the low-income category has shrunk to 847 million, down from 2.5 billion in 2000, the figure listed in the previous edition of this book.

per cent. Poverty is not restricted to the poorest countries. In developing countries with a higher average income, there are also large numbers of extremely poor people as a result of the unequal distribution of incomes.[7] The greater the income inequality, the higher the incidence of poverty at a given level of average income per capita.

The simplest indicator of poverty is the *headcount*, the numbers of persons in a given country with incomes or consumption expenditures lower than a given poverty line. A more complex indicator is the *poverty gap*, the amount of money needed to bring persons below the poverty line up to the level of the poverty line (Sen, 1981). A comprehensive study by Chen and Ravallion (2008) provides new recalibrated international poverty lines which allow us to assess trends in poverty. The more recent estimates of the numbers of people in poverty are higher than the older ones from previous studies (see Chen and Ravallion, 2001). Their estimate of people in absolute poverty in 2005 is no less 1.4 billion persons. However, the study concludes that the downward movements in poverty are confirmed by the recent estimates. In Table 1.5 two poverty lines are reproduced, one of 1.25 2005 PPP dollars and one of 2.00 2005 PPP dollars. Their results for the headcount are reproduced in Table 1.5.

In 2005, the number of poor persons living on an income below the poverty line of 1.25 dollars a day was 1.4 billion. 2.5 billion persons had to survive on less than 2.00 dollars a day. Expressed as percentage of the population, poverty is declining substantially. In 1981, 52 per cent of the global population was living in absolute poverty. By 2005, this number had declined to 25 per cent. The absolute numbers are also on the decline, though the extent of poverty remains shocking.

One of the most distressing aspects of poverty in developing countries is absolute malnutrition. Estimates of the numbers of undernourished people differ greatly, but the numbers are certainly high. According to estimates by the FAO, 923 million persons were undernourished in 2008. This comes to 17 per cent of the total population of developing countries (FAO, 2008). In percentage terms, the percentage of undernourished people had declined from 20 per cent in 1990–2 to 16 per cent in 2003–5. But a sudden rise in food prices in 2007–8 reversed this declining trend. The number of undernourished persons in 2008 was 80 million higher than in 1990–2. On top of the rising food prices, the economic crisis of 2008 added to the number of malnourished, which peaked at 1.02 billion in 2009 (FAO, 2009). Absolute malnutrition is associated with high death rates, low life expectancy, bad health, impairment of mental capacities and low productivity.

Large shares of agriculture

In developing countries the share of agricultural production in the total production is much higher than in affluent countries. Labour productivity in agriculture is much lower than in the industrial sector. The share of the agricultural labour force in the total labour force is therefore even larger than the share of the agricultural production in the total production. This means that in developing countries a much larger proportion of the labour force is active in the agricultural sector than in the affluent countries. Conversely, the share of the industrial sector in production and employment is smaller.

---

[7] 'Data on income distribution should be interpreted with caution.' (*World Development Report 1995*, p. 220.) International comparisons of income inequality are not yet very reliable.

Table 1.5: World poverty
Population living below poverty lines, 1981, 1993 and 2005

Region	$1.25 per day						$2.00 per day					
	Head count Index (%)			Number of poor (million)			Head count Index (%)			Number of poor (million)		
	1981	1993	2005	1981	1993	2005	1981	1993	2005	1981	1993	2005
East Asia,	77.7	50.8	16.8	1,071.5	845.3	316.2	92.6	75.8	38.7	1,277.7	1,262.1	728.7
of which China	84.0	53.7	15.9	835.1	632.7	207.7	97.8	78.6	36.3	972.1	926.3	473.7
Eastern Europe and Central Asia	1.7	4.3	3.7	7.1	20.1	17.3	8.3	10.3	8.9	35.0	48.6	41.9
Latin America and Caribbean	11.5	9.1	8.2	42.0	41.8	46.1	22.5	19.3	16.6	82.3	88.9	91.3
Middle East and North Africa	7.9	4.1	3.6	13.7	9.8	11.0	26.7	19.8	16.9	46.3	48.0	51.5
South Asia,	59.4	46.9	40.3	548.3	559.4	595.6	86.5	79.7	73.9	799.5	950.0	1,091.5
of which India	59.8	49.4	41.6	420.5	444.3	455.8	86.6	81.7	75.6	608.9	735.0	827.7
Sub-Saharan Africa	53.7	57.1	50.9	213.7	318.5	390.6	74.0	76.0	73.0	294.2	423.8	556.7
Total	**51.8**	**39.1**	**25.2**	**1,896.2**	**1,794.9**	**1,376.7**	**69.2**	**61.5**	**47.0**	**2,535.1**	**2,821.4**	**2,561.5**
Total, excl. China and India	**39.8**	**34.1**	**28.2**	**1,061.1**	**1,162.3**	**1,169.0**	**58.6**	**55.6**	**50.3**	**1,563.0**	**1,895.3**	**2,087.9**

Note:
Poverty lines defined at 2005 dollars using 2005 PPPs.

Source:
Chen and Ravallion (2008).

Dualism and inequality

In developing countries there is a wide gap between the modern sector – which includes mining, manufacturing, commercial crop production, and modern services – and the traditional sector – which uses primitive and low-productivity techniques, e.g. traditional agriculture, in particular food production and the informal sector in the cities and the countryside. The modern sector is an enclave closely linked to the international economy, but isolated from the remainder of the domestic economy. The principal problem of *dualism* is the absence of technological diffusion from the modern technologically advanced sector towards the rest of the economy. Apart from technological dualism, other forms of dualism can also occur such as regional dualism (the traditional and the modern sector have also been divided spatially), cultural dualism and ethnic dualism (some ethnic groups are active in the modern sector, others in the traditional sector). When all dualisms coincide, problems can be quite extreme, and dualism may lead to social conflicts or even to civil wars (Higgins and Higgins, 1979).

Dualism goes hand in hand with very high levels of income inequality. In developing countries, inequality is much higher than in advanced economies and it is on the increase, not in the least in rapidly growth Asian economies such as China (see Table 1.2, p. 28).

Rapid population growth

As a result of a decrease in death rates and a continued high level of birth rates, there is a large excess of births over deaths. Between 2000 and 2012, the average rate of population growth in low-income countries was growing at a little over 2.2 per cent per year. In developing countries as a whole the rate of growth was gradually slowing down, but was still 1.3 per cent per year (World Bank-WDI, 2014).

Rapid urbanisation

Most developing countries experience large-scale migration from rural to urban areas as well as rapid growth of the existing urban population. Urban population growth exceeds the absorption capacity of the urban economy, the urban labour market and the urban infrastructure. Thus, widespread slums and uncontrollable megacities come into being; the best-known example of this is Mexico City. In turn, the growth of the cities and the relative depopulation of the rural areas reinforce existing dualism. Within urban society, too, there is dualism between the modern formal sector and the small-scale informal sector.

Underutilisation of labour

Open unemployment is relatively low in most developing countries. Given the absence of formal systems of social security few people can afford to be out of work. If they cannot get a job in the formal sector, they will work in the informal sector. However, there is widespread underutilisation of labour. Underutilisation of labour means either that only part of available labour is utilised, or that labour is being used so unproductively that labourers can hardly make a living despite working very long hours.

Political instability and pervasive corruption

The nation-state in developing countries is weakly developed. There is a lack of national integration. Feelings of solidarity with a common national culture and society are not fully developed. Loyalties are primarily oriented to a specific area, tribe, ethnic group, family or religious community. Many developing countries are wracked by ethnic or religious conflicts, which are a threat to national unity. The rule of law is poorly developed. There are insufficient guarantees for human rights. The military play a disproportionately large role in politics. Corruption is rife and transparency of the rules and regulations is limited.

Environmental degradation

The pressure of population on natural resources results in severe environmental degradation. Pollution laws are lax and in countries where industry is growing rapidly, waste water, toxic substances and effluents are indiscriminately dumped into the environment. The concentration of populations in the burgeoning cities with inadequate sewerage and sanitation imposes heavy burdens on the environment, in particular on water resources. Expansion of agricultural land, logging and the use of fuelwood results in rapid deforestation. Environmental unfriendly types of industrial production and waste disposal are relocated to developing countries. Finally, population pressure, more intensive cultivation and fertilisation frequently result in land degradation, desalination and even desertification in large parts of the developing world (World Bank, 1992; World Bank-WDR, 2010).

Though the advanced economies together with China and India contribute most to global environmental problems such as CO_2 emissions and global warming, localised environmental degradation is typically concentrated in developing countries. Poverty contributes to environmental degradation – for instance, through the use of fuelwood – and the poor are most likely to be victims of environmental pollution (World Bank-WDR, 2000b).

Low levels of technology capabilities

Improvement of productive capacity in developing countries depends to a considerable extent on technological change, as is the case in the world economy at large (see Chapter 4). Worldwide, most technological change is still generated in the advanced economies. Developing countries continue to import much of their technology from abroad. The successful use of imported new technologies depends on the technological efforts and capabilities of individuals and organisations. New technologies have to be selected, adapted, implemented and further developed in mining, manufacturing, agriculture and services. In later stages of development indigenous design and development can substitute for imported technologies. However, many developing countries are presently still handicapped by very low levels of technological capabilities, due to inadequate schooling, training and experience (Lall, 1990; Romijn, 1999). Low levels of technological capabilities limit the rate of technological change and economic growth and keep developing countries dependent on outside knowledge and expertise.

Together these common characteristics provide a loose characterisation of what constitutes a 'developing country'. Of course, the degree to which these characteristics are present in different developing countries or regions varies. For example, in Tanzania or Ethiopia the share of agriculture in employment is much higher than in Brazil or Argentina; political instability and ethnic tension is more pronounced in Congo or Sudan than in Brazil Morocco. Technological capabilities are much more developed in Malaysia than in Tanzania. Besides, one should not forget that the differences between developing and economically advanced countries are also differences of degree. Still, the list of common characteristics in Box 1.5 does helps us in identifying the present-day developing countries and their problems.

1.10   The framework of proximate, intermediate and ultimate sources of growth and development

In this introductory chapter, we have argued for a broad approach to development which includes both economic and social dimensions. In this broader approach, we do however see a central role for economic growth. In the long run it is the growth of productive capacities that enables countries to fulfil a wider range of social needs of their citizens such as housing, nutrition, primary healthcare, education and social protection. Next, there is an ongoing interaction between economic and social developments in the wider development process, which will be systematically highlighted in this book.

In our analysis of development, we will make use of the framework of proximate, intermediate and ultimate sources of growth and development (Abramovitz, 1989a; Maddison, 1988; Rodrik, 2003; Szirmai, 2008, 2012b, 2013). The framework will be elaborated in Chapter 3 and will be briefly introduced here (see Figure 1.1).

At the proximate level, we analyse the *measurable economic determinants* of economic growth, such as labour supply (L), capital inputs (K), the supply of land and natural resources (R) and the efficiency with which these resources are used (e). We also look at the quality of labour (health, education) and the quality of capital (embodied technological change). Efficiency depends on a wide range of factors including structural change and technological advance.

At the proximate level we also look at the *actors* who are responsible for the supply of inputs. These actors include households, firms, inventors, government organisations, entrepreneurs or financial organisations. By including actors we can try to bridge the gap between macro- and micro-analysis. Thus, it is households that decide to invest time and energy in education or entrepreneurs that make investment decisions or promote technological change.

The ultimate sources of growth and development refer to more fundamental factors such as geographic conditions, institutional characteristics, culturally defined attitudes, historical developments, political conditions, class and power relationships, demographic trends and historical shocks. The ultimate sources illustrate that even if one limited oneself to the study of economic growth, a multidisciplinary approach is still required.

At the intermediate level, the framework highlights factors such as economic, technological and social policies and national and international demand conditions. On the one hand policies and demand conditions influence the proximate sources of growth, by providing incentives and constraints to economic actors. On the other hand, policies themselves are shaped and constrained by more ultimate social forces. The same holds for trends in demand, which on the one hand are shaped by long-run changes in technology, demography, culture and preferences and not least by historical shocks and economic crises. On the other hand they are affected by short-term fluctuations of economic activity at the proximate level.

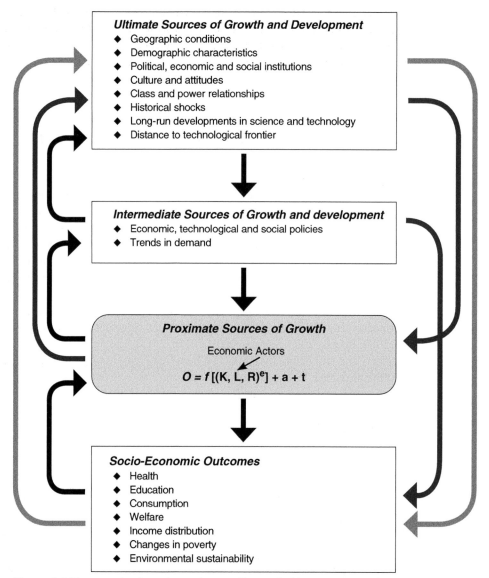

Figure 1.1 Framework of proximate, intermediate and ultimate sources of growth and development

Economic growth provides the resources which can potentially be invested in development: better health, better education, reduction of poverty, reduced inequality and environmental sustainability. Growth can be transformed into the socio-economic outcomes which are represented in the bottom box of Figure 1.1. Whether the development potential of growth of productive capacity is realised depends on the nature and effectiveness of socio-economic policies and the underlying ultimate characteristics of a society. In turn better health, high levels of education and lower levels of poverty feed back into the proximate sources of economic growth in the form of human capital.

The framework is summarised in Figure 1.1. The circular arrows illustrate the feedback loops operating at all levels. A more detailed discussion of the framework will be provided in Chapter 3. From Chapter 4 onwards, every chapter starts with a version of the figure, highlighting the place of the chapter within the larger framework.

Questions for review

1. Discuss the relationships between 'economic growth' and 'development'.
2. Is development conceivable without economic growth?
3. Why are Saudi Arabia and Kuwait still considered to be developing countries?
4. What are the main drawbacks of the use of GNP per capita as an indicator of economic development?
5. What are the most important dimensions along which developing countries differ from each other? Is the use of the term 'Third World' justified in the light of these differences?
6. Is the inequality between rich and poor countries increasing or decreasing over time?
7. To what extent is there an unsurmountable gap between rich and poor countries in the world economy?
8. What are the most important common problems and characteristics of developing countries?
9. Why is the degree of world income inequality measured at PPPs lower than that measured at exchange rates?
10. What are the main trends in global poverty, and how do these trends differ from region to region?

Further reading

Asian Drama by Gunnar Myrdal (1968) provides a useful discussion of the value laden nature of the concept of development. In his classic study, *The Theory of Economic Growth* (Lewis, 1950), Arthur Lewis gives an excellent early treatment of the desirability of growth and development. An influential article by Dudley Seers on the *Meaning of Development* (Seers, 1979) criticises narrow post-war concepts of development. His prerequisites for development include criteria such as poverty reduction, employment creation and equality. In *Development as Freedom*, Amartya Sen (1999) defines development as an expansion of substantive freedoms. Critical perspectives on the concept of development are provided by Peter Bauer in *Dissent on Development* (Bauer, 1976), and Deepak Lal in the *Poverty of Development Economics* (Lall, 2000). Important sources on global inequality are *Worlds Apart. Measuring International and Global Inequality* by Branco Milanović (2005), and a series of papers by Chen and Ravallion on poverty lines (e.g. Chen and Ravallion, 2010). The approach of the Millennium Development goals is explained in Jeffrey Sachs, *The End of Poverty* (Sachs, 2005). The plight of the poorest countries is brilliantly analysed by Paul Collier in *the Bottom Billion* (Collier, 2007).

An important source of information for students of development is the *WDR* published every year by the World Bank. Each issue focuses on a different topic, such as population growth, poverty, institution building, human capital, climate change or jobs. The statistical annex of the

WDR presents a wide range of development indicators, available online at World Bank, *World Development Indicators*, http://data.worldbank.org/data-catalog/world-development-indicators. The UNDP publishes the annual *HDR*, with a wide range of social indicators (for instance UNDP, 2009). This report includes the Human Development Index (HDI), which ranks countries on a combination of economic and social indicators.

A valuable compendium of original articles on many aspects of development is the six-volume *Handbook of Development Economics* edited by Chenery, Srinivasan and Behrman, Schultz and Strauss, Rodrik and Rosenzweig, published between 1988 and 2010. Important journals on development include *World Development*, the *World Bank Research Observer,* the *Journal of Development Economics, Economic Development and Cultural Change,* the *Journal of Development Studies, Development and Change, the Review of Development Economics, the Journal of International Development* and *Oxford Development Studies.*

2 Development of the international economic order, 1450–2015

The differences in income levels, which characterise the present-day international economic order, are not self-evident. In the past these differences used to be much smaller. Around 1500 by far the greater part of world population made its living in agriculture. Although some countries were richer than others, most people in most countries lived close to subsistence levels. The distribution of world income by region was therefore relatively equal (Bairoch, 1980; Cipolla, 1981: 220; Clark, 2007; Maddison 2001). In contrast, in the year 2012, the average income per capita in the thirty-five richest countries was no less than 35 times that in the thirty-five poorest countries in PPP dollars (see Table 1.1, p. 16).

How did the present diversity of levels of economic development and welfare in the world economy come about? In order to examine possible answers to this question, this chapter will offer a rough outline of the history of European expansion and the development of the international economic order associated with it.

In the framework of proximate and ultimate causality, this chapter focuses on the ultimate factors influencing growth and development, namely the role of the international economic and political order.

2.1 International economic order

Instead of presenting a formal definition of the slippery concept of international economic order, Box 2.1 identifies some of its important characteristics (Goldin and Reinert, 2012; Lewis, 1978b; Maddison, 1985, 1989; Streeten, 1984).

2.2 Economic breakthrough and external expansion from Western Europe

Since the middle of the fifteenth century, Western Europe has experienced a dual process of internal economic growth and external economic and political expansion. This process of development is unique in two respects. First, in a limited part of the world the age-old vicious circle of struggle for survival at near-subsistence level was broken. Second, the European expansion led to the formation of a world economy in which all countries and regions in the world are interrelated in networks of interdependence. Both statements are in need of clarification and qualification.

BOX 2.1 : **Characteristics of international economic orders**

- **Flows of goods** (final products, capital goods, primary products, semi-finished goods and services).
- **Financial flows** (investments, loans, transfer payments, levies and taxes).
- **Flows of people** (voluntary migration, indentured labour, slave trade, migrant labour).
- **Flows of knowledge** (diffusion of science, knowledge, information and technology).

Other important characteristics of the international economic order include:

- The **intensity of the economic relationships** between the various regions which together form the international economic order. Trade flows, for example, were small until the second half of the nineteenth century (Lewis, 1978b). The different parts of the world economy were not yet closely related.
- **Relations of dependence between countries and regions**. Economic relationships create mutual interdependence. However, some areas are more dependent than others. Dependence on advanced economies is a problem for developing countries.
- The **institutional framework** of the economic and political relations between countries and regions. Is it an area under direct political domination as a result of colonial rule or is it being influenced indirectly through foreign economic interests? Is the trade regime characterised by free trade or protectionism? What is the role of international organisations and international treaties?
- **Differential patterns of growth and stagnation** in various parts of the world economy which together make up the international economic order.
- The **size of the income gaps** between countries and regions.

2.2.1   Economic growth before 1500

In the first place, economic history prior to the sixteenth century is by no means exclusively a history of stagnation. It is the rule rather than the exception that, in the long run, production increased sufficiently to maintain a slowly growing population (Boserup, 1981; Jones, 1988; Maddison, 1982a). This is referred to as *extensive growth* (Reynolds, 1986: 7–10). There have also been periods in pre-modern history when total production grew faster than population, leading to growth of per capita income (*intensive growth*). This, for example, was the case in China under the Sung dynasty from the tenth to the thirteenth century.

Nevertheless, economic growth in the Western world since the sixteenth century is distinguished by the long duration of growth and its rapid and accelerating pace.[1] For example, per capita income in the rich capitalist countries is now at least nineteen times as

---

[1] Earlier estimates date the beginning of European growth from the second half of the fifteenth century onwards. According to estimates by Maddison (2001), European growth started even earlier, around the eleventh century, with no sharp acceleration around the year 1500. What is new after the fifteenth century, however, is the combination of long-term growth with external expansion.

high as in 1820 (Maddison, 2001). Already in the first part of the eighteenth century, on the eve of the Industrial Revolution, the average level of prosperity in countries like England and the Netherlands was substantially higher than in the rest of the world (Broadberry *et al.*, 2006; Landes, 1969, 1998; Maddison, 1983, 2001, 2007). Per capita incomes in Europe and the European offshoots were twice as high as in the non-European world.[2] Growth in Europe has led to an unprecedented and lasting increase in prosperity for great numbers of people, whereas in pre-modern societies malnutrition and starvation were never far round the corner, even in more prosperous periods and regions. Although economic development in Europe was often attended by impoverishment and disruption, in the long run the masses of the poor also profited from the increases in average per capita income. It is in this sense that one may speak of a breakthrough from the vicious cycle of poverty.

2.2.2   Pre-modern international orders

Second, the European expansion since the fifteenth century has been preceded by many other processes of political, economic and cultural expansion. To list but a few examples: the formation of the Hellenistic and the Roman empires, the long-lasting Chinese empire, the spread of the Arab/Islamic sphere of influence under the Umayyad and Abbasid caliphs from 760 to 1100, the Mongolian conquests between 1200 and 1350 which unified the Eurasian landmass and stretched from the Pacific to southern India, China, Russia and Central Europe, and the formation of the Ottoman empire between 1300 and 1550. Two international orders have been of key importance in the history of the development of the global economy (Findlay and O'Rourke, 2007): the Islamic International Order (750–110) and the *Pax Mongolica* (1200–1350).

Between 660 and 750 there was a rapid expansion of the Umayyad Caliphate to North Africa and Spain to the West and via Southwest Asia all the way to Persia in the East. In 751 the Arab armies defeated the Chinese army at the battle of Talas river, defining the future boundaries of Chinese and Islamic civilisations and spheres of influence. During the golden age of Islam from 750 to 1100 there was a flowering of science, technology and culture. The Islamic world was the hub that maintained trade relations with all other regions of the world order: Western Europe, Eastern Europe, Central Asia, South Asia, East Asia and Southeast Asia and Sub-Saharan Africa. Trade relations were accompanied by flows of knowledge and technology, including the Arabic numeral system which displaced Roman numerals in Europe.

Between 1200 and 1350, the Mongolian expansion initiated by Genghis Khan unified the whole of the Eurasian landmass. The Mongolian empire extended from China and Korea in the East to Russia and parts of Central and Eastern Europe in the West. In the Middle East and Central Asia, the Mongols gained control of Anatolia, Persia and Iraq. Though the Mongol expansion is usually seen as highly destructive, Findlay and O'Rourke argue that there was a *Pax Mongolica* which allowed for safe trade routes all the way from the Far East to the Far West. *The Pax Mongolica* also allowed for the migration of germs which later caused the Black Death in fourteenth-century Europe and the Middle East. According to Findlay and O'Rourke the Mongol expansion laid the foundations for later globalisation.

---

[2] For a dissenting view see Bairoch (1980), who argues that on the eve of the industrial revolution developing countries were about as rich as the presently affluent countries at that time. See also Frank (1998) and Pomeranz (2000).

Nevertheless, the process of European expansion is different from previous processes of expansion in at least three respects. First, the European process of expansion was characterised by the absence of political centralisation within the core area of Europe. Europe was a multitude of rival nation-states in the making, rather than an integrated empire. Second, the ties between the European countries and the rest of the world were not only political, but also economic (Braudel, 1978; Wallerstein, 1974). The European-based international economic order was not the first international economic order in history. Thus, both the Islamic and the Chinese empires formed the core of large and wide-ranging international trading systems (Abu-Lughod, 1989; Findlay and O'Rourke, 2007; Isichei, 1997; Klein, 1999). However, the European world system was characterised by a long-run extension and intensification of international economic relationships, which in time came to span the whole globe. From the 1490s onwards, the international economic order included the Americas and Australasia. Third, the process of interweaving the world economy and the world society, which was a consequence of the European expansion, is characterised by irreversibility. With the partial exception of the Chinese Empire, the history of all ancient empires, processes of expansion and world systems is characterised by rise and fall, centralisation followed by decentralisation, contraction and disintegration (Goldstone, 2002). The European expansion from the second half of the fifteenth century onwards, on the other hand, has resulted in a single global economic order of which the constituent parts have become permanently interdependent – for better or worse. They will remain closely interrelated long after the role of the West in the global order has come to its term and other leading centres of power and technology have emerged.[3]

2.2.3 China in the fourteenth and fifteenth centuries

If an early fourteenth-century observer could have taken a look at the twenty-first century, he would have been very surprised at the present position of Western countries in the world economy. Around the year 1400, little indicated that drastic economic breakthroughs and processes of external expansion would take place especially in Europe. From a military point of view it was by no means obvious that Europe would expand its sphere of influence in the world (Kennedy, 1989). The Moors were not driven out of Spain until 1492. Constantinople fell to the Ottoman Turks in 1453. Towards the end of the fifteenth century the Ottoman empire had occupied Greece, the Ionian Islands, Bosnia, Albania and large parts of the Balkan Peninsula. In 1526, the Ottomans conquered large parts of Hungary; in 1529 they besieged Vienna. In naval technology, European nations gained ascendency in the seventeenth century. But it was not until the late eighteenth and early nineteenth century that military superiority on land was gained over Asian regimes (Fieldhouse, 1982: 10; McNeill, 1989).

If our observer had ventured to predict the prospects of economic development in 1400, he would probably have put his money on the ancient and highly developed societies in Asia, the Middle East and, in particular, on China. In the fourteenth century, China was the

---

[3] In his book, *Global Economy in the Asian Age*, Frank (1998) has attacked the notion of Western exceptionalism. He reinterprets the period of Western expansion as an intermezzo between an earlier Asian age and the present rise of Asian economies. It is useful to emphasise the continuity between the European period and what has gone before. However, the rates of internal growth in Europe in combination with global expansion remain a unique phenomenon. Frank presents no new empirical evidence to contradict this view.

most advanced society in the world in terms of technology (Boserup, 1981; Castells, 2000; Elvin, 1973; Mokyr, 1990; Needham *et al.*, 1954). China knew firearms, blast furnaces, gunpowder, hydraulic clocks, magnetic compasses, advanced seagoing ships with moveable sails, navigation techniques, the arts of printing and paper making. Transportation technology was well developed; there were roads and extensive systems of canals and waterways. Money came into circulation at an early stage, along with market relationships. Intensive agriculture was practised, the techniques of which were recorded in handbooks (Perkins, 1969). Complicated irrigation systems were in use. In 1078 Sung China produced 150,000 tons of iron per year (Findlay and O'Rourke, 2007). By the twelfth century there was already mass production in manufacturing. Elvin (1973) estimates that in the thirteenth century some 20 per cent of the population lived in towns. There was a highly developed bureaucratic administrative system, which would much later serve as a model for the British civil service. China was the first country in the world to have a national system of education, with competitive examinations providing for entry into positions in the Mandarin bureaucracy. Nevertheless, China was not the first country to experience a major economic breakthrough and nor was it the country from which the rest of the world was penetrated. The penetration of world society started from an insignificant and relatively sparsely populated country in the southwest of Europe: Portugal (Wallerstein, 1974: 38 ff.).

It is fascinating to note that at the same time as Europeans set out upon their expeditions at the beginning of the fifteenth century, a similar process of expansion was already taking place from China. From 1405 to 1433 the famous eunuch admiral Cheng Ho undertook a series of expeditions which took the Chinese to the Indian Ocean, Java, Ceylon, Persia and even to the African east coast. However, after Cheng Ho died in 1433, these expeditions were stopped abruptly as a result of changes in Chinese policy. In 1435 shipbuilding was even prohibited by imperial decree. The Chinese fleet was dismantled, and overseas trade was discouraged as much as possible. By 1477 the logs of the naval expeditions had been confiscated, hidden, or burned. By 1500, the death penalty was imposed for building ships with more than two masts. The empire turned inward (Elvin, 1973; Jones, 1988; Kennedy, 1989; Lin, 1995; McNeill, 1989; Wallerstein, 1974). Traffic along the grand canal connecting North and South China replaced foreign exploration. Scientific and technological development faltered. The empirical and experimental attitude in science and technology was abandoned for a more mystical and contemplative set of attitudes (Elvin, 1973).

The Chinese economy, which had flourished until the middle of the fourteenth century, got caught up in a centuries-long process of stagnation lasting until the communist takeover in 1949. On the other hand, the expansion from Europe continued, filling the vacuum left by the discontinuation of the Chinese expansion. Portugal gave the initial impetus to the European penetration of the world and the gradual formation of a coherent world economy of which the constituent parts would become progressively ever more interrelated in the course of time.

2.3 Why expansion from Europe instead of from China?

10 Jan

These historical developments led Immanuel Wallerstein to pose a series of interesting questions which touch upon the very essence of development (Wallerstein, 1974: 36–63): why did the breakthrough of capitalism and the process of economic growth associated with it, take place in Europe? Why did the Chinese economy stagnate from the fourteenth century onwards despite the initial conditions that seemed so promising? Why was there a process of external European expansion, starting in the fifteenth century? Why did the external expansion of China come to a stop after 1433 and why did China develop in an inward-looking fashion?

Following Max Weber (1920a), Wallerstein seeks the answer to such questions in the difference between the centralised Chinese empire and the decentralised feudal system in medieval Europe, which would later generate strong national states and within which capitalist institutions and property rights could develop and flourish. Maintenance of an empire involves a multitude of military and administrative expenses, the burden of which may eventually stifle economic development – *imperial overstretch* in the terminology of Kennedy (1989). In the world economic system that developed in Europe after 1500, economic relations were more important than direct political control radiating from a single administrative centre. The European centre of this 'world system' gave rise to powerful national states in fierce competition with each other. These states offered support to enterprising groups and classes that contributed to internal economic development and external expansion. Landes (1969) points to two distinctive characteristics of European development, namely a pattern of political institutional and legal development that provided an especially effective basis for the operation of private economic systems and the high value placed upon the rational manipulation of the environment (see also North, 1990).

Wallerstein seeks the incentives for external European expansion in the crisis of feudalism from the fourteenth century onwards. This crisis offered motivations for expansion to several social groups: the nobility, whose traditional sources of revenue were threatened by the crisis; the rising middle classes; the state apparatus that considered external expansion as a source of revenue and prestige; and members of the new urban semi-proletariat who were available for work as soldiers and sailors.

Incentives for expansion, discussed by Wallerstein, include: the demand for gold, silver and precious metals; spices; food; fuels and raw materials; and the search for new sources of income and employment. Gold and silver was needed to pay for luxury imports from Asia such as jewels and spices. The need for food, fuels and raw materials stimulated expansion to the Mediterranean countries, the Atlantic islands, North and West Africa, Eastern Europe, the Russian steppes and Central Asia. Population growth led to a modest intensification of agriculture which involved the introduction of cash crops, cattle-breeding and horticulture (see Chapters 5 and 10). There was an increasing demand for corn imports from less densely populated areas. From the fourteenth century onwards England and the Netherlands imported corn from the Baltic and Mediterranean. Cultivation of sugar cane was the motivation for expansion towards the eastern Mediterranean and the Atlantic islands. The need for labour for sugar cane processing led to the emergence of the Atlantic slave trade (Klein, 1999). Owing to increasing deforestation, there was a shortage of wood for fuel and for shipbuilding. The textile industry required materials such as pigment and gum.

All these factors played a part in the development of various European states. But several factors were specific to Portugal. According to Wallerstein, they may explain why expansion originated from there. He mentions, for example, the absence of alternative options for the Portuguese nobility, Portugal's location by the sea, its previous experience with long-distance trade, the availability of capital from the Italian city-states and the strength and stability of the state machinery. There was a convergence of interests. The sovereign, the nobility, the commercial middle classes and the urban semi-proletariat that had fled the countryside all benefited from external expansion.

To explain the contrast between Chinese inward-looking development and European expansionism, Wallerstein points to the absence of a similar convergence of interests in China, the intensification of food production and the political characteristics of a centralised Chinese empire.

The absence of converging interests

In China, no consensus existed with respect to the benefits of external expansion. The Confucian mandarins in the state bureaucracy opposed the eunuch admirals whose interests lay in expansion. The central bureaucracy had a great dislike for the expense involved in these foreign expeditions. They preferred to invest in major fortifications against invasions from the North and canals. In due course, the emperor sided with the central bureaucracy. The lack of a colonising mission also played a part. In the Chinese world view China was the centre of the world, and the Chinese empire already contained everything of importance in the world. The Chinese were not interested in communication with barbarians, including barbarians from faraway Europe. This world view was to play an important role until the nineteenth century. It is often put forward as an explanation for the half-heartedness of Chinese attempts at modernisation in the face of Western challenges in the nineteenth century.

Intensification of food production

In Europe, increasing population density led to a pattern of agriculture in which more densely populated areas concentrated on cattle farming, horticulture and cash crops, while importing corn from less densely populated areas in Eastern Europe. Compared to crop production, cattle farming is a less efficient way of producing calories. It is only feasible if foodstuffs can be imported from elsewhere (Boserup, 1981). Population growth provided an impulse for external expansion for the purposes of importing corn from less densely populated peripheral regions in the Baltic and Eastern Europe. Subsequently, the availability of animal power in Europe, lacking in China, was a stimulus to further economic development.

In southeastern China an extremely labour-intensive type of agriculture developed causing a shortage of labour (Perkins, 1969). The high level of agricultural and irrigational technology allowed for intensive agriculture – in particular cultivation of rice. The increasing demand for labour was an impediment to external expansion.

Political centralisation

After the fall of the Roman empire, a highly decentralised feudal system came into being in Europe (Elias, 1969b; Maddison, 2001; Wolf, 1982).[4] Money played a relatively small part in this feudal economy, which stagnated economically up until the eleventh century. Economic entities were highly self-sufficient. The feudal system, with its landowners living on the surplus of agricultural production, was inimical to the rising groups based on trade

---

[4] It may be useful to remind readers that European feudalism was not some sort of primitive initial condition. It came into being after the dissolution of a centralised empire.

and industry. In Europe, capitalism had to struggle for survival, which accounts for its strength in later periods. Capitalist activities were centred in the cities, which managed to preserve their autonomy due to the decentralised nature of the feudal system. If political pressure became too severe in one region, entrepreneurs and merchants could always move to other places where taxes were lower and economic activities less constrained (McNeill, 1989).

Paradoxically, in the long term the decentralised feudal system gave birth to the highly centralised states of Europe. Some political centres started dominating surrounding regions and, once processes of centralisation were well under way, the feudal mystique was transferred to the central authorities. The mystique surrounding power strengthened the centralising tendencies in the emerging absolute monarchies. We should emphasise here that the tendencies towards centralisation in Europe did not result in the rise of another centralised empire, but rather in a multitude of internally highly centralised nation-states competing with one another. In this environment the emerging states were also dependent on the support offered them by the financial and commercial bourgeoisie, which in turn succeeded in consolidating its position and independence. Revenues from external expansion were also crucial to competitive survival of states (Findlay and O'Rourke, 2007).

Competition between states also contributed to the rapid development of military technology. Technological or organisational innovations were quickly adopted by other states. In the centralised Chinese, Indian and Ottoman empires the spread of firearms and cannon led to the strengthening of central authorities. But the monopolisation of technology by these central authorities hampered further technological development. From the middle of the seventeenth century onwards this would result in an increasing military supremacy of the Western powers in comparison with the Asian empires, initially in naval technology, later in land-based technology (Kennedy, 1989; McNeill, 1989).

Justin Yifu Lin (1995) introduces another interesting explanation of Chinese stagnation, namely the role of classical literary training as prerequisite for entry into the mandarin bureaucracy. This created a disincentive for investments in human capital of the kind required for 'modern' scientific research. As a result, China failed to make the transition from traditional experience-based science and technology to modern mathematically and experimentally based science. 'Therefore, despite her early lead in scientific achievement, China failed to have an indigenous scientific revolution' (Lin, 1995: 285).

The Roman empire fell apart in the fifth century in Western Europe in a process of feudalisation. The Chinese empire survived major periods of upheaval and succeeded in maintaining its continuity for over two thousand years (Elvin, 1973). Chinese feudal rulers lived off the land and used serfs as foot soldiers in their military rivalries. Time and again they tried to assert their independence from central authorities. But the central authorities successfully managed to resist decentralising tendencies. Instead of a feudal structure, China developed a *prebendal structure* (Weber, 1920b) in which the central authorities appointed 'officials' to administer far-off regions. These officials did not earn a salary but had to live off the revenues collected in their region. Naturally, there were constant tendencies towards feudalisation and autonomy, with officials trying to turn their positions into hereditary ones. These tendencies, however, were countered by the central authorities, who developed a system of regularly transferring officials in order to weaken the ties between them and the regions they had to manage. The emperor and the central authorities succeeded in maintaining a loose form of imperial centralisation.

The instinct of an imperial power is to defend its territory. 'This drains attention, energy and profits which could be invested in capital development' (Wallerstein, 1974: 60). In the long term, centralisation will be at the expense of external expansion. All energy is frittered away in the construction of defensive fortifications like the great Chinese Wall. Thus decentralisation was one of the preconditions for expansion in Europe, which was lacking in China. European expansion was furthered by the competition between states. '[W]hen the Turks advanced in the east, there was no emperor to recall the Portuguese expeditions' (Wallerstein, 1974: 70). The degree of centralisation in the Chinese Empire was also quite low in comparison with the centralisation of the later European nation-states. The absence of a feudal mystique in prebendalism made it easier to resist tendencies towards centralisation around the person of an absolute ruler.

Initially, the contractual nature of prebendalism was conducive to the development of capitalist groups and activities. However, in part because of this, capitalist tendencies in China did not unfold as fully as they did in Europe, where the rising middle classes had to wage a fierce struggle for survival. As opposed to European cities, which developed into independent and autonomous enclaves in feudal society with their own municipal rights, Chinese cities never became completely independent from the central authorities. Capitalist impulses were thus smothered in a non-feudal bureaucratic environment which was initially far from hostile to capitalist impulses. In centralised empires there was an irresistible tendency to tax and regulate economic activities in order to cover the expenses of the central administrative apparatus (Jones, 1988).

Of course, it is not possible to discuss the voluminous literature on these classical questions adequately in a nutshell.[5] But the very posing of such questions advances our understanding of the sources of development and stagnation in the very long term.

2.4 European expansion in the world

Western expansion in the world proceeded unevenly. Some areas were penetrated very early, others much later; some areas regained their independence long before colonisation even reached other parts of the world.

In his standard work on the history of European colonisation, Fieldhouse distinguishes between *settlement colonies* and *colonies of occupation* (Fieldhouse, 1982). Settlement colonies involve immigrants from the mother country settling permanently in a colony; these immigrants attempt to build a society resembling as much as possible the society in their country of origin. Settlement colonies can be subdivided into 'pure' settlement colonies, 'mixed' colonies and 'plantation' colonies. In 'pure' settlement colonies such as the USA, Canada and Australia the original inhabitants with pastoral or hunting and gathering modes of production – Indians, Aborigines – were completely crowded out and destroyed by immigrants from Europe who built another European society in the new world and imported European institutions. In 'mixed' colonies (for example, the Spanish colonies in Mexico and Peru) a substantial minority of Europeans settled in the colony, trying to absorb the local population. In 'plantation' colonies a tiny minority of Europeans settled

---

[5] An important source for these paragraphs was Wallerstein (1974), who in turn offers a excellent synthesis of the earlier literature on this subject. A brilliant recent synthesis is offered by Findlay and O'Rourke (2007).

permanently; they imported slave labour from elsewhere in order to establish a plantation economy (e.g. the Portuguese in Brazil).

Colonies of occupation are characterised by an extremely small elite of foreign colonial officials sent out to rule over native inhabitants with a completely different language and culture.

Finally, apart from settlement colonies and colonies of occupation the Europeans also founded many trading posts all over the world. Types of colonies and phases of expansion and contraction are summarised in Box 2.2.

BOX 2.2 Western expansion and contraction

Types of colonisation
Colonies of settlement

- Pure colonies of settlement (e.g. USA)
- Mixed colonies of settlement (e.g. Mexico)
- Plantation colonies (e.g. Brazil)

Colonies of occupation (e.g. India, Indonesia, Vietnam)
Trading posts

Phases of expansion and contraction
1400–1815: *first wave of expansion*

- Colonies of settlement in the Americas
- Trading posts in Africa and Asia

1776–1824: *first wave of decolonisation in North and South America*
1815–1913: *second wave of expansion*
Colonies of occupation in Africa, Asia and the Middle East
1930–80: *Second wave of decolonisation*
The second wave of decolonisation starts in the Middle East in 1930 and accelerates after 1945.

Before the beginning of the nineteenth century, European expansion in Africa and Asia primarily took the form of the establishment of trading posts by the Portuguese, the Dutch and the British. On the American continent the Spanish, the Portuguese, the British, the French and the Dutch founded settlement colonies. Between 1776 and 1824 almost all the colonies in the Americas gained their independence. The second phase of the European expansion started around 1815 after the Napoleonic Wars and was directed towards Asia and later also towards Africa. During this period the colonies that were carved out were mainly colonies of occupation, where alien peoples were dominated by colonial rulers whose prime loyalties lay in their faraway homelands.

The type of colonisation is influenced by two major factors: settler mortality and military technology. The higher the settler mortality the less likely the colonisers were to establish colonies of settlement (Acemoglu, Johnson and Robinson, 2001). The stronger the military technology of the indigenous societies, the less likely were the Europeans to move beyond coastal enclaves. Acemoglu *et al.* argue that the most extractive institutions were imposed on colonised areas with lowest degrees of settlement.[6]

2.4.1   Types of international economic orders

Western expansion has led to economic relations between the Western and the non-Western world, each of which affected non-Western countries in different ways. Following Maddison, one can distinguish six international economic orders since 1500 (Maddison, 1982b, 1983, 1985, 1989): conquest imperialism; merchant capitalism; free trade imperialism; conflict and autarky 1913–50; the post-war golden age; and the economic order since the 1973 oil crisis. Each order is characterised by a specific kind of relationship between the rich Western countries and developing countries. These orders are ordered in chronological sequence, but different orders can overlap (see Box 2.3). The characteristics of the six orders will only be briefly touched upon here. They will be discussed in more detail later in this chapter and elsewhere in this book.

BOX 2.3 : **Types of international economic orders**

1. **Conquest imperialism**
   Spain in Latin America: 1500–1820
2. **Merchant capitalism**
   Portugal in Brazil: 1500–1870
   The Netherlands in Indonesia: 1600–1949
   The UK in India: 1850s–1946
   Beginning of period of capitalist accumulation and development: 1820
3. **Free trade imperialism: 1870–1913**
4. **Defensive autarky: 1913–50**
5. **The golden age of growth: 1950–73**
6. **Differential patterns of growth and stagnation: 1973–2015**

In *conquest imperialism* the relations between Western countries and the colonies are characterised both by straightforward plundering of the colonised areas' resources and by a transfer of economic surpluses by means of taxation and tribute payments. Such destructive relations existed, for example, between Spain and Mexico from 1500 to 1820. 1521~1821

Merchant capitalism is characterised by the European powers' search for monopolistic profits on the production and export of luxury goods from the penetrated areas. Where Western expansion resulted in direct colonial domination, taxation, in addition to monopolistic profits, served to transfer economic surpluses to Western countries. These relations can

---

[6] In their frequently cited article, Acemoglu *et al.* (2001) focus on settler mortality to the exclusion of all other factors such as military technology and the strength of indigenous institutions.

be found in the areas penetrated by the Portuguese, the French, the Dutch and the British from 1500 to 1870.

The international order of *free trade imperialism* reached maturity in the period 1870–1913 and is characterised by far-reaching liberalisation of international trade. In developing countries such liberalisation was imposed by force or by the threat of force. During this period the typical colonial pattern of international trade emerged, in which developing countries exported primary products to the rich industrialised countries and the industrialised countries exported finished manufactured goods to developing countries.

Between 1913 and 1950 two world wars and an economic depression took place. In this period of *defensive autarky* free trade was abandoned, and protectionism prevailed. Each country tried to isolate itself from the consequences of the economic crisis at the expense of its trading partners. Partly as a result of this, the volume of world trade fell off, and investment in developing countries decreased dramatically. Economic growth stagnated in both rich countries and developing countries most involved in international trade. In many colonies, policy attempts to cope with the economic crisis were hampered by colonial constraints.

During the *post-war golden age* from 1950 to 1973 there was an increase in per capita income in rich as well as in developing countries. Indeed, per capita income grew more rapidly than ever before. International trade was highly liberalised, though manufacturing sectors in developing countries remained highly protected. The volume of international trade increased sharply, as did international capital flows. Developing countries received a considerable net inflow of capital consisting of direct investments, loans and development aid.

Between 1820 and 1973 the world economy moved in phase, with accelerations in the rich countries being mirrored in accelerations in the developing world. Since the oil crisis of 1973, the growth of the world economy as a whole has slowed down and differences between patterns of economic performance in various parts of the world have increased. We therefore refer to this period as a period of *differential patterns of growth and stagnation*. There were recurrent major crises which affected different regions in very different ways. After 1982, economic growth in Latin America stagnated for ten years in the aftermath of the debt crisis. In some developing countries the debt crisis resulted in a substantial net capital outflow to the rich countries. In Sub-Saharan Africa a long period of economic stagnation followed lasting from 1973 till 2000, with substantial recovery only after 2000. In major Asian economies growth continued to be rapid from 1973 onwards and there was substantial catch-up relative to the advanced economies. In 1997 Asian growth was interrupted by a major financial crisis – the Asian financial crisis – which dramatically affected real growth rates in the short run. The Asian crisis emphasised the vulnerability of developing economies to massive global inflows and outflows of capital. But the effects of the Asian crisis were not lasting and most countries recovered quickly. The global financial crisis of 2008 hit hardest in the Western countries, where growth turned sharply negative in 2009. Growth in developing countries in Africa, Latin America and Asia was much less affected by this crisis. In the post-1973 period, there were tendencies towards revival of protectionism but on the whole the principles of free trade have prevailed, though they are presently under severe pressure in the aftermath of the crisis of 2008–9.

In the following sections the historical developments in international economic relations will be discussed in more detail, combining the discussion of economic orders with that of colonial expansion and contraction.

2.4.2 The first wave of expansion, 1400–1815

In the fifteenth and sixteenth centuries Portugal and Spain initiated the first wave of expansion directed towards Africa, Asia and Latin America. The Portuguese were the pioneers. They started to found trading posts and bases along the African west coast from 1415 onwards and along the African east coast in India and the Far East from the late fifteenth century onwards. From these trading posts luxury goods such as gold, ivory, pepper and spices were shipped to Europe. From the second half of the fifteenth century African slaves were transported to sugar plantations on the Atlantic islands and later to plantations in the Caribbean and the American continent. There was no direct colonial rule. Native societies, political systems and the economy were initially left undisturbed. Especially in Asia, the impact of Western penetration would be limited for quite some time. From the beginning of the sixteenth century onwards the Dutch pushed the Portuguese out of the Far East; however, the impact of Dutch presence on local societies was initially also rather limited.

The Spanish colonisation of Latin America from the late fifteenth century onwards was of an extremely destructive nature. Initially, straightforward plunder of gold and silver treasures was predominant. Later, large estates were created for the *conquistadores,* on which the Indians were forced to work. A major part of the economic surplus was transferred to Spain by means of taxation and tribute payments. The ancient Aztec and Inca civilisations were completely erased. Catholicism was imposed by force. The demographic consequences of the Spanish colonisation were disastrous. The Indian population was exposed to new germs against which it had no natural immunity (Diamond, 1998).[7] As a result of wars, heavy labour in mines and on plantations and especially contagious diseases, the original population was decimated (Furtado, 1976).

Present-day Brazil was primarily colonised by the Portuguese after its discovery in 1500 by Pedro Cabral.[8] The Portuguese discovered an extremely sparsely populated area. They founded plantations and initiated exports of wood and other primary products. The demand for labour was met by African slave imports. Portuguese colonialism very much focused on making monopolistic profits through trade. In comparison to Spanish colonialism, which was actually a form of organised plunder, Portuguese colonialism was less destructive since new technologies and products were introduced as well. However, neither the slaves nor the original Indian inhabitants benefited much from these new technologies. After an initial increase in per capita production as a result of the introduction of a plantation economy based on slave labour into a society of hunters and gatherers, per capita income remained unchanged for three centuries (Maddison, 1985).

Slaves were also imported to Spanish colonies, where the Indian population proved to be unwilling or unsuited to do the heavy work in mines and on plantations. In the nineteenth century the demand for labour in Latin America was also met by the recruitment of indentured labourers from China, India and Java.

---

[7] One might even argue that the migration of germs is a fifth characteristic of international economic orders, in addition to the four dimensions discussed above: people flows, money flows, goods flows and knowledge flows (see McNeill, 1976).

[8] For a brief period in the seventeenth century, the Dutch also played an important role in Brazil. However, their role had been played out by 1655.

The economic history of Latin America is the model for theories of exploitation and underdevelopment; in this model the negative effects of colonialism, neocolonialism and capitalist exploitation account for the backwardness of the poor countries. Not only had economic surpluses been transferred to Europe for centuries, but also regressive social institutions such as landlordism and slavery were introduced, which were to form obstacles to economic development long after political independence had been achieved. That exploitation has played an important part in the development of Latin America is beyond dispute. There is, however, a debate on the degree to which all present-day economic problems can be explained by adverse colonial experiences and postcolonial foreign influences.

Marxist and radical theorists tend to explain the successful economic development of Western Europe from the perspective of colonial exploitation. It is suggested that gold and silver from Latin America, colonial taxation, monopolistic profits from trade and the revenues of the slave trade figured decisively in the 'original accumulation' which was a prerequisite for the Western European economic breakthrough in later years (Baran, 1957; Williams, 1964). This theory, however, is not very tenable. Domestic savings, advances in knowledge and technology and a gradual increase in productivity in handicrafts and agriculture have been of more importance to European development than external plunder, taxation and foreign profits (Jones, 1988; Landes, 1969; Maddison, 1982a, 1995, 2001; North and Thomas, 1973). Colonial exploitation undoubtedly contributed to Western prosperity and growth. But the key question is whether economic surpluses and savings could be transformed into productive investments (Wolf, 1982: 120). Modern quantitative historical research supports the view of David Landes that 'Western Europe was already rich before the Industrial Revolution – rich by comparison with other parts of the world of that day. This wealth was the product of centuries of slow accumulation, based in turn on investment, the appropriation of extra-European resources and labour, and substantial technological progress, not only in the production of material goods but in the organisation and financing of their exchange and distribution' (Landes, 1969: 13–14).[9] Distinctive characteristics of European development include a pattern of political institutional and legal development (property rights) that provided an especially effective basis for the operation of private economic systems. Also of importance were the European receptivity to new technologies and the capacity to assimilate them, a capacity as important as inventiveness itself (Rosenberg, 1982).

It is consistent with this view that the countries that first profited from colonial revenues and plunder – Spain and Portugal – were not capable of converting economic surpluses into productive domestic investments. After the sixteenth century, their role soon came to an end.

In the seventeenth century, economic and political supremacy shifted from southwestern Europe to northwestern Europe. In terms of technological capacity as indicated by per capita income, the Netherlands was the leading economy. For a short period of time the Dutch republic was also the dominant power in world politics (Israel, 1995). The Dutch penetrated Indonesia where they ousted the Portuguese and established trade monopolies. Dutch expansion was of a mercantilist nature. They did not strive for direct colonial domination but rather for lucrative trade by means of the Dutch East India Company,

---

[9] For a dissenting view see Bairoch and Levy-Leboyer (1981). Bairoch and his associates argue that income levels before the industrial revolution are rather similar and that increase in income levels since then is due to exploitation of developing countries.

founded in 1602. The Dutch also penetrated into the western hemisphere. They founded settlement colonies in North and South America and in the Caribbean.

In addition to the Dutch republic, France and England also started colonising North America and the Caribbean in the seventeenth century. In the Caribbean the colonial powers primarily founded plantation economies where sugar was grown with slave labour.

Dutch colonisation in Brazil was not granted a long life. It came to an end in 1665. On the North American continent the Dutch had already been ousted by the British in 1667, exchanging New Amsterdam for Suriname. The French and the British continued to compete for control over North America. In the eighteenth century this conflict resulted in a series of Anglo-French wars from which the British arose as the dominant power on the North American continent. At the end of the Seven Years' War in 1763 the role of France in North America had come to an end. Today only Francophone Quebec reminds one of the French expansion in this part of the world.

In the course of the eighteenth century the leading economic and technological position of the Netherlands was taken over by Great Britain. In the second half of the century rapid industrialisation took place in Great Britain, often referred to by the dramatic term 'Industrial Revolution'.[10] In the early nineteenth century the Netherlands were outdistanced by England in terms of per capita production (Maddison, 2001, Table B-21). The other Western European countries became the followers of British leadership, profiting from diffusion of technology from the lead country.

In the eighteenth century the British penetration into India gathered momentum. In the seventeenth century the British had already founded trading posts and cities along the Indian coastline. Trade was controlled by the British East India Company, founded in 1600. Until the early eighteenth century India was still a powerful Asian empire, somewhat past its prime after a glorious flowering in the sixteenth century under Akbar (1556–1605). In 1757 Bengal was conquered after the battle at Plassey and was henceforth governed by the East India Company as a satrapy. The French, who penetrated into India at the same time as the British, were eclipsed. However, there still was no question of direct colonial control over the entire Indian subcontinent.

From the late eighteenth century onwards Australia was penetrated by the British, starting with the foundation of a penal colony in Sydney in 1788. Convicts were soon followed by voluntary migrants who would eventually turn Australia into a prosperous settlement colony like the USA and Canada, once again at the expense of the indigenous inhabitants.

As can be seen above, the patterns of penetration in various parts of the world differ widely during the first phase of European expansion (Fieldhouse, 1982). In Asia the Europeans were faced with ancient established civilisations that were initially neither technologically nor militarily inferior to the Europeans. The Europeans had the advantage at sea; but on land they were initially not stronger than their opponents. The Europeans were concentrated in enclaves along the coasts. Their influence on the native society was relatively unimportant. On the North American continent the hunting and gathering Indian peoples were totally unable to withstand the European onslaught. The same holds for the large Indian civilisations in Latin America that succumbed to the force of small numbers of

---

[10] The term 'Industrial Revolution' tends to misrepresent the gradual nature of the long-term increase in economic productivity.

determined and unscrupulous Spaniards and European germs against which they had no resistance. European immigrants settled on the American continent. The language and culture of their countries of origin would leave a lasting imprint on the development of colonial and postcolonial society. On the African continent there were initially no permanent settlements with the exception of Cape Colony and Angola. None of the African empires – not even the most developed ones like Benin, Mali or Songhai in West Africa – were militarily a match for the European intruders. However, climate, disease and severe conditions of life were obstacles to permanent European settlement (Acemoglu *et al.*, 2001; Isichei, 1997). Trading posts predominated.

2.4.3 The first wave of decolonisation

Decolonisation is not a recent phenomenon. The process of Western expansion would continue in many parts of the world during the nineteenth century, but in other areas direct European political control was on the decline. The British colonies in America declared their independence in 1776 and formed the United States of America. The Napoleonic Wars sounded the death knell for Iberian colonialism. From 1814 to 1824 all Spanish colonies on the American continent became independent. Brazil declared its independence in 1822, although a son of the Portuguese king was crowned as emperor.

The decolonisation of the English-speaking colonies in Australia, Canada, New Zealand and South Africa took place more gradually. Traditionally, English colonies used to have virtual autonomy with respect to their mother country. From the middle of the nineteenth century onwards this autonomy was gradually transformed into a *de facto* independence within the framework of the British Commonwealth. The attainment of formal independence can best be dated *circa* 1931 when a statute was passed stating that dominions were no longer subject to decisions of the British parliament.

2.4.4 The second phase of European expansion, 1815–1913

The nineteenth century was the apex of Western expansion and Western political, economic, military and cultural dominance. Per capita production increased sharply (Maddison, 1982a) among other things owing to a rapid increase in the amount of capital goods per head of population and acceleration of technological progress. The differences in the levels of prosperity between the rich and developing countries increased dramatically. Industrialisation also consolidated the Western military lead. Formerly powerful empires in Asia and the Middle East were now no longer a match for the Western powers. Western expansion progressed more rapidly than ever before. In 1800 Europe, together with its overseas possessions and former colonies, controlled 55 per cent of the surface of the earth. By 1878 this percentage had risen to 67 per cent and by 1914 to 84.4 per cent (Fieldhouse, 1982: 178).

The political and economic relationships between the colonial powers and the colonised areas were intensified. In India, Indonesia and other Asian countries indirect influence through commercial relations was transformed into formal political domination of colonies of occupation by the mother countries. The consolidation of colonial domination was attended by a series of military conflicts such as the Indian Mutiny in 1857 and the Diponegoro rebellion on Java (1825–30).

Colonies founded by white migrants in Canada, South Africa, Australia and New Zealand expanded inland at the expense of the native inhabitants. Economic growth in the USA went hand in hand with strong expansionist tendencies. This did not lead to the founding of new colonies, but rather to the annexation of vast Spanish-speaking areas which became states in the American union. In the mid nineteenth century tsarist Russia expanded eastward to Central Asia and the Far East.[11] France, which had an insignificant colonial empire before the nineteenth century, penetrated into North Africa and Indochina. Algiers was conquered in 1830, and in the fifty years that followed the whole of Algeria was colonised. The French colonisation of Indochina in the second half of the nineteenth century started in 1859 with the occupation of Saigon on the Mekong Delta. Between 1829 and 1914 the far-flung Ottoman empire, heir to the medieval Arab caliphates and the Mameluk empire, contracted. The Ottomans had to recognise the southern and southeastern European Balkan States of Albania, Bulgaria, Greece, Romania and Serbia as independent states.

For the better part of the nineteenth century Great Britain was the leading world power economically, politically and technologically. In Great Britain industrialisation had proceeded furthest and British maritime power was undisputed until the 1890s. As a result of British dominance there were few conflicts between colonial powers. This was the era of *Pax Britannica*.

After 1830, free trade became predominant in English international trade policy. Tariff rates declined steadily in the course of the century, reaching very low levels after 1870. Colonial monopolies on trade were abolished. Colonies could now also trade with countries other than their mother country. England lowered numerous tariffs on imports from colonies. But it also demanded free access for its industrial exports to both colonial and non-colonial markets. These exports competed with handicraft and infant industrial production in developing countries and retarded industrialisation outside Europe. The case of the Indian textile industry is frequently mentioned as an example of the negative effects of colonial rule on industrialisation.

Establishing free trade involved considerable force and coercion. By means of gunboat diplomacy monarchs and rulers, accustomed to financing their expenditures through royal monopolies on trade, were forced to lower tariffs and to open up their countries to Western exports. Maddison has used the term 'free trade imperialism' to describe the economic order of 1870–1913 (Maddison, 1985). Furthermore, Great Britain tried to impede industrialisation in the colonies wherever her influence reached.

Not all colonial powers immediately adopted the policy of free trade. In Java, the Dutch governor Van den Bosch introduced the 'culture system' in 1830. In this system the key element was compulsory production of cash crops for the benefit of the colonial rulers. This 'culture system' may be considered as a nineteenth-century continuation of the international economic order of merchant capitalism.

Around 1890 the USA, once a British colony, took the economic and technological lead and has held that position ever since. It innovated in standardised industrial production for mass markets. Western Europe, Australia, Canada, New Zealand and Japan became the followers in the race for technological and economic development. It was not until after the

---

[11] The conquest of Siberia dates back to the late sixteenth century (1580–1639). But until the nineteenth century Siberia remained a sparsely populated and isolated area. Between 1801 and 1913 some 7 million settlers moved from European Russia to Siberia. The Trans-Siberian railway was constructed between 1891 and 1913 and served to integrate Siberia into Russia.

Second World War that the USA emerged as the dominant power in world politics. However, it did claim the right to intervene in Latin American affairs as early as the nineteenth century. In 1823 the Monroe Doctrine proscribed any intervention by powers other than the USA on the entire American continent.

By the end of the nineteenth century all European powers rushed to obtain new colonies. In doing so, they became more and more entangled in fierce rivalries. Until then, the African continent had hardly been penetrated by white people. Now it was rapidly colonised in what has come to be known as the 'scramble for Africa' (Davidson, 1992). At international conferences, the colonial powers drew straight lines on the map in order to demarcate their possessions. These artificial borders disregarded geographical characteristics and ethnic, cultural and historical dividing lines. Much of the present-day instability of African states has to do with the arbitrariness of these colonial borders (see Chapter 11).

2.4.5 The period 1870–1913

The abolition of forced cash crop production in the Indonesian 'culture system' in 1870 marked the demise of the international economic order based on monopolistic trade relations. Free trade became the predominant characteristic of the international economic order. Since the mid nineteenth century developing countries had opened their borders to international trade – at times under threat of military force. Leading countries such as England, France and the Netherlands had also lowered their tariff rates on imports.

From 1870 to 1913 economic relations between rich countries and developing countries intensified; this was a new phenomenon. As Arthur Lewis argues convincingly, economic relations between the Western countries and the rest of the world were weak before the second half of the nineteenth century (Lewis, 1978a, 1978b). Initially most of the raw materials needed for industrialisation were available in Europe. The volume of trade between rich industrialised countries and developing countries was negligible. 'Even in 1883 total imports into the United States and Western Europe from Asia, Africa and Tropical Latin America came to only about a dollar per head of the population of the exporting countries' (Lewis, 1978b: 5).

Improvements in transportation and communication – railways, iron ships, the telegraph – and the opening of the Suez Canal in 1869 changed all this. Both the continuous growth of the population of rich countries and the growth of industrial production caused an increase in the demand for agricultural and mining products. The tropics reacted to this growing demand by greatly increasing the export of primary products (e.g. coffee, tea, palm oil, groundnuts, tropical fruit, jute, sisal, rubber, tobacco, cotton, sugar and mining products). On the one hand, small peasants cultivated surplus land and used part of their surplus labour for the production of cash crops. On the other hand there were Western investments in plantations and mines (Lewis, 1970, 1978b; Myint, 1980). The revenues from exports created a market for industrial products from industrialised countries. There was thus a sharp increase in the volume of international trade.

The modern world economy came into being between 1870 and 1913. Western influences were felt everywhere, even in those places where the native life styles had remained unaffected until then. The poor countries became involved in the world economy through their exports of agricultural and mining products. They became acquainted with the industrial consumer goods that were exported by the industrialised countries. The money economy arose when native inhabitants embarked on the production of commercial crops in addition to the cultivation of food products for their own consumption.[12] Large migration flows established new relationships between the various parts of the world and led to drastic changes in the structure of populations (see section 2.4.6). In many developing countries there was a vast increase in investment by rich countries. This investment focused on plantations, mines and the creation of an infrastructure of railways, roads and harbours for the benefit of exports and imports. Investment flows also increased among the rich countries themselves. According to Lewis (1970, 1978a, 1978b) and Maddison (1989), the 1870–1913 period was one of increasing per capita income in both developing and rich countries. However, as a result of a complex of factors – among which were colonialism and the overwhelming attractiveness of primary exports – developing countries did not succeed in using the revenues from exports to achieve industrialisation and lasting economic development (Lewis, 1970).

In summary, in the 1870–1913 period an integrated world economy came into being, in which the volume of international trade underwent a sharp increase. International trade was of an asymmetric nature. Poor developing countries exported primary agricultural and mining products. Rich and politically powerful countries exported industrial products. After the Second World War 'industrialisation' became strongly associated with 'economic development', partly because of the historical experiences of the 1870–1913 period. Dependence on primary exports was more and more seen as a symptom of economic weakness. However, this is not always true. As will be shown in Chapter 8, countries like the USA, Canada and New Zealand benefited very much from agricultural exports at some stage in their development.

2.4.6 Migration flows

Following Arthur Lewis, we have argued that Western economic influence on the rest of the world was limited before the second half of the nineteenth century. Western powers may have had trading posts all over the world yet in many parts of the world native societies continued to exist unchanged alongside European enclaves. Also the volume of international trade was relatively small. Only in the course of the nineteenth century did political penetration intensify and international trade relations become more important.

In at least three respects, however, Lewis' argument may lead to an underestimation of the importance of Western penetration in the world before 1870. First, the enormous impact of Iberian colonialism in Latin America has received insufficient emphasis. Secondly, even though the volume of trade may have been small, its impact on European development was large (Findlay and O'Rourke, 2007). It was associated with flows of knowledge and transfers of technology which contributed to subsequent economic development in the Western countries. The revenues from international trade and colonial exploitation also helped to finance powerful national states in Europe. Finally, not enough attention has been paid to the Atlantic slave trade, which transformed the entire population structure of Latin America and the Caribbean and has left deep scars on the African continent.

---

[12] Both long-distance trade and the use of various kinds of money, of course, preceded European penetration (e.g. Hill, 1986; Klein, 1999; Isichei, 1997; Wolf, 1982). But production for own consumption did play a much greater role in pre-modern economies and monetary transactions tended to be limited to more ceremonial transactions, such as bridewealth.

In this section, we examine migration flows as an important aspect of the international economic order, paying attention to the Atlantic slave trade from 1500 to 1870 and migration flows at the end of the nineteenth century.

The Atlantic slave trade

Table 2.1 and 2.2 present quantitative estimates of the Atlantic slave trade and its importance for the development of African and Latin American populations. Table 2.1 shows the numbers of slaves imported into different parts of the Americas in different periods. Table 2.2 shows the numbers of slaves exported from Africa by region of origin in different periods.

According to the latest revisions of Curtin's authoritative 1969 estimates (Curtin, 1969; Klein, 1999), in total 11.1 million African slaves were shipped to America between 1500 and 1870.[13] This number does not include the 175,000 slaves who were exported to

Table 2.1: Slave imports into the Americas, 1451–1870 (thousands)

	North America[a]	Spanish America[b]	Caribbean[c]	Brazil	The Americas	Old World	Total
Imports 1451–1500						25	25
Population 1500		9,350	300	1,000	10,650		
Imports 1501–1600		75		50	125	116	241
Population 1600		6,900	200	1,000	8,100		
Imports 1601–1700		293	464	560	1,316	25	1,341
Population 1700	370	7,600	500	1,250	9,720		
Imports 1701–1800	391	513	3,110	1,700	5,715		5,715
Population 1800	6,040	10,400	2,000	2,500	20,940		
Imports 1801–1870	169	782	247	1,720	2,917		2,917
Population 1900	23,700	29,600	6,500	18,000	77,800		
Total 1501–1870	560	1,662	3,821	4,030	10,073	142	10,214

Notes:

[a] North America includes Delaware, Georgia, Maryland, North Carolina, South Carolina, Virginia, Kentucky, Mississippi, Alabama, Missouri, Arkansas, Tennessee and Texas. There are no data on Louisiana population. Slave imports into Louisiana have been included in totals for North America.

[b] Spanish America includes Mexico, Central America, Cuba, Peru, Colombia and Venezuela.

[c] The Caribbean includes Jamaica, Barbados, Leeward Island, St Vincent, St Lucia, Tobago, Dominica, Trinidad, Grenada, the other Leeward Islands, Santo Domingo, Martinique, Guadeloupe, Guyana, the Netherlands Antilles, the Danish West Indies.

Sources:

Data on population in McEvedy and Jones (1978), and Darby and Fullart (1970). Slave imports from Curtin (1969). The period 1781–1870 revised by Eltis (1989).

[13] Curtin's estimates of the Atlantic slave trade have subsequently been revised and refined by later researchers such as Eltis (1989, 2001); Eltis *et al.* (1998); Klein (1999); and Lovejoy (1982) but the overall magnitudes have by and large remained the same. We primarily use the revised estimates reported in Klein (1999).

Table 2.2:   Slave exports from Africa to the Americas, by region of origin, 1500-1870 (thousands)

| | Exports by region of origin | | | | | |
	West Africa[a]	Western Central Africa[b]	Southeast Africa[c]	Total	Mortality in transit	Arrived in America
Population 1500	11,000	8,000	7,000	26,000		
Exports 1500–1600		150		150	25	125
Population 1600	14,000	8,500	8,250	30,750		
Exports 1600–1700[d]	526	1,053		1,579	263	1,316
Population 1700	18,000	9,000	9,500	36,500		
Exports 1700–1800[e]	3,824	2,242		6,066	351	5,715
Population 1800	20,000	10,000	12,000	42,000		
Exports 1800–1870	1,315	1,598	386	3,299	382	2,917
Population 1900	27,000	15,000	16,000	58,000		
Total 1500–1870	5,665	5,042	386	11,094	1,021	10,073

Notes:

[a] West Africa includes the coastal areas from Senegal to Benin, and Nigeria.

[b] Western Central Africa includes Cameroon, the Central African Republic, Gabon, Democratic Republic of Congo and Angola.

[c] South East Africa includes Uganda, Kenya, Tanzania, Rwanda and Burundi, and Mozambique.

[d] The slave exports to the Old World have not been included. Since most slaves were of Western Central African origin until 1650, we assumed that between 1500 and 1600 Atlantic slaves were exported from Western Central Africa only. It is assumed that in the seventeenth century two-thirds of the slaves were natives of Western Central Africa, and that one-third was of West African origin. This rough assumption is borne out by detailed figures for the years 1662–1700 from Klein (1999), Appendix Table A.1.

[e] Discrepancies between exports and arrivals are a rough indication of mortality in mid-passage. However recent estimates of mortality in passage in the literature are around 7.5 per cent (Klein, 1999: 130 ff.). This is lower than the percentage 9.2 calculated from the discrepancies in Table 2.2.

Sources: Population, see Table 2.1; pre-1700 totals of slave exports from Curtin, 1969, p. 268. Post-1700, Klein (1999), Appendix Table A.I.

the Old World in the sixteenth and seventeenth centuries and some 7 million slaves exported to the Islamic world (Klein, 1999). To this should be added widespread slavery within African societies. The slaves for the Atlantic slave trade were collected by African states along the coast through warfare, systematic raiding and tribute. These states prospered thanks to the revenues of the slave trade. Slaves were among the most important export products along with gold, ivory, hides, pepper, beeswax and gum.

Trade and transportation of slaves across the Atlantic was completely controlled by white people (first the Portuguese and later also the Dutch, the British, the French and even the

Spanish). The expansion of the Atlantic slave trade was highly correlated with the Western conquest of the American hemisphere. The demand for slaves on the American continent increased rapidly. In the fifteenth century 150,000 slaves were shipped to the Americas; in the sixteenth century their number had risen to 1.6 million. The slave trade reached its zenith in the eighteenth century when no fewer than 6.1 million slaves were transported overseas.

In 1807 the British parliament passed a bill prohibiting the slave trade. The holding of slaves in areas controlled by the British was forbidden in 1833. Other nations followed hesitantly, sometimes under British pressure: France in 1848, the Netherlands and the USA only in 1863. In spite of abolition, no less than 3.3 million slaves were transported to America in the course of the nineteenth century, mainly to work on sugar cane and coffee plantations (Hopkins, 1973). The Portuguese accounted for 46 per cent of total slave exports, the British for 31 per cent, the French for 13 per cent, the Dutch and Spanish for 5 per cent each (Eltis, 2001).

Nowadays there are, fortunately, no differences of opinion regarding the ethical repulsiveness of the slave trade. There is, however, a lively academic debate on the effects of the slave trade on economic and demographic development on the African continent. It is clear that there has been a considerable demographic bloodletting. The total number of slaves exported over the eighteenth century was no less than 14.4 per cent of the combined population of the exporting regions in the year 1800. Besides, it was young strong males in particular who were sold as slaves. West Africa was the most important slave-exporting region. In the course of the eighteenth century 3.8 million people were forcibly removed; this amounts to no less than 19 per cent of the West African population in the year 1800. Klein estimates that the population growth rate in areas exposed to the slave trade was reduced from 0.5 to 0.2 per cent per year. Allowing for births forgone, Maddison estimates that population growth in Sub-Saharan Africa would have been three times as high, in the absence of slavery (Findlay and O'Rourke, 2007; Maddison, 2001). If one realises that even within West Africa specific regions and ethnic groups were targeted by slave expeditions, then the impact in these regions must have been devastating. Fertile agricultural areas were abandoned by populations subject to slave raids. The increasing demand for slaves fuelled internal warfare, banditry and conflict. Resources were diverted from productive activities to military activity, with negative effects on West African economic development.

On the other hand, authors like Fage and Hopkins (Fage, 1969, 1977; Hopkins, 1973) have pointed out that the annual exports of slaves were less than the natural growth of the population. Even in West Africa there was an absolute increase in the population in the eighteenth century. In the nineteenth century several European countries were faced by even larger out-migrations, than those endured by African societies. These authors emphasise that the European slave trade fits into pre-European patterns of internal slavery and slave exports to the Islamic world (see also Wolf, 1982, Chapter 7). They state that several African kingdoms prospered thanks to the Atlantic trade of which the slave trade was a part. Therefore, the effects of the trade varied greatly from region to region. On balance, it cannot be denied that the Atlantic slave trade has had a profoundly demoralising impact on African societies and has been one of the obstacles to the economic development of Sub-Saharan Africa.

In Latin America the slave trade has transformed the entire structure of the population and thus the entire social structure. Most slaves have been imported into the Caribbean. In

1700 the entire population in the Caribbean was around 0.5 million persons. In the course of the eighteenth century no less than 3.1 million slaves of African descent were added to this total. In Brazil in the eighteenth century, 1.7 million slaves were added to a total population of 1.25 million in the year 1700. In Spanish America the demographic impact of slave imports has been less extreme. Here, the primary demographic impact of Iberian colonial rule consists of the decline in total population. This can be seen by comparing the population figures for 1500 and 1600.

Both demographic data and data on the slave trade are surrounded by many uncertainties. The estimates of the entire Indian population in Latin America in 1492 range between 7.5 million and 100 million (Slicher van Bath, 1989). Slicher van Bath estimates the number of Indian inhabitants at 35–40 million. Towards the middle of the seventeenth century he estimates that only 10 per cent of the original inhabitants had survived. If this were true, the negative effects of the Spanish colonisation on the native inhabitants would be much greater than shown in Table 2.1. In spite of all these uncertainties, the data in Tables 2.1 and 2.2 serve to illustrate the profound demographic significance of the slave trade.

Migration flows from Europe and Asia in the late nineteenth century

During the second half of the nineteenth century two enormous migration flows occurred which were characteristic of the international economic order of 1870–1913. One of these flows originated in Europe and was destined for regions with a temperate climate. From 1846 to 1932, 58.6 million people left Europe, of whom one-fifth returned home after some time (Palmer and Colton, 1978).[14] Most immigrants – 34 million – left for the USA. Between 1871 and 1915 European emigration amounted to 36 million people, two-thirds of whom emigrated to the USA (Lewis, 1978a: 181). Other popular destinies were Argentina, Canada, Brazil, Australia, South Africa and New Zealand.

These 'new worlds' had an abundance of land and were sparsely populated. Everywhere the original inhabitants – Indians, Aborigines, Maoris, Africans – were pushed aside by the immigrants. Tempted, among other things, by the higher wages in these new countries, European migrants left their technologically advanced homelands. Scarcity of labour and the relatively high education of the migrants led to a high capital–labour ratio in the new territories. Therefore productivity of labour was high and incentives for labour replacing technological advance were strong. European migration was accompanied by international technology transfers. Many of the countries where European immigrants arrived were originally exporters of primary products. Today these are among the world's richest countries.

The other great migration flow consists of migrants who left very densely populated areas in India, China and Java; they migrated to tropical areas in the Caribbean, Africa and Asia where they were employed in mines, construction works and on plantations. In the Caribbean, the import of indentured labourers from Asia was the alternative to slavery which had been banned by the British in 1833. Quantitatively, however, migration from densely populated areas to sparsely populated areas within Asia was most important.

The estimates of the volume of this second migration flow differ widely. This is also because only some of the migrants settled permanently in a new country. Considerable

[14] This total includes 7 million migrants who left for Asian Russia. Basing themselves on Ferenczi and Willcox (1929) and Hatton and Williamson (2005) provide estimates of annual emigration from Europe between 1846 and 1924. Summing these estimates results in a total of between 47.4 million and 50 million persons.

numbers of people returned to their homeland, whether voluntarily or not, after varying periods of time. Besides, some studies are concerned with migration between countries, whereas other studies also deal with internal migration flows within a particular region. The highest estimate is by Lewis (1978b) who – without mentioning any sources – states that the entire migration flow involved about 50 million people. A frequently quoted source is Kingsley Davis (1951), who calculated the gross migration from India between 1846 and 1937 at more than 30 million people – 6 million of them actually settling abroad permanently. Only a minor part of this migration took place before 1871, and not all migrants were indentured labourers. The most important migration flows went to Burma, Ceylon and Malacca. Migrants from India also ended up in the south and east of Africa where they later came to play an important role in trade and commerce. Between 1880 and 1922 the number of Chinese settling in tropical areas outside China increased by 5 million – from 3 million to 8 million. Taking into account remigration, gross migration must have been much greater (Lewis, 1978b: 185; see also Baker, 1981). Chinese migrants ended up especially in the Netherlands East Indies, Thailand, Malacca and other parts of Southeast Asia. Finally, there was also a migration flow from Java, which was densely populated, to several other islands of the Indonesian archipelago. Like slavery, the migration of indentured labour has changed the demographic composition of many Asian, Latin American and African countries.

Breman stresses the involuntary nature of indentured labour (Breman, 1985). Press gangs, deception and coercion played an important role in the recruitment of indentured labourers. Often migrant labour was the only way to pay the taxes imposed by colonial governments and to pay off debts to landlords. Other authors, however, emphasise the appalling conditions of life in the densely populated rural areas of China or India, which provided incentives for voluntary migration. According to Lewis, a salary just above subsistence level was enough to attract an 'unlimited supply of labour' from the densely populated areas (Lewis, 1978b). Migrants made a conscious choice to improve their lot (Emmer, 1986). According to Engerman (1986), the truth lies somewhere in the middle: indentured labour had both voluntary as well as involuntary aspects.

The availability of large numbers of uneducated and cheap labourers has had a negative effect on the development of productivity in mines and on plantations. Western entrepreneurs invested little in schooling and educating their inexpensive raw labour power. The amount of capital per worker was limited. According to a well-known theory of Lewis, the availability of an unlimited labour supply forced down the prices of exports from tropical developing countries. This explains why these countries benefited so little from their primary exports (Lewis, 1954, 1978a, 1978b).

Migration flows from developing to advanced economies since 1950

A third wave of migration occurred after the Second World War, in this case from developing countries to advanced economies. One of the typical characteristics of the post-war economic order is a large flow of people from former colonies and developing countries to the advanced economies. This includes inhabitants of former colonies who moved to the former colonial countries such as Algerians to France, Indians and Pakistanis to the UK, Congolese to Belgium, Indonesian and Surinamese to the Netherlands. It also includes large numbers of migrants from Mexico and other Latin American countries to the USA, or from Turkey, Morocco and other North American and African countries to Europe. Including migration of Koreans to Japan the total migration flow amounts to approximately 67.5

million persons between 1950 and 2007.[15] These flows have markedly changed the demographic composition of Europe, Canada and Australia. They have also imposed a heavy burden on developing countries in the form of a drain of skilled labour and entrepreneurial talent.

2.4.7 Non-colonised areas

Some countries – China, Tibet, Afghanistan, Korea, Turkey, Iran, Thailand, Mongolia and Japan, to name but a few – were never colonised by the West. With the possible exception of Tibet and Mongolia, the non-colonised countries were, however, also confronted with the Western challenge and the need to respond to it. Using gunboat diplomacy, the British forced Thailand to open up to foreign trade in the Bowring Treaty (1855). In 1853, Japan was faced with the American fleet of Admiral Perry who forced the shogun to open up Japan to foreign trade. The humiliating experience of Western military supremacy has, of course, been one of the reasons for the initiation of a large-scale process of modernisation in Japan which has led to rapid economic growth. By the end of the nineteenth century Japan already proved capable of joining the Western game of imperialism (Myers and Peattie, 1984). After the Sino-Japanese war (1894–5), Taiwan and part of Manchuria was ceded to Japan. In 1905 Japan defeated Russia. In 1910 Korea was officially colonised, and in 1932 the Japanese puppet state of Manchukuo was set up in Manchuria. It was not until the end of the Second World War that the period of Japanese imperial expansion in Asia was concluded.

During the nineteenth century a substantially weakened China was penetrated from all sides by colonial powers. From 1840 to 1842 the British waged war against China – in the name of free trade – because the Chinese government refused to allow the import of opium from India. Great Britain thus was one of the first narco states in history. The Chinese were forced to pay the costs of the war and to accept the imports of opium. In addition, they had to cede Hong Kong to the British. After the Opium Wars 'treaty ports' were created along the Chinese coast, where the right of foreigners to trade was guaranteed by treaties. In the treaty ports, Chinese jurisdiction over Western subjects was restricted (extraterritoriality). Towards the end of the nineteenth century several imperial powers, including Great Britain, France, Russia and Japan, had carved out spheres of influence in China. It is mainly owing to colonial rivalry that China was not completely colonised in this period. It is an interesting question as to why Japan reacted to the Western challenge with wholesale modernisation whereas Chinese attempts of modernisation in the face of similar challenges were half-hearted (Boserup, 1981; Spence, 1990).

2.4.8 Latecomers in the process of economic development

Russia and Japan are well-known latecomers to the process of economic development. During the last quarter of the nineteenth century these two countries began a dramatic modernisation of their economies. In a relatively short time they succeeded in building up a large industrial sector and ranged themselves among the important industrialised nations. Japan, in particular, emerged as a new industrial superpower in a short period of time.

---

[15] Own calculations based on OECD, *International Migration Statistics Database Edition* (ISSN 1608–1269), issues 2009 and 2006.

With regard to the economic development of Russia, Alexander Gershenkron has pointed out the 'advantages of backwardness' (Gershenkron, 1962). A technological leader has to pay all costs of R&D of new technologies; its followers may copy the newly developed theories at little cost. Under certain circumstances the follower countries can experience a process of rapid catch-up. After 1945 the advantages of backwardness contributed to rapid productivity growth in Japan and Western Europe. More recently, South Korea, Taiwan, Singapore, Hong Kong, China and India have been experiencing explosive growth and catch-up. The Russian Federation has fallen behind after the collapse of the Soviet Union. Its industrial base has shrunk and its economy is now based on primary energy exports.

2.4.9   The period 1913–50

Maddison (1989) describes the international order between 1913 and 1950 as a period of conflict and autarky. The international economic order underwent dramatic changes as a result of two world wars and a deep economic crisis (1929–32). After the Communist Revolution of 1917 the Soviet Union seceded from the world economy and strove for further industrialisation and economic development by means of a centrally planned economy. Attempts to reconstruct the liberal international economic order after the First World War did not meet with success.

In many respects the 1913–50 period was the reverse of the economic order of 1870–1913. Economic growth slackened in both rich countries and in developing countries. Investment flows to developing countries dried up. Latin American countries defaulted on their debts, and the international financial system, based on the gold standard, was disrupted. Strong protectionism replaced free trade. Especially after 1929, each country tried to protect its own economy and to saddle other countries with the consequences of the economic crisis. As a result international trade spiralled downwards. Developing countries most involved in international trade from 1870 to 1913 were the most affected. The demand for primary exports of developing countries collapsed; the development of their prices was unfavourable compared with the development of the prices of industrial imports ('deteriorating terms of trade'). In some Latin American countries – Brazil, for example – domestic industries benefited from the fact that industrial imports from the Western countries could no longer be paid for. Moreover, domestic industries were actively stimulated and protected by the government (import substitution).

One of the important ideas rooted in the experiences of developing countries during this period of time is that of 'export pessimism'. Export pessimists argue that primary exports will not lead to lasting economic development since the global demand for these products is not stable and terms of trade with respect to industrial products tend to decline in the long term. Developing countries ought to isolate themselves more from the international economy and they should strive for industrialisation with the aid of government intervention. These notions will be discussed in more detail in the chapter on industrialisation strategies (Chapter 9).

2.4.10   The period after the Second World War

From a political point of view the period after 1945 marks the end of the process of Western expansion. Rapidly, one colony after the other achieved independence – sometimes through negotiation, sometimes through bloody wars as was the case in Algeria, Vietnam and Indonesia. However, the end of Western supremacy over vast colonial empires did not constitute the end of international relations of dependence. As has already been argued above, Western expansion led to the formation of an integrated world economy with interdependence among its components.

This period also marks the resurgence of industrialisation in part of the developing world. In the nineteenth century moves towards industrialisation were scarce and hesitant (Pollard, 1990). Industrialisation took place in Europe and the USA. Developing countries remained predominantly dependent on agriculture and mining. Only after 1945, after a pause of fifty years, did the industrialisation of developing countries – or some of them – begin in earnest (see Chapter 9).

The period 1950–73 is characterised by growth rates of the national income unprecedented in economic history. In both developing and rich countries there was a strong growth, though not everyone benefited from it to the same degree. One after another, obstacles to international trade were eliminated in rich countries, with the notable exception of agriculture. Liberalisation of international trade resulted in a considerable growth of the volume of international trade. International trade benefited from a stable monetary system based on fixed exchange rates, gold and the dollar. Developing countries used their newly achieved autonomy to systematically pursue economic development. A number of developing countries experienced rapid processes of industrialisation. Some of them even succeeded in producing competitive industrial products for the global market. Almost without exception, industrialisation in developing countries involved protection of the young industrial sector. This constituted an exception to the general trend towards liberalisation of the international economic order. The volume of investment and capital flows increased sharply. Developing countries benefited from a net capital inflow, in contrast to the period before the the Second World War.

The 1973 oil crisis heralded an era of increased uncertainty for both rich and developing countries (Maddison, 1985, 1989). The growth rate of the world economy slackened in comparison with post-war years. Protectionist tendencies re-emerged, though there was no return to pre-war protectionism. Increasingly, economic trends in different parts of the global economy started to diverge. After a period of continued growth in the 1970s, Latin American economic development stagnated for ten years in the wake of the debt crisis of 1982. Most African countries experienced economic declines or at best sluggish growth between 1973 and 2000, with growth only picking up after 2000. The dissolution of the Soviet Union in 1991 and the transition to the market was accompanied by an economic collapse, with GDP in the Russian Federation dropping to 58 per cent of its 1991 level by 1998 (Maddison, 2001: 157). After 1998 there was a strong recovery based on primary exports. Many of the former Soviet Republics in central Asia which have become independent show strong similarities with the poorest developing countries elsewhere in the world.

Several countries in South and East Asia including China, India, Indonesia, Malaysia, South Korea, Taiwan, Thailand and Vietnam experienced very rapid growth and catch-up. They have all tended to liberalise their economies, opening up to FDI and pursuing policies for labour-intensive industrial growth. They achieved considerable success in industrial exports to world markets. A distinction is often made between the Asian tigers: South Korea, Taiwan, Singapore and Hong Kong and the late late developers such as Malaysia, Thailand, Indonesia, China and India.

The Asian resurgence was rudely interrupted by the Asian financial crisis of 1997, which led to a sudden collapse of economic growth in Thailand, Indonesia, Malaysia, South Korea and the Philippines and slowdown in many other Asian countries. After the Asian crisis, most Asian countries including China, Korea and Malaysia recovered surprisingly rapidly. But in Indonesia and the Philippines the effects of the crisis were more long-lasting and it took up to seven years to reach to pre-crisis levels of GDP per capita. Their recovery was made more difficult due to the worldwide recession of 2001.

The global financial crisis of 2008 hit hardest in Western countries, where growth turned sharply negative in 2009. Growth in Asia, Latin America and also in Africa was much less affected. Growth continued to boom in the giant countries India and China, perhaps heralding the new age of Asia in the world economy. The post-war period will be discussed in more detail in Chapter 13.

2.4.11 Two perspectives on developments in the world economy, 1450–2015

The development of the world economy since the fifteenth century can be viewed from two distinctive perspectives, each of which raises different questions. The first perspective is that of the formation and dynamisation of the world economy; the second perspective is that of exploitation and increasing inequality in the world economy.

The perspective of the formation and dynamisation of the world economy

Since 1500 we have seen the first instance of a sustained breakthrough from recurring cycles of poverty in economic history. In most periods in history the majority of the people never lived far above subsistence levels. A bad harvest – as a result of war, drought or flooding – could easily result in famine. The time horizon was short. Most individuals could not even contemplate investing in long-term improvement of their living conditions; their first priority was survival in the short term.

In this respect the process of economic growth, which started in Europe, was a mysterious breakthrough, a puzzle that demands an explanation. This growth, combined with external expansion, challenged peoples and societies in other parts of the world. It induced processes of change everywhere. The example of Western economic development and the threat of Western penetration and domination called forth an almost universal pursuit of development in other parts of the world. There would be no concept of development if the breakthrough had not taken place.

The perspective of exploitation and increasing inequality in the emerging world economy

Around 1450 there were no great differences in the level of prosperity between the various countries and regions of the world. In subsequent centuries there was a growth of per capita income in Western countries such as the Netherlands, France and Great Britain. At the same time per capita income stagnated in most developing countries such as, for example, China, India, Indonesia and Mexico. The increasing inequalities went hand in hand with exploitation of poor areas by rich – the rich countries appropriating part of the economic wealth of the poor areas they penetrated.

The income differences increased sharply in the nineteenth and twentieth century when growth accelerated in Western countries. Even when per capita income in developing countries increased, growth in rich countries was faster, at least until 1973. As a result income differentials between the rich and the poor countries increased further.

From this gloomy point of view, the formation of the world economy involved a truly explosive growth of global income inequality. The gap that divides rich and poor countries has increased. From this perspective, what needs to be explained is the lack of development in developing countries. The emphasis is on understanding centuries of relative economic stagnation and analysing the role of colonial and neo-colonial exploitation in such processes of stagnation.

There are important elements of truth in both perspectives. It is neither necessary nor possible to make an absolute choice between them. Advocates of each perspective should realise that there are alternative ways of looking at issues of development and stagnation and that different perspectives raise different kinds of interesting questions.

2.5   Key issues in development

The contrast between the world economy of 2015 and that of 1450 raises several fascinating questions which may help to bring some order in the multitude of schools, theories and approaches concerned with development issues. Three kinds of questions will be distinguished here.

1. *How is it possible that a certain part of the world has experienced a historically unprecedented process of economic growth and development since 1450?*

Two types of explanations can be offered: *internal* and *external* explanations. Internal explanations seek the causes of the Western economic breakthrough in typical factors and conditions which distinguish Western from non-Western countries: culture, religion, mentality, institutions, population density, climate, natural circumstances, geographical location and political characteristics. They also devote considerable attention to the economic and social policies pursued by governments. External explanations seek the causes of Western prosperity in the success of Western exploitation of other parts of the world. These explanations see the drain of revenues and wealth resulting from colonial penetration as the decisive factor which put the West and the developing world on different paths of development.

2. *Why have other parts of the world lagged behind the rich Western countries in their economic development since 1450? Why did developing countries not experience processes of development similar to those in the West?*

In answering these questions, one can again distinguish *internal* and *external* explanations. Internal explanations focus on the specific factors that have been obstacles to economic development in developing countries: traditional cultural orientations, attitudes towards work, risk, saving or education; institutions that are not conducive to technological progress, patterns of saving and investment, unfavourable natural circumstances such as climate or whether countries are landlocked (Collier, 2007; Naudé, 2007; Sachs *et al.*, 2004); characteristics of the political system (North *et al.*, 2009); misguided or ineffective economic and social policies.

External explanations emphasise the negative effects of Western penetration of the world. The lack of economic growth in developing countries is seen as a result of colonial and neocolonial exploitation or the structure of the world economic order. Moderate versions of this perspective tend to emphasise the disadvantages of backwardness. In a global economy dominated by established economic powers latecomers will find it ever more difficult to initiate successful development.

3. *Is it possible for developing countries today to undergo processes of development similar to those experienced by rich countries in the past?*

The answers to this last question of course, depend on the answers to the previous ones. Three types of answers are possible:

1. In principle, developing countries can undergo processes of economic and social development similar to those experienced by the rich countries in the past. This answer was primarily given by the modernisation theorists of the 1950s and 1960s. They emphasised the necessity of breaking through the traditional structures, attitudes and institutions that hamper development. Advanced countries may help by providing education, information and the financial means for investment in new infrastructures and capital goods.

2. In principle, developing countries cannot pursue the same path as rich countries, since the development of rich countries is based on the (capitalist) exploitation of the rest of the world. Such answers are given by Marxists and radical critics of modernisation theories and orthodox development theories. Underdevelopment of the poor countries is the other side of the coin of development in the West. Only by liberating themselves from the capitalist world economy and by finding their own – different – paths, do underdeveloped countries have a chance of attaining development.

3. There is no reason to believe that developing countries are in principle incapable of reaching higher levels of prosperity. However, it is unlikely that the path to a higher per capita income will be the same as the path rich countries have followed in the past. Initial conditions for development differ in every historical period and every phase of development of the international economic and political order. Different conditions call for different development paths, strategies and policies. Lessons can be learned from past experiences, but they have to be adapted to new conditions. This is the perspective that informs this book.

Initial conditions have to do with demographic characteristics, the development of the world trade, the nature of international competition in a global economy, the state of science and technology, the international balance of power, and the nature of the relationships with established advanced economies. Latecomers to development may face both major disadvantages and potential advantages. Apart from the differing initial conditions over time, there are also differences in circumstances between various countries and regions. Finally, the policy choices made in developing countries themselves are of great importance.

Questions for review

1. List the most important characteristics of the concept of international economic order. Discuss the six types of international economic order which can be distinguished since 1450.
2. Explain the unique features of the Western process of development since the beginning of the sixteenth century, compared to earlier processes of socio-economic development.

3. Why did Chinese economic development stagnate from the fourteenth century onwards, in spite of initial conditions which seemed so promising?
4. Discuss the differences between colonies of settlement and colonies of occupation.
5. What were the characteristics of the international division of labour between rich countries and poor countries which evolved in the period 1870–1913?
6. Discuss the impact of major migration flows on the demographic characteristics of developing countries.
7. Discuss the contrasting perspectives on the role of Western expansion in the formation of the modern world economy.
8. What lessons can Sub-Saharan African countries derive from the post-war experiences of the East Asian countries?

Further reading

There is a very large literature on the evolution of the international economic order, which includes works by economists, historians, sociologists and anthropologists. The following suggestions are inevitably incomplete. The foundations for the modern quantitative study of growth and development have been laid by Simon Kuznets in a long series of studies, including *Modern Economic Growth: Rate, Structure and Spread* (1966) and *Economic Growth of Nations: Total Output and Production Structure* (1971). A short book by Arthur Lewis on *The Evolution of the International Economic Order* (1987b) gives a brilliant summary of important changes in international order since the nineteenth century. The same topics are dealt with in a more quantitative fashion in his *Growth and Fluctuations, 1870–1913* (1978a).

A source of inspiration for the discussion of the differences between Chinese and European development in this chapter is Immanuel Wallerstein's *The Modern World System* (1974). This is the first of four large volumes on the modern world system from a centre–periphery perspective. China's early technological lead is documented in J. Needham *et al.*'s monumental study, *Science and Civilisation in China* (1954). A well-written overview of Chinese economic development is Mark Elvin's, *The Pattern of Chinese Past* (1973). China's agricultural development is documented by Dwight Perkins in *Agricultural Development in China 1368–1968* (1968). Angus Maddison also analyses the modern economic development of China in historical perspective in his *Chinese Economic Performance in the Long Run* (1998).

Valuable sources for the historical study of the European breakthrough are David Landes, *The Unbound Prometheus: Technological Changes and Industrial Development in Western Europe from 1750 to the Present* (1969) and his provocative and enjoyable study, *The Wealth and Poverty of Nations: Why Some Are So Rich and Some so Poor* (1998). Another study offering a long-run perspective is Ernest Jones' *Growth Recurring: Economic Change in World History* (1988).

An impressive series of quantitative studies by Angus Maddison charts the long-run growth of the Western and non-Western world in comparative perspective. These studies include his *Phases of Capitalist Development* (1982a), his comparative study *Two Crises: Latin America and Asia, 1929–1938 and 1973–1983* (1985), his *Monitoring the World Economy* (1995) and his magnum opus, *The World Economy: A Millennial Perspective* (2001) and *Contours of the World*

Economy (2007b). Maddison makes the case for the early forging ahead of Europe relative to Asia. The opposite view on this issue is argued by Paul Bairoch and M. Lévy-Leboyer, in *Disparities in Economic Development since the Industrial Revolution* (1981) and for China by Kenneth Pomeranz, *The Great Divergence* (2000). Two economic historians, Ronald Findlay and Kevin H. O'Rourke published an inspiring volume on the history of world trade from the year 1000 to present: *Power and Plenty: Trade, War and the World Economy in the Second Millennium* (2007).

On the Atlantic slave trade, the classic study is Curtin's book, *The Atlantic Slave Trade: A Census* (1969). Curtin's estimates have been revised in an article by Lovejoy, 'The Volume of the Atlantic Slave Trade: A Synthesis' (1982). The various revisions of Curtin's estimates are summarised in H.S. Klein, *The Atlantic Slave Trade* (1999). The quantitative data on the slave trade are now available on CD-ROM (Eltis *et al.*, *The Transatlantic Slave Trade, 1562–1867: A Database CD-ROM* (1998).

An good overview of the political history of European expansion is offered in Fieldhouse's *The Colonial Empires: A Comparative Survey from the Eighteenth Century* (1982). From an anthropological and historical perspective Eric Wolf's *Europe and the People without History* (1982) provides interesting and sometimes unexpected insights in the relations between European expansion and non-European societies. For African history, useful studies include: J.D. Fage, *A History of West Africa: An Introductory Survey* (1969); A. G. Hopkins, *An Economic History of West Africa* (1973); and E. Isichei, *A History of African Societies to 1870* (1997). For the economic history of Latin America, a good starting point is Celso Furtado's *Economic Development of Latin America* (1976).

3 Growth and stagnation: theories and experiences

As discussed in Chapters 1 and 2 of this book, there has been long-run divergence in the world economy. In the fifteenth century disparities in per capita incomes between countries and regions were small. Since then some economies have moved ahead and others have fallen far behind. After 1820, capital accumulation and technological change accelerated. The rate at which income levels diverged increased, resulting in the wide global disparities of the present international economic order. We have also noted that the ranking of countries was not immutable. Former British colonies such as the USA, Canada and New Zealand or Asian economies such as Japan, Singapore and Korea grew so rapidly that they moved far up the income ladder. Other countries such as Argentina, the Ottoman empire or the Russian Federation slipped downward. For a better understanding of development, we are interested in why some countries or societies forge ahead in given periods, while others stagnate or fall behind (Abramovitz, 1989b). We are especially interested in the conditions under which growth and catch-up can be realised in developing countries of today. Sections 3.1–3.6 of this chapter offer a brief introduction to theories of growth and stagnation. Section 3.7 presents theoretically relevant empirical information on long-run economic trends in developing countries.

3.1 What are the sources of growth and development?

The key challenge to our theoretical and empirical understanding of development is to understand why some developing countries experience accelerated growth, catch-up and socio-economic development while others become mired in stagnation. Let us start with the question of what are the immediate or proximate sources of economic growth. In simplified form, these are summarised in Box 3.1.

The factors in Box 3.1 can be represented in the form of a basic production function, which relates output to the so-called *proximate sources of growth* (Denison, 1967; Maddison, 1987, 1988):

$$O = F(K, L, R)^e + A + P.$$

In this equation O refers to output, K, L and R refer to the primary factors of production capital, labour and natural resources. The exponent e refers to the efficiency with which the primary factors are used to transform intermediate inputs into final goods and services. The concept of 'efficiency' as used here refers to everything that increases output per unit of primary input. It includes a number of important elements mentioned under points **6–9** in Box 3.1, such as economies of scale, efficient allocation of the factors of production within

BOX 3.1 : Sources of growth of GDP

Economies grow and societies become more prosperous through:

1. Discovery and exploitation of riches and natural resources

Discovery of natural resources – gas, coal, oil, gold, minerals and so forth – can promote growth. However, such growth will not be sustainable unless the revenues from windfall discoveries are transformed into more durable sources of growth.

2. Effort

Working harder, increasing hours worked per year, increasing labour market participation, greater effort and discipline.

3. Saving and accumulating capital

Being sober and abstaining from current consumption in order to save; investing these savings in order to accumulate capital goods, which increase the productivity of labour.

4. Investing in education and human capital

Abstaining from current consumption in order to invest in education, training and health in order to improve the productivity of labour.

5. Theft

Appropriating resources from other societies and using these to accumulate capital. If resources are appropriated, but not reinvested they will have the same non-sustainable effects as windfall discoveries.

6. Efficiency

Becoming more efficient and effective in the use of capital, labour, land, intermediate inputs and the ways in which these can be combined in production. Efficiency includes: choosing the right combinations of capital and labour, specialising on what a country is good at in production and international trade, shifting resources from less productive to more productive sectors of the economy and better utilisation of capacity.

7. Structural change

Shifting resources to new sectors which are more dynamic than the existing ones and which have positive effects on the whole economy. This goes beyond the static efficiency effects mentioned under **6** above.

8. Economies of scale

Increasing the scale of production to profit from economies of scale. Producing on a larger scale creates opportunities for cost reduction. Related concepts are economies of scope and agglomeration effects. Economies of scope refer to the cost reductions which are achieved by producing a wider range of related products. Agglomeration effects refer to advantages of concentrating production in large urban centres.

9. Technological change

Developing or acquiring new knowledge about how to produce valued goods and services and applying such knowledge in production.

sectors (*appropriate choice of technology*), efficient allocation between less productive and more productive economic sectors (*structural change*), reallocation of resources towards more dynamic sectors (*structural change*), efficient allocation between countries (*specialisation and comparative advantage*), utilisation of capacity and, last but not least, disembodied technological change.[1] The term A denotes net income from capital investments and labour abroad (net factor income) and P refers to colonial plunder and expropriation (negative) or voluntary transfers and development aid (positive).[2] Several of these proximate factors will be further examined in the coming chapters. Economic historians have made efforts to quantify and measure them. Economists have modelled the relationships between inputs and outputs in a great variety of production functions.

Once we have quantified the proximate sources of growth, we can subsequently explore their links with the wider economic and social sources of growth and development. For instance, one can explore the social, historical and institutional roots of the high rates of savings which result in rapid growth of the capital stock in Asia. Or one can explore the policies which accelerate or slow down technological advance.

Based on the time scale, we can make a distinction between *intermediate sources of growth and development* and *ultimate sources of growth and development*. The framework of proximate and ultimate sources of growth has been developed by authors such as Maddison (1988), Abramovitz (1989b) and more recently by Rodrik (2003). It is very useful for the systematic and comprehensive analysis of economic development. Figure 3.1 provides a further elaboration of this framework (Szirmai, 2008, 2012b, 2013). Four levels are distinguished: ultimate sources of growth and development, intermediate sources of growth and development, proximate sources of economic growth and socio-economic outcomes.

Proximate sources refer to directly measurable sources of output growth. These have already been summarised in Box 3.1. One of the most important sources of growth is *disembodied technological change.* This refers to advances in our technological knowledge concerning products and production processes. It involves the development of new production processes, new types of machinery, new forms of organisation, use of new inputs, new products and services, new ways of distributing products and services, and new knowledge that can be transferred through education. It also involves a variety of knowledge spillovers between economic actors and between countries. With regard to technological change, it is important to distinguish between change at the frontiers of knowledge in the lead economies and diffusion and absorption of technology in the follower countries. The latter is of vital importance for developing countries (see Chapter 4).

It is long known (Abramovitz, 1989b; Nelson, 1996; Rodrik, 2003) that one should be careful in giving the sources of growth equation a strong causal interpretation. As Rodrik notes, for instance, capital accumulation and efficiency in the use of resources are themselves *endogenous*. Causality may well run backwards from growth to accumulation and productivity (Rodrik, 2003: 4). These circular relationships are indicated by the

---

[1] Advances in technological knowledge can be *embodied* in capital goods which reflect the latest stages of technological knowledge or in workers who have been exposed to up-to-date knowledge through education and training. *Disembodied* technological change refers to changes in the state of our knowledge which cannot be measured through changes in the quality of capital and labour.

[2] When net factor payments from abroad are included, economists speak of national income (e.g. GNP), when they are excluded they speak of domestic income (e.g. GDP). When we are interested in productive capacity as such, domestic product is the more relevant concept. When we are interested in standards of living and the the resources available to a country, national income is more appropriate.

feedback arrows in Figure 3.1. Nevertheless, the proximate sources of growth formulation is indispensable for a systematic empirical examination of the sources of growth and development.

A new element in Figure 3.1 is that the proximate sources of growth also include the behaviour of the economic actors that are responsible for the changes in the immediate sources of growth, such as saving and capital accumulation, investment in human capital, investment in R&D, efficiency improvements, inventions and innovations, and entering new economic sectors. Economic actors provide the link between the macro-economic analysis of the production function and the burgeoning micro-economic and sociological literature on firm-level analysis, household surveys, entrepreneurship and innovation studies

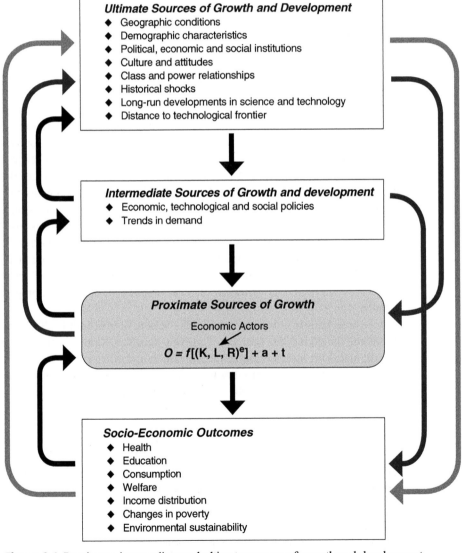

Figure 3.1 Proximate, intermediate and ultimate sources of growth and development

(Szirmai, Naudé and Goedhuys, 2011). It also allows us to examine the relationships between proximate sources of growth such as capital accumulation and ultimate sources such as culture and institutions. Culture and institutions provide the incentives and mindsets for saving, investment and entrepreneurial behaviour by economic actors, which can result in accumulation of capital or technological advance.

Intermediate sources of growth and development include three types of factors: (1) trends in domestic and international demand, (2) economic policies, social policies and technology policies, and (3) changes in the terms of trade (Williamson, 2011). Adding demand and terms of trade as intermediate sources of growth is an attempt to respond to the criticism that the sources of growth framework is an exclusively supply-side approach. Taking patterns of demand into account is important for the understanding of the path-dependent nature of processes of economic development. Thus when world demand or domestic demand are growing rapidly, when a country's market shares are expanding or its terms of trade are improving, this will encourage economic actors to accumulate human and physical capital, which results in further growth and competitiveness.

Policies include a wide range of factors such as trade policies, macro-economic policies, industrial interventions or subsidies to stimulate innovation. They also include social policies in the area of social protection and welfare, which affect the distribution of the fruits of economic development.

Interpreting national and international socio-economic policies as intermediate factors emphasises that policy is in turn influenced and constrained by more ultimate factors such as economic interests and power structures. This is increasingly being rediscovered in recent research in political economy (e.g. Acemoglu *et al.*, 2001; Acemoglu and Robinson, 2006; Shleifer and Vishny, 1993; Glaeser *et al.*, 2004). This research takes policy itself as an endogenous variable, to be explained by more ultimate factors such as the balance of power between classes or between elites and masses.

Underlying both the proximate and intermediate sources, there are more basic social factors, which we call the *ultimate sources of growth and development*. These include external shocks, geographic conditions, long-run trends in scientific and technological knowledge, demographic conditions and trends, economic, political and social institutions, historical developments, social attitudes and capabilities, changes in the class structure and the relationships between social groups, and developments in the international economic and political order and international balance of power, such as discussed in Chapter 2. The ultimate sources of growth and development are summarised in Box 3.2.

The final element of the framework consists of *socio-economic outcomes*. Socio-economic outcomes include health, education, literacy, levels of consumption, the number of people living in poverty, changes in the distribution of income and resources and environmental sustainability. Outcomes are what ultimately matter in development. If a country has rapid growth but no improvement in the living conditions of its people, we cannot speak of development. However, in contrast to much of modern development discourse, the framework of proximate and ultimate causality does emphasise the crucial importance of increases in productive capacity.[3] Improvements in social outcomes are not

---

[3] A recent example of facile anti-growth rhetoric is the report of the Sarkozy Commission on economic performance and progress (Stiglitz, Sen and Fitoussi, 2009).

BOX 3.2 : Ultimate sources of growth and development

1. **Geographic location, climate and natural resources.**
   Geographic location and climate determine the challenges which the people in a country have to face: rich versus poor soils, landlocked versus seaboard location, extreme versus moderate climate, availability of natural resources.
2. **Demographic conditions and trends.** These include the size of population, population density, the rate of population growth and the age structure of the population.
3. **The history of political centralisation, state formation and external domination.**
4. **The dynamics of class relationships and the balance of power between elites and the mass of the population.**
5. **Culture and values.** The evolution of culturally and religiously sanctioned values and attitudes affecting economic behaviour (attitudes towards work and effort, saving and risk, entrepreneurship, science, technology and innovation, rent seeking).
6. **Evolution of institutions which provide incentives for economic behaviour. These include:**
   a. Political institutions for conflict management and the maintenance of law and order
   b. Economic institutions such as private property rights, public ownership of the means of production, intellectual property rights (IPRs), joint stock companies, central planning institutions, banking institutions and other institutions for financial intermediation, and inheritance institutions affecting the intergenerational transfer of wealth
   c. Labour market institutions
   d. Institutions regulating social protection.
7. **Developments in the international order such as changing international trade regimes or migration flows.**
8. **Long-run developments in science and technology.** These determine the limits and possibilities of technological advance in economic production.
9. **The distance to the technological frontier.** This influences the catch-up potential of a country.
10. **Absorptive capacities and the evolution of technological and social capabilities.** These determine the extent to which a country and its firms can benefit from international knowledge flows.

possible without long-run increases in productive capacity, as indicated by growth in GDP per capita. Economic growth is one of the essential preconditions for improvements in social outcomes. There can be no expansion of a healthcare system or an educational system or a system of social protection without a sustained increase in productive capacity.[4]

---

[4] The growth equation can easily be transformed into a productivity equation, by dividing inputs and outputs by labour input. We then get GDP per capita as the dependent variable and the amount of capital per worker, the

Improving the living conditions of the poor, while moving towards more sustainable systems of production, also requires advances in productive capacity.

But, on the other hand, the degree to which productive capacity is transformed into desired social outcomes depends on the nature of social and economic policy (intermediate causality) and the incentives provided by the institutional framework and initial levels of socio-economic inequality (ultimate causality). In Figure 3.1 socio-economic outcomes are not only influenced by an arrow running from the proximate sources of growth to outcomes, but also by arrows connecting ultimate conditions and intermediate policies with socio-economic outcomes.

The use of the term 'ultimate', 'intermediate' and 'proximate' is not meant to imply a linear model of causality. Causality is circular at all levels, as indicated by the feedback arrows in Figure 3.1. For instance, improved health and education (social outcomes) result in higher quality of labour inputs (proximate causality), but also in the longer run in changes in absorptive capacity (ultimate causality). Changes in the distribution of income and wealth (social outcomes) change the incentives for economic actors in the growth equation. Growth of per capita incomes affects demographic and epidemiological transitions (see Chapters 5 and 6). In the long run even cultural values and institutions are shaped and reshaped in the course of economic development (Harrison, 1985; Harrison and Huntington, 2000).[5]

The difference between the more ultimate and more proximate sources of causality lies mainly in the ease of quantification and the time span of the chains of causality. It also provides a research strategy, which starts with the measurable economic factors and then goes beyond them to broader social and historical determinants. It also provides a framework for multidisciplinary analysis of socio-economic development.

It is important to emphasise that Figure 3.1 is a framework for the analysis of development rather than a theory of development as such. There is no monocausal model of development, where one crucial variable always explains development. There is no checklist of factors which have to be ticked off to explain development (Hirschman, 1988; Szirmai, 2013; Von Tunzelmann, 1995). In different historical periods, different configurations of factors operate and there is a great variety of development paths. On the other hand, one can learn much from a systematic analysis of the factors that play a role in development and their interactions. At the minimum one can say that a common element of successful development involves positive feedback loops whereby initial success creates conditions for further success and rapid economic growth removes obstacles to further growth and development in a virtuous cycle (Myrdal, 1971).

The remainder of the chapter discusses theories of economic growth and development, which involve ultimate, intermediate and proximate factors. Chapters 6 and 7 zoom in on social outcomes in the important areas of health and education.

---

amount of education per worker and natural resources per worker as inputs. As long as GDP is growing more rapidly than population, GDP per capita (our measure of productive capacity) will increase.

[5] Ester Boserup has argued that even the seemingly ultimate factor of 'natural' environment has been shaped by the impact of human interventions in socio-economic development.

3.2 Classical thinking about growth, development and stagnation

Since the eighteenth century, classical economists and sociologists have concerned themselves with the mystery of breakthrough and economic growth in the capitalist West. Their work is primarily concerned with the ultimate sources of growth and development, and many of their ideas still play a prominent role in topical discussions of problems of development. Without doing justice to the complexities in the thought of these authors, we shall briefly touch upon a number of important themes in classical thought, which have retained their relevance for present-day discussions.

3.2.1 Adam Smith

In *The Wealth of Nations* (1961), Adam Smith (1723–90) ranked countries according to their economic performance. The most modern and prosperous country was the Republic of the United Netherlands, followed by England, France, North America, Scotland, China, with Bengal coming in last place. Smith was interested in how differences between countries had come about and how knowledge about the causes of prosperity could help England improve its relative standing *vis-à-vis* the Netherlands. Smith attacked traditional obstacles to free trade and free competition, such as guilds and royal monopolies. The more individuals were left free to pursue their own interests, the more the 'invisible hand' of the market would promote collective welfare. In addition, Smith emphasised the importance of the division of labour in the production process, the increase of worker skills owing to the dividing up of tasks, and specialisation and economies of scale. The division of labour within firms and the increase in the scale of production associated with specialisation, trade and expanding markets would lead to dramatic increases in productivity.

3.2.2 The classical economists Ricardo, Malthus and Mill

The classical economists David Ricardo (1792–1823), Thomas Malthus (1766–1834) and John Stuart Mill (1806–73) shared Smith's preference for free markets and *laissez faire* policies. The government should intervene as little as possible in the economic process. One might say that the classical economists offered an *institutional explanation* of economic growth. People have an innate tendency to engage in exchange and trade. If social institutions give free play to such tendencies, individual self-interest will stimulate efforts, which contribute to economic growth and increasing prosperity for all.

Compared to Smith, the classical economists placed more emphasis on capital accumulation, the importance of the stock of capital goods used in the production process and on the importance of international trade. Ricardo formulated his famous *law of comparative advantage*. This law states that all countries entering into international trade will profit from such trade if they concentrate on the production of those products in which they are relatively most efficient. This law is still the keystone of modern arguments for liberalisation of international trade and an international division of labour in production. Comparative advantage enters our framework as one of the proximate sources of growth.

There are also some pessimistic elements present in the work of the classical authors. Malthus was afraid that food production would not be able to keep up with population growth. In the long run, this would result in starvation and widespread famine, which would serve as a check to further population growth. Malthusianism has become the general term for all modern pessimistic perspectives emphasising the limits to economic growth.

Ricardo feared that economic development would stagnate in the long run. As more and more people work in agriculture owing to population growth, less and less fertile soils are taken into production and diminishing returns set in. When the marginal product in agriculture declines, food will become scarce and prices will go up, in turn exerting an upward pressure on wages in industry. Rising food prices are translated into higher wage costs. In due time increasing wages cut into profits and thus into future investment. The engine of economic growth grinds to a halt. Ricardo's theory is a predecessor of modern *two-sector models*, which analyse the relationships between agriculture and industry in economic development (Fei and Ranis, 1964; Lewis, 1954). Ricardo was in favour of abolishing tariffs on food imports, to keep food prices from rising. This would postpone the slowdown of growth.

3.2.3 Friedrich List

Ricardo, Malthus and Mill all lived and wrote at a time when the dominant power in the world economy, England, propagated international free trade. They were convinced of the advantages of free trade, but Friedrich List (1789–1846), German by birth and founder of the 'historical school' in economics was less enthusiastic about its blessings. According to him, it was the dominant powers that primarily profited from free trade. Latecomers to economic development such as the German states were hindered in their development by competition from economically advanced countries. List argued for tariff protection of newly founded German industries against murderous international competition. This so-called *infant industry argument* would play an important role in the development strategies of developing countries in the twentieth century. He also saw an important role for public measures in promoting and supporting industrialisation.

List identified four stages of development through which all countries in the temperate climatic zone will pass: (1) Pastoral life, (2) Agricultural societies, (3) Agriculture combined with manufactures, and (4) A final stage where agriculture, manufactures and commerce are combined. List was convinced that active government intervention was necessary to build up an industrial sector in late-developing economies and to further the structural transformation of agrarian into agrarian/industrial societies. He explicitly discusses the role of intermediate factors, namely trade policies and industrial policies. All successful catch-up economies in the twentieth century have followed List's policy prescriptions.

3.2.4 Classical sociologists: Spencer, Tönnies and Durkheim

Like the classical economists, the classical sociologists also focused on the major developmental trends associated with the rise of modern capitalist societies.[6] The classical economists' preference for free markets was mirrored in the Social Darwinism of Spencer (1820–1903) and his followers. Applying metaphors from biological evolutionism to social evolution, Herbert Spencer argued that societies evolve, adapting to changing environmental conditions.[7] Social evolution is seen as a process of increasing size, differentiation

---

[6] The modern division of labour between the social sciences only emerged in the course of the nineteenth century. Many early authors, including Adam Smith, combined sociological and economic perspectives in their work.

[7] Spencer actually formulated his theories well before Darwin published *The Origin of Species* in 1859.

and complexity, but also increasing interaction and integration of differentiated functions. Social regularities emerge as the unanticipated consequences of individual actions and choices. Industrial societies represent later stages of social evolution, militant hierarchical societies represent earlier states. Markets and market exchange emerge as part of the process of social differentiation. Market competition is seen as promoting the survival of the fittest – i.e. the most efficient – firms and thus contributes to further social change and increasing welfare. Governments should abstain from intervening in the markets. Social Darwinism can have some rather crude social implications such as the rejection of all welfare systems, minimum wage regulations and imputations of evolutionary superiority of dominant civilisations or ethnic groups. But the analytic elements of variety and selection environments resurface in modern evolutionary economic theories of development (Nelson and Winter, 1982).

While the economists primarily focused on the sources and dynamics of growth, many of the classical sociologists focused on the changes in social relationships that accompanied economic growth. Ferdinand Tönnies (1855–1936) highlighted the change from more communal social patterns (*Gemeinschaft*) to more individualistic, specialised and impersonal relationships (*Gesellschaft*). Among others these involved the decline of extended families and communities and the rise of nuclear families which interacted with other nuclear families through markets. While communal relationships based on family, kinship, clan and local community are multistranded and complex, *Gesellschaft*-type relationships are single-stranded, rational and anonymous. People are bound together by contractual relationships focusing on well-defined exchanges. These polarities will later surface in the so-called modernisation theories of development and in many comparisons between 'developing' and 'more developed' societies.

One of the greatest of the classical sociologists, Émile Durkheim (1858–1917) analysed the potentially negative social effects of such social transformations in the course of development. In his early work he distinguished between more communal societies characterised by *mechanical solidarity* (well-integrated local communities rather isolated from each other) and modern societies characterised by *organic solidarity* (extended networks of interdependence and exchange between individuals performing specialised actions). In his later works he pointed to the erosion of common norms (*anomie*) and the rise of divorce rates and suicides in highly individualistic modern societies. The discussion about the disruptive social effects of global economic transformations is still central to all modern debates about development.

3.2.5   Karl Marx

Karl Marx (1818–83) focused on the dynamic role of capitalism as an explanation of economic developments in the West. Just like List and other representatives of the historical school of economics, Marx postulated a unilineal theory of stages of development, in which every society sooner or later passes through the same stages. His stages of development were: primitive original communism, slavery, feudalism, capitalism and socialism, each characterised by a different mode of production and by typical conflicts between the dominant classes, who own the means of production and the subordinate classes, who do not. Each stage was characterised by internal contradictions between the development of the production forces (the production technology) and the social relations of production (class relationships, the social organisation of production). These internal contradictions were the ultimate drivers of socio-economic change and development.

Each subsequent stage represented a higher level in the development process. In the West, the contradictions within feudalism had for the first time led to the overthrow of an economic system based on ownership of land and its replacement by an economic system based on the ownership of capital goods. Sooner or later societies in other parts of the world would inevitably go through the same transition. Such stage theories were the foundation of the negative attitude of many twentieth-century Marxist regimes towards agriculture, which was seen as representing an outmoded stage of development.

In Marxist theories, class contradictions – conflicts of interest between social groups that own the predominant means of production and social groups that do not – play a central role in the explanation of social dynamics. Under capitalism, competition between the owners of the means of production provides the incentive for accumulation of capital and technological progress. But it also results in an ever-increasing exploitation of the newly created industrial working classes by the capitalist classes.

Marx agreed with the classical economists that capitalism had led to a revolutionary increase in productive capacity. The capitalist system was seen as a dynamic and successful system promoting both capital accumulation and technological change. Productive potential was liberated from the shackles of feudalism. In due course, however, these liberating tendencies of capitalism were superseded by repressive tendencies. The capitalist system, in the grip of competitive forces and conjunctural fluctuations, was no longer able to make an efficient use of the newly unchained productive capacities. Competition led to increasing exploitation of workers. Impoverishment of workers led to decreasing purchasing power of the working class. The economic result was overproduction, declining profit margins and ever-deepening economic crises. The social result was pauperisation and increasing revolutionary class consciousness. In the long run, the increased polarisation between the capitalist class and the working class would inevitably lead to revolution and the collapse of capitalism. Marx predicted that these revolutions would take place in the most advanced capitalist societies.

According to Marx, the essence of capitalism is production for profit and reinvestment, rather than production for the satisfaction of human needs. Competition forces entrepreneurs to invest continuously in more and qualitatively better means of production. Thus, just as in classical economic thought, accumulation of capital has a central place in Marxist theory. However, in contrast to the classical economists, Marx did not see capital accumulation and economic growth as a harmonious process leading to increased collective welfare.

Economic development is characterised by continuous exploitation, appropriation of surpluses for the purposes of reinvestment, and social conflict. Competing entrepreneurs can only make a profit by paying their workers no more than a subsistence wage, which barely keeps them alive. One of the Marxist ideas which continues to have considerable relevance for modern thinking about economic development, is the relationship between appropriation of economic surplus by certain social groups – capitalists, governments – and the process of reinvestment, accumulation of capital and economic growth. Successful economic development in the second half of the twentieth century was invariably associated in its earlier phase with the ruthless exploitation of cheap labour.

3.2.6 Theories of imperialism

Marxist stage theory predicted that socialist revolutions would only take place in the most advanced capitalist countries. These predictions have failed to come true, creating a crisis in Marxist theory. When Communist revolutions materialised, they invariably took place in agrarian societies, with low levels of industrial development, such as Tsarist Russia, China, Vietnam, Cambodia or Cuba. A later generation of theorists (Hilferding, 1877–1943; Hobson, 1858–1940; Lenin, 1870–1924; Luxemburg 1870–1919) tried to explain the absence of the predicted revolutions in advanced countries with various theories of imperialism. Such theories state that the Western world succeeded in transferring its internal contradictions and conflicts to the world economy and developing countries. In the process of imperialist expansion in the second half of the nineteenth century, these countries were colonised and exploited.

Theories of imperialism come in many guises. Some explained imperialist expansion by pointing to the lack of investment opportunities in the advanced countries and the search for new investment possibilities in the colonies. Others pointed to factors such as the safeguarding of the flow of raw materials as inputs for industrial development or the search for new markets for industrial products which could no longer be sold in saturated home markets because of overproduction. Theories of imperialism were drawn up at a time when the Western expansion in the world was at its apex. Without exception, these theories stressed the negative effects of imperialism on the development chances of the poor countries.

Nowadays, the empirical evidence for economic explanations of imperialism is considered to be weak (Chirot, 1977; Fieldhouse, 1973; see also Schumpeter, 1976). Nevertheless, these theories have been a source of inspiration for twentieth-century theorists of underdevelopment.

3.2.7 Max Weber and Joseph Schumpeter

To conclude this short excursion through the history of ideas, we will briefly discuss some ideas of two important post-Marxist scholars Max Weber and Joseph Schumpeter. Both of these authors follow Marx in his emphasis on the importance of class conflict, and the analysis of the dynamics of capitalism. But they also offer fundamental criticisms of the Marxian legacy.

While Marx saw the profit motive as the essential characteristic of the capitalist system, Max Weber (1864–1920) emphasised the principle of rational calculation of means and ends. According to Weber, the development of capitalism was part of a wider long-run social trend of rationalisation and bureaucratisation in Western societies. The profit motive is common to all times; it cannot differentiate capitalism from other economic systems. New in capitalism is the rational organisation of production for the purposes of sustained profitability, making use of systematic accounting methods. The emergence of markets is also part of the long-run rationalisation trend. Production for the market stimulates businesslike rational thinking about means and ends and the calculation of financial costs and benefits, irrespective of the personal relationships involved in the transactions. The rise of bureaucracy was seen by Weber as the rise of a radically new and highly efficient form of organisation, systematically harnessing human capabilities to organisational goals. Not only government bureaucracies, but also big capitalist firms, successfully made use of efficient, impersonal bureaucratic forms of organisation. This idea has had a major impact on modern scholarship. For instance, the economic historian David Landes (1969, 1998) sees the high value placed on rational manipulation of physical and social environment as one of the distinguishing characteristics of European economic development.

Weber explicitly posed the question of why capitalism had broken through in Western Europe, rather than elsewhere in the world. Marx saw developments in the economic sphere of society, the 'substructure', as determining developments in culture, religion, politics and law (the 'superstructure'). In contradiction to this, Weber sought the explanation of the rise of capitalism in religious influences. He noted that the first capitalist countries were predominantly Protestant. His famous hypothesis – known as the Weber thesis – states that the Protestant Ethic favoured economic development. The combination of diligent and disciplined work in one's professional 'calling' and religiously motivated sobriety in consumption promoted high levels of savings and the accumulation of capital (see Chapter 9). According to Weber, the Protestant Ethic was the factor that distinguished the Western world from other regions where the breakthrough of capitalism did not take place. Thus the Protestant Ethic is the determining factor in the rise of capitalism and process of economic growth in the West (Weber, 1969). Though the Weber thesis has since been heavily criticised for its simple one-directional causality, Weber's emphasis on the attitudinal foundations of economic performance remains of lasting importance.

A third difference with the Marxist tradition lies in the greater importance of the political sphere. According to Marx, developments in the political sphere (part of the superstructure of society) are determined by developments in the economic sphere (the substructure). According to Weber, economic development presupposes the rise of highly centralised state apparatuses, which are able to maintain internal peace and order in a country. Without internal peace, centralisation and standardisation of rules and regulations, markets will never be able to function. If trade is unpredictable, if there are all sorts of capricious local rules, taxes and tithes and if the safety of trade is not guaranteed, a rational assessment of the costs and benefits of long-term investments is impossible. Thus, the formation of stable centralised states precedes the rise of capitalism. In line with the Weberian tradition, state formation is seen as one of the ultimate sources of growth and development in Figure 3.2. It will be discussed in Chapter 11.

While Weber focused on the origins of the capitalist breakthrough, Schumpeter (1883–1950) was primarily interested in twentieth-century capitalism. From Marx he derived the idea of capitalism as an economic system, riven by deep class conflicts. This system was both destructive and extremely dynamic. However, in contradiction to Marx, Schumpeter did not believe capitalism would be destroyed by its own inefficiencies. In the middle of the Great Depression of the 1930s, Schumpeter correctly predicted a golden age of more than fifty years of economic growth in the Western world (Schumpeter, 1976).

According to Schumpeter, capitalism is characterised by a 'gale of creative destruction'. Old production techniques are continuously becoming obsolescent and are being replaced by new ones. Schumpeter emphasises the importance of technological progress. Long cycles of economic growth were driven by major technological breakthroughs such as textile spinning and weaving, steam power (1780–1842), railways (1842–97) and chemicals, electrical power and automobiles (1898–1930s). The hero of technological progress is the entrepreneur who realises 'new combinations': new forms of organisation, new production techniques, new products, new markets, new sources of raw materials (Schumpeter,

2000). Capitalism as a system gives free rein to the entrepreneur and thus creates incentives for an ample supply of entrepreneurship.

In the long run, however, Schumpeter thought that capitalism would be undermined by its successes rather than its failures. The process of innovation would become routinised. The role of the creative entrepreneur would be taken over by staff departments and research laboratories of large monopolistic enterprises. Gradually and unnoticeably the system would be transformed into something akin to a socialist planning system, through the planning and managerial procedures of the very large capitalist firms. At the same time, the uncertainties involved in the process of creative destruction and the disappearance of feudal classes, which acted as a political buffer, would undermine political support for capitalist institutions.

On the basis of Schumpeter's later work two forms of Schumpeterian competition can be identified: Schumpeter Mark I, where small innovative entrepreneurial firms dominate, and Schumpeter Mark II where giant corporations have taken over the innovative function and engage in oligopolistic competition (Schumpeter, 1976). The respective roles of small and medium-sized enterprises (SMEs) and giant corporations in innovation and growth are debated to this day.

It is not clear whether Schumpeter would consider the present-day Western mixed economies as capitalist or socialist. But the question whether developing countries have a sufficient supply of entrepreneurship is one of the classical questions, which keep cropping up in post-war theorising on development. A related question is whether developing countries provide a sufficiently stimulating atmosphere for the emergence of entrepreneurial and innovative behaviour (Naudé, 2010; Szirmai, Naudé and Goedhuys, 2011).

3.3 Internal and external approaches

The classical authors were primarily concerned with explanations of the economic breakthrough and growth of the presently prosperous Western countries. Without exception they emphasised the importance of the rise of capitalist institutions, markets and property rights in explaining growth. The post-war discussion of development focuses more on the reasons why the poorer countries could not keep up with the richer ones.

At the end of Chapter 2 a distinction was made between internal approaches and external approaches to economic development. Both the internal and the external approaches start with the empirical observation that economy and society in developing countries are characterised by *dualism*. The term refers to the existence side by side of a modern and a traditional sector. The modern sector is technologically developed, commercialised and is located in and around urban centres. The traditional sector is characterised by traditional technologies, low productivity, production for own consumption and is predominantly rural. Dualist structures in developing countries came into being at the end of the nineteenth century, when these countries were drawn into international trade. Capitalist enclaves emerged within non-capitalist economic systems.

The main problem of dualism is the economic and social gap between the modern and the traditional sector. The modern sector is oriented to the outside world, rather than to domestic society. There are few linkages between the modern sector and the rest of the economy and society. Thus, a developing country as a whole does not profit much from technological and economic development in the modern sector. Also, a traditional hinterland can form an obstacle to the further development of a modern sector which is relatively small in size.

Internal approaches emphasise the factors within a society which promote or hinder development. Thus one of the founding fathers of development economics, J.H. Boeke, explained the lack of development of the traditional sector in Indonesia by pointing to the characteristics of oriental man and oriental culture, in which individual economic incentives were not operative. Needs were limited; social needs dominated individual needs (Boeke, 1961a, 1961b). The continuation of a traditional economy alongside the modern enclave was thus explained by internal cultural and institutional characteristics.

External approaches try to explain the situation in developing countries by reference to negative influences from the advanced economies. Dualistic structures are created by external economic and political penetration and exploitation. These external influences also maintain the dualistic structures. The external and internal perspectives will be discussed in more detail in the following sections.

3.4 Explanations of economic backwardness

Internal approaches to the problems of development draw our attention to the unfavourable circumstances and factors within a society which form an obstacle for development. These obstacles explain *economic backwardness*. In the pessimistic perspective of Boeke there was little chance of overcoming the internal obstacles to development. However, most representatives of internal approaches are more optimistic. The modernisation theorists of the 1950s and 1960s believed that a long-run process of modernisation has set in, in which all societies gradually move from traditionality in the direction of modernity. Dualism exists because modernisation has taken place in one part of society, but not yet in society as a whole. The key words are 'not yet'. Less developed countries have a 'lag' compared to more developed countries, just as the less developed traditional sectors lag behind the modern sectors. Once the internal barriers to development have been overcome, the laggards can start overtaking the leaders.

3.4.1 Rostow's theory of the stages of economic growth

One of the most well-known representatives of modernisation theory is W. W. Rostow. In *The Stages of Economic Growth* (1960) he sketched a stage theory of growth in which each society sooner or later passes through the same five stages: (1) traditional society, (2) preconditions to take-off, (3) take-off, (4) 'drive to maturity', and (5) mass consumption society. In this development process some countries take the lead, others lag behind. Just as in Marxist theory, however, the path of development is the same for all societies. All trains stop at the same stations.

In the *traditional society* (Stage 1) fatalistic patterns of thought predominate, in which people feel at the mercy of external forces of nature, higher powers, or political rulers. The production technology is static.

In the *precondition* stage (Stage 2) the stability of the traditional society is undermined, usually as a result of external threats or challenges. In this stage the idea emerges that people can improve their living conditions or those of their children by their own efforts. A beginning is made with the translation of the insights of modern science into production technologies.

In the economic sphere the conditions for industrialisation are created in this period. The most important condition is an increase in productivity in one of the non-industrial sectors such as agriculture or mining. This creates a surplus above subsistence, which is potentially available for investment in the industrial sector. Especially in agriculture, such an increase in productivity is of the greatest importance. Productivity growth in agriculture frees labour for employment in the industrial sector and fulfils the food requirements of a growing population. Increased earnings in the agrarian sector provide a market for industrial goods, while financial surpluses from agriculture can be invested in industry.

In the precondition stage investments are realised in infrastructure (railways, canals, roads, energy supply, harbours and so forth), which are a prerequisite for industrialisation. In the social–political sphere, the pre-condition stage is characterised by the emergence of modernising elites, which deliberately strive for development and industrialisation. Socially, the horizon of expectations expands.

The crucial stage is the *take-off* stage (Stage 3). The analogy is that of an aeroplane which gains sufficient speed on the runway to take off into flight. In the take-off stage the structure of the economy changes very drastically in a short period of ten to twenty years, after which sustained growth can set in. In the take-off stage the level of investment needs to be increased substantially to boost growth. Echoing earlier publications by Lewis (1950, 1954), Rostow writes that investment should increase from less than 5 per cent to more than 10 per cent of net national income (NNI).

In the take-off stage, investment should be directed towards industrial sectors, with the strongest linkages with the rest of the economy. In the past the role of 'leading sector' has been played by the textile industry, the military industry, the railway industry and the chemical industry. The current development literature identifies the ICT sector as one of the leading sectors in the modern world (Fagerberg, 2000). Other characteristics of the take-off stage are a sufficient supply of entrepreneurship and a sufficient supply of loanable funds, which can be channelled into the industrial sector, either voluntarily or involuntarily.

In the subsequent '*drive to maturity*' stage (Stage 4), new production techniques spread from the leading sectors to the rest of the economy. In the last stage, *mass-consumption society* (Stage 5), which looks suspiciously like Rostow's North American society, the whole population benefits from the increased opportunities for consumption.

Parallel with Rostow's primarily economically oriented theories, the 1950s and 1960s witnessed the rise of various sociological theories of modernisation (Hagen, 1962; Hoselitz, 1960; Inkeles, 1969; Inkeles and Smith, 1974; Lerner, 1958; Moore, 1963). These theories take up themes from classical sociology and chart the social changes which accompany economic growth, including: urbanisation, the transition from extended family structures to nuclear families, the increasing division of labour and occupational specialisation, the rationalisation in attitudes, the increasing social mobility, and the transition from ascription to achievement as the determining principle of social stratification,[8] increasing levels of schooling and individualisation. Like Rostovian theory and classical stage theories,

---

[8] In an ascriptive society a person's position in the social hierarchy is determined at birth by the position of his or her parents and does not depend on effort, talent, or performance.

modernisation theories usually conceive of development as a unilinear path from a traditional to a modern society. Some sociological modernisation theories focus on the social disruption accompanying rapid technological and economic change. These theories hark back to the classical Durkheimian tradition in sociology, which analyses the increasing normlessness (*anomie*) of modern social life (Durkheim, 1973).

An important policy recommendation deriving from Rostovian analysis is the requirement of large-scale investment in industry in the take-off stage. Foreign investment, loans and development aid can help compensate for the shortfalls in domestic savings and foreign currency requirements, compared to investment needs. Development aid, training and education can also help surmount the traditional obstacles to growth and contribute to the realisation of the preconditions for take-off. From the economic perspective, Rostow represented a wider intellectual climate of the 1950s and 1960s focusing on the need for massive investment, the mobilisation of savings and seeing capital as the missing link in development.

Similar ideas have been formulated by the early development economists Rosenstein-Rodan (1943) and Nurkse (1953), who called for a 'Big Push' in investment to escape from vicious circles of poverty. The 'Big Push' approach will be discussed in more detail in the chapter dealing with industrialisation (Chapter 9).

Rostow's theory of stages of development has been severely criticised in the course of time, just like modernisation theory in general. Nevertheless, it is striking how many traces of his theory can be found in the work of later authors. A recent example of Rostovian unilineal thinking is the dichotomy between limited access orders and open access orders made by Douglass North and his co-authors (North *et al.*, 2009).

3.4.2   Kuznets' preconditions for industrialisation

According to Simon Kuznets (1965) it is not possible to distinguish Rostow's stages of growth empirically. The changes in investment and growth rates are more gradual than the dramatic term 'take-off' suggests. The concept of traditional society does not do justice to the great diversity of social and economic circumstances in pre-capitalist societies. Finally, Kuznets, along with many authors, has serious objections to the unilinear concept of development, the idea that every society follows one and the same path of development. It makes a big difference, for instance, whether a country is an early or a late industrialiser, whether industrialisation takes place in a large country with a large domestic market, a small country with a small domestic market, a resource-rich or a resource-poor country (e.g. Chenery *et al.*, 1986). Also, there is nothing inevitable about stages of development. Countries can move backward as well as forward (Kuznets, 1965).

Nevertheless, there are also some important similarities between Kuznets and Rostow. Like Rostow, Kuznets emphasises the importance of industrialisation in development. *Changes in the structure of production* are among the main characteristics of modern economic development.[9] Furthermore, Kuznets identifies conditions for industrialisation, which are similar to those mentioned by Rostow: productivity increases in other sectors such as mining, agriculture or transport, sufficient supply of labour, capital and entrepreneurship and sufficient effective demand for industrial products.

---

[9] The importance of structural change is also emphasised by authors such as Lewis and Fei and Ranis, whose work will be discussed in Chapters 8 and 9.

According to Kuznets (1955) industrialisation and urbanisation in developing countries are accompanied by increasing income inequality. This is caused by two factors. First, urban/industrial incomes are higher than rural incomes. Second, urban income inequality is higher than rural income inequality. At later stages of economic development, the income distribution becomes more equal as a result of demographic factors, democratisation and the rise of trade unions and political pressure groups. This is referred to as the *inverted U-curve hypothesis*, which is still being hotly debated in current international comparative research. There seems to be agreement about increases in inequality when growth accelerates in poor countries. But recent findings indicate that there is no automatic tendency for inequality to decline at higher levels of national income per capita. On the contrary, income inequality in most of the advanced economies has been increasing since around 1980 (see Atkinson *et al.*, 2010).

3.4.3 Neoclassical theories of growth

Neoclassical economic theories of growth analyse the relationships between the growth of inputs (capital, land, labour, technology) and growth of output, in the form of mathematical models of growth.[10] Compared to the theories discussed so far the neoclassical economic theory of growth as formulated by Solow (1956, 1957) focuses primarily on the proximate sources of growth. It has little or nothing to say about the more fundamental social mechanisms and institutions underlying accumulation of capital, technical change and growth.

The Solow model makes use of the so-called Cobb–Douglas function, which takes the form:

$$O = AK^{\alpha}L^{1-\alpha}.$$

Output is a function of the stock of capital and the amount of labour, with α and $1-\alpha$ representing the elasticity of output to capital and labour and A reflecting the state of knowledge (technology). This draws our attention to the contribution to growth of the accumulation of factors of production and of changes in the quality of factors of production. Changes in K are determined by investment decisions, changes in L by labour market decisions of households and firms. Solow and his contemporaries found that accumulation of physical capital (K) and labour (L) accounted for less than 50 per cent of growth. The rest was due to technological advance (A) which was an exogenous factor.

The Solow model emphasises the importance of an efficient allocation of factors of production in processes of economic development. Capital and labour can be substituted for each other. If labour is cheap and abundant, as in many developing countries, than efficient allocation implies a choice for labour-intensive forms of production. Free markets and perfect competition are the mechanisms which make for such efficient allocation.

The Solow model of growth assumes profit-maximising behaviour on the part of economic actors. Firms will continue to use more and more capital and labour in production, as long as the marginal costs of these factors of production are less than their marginal returns. Under competitive conditions and perfect information, this will result in equalisation of

[10] For accessible introductory expositions see Jones (1998) and Ray (2000).

marginal costs and marginal returns. The model assumes constant returns to scale – implying, for instance, that if the amount of both capital and labour is doubled, output will also double. If one factor of production is held constant, while the other increases, the marginal returns to the increasing factor will diminish. The model assumes that the growth of labour depends on population growth and is thus given. The growth of the capital stock is determined by the savings rate. The share of savings in national income is assumed constant.

Now as the savings are used to accumulate more and more capital per worker, labour productivity will go up. But as the marginal returns to capital are declining because of diminishing returns, the rate of increase in labour productivity will decline and productivity growth in the long run will become zero. Per capita income growth will then come to a stop as the economy reaches its steady state. In the steady state output grows at the same rate as population and the level of per capita income is fixed.

The only factor which counterbalances diminishing returns is technological change, the rate of which is determined outside the model (i.e. exogenously) and is not explained. Technological change shifts the production function upwards. In the long run, therefore, the growth rate of labour productivity depends on technological change. Technological knowledge is assumed to be freely available to all countries in the world economy. Therefore, assuming perfect information and in absence of institutions blocking the diffusion of technology, all countries are assumed to have the same rate of technological change.

As developing countries have less capital per worker than rich countries, the marginal productivity of capital should be higher and labour productivity growth will therefore be more rapid than in rich countries. In the long run, per capita incomes in rich and poor countries will tend to converge. This is referred to as the hypothesis of *unconditional convergence*. This tendency towards convergence in neoclassical theory is strengthened by the assumption that capital moves freely across the world economy. If returns are higher in developing countries, capital will move there, making for convergence. Technology is also conceived of as a public good, which is available to all economies. Therefore in the long run rich and poor countries should converge in per capita incomes and in growth rates and their steady state growth rate of per capita income should be determined by the rate of technological change.

Neoclassical theory does not focus explicitly on developing countries. Implicitly, however it predicts that, if markets function smoothly and the factors of production can move freely across the world economy, sooner or later rich and poor countries will converge and developing countries will catch-up.

As discussed in Chapters 1 and 2, there is no empirical support for convergence between rich and poor countries in the world economy. On the contrary, world income differentials have been increasing. Within the framework of neoclassical growth theory, the absence of unconditional convergence can be explained by differences in savings rates. If savings propensities differ and population growth rates are similar, than the theory states that countries will tend to converge to the same growth rate, but not to the same long-run per capita incomes. Per capita incomes in groups of countries with similar initial savings rates will still tend to converge, countries with lower incomes growing more rapidly than countries with higher initial incomes within a given group. But, countries with different initial savings rates do not have to converge to the same income levels.

A further extension of the notion of conditional convergence is that of convergence clubs. Convergence clubs are countries that have similar initial conditions not only in terms of savings but also in levels of education, technological capabilities and absorptive capacities. The *conditional convergence hypothesis* states that countries within a convergence club will tend to converge to common growth rates and income levels, but the steady state growth rates of the different convergence clubs may be very different. Thus convergence within groups can coexist with divergence in the whole world economy. In cross-country regression analyses a wide range of initial conditions have been taken into account, including savings rates, population growth rates, initial levels of capital per worker, educational levels and political variables (see Barro, 1991; Barro and Sala-i-Martin, 1995; Baumol *et al.*, 1989; Mankiw *et al.*, 1992).

3.4.4 Growth accounting

Parallel with the rise of neoclassical growth theory, there is the rise of the growth accounting tradition, pioneered by authors such as Abramovitz (1989a), Denison (1967), Jorgenson (1995), Kendrick (1961), and Maddison (1970, 1987). Growth accounting focuses on the empirical measurement and quantification of the contributions of different proximate sources of growth, taking the neoclassical production function framework as an initial point of departure. It asks questions such as: how much of growth is explained by capital accumulation, how much by education, how much by efficiency, how much by technological change? Step by step growth accountants try to increase the percentage of growth explained by the various proximate sources. Thus, capital is 'augmented' by taking the quality change of capital goods into account and labour is augmented by adjusting labour input for its human capital (health, education).

While growth theory tends to focus on formal modelling, growth accounting has a much stronger empirical orientation. Theoretically it is more eclectic. Measurement of the proximate sources of growth and their contribution allows one to link up these sources with institutional and historical analysis.

Growth accounting makes a distinction between the growth of inputs (increase in the quantity and quality of capital and labour) and the growth of output per unit of input (see Maddison, 1987). Like the Solow model, growth accounting shows that a considerable part of growth cannot be accounted for by increases in the amount of inputs of capital and labour, even after these have been adjusted for increases in quality and education. Growth accounting goes on to explain the growth of output per unit of input (or total factor productivity) by various factors, for example structural shifts from low-productivity sectors such as agriculture to high-productivity sectors such as manufacturing, economies of scale and technological change. An important part of growth can only be explained by technological advance, which is the interpretation of the residual part of growth that cannot be accounted for by other factors. One of the important debates in the 1990s was whether rapid growth in some Asian economies was primarily owing to technological change and rapid increases in total factor productivity (World Bank, 1993) or rather, as argued by Young (1995), whether it was primarily due to enormous efforts to accumulate more capital and improve education. The focus of both neoclassical theory and growth accounting on the accumulation of capital, education and technological change, places these approaches squarely within the internal tradition in the analysis of backwardness.

New growth theory

A new version of neoclassical growth theory emerged in the mid 1980s. One of the main criticisms of older neoclassical growth models is that technological change was conceived of as 'exogenous'. The rate of technological change itself was not explained. It came as manna from heaven. New growth theory tries to explain technological change as a result of human efforts. Economic actors not only invest in physical and human capital. They also invest in knowledge. New growth theories pay special attention to investments in knowledge, R&D technology and schooling.

New growth theories try to endogenise[11] technological change in two ways (Lucas, 1988; Romer, 1986, 1990; for an overview see Fagerberg, 1994). In the first place it is assumed that technological change (changes in the stock of knowledge about production) is automatically associated with investment in capital goods and education, through a process of learning by doing. Investment in capital and education creates technological advance, which counteracts the diminishing returns to scale of the older neoclassical growth model.

In the second place, one can conceive of investment in a separate sector producing technology and knowledge through investments in R&D and knowledge. These technologies become available for all firms engaged in production of goods and services, not only for the firms that initially developed the technology. Knowledge spills over from one firm to another. Thus, the production of goods and services through the application of increasing amounts of knowledge and technology in production is subject to increasing returns to scale owing to the positive external effects of knowledge in production (spillover effects).

The greater the level of initial investment in knowledge and human capital in a country, the greater the spillovers and the higher the returns to further investment. Advanced economies will profit more from investment in technology than developing countries. Firms in developing economies are less well prepared to profit from spillovers. Thus, new growth theory offers an explanation of the divergence in economic performance between rich and poor countries in the world economy. Countries with a head start in the accumulation of physical capital, human capital and knowledge will tend to forge ahead. Countries which are backward will tend to stagnate further. The only limit to unrestricted growth in advanced economies is that the production of knowledge at some point is subject to decreasing returns (in other words, technological advance becomes ever more difficult).

One of the reasons for the emergence of new growth theories was that older neoclassical theories predicted convergence between rich and poor countries. In reality, rich and poor countries diverged rather than converged. New growth theory provides an explanation for global divergence.

In Chapters 1 and 2, we showed that in spite of global divergence, some developing countries have had spectacular success in catching up. Countries starting at very low levels can leap upwards on the world income ladder in the course of one or two generations. New growth theory has great difficulties in accommodating the occurrence of catch-up. Such processes are better explained by theories of the advantages of backwardness and by evolutionary economics (see sections 3.6.1 and 3.6.2).

---

[11] To endogenise is to explain something within a model instead of taking it as exogenous, or given outside the model.

Though the ideas contained in new growth theory are stimulating, the empirical verification of these models has run into difficulties (Pack, 1994). It turns out to be almost impossible to discard one model in favour of another, on the basis of statistical tests. Even at a theoretical level, Solow, one of the founding fathers of neoclassical growth theory, has pointed out that neoclassical growth theory can also accommodate divergence (Solow, 1991). He argues that the availability of modern technology does not automatically mean that technological diffusion to less developed economies will indeed take place. In the absence of institutional changes, these economies may simply be unable to assimilate new technologies. This brings the argument back to more ultimate institutional and structural factors.

3.4.6   North and Thomas: efficient institutions

One of the less satisfactory aspects of modern theories of backwardness discussed so far is how the transition from a traditional to a modern economy takes place. This transition is the central theme of a beautiful study by two economic historians, Douglass C. North and Robert P. Thomas. In *The Rise of the Western World: A New Economic History* (1973) they focus on the emergence of efficient institutions. Efficient institutions are defined as institutions which motivate self-interested individuals to act in ways that contribute to collective welfare. Among the efficient institutions discussed by North and Thomas are well-defined property rights, which guarantee that individuals will profit from the fruits of their own exertions. Only under such conditions will individuals be willing to make risky investments in future productive capacity. Protection of intellectual property (patent rights) is one of the conditions for a continuous stream of innovations (1973: 154). The institution of the joint stock company diminishes the risks of large-scale investments for individuals. Land reforms – such as the enclosure movements in Great Britain in the fifteenth and sixteenth centuries – that create well-defined individual rights to land, motivated farmers to invest in increased land productivity.

Efficient institutions do not emerge automatically. The rise of efficient institutions depends on the costs and benefits involved in the creation and maintenance of such institutions for different individuals and groups. When population density increased in Europe at the end of the Middle Ages, this facilitated the development of interregional trade. Production for the market and the money economy become viable alternatives to the traditionally determined exchange relationships of feudal economic systems. Previously these traditional institutional arrangements had been more efficient, because the *transaction costs* of market exchanges were too high.

Governments were able to guarantee property rights at lower costs per person than private groups, because the costs could be distributed over larger numbers of people. Also, government intervention avoided the problems of *free ridership*. Therefore the development of individual property rights went hand in hand with the increasing importance of state apparatuses in societies. Not all governments, however, promoted more efficient institutions. In Northwest Europe they did, in Spain and Portugal they did not, and this explained the divergence in economic development of the two regions. In the Iberian peninsula, government policy was shaped by social classes, whose interests lay in the preservation of inefficient institutions. The influence of governments on the development of institutions in its turn was influenced by the power relationships between different classes in society. Thus North and Thomas succeed in an ingenious fashion in combining the neoclassical economic analysis of institutional changes in terms of costs and benefits with the historical study of the power relationships between classes and interest groups. This analysis is a brilliant example of the interplay of ultimate and intermediate causation in economic development.

In later publications North (1990, 1993) warns us that efficient institutions do not automatically supplant less efficient institutions. When a society has embarked on a certain institutional path, later developments depend on choices made earlier on in the development process. Such *path dependence* is one of the explanations for the increasing divergence of richer and poor societies in the world economy.

3.4.7 Myrdal: institutional reforms

As a last representative of the internal approach to development we now discuss Gunnar Myrdal. Even more than Kuznets, Myrdal (1968) emphasises that simple unilinear development schemes are misleading. They do not take into account the important differences in institutional structures in different countries, regions and historical periods. They can give rise to fundamentally mistaken policy recommendations. Myrdal attaches considerable importance to differences in initial conditions. The initial conditions in developing countries – climate, demography, technology, position in the international economic order – are so different from those of the currently rich countries that copying earlier development experiences of Western countries is not a viable option. His approach to initial conditions is much more historical than the a-historical formulations of neoclassical theorists. He pays more attention to ultimate causality, but pays a price in terms of weaker quantification of the proximate sources of growth.

In formulations which predate the literature on path dependence, Myrdal formulated the principle of interlocking interdependencies within a process of cumulative causation (1957). This principle states that in the absence of major social, political or policy changes, initial differences in levels of performance tend to increase.

In spite of his criticisms of Rostow and his recognition of the importance of international power relationships, Myrdal should nevertheless be considered as a representative of the internal approach to development. This is because he considers domestic reforms in developing countries among the most important preconditions for development. One of Myrdal's intellectual contributions is the thesis that extreme social inequality is a powerful obstacle to economic development in poor countries. The unequal distribution of rights to land and large landownership hinders the modernisation of agriculture. Poverty and hunger undermine the productivity of workers and peasants. Wealthy unproductive elites consume more than they invest. Both the content and the accessibility of education are geared to the requirements of elites rather than the real developmental needs of societies. Finally, inefficient and ineffective state bureaucracies and widespread corruption (for which Myrdal coined the term *soft state*) form a serious obstacle to all developmental efforts. Without drastic internal reforms, therefore, development will stagnate. According to Myrdal, redistribution of income and productive assets and equalisation of social and political power is an important aspect of such reforms.

3.4.8 Rodrik: identifying the binding constraints to growth

In the context of a discussion of policy reform and institutional reform, Dani Rodrik (2006) has made a very important distinction between initiating growth and maintaining growth. He criticises what he calls 'institutional fundamentalism', the notion that economic development is only possible if a wholesale catalogue of institutional reforms put forward by international organisations such as the World Bank and the IMF, is adopted. This catalogue includes good governance, accountability and elimination of corruption, rule of law, well-defined private property rights, protection of intellectual property rights, tax reform, getting rid of excessive government intervention, liberalisation of domestic markets, liberalisation of trade regimes and capital markets. In a statistical analysis of growth accelerations, Hausmann, Pritchett and Rodrik (2005) show that there have been many growth accelerations in developing countries since 1950 which have not been preceded by comprehensive reforms.[12] Examples include India where growth accelerated before major reforms were implemented and China. In China, private property rights are ill-defined, the boundaries between state and private ownership are murky and intellectual property rights are not well-protected. This does not prevent the economy growing at breakneck speed (Qian, 2003).

The factors that initiate growth may not be the same as those important for maintaining growth. In order to initiate growth, one needs to identify the most binding constraints facing a specific country. These will differ from country to country, so that policy reforms which are successful in one setting may completely backfire in another. Hausmann, Velasco and Rodrik have developed a growth diagnostic framework, which helps us in identifying the most binding constraints facing a specific country. At the first level they distinguish countries hampered by a too high cost of financing domestic investment and countries with low return to domestic private investment. At the second level, the high cost of financing investment can be caused by bad international finance (too high country risk and unattractive investment conditions) or bad local finance (when domestic capital markets function badly). A low private return to investment can be caused by a variety of factors including high risk of expropriation, excessive taxation, lack of human capital, large externalities and too low productivity. One cause of low productivity is a weak physical infrastructure.

Each of these constraints call for different policy responses. For instance, it is no use providing additional foreign finance if low returns to private investment are the main problem. Policy reforms should start by targeting the most binding constraints, rather than aiming at a total overhaul of policy which is likely to fail. If the binding constraints can be identified and appropriate targeted reforms can be put in place, growth accelerations can take hold. But, there are no standard recipes for kick-starting growth. This explains why so many of the cross-country regressions with growth rates as dependent variables and policy or institutional variables as explanatory variables give inconclusive results.

Once growth is underway, the question becomes how to maintain rapid growth in the longer run. Here more fundamental institutional changes, which may not have been a binding constraint for kickstarting growth, become more important. One might say that growth buys time for more comprehensive and deeper institutional reforms, which can sustain growth and development over longer periods of time, beyond the initial growth acceleration. In absence of deeper reforms, an emerging economy for instance remains

---

[12] Growth accelerations are defined as an increase in an economy's per capita GDP growth of 2 percentage points or more (relative to the previous five years) that is sustained over at least eight years. There have been eighty-three such growth accelerations between the mid 1950s and 1992 (Hausmann et al., 2005).

vulnerable to external shocks, which may put a country off an accelerating growth path and put it on a stagnating trajectory. Examples of such external shocks are major wars such as the First and Second World War, financial crises such as the Asian crisis of 1997 or the debt crisis of 1982. Examples of rapidly growing countries being negatively affected by external shocks include Indonesia or Ireland.

The distinction between kickstarting growth and maintaining growth explains the paradoxical finding that there is hardly any statistical correlation between growth rates and institutional characteristics, while there are highly significant correlations between levels of per capita incomes and institutional characteristics (De Crombrugghe and Farla, 2012; Rodrik, 2006). The latter correlations suggest that in the very long run institutions do determine the prospects of economic growth.

3.5 Explanations of underdevelopment

In spite of all their differences of opinion, theorists of backwardness are primarily searching for the internal characteristics of societies – geographic conditions, institutional characteristics, initial conditions, culturally shaped attitudes, policy regimes – that form obstacles to development, and for the internal factors and policies that promote development. This is not to say that these theorists are blind to the outside world. Rather they are convinced that it depends primarily on internal characteristics, institutions and policies how a country will respond to external threats, challenges and opportunities.

Proponents of the external perspective on development believe that developments in different countries and regions are mutually interrelated in the context of the international economic and political order. The possibilities for development in poor countries depend first and foremost on their relationships with rich countries. These relationships are sometimes conceived of as advantageous; thus the theory of comparative advantage states, for instance, that developing countries profit from entering into international trade. The possibility of taking over technology from advanced countries also belongs to the advantages of international relationships.

A prominent group of development theorists argues, however, that relationships between rich and poor countries are intrinsically detrimental to the developmental prospects of the economically and politically weaker parties. The most extreme version of such perspectives is *underdevelopment or dependency theory.*

The choice for the term *underdevelopment* implies that the low level of development in developing countries is the result of active negative influences from outside. One cannot speak of backwardness, because poor countries do not have the chance to follow the same path of development as the currently prosperous countries. Prosperity in the rich countries is even based on past and present exploitation of developing countries. Poverty in developing countries is the result of such exploitation. The underdevelopment of the non-Western world is thus the other side of the coin of economic development in the West. The internal obstacles to development are seen as the product of negative interaction with advanced countries in the world economy. Economic historians such as Bairoch (1975, 1981) and Pomeranz (2000) are also associated with the underdevelopment perspective. They argue that levels of per capita income in Western and non-Western countries were largely similar prior to the industrial revolution. The spectacular forging ahead of Western countries was closely associated with the stagnation and underdevelopment of the non-Western world.[13]

The term *dependence* implies that development in poor countries is subordinated to development in affluent countries. A summary of the characteristics of dependent development, derived from Colman and Nixson (1985) is presented in Box 3.3.

BOX 3.3 : Characteristics of dependent development

1. **Importance of export of primary commodities**. The exports of a dependent economy consist in large part of primary products. The export sector, consisting of mines and plantations, is an enclave within the economy. All its products are exported abroad. Capital equipment is imported from abroad. The infrastructure of a dependent economy is completely oriented towards the interests of the export sector. There are few backward and forward linkages between the export sector and local producers and buyers.
2. **Dependence on imports of manufactured goods**. Most industrial products are imported from the affluent countries. Western-oriented elites consume imported products on a large scale.
3. **Dependence on imports of intermediate goods, capital goods and technology**. Even if a dependent economy succeeds in building up its own consumer goods industry via import substitution, it remains dependent on the advanced countries for imports of and intermediate goods, capital goods and technology.
4. The modern sector of the economy is dominated by **foreign firms and TNCs**.
5. **Surpluses** are repatriated abroad, either through direct transfer of profits or through mechanisms of unequal exchange and transfer pricing.
6. **Dependence** is not limited to the economic sphere. There are also cultural, psychological and political relations of dependence with the advanced nations.

It is clear that from the perspective of underdevelopment the dualistic structure of the economy in developing countries was not only the consequence of Western penetration in the past. It is also maintained by the relationships with the rich Western countries in the present. Dependence does not end with political decolonisation. In the postcolonial period, economic development is still determined by neocolonial influences from abroad. The only chance to realise goals such as development, growth and industrialisation is to withdraw from the global network of dependency relations characterising the capitalist international economic order and to seek alternative paths of development.

Within the underdevelopment theory one can distinguish two partly overlapping theoretical traditions:

---

[13] Most of the recent empirical evidence does not support the assertion that per capita GDP was approximately the same in the Western and non-Western world. There was already a substantial gap prior to the Industrial Revolution, resulting from centuries of gradual accumulation in Western Europe (Broadberry and Gupta, 2006; Landes, 1998; Maddison, 2007).

1. Neo-Marxist theories of underdevelopment.
2. Structuralism and theories of unequal exchange.

3.5.1   Neo-Marxist theories of underdevelopment

In their criticisms of capitalist relations of exploitation, neo-Marxist theories of underdevelopment build on the Marxist tradition and theories of imperialism. They analyse class relationships within developing countries in the context of class conflicts in the global economy.

However, classical Marxism was a typical stage theory in which capitalism was considered to be a higher stage than the preceding feudal stage. Therefore, in classical Marxism, Western capitalist penetration in developing countries was considered as a progressive force on the way to the highest stage which would succeed capitalism, namely socialism. This aspect of classical Marxism is rejected by neo-Marxist thinkers. One of the first theorists of underdevelopment, Paul Baran, argues that capitalism in developing economies functions differently from capitalism in the advanced countries. In the advanced countries, capitalism generates an economic surplus which is appropriated by the capitalist class and subsequently reinvested (Baran, 1957). This process of reinvestment promotes economic growth and dynamism. In poor countries, the economic surplus is transferred to rich countries by monopolistic firms or is squandered away in luxurious consumption by wasteful elites. There is a lack of dynamic investment incentives which can fuel domestic economic growth. The absence of a stream of investments and reinvestments in the domestic economy makes for economic stagnation. Only those investments, which benefit the rich countries are realised. Thus what development there is, is dependent development.

Capitalist penetration in developing countries thus leads to a distorted form of capitalism: dependent capitalism. Domestic handicraft production is undermined by competition from imported products. Economic surpluses are transferred to rich countries. Simultaneously, a wealthy domestic 'comprador class' is created, which is involved in import and export trade and whose interests are closely aligned with the interests of the rich capitalist countries. According to Dos Santos (1970), dependence does not only refer to the external economic relations of a country. The class relations within a country are also determined and reinforced by the external dependency relationships. Therefore a country cannot simply withdraw from relations of dependency. This also requires dramatic changes in internal relationships between groups and classes. Domestic reforms, however, can bring about confrontations with rich countries, whose interests are threatened by reform. Latin American history offers many examples of such confrontations.

One of the most developed versions of underdevelopment theory has been put forward by André Gunder Frank (1969, 1971, 1998). Frank analyses a chain of exploitative relationships running from the centre of the world economy to the rural sector in developing economies. He makes a distinction between rich countries at the core or *centre* of the world economy and poor countries at the *periphery*. In between are countries of the semi-periphery. The centre appropriates surplus from the semi-periphery and the peripheral countries. The semi-periphery exploits the periphery. Within dependent peripheral economies, dominant elites emerge, whose interests coincide with those of the centre countries. These elites within the modern sector of the economy exploit the peripheral sectors in their own countries. The last link in the chain of exploitation is at the level of the rural sector, where landowners, whose interests coincide with those of members of the urban elites, exploit small peasants and landless rural labourers.

The emphasis on relationships of exploitation within developing countries makes the centre-periphery theory into a theory of regional inequality as well. It offers an alternative explanation of the dualistic structure of developing economies, discussed in section 3.3. From this perspective, the traditional sector is not a lagging sector which has yet to catch-up with the modern sector. It comes into being as a result of exploitation by the centre. The so-called traditional sector is artificially maintained as a source of cheap labour, foodstuffs and other products required by the modern sector.

The more a poor country is integrated into the capitalist world economy, the more it becomes underdeveloped. An autonomous process of industrialisation is only possible in periods in which the economic ties with the centre are loosened or in which the rich countries are in economic crisis.

Among the most valuable aspects of Frank's thought is his criticism of the treatment of 'traditional society' in theories of modernisation (Frank, 1969, 1971). Like classical Marxism, modernisation theories conceive of traditional feudal societies as a stage preceding modern economic development. Feudal societies contain various cultural and institutional obstacles to development, which have to be overcome for development to take place. Dualistic structures are explained by the fact that these traditional obstacles and barriers have not yet been transcended in some parts of the economy and society. Frank gives many interesting counterexamples from Latin American history which show that the traditional society, which is called feudal, is in reality the product of Western and capitalist penetration. The Spaniards and Portuguese newly introduced forms of large landownership and serfdom which had not existed before. As we saw in Chapter 2, even the population mix is a product of Western penetration. For instance, almost the whole population of Suriname was imported by the Dutch from Africa and Asia to work on capitalist plantations as slaves or bonded labourers. If one rereads Rostow, after reading Frank, Rostow's use of the term 'traditional society' which precedes higher stages makes a very a-historical impression. The main value of theories of underdevelopment is that they show how 'internal' characteristics and institutions of developing countries have been deeply influenced and shaped by past and present external forces such as colonialism, imperialism, the Cold War and international economic trends and relationships.

The conclusion of neo-Marxists such as Baran and Frank is that the bourgeoisie cannot play the same dynamic role it played in the earlier development of the presently affluent countries. They argue that socialist revolutions are a necessary condition for development and that developing countries should extricate themselves from international trade and the international division of labour. Similar arguments are advanced by modern exponents of the anti-globalist movement of the late 1990s.

3.5.2 Structuralism and theories of unequal exchange

Theories of unequal exchange have been formulated both by neo-Marxists such as Samir Amin and Arghiri Emmanuel and by non-Marxist theorists such as Raul Prebisch and Hans Singer (Hunt, 1989, Chapters 5–7; Prebisch, 1950). Theories of unequal exchange reject the orthodox economic proposition that differences in factor endowments in different regions result in mutually advantageous patterns of international trade based on comparative advantage. According to orthodox views, free trade and specialisation in those lines of production in which a country is relatively most efficient will increase all countries' welfare. In the long run free movements of factors of production will also result in a gradual equalisation of returns to the factors of production in rich and poor countries. Theories of unequal exchange, however, state that participation of developing countries in the international division of labour is detrimental to their chances of economic development. Only the rich countries profit from international trade.

These theories emphasise the structural characteristics of the economies of developing countries that hinder the operation of free market incentives in the domestic economy and comparative advantage in international trade. Therefore these theories are often called *structuralist theories*.

Various arguments are put forward by theorists of unequal exchange to explain why developing countries are at a disadvantage in international trade. In the first place, many developing countries have a comparative advantage in primary products (agricultural products and raw materials). The income elasticity of world demand for these products is low. This means that as per capita incomes in the world economy go up, the demand for primary products will lag behind. (For instance, as people become more prosperous they will buy more manufactured goods and services. But there are limits to how much more bread they can consume.) Prices of primary exports will therefore not keep up with prices of industrial exports for which world demand is much more buoyant. In the second place, high wage levels in the affluent countries stimulate investments in capital and technological development so as to increase labour productivity. In poor countries, the abundance of cheap labour will limit technological advance. The technological gap between rich and poor countries will tend to increase. In the third place, orthodox neoclassical economic theory does not take into account the fact that most investment in developing countries is in foreign hands. Therefore investment behaviour is determined by foreign rather than by national interests. In the fourth place, Prebisch and Singer state that both well-organised trade unions and monopolistic corporations in the rich countries prevent productivity gains in these countries from being passed on to consumers in poor countries in the form of lower export prices. The absence of such institutions in developing countries means that productivity gains in these countries are passed on to consumers in rich countries. For all these reasons the terms of trade between export and import prices of developing countries show a structural decline over time.

An influential version of the theory of the declining terms of trade was formulated by Nobel Prize winner Arthur Lewis (1954, 1978a, 1978b). He argues that disguised unemployment in the traditional sector of the economy makes for a large flow of cheap labour towards the export sector. This flow of cheap labour has a depressing effect on the export prices of agrarian products from developing countries and the incomes of agrarian workers. In the mining sector high productivity and low wages make for large profits. As mines are mostly foreign owned, the profits will flow out of the country, which therefore benefits but little from mining exports. According to Lewis, international trade offers poor countries an opportunity to stay poor, as incomes earned in export production remain low. Only if productivity in the traditional food-producing sector goes up, will the unlimited supply of extremely cheap labour, with its depressing effects on wages and export prices, come to an end. The evolution of the terms of trade will be discussed further in Chapter 8.

Non-Marxist structuralists draw less radical conclusions than the Marxists with regard to the need for domestic political and economic changes. However, following the classical prescriptions of Friedrich List, they do argue for a development strategy which would make developing countries less dependent on international trade (Sunkel, 1993; Urquidi, 1993). To achieve this, they have to build up and protect a domestic industrial sector which can replace imports of industrial goods by domestic production. This strategy, known as the *import substitution strategy*, has been applied with a certain measure of success in Latin American countries between the 1930s and 1960s, and elsewhere in Africa and Asia. After the 1960s this strategy ran out of steam. Asian countries which made an earlier switch towards export orientation performed much better than African and Latin American countries which continued inward-looking import substitution policies (see Chapters 8 and 9).

Structuralists believe that free market policies will not work in developing countries due to a variety of structural constraints. These include: the absence of an adequate transport and communications infrastructure; the underdevelopment of the financial system; the limited extent of the market; the lack of market information; the lack of free choice for subordinate classes; and the monopolistic structure of the economy. Both Marxists and structuralists are in favour of government planning and a leading role of the state in the development process. It is the state that has to breakthrough the structural constraints to development. This recommendation is a corollary of their critique of the workings of capitalism and the free market. Finally, structuralists are among those calling for regulation of international trade and the creation of an NIEO, in which developing countries would have better chances.

In the 1960s and 1970s there was a widespread surge of interest in a new, more regulated international order. This completely disappeared from the agenda in the 1980s and 1990s, when resurgent economic liberalism challenged the tenets of national and international planning and regulation. In a rather inchoate form the call for a new international order re-emerged at the beginning of the twenty-first century in the political and academic criticisms of globalisation. The modern critics of globalisation point to financial instability and loss of national independence as negative consequences of participation in the global world economy. The debate on globalisation will be taken up again in Chapter 13.

A recent version of underdevelopment theory is found in the work of Acemoglu, Johnson and Robinson (2001, 2006). These authors relate settler mortality to the kind of institutions they implanted in colonies of settlement. The higher the mortality rates, the more extractive the institutions will be. These extractive instititions persist to the present. Using mortality rates as a proxy for institutional characteristics, the authors find strong correlations between institutional quality and levels of per capita income.

3.5.3   Underdevelopment theories: an evaluation

Theories of underdevelopment have been primarily formulated with reference to the development experiences of Latin America. In the history of this subcontinent, colonial and neocolonial exploitation by Spaniards, Portuguese, English, Dutch, Americans and others has played an important role. The artificial creation by Iberian colonists of large landholdings and plantations on the one hand and a poor rural population of landless labourers, serfs and very small farmers, on the other hand, is prominent in history. The slave trade and the import of bonded labourers have changed the whole population profile. After the achievement of independence in the early nineteenth century, foreign interests continued to play an important role. Military interventions by the English and later by the Americans occurred frequently and continued to do so until late in the twentieth century. The dualist development of the economy went hand in hand with extreme income inequality. Thus, rapid economic growth could coexist with continued widespread poverty.

Theories of underdevelopment have undoubtedly increased our insight into the negative aspects of Western penetration in the world. They form a valuable counterweight to the often a-historic blueprints of modernisation theorists or the bland prescriptions of market enthusiasts. One of the important insights deriving from the underdevelopment tradition is that Western influences can give rise to institutions and constellations of interest groups, which form serious obstacles to development in subsequent historical periods. Theories of underdevelopment also help us understand how rapid capitalist growth in Latin America can sometimes coexist with continued poverty of large masses of the population.

Nevertheless, underdevelopment theories also have a number of important shortcomings. The most basic is the deterministic nature of many of their propositions. From the perspective of underdevelopment theory it is hard to understand how and why former colonies such as the USA, Canada, Australia or New Zealand have achieved such economic success. Neither do the experiences of dynamic capitalist developments in South Korea, Taiwan, Singapore, Thailand, Hong Kong, Malaysia, Indonesia, China, India and other NICs fit the underdevelopment mould.

Many of the empirical propositions of underdevelopment theory are unfounded. For instance, as we shall see in section 3.7.5, it is simply not true that there is always a net outflow of capital from poor to rich countries. Also, empirical data do not invariably support a law of declining terms of trade for developing countries. Sometimes the terms of trade deteriorate, sometimes they improve. Finally, the proposition that the economic breakthrough in the West should primarily be explained by colonial exploitation and plunder is not supported by empirical historical research, which emphasises the importance of centuries of internal pre-capitalist accumulation and gradual increases in productivity.

In the present economic situation, underdevelopment theory has little to offer in the way of policy recommendations. Socialist central planning of industrial development is increasingly considered a highly inefficient development strategy. There is indeed a renewed debate about the role of industrial and technology policy in Asian economic growth, which some authors refer to as neostructuralist (Sunkel, 1993, see also Cimoli et al., 2009). But, this debate focuses on how developing countries can profit from participation in the international division of labour rather than how they can extricate themselves from international trade. The disadvantages of extreme import substitution and the related neglect of agriculture are now widely recognised (see Chapters 9 and 13). The advantages of participation in international trade are underlined by the positive development experiences of those developing countries which have shown the strongest export orientation.

Thus, though underdevelopment theory has contributed to our understanding of historical development processes, it has little to offer for the formulation of adequate development strategies in the present. The study of historical questions of guilt and responsibility for underdevelopment cannot substitute for the search for appropriate development strategies in the present.

3.6   Combining internal and external influences

The sharp analytic distinction between external and internal explanations does not do full justice to the nuances of the different theories. For instance neoclassical growth theories do make assumptions about – benign – external influences such as free access to international technology flows, the flow of capital to capital scarce countries and international trade. Structuralist theories also pay attention to internal characteristics. The distinction makes sense in that it focuses on the prime sources of growth and stagnation emphasised in different theories. In some theories external and internal influences are explicitly combined. Here we discuss two such theories, namely the theory of the advantages of backwardness and evolutionary growth theory.

3.6.1   Advantages of technological backwardness

The economic historian Alexander Gerschenkron formulated his theories about the advantages of backwardness on the basis of the rapid growth and catch-up of the latecomer countries Russia and Japan after the last quarter of the nineteenth century (Gerschenkron, 1962). These countries were able to profit from copying and taking over technologies developed elsewhere, without bearing the full cost of their development. Their technological backwardness created a potential for accelerated growth.

To some extent, Gerschenkron makes assumptions similar to those of Solow, namely that international technology and knowledge are freely available. However, as a historian, he pays much more attention to the conditions under which certain countries can profit from diffusion of technology. Diffusion is certainly not automatic as in the Solow model. It depends on changes in the social structure and modernisation of society and calls for a greater role of governments and large financial institutions in mobilising resources.

Like Rostow, Gerschenkron emphasises the importance of overcoming internal institutional obstacles to industrialisation for a country to embark on growth and catch-up. For nineteenth-century Russia, such obstacles included serfdom and the absence of a disciplined, reliable and stable supply of industrial labour.

When industrialisation takes off and absorptive capacities are sufficiently developed in late-developing economies, growth happens in leaps or in rapid spurts, concentrated in certain leading sectors of the economy (Gerschenkron, 1962).

In two respects Gerschenkron disagrees with Rostow. In the first place there are important differences between the patterns of industrialisation in different countries and different historical periods. There is no uniform, unilineal sequence of stages of development. In early processes of industrialisation in the UK in the eighteenth century, self-financing by firms was the most important source of investible funds. In the economic development of Germany in the nineteenth century, banks and financial institutions played a far more important role than earlier in England and France. In late nineteenth-century Russia, only the government was able to mobilise sufficient amounts of financial capital for massive investment in industry and infrastructure. As time went by, technological change required investment on an ever-larger scale. This explains why the role of banks, financial institutions and governments becomes more and more important in late industrialisation. Increasing scale also explains the explosive nature of industrialisation processes. For industrialisation to succeed in late industrialisation, very many changes in the economy have to take place simultaneously, in a short period of time. If changes are only partial or limited, the required scale of investment will not be attained and the process of industrialisation will stagnate.[14]

---

[14] This notion is not incomparable to the Rostovian notion of take-off, but Gerschenkron differs from Rostow in not making use of a unilinear stage theory.

In the second place, Gerschenkron argues that the economic development of a country can only be understood in a context of international technology transfer. In this respect Gerschenkronian theory transcends the limits of internal perspectives. It combines both internal characteristics and policies and interactions with the technologically advanced countries in the world economic order. In Gerschenkron's theory, latecomers in economic development have the opportunity to take over technological know-how from economically advanced countries, without having to bear the burden of the costs of R&D of new technologies. Developing countries can choose from a huge arsenal of new production techniques, which were not available previously. Thus if the economy and the society is able to absorb new technologies, latecomers in development can experience much faster economic growth than early developers, because they profit from the *advantages of backwardness*.

Gerschenkron's theories bear some interesting resemblances to earlier writings of Torstein Veblen on the rise of imperial Germany (1915) and the theories of the Dutch Marxist historian Jan Romein (1937). Romein and Veblen called attention to potential dangers and disadvantages of technological leadership. Lead countries may have invested too heavily in given technologies and their surrounding infrastructure and may be unable to move to new generations of technology. In modern theorising this is referred to as '*technological lock in*'. The loss of technological leadership of the UK since the end of the nineteenth century is explained in these terms. The combination of the advantages of backwardness and the penalties of leadership can result in rapid catch-up. However, Gerschenkron does not suggest any tendency to global convergence. Rather, he highlights the possibilities of rapid catch-up in individual developing countries. In the post-war period this reflected in the experiences of Asian countries such as Japan, South Korea, Taiwan, Hong Kong, Singapore, and currently India and China.

Abramovitz (1989b) has further developed the notion of advantages of backwardness. The capacity of developing countries to profit from technologies developed in the advanced economies depends on the social capabilities of a developing country and the congruence between technologies developed in the lead countries and conditions in the follower countries. 'Social capability' refers to the use a country can make of advanced technology and its capacity to acquire it in the first place. Social capability depends on the technical competence of a country's people, indicated among other things by levels of general education and the share of population with training in technical subjects. It also is influenced by the degree of experience of managers with large-scale production, the availability of financial institutions and supporting services and so forth. Once certain threshold levels of capabilities have been achieved, backward countries can grow very rapidly as they take over technology from elsewhere. But if they fail to achieve these threshold levels, gaps will tend to widen. Absorptive capacity is one of the very important ultimate sources of growth.

In recent years Mike Hobday has provided a further elaboration of the Gerschenkronian framework in a series of publications focusing on the successful development of East Asian economies. Different countries have followed different kinds of policies. For instance, Taiwan nurtured SMEs while South Korean development was based on large-scale conglomerates, the *Chaebols*. A common characteristic of East Asian development is close cooperation and interaction between government and the private sector, economic growth driven by manufactured exports and a focus on learning and technological upgrading. These policies have resulted in rapid catch-up (Hobday, 1995, 2013)

3.6.2　Evolutionary theories of economic change

Evolutionary theories of economic change refer to a relatively recent strand of theories building on the Schumpeterian tradition. Like Schumpeter, evolutionary theories focus on the central role of technological change and innovation in growth and development (Dosi, 1988; Freeman and Soete, 1997; Nelson and Winter, 1982; Verspagen, 1993, 2001). Investment in new technology is associated with major uncertainties and risks. These uncertainties and risks are not easily dealt with in the neoclassical approaches which assume perfect information, rational profit maximisation and movements towards equilibria and steady states.[15]

Evolutionary theory rejects the notion of rational choice underlying neoclassical theory. Economic agents have to deal with imperfect information. They have to search for information, and their decisions are made on the basis of rules of thumb. Evolutionary theory starts with the twin notions of heterogeneity of economic agents and selection environments. Heterogeneity implies that different economic actors faced with uncertainties will use different decision rules and different search strategies and will arrive at different decisions. In other words, there is no representative actor as in neoclassical theory. Given the selection environment, some choices of some firms turn out to be successful and they and their decision rules are subsequently reinforced. The collective outcomes of these choices and selection processes can put an economy onto a dynamic growth path, which distinguishes it from other economies. This is referred to as path-dependence (David, 1975), where relatively small initial differences can be greatly reinforced in the long run, as in Myrdal's cumulative causation.

Thus, like new growth theory, evolutionary theory is well equipped to deal with divergence of economic performance in the world economy. But evolutionary theory also incorporates the Gerschenkronian notions of international flows of technology and knowledge from advanced economies to less advanced economies and the associated advantages of technological backwardness. Also, in evolutionary economics, disequilibrium reigns rather than equilibrium. New technological developments, shocks and changes in the environment can make past successful paths irrelevant, and can open new opportunities for dynamic growth for low-income economies which did not exist before. Thus, evolutionary theory can also accommodate processes of catch-up.

Like new growth theory, evolutionary theory endogenises technological change by focusing on investment in and creation of knowledge (Verspagen, 2001). Technology does not develop automatically or exogenously as in the earlier neoclassical theories. It depends on deliberate efforts, investments in science, R&D, education and training by firms, governments and universities. Evolutionary theory suggests that there are increasing returns to investment in technology. But whether or not this leads to increased divergence depends on whether the advanced countries appropriate all the returns to new technology or whether technology diffuses or spills over to developing countries. This depends on the one hand on how IPRs are protected (the IPR regime). On the other hand, it depends on the internal

---

[15] Note, however, that modern neoclassical theory increasingly takes imperfect information and information asymmetries into account. In this sense, the difference between competing strands of theory are less pronounced than they seem at first sight.

technological capabilities and absorptive capacities in developing countries – capabilities to identify, select, absorb and adapt technologies.

Developing countries with strong technological capabilities are better placed to profit from the Gerschenkronian advantages of backwardness. But, when technological capabilities are weak and the technology gap separating advanced from developing economies is too wide, then there are insufficient possibilities for diffusion and international spillovers and countries will fall further behind. The concept of technological capabilities emphasises that technology is not freely available, but requires major creative efforts and costs to acquire and master.[16]

Evolutionary theories of growth try to combine the contradictory forces of increasing returns in lead countries and the advantages of technological backwardness. New technologies are primarily developed in the advanced economies and specifically in the lead countries among the advanced economies. But technologies can diffuse from lead countries to follower countries and to developing economies. Evolutionary theory, like Gerschenkronian theory, incorporates both internal and external factors and forces.

The outcome of the race between technological advance and the international diffusion of technology is not given in advance. Whether countries catch-up or fall behind depends on the balance between the generation of new technology and increasing returns in lead countries, and diffusion of technology and spillovers to follower countries (Verspagen, 1993). However, the larger the technology gap between leader and follower, the more difficult technology diffusion will become. Beyond some threshold levels, income gaps will tend to increase and countries will fall behind. Developments in Sub-Saharan Africa between 1973 and 2000 are an illustration of this tendency (see also James, 2002). But when the gap is not too large and absorptive capacities are highly developed, very rapid catch-up can take place, as is evidenced by the East, South East and South Asian experiences of recent decades.

3.7 Empirical study of development experiences

In the following sections we discuss empirical data on long-run economic development in poor countries. We show how such empirical data are of relevance for some of the theoretical questions raised in the first half of this chapter. The data primarily derive from Angus Maddison's publications, *The World Economy: A Millennial Perspective* (2001) and *Monitoring the World Economy* (1995), his database *Statistics on World Population, GDP and per Capita GDP, 1–2008 AD* (2010), supplemented by information from a variety of other sources. In this chapter, we only present selected economic indicators for the total economy. Information about demography, education, health, nutrition, industrialisation, agricultural development and other aspects of economic and social life will be presented in the following chapters.

Much of the literature on development and development studies is based on examples, case studies, or metaphors. It is our conviction that the systematic empirical study of long-term trends in economic and social indicators and systematic comparisons of

---

[16] The tacit nature of much technological knowledge is one of the factors which impedes the effortless adoption of technology by developing countries.

such trends can contribute to a less ideological and more analytical approach to the emotionally highly charged field of development studies and to a strengthening of its empirical foundations.

The data in this section refer to a sample of thirty-one developing countries. Nevertheless the 4.5 billion inhabitants of these thirty-one countries represented 78 per cent of the total developing country population in 2010. This means that developments in the selected countries do represent changes in the economic circumstances of a large portion of developing country population.

The choice of countries is primarily determined by the quality and availability of empirical data and by the size of the countries. The sample contains thirteen Asian countries, seven Latin American countries and eleven African countries. For African countries the data can usually not be traced back as far as those for other countries. In many tables developing countries are compared with sixteen advanced countries.[17]

3.7.1   Growth of income per capita: can developing countries escape stagnation?

Table 3.1 presents data on the average growth rates of GDP per capita since 1870. This table shows us that average income per capita in developing countries has been increasing ever since the late nineteenth century. This effectively contradicts the myth that growth of per capita income in developing countries is impossible owing to vicious circles of poverty. Several developing countries show considerable economic dynamism. The increase in production per capita has been realised in spite of very rapid population growth, particularly since 1950.

The periodisation of the data in Table 3.1 is the same as that discussed in Chapter 2. Between 1870 and 1913 there was substantial foreign investment in developing countries and the exports of agricultural and mining products increased rapidly. There was growth in both rich and poor countries, with Asia lagging behind other regions and Latin America growing at the same rate as the advanced economies.

From 1913 to 1950 growth in the world economy stagnated as a result of wars and economic depressions. Developing countries were heavily hit by the economic crisis of 1929, especially the Asian countries, which were most deeply involved in international trade.

The period between 1950 and 1973 was a golden age of dynamic development, with growth of per capita incomes in the world economy higher than ever before in economic history. Both rich and poor countries profited from the liberalisation and growth of world trade and the increase in investment and capital flows. Growth in the advanced economies was more rapid than in developing countries.

For the period between 1870 and 1973, the figures in Table 3.1 illustrate that economic developments in rich countries and developing countries tend to run parallel. Otherwise than suggested by theories of underdevelopment, growth in the rich countries was not

[17] The sixteen advanced economies are Australia, Austria, Belgium, Canada, Denmark, Finland, France, Germany, Italy, Japan, Netherlands, Norway, Sweden, Switzerland, UK and USA. Germany refers to the united Germany. Since 2000, South Korea and Taiwan have become high-income economies. In all subsequent tables they will be included in the advanced country averages for the periods after 2000. They can no longer be considered as developing countries. South Korea and Taiwan are included in the Asian and developing country averages for the earlier periods.

Table 3.1: Growth of GDP per capita, 1870–2013 (annual average compound growth rates, %)

	1870–1913	1900–13	1913–50	1950–73	1973–2013
Bangladesh	0.5	0.9	−0.4	−0.4	2.5
China	0.1	0.1	−1.3	2.8	6.1
India[a]	0.5	0.9	−0.3	1.4	3.5
Indonesia	1.0	1.7	−0.2	2.7	2.6
Iran	0.8		1.5	5.2	1.4
Malaysia			1.5	2.2	2.7
Pakistan	0.6	0.9	−0.4	1.7	2.0
Philippines	1.1	3.0	0.2	2.7	0.9
South Korea	0.9	0.8	−0.05	5.3	4.3
Sri Lanka	0.9	−0.3	0.04	0.8	3.1
Taiwan	0.7	1.4	0.6	5.9	3.9
Thailand	0.8	0.3	-0.1	3.7	3.4
Turkey	0.9		0.8	3.4	2.0
Argentina	2.5	2.5	0.7	2.1	0.9
Brazil	0.3	1.4	2.0	3.7	0.9
Chile	1.7	1.5	0.9	1.4	2.4
Colombia		1.9	1.5	2.1	1.5
Mexico	2.2	1.8	0.8	3.2	0.5
Peru		3.2	2.2	2.4	1.1
Venezuela	1.6	2.3	5.3	1.5	0.2
Congo, Dem. Rep.				1.6	−0.1
Côte d'Ivoire				2.6	−1.4
Egypt	0.8	−0.02	0.02	1.5	2.0
Ethiopia[b]				2.1	1.5
Ghana	1.3	2.6	1.0	1.0	1.8
Kenya				1.8	0.5
Morocco	0.5	2.6	2.0	0.7	1.8
Nigeria				2.3	1.5
South Africa	1.5	2.6	1.2	2.2	0.6
Tanzania				1.5	1.4
Zambia				2.1	0.03
Weighted averages[c]					
Asian countries	0.4	0.8	−0.2	2.7	4.7
Latin American countries	1.6	2.2	1.4	2.7	0.9
African countries	1.1	1.4	1.0	1.9	1.2
Average developing countries	0.6	1.0	0.3	2.8	3.7
Average 16 advanced economies[d]	1.6	1.7	1.2	3.6	1.7

Notes:

[a] India prior to 1950 refers to undivided India, including Bangladesh and Pakistan.

[b] Ethiopia pre-1992: Ethiopia and Eritrea, post-1992 Ethiopia.

[c] Population weighted average of countries in the table.

[d] Advanced economies: Australia, Austria, Belgium, Canada, Denmark, Finland, France, Germany, Italy, Japan, Netherlands, Norway, Sweden, Switzerland, UK and USA. Germany refers to united Germany. Population weighted average.

Sources:

1870–1950: Maddison, *Historical Statistics of the World Economy: 1–2008 ad* (2010), www.ggdc.net/maddison/oriindex.htm. 1950–2013: Conference board/Groningen Growth and Development Centre, *Total Economy Database*, www.conference-board.org/data/economydatabase/, downloaded September 2010, 2010–13 downloaded March 2014. The *Total Economy Database* originally derives from the Maddison database, but after 1990 there are differences.

accompanied by stagnation in developing countries. On the contrary, if the heart of economic growth in the rich countries started beating at a slower pace, this had negative consequences in other parts of the world economy. If growth in rich countries accelerated, growth in developing countries tended to respond.

This does not mean that the discussion of underdevelopment theories can be concluded. In the first place, Table 3.1 refers to GDP rather than GNP. It is conceivable that part of the GDP of developing countries drains away in the form of factor payments to foreign owners of capital. Not only will national product then be lower than domestic product, but economic growth will also be lower than if all economic surpluses had been reinvested in the domestic economy. In the second place, income per capita is an average figure, which disregards the income distribution within a country. Rapid growth can go hand in hand with rapidly increasing inequality and can even be accompanied by immiseration of large segments of the population. Even when developing countries are catching-up, the world household income distribution may not be becoming more equal (see e.g. Table 1.3). In the third place, between 1913 and 1950, the development experiences of some Latin American countries were not inconsistent with underdevelopment theory. In this period industrial imports from Europe stagnated due to wars and economic crises. This gave Latin American countries such as Brazil a chance to build up a domestic manufacturing sector. Growth in Latin America was higher than elsewhere in the developing world and also higher than in the advanced economies.

After the oil crisis of 1973, there was a slowdown of global growth relative to the period 1950–73 (Maddison, 1989) and many individual countries, especially in regions other than Asia, showed lower growth rates than in the golden age. However, because of accelerated dynamic developments in some very large Asian countries, the total weighted growth rate in developing countries from 1973 to 2013 was higher than in the period 1950–73.[18] Between 1950 and 1973, income per capita in the advanced economies was growing more rapidly than in developing countries, so that the gap between rich and poor countries became ever larger. Since 1973, the average growth in our sample of developing countries was higher than that in the advanced economies. This primarily reflected accelerating growth in large Asian economies, including China and India. But the average figures mask highly divergent trends between regions. Asia was growing much more rapidly than the advanced economies, while both Latin America and Africa experienced very sluggish growth rates.

In Table 3.2, the period 1973–2013 is broken down into five subperiods in order to highlight the effects of four major historical shocks – the oil crisis of 1973, the debt crisis of 1982, the Asian financial crisis of 1997 and the global financial crisis of 2007–8. The subperiods are 1973–81, 1981–96, 1996–2000, 2000–7 and 2007–13. From 2000 onwards, South Korea and Taiwan are included in the advanced country averages. They have become high-income economies and can no longer be considered as developing countries.

After the oil crisis of 1973, growth in the advanced economies slowed down markedly compared to the golden age. Initially, Latin America was able to sustain its growth

---

[18] The averages in Tables 3.1 and 3.2 are weighted with population size, giving large countries a heavy weight. Using population weighted averages gives very different results than the use of unweighted averages. One should realise that the population of India is about twice as large as the total combined population of Sub-Saharan Africa.

Table 3.2: Growth of GDP per capita, 1973–2013, (annual average compound growth rates, %)

	1973–81	1981–96	1996–2000	2000–7	2007–13
Bangladesh	1.3	2.0	3.6	4.0	4.5
China	3.6	6.6	4.3	11.7	8.4
India	1.7	3.5	3.9	5.7	5.2
Indonesia	3.5	4.1	−2.5	3.7	4.6
Iran	−4.8	0.6	2.3	5.0	0.6
Malaysia	5.1	4.7	0.9	2.9	2.6
Pakistan	3.0	2.9	0.8	3.2	1.6
Philippines	2.5	−0.4	0.7	2.8	3.0
South Korea	5.4	7.6	3.9	4.3	2.7
Sri Lanka	3.2	3.2	4.1	3.8	5.5
Taiwan	6.0	6.5	4.3	3.7	2.5
Thailand	4.4	6.5	−1.4	4.6	2.4
Turkey	2.0	2.7	2.1	3.3	1.7
Argentina	−0.6	0.4	0.9	2.2	1.9
Brazil	2.8	0.6	0.4	2.1	1.8
Chile	2.1	3.1	2.0	3.3	3.1
Colombia	2.5	1.7	−0.6	3.2	2.7
Mexico	4.1	0.5	4.0	1.3	0.4
Peru	1.0	−1.2	0.9	4.1	5.2
Venezuela	−1.0	−0.9	−0.7	2.9	0.3
Congo, Dem. Rep.	−3.9	−1.8	−0.9	0.6	4.0
Côte d'Ivoire	1.1	−3.3	−0.1	−1.9	1.2
Egypt	6.1	2.6	3.0	2.4	1.7
Ethiopia	0.1	−0.7	−0.3	4.7	6.6
Ghana	−2.5	0.4	2.5	3.1	6.1
Kenya	0.8	0.1	−0.8	1.6	1.3
Morocco	3.1	1.6	0.4	3.8	3.3
Nigeria	−1.0	−0.8	0.3	6.8	4.0
South Africa	0.9	−1.2	1.1	3.3	2.2
Tanzania	−0.3	0.1	1.4	3.9	3.9
Zambia	−1.6	−2.2	−1.1	2.5	3.7
Weighted average:					
Asian countries[a]	2.7	4.7	2.8	7.7	6.2
Latin American countries	2.1	0.3	1.3	2.2	1.7
African countries	1.0	−0.1	0.9	3.1	2.6
Average developing countries	2.4	3.1	2.3	6.2	5.1
Average advanced economies[b]	1.8	2.0	2.7	1.7	0.3

(handwritten annotations near Mexico row: "JLP" by 1973–81 column; "MMH CSG" by 1981–96 column; "Zedillo" by 1996–2000 column; "Fox" by 2000–7 column; "Calderon" by 2007–13 column)

Notes:

[a] Averages for Asia and developing countries after 2000 excluding South Korea and Taiwan.

[b] From 2000 onwards, advanced country averages include South Korea and Taiwan.

Sources:

See Table 3.1.

momentum until around 1981, through highly expansionary fiscal and monetary policies. The average Latin American growth rate for this period was 2.1 per cent. After 1981, Latin American economic development stagnated severely as a result of misguided policies, hyperinflation and the impact of the 1982 debt crisis (Maddison, 1989). Negative growth in Congo, Côte d'Ivoire, Ethiopia, Nigeria, South Africa, Tanzania and Zambia reflected the onset of economic stagnation on the African continent after 1973. The African economies continued to stagnate until around 2000. In contrast, growth started to accelerate in Asia from 1973 onwards. The average growth rate of 2.7 per cent between 1973 and 1981 was higher than in the advanced economies or Latin America.

The impact of the 1982 debt crisis was particularly severe in Latin America. Many economies experienced contraction of GDP in the 'lost decade' of the 1980s (Hoffman, 1998), only really starting to recover after 2000. African countries also suffered heavily in the wake of the 1982 debt crisis. Between 1981 and 1996 average per capita output contracted by 0.1 per cent per year. In contrast, Asian countries surged ahead, growing at 4.7 per cent per year, providing an example of catch-up relative to the advanced economies.

The euphoria of Asian growth was temporarily shaken by the Asian financial crisis of 1997, which dramatically interrupted growth in countries such as Thailand and Indonesia. Other Asian countries recovered quickly or were less affected, but average growth in the Asian countries declined from 4.7 per cent to 2.8 per cent between 1996 and 2000.

After 1981, Latin America lost much of its earlier gains, while Asia continued on a catch-up trajectory. Between 1973 and 2000, Africa provided an example of falling behind, with many countries experiencing real declines in per capita GDP over long periods. In sum, between 1973 and 2000 we see divergent trends in the developing world with catch-up in Asia, stagnation in Africa and a mixed record in Latin America.

After 2000, growth started to accelerate in the developing world. The Asian economies were growing very rapidly, in particular those of China and India. Latin America was finally recovering from the long period of stagnation since 1980, though growth was still slower than elsewhere in the developing world. The most amazing changes were to be found in Africa, where average growth was 3.1 per cent per annum between 2000 and 2007. This growth was mainly driven by primary exports.

The final column of Table 3.2 shows the effects of the global financial crisis of 2007. It is too early to assess the long-run effects of this crisis, but it is clear that the advanced economies suffered much more than developing countries. In the advanced economies, GDP per capita contracted by almost 2 per cent in 2008 and 2009. A hesitant recovery has now set in and average growth in the advanced economies between 2007 and 2013 was 0.3 per cent. During the same period average growth in developing countries was 5.1 per cent, slower than the 6.2 per cent of the years 2000–7, but still very rapid. The average is driven by high growth in Asia. After a long period of catch-up in Asia since 1973, we seem to be witnessing a sea change in the international economic order.

3.7.2   Investment: how important is capital?

One of the issues in classical and modern theories of economic development has to do with the rate of capital accumulation and the contribution of capital to growth. Along with education, capital is one of the most important proximate sources of growth in Figure 3.1.

In post-war thinking about development, capital accumulation was seen as the key to growth and development. Inability to save and too low levels of capital per worker explained low levels of development.

A well-known theory of Lewis and Rostow, discussed briefly in section 3.4.1, states that sustained economic growth will occur when the rate of saving and investment increases from 5 per cent or less to more than 12 per cent of NNI. Have developing countries been able to save enough to meet the requirements of this theory?

Table 3.3 presents data on gross domestic income as a percentage of GDP. The data refer to gross investment (i.e. before subtraction of depreciation) rather than net investment. However, one may assume that 5 per cent net roughly corresponds to 8 per cent in gross terms (Maddison, 1989). This implies that most of our developing countries were already investing more than the Lewis–Rostow lower bound of 5 per cent in 1950. Since then, most developing economies have succeeded in increasing investment to levels in percentage terms exceeding those of the rich countries. Between 1950 and 1973 investment rates increased from 13.7 to 20.6 per cent, while investment rates in the advanced economies reached their peak level of 27.2 per cent. By 1981, the average investment rate in developing countries was higher than in the advanced economies. After the 1982 debt crisis, investment rates in six of the seven Latin American and eight of the eleven African countries declined sharply. The investment rates in many Asian countries continued to increase, reaching peak levels in the 1990s (an average of 28.9 per cent of GDP in 1990). By 2012, investment levels in developing countries were substantially higher than in the advanced economies (25.7 per cent against 20.2 per cent).

The data in Table 3.3 can be interpreted in two ways. First, it seems clear from a comparison of Table 3.1 and Table 3.3 that on average high rates of investment and capital accumulation are associated with rapid economic growth since 1950. Capital is an important proximate source of growth. Yet the causal relationship between investment and growth is not unambiguous. Differences in growth performance between individual countries are not directly related to differences in investment efforts. Similar investment rates can result in very different growth outcomes. Some countries use investments much more effectively and productively than others. Wasteful investment in prestige projects, for instance, results in high investment rates but low growth. The African economies between 1973 and 1997 provide ample illustration of the combination of rather high investment rates and low or even negative growth. The 'capacity to absorb investment' is of the greatest importance for the contribution of investment to economic development (Myint, 1980). This capacity depends on a variety of complementary economic, political, cultural and institutional factors.

3.7.3 Export performance

Tables 3.4 and 3.5 give a picture of export performance in developing countries. Table 3.4 presents data on the growth of exports between 1870 and 2012. The characteristics of the main phases are clearly distinguishable. Exports were growing at just below 5 per cent per year from 1900 to 1913. Between 1913 and 1950 growth rates slumped, especially in Asian countries heavily involved in world trade. In four Asian countries export growth was even negative. Between 1950 and 1973 exports from the advanced economies grew at 8.6 per cent per year. Average export performance in developing countries was also much higher than in the pre-1913 period, though still lower than in the advanced economies.

Table 3.3: GDI as a percentage of GDP, 1950–2012 (at current market prices)

	1950	1973	1981	1990	1997	2012
Bangladesh	5.5	12.9	23.5	17.1	20.7	26.5
China	10.4[a]	29.4	32.5	36.1	37.9	48.8
India	9.9	18.2	23.8	24.2	23.9	35.6
Indonesia	11.5	20.8	26.7	30.7	31.8	36.0
Iran		25.5	27.1	37.2	35.7	33.2[d]
Malaysia		25.5	35.0	40.4	33.8	25.8
Pakistan	5.5	12.9	18.8	18.9	17.9	14.9
Philippines	15.0	21.8	27.5	24.2	24.8	18.5
South Korea	5.7	25.4	29.4	37.5	36.0	27.6
Sri Lanka	11.8	13.7	27.8	22.2	24.4	30.3
Taiwan	14.5[b]	29.1	29.9	23.9	22.7	19.6
Thailand	11.8	27.0	29.7	40.4	33.8	29.7
Turkey	11.3	14.7	17.9	22.9	26.4	20.3
Argentina	13.3	20.9	22.7	14.0	19.4	21.8
Brazil	12.3	23.2	23.1	20.2	17.4	17.6
Chile	8.0	10.5	22.7	25.2	27.7	25.0
Colombia	16.9	18.3	20.6	18.5	20.9	23.4
Mexico	14.1	20.0	27.5	23.1	26.0	22.9
Peru	17.1	20.3	34.3	16.1	23.8	28.2
Venezuela		31.0	24.4	14.1	25.5	26.6
Congo, Dem. Rep.		16.8	10.5	12.8	2.5	26.5
Côte d'Ivoire		23.2	25.9	6.7	14.4	10.1[d]
Egypt	11.8	13.1	29.5	28.8	17.6	16.4
Ethiopia	11.8	13.1	14.5	12.9	19.8	34.6
Ghana	15.1	9.0	4.6	14.4	24.8	30.9
Kenya		25.8	27.7	24.2	15.1	20.1
Morocco		16.9	26.1	24.0	20.7	35.3
Nigeria	7.2	22.4	23.3	14.7	22.0	8.2
South Africa		27.7	34.2	17.7	16.6	19.4
Tanzania		21.4	24.6	26.1	14.9	36.7
Zambia		28.9	19.3	17.3	14.6	25.0[d]
Average Asian countries[c]	10.3	21.3	26.9	28.9	28.4	28.2
Average Latin American countries	15.6	20.6	25.0	18.8	23.0	23.6
Average African countries	16.0	19.8	22.6	20.0	18.0	25.2
Average developing countries[c]	13.7	20.6	24.7	22.8	23.0	25.7
Average advanced economies	21.6	27.2	23.0	23.9	20.9	20.2

Notes:
[a] 1952;
[b] 1951;
[c] averages 2012 excluding South Korea and Taiwan;
[d] No data for 2012, we used latest available year: Iran, 2007; Côte d'Ivoire, 2008; Zambia, 2011.
Sources:
1950: Maddison (1989), Table 6.6, except for Egypt, Ghana, Kenya, Nigeria, South Africa, Sri Lanka, Turkey, Venezuela and all advanced economies except France, Germany, Japan, UK and USA: World Bank, *World Tables 1980*. 1973–81: World Bank, *World Development Indicators*, CD-ROM, 1999, except: Tanzania: 1973–83, *World Tables 1995*. 1990–2012 and Iran: 1950–2007, World Bank, *World Development Indicators Online, 2010*, http://databank.worldbank.org, downloaded March, 2014. Taiwan 1950–2012: DGBAS, *Statistical Yearbook of the Republic of China, 2009 and 2012*.

Table 3.4: Export performance, 1870–2012 (annual average growth rates, %)

	1870–1913	1900–13	1913–50	1950–73	1973–98	1998–2007	2007–12
Bangladesh	2.4	4.2	−1.5	2.0	9.3	11.2	8.5
China	2.6	4.7	1.1	2.7	11.8	21.6	3.4
India	2.4	4.2	−1.5	2.5	5.9	13.1	9.7
Indonesia	4.2	4.0	2.3	6.5	7.3	8.2	5.7
Iran				*5.6*	1.2	3.8	
Malaysia				6.3	10.2	7.3	1.0
Pakistan	2.4	4.2	−1.5	3.6	7.5	8.9	−1.5
Philippines	2.8	2.8	3.7	5.9	9.0	8.6	2.8
South Korea		8.0	−1.1	20.3	13.9	11.8	6.6
Sri Lanka				1.2	4.0	5.6	1.3
Taiwan		7.4	2.6	16.3	12.1	8.5	1.9
Thailand	4.1	5.0	2.3	4.4	11.7	9.8	3.5
Turkey						12.5	5.0
Argentina	5.2	4.2	0.2	3.1	7.1	5.6	1.1
Brazil	1.9	*0.4*	1.7	4.7	6.6	8.0	1.4
Chile	3.4	3.8	1.3	2.6	9.2	6.8	0.6
Colombia	2.0	7.8	3.9	3.8	5.9	8.9	4.1
Mexico	5.4	4.6	−0.5	4.3	10.9	4.7	3.4
Peru	1.7	6.7	2.9	5.8	1.5	8.1	5.7
Venezuela			5.4	4.0	0.9	−2.1	−4.6
Congo, Dem. Rep.				*3.1*	0.1	9.9	18.9
Côte d'Ivoire				*8.6*	4.1	4.9	
Egypt				*2.0*	5.9	13.7	1.1
Ethiopia					*2.3*	6.7	10.9
Ghana			3.1	2.8	0.9	5.4	
Kenya				*5.3*	2.0	6.6	5.0
Morocco				*4.4*	3.3	8.2	2.3
Nigeria				7.4		5.8	13.2
South Africa				7.4	2.8	1.3	−0.7
Tanzania				6.3	*9.4*	8.9	−1.5
Zambia				*1.4*	−0.3	16.0	5.7
Average Asian countries	3.0	4.9	0.7	6.4	8.7	10.1	4.0
Average Latin American countries	3.3	4.6	2.1	4.0	6.0	5.7	1.7
Average African countries				4.6	3.3	8.1	4.5
Average developing countries	3.1	4.8	1.4	5.3	6.1	8.3	4.1
Average advanced economies	3.9	4.8	1.1	8.6	5.0	5.0	5.1

Notes:

Figures in italics refer to different periods: Brazil, 1901–13; Iran, 1961–73; Kenya, 1954–73; Malaysia, 1952–73; Philippines, 1998–2006; Congo, Côte d' Ivoire, Egypt, Morocco and Zambia, 1960–73; Ethiopia, 1981–98; Tanzania, 1990–8.

Figures in current dollars deflated with US GDP deflator.

Sources:

1870–1998, unless indicated otherwise from Maddison (2001), Table F-2; 1900–13 from Maddison, 1989, Table 6.1; Sri Lanka, Turkey, Morocco, South Africa, 1950–98, Malaysia, 1952–98, Iran, 1961–98, Kenya, 1954–96 from IMF, IMF, *International Financial Statistics Database*, downloaded, October 2010, www.imfstatistics.org/imf/; Congo, Democratic Rep., Côte d'Ivoire Egypt, Ethiopia, Ghana, Tanzania and Zambia, 1960–98 from World Bank, *World Development Indicators Online*, downloaded October 2010, http://databank.worldbank.org/ddp/home.do?Step=12&id= 4&CNO=2; 1998–2012 from WDI, World Bank, *World Development Indicators Online*, downloaded April 2014; Taiwan from DGBAS, *Statistical Yearbook for the Republic of China*, 2012, http://ebook.dgbas.gov.tw/public/Data/3117141132EDNZ45LR.pdf; Ghana, World Bank, *WDI*, downloaded October 2010; 1998–2007, India, Indonesia, Philippines, Thailand, Turkey, Brazil, Colombia, Congo, Zambia from IMF, *International Financial Statistics Database*, downloaded October 2010, www.imfstatistics.org/imf.

After the 1973 oil crisis, export growth from the advanced economies slowed down to 5 per cent per year between 1973 and 1998. In this period, the growth of exports from developing countries became higher than from the advanced economies. Asian countries showed exceptionally high growth rates of 8.7 per cent, while exports from African countries grew more slowly at 3.3 per cent. The worst performers were Congo and Zambia.

In the period between the Asian crisis of 1997 and the financial crisis of 2007, exports from developing countries grew at breakneck speed. The Asian growth rate was 10.1 per cent per year, the African growth rate was 8.1 per cent per year and Latin America was growing at 5.7 per cent per year. Developing country exports were growing much more rapidly than exports from the advanced economies. Since the financial crisis, there has been a dramatic slowdown in developing country exports from 8.3 to 4.1 per cent.

3.7.4   Can primary exporters become manufacturing exporters?

Table 3.5 effectively demolishes the stereotype of developing countries as exporters of primary agricultural or mining products. This stereotype derives from the colonial division of labour in the world economy in the period 1870–1913, when developing countries specialised in primary exports. It is no longer relevant for large parts of the developing world. From 1953 to 2000 the average share of manufactured exports in total merchandise exports in developing countries increased from 6 per cent to 49 per cent. In Asian developing countries the increase was even more dramatic, from 7 per cent in 1950 to 77 per cent in 2000. This share exceeds that of the advanced economies. After 2000, the share of manufactured exports declined, in particular after the 2007–8 financial crisis. In 2012, it stood at 39 per cent.

3.7.5   External finance: does money flow from poor to rich countries?

Theories of underdevelopment and dependence suggest that there is a permanent drain of resources from poor countries to rich. This net outflow of resources reduces the possibilities for domestic investment, capital accumulation and growth and keeps poor countries poor and dependent. This is an example of a theory about more ultimate causality, where characteristics of the international order act as obstacles for development.

Table 3.6 provides some empirical information about the role of foreign finance in developing countries. At the beginning of the twentieth century, a typical colony would normally export primary products. It would export more than it imported. The surplus on the trade balance would be compensated by an outflow of profits, interest payments, salaries of colonial officials, gold and reserves to banks in the colonial mother country. This drain limited developing country growth potential, as suggested by dependency theories.

Compared to the pre-war period, one of the salient characteristics of the international economic order since 1950 is that financial flows were reversed. In most countries and most periods, a net influx of financial capital compensated for deficits in the trade balances and the current account balances. During much of the post-war period, developing economies were able to import more consumer goods, capital goods and intermediate goods than they could have financed from their export revenues. The capital flows consisted of commercial loans, direct investment, portfolio investment and development aid. Net capital inflows served to finance imports. A part of the net inflow was used to service dividend and interest payments on earlier loans and investments.

Table 3.5: Manufactured exports as a percentage of total merchandise exports, 1953–2012

	1953	1990	2000	2007	2012
Bangladesh	1	77	91	88	
China		72	88	93	94
India	48	71	78	64	65
Indonesia	0	35	57	43	36
Iran			7	_10_	12[d]
Malaysia		54	80	71	62
Pakistan	1	79	85	80	76
Philippines	8	38	92	85	83
South Korea	0	94	91	89	85
Sri Lanka		54	75	68	69
Taiwan	6	93	95	99	99
Thailand	2	63	75	77	74
Turkey	1.1	68	81	82	78
Argentinia	10	29	32	31	32
Brazil	2	52	58	48	35
Chile	2	11	16	12	14
Colombia	1	25	32	40	17[d]
Mexico	(8)	43 NAFTA	84	72	74
Peru	3	18	20	14	14[d]
Venezuela[a]	0[a]	10	9	5	2[d]
Congo, Dem. Rep.			10	10	
Côte d'Ivoire	1[a]	11	14	14	10[d]
Egypt	4.2	42	38	19	45
Ethiopia		7	10		10[d]
Ghana	10[a]	8	15	21	9[e]
Kenya	12[b]	29	21	37	35[e]
Morocco		52	64	67	66
Nigeria	3[a]	1	0	2	3[d]
South Africa		29	54	52	45
Tanzania	13[a]	8	20	23	25[d]
Zambia		5	11	7	10[d]
Average Asian countries[c]	7	67	77	69	59
Average Latin American countries	4	27	36	32	27
Average African countries	8	20	26	25	26
Average Developing countries[c]	6	41	49	44	39
Average advanced economies		72	72	70	67

Notes:

[a] 1960;

[b] 1961;

[c] averages 2007 and 2012, excl. S. Korea and Taiwan.

Sources:

1953: Maddison (1989); Egypt and Turkey derived from Maddison (1970); Venezuela, Côte d'Ivoire, Ghana, Kenya, Nigeria and Tanzania from World Bank, *World Development Report 1983*; 1990: World Bank, *World Development Indicators 2001*; 2000–12: World Bank, *World Development Indicators Online, 2010 and 2014*.

Together with imports and exports of goods and services and transfer payments, dividends and interest payments figure on the current account of the balance of payments. Deficits or surpluses on the current account are balanced by capital flows on the capital account or changes in the gold and foreign currency reserves of a country.

In principle, it is more advantageous for a developing country to use net capital inflows to finance imports of goods, especially capital goods, than for the payment of dividends and interest. But dividend and interest payments should not be exclusively interpreted as a detrimental drain of resources. If investments and loans make a positive contribution to the productive potential of a country, then factor payments represent payments for the productive services of foreign capital. Less favourable is the case in which interest is paid on loans that have been used for purely consumptive purposes, while new inflows of capital are required to service the interest payments. Then a country can get caught up in an increasing spiral of indebtedness, without any improvement of its productive potential.

Table 3.6 offers a rough picture of the importance of external finance in developing countries. 'External finance' is defined here as the net balance of exports and imports of goods and non-factor services, with the sign reversed.[19] This concept shows to what extent inflows of capital allowed developing countries to import more goods and services than they were exporting.[20]

Between 1950 and 1981 there was an unmistakable though modest net inflow of capital in developing economies, averaging between 1.1 and 2.6 per cent of GDP. Between 1950 and 1973, twenty-six of our thirty-one countries had a net inflow. This inflow is inconsistent with underdevelopment theories, which assume that there is a permanent outflow of capital from poor to rich countries. The exceptions were typically primary exporters such as Zambia, Venezuela and Côte d'Ivoire with a surplus on their balance of payments owing to exports of products such as copper, oil and groundnuts. Between 1974 and 1981 twenty-one of the thirty-one countries had a net inflow of capital. Many of the countries with a net outflow were oil exporters such as Indonesia, Iran, Nigeria and Venezuela.

The debt crisis of 1982 caused the inflow of capital, in particular the inflow of private capital, to stagnate in Latin America. An increasing number of countries were faced with net outflows of capital, creating the paradoxical situation that developing countries were financing the advanced economies. The net outflow of capital was most marked in Latin American countries, between 1982 and 1990. Outflows from Taiwan, South Korea can be interpreted in a more positive sense. They represent repayment of past debts or new outward FDI by rapidly growing economies which have attained surpluses on the balance of payments through success in manufactured exports. The same holds for China, which has had a net outflow of capital since 1991. This capital flows not only to the advanced economies such as the USA, but also to developing countries in Africa and elsewhere.

---

[19] This concept is referred to in the literature as a 'resource balance'. Factor services are excluded from the resource balance. These factor services refer to the services of the production factors labour and capital. They include wages for workers working outside their own country, dividends, profits and interest payments.

[20] An alternative concept is external finance as the net balance of the current account of the balance of payments with the sign reversed. This concept includes among others payments for factor services. In Table 3.6 the data for 1950–66 from Maddison (1989) refer to this concept of external finance. After 1966 the data in the table refer to the resource balance concept.

Table 3.6: External finance as percentage of GDP, 1950–2012 (at current market prices)

	1950–73	1974–81	1982–90	1991–7	1998–2012
Bangladesh	2.5	8.9	8.1	5.8	6.5
China	0.2[a]	0.1	0.3	−2.0	−4.1
India	1.8	1.1	1.7	0.7	3.2
Indonesia	3.1[b]	−6.4	−1.4	−0.9	−4.9
Iran	3.1[f]	−5.6	4.9	−2.1	−4.7[h]
Malaysia	−4.0[d]	−3.5	−3.4	0.8	−19.5
Pakistan	4.4	10.1	9.9	3.7	3.9
Philippines	2.1	4.4	1.5	7.1	3.5
South Korea	8.4	5.8	−1.9	1.3	−3.2
Sri Lanka	1.0	8.6	11.4	9.6	9.3
Taiwan	3.1[c]	−0.6	−9.9	−2.2	−5.5[i]
Thailand	1.8	4.8	2.7	4.5	−6.6
Turkey	1.8[d]	5.3	2.7	3.9	2.5
Argentina	0.6	−0.9	−3.5	1.3	−4.2
Brazil	1.3	2.3	−3.1	0.1	−0.4
Chile	1.3	2.4	−2.6	−0.6	−4.2
Colombia	2.0	−1.2	−1.9	2.4	2.4
Mexico	1.9	1.6	−4.2	1.7	1.6
Peru	2.6	3.1	−0.3	3.8	−1.8
Venezuela	−4.3	−3.1	−4.8	−5.5	−8.9
Congo, Dem. Rep.	2.2[d]	2.7	0.5	−1.2	6.0
Côte d'Ivoire	−3.6	−0.2	−5.5	−6.6	−8.9[j]
Egypt	4.0	15.2	12.9	5.3	5.0
Ethiopia		0.5	5.1	6.4	16.2
Ghana	0.9	0.8	4.3	12.1	16.0
Kenya	0.0[d]	4.2	4.9	2.3	10.4
Morocco	1.4[d]	12.5	6.3	5.2	7.1
Nigeria	4.5[d]	−1.3	−2.2	−5.1	−10.5
South Africa	−2.4[d]	−2.9	−5.6	−2.7	−0.2
Tanzania	3.3[d]	9.9	14.9	21.5[e]	10.8
Zambia	−12.9[d]	2.3	0.5	5.3	3.4[i]
Average Asian countries[g]	2.2	2.5	2.0	2.3	−1.0
Average Latin American countries	0.8	0.6	−2.9	0.4	−2.2
Average African countries	−0.2	4.6	4.6	5.6	6.5
Average developing countries[g]	1.1	2.6	1.4	2.4	1.0

Notes:

[a] 1953–73; [b] 1966–73; [c] 1951–73; [d] 1960–73; [e] 1990–6; [f] 1965–73; [g] 1998–2012, averages excluding S. Korea and Taiwan; [h] 1998–2007; [i] 1998–2001; [j] 1998–2008.

Sources:

'External finance' is the resource balance (net balance of all exports and imports of goods and non-factor services) divided by GDP at market prices, with sign reversed. 1950–73: Maddison (1989), Table 6.7 except for countries denoted by footnote d. Sri Lanka, Venezuela, Côte d'Ivoire 1950–9 from Maddison, 1970. Countries denoted by footnote d. 1960–73 and all countries 1973–2000 from World Bank, *World Development Indicators Online, 2010.* 2000–12 from World Bank-WDI (2014). Tanzania 1960–86 from *Tanzania National Accounts*; Taiwan 1974–81 from Maddison (1970), Taiwan 1982–2012 from DGBAS, *National Statistics of Taiwan*, The Republic of China, *National Accounts*, http://eng.stat.gov.tw/ct.asp?xItem=25763&CtNode=5347&mp=5.

The figures for the period 1991–7 illustrate a resumption of capital flows into most developing countries, with an average inflow of 2.4 per cent for all developing countries. The impact of the Asian financial crisis of 1997 and the global financial crisis of 2007–8 is clearly visible in the figures for the period 1998–2012. For instance, there are massive outflows of capital in the hard-hit Asian economies of Indonesia, Malaysia, South Korea and Thailand. On the other hand, the outflow from China is an indication of the increasing strength of the Chinese economy. In general one may conclude that the period of net inflows of capital to developing countries came to an end in 1997. However this is not true for developing countries on the African continent, many of which continue to profit from large inflows of capital in the latest period.

3.7.6   Are developing countries dominated by foreign interests?

Table 3.7 presents data on the total value of foreign capital in developing countries from 1870 to 2008. This table provides an indication of globalisation trends and of the importance of foreign presence in developing countries. Between 1870 and 1914 investment in developing countries increased rapidly, as FDI developed harbours, roads and infrastructure to exploit the possibilities of primary exports. The real value of foreign capital in this period increased almost sixfold. After 1914 there was a decline in the stock of foreign capital in developing countries as the world economy slowed down. In real terms the value of foreign capital in 1950 was only 27 per cent of that in 1914. As a proportion of GDP it was down to half its 1870 level. After 1950, we see an explosive increase in the value of foreign capital from 63.2 billion dollars in 1950 to 7,884 billion dollars in 2012.

How to interpret these figures? It is clear that in the long run the stock of foreign capital has increased, indicating net inflows of capital. This contradicts the predictions of dependency theory. However, a negative interpretation of these trends is that the value of foreign capital is a measure of the degree of foreign domination of the economies of developing countries. This domination is increasing. There is an element of truth in this interpretation, especially when domestic economic and political structures are weak and governments are

Table 3.7:   Gross value of foreign capital in developing countries, 1870–1998 ($ billion)

	1870	1914	1950	1973	1998	2000	2008	2012
Total in current prices	4.1	19.2	11.9	172	3242	3715	7407	12855
Total in 1990 prices	40.1	235.4	63.2	495.2	2743	3032	4851	7884
Stock as % of developing country GDP	8.6	32.4	4.4	10.9	51.9	53.8	43.0	50.5

Notes:
The gross value of foreign capital is the sum of the stock of inward FDI, long- and short-term loans and portfolio equity. The share of foreign capital to GDP is calculated at constant 1990 prices until 1973, and as a percentage of current GDP thereafter. Foreign capital in current prices is deflated to 1990 prices with the US GDP deflator.
Sources:
1870–1973 from Maddison (2001), Table 3–3. FDI stock and GDP shares 1998–2008 from UNCTAD, *World Investment Report, 2009*, 2012 from *WIR, 2013*. External debt stocks and GDP deflator from World Bank, *World Development Indicators Online*, November 2013.

unable to bargain with powerful multinational firms. However, by the same criterion, many European advanced economies are also dominated by foreign capital.

From our macro-perspective the figures can be given a more positive interpretation. A net inflow of foreign capital provides a positive impulse to the economic development of a country. An inflow of foreign capital can contribute to rapid growth and economic dynamism. Periods when the inflow of capital stagnates, such as 1914–1950, are usually periods of weak growth performance. Rapid growth in the booming economies in South East Asia goes hand in hand with massive foreign investment, which transfers much-needed capital, technology and know-how to the receiving economy.[21] Of course the impact of foreign capital and foreign firms in developing countries needs to be studied in more detail. A positive evaluation of foreign investment does not mean that developing countries should not set conditions for the operation of multinational firms and foreign investors in the domestic economies. The Asian crisis has made us more conscious of the potential disadvantages of extreme openness to foreign capital. This debate about FDI and multinational companies will be taken up again in Chapter 13.

3.7.7   Are developing countries capable of structural change?

Nobel Prize winner Simon Kuznets has emphasised that modern economic development implies changes in the structure of the economy. In the process of *structural change*, the importance of the agrarian sector declines, while that of the industrial sector increases. The industrial sector offers more scope for accumulation of capital per worker and technological change. Productivity per worker in industry is much higher than in traditional agriculture. Therefore structural change is one of the major forces contributing to productivity growth and economic dynamics in development. This is referred to as the *structural change bonus*. At a later stage of development the service sector overtakes the industrial sector and becomes the most important sector in terms of its share in employment and production.

There is an ongoing debate about productivity growth in the service sector. Baumol (1986) suggests that in many service sectors opportunities for productivity growth are constrained, owing to the personal and inherently labour intensive nature of many services (haircuts, restaurants, tourism, medical services, counselling). Therefore, productivity growth will slow down as the service sector increases in size (the *structural change burden*). However, the service sector is an extremely heterogeneous sector. Some subsectors such as financial services, software, or transport do exhibit substantial technological change and productivity growth. In the recent literature, the dynamic nature of the service sector receives more emphasis. It is also seen as a sector which enables productivity growth in other sectors such as manufacturing (Marks, 2009).

Table 3.8 presents information on changes in the structure of employment between 1950 and 2012, Table 3.9 on changes in the structure of production. Both tables show that there have been major structural changes in developing countries. The share of agriculture in both employment and value added declined between 1950 and 2012. The shares of industry and services increased. As labour productivity in industry is higher than in agriculture, the share of industry in production is always higher than its share in employment. High labour productivity is one of the reasons why the modern industrial sector in developing countries

---

[21] South Korea is an interesting exception. Until recently domestic investment predominated.

Table 3.8: Structure of employment by sector, 1950–2012 (%)[a]

	1950[b]			1980			2000[c]			2012[d]		
	Ag	Ind	Serv	Ag	Ind	Serv	Ag	Ind	Serv	Ag	Ind	Serv
Bangladesh	77	7	16	75	6	19	63	10	25	48	15	37
China	77	7	16	74	14	12	48	22	13	35	30	36
India	72	10	18	70	13	17	67	13	20	47	25	28
Indonesia	75	8	17	57	13	30	45	16	20	36	21	44
Iran										23	32	45
Malaysia	63	12	25	50	16	34	18	32	50	13	28	59
Pakistan	77	7	16	54	16	30	47	17	36	45	20	35
Philippines	71	9	20	51	16	33	39	16	45	32	15	53
South Korea	73	3	24	36	27	37	11	28	61	7	17	76
Sri Lanka	56	14	30	54	14	32	42	23	33	39	18	42
Taiwan	57	16	27	22	38	40	10	29	62	5	36	59
Thailand	82	3	15	71	10	19	49	18	33	40	21	39
Turkey	77	8	15	58	17	25	46	21	34	24	26	50
Argentina	25	31	44	13	34	53	12	32	56	1	23	75
Brazil	60	18	22	31	27	42	23	20	57	15	22	63
Chile	36	30	34	17	25	58	14	26	60	10	24	66
Colombia	57	18	25	34	24	42	34	24	42	17	21	62
Mexico	61	17	22	36	29	35	21	25	53	13	24	62
Peru	58	20	22	40	18	42	40	18	42	26	17	57
Venezuela				16	28	56	11	24	65	8	21	71
Congo, Dem. Rep.							68	13	19			
Côte d'Ivoire				65	8	27	65	8	27			
Egypt	64	12	24	46	20	34	30	22	48	29	24	47
Ethiopia							89	2	8	76	8	16
Ghana	62	15	23	56	18	26	62	10	28	42	15	43
Kenya				81	7	12	81	7	12	49	16	35
Morocco							45			39	21	39
Nigeria				68	12	20	45	7	48	59	6	35
South Africa							14			5	24	72
Tanzania				86	5	10	84	4	12	74	6	20
Zambia				73	10	17	75	8	17	75	5	20
Average Asia[e]	71	9	20	52	15	25	40	20	36	30	23	46
Average Latin America	50	22	28	27	26	47	22	24	54	13	22	65
Average Africa							60	9	24	50	14	36
Average developing countries[e]	64	13	23	49	17	30	43	18	37	32	20	48
Average 16 advanced economies	25	36	39	7	34	59	4	26	70	3	22	74

Notes:

[a] 'Agriculture' includes agriculture, forestry and fisheries; 'Industry' includes mining, manufacturing, construction, gas, water and electricity; 'Services' include wholesale and retail trading, trade, transport and communication, financial and business services, and community and personal services.

[b] 1950 except Egypt, South Korea, 1951; China, 1952; Indonesia, Malaysia and Ghana, 1960.

[c] Data for years between 1995 and 2000, except Argentina, Colombia, Peru, Ghana, Ivory Coast, Kenya, Morocco, Congo and Zambia, 1990; Tanzania, 1991 and Nigeria, 1986.

[d] Data for 2012, except for Iran, 2007, China, Brazil, Mexico, Peru, Egypt, 2011; Pakistan, 2008; South Korea, Ethiopia, Ghana, Kenya, Nigeria, Tanzania and Zambia, 2010; Australia, 2009; Canada, 2008; Japan and UK, 2010.

[e] 2012 averages, excluding S. Korea and Taiwan

Sources:

1950: Maddison (1989), Table C-11, except for Ghana and Egypt from Mitchell (1982) and Turkey from Maddison (1986). 1980: Maddison (1989), except for Turkey, Venezuela, Côte d'Ivoire, Egypt, Ghana, Kenya, Nigeria, Tanzania and Zambia from World Bank-WDR (1988). 1990–2000: from ILO (2002), except Argentina, Colombia, Peru, Côte d'Ivoire, Kenya and Nigeria from World Bank-WDR (1995). Morocco and South Africa from World Bank, *World Development Indicators*, 1999; Congo from ILO, 2002; Ethiopia from World Bank, *World Development Indicators Online, 2010*; 2012 from *World Development Indicators Online*, downloaded April 2014. Except: Indonesia, Taiwan, Turkey, Chile, South Africa from ILO website, Ethiopia, Kenya, Nigeria, Tanzania and Zambia from *Africa Sector Database* 2013, www.rug.nl/research/ggdc/data/africa-sector-database.

is unable to provide a rapidly growing population with sufficient employment. This is one of the crucial differences between industrialisation processes in the nineteenth-century and present-day processes of industrialisation.

Table 3.8 illustrates the changes in the structure of employment. The share of agriculture decreased from 64 per cent to 32 per cent between 1950 and 2012.[22] In Africa, agriculture was still by far the largest sector in terms of employment in 2012, but in Asia and Latin America, the service sector had become the large sector in terms of employment. The speed of structural change is striking. Between 2000 and 2012, the share of agriculture in developing countries declined from 43 to 32 per cent. Nevertheless, the average share of agriculture was still more than ten times as high as that in the advanced economies, indicating that there is still scope for further structural change in developing economies. In countries such as Bangladesh, India, Pakistan, Thailand, Congo, Côte d'Ivoire, Ghana and Kenya agriculture is still the largest source of employment. In Ethiopia, Tanzania and Zambia agrarian employment even accounted for around 75 per cent of total employment. On average, the share of agriculture in total employment in Latin American countries (13 per cent) was much lower than in the more densely populated Asian countries (30 per cent) and the African countries (50 per cent). Between 2000 and 2012 every country for which we have data showed marked decreases in the shares of agriculture. In most countries, the share of services increased substantially. These changes are an indication of the rapidity of structural change in recent years.

For the structure of production, Table 3.9 shows that the share of agriculture in total GDP in developing countries declined from 42 per cent around 1950 to 16 per cent in 2012. Compared to the advanced economies, however, the share of agriculture in developing economies is still sixteen times as high. The share of manufacturing increased

---

[22] The averages for 2012 are biased downward because data for many developing countries with high shares of agriculture are missing.

Table 3.9: Structure of production, 1950–2012 (value added in agriculture, industry and services as percentage of GDP)

	1950[a]				1980[b]				2012[c]			
	Ag	Ind	Man	Serv	Ag	Ind	Man	Serv	Ag	Ind	Man	Serv
Bangladesh[d]	61	7	7	32	32	21	14	48	19	28	18	53
China	51	21	14	29	30	49	40	21	10	47	32	43
India	55	14	10	31	36	25	17	40	17	26	14	57
Iran	58	9	7	33	24	42	13	34	14	47	25	38
Indonesia	32	31	9	37	16	31	8	53	10	44	11	45
Malaysia	40	19	11	41	23	41	22	36	10	41	25	48
Pakistan	61	7	7	32	30	25	16	46	24	21	14	55
Philippines	42	17	8	41	25	39	26	36	12	33	21	55
South Korea	47	13	9	41	16	37	24	47	3	39	30	59
Sri Lanka	46	12	4	42	28	30	18	43	11	29	18	58
Taiwan	34	22	15	45	8	46	36	46	2	29	32	66
Thailand	48	15	12	37	23	29	22	48	12	45	36	43
Turkey	49	16	11	35	27	20	17	54	9	27	18	63
Argentina	16	33	23	52	6	41	29	52	9	31	20	60
Brazil	24	24	19	52	11	44	33	45	5	26	13 ·	68
Chile	15	26	17	59	7	37	22	55	4	36	11	61
Colombia	35	17	13	48	20	32	24	48	7	38	13	56
Mexico	20	21	17	59	9	34	22	57	4	36	17	61
Peru	37	28	15	35	12	43	20	45	7	35	14	58
Venezuela	8	48	11	45	6	46	16	49	6	52	14	42
Congo, Dem. Rep.	31	34	9	35	27	35	15	38	45	22	5	33
Côte d'Ivoire	48	13		39	26	20	13	54	25	26	18	49
Egypt	44	12	8	44	18	37	12	45	14	39	15	46
Ethiopia	68	9	6	23	61	11	5	29	49	10	4	41
Ghana	41	10		49	58	12	8	30	23	27	7	50
Morocco	44	17	11	39	33	21	13	47	30	17	10	53
Kenya	37	30	15	33	18	31	17	50	15	30	15	56
Nigeria	68	10	2	22	21	46	8	34	33	41	2	26
South Africa	19	35	16	47	6	48	22	45	3	28	12	69
Tanzania	68	10	4	22			12		28	25	10	47
Zambia	9	71	3	19	15	42	19	43	20	37	8	43
Average Asia[d]	48	16	10	36	24	33	21	42	14	35	21	51
Average Latin America	22	28	16	50	10	40	24	50	6	36	15	58
Average Africa	47	18	9	35	28	30	13	42	26	28	10	47
Average developing countries[d]	42	19	11	39	22	34	19	44	16	33	15	51
Average 16 advanced economies	16	41	31	43	4	36	24	59	1	26	14	73

Notes:

[a] Earliest year for which data are available: 1950, except for Morocco, Taiwan and Thailand, 1951; China and Tanzania, 1952; South Korea, 1953; Malaysia and Zambia, 1955; Iran, 1959; Ghana, Ivory Coast, 1960, Ethiopia 1961; Australia, 1953; Belgium, 1953; West Germany, Italy and Norway, 1951; Japan, 1952; Bangladesh, same figures as Pakistan.

[b] Tanzania, 1978 instead of 1980; Ethiopia, 1981.

[c] China, Venezuela, 2010; Iran, 2007; Côte d'Ivoire, 2008; Zambia, 2011.

[d] 2012 average, excl. S. Korea and Taiwan.

Sources:

General: UN, *Yearbook of National Accounts Statistics*, 1957, 1962 and 1967; Groningen Growth and Development Centre, *10 sector database,* www.ggdc.net/index-dseries.html; OECD, *National Accounts 1956–68*, 1971; World Bank, *World Development Indicators Online*; BEA, *National Income and Product Accounts*, www.bea.gov/national/nipaweb/TableView.asp#Mid.
Specific country sources: IBGE – Diretoria de Pesquisas – Departamento de Contas Nacionais (Brazil, 1950–9); NBS, *China Statistical Yearbook 2000*, Table 3–1 (China); Van der Eng, 2008 (Indonesia); Prins and Szirmai (1998) (Tanzania); *UNIDO Yearbook*, 2000 (Peru). Yamfwa *et al.*, 2002, (Zambia); UN Statistical Division, *National Accounts Online*, downloaded November 2011: http://unstats.un.org/unsd/snaama/dnlList.asp. For detailed source notes see: www.dynamicsofdevelopment.com.

from 11 per cent in 1950 to a peak of 19 per cent in 1980, followed by a decrease to 15 per cent in 2012. In Asia the share of manufacturing peaked in 2005 at 23 per cent in 2005 and then declined to 21 per cent in 2012. The highest manufacturing shares were registered in China (32 per cent in 2012). In the advanced economies the share of manufacturing steadily declined from 31 per cent in 1950 to 14 per cent in 2012. Both the developing world and the advanced economies are experiencing deindustrialisation. In 2012, the average share of manufacturing in developing countries was somewhat higher than in the advanced economies.

It is striking how important the service sector has become in developing countries. Even in the 1950s, services were almost as large as agriculture in terms of value added. Developing countries have not followed the classical sequence of shifts from agriculture to industry, followed by later shifts from industry to services. Rather the service sector developed parallel to the industrial sector, as the shares of agriculture declined. By 2012, the service sector accounted for more than 50 per cent of total value added and around 48 per cent of total employment.

In part the early growth of the service sector can be explained by the expansion of the government sector in developing countries in the post-war years. As the government sector was characterised by low productivity, the large share of services acted as a brake on growth. But in recent years, the expansion of services has been driven by market services. At present there is a lively debate about whether the service sector might supplant the manufacturing sector as an engine of growth in developing countries (Szirmai, 2012a).

3.7.8   How unequal is the income distribution?

There is a widespread view that inequality tends to increase in the course of economic development. As discussed in section 3.4, Kuznets has argued that income inequality will tend to increase in the course of industrialisation but then tends to decrease as societies become more prosperous and more modern. This is referred to as the *inverted u-curve of inequality* hypothesis (see Szirmai, 1988, Chapter 2). Most older economic theories of backwardness emphasise the positive economic functions of inequality, in line with Keynesian economic theories. As the poor consume most of their incomes, while rich people can save part of their income, increasing inequality will increase aggregate savings (see Thirlwall, 1999, Chapter 12). Higher saving rates contribute to growth of per capita incomes and, in the longer run, to a reduction of poverty. As income per capita increases, the bargaining power of the poorer sections of the population will increase and income inequality will start to decline. Cross-country research on the relationship between levels of income per capita and the degree of inequality tends to support this hypothesis (Bacha, 1979; Deininger and Squire, 1996), but time series analysis is much less conclusive (Deininger and Squire, 1998; Ferreira, 1999; Thorbecke and Charumilind, 2002). In fact, in the advanced economies, income inequalities have been increasing since 1980 (Atkinson, Piketty and Saez, 2010), after a long period of declining inequality from the 1930s onwards.

Radical and underdevelopment theorists agree that income inequality is increasing, but evaluate this much more negatively. They do not believe that inequality will necessarily lead to higher savings and more growth. They even argue that a combination of increasing average incomes and increasing inequality can lead to impoverishment of the bottom 40 per cent of the population.

The answers to these questions are ultimately empirical rather than ideological and may differ from country to country and region to region. We will return to this debate in subsequent chapters, arguing that on average there is strong evidence that growth of per capita incomes tends to reduce poverty. However, distributive policies can be very important. Similar levels of income per capita can coexist with very different degrees of inequality, poverty and immiseration. This is an important example of how intermediate factors interact with the proximate sources of growth to produce different socio-economic outcomes.

Table 3.10 presents some extremely rough empirical information on income inequality, primarily based on primary household survey data. The table presents information on the Gini index (an index running from zero for complete equality to one for complete inequality),[23] the share in income or consumption of the bottom 40 per cent of the population and the share of the top 10 per cent of the population for the period 1980–2010.

The table provides ample evidence of the high degree of inequality in present-day developing countries. On average, the bottom 40 per cent of the population had 19 per cent of total income in 1980, while the top 10 per cent had 33 per cent. The degree of inequality in developing countries is much higher than in the advanced economies – as measured by the Gini index as well as by the shares of the top 10 per cent and bottom 40 per cent. This is consistent with cross-section research on the Kuznets hypothesis. Inequality is by far the highest in Latin America, whether measured by the Gini index or by income shares. In 2010, the top 10 per cent of income recipients enjoyed 40 per cent of total income. For our sample countries, the correlation coefficient between income per capita in 2000 and the percentage of the population earning less than 1 dollar a day is –0.50.[24] This provides a first indication of the inverse relationship between level of income per capita and poverty. It also confirms that

---

[23] The Gini Index is defined as half of the sum of all possible differences between the incomes of units, divided by the mean income (μ) times the square of the number of units (n^2):

$$G = \left(\sum_{i=i}^{n} \sum_{j=1}^{n} |y_i - y_j| \right) / (2n^2 \mu)$$

[24] Income per capita from Table 3.1, the percentage of the population earning less than 1$ a day from World Bank-WDI (2001, Table 2.6).

Table 3.10: Distribution of income or consumption, 1980–2010

	Gini Index			bottom 40%			top 10%		
	1980	1995	2010	1980	1995	2010	1980	1995	2010
Bangladesh	25.9	33.6	32.1	24.0	20.7	30.2	21.9	28.6	27.0
China		40.3	42.1		16.1	27.9		30.4	30.0
India	32.1	37.8	33.9	21.0	19.7	29.4	26.4	33.5	28.8
Indonesia	40.4	31.7	35.6	19.0	21.5	29.5	28.3	26.7	28.2
Iran	47.4	44.1	38.3	25.4	26.7	28.6	36.9	33.8	29.6
Malaysia	48.6	49.2	46.2	25.7	12.5	26.2	36.4	38.4	34.7
Pakistan	33.4	31.2	30.0	20.6	22.4	30.7	27.8	27.6	26.1
Philippines	41.0	46.2	43.0	16.6	14.2	27.0	32.7	36.6	33.6
South Korea	36.7	31.6	31.0	18.2	20.4		28.1	24.3	
Sri Lanka	32.5	34.4	36.4	20.7	19.8	28.7	26.4	28.0	30.0
Taiwan	27.7	31.7	34.2	20.7	20.2	18.7	24.0	24.4	
Thailand	45.2	41.4	39.4	15.0	16.2	28.2	35.5	32.4	31.0
Turkey	43.6	41.5	40.0	15.7	16.0	27.9	35.3	32.3	30.1
Argentina	44.5	48.6	44.5	26.5	25.4	26.6	34.0	36.6	32.3
Brazil	57.5	59.2	55.0	21.7	21.3	21.9	47.3	46.7	42.9
Chile	56.4	57.5	52.1	10.0	9.7	22.6	45.7	46.9	42.8
Colombia	59.1	57.1	55.9	20.8	9.6	21.8	41.2	46.1	44.4
Mexico	46.3	51.9	47.2	26.0	11.6	25.1	44.0	41.1	37.5
Peru	45.7	46.2	48.1	14.0	13.5	25.4	35.5	35.4	36.1
Venezuela	55.6	46.8	43.4	9.6	25.8	27.0	43.5	35.5	32.7
Congo, Dem. Rep.			44.4			26.4			31.8
Côte d'Ivoire	41.2	36.7	41.5	15.8	18.3	27.4	31.4	28.8	
Egypt	37.4	28.9	30.8	17.6	23.0	30.3	28.8	25.0	26.6
Ethiopia	32.4	40.0	33.6	17.6	27.0	30.6	28.8	33.8	27.5
Ghana	35.4	39.6	42.8	18.7	16.3	27.1	27.3	29.5	32.5
Kenya		44.5	47.7		14.7	25.0		34.9	37.8
Morocco	39.2	39.5	40.9	17.7	17.1		31.8	30.9	
Nigeria	38.7	50.6	48.8	16.4	12.6	24.7	28.2	40.8	38.2
South Africa		56.6	63.1		22.0	19.0		45.1	51.7
Tanzania		38.2			17.8			30.1	
Zambia	51.3	52.6	57.5	11.2	10.9	21.1	38.5	41.0	47.4
Average Asian countries	37.9	38.1	37.9	20.2	19.0	28.6	30.0	30.5	29.9
Average Latin American countries	53.4	53.1	50.3	17.0	15.2	24.0	42.9	41.9	39.4
Average African countries	39.4	42.7	45.1	16.4	18.0	25.7	30.7	34.0	36.7
Average developing countries	42.1	43.0	41.9	18.7	18.1	24.7	33.3	34.2	30.7
Average advanced economies	29.0	29.8	29.5	22.6	21.6	22.9	22.6	23.5	22.4

Note:
The data refer either to inequality of personal income or consumption expenditures. 1980: 1980 or earliest year in period 1980–90; 1995: 1995 or year closest to 1995 in period 1990–2000; 2010: 2010 or latest year in period 2005–10. The Gini Index has been multiplied by 100. The averages for Asia and developing countries 2010 exclude S. Korea and Taiwan.
Sources:
World Bank Global Poverty Monitoring Website, www.worldbank.org/research/povmonitor/index.htm;
WIDER, *World Income Inequality Database*, downloaded November 2010, www.wider.unu.edu/ research/T 2.8; World Bank, *World Development Indicators Online*, downloaded November 2010 and 2014, http://databank.worldbank.org/ddp/home.do?
Step=3&id=4; DGBAS, *National Statistics of Taiwan*, www129.tpg.gov.tw/mbas/doc4/89/book/77.xls (Taiwan); for detailed source notes, see www.dynamicsofdevelopment.com.

the importance of the income distribution for poverty, as much of the variation in poverty remains unexplained by average levels of income per capita.

It should be noted that distribution data are notoriously difficult to compare across countries and even more so over time. The income concepts are not standardised: some surveys focus on household consumption, others on income. Some surveys use household equivalent incomes (standardised for household composition), others do not. Some surveys focus on the distribution over persons, rather than households. The estimates of inequality vary from year to year and from survey to survey. One therefore needs to be very careful in drawing premature conclusions. This being said, Table 3.10 shows no conclusive evidence of increasing inequality in developing countries between 1980 and 2010. This runs counter to the prevailing view in development economics that inequality is increasing in the rapidly growing Asian economies. The average Gini index for all developing countries declined minimally from 0.421 in 1980 to 0.419 in 2010. The only region where the Gini index is going up sharply is Africa, but even here the average share of the bottom 40 per cent of the population is improving, as in the other regions. In the advanced economies we do not see much change in average inequality between 1980 and 2010, in contrast to the increasing inequality emphasised in most of the secondary literature. But there it is clear that there is no decline in inequality as suggested by the Kuznets hypothesis for the advanced economies decreases. Also, much of increasing inequality is due to increases in the share of the top 1 per cent of the income distribution, which is not captured in this table.

Questions for review

1. Compare the internal and external explanations of development and stagnation. Is the use of the term 'less developed' associated with internal or external explanations of the situation of development?
2. What are the main elements of classical liberal explanations of growth and development?
3. How do economic theories of imperialism explain economic stagnation in developing countries?
4. Discuss the concept of dualism. Why is dualism an obstacle to development?
5. Which stages of economic growth are distinguished by Rostow and what are their main characteristics?
6. What are the potential advantages of backwardness?
7. How do North and Thomas define efficient institutions? Give examples of institutions which are considered to be efficient.
8. Discuss the characteristics of dependent development, as emphasised by dependency theorists.
9. To what extent can a lack of savings and investment be considered as an obstacle to growth?
10. Discuss Frank's criticism of the use of the concept of 'traditional society' in theories of modernisation.
11. Why do neoclassical theories of growth predict convergence of levels of income per capita and new growth theories predict divergence of levels of income per capita?
12. What are the main phases of development since 1870, and what are the most important characteristics of the different phases?

13. How do structuralist explanations of development differ from those of liberal and neoclassical theories?
14. Discuss the theoretical and empirical relationships between growth and inequality.
15. To what extent do the empirical data in Table 3.10 provide support for Kuznets' inverse U-curve hypothesis?

Further reading

One of the most important sources for the empirical study of long-run comparative development is the monumental study by Angus Maddison, *The World Economy: A Millenial Perspective* (2001) and its sequels *The World Economy: Historical Statistics* (2003) and *Contours of the World Economy* (2007b). Other useful sources include the website of the Groningen Growth and Development Centre (www.rug.nl/research/ggdc) and the website of the Penn World Tables (www.ggdc.net/pwt/pennhome.htm). An indispensible source for the comparative study of development is the World Bank online database *World Development Indicators Online*. *World Development Indicators Online* contains time series for around 575 social and economic indicators for 225 countries for the period since 1960. It synthesises data from a variety of international publications such as the annual *World Development Reports*, the *Human Development Reports* and *World Tables*, a publication which was discontinued after 1995.

The literature on development theories is almost impossible to summarise. We selectively mention a few of the older and newer studies which have been consulted in writing this chapter. Everyone interested in development theory can still profit from reading Arthur Lewis' *Theory of Economic Growth* (1950) and his pathbreaking article 'Economic Development with Unlimited Supplies of Labour' (1954). The starting point for the modern debates on multi-sector models lies with Fei and Ranis' book, *Development of the Labor Surplus Economy: Theory and Practice* (1964). Key publications for modernisation theory and underdevelopment theory respectively are Rostow's *The Stages of Economic Growth* (1960) and André Gunder Frank's, *Capitalism and Underdevelopment in Latin America* (1969). For structuralism and unequal exchange an early article entitled *The Economic Development of Latin America and its Principal Problems* by Raul Prebisch (1950) has been very influential. A more recent discussion of structuralism and neo-structuralism can be found in Sunkel's *Development from Within: Toward a Neostructuralist Approach for Latin America* (1993).

For the potential advantages of backwardness, the work of Gerschenkron and Abramovitz remains as relevant as ever. Useful books are Gerschenkron's *Economic Backwardness in Historical Perspective* (1962), Abramowitz's *Thinking about Growth and Other Essays on Economic Growth and Welfare* (1989c). For evolutionary theory the classic study is Nelson and Winter's *An Evolutionary Theory of Economic Change* (1982). The role of institutions is emphasised in major studies by North and Thomas, *The Rise of the Western World: A New Economic History* (1973), North's *Institutions, Institutional Change and Economic Performance* (1990) and Myrdal's *Asian Drama: An Inquiry into the Poverty of Nations* (1968). Acemoglu has developed an interesting research tradition on the role of institutions in growth. A good example of this is found in Acemoglu and Robinson, *Economic Origins of Dictatorship and Democracy* (2006).

Overviews of theories of economic development theory are also found in a variety of text-books, of which we should mention Ray's *Development Economics* (2000), which has a micro-focus on the imperfect functioning of markets in developing countries owing to institutional constraints, Thirlwall's excellent textbook on *Growth and Development, With Special Reference to Developing Economies* (2003), which has a macro-perspective, and Hunt's overview of development theories in *Economic Theories of Development: An Analysis of Competing Paradigms* (1989). New developments are touched upon in an interesting collection edited by Meier and Stiglitz, *Frontiers of Development Economics: The Future in Perspective* (2000). A delightful older textbook is Myint's, *The Economics of the Developing Countries* (1980). One of the most original writers on growth in recent years is Rodrik. A collection of his papers is published in *One Economics, Many Recipes: Globalization, Institutions, and Economic Growth* (2007). Also of interest is his edited volume of country studies *In Search of Prosperity. Analytic Narratives on Economic Growth* (2003b).

4 Technology and development

In Chapter 3, we discussed a range of development theories. Technological change was identified as one of the important sources of growth and development. This chapter singles out such change as one of the key issues in the study of development. Two main questions will be raised: (a) to what extent is technological change really one of the driving forces in growth and development?(b) What are the consequences of accelerating global technological change for developing countries? Does technological change constitute a threat to their chances for development? Does technological change offer new opportunities for development?

In the framework of proximate and ultimate causality, technological change can be studied at the proximate level of the production function: changes in knowledge; at the intermediate level of science, technology and innovation policy; and at the ultimate level of the institutions governing science, technology and innovation, systems of innovation, distance to the technological frontier and long-run developments in science and technology (Figure 4.1).

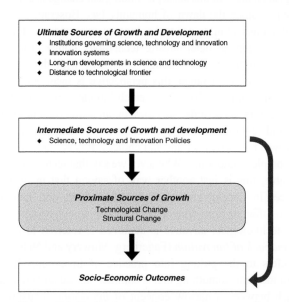

Figure 4.1 Technological change as a source of growth and development

4.1 The role of technology

'Technology' refers to the state of knowledge about how to do things, in particular how to produce valued goods and services for the satisfaction of human needs (Evenson and Westphal, 1995). Without offering a formal definition, one may say that technology stands halfway between science (abstract knowledge about the fundamental laws and regularities of the natural environment) and production techniques (specific applications of technology in products or processes, singular ways of doing particular things). Prior to the twentieth century many technological advances were not based on scientific knowledge, but on practical experience, on the job tinkering and experimentation. Today more and more technology is science based.

In Chapters 1 and 3, we argued that while development is a much broader concept than economic development, growth of income per capita was one of the core dimensions of development. 'Economic growth' refers to increases in the productive capacity of a society. Productive capacity is a potential, which can be used to achieve socio-economic outcomes. It can be wasted for destructive purposes or for conspicuous consumption of elites. It can also be used to improve a broad range of living conditions of the masses of people living in poverty in developing countries. It is one of the necessary conditions for wider socio-economic development.

The concept of productive capacity indicates that socio-economic development is closely connected with technological change. In this sense, technological change is a driving force in development and has been so since the dawn of humanity (see Boserup, 1981; Lapperre, 1992). At the same time it is misleading to see technology as an exogenous force. The term 'driving force' suggests technological determinism: technology comes from outside and drives us inexorably in certain directions. Though consistent with the ways in which most people experience technological change, this perspective is incorrect. Technological change is the result of focused human efforts in research laboratories, scientific institutes, small and large firms, or inventors' backyards. Societies, organisations and individuals invest in knowledge, schooling and research, just as they invest in physical capital goods. Thus, technological change is driven by human actions and choices. It is not an external phenomenon, which develops in complete autonomy. Whenever we say that technological change is uncontrollable and inevitable, this is just another way of saying that many outcomes of human actions and choices in general are relatively autonomous and hard to control. Technological change is no different from other spheres of human behaviour.

The process by which technological advance is achieved is referred to as innovation. Following *The Oxford Handbook of Innovation* (Fagerberg, Mowery and Nelson, 2005), the concept of innovation refers to the putting into practice of inventions. This involves developing an invention or idea into something that is commercialised and creates economic value. One can distinguish between a narrow concept of innovation focusing on strictly technological innovations in new products or new methods of production. But in the Schumpeterian tradition (Schumpeter, 2000, see section 3.2.7 of this book) there is also a broader notion of innovation including the development of new types of organisation and the discovery of new marketing techniques, new markets, or new sources of raw materials. It is very important to note that innovation does not only refer to the first introduction of novelty by a first mover, but also to the diffusion of the innovation to other actors in the national and international economy.

4.2 The technology race

If we interpret changes in productive capacity as a rough indicator of technological change, we can use labour productivity as a rough indicator of technological performance. We can then conceive of development as a long-run race between leaders and followers in technology and productivity.

As briefly sketched in Chapter 2, a technological breakthrough occurred in Western Europe since the fifteenth century. This breakthrough resulted in a historically unique process of internal growth and external political, economic and cultural expansion (e.g. Landes, 1998). The European expansion resulted in the formation of an interdependent world economy, characterised by competition between technological leaders and technological followers. This competition involved both dynamic challenges and the creation of new opportunities and a simultaneous increase in global disparities.

The increase of global inequality between rich and poor economies should not be seen as a static process. At the frontier, one leader succeeded another. One of the first technological leaders on the Eurasian and African continents – in terms of both productivity and science and technology – was the Islamic World during the flowering of Islam between 750 and 1100. In the fourteenth century China was the indisputable global technological leader (Needham *et al.*, 1954). From then onwards, technological leadership successively shifted from China to Italian City States, the Iberian Peninsula, the Dutch Republic, Great Britain and subsequently the USA.

There was also considerable change behind the technological frontier. Since the end of the nineteenth century, dynamic processes of catch-up took place in countries such as Japan, Germany, Russia and its successor the Soviet Union, South Korea and Taiwan. Relatively advanced countries or political units such as Argentina, the Ottoman empire and the constituent parts of the former Soviet Union experienced relative decline. The boundaries between more and less technologically advanced countries are continuously shifting.

Since the Second World War, the USA has been the undisputable world technological leader. Until the middle of the 1970s, Western Europe and Japan were engaged in a process of catch-up. Large countries in Latin America experienced some catch-up till around 1979, followed by ten years of stagnation during the 'lost decade' following the 1982 debt crisis. Asian NICs such as South Korea, Taiwan, Singapore and Hong Kong developed at breakneck speed. Second-tier Asian NICs such as Indonesia, Thailand, Malaysia and the Philippines grew rapidly prior to the financial crisis of 1997. China forms a case apart. This enormous country has experienced very rapid growth since the reforms and liberalisations of 1978, in both agriculture and industry. The other Asian giant, India, showed sluggish growth for a long time. It lagged behind the Asian tigers. But in the 1990s it started liberalising and growth started accelerating. African countries showed long-run stagnation since the oil crisis of 1973, even though the initial levels of income around 1950 were very similar to those of the Asian economies (Lal and Myint, 1996). It is only after 2000 that growth re-emerged on this continent. The Soviet Union experienced growth up to 1973. After that stagnation set in. After the collapse of communism in 1989, most former Soviet

Republics become caught up in a dramatic process of economic and technological decline, with an accompanying deterioration of social indicators such as health and life expectancy.[1] In recent years, growth has resumed in Russia on a narrower economic base, primarily driven by natural resources.

Figure 4.2 provides an exciting illustration of the technology race in manufacturing. It presents real value added per worker relative to the USA in ten selected countries. The figure shows spectacular catch-up in Korea and Taiwan, with Korea equalling Japan in 2007. It reveals the acceleration of productivity growth in China, India and Indonesia in the 1990s. China went from around 5 per cent of the US level in the 1980s to almost 20 per cent in 2007. But, contrary to popular impressions, there is still a vast productivity gap to be bridged (Szirmai and Ren, 2007). Next, it is interesting to note that in the 1960s productivity levels in the African economies (Tanzania and Zambia) were higher than in Asia. After 1973, however, productivity levels in Africa showed spectacular long-run decline both in absolute and in relative terms (see Szirmai *et al.*, 2001). Only in the most recent years has there been some recovery, in particular in Tanzania. Productivity levels in the poor Asian economies kept pace with the USA during most of the period – a phase of productivity growth without catch-up. They only started to narrow the gap in the 1990s. The perform-ance of Japan is rather interesting. Japan is one of the famous examples of catch-up in modern economic history. But this process came to an end around 1990, when Japan failed to make the transition from imitating technology to innovating at the technological frontier. In the US economy productivity growth accelerated, while Japan got caught up in a slump from which it has still not recovered. Brazil epitomises the ups and downs of Latin American industrialisation. Up until 1980, productivity was improving rapidly, but after the economic turmoil of the 1980s there was a loss of technological capabilities and productivity declined dramatically to around 30 per cent of the US level.[2]

4.3 Technological change and increases in productive capacity

In the previous section, the technology race was discussed in terms of comparative productivity trends. This perspective on technology will be further elaborated in this section.

To provide in their daily needs, humans need to transform natural resources into goods and services. Labour, capital goods and land – the primary factors of production – are used to transform raw materials and semi-fabricated goods – the intermediary inputs – into outputs. The transformation process makes use of the technologies available at a given point in time in given societies. The level of technological capacity of a society is ultimately expressed in the labour productivity per hour worked.

---

[1] The recent history of the Russian Federation and other Former Soviet republics provides one of the most powerful examples of the strong correlations between growth collapse and worsening social indicators such as life expectancy, education or health.

[2] It is sometimes argued that the national state is increasingly losing its relevance as the main unit of analysis. Transnational regions and clusters and groupings of countries are becoming more important. However, Kuznets (1966) and Abramovitz (1989b) have made a convincing case for the continued importance of the national setting in studying differences in economic performance.

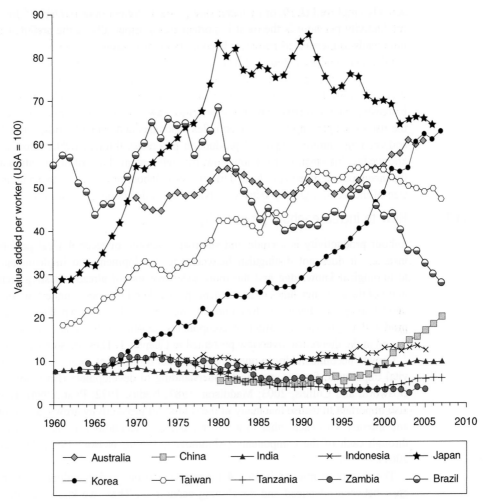

Figure 4.2 The technology race in manufacturing, 1960–2007
Source: Own calculations from Groningen Growth and Development Centre data, using country working papers, 10-sector database, EUKLEMS database, supplemented with data from WDI, ILO, Laborsta and UNIDO industrial statistics yearbooks. For details see www. dynamicsofdevelopment.com.

Together with average hours worked per person per year (*H/L*) and the share of the actually working population in total population (*L/P*), labour productivity determines GDP per capita (*GDP/P*) as follows:

$$\frac{GDP}{P} = \frac{GDP}{H} * \frac{H}{L} * \frac{L}{P}$$

As the equation indicates, per capita output (and potential welfare) can be increased by working more hours per person (*H/L*), by increasing the proportion of the population that is actively employed (L/P), or by increasing productivity per hour (GDP/H).[3] In the long run productivity per hour is the most important factor, especially as the preference for leisure time tends to increase as countries become more prosperous.

GDP per hour is the broadest measure of technological performance.[4] In the remote past and in traditional agriculture, labour was the only factor of production and output per hour was very low. In the broadest sense of the word, technological change has to do with increasing the productive capacity of unskilled raw labour power. This can be done through the use of simple implements or complex machines and capital goods, through education and training, through improved production processes, through R&D, through changes in knowledge, information and know-how, through new methods of organisation and through the development of new products. Differences in labour productivity are an indication of the size of the *technology gap* between advanced and developing economies.

4.3.1   How to increase labour productivity?

Labour productivity is a crude and summary measure of technological performance. For instance, it does not distinguish between the development and implementation of new technological knowledge and the more extensive use of already existing technologies – more of the same machines or implements per worker. For a better understanding of the role of technological change in development, we need to break down the sources of labour productivity growth into different components. Several of these have already been mentioned in the theoretical overview presented in Chapter 3. They are summarised in Box 4.1.

Growth accountants try to quantify the impact of different sources of growth. This is of vital importance for our empirical understanding of development (Bosworth *et al.*, 1995; Bosworth and Collins, 2003; Maddison, 1987; Nadiri, 1972; Pilat, 1994). However, it is also important to realise that many of the sources of productivity growth are complementary and interact with each other in a wider process of technological change, which operates through each of the components (Abramovitz, 1989b; Nelson, 1996; Pack and Paxson, 2001).

The factors mentioned in Box 4.1 contribute to our understanding of the productivity gaps between advanced and developing economies. Thus, we know that the amount of physical capital per worker in developing countries is much lower than in advanced economies. In Chapter 7, we show that the amount of schooling per person in developing countries is lower than in advanced economies. Later in this chapter we will discuss knowledge gaps.

With regard to efficiency, two issues are of special interest. In the first place due to a variety of institutional, educational and infrastructural factors, the technical efficiency of production in developing countries is lower than in the advanced economies. Even the same machinery, operated with a similar number of workers will deliver a lower output (Pack, 1987).

A second issue is that of the choice of technology (e.g. Pack, 1987; Stewart, 1972, 1974, 1987). It has often been argued that developing countries with an abundance of cheap labour

---

[3] L/P depends on the proportion of the population of working age being actively employed. It also depends on the age structure of the population.

[4] GDP per hour figures are not always available. Therefore, as a first step we frequently use GDP per person engaged as a proxy (see Figure 4.2).

BOX 4.1 : Sources of increase in labour productivity

- **Capital accumulation**. Labour productivity is increased by adding implements, machines and capital goods. The amount of capital per worker – capital intensity – increases. Not only the amount of capital matters, but also the quality of capital. Younger generations of capital goods embody the latest state of knowledge. They tend to be more productive.
- **Increased scale of production**. Large-scale production of standardised products is usually more productive than small-scale production. Such scale effects can be more easily realised in industry than in spatially dispersed agriculture. This is why industrialisation is important in economic development.
- **Accumulation of human capital**. Human capital theory suggests that schooling and education makes workers more productive. Accumulation of human capital may take place through formal schooling, but also through on-the-job training, learning by doing and by using new technologies. Health is also an aspect of human capital. Investing in health makes for more productive workers.
- **Increased technical efficiency**. Increased efficiency covers a wide range of factors such as higher capacity utilisation and better use of production technologies.
- **Increased economic efficiency**. Productivity improves if one uses appropriate combinations of labour and capital and other inputs into the production process.
- **Changes in the organisation of production**. This aspect of efficiency improvement deserves separate attention. It involves aspects such as the division of labour, flexible production systems, systems of motivation, monitoring systems and changes in the logistic organisation of production.
- **Increased allocative efficiency through structural change**. Structural change is also an aspect of increased efficiency. Structural change involves shifting resources from sectors with lower productivity to sectors with higher productivity such as manufacturing.
- **Increased allocative efficiency through specialisation in international trade**. This involves international specialisation according to comparative advantage. This specialisation is also related to structural change.
- **Disembodied technological change**. This involves advances in our technological knowledge concerning products and production processes: the development of new production processes, new types of machinery, new forms of organisation, use of new inputs, new products and services, new ways of distributing products and services, new knowledge that can be transferred through education.

should choose more labour-intensive technologies. Capital-intensive technologies developed in the advanced economy may not be appropriate to conditions in developing countries and need to be adapted. Also, it may be easier to transfer mature well-developed technologies to developing countries, rather than the most advanced generations of state-of-the-art technology.

In the long run, however, the key question is whether developing countries can participate in global processes of technological change and close the knowledge and technological gaps relative to the advanced economies. This involves learning mechanisms, which will allow developing countries to move up the technological ladder over time.

A factor of particular importance is *structural change*. This has a static aspect. A country can profit in the short run from shifting labour and capital to more productive uses. It also has a dynamic aspect: discovering which high-potential sectors will be profitable for a country in the future. In a much-cited article on 'Economic Development as Self-Discovery', Hausmann and Rodrik have shown how entrepreneurs may have a very special role in discovering what a developing country could be good at producing in the future (Hausmann and Rodrik, 2003).

4.3.2   Investing in technological change

Just as one can invest in physical capital goods, one can invest in knowledge and technology, through R&D. Investments in knowledge, however, have some special characteristics. It is easy to own physical machines and to exclude others from access to these machines in order to appropriate the fruits of investment in machinery. It is less easy to appropriate the results of investments in knowledge, even though inventors and investors try to protect their intellectual property through patents, trademarks, secrecy and other strategies. Knowledge is *non-rival*: use of knowledge by one person does not diminish the possibilities of use by other people. Knowledge is *non-excludable*: it is hard to prevent others from using knowledge. Once it is there, knowledge has a tendency to diffuse or spread ('knowledge spillovers'). Other individuals, other firms and other countries can make use of new knowledge and technology without having to pay for the complete costs of its development. Referring to countries, this is what Gerschenkron called the potential 'advantages of backwardness'. Under certain conditions, developing countries can profit from technological investments in the lead countries, without bearing the high risks and costs of R&D. Given the right conditions, international technology spillovers can result in explosive growth. Examples of catch-up based on such processes in the second half of the twentieth century are provided by Western Europe, Japan and the Asian NICs.

4.3.3   Diffusion of technology and absorptive capabilities

On the one hand it is hard to stop knowledge and technology from flowing, from diffusing. On the other hand not all developing countries and economic actors in developing countries are able to profit equally from the international diffusion of technology. Whether or not a country or an actor can profit from international technology flows depends very much on its absorptive capacities.

Technology and knowledge are difficult to absorb for a variety of reasons. Technological changes seldom occur in isolation. They are interrelated and of a systemic nature (Hughes, 1983; Rosenberg, 1982). Technologies such as steam power, the internal combustion engine, electrification, plastics or information and communication technologies are embedded in far wider systems of complementary technologies, social conditions and infrastructures. Transfer of technology to developing economies frequently fails because the relationships between new technologies and the wider environment in which they are to function are neglected. Technologies have to be appropriate to new settings in the sense that they make use of existing factor proportions (availability of labour, skills, capital, or natural resources), market conditions, available infrastructure and climatic conditions. Absorbing technology successfully therefore requires considerable effort, capabilities and creativity.

Developing countries differ greatly in their capacity to absorb technology. In developing countries with well-developed absorptive capabilities, there are ample opportunities for catch-up. If such capabilities are weak then technological gaps will tend to increase and countries will fall behind. The international technology race is thus characterised by two contradictory tendencies. On the one hand, lead countries have the most developed technological capabilities and are best placed to profit from new technological developments. On the other hand, follower countries with adequate and improving capabilities can profit from transfer and acquisition of technologies developed elsewhere and can experience explosive growth. Further discussion of absorptive capacities is to be found in section 4.7.3.

4.3.4   The knowledge economy: technology, productivity and competitiveness

In the modern world economic competitiveness depends more and more on technology and innovation. On the one hand, technological advances in process technologies contribute immediately to increases in productivity. Along with costs, quality, reliability, speed of delivery and flexibility, productivity is one of the determinants of competitiveness. On the other hand, modern firms in the world economy increasingly compete through innovation itself. Competitiveness depends on a continuous flow of new products and services and the emergence of new production processes (James, 2002). In the global knowledge economy the distinction between traditional low-tech and modern high-tech sectors is becoming eroded. Even so-called traditional labour-intensive sectors such as agriculture, beverages, textiles or shoemaking are experiencing rapid technological change in the form of biotechnology, weather satellites and computer-aided design and manufacturing (von Tunzelmann and Acha, 2005). Also the direction of global technological change is skill-biased, creating an increasing global demand for high-skilled workers.

Since the rise of large research laboratories and R&D departments in the second half of the nineteenth century, organised R&D has become more and more important as a source of technological change. Knowledge has become one of the most important factors of production. This makes it more difficult for latecomers to compete on product markets. Acceleration of technological change in the advanced economies means that developing countries have to grow more rapidly if they are not to fall further behind.

Technological change is not only rapid, there are also major shifts in the technological paradigms that drive growth in different historical periods (Dosi, 1988; Freeman and Perez, 1988; Freeman and Soete, 1997). In the industrial revolution, rapid technological change took place in weaving and in steam-driven machinery. In the second industrial revolution of the nineteenth century the locus of technological change was in chemical engineering, and also in railways. In the first half of the twentieth century the major drivers of growth were advances in automobile technology, standardised mass production and electrification. In the second half of the twentieth century the revolutionary technologies were electronics, and biotechnology. Presently we are seeing the emergence of nanotechnology. These technological paradigm shifts mean that an economy trying to get closer to the technological frontier is shooting at a moving target. Not only is technological progress at the frontier accelerating, but there are also radical changes in technology. These shifts are a challenge, but can also create new opportunities for catch-up.

Simultaneously the world economy is becoming more and more interdependent. Between 1960 and 1995 international trade (as the sum of exports and imports) increased from 24 to 42 per cent of world GDP. According to the WTO the top 500 largest multinational enterprises (MNEs) account for one-third of global trade (UNDP, 2001). Other estimates put the total share of all MNEs in global exports of goods and services as high as 67 per cent (Dunning, 2003). There is a growth of international investment flows, migration flows, tourism and last but not least information flows. Increasing interdependence implies that developing countries are more and more influenced by international technological trends. Even in traditional labour-intensive sectors such as textiles or footwear, developing countries are now faced by technological advances in the advanced economies (Cooper, 2001). At the same time, technologically driven reorganisation of production creates new possibilities for locating part of global production chains in developing countries.

4.4   Indicators for science, technology and innovation[5]

For measurement purposes the following indicators can be distinguished.

R&D-based indicators

R&D refers to creative work undertaken on a systematic basis in order to increase the stock of knowledge, including knowledge of man, culture and society and the use of this stock of knowledge to devise new applications. Data on R&D are usually collected in separate R&D surveys, which are based on the standards and procedures of the Frascati manual (OECD, 2002). The Frascati manual distinguishes basic research (aimed at new knowledge without application or use in view, applied research (aimed at new knowledge with practical aims and objectives) and experimental development (aimed at applying existing knowledge to new applications or substantially improving existing applications).

Well-known indicators based on R&D surveys are:

- Gross domestic expenditure on R&D (GERD). These data are often expressed as a percentage of GDP. An important distinction is that between public R&D and R&D expenditures in the private sector.
- Gross national expenditure on R&D (GNERD). These data are also often expressed as a percentage of GNP.
- Head counts of R&D personnel, e.g. the number of scientists and engineers per million population.

An important shortcoming of R&D indicators is that not all innovation is based on formal R&D and formal R&D expenditures. This is especially important for developing countries. Next, R&D statistics are usually collected for larger manufacturing establishments, while activities of SMEs and enterprises in the service sector are less well captured.

---

[5] This section is based on a presentation given in September 2011 by my colleague Norbert Janz in a UNU-MERIT workshop on innovation policy in Bogotá, Colombia, in September 2011, and on Gault (2010).

Innovation surveys

Innovation surveys can be seen as a response to the criticism that not all innovative activities are pursued by scientists and engineers in formal R&D departments. Innovation surveys started in the European Union with successive waves of the Community Innovation Surveys (CIS). They have since spread to developing countries in Latin America, Africa and Asia (Gault, 2010). Innovation surveys ask a variety of questions about innovative performance of firms. Innovation is defined in a very broad sense (see also section 4.1) as the implementation of a new or significantly improved product (good or service), or process, a new marketing method or a new organisational method in business practices, workplace organisation or external relations (OECD, 2005). Firms are asked how many innovations they have generated in a given period (usually three years). A very interesting distinction is between innovations that are new to the world, innovations that are new to the market and innovations that are new to the firm. In a developing country context, most innovations will be new to the firm or at best new to the domestic market. Indicators based on innovation surveys include:

- Innovative performance measured as the average number of innovations in a given period.
- Innovative performance measured as the average percentage of innovative products in firm sales.

The innovation surveys also include questions about how firms access new knowledge and what linkages they have with other actors (other firms, public or private research institutes, universities). Thus innovation surveys also provide interesting information about formal and informal linkages between actors and the systemic nature of innovation.

Other indicators

Other indicators for science technology and innovation include:

- *Patent statistics* (patents granted, patent applications, the stock of patents). Patent statistics provide an indication of the outcomes of the innovation process. But the fact that a patent has been granted does not necessarily mean that an innovation has successfully been implemented. Patent statistics are widely used in research, but patents are not the only manner in which IPRs are protected. Other IPR strategies include the use of secrecy, trademarks, brand names and petty patents.
- *Publication and citation statistics*. These statistics measure the publication output of a country and the frequency with which its publications are cited.

4.5 Economic theories about the role of technological change revisited

In Chapter 3, we discussed theories of growth and development. The core theoretical challenge that every economic theory of long-run growth performance has to meet is that it should be able to account for the paradox of increasing upward mobility of a few developing countries in the context of the increasing disparities of global income per capita discussed in Chapter 1. We have to account for two stylised facts, between which there seems to be a considerable tension. On the one hand, the degree of inequality between rich and poor countries has vastly increased over time from 2.1 in 1820 to 20.1 in 2008

(Maddison, 2009; World Bank-WDI, 2010). On the other hand, the speed of catch-up in selected developing countries has greatly accelerated.

Technological change is crucial to understand and explain these patterns. Three sets of theories were singled out as especially relevant: new growth theory, Gerschenkron's theory of the advantages of technological backwardness and evolutionary theory. New growth theory argued that there were increasing returns to investment in knowledge, which explains why advanced countries tend to forge ahead and poor developing countries tend to fall behind. Publications in the Gerschenkronian tradition explained how and why some countries can accelerate their growth and development in a spectacular fashion starting from a position of technological backwardness by copying and imitating and absorbing technology and know-ledge from technological leaders, without paying the full costs or bearing the full risks of investing in technological advance. From this perspective, technological backwardness is a potential for growth, rather than a drawback. But whether this potential is realised depends on the absorptive capacities of economies and societies. Like the Gerschenkronians, evolutionary economic theorists try to combine the trends toward divergence and catch-up in a comprehensive framework. An important difference between new growth theory and evolutionary theory is that evolutionary theories also allow room for the penalties of leadership.

Technological change is characterised by extreme uncertainties and shifts. Once a lead economy has made a choice for a certain technological trajectory, it may get locked into it. When external circumstances change, and new techno-economic paradigms emerge (Freeman and Perez, 1988), the lead countries may find it more difficult profit from them than follower countries. Follower countries, which had invested less in former generations of technology, may suddenly be better placed to profit from new developments. Thus, there is nothing inevitable about falling behind. Changes in external circumstances and the emergence of new technological paradigms can lead to rather sudden changes in patterns of divergence and convergence, stagnation or catch-up. One of the ongoing changes is the improvement of global communication systems, which can facilitate the international transfer of technology and lower international transaction costs.

Divergence between rich and poor countries is driven by two sets of factors: (1) There is much more investment in science, technology and innovation in the advanced economies than in developing countries. (2) Firms in advanced economies profit more from investment in R&D and innovation because knowledge flows so much more easily from firm to firm in an advanced economy. This is what is referred to as the *system of innovation*, which will be discussed further in section 4.6.3. In developing countries, knowledge and technology do not flow very easily. Innovations and best practices do not diffuse quickly from leading firms to other firms.[6] These two factors together contribute to rapid divergence in the global economy.

But in some countries the forces driving divergence are more than compensated for by the advantages of technological backwardness: the ability to copy, imitate, steal and absorb advanced technology. If the right capabilities and absorptive capacities are present, the advantages of technological backwardness outweigh the increasing returns of the leaders and a country can experience very rapid growth and catch-up. The countries that achieve this are those that invest heavily in their absorptive capacities (education, training, increased investment in R&D, acquisition of technology, learning). Over time, as these catch-up economies grow, they also rapidly upgrade their own investment in R&D, quickly reducing technology gaps.

---

[6] See also the discussion of dualism in Chapter 1.

4.6 ⊙   Consequences of the acceleration of technological development for developing countries

4.6.1   Acceleration of global technological change

The rate of technological change is increasing very rapidly. For instance the global number of patent applications increased from 1.4 million to 2 million in the four years between 1989 and 1993 (World Bank-WDR, 1999). Table 4.1 shows the acceleration of patent applications in the lead country (the USA) since 1870.[7] Since 1870 the number of patents annually granted in the USA has increased twentyfold. For recent years, the table also documents the marginal role of the developing world in global technological change. There are a few exceptions. The catch-up countries Taiwan and especially South Korea have dramatically increased their patent shares. Since 2000, India and China have also suddenly entered the stage. But excluding these four countries, the share of developing country patents in total patents granted in the USA in 2010 does not exceed 0.7 per cent.

There has been a veritable explosion of technological changes in ICT. These in turn spill over to a great variety of production technologies, through automation, robotisation and computerisation. They also result in rapid changes in the service and communication sectors, including the rise of the World Wide Web. They allow for global dispersal and integration of production activities by multinational corporations (MNCs). They create global information networks that increase global interdependence in terms of trade, investment and cultural exchanges (Castells, 2000).

Another area of rapidly accelerating technological change is that of biotechnology, with applications in the spheres of health, reproductive practices, agricultural production and food processing. These changes have wide-ranging impacts not only on production, but also on human reproduction and human living conditions.

In the OECD countries the importance of high-tech sectors is rapidly increasing (World Bank-WDR, 1999: 23). These sectors account for an increasing portion of productivity growth. In some Asian economies such as Malaysia, the ICT sectors have also been important sources of growth and catch-up. Product cycles and time to market become shorter and shorter through a continuous flow of innovations. Production systems become more flexible and have to react very quickly to changes in and diversity of consumer preferences.

4.6.2   Knowledge gaps

In the world economy there is great inequality in technological efforts. An overwhelming proportion of scientific, research and development activities takes place in the advanced economies. As can be seen in Table 4.1, almost all patent applications are concentrated in these countries. The same holds for scientific publications.

---

[7] As all important innovations tend to be patented in the USA, the US data provide an indication of trends in world technological advance. Figures on the number of world patents can be misleading: important innovations are patented in many countries, resulting in double counting.

Table 4.1: US patent activity, 1870–2010

	Patent appli-cations	Patents granted	Foreign patents	Developing country patents	Share of patents granted: South Korea	Taiwan	China	India	Developing countries, excl. col. 5–8
Year	(1)	(2)	(3)	(4)	(5)	(6)	(7)	(8)	(9)
1870	19171	12 157							
1900	39673	24 656							
1913	68117	33 915							
1950	67264	43 039							
1973	103695	74 139							
1990		99 220	46.6	1.7	0.3	0.9	0.05	0.02	0.4
1991		106 842	45.9	1.9	0.4	1.0	0.05	0.02	0.4
1992		107 511	45.3	2.1	0.5	1.2	0.04	0.02	0.4
1993		109 890	44.3	2.6	0.8	1.4	0.05	0.03	0.4
1994		113 704	43.4	3.0	0.9	1.6	0.04	0.02	0.4
1995		113 955	43.4	3.4	1.1	1.8	0.1	0.03	0.4
1996		121 805	43.0	3.8	1.3	2.0	0.04	0.03	0.4
1997		124 146	43.7	4.2	1.6	2.1	0.1	0.04	0.5
1998		163 209	44.4	5.0	2.1	2.3	0.1	0.1	0.5
1999		169 146	44.4	5.5	2.2	2.7	0.1	0.1	0.5
2000		176 084	44.9	6.0	2.0	3.3	0.1	0.1	0.5
2001		184 051	46.4	6.4	2.0	3.6	0.1	0.1	0.5
2002		184 424	47.3	6.7	2.2	3.6	0.2	0.1	0.5
2003		187 048	47.3	6.8	2.2	3.6	0.2	0.2	0.6
2004		181 320	48.1	7.6	2.6	4.0	0.3	0.2	0.5
2005		157 741	47.6	7.9	2.9	3.8	0.4	0.3	0.5
2006		196 437	47.9	8.6	3.3	4.0	0.5	0.3	0.6
2007		182 928	48.8	9.6	4.0	4.1	0.7	0.3	0.6
2008		185 244	50.3	10.9	4.7	4.2	1.0	0.4	0.6
2009		191 933	50.5	11.2	5.0	4.1	1.2	0.4	0.7
2010		244 358	50.4	11.6	5.1	3.9	1.4	0.5	0.7

Sources:
1870–1973: US Department of Commerce, Patent and Trademark Office (1977), Table AI. 1990 and later: US Patent and Trademark Office (2002, 2004, 2006, 2009).

Large multinational companies take the lead in innovation. Thus the fifty largest multi-national companies alone account for 26 per cent of all patents in the USA. According to estimates by the World Health Organisation (WHO), 95 per cent of all medical research focuses on health problems of the advanced countries (World Bank-WDR, 1999).

Developing countries invest a much lower fraction of GDP in R&D than the advanced countries. Table 4.2 provides some information about the R&D efforts of developing countries between 1990 and 2008. In 2000, developing countries on average invested 0.6 per cent of GDP, against 2.7 per cent in the advanced economies. The technological gaps in terms of researchers and R&D per head of population are even greater than in terms of R&D percentages. As a percentage of GDP, advanced economies spent more than four times as much as developing economies in 2008. The number of researchers per million inhabitants in the advanced economies was eight times as high as in developing countries in 2007. The ratio of per capita expenditures in 2009 was no less than 25 to 1.

The nature of R&D efforts is also very different. Much of R&D in developed countries is directed at technological breakthroughs. R&D in developing countries is more defensive in nature. It functions as an investment in order to keep up with developments elsewhere. In the poorest developing countries the quality of R&D efforts leaves much to be desired (see Bongenaar and Szirmai, 2001).

Table 4.3 provides some rough information about differences in technological level in the ICT field. There are vast technology gaps between in particular the least developed countries and low-income countries on the one hand and the advanced economies on the other. Even the upper-middle-income countries lag far behind the advanced economies. The only partial exception is that of mobile phones, which have experienced a spectacular expansion even in the very poorest countries.

4.6.3   New opportunities offered by technological development

Rapid technological change offers new opportunities for development. In the area of health, advances in medical technology such as vaccines and antibiotics have contributed to an unprecedentedly rapid decline in death rates and improvements in life expectancy in developing countries (see Chapter 6), irrespective of per capita income.[8] Advances in reproductive technology offer families new opportunities for realising their preferred family size and offer countries new opportunities for birth control and limiting the rate of population growth.

Breakthroughs in agrarian technologies have led to impressive productivity improvements in agriculture and reductions in undernutrition (see Chapter 10). Through technological breakthroughs in plant breeding, fertilisers and pesticides world cereal yields doubled since the 1960s.

Information technologies have enhanced the ability of multinational companies to coordinate cross-border activities. Thus, ICT create new possibilities for relocating parts of global production chains to developing countries, to profit from abundant labour. Surprisingly they also allow multinational companies to decentralise R&D activities, in order to profit from the availability of relatively cheap highly skilled labour in developing countries such as India, Brazil or Korea (James, 2002).

---

[8] The HIV/AIDS epidemic in Africa and Asia has impacted negatively on these positive trends.

Table 4.2: R&D efforts, 1990–2009[a]

	R&D as % of GDP[b] 1990	R&D as % of GDP[b] 1997	R&D as % of GDP[b] 2008	R&D per capita 2005 PPP $ 1996	R&D per capita 2005 PPP $ 2009	Researchers in R&D per 1,000 1996	Researchers in R&D per 1,000 2007
Bangladesh		*0.3*	*0.6*			51	*30*
China	0.7	0.7	1.7	11.4	83.7	447	1071
India	0.8	0.8	0.8	9.6	19.5	153	137
Indonesia	*0.2*	0.1	0.09	*1.8*	3.1	*182*	205
Iran			0.8	*42.3*	82.0		706
Malaysia	*0.1*	0.2	0.6	21.2	76.2	90	372
Pakistan		0.2	0.5	*2.8*	10.9	74	152
Philippines	0.2		0.1	*2.1*	3.6	*157*	81
South Korea	2.0	2.8	3.8	410.3	873.3	2,190	4627
Sri Lanka		0.2	0.2	4.7	4.7	189	93
Taiwan	1.7	1.9	*2.7*			3,337	6601
Thailand	*0.2*	0.1	0.3	7.2	15.5	100	281
Turkey	0.2	0.4	1.0	41.6	99.1	283	680
Argentina	*0.4*	0.4	0.6	41.8	69.5	650	980
Brazil		0.6	1.3	55.5	103.6	*168*	629
Chile	*0.7*	0.5	0.7	51.0	78.6	390	833
Colombia		0.3	0.2	20.4	13.1	72	151
Mexico	*0.2*	0.4	0.4	31.5	48.2	213	417
Peru		0.1	0.2	*4.6*	9.0	229	
Venezuela	0.5	0.5	0.2			116	122
Congo, Dem. Rep.			0.5	*0.7*	1.3	..	
Côte d'Ivoire						..	66
Egypt	0.8	0.2	0.2	7.7	11.4	493	617
Ethiopia			0.2	*0.6*	1.3		21
Ghana				*1.5*	3.0		
Kenya				*3.0*	6.1		
Morocco		0.3	0.7	*8.5*	24.1		647
Nigeria				*2.1*	4.1	*15*	

Table 4.2: (cont.)

	R&D as % of GDP[b] 1990	R&D as % of GDP[b] 1997	R&D as % of GDP[b] 2008	R&D per capita 2005 PPP $ 1996	R&D per capita 2005 PPP $ 2009	Researchers in R&D per 1,000 1996	Researchers in R&D per 1,000 2007
South Africa	*0.8*	0.7	1.0	*43.8*	87.5	*337*	382
Tanzania				*2.4*	4.9		
Zambia		0.01	0.3	0.13	4.42	47	
Average Asian countries		0.3	0.7	15.8	39.8	173	200
Average Latin American countries		0.4	0.5	34.1	53.7	263	522
Average African countries				7.0	14.8		
Average developing countries	0.5	0.4	0.6	16.8	34.7	434	510
Average 16 advanced economies[b]	2.1	2.3	2.7	606.5	873.4	2,912	4327

Note:

[a] If no data exist for the year specified, we use the closest year in a five-year range for which data are available (in italics).

[b] The R&D data from UNESCO for developing countries are more inclusive than the R&D data from the OECD source for advanced economies.

Sources:

R&D expenditures from UNESCO, Institute of Statistics (2008, 2011); 1990 from: UNESCO, *Statistical Yearbooks* (various years); R&D % of GDP, Advanced economies, 1990 from OECD (1998a); R&D, Taiwan, DGBAS (1994, 2009); GDP and PPP converters from WDI online (2009). Population, see the sources for Table 5.2.

Researchers in R&D from *World Development Indicators Online (2011)*, supplemented by data from by UNDP, *Human Development Report* (2001, 2005, 2007/8). Taiwan, from DGBAS (2002, 2009); India, Department of Science and Technology (2006).

Table 4.3: ICT indicators

	Telephone lines per 1,000 people			Mobile phones per 1,000 people			Personal computers per 1,000 people	
	1992	2000	2008	1992	2000	2008	2000	2005
LDCs	2.9	5.6	10.8	0.004	2.8	214.2		
LICs	4.9	6.6	11.5	0.004	3.0	220.1	5.1	9.3
LMICs	13.9	67.5	135.1	0.2	33.5	472.2	20.1	27.7
UMICs	99.8	173.1	223.1	1.0	107.6	917.6	69.9	98.9
HIEs[a]	445.7	553.8	462.1	21.9	498.2	1063.4	392.7	562.1

	Internet users per 1,000 people			Secure servers per million people		
	1997	2001	2008	2001	2004	2008
LDCs	0.1	1.7	22.4		0.1	0.3
LICs	0.1	2.1	23.1		0.1	0.3
LMICs	0.7	16.8	136.7	0.2	0.5	1.5
UMICs	6.1	53.0	298.8	3.9	7.4	19.0
HIEs	108.0	365.0	683.3	110.7	290.4	638.7

Note:
HIE = high-income economy.
Source:
World Bank-WDI (2002, 2011).

In the field of education, ICT offer new developments in distance learning and multi-media technologies. The declining costs of communication lower the thresholds for diffusion of scientific, technical and statistical information, especially in countries such as India and China, but also in Sub-Saharan Africa. In this respect, information and communication technologies contribute to a reduction of international technology and knowledge gaps.

Some technological developments offer possibilities of leapfrogging. For example, mobile telephony can compensate for inadequate fixed communication infrastructure in Tanzania. In India, wireless technologies have been developed to connect rural users with switch exchanges at low costs, thus opening up rural areas. Some developing countries have been able to install new digital telephone networks, where advanced countries have invested heavily in older analog technologies. India and Brazil have developed new low-cost computers costing 200–400 dollars, with associated savings in software (James, 2002). In developing countries, access to use of ICT facilities is more important than ownership. New institutional arrangements result in rapid improvements in access. For instance, Dar es Salaam now has numerous internet cafés. In Africa, the growth of mobile telephony is proceeding at a phenomenal speed.

Finally, there is the emergence of a new set of innovative products which are specifically aimed at poor households at the bottom of the global pyramid (Prahalad, 2006). Though one should be sceptical about the present hype surrounding pro-poor innovation, there are examples of innovations in healthcare, in water treatment and in nutrition which are of potential interest for combating poverty.

4.6.4   New threats

If a country is unable to keep up in the technology race and is unable to profit from technology transfers, it is threatened with increasing marginalisation in the world economy. The larger the initial knowledge gap, the less adapted or congruent technologies will be to local needs and competences. This makes it ever more difficult to start bridging the gap. This further erodes the capacity to compete on international markets and reduces the attractiveness of a country for FDI.

Another threat is that technology transfer – in so far it takes place – may lead to increased inequality within developing countries, between groups with access to new technology and groups without access. These problems have been noted in agriculture and in access to ICT.

Finally, the emergence of global labour markets means that developing countries stand to lose some of their most skilled and highly trained members of the workforce due to brain drain (see Chapter 7).

4.7   International technology transfer and technology diffusion

Technological advance in developing countries can take place in two ways: through investments in new technology or through copying new technology. As we showed in Table 4.2, most R&D takes place in the advanced economies. This R&D results in innovations and in advances at the frontiers of technological knowledge. For most developing countries, copying and adapting internationally available technologies is the only realistic path towards technological advance.[9] It should be emphasised, however, that such copying is a form of innovative behaviour that requires considerable efforts on the part of countries, firms and individuals (Evenson and Westphal, 1995). A second point that needs to be made is that international technology transfer has to be complemented by domestic technology diffusion. If new technologies remain completely locked in enclaves of a few large (multinational) firms and do not diffuse through the economy, the impact of technology transfer will remain limited.

4.7.1   International technology transfer

Firms in developing countries can make use of a wide range of channels for international technology transfer. These are summarised in Box 4.2.

Whether each of these mechanisms actually contributes to reducing international technology gaps depends on a variety of supporting factors. Thus, if sending personnel abroad for training and schooling leads to a brain drain because there are no adequate employment prospects, as in many African countries, then efforts to reduce the technology gap will be frustrated. When foreign owners of technology maintain complete control over the technology and prohibit its spread into the domestic economy, the impact of technology transfer

---

[9] Important exceptions are countries such as Brazil, China, India, South Korea and South Africa which engage in innovative R&D activities. As countries develop they can gradually shift their R&D efforts into more innovative channels.

BOX 4.2 : **Mechanisms of technology transfer**

- Acquisition of technology licences.
- Technology transfer as part of a package of FDI or joint ventures.
- Reverse engineering: acquisition of technology through imports of new products, which are copied through reverse engineering.
- Competing on international export markets and having to meet international quality standards has important learning effects.
- Original equipment manufacturing (OEM): producing for foreign firms, according to specifications supplied by these firms.
- Subcontracting for advanced domestic firms.
- Outsourcing of software design and business processes.
- Acquisition of technological know-how through the hiring of expatriate experts.
- Sending own personnel abroad for training and schooling: this was the path followed by Japan at the beginning of the twentieth century.
- Accessing patents, international technological literature and digital resources.
- Sending own personnel to participate in trade fairs, conferences and international meetings.
- Tapping into the diaspora of highly educated nationals living abroad.

will be limited. On the other hand, many developing countries have made very effective and successful use of these transfer mechanisms in the past (Hobday, 1995, 2013; Lall, 2000). Examples include Japan, Korea, Taiwan, India and Western Europe. Technology acquisition can lead to explosive growth.

As discussed previously, the success of technology transfer depends both on the conditions under which it is supplied and on the characteristics and policies of the receiving countries, such as education levels, infrastructure, political stability, capabilities of using new technologies and the size of the technology gaps.

In the following paragraphs we discuss some further aspects of diffusion of technology and technology transfer.

4.7.2   Intellectual property rights

How knowledge develops and diffuses is influenced by property right regimes. Knowledge, technology and information are public goods. They are *non-rival* (the same knowledge can be used simultaneously by different people) and *non-excludable* (it is difficult to prohibit the use of knowledge by others).[10] In a market economy, this reduces the incentives for firms and individuals to invest in the development of new knowledge. They cannot appropriate all the returns to their investment. Throughout economic history, protection of IPRs has proved to be one of the engines of technological change and economic growth. Instruments such as patents, trademarks, brand names and breeders' rights allow inventors, innovators and

---

[10] This section is based in part on a recent presentation on intellectual property rights by Bart Verspagen, at a UNU-MERIT workshop on innovation policy in Bogotá, Colombia, in September 2011.

investors to profit from their efforts to generate new knowledge and technology. Furthermore, patents describe the content of new knowledge and can thus serve as a mechanism for disclosure and spreading of knowledge.

Protection of IPRs, however, also has the potentially negative effect of restricting access to knowledge and slowing down the diffusion of technology. Owners of technology can prohibit the use of technology by others, or charge prohibitive fees for its use. Thus, a patent provides the patent holder with a monopoly which restricts knowledge flows and technology spillovers, which are one of the most attractive and growth-promoting features of investment in knowledge. A fine balance needs to be struck between the strength of protection (the length of patent protection; how novel does the invention have to be?; how much knowledge is covered by the protection?) and the desirability of knowledge spillovers (Nordhaus, 1969).

In this respect, developing countries are in a potentially vulnerable situation. We have argued that catch-up is based on accessing and imitating state of the art technology from technologically leading countries, without needing to pay the full price for the development of technology. Too strong IPR protection will act as an obstacle to catch-up. A second potential disadvantage of profit-driven investment in knowledge is that firms and commercial organisations will tend to underinvest in areas where the private returns are less than the social returns. Examples of sustained underinvestment are to be found in the field of research on AIDS/HIV, malaria and global warming. In the case of health, sick people in developing countries cannot afford expensive medicines so that the pharmaceutical industries will gear their research to markets in the advanced economies. There has been insufficient investment in agricultural research for semi-arid agriculture in Sub-Saharan Africa. Where there is underinvestment in socially important areas of knowledge and technological change, there is a special task for public support by governments, non-profit organisations and international organisations.

When the WTO was set up in 1995, the Trade-Related Aspects of Intellectual Property Rights (TRIPS) Agreement was one of its essential components (Granstrand, 2005). Developing countries that wanted to join the WTO had to accept the provisions of TRIPS. This meant that they had to implement minimum standards in all areas of IPR protection. This resulted in a considerable strengthening of the international IPR regime.

There is an ongoing debate on the advantages and disadvantages of such strengthening (Verspagen, 2003). For the poorer developing countries stronger IPR protection is a serious disadvantage, as it limits their access to knowledge. Also, the new IPR regimes had the possibly unintended consequence that MNCs started patenting indigenous knowledge about the herbs used in traditional medicines, or local gene varieties of plants and crops. Improved protection of IPRs may be less negative for the more advanced developing countries. It can result in increased FDI and accompanying inflows of technology. Firms would not be willing to risk their advanced technological knowledge base in developing countries without adequate protection. Finally, better protection can provide incentives for more R&D efforts in developing countries such as China and India, where more and more domestic firms are starting to engage in research and development.

4.7.3   Absorptive capacity

As emphasised in section 4.2.3, technology acquisition requires considerable effort. It does not take place automatically. It requires highly developed absorptive capabilities and these capabilities have to be developed over time. For instance, it is not enough to import advanced machinery. Much of the technological knowledge embodied in this machinery is implicit and tacit. It exists in the minds of users, and is not captured adequately in blueprints or handbooks. Many of the disappointing effects of development projects aimed at technology transfer in the past stem from disregard of this basic fact. In the following paragraphs we will discuss three separate strands in the literature which, in our view, capture different aspects of absorptive capacity. One of the challenges for development theory is to synthesise these different literatures into a more comprehensive view of absorptive capacities.

Technological congruence and social capability

In Chapter 3, mention was made of the work of Abramovitz (1989b), who argued that technological backwardness could be seen as a potential for accelerated growth and catch-up, if a country succeeded in tapping into global technology flows. Whether a country succeeded in doing so depended on two factors: technological congruence and social capabilities. *Technological congruence*, or technological distance, refers to the degree to which foreign technologies are adapted to conditions in the receiving countries. One can think of differences in the physical environment (temperature, humidity, precipitation, dust, available resources such as water, sunlight, fertile soils and so forth), the availability of complementary schooling and skills, the organisation of local production, local market size and market conditions. Abramovitz has argued that much of modern technology in the second half of the twentieth century was developed in the context of standardised mass markets in the USA. It cannot automatically be transferred to low-income economies where markets are smaller and more fragmented. Only if the problems of technological congruence can be overcome through creative adaptation of technology to local conditions, or by the broadening of markets, does technological backwardness offer potential advantages.

Whether such advantages can be realised also depends on what Abramovitz has called the *social capabilities* of a national society (Abramovitz, 1989b). 'Social capabilities' refers to the use a country can make of advanced technology and its capacity to acquire it in the first place. The opportunities offered by technological backwardness can be offset by lack of sufficient social capabilities (Box 4.3).

BOX 4.3 : Social capabilities

- Technical competence of a country's people.
- Levels of general education.
- Share of the population with training in technical subjects.
- Managerial experience with large-scale production.
- Availability of supporting services for the use of advanced technology (in the fields of merchandising and distribution, legal services, accounting, statistical and personnel management).
- Quality of the financial system and financial services, ability to mobilise capital.
- Pool of dynamic entrepreneurship.
- Availability of adequate infrastructure devoted to power, transport and communication.

Source: Abramovitz (1989b).

Technological capabilities

Development economists have formulated a related but somewhat more narrowly defined concept of *technological capabilities* (Lall, 1987, 1992, 1996; for an overview see Romijn, 1999). The term 'technological capabilities' refers to the capability to select and acquire appropriate new technologies and capital goods (investment capabilities), the capabilities to operate new capital goods (production capabilities) and the capabilities to adapt and further develop technologies (innovation capabilities). Technological capabilities operate at the micro-level of firms (Biggs *et al.*, 1995; Cohen and Levinthal, 1990; Figueiredo, 2003; Romijn, 1997), but also at the level of national societies (Lall, 1992; van Egmond, 2000).

Technological capabilities include skills, experiences, attitudes and schooling. Technological capabilities are necessary to select and acquire the adequate technologies, to adapt them to local circumstances, to operate them and to develop them further. In cases of successful development, there is a gradual shift from adaptation of imported technology to indigenous development of technology. Japan, Taiwan, Korea, India and China are well-known examples in this respect.

In the capability literature, learning is one of the key issues. Learning can be seen as an effort to improve capabilities. Learning refers to formal schooling and professional training on the one hand, and to on-the-job training, experience and internal training on the other. Learning by doing (producing capital goods) and learning by using (using capital goods in production) are extremely important (Tunzelmann, 1995). Such learning will not take place if there is no parallel inflow of new capital goods and technologies. This is why investment in human capital alone will have disappointing results (see Chapter 7). Education and schooling primarily work when they are complementary to technological change.

An important lesson to be derived from the technological capability literature is that acquisition of technology is neither easy nor costless, as suggested by older neoclassical theories of growth. Acquisition and use of existing technology requires skills, effort and capabilities. The adaptation of international technology to local conditions requires considerable creativity. It is innovation rather than pure imitation. Such creative capabilities themselves have to develop or to be developed through education, training, experience and investment in human capital (see Chapter 7).

National systems of innovation

One can also link the notion of absorptive capabilities to the burgeoning literature on national systems of innovation (Freeman, 1987; Lundvall, 1992; Lundvall *et al.*, 2009; Malerba, 2002; Nelson, 1993). Authors such as Lundvall (1992) and Nelson (1993) have emphasised that the innovativeness of an economy does not simply depend on the sum of innovative actions by separate actors, but also on their interrelationships. For innovation, firms depend not only on their own efforts, but also on their abilities to profit from resources and efforts of other actors: suppliers, competitors, customers, research institutes, government organisations and so forth. Innovative countries are characterised not only by the volume of their R&D efforts and human capital, but also by strong interrelationships between firms, private and public research institutions, fundamental and applied researchers and governments. These networks promote the flow of knowledge and diffusion of technology within an economy and contribute to the production of new knowledge (Box 4.4).

BOX 4.4 : **The innovation system approach**

- Focus on innovation as an interactive and adaptive process within a broad systems context.
- Learning and linkages are central to innovation processes.
- The following linkages and interactions are of special interest:
  - Between producing and using firms
  - Between competing firms
  - Between firms and final customers
  - Between universities and firms
  - Between universities, firms, public research organisations and government.
- Importance of the role of the home market for innovation.
- Attention for non-price relations including power, trust and loyalty; interactive learning instead of transactions.
- Importance of feedbacks and learning, as opposed to the traditional linear innovation model, which emphasises the sequence running from pure science, via applied technology to introduction of innovations in the market.

The function of an innovation system in a developing country is different from that in an advanced economy (Lundvall *et al.*, 2009). In an advanced economy, the innovation system contributes to advances of knowledge at the knowledge frontier. In a developing country context, the main function is that of absorption of technology. One of the reasons that international technology transfer has often had disappointing results is because the national systems of innovation of many developing countries are weakly developed and are unable to absorb knowledge effectively and diffuse it throughout the domestic economy.

In spite of all advances in communication, technology flows also have a strongly localised nature (Caniëls, 2000). Technology diffusion within an economy operates more effectively in localised clusters, where people can experience face-to-face interaction and transfer the tacit elements of technology, which are not captured in blueprints and manuals or embodied in machinery. Thus the national systems approach has been further developed to include regional systems of innovation. A further extension is to study the systems of innovation that are specific to economic sectors such as chemicals, textiles or aerospace (sectoral systems of innovation, see Malerba, 2002, 2004; Vertesy, 2011).

Many developing countries have made serious efforts to invest in higher education, research and R&D institutes. However, the diffusion of technology from these systems to the wider economy remains limited, due to shortcomings in the innovation system. In Tanzania, for example, a whole set of R&D institutes was set up in order to promote innovation in various sectors of the economy. A detailed study of an R&D institute focusing on industry (Bongenaar and Szirmai, 2001) concluded that some degree of success had been achieved in acquiring, adapting and developing useful small-scale technologies. However, it turned out there was not a single case of successful technology transfer to any enterprise in a period of twenty years. All attention of the institute was focused on generating technology. Little or no attention was paid to early contacts with potential users, needs assessments or market research, which feed into the research effort and increase the chances of successful technology diffusion. Unfortunately, this linear approach is not a-typical for developing countries in general.

Kline and Rosenberg have emphasised that successful innovation requires combining technical and economic factors and technology push and market pull in an interactive model which they refer to as the chain-linked model (Kline and Rosenberg, 1986; Rosenberg, 1990).

4.8   Biotechnology and information and communication technology

In the following section, we will discuss the impact of recent developments in biotechnology and ICT in developing countries (see UNDP, 2001).

4.8.1   Biotechnology

Biotechnological research has contributed to very substantial increases in land productivity in developing countries. Without these increases global food production would not have been able to keep up with global population growth (see Chapter 10). Nevertheless, one always has to ask who profits from technological change. In developing countries, the so-called 'green revolution' has sometimes led to increasing rural inequality. Internationally, technological development has made farmers more dependent on biotechnological MNEs. Intellectual protection of new seed varieties prohibits farmers and peasants from using their own seed; they are required to buy their seed from MNCs. Genetically manipulated seeds cannot usually be reproduced by farmers.

We have already mentioned the tendency of patenting and appropriating indigenous plant varieties for medicinal purposes by MNEs from the advanced economies. According to the 1989/99 *World Development Report* (World Bank-WDR, 1999), 43 billion dollars' worth of medicines are sold annually which are based on plant varieties indigenous to developing countries.

Commercial incentives in agrarian research have resulted in underinvestment in agrarian technologies for semi-arid agriculture in Africa. Here there is an urgent need for new agricultural green revolutions. Realising such breakthroughs requires public investment in R&D, as has been done in the past for rice and wheat.

In the field of medical technology there are similar problems. Quite modest investments can result in radical improvements in health conditions. Think of vaccinations against child diseases, oral rehydration packages for diarrhoea, investments in hygiene and clean water, and education about the importance of hygiene.

One of the shortcomings of international research efforts is lack of sufficient research on diseases such as HIV/AIDS in their African and Asian context, malaria and river blindness. There is no effective market demand for medicines, because people simply cannot afford to pay for them. Here lies a real challenge for guiding international research efforts into socially desirable directions.

4.8.2   Information and communication technology

The rapid evolution of ICT provides the most telling example of both the opportunities and the challenges of technological change for development (see James, 2002; UNDP, 2001).

Thus, new developments in telecommunication provide possibilities for improving both the access to and the quality of education. Through distance learning large groups of people can be reached, who until now had no access to education. Distance learning is suitable both for school children and for adult education. It is relatively cheap. An example of successful distance learning is provided by the Monterrey Institute of Technology in Mexico. This virtual university has 9,000 students studying for a university degree and 35,000 students enrolled for shorter courses. Other countries investing in distance education include Indonesia and South Africa. Especially where population is geographically dispersed, distance learning can be an excellent solution. The development of the internet improves access to knowledge in developing countries and facilitates international knowledge diffusion and transfers.

Jeffrey James has made an interesting analysis of the possibilities and challenges of ICT technology (James, 1999, 2002). His conclusion is in line with the discussion in this chapter. Global technological developments lead either to further integration of developing countries into the world economy or to further marginalisation or even exclusion. On the one hand, ICT leads to geographically dispersed chains of production, both within MNCs and in the form of strategic alliances between corporations, including corporations in developing countries (Duijsters and Hagedoorn, 2000). This offers new opportunities for developing countries. On the other hand, countries with insufficient technological capabilities will not be included in and profit from these global production chains. They will be further marginalised.

James distinguishes four categories of developing country which have profited from technological developments in ICT: first-generation NICs such as Korea or Taiwan, second-generation NICs such as Malaysia and the Philippines; large developing countries such as India and Brazil with a well-developed scientific and technological infrastructure; and countries localised close to large developed country markets such as Mexico.

James makes a systematic analysis of the mechanisms through which technology affects developing countries. Negative factors include: an abundance of small-scale enterprises in rural areas, low rates of investment, weak technical capabilities, high labour costs in relation to levels of schooling, the lack of an adequate technological or scientific infrastructure, long distance from advanced markets and the lack of research competence in the ICT field. Countries with these characteristics are being marginalised in the world economy. Their technological and economic backwardness increases. Technological development does not result primarily in a gap between the advanced and developing world, but rather in a parting of the ways among developing countries themselves.

4.9   National and international policy

There is a wide range of policy instruments which can be used to promote innovation and technological change. They are summarised in Box 4.5.

These measures should not be seen in isolation. In thinking about technology policy there has been a movement from linear science and technology policies aimed at increasing the supply of university graduates, the volume of R&D expenditures or the output of universities,

BOX 4.5 : Policies to support innovation

- R&D subsidies.
- R&D tax policies.
- Cluster policies which promote the emergence of firm clusters to profit from agglomeration effects.
- Regional policies (agglomeration effects).
- Incubators and science parks which promote knowledge flows between research institutions and private enterprises.
- Design of appropriate IPR regimes.
- Educational policies to increase the supply of skilled labour.
- Research policies (subsidies and grants), promoting both basic and applied research.
- Public procurement policies which support innovative products.
- FDI policies aimed at maximising spillovers from multinational firms to the domestic economy.
- Investment incentives for SMEs and large firms.
- Policies promoting the financing of innovation and the emergence of venture capital.
- Industrial policies promoting structural change and industrial upgrading.
- Sectoral policies supporting specific sectors.
- Agricultural extension policies.
- Business support policies.

to a more systemic view based on complementarities and interactive learning. Policy should contribute to the development of more effective national systems of innovation and research systems. One of the important issues is strengthening linkages and interaction between publicly funded research institutes and the needs of private and public production units.

In a developing country setting, the function of R&D is not primarily to contribute to advances at the frontiers of knowledge, but rather it is an investment in order to be able to profit from technological developments elsewhere and develop new appropriate adaptations. A consensus has developed that stronger export orientation contributes to the development of the technological capabilities of the export firms. Competing on international markets requires meeting international technology and quality standards. An outward-oriented trade policy will thus contribute to learning.

Some types of FDI can contribute to the building of technological capabilities, if technology transfer is accompanied by schooling and training efforts and technological knowledge is diffused through the domestic economy. But if the foreign investor retains complete and restrictive control of technology, the learning impact will be limited. This is also an area where policy can have a major impact.

The complementarity of technological capabilities and acquisition of new technologies and new capital goods is important. New technologies and imported capital goods will have little impact without appropriate capabilities. But investing in education and technological capabilities will be useless if there is no simultaneous inflow of new technologies in a country.

In the international context, research efforts should be better oriented to the needs and problems of developing countries (UNDP, 2001). Areas which require urgent attention from the international research community include HIV/AIDS research for developing countries, malaria research, water management, agricultural and biotechnological research and research on the economic impacts of climate change. Where market incentives result in underinvestment in socially important avenues of research, public research institutes should directly or indirectly try to influence the direction of research efforts.

Questions for review

1. Discuss the main changes in economic and world technological leadership since the fifteenth century.
2. Discuss examples of catch-up in developing countries in the twentieth century.
3. Under which conditions could a developing country profit from international technology transfer?
4. Under which conditions will the acceleration of technological change result in further marginalisation of a developing country?
5. What is a national innovation system?
6. Identify possible weaknesses in the innovation systems of developing countries, which hinder technological change and the diffusion of technology.
7. What are the shortcomings of a linear perspective on technological change?
8. Discuss the most important mechanisms for international transfer of technology. To what extent can these be influenced by policy measures?
9. Discuss the relationships between technological change, productivity increases and competitiveness.
10. Discuss the role of IPRs in the national and international diffusion of knowledge.

Further reading

A nice overview of the debates on technology and development is provided by Evenson and Westphal in their article 'Technological Change and Technology Strategy', in Volume IIIA of Behrman and Srinivasan (eds.), *Handbook of Development Economics* (1995). Many of the topics and theories discussed in this chapter are treated in a collection of both older and new articles on growth, innovation and technology by Richard Nelson, *The Sources of Economic Growth* (1996) and a volume edited by Kim and Nelson, entitled *Technology, Learning and Innovation: Experiences of Newly Industrializing Economies* (2000). The relationship between technology and productivity is explored in an important study by Howard Pack, *Productivity, Technology and Industrial Development* (1987). This book focuses on the textile industry and is unique in combining economic analysis with engineering information. It presents detailed case studies for textile firms in the Philippines and Kenya. Frances Stewart has written widely on the choice of technology from the perspective of developing countries. We mention the articles 'Choice of Technique in Developing Countries' (1972), 'Technology and Employment in Less

Developed Countries' (1974) and an interesting edited volume *Macro-Policies for Appropriate Technology in Developing Countries* (1987). A historical perspective on the choice of technology in textiles in India and Japan is provided in a brilliant study by Otsuka, Ranis and Saxonhouse, *Comparative Technology Choice in Development* (1988). The impact of changes in technological paradigms is explored by Freeman and Perez in 'Structural Crises of Adjustment, Business Cycles and Investment Behaviour' (1988) and Dosi in 'Technological Paradigms and Technological Trajectories' (1988). The concept of national systems of innovation was discussed by Lundvall in *National Systems of Innovation: Towards a Theory of Innovation and Interactive Learning* (1992). Another important source for systems of innovation is a volume edited by Nelson entitled *National Innovation Systems: A Comparative Analysis* (1993). More recently, the concept has been applied in a developing country context in the *Handbook of Innovation Systems and Developing Countries: Building Domestic Capabilities in a Global Setting* (Lundvall et al., 2009). In a series of books and articles Sanjaya Lall has focused on the role of technological capabilities in development. We mention *Learning to Industrialise: The Acquisition of Technological Capabilities in India* (1987), an article in World Development on 'Technological Capabilities and Industrialization' (1992) and *Learning from the Asian Tigers: Studies in Technology and Industrial Policy* (1996). Jeffrey James has explored the impact of the spread of ICT on the integration or marginalisation of developing countries in the global economy in *Technology, Globalization and Poverty* (2002). The challenges and opportunities offered by technological change are also explored in the 1989–99 edition of the *WDR*, *Knowledge for Development* (World Bank-WDR, 1999) and the 2001 *HDR*, entitled *Making New Technologies Work for Human Development* (UNDP, 2001). An excellent collection of articles on the role of innovation in both advanced economies and developing countries is presented in *The Oxford Handbook of Innovation*, edited by Jan Fagerberg, David C. Mowery and Richard R. Nelson (2005). Journals with a specific focus on technology and innovation include *Research Policy, Industrial and Corporate Change* and the *Economics of Innovation and New Technology*.

5 Population and development

Chapters 5–7 focus on the various relationships between population, human capital and socio-economic development. Chapters 6 and 7 deal with health and education. In this chapter, we discuss the relationships between population growth and economic development.

The chapter opens with a discussion of global demographic trends, which indicate that in the next ninety years world population will increase by a further 2.4 billion people, stabilising around 2100 at 10.1 billion. Subsequently, we discuss the economic consequences of population growth and demographic change. We contrast pessimistic Malthusian perspectives, which argue that population growth is a threat to sustained economic development, with more optimistic assessments which indicate that technological change has the potential to outpace the growth of population. We pay special attention to the challenge of global warming. The second half of the chapter focuses on explanations of why families in developing countries have so many children. These explanations serve as guidelines for the formulation of population policies, which are the topic of the last section of this chapter.

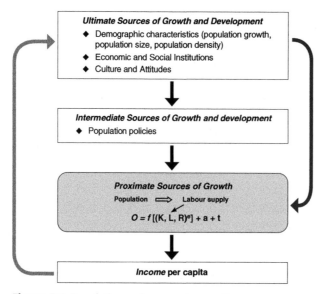

Figure 5.1 Population and economic growth

In the framework of proximate and ultimate causality, major population trends and characteristics figure among the more ultimate sources of growth and development, as indicated in Figure 5.1. At the proximate level, population trends affect labour input. There are also strong feedback loops from increasing levels of per capita income to population dynamics.

5.1 Introduction

As an introduction to this chapter on population and development, we distinguish eight types of relationships between demographic and economic developments, which are summarised in Box 5.1.

Apart from population growth, population size and population density are also important demographic variables. Several countries in Latin America and Africa have rapid population growth, but relatively low population density. Low population density discourages large-scale investment in infrastructure. Population size influences the absolute volume of required investment and the size of domestic markets. Countries with large domestic markets can better afford to follow an inward-looking path of economic development than small countries (Myint, 1980).

BOX 5.1 : Relationships between population change and economic development

1. Population growth supplies the **labour**, which is available as an input into economic production (see Figure 5.1). The availability of labour with various qualifications, and levels of education and health, influences the productive potential of a society.
2. The growth of population, on the other hand, also gives rise to **employment challenges**. Can economic development provide a rapidly growing labour force with sufficient productive and paid employment, or does open or disguised unemployment increase?
3. A rapidly growing population can stimulate the **growth of production** by providing an expanding market for goods and services.
4. The **level of consumption** in a society depends in part on the relationship between population growth and growth of production. Is the growth of production of goods and services sufficient to provide a growing population with an acceptable standard of living?
5. A growing population creates opportunities for **productive investment and can stimulate savings**.
6. The size and growth of the labour force is one of the determinants of the need for **savings and investment**. If investment lags behind the growth of the labour force, then – with given technology – labour productivity will tend to decline and the growth of production will not be able to keep up with the growth of population.
7. In the absence of technological change, growth of population increases the pressure on the **national environment**, especially when combined with increased output per capita.
8. Growth of population and increasing pressure on **scarce resources** can stimulate technological change.

5.2   Perspectives on population growth

In post-war debates on the population problem Malthusian views predominated up to the 1970s. It was thought that rapid growth of population in developing countries threatened their chances of economic development. Researchers and representatives of international organisations warned about the consequences of the 'population explosion' and pleaded for vigorous family planning programmes (Coale and Hoover, 1958).

Representatives of developing countries countered that an overemphasis on population policy deflected attention from the core of development problems, namely economic underdevelopment. Once economic development accelerated, population growth would automatically slow down, as it had done earlier in the Western countries. In addition, they argued that one-quarter of world population was using more than 80 per cent of global natural resources. The question was not scarcity of world resources, but their unequal distribution (Keating, 1993; Todaro, 1981, Chapter 6).

There is no firm empirical support for the conclusion that the effects of population growth on a country's economic development are always negative. In some instances, population growth can even have positive effects on factors such as technological change and growth of output (Birdsall, 1988; Kelley, 1988; World Bank-WDR, 1984). High population growth rates notwithstanding, some countries have succeeded in substantially raising their per capita incomes. Rapid growth results in a young labour force, which is often seen as a demographic window of opportunity. But, other countries with rapid population growth show slow growth or even declines of per capita income. The poorest countries in Sub-Saharan Africa are the countries with the highest rates of population growth.

In both the political debate and in the empirical scientific discussion the contours of a new consensus have become visible: very rapid growth of population can seriously exacerbate existing economic problems in very poor societies. But these economic problems are usually not primarily caused by population growth. Therefore population policy should not be discussed in isolation. Rather it should be integrated into a wider framework of policies aimed at overall economic and social development (Bengtsson and Gunnarsson, 1994; Keating, 1993, Chapter 5; United Nations Population Division, 1994). At the macro-level the question of controlling the growth of global population is becoming increasingly urgent in the light of issues such as global warming and global pollution (IPCC, 2007a; Nordhaus, 2007; Raupach et al., 2007; Stern, 2007; Tol, 2009; World Bank-WDR, 2010). Here, Malthusian concerns are justified.

5.3   Growth of world population

Table 5.1 presents estimates of world population in the very long run. This table shows that there has always been some measure of global population increase, even in pre-historic times. There was no such thing as a Malthusian equilibrium in which world population remained stable due to the checks of famine and disease. There was *extensive growth*, with increases in production sustaining a growing population. However, the growth of population before 1750 was very slow. After this date there was a dramatic acceleration of growth, which

Table 5.1: Growth of world population

Year	Estimated world population (low and high estimates)[a] (million)	Estimated world population (million)	Average annual growth rate[b] (%)	Population developing countries (million)	Average annual growth rate developing countries[b] (%)
10,000–8,000 BC	5–10	7.5			
0–14 AD	270–330	300	0.04		
1000	275–345	310	0.00		
1250	350–450	400	0.10		
1500	440–540	490	0.08		
1750	735–805	770	0.18		
1850	1,100–1,300	1,200	0.44		
1900	1,650–1,710	1,680	0.68		
1950		2,532	0.82	1,721	
1970		3,696	1.91	2,690	2.26
1975		4,076	1.98	3,030	2.41
1985		4,863	1.78	3,750	2.16
1990		5,306	1.76	4,162	2.10
1995		5,726	1.53	4,557	1.83
2000		6,123	1.35	4,934	1.60
2005		6,507	1.22	5,296	1.43
2010		6,896	1.17	5,660	1.34
2020		7,657	1.05	6,383	1.21
2030		8,321	0.84	7,025	0.96
2050		9,306	0.56	7,994	0.65
2060		9,615	0.33	8,305	0.38
2070		9,827	0.22	8,518	0.25
2080		9,969	0.14	8,655	0.16
2090		10,062	0.09	8,738	0.10
2100		10,125	0.06	8,790	0.06
2150		9,488	−0.13	8,125	−0.16
2200		9,493	0.00	8,079	−0.01

Notes:

[a] Durand (1977) presents the upper and lower limits of estimates that have the same degree of plausibility. In the second column we have taken the midpoint of the upper and lower boundaries of Durand's indifference ranges.

[b] Average growth rates in the period since the year listed in the previous row.

Sources:

10,000 BC–AD 1750 and 1900: Durand (1977); 1850: Cipolla (1978); 1950–2100: United Nations Population Division, *World Population Prospects, The 2010 Revision*, CD-Rom edition (2011a), http://esa.un.org/unpd/wpp/Excel-Data/population.htm (2110–2100 projections, medium variant); 2100–2200: 2100 figures extrapolated with growth rates from United Nations Population Division, *World Population to 2300* (United Nations Population Division, 2004).

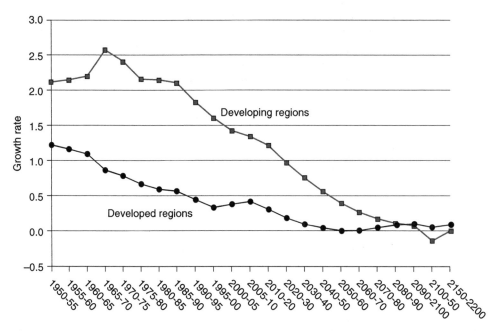

Figure 5.2 Population growth, 1950–2200
Sources: See Table 5.1.

reached its peak in the period 1970–5. During this period world population increased at 2 per cent per annum. At such a growth rate world population would double every thirty-five years.

Figure 5.2 shows that most of population growth takes place in developing countries. In the rich countries population growth is low and is projected to reach zero by 2040. Current growth rates in the advanced economies are driven for an important part by immigration. Between 2005 and 2010 world population increased by some 389 million persons. The population of the more developed countries increased by 25 million, the population of developing countries by 364 million, or around 73 million per year.

After 1975, the rate of population growth began to slow down. But growth remained very high in historical perspective.

The projected world population for 2050 is 9.3 billion people, of which 86 per cent will be in developing countries. UN medium projections (United Nations Population Division, 2011a) suggest that world population will stabilise around 10.1 billion people in 2100, declining somewhat after that year. In previous projections (United Nations Population Division, 2002a), population was expected to stabilise at a similar figure of 10.2 billion fifty years earlier, in 2050. Extrapolations of the 2100 estimates with growth rates from long-run projections (United Nations Population Division, 2004) suggest that world population could ultimately stabilise at 9.5 billion in 2150. Most of the increase in population will be added in the years between 2015 and 2060. India is expected to be by far the largest contributor to world population growth, adding around 570 million persons by 2050, followed at a distance by countries such as Pakistan (160 million), Nigeria (141 million), Congo (127 million) and China (142 million) (estimates from United Nations Population Division, 2005). After 2060, projected population growth will slow down, in both percentage terms and in absolute numbers.

One should realise, however, that these long-term projections depend heavily on assumptions concerning fertility rates (see section 5.4). Under the assumption that present fertility rates remain unchanged, a world population of 10.3 billion people could already be reached by 2045. In 2100 world population would then reach a staggering 26.8 billion. Based on low and high assumptions about fertility decline, population projections for 2100 vary from 6.2 billion in the low-fertility scenario to 15.8 billion in the high-fertility scenario. The medium variant reproduced in Table 5.1 and Figure 5.2 assumes that fertility rates will continue to decline until the replacement fertility rate is achieved. After that they stabilise (United Nations Population Division, 2011b). The low variant assumes half a child per woman less than the medium variant; the high variant assumes half a child more. Projections are heavily influenced by developments in the two most populous countries in the world, India and China. When the decline in fertility rates in China was reversed in the late 1980s, projections were revised upwards. In the early 1990s, fertility rates dropped again, resulting in lower global projections. The most recent projections also incorporate the negative effects of HIV/AIDS on mortality and life expectancy.

5.4 The demographic transition

The growth of population is determined by the relation between *birth rates* and *death rates*. Acceleration of world population growth is caused by what is optimistically called the *demographic transition*. Figure 5.3 presents a schematic representation of the demographic transition which has earlier taken place in Europe.

Before the demographic transition both birth rates and death rates were high. The so-called *crude birth rate* – the annual number of births per 1,000 inhabitants – was around 35 per 1,000, the crude death rate – the annual number of deaths per 1,000 inhabitants – was around 25–30 per 1,000. The net excess of births over deaths caused a slow increase of population. In the nineteenth century the death rate gradually declined in the presently prosperous countries, principally as a result of improved nutrition, increases in the overall standard of living and improved sanitation and hygienic circumstances. As the birth rate did

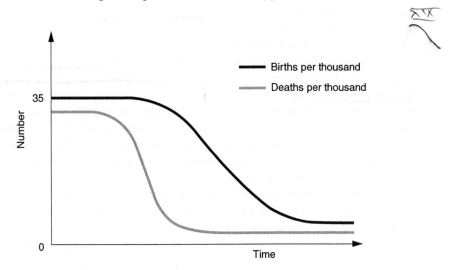

Figure 5.3 The demographic transition

not decline along with the death rate, the excess of births over deaths increased. Population growth in Europe accelerated to the hitherto unknown level of 1 per cent per year. In due course, however, birth rates also started to decline, under the combined influence of urbanisation, modernisation and improving standards of living. In the twentieth century a new equilibrium was reached between low death rates and low birth rates.

A similar process took place in developing countries in the second half of the twentieth century, though even more dramatically. Death rates declined much faster than they did in Europe in the nineteenth century, primarily due to medical progress. Developing country birth rates of around 45 per 1,000 inhabitants in the 1950s were higher than they were in nineteenth-century Europe. For much of the twentieth century birth rates remained high. The result was an unprecedented rate of population growth. If the earlier pattern of the demographic transition repeats itself, birth rates in developing countries will decline in the long run in developing countries and a new equilibrium between birth and death rates will be achieved at a lower level.

There is evidence that this is happening at the moment, though the characteristics of the demographic transition differ substantially from region to region (Lee and Reher, 2011a, 2011b; McNicoll, 1994, see also the next section). Caldwell (1997) argues that there is a single global fertility transition which started in nineteenth-century Europe and which diffused step by step to the rest of the world. Caldwell and Caldwell (1997) emphasise the importance of the diffusion of the intellectual notion of birth control in an increasing globally interconnected social system.

In addition to the 'crude birth rate' and the 'crude death rate' two other concepts are important for an understanding of demographic developments, namely the *total fertility rate* and *life expectation*.

The total fertility rate is the average number of children a woman will bear in the course of the fertile period of her life (World Bank-WDR, 1984: 66). Together with the age structure of the population, the total fertility rate determines the crude birth rate. A low fertility rate in combination with an age structure comprising many young women in the fertile period of their life could result in the same crude birth rate as a high fertility rate with relatively few women in their fertile years. Rapid population growth in developing countries results in a youthful age structure. This means that population will continue to grow for quite a long time, even if the average number of children per woman has declined to the *replacement level* of two children per woman.

The crude death rate also depends on two factors: the life expectation and the age structure. The life expectation is the average number of years a child is expected to live from birth onwards. In countries with high child mortality, average life expectancy is strongly influenced by mortality in the first five years of life. Other things being equal, a young population with a high life expectation will make for very low death rates. An old population with high life expectations will have higher death rates. Many affluent countries have an increasing number of elderly people in their population, leading to higher death rates in spite of high life expectation.

As child mortality declines, *adult mortality* – defined as probability of a fifteen-year-old dying before the age of sixty – becomes more and more important. As a result of declines in child mortality rates in developing countries, the under-five mortality rate is less important as determinant of total mortality than it was in the past. Further increases in life expectation in the developing world will increasingly depend on success in reducing adult mortality rates (Kuhn, 2010).

5.5   Demographic developments in developing countries

Table 5.2 and Table 5.3 offer a picture of demographic developments in developing countries. Table 5.2 presents growth rates for thirty-one countries, where possible traced back to 1820. These growth rates are compared with those of sixteen advanced economies. Between 1950 and 1973, population growth in our sample of thirty-one developing countries is more than twice as high as in the advanced economies, between 1973 and 2000 even three times as high. Since 1973 the rate of growth in developing countries has started to decelerate. In all but five countries, average population growth after 2000 is lower than before 2000. But growth still remains very rapid in historical perspective.

The post-war rates of growth of total population in developing countries are more than twice as high as population growth rates in the advanced economies in the nineteenth century. We may therefore conclude that the demographic challenge for developing countries in the twentieth century was much greater than that which faced the presently rich countries in the nineteenth century. The acceleration of population growth in the nineteenth century was paralleled by a substantial increase in the demand for industrial labour. Emigration also provided a potential outlet for surplus population.

In many developing countries today the industrial sector is unable to provide the massive influx of new entrants to the labour market with sufficient paid employment. With a few exceptions, manufacturing is characterised by jobless growth (see Tregenna, 2013). On the one hand, entry into the labour market by young persons is much greater than in the past. On the other hand, increasing capital intensity in production and labour-saving technological change diminishes the demand for labour. Employment will have to be created in other sectors of the economy, such as agriculture, services, or the informal sector.

Population pressure in poor developing countries results in large-scale emigration to the advanced economies (Hatton and Williamson, 2005, see also Chapter 2). As a result almost 10 per cent of the population of the advanced economies in 2000 was made up of international migrants (United Nations Population Division, 2005: 23). But in the face of the large increase in population, emigration does not provide relief from population pressure and the resistance to continued immigration in the advanced economies is on the increase.

Table 5.3 contains a number of important demographic indicators for the post-war period. This table indicates that the developing world is moving into the stage of demographic transition characterised by declining fertility rates. Even in Africa, fertility rates are starting to decline, though they are still much higher than in other regions. Wilson (2001) concludes that a global demographic convergence is taking place.

The demographic transition in developing countries lags some 100 years behind the transition in presently affluent countries. But there are a number of interesting differences between present day and historical processes of transition (Kelley, 1988; Reher, 2011; World Bank-WDR, 1984).

In the first place, aggregate birth rates in developing countries in the 1950s were substantially higher than they were in the past. Even at their peak, birth rates in the nineteenth century were never above 40 births per 1,000 inhabitants. Between 1950 and 1955 the birth rate in developing countries was no less on average than 44 per 1,000 inhabitants.

Table 5.2: Population growth in selected developing countries 1820-2010 (%)

	1820–70	1870–1913[b]	1913–50	1950–73	1973–2000	2000–10
Bangladesh[a]	0.4	0.4	1.0	2.6	2.1	1.7
China	−0.1	0.5	0.6	2.0	1.2	0.7
India	0.4	0.4	0.5	2.1	1.9	1.6
Indonesia	1.2	1.1	1.0	0.9	1.0	1.3
Iran	0.5	0.6	1.1	2.5	2.5	1.5
Malaysia	2.1	3.2	2.0	2.9	2.2	2.3
Pakistan[a]	0.4	0.4	1.9	2.4	2.6	2.1
Philippines	1.7	1.4	2.2	3.3	2.3	2.1
South Korea	0.1	0.2	1.8	2.4	1.1	0.5
Sri Lanka	1.7	1.3	1.2	2.1	1.2	0.9
Taiwan	0.3	0.9	2.1	3.2	1.3	0.4
Thailand	0.4	1.0	2.3	3.0	1.5	1.1
Turkey	0.3	0.6	0.9	2.5	1.7	1.4
Argentina	2.5	3.4	2.2	1.7	1.3	1.0
Brazil	1.6	2.1	2.2	2.9	1.7	1.4
Chile	1.9	1.3	1.6	2.2	1.4	1.2
Colombia	1.4	1.8	2.2	2.8	1.8	1.6
Mexico	0.7	1.1	1.8	3.1	1.9	1.4
Peru	1.4	1.2	1.6	2.8	2.0	1.4
Venezuela	1.7	1.3	1.5	3.7	2.4	1.9
Congo, Democratic Rep.		1.1	2.8	2.6	2.7	2.7
Côte d'Ivoire		1.0	1.9	3.8	3.4	2.0
Egypt	1.0	1.3	1.5	2.6	1.9	1.8
Ethiopia				2.4	2.3	2.6
Ghana		0.6	2.6	2.8	2.3	2.4
Kenya		0.7	2.5	3.2	3.0	2.6
Morocco	0.7	0.7	1.6	2.7	1.9	1.2
Nigeria		0.8	2.2	2.1	2.3	2.4
South Africa	1.0	2.0	1.8	2.5	2.1	1.4
Tanzania		0.2	1.8	3.0	2.7	2.6
Zambia				3.0	2.6	2.5
Average Asian countries	0.7	0.9	1.4	2.5	1.7	1.4
Average Latin American countries	1.6	1.7	1.9	2.8	1.8	1.4
Average African countries	0.9	0.9	2.0	2.7	2.3	2.2

Table 5.2: *(cont.)*

	1820–70	1870–1913[b]	1913–50	1950–73	1973–2000	2000–10
Average developing countries	1.0	1.1	1.7	2.6	2.0	1.7
Annual growth total population in developing countries	0.2	0.6	0.9	2.3	1.7	1.4
Annual growth total population in 16 advanced economies[c,d]	0.9	1.1	0.8	1.1	0.5	0.6

Notes:

[a] Growth rates of Bangladesh and Pakistan before 1913 equal the Indian growth rate.

[b] The following African countries' growth rate 1900–13 instead of 1870–1913: Côte d'Ivoire, Kenya, Nigeria, Tanzania.

[c] Australia, Austria, Belgium, Canada, Denmark, Finland, France, Germany, Italy, Japan, Netherlands, Norway, Sweden, Switzerland, UK and USA.

[d] For developing countries both average growth rates and the growth rate of total population have been calculated. For OECD countries only the growth rate of total population has been represented.

Sources:

1820–1950, unless otherwise indicated from Maddison (2010), http://www.ggdc.net/MADDISON/oriindex.htm, downloaded 7/9/ 2010; 1820–1913: Bangladesh, Pakistan, Côte d'Ivoire, Ghana, Kenya, Morocco, Nigeria, Tanzania and Zaire/Congo from Maddison (1995); Egypt, 1900: Hansen and Marzouk (1965); 1950–2010: United Nations Population Division (2011a), http://esa. un.org/unpd/wpp/Excel-Data/population.htm, except Taiwan from Maddison (2010).

This figure had declined to 22.9 births per 1,000 by 2005–10. This birth rate is comparable to that in many European countries in the 1950s. Present-day birth rates are lowest in China, which has experienced an astounding decline of birth rates as a result of its harsh birth-control policies. Latin America is in second place. With 35.6 births per 1,000 inhabitants, the African continent has by far the highest birth rates.

In the second place, death rates in developing countries have been declining much faster than in the past. Historically, death rates declined as a corollary of a general increase in the standard of living, improved nutritional intake, economic growth and modernisation of society. Nowadays death rates are declining in most developing countries, irrespective of their standards of living or economic growth rates. Since 1950, the death rate in developing countries has decreased from 22.6 deaths per 1,000 inhabitants to 8 per 1,000, even after accounting for the impact of the HIV/AIDS epidemic on death rates. It is now 2 per cent lower than in the more developed countries, primarily due to a different age structure. The decline of the death rate proceeded four to five times as fast as in Europe in the nineteenth century (Kelley, 1988; Kuznets, 1980; Reher, 2011). This decline is not primarily due to an overall improvement in standards of living. Rather, it is explained by medical technical progress – in the treatment of infectious diseases, vaccination, antibiotics, combating animal bearers of diseases (vectors) – and by improvements in curative healthcare, medical services, education, transport and communication.

In the last quarter of the twentieth century, population growth in developing countries was still higher than it had ever been in the presently prosperous countries (cf. Table 5.2). Population growth increased throughout the 1950s and 1960s, peaking between 1965 and

Table 5.3: Indicators of demographic changes, by region, 1950–2010

	Africa	Latin America & Caribbean	Asia[a]	China	India	Developing countries	More developed countries[b]	World
Population (million)								
1950	230	167	399	551	372	1,721	811	2,532
1980	483	362	838	983	700	3,372	1,081	4,453
2010	1,022	590	1,472	1,341	1,225	5,660	1,236	6,896
Annual growth rate of population (%)								
1950–5	2.1	2.8	2.3	2.0	1.8	2.1	1.2	1.8
1980–5	2.8	2.1	2.4	1.5	2.3	2.2	0.6	1.8
2005–10	2.3	1.2	1.4	0.5	1.4	1.3	0.4	1.2
Birth rate per 1,000								
1950–5	47.7	42.7	43.6	42.1	43.3	43.5	22.4	36.9
2005–10	35.6	19.3	21.3	12.6	23.1	21.9	11.4	20.0
Death rate per 1,000								
1950–5	26.2	15.6	21.4	22.2	25.5	22.6	10.3	18.7
2005–10	11.9	5.9	6.7	7.2	8.3	8.0	10.0	8.4
Net migration rate per 1,000								
1950–5	−0.5	0.1	−0.02	0	0	0	0.1	0
2005–10	−0.7	−1.8	−0.48	−0.3	−0.5	−0.6	2.7	0
Fertility rate								
1950–5	6.6	5.9	5.9	6.1	5.9	6.1	2.8	5.0
2005–10	4.6	2.3	2.6	1.6	2.7	2.7	1.7	2.5
Net fertility rate								
1950–5	1.9	2.1	1.9	2.0	1.7	1.9	1.3	1.7
2005–10	1.8	1.1	1.1	0.7	1.2	1.1	0.8	1.1
Percentage of urban population								
1950	14.4	41.4	18.1	11.8	17.0	17.6	52.6	28.8
2010	40.0	79.6	45.8	47.0	30.0	45.1	75.2	50.5
Percentage of population under 15 years								
1950	41.6	40.2	39.0	34.2	37.5	37.6	27.3	34.3
2010	40.3	27.9	28.9	19.5	30.6	29.0	16.5	26.8
Percentage of population over 65 years								
1950	3.3	3.5	4.3	4.5	3.1	3.9	7.9	5.2
2010	3.5	6.9	5.5	8.2	4.9	5.8	15.9	7.6
Youth dependency ratio (%)[c]								
1950	75.5	71.4	68.7	55.8	63.1	64.3	42.1	56.7
2010	71.7	42.8	44.0	27.0	47.4	44.5	24.4	40.9
Aged dependency ratio (%)[c]								
1950	60	6.2	7.6	7.3	5.2	6.7	12.2	8.6
2010	6.2	10.6	8.3	11.3	7.6	8.9	23.5	11.6

Table 5.3: *(cont.)*

	Africa	Latin America & Caribbean	Asia[a]	China	India	Developing countries	More developed countries[b]	World
Total dependency ratio (%)[c]								
1950	81.15	77.6	76.3	63.1	68.4	70.9	54.3	65.3
2010	77.9	53.4	52.3	38.3	55.0	53.4	47.9	52.4

Notes:

[a] Excl. Japan, China and India.

[b] Europe, Russian Federation, North America, Japan, Australia and New Zealand.

[c] Youth dependency rate: population of less than 15 years of age as percentage of population aged 15–64; aged dependency ratio: population of 65 years and over as percentage of population aged 15–64. Total dependency rate: population aged less than 15 years or 65 years and over as percentage of the population aged 15–64.

Sources:

United Nations Population Division (2011a), *World Population Prospects: The 2010 Revision*; Urban population from United Nations Population Division (2009), *World Urbanization Prospects: The 2009 Revision*, http://esa.un.org/unpd/wup/index.htm.

1975. After the 1960s a decline set in Asia and Latin America, while growth rates continued to accelerate in Africa till 1985. Between 2005 and 2010, the African population was growing at 2.3 per cent per year. Fears that the slowdown in the growth of population in Asia was being reversed (World Bank, 1994), have not materialised. Since 1990–5, Asian growth rates have declined from 1.64 to 1.2 in the period 2000–5 (see www.dynamicsofdevelopment.com, Table 5.3). In the period 2005–10 the growth rates for Asia excluding Japan, China and India were 1.43, 0.85 percentage points lower than in 1950–55. In China growth dropped to 0.5 per cent per year.

Between 1973 and 2000, most rapid population growth was found in Africa, with growth rates of around 2.3 per cent per year (extreme cases being Congo, Côte d'Ivoire, Kenya, Tanzania, and Zambia). Latin America and South Asia came second. The lowest growth was to be found in East and Southeast Asia, in particular in populous China. But even for China, the growth rate of 1.2 per cent since 1973 was higher than the peak growth rates of European countries in the nineteenth century.

High fertility and rapid population growth result in a very youthful age structure of the population. This implies a high *dependency ratio* – the proportion of the population belonging to age groups that do not make an economically productive contribution.[1] The youthful age structure also means that a large proportion of women will be in a reproductive age category in coming years. Thus, even if the fertility rates per woman would go down, birth rates would continue to be high for quite a long time. The increase of young age categories peaked around 1975. In this year no less than 42 per cent of the population of developing countries was less than fifteen years old (www.dynamicsofdevelopment.com). Declines in fertility and the slowdown of population growth have reduced the share of

[1] The total dependency ratio depends both on the share of young people and the share of old people relative to the population of working age. In developing countries, the share of young people is still the primary determinant of the total dependency rate.

young people in the total population. Nevertheless in 2010, the share still stood at 29 per cent, compared to 16.5 per cent in the advanced economies.

In developed countries the share of people of sixty-five years and over in total population increased from 8 per cent in 1950 to 16 per cent in 2010. The share of the aged in developing countries is still much lower, but as fertility rates decline, the world population and the population of developing countries will age. Aging provides major new challenges to policy. The process of aging is proceeding much more rapidly in developing countries than previously in the more developed countries (Reher, 2011).

Another interesting indicator is the *net fertility rate* (or net reproduction rate). This indicator refers to the number of female children born to a woman in the fertile period of her life. The net fertility rate in the developing world has now dropped to close to one, indicating that the number of females is stabilising.

Total changes in population are the net result of the crude birth ratio, the crude death ratio and migration. Table 5.3 shows that in 2000–10 there has been a quite substantial flow of population from developing countries to the advanced economies (0.6 per 1,000). But compared to crude death rates and crude birth rates, the figures for net migration remain modest, indicating the relative unimportance of emigration for population growth in the developing world. On the other hand, net immigration into the more developed countries is quite substantial, at 2.7 per 1,000. In the absence of this net inflow, population growth in the advanced economies would now be close to zero.

Finally, Table 5.3 also contains information on trends in urbanisation. The net international migration flows discussed in the preceding paragraph exclude vast internal migration flows within countries. Most of this migration is from rural to urban areas, contributing to rapid urbanisation (Dyson, 2011). Latin America is the most urbanised region, with an urban population of 80 per cent, exceeding the share of urban population in the developed world (75 per cent). According to Kelley, urbanisation trends in developing countries deviate less from historical patterns than is sometimes suggested. The increase in the share of urban population from 18 to 40 per cent since 1950 is comparable to the speed of urbanisation in earlier historical periods. However, in absolute terms the growth of urban population has proceeded at a much faster pace. The growth of mega cities such as São Paulo and Mexico City or African capitals such as Dar es Salaam confronts policy makers with historically unprecedented challenges in terms of water supply, sanitation, housing and infrastructure. The growth of urban population is not only caused by migration from rural to urban areas, but increasingly by growth of the urban population itself (Kelley, 1988). On average 45.1 per cent of developing country populations live in urban areas. More than half of total world population is now urbanised.

The demographic characteristics of developing countries are summarised in Box 5.2.

5.6   Socio-economic consequences of population growth

5.6.1   Pessimistic and optimistic perspectives

Since Thomas Malthus wrote his *Essay on the Principles of Population* in 1798 a debate has raged on the perceived consequences of population growth. Malthusian pessimists believe that population growth threatens human welfare and that there are physical limits to

....
BOX 5.2 : **Demographic characteristics of developing countries**
....

1. **Rapid population growth**:
   - Faster than nineteenth-century growth in the currently rich countries.
   - Highest in the poorest countries.
   - Declining since 1970.
2. **Very rapid decline in mortality, irrespective of income *per capita***:
   - Faster than in the nineteenth century.
   - Related to advances in medical technology.
   - Increased life expectation.
3. **High birth rates, high fertility rates**:
   - Higher than previously in the currently rich countries.
   - Much lower age of marriage than in nineteenth-century Europe.
   - Beginning decline in developing countries, especially in Asia; some decline in Africa, but African fertility rates remain very high.
4. **Population growth out of step with the demand for labour**
5. **Emigration opportunities not sufficient to absorb excess population**
6. **Rapid urbanisation**:
   - Share of rural population declining; numbers of rural population remaining stable.
   - Urbanisation caused both by rural–urban migration and internal population growth.
7. **High dependency ratios**
8. **More rapid process of aging than previously in the currently rich countries**
9. **Shorter duration of the demographic dividend of an increasing population of working age than previously in the presently rich countries**

the increase in production, such as availability of land, scarcity of energy and raw materials and the carrying capacity of the global environment (e.g. Brundtland *et al.*, 1987; Clark, 2007; Ehrlich and Ehrlich, 1990; IPCC, 2001, 2007a; Keating, 1993; Meadows *et al.*, 1972; United Nations, 1994; World Bank-WDR, 2003; World Bank-WDR, 2010). Optimists argue that scarcity provides a challenge to human creativity. In this view, people will always find new technological solutions to the problems of scarcity. For instance, if the prices of raw materials such as oil go up, it becomes economically feasible to develop alternative sources of energy. Limits to growth are not fixed, but are shifting all the time. Well-known representatives of the optimistic perspective are Ester Boserup, Bjørn Lomborg and Julian Simon (Boserup, 1965, 1981, 1983; Lomborg, 2001, 2004, 2007; Simon, 1982). Optimists and pessimists not only differ in their analysis of causal mechanisms, but also in their empirical estimates and projections. It is important for the reader to realise that almost every single empirical estimate is hotly debated. This holds for global warming, greenhouse effects, population projections, or seemingly incontrovertible facts such as deforestation.

5.6.2   ## Malthusian analyses

Central to Malthusian thought are two mechanisms, namely the influence of increasing welfare on population growth on the one hand, and the law of diminishing marginal returns in food production on the other. If the standard of living improves, people will tend to have more children. If increasing numbers of people have to cultivate limited amounts of land, marginal returns will have to decline in the longer run. Food production will be unable to keep up with the growth of population. Famines, malnutrition and epidemics will finally serve as a check on the growth of population.

As we shall show in Chapter 10 on agrarian development, long-run developments since the eighteenth century clearly contradict Malthusian predictions. In the past there may often have been major fluctuations in population size in given regions. Also, in some periods famines and epidemics may have led to depopulation of whole areas. But at a global level, world population never stabilised at any fixed level. In Table 5.1, we saw that world population has been growing since pre-historic times, albeit at a very slow pace (Boserup, 1981, Chapter 4). Since the acceleration of population growth in the nineteenth century, food production has been increasing even more rapidly than population (van der Meer, 1983; World Bank-WDR, 1984; see also Chapter 10).

The crucial factor generally neglected in Malthusian thought is *technical change*. If there were no technical change, it would be correct to assume that marginal returns to labour in agriculture would decline as the person–land ratio goes up. But so far, the threat of declining marginal returns has always stimulated people to develop new production techniques.

5.6.3   ## The Neo-Malthusian trap

In the 1950s, Leibenstein and Nelson wrote that developing countries were in danger of getting caught in an equilibrium at a low level of economic development (Leibenstein, 1954; Nelson, 1956). This low-level equilibrium, known as the *neo-Malthusian Trap*, is represented in Figure 5.4.

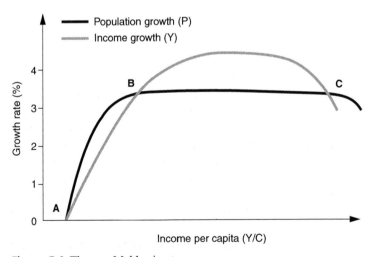

Figure 5.4 The neo-Malthusian trap

The horizontal axis of Figure 5.4 refers to per capita income (Y/C), the vertical axis to growth of population (P) and growth of national income. As per capita income goes up, Malthusian lore states that population growth (P) will increase till the biological maximum of around 3 per cent growth per year is reached. Growth of national income (Y) also depends on per capita income. As people become more prosperous, they are better able to save and invest. Higher investment rates in turn have a positive influence on the rate of growth.

Between points A and B population is growing faster than income. As a result income per capita will decline, until a low-level equilibrium is reached at point A. At this point the economy stagnates at a minimum subsistence level. Beyond the intersection point B, national income grows more rapidly than population. Per capita incomes will tend to increase, with a positive influence on the savings rate and further economic growth. Thus, economic growth becomes self-sustaining. In the very long run, diminishing returns may stabilise per capita incomes at a high level equilibrium point C. But in the context of developing economies, we are primarily interested in the trajectory between points A and B. Here we see that a small increase in per capita incomes is not sustainable. The economy will be forced back to its low-level equilibrium point. Only if the whole economy can jump beyond point B will it be able to realise spontaneous and sustainable economic growth of per capita income. The policy recommendation deriving from this model is that of the 'Big Push', the attempt to jump over the neo-Malthusian trap by a gigantic investment programme (see Chapter 9).

Just as in classical Malthusianism, the neo-Malthusian model in Figure 5.4 disregards technical change. As production techniques change, line Y will shift upwards. The intersection point B may even disappear (Myint, 1980: 90). Furthermore, we have seen in section 5.5 that the relationship between demographic change and income per capita does not necessarily obey a-historical Malthusian laws. On the contrary, the poorest developing countries are those with the highest population growth rates. Birth rates and fertility rates tend to decline rather than increase, as per capita income goes up. These declines are visible in most developing countries. In the post-war period, death rates have been declining irrespective of income levels. This decline can be seen even in the poorest of developing countries.

5.6.4 Growth of national income, growth of per capita income and the dependency ratio

In an arithmetic sense it is obvious that, given the growth rate of national income, a higher figure for population growth implies a lower growth rate of per capita income. If one compares the growth rates of GDP per capita in Table 3.1 with the population growth rates in Table 5.2, it is clear that production in developing countries grew much more rapidly than production per capita. But one may not conclude automatically that population growth has had a negative effect on the growth of national income per capita. For instance, a growing population may provide incentives to increase production or to work more efficiently. Nevertheless we may safely assume that the challenges with which developing countries are confronted become greater as population growth becomes higher.

A rapidly growing population is associated with high percentages of young persons in the age structure of the population. Children do not usually contribute fully to production, while they participate in consumption. The higher the so-called *dependency ratio* – the proportion of economically non-active to economically active persons – in an economy, the more the active members of the labour force have to produce to attain a given level of welfare.[2] Several theories state that population growth, working through the dependency ratio, has a negative effect on overall economic development.

5.6.5 Changes in the age structure and the demographic dividend

Changes in the age structure of the population affect dependency ratios. Initially, the decline in fertility in developing countries might create a window of opportunity. As large younger generations become older, they enter the labour market, while the slowdown in fertility rates translates into a declining share of the population of younger than fifteen years old. As a result, the share of the population of working age (fifteen to sixty-five) relative to the young population increases. This is referred to as the *demographic dividend* and allows for accelerated rates of economic growth, if the expanding job opportunities can absorb a growing working age population. Thus, the dynamic economies of East Asia have profited from a demographic dividend (Kelly and Schmidt, 2007).

Note, however, that the demographic dividend disappears if the economy cannot absorb a growing working age population. The demographic dividend can be swamped by too rapid population growth (Reher, 2011). Where this happens one sees a youth bulge of unemployed people, which has major implications for political stability.

Unfortunately for countries profiting from the demographic dividend, it is at best only temporary. It persists until the aging of the population at a later stage results in increasing dependency due to the increasing shares of people of sixty-five and over in the total population (United Nations Population Division, 2005; World Bank-WDR, 2003). As indicated in Table 5.3, even in developing countries share of the aged is starting to rise.

While the presently advanced countries have profited from a demographic dividend for almost a century, there are indications that the demographic dividend in developing countries will only last for some ten–thirty years (Reher, 2011). This is due to the more rapid aging of the population. The only country with a longer window of opportunity is China (some forty years).

5.6.6 Dependency ratio and savings

If there are many small children in a household, the consumptive expenditures of the household will tend to be greater and the proportion of household income saved will be smaller. A well-known hypothesis states that a high dependency ratio will result in a low savings rate in an economy.

Surprisingly, however, empirical research provides but little support for this hypothesis (Birdsall, 1988; Kelley, 1988; World Bank-WDR, 1984). There are several reasons for this. In the first place, the private household is but one of the sources of savings along with firms,

---

[2] Here we interpret the dependency ratio as the ratio of young people in the age category one to fourteen years to persons in the age category of fifteen to sixty-five years. Another possible measure is the ratio of all persons under fifteen or over sixty-five to the population aged fifteen to sixty-five.

financial institutions and government. The savings decisions of firms and financial institutions are not influenced strongly by the dependency ratio. In the second place, the level of financial savings by households is negligible in poor economies. What savings there are take a physical form, like using family labour to produce tools and implements, clearing land or reserving part of output for feed and seed. These kinds of savings will not show up in statistics. Furthermore many children in poor families often result in lower consumption, rather than lower savings. Finally, large numbers of children can provide incentives to work harder and to produce more, in order to be able to feed more mouths. Nevertheless the World Bank concludes tentatively that a large family size forms a heavy economic burden for a family and may indirectly have negative effects on its long-run capacity to save (World Bank-WDR, 1984). Also, there is ample evidence that the life chances of children from very large families are less favourable than those of children from smaller families (World Bank-WDR, 2003).

In the more developed economies, the debate has now shifted to consequences of aging. The pension schemes and arrangements developed in the years of the demographic dividend are no longer sustainable when the aged dependency ratio continues to grow as a result of slower population growth and increasing life expectation.

5.6.7 Population growth and investment

Population growth results in an increased number of entrants to the labour market (see section 5.6.9). This can cause a decline in the amount of capital goods available per person engaged (Coale and Hoover, 1958). If one invests a given percentage of national income, while the supply of labour is increasing, the amount of capital per person engaged will decline. In the absence of technical change, output per worker will also decline. In such a situation, one has to invest a higher percentage of national income to forestall a decline of the amount of capital goods (implements, machines, and so forth) per worker. In other words, one has to run harder to stay in the same place. A slower rate of population growth would free resources, which could be used for an increase in the investment per worker.

Furthermore, the increasing share of young people in the population structure might create a competition between resources available for investment in capital goods and resources available for investment in schooling and health services (Coale and Hoover, 1958).

Empirical research does not give unequivocal answers to the questions raised here. Theoretically, the effects of population growth on savings and investment depend on numerous assumptions – e.g. assumptions with regard to economies of scale and the degree of substitutability of capital and labour in the production process. According to Birdsall (1988), the effects of population growth on capital accumulation are negligible compared to the effects of the level of national income. Given an investment rate of 18 per cent of national income in 1980, the USA invested $189,000 for every new job. In the same year, Kenya invested 22 per cent of its national income. Per new job, this only amounted to $4,700 (World Bank-WDR, 1984: 87).

Empirical uncertainties notwithstanding, we may nevertheless conclude that rapid population growth places additional burdens on already strained economies by increasing the need for investment. This is especially relevant for the poorest countries with the highest population growth rates.

5.6.8   Population growth, education and healthcare

A high youth dependency ratio means that a rapidly increasing youthful population has to be supplied with education. Even if nothing is done to improve the present quality of education, this means more money needs to be spent. Once again, developing countries have to run harder just to stay in the same place.

Since the Second World War, developing countries have succeeded in substantially increasing educational participation, in spite of rapid population growth. Since the period of structural adjustment, there is a tendency for educational expenditures per student to decline (see Chapter 7). This threatens the quality of education, which is not very high as it is. If the number of pupils were increasing less rapidly, it would be possible to reserve more funds for quality improvement. The difficult choices between educational expenditures and investment in physical capital would also become less pressing.

Similar dilemmas exist with regard to healthcare. Rapid population growth means that existing health facilities have to be spread over more and more people, creating new dilemmas with regard to government expenditures.

At a family level, finally, the negative effects of population growth are clearly discernible. Children from larger families do less well at school and, due to the pressure on family budgets, have less prospects of enjoying good health (Kelley, 1988; World Bank-WDR, 2003).

As the population of developing countries starts to age, these pressures will tend to be reduced. However, they will be replaced by similar pressures and dilemmas with regard to health and social protection expenditures for the aged, versus investments in productive capital.

5.6.9   Employment, income distribution and poverty

With a delay of some fourteen to twenty-four years, births manifest themselves as new entrants on to the labour market. High fertility rates, decreasing infant mortality and a youthful age structure result in rapid increases in the supply of labour. Between 1990 and 1999, the labour force in low-income countries grew at no less than 2.4 per cent per year. The growth rate of the labour force even exceeded the average rate of population growth of 2 per cent per year. In MICs the labour force grew by 1.5 per cent per year (World Bank-WDR, 2000, Table 3). When accelerated growth and catch-up takes hold, as in the East Asian economies, the increasing supply of labour is a bonus which facilitates the growth process. But in other developing countries the growth of jobs lags behind population and the youth bulge creates huge employment problems. The influx of large numbers of – unskilled – young people on to the labour market depresses wages and increases unemployment, thereby contributing to increased poverty. The modern formal sector (comprising the capital-intensive industrial sector, government and commercial services) is unable to supply an ever-growing labour force with sufficient employment (e.g. Tregenna, 2013).

Unemployment can take two forms: open unemployment and underutilisation of labour. Open unemployment – not being able to find any gainful employment – is not very common in the poorest developing countries, where systems of social security are rudimentary or non-existent. This is especially true in rural areas (World Bank, 1995). We speak of *underutilisation of labour* when people work shorter hours than they would prefer to work, or when labour productivity is so low that people can hardly earn enough to survive, in spite of working very long hours.

Labour statistics are notoriously difficult to compare between developing countries, due to differences in concepts, coverage and methods of data collection. Table 5.4 provides some rough estimates of unemployment and informal employment derived from the database of the International Labour Organisation (ILO, 2002, 2011). Most ILO data refer to urban areas, where formal unemployment rates tend to be higher than at national levels. Direct estimates of the underutilisation of labour are not available. The table serves to illustrate the extent of informal employment. The informal sector contains a wide variety of economic activities, some of which can be quite dynamic and profitable (Gaillard and Beernink, 2001), but by and large the informal sector is a proxy for underutilisation of labour (see Chapter 9).

Many people are forced to make a living by engaging in low-productive activities in the traditional agrarian sector or in the urban and rural informal sectors of the economy. Thus, the large supply of labour promotes increasing income inequality. In the first place, the abundant labour supply weakens the position of employees *vis-à-vis* the owners of capital. In the second place income inequality between various categories of workers is also increased. Incomes of unskilled labourers in low-productivity sectors (in the informal sector or traditional agriculture) lag behind incomes in the formal sector of the economy.

The direct determinants of poverty are twofold:

1. *Lack of growth of average* per capita *income*. This occurs when the rate of growth of national income does not exceed population growth. Other things being equal, growth of per capita income will result in reductions in poverty. Negative growth results in increased poverty. There is overwhelming evidence that growth is important for poverty reduction (e.g. Kraay, 2006). Famous examples are China and Indonesia, where rapid growth has dramatically reduced the number of households below the poverty line.

2. *Large and increasing income disparities within countries*. The positive effects of growth of average per capita income on poverty may be neutralised by increasing income inequality. As a result, the poor may not share sufficiently in the benefits of growth. The worst scenario is when economic stagnation goes hand in hand with increasing inequality. There is ample evidence that declines in per capita income do indeed weigh disproportionately on the poor (Ravallion, 2001).

Analytically we saw in sections 5.6.3 and 5.6.4 that rapid population growth can depress per capita income in the absence of technological change, increased effort, or increased efficiency. We argued that this was not the inevitable consequence of population growth, but only a possible outcome. Between 1973 and 2000, the neo-Malthusian scenario does seem to be valid for much of Sub-Saharan Africa.

A second analytical impact of rapid population growth operates indirectly through the labour market. When population grows more rapidly than gainful employment, the share of open and disguised unemployment in the labour force increases. Average income per worker declines and the unemployed and underemployed inflate the ranks of the poor. The influx of labour leads to increased income inequality, further increasing the numbers in poverty and further depressing their incomes.

Table 5.4:   Unemployment and informal employment, 1988–2009 (selected countries, %)

		Informal sector employment as % of total employment		Unemployment as % of the labour force
Bangladesh	1993	16[a]	2005	4
China			2007	4[a]
India	2000	56[e]	2005	4
Indonesia	1999	63	2009	8
Iran	1996	18[a]	2008	11
Malaysia			2009	4
Pakistan	2004	40[a]	2008	5
Philippines	1995	17[a d]	2009	8
South Korea			2009	4
Sri Lanka			2009	8
Taiwan			2009	6
Thailand	2002	72	2009	1
Turkey	2000	11	2009	14
Argentina	2001	42[a]	2009	9[a]
Brazil	2001	47[a]	2009	8
Chile	2000	33	2009	10
Colombia	2004	58[a]	2009	12
Mexico	2005	28[e]	2009	5[d]
Peru	2006	55[a]	2008	7[a]
Venezuela	2006	49[a]	2009	8
Côte d'Ivoire	1996	53[a d]	1998	4
Egypt	2003	44	2009	9
Ethiopia	1999	50	2006	17[a]
Ghana	1997	79[a]	2000	10
Kenya	1999	36	1999	10
Morocco	1988	28[a e]	2009	10
Nigeria			1986	4
South Africa	2004	14	2009	24
Tanzania	1995	67[d]	2006	4
Zambia	1993	81	2000	13

Notes:
[a] Urban; [b] Manufacturing sector; [c] Punjab/North–West Pakistan; [d] Capital region; [e] Excluding agriculture.
Sources:
ILO (2002); ILO (2011), http://kilm.ilo.org/KILMnetBeta/default2.asp, downloaded 2011. Informal sector employment as percentage of total employment. Unemployment as percentage of the labour force. Latest year between 1986 and 2006.

In Table 1.3 in Chapter 1, we presented data on the evolution of global poverty using the simplest measure available, the head count of people living below a given poverty line.[3] In a nutshell, these figures do not support the most pessimistic Malthusian predictions. The global percentage of people below the absolute poverty line of 1.25 dollars per day has declined from 52 to 25 per cent between 1981 and 2005. The absolute numbers of people in poverty have declined from 1.9 billion to 1.4 billion. Some regions such as Sub-Saharan Africa and South Asia do continue to have very high rates of poverty. It is interesting to note the dramatic decline of poverty in East Asia and the Pacific (including China), in spite of rapid increases in inequality. These are typically regions with marked slowdowns in population growth, which have profited from the demographic dividend.

5.6.10   Population growth and the environment

Human impacts on the environment include the use and depletion of natural resources and the emission of pollutants into the ecosphere. The environmental effects of human actions can be decomposed into four elements, also referred to as the Kaya equation (Girod *et al.*, 2009; Raupach *et al.*, 2007; United Nations, 1994a: 27 ff.): pollution per unit of output of energy (F/E); energy per unit of output (E/GDP); output per capita (GDP/P); and population size (P).

$$F = \left[\frac{F}{E}\right] * \left[\frac{E}{GDP}\right] * \left[\frac{GDP}{P}\right] * P.$$

The symbol F refers to environmental impacts. In principle, this can include any environmental effects, such as soil pollution, air pollution, water pollution, environmental degradation, or declining biodiversity. Frequently the Kaya equation is used to decompose global emissions of greenhouse gases (GHGs) which contribute to anthropogenic global warming. The first term of the equation (F/E) measures emission intensity per unit of energy. This depends on technology. Technological progress (in use of more sustainable energy sources, resource use, process technology, product technology, environmental technology) reduces the environmental impact per unit of energy used. The second term E/GDP refers to energy intensity. Energy intensity depends on energy efficiency as well as technology. Output per capita reflects the affluence effect and population growth the demographic effect.

The decomposition technique can be used to analyse various specified environmental effects. It can highlight the contributions of technological change, energy intensity, economic growth and population growth. It can also analyse the contributions of different economic sectors and activities, as well as the contributions of countries and regions. A simplified version of the Kaya equation merges pollution intensity (F/E) and energy intensity (E/GDP) into a single equation, where F/GDP stands for pollution intensity per unit of production.

---

[3] The two simplest measures of poverty are the headcount measure (the number of people living below an absolute poverty line) and the income gap measure (the percentage of GDP required to lift all people above a given poverty line). One should also realise that poverty is a multidimensional concept including not only income, but deprivation in terms of health and education, vulnerability to changes, lack of access to services (World Bank-WDR, 2000b).

$$F = \left(\frac{F}{GDP}\right) * \left(\frac{GDP}{P}\right) * P.$$

In the prosperous countries the environmental effects of the population factor are limited, as population growth in these countries is by now very slow. The most important factor is the growth of production and consumption per person. Technological progress tends to make for less pollution per unit of output. In developing countries the decomposition studies summarised in United Nations (1994a) suggest that one-quarter to one-third of increases in pollution are due to population growth. However, the indirect effects of population growth may be even higher and the negative environmental effects tend to weigh disproportionately on the poorest population groups.

Since 2000 global emissions of CO_2 have been increasing, in spite of international efforts to reverse this trend. Raupach *et al.* (2007) use the Kaya equation to analyse these trends. In the advanced economies moderate GDP growth and very slow population growth were to some extent compensated by decreasing energy intensity of production and a slight decrease in pollution intensity per unit of energy. However the trends with regard to energy and pollution intensity have been reversed since 2000.

In recent years, developing countries are increasingly responsible for a large share of global emissions. Thus in China very rapid growth of GDP per capita and moderate population growth increases emissions and there has been a reversal of earlier declines in energy intensity. Due to its sheer population size China has become the world's largest polluter. In countries like India increases in GDP per capita go hand in hand with more rapid population growth.

In the analysis of environmental effects of population growth and economic development it is useful to distinguish scarcity of natural resources, localised environmental effects and global environmental effects.

Scarcity of natural resources

Otherwise than predicted by the Club of Rome in 1972 and other neo-Malthusian authors, there is presently no scarcity of raw materials. Where shortages of raw materials occur in the short run, prices are driven up. In the longer run this discourages the use of these raw materials, while making alternative techniques of resource extraction and alternative materials economically more profitable. Thus, price increases of fossil fuels will ultimately make renewable energy sources such as solar energy, wind energy and biofuels competitive. However, the transition from non-renewable to renewable energy sources is not easy, as economies are locked into established modes of energy use.

Localised environmental effects

It is also not obvious that there has to be a negative relationship between growth of production per capita in given countries and regions and localised deterioration of the environment. Of course, growth of production implies the emission of various noxious wastes in air and water, which put a severe burden on the environment. On the other hand, however, research indicates that pollution of air and surface waters in urban areas of developing countries is far worse than in richer countries (see World Bank, 1992: 44–63). Rich countries can afford to reserve an increasing part of their national income for purposes of environmental protection, provision of clean drinking water, disposal of solid wastes, sewage systems and soil decontamination, which are too expensive for developing countries. Concentrations of solid matter and SO_2 in the air above cities in developed countries are generally declining, as is pollution of surface waters.

This has given rise to the notion of the 'environmental Kuznets curve' in which economic growth initially results in increasing local environmental deterioration, followed by environmental improvement at higher income levels (Beckerman, 1992; Brock and Taylor, 2005; de Bruyn, 1997; Ezzati *et al.*, 2001; Stern, 2007).[4] This is due to technological advance, changing consumer preferences, environmental policies and shifts in the structure of production towards less polluting sectors, processes and products, such as services.

In developing countries localised environmental effects are presently very severe and many pollution indicators are on the increase. In 2010, 780 million persons in developing countries had no access to clean water; 2.5 billion people were not served by adequate sanitary facilities, with tremendous health hazards as consequences (UNICEF/WHO, 2012). Most urban settlements in developing countries have no sewerage system; 90 per cent of sewage is discharged without treatment. Air pollution is on the increase (United Nations, 1994a). These localised environmental influences, however disastrous, can be tackled in the long run by technological change and increased investment in pollution abatement, which are positively associated with economic growth.

But can we afford to wait? The 2003 *World Development Report* (World Bank-WDR, 2003) argues that developing countries should not automatically copy the path of 'growing first and cleaning up later', implied by the Kuznets curve. 'Cleaning up later' may be more expensive than taking preventive measures. New technologies have been developed in the advanced economies, which could lessen the conflict between growth and environment in developing countries. Also, some forms of environmental deterioration may be irreversible, which would strengthen the case for simultaneously addressing growth and environmental concerns. Dasgupta, Folke and Mäler (1994) argue that environmental resources should not simply be conceived of as a stock, which can be used or replaced at will. Many environmental processes are non-linear. When the carrying capacity of an ecological system is exceeded it might suddenly and irreversibly flip to a vastly different state.

Global environmental effects

The global environmental effects of economic development are the most problematic ones. There are ever stronger indications that the growth of world population, and the associated growth of world production, pose a threat to the environment at a global level, with consequences that may be irreversible. These indications include deforestation, dilution of the ozone layer, declining biodiversity, land degradation, salination and desertification, global pollution and climate change.

---

[4] The environmental Kuznets curve is named after the inverted U-curve hypothesis of Kuznets (1955), which states that income inequality first increases and then decreases in the course of economic development.

DEFORESTATION   Under the influence of human exploitation, expansion of agricultural land area, logging and acid rain effects, tropical rain forests are rapidly disappearing (see Chapter 10). According to some estimates 1.1 billion square kilometres of forest were lost between 1973 and 1988 (World Bank, 1994). The most important single cause of deforestation was the expansion of agricultural land area under the influence of increasing population pressure. Other important causes include the cutting of trees for fuel wood in poor countries and logging. In the industrial world acid rain contributes to a serious deterioration of the quality of forests. Deforestation contributes to increased CO_2 emissions and declining biodiversity. Land clearing in highland areas leads to land erosion and downstream flooding.

However deforestation is not inevitable or irreversible. According to an interesting study for West Africa by Leach and Fairhead (2000), neo-Malthusians tend to exaggerate the rate of deforestation. In the advanced countries, forest coverage is increasing. Some recent publications suggest that declining demand for croplands may free land for reforestation in the period till 2050 (Waggoner and Ausubel, 2001; see also Chapter 10). On the other hand, climate change could contribute to further deforestation.

DILUTION OF THE OZONE LAYER   The dilution of the ozone layer increases the danger of skin cancers and related diseases. Chlorofluorocarbons (CFCs) and related substances are responsible for the dilution of the ozone layer. In 1989, CFCs were banned when the Montreal Protocol entered into force. Since then, ozone dilution has stabilised and the ozone layer is expected to recover.

DECLINING BIODIVERSITY   Biodiversity should be seen as a genetic insurance policy against unknown future risks. Declining biodiversity not only means that interesting species are disappearing from the world at an alarming rate. It may also pose a threat towards continued human existence in the longer run.

LAND DEGRADATION, SALINATION AND DESERTIFICATION   It is estimated that between 1945 and 1990 1.2 billion hectares, almost 11 per cent of the earth's vegetated surface, have suffered moderate to extreme soil degradation over the past forty-five years (Oldeman, van Engelen and Pulles, 1990). Irrigation can lead to salination. Inappropriate agricultural technologies can promote desertification. Land degradation is estimated to cause loss of 12 million tons of grain output per year, equivalent of half the annual increase in production (Brown and Young, 1990). This is all the more urgent, as a growing world population requires 2–3.6 billion tons of additional cereals until 2030 (Birdsall, 1994). The modest impact of land degradation on overall growth tends to obscure the fact that it is the poorest cultivators who are hardest hit by land degradation.

GLOBAL POLLUTION AND CLIMATE CHANGE   The situation is most alarming with regard to global emissions of GHGs and climate change (World Bank-WDR, 2010). There is now a broad consensus among researchers that global warming is actually taking place due to greenhouse gas emissions, resulting from human economic activity (IPCC, 2007b, 2007c; Naudé, 2012; Tol, 2009). The greenhouse effect may lead to irreversible climatic changes, such as global warming, which entail major risks for human societies.

Average temperatures have increased by 1 per cent since the beginning of the industrial period and are continuing to increase. The fourth assessment report of Working Group I of the Intergovernmental Panel on Climate Change (IPCC, 2007a, 2007b) estimates that in coming years global warming will raise average temperatures by 0.2 degrees Celsius per decade. Depending on different scenarios for population growth and pollution intensity (see the Kaya equation, p. 181), global temperatures are projected to rise between 1.8 and 4 degrees Celsius by 2099. Sea levels are projected to rise by between 0.18 and 0.59 metres.

Global warming has major negative economic effects, ranging from rising sea levels and flooding of coastal areas, land degradation, declining agricultural productivity, increasing water shortages, droughts, increased weather variability, possible melting of permafrost and dislocations of ecosystems. Not all regions of the world are equally affected. But poor developing countries are especially vulnerable to the consequences of climate change (World Bank-WDR, 2010). Climate change further worsens the trends with regard to deforestation, land degradation and loss of biodiversity discussed above.

One of the stated policy targets of the IPCC and successive climate conventions is to constrain global warming to a maximum of two degrees Celsius, compared to the beginning of the industrial era. Higher rates of warming of up to 5 degrees may well have catastrophic consequences. Achieving the 2 degrees target requires a return of global CO_2 emissions to their 2000 levels by 2030 and a reduction of emissions by more than 20 per cent relative to the 2000 level between 2030 and 2050 (Word Bank-WDR, 2010, Figure 8). Presently there is no progress towards achieving these targets and emissions. Emissions of CO_2 and other GHGs are continuing to increase, in spite of all international attempts to reduce them. Here the outlook is a truly Malthusian one.

In the meanwhile, the debate about global warming has shifted. Most scientists now accept that global warming takes place and that it is indeed anthropogenic. The discussion focuses on how much should be invested in prevention and mitigation, how soon these investments should be made and what policy instruments should be used. Much depends on the rates used to discount the value of future damages to the environment and the economy to the present. If close to zero discount rates are used, the present value of future losses in GDP and economic welfare is very high and massive early policy interventions are required (Stern, 2007). If higher discount rates are used, the present value of damages is lower and investment in prevention and mitigation can be deferred to later years (Nordhaus, 2007; Tol, 2009).

Critics of Malthusianism such as Beckerman (1993) and Lomborg (2001) have warned that we should balance the unknown future effects of climatic changes against the known huge costs of draconian measures to control CO_2 emissions. On the other hand, the risks of not taking policy measures are so high that governments and international organisations have been gradually shifting towards policies aimed at controlling the increase of CO_2 emissions. This is indicated by the adoption of the Framework Convention on Climate Change adopted at the international UN conference of world leaders on environment and development in Rio de Janeiro in 1992 and the adoption of the Kyoto Protocol in 1997. In a recent volume even Bjørn Lomborg (2010) has come to recognise that global warming poses a huge risk, which needs to be dealt with.

In practice, countries have been slow to implement the proposed measures. In 2001, international agreement was reached on a watered-down version of the Kyoto Protocol to reduce greenhouse emissions. But one of the major polluters, the USA, withdrew from the climate convention in 2002. Most of the emission targets of Kyoto have not been realised, even by the countries that have adopted these targets. The Kyoto Protocol expired in 2012. At the time of writing, international negotiations to reach agreement on future reductions of global emissions are still stalled, partly because of conflicts of interest between developing countries and the advanced economies.

The debates on this issue continue, but one should realise that it is hard enough to get the engine of economic development moving in low-income countries. It may be asking too much to assume that this can always be done in environmentally friendly ways, however desirable this may be. The initiative in pollution prevention and abatement should be taken by the advanced economies that have contributed most to the present stock of pollution through their past actions (Gries, 2013).

From the preceding it is clear that the global environmental effects pose the most serious limits to unchecked population growth and growth of per capita income. There are limits to the carrying capacity of the global environment (Brundtland *et al.*, 1987; IPCC, 2001, 2007a, 2007c; Keating, 1993; United Nations Population Division, 1994). This insight provides powerful arguments for a policy mix which includes effective population policies aimed at reducing population growth rates and stabilising world population, along with policies focusing on prevention or mitigation of climate change.

Even so, one should not forget that even global environmental effects also depend on the rate of technological change. For instance, as mentioned, land degradation does not have to be irreversible, if intensification of land use is accompanied by technological change, which maintains or improves the productive capacity of land.

To a considerable extent the present global environmental effects mentioned under these points are the consequences of past industrial growth in the rich countries. However, if one thinks of the billions of people in developing countries striving to attain standards of living comparable to those in the rich countries, the fundamental threat to the global environment in the absence of technological change is obvious.

It would be incorrect to blame environmental problems exclusively on growth of population and production. Imperfect institutions are also important. For instance, desertification and deterioration of agricultural land also have something to do with poorly defined property rights. In many parts of Africa there are still traditionally defined common rights of land use. Where individual property rights do not exist or are not enforced, individual users of land have little incentive to invest in maintaining or improving land quality. As a result farmers may continue to apply inappropriate technologies deriving from historical periods with lower population densities.

In the case of air pollution, water pollution and deforestation, market imperfections also play an important role. In the market the costs of environmental deterioration (external effects) are not charged to producers and consumers. Individual cost-benefit calculations result in outcomes which are socially unacceptable. Changes in market institutions, leading to internalisation of external costs, could contribute to solutions for environmental problems (Birdsall, 1988). Institutions which give voice to the poorest segments of the population, can help tackle poverty-related causes of environmental degradation (World Bank, 2003a, 2003b).

Environmental problems are thus not only caused by population growth and economic growth but also by inefficient institutional arrangements. This being said, rapid population growth does exacerbate existing environmental problems. It leaves less breathing space in which to search for adequate solutions and responses to environmental problems.

5.6.11   Population growth and technological progress

In two books, which have received considerable acclaim – *The Conditions of Agricultural Growth* and *Population and Technology* – Ester Boserup (1965, 1981) has drawn attention to the potentially stimulating effects of population growth on economic and technological development. She argues that increasing *population pressure* is a condition for productivity growth in agricultural and for industrialisation and technological progress in general. In particular in the period before 1750, when transport and communication were not so well developed, there was a strong correlation between the level of technological development and population density. But even today population pressure can exert a positive influence on technological development.

According to Boserup, there are two countervailing influences. On the one hand an increase of population leads to increasing pressure on natural resources. If technology does not change, there are diminishing returns. The economic surpluses available for investment and technological change will decline. On the other hand, population pressure is an incentive to develop new productivity-enhancing technologies (*innovation*) or take them over from elsewhere (*diffusion*).

Especially in agriculture, population pressure has had a stimulating influence, according to Boserup. As long as population is sparse, people can provide for subsistence by hunting, gathering, or by very extensive use of land. As population pressure increases, people are forced to switch to settled agriculture and to the ever-more intensive use of land. Intensification implies that one has to work ever harder to increase output per hectare, while maintaining land fertility by weed control, fertilisation and water control. The number of harvests per land area also increases gradually from one harvest in fifteen to twenty-five years in forest fallow agriculture to several harvests per year in areas with high population density. Intensification allows for considerable increase in output per hectare. But it requires so much extra labour input that there is a strong incentive to develop labour-saving and output-increasing production technologies. In a neo-Boserupian study, Leach and Fairhead have even shown that in given institutional settings increasing population density in West Africa can result in reforestation rather than deforestation (Leach and Fairhead, 2000).

Furthermore, without large population size and fairly high population density, it does not pay to invest in agricultural infrastructure. Infrastructural investment in water control and irrigation is a condition for further development of agriculture. Infrastructural investment in transport and communication facilities is even one of the necessary conditions for industrialisation (see Chapter 8) and modern economic growth.

Population size and growth are also preconditions for urbanisation. Prior to the development of modern transport technologies, only regions which were rich in population could afford to maintain and feed urban centres. These urban centres were the breeding grounds for subsequent technical and scientific progress.

Though the interconnections between population and technology have become less tight since the eighteenth century, Boserup is convinced that population pressure can still exert positive effects on development in present times. For instance, she suggests that the economic problems of many African countries are to some extent related to low population pressure. Low population pressure offers an insufficient basis for the necessary renewal and extension of infrastructure. In such a situation Malthusian mechanisms operate, where a growing population, using traditional agricultural technologies, is confronted with diminishing marginal returns.

Boserup's hypotheses are open to criticism. For instance, there are countries where the hypothesised relationships between population and technological development do not obtain. Nevertheless, her most important contribution is the concept of a race between Malthusian mechanisms of diminishing returns and increasing productivity as a result of technological change. These mechanisms are most clearly visible in the agrarian sector (see Chapter 10).

5.6.12 Consequences of population growth: concluding remarks

As we have shown, there are different schools of thought with regard to the consequences of population growth. The orthodox view emphasises the dangers of population growth. The 'revisionists' argue that high population growth is not necessarily associated with economic stagnation. They provide empirically founded criticisms of the pessimistic predictions of the Malthusians. Nevertheless, none of the participants in the discussion denies that dramatic population growth provides major challenges to developing countries. Control of population growth is still high on the political agenda, though it is now seen as but one of many aspects of the development problem.

In the final analysis, the exponential growth of world population is the most convincing argument in favour of control of population growth. Many pessimistic predictions concerning the negative consequences of population growth have drawn justifiable criticism. Nevertheless, it is obvious that if we want to provide an ever-growing world population with an adequate standard of living, the carrying capacity of the natural environment will sooner or later be exceeded.

5.7 Why do people in developing countries have so many children?

5.7.1 Introduction

In section 5.4, we saw that the high rate of population growth in developing countries can be explained by rapid declines in mortality in combination with continued high birth rates. The high birth rates in turn are determined by the youthful age structure of the population and the high number of births per women (high fertility). For an adequate understanding of the population problems of developing countries, it is important to find out why women in poor countries have so many children, in spite of the fact that large families strain family budgets and reduce the ability of families to invest in their children's health and education (Birdsall, 1994).[5]

In this context, Bongaarts has made a useful distinction between the intermediate determinants of fertility and the underlying economic, social and cultural determinants of fertility (Bongaarts, 1982; Bongaarts and Potter, 1983). The intermediate determinants refer to factors such as age of marriage, breastfeeding, contraception, or abortion, which exert an immediate

---

[5] This section has benefited from advice from Harry van Vianen and Bert van Norren.

influence on the biological processes of reproduction. The more ultimate determinants include factors such as the cultural appreciation of children, sexual attitudes, female–male relationships and institutional arrangements, as well as the conscious or unconscious economic considerations which play a role in determining family size. The ultimate determinants do not affect fertility directly. They always work through the intermediate determinants, which Bongaarts calls '*intermediate fertility variables*'. The relationships are summarised in Figure 5.5.

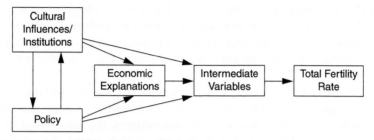

Figure 5.5 Determinants of fertility

In section 5.7.2 the Bongaarts model of the effects of intermediate fertility variables is discussed. Section 5.7.3 deals with economic explanations of family size. Section 5.7.4 discusses the underlying cultural and institutional determinants of fertility.

5.7.2   Intermediate determinants of fertility: the Bongaarts model

The point of departure for the Bongaarts model of fertility is the biological maximum number of childbirths a woman could experience in the course of the fertile period of her life. The intermediate fertility variables determine the extent to which realised fertility deviates from this biological maximum.

Bongaarts distinguishes seven intermediate fertility variables:

1. The percentage of women in the fertile period of their lives, who are married (or who have a stable sexual relationship).
2. The use and the effectiveness of birth control techniques.
3. The practice of induced abortion.
4. The duration of the infertile period after the birth of a child due to lactation and *post-partem infecundability*.
5. Frequency of sexual intercourse (*fecundability*).
6. Occurrence of spontaneous intra-uterine abortion.
7. The prevalence of permanent infertility.

Empirical research has shown that the first four variables are by far the most important in explaining variation in fertility.[6] The effects of these four variables are measured in relation to *total fecundity* (TF), which concept measures the combined effects of the last three fertility-inhibiting variables (fecundability, spontaneous abortion and infertility). Total fecundity varies from 13 to 17 births per woman, with an average of 15.3. The Bongaarts model can be summarised in the following equation:

---

[6] Bongaarts mentions two criteria for the selection of important factors: (1) variations in a factor should be clearly associated with variation in fertility; (2) factors should vary from society to society. If they do not vary, they will not contribute to explanation of differences in fertility between countries and regions.

$$TFR = \{C_m * C_c * C_a * C_i\} * TF.$$

Total fertility (*TFR, total fertility rate*) equals the biological maximum of fertility (*TF, total fecundity*), multiplied by four indexes, varying in value from 0 to 1. If an index has a value of 1, fertility will not deviate from TF due to this factor. If any of the indices has a value of 0, TF will equal 0.

C_m is the *marriage index*. If all women in fertile age groups are married, then the value of this index is 1. If everyone is single, the value is 0. An important determinant of the marriage index is the age of marriage. In nineteenth-century Europe late marriages were the norm, so that substantial numbers of women in fertile age groups remained single. In Sub-Saharan Africa, people marry very young, which contributes to high realised fertility.

C_c is the *contraception index*, which measures the use and effectiveness of birth-control techniques. If all fertile women and their sexual partners used modern and effective birth-control techniques under all circumstances, the index would take the value 0. The TF rate would also be 0. If nobody practices birth control, the value of the index would be 1.

C_a is the index for *induced abortion*, again running from 1 (abortion is never practised) to 0 (all pregnancies are terminated by abortion).

C_i is the index for the period of infertility after the birth of a child (*post-partem infecundability*). This infertile period lasts a minimum of two months, but can be substantially longer when women breastfeed their children. Also the cultural practice of sexual abstinence after the birth of a child can contribute to a lengthening of post-partem infecundability. The index has a value of 1 in case of complete absence of both breastfeeding and sexual abstinence. It takes a value of 0 in case of complete abstinence by women during their whole fertile life.

This Bongaarts model has two important advantages. In the first place, it stimulates systematic empirical research concerning the intermediate determinants of fertility in different societies, social classes and historical periods. In the second place, the model structures the investigation of the various underlying economic and cultural variables. These underlying factors can only exert influence on fertility via the intermediate factors. For instance, changes in cultural norms concerning the age of marriage influence the marriage index, which in turn influences fertility. With the help of Bongaarts' analytical model it is possible to analyse, for instance, the extremely high fertility in a country such as Kenya. Here social–cultural changes have led to the disappearance of traditional barriers to high fertility such as lengthy breastfeeding and the practice of sexual abstinence by women after childbirth. The disappearance of traditional obstacles to high fertility is insufficiently compensated by an increase in the use of modern anti-conceptive techniques.

5.7.3   Economic explanations of fertility

Economic explanations of fertility assume that people to a certain extent weigh the costs and benefits of having children, whether consciously or unconsciously. Having and raising children costs parents a lot of time, energy and money. If couples have many children, this means they may have to sacrifice other valued things in life. As most people want to have some children anyway, cost-benefit considerations usually only start playing a role after the birth of a second child.

The following seven factors can influence the decision whether or not to have another child (Becker, 1960; Birdsall, 1988; Easterlin, 1978; Schultz, 1997; Willis, 1973, 1994):

1. *Costs of educating children.* Structural changes in the economy require more skilled labour. The longer children have to go to school and the higher the parents' contribution to the costs of schooling, the higher the costs of children.
2. *Contributions of children to household income.* The earlier children start working – for instance, by helping their parents in agriculture – the greater their economic advantages. In many African societies, women need the help of their children in food production.
3. *Financial sacrifices made by parents.* Mothers especially face high opportunity costs, when they are unable to take paid jobs outside the home because they have to take care of many children. However, if the opportunities for paid work outside the home are scarce, the sacrifices will be correspondingly lower.
4. *Educational opportunities for women.* The greater the educational opportunities for women, the higher the costs of bearing and raising children. Given prevailing male–female relationships, it is difficult for women to participate in education when they have many children. A low level of education in its turn diminishes the chance of a woman finding well-paid work on the labour market.
5. *Distribution of costs and benefits between men and women.* This depends on the nature of relationships between men and women, on family structures and patterns of social organisation. Often the costs of children are not borne by the biological fathers, but by the mothers or by the extended family system. In such situations biological fathers have little incentive to limit family size.
6. *Provisions for old age.* Children function as a provision for old age in societies where publicly guaranteed systems of old age pensions are lacking. Also, the absence of well-developed financial markets and markets for land in many developing societies makes it difficult to save for one's old age. As traditional communities are opened up in the course of development and the geographic mobility of younger generations increases, the value of children as an investment in old age social security may decrease.
7. *Child mortality.* The higher child mortality, the more children couples will have, in order to ensure a sufficient number of surviving children.

Generalising broadly, one can reach the following conclusions on the basis of an economic analysis of fertility. The higher the household income, the more children as well as other desirable things in life one can afford. In this respect, higher incomes make for higher fertility. On the other hand, the higher the level of income and education, the higher the opportunity costs of children become, compared to the costs of other valued goods and services. Usually, the latter effect dominates the former. Members of wealthy and highly educated social classes tend to opt for a smaller number of better-educated children (Birdsall, 1988). At lower income levels and in societies with underdeveloped markets, the advantages of children will be relatively greater and the opportunity costs lower. In such contexts, people tend to choose a large number of children. This implies that large families are related to poverty and that a decline in poverty will contribute towards lower fertility.

According to Caldwell (1976), low-income economies are characterised by an *upward flow of wealth* from younger to older generations. One aspect of the demographic transition is a shift from an upward flow of wealth to a downward flow in which older generations invest in their children.[7]

Of course, the economic analysis of fertility is open to criticism. One may doubt whether parents have sufficient information about costs and benefits. It is far from certain whether they consciously weigh the costs and benefits of children. Nevertheless, the model of economic choice focuses our attention on a number of variables which can be important for population policy. Thus, it seems clear that increasing educational opportunities for women makes for lower fertility. Increased educational opportunities for children tend to have the same effects.

5.7.4   Cultural and institutional explanations of fertility

The economic model of rational choice can increase our understanding of the considerations affecting family size. However, the model of economic choice is no more than an empty vessel. Decisions and choices are always made within a matrix of institutional constraints and cultural preferences of men and women, which directly or indirectly influence the outcomes of their decision making processes. With no knowledge of culturally determined preferences, we can say little or nothing about the outcomes of processes of economic choice. To give a very simple example, if the cultural value of children is higher in one society than another then, other things being equal, fertility will be higher in this society.

Cultural factors not only influence choices, they also operate via the intermediate fertility variables. If cultural norms and institutions make for early marriage, fertility will be higher than in societies where late marriage is the rule. If there is a religious taboo on the use of contraceptives, fertility will be higher than in societies where such taboos are absent.

In an interesting review article Caldwell and Caldwell have shown how cultural factors contribute to the extremely high levels of fertility in Sub-Saharan Africa (Caldwell and Caldwell, 1987, see also Caldwell and Caldwell, 1985; McNicoll, 1994). Their central thesis is that traditional belief systems based on ancestor worship and the continuity of tribe and lineage continue to be important to the present day, in spite of the influences of Christianity and Islam. These cultural systems form a major obstacle to the successful introduction and diffusion of modern birth-control technologies.

Caldwell and Caldwell discuss seven factors:

1. *Ancestor worship.* After their death, the spirits of the deceased have to be tended by their descendants. This guarantees the continued existence of both the spirits and the kinship group. Large numbers of children are among the most important conditions for such continuity.
2. *Social prestige.* High fertility is seen as a reward of higher powers and proof of virtuous behaviour in one's life. The social prestige of women is dependent on having large numbers of children. Infertility is associated with witchcraft, adultery, or manifestations

---

[7] Willis (1994) shows that this does not mean that parents in low-income societies are necessarily less altruistic than in high-income societies. The change in the direction of the flow of wealth can also be explained by the relative poverty or affluence of the parents. A completely different perspective is offered in a paper by Lee and Mason, measuring net aggregate income flows between generations (Lee and Mason, 2011). They argue that net flows are downward in low-income countries and upward in rich countries as a result of aging. The difference between the older perspective could be that in the recent work all public and tax transfers are now also included in the calculations. From a perspective of private household expenditures, it is clear that in advanced economies families still invest very heavily in the education of a small number of children.

of evil. Contraceptive techniques in turn are associated with infertility and are therefore rejected. Fear of infant mortality and concern with the continuity of the lineage forms a further legitimisation of large numbers of births.

3. *Respect for elders*. Ancestor worship is associated with respect for elders in lineage groups. Traditional African societies provide a typical example of the upward flow of wealth from younger to older generations. Therefore parents profit from large numbers of children.

4. *Male dominance*. Decisions concerning reproductive behaviour frequently rest with the males, while the burden of upkeep of the children is on the females. This divorce between benefits and costs makes for high fertility.

5. *Kinship relationships*. In several societies, women are not considered to be part of the kinship group of their husbands. Though responsible for the cultivation of the food crops, they have no independent rights to land. Their access to land depends on having children, who can also be used as labour. In this way, women also have an interest in high fertility.

6. *Shared costs of raising children*. In traditional societies the costs of raising children are spread over many relatives in the extended family: aunts, grandmothers and so forth. Adoption is also a frequent phenomenon. Once again, this weakens the links between having children and bearing the costs and responsibilities of their education.

7. *Sexual abstinence*. Lengthy sexual abstinence by women after the birth of a child or grandchild is a traditionally accepted practice. This is sometimes used as a reason for rejecting modern birth-control techniques.

According to Caldwell and Caldwell, all these factors together make for high fertility and culturally legitimised opposition to birth control. Cultural barriers explain why birth-control programmes in countries such as Kenya and Ghana have met with so little success. They also explain why governments in African countries are so hesitant to start large-scale birth-control programmes. In another article (Caldwell and Caldwell, 1997), the authors argue that the world diffusion of cultural notions of birth control have been an important contributor to the global process of demographic transition.

In the long run cultural factors themselves are in turn also influenced by changes in economic and social conditions and policies. Bengtsson and Gunnarsson (1994) argue that where economic and political institutions provide insufficient basic security for large segments of the population, seemingly 'traditional' fertility patterns and family institutions should be seen as rational responses. Cultural elements and institutions are not autonomous. If equitable economic growth leads to more basic security for large segments of the population, this may ultimately be reflected in institutional changes and choices for smaller families.

Of course, cultural and institutional influences vary from society to society. Nevertheless, we can derive at least four lessons from the studies discussed above:

1. *Birth-control programmes* which go against the grain of strong culturally determined attitudes have little chance of success.

2. *Cultural factors* influence both the intermediate determinants of fertility and the economic considerations which consciously or unconsciously play a role in determining family size.

3. Culturally buttressed attitudes concerning *male–female relationships* are of great importance in explaining fertility levels and trends. Conversely, one may say that, whatever the cultural context, improvements in the social position of women – in terms of education,

economic and social independence, or equality between sexes – contribute to a lowering of birth rates.

4. Cultural factors and institutional arrangements affecting *fertility* can in turn be seen as responses to the risks and uncertainties to which people are exposed over time in stagnant low-income economies.

5.8   Policy

In the 1990s around 5 billion US dollars per year were available for population policies. The bulk of these resources was directly or indirectly devoted to family-planning programmes (Bongaarts, 1997). This raises the question of the importance and impact of these and other policies.

In the long run, one may expect fertility rates in developing countries to decline spontaneously under the influence of economic and social development, as has happened in the presently prosperous countries. Indications of declining fertility are now becoming visible in the developing world (see Table 5.3, p. 170). Improving standards of living, the penetration of the money economy, urbanisation and industrialisation all change the cost-benefit ratios of children and make the advantages of large family size less obvious. Culturally legitimised preferences for high fertility are gradually eroded in the process of development. Such patterns of spontaneous fertility decline manifested themselves in the 1960s in countries such as South Korea, Singapore and Hong Kong (World Bank, 1984: 106).

In economic development it is not only the growth of per capita income that is important, but also the distribution of incomes and life chances. Success in combating widespread poverty, improvements in the health situation, increasing life expectations, rising educational levels and declining illiteracy are all conducive to declines in the fertility rate. Thus, between 1965 and 1975 the fertility rate in countries such as Sri Lanka, Thailand and Turkey declined faster than could have been expected on the basis of average economic growth rates.

One may conclude that policies aimed at overall socio-economic development will also contribute to a much-needed decline in fertility, especially if the benefits of development are evenly distributed over the whole population. However, present birth rates are too high for policy makers to wait till spontaneous declines set in. Direct measures aimed at limiting the rate of population growth are still urgently required.

There is an interesting debate about the relative contribution of population policies to past and future fertility declines. Critics such as Pritchett (1994) and McNicoll (2006) have argued that the claims of advocates of birth-control policies have been overstated. Declines in desired fertility have been more important than catering to unmet demand for contraception through family-planning policies. In an overview of this debate, Bongaarts (1997), acknowledges the validity of some of these criticisms. But he concludes that past investments in family planning programmes have nevertheless substantially accelerated fertility declines. As a consequence, world population is expected to stabilise at an earlier date and at a lower level than in older population projections (see section 5.3). Though the future impact of family-planning policies will be more modest than in the past, they remain important. The slowdown in population growth rates in the medium projections depends on assumptions concerning continued fertility decline. The medium projections are based on the assumption that programme efforts will be maintained at current levels.

Among the determinants of fertility, the cultural determinants are most resistant to policy influences. At best one can hope that if governments show sufficient conviction in propagating birth control, this may in the long run contribute to a gradual erosion of culturally and religiously founded objections to population control. What policy can do most effectively is change the balance of costs and benefits involved in individual choices with regard to family size. Policy can also directly influence the intermediate determinants of fertility.

Table 5.5 summarises the ways in which policy makers can try to influence reproductive behaviour. In this table a distinction is made between (1) Policy and legislation, (2) Government expenditures and (3) Tax programmes (World Bank-WDR, 1984: 106).

Table 5.5: Government policies and birth control

Policies and legislation	Government expenditures	Tax programmes
• Minimum marriage age	• Education	• Family allowances
• Promoting breastfeeding	• Primary healthcare	• Tax penalties for larger families
• Improving the status of women	• Family planning	
• Children's education and work	• Incentives for fertility control	
• Active encouragement of birth control	• Old age security	

Source: World Bank-WDR (1984: 106).

Of the policy measures set out in the table, the following primarily affect the intermediate determinants of fertility:

1. *Policies or legislation aimed at increasing the minimum age of marriage.* Late marriages lead to lower fertility rates.
2. *Abortion legislation.* Legislation can have a direct influence (positive or negative) on Bongaarts' abortion index.
3. *Policies aimed at promoting breastfeeding.* Breastfeeding lengthens the period of infertility after childbirth.
4. *Government expenditure on and government policy concerning birth control.* There is a clear relationship between the use of modern birth-control techniques and family size. Expenditure and policy can increase the availability of modern contraceptives and lower the costs for their users. Such policy is especially effective if there is an unmet demand for birth control. This is the case when many couples have more children than they would prefer to have. Contraceptive use increased rapidly between 1990 and 2005, from 54 per cent to 63 per cent in 2005, with the fastest increases in Africa, Latin America and the Caribbean (United Nations Population Division, 2005).

Policy can also aim at influencing the choices parents make. The following areas of policy are of interest in this respect:

1. *Improvement in the socio-economic status of women.* There is a strong correlation between improvement in the social status of women and a decline in fertility rates. Status improvement has to do with both educational opportunities and labour market opportunities of women and with more equality in relationships between men and women in general.

2. *Improved educational opportunities for children.* Investment in education increases the costs of having children. When educational opportunities are available, parents will tend to opt for a smaller number of more highly educated children.

3. *Regulating or even prohibiting child labour.* This restricts economic activities by children and diminishes their potential economic benefits.

4. *Expenditures for old age pensions and provisions.* The better old age provisions are, the less parents will depend on their children for old age security.

5. *Improved functioning of capital markets.* Capital markets make it possible to set aside savings for old age provisions.

6. *Educational expenditures.* The greater the educational opportunities for women, the greater the sacrifices they have to make in order to have many children. In addition, education increases knowledge of and receptivity to modern birth-control techniques among both women and men.

7. *Expenditures for primary healthcare.* Such expenditures contribute to lower child mortality. The higher child mortality, the more families will tend to insure themselves against the risk of losing children by having many children.

8. *Affordability of contraceptive techniques.* Expenditures for birth control can lower the costs of contraception. This is especially important where there is an unmet need for contraception.

9. *Rewards and sanctions.* One of the most important ways in which governments can influence choices with regard to family size is through material rewards and sanctions. Positive rewards for families with few children can consist of tax cuts, subsidies, better educational opportunities and better housing. Negative sanctions include the loss of tax advantages and subsidies or even tax levies on children. Negative sanctions also include social pressure by local authorities, as in the case of the one-child policy in China.

Rewards and sanctions change the balance between the costs and benefits of children and can stimulate people to have smaller families. But there are all kinds of ethical objections to the too blatant use of rewards and sanctions. In the first place, the sanctions tend to place an additional burden on the children from large families, who will be even worse off than before. In the second place, for very poor people incentives and sanctions can end up in a form of coercion, which violates elementary human freedoms. In the case of China, the pressure for smaller families in combination with the preference for male descendants has led to an increasing imbalance between male and female births. Research suggests that this is due to sex-selective abortion (Junhong, 2001). The use of incentives and sanctions to promote irreversible interventions such as sterilisation raises fundamental moral issues. This is even more the case if there are insufficient guarantees that participation in birth-control programmes is entirely voluntary, as was sometimes the case in countries such as India and China. Thus the World Population Plan of Action, adopted in September 1994 by the UN Conference on Population and Development in Cairo, reaffirmed the basic right of individuals and couples 'to decide freely and responsibly the number and spacing of their children and to have the information, education and means to do so' (United Nations Population Division, 1994).

Conversely, population pressure in densely populated countries such as China, India, Bangladesh and Indonesia is so excessively high that a system of incentives can well be defended. Some experts argue for the use of 'deferred incentives' in the form of pension schemes for people with small families. With deferred incentives, the burden of the decision rests on the parents rather than on the children.

Of great importance is the conviction with which governments pursue birth-control policies. In India, the Middle East and Africa, government efforts to promote birth control have been half-hearted at best. Cultural and religious factors not only impede the execution of existing policies. They also form obstacles to the formulation of new policies.

In most Asian countries, population policy has received greater priority than in Africa and Latin America. Especially in China, a marked decline in fertility has been realised since 1979 in the context of the 'one child per family' programme (Goodstadt, 1982). In this programme extensive use has been made of systems of incentives and sanctions as described above. But the onset of the fertility decline from 1970 onwards actually preceded the introduction of this programme (Reher, 2011).

Questions for review

1. Discuss the concept of the demographic transition. How does it explain the changes in population growth?
2. Analyse the effects of changes in the age structure of the population on economic development.
3. Compare demographic developments in developing countries with earlier demographic developments in the presently rich countries of Western Europe.
4. Why do families in developing countries frequently have so many children?
5. Is rapid population growth a threat to economic development? Give an overview of the various ways in which population growth could affect the prospects for economic growth.
6. What is the demographic dividend, and why is it a temporary phenomenon?
7. Why is technical change important in assessing the consequences of population growth?
8. Why should rapid population growth result in increasing economic and social inequality?
9. What is the difference between localised and global environmental effects of growth?
10. Summarise the debate on the issue of 'growing first and cleaning up later'.
11. Analyse the different factors affecting emissions of GHGs using the Kaya equation.
12. What is the relationship between poverty and fertility?
13. Give examples of how government policies can affect the intermediate determinants of fertility.
14. Give examples of how government policies can affect the choices families make with regard to family size.
15. How does population growth affect technological change?

Further reading

An important source of demographic statistics is the website of the Population Division of the Department of Economic and Social Affairs, www.un.org/esa/population. This organisation is the authoritative source for long-run population projections. The latest version of these projections is: *World Population Prospects, the 2012 Revision,* CD-Rom edition, http://esa.un.org/unpd/wpp/Excel-Data/population.htm. Useful summaries of population data are also to be found in Maddison's *The World Economy Historical Statistics* (2010) and the website of the Groningen Growth and Development Centre (www.rug.nl/research/GGDC/). Other relevant statistical publications are: United Nations Population Division *World Population to 2300* (2004) and United Nations Population Division *World Population Prospects, The 2012 Revision* (2011a), CD-Rom edition, http://esa.un.org/unpd/wpp/Excel-Data/population.htm.

The following three publications provide a comprehensive introduction to the study of the relationships between demography and economic development: Birdsall's article 'Economic Approaches to Population Growth', in Chenery and Srinivasan (ed.)'s *Handbook of Development Economics,* Vol. I (1988), Kelley's review article 'Economic Consequences of Population Change in the Third World' (1988), in the *Journal of Economic Literature,* and the excellent edition of the *WDR* entitled *Population Change and Development* (World Bank-WDR,1984), which is still relevant today.

Interesting works on the demographic transition in developing countries are Caldwell's article 'Toward a Restatement of Demographic Transition Theory' (1976), his article 'The Global Fertility Transition: The Need for a Unifying Theory' (1997) and Wilson's article 'On the Scale of Global Demographic Convergence, 1950–2000' (2001). All these have appeared in the *Population and Development Review,* which is the most prominent journal for the study of population issues in developing countries. Also of interest is a collection of papers on *The Continuing Demographic Transition* (1997) edited by Jones *et al.* A recent special issue of the *Population and Development Review* edited by Lee and Reher (2011) provides an overview of the present state of the art and revisits many of the classical debates about the demograhic transition and fertility decline. An interesting study of global migration is Hatton and Williamson, *Global Migration and the World Economy: Two Centuries of Policy and Performance* (2005).

The term 'sustainable development' was introduced to a wider public in Brundlandt Report, *Our Common Future* (Brundtland *et al.,* 1987). One of the main sources for global warming consists of the reports of the Intergovernmental Panel on Climate Change (IPCC), such as *Climate Change 2001: The Scientific Basis* (2001) and *Climate Change 2007 – The Physical Science Basis* (2007). Sustainability is the theme of the 2003 *WDR, Sustainable Development in a Dynamic World* (World Bank-WDR, 2003). An important milestone in the discussion of global warming was the Stern Report, *The Economics of Climate Change: The Stern Review* (2007). The challenge of climate change is discussed in the 2010 edition of the *WDR, Development and Climate Change* World Bank-WDR, 2010).

The anti-Malthusian perspective is represented by Boserup's *Population and Technology* (1981), Julian Simon's *The Ultimate Resource* (1982) and Bjørn Lomborg's, *The Skeptical Environmentalist: Measuring the Real State of the World* (2001).

The intermediate sources of fertility are discussed in the classical article by Bongaarts, 'The Fertility-Inhibiting Effects of the Intermediate Fertility Variables' (1982) and in *Fertility, Biology and Behavior: An Analysis of the Proximate Determinants* (1983) by Bongaarts and Potter. For the economic analysis of fertility, one can consult an article by Schultz, 'Demand for Children in Low Income Countries' (1997), in Rosenzweig and Stark, *Handbook of Population and Family Economics,* an edited volume. An interesting discussion of the cultural aspects of fertility is provided in Caldwell and Caldwell's article 'The Cultural Context of High Fertility in Sub-Sahara Africa' (1987).

6 Health, healthcare and development

Health and education are important aspects of development. They belong to the basic needs that every development strategy tries to meet (Deolalikar, 1988). Improving the state of health and the level of education also contributes to the realisation of other developmental objectives such as economic development, labour productivity growth, responsiveness to innovation and future orientedness. From the perspective of economic development, investment in education and healthcare can be regarded as an investment in human capital. In turn, economic growth and development feed back into improvements and health, education and other indicators of human development (Ranis, Stewart and Ramirez, 2000).

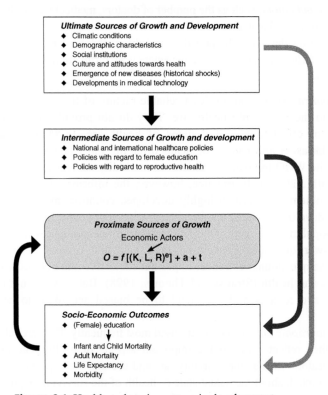

Figure 6.1 Health and socio-economic development

In this chapter the main focus is on the discussion of health-related issues. We document long-run trends in child mortality, average life expectancy and the changing global patterns of morbidity and health. The factors that determine developments in health are identified. In the light of these factors, we pay attention to health policies.

In the framework of proximate and ultimate causality this chapter specifically focuses on five relationships: (1) The relationship between economic development and changes in the patterns of health, morbidity and mortality; (2) The feedback from health as an aspect of human capital to economic growth and development; (3) The relationships between two social outcomes, education and health; (4) The role of health policy in improving health; and (5) The role of advances in medical technology in improving health. These relationships are summarised in Figure 6.1.

6.1   The state of health in developing countries

6.1.1   Quantitative indicators of the state of health

We can distinguish three main types of indicators of the state of health (Hardiman and Midgley, 1982):

1. *Health service indicators,* such as the number of doctors, medical staff or hospital beds, or financial resources devoted to health and healthcare.
2. *Morbidity statistics* that chart the prevalence of different types of diseases.
3. *Demographic indicators* such as life expectancy at birth, mortality rates and child mortality rates.

Health service indicators present the least reliable picture of the state of health. These indicators refer to the inputs into healthcare. They do not provide any information on the functioning or effectiveness of systems of healthcare. In theory, *indicators of morbidity* (i.e. diseases) and causes of death offer the most complete picture of the state of health. The WHO publishes estimates of morbidity and causes of mortality (e.g. WHO, 2008a, 2011, 2012a). In practice, however, the information on the prevalence of diseases is problematic. Even in highly developed countries morbidity registration is unreliable; in developing countries the situation is even worse. Here no full medical records of the population are kept. One has to rely on questionnaires in which people subjectively answer questions concerning their past and present health. The data derived from these questionnaires reflect important subjective and culturally determined aspects of illness and health (Strauss and Thomas, 1998). But they are not comparable across countries and regions and they tend to be biased according to age, sex and education.

Therefore, *demographic indicators* are still used most frequently. They are relatively easy to register and they reflect some of the important aspects of health. The drawback of demographic indicators, such as the mortality rate and average life expectancy, is that they do not tell us very much about the actual state of health of the surviving population. Many diseases in developing countries are chronic. They undermine health and welfare even when they do not result in death.

Demographic indicators also need to be employed with some caution. Data on many developing countries are often incomplete or insufficiently reliable (United Nations, 1988a, 1988b; Walsh, 1990). Only 108 countries presently have at least 90 per cent coverage of vital mortality statistics (United Nations, 2012a).

In recent years, demographic indicators have been merged with information about morbidity into indicators measuring *quality adjusted life years* (QUALYs). One such indicator is years of *healthy life expectancy* (HALE). This indicator deducts average years spent in ill health from average life expectancy (WHO, 2002a). An important related indicator is *disability adjusted life years* lost (DALY). This indicator measures the number of healthy years of life lost due to premature mortality or due to diseases, poor health or disabilities, relative to an ideal yardstick (the ideal number of years that the population lives to an advanced age, free of disease and disability).[1] First, years of life lost due to premature mortality (YLL) are estimated. Next, years lived in bad health or disability are estimated (Years of life lost to disability, YLD). To get an estimate of YLD, diseases are weighted with a disability weight on a scale from 0 (perfect health) to 1 (death). DALY equals the sum of YLL and YLD. Expected reductions in DALYs can be used for policy purposes to measure the benefits of different kinds of health interventions (Murray and Acharya, 1997; Murray and Lopez, 1996; WHO, 2008a).[2] These are valuable new indicators. But the data requirements for the calculation of these indexes are enormous and the choice of standardised weights for different disabilities across the world is highly debatable. The same holds for different age weights.

The folllowing sections will pay special attention to the following indicators: infant and child mortality; average life expectancy at birth; patterns of illness as reflected by causes of death.

Infant and child mortality

Mortality is distributed bimodally, with high probabilities of dying in the first years of life (in particular at birth and immediately afterwards) and gradually increasing chances of dying after the age of thirty. High mortality among infants and children under the age of five is one of the important characteristics of the general state of health in developing countries. This, in turn, affects average life expectancy. For these reasons, the literature on health issues pays a lot of attention to the topic of infant and child mortality.

Table 6.1 presents data on infant and child mortality. Infant mortality is defined as the chance of dying between the age of 0 and 1 per 1,000 births. Child mortality is defined as the chance of dying between the age of 0 and 5 per 1,000 births.

In the 2005–10 period, the average infant mortality rate per 1,000 live births in developing countries was 50 against six in the more developed countries. The mortality rate for children under the age of five was 72 per 1,000 in developing countries and eight per 1,000 in more developed countries.

It is not just the contrasts between developing and more developed countries that stand out. There are also great differences among developing countries themselves. For example, the infant mortality rate in countries like Congo, Côte d'Ivoire, Ethiopia, Nigeria, and

---

[1] The yardstick is somewhat arbitrary. It is usually based on conditions in the advanced economies. A figure of seventy-five years is often taken as the yardstick.

[2] In addition, one can weight the years lost by age, for instance giving less weight to years lived at very young and at older ages. This reflects the economic aspect of the burden of disease. Also, the DALYs reported in the *WHR*s use a 3 per cent discount rate per year. A health year saved now will have a higher weight than a health year saved later.

Table 6.1: Infant and child mortality, 1950–2010 (probability of dying per 1,000 births)

	1950–5 Probability of dying		2005–10 Probability of dying	
	between 0-1 years	between 0-5 years	between 0-1 years	between 0-5 years
Bangladesh	165	312	49	61
China	122	266	22	26
India	165	332	53	72
Indonesia	192	270	29	36
Iran	262		27	37
Malaysia	96	147	8	10
Pakistan	177	332	71	94
Philippines	97	178	23	30
South Korea	138	164	4	5
Sri Lanka	104	151	12	14
Taiwan			5	5
Thailand	130	195	12	14
Turkey	167	318	24	28
Argentina	66	84	13	16
Brazil	135	187	23	29
Chile	120	162	7	9
Colombia	123	189	19	26
Mexico	122	193	17	20
Peru	164	268	21	33
Venezuela	107	148	17	22
Congo, Dem. Rep.	167	266	116	192
Côte d'Ivoire	167	350	77	122
Egypt	201	350	26	30
Ethiopia	199		72	113
Ghana	150	250	50	74
Kenya	147	254	65	101
Morocco	170	310	34	38
Nigeria	189	345	96	156
South Africa	96	217	55	79
Tanzania	153	270	64	101
Zambia	148	254	95	156
Average 31 developing countries	148	242	39	56
Africa	180	322	79	125
Latin America	127	189	22	28
Asia	145	278	41	54
East Asia, excl. Japan	126	266	21	26
Southeast Asia	165	244	27	35
South-central Asia	171	327	56	76
West Asia	167	307	29	35
Developing countries	151	281	50	72
Developed countries	60	73	6	8

Source:
United Nations Population Division (2011a), except Mortality under age 50, 1950–5, from: United Nations (1988b) and Taiwan: DGBAS (2012).

Zambia is over 70. In countries such as Argentina, Chile, Malaysia, Sri Lanka and Thailand it is less than 14. Africa has by far the highest infant mortality (79). The lowest infant mortality rates are found in Latin America (22) and East Asia (41). The regional distribution of child mortality under the age of five shows similar patterns.

Since the Second World War, infant and child mortality has decreased dramatically in developing countries (Vallin, 1989). Infant mortality in the most recent period (2005–10) is one-third of what it was in 1950–5. Child mortality is one-fourth. Even in Africa, which lags behind other developing regions, infant mortality dropped from 180 in 1950–5 to 79 in 2005–10. During the same period child mortality declined from 281 to 72 per 1,000. In other parts of the world, especially in Asia, the decrease was even more dramatic.

In *Global Strategy for Health for All by the Year 2000* (WHO, 1981) one of the stated objectives was that infant mortality in the year 2000 should be no higher than 50. Under-five mortality should be below 70. Table 6.1 shows that by 2005–10 these goals have more than been realised in Latin America and large parts of Asia. However, this is not the case for Africa, where mortality rates remain high in spite of spectacular long-run declines.

Fears that the decrease in infant mortality was slowing down since the 1980s (Caldwell, 1986; United Nations, 1984) have proved to be unfounded. From year to year, infant and child mortality continue to decline. Thus, infant mortality in 2005–10 is 50 per 1,000, compared to 71 per 1,000 in 1985–90. Child mortality in 2005–10 is 72, against 97 in 1995–2000 (United Nations, 2012a). In the African countries hardest hit by HIV/AIDS (Botswana, Lesotho, South Africa, Swaziland and Zimbabwe) mortality estimates have been revised upwards (United Nations, 1994b; WHO, 2002a). But so far this primarily affects older age groups, rather than infant and child mortality.

Despite positive trends, present levels of infant and child mortality in developing countries are still unacceptably high. In the Millennium Declaration, the target for 2015 was that child mortality be reduced to one-third of its 1990 level. In fact, child mortality has only fallen by one-third since 1990. This progress is too slow to reach the MDG targets (United Nations, 2012b). In relative terms the gap between developing and rich countries has even widened. In 1950, the probability of an infant in a developing country dying before the age of one was two and a half times as high as in rich countries; today the probability is 8.3 times as high. The probability of a child dying before it reaches its fifth birthday in a developing country is almost nine times as high as in more developed countries.

As progress is achieved in reducing infant and child mortality, reductions in adult mortality are becoming more and more important for further overall reductions in mortality rates (Kuhn, 2010).

6.1.3   Life expectancy

Table 6.2 and Table 6.3 present data on life expectancy at birth in developing countries. Table 6.2 focuses on our sample of developing countries. Table 6.3 presents aggregate data for regions and compares developing countries with more developed countries. The rapid increase of life expectancy in developing countries is one of the most marked manifestations of the dynamics of development. On average, a child born between 2010 and 2015 will live twenty-five years longer than a child born three generations earlier in the 1950s. This is primarily due to reductions in infant and child mortality. In the thirty-one countries included in Table 6.2, life expectancy has increased from 46 to 69 years. In the developing world as a whole it has increased from 42.3

Socio-Economic Development

Table 6.2: Life expectancy at birth, selected developing countries, 1920–2015 (years)[a]

	1920	1930	1940	1950–5	1970–5	1990–5	2010–15
Bangladesh	20[b]	27[c]	32[d]	45	36	61	69
China				45	65	70	74
India		27[e]		38	51	59	66
Indonesia				39	53	63	70
Iran				38	53	66	73
Malaysia				55	65	71	75
Pakistan	20[b]	27[c]	32[d]	41	55	61	66
Philippines				55	61	66	69
South Korea		38	41	48	63	73	81
Sri Lanka				53	64	70	75
Taiwan			43	52[f]	70[g]	74	79
Thailand				51	61	72	74
Turkey				48	51	64	74
Argentina				63	67	72	76
Brazil	37			51	60	67	74
Chile		37	39	55	64	75	79
Colombia		33		51	62	69	74
Mexico			39	51	63	72	77
Peru				44	55	67	74
Venezuela				54	65	71	75
Congo, Dem. Rep.				39	45	47	49
Côte d'Ivoire			39[h]	39	46	52	56
Egypt				43	52	64	74
Ghana				34	44	48	60
Ethiopia				42	50	58	65
Kenya				42	54	58	58
Morocco				43	53	65	73
Nigeria				36	43	45	53
South Africa				45	54	61	54
Tanzania				41	48	50	59
Zambia				42	50	45	50
Average 13 Asian countries				47	57	67	73
Average 7 Latin American countries				53	62	70	73
Average 11 African countries				41	50	55	60
Average developing countries				46	55	63	69
Average Russian Federation				64	69	67	69
Average 16 advanced economies				69	72	77	81

Notes:

[a] Data for 1950 and before are mostly five-year averages. The figures in the table are simple interpolations. [b] 1921; [c] 1931; [d] 1941; [e] average 1921–31; [f] Taiwan, 1950 interpolated with growth rate 1940–60; [g] 1971: the average of male and female life expectancy; [h] average 1936–8.

Sources:

1920, 1930, 1940: United Nations (1953); except Bangladesh, Pakistan, South Korea: UN/ESCAP (1985).

1950–2010 from: United Nations Population Division (2011a), except advanced economies 1950 from *World Population Prospects, The 2000 Revision*, 1970–95 *World Development Indicators Online*. Taiwan, 1940–55, United Nations (1963), 1966–2000: DGBAS (2012a), www.stat.gov.tw; Taiwan specific years, not five-year averages.

Table 6.3: Life expectancy at birth, by region, 1950–2015

	1950–5	1985–90	1995–2000	2010–15[a]
Africa	38.2	51.2	51.6	57.4
Sub-Saharan Africa	37.1	49.1	48.9	55.0
Latin America	51.3	67.1	70.6	74.7
Asia, excl. Japan	41.7	62.9	65.7	70.0
East Asia, excl. Japan	44.2	69.0	71.0	74.3
Southeast Asia	46.4	69.9	71.9	71.1
South Central Asia	39.0	57.9	61.1	66.2
West Asia	46.9	64.4	68.8	73.1
Developing countries	42.3	61.2	63.3	67.5
Least developed countries	37.2	50.2	52.5	58.8
More developed countries	65.9	74.0	74.8	78.0
Advanced economies	67.6	75.8	77.9	80.6

Note:

[a] 2010–15 medium projections.

Source:

United Nations (2011a), except OECD 1950–2000 from: *World Population Prospects: The 2006 Revision,* http://esa.un.org/unpp/p2k0data.asp, downloaded December 2007.

to 67.5 years (Table 6.3). Today, on average people in economically advanced countries live 13.1 years longer than people in developing countries (80.6 versus 67.5 years). In 1950, the difference was no less than 25.3 years. In this important respect, there is a substantial narrowing of the gap between economically advanced countries and developing countries.

There are marked differences between regions (see Table 6.3). Particularly in Africa, life expectancy is still low. In Table 6.2 this is illustrated by the data for countries like Congo, Nigeria, South Africa and Zambia. In the period 2010–15, the average life expectancy in Sub-Saharan Africa is 55 years. In South Asian countries average life expectancy is also comparatively low: 66.2 years. In Table 6.2 this region is represented by India, Pakistan, and Bangladesh. The highest life expectancy can be observed in Latin America (74.7) and East Asia (74.3 years). In 2010–15, life expectancy in China is 74 years.

Between 1985 and 2000, the increase in life expectancy in Sub-Saharan Africa stagnated as a result of the AIDS epidemic. In countries heavily affected by HIV/AIDS, such as South Africa and Zambia, life expectancy even declined substantially. On average, life expectancy at birth in Sub-Saharan Africa in 2000 was six years lower than it would have been in the absence of HIV/AIDS for males and seven years lower for females (WHO, 2002a, Table 6). After 2000, however, life expectancy in this region resumed its upward trend, as HIV/AIDS mortality was reduced through more effective medicines (see section 6.1.5). In the Russian Federation, life expectancy declined rapidly in the period of economic and political chaos following the dissolution of the Soviet Union. In 1985–90, life expectancy was 69 years.

By 2000–5 it had dropped to 65 years. Similar declines have been registered in many other former Soviet Republics, especially during the period 1989–95 (Becker and Hemley, 1998; Brainerd, 1998). But as economic conditions improved in the Russian Federation after 2000, life expectancy bounced back. In the current period it has again reached 69 years. The reversals in Africa and the Soviet Union provide an illustration of the fragility of developmental gains.

6.1.4   Patterns of disease and health

It is difficult to obtain reliable data on the causes of death in developing countries. There is no complete and systematic registration, and it is often hard to determine the disease a person has died of. Still, some clear patterns can be discerned. In poor developing countries infectious diseases are the most important cause of death (respiratory infections, diarrhoeal diseases, HIV/AIDS, neonatal infections and tuberculosis, TBC). In rich countries and MICs, cardiovascular diseases (CVD), neoplasms (cancer) and degenerative diseases rank high among the causes of death (WHO, 1987, 2008a: 13; WHO, 2011). Many of these diseases are age-related, life style-related or both.

Table 6.4 presents a broad survey of the most important causes of death in different parts of the world for the period 1980–2008. This table indicates that infectious and parasitic diseases caused about 40 per cent of all deaths in developing countries in 1980. Other sources present even higher estimates. According to Hardiman and Midgley (1982), infectious diseases caused 40–50 per cent of all deaths in developing countries. In a study by Walsh (1990), the share of infectious and parasitic diseases in 1986 was estimated to be 35.4 per cent and the share of respiratory diseases 26.8 per cent, adding up to a total 62.2 per cent of all deaths. In 1990, WHO statistics indicated that 44.2 per cent of all deaths in developing countries were due to infectious and parasitic diseases. After 1990 the share of infectious diseases in developing countries declined and the share of cardiovascular and degenerative diseases rapidly increased. But infectious diseases remain important. In 2008, infectious and parasitic diseases accounted for 32.2 per cent of all deaths.

Infectious and parasitic diseases in particular claim lives of children under the age of five. In 2008, pneumonia accounted for no less than 18 per cent of all deaths of children, followed by diarrhoea, which was responsible for 15 per cent of child mortality (WHO, 2011). Even if these diseases do not result in death, they may permanently impair the development, welfare and general state of health of their victims.

The statistics from 2000 onwards distinguish a special category for HIV/AIDS-related mortality. For all developing countries, HIV/AIDS accounted for 6.9 per cent of all deaths in 2000. In the African region, it accounted for no less than 22.6 per cent of total mortality. Including HIV/AIDS, infectious diseases in 2000 accounted for 63.8 per cent of mortality in Africa. After 2000, HIV/AIDS-related mortality started declining rapidly as treatment with retroviral therapies became more widely available. By 2008, the share of HIV/AIDS in developing country mortality had dropped to 3.7 per cent and to 12.9 per cent in Africa.

Table 6.4 shows that in 2008 cardiovascular diseases, other degenerative diseases and neoplasms caused 80 per cent of all deaths in the economically more developed countries.

Cardiovascular diseases and degenerative diseases caused 53 per cent of all deaths, and neoplasms about 27.2 per cent. These diseases are very much age-related, that is, they gain in importance as the population grows older. The share of cancer increased rapidly between 1980 and 2008. Cardiovascular diseases and cancer are typically related to age, life style, stress and unhealthy eating habits.

Until recently, these classes of diseases used to be much less important in developing countries, than in the more developed countries. The infectious diseases characteristic of developing countries manifest themselves primarily among children. The diseases characteristic of more developed countries typically occur at more advanced ages. Deaths in these countries are concentrated in the higher age groups. The difference in age-related patterns of morbidity is one of the reasons why life expectancy in developing countries is lower than in more developed countries. However, it also explains why the differences in average death rates per 1,000 people are not so pronounced (see Chapter 5, Table 5.3, p. 170); in more developed countries there are more elderly people among whom the death rate is obviously much higher than in younger age groups.

Since the 1980s, important new trends have become visible in developing countries (WHO, 1993, 1998, 1999, 2004, 2011). Since 1980, the HIV/AIDS epidemic has emerged as one of the most serious diseases in the developing world, especially but not exclusively in Africa. HIV/AIDS mortality peaked around 2000. In recent years, mortality due to HIV/AIDS, though still high, is starting to decline. Cardiovascular diseases and cancer are rising rapidly as a proportion of all deaths. By 2008, they accounted for 39.9 respectively, 11.1 per cent of all mortality in developing countries. More than half of all new cancer cases now occur in developing countries. The relative rise of cancer is related to both tobacco use and progress made in tackling other major causes of death. Since 2000, cardiovascular diseases have replaced infectious diseases as the most import causes of mortality in developing countries. As cardiovascular diseases and cancer are far more difficult and costly to treat than infectious diseases, this will pose new challenges to the health systems of developing countries (Schultz, 2010).

A category of morbidity receiving more attention in recent years is that of mental disorders (WHO, 2001). Worldwide 45 million people are affected by schizophrenia, 29 million people suffer from dementia and 40 million people suffer from different types of epilepsy (WHO, 1997). Depression is one of the major diseases burdens. Mental health problems have been underestimated in developing countries, where increasing numbers of adults and children are traumatised by warfare, civil strife, violence and hunger.

6.1.5   Common infectious and parasitic diseases in developing countries

Infectious and parasitic diseases deserve special attention, for at least two reasons. In the first place they are still one of the most important causes of death in developing countries. In the second place, many of these deaths of young people are unnecessary and could relatively easily be prevented through adequate and not too costly health interventions. In this section infectious and parasitic diseases have been categorised on the basis of the way they are passed on. Diseases can be transmitted through (a) contaminated food and drinking water; (b) air; (c) direct physical contact; (d) parasites; and (e) animal bearers of diseases (vectors).

Table 6.4: Causes of death, by region, 1980–2008 (%)

	Africa			Latin America			South and Southeast Asia		
	1980	2000	2008	1980	2000	2008	1980	2000	2008
Infectious and parasitic diseases	49.7	63.8	56.0	31.2	20.6	17.6	43.9	34.3	36.4
– *excluding AIDS*		*41.2*	*43.1*		*18.8*	*15.8*		*31.7*	*34.7*
– *AIDS*		*22.6*	*12.9*		*1.8*	*1.7*		*2.6*	*1.7*
Neoplasms, cardiovascular and degenerative diseases	2.9	5.1	4.2	8.9	12.4	16.1	4.3	8.0	8.0
	11.7	14.6	20.6	24.5	45.4	48.7	15.6	38.4	36.6
Conditions related to the perinatal period	8.5	5.5	8.8	8.3	4.3	3.1	8.3	7.1	6.5
Injuries and poisoning	3.8	7.1	6.8	6.4	12.3	11.7	4.3	9.7	10.7
Other causes (ill-defined or unknown)	23.4	3.9	3.7	20.7	4.9	2.8	23.5	2.5	1.9
Total	100	100	100	100	100	100	100	100	100
N (x 1,000)	7,180	10,572	10,125	3,140	3,097	3,300	15,430	14,157	14,498

Notes:
[a] Incl. Libya, Morocco, Somalia, Sudan and Tunisia, excluding former Soviet Asian Republics.
[b] Excl. Japan, Australia and New Zealand.
[c] Incl. former Soviet Republics in Asia.
Sources: 1980: WHO (1987), p. 72; 1990: WHO (1993); 2000: WHO, 2001; 2008: WHO (2012a); *Global Health Obsevatory Data Repository.*

Diseases transmitted through contaminated water or food

Infectious diseases are often transmitted faecally, through direct contact with faeces or through contaminated food or drinking water. Insects and other animal bearers of infections – *vectors* – cause food to rot or water to be contaminated. Poor hygiene, therefore, is among the most serious pathogenic factor. Infectious diseases that are passed on in these ways include (Hardiman and Midgley, 1982; Maurice and Pearce, 1987; WHO, 1987):

- *Diarrhoea.* Diarrhoea is a collective name for infections of the digestive system. It is one of the most important causes of death among children in developing countries: 23.3 per cent of child mortality in 1990 was caused by diarrhoea (WHO, 1993). In 2008, 2.4 million persons died of this easily preventable disease (WHO, 2012a).
- *Bacterial and viral diseases: cholera, poliomyelitis (polio), hepatitis and typhus.* Faecally transmitted diseases like cholera and poliomyelitis are less common as a consequence of vaccination schemes, although they are far from being eradicated. Cholera re-emerged in South America in 1991. It is still prevalent in many countries, with between

Eastern Mediterranean/ West Asia[a]			East Asia/Western Pacific[b]			Developing countries				More developed countries[c]			
1980	2000	2008	1980	2000	2008	1980	1990	2000	2008	1980	1990	2000	2008
44.4	35.7	29.2	27.2	27.4	20.5	39.9	44.2	39.2	32.2	7.6	4.4	10.6	11.8
	34.4	28.6		27.1	20.0			32.3	28.6			10.4	11.6
	1.3	0.6		0.3	0.5			6.9	3.7			0.3	0.2
4.0	6.1	7.9	8.6	17.2	20.2	5.5	7.0	9.7	11.1	19.2	21.2	21.9	27.2
14.1	38.0	40.3	30.0	40.2	46.9	19.0	16.9	33.3	39.7	53.5	47.5	58.0	53.0
9.8	7.5	8.5	4.9	3.1	2.0	7.7	9.1	5.6	5.4	1.6	0.8	0.7	0.4
4.0	8.4	10.6	6.7	11.2	9.7	4.9	6.8	9.5	9.6	6.5	7.6	7.9	6.2
23.5	4.2	3.4	22.5	0.8	0.6	23.0	16.1	2.8	2.1	11.6	18.6	0.8	1.4
100	100	100	100	100	100	100	100	100	100	100	100	100	100
3,960	4,036	4,198	9,630	10,238	11,344	40,140	38,500	42,100	47,817	10,670	11,440	13,594	9,071

100,000 and 120,000 deaths a year (WHO, 2012b). Polio is now close to eradication (WHO, 1996, 2011).

Airborne diseases

Diseases transmitted by air – e.g. pneumonia, tuberculosis, diphtheria, small pox, meningitis, pertussis (whooping cough) and measles – cause between a fourth and a third of all deaths in developing countries (Hardiman and Midgley, 1982; WHO, 2001, Annex Table 2). In 1990, 27.6 per cent of total child mortality was caused by acute infections of the respiratory system (WHO, 1993). In 2008 pneumonia alone caused 18 per cent of child mortality (WHO, 2011). Smallpox was officially eradicated by 1980; the last case was reported in Somalia in 1977 (WHO, 1996). TBC was once regarded as under control. But it has made a comeback due to policy neglect and increased drug resistance. In 2004, 31.4 million people worldwide were suffering from TBC, often in combination with HIV/AIDS (WHO, 2008a). Most cases are found in Africa. In 2009, the prevalence of TBC was estimated at 12–16 million cases, with an estimated 9.4 million new cases

(WHO, 2011). But mortality due to this disease has fallen by more than a third since 1990, due to high treatment success rates. Multidrug-resistant TBC, however, poses a serious problem. The number of deaths from diphtheria dropped to 8,000 deaths annually in 2008 (WHO, 2012a). With all these diseases a vicious circle of poverty, undernourishment and infection plays a significant role.

Diseases transmitted through direct physical contact

Other contagious diseases are transmitted through direct physical contact; for example, leprosy (10–12 million cases in the 1980s, see Maurice and Pearce, 1987), framboesia and sexually transmissible diseases. Leprosy can easily be treated. Between 1985 and 2011, prevalence has been reduced by 90 per cent worldwide and more than 15 million patients have been cured (WHO, 1997, 2011).

Within the category of physically transmitted diseases, HIV/AIDS is the most important. In several countries, in particular in Southern Africa, HIV/AIDS infections have reached epidemic proportions. The joint United Nations Programme on HIV/AIDS publishes global estimates of the incidence and impact of the disease (UNAIDS, 2002, 2011). The dramatic impact of this disease is illustrated by the figures reproduced in Table 6.5.

Globally, in the year 2010 some 34 million persons were infected with HIV/AIDS. Of these 34 million cases, no less than 23 million occurred in Sub-Saharan Africa, the region hardest hit by this disease: 17 African countries have the highest incidence of AIDS. In these countries between 3.4 and 25.9 per cent of the adult population is infected. In six countries, Botswana, Zimbabwe, Swaziland, Lesotho, Namibia and South Africa, the prevalence among the adult population is above 15 per cent. Some of these countries have small populations. In terms of absolute numbers, the greatest number of cases is found in South Africa (5.6 million), Nigeria (3.3 million), India (2.4 million) and Mozambique (1.4 million).

In 2010, HIV/AIDS-related deaths numbered 1.8 million, of which 1.2 million were in Sub-Saharan Africa. The majority of HIV/AIDS infections in adults are transmitted through unprotected sexual intercourse, of which 70 per cent are heterosexual (WHO, 1997). But HIV/AIDS is also being transmitted from infected mothers to their children. In 1997, no less than 590,000 children under the age of fifteen became infected.

Many infectious diseases primarily affect children. HIV/AIDS is the exception. In spite of mother–child transmission, HIV/AIDS is most common within the economically most productive age group (25–49). AIDS has serious economic consequences because the most productive and often highly educated segment of the labour force is most seriously affected. Agricultural production is also negatively affected. HIV/AIDS infections will have negative impacts on childcare and care for the elderly. Moreover, the large numbers of HIV/AIDS patients are an enormous burden on the healthcare system. Nevertheless, the fears of an economic collapse due to HIV/AIDS have not materialised, in part because of the increasing effectiveness of treatment.

Until very recently the outlook for HIV/AIDS was persistently gloomy. The numbers of infections and deaths were increasing, there were no breakthroughs in vaccine research and treatment was so expensive that most people in poor countries did not have access to it. Also, in Africa many governments continued to deny the seriousness of the threat: South Africa is one of the saddest examples of this. Recent publications are much more optimistic.

Table 6.5: Prevalence of HIV/AIDS, developing countries, 2001–10[a]

Region	Number of people with HIV/AIDS		% of total population with HIV/AIDS		% of adult population with HIV/AIDS		AIDS deaths	
	2001	2010	2001	2010	2001	2010	2001	2010
Sub-Saharan Africa	20,500,000	22,900,000	3.0	2.7	5.9	5.0	1,400,000	1,200,000
North Africa and Middle East	320,000	470,000	0.0	0.1	0.2	0.2	22,000	35,000
Eastern Europe and Central Asia	410,000	1,500,000	0.1	0.5	0.3	0.9	7,800	90,000
South and South-East Asia	3,800,000	4,000,000	0.2	0.2	0.3	0.3	230,000	25,000
East-Asia and Pacific	380,000	790,000	0.0	0.1	<0.1	0.1	24,000	56,000
Latin America	1,300,000	1,500,000	0.3	0.3	0.4	0.4	83,000	67,000
Caribbean	210,000	200,000	0.5	0.5	1.0	0.9	18,000	9,000
Oceania	41,000	54,000	0.1	0.1	0.2	0.3	1,800	1,600
Western Europe and Central Europe	630,000	840,000	0.1	0.2	0.2	0.2	10,000	9,900
North America	980,000	1,300,000	0.3	0.4	0.5	0.6	9,000	20,000
World	28,600,000	34,000,000	0.5	0.5	0.8	0.8	1,900,000	1,800,000
Countries with 400,000 or more HIV infected persons or more than 5 per cent of the adult population with HIV/AIDS, ranked by HIV/AIDS as per cent of adult population								
Swaziland	130,000	180,000	12.8	17.2	23.6	25.9	6,800	7,000
Botswana	270,000	320,000	15.1	16.1	26.3	24.8	15,000	5,800
Lesotho	240,000	290,000	12.1	13.5	24.5	23.6	14,000	14,000
South Africa	4,600,000	5,600,000	10.2	11.4	17.1	17.8	220,000	310,000
Zimbabwe	1,700,000	1,200,000	13.5	9.6	23.7	14.3	130,000	83,000
Zambia	830,000	980,000	7.9	7.7	14.3	13.5	68,000	45,000
Namibia	160,000	180,000	8.3	8.0	16.1	13.1	8,100	6,700
Mozambique	850,000	1,400,000	4.5	6.1	9.4	11.5	43,000	74,000
Malawi	860,000	920,000	7.5	6.4	13.8	11.0	68,000	51,000
Uganda	980,000	1,200,000	3.9	3.7	7.0	6.5	89,000	64,000
Kenya	1,500,000	1,500,000	4.7	3.8	8.4	6.3	120,000	80,000
United Republic of Tanzania	1,400,000	1,400,000	4.0	3.2	7.1	5.6	110,000	86,000
Cameroon	480,000	610,000	3.0	3.2	5.5	5.3	31,000	37,000
Gabon	36,000	46,000	2.8	3.1	5.3	5.2	2,000	2,400
Equatorial Guinea	5,700	20,000	1.1	2.9	1.9	5.0	<500	<1000
Nigeria	2,700,000	3,300,000	2.1	2.1	3.8	3.6	210,000	220,000
Côte d'Ivoire	630,000	450,000	3.7	2.3	6.5	3.4	51,000	36,000
Thailand	640,000	530,000	1.0	0.8	1.7	1.3	52,000	28,000
Russian Federation	1,700,000	1,200,000	1.2	0.8	0.5	1.0		
USA	940,000	1,200,000	0.3	0.4	0.5	0.6	17,000	17,000
India	2,500,000	2,400,000	0.2	0.2	0.4	0.3	140,000	170,000
China		740,000		0.1	...	0.1		26,000

Notes:

[a] Regional data for 2010, country data for 2009.

[b] The *Global Health Observatory Data Repository* and the *World Aids Report* provide uncertainty ranges for each estimate. In 2010 the range for the world total of people with HIV/AIDS was between 31.6 and 35.2 million; for Sub-Saharan Africa the range was between 21.6 and 24.1 million.

Sources:

Country data 2001–9: WHO (2012a); *Global Health Observatory Data Repository*; regional data from: UNAIDS (2011), *World AIDS Day Report 2011: How to Get to Zero. Faster, Smarter, Better*; regional population data from United Nations Population Division (2011a); *World Population Projections: The 2010 Revision*; country population data from World Bank, *World Development Indicators Online*, downloaded August 2012.

The 2011 World AIDS day report (UNAIDS, 2011) argues that we are on the verge of a significant breakthrough in the response. The primary reason is the increased effectiveness and rapidly declining cost of retroviral therapies. In 2011 more than 8 million people were receiving treatment for HIV/AIDS in LICs and MICs and efforts were being made to increase these numbers to 15 million people by 2015 (UNAIDS, 2012). The number of people suffering from HIV infections has increased since 2001 (see Table 6.5), but this reflects the fact that fewer people are dying from HIV/AIDS due to effective treatment. The number of HIV/AIDS-related deaths peaked in 2005 and has actually declined since then so that the numbers are now lower than in 2001. The number of new infections has gone down by 21 per cent since 1997. New infections among children declined dramatically from 590,000 in 1997 to 390,000 in 2010. But the numbers remain unacceptably high. The challenge for the coming years is to finance and organise the further roll-out of effective treatment and prevention.

Parasitic diseases

Parasitic intestinal diseases are also quite common. Approximately 1 billion people suffer from ascariasis (caused by roundworms) and ancylostomiasis (caused by hookworms). In 2004, 151 million people suffered from parasitic infections (WHO, 2008a).

Diseases transmitted by animal vectors

Very important diseases are transmitted by insects or other animal vectors. These include:

- *Malaria* (transmitted by the malaria mosquito). In the past, the incidence of malaria had been reduced strongly due to the use of pesticides like DDT and effective treatment. However, in the course of time mosquitoes have become immune to pesticides, DDT is now banned for environmental reasons and the rapid spread of resistance to antimalarial drugs presents a threat to effective treatment. In the 1980s, the number of malaria cases was estimated to be about 100 million per year (Maurice and Pearce, 1987). By 1998, no less than 273 million persons were suffering from malaria and 1.1 million persons had died from this disease (WHO, 1999, Chapter 4). Since 2000 there have been decreases in the number of cases of malaria and malaria-related deaths. In 2009, the estimated number of deaths was 781,000. The estimated number of cases of malaria decreased to 225 million in 2009 (WHO, 2011).
- *Bilharzia* (schistosomiasis, an infectious disease of the intestines and the urinary tracts caused by worms). Bilharzia can be found in watery areas and is transmitted by snails. Between 500 and 600 million people are exposed to schistosome infection and 200 million are actually infected (Maurice and Pearce, 1987). In 2008, 44,000 deaths were related to this disease (WHO, 2012a).
- *Sleeping sickness* (trypanosomiasis). Sleeping sickness occurs in many Sub-Saharan African countries and is passed on by tsetse flies. In thirty-six countries 50 million people were exposed to infection (Maurice and Pearce, 1987) and 16–18 million people were actually infected (WHO, 1993).
- *Filariasis* (a category of parasitic infectious diseases, transmitted by mosquitoes, flies, and worms). The most important diseases in this category are lymphatic filariasis (its most serious form being elephantiasis), and river blindness (onchocerciasis). In the 1980s an estimated 905 million people were exposed to lymphatic filariasis and 90 million were actually infected. River blindness is common especially in tropical African countries

where 17 million persons were actually infected and 78 million were exposed to infection in the 1980s (Maurice and Pearce, 1987). Substantial progress has been made in combating filariasis. For instance, fifty-three countries were implementing mass treatment programmes for lymphatic filariasis, treating 546 million people in 2007.

- *Trachoma* (inflammation of the eye membrane). Hundreds of millions of people suffer from this disease, which is passed on by flies and through direct physical contact. Trachoma can result in blindness.

Among infectious diseases, the so-called undernourishment-infection syndrome merits special attention. Infectious diseases interact with undernourishment. Undernourishment increases susceptibility to infection. Infectious diseases, in particular diarrhoea, cause further undernourishment, thus creating a vicious circle. In the end, diseases that are not dangerous in themselves, may result in death (Mosley, 1985a; Van Norren and van Vianen, 1986). This will be discussed in more detail in section 6.2.5.

6.1.6   Epidemiological transition

The fact that people all over the world live longer today than they did thirty to forty years ago is very much related to the reduction of infectious diseases of the intestines and the respiratory tracts. These are diseases that mainly kill young people. In the affluent countries of today infectious diseases have gradually been reduced from the eighteenth century onwards. At present they are no longer very important. Similar trends are emerging in today's developing countries.

Such developments are often discussed in the context of the so-called *epidemiological transition*, which is seen as an integral part of an overall process of economic and social development. The transition involves changes from situations characterised by infectious diseases, high fertility rates, high child mortality rates, and low life expectancies to situations characterised by low child mortality rates, few infectious diseases, low fertility rates, high life expectancies and the predominance of cancer and CVDs (Frederikson, 1969; Omran, 1971; WHO, 1999). This epidemiological transition is seen as closely interlinked with the wider process of modernisation characterised by increases in prosperity, improvements in nutrition, hygiene and water supply, higher levels of education and improvements in medical technology.

Omran (1971) distinguishes three models of the epidemiological transition:

(a) *The classical Western model*, characterised by a gradual decrease of the death rate associated with modernisation, improved nutrition and hygiene. By the beginning of the twentieth century infectious diseases were outstripped by other diseases. The decline in the death rate accelerated.

(b) *The accelerated model*. The difference from the classical model is mainly that the death rate declines more rapidly and that public hygiene, sanitation and medical factors play a more important role. The pattern of change is similar, however. A typical example of this model is twentieth-century Japan.

(c) *The decelerated model*. This model refers to today's developing countries and indicates that the transition from older to newer patterns of disease is still unfinished.

Like other modernisation theories that assume a unilinear development from a traditional to a modern stage, the simple model of epidemiological transition has proved to be untenable. Changes of patterns of sickness and health never develop along the same path in different societies and during different historical periods (Frenk *et al.*, 1989). For example, in many developing countries CVDs, cancer, diabetes and other chronic conditions are on the increase, while infectious diseases continue to remain important (WHO, 1993, 1999, 2012a). In 2008, no less than 51 per cent of deaths in developing countries were due to either cancer or cardiovascular diseases, up from 24 per cent in 1990 (Table 6.4).

In the more developed countries, recently life style- and age-related diseases such as cardiovascular diseases and degenerative diseases and cancer were among the most important causes of death. Interestingly, in Japan cardiovascular diseases have shown a downward tendency since the Second World War. They do not rank first among the causes of death as they do in other rich countries. Also, life expectancy – 83.7 years in the period 2010–15 – is higher than in any of the other rich countries (United Nations Population Division, 2011a).

Japan is different in other respects, too. In 1900, Japanese life expectancy was similar to the life expectancy in England, whereas per capita income was much lower. According to Johanson and Mosk, this is explained by the exceptional emphasis on public hygiene in Japan in the late nineteenth century. Between 1900 and 1940 life expectancy in Japan hardly changed, whereas in England and in other Western European countries it rose to approximately sixty years. After the Second World War, Japan embarked on a dramatic process of epidemiological catch-up, which paralleled its economic performance. In health terms it succeeded in overtaking Western Europe and the USA (Johansson and Mosk, 1987; Vallin, 1989).

Nevertheless, the various patterns of health development have some important elements in common. The share of deaths caused by infectious intestinal and respiratory diseases tends to decrease over time, whether gradually or rapidly. The share of deaths caused by non-infectious diseases tends to increase. What comes in the place of infectious diseases can differ, but the decline in infectious diseases itself is certainly an 'epidemiological transition'.

Table 6.4 provides clear indications that a kind of epidemiological transition is indeed taking place in developing countries today. Non-communicable diseases such as diseases of the circulatory system, heart diseases and cancer have rapidly increased. Traditional infectious diseases are declining, but are still very important. Within the category of infectious diseases, HIV/AIDS has exploded into prominence, though HIV/AIDS-related deaths are finally on the decline. Finally, injuries as results of accidents as well as intentional injuries as a result of crime, war and civil unrest increased between 1980 and 2000 and stabilised thereafter. In 2008, they accounted for almost 10 per cent of mortality in developing countries.

6.2　Theoretical explanations of changes in health and morbidity

To pursue adequate healthcare policies, we need to identify the determinants of health and morbidity. We will discuss this issue from two different points of view. First, we will concentrate on the various factors that may be of importance to the improvement of the state of health. Next, we will consider several important theoretical ideas. Finally, we will attempt a cautious synthesis.

6.2.1   Factors affecting the state of health

The following factors may affect the state of health in a particular country:

1. *Improvements in medical technology.* Improvements in curative medicine and the development of effective medicines make it possible to treat diseases which were previously untreatable. Extremely important are, for example, the antibiotics that are used to combat various infectious diseases. Preventive medicine based on vaccination is also part of medical technology. Several diseases can be eradicated at relatively modest cost by means of large-scale vaccination schemes. For example, vaccination against smallpox has already been very successful. Most countries have schemes for vaccinating children against diphtheria, whooping cough, tetanus, poliomyelitis, measles, and tuberculosis (WHO, 1987: 76). Still, millions of children continue to die of these diseases, and millions are crippled for life. More vaccination could have prevented this.

2. *Improvements in water supply, hygiene, and sanitary facilities.* Many diseases are passed on through contaminated water, unhygienic treatment of excrements and unhealthy living conditions. In developing countries hundreds of millions of households do not have access to clean drinking water. Facilities for the hygienic treatment of excrements are often woefully inadequate.

3. *Combating animal carriers of diseases (vectors).* An important aspect of healthcare policy is controlling the vectors that transmit diseases, e.g. flies, mosquitoes, worms, slugs, snails, or rats. Chemical substances are often used in combating vectors, although biological methods are applied as well.

4. *Improved nutrition.* According to some theorists, the importance of medical technology is overrated (McKeown, 1976). Nutrition is the most important factor reducing susceptibility to diseases and reinforcing natural resistance against diseases contracted. In this respect, improvement of the state of health primarily depends on the overall improvement of the economic situation, the standard of living and the food supply.

5. *Increased birth spacing.* When intervals between births and successive pregnancies are too short, there are increased risks for maternal, perinatal and infant health and mortality. A minimum period of twenty-four months between a birth and a successive pregnancy is recommended by a panel of WHO experts (WHO, 2006). Periods of less than six months pose severe risks to maternal health.

6. *Demographic factors such as population density and migration.* Very dense urban populations provide an ideal setting for transmission of infectious diseases (Schultz, 2010). Migration patterns contribute to the international spread of diseases. Thus, in Southern Africa, truckers have been instrumental in the spread of HIV/AIDS.

7. *Education.* Other authors like Mosley (1983, 1985a) and Caldwell (1984, 1986) emphasise the importance of education, especially the education of mothers. Improving educational levels is positively associated with practices favourable to children's chances of survival – both from a preventive viewpoint, e.g. hygiene, vaccination, food, and in a curative sense, e.g. making better use of the possibilities of the health facilities.

8. *Healthcare policy.* Countries that make greater efforts with respect to basic healthcare are relatively more successful in combating diseases, reducing the child mortality rate and increasing life expectancy. Policy is an important autonomous factor.

9. *Egalitarian patterns of growth.* In developing countries where large segments of the population share in the fruits of growth, this is reflected in improvements in health, irrespective of healthcare policies (McQuire, 2001).

The first six factors are of a medical–biological nature. They have direct impacts on processes of disease and treatment. The last three factors are of an indirect nature. They influence the availability of direct factors and the ways in which people deal with the direct factors that influence sickness and health. There are many differences of opinion concerning the relative importance of these different factors. Some of the most pronounced theories and models will be discussed in the following section.

6.2.2   Preston: per capita income and life expectancy

In a pioneering article published in 1975 Samuel Preston studied the relation between average per capita income and life expectancy (Preston, 1975; see also Preston, 1980). At a given moment in time, the level of income and the average life expectancy are closely related. In poor countries, life expectancy is much lower than in rich countries. However, in the course of time life expectancy in all countries increases regardless of the level of income. This is illustrated in Figure 6.2 in which the average life expectancy in a country (on the vertical axis) is set out against per capita income (on the horizontal axis). In this figure there is a positive relation between per capita income and life expectancy in both 1930 and in 1960. However, the 1960 curve lies above the 1930 curve.

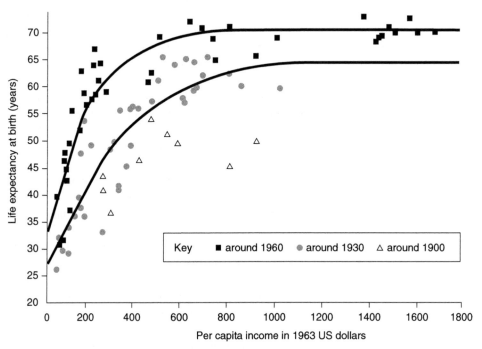

Figure 6.2 Life expectancy at birth, 1900, 1930 and 1960
Source: Preston (1975).

On the basis of his statistical analysis Preston comes to the conclusion that factors other than per capita income account for the 75–90 per cent increase of global life expectancy. Factors like improved nutrition and a higher level of education cannot explain the increase in the average life expectancy either. According to Preston, the rise of life expectancy is explained to a great extent by improvements in health technology. This includes not only vaccination technology, antibiotics and sulphonamides, but also health policies with respect to vectors, public hygiene, health education and health facilities for mothers and their children. Preston's analysis has frequently been replicated with comparable results. Thus the WHO documents an upward shift of the life expectancy curve between 1975 and 2005 (WHO, 2008b, Figure 1.4). Strauss and Thomas (2008) have re-estimated Preston, adding data for 2004. Their study also identifies negative outliers in 2004 in Sub-Saharan Africa, with exceptionally lower life expectancy due to the incidence of HIV/AIDS.

The conclusion often drawn on the basis of Preston's analysis is that a low level of prosperity does not necessarily hinder improvements in healthcare and the state of health by application of modern medical technology (e.g. see WHO, 1999; World Bank-WDR, 1984: 69). However, Preston also stresses the fact that – after the upward shift of the curve – the relation between per capita income and life expectancy for the poorest developing countries is even closer than before. This may be because when life expectancy increases, the diseases that remain are those most closely related to standard of living – like diarrhoea and other infectious diseases.

6.2.3   McKeown: the importance of nutrition

In a long series of influential publications, Thomas McKeown comes to radically different conclusions (McKeown, 1976, 1978, 1979, 1988; see also Fogel, 2004). McKeown concentrates on the history of health and healthcare in Great Britain in the eighteenth and nineteenth century. He shows that declines in the number of deaths due to diseases preceded important medical breakthroughs in the treatment of these diseases. This is especially marked in the case of TBC, the leading killer of nineteenth-century Britain. McKeown believes that nineteenth-century hospitals contributed more to the spread of diseases than to their effective treatment. He claims that the role of medical technology and medical progress is highly overrated and that one should look for other possible sources of the decline in the death rate and the increase of life expectancy. McKeown stresses the importance of nutrition. He argues that the decreasing death rate in Great Britain in the eighteenth and nineteenth century was caused to a large extent by increasing immunity against airborne infectious diseases. This immunity was caused by better nutrition.

On the basis of these analyses McKeown and his followers claim that the state of health in developing countries cannot be improved without overall improvement in the standard of living and levels of nutrition. In other words, economic factors are of crucial importance.

6.2.4   Preston and McKeown

It is by no means easy to make a choice between the incompatible perspectives of Preston and McKeown and their followers. Still, an attempt will be made.

First, McKeown's thesis that only nutrition is of importance can be qualified. Sreter (1988) has convincingly shown that the so-called 'public health movement' in nineteenth-century Great Britain contributed greatly to an improved state of health. This movement focused on the amelioration of hygienic conditions, sewers, supplies of clean drinking water, inspection of food quality and housing conditions and the improvement of preventive medicine. Improvements in urban health infrastructure were responsible for mitigating the urban health problems associated with rising population densities (Schultz, 2010). McKeown underestimated the importance of preventive medical technology, in particular vaccination and inoculation. Further, Sreter criticises McKeown for generalising on the basis of the healthcare history of a single country. On the basis of further historical statistical analysis, Fogel (1986) concludes that the contributions of improvements in nutritional status can be identified. But they are not overwhelming. After 1930, the impacts of advances in medical science and technology became more and more important (Fogel, 2004).

Next, the difference between Preston and McKeown is not as great as it seems (Vallin, 1989). In Preston's data there is also a clear relation between the level of prosperity and life expectancy at a given moment in time. This relation is especially strong in the case of the poorest developing countries. The economic factor clearly does matter.

One of McKeown's valuable contributions is that he puts the claims of curative medical technology in perspective and stresses the significance of nutrition and undernourishment. The interaction between undernourishment and infectious diseases, in particular, is very important for a good understanding of the health problems of developing countries. The scepticism about the role of curative medicine may have contributed to the rise of the primary healthcare movement (see section 6.4).

On the other hand, the conclusion that medical technology and medical progress are unimportant for developing countries is not justified. We should realise that progress of medical knowledge not only encompasses better techniques of curative treatment for diseases contracted, but also the whole complex of preventive healthcare, better sanitary conditions, knowledge of the causes of diseases, vaccination, vector control and medication.

6.2.5   The Mosley model and the importance of education

Mosley (1983; see also Mosley, 1984, 1985a, 1985b) has made a significant contribution to the debate on the importance of medical versus socio-economic factors. He concentrates on explanations of child mortality. Like the Bongaarts model presented in Chapter 5, Mosley makes a distinction between underlying social and economic determinants and the intermediate (biological) factors that directly influence the chances of contracting disease and dying. The basic principle is the notion that in a well-protected environment 98 per cent of all children under the age of five ought to survive, as in the economically advanced countries. The extent to which this survival rate is not realised should be explained systematically.

A decrease in the chances of survival is the result of primary social and economic determinants. These primary determinants, however, operate through intermediate biological mechanisms, which influence the chances of contracting disease and determine the outcomes of processes of illness. In Mosley's model, death is the ultimate result of the multiple episodes of morbidity. It is seldom the result of one isolated instance of illness. The essence of the model is the identification of intermediate variables, in order to analyse how primary determinants influence child mortality through the intermediate variables (see also van Norren and Van Vianen, 1986).

Mosley's model consists of the following five intermediate variables:

1. *Maternal fertility factors*:
   (a) *Age of childbearing*. When mothers are either too young or too old, the children may be at risk.

(b) *Number of children per woman*. Large families reduce the health prospects of children.

(c) *Birth intervals*. If intervals between births are short, this may have adverse effects on the state of health. In general, children from large families are more likely to contract diseases than children from small families.

2. *Environmental contamination by infectious agents*:
   (a) Contamination of the air.
   (b) Contamination of food, water, or fingers.
   (c) Contamination of the skin (caused by soil or mites).
   (d) Contamination by vectors.

3. *Availability of nutrients for foetus and child*:
   (a) Calories.
   (b) Proteins.
   (c) Vitamins.
   (d) Minerals.

4. *Injuries*:
   (a) Accidents.
   (b) Injuries inflicted intentionally.

5. *Personal disease control factors*:
   (a) Personal preventive measures.
   (b) Treatment of illnesses once they are contracted.

Figure 6.3 summarises the model consisting of the five intermediate variables and a set of behavioural practices. The behavioural practices affect health through the intermediate variables. Thus, the availability and distribution of food within the household affects the

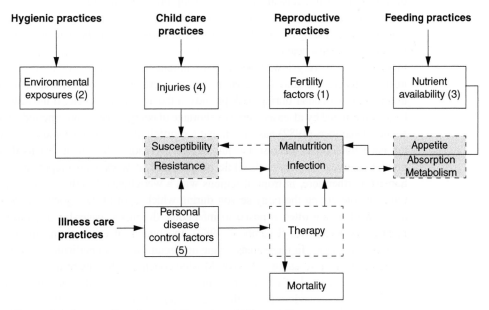

Figure 6.3 Intermediate factors influencing child mortality
Source: Mosely (1983).

malnutrition of mothers and their children. Hygienic conditions and circumstances affect susceptibility and resistance to diseases. Hygienic conditions in turn are influenced by hygienic practices and policies.

The central element of Figure 6.3 is the malnutrition–infection syndrome. Malnutrition increases susceptibility and decreases resistance to a variety of (infectious) diseases. Infectious diseases result in metabolic changes and in loss of appetite among children. This causes a decreasing capacity to absorb nutrients, which results in further undernourishment. Child mortality is not the result of any one single factor. Most often there has been a long history of illness leading to retardation of growth, undernourishment and undermining of a patient's resistance. At the end of the sequence non-lethal diseases like respiratory infections or diarrhoea may result in death.

Curative healthcare (therapy) is only one of the many factors in the model. It does not prevent malnutrition or tackle the malnutrition–infection syndrome, but only tries to deal with diseases once they have emerged. Often illnesses are not treated until very near the end of a long sequence of sickness. Many kinds of medication only affect one specific ailment while several diseases in combination contribute to child mortality. Only if a single disease causes high mortality can medical treatments have a substantial, demographic influence (this is the case with combating malaria or vaccinating against tetanus). Although Mosley does not take an explicit stand in the debate on the role of medical technology, he tends to play down the importance of treating specific diseases by means of medical interventions.

Mosley gives two good examples that may serve to put curative medical interventions into perspective. Vaccination against measles prevents people from contracting measles. However, measles is quite a harmless disease unless one's resistance has already been affected. Treating diarrhoea by means of 'oral rehydration' may prevent children from dying of the disease. Still, this technique does not halt the gradual deterioration and undermining of a patient's health caused by ever-recurring bouts of diarrhoea.

Mosley's model refers especially to infant and child mortality. Yet, it gives us a more general understanding of the effects of social circumstances on the state of health. De Kadt and Lipton indicate that health risks are greatest in rural areas (De Kadt and Lipton, 1988). Income in rural areas is very low, food supplies unreliable, especially for those households with insufficient access to land. At the same time the energy requirements for agricultural labour are immense, in particular during peak periods in the agricultural cycle. If the state of health has been undermined by disease, there is a shortage of energy, just in those periods when it is most needed. Chambers (1982) has shown that a shortfall of food supplies most often occurs when the need for food is greatest, i.e. just before harvesting. It is then that food stocks of the previous harvest are depleted, while people need to work hard preparing for the coming harvest. Furthermore, in tropical regions with a wet climate health conditions are extremely unfavourable during the rainy season during which a lot of the agricultural work has to be done. Workers are often exposed to infections, diarrhoea, water-borne parasitic infections, malaria and snakebites (Chambers, 1982). Inhabitants of urban slums are also exposed to serious health risks. In these areas, hygienic circumstances in particular are very poor.

On the basis of research in Kenya, Mosley concludes that the prime determinant of child mortality is the level of education of the mother. The level of education operates through several of the behavioural practices and intermediate variables. It positively influences hygienic practices; it affects the distribution of food within the family so that children receive their fair share of food (nutrition practices); it operates through reproductive practices such as birth spacing and birth control; and it affects the way in which preventive and curative medical services are made use of (personal health control factors).

Therefore, a 'primary healthcare' system should not concentrate merely on medical facilities but rather on the entire complex of nutrition, educational practices, water supply, hygiene, counselling of parents, family planning and so forth. Mosley's argument should not be considered an attack on healthcare but rather a plea for considering preventive healthcare in a broad sense including education and information about health, contraception and nutrition. More attention will be paid to healthcare policy in section 6.4.

6.2.6   Caldwell: the importance of healthcare policy

In an interesting article published in 1986 Caldwell raises the question why some developing countries have high scores on health indicators despite relatively low levels of prosperity, while other developing countries with relatively high levels of prosperity have relatively low scores on health indicators (Caldwell, 1986). Caldwell compared the ranking of countries by their average per capita income in 1982 to their ranking by infant mortality per 1,000 live births, and their ranking by average life expectancy.

Caldwell focused on countries whose ranking on health indicators compared favourably with their ranking by per capita income (*superior health achievers*) or unfavourably (*poor health achievers*). Among the *superior health achievers* Caldwell found four important countries with a Buddhist tradition (Thailand, Vietnam, Sri Lanka and Burma). In the category of *poor health achievers* there were a strikingly large number of Islamic countries. Caldwell associated the health achievements of the Buddhist countries with the positive evaluation of education in Buddhism and the Buddhist concept of 'enlightenment'. According to Caldwell, the poor scores of Islamic countries were closely associated with the low social status of women and the relatively low appreciation of education in general and female education in particular (see also UNDP, 2002).

In general, Caldwell, like Mosley, sets great store by the educational level of women. Education leads to greater openness with respect to preventive healthcare measures and a more effective use of existing health services:

> The key factor seems to be that a woman who goes to school is increasingly seen by both herself and others as being part of a global society with an accepted attitude towards bacterial contamination and corresponding hygienic methods, the use of modern medical facilities and persistence in recommended treatments ... [such women] are more likely to insist that health centres should provide them with adequate treatment. Educated mothers distribute food within the family in closer accord with needs ... they are more likely to behave in accordance with beliefs in bacterial rather than religious pollution.   (Caldwell, 1984: 108)

Sri Lanka, Costa Rica and the South West Indian state of Kerala are well-known examples of poor societies with relatively good results with respect to health. Caldwell analysed the demographic history of these entities and considered the factors that might explain a lower death rate. The factors he identified as important were: autonomy of women, a positive evaluation of education, a relatively open political system and a tradition of political egalitarianism and radicalism. For Caldwell, the degree of female autonomy is the central factor in mortality declines in poor but open societies. Female autonomy has very positive effects on the quality of childcare. The combination of education and political radicalism puts pressure on the political system to develop and maintain good healthcare systems. According to Caldwell, investments in the healthcare system and progress in medical technology and medical knowledge have contributed greatly to increases of life expectancy, especially in combination with wider social and economic changes. Centrally planned economies like China, Cuba and Vietnam also score high on health indicators. In their policies high priority is given to the realisation of effective primary healthcare systems, accessible to large sections of the population.

In Table 6.6, Caldwell's analysis has been reproduced using data for 2010. Caldwell had arranged countries in order of their infant mortality rate and studied those countries whose ranking by infant mortality deviated at least 25 points from their ranking by per capita income. In Table 6.6 the criterion is a rank difference of at least 30 points for either of the two health indicators (infant mortality and life expectancy). Also the new table uses PPP-converted national income per capita as the income measure, rather than exchange rate-converted national income.[3]

Compared to 1982, three countries continue to be superior health achievers: Sri Lanka Thailand and Costa Rica.[4] China and India no longer figure amongst the superior health achievers. This is not because their health performance has deteriorated, but because they have experienced rapid economic growth. As a result their ranking in PPP-converted income is higher than before.

Among the superior health achievers in 2010, Cuba and Costa Rica are well-known examples of countries that give a very high priority to health. Quite prominent in the list of superior health achievers in 2010 are a number of former Soviet republics (Moldova, Belarus, Ukraine, Kyrgyz Republic, Armenia and Georgia). Here, the discrepancy between health and income rankings is caused by the weak growth performance in the wake of the collapse of the Soviet Union.[5]

Among the inferior health achievers of 2010, we find six middle-eastern Islamic countries (Iran, Kuwait, Oman, Qatar, Saudi Arabia and United Arab Emirates) and a large number of countries from Sub-Saharan Africa, of which Angola, Botswana, Equatorial Guinea, Gabon and South Africa are prominent examples. Interestingly, both the Russian Federation and the USA are inferior health achievers.

The most important conclusion that can be derived from Caldwell's analysis and from Table 6.6 is that health policy itself is an important explanatory factor of health. Societies giving high priority to the realisation of good healthcare systems in the broadest sense were able to achieve excellent results even at a low income level. A given income level is associated with varying levels of health performance. In this respect, McKeown's idea that only the level of prosperity is of importance proves to be incorrect. On the other hand, one should realise that in countries where per capita income shows secular stagnation, sooner or

---

[3] PPP-converted income gives a more realistic idea of real differences in standards of living than exchange rate converted income.

[4] The tables are not strictly comparable, because the number of countries ranked in 2010 is much greater than in 1982.

[5] Note that superior health achievement is a relative concept. In absolute terms, a superior health achiever might have quite low health scores.

Table 6.6: Comparisons of levels of per capita income, infant mortality and life expectancy at birth, 2010

	Per capita GNI (PPP $)	Infant mortality (per 1,000 live births)	Difference in ranking	Life expectancy at birth (years)	Difference in ranking
Superior health achievements in relation to level of income[a]					
Cuba	8,852	4.6	57	78.96	55
Eritrea	540	42.3	49	60.99	36
Moldova	3,370	16.3	42	68.90	15
Madagascar	950	43.1	39	66.47	43
Belarus	13,590	4.0	38	70.40	−41
Bosnia and Herzegovina	8,870	7.5	38	75.40	32
Syrian Arab Republic	5,090	13.8	36	75.70	59
Nepal	1,210	41.4	35	68.39	42
Ukraine	6,590	11.4	35	70.28	−9
Vietnam	3,060	18.6	35	74.83	73
Serbia	11,090	6.1	33	73.94	6
Sri Lanka	5,040	14.2	31	74.72	50
Thailand	8,150	11.2	30	73.93	20
Bangladesh	1,810	38.0	28	68.63	35
Nicaragua	2,660	22.6	27	73.73	58
Kyrgyz Republic	2,070	32.8	24	69.37	34
Honduras	3,750	20.3	21	72.83	29
Costa Rica	11,290	8.7	20	79.19	43
Armenia	5,640	17.5	13	73.78	32
Georgia	4,950	20.0	13	73.33	31
Albania	8,570	16.4	3	76.90	50
Ecuador	7,850	17.6	0	75.46	40
Inferior health achievements in relation to level of income[b]					
Lithuania	18,010	5.4	13	73.27	−32
Russian Federation	19,210	9.1	−7	68.80	−66
Oman	25,770	7.8	−15	73.12	−51
Namibia	6,270	29.3	−16	62.07	−37
Nigeria	2,140	88.4	−28	51.41	−22
Iran, Islamic Rep.	11,400	21.8	−31	72.75	−22
United Arab Emirates	46,990	6.1	−31	76.57	−29
Brunei Darussalam	49,790	5.8	−32	77.93	−28
USA	47,310	6.5	−34	78.24	−25
Lebanon	13,820	18.8	−36	72.41	−34
Swaziland	5,570	55.1	−37	48.34	−67
Kazakhstan	10,620	29.1	−37	68.30	−42
Turkmenistan	7,460	46.9	−37	64.86	−34
Saudi Arabia	23,150	15.0	−41	73.85	−30
Azerbaijan	9,240	39.4	−41	70.51	−22
Qatar	76,470	6.7	−42	78.10	−33
South Africa	10,330	40.7	−46	52.08	−84

Table 6.6: (*cont.*)

	Per capita GNI (PPP $)	Infant mortality (per 1,000 live births)	Difference in ranking	Life expectancy at birth (years)	Difference in ranking
Kuwait	53,820	9.6	−50	74.60	−55
Botswana	13,640	36.1	−58	53.11	−98
Angola	5,170	97.9	−66	50.65	−60
Trinidad and Tobago	24,400	24.0	−70	69.76	−70
Gabon	13,070	54.4	−73	62.29	−69
Equatorial Guinea	21,980	80.5	−121	50.84	−123

Notes:

[a] 177 MICs and LICs have been ranked by income per capita, infant mortality and life expectation. Superior health achievers are countries with a positive rank difference of 30 or more points between the ranking on infant mortality and the ranking on income per capita, and/or between the ranking on life expectation and the ranking on income per capita. The sample of countries excludes countries with less than 1 million inhabitants.

[b] Inferior health achievers are countries with a negative rank difference of 30 or more between the rankings on either of the two health indicators and income per capita.

Sources:

GNI/per capita (PPP dollars), infant mortality and life expectancy from *World Development Indicators Online*, downloaded August 2012. For Cuba, figures in current dollars were converted to PPP dollars, using the average ratio of PPP dollars to current dollars for Latin America.

later the economic basis for the maintenance of a good healthcare system will inevitably be undermined.[6]

Mosley's thesis that education is more important than medical interventions is also slightly exaggerated. Education – especially education of women – is indeed of great importance. However, the direct effect of education is that the facilities of a healthcare system are utilised more effectively. If no healthcare facilities are available, education alone will be of less significance.

Some authors argue that underlying factors such as religion and culture are highly important since these factors determine attitudes towards education, the status of women, family planning and a scientific approach to health issues. In an interesting article on the relatively unfavourable state of health in Africa, Vallin has paid a great deal of attention to religious and cultural factors as ultimate determinants of the state of health. Unlike Asian and Latin American societies, which were penetrated by great unitary religions like Islam, Christianity, or Buddhism, African societies never experienced the predominance of one single religion or civilisation. Rather there is a patchwork of animistic, Islamic and Christian influences. The extreme cultural, religious and ethnic diversity in Sub-Saharan Africa hampers the effective development of healthcare services (Vallin, 1989). As adequate knowledge of the cultural backgrounds is lacking, it is difficult to integrate healthcare systems into local cultures.

[6] One would expect that time series of health performance and GDP per capita would be cointegrated in the long run.

In a more recent article, Kuhn (2010) has revisited the work of Caldwell and has re-estimated the 1982 table with data for 2007, in a similar fashion as was done here. He rightly concludes that the results are definitely not stable.[7] The superior health achievers of 1982 tend to have more rapid economic growth. The inferior health achievers tend to improve their health status. On balance there has been convergence in health performance over time. The strong relationship between a majority Muslim population and poor health achievement has weakened over time; there are steep mortality reductions in a wide range of Muslim countries. Tackling adult mortality has become more important. Kuhn concludes that Caldwell's grand cultural explanations fail to explain how inferior and superior performance of countries shifts over time. What remains is the interesting phenomenon that countries at given levels in income per capita have widely varying health performance. This points to the key importance of health policy and health systems as an intermediate factor explaining health performance.

6.2.7   Standards of living, education, medical technology and healthcare systems: a synthesis

The *World Health Report 1999* (WHO, 1999) presents an interesting synthesis of the different perspectives discussed here. In an analysis similar to that of Preston, the report analyses the relationships between infant mortality and income per capita. Cross-section regression analysis shows that at one point in time there is a relationship between GDP per capita (in 1985 PPP dollars) and infant mortality. The higher the income, the lower the infant mortality. But between 1952 and 1992 the whole curve shifts downwards. This means that in 1992 the same level of real income as 1952 is associated with much lower rates of mortality. This shift is due to changes in medical technology and knowledge.

The report cites research by Preker *et al.* (1999), who have decomposed the changes in mortality and life expectancy between 1960 and 1990 in 115 developing countries. They conclude that 45 per cent of the reduction in under-five mortality is due to generation and utilisation of new medical knowledge, 38 per cent is due to improved education of adult females and 17 per cent is due to changes in income (standard of living, nutrition). In the case of life expectancy, around 50 per cent of the improvement is due to new knowledge and around 30 per cent is based on the educational level of adult females. Thus the analysis integrates standards of living, education and technological change.

The *World Health Report 1999* concludes that 'typically half the gains in health between 1952 and 1992 result from access to better technology. The remaining gains result from movement along the curve (income improvements and better education)' (WHO, 1999: 7).[8]

It is also plausible to argue that, compared to past changes, changes in medical technology and its application have become more important. In the nineteenth century, there is support for the McKeown thesis that knowledge and tools for improving health played a limited role in mortality decline. In the twentieth century these technology related factors became much more important. The recent history of eradication or reduction of major diseases provides ample examples of the importance of medical technology, especially

---

[7] We have redone the Caldwell estimates for 2000 in the 2005 edition of this book and found very different results than for 2010.

[8] To the extent that education is related to income, education shows up as movement along the curve. However, like health, education can also improve irrespective of income level. Then it will show up in the shift of the curve.

of a preventive nature. It shows that the use of medical technology is intimately related to health policy. The *World Health Report 1998* (WHO, 1998) provides a summary of progress. Here we mention only a few examples.

By 1995, 80 per cent of the world's children had been immunised against diphtheria, tetanus, whooping cough, polio, measles and tuberculosis, compared to less than 5 per cent in 1974. In India, more than 120 million children were immunised against polio on a single day in 1996 (World Bank-WDR, 1997). Polio is now close to eradication. The use of simple oral rehydration therapies has reduced child mortality due to diarrhoea. Drugs such as Mectizan and have become available to limit the transmission of onchocerciasis (river blindness). In Africa some 70 million people have received treatment so that for the first time there is a perspective on eliminating this disease.

Two cautionary remarks are in order. First, there are no simple technological fixes. Success in combating diseases depends on an integrated intersectoral approach. Health systems provide access to new medical technology and knowledge. But health systems and medical technologies interact with improved nutrition, improved sanitation and water supply, improved education and social protection.

Second, in the future existing medical technologies cannot be relied on to the same extent as in the past. New strains of TBC, malaria and pneumonia are rapidly becoming drug resistant. These diseases are re-emerging. Major new diseases such as HIV/AIDS or avian flu have emerged. Finally, the increasing global mobility of people creates new dangers of infection.

The synthesis suggests three main avenues towards improving health: (1) Shifting the income–health curve through advances in technology; (2) Moving along the curve by increasing income per capita; (3) Changing the position relative to the curve by healthcare policy and improving the effectiveness of health systems.

As countries improve their standards of living and levels of education, they will tend to move along the curve. New medical knowledge and its applications will shift the curve downwards (lower average mortality irrespective of average incomes). At the same level of income, some countries will perform worse than average (above the curve), others better (below the curve). Improving health system development should enable countries to join or even exceed the curve (WHO, 1999, Chapter 1). Finally, at the same level of income, a more equal distribution of income will also translate into better health conditions, as the poorer segments of the population share in the fruits of growth. This is illustrated by the experiences of Taiwan and Korea, where health conditions improved in spite of the absence of specific large-scale efforts in health policy (McQuire, 2001).

6.3   Health and economic development

There is a considerable literature on the relationships between investments in healthcare and economic development (see Baldwin and Weisbrod, 1974; Barlow, 1979; Fogel, 1994, 1997, 2004; Keyzer, 1993; Mayer, 2001; Mushkin, 1962; Popkin, 1978; Schultz, 2010; Strauss and Thomas, 1998; Walsh, 1990; WHO, 1999). Health is an important aspect of human capital. Investments and improvements in health are seen as having positive impacts on economic growth and development.

One can distinguish micro-level and macro-level relationships between health and economic performance. Studies at the micro-level focus on the causal mechanisms through which health affects the economic behaviour and performance of individuals and households. Studies at the macro-level analyse the statistical relationships between investments in health, health status and economic development.

The quantification of the relation between improvements in the health situation and changes in economic output is fraught with difficulties. At the macro-level, health interacts with a great variety of other proximate and ultimate determinants of growth. Also, growth itself contributes to better health through factors such as improved nutrition, improved sanitation and more scope for medical expenditures in a circular process. Therefore, it is hard to isolate the specific contribution of health indicators to economic growth.[9] Next, researchers may attempt to quantify the losses in output and productivity caused by illness and reduction of hours worked due to premature death. But, we also know that there is widespread unemployment and underutilisation of labour in most developing countries. Therefore, better health outcomes do not automatically result in higher employment or output. Moreover, workers may compensate for low productivity due to illness by working longer hours.

At the micro-level, illness undermines the productive capacity of individuals and households. The following two relationships can be distinguished:

1. *Reduction of labour input.* Illness results in a decrease of the number of hours a person is capable of working per year. Absence from work due to illness is included under this heading. Downright disablement or invalidity makes it impossible to work.

2. *Reduction of labour intensity.* Illness and malnutrition often lead to loss of body weight, body length and a decrease in human energy and productivity. Undernourished and unhealthy people become listless, lethargic and passive. Protracted illness and malnutrition in youth can lead to lifelong impairment of mental functions, creativity and learning potential. All this implies direct negative effects on labour productivity and labour income. Thus, in Indonesia men with anaemia were 20 per cent less productive then men without anaemia (Basta *et al.*, 1979). In Tanzania it was shown that schistosomiasis reduced the productivity of sugarcane workers (Strauss and Thomas, 1998). In a study for Ghana and Côte d'Ivoire, Schultz and Tansel (1997) found that wages declined significantly for each day of disability. Gallup and Sachs (1998) found a significant negative relationship between the incidence of malaria and economic growth. Schultz (2010) summarises the findings of studies that estimate the effect of health status (often approximated by the body mass index, BMI) on wages. In these studies, health is entered into an earnings function that also includes education, innate ability, capital and technology. Schultz concludes that on balance improvements in health status have a positive and independent effect on earnings. Higher incomes in turn will affect the ability of households to invest in the future health of their members.

3. Another effect of health on productivity runs via *infant and child mortality.* High infant and child mortality leads to *replacement fertility.* This involves a

---

[9] In econometric terminology, health is a so-called endogenous variable. If one does not control for endogeneity using instrumental variables, the effects of health on economic growth will tend to be overestimated.

decrease in the productive potential of women during pregnancy and the period of breastfeeding.

4. *Choice of less productive activities*, requiring less energy and effort. Illness and malnutrition may force people to choose less productive work and lower incomes (Popkin, 1978).

The so-called *efficiency wage theory* can also be applied to the relationships between earnings health and productivity in a developing country context (Bardhan, 1993; Leibenstein, 1957; Keyzer, 1993). The efficiency wage theory states that earnings contribute to workers' productivity, as a result of which wages will be set above the minimum market clearing wage level. In a labour-surplus developing economy the market-determined wage rate may be too low to guarantee sufficient food, nutrition and health, so that the labour productivity of workers is undermined. Thus it may be economically efficient to set minimum wages above free market rates.

Labour productivity is especially important for households that depend on their own labour for their livelihood. Illness leads to reduced production in subsistence agriculture (Chambers, 1982; De Kadt and Lipton, 1988), lower revenues for the self-employed and lower wage incomes for labourers. It is not hard to imagine the disastrous effects of serious illness on the life chances of a household trying to survive at subsistence level.

At the macro-level, the focus is on the relationships between the state of health of a population and aggregate growth and productivity indicators. The following direct and indirect relationships can be distinguished:

1. *Health improvements result in declining child mortality and increasing life expectancy.* In the early stages of the demographic transition (before the population starts to age) this results in an increase in labour supply and a reduction in the dependency ratio. In East Asia this has contributed to accelerated growth of income per capita. Fogel (1986) estimated that 30 per cent of per capita growth since 1780 in Western countries was due to improvements in health and nutritional status. These mechanisms, however, only operate if a dynamic economy is also able to provide paid employment for the increased supply of labour (WHO, 1999, Chapter 2).

2. Conversely, high child mortality and a low life expectancy can result in *reductions in total labour supply.* A short life expectancy implies that the number of years a worker can be active is reduced (United Nations, 1984: 4; WHO, 1999). In the light of widespread underutilisation of labour in many developing countries this does not inevitably lead to reduced growth of production. However, if mortality is highly concentrated in certain occupational groups, there can be negative effects on production. For instance, this is the case with HIV/AIDS, which primarily affects young adults with relatively high schooling.

3. *Low life expectancy is also not conducive to future-oriented attitudes.* Increases in life expectancy make for higher rates of collective saving and investment.

4. *Illness may lead to a decrease in learning potential.* As a result, investments in education and human capital become less attractive. Improvements in infant health and nutrition directly increase the benefits of education (Glewwe and Miguel, 2008; Mayer, 2001). Conversely, investment in education may lead to higher productivity of investment in healthcare (Mushkin, 1962). Schultz (2010: 4819) concludes that early health shocks are associated with decreased cognitive scores, lower occupational status

and earnings and increased adult morbidity. Thus one should expect that improved infant and child health will affect the productive potential of the workforce after a lag of several decades.

5. *The prevalence of diseases such as onchoceriasis* may make it impossible or unattractive to open up certain fertile areas for agriculture. Eradication of such diseases can lead to improvements in productive potential in the very short term (Hardiman and Midgley, 1982; WHO, 1999).

The role of health in economic growth is highly contested. On the one hand, there are high claims made for the positive role of health. Thus, Fogel claims that about one-third of economic growth in England in the past 200 years is due to improvements in nutrition and health (Fogel, 1986, 1994, 1997). Mayer (2001) summarises the literature on this topic and concludes that the percentage of total growth attributed to the various health variables lies between 26 and 40 per cent. On the other hand, Acemoglu and Johnson (2006) sound a cautionary note. Using instrumental variables for increases in life expectancy, they conclude that the instrumented increases in life expectancy do not account for the levels or growth rates of GDP per capita since the Second World War. Acemoglu and Johnson argue that it is not so much poor health that is a root cause of poverty, but poor institutional arrangements (Acemoglu *et al.*, 2001, see Chapter 12 for a further discussion).

In the debates surrounding the Millennium Development Goals (MDGs), it is often argued that investing in health will have an immediate positive feedback into the process of economic development, through improvements in human capital. On the basis of the literature reviewed in this chapter, we would conclude that this is overoptimistic. Positive feedbacks do exist, but they are far from automatic, simple and direct. They depend on many other complementary factors, the effects of improved health may only emerge after decades and one should be aware of the circular relationships between health and economic development.

6.4   Healthcare policy

In building healthcare systems after the Second World War, many developing countries initially copied Western medical institutions. Attention and resources were heavily invested in educating qualified doctors and specialists and in the realisation of a system of medical faculties, hospitals and curative medicine. The attitude towards native, traditional medicine was negative; it was considered non-scientific (Hardiman and Midgley, 1982; Mosley, 1983). Most hospitals were located in national and provincial capitals and were insufficiently accessible to the rural population and to some extent also to the inhabitants of urban slums. Major urban hospitals and clinics received around two-thirds of the government health budget, while serving just 10 to 20 per cent of the population (WHO, 2000). In addition, there were 'vertical' campaigns – outside the hospital system – against particular diseases, e.g. malaria, river blindness, TBC and whooping cough (Netherlands Development Cooperation, 1988). These campaigns focused on combating the vectors of diseases and on preventive vaccination. Many of these campaigns were quite successful in the short term. But they were initially not integrated sufficiently into healthcare policy as a whole.

There are several objections to a predominantly curative approach to medicine. First, there is too much emphasis on the treatment of diseases (curative medicine) rather than on their prevention. As illustrated by Mosley's model, medical treatment is just one of the many factors influencing disease and death. A second objection is the fact that medical facilities are both expensive and inaccessible to large segments of the population. Medical facilities are heavily concentrated in big cities. Well-trained doctors are seldom willing to work in remote rural areas. Even in urban areas, medical services tend to be restricted to the more well-to-do sections of society. Paradoxically, there is also an outflow of well-trained doctors and medical specialists to rich countries. Many doctors trained in developing countries are unable or unwilling to find positions in their own country and look for jobs in the affluent countries.

In the course of the 1970s there was increasing criticism of the health strategies pursued up until then. At a landmark international conference in Alma Ata in 1978, a plea was made for a system of *primary healthcare*. At this conference it was stated that health is a basic human right and that healthcare ought to be accessible, affordable, and socially relevant (WHO, 1978).

In the Alma Ata resolutions primary healthcare is interpreted in a very broad sense – and rightly so, in the light of the theories discussed in section 6.2. It includes health education and information, provision of adequate food supplies and nutritional supplements such as school milk, provision of clean water, measures to promote hygiene (sanitation), healthcare for mothers and their children, information about birth control, vaccination against infectious diseases, prevention and control of endemic diseases like malaria, treatment of diseases, adequate supply of medicines, and the promotion of mental health (WHO, 1978: 24).

Furthermore, the primary healthcare approach emphasises the reallocation of medical funds to improve the accessibility of medical services. It advocates replacing investments in costly hospitals and medical specialists by investments in cheaper local healthcare centres and simply trained paramedic personnel. Healthcare policy is seen in relation with other aspects of socio-economic policy. Where the benefits of economic development are distributed more equally, the chances of improving primary healthcare are greater.

Another important aspect is the participation of the local population in the preparation and execution of healthcare policies. Thus healthcare workers recruited from the local population will function more effectively. Healthcare facilities supported and monitored by the local population will tend to be more effective than facilities administered from some inaccessible bureaucratic centre.

For the social relevance and acceptance of primary healthcare, it is seen as important that health services are adapted to the local culture. Traditional medicine should not simply be eradicated or devalued. It should be merged with newer medical insights. Many people consult both traditional and modern healers. It pays to train traditional healers in order to narrow the gap between various medical approaches. For example, retraining programmes for traditional midwives have been quite successful. On the other hand, unquestioning acceptance of traditional values may also involve the acceptance of female circumcision or entrenched gender disparities (e.g. Lawn *et al.*, 2008).

The Alma Ata conference has been extremely influential. In a series of resolutions of international organisations, the recommendations made have been adopted. National authorities have been urged to implement them. In 1979, the United Nations Assembly endorsed the Alma Ata recommendations. In 1981 the WHO adopted the *Global Strategy for Health for All by the Year 2000* (WHO, 1981). Moreover, the WHO makes use of indicators to monitor the degree to which authorities meet their commitments with respect to health policy (see WHO, 1987, 1993, 2000, 2008b). The commitment to the Alma Ata goals has been reaffirmed in *Health for All in the 21st century*, adopted by the World Health Assembly in May 1998 (see www.who.int/trade/glossary/story039/en/), and in a more restricted sense by the MDGs, which include three specific health-related objectives for child survival (MDG 4), maternal health (MDG 5) and HIV, TBC and malaria (MDG 6). The *World Health Report 2008*, entitled *Primary Healthcare: Now More Than Ever* (WHO, 2008b), revisited and reaffirmed the Alma Ata goals in the light of changed circumstances, new challenges and lessons from past experiences.

In detailed evaluations published in 1987, 1993 and in the subsequent editions of the *World Health Report* (e.g. WHO, 1998, 1999, 2008b, 2010), the WHO has monitored the degree to which the objectives of the *Global Strategy for Health for All by the Year 2000* were being realised. As shown in Tables 6.1, 6.2 and 6.3, there have indeed been substantial declines in infant and child mortality and increases in life expectancy – especially in Asia and Latin America.

The WHO monitoring reports document slow improvements in the percentage of populations covered by elements of primary healthcare and in the commitment of governments to primary healthcare objectives. The availability of safe drinking and sanitary facilities (excreta disposal, waste treatment, sewer systems and so forth) has improved. In 2000, 1.1 billion people still lacked access to clean water supplies and 2.4 billion lived without adequate sanitation (WHO, 2004). By 2008, the number of people without access to improved water sources had dropped to 0.87 billion people (13 per cent of global population against 23 per cent in 1990) (WHO, 2011). The vaccination of children against six targeted diseases (diphtheria, tetanus, measles, poliomyelitis, TBC and whooping cough) has clearly improved. There have been noticeable expansions of local community health services. The numbers of health workers, health volunteers and trained traditional midwives has increased. In some countries there is even an oversupply of medical personnel.

On the other hand, progress has been uneven. In the 1980s, the economic crisis and cuts in government expenditures resulting from the structural adjustment programmes advocated by the World Bank and the IMF affected healthcare and education budgets negatively (Cornia, 1984). Whatever doubts one may have concerning the blessings of economic growth, it is obvious that economic stagnation had deeply unfavourable effects on provisions for healthcare and for the state of health, in particularly in Africa. In many post-communist societies, universally accessible collective healthcare systems were dismantled. For instance, China has dismantled and partially privatised its rural primary healthcare system.

After cutbacks in health expenditures during the years of structural adjustment in the 1980s, governments started re-engaging in health in the late 1990s. Global expenditures on health have since expanded substantially. In 2005, public expenditure on health ranged from just under 2 per cent of GDP in the poorest countries to 6.6 per cent in the advanced economies, with the middle-income economies spending between 2.5 and 3.5 per cent of GDP. Private expenditures on health are often even higher than public expenditures (WHO, 2008b, Figure 5.1). Global health expenditures have been increasing more rapidly than

GDP, raising their share in global GDP from 8 to 8.6 per cent between 2000 and 2005 (WHO, 2008b). Also we have seen the entry of large private donors such as the Gates Foundation into the health field.

In spite of progress, the Alma Ata goals of universal access to affordable basic healthcare have not been fully realised (Lane *et al.*, 2008; WHO, 1999, 2008b, 2010). There are still significant problems. In 2011, there were 6.9 million deaths of children under five (UNICEF, 2011). Most of these deaths were preventable. Diarrhoea, acute respiratory infections, undernourishment, and vaccination preventable diseases such as measles are still the most important causes of death for infants and children (UNICEF, 2012; WHO, 1998). In 2010 the probability of dying before the age of five in developing countries was still 72 out of 1,000 births.

Though the percentage-wise availability of elements of primary healthcare has improved, this does not mean that coordinated systems of primary healthcare have been developed. Specialised vertical interventions for specific diseases such as AIDS, river blindness, or malaria are not well integrated into the overall healthcare system. The command and control approach to disease control, characteristic of vertical interventions, is focused on short-term results and is threatening to fragment overall health service delivery. One the other hand, primary healthcare itself is not sufficiently integrated into a wider healthcare system, including curative healthcare facilities (WHO, 2008b). Primary healthcare should be a hub from which patients are guided through the health system, not a stand-alone isolated facility.

Increasing reliance of out-of-pocket payments for healthcare services threatens to plunge millions of poor households into poverty (WHO, 2010). Also, due to population growth the absolute numbers of people without access to healthcare facilities are increasing, rather than decreasing. Though there is progress in access to clean water supplies the situation is worse with regard to sanitation. In 2008, 2.6 billion people still lacked access to improved sanitation facilities and 1.1 billion did not have access to toilets or sanitation facilities of any kind (WHO, 2011).

There is a continued outflow of highly skilled medical personnel to more developed countries. There is a serious maldistribution of health personnel and health resources. It is still exceedingly difficult to get well-qualified doctors to work in rural areas. Semi-skilled medical personnel (community health workers, village counsellors, traditional healers) are paid poorly, and their motivation is often minimal. Moreover, expectations with respect to briefly trained paramedics were unrealistically high (Netherlands Development Cooperation, 1988).

The ideals of community participation in and democratic control of health services have been insufficiently realised (WHO, 2008b). Local power structures frequently stand in the way of real community participation (Mosley, 1983). The organisation of medical systems is still highly centralised and hierarchical. The efficiency of medical systems is low. The *World Health Report* 2010 (WHO, 2010) argues that efficiency increases alone could reduce waste in the health system by 20 to 40 per cent. The *broad* concept of primary healthcare – in which healthcare is integrated into overall economic and social development policy – is more rhetoric than reality. In so far as primary healthcare services have been established, they remain restricted to medical facilities and services in the *narrow* sense. Even today insufficient attention is being paid to preventive healthcare and early detection of diseases. Health services for poor and marginalised groups are often highly fragmented and severely under-resourced, while development aid often adds to further fragmentation (WHO, 2008b).

In addition to the problems mentioned above, health systems in developing countries are challenged by the emergence of new infectious diseases such as HIV/AIDS and avian flu and the re-emergence of old ones such as TBC, pneumonia and malaria, which are becoming drug resistant. The pattern of diseases in developing countries is changing, in part due to the success in reducing child mortality. There is a far greater prevalence of cancer, CVDs, degenerative diseases and mental health problems, all of which are much more difficult and costly to tackle than infectious diseases.

In recent years, important new elements have emerged in the thinking about healthcare policy (WHO, 2000, 2008b, 2010). These can be summarised in three terms: *effectiveness*, *new universalism* and the *balance between public and private efforts*.

Effectiveness

The importance of primary healthcare is still central to policy thinking and has been reaffirmed in recent publications (particularly WHO, 2008b). But the new emphasis is on making healthcare systems more effective. *Effectiveness* implies trying to target diseases with the most negative impacts on health and welfare. It also involves paying increased attention to people's demand for health. In earlier healthcare policy, funds were channelled to suppliers of healthcare, based on assumptions about people's needs. Presumed needs may not reflect real demands. Effectiveness requires service delivery reforms focusing on people's needs and expectations. Further, one needs to go beyond the older polarity of thinking in terms of an opposition between primary healthcare and curative health facilities. Primary healthcare needs to be integrated into a broader district healthcare system, which includes rural and urban healthcare facilities (Lawn *et al.*, 2008).

New universalism

The emphasis on effectiveness is mirrored in the emergence of new indicators trying to measure the burden of disease, such as the DALYs discussed in section 6.1.1 of this chapter (Murray and Lopez, 1996). Older ideals of providing everything medically useful to the whole population are being abandoned as unrealistic. Health policy should try to identify diseases that account for large, avoidable burdens of ill health. On the other hand, it should try to identify health and nutrition interventions that have the largest impacts at the lowest cost. This results in a cost-effective package of basic or essential interventions, which should be available for everybody. This *new universalism* contrasts with policies focusing only on the poor and unrealistic older ideals of providing total medical care for everybody (WHO, 2000, Chapter 1). However, it is a severe misconception that primary healthcare should focus only on a few 'priority diseases'. Primary healthcare should continue to address a wide range of health problems.

Balance between private and public healthcare provision

A third element of the new policy debate refers to finding an appropriate *balance between private and public healthcare provision*. Berman (1998) argues that thinking about healthcare systems in the past has overwhelmingly focused on government policies. In fact, even in a country with a statist tradition such as India, private expenditures account for more than

75 per cent of total health expenditures in 2005 (WHO, 2008b, Figure 5.1). Government expenditure accounts for a modest proportion of health expenditure except in the case of preventive primary healthcare, where government accounts for 50 per cent. Private expenditures also combine and mix expenditures on 'traditional medicine' and modern 'allopathic' medicine in an interesting fashion. Berman calls for a new balance between private and public provision of medicine. Governments should not try to replace private by public provision but should focus on regulation, health standards, access to healthcare and combating abuses. This debate is still continuing. Proponents of public provision point to the danger that privatised medicine primarily benefits those that can pay. They also point to the effectiveness of collective-based health insurance systems. Health insurance systems do not necessarily have to be public. They can be financed for a large part by private contributions. But they do not involve out-of-pocket payments for health services. In the *World Health Report 2010*, out-of-pocket payments for medical treatment are seen as one of the most important obstacles to universal access to healthcare. In some countries 11 per cent of the population suffers severe financial hardship and 5 per cent are pushed into poverty due to out-of-pocket payments. Globally 150 million people suffer financial hardship and 100 million are pushed below the poverty line (WHO, 2010). In recent years, a hands-off *laissez-faire* approach to governance of healthcare has allowed unregulated commercialisation of healthcare to flourish, with negative results. Thus there is a dual challenge for healthcare reform to reduce disproportionate reliance on command and control methods of management on the one hand, and avoid a *laissez-faire* disengagement of the state on the other.

Questions for review

1. What are the characteristics of the epidemiological transition? Do the patterns of disease and health change in the same way in all societies, in the course of development?
2. Discuss the relationships between standards of living and nutrition on the one hand and life expectation and child mortality on the other.
3. Do advances in medical technology provide an adequate explanation of the overall decline in death rates and increases in life expectation in developing countries?
4. What is the malnutrition-infection syndrome? How can Mosley's model of this syndrome be used to explain how relatively mild diseases such as diarrhoea can result in death?
5. Why is education considered to be an important factor in combating child mortality?
6. What are the most important differences between preventive healthcare and curative healthcare in the context of developing countries?
7. Discuss some of the drawbacks of morbidity indicators.
8. To what extent do investments in health contribute to economic growth?
9. Discuss and evaluate new directions in thinking about health policy.
10. What are the effects of out-of pocket-payments for medical treatment?
11. Explain the concept of superior health achiever. What are the lessons one can derive from the existence of superior and inferior health achievers?
12. To what extent can cultural factors explain the differences between superior health achievers and inferior health achievers, in the light of the available empirical information?

Further reading

Data on indicators such as life expectancy and mortality can be found in the *Population Data Base* of the United Nations Population Division, http://esa.un.org/unpd/wpp/index.htm. Data on health, morbidity and causes of death can be found in WHO publications such as *World Health Statistics 2011* (WHO, 2011) and *The Global Burden of Disease. 2004 Update* (WHO, 2008a), as well as in the WHO *Global Health Observatory Data Repository*, which provides access to over fifty datasets on health topics. Every year the WHO publishes the *World Health Report* (*WHR*), which has an annex with data on health indicators. Two interesting editions of the report are *Life in the 21st Century – A Vision for All* (1998) and *Health Systems Financing: The Path to Universal Coverage* (2010). The World health reports can be downloaded from the WHO website: www.who.int/publications/en/. Information about the spread of HIV/AIDS can be found in the *World AIDS Day Report 2011. How to Get to Zero: Faster, Smarter, Better*, published by the Joint United Nations Programme on HIV/AIDS (UNAIDS, 2011) and in *Together We Will End AIDS* (UNAIDS, 2012). The programme maintains a special website on HIV/AIDS: www.unaids.org/en/. Statistical data on HIV/AIDS are included in the *Global Health Observatory Data Repository*.

McKeown has written several books arguing the case for the importance of nutrition in health. These include *The Role of Medicine* (1979) and *The Origins of Human Disease* (1988). Another important contribution about nutrition is R.W. Fogel's book, *The Escape from Hunger and Premature Death, 1700–2100* (2004). Two publications by Preston focus on the role of advances in medical technology: *Mortality Patterns in National Populations* (1976) and an article entitled 'The Changing Relation between Mortality and Level of Economic Development' (1975), in *Population Studies*. Preston's analysis has been updated by Strauss and Thomas, in their article 'Health over the Life Course' (2008). Mosley's influential model of the determinants of child mortality is summarised in 'Biological and Socio-Economic Determinants of Child Survival: A Proximate Determinants Framework Integrating Fertility and Mortality Variables' (1985a). An interesting attempt at quantitative synthesis of the different theories and approaches is presented in the 1999 edition of the *WHR*, *Making a Difference* (WHO, 1999). For the epidemiological transition, two classic articles are Omran's 'The Epidemiological Transition: A Theory of the Epidemiology of Population Change' (1971) and Frederikson's 'Feedbacks in Economic and Demographic Transition' (1969).

For a discussion of disability adjusted life years (DALYs), see Murray and Lopez, *The Global Burden of Disease: A Comprehensive Assessment of Mortality and Disability from Diseases, Injuries and Risk Factors in 1990 and Projected to 2020* (1996), Murray and Acharya, 'Understanding DALYs' (1997), in *Journal of Health Economics* and Mathers *et al.*, 'The Burden of Disease and Mortality by Condition: Data, Methods and Results for 2001' (2006).

In a stimulating article 'Routes to Low Mortality in Poor Countries' (1986), in the *Population and Development Review*, Caldwell shows how healthcare policy can affect the health achievements of countries. This article has been updated by Kuhn in 'Routes to Low Mortality in poor Countries Revisited' (2010). The vast literature on the relationships between health and economic development is reviewed in an article by Strauss and Thomas, 'Health, Nutrition and Economic Development' (1998), in the *Journal of Economic Literature*, and more recently by Schultz in an article, 'Population and Health Policies' (2010), in Volume 5 of Rodrik and

Rosenzweig (eds.) *Handbook of Development Economics*. In 'Disease and Development in Historical Perspective' (2003), Acemoglu, Johnson and Robinson question the relationship between investments in health and economic growth.

For a discussion of primary healthcare, see Mosley 'Will Primary Healthcare Reduce Infant and Child Mortality? A Critique of Some Current Strategies, with Special Reference to Africa and Asia' (1985b) and the WHO Report, 'Primary Health Care: Report of the International Conference on Primary Health Care' (1978). This report was the first of a long series of reports in the *Health for All Series* published by the WHO. More recently, there have been interesting reassessments of primary healthcare approaches in an article by Lawn *et al.*, 'Ama-Ata 30 Years on: Revolutionary, Relevant and Time to Revitalise' (2008), in *The Lancet*, and in the *WHR 2008*, *Primary Healthcare: Now More than Ever* (WHO, 2008b).

7 Education and development

Like health, education is both an end and a means. It is one of the basic human rights and a developmental goal in its own right. But, education also contributes to the realisation of other important developmental goals (UNESCO, 2002c). The functions and tasks generally ascribed to education include the following:

1. *Promotion of economic growth and development. Investment in the physical capital stock is not sufficient for economic development. Investment in 'human capital' is also required.*
2. *Modernisation of attitudes and mentalities in society.*
3. *Contribution to important developmental goals such as increased life expectancy, improved health and reduced fertility. Education of mothers, in particular, makes important contributions to better health of children and reductions in fertility. These are among the important non-economic benefits of education. These relationships have been discussed in Chapters 5 and 6 on population and health.*
4. *Political socialisation, promotion of a sense of civic responsibility, contributing to national integration and national political consciousness in developing countries.*
5. *Reduction of social and gender inequality and increasing social mobility.*
6. *Contribution to personal growth, development and emancipation.*

In the context of the framework of proximate, intermediate and ultimate causality, these relationships are summarised in Figure 7.1.

Immediately after the Second World War, expectations concerning the role of education in development were high. Expansion and improvement of education were generally considered as essential to development. Governments in developing countries were prepared to invest heavily in education. Families saw education as the main way to improve their children's chances in life. International organisations were eager to provide financial and technical support for the construction of new educational systems.

However, since the 1970s, optimism about the contributions of education has been shaken. Not all investment in education proved beneficial to development. Resources were often insufficient and the quality of education was disappointing. Nevertheless, education remains high on the policy agenda. One of the MDGs was to achieve universal access to primary education by 2015.

This chapter presents a survey of important debates and theories concerning the role of education in development (section 7.1). It will also discuss the educational performance of developing countries in the post-war period (sections 7.2 and 7.3). Important problems and bottlenecks in education are the subject of section 7.4. Throughout the chapter, special attention will be paid to the role of education in the process of economic growth and development.

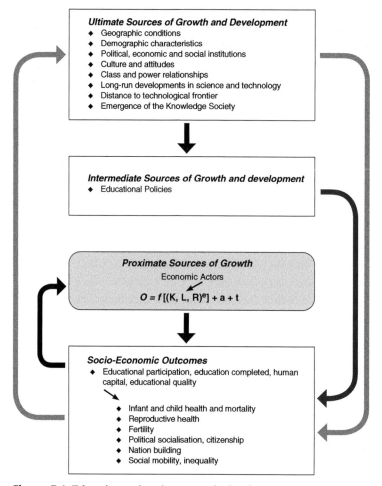

Figure 7.1 Education and socio-economic development

7.1   Theories of the contribution of education to economic development

7.1.1   'Human capital' theory

The notion of education as an investment in economic growth arose in the late 1950s in the USA. Economists such as Abramovitz, Solow, and Denison found that the growth of national product in economically advanced countries could not be adequately explained by the growth of the physical capital stock and the growth of the labour force. Considerable part of growth remained unaccounted for (Abramovitz, 1989a; Denison, 1962, 1967; Kendrick, 1961; Solow, 1957). These authors adjusted the growth of the labour force for increases in labour quality due to education. In addition to the growth in physical capital stock, the increase in human capital turned out to be of great importance as well. As people became more and more educated, developed more skills, and improved their reading and writing abilities, it was argued they became more productive and they were better able to handle existing and new production techniques. The inclusion of human capital in growth accounting studies substantially reduced the unexplained residual in growth (Maddison, 1987; Pilat, 1994; Timmer, 2000).

Human capital theory developed this line of thought further, particularly at a micro-level (Becker, 1964; Blaug, 1972, 1976, 1990; Mincer, 1970, 1974; Schultz, 1961, 1971, 1988). The empirical foundation for this theory was the close relationship observed in many societies between the number of years of education received and a person's income level. The essence of human capital theory was the notion that individuals (supported by their parents) were willing to invest in their own education so that they would be able to earn a higher income in the future. These investments consisted of educational expenses and income forgone due to delayed entry into the labour market. The theoretical link between investment in education and the level of income was labour productivity – just as in the macro-approach. Increasing the level of schooling would lead to higher labour productivity. In line with neoclassical economic theory, greater labour productivity would result in higher incomes for the categories of employees concerned.[1]

Not only individuals would benefit from investment in education. Society as a whole would also benefit from an increasing supply of better-educated workers and citizens. *External effects* of education included more rapid technological change, productivity spill-overs, lower crime rates, higher civic participation, reduced fertility and higher infant health (e.g. Lloyd *et al.*, 2000; Patrinos and Psacharopoulos, 2011). Such positive external effects are a justification for public subsidies to education. In almost every country in the world a considerable part of the cost of education is subsidised by the government.

In the mid 1980s and 1990s, these ideas resurfaced in macro-economics in the context of 'endogenous growth theory' (Barro, 1991; Lucas, 1988; Romer, 1986, see also Chapter 3, section 3.4.5). Endogenous growth theory suggests that investments in technological change, R&D, physical and human capital are subject to increasing returns, due to spillover effects through which firms profit from each others' investments. The more a country has previously invested in technology and in human and physical capital, the more it will profit from additional investment. Such theories thus offer an explanation of increasing divergence of economic performance in the world economy.

Another version of human capital theory is contained in the notion of 'conditional convergence' (Barro, 1991; Mankiw, Romer and Weil, 1992; Wolff and Gittleman, 1993). Given characteristics such as a country's initial investment rate and educational attainment, countries will tend to converge to common productivity levels and growth rates, with countries with lower initial productivity growing more rapidly and countries with higher productivity growing more slowly. However, countries in different convergence groups do

---

[1] According to neoclassical economic theory, employers will continue to attract labour as long as the marginal returns of additional workers are higher than their gross wages. For the last worker employed, the marginal costs will be equal to the wage rate.

not converge on each other. Countries with higher initial levels of education will tend to converge to higher growth rates and levels.

As usual, the econometric literature on the impact of education on growth is not unanimous. Some studies (such as Benhabib and Spiegel, 1994; Easterly, 2001a; Pritchett, 2001, 2006) do not find significant effects of education. But most recent studies tend to confirm the importance of education as one of the factors with a positive influence on growth, in both advanced and developing economies (for reviews see De la Fuente and Doménech, 2006; Hanushek and Wößmann, 2008; Krueger and Lindahl, 2001; Patrinos and Psacharopoulos, 2011). The reasons why it is hard to make unambiguous statements about the impact of education as a factor on its own will be elaborated on below. But this does not detract from the importance of education.

Though human capital theory was initially developed in the USA and Europe, it was soon applied to developing countries as well. The idea of furthering development by means of education had already achieved considerable popularity, well before the rise of this theory (Foster, 1965a; Krieger, 1988). Many members of the new elites in developing countries had received their education during the colonial period. It was often via education that they had been exposed to ideas about human rights, nationalism and development. At the same time, colonial educational systems had offered them insufficient opportunities to develop their talents. Independence provided an opportunity for rapid improvements in access to education. Education was also regarded as a modernising force. It would help detach people from traditional cultural influences and social relationships that were seen as obstacles to modernisation.

Human capital theory – in both its micro-economic and its macro-economic guise – provided an additional justification for increased efforts in the field of education. National and international policy makers embraced the theory wholeheartedly.

Human capital theory provides a framework for the systematic evaluation of the costs and benefits of different kinds of education for households. The costs include:

1. School fees, costs of books, teaching materials, school uniforms and so forth.
2. Income forgone while receiving an education. One of the major costs of formal education is that the entry of a person to the labour market is delayed for years. During this period, the individual or the household not only has to bear the costs of education, but also loses the income which could have been earned in this period.

The benefits consist of the difference between the lifetime income of an individual with a given amount of education and the lifetime income he would receive if he had not had this education. On the basis of the discounted total costs and benefits one can calculate the average annual return on an educational investment, the so-called *rate of return*. In addition to the private rates of return, social rates of return can be calculated for society as a whole. Here the benefits include the whole range of positive economic and social external effects of education for society. The social costs refer to the total costs of education including public subsidies and the production forgone by society because individuals do not produce while being educated.

One of the interesting research findings was the fact that in developing countries the rate of return on investment in education was higher than the rate of return on investment in physical capital (Psacharopoulos, 1985; Psacharopoulos and Patrinos, 2002). The rates of return in developing countries were substantially higher than those in HICs. The highest rates were found in the poorest countries. Another interesting finding was that the rates of return for primary education were consistently much higher than those for secondary and higher education (Blaug, 1976; Psacharopoulos, 1985; Psacharopoulos and Patrinos, 2002; Schultz, 1988). On these grounds developing countries should give higher priority to investment in primary education. In recent years, this accepted wisdom has been challenged. A case has been made for a reorientation of education investment to higher education in the context of the rise of the knowledge society (see further section 7.4.7).

Since governments usually bear the greater part of the costs of education, individual calculations of costs and benefits will differ substantially from social calculations of costs and benefits. Without exception, individual rates of return are higher than social rates of return (Coombs, 1985).[2] This is one of the factors which has contributed to the explosive growth in the demand for secondary and higher education in developing countries.

Prior to a discussion of criticisms of human capital theory, the question should be raised why investment in human capital (education) should lead to higher productivity and economic development. The possible answers to this question are summarised in Box 7.1.

BOX 7.1 : Education, productivity and economic development

1. **Professional skills**. Education teaches specific professional skills required for professional practice (for mechanics, plumbers, nurses, or doctors).
2. **The three Rs**. Workers who have mastered the three Rs – reading, writing and arithmetic – are more productive than those who have not. Literate employees are able to read instructions, keep records, make calculations and so on.
3. **Commercial and financial aptitudes**. Education and literacy contribute to the development of commercial and financial activities. These activities require people who can work as book-keepers, clerks, who can write letters, file papers, or manipulate numbers. Literate people are more likely to utilise paper money, hold bank accounts and use other financial instruments. Literacy is a prerequisite for the development of financial systems and it influences the supply of savings (Sandberg, 1982).
4. **Change in attitudes**. Education and literacy lead to changed attitudes, which indirectly result in higher productivity (Anderson and Bowman, 1976). For example, increased literacy and education changes peoples' perceptions of the alternatives open to them.
5. **Geographic and occupational mobility**. Education and literacy promote geographic and occupational mobility. People will start becoming aware of geographic locations or occupations, where the earnings and opportunities are better than in their present jobs. (Easterlin, 1981; Sandberg, 1982). Job and labour markets will function better. This contributes to a more efficient allocation of productive resources and thus to increases in productivity. Some authors even consider the loosening of age-old ties to village or ancestral occupation as a prerequisite for modernisation. Of course, increased mobility also has drawbacks, such as unrestricted migration to urban areas.

[2] The comparison between social and private rates of return is biased because social costs can be measured, while external effects are usually not measured (Psacharopoulos and Patrinos, 2002).

6. **Functioning of product markets**. For market mechanisms to function, people have to be able to acquire information about prices, the quality of goods and services, market demand and to be able to orient themselves among alternatives. Education contributes to this. Effectively functioning product markets in turn contribute to the more efficient allocation of productive resources.

7. **Openness to innovation**. Technological development proceeds at an ever-faster pace. The modern knowledge society needs well-educated employees to understand and apply the continuous flow of new production techniques. A more educated population is likely to be more innovative, which speeds the adoption of new technology (Nelson and Phelps, 1966). This applies not in the least to agriculture where new techniques can lead to dramatic increases in productivity (Schultz, 1988).[3]

8. **Dissemination of new ideas and technologies**. In general, literacy has positive effects on the dissemination of new ideas and technologies in a society.

9. **The rate of technological change**. In modern society the rate of technological development itself depends on continued investment in education, research and development (Nelson, 1981). A sufficient supply of scientific and technical personnel is needed to adapt existing technologies from abroad and develop new ones. Highly trained engineers and scientists are essential for R&D (Pavitt, 1980; World Bank, 2002b). Technological sophistication of management is needed to make decisions about allocation of resources for R&D and acquisition of technology.

7.1.2   Criticisms of human capital theory

Though highly influential, human capital theory has also been severely criticised (Blaug, 1976, 1985). The basic points of criticism are summarised in Box 7.2.

7.1.3   Screening theory

The most radical version of preceding criticisms of human capital theory is contained in *screening theory* (Berg, 1970; Blaug, 1985; Dore, 1976; Spence, 1973). This theory argues that education in itself does not contribute to a person's productivity. The knowledge and skills acquired in educational institutions are not applied in one's later career. The specific skills required in a profession are learned on the job rather than at school.

Why then are higher-educated employees paid more than less well-educated employees? Screening theory states that employers find it hard to predict the future performance of job applicants. They use educational qualifications and diplomas as a screening system for ability, achievement motivation, social background and the right personality traits. Schooling is an indication of trainability itself. Actual training starts on the job when one starts working.

---

[3] This issue is nicely summed up in a quote from the Economist: 'What use is modern technology if a poor country's workers cannot read the instructions on a bag of fertiliser?' (Economist, 1996: 16).

. . . .

BOX 7.2 **Criticisms of human capital theory**

. . . .

- **Marginal productivity is difficult to measure**. The high correlation between education and personal income does not necessarily mean that education makes workers more productive. Nothing is more difficult to measure than marginal productivity (Blaug, 1990).

- **Difficulty in measuring costs and benefits**. We may have sufficient information on income inequality at a given moment in time. But it is very difficult to draw any conclusions from this concerning the distribution of *lifetime incomes*. Next, it is hard to estimate the income forgone while individuals are being educated. Finally, if we want to calculate the social rate of return of education, we will find the external effects of education difficult to estimate. With so many uncertainties, the whole notion of a cost-benefit analysis of educational investment becomes rather problematic.

- **The benefits of education are not merely economic**. Education also increases one's social status and may lead to greater work satisfaction.

- **Disregard of quality and type of education**. In most cost-benefit analyses of education, only the number of years of education is taken into account. The quality of education and the type of education (e.g. technical education, humanities) is disregarded.

- **Insufficient attention for the ability to pay**. The demand for education does not only depend on costs and benefits, but also on the ability to pay for education.

- **Importance of perceptions of costs and benefits**. It is not just the objective relation between costs and benefits that matters, but also the *perception* of this relation. If people believe that education will increase their opportunities, they are more likely to make sacrifices for it.

- **Innate abilities and family background may determine rewards**. Education in itself is not important. Individual innate talents and characteristics of the parental family are the crucial determinants of both one's future income and future income. Education merely translates these characteristics into diplomas. Education is rewarded because it is a signal of innate ability (Spence, 1973).

- **Education is not only investment, but also consumption**. Many people study because they find it enjoyable or intrinsically interesting. This makes it difficult to determine the direction causality. Education can be both cause and consequence of economic growth. The correlation between educational levels and growth may in part be driven by increases in the demand for education as countries and their inhabitants become richer (Bils and Klenow, 2000; Harbison and Myers, 1965).

Thus radical versions of the screening theory argue that education merely 'reproduces' social inequality from generation to generation (Williamson, 1979). The main function of education for the masses is to teach them discipline, respect for authority, punctuality, obedience, ability to cooperate and concentration (Bowles and Gintis, 1976). Education prepares labourers for inferior-level, routine tasks in productive organisations. People from higher social strata are prepared for top-level positions in the hierarchical structure. Their education develops personal qualities such as self-reliance, self-esteem, autonomy, flexibility, capacity to assume leadership roles, managerial qualities and initiative.

The screening theory suggests that much of education in developing countries is irrelevant. Expanding the educational system merely results in diploma inflation and a scramble for the highest diplomas (*credentialism*). The diploma is the ultimate goal. Students are not interested in the content of what is taught. On the labour market, people with higher diplomas displace people with lower educational qualifications without any improvement in productivity. For example, university graduates displace graduates of polytechnics; graduates of polytechnics displace workers with a secondary education. The latter in turn displace people with a primary education. This process is referred to as *bumping down*.

7.1.4 Criticisms of screening theory

Like human capital theory, screening theory is also open to criticism (Blaug, 1985; Hanushek and Wößmann, 2008):

1. If screening theory is valid and education does not contribute to productivity, it is hard to explain why self-employed people with a higher education usually have higher earnings than self-employed people with less education (Wolpin, 1977).
2. In screening theory, educational qualifications explain differences in initial earnings. In later stages of a career the relation between education and income should become weaker, as employers gain first-hand experience of an employee's productivity. In fact, however, the correlation between education and income persists throughout people's working lives.
3. If selection is the only real function of the educational system, one might as well use less laborious and less expensive methods of selection and recruitment. Psychological tests would serve just as well to identify the right personality traits. However, in practice, applicants are never selected exclusively on the basis of psychological tests.

7.1.5 An evaluation of the human capital debate

The debate between the proponents and critics of human capital theory is still very much open. In particular, the more extreme positions in the debate are based on faith and ideological conviction rather than on empirical evidence.

Since Émile Durkheim, sociologists have emphasised that one of the important functions of education is the transmission of values, standards, attitudes and knowledge to successive generations. In this sense, education has always had a conserving function and will tend to maintain existing structures of inequality. Yet, we also know that education may often lead to change. A well-known example is the colonial educational system, within which members of future nationalist elites received their education. They later rebelled against colonialism in the name of the very political and humanistic ideals transmitted by Western-style education. Education can also be an important means of upward social mobility. Groups with few chances of upward mobility within traditional societies were now offered opportunities to improve their positions by way of education.

It is an interesting empirical question which of these influences – the conserving or the change-oriented – predominated in different societies and historical periods. As we will argue below, the dynamic, change-oriented functions of education predominated in developing countries in the post-war period. Here, we would like to make a preliminary evaluation of the debate between advocates of the human capital theory and those of screening theory.

Screening theory – sometimes also referred to as signalling theory – has drawn our attention to several aspects of education that are also of major importance to developing countries. These are summarised in Box 7.3.

BOX 7.3 : Key elements of screening theory

- **Learning by doing**. On the job many employees do not use any of the cognitive knowledge they learned in school. For low-skilled workers, most skills needed in modern industries can be acquired within a few weeks. For high-skilled workers, their real training starts when they are hired by large modern firms. In this respect 'on-the-job training' and 'learning by doing' are of great importance.
- **Screening**. Screening is one of the social functions of education. Given insufficient information, it is plausible to conclude that educational qualifications serve as an important screening device for job applicants.
- **Diploma inflation**. Expanding the educational system does not always contribute to economic development. Especially the rapid expansion of secondary and higher education may lead to 'diploma inflation'. Of course, it remains perfectly rational for every individual to try to improve his or her life chances by gaining as many educational degrees as possible.
- **Standardised testing of educational performance**. Standardised testing may orient teachers and students towards the preparation for the tests and away from intrinsic learning.

The conclusion of screening theory that education adds 'nothing' to already existing personality traits and thus has no autonomous influence on productivity is not tenable. The most important contribution of education is indeed 'learning to learn'. Reading, writing and arithmetic are basic requirements for being able to learn later on in life.[4] At higher educational levels, learning to think analytically and evaluate information independently are important preconditions for future learning on the job. On-the-job training is possible in part thanks to the capacity to learn, which has been developed in the formal schooling system. Nelson argues that there is a lot about semi-conductor design or the production of chemicals

---

[4] Too much emphasis on the insignificance of cognitive skills may lead to the neglect of these essentials, in both developing countries and economically advanced countries.

that cannot be taught at school because the details are too specialised. These details can only be acquired in on-the-job courses, apprenticeships and training programmes, which are usually part of technology-transfer agreements. But, at various levels on-the-job training requires prior engineering, scientific and academic training (Nelson, 1981).

Evidently, social background and inherited talents also determine one's educational career and later income. However, inherited talent and high status are not sufficient for success in modern societies. It is the schooling system that translates such factors into qualities that are useful for society. An important review article by Hanusek and Wößmann (2008) suggests that the quality of education has an independent impact on earnings and performance, irrespective of innate ability. Education is more than a signalling device (Krueger and Lindahl, 2001). Focusing specifically on studies in developing countries Glewwe (1996, 2002) comes to the same conclusion. Cognitive skills learned at school increase wages and are direct determinants of productivity, irrespective of innate ability.

With regard to developing countries, one may even argue that education today is even more important than it used to be in the presently more advanced countries. The modern global economy is a knowledge economy. New production techniques in the industrial and agricultural sector require ever-more knowledge and understanding. The pace of technological development is increasing. Only a well-trained labour force can benefit from the opportunities of adopting modern technologies from abroad and adapting these to domestic production processes. Educational investment thus contributes to the building of technological capabilities of a country which are essential to achieve accelerated catch-up (Aubert, 2005; Evenson and Westphal, 1995; Hobsbawm, 1969; World Bank, 2002b).

Though much criticism of human capital theory is justified, we therefore conclude that it is worthwhile for developing countries to invest in further development of their educational systems.

7.1.6 Education as a necessary but not sufficient condition for development: thresholds and complementarities

Human capital theory takes neoclassical micro-economics as its point of departure and focuses on the costs and benefits of education in a country. An alternative approach is the historical and comparative study of the role of education and schooling in the different processes of economic development. Two important insights emerge from this literature. First, there are *threshold levels* of human capital and literacy which need to be reached before economic growth takes off with shorter or longer delays. Second, human capital only has significant effects on economic development if complementary factors such as capital investment, technology and growth enhancing institutions are in place.

In a classic study based on international comparisons of indicators of literacy and economic development, Bowman and Anderson (1963) conclude that economic development only starts when the level of literacy among the adult male population has reached at least 40 per cent. Analogous to Rostow's theory of the stages of economic growth (see Chapter 3) – which argues that modern economic growth will set in only if physical investment exceeds a certain threshold value – Bowman and Anderson argue that reaching a threshold level of literacy is a *necessary condition* for economic growth. Especially in European and North American history, the growth of human capital has been more important than has been hitherto recognised. Education, however, is not a *sufficient* condition for growth and development. Without investment in physical capital and the rise of institutions that provide positive incentives to productive efforts there will be no economic development.

Once the 40 per cent threshold has been reached further development of literacy has little impact, according to Bowman and Anderson. It is not until literacy exceeds the 70 per cent level, that it will have positive effects on further economic development.

As with human capital, an interesting debate developed around the Bowman and Anderson hypothesis (Tortella, 1990). The essential problem is how to determine the direction of causality empirically. It is indisputable that on average more affluent societies are also more literate and have more training per head of the population. However, this may be explained by the fact that people with higher incomes are willing to pay more for education than people at lower income levels (*reverse causality*). According to Schultz (1988), the income elasticity of education is 1.4. This means that if the national income rises by 1 per cent, expenditure for education goes up 1.4 per cent.

Some authors try to solve this problem by examining the relations between literacy at an earlier moment in time (A) and national income at a later moment in time (B). For Spain, Nuñez has estimated that the level of literacy affects provincial per capita income with a thirty-five-year lag (Nuñez, 1990). Sandberg (1982) even states that for European countries the degree of literacy in 1850 is the best predictor of national income in 1970. In the short run, however, there is no connection between literacy and economic growth.

For Sandberg, too, education is only one of the relevant factors in economic development. The volume of investment in physical capital is also of great importance. Sandberg argues that countries will benefit more from physical capital accumulation when their initial level of education is higher. There is a complementarity between human and physical capital. The currently affluent Scandinavian countries, Sweden and Finland, provide examples supporting this proposition. In the nineteenth century these countries were quite poor but at the same time they had high levels of literacy, which were the foundation for their later growth when they started to accumulate capital.

Japan can also be quoted as an example supporting Sandberg's theory (Hanley, 1990; Pilat, 1994). Around 1869 the Japanese were already highly educated. Since then Japan has continued to invest in education as part of its national development and modernisation strategy. The investment in physical capital, which started after the Meiji Revolution in 1869, enabled Japan to experience rapid economic growth from the late nineteenth century onwards, especially in the period 1950–70. In an excellent analysis of the Japanese catch-up experience, Godo and Hayami (2002) combine the notions of *complementarity* and *threshold*. Initially, the early increase in education had little impact on growth, because capital per worker was growing so slowly that there was little complementarity. After the Second World War, a threshold level of education had been reached and rapid capital accumulation combined with further advances in human capital to promote explosive growth and catch-up. Finally, the rapidly industrialising East and Southeast Asian countries such China, South Korea, Singapore and Taiwan also achieved high levels of literacy and education at a relatively early stage prior to their economic take-off (World Bank, 1993). The Bowman and Anderson notion of threshold levels of education has received further support in more recent economic research of authors such as Azariadis and Drazen (1990) and Benhabib and

Spiegel (2005). This strand of research is consistent with the notion of 'conditional convergence' discussed in Chapter 3, in which a high level of education is seen as one of the necessary conditions for catch-up (Mankiw, Romer and Weil, 1992).

Other authors object to the notion of education as a necessary condition for development. Mitch argues that the level of literacy is not as essential to agricultural and industrial development as Bowman and Sandberg suppose (Mitch, 1990). Like the critics of the human capital theory, Mitch argues that during the Industrial Revolution it was not important for the working masses to be able to read or write. Literacy only mattered for a limited number of clerks, engineers, book-keepers, managers and foremen. Before the twentieth century literacy did not play a major role in agricultural development either. The development of human capacities is important, but this does not always require a formal education. There are 'functional alternatives' such as working experience, 'on-the-job training' and 'learning by doing'.

It is also argued that in England and elsewhere the labour force was actually 'deskilled' in the course of the Industrial Revolution. Traditional craftsmanlike skills became obsolete due to the development of mass production (Nicholas, 1990; Thompson, 1963). The educational level of labourers remained unchanged at best. Nicholas, however, does acknowledge the fact that on the eve of the Industrial Revolution England had a high level of education. In an interesting attempt at synthesis, Sandberg argues that while education has been an important factor in the history of modern European development, there have always been alternatives to education (Sandberg, 1990). Russia, for example, had an extremely low level of education during the nineteenth century. In part it compensated for this by using highly capital-intensive methods of production, which reduced the need for skilled labour. In a like fashion, the increased role of government in the mobilisation of financial resources compensated for underdeveloped financial markets (Sandberg, 1982).

Authors such as Easterly (2001a) and Pritchett (2001, 2006) also voice their scepticism about the contributions of education in a developing country context. Basing themselves on modern econometric analysis, they find no systematic effects of education on economic development. Easterly, in particular, concludes that education will only have positive effects in conjunction with appropriate institutions.

One of the powerful arguments in this literature refers to the Sub-Saharan African experience, where impressive improvements in educational performance were not accompanied by economic growth between 1973 and 2000. An article by Pack and Paxson confronts precisely this puzzling question: why did African economies stagnate in spite of impressive advances in educational performance (Pack and Paxson, 2001)? They conclude that investment in education in itself does not promote economic growth. Education will only have major positive impacts if improved education is complemented by inflows of new capital goods and technology, which make use of the new skills acquired through education. If such inflows are not forthcoming there will be no learning through experience and people will quickly lose their skills.

This notion of the complementarity of human capital investment, physical capital accumulation, technological change and growth-promoting institutions is one of the key insights of much modern research on economic growth and technological change discussed in Chapters 3 and 4 (see e.g. Abramovitz, 1989b; Fagerberg et al., 2005; Godo and Hayami, 2002; Grier, 2002; Kim and Nelson, 2000; Nelson, 1996). Capital accumulation without complementary improvement of capabilities and knowledge will be wasted. Accumulation of human capital without capital accumulation or technological change will be useless. This reads very much like the conclusions arrived at by economic historians such as Sandberg.

However, there is one interesting area of disagreement. Sandberg and other economic historians argue that educational investment precedes other types of investment with long lags and may affect growth with great delay. This implies that even if educational improvement has not led to economic dynamics in Africa, it may still do so in the future if other complementary factors are forthcoming.

Reflecting on the previous debates, we arrive at the following conclusions:

1. Since the mid nineteenth century *education has become increasingly important*, as the scientific and technological basis of economic development became more prominent. In an earlier era, formal schooling may not have been of particular value for learning to master a technology. Now, for many technologies, education is virtually a prerequisite for high-level competence. Investment in education and technology since the late nineteenth century is considered one of the crucial factors in the rise of Germany and Japan as economic powers. Insufficient investment in education in England – particularly in technical and vocational training – is seen as contributing to the relative decline of the former economic leader.

2. In developing countries today *education is more important than in Western countries in the past*, because it increases the potential to adopt and adapt new technologies. The pace of international technological change is much higher than before. Developing countries have both the opportunity and the necessity to adopt technological innovations very rapidly in order to realise catch-up. Again, we conclude that investment in human capital remains one of the crucial ingredients of a successful development strategy for developing countries today.

3. There are *important complementarities between investment in human and physical capital*. Only when investments in one type of capital are matched by investments in the other will they have sustained positive effects on growth. There are also complementarities between educational investment and the institutional environment.

4. On the basis of the historical record, we would argue that there is not a single case of successful catch-up in the world economy since the last quarter of the nineteenth century, where *advances in educational levels did not precede subsequent economic growth*. Education is indeed one of the necessary conditions for economic development.

7.2 Indicators of educational development

Before discussing empirical developments in education in developing countries, the following section will provide a brief discussion of several well-known indicators of educational development (Coombs, 1985; UNESCO, 2000a).

7.2.1 Indicators of educational enrolment

The *gross enrolment ratio* is the ratio in a given year of the total enrolment at a given educational level (primary, secondary, or tertiary) and the total estimated population in the corresponding age bracket. It is a rather rough criterion, which does not take into account that the numerator includes children outside the relevant age category (e.g. pupils of secondary school age still enrolled in primary education). The gross enrolment ratio, therefore, presents too rosy a picture of primary educational enrolment. Frequently, it even exceeds 100 per cent. Experts suggest that this indicator overestimates actual enrolment in primary education by 10–30 per cent (Colclough and Al-Samarrai, 2000; Coombs, 1985).

The *net enrolment ratio* is a better criterion of enrolment. This ratio indicates what percentage of each school age group is actually somewhere in the school system. The problem with this concept is that it does not show where in the educational system the pupils actually are. Since 1995, the UNESCO definition of net enrolment has been adjusted to take this into account (UNESCO, 2002a). Net enrolment is now defined as the percentage of an age group enrolled in the education level appropriate for the age group. Of course, the new enrolment figure will be lower than the old one, because part of the age group is left out of consideration. The change in definition means that it is no longer possible to construct consistent long-run time series of net enrolment.[5]

Indicators of educational enrolment are frequently used. Still, they have several important shortcomings (Coombs, 1985; Hardiman and Midgley, 1982). These are summarised in Box 7.4.

BOX 7.4 : Shortcomings of indicators of educational enrolment

1. **Overreporting**. Enrolment data are inflated since schools have an interest in high enrolment figures in order to receive more subsidies. The same applies to reports to UNESCO on educational enrolment by national ministries of education.

2. **Enrolment versus completion**. Enrolment data do not show how many students actually finish a particular cycle of education. In fact, not more than 60 per cent of all students actually complete the educational cycle in which they are enrolled. Dropping out of school is quite common. Between 20 and 75 per cent of all students do not continue beyond the fourth year of primary school (Coombs, 1985; see also Table 7.3, p. 258).

3. **Enrolment data provide no information about the quality of education**. At many schools there is substantial absenteeism. Especially in rural areas school children are expected to work in the fields during agricultural peak periods. Often children are absent for more than one-third of the school year. Besides, the data do not tell us anything about the size of school classes, the quality of the teaching materials and the usually low level of qualification and poor motivation of the teaching staff. Recent research shows that the quality of education as reflected by measurement of cognitive skills is much more important in explaining earnings and growth than enrolment or attainment statistics (Hanushek and Wößmann, 2008).

4. **Data seems to be deteriorating over time**. In recent years less data are available on secondary and tertiary education. Data on net enrolment in higher education have been discontinued.

---

[5] The old NER indicator resurfaces as the Age Specific Enrolment Rate (ASER), but there are no ASER statistics in the UNESCO publications.

7.2.2   Educational attainments

Data on enrolment tell us something about the efforts made by a society to educate its people. However, they provide little information on the outcomes of the educational process, by the time people leave school and enter the labour market. A useful indicator of educational attainments is the average number of years of schooling completed by people in different age categories. This indicator provides information on the quantity of human capital per person. Thus, one could look at years of schooling completed for all persons over fifteen years of age or all persons over twenty-five years of age.

Psacharopoulos and Arriagada (1986) have made estimates of years of schooling in the labour force, based on labour force surveys and population censuses. With some justice, they argue that this is one of the best indicators of the stock of human capital. But their exercises have not been updated. Most human capital estimates focus on educational attainment of the total population of a given age (e.g. 15+ or 25+), rather than on the labour force. The general approach is to use enrolment ratios of successive years to calculate a stock estimate of the average years of education of the population in a given year. The most frequently used dataset is the Barro and Lee dataset (see Barro and Lee, 1993, 2000, 2010, 2011). Alternative estimates are provided by Cohen and Soto (2007); De La Fuente and Doménech (2006); Lutz *et al.* (2007); Nehru, Swanson and Dubey (1995). In Table 7.4 (p. 272), we will use the most recent version of the Barro and Lee dataset.

7.2.3   Financial indicators

Financial indicators give us an idea of the efforts of governments and societies to develop educational systems and the resources available for education.

Well-known indicators are:

1. Government educational expenditures as a percentage of national income.
2. Government educational expenditures as a percentage of total government expenditures.
3. Government expenditure per pupil at different levels of education.

These data refer to government expenditure only. Private expenditure on education is not included. In fact, households are responsible for sizable proportions of educational expenditures. It should be noted that financial indicators are input indicators rather than output indicators. Different countries may achieve very different educational outcomes for similar levels of educational expenditures.

7.2.4   Physical indicators

Physical indicators refer to numbers of teachers, pupil–teacher ratios, numbers of buildings and so on. These indicators are also input indicators.

7.2.5   Educational outcomes: literacy

Most of the indicators discussed above refer to educational inputs: enrolment, numbers of teachers, amounts of money, years of education. Far less is known about the results of the educational process. Apparently, it is possible to attend school for years without learning to read, write, or calculate – even in economically advanced countries.

One of the important indicators of educational outcomes is the degree of literacy. Even here, though, one should be careful. Too often literacy is determined by means of survey questions about literacy to which one can answer 'yes' or 'no', without any testing of the actual skills themselves. In other estimates of literacy it is assumed that a person is literate when he or she has attended primary school for at least four years. Moreover, literacy itself had been defined in very different ways (Ooijens and van Kampen, 1989; UNESCO, 2002c). According to UNESCO, a person is functionally literate 'if a person is able to engage in all those activities in which literacy is required for effective functioning of his group and community and for enabling him to continue to use reading, writing and calculation for his own and the community's development' (Ooijens and Van Kampen, 1989: 2; UNESCO, 2002c: 66). The functional definition captures the ability of people to use literacy to carry out everyday tasks. But as common tasks differ across cultures, the comparative measurement of literacy is not easy. The best measures of literacy are based on tests for reading, writing and simple arithmetic calculation. Most often literacy is expressed as a percentage of the population over fifteen years of age.[6]

7.2.6   Educational outcomes: cognitive skills

In the past ten years there has been a proliferation of standardised international tests of cognitive skills. These include the TIMMS (Trends in International Mathematics and Sciences Studies) and the PIRLS (Progress in International Reading and Literacy Studies). Since 2000 the OECD has developed the Programme for International Student Assessment (PISA). PISA is a comprehensive set of tests for fifteen-year-olds, which include reading skills, mathematical skills and science skills. The survey is conducted every three years. Originally the focus was on advanced economies, but gradually PISA has been extended to developing countries. The 2012 PISA includes sixty-five countries (see www.oecd.org/pisa/).

7.3   Educational performance in developing countries

7.3.1   The initial situation after the Second World War

In most developing countries the state of education after the Second World War was very poor. The colonial authorities had never invested much in education (Altbach, 1982; Altbach and Kelly, 1978; Heinink and Koetsier, 1984). Under colonialism there were two dominant motives for providing education:

1. Religion: missionary work was important in primary education.
2. Educating native elites to fulfil subordinate positions in colonial administration. For members of native elites a limited number of secondary and higher educational institutions were created, modelled on Western educational institutions. The language of education was the colonial 'mother tongue'. The substance of the curriculum was Western-oriented.

---

[6] Ooijens and Van Kampen argue in favour of also including 11-to-15-year-olds in estimates of literacy (Ooijens and van Kampen, 1989).

The educational system had a dual structure (Heinink and Koetsier, 1984). Primary education in rural areas emphasised practical and moral training under missionary influence. In addition, there was academically oriented primary, secondary and higher education for children of the foreign colonial elites. This education was also open to very restricted numbers of children of native elites. In academically oriented education the emphasis was on preparing pupils for employment in the small modern sector of the economy. It was a weak imitation of Western educational systems. In the curriculum the humanities and in particular languages, predominated. Little attention was paid to the natural sciences and to native languages and cultures.

Of course, there were differences between the colonial educational systems. More than the British, the French tried to create small elites of assimilated 'coloured French individuals' by means of education (Altbach, 1982). Of all the colonising powers, the British paid most attention to education, the Belgians and the Portuguese the least. At the eve of independence there were hardly any graduates of higher education in the Belgian Congo.

In non-colonised countries such as China and Thailand educational opportunities were also rather limited until the Second World War. In India and in the Islamic world precolonial religiously oriented educational systems persisted alongside colonial education. But their importance tended to decline under colonialism. The most favourable situation was to be found in Latin America, where decolonisation had been completed early in the nineteenth century and formal education had been developed furthest. Even here, the level of education in the 1950s was still very low.

In the sections below empirical data will be presented on developments in education since the Second World War. The educational performance of developing countries should be judged in the light of very poor initial conditions.

7.3.2 Increases in educational enrolment

The data on gross enrolment in Table 7.1 indicate that enrolment in developing countries increased very substantially since 1960. Educational performance in developing countries has been very dynamic. With respect to primary education developing countries seem to be well on the way to achieving the goal of primary education for all. Gross enrolment figures in Asia, Latin America and Africa exceed 100 per cent. The greatest long-run progress has been made on the African continent. Though enrolment growth declined for ten years after 1980, due to economic stagnation and budget retrenchments (Colclough and Al-Samarrai, 2000), it picked up again after 1990, reaching 100.9 per cent in 2010. The data indicate an unambiguous narrowing of the gap between educational levels in developing countries and in more affluent countries.

Since 1960, the growth rate of enrolment in secondary and post-secondary education has been far higher than in primary education (Coombs, 1985; UNESCO, 1983). Between 1960 and 2010 the number of students enrolled in post-secondary education in developing countries increased by a factor of 1.4, in secondary education by a factor of 4.1 and in tertiary education by a factor of 10.2 (Table 7.1).

Gross enrolment data give a far too optimistic picture of primary educational enrolment, as many children over the age of eleven are still in primary school, due to grade repetition or late enrolment. The net enrolment data in Table 7.2 show that the percentage of pupils enrolled for the six–eleven-year age bracket tends to be much lower in all regions. The gross enrolment data seem to suggest that by 2010 all developing regions had achieved full

Table 7.1: Gross enrolment ratios, by educational level, country and region, 1960–2010[a]

Country/region	Primary education		Secondary education		Higher education	
	1960	2010	1960	2010	1960	2010
Bangladesh	47	96	8	51	1	11
China		111		81		26
India	41	116	23	63	2	18
Indonesia	67	118	6	77	1	23
Iran		114		91		43
Malaysia	96	96	19	68	1	40
Pakistan	30	95	6	34	1	5
Philippines	95	106	26	85	13	29
South Korea	94	106	27	97	5	103
Sri Lanka	95	99	27	87	1	15
Taiwan[b]		100		100		60
Thailand	136	91	8	77	2	46
Turkey	75	103	14	78	3	46
Argentina	98	118	31	89	11	71
Brazil	95	137	11	106	2	26
Chile	109	106	24	88	4	59
Colombia	77	115	12	96	2	39
Mexico	80	114	11	89	3	28
Peru	83	108	18	91	4	43
Venezuela	100	103	97	83	4	78
Congo, Dem. Rep.	60	94	3	38	0.1	6
Côte d'Ivoire	46	79	2		0.0	9
Egypt	66	101	16	72	5.0	32
Ethiopia		102		36		5
Ghana	59	106	3	59	0.0	9
Kenya	47	113	2	60	0.0	4
Morocco	47	111	5	56	0.5	13
Nigeria	36	83	3	44	0.0	10
South Africa[c]	89	102	15	94	3.1	16
Tanzania	24	102	2		0.1	2
Zambia	48	115	1	28	0.0	
Average 31 countries	71.9	105.1	15.6	73.1	2.6	30.6
Sub-Saharan Africa[d]	40.4	100.9	3.5	39.7	0.3	6.8
Asia[e]	85.6	104.1	20.9	68.0	2.6	21.4
Arab countries	48.3	98.2	10.2	68.8	2.0	23.7
Latin America & Carib.	72.7	113.9	14.6	89.6	3.0	40.6
Developing countries	75.8	107.8	15.7	64.0	2.1	21.4
Developed countries[f]	105.6	101.4	61.1	100.2	13.5	69.7

Notes:

[a] The number of students enrolled per educational level regardless of their age, as a percentage of the number of persons in the relevant age bracket. The age brackets for educational levels differ per country. Percentages over 100 per cent indicate that persons outside the relevant age bracket are also enrolled.

[b] For tertiary education Taiwan only publishes enrolment data for 18–21 years. We have calculated rough gross enrolment ratios for the 18–23 age bracket.

[c] Tertiary enrolment 2007 instead of 2010.

[d] Sub-Saharan Africa, excluding North African Arab countries.

[e] Asia, excluding Arab countries, own calculation based on country enrolment figures weighted by school age population.

[f] 2009 instead of 2010.

Sources:

1960: UNESCO, *Statistical Yearbook, 1976* and *1978–99*; 2010: UNESCO Institute of Statistics: http://stats.uis. unesco.org/unesco/TableViewer/tableView.aspx, downloaded June 2012. Totals for developing and developed countries from: World Bank, *World Development Indicators Online*, downloaded June 2012. Taiwan from: DGBAS, *Monthly Bulletin of Statistics*, November 2012 and *Statistical Yearbook, 2011*. Tertiary enrolment South Africa 2007 from: *Trends in Education Macro Indicators*, South Africa, Republic of South Africa, Department of Education, 2009.

primary school enrolment. However, the net enrolment data indicate that 13 per cent of all six-to-eleven-year old children in developing countries did not attend primary school in 2010. The objective of primary education for all has not yet been realised, particularly not in Sub-Saharan Africa. Here, 24 per cent of the age group was not attending primary school in 2010.

In Sub-Saharan Africa, structural adjustment programmes (SAPs) resulted in a temporary decline in net enrolment rates for all school levels between 1987 and 1992 (see Colclough and Al-Samarrai, 2000). But by 1999, primary enrolment had recovered to its 1987 level. The much lower secondary net enrolment figures in 1999 and 2010 are not comparable with the older data due to the change in the definition of net enrolment ratios after 1995.[7]

One should realise that even the more realistic net primary enrolment data tend to exaggerate educational performance (see section 7.2.1). For instance, household surveys in Sub-Saharan Africa indicate that the numbers of pupils, who actually attend school, are substantially lower than the enrolment figures indicate (UNESCO, 2002c, Table 2.6).

Although not all educational objectives have been realised, the long-run educational achievements of developing countries have been very impressive. Despite considerable population growth, they realised very substantial increases in enrolment rates since 1960. The educational gap between developing and rich countries has been unmistakably narrowed. As early as 1960, considerable progress had already been made in comparison with the unfavourable initial conditions after the Second World War. Latin America and East Asia are on course to achieving universal access to primary education and have net primary enrolment levels comparable to those of developed countries. Other regions such as Sub-Saharan Africa and the Arab countries have also taken rapid strides forward.

[7] Recent secondary net enrolment data are not consistent with older ones, as the definition changed in 1995. The dramatic drop in secondary enrolment in Africa is in large part due to this change in definition. The new net enrolment concept is defined as the number of pupils actually enrolled in a given level of education divided by the number of people in the corresponding age bracket. For secondary education, this is substantially lower than the old net enrolment concept, which was defined as the number of pupils of a given age bracket enrolled anywhere in the educational system divided by the number of people in that age bracket.

Table 7.2: Net enrolment ratios, by region, 1960–2010 (percentage of persons enrolled, by age bracket and region)[a]

Region[b]	6–11 years					12–17 years					18–23 years			
	1960	1987	1992	1999	2010	1960	1987	1992	1999	2010	1960	1987	1992	2010[c]
Sub-Saharan Africa	29	56	51	58	76	17	46	41	19	29	1	9	7	7
Arab countries	39	73	77	77	86	18	51	52	51	61	4	20	20	24
Asia[d]	53	80	81	85		41	43	47	46		9	14	14	21
Central Asia				91	90				77	87				25
East Asia				94	95				57	73				29
South Asia				74	88				40	51				17
Latin America	58	86	88	92	94	36	68	68	59	74	6	25	25	41
Developing countries	48	76	77	80	87	35	45	47	47	56	8	15	14	21
Developed countries	91	92	92	96	95	69	87	86	88	90	15	35	40	70

Notes:

[a] After 1995 the definition of NER changed. The new definition is the enrolment of the official age group for a given level of education expressed as a percentage of the corresponding population. The 1999 and 2010 figures are therefore not comparable to the earlier figures.

[b] Africa and Asia exclude the Arab countries. Latin American includes the Caribbean.

[c] Since 1992, UNESCO does not provide tertiary net enrolment data. For 2010 we used GER.

[d] Prior to 1999 Asia excludes Central Asia. Totals for Asia 1999 calculated with population weighted country figures.

Sources: 1960, 1987 and 1992: UNESCO, *Statistical Yearbook, 1989* and *1994*.

1999–2010 from: UNESCO Statistical Institute, downloaded June 2012, except developing countries and developed countries from World Bank, *World Development Indicators Online*, downloaded June 2012. Tertiary enrolment 2010 from the sources documented in Table 7.1.

7.3.3   Education completed

One of the reasons that enrolment data give a too rosy picture of educational performance is that large numbers of students leave school prematurely without a degree. This is well illustrated by the data in Table 7.3. For selected years, this table shows what proportion of the population of twenty-five years and older has a completed primary, secondary, or tertiary education. Though the data derive from various years and statistical practices differ from country to country, it is useful to compare these percentages with the gross enrolment data in Table 7.1, which sometimes exceed 100 per cent. The completion data are generally far lower. In the period 2000–10, there were several countries where very large fractions of the 25+ population had no education at all, such as Pakistan (52.5 per cent), Bangladesh (51 per cent), Tanzania (34.9 per cent), or Ethiopia (71.8 per cent).[8] Six countries in Table 7.3 had non-completion rates of primary education of above 25 per cent.

[8] In the same year the percentages for the age bracket 15–19 were higher, reflecting ongoing improvements in education from generation to generation. But even for this age group only 31.7 per cent had more than a completed primary education.

Some countries do not distinguish a separate category for completed primary education. We may assume that all pupils with complete or incomplete secondary education have completed primary education. To increase the comparability between countries, we have calculated the percentage of pupils with more than a completed primary education.[9] Countries that score high in this respect in the period 2000–10 are South Korea, Sri Lanka, Taiwan, Chile and South Africa. Table 7.3 also documents the huge progress made between 1980 and 2010.

7.3.4   Years of education per member of the population

Table 7.4 shows that the average number of years of schooling received by members of the population aged twenty-five years or more in our sample of developing countries has increased by a factor of 4 between 1950 and 2010 – from 1.8 years in 1950 to 7.1 years in 2010. The African countries have experienced the most rapid increase. Latin America is the region with the highest levels of human capital. The gap relative to the advanced economies has become smaller over time, but there is still a four-years gap in schooling levels in 2010.

7.3.5   Educational expenditures

The following Tables 7.5 and 7.6 refer to public expenditures on education. In spite of a host of economic problems, the real expenditures per pupil in primary education in most countries show a clear upward trend in the long run. Exceptions to this trend are Congo and Zambia.

Table 7.5 brings out clearly how much more is being spent per student in higher education than in primary education. Extreme cases in 1965 were Côte d'Ivoire, Ghana, Kenya, Nigeria and Zambia. In these countries tertiary expenditures per pupil ranged from 107 to 1 (Kenya) to 216 to 1 (Ghana). South Korea is the only exception to this skewed pattern for tertiary expenditures. Expenditures in secondary education are also higher than those in primary education, but the differences are less pronounced. Over time the skewdness of educational expenditures has declined, with expenditures per primary student increasing at the expense of secondary and tertiary levels. By 2010 the average ratio of tertiary to primary expenditure had decreased to around 5 to 1, from 50 to 1 in 1965. The ratio of secondary to primary expenditure was around 1.3 to 1 in 2010, with several countries even spending more per pupil in primary education than in secondary education. These changes are consistent with the finding that returns to primary education are higher than those to secondary education and tertiary education (Psacharopoulos and Arriagada, 1992; Psacharopoulos and Patrinos, 2002). Educational expenditures seem to be responding to policy advice in this respect.[10]

---

[9] Some countries only publish data on entry into secondary education. These data probably also include those students that have completed primary school but do not continue their education. Other countries distinguish between finishing primary school and enrolment in secondary education. The percentage of people with more than a completed primary school education equals 100 minus the percentage with 'no education', the percentage with 'uncompleted primary education' and the percentage with 'completed primary education'.

[10] In recent years the debate about the importance of investing in tertiary education versus primary and secondary education has picked up again. Advocates of tertiary expenditures base themselves on the requirements of a knowledge economy (see section 7.4.7).

Table 7.3: Highest diploma obtained (as percentage of 25+ age bracket), 1980–2010

	Year	No schooling	Primary education		Secondary education		Higher education	More than primary
			Incomplete	Complete	Incomplete	Complete		
Bangladesh	1981	70.4	16.7	→	7.4	4.2	1.3	12.9
China	1990	29.3	34.3	→	34.4	→	2.0	36.4
India	1981	57.5	28	→	7.2	→	7.3	14.5
Indonesia	1990	54.5	26.4	→	16.8	→	2.3	19.1
Iran								
Malaysia	1980	16.7	13.0	20.7	19.4	23.6	6.9	49.6
Pakistan	1990	73.8	9.7	→	5.8	8.2	2.5	16.5
Philippines	1990	3.8	20.8	15.1	17.3	21.2	22.0	60.3
South Korea	1995	8.7	0.9	17.3	15.7	36.2	21.1	73.1
Sri Lanka	1981	15.9	48.9	→	34.1	→	1.1	35.2
Taiwan	1987	→	→	55.8	→	32.5	11.8	44.2
Thailand	1990	20.5	67.3	2.4	4.5	2.3	2.9	9.8
Turkey	1993	30.6	6.6	40.6	21.9	→	→	22.2
Argentina	1991	5.7	22.3	34.6	25.3	→	12.0	37.4
Brazil	1989[a]	18.7	57.0	6.9	11.9	5.5	→	17.4
Chile	1992	5.8	48	→	33.9	→	12.3	46.2
Colombia	1993	11.9	27.3	18.3	13.3	16.7	10.4	42.5
Mexico	1990	18.8	28.6	19.9	12.7	10.7	9.2	32.7
Peru	1993	16.4	34.7	→	27.2	→	20.5	48.9
Venezuela	1990	21.2	55.0	→	12	→	11.8	23.8
Congo, Dem.R.	1984	52.4	30.3	→	14.6	→	1.3	17.3
Côte d'Ivoire	1992		48.2	→	43.1	→	8.7	51.8
Egypt	1986	64.1	16.5	→	14.8	→	4.6	19.4
Ethiopia								
Ghana	1970	77.7	5.8	→	12.8	3.3	0.4	
Kenya	1979	58.6	32.2	→	7.9	1.3	→	9.2
Morocco	1971	92.5	1.9	1.2	4.4	→	→	4.4
South Africa	1995[b]	13.0	17.1	6.9	26.7	25.7	8.8	63.0
Tanzania	1988		89.7	→	7.8	0.6	2.0	10.3
Zambia	1993	40.2	37.3	→	5.8	15.5	0.3	22.5

Notes:
[a] 10+; [b] 20+; [c] From Barro and Lee (2010). →included in next column: ←included in previous column.
Sources: Left panel from UNESCO, *Statistical Yearbook, 1999*, except for Ghana, Ivory Coast, Morocco, South Africa (1996) and Congo: UNESCO Institute for Statistics, Education Statistics, 2002 and Taiwan: *National Statistics of Taiwan*, the Republic of China. Right panel from: UNESCO Institute of Statistics, *Global Education Digest 2012*, Table 15, UIS: http://stats.uis.unesco.org/unesco/ ReportFolders/ReportFolders.aspx. Taiwan from DGBAS, *Statistical Yearbook of Republic of China, 2011*, Table 45, http://eng.dgbas.gov. tw/public/data/dgbas03/bs2/yearbook_eng/y045.pdf. India, Congo, Côte d'Ivoire, Egypt, Kenya, Morocco and Zambia from Barro and Lee (2010, 2011), www.barrolee.com/. The Barro and Lee categories have been reclassified as follows: BL total primary minus completed primary = incomplete primary education. BL total secondary education minus completed secondary education = incomplete secondary education, BL total tertiary minus completed tertiary = post-secondary education.

Year	No schooling	Primary education		Secondary education		Post secondary education	Tertiary	Un-known	More than primary
		Incomplete	Complete	Lower	Upper				
2001	51.0	1.8	20.5	9.6	12.9	0.0	4.2		26.7
2010	6.6	←	28.1	43.0	13.5	5.2	3.6		65.3
2010^c		2.5	16.6			2.2	3.7		
2009	9.5	17.7	30.6	14.4	20.3	na	7.5		42.3
2010	→	→	37.5	20.0	24.0	→	18.5		62.5
2010	8.8		23.0	17.3	34.5	→	16.4		68.2
2009	52.5	2.6	12.8	8.9	16.6	0.0	6.7		32.2
2008	3.4	→	31.7	→	35.1	5.5	24.2	0.1	64.8
2010	4.7	1.0	11.4	10.2	37.4	na	35.3		82.9
2009	5.4	→	20.6	44.4	→	15.5	14.1		74.0
2010	0.0	0.0	21.8	0.0	43.8	0.0	34.4	0.0	78.2
2006	6.1	42.3	18.9	9.7	9.6	0.0	12.8	0.5	32.2
2009	10.7	5.7	43.7	8.3	16.1	na	10.1	5.4	34.5
2003	1.1	8.9	33.5	14.2	28.4	na	13.7	0.2	56.3
2010	→	→	49.3	14.7	24.6	na	11.3	0.3	50.5
2010	2.9	12.3	9.6	22.1	34.7	na	18.0	0.4	74.8
2011	7.9	→	35.7	14.5	22.1	na	19.7		56.3
2010	9.3	15.8	18.3	23.7	14.8	na	17.6	0.5	56.0
2010	6.8	15.1	18.9	6.2	32.0	0.0	20.9	0.1	59.1
2009	6.6	10.6	28.9	10.8	27.0	na	15.9	0.2	53.7
2010^c		21.9	6.8	10.2	11.8	0.5	0.7		
2010^c		12.9	18.0	10.2	6.9	1.8	3.2		
2010^c		5.8	8.1	33.0	17.6	1.2	2.0		
2007	71.8	1.0	17.8	0.2	4.5	1.8	0.5	2.4	7.0
2010^c		4.5	50.0			1.2	2.0		
2010	21.1	18.0	17.5	5.6	30.0	6.3		1.4	41.9
2010^c		3.6	17.5	8.7	10.0	3.3	6.0		
2011	7.7	12.9	5.9	13.9	45.7	6.5	6.1	1.2	72.2
2002	34.9	16.2	42.9	4.4	0.7	←	0.9		6.0
2010^c		16.8	29.8	14.2	19.2	0.6	1.0		

Table 7.4: Average years of education of the population of twenty-five years and over, 1950–2010

	1950	1960	1970	1980	1990	2000	2010
Bangladesh	0.9	0.9	1.2	2.0	2.9	3.7	4.8
China	0.7	1.4	2.5	3.7	4.9	6.6	7.5
India	0.9	0.9	1.2	1.9	3.0	3.6	4.4
Indonesia	0.7	1.1	2.3	3.1	3.3	4.8	5.8
Iran	0.3	0.6	1.2	2.1	3.8	6.0	7.8
Malaysia	1.8	2.3	3.0	4.4	6.5	8.2	9.5
Pakistan	0.8	0.9	1.3	1.8	2.3	3.3	4.9
Philippines	2.3	3.7	4.8	6.1	7.1	8.0	8.7
South Korea	4.0	3.2	5.4	7.3	8.9	10.6	11.6
Sri Lanka	3.2	3.6	5.1	5.9	6.5	6.7	6.3
Taiwan	4.1	4.6	5.0	6.4	8.0	9.6	11.0
Thailand	2.2	3.4	3.0	3.7	4.6	5.4	6.6
Turkey	1.0	1.5	2.0	2.9	4.5	5.5	6.5
Argentina	4.6	5.3	5.9	6.7	7.9	8.6	9.3
Brazil	1.4	1.8	2.5	2.6	3.8	5.6	7.2
Chile	4.7	5.0	5.8	6.4	8.1	8.8	9.7
Colombia	2.2	2.8	3.4	4.3	5.5	6.5	7.3
Mexico	2.4	2.6	3.1	4.0	5.5	7.4	8.5
Peru	2.7	3.2	3.9	5.5	6.6	7.7	8.7
Venezuela	2.0	2.5	2.9	4.9	4.8	5.6	6.2
Congo, Dem. Rep.	0.3	0.5	0.8	1.2	2.0	3.2	3.5
Côte d'Ivoire	0.4	0.5	0.7	1.3	2.0	3.2	4.2
Egypt	0.5	0.7	1.0	2.1	3.5	4.7	6.4
Ghana	0.6	0.7	2.1	3.6	5.3	6.3	7.0
Kenya	0.9	1.3	1.4	2.7	4.2	5.9	7.0
Morocco	0.2	0.3	0.3	1.2	2.2	3.4	4.4
South Africa	4.0	4.2	4.4	4.8	6.5	7.2	8.2
Tanzania	1.5	1.6	1.8	2.5	3.6	4.6	5.1
Zambia	1.4	1.8	2.8	3.3	4.7	5.9	6.7
Average Asia	1.8	2.2	2.9	3.9	5.1	6.3	7.3
Average Latin America	2.9	3.3	3.9	4.9	6.0	7.2	8.1
Average Africa	1.1	1.3	1.7	2.5	3.8	4.9	5.8
Average developing countries	1.8	2.2	2.8	3.7	4.9	6.1	7.1
Average advanced economies	6.2	6.5	7.5	8.6	9.4	10.3	11.1

Source: Barro and Lee, *Educational Attainment Dataset*, 2011, www.barrolee.com/.

Table 7.5: Government expenditure, per pupil, selected countries, 1965–2010 (in 1995 $)

	1965			1980			2000			2010		
	Primary Education	Secondary Education	Tertiary Education	Primary Education	Secondary Education	Tertiary Education	Primary Education	Secondary Education	Tertiary Education	Primary Education	Secondary Education	Tertiary Education
Bangladesh	9	15		11	18	102	**26**	35	141	*43*	*74*	*135*
China				6	102	416	45	93	728	*51*	101	510
India	8	47	294	23		190	60	103	395	111	92	243
Indonesia							**41**	**81**	**235**			
Iran							*135*	*147*	*516*	*300*	*421*	*441*
Malaysia				274		3,399	461	804	2,999	726	1,014	2,827
Pakistan	19	24	323	27	*73*		115		*483*			
Philippines	*102*		*174*	68	50	161		98	138	*108*	110	*116*
South Korea	85	118	504	356	315	544	1,689	2,177	810	3,272	3,347	*1,850*
Sri Lanka	37	95	492				**90**	**101**	**393**	82		
Taiwan	48	134	852	364	690	1,984	**2,484**	**3,265**	**3,563**			
Thailand				92	102	671	322	291	651	565	384	439
Turkey				126		1,876	418	374	1,232			*1,272*
Argentina	843	1,648	3,730	547		2,463	901	1,243	1,251	1,534	2,466	*1,737*
Brazil				385	486	2,592	363	350	1,884	818	833	*1,153*
Chile	133		3,313	229		2,682	680	700	914	918	959	1,012
Colombia	40	70	1,274	106	130	899	273	297	681	463	449	865
Mexico	81		1,330	140	222	837	708	873	2,211	779	842	2,362
Peru	232	580	1,793	186	148	907	*130*	171	393	247	301	267
Venezuela	*374*	*836*	*4,377*	230		2,877	76	**166**		477	425	
Congo, Dem.Rep.	82	635	5,204			1,170		51	*166*	5	16	
Côte d'Ivoire	55	419	6,064	158		7,296	78	192	770			579
Egypt			611			359	**126**	**272**	**714**			
Ethiopia	35			14						36	20	47
Ghana	42		7,501	51		3,041	43	98	*801*	36	82	
Kenya		70	4,542				80	54	775	90	85	
Morocco	157	430	1,491	169	593	1,681	211	523	1,307	279	594	*1,373*
Nigeria	22	*129*	*2,485*	*11*		*1,221*						
South Africa							384	491	**2,201**	605	681	
Tanzania				83	1,264					84	72	
Zambia	59		8,536	55		14,688	20	42	**469**	18		3,653

Note:

[a] Figures in *italics*, closest year in period, in **bold** data from World Bank-WDI (2004).

Sources: 1965 and 1980: World Bank, *World Development Indicators, 1999*; Missing countries, 1980 supplemented from Komenan (1987), recalculated into 1995 $. 2000 and 2010 from UNESCO Institute of Statistics, http://stats.uis.unesco.org/unesco/ReportFolders/ReportFolders.aspx, downloaded January 2013, supplemented by data from World Bank, World Bank-WDI (2004). Taiwan: *National Statistics of Taiwan*, the Republic of China, DGBAS.

Table 7.6: Government expenditure on education as a percentage of GNP, 1960–2010[a]

	1960/61	1965	1970	1980	1990	2000	2010
Bangladesh		1.3		1.1	1.5	2.4	*2.2*
China			1.3	2.5	2.3	*1.9*	
India	2.3	2.6	2.6	3.0	3.9	4.3	3.3
Indonesia			2.6	1.7	1.0	2.5	3.0
Iran			*2.9*	*6.0*	4.0	4.4	4.7
Malaysia			4.2	*6.0*	5.5	6.0	*6.3*
Pakistan	0.9	1.5	1.7	2.1	2.7	1.8	2.4
Philippines	2.6	2.7	2.8	1.7	2.9	3.3	*2.7*
South Korea, Rep.	3.2	1.8	3.4	3.7	3.5	*3.9*	*5.0*
Sri Lanka			4.0	2.7	2.7	*3.1*	*2.1*
Taiwan					4.7	3.7	3.8
Thailand	2.5	3.1	3.2	3.4	3.6	5.4	3.8
Turkey	2.4	3.5	2.1	2.2	2.1	2.6	2.9
Argentina	2.0	3.0	2.5	2.7	3.4	4.6	*6.0*
Brazil	2.3	1.1	2.9	3.6	4.5	4.0	*5.6*
Chile	2.7	2.7	5.1	4.6	2.7	3.9	4.2
Colombia	1.8	2.3	1.9	2.4	2.6	3.5	*4.8*
Mexico	1.3	1.9	2.3	4.7	3.7	4.9	*5.3*
Peru		5.0	3.3	3.1	2.3	*3.1*	2.7
Venezuela		3.9	4.1	4.4	3.1		3.6
Congo, Dem. Rep.				2.6	*0.8*		2.5
Côte d'Ivoire	4.2	5.4	5.3	7.2	7.7	3.8	*4.6*
Egypt	4.9	4.6	4.8	5.7	3.8	4.1	*3.8*
Ethiopia				*2.1*	*2.4*	3.9	4.7
Ghana	3.4	4.1	4.3	3.1	3.3	*4.7*	5.5
Kenya		4.6	5.0	6.8	7.1	5.2	6.7
Morocco			3.5	6.1	5.5	5.8	5.4
Nigeria		2.3	*3.2*	*3.6*	1.0	0.7	
South Africa					6.5	5.6	6.0
Tanzania					3.4	*2.1*	6.2
Zambia	1.8	6.0	4.5	4.5	2.6	2.0	1.3
Sub-Saharan Africa[b]		2.5	3.4	5.0	4.6	3.5	4.4
Asia[c]		3.5	3.5	3.2	3.2	3.5	3.6
Arab countries and North Africa		4.2	4.7	4.1	4.9	*5.6*	*4.2*
Latin America and the Caribbean		3.1		3.9	4.0	4.0	*4.4*
Developing countries		3.0	3.3	3.8	3.8	3.8	*3.9*
Developed countries		5.2	5.6	5.1	5.0	5.0	*5.6*

Notes:

[a] Where data for the selected year are lacking, data for the preceding or subsequent year were used, if available (21 observations, figures in italics). From 2000 onwards the percentages refer to GDP rather than GNP.

[b] Excl. North Africa and the Arab countries.

[c] Asia: calculated as GNP weighted average for East and South Asia. For 2000 and 2010, excl. Arab countries. After 2000, unweighted average of Asian countries, incl. the former Soviet Republics in Central Asia.

Sources:

UNESCO, *Statistical Yearbook, 1972, 1976, 1995, 1997* and *1999*. 2000–10 from UNESCO Institute for Statistics, http://databank.worldbank.org/ddp/home.do?Step=3&id=4, downloaded January 2010, except Egypt and Nigeria 1999/2000 from UNESCO, Institute for Statistics, downloaded 2002, and Tanzania, 1998 from UNESCO, *Statistical Yearbook, 1999*. Ethiopia, 1980–2000, and Iran 1970–2000 and regional data 2000–10 from World Bank, *World Development Indicators Online*, downloaded January 2013. Taiwan from DGBAS, Taiwan: www.dgbas.gov.tw, Table 47, Table 48; from 2000 onwards from DGBAS, *Social Indicators*, 2011.

The financial sacrifices developing countries are willing to make for education are represented in Table 7.6. In 1965, developing countries invested on average 3 per cent of their GNP in education. By 1980 this percentage had increased to 3.8 per cent, subsequently remaining stable until 2010. In Sub-Saharan Africa, the percentages increased significantly reaching 4.4 per cent in 2010. In that same year, the rich countries invested 5.6 per cent of their GDP in education. Since per capita GDP in developing countries is much lower, this of course means that developing countries can spend less on education per head of the population.

It is interesting to note that the two regions with the lowest net primary enrolment figures, Sub-Saharan Africa and North Africa and the Arab states, have the highest proportional public investment in education. In a comparison of educational expenditures between South Asia and Sub-Saharan Africa, Colclough and Al-Sammarai (2000) conclude that the efficiency of educational expenditures in Africa is low. More could be achieved within given budgetary constraints.

7.3.6   Cognitive skills

Table 7.7 reproduces PISA rankings for the still limited number of developing countries included in this exercise. Exceptionally high rankings are found for Singapore, Korea, Taiwan and three Chinese regions. Other developing countries in Latin America, Asia and the Arab world have significantly lower scores than the OECD average. Scores of 400 and lower are considered to be indications of exceptionally weak performance. Overall, the low rankings of most developing countries provide a valuable illustration of the quality problems that still face most of them in education.

7.3.7   Non-formal and informal education

All officially registered indicators refer to formal education. However, there are all kinds of education and schooling that fall outside the scope of formal education. For these terms such as 'non-formal education' and 'informal education' have come into use.

Non-formal education comprises all forms of organised education that are not included in the regular schooling system; adult education, education for dropouts, literacy projects, agricultural extension or information, occupational training, in-firm training programmes, health education, education for family planning and so on (Coombs and Ahmed, 1974). Advocates of non-formal education believe that it is more suited to practical everyday needs and requirements than formal education. They claim that it offers opportunities to integrate education into wider development strategies.

It is difficult to obtain hard data on non-formal education, as it includes such a variety of educational activities financed by various ministries, institutions and private organisations. Still, studies conducted by UNESCO indicate an upward trend in enrolment in non-formal education. Rapid advances in ICT have created new opportunities for education in the form of distance learning. Distance-learning techniques range from simple correspondence courses to modern multimedia applications and videoconferencing techniques using the internet. Potentially distance-learning technology can reach dispersed students in rural areas which cannot adequately be served through traditional formal schooling institutions. In developing countries such as Indonesia, Mexico or South Africa hundreds of thousands of students are involved in distance-learning programmes (Perraton, 2000). Distance learning can supplement the formal educational system, offering the same degrees to the same age groups or supplementing classroom teaching. But there is also a great variety of non-formal

Table 7.7: Cognitive performance of developing countries, 2009

| | On the overall reading scale | On the reading subscales | | | | | On the mathematics scale | On the science scale |
		Access and retrieve	Integrate and interpret	Reflect and evaluate	Continuous texts	Non-continuous texts		
Azerbaijan	362	361	373	335	362	351	431	373
China, Hong Kong	533	530	530	540	538	522	555	549
China, Macao	487	493	488	481	488	481	525	511
China, Shanghai	556	549	558	557	564	539	600	575
Indonesia	402	399	397	409	405	399	371	383
Kazakhstan	390	397	397	373	399	371	405	400
Korea	539	542	541	542	538	542	546	538
Kyrgyzstan	314	299	327	300	319	293	331	330
Singapore	526	526	525	529	522	539	562	542
Taiwan	495	496	499	493	496	500	543	520
Thailand	421	431	416	420	423	423	419	425
Turkey	464	467	459	473	466	461	445	454
Argentina	398	394	398	402	400	391	388	401
Brazil	412	407	406	424	414	408	386	405
Chile	449	444	452	452	453	444	421	447
Colombia	413	404	411	422	415	409	381	402
Mexico	425	433	418	432	426	424	419	416
Panama	371	363	372	377	373	359	360	376
Peru	370	364	371	368	374	356	365	369
Uruguay	426	424	423	436	429	421	427	427
Dubai (UAE)	459	458	457	466	461	460	453	466
Jordan	405	394	410	407	417	387	387	415
Qatar	372	354	379	376	375	361	368	379
Tunisia	404	393	393	427	408	393	371	401
OECD average	493	495	493	494	494	493	496	501

Note:
Scores of 400 and lower are considered to be indications of exceptionally poor performance.
Source: OECD, PISA 2009 database, www.oecd.org/pisa/.

programmes which can be combined with work. These include courses for upgrading teacher skills, vocational education, language and literacy programmes, reproductive health, agricultural education and so forth.

It is well known that schooling and socialisation are not limited to schools. Families, churches, associations, work experience and peer groups can also be very important. *Informal education* refers to the lifelong process of accumulation of knowledge and skills, through experiences in daily life – at work, at home, at play or otherwise (Coombs, 1985: 24; Coombs and Ahmed, 1974). There is no point in considering informal education as part of the educational system. But the rapid rise of new mass media and means of communication, such as newspapers, radio, cinema, television, books, magazines, the internet, social media and mobile phones are very important. They can serve as mechanisms of information transfer, influence, education, or indoctrination. In particular, radio, television and the internet provide major opportunities for new modes of education, teaching and dissemination of information.

7.3.8   Literacy

In a discussion of education, the issue of literacy merits special attention, since it is one of the essential outcomes of the educational process. As noted in section 7.1.6, many authors consider a certain threshold level of literacy as a prerequisite for economic development. In pre-literate societies, families were the main vehicle of transmission of knowledge and skills to successive generations. As the task of transferring knowledge and skills shifts from families to formal educational institutions in ongoing processes of social differentiation, literacy becomes more and more important (Hardiman and Midgley, 1982).

There are several reasons to strive for literacy. Apart from increasing economic productivity, literacy can promote social participation. It can contribute to cultural education, to the realisation of humanist goals and to personal awareness.

In the past, religious groups were particularly active in spreading literacy. An important objective of much religiously oriented education was to teach people to read sacred texts. For example, in Scandinavia Protestantism led to widespread literacy as early as the end of the nineteenth century. In developing countries missionaries played an important role. Ideological movements such as communism also set great store on literacy, as it would enable people to study Marxist writings.

Since its foundation, UNESCO, the UN organisation for education, science and culture, has placed great emphasis on the battle against illiteracy (Jones, 1988). Between 1946 and 1958, one of the main objectives of UNESCO was *fundamental education*. The essence of fundamental education was that every person had a right to learn the three Rs, reading, writing and arithmetic. But fundamental education was not limited to 'literacy' alone; it also included vocational skills, domestic skills, knowledge of hygiene, knowledge of the principles of science, artistic skill, an understanding of one's social environment and the development of personal skills and moral traits. In the early years it was assumed that there were close links between fundamental education and formal schooling.

Within UNESCO there was a lively debate on the scope of educational objectives. Gradually, the notion of fundamental education was broadened to include development in general. Literacy in the narrow sense was seen as one of the instruments to achieve wider developmental objectives. In practice, however, the main emphasis remained on the formal schooling system, which was being rapidly expanded during this period.

Between 1958 and 1966 the concept of fundamental education was dropped altogether from international rhetoric. Education was no longer to be considered a separate issue.

It should be integrated into wider development policies. The new catch phrase was *community development*. In this new context, formal education became less important. The focus shifted to various kinds of adult education. Literacy was also seen as contributing to community development as a whole.

At the second world conference on adult education in Montreal in 1960 the idea emerged for the first time that illiteracy was a manageable problem and that it could be eliminated within a limited number of years (Jones, 1988). The world conference of education ministers in Tehran in 1965 explicitly adopted the objective of eradicating illiteracy. In 1996, UNESCO launched the 'Experimental World Literacy Program' (EWLP).

Both at the 1965 conference and in the EWLP the notion of *functional literacy* was paramount. Functional literacy is not just about reading, writing and calculating, but rather about the contribution of these skills to the economic and social welfare of the individual and the community. In contrast to the concept of fundamental education, which related to individual and social welfare in the broadest sense, functional literacy was given a more limited economic interpretation. Literacy should contribute to the productivity and earning capacity of workers. To realise this, literacy education should be related to work practices and vocational training programmes. It should be aimed at specific groups of urban and rural workers. Pupils should learn skills which would be useful for their work and their future careers. It is clear that non-formal education would receive more emphasis in the context of functional literacy.

Between 1966 and 1974 more than 1 million students participated in the EWLP in one form or other (Coombs, 1985). On balance, the programme turned out to be a complete failure. The gap between the high-flown rhetoric of international organisations and the intractable problems in the field proved to be to too wide. The main problem was the lack of success in integrating literacy projects into economic and social practice. Despite its disappointing results, several noteworthy lessons can be derived from the EWLP (Coombs, 1985; Ooijens and van Kampen, 1989). These are listed in Box 7.5.

BOX 7.5 : Lessons of the experimental world literacy programme

1. Literacy programmes are most likely to be successful for people who **need literacy in their daily life**. Literacy is often most effectively learned in the context of acquiring some other skill to which literacy is incidental (Curle, 1964, quoted in Jones, 1988).
2. Literacy requires that reading materials (newspapers, books, information material) continue to be available **after completion of the literacy programmes**. Maintaining reading skills requires post-literacy programmes either through formal or non-formal education.
3. Teaching materials should be tailored to the students' **environments and interests**.
4. Literacy should not be taught **in isolation from other subjects**. Literacy training should be linked with subjects of strong immediate interest and concern to particular learners. The EWLP did not implement these objectives adequately. It made too much use of standardised teaching programmes and teaching materials in a classroom setting.

Socialist countries, such as the Soviet Union (in the 1920s), Cuba, Nicaragua, China and Vietnam, have had considerable success with large-scale, politically motivated literacy campaigns. In these programmes the advancement of literacy was closely linked with political mobilisation and ideological propaganda. Adult literacy rates in present-day Cuba and Vietnam are above 90 per cent. The pedagogical experiments of Paulo Freire in Latin America are also worth mentioning; Freire linked literacy education to political awareness, political mobilisation and the emancipation of oppressed groups. Most of these literacy campaigns are very much rooted in a particular political and social context. They cannot be used as standard recipes irrespective of time and place. They do illustrate the crucial importance of motivation. If people can be motivated to participate in literacy programmes, impressive results can be achieved in very short periods of time.

Ooijens and van Kampen (1989) rightly point out that the best guarantee for literacy is a well-functioning and accessible system of primary education. This implies that the main function of non-formal education is to maintain literacy after students have left school. Once again, formal and non-formal education are complementary. There is a clear correlation between the expansion of primary education and increases in literacy (UNESCO, 2002c: 66).

Since 1990, the concepts of literacy have evolved further (UNESCO, 2002c, Chapter 2). More attention is paid to the varying contexts in which literacy can be used, such as work, personal life, different languages and so forth. Situations can differ substantially in their need for literacy. Literacy is now interpreted as one of many ways of communication. Illiteracy is redefined as the inability to interact adequately with the wider society through reading and writing. All these terminological refinements, however, are not really reflected in literacy indicators. We still measure literacy in terms of whether persons are able to read and write.

Despite disappointing results of some literacy programmes, illiteracy shows a clear downward tendency as a joint result of efforts in formal education and non-formal national and international literacy programmes. Since 1946, the percentage of illiterates in the population over fifteen years has declined sharply in all countries. The literate share of the adult world population in developing countries increased from 57.4 per cent in 1970 to 81.2 per cent in 2010 (see Table 7.8), but the pace of advance has been slackening. In absolute numbers the total number of illiterates worldwide declined by 95 million between 1980 and 2010, from 870 million to 775 million. Illiteracy is still much more widespread among women: 64 per cent of all illiterates are female.[11]

In Latin American countries, in particular, the rate of illiteracy has been reduced drastically. In no less than twenty Latin American countries (including Argentina, Chile, Colombia, Costa Rica, Cuba, Mexico, Panama, Paraguay, Uruguay, Trinidad and Venezuela) the adult illiteracy rate is below 10 per cent (UNESCO Institute of Statistics, 2013). High rates of literacy have also been achieved in East and Southeast Asia. Lower levels of literacy are found in the Arab States, South Asia and Sub-Saharan Africa. But even here the declines in illiteracy have been striking. The decline in illiteracy in developing countries is much more rapid than previously in European development (Fägerlind and Saha, 1989: 46).

For selected countries, Table 7.8 documents the long-run decline in illiteracy. It also shows, however, that the problems of illiteracy are still far from being solved. In many

[11] UNESCO, Institute of Statistics, Homepage: http://stats.uis.unesco.org/unesco/TableViewer/dimView.aspx.

Table 7.8:   Illiterates as a percentage of the population of fifteen years and over, 1946–2010

	1946–55[d]	1956–65[d]	1970	1980	1990	1995	2000	2010[e]
Bangladesh		78.4	75.4	71.1	65.8	62.9	60.0	43.2
China			47.1	32.9	21.7	18.1	14.8	5.7
India	80.2	72.2	66.9	59.0	50.7	46.7	42.8	37.2
Indonesia		84.6	43.9	31.0	20.5	16.5	13.2	7.4
Iran				*63.5*	*34.5*	*26.9*	*23.4*	15.0
Malaysia			41.9	28.8	19.3	15.7	12.6	6.9
Pakistan		84.6	79.1	72.2	64.6	60.7	56.8	45.1
Philippines	40.0	28.1	18.2	12.2	8.3	6.5	5.1	4.6
South Korea	23.2	29.4	13.2	7.1	4.1	3.1	2.2	
Sri Lanka			19.5	14.7	11.3	9.8	8.4	8.8
Taiwan[a]				23.7	13.7		8.9	*2.5*
Thailand	48.0	32.3	19.8	12.5	7.6	5.9	4.5	6.5
Turkey	68.1	61.9	43.5	31.6	22.1	18.2	15.0	9.2
Argentina	13.6	8.6	7.0	5.6	4.3	3.7	3.2	2.2
Brazil[b]	50.6	39.0	31.6	24.0	18.0	15.3	13.1	9.7
Chile	19.8	16.4	12.4	8.6	6.0	5.1	4.2	1.4
Colombia	37.7	37.7	22.2	16.0	11.6	9.9	8.4	6.6
Mexico	43.2	34.6	26.5	18.7	12.7	10.5	8.8	6.9
Peru		38.9	28.5	20.6	14.5	12.2	10.1	10.4
Venezuela	47.8	36.7	23.7	16.1	11.1	9.1	7.5	4.5
Congo, Dem. Rep.			77.2	65.9	52.5	45.4	38.6	33.2
Côte d'Ivoire		95.0	79.0	70.5	61.5	56.4	51.4	43.8
Egypt	80.1	74.2	68.4	60.7	52.9	48.9	44.7	28.0
Ethiopia						73.0		61.0
Ghana		80.6	70.5	56.2	41.5	34.8	28.4	32.7
Kenya		80.5	59.4	43.8	29.2	23.0	17.6	12.6
Morocco			80.2	71.4	61.3	56.1	51.2	43.9
Nigeria		84.6	79.9	67.1	51.3	43.6	36.0	38.7
South Africa			30.3	23.9	18.8	16.7	14.8	11.3
Tanzania		90.5	64.4	51.0	37.1	30.8	25.0	26.8
Zambia			52.3	41.4	31.8	26.7	21.8	28.8
Average Asian countries		56.0	42.6	33.1	25.8	24.0	20.4	16.0
Average Latin American countries		30.3	21.7	15.7	11.2	9.4	7.9	6.0
Average African countries		82.1	63.2	51.9	40.5	35.1	29.9	32.8
Average developing countries		55.5	44.7	35.3	27.1	24.1	20.3	19.8
Average developed countries[c]			5.5	3.6	2.3	1.8	1.4	0.9

Notes:

[a] 25 years and over, 1999 instead of 2000.

[b] 13 years and over.

[c] Until 2000, incl. former Soviet Asian republics in transition.

[d] Figures refer to the most recent data within the period.

[e] 2010 or closest year for which data are available (in *italics*).

Sources:

1946–65: UNESCO, *Statistical Yearbook, 1976, 1984, 1989* and *1994*. Figures refer to the most recent data within each period; 1970–2000: UNESCO Institute of Statistics, downloaded 2002; 2010 and Iran all years: UNESCO Institute of Statistics, http://stats.uis.unesco.org/unesco/TableViewer/tableView.aspx, downloaded June 2012. Taiwan: ADB, *Key Indicators 2001: Growth and Change in Asia and the Pacific*, www.adb.org, and Ministry of Education, Education Statistics, http://english.moe.gov.tw/ct.asp?xItem=7444&ctNode=1184&mp=1, downloaded January 2013.

countries, such as Bangladesh, India, Pakistan, Côte d'Ivoire, Ethiopia, Nigeria and Morocco, levels of illiteracy in 2010 were still unacceptably high.

7.3.9.   Nation building

Apart from the economic functions of education, its political functions are also of great importance. After the Second World War, education was expected to contribute to state formation and the creation of a national identity in developing countries. In many of the newly independent states people identified more with tribe, region, lineage, or ethnic group, than with the national state. New political values stood in sharp contrast to traditional ideas about politics. Nationalist leaders fervently hoped that education would contribute to a sense of national awareness and political integration (Fägerlind and Saha, 1989; Hardiman and Midgley, 1982; Krieger, 1988; Psacharopoulos, 1989). Education would further the development of a joint culture and joint political values. Education would familiarise young people with the idea of participation in national political processes. Also, in many countries – particularly those with socialist regimes – education was regarded as a means to achieve political mobilisation and increased social consciousness.

In practice, education is often a two-edged sword. Under certain conditions, it can contribute to a sense of national identity. But it can also have very divisive effects. In some states in India education strengthened feelings of regional identification. Unequal access to education for members of different ethnic, cultural, or religious groups may lead to political frustrations and conflicts. It may undermine the loyalty of underrepresented groups to national institutions. In settings of conflict, different groups can use education to strengthen their own identities and to emphasise their differences. Finally, universities are often hotbeds of political opposition and resistance. Educated unemployment in particular is frequently a politically destabilising factor.

In many former colonies in Africa and Asia the choice for a language of instruction posed a distinct problem. During the colonial period the language of instruction was the language of the colonial power. In view of national integration and national consciousness it would have been preferable to replace this language with a national language. Yet this often proved to be impossible. In many new states several languages were spoken. To adopt one of these languages as the national language would lead to serious opposition from members of the other language groups. Therefore, English, French, or Portuguese were often maintained as the language of instruction, especially in secondary and higher education. In some countries such as Tanzania, Malaysia and Indonesia, there is a tendency to replace English as the language of instruction in secondary education by the national language. This however raises fears of declining English language skills and weakening connections with global science and technology.

Only in a few multilingual countries was a single language accepted as the national tongue. For the national language one chose trade languages that were acceptable to many groups in society: in Indonesia Bahasa Indonesia, in Tanzania Kiswahili.

In the long run education should try to take ethnic, cultural and linguistic diversity into account. This should have more positive results than the forced propagation of a yet weakly developed national culture and identity. An overemphasis on national unity could well have adverse effects. A national political system, which is open to regional diversity, may well achieve more stability. But, of course, this is far from certain. If education does not succeed in creating some sense of national belonging, regional diversity in education, language and culture will end up undermining fragile national unity.

7.3.10   Summary: comparison with developments in more developed countries

In 1870, there was a huge educational gap between the rich countries and the developing world (Morrisson and Murtin, 2009), which persisted well until 1950 (see Table 7.4, p. 260). In the twentieth century the USA established its leadership in education performance (Acemoglu and Autor, 2012; Goldin and Katz, 2008). American exceptionalism in education went hand in hand with its economic, technological and productivity leadership. By the 1930s the USA had provided widespread access to mass secondary education and took the lead in the large-scale expansion of tertiary education, especially after 1950. Other Western countries followed more gradually.

The post-war period was a period of educational catch-up in the developing world. Developing countries have given high priority to expanding their educational systems. The increase in schooling and decline in illiteracy proceeded more rapidly than previously in European countries, where primary education expanded very gradually, resulting in universal primary education by the end of the nineteenth century. Developing countries today are on the way to universal primary education. Participation in secondary and higher education today is substantially higher than it was in France, England, and Germany in 1950 (see Tables 7.1 and 7.2, pp. 254 and 256). In Europe democratisation of higher education did not make much headway until after 1945. Before that time, entry to higher education was by and large restricted to the offspring of the upper classes.

One of the characteristics of the educational expansion in developing countries is that enrolment in secondary and higher education started increasing long before the realisation of universal primary education. In this respect, the educational performance of developing countries not only differs from Western development experience, but also from that of the late-developers Japan and the Soviet Union. Both Japan and the Soviet Union experienced an explosive expansion of education from the late nineteenth century onwards (Morrisson and Murtin, 2009). But they gave more priority to universal primary education. After the Bolshevik revolution large-scale literacy campaigns were organised in the Soviet Union and primary education was expanded very rapidly. Secondary education was only developed after universal primary education had been realised. Higher education was expanded at an even later stage (Lind and Johnston, 1986). In developing countries, however, expansion of secondary and higher education received higher priority.

Despite differences in the patterns of educational development one may conclude that developing countries are engaged in a process of successful educational catch-up. They have succeeded in training their own educational staff, in decreasing their dependence on foreign teachers and educators, and developing an educational infrastructure. In the light of the unfavourable initial state of education after 1945, the educational performance of developing countries is quite impressive. In 1950, the average adult in a developing country had 1.8 years of education (30 per cent of the level in the advanced economies). In 2010, this had increased to 7.1 years, 63 per cent of the advanced country level (see Table 7.5; see also Morrisson and Murtin, 2009).

7.4   Problems and challenges

From the mid-1970s onwards important qualitative shortcomings in the educational systems became more and more visible. In their enthusiasm to create new educational facilities as fast as possible, authorities in developing countries had paid little attention to educational content. The Western-oriented educational systems inherited from the former colonial period were expanded with little or no change. Coombs (1985) calls this a process of 'linear expansion'. In Latin America – where decolonisation had been completed early in the nineteenth century – educational systems were also copies of Western models. As a result, educational systems were in many aspects ill adapted to the conditions and needs of developing countries. The following section will address some of the most important deficiencies in educational systems.

7.4.1   Discrepancies between educational needs and financial resources

Since the late 1970s the pace of growth in educational facilities has declined. The scarcity of financial resources increased as a result of the economic problems of the early 1980s and the cutbacks in government spending in the context of structural adjustment programmes. At the same time the demand for education continued to increase due to population growth and the youthful age structure of the population (Coombs, 1985; Hallak, 1990). The problems are especially acute in South Asia and Sub-Saharan Africa, where growth of numbers of pupils enrolled has outpaced growth of educational expenditures, sometimes leading to declining expenditures per student.

Even without an increase in enrolment, the cost of education tends to rise autonomously. First – if policies are not adjusted – fixed salary structures will lead to increasing salary costs as the teaching staff gets older and as more qualified teachers replace less qualified teachers. Secondly, the costs per student are much higher in secondary and higher education than in primary education. As more students enrol in secondary and higher education, the average expenditure per student increases.

In the coming years, the gap between the demand for education and the available resources is expected to widen even further, before declines in fertility rates result in a drop in the dependency rates and ease the pressures on the schooling system in some ten–fifteen years. In regions where fertility rates have not yet started declining, such as Sub-Saharan Africa, the pressures on the educational system will continue unabated.

Increasing the provision of education, however, is not only a question of more funding. It also has to do with the effectiveness of educational expenditure. Colclough and Al-Samarrai (2000) argue that Sub-Saharan Africa has relatively high unit costs compared to other regions and could increase enrolment and improve education by increased effectiveness. Another route to improved education is by private contributions, which are becoming more and more important in various developing countries. But, as will be argued in the next section, increases in funding without changes in the institutions and incentives with regard to educational quality may have disappointing results.

7.4.2   The quality of education

The success of developing countries in reducing the education gaps relative to the advanced economies in quantitative terms obscures that fact that there are still very large quality gaps. The quality of education in developing countries has come under increasing criticism. Classes are very large, with class sizes sometimes even reaching extremes of 70 to 100 pupils. Students are often absent from school, grade repetition and dropout rates are high (UNICEF, 2012). In some countries only 10 per cent of all students complete the educational cycle in which they are enrolled. Teachers are underpaid; their training is often insufficient and their motivation is low. Teaching materials are of poor quality, if available at all. Sanitary conditions are frequently unspeakable. Education is very much focused on preparing for examinations and learning by rote. Independent thinking and creativity is insufficiently encouraged. Pupils are primarily expected to replicate what is taught to them by their teachers. Even when educational cycles are completed, it is not always clear how much the pupils have actually learned. *Educational attainment* does not guarantee *educational achievement*. Standardised assessments such as PISA are starting to provide us with an idea of the extent of the quality problem, but so far only a limited number of countries participate in these exercises. After the relative neglect of quality issues in the preceding decades, improving educational quality was included among the six major educational goals formulated for 2015, at the World Education Forum in Dakar in 2000 (UNESCO, 2002c).

In two important publications, Hanushek and Wößmann (2007, 2008) highlight the key importance of cognitive skills in the human capital debate. When measures of educational quality such as cognitive skills are introduced into human capital regression equations explaining income or economic growth, the coefficients of school enrolment or educational attainment become insignificant or less significant. They show that the quality of educational institutions affect cognitive skills irrespective of innate ability. Therefore attention should focus on increasing teaching quality. In particular teacher quality has powerful impacts on student outcomes.

Hanushek and Wößmann argue that simply increasing financial resources for smaller classes, better facilities or better teacher remuneration will not do the job.[12] What has to change are the institutions and incentives that affect quality improvement. Hanushek and Wößmann single out three sets of policy measures to promote strong schools and high-quality teachers: (1) Introducing more competition between schools so that parental demand will create strong incentives for schools to improve quality. (2) Increased autonomy in local decision making. This is a factor which is obviously lacking in many developing countries, where educational systems are extremely centralised and bureaucratised. (3) Introduction of accountability systems – including standardised testing of the cognitive performance of pupils – that identify good school performance and lead to rewards for schools and teachers based on good performance.

7.4.3   Lack of relevance

Educational systems in developing countries were often set up as copies of Western educational models. The content of education was Western-oriented; textbooks were Western; examination requirements were derived from Western exams. Little attention was paid

---

[12] They qualify this statement for situations where school systems are not even able to provide the most minimal resources such as basic textbooks, teaching materials or class rooms. Increasing funding in those – not uncommon settings – will have positive impacts.

to the indigenous history, culture and society. In many countries the language of instruction was – and frequently still is – the language of the former colonial power. Education tends to be academically oriented and has little relationship with the life situations of most students.

In the 1970s, radical authors went so far as to characterise Western-oriented education in Africa, Asia, and Latin America as an instrument of oppression and alienation (Carnoy, 1974; Freire, 1970; Illich, 1974). At school people learn to look down on their own culture. The more successful their educational career, the more students tend to become alienated from their own social backgrounds (Altbach, 1982).

It is indisputable that education has alienating effects and can contribute to the formation of rootless elites. Still, it is important to realise that education as an instrument of modernisation, technology transfer and social change is always a reflection of the educational systems of the dominant nations in world society.[13] An educational system that was in complete harmony with the requirements of a traditional society would not contribute much to 'development'. A modern educational system cannot but be 'alienating' in a partly traditional society (see the debate on westernisation and modernisation in Chapter 1). The tendency to shift away from English as a language of instruction to indigenous language in countries such as Tanzania, Malaysia or Indonesia may isolate pupils from the international community of learning. The challenge is to develop educational systems that are both relevant to the life situations of people in developing countries and provide meaningful entry into the modern international world of science and technology.

One of the important shortcomings of education in developing countries is the insufficient attention to agriculture. Many students in the least developed countries will spend the rest of their lives in an agricultural or rural environment. Nevertheless, the educational curriculum is oriented almost exclusively to the modern urban sector of society. Primary education is little adapted to the educational needs of rural young people. In secondary and higher education courses with agricultural content are rarely taught. Education reinforces the already low status of physical labour and in particular agricultural labour. It contributes to mass migration to urban areas. Almost all authors argue for a more practical orientation of education, with more emphasis on vocational training, work experience and agricultural content.

Most reforms of this nature – however justified – are likely to meet with fierce resistance on the part of students. They rightly consider education as an important means of upward social mobility. This path leads from lower to higher educational levels, which become progressively more academic. In order to gain access to higher educational levels students have to be able to pass academically oriented examinations. Lower vocational education is seen as an obstacle to upward educational mobility – *the vocational education trap* – though in fact only a minority of students has a realistic chance of entering higher educational levels (Abernethy, 1969; Foster, 1965a, 1965b). Vocational and practical oriented education are regarded as second rate by students and their parents, in both developed and developing countries (Psacharopoulos, 1989). The major challenge to educationalists in developing countries is how to make education more relevant for the masses of rural children, who will never go on to higher education, without diminishing the possibilities of upward educational mobility (Hardiman and Midgley, 1982).

---

[13] In Europe, too, modernisation of educational systems has always been based on foreign models that are considered successful.

It should be noted that actual experiences with vocational education have often been rather disappointing. The specific occupational skills learned at school are hardly applied in later working life (Foster, 1965b; Psacharopoulos, 1989).

An alternative, presently much in prominence, is so-called non-formal education (see section 7.3.7). Among other things, non-formal education comprises adult literacy programmes, agricultural extension, on-the-job training programmes, education of school leavers, health education and education about family planning and distance learning. Non-formal education offers an opportunity to relate both the form and content of education to the immediate needs and problems of students.

However, it is an illusion to believe that non-formal education could ever replace formal education (Hallak, 1990). The ability to profit from non-formal education and on-the-job training depends on prior formal education. Non-formal education supplements formal education rather than providing an alternative to it. The more formal education people have received, the more likely they are to enrol in non-formal programmes and the more likely they are to profit from them. Besides, the costs of non-formal education are by no means lower than those of formal education.

7.4.4   Unequal access to education

Access to educational facilities is distributed very unequally (Coombs, 1985; Hardiman and Midgley, 1982; Ooijens and van Kampen, 1989; Williamson, 1979). In particular, there are great differences between urban and rural areas. In rural areas schools are scarce and of poor quality. Students have to travel great distances to get to school and means of transport are lacking. Both educational participation and the quality of education lag far behind those in urban areas. In the cities there is almost universal primary education. Furthermore, secondary and higher educational institutions are concentrated in urban regions. Rural young people have far less opportunities to follow secondary and higher education than their urban counterparts.

Since 1950 one of the significant inequalities in educational participation was that between males and females (Coombs, 1985; Fägerlind and Saha, 1989; Schultz, 1988; UNESCO, 2002c). This was particularly pronounced in secondary and higher education. In the chapters on population (Chapter 5) and health (Chapter 6) we have seen that the education of women was a crucial factor in improving the health situation and in the success of family planning efforts. Research by Nuñez has indicated that education of women is also of importance to economic development. In a study of economic development in Spain, she found that the regions where male–female differentials in education were smallest were the regions with most rapid growth of income per capita. Also, improvements in female literacy tended to have more positive effects on economic development than improvements in male literacy (Nuñez, 1990).

Over time the educational status of women has shown substantial improvement. In the past thirty-five years female participation in all cycles of education has increased. The slowdown in the increase of primary enrolment ratios in the 1990s affected boys more than girls. In primary education, the *Gender Parity Index (GPI)* – defined as female enrolment ratios divided by male enrolment ratios – was 0.92 worldwide in 1999. It increased to 0.97 by 2010 (UIS, 2013). Presently the largest gender gaps in primary education are still found in the Arab states (0.93), and Sub-Saharan Africa (0.93). At tertiary level females are presently even overrepresented in most regions, with the exception of Sub-Saharan Africa (0.62) and South and West Asia (0.76). But gender disparities go beyond the simple numbers (Fägerlind and Saha, 1989; Schultz, 1988; UNESCO, 2002c). For instance, in terms of literacy women are still at a serious disadvantage in the Arab states. In 2010 female illiteracy in the Arab states was twice as high as male illiteracy.[14]

A third significant form of educational inequality derives from the socio-economic status of the parental family. As in Western societies, children from upper social strata, income groups, or from dominant ethnic groups are significantly more likely to participate in the highest levels of education. However, in the African context, Foster emphasises that access to modern education is relatively open. Education has promoted rather than hampered upward social mobility (Foster, 1980).

7.4.5　Mismatch between education and the labour market

One of the most important points of criticism of education in developing countries is the mismatch between education and the labour market. We have already pointed out that agricultural education is almost non-existent in many countries, where agriculture provides the main source of employment and livelihood.

Next, secondary and higher educational enrolment has increased more rapidly than the demand for higher-educated persons on the labour market (Blaug, 1979; Gillis et al., 1992). From the 1960s onwards, many countries trained more doctors than nurses, more engineers than mechanics and so on. People with higher degrees displaced people with lower degrees (see section 7.1.3 on screening theory). As a result many employees were overqualified for their work.

In the 1950s, there were great shortages of well-educated personnel in the civil service, schools and firms. A task of the educational system was to solve these shortages in a brief period of time. Soon, however, shortages turned into surpluses. Today swollen government bureaucracies are no longer able to provide jobs for the growing flows of graduates. Almost all developing countries have extensive academic unemployment. Thus, scarce resources are wasted on a large scale on investment in higher education which could be invested more productively in primary education. Academic unemployment and overqualification can lead to great frustration of students and graduates. Universities are often hotbeds of political turmoil and instability. One of the most paradoxical results of overschooling is the *brain drain*, the exodus of highly qualified doctors, experts and scientists from developing to rich countries. Many of the social benefits of educational investment are thus not realised.

Despite widespread educated unemployment, there are still severe shortages in specific occupations, especially those requiring technical skills (Psacharopoulos, 1989). Education is still oriented too much to the humanities and social sciences – languages, law, history, sociology, economics – rather than to technical, scientific and agricultural disciplines. In these areas the services of expatriate experts are still often called upon.

To improve the match between education and the labour market, it is often argued that vocational education and on-the-job training should receive more emphasis in educational policy (see section 7.3.7 on non-formal education). However, students still have a clear preference for academically oriented education. Regardless of high educated unemployment rates, academic education still seems to offer the best career prospects from an individual point of view.

One of the most important recommendations of educationalists is to give higher priority to primary education. Extensive research has shown that both the private and the social returns to investment in primary education are much higher than the returns to investment in secondary and tertiary education (Psacharopoulos and Arriagada, 1992; Psacharopoulos and Patrinos,

---

[14] Calculated by dividing female illiteracy rates by male illiteracy rates from UIS (2013).

2002). In primary education, more could be achieved with fewer resources. Such a policy switch, however, encounters considerable opposition on the part of politically influential groups, who are defending the educational opportunities of their offspring. Nevertheless, the statistics in Table 7.5 (p. 261) show that primary education is indeed gaining some ground.

Blaug (1979) argues in favour of loosening the ties between educational certificates and paid jobs. Credentialism on the labour market leads to the displacement of people with lower educational qualifications by people with higher qualifications, irrespective of the nature of the jobs involved. It also has very negative effects on the quality of education. All attention is focused on the mechanical preparation for centrally set academic examinations. The content of education is relegated to second place.

7.4.6 Education and the national innovation system

During much of the post-1950s educational policy concentrated on increasing the supply of education and raising the skills of the population. The emergence of the concept of systems of innovation since 1990 (see Chapter 4) has changed our perception of the role of education. Innovation systems focus on the strength and quality of interactions between actors such as innovating firms, educational institutions, public research laboratories and government organisations. It is not enough to simply increase the supply of education. One should strengthen the connections and linkages between the educational and the productive system, so that knowledge flows can take place more easily (Aubert, 2005).

There is a whole range of initiatives to strengthen the relationships between educational institutions and the productive sector. These include:

- Establishing science parks and incubators in and around universities.
- Strengthening ties and linkages between secondary and tertiary educational institutions and small and large economic actors.
- Increasing the opportunities for practical training of students at secondary and tertiary level to bridge the gaps between the worlds of learning and the needs of economic actors.
- Introducing entrepreneurship training into the curriculum. In the past the mindset of pupils was that education would automatically provide entrance to good jobs in government and the formal sector. This is no longer the case. Employment opportunities are inevitably limited. Entrepreneurship training encourages students to go out and create their own small enterprises, apply their newly acquired knowledge and thus contribute to economic dynamics.
- Encouraging and supporting on-the job-training and strengthen its connections to formal education.

7.4.7 The knowledge economy: the increased importance of tertiary education

The increasing importance of knowledge as a key factor of production in the knowledge economy poses new challenges for tertiary education. Universities are becoming increasingly important in supplying the economy and society with highly trained engineers, software developers, researchers, professionals and innovators. University research capabilities have to be upgraded in order to make a contribution to the generation and absorption of knowledge in the process of economic growth and catch-up. For cash-strapped developing countries, these mean that one has to choose to focus on a limited number of centres of excellence in a limited number of areas, rather than spreading expenditures across all institutions. It is through such centres that the system of innovation interacts with the international research community.

The requirements of the knowledge economy are starting to call the received wisdom of priority for primary education in question. One may need to strike a new balance. On the one hand it remains an important goal to achieve universal access to primary education. On the other, tertiary education and research capacity need to be strengthened. A World Bank report on challenges for tertiary education (World Bank, 2002b) provides some useful rules of thumb. Total educational investment should be between 4 and 6 per cent of GDP. Public investment in tertiary education should be in the range of 15–20 per cent of all public expenditures on education. If it is far above this range, primary education should receive a higher priority, but if it falls short of this range, funds should be reallocated to higher education.[15]

7.4.8   Brain drain versus brain circulation

One of the consequences of globalisation is increased international mobility of labour. In the advanced economies there are increasing shortages of highly skilled labour. In developing countries the mismatch between education and the labour market provides strong incentives for skilled and highly educated workers to migrate to the advanced economies. The number of individuals migrating from the South to the North increased from 14 million in 1960 to 60 million in 2000 (cf. our rather similar estimates in section 2.4.6 of Chapter 2). Within this migration flow there is a huge increase in the proportion of adult migration with tertiary education (Gibson and McKenzie, 2011).

There is a long and fierce debate about the implications of the migration for developing countries (summarised in Docquier and Rapoport, 2012). One strand of thought emphasises the welfare losses for developing countries. Poor countries invest scarce resources in training highly skilled workers. When these workers – doctors, IT specialists, engineers, biotechnical researchers or accountants – migrate to the advanced economies, the investments in human capital made by developing countries are wasted (Bhagwati and Hamada, 1974; Haque and Kim, 1995).

Since the 1990s, a more positive view of migration has emerged (Beine, Docquier and Rapoport, 2001; Clemens, 2011; Gibson and McKenzie, 2011). Migrants are a very important source of remittances and foreign investment from which the countries of origin can benefit. Highly skilled migrants working in the advanced economies can also act as a source of knowledge spillovers. In this respect, the emergence of a successful Indian IT sector has profited greatly from the links with the Indian diaspora in Silicon valley in the USA. Countries can also profit from the experiences and knowledge that migrants have gained in other countries, in the case of return migration.

We would nevertheless argue that the threat of a permanent loss of the best and the brightest should remain a serious concern for policy makers in developing countries, irrespective of certain compensating advantages. In recent policy debates the emphasis has therefore shifted to the relatively new concept of *brain circulation*. Efforts to prohibit or restrict skilled migration are clearly counterproductive, but developing countries can encourage all kinds of voluntary temporary or permanent return migration of skilled

---

[15] Such rules of thumb should never be applied mechanically, but they do serve as signposts for the debate about educational priorities in a country.

workers, or other kinds of active involvement of the diaspora in the domestic economy. China and India are the leading examples in this respect. China has been successful in recruiting top Chinese researchers and academics working in the USA and elsewhere to accept part-time or full-time positions at leading Chinese research institutions. India has been successful in attracting entrepreneurship. The more dynamic the domestic economy, the greater the chance of profiting from brain circulation.

7.5   Policy

During the first few years after the Second World War educational policy was mainly concerned with the quantitative expansion of educational facilities. Not much thought was given to the content of the educational curriculum. Education was seen as a driving force in economic development. In this respect, the rapid expansion of education was the counterpart of capital accumulation in the industrialisation strategy. In addition, education would contribute to social modernisation and political integration.

Since the early 1970s the debate on educational policy has shifted in two directions. On the one hand, as educational performance improved in developing countries increasing attention was paid to achieving education for all. On the other hand, the educational debate increasingly shifted from an emphasis on quantitative expansion to a focus on the content and quality of education.

Following the example of the WHO, the World Conference on Education for All, held in Jomtien, Thailand in 1990 formulated the global objective of education for all. In 2000, this was followed by the World Education Forum on Education for All, held in Dakar in 2000 (UNESCO, 2000a). This meeting focused both on quantitative and qualitative issues. On the one hand, it specified clear-cut quantitative targets such as universal primary education and a 50 per cent reduction in illiteracy, to be realised by 2015. On the other hand, attention was paid to issues of content and educational quality. Progress towards the goals was monitored in annual monitor reports.

These debates resulted in a series of proposals and recommendations for reform that will dominate the educational agenda in the coming years. In conclusion to this chapter, we will summarise the most important recommendations emerging from the literature and the policy debates:

1. *There is a need to find an appropriate balance between primary and tertiary educational investment.* Achieving universal access to primary education remains an important policy goal, but it should be balanced by policies aimed at expanding and improving tertiary education in the light of the needs of the knowledge economy.
2. *Improving educational quality at all levels is an urgent priority.* Increasing emphasis should be place on measuring the outcomes of the educational process, rather than focusing on enrolment.
3. *The key to improving educational quality is teacher quality.* Improving teacher quality depends on institutions and incentives. Important policy tools to improve quality are school competition, school autonomy and accountability for the results of the schooling process (Hanushek and Wößmann, 2008).

4. *Education should be made more relevant to the needs of the labour market.*
5. *Primary schools in rural areas should pay more attention to subjects that are relevant to the rural population.* In secondary and higher education more attention should be paid to agricultural education.
6. *In the curriculum more attention should be paid to technical subjects and the natural sciences* and less to the humanities and the social sciences.
7. *On the labour market educational certificates and diplomas should receive less emphasis.* Credentialism results in overschooling. It is no use discussing the content of education without paying attention to the form and content of examinations. Less emphasis in education on the preparation for academically oriented examinations would have positive effects on educational content and relevance.
8. *Non-formal education should be further developed as a supplement to and in close relationship with formal primary education.* Non-formal education can contribute in particular to further training of people who already have jobs and to increased literacy among adults and school leavers.
9. *Educational institutions should be seen as part of the national system of innovation.* Links between educational institutions and the productive sector should be strengthened.
10. *Brain drain can be both a burden and a source of advantage for developing countries.* Policies aimed at brain circulation can maximise the advantages of a skilled diaspora for a country.

Despite the scarcity of financial means, developing countries should try to provide adequately for the increasing need for education in coming years. Scarce resources should be utilised as efficiently as possible, with due regard for costs. Repetition of past mistakes should be avoided. As shown in this chapter, education is no guarantee for development. The high hopes for education have often not been fulfilled. Nevertheless, education is still one of the important links in the process of development. Developing countries are well advised to continue to invest in it.

Questions for review

1. What are the most important problems presently facing educational systems in developing countries?
2. Discuss the non-economic functions of education.
3. Give an overview of human capital theory. Explain the role of productivity in this theory.
4. Why are expenditures in education skewed towards higher education, in spite of the fact that returns to primary education are higher than to tertiary education?
5. Discuss the criticisms of human capital theory put forward by proponents of screening theory.
6. Does innate ability explain the cognitive performance of students or does school quality matter. If so, how?
7. Discuss the most common indicators of educational performance, and their strengths and weaknesses.
8. What is non-formal education? To what extent is non-formal education an alternative to formal education?
9. To what extent is investment in education a necessary condition for economic development?

10. What part can universities and educational institutions play in the national system of innovation?
11. Should governments give priority to primary or tertiary education? Discuss the various arguments in favour of different priorities.
12. What is meant by the complementarities between investment in physical and human capital? Why are these important?
13. Discuss the factors that influence the success or failure of literacy programmes.

Further reading

The main sources of data on comparative educational performance are UNESCO publications and statistics. A wealth of educational statistics and reports can be found on the website of the UNESCO Institute of Statistics: http://stats.uis.unesco.org/unesco/tableviewer/document.aspx?ReportId=143. Useful statistical publications by UNESCO include the *Statistical Yearbook*, published on an annual basis until 1999; *Education for All: Year 2000 Assessment. Statistical Document* (UNESCO, 2000a); *The 2002 Global Education for All Monitoring Report: Is the World on Track?* (UNESCO, 2002c); and the *Global Educational Digest*, published from 2003 onwards. The comparative data on student performance of the OECD *Programme on International Student Assessment* (PISA) can be accessed at www.oecd.org/pisa.

Seminal publications on human capital theory include Becker's *Human Capital: A Theoretical and Empirical Analysis, with Special Reference to Education* (1964), Schultz's *Investment in Human Capital: The Role of Education and Research* (1971) and Mincer's *Schooling, Earnings and Experience* (1974).

An overview of human capital theory is provided by Schultz in an article in Volume I of Chenery and Srinivasan (eds.) *Handbook of Development Economics*, 'Education, Investment and Returns' (1988). Blaug has provided an excellent critical evaluation of human capital theory in his article 'The Empirical Status of Human Capital Theory: A Slightly Jaundiced Survey', in the *Journal of Economic Literature* (1976), and his NIAS lecture entitled *The Economic Value of Higher Education* (1990). Empirical estimates of returns to different types of education are provided in a long series of valuable papers by Psacharopoulos and his associates. These include three World Bank Policy Research papers, *Returns to Investment in Education: A Global Update* (Psacharopoulos, 1993), *Returns to Investment in Education: A Further Update* (Psacharopoulos and Patrinos , 2002) and *Education. Past, Present and Future Challenges* (Patrinos and Psacharopoulos , 2011). Recently, a more technical review of the human capital literature by Behrman, 'Investment in Education – Inputs and Incentives', has appeared in Volume 5 of Rodrik and Rosenzweig (eds.) *Handbook of Development Economics* (2010).

There has been a proliferation of datasets on human capital. One of the most-often used is the Barro and Lee dataset on years of education per member of the population (15+ and 25+). The most recent version was published in 2010 (Barro and Lee, 2010; see also www.barrolee.com). Another dataset is that of De la Fuente and Doménech (2006). Long-run global trends in human capital accumulation are analysed in *The Century of Education* by Morrisson and Murtin (2009).

Interesting historical publications on the role of education in development are Anderson and Bowman, 'Education and Economic Modernization in Historical Perspective' (1976), Bowman and Anderson, 'Human Capital and Economic Modernisation in Historical Perspective' (1973) and Sandberg's outstanding article, 'Ignorance, Poverty and Economic Backwardness in the Early Stages of European Industrialisation: Variations on Alexander Gerschenkron's Grand Theme' (1982). This tradition is continued in Godo and Hayami's paper 'Catching Up in Education in the Economic Catch-up of Japan with the United States, 1890–1990' (2002), in *Economic Development and Cultural Change*.

For a comprehensive overview of educational problems and issues in developing countries a useful, though somewhat dated source is Philip Coombs, *The World Crisis in Education: The View from the 1980s* (1985). The current state of the debates on the role of education in economic development is well represented in several good review articles: Glewwe, 'Schools and Skills in Developing Countries: Education Policies and Socioeconomic Outcomes' (2002), Krueger and Lindahl, 'Education for Growth: Why and for Whom?' (2001) and Pritchett's critical articles 'Where has All the Education Gone?' (2001) and 'Does Learning to Add Up Add Up? The Returns to Schooling in Aggregate Data' (2006).

Hanushek and Wößmann provide a masterly overview of 'The Role of Cognitive Skills in Economic Development' (2008). Their article represents the shift from education quantity – years of education – to educational quality in the literature.

For the debate on migration and brain drain one can consult the review articles of Docquier and Rapoport, 'Globalization, Brain Drain and Development' (2012), in the *Journal of Economic Literature*, and Gibson and McKenzie, 'Eight Questions about Brain Drain' (2011), in the *Journal of Economic Perspectives*.

8

Economic development, structural change and industrialisation

As long as people work with their bare hands, their daily production will remain low. This sets a limit to the attainable level of economic welfare in a traditional agriculture-based economy. Higher standards of living can only be realised if production per worker increases. One of the principal ways to raise labour productivity is by providing workers with tools, implements and machines – in other words through capital accumulation.

Some sectors offer better opportunities for capital accumulation and productivity increases than others. Therefore, economic development and capital accumulation are linked to structural change. Since the mid eighteenth century, capital accumulation and accelerated growth have been intimately associated with the emergence of the industrial sector, i.e. with industrialisation. This chapter focuses on structural change and the relationships between agriculture and industry in the course of economic development. It provides a setting for the discussion of industrialisation in Chapter 9 and agricultural development in Chapter 10.

Structural change is not limited to industrialisation. It also refers to other changes in the structure of the economy. One of the interesting questions raised in this chapter is whether manufacturing will continue to play the leading role it has played in the past two-and-a-half centuries. Services seem to be becoming more important over time. But manufacturing will continue to be one of the important engines of growth in developing countries in the years to come.

In the framework of proximate, intermediate and ultimate causality, structural change operates at the level of proximate causality. The debates about the roles of industrial policy and comparative advantage are typically situated at the level of intermediate causality. At the ultimate level patterns of comparative advantage are influenced by resource endowments. In highly simplified form these relationships are depicted in Figure 8.1.

Structural transformation can be pursued in different ways. In one strategy, primary exports and international trade provide the resources for structural change and capital accumulation in the industrial sector. In another, resources are transferred directly from one sector to another in the context of a closed economy.

This chapter opens with a brief discussion of patterns of structural change in section 8.1. Section 8.2 explains the connections between capital accumulation, structural change and industrialisation. Section 8.3 is devoted to the debate about engines of growth. Sections 8.4 – 8.7 distinguish between structural change in closed models and structural change in open models of the economy. Section 8.4 discusses closed models at early stages of development. Section 8.5 focuses on open models and discusses the role of primary exports in development. It contrasts the views of export optimists who see primary exports as an engine of growth and export pessimists, who focus on disadvantages of primary exports. The notion of a balance between agriculture and industry in the context of a closed

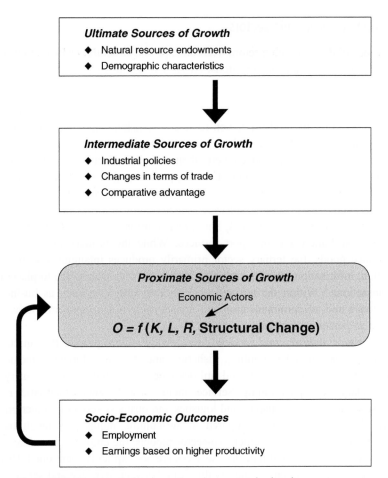

Figure 8.1 Structural change and socio-economic development

model is discussed in section 8.6. Section 8.7 returns to open economy models and introduces labour-intensive manufactured exports.

8.1 Economic development and structural transformation

Economic development is broader than economic growth. It involves a qualitative change in the structure of the economy, shifting resources from activities with low productivity in traditional agriculture to sectors with higher levels of productivity and more potential for productivity growth. In the course of the process, the economy also becomes more diversified, producing a wider range of goods and services (Saviotti, 1996; Saviotti and Pyka, 2009). If structural change has the effect of increasing the importance of productive activities it is growth-enhancing. But if the importance of less productive activities increases, structural change may even become growth-reducing (McMillan and Rodrik, 2011).

8.1.1	Definitions of economic sectors

Discussions of dualism, intersectoral relationships and structural change often suffer from a lack of clarity in sectoral demarcations. At least four kinds of sectoral distinctions can be distinguished:

1. *The primary, secondary sector and tertiary sectors.* The primary sector includes the production of foodstuffs, non-food crops, fishing, hunting, forestry and mining (Lundahl, 1985). The secondary sector uses primary products, which are directly extracted from nature, and converts them into manufactured products. It consists of manufacturing and construction. Utilities, providing gas, water and electricity, are also included in the secondary sector. The tertiary sector consists of a great variety of service activities, including software, telecommunication services, financial and busi-
   [...] s, hotel, restaurant and tourism services, wholesale and [...] rt services. While the primary and secondary sectors [...] ctor primarily produces intangibles such as communi- [...]; of goods and persons from place to place, or financial [...] ry sector, some subsectors such as business services, [...] and transport are much more productive than others [...]

   [...] es. Besides agriculture proper, the agricultural sector [...] fisheries and forestry. Industry includes mining, [...] utilities (see ISIC, 1990). Thus industry equals the [...] rvices include a wide range of activities ranging from [...] logistics and business services. Government services [...] ed to agriculture, industry is much more capital- [...] o-sector models, the emphasis is on the relationships [...] Services are not explicitly mentioned. However, with [...] iding line between industry and services is blurred. [...], which are part of the service sector, are just as [...]...ve as utilities, which belong to the industrial sector. On the other hand, parts of the service sector such as personal care and personal services are extremely labour-intensive, sometimes even more so than agriculture.

3. *The traditional sector versus the modern commercial sector.* The traditional sector includes subsistence agriculture, traditional crafts production, and the rural and urban informal sector. The modern sector includes manufacturing, construction and mining, but also commercial agriculture (including plantations) and formal service activities. In recent decades developing countries have frequently developed new agricultural based exports such as cut flowers, vegetables, brand wines and coffees, or salmon. These are referred to as non-traditional exports and are also part of the modern sector (Iizuka and Gebreeyesus, 2012). The modern sector is characterised by a monetary economy, production for the market and higher levels of productivity and technological sophistication.

---

[1] While secondary activities result in goods, services activities result in changes, transformations, or movements. For a critical discussion of service sector definitions see Glassmeier and Howland (1994). The authors note that some modern service activities such as software development result in tangible and permanent outputs.

Handwritten annotations:

Economic Development:
- Growth-enhancing: if structural changes increase productive activities
- Growth-reducing: less productive activities increase

Economic Sectors:
1) production of foodstuffs (Primary), manufactured products (secondary), diverse service activities (Tertiary)
2) Services: include gov. services; industry: capital-intensive
3) non-traditional exports in developing c.
4) Spatial distinction

4. *The rural sector versus the urban sector.* The distinction between the countryside (rural areas) and the urban sector is a spatial one. Cities and towns are locations characterised by higher population densities than rural areas. Industrial activities are more important in the urban sector and agricultural activities more important in the rural sector. In rural areas one finds both subsistence agriculture and commercial agriculture. But the rural sector is not exclusively agricultural (see Chapter 10). In rural areas one also finds rural industries, traditional crafts production, wage labour, sometimes mining, services, and a rural informal sector.

The various sectoral distinctions are summarised in Table 8.1.

Table 8.1: Sectoral distinctions

Primary sector	Secondary sector	Tertiary sector
Food production	Transformation of primary	Wholesale and retail trade
Cash crops	and semi-finished goods	Tourism
Mining	Manufacturing	Transport
Fishery	Construction	Communication
Logging/forestry	Utilities (electricity, gas, water)	Finance
		Education and health
		Government services
		Personal services

Agriculture	Industry	Services
Agriculture	Mining	See above
Fishery	Manufacturing	
Logging/forestry	Construction	
	Utilities	

Traditional sector		Modern/Commercial sector
Subsistence agriculture		Modern industry, incl.
Informal manufacturing		mining, construction and utilities
Handicrafts		Plantations, non-traditional exports
Informal services		Commercial agriculture
		Market services

Rural sector		Urban sector
Subsistence agriculture		Urban industry
Commercial agriculture		Formal services/government
Rural handicrafts		Urban informal sector
Rural wage labour		
Rural informal sector		
Rural industry		

The four classifications differ considerably. But in the literature on structural change they are often used in a loose and careless manner. For some two-sector models (e.g. the Lewis model of economic development with unlimited supplies of labour to be discussed in Chapter 9) the distinction between the traditional sector and the modern commercial sector seems to be the most important one. But two-sector models also frequently refer to the relationships between agriculture and manufacturing. Other theories focus on the relationships between primary and secondary production. When one is talking about the *urban–industrial bias* (Lipton, 1977), the important distinction is between urban and rural communities. The term *rural development* is also based on the rural–urban distinction. It indicates that the rural community comprises more than agricultural activities only (see Chapter 10). In a paper by McMillan and Rodrik (2011) the distinction is between low-productivity and high-productivity sectors, the latter implicitly being associated with manufacturing.

In sections 8.2.2, 8.4.1 and 8.6 of this chapter, the emphasis is on the relationships between agriculture and manufacturing in the course of economic development. Agriculture consists of subsistence production and market production of foodstuffs and other agricultural products by both smallholders and large commercial farms and plantations. Forestry and fishing will not be dealt with explicitly, although they also belong to the agricultural sector. In section 8.5, which discusses the role of primary exports in economic development, the focus shifts to the distinction between the primary and the secondary sector. Of course, agricultural exports are important primary exports and much of the argument in this chapter will focus on agricultural exports, but primary exports also include mining exports.

8.1.2   Structural change

'Structural change' is a neutral term which can refer to all sorts of changes in the structure of employment and output. It can refer to the emergence of manufacturing, the emergence of non-traditional exports, or the increasing importance of services. It can also refer to process of de-industrialisation.

Since the middle of the eighteenth century modern economic growth has been closely associated with a specific type of structural change, namely industrialisation (Allen, 2009; Clark, 1940; Chenery *et al.*, 1986; Kuznets, 1966; Maddison, 1991; Syrquin, 1988, Williamson, 2011). In industry it is possible to employ much more capital per worker, so that productivity per person and per hour is much higher than in agriculture. Economies of scale are also of major importance. In the concentrated large-scale production processes characteristic of industry, one can produce more efficiently than in the decentralised small-scale production units characteristic of traditional agriculture.

As emphasised in the seminal writings of Colin Clark and Simon Kuznets, economic development involves a *structural transformation* in which factors of production are transferred from the sector with the lowest productivity, agriculture, to the industrial sector where productivity is much higher and the pace of technological change and productivity growth is more rapid.[2] In the course of this process of structural change, the share of

---

[2] In discussions of industrialisation, the main emphasis is on the most dynamic sector: manufacturing. The construction sector is quite large, but is usually not seen as a driving force in economic development. The terms 'structural change' and 'structural transformation' are used interchangeably.

agriculture in the total labour force declines, and the share of industry increases. The importance of the agricultural sector also declines in terms of its share in GDP, while the importance of industry increases. Structural transformation involves more than changes in the sector structure alone. It also refers to increases in savings and investment rates, changes in the quality and variety of goods and services, rapid urbanisation, demographic transitions with declining death rates followed by later declines in birth rates, epidemiological transitions, changes in income inequality[3] and changing social institutions, attitudes and beliefs without which modern economic growth would be impossible (Caldwell, 1997; Frederikson, 1969; Kuznets, 1971; Syrquin, 1988).

Apart from the productivity differential, a low income elasticity of the demand for agricultural products also plays an important role in the transformation process. As societies become richer, people tend to spend an ever-smaller part of their additional income on agricultural products. There is a limit to the amount of food people can consume. Once the basic need for food has been met, people tend to spend more on manufactured goods as their incomes go up. The share of food consumption in total expenditure will tend to decrease.[4] Thus structural change is also tied up with changes in the pattern and composition of demand.

Following the rise of the industrial sector in the advanced economies, the service sector started to increase. By the 1940s the share of industry in GDP in the advanced economies had already reached its peak. Note that industrial value added never exceeded 40 per cent of GDP, while manufacturing peaked at around 30 per cent. Since then, the share of services has steadily been on the increase. They now account for more than 70 per cent of GDP and employment in the advanced economies. Modern economies are predominantly service economies. However, the manufacturing sector still plays a key role as an important source of technological change.

The process of structural transformation away from agriculture that took place in the presently rich countries in the past, is now taking place in developing countries. In Chapter 3, we presented data on changing sectoral shares in employment and output for our sample of thirty-one countries. In Tables 8.2 and 8.3 we present similar sectoral shares in value added for a broader sample of eighty-nine countries.

Table 8.2 shows how the share of the agricultural sector in developing countries dramatically declined from 37 per cent in 1950 to 16 per cent in 2005. Benjamin Higgins, one of the early advocates of large-scale industrialisation strategies, wrote that 'the basic formula for development ... was "getting rid of farmers"' (Higgins and Higgins, 1979: 12). Figure 8.2 shows that there is an important element of truth in this provocative statement. The figure shows that there is a strong correlation between the level of GNP per capita (in current 2011 dollars) and the shares of agriculture in GDP. The poorest countries are the countries that continue to have large shares of agriculture.

---

[3] The Kuznets hypothesis of the inverted U curve suggests that income inequality increases in earlier stages of industrialisation and decreases in later stages (Kuznets, 1955). See for further discussion Chapters 3 and 9.

[4] This is referred to as Engel's law. The income elasticity of the demand for agricultural products is the percentage increase in the consumption of agricultural products divided by the percentage increase in real income per capita. If income elasticity is less than one, the share of agricultural products in total expenditure will decrease as per capita income rises.

In spite of the common trend of a shrinking agricultural sector, it is important to emphasise that there is no standard pattern of structural change. Developing countries cannot simply copy earlier development experiences. One striking difference with earlier experiences is that service sectors have expanded much earlier in developing countries. In Table 8.2, we see that the shares of the service sector in developing countries already exceeded those of both industry and agriculture in the 1950s and 1960s. Another crucial difference is that the Western countries were the first to industrialise, whilst developing countries had to compete as latecomers in a highly competitive world economy dominated by giant industrial corporations and powerful advanced economies.

With regard to industrialisation we see interesting regional differences. In Latin America, the Middle East and Africa, the share of manufacturing peaked around 1980, followed by a process of de-industrialisation. In Asia the share of manufacturing continued to be high, reaching 22 per cent in 2005, much higher than the average of 16.1 per cent in the advanced economies. While de-industrialisation is normal at higher levels of per capita GDP, what we observe in Africa and Latin America is a pattern of de-industrialisation at lower and medium levels of per capita income. Fiona Tregenna (2013) refers to this as 'pre-mature de-industrialisation'. One should also note that this is not the first instance of de-industrialisation in the developing world. Jeffrey Williamson (2011) and Paul Bairoch (1982) argue that the countries on the periphery of the world economy experienced an earlier process of comparative de-industrialisation in the course of the nineteenth century.

In a variety of publications Chenery and his co-authors have emphasised the differences in patterns of structural change (Chenery, 1979; Chenery and Taylor, 1968; Chenery, Robinson and Syrquin, 1986; Kirkpatrick, 1987; Syrquin, 1988; see also Haraguchi and Rezonja, 2013). Thus in developing countries with an abundance of natural resources the shift away from agriculture and mining will be delayed. As wages in these countries are higher, they are likely to choose more capital-intensive production techniques in manufacturing. They will also focus on resource-processing manufacturing activities. Countries that are unable to export primary products will industrialise earlier and are more likely to concentrate on labour-intensive export production. In small countries the share of trade and capital imports in GDP will tend to be high. These countries will tend to specialise in a few lines of industrial production. In countries with large domestic markets such as China, Brazil, India, or Indonesia the pattern of industrialisation will be more diversified. There are greater opportunities for developing a domestic intermediate goods and capital goods sector. The nature of industrial policies also affects the pattern of industrialisation. Finally, the timing of industrialisation is of importance. Countries such as Brazil, China, India, and Egypt had at least sixty–seventy years' experience with large-scale industry prior to 1950, especially in food processing and textiles. Countries in Sub-Saharan Africa had hardly any experience with industrialisation before the Second World War. This is one of the reasons why post-war industrialisation in these countries was initially rather unsuccessful (Szirmai and Lapperre, 2001). The countries with rapid industrial growth in the post-war period all had substantial industrial experience before the Second World War (Pack, 1988). By now Sub-Saharan Africa has had over fifty years experience with – failed – industrialisation. Together with much higher present levels of human capital and accelerating growth after 2000, there may be a new window of opportunity for African industrialisation.

Table 8.2: Structure of production, 1950–2005
(Gross value added in agriculture, industry, manufacturing and services as percentage of GDP in current prices, regional averages)

Average	1950				1960				1980				2005			
	AG	IND	MAN	SERV	AG	IND	MAN	SERV	AG	IND	MAN	SERV	AG	IND	MAN	SERV
15 Asian countries	49	14	10	36	37	22	14	41	23	33	22	44	14	33	22	53
25 Latin American countries	29	25	15	46	23	29	17	48	16	32	20	51	10	31	15	59
10 Middle Eastern and North African countries	31	23	9	46	23	27	11	49	12	39	14	49	11	33	13	52
18 African countries	43	22	11	34	42	21	8	37	29	28	12	43	28	27	10	45
68 Developing countries	37	22	12	42	31	25	13	44	21	32	17	47	16	31	15	53
21 Advanced economies	16	40	29	45	12	41	30	47	4	35	23	60	2	27	16	71

Source:
Szirmai *et al.* (2013a), Table 1.2. Original source World Bank, *World Development Indicators*, supplemented by country sources documented in Szirmai (2009).

Table 8.3: Share of manufacturing in value added, 1950–2005 (gross value added in manufacturing as percentage of GDP in current prices, regional averages)

Average	1950	1955	1960	1965	1970	1975	1980	1985	1990	1995	2000	2005
15 Asian countries	9.8	13.7	14.3	15.9	18.9	19.9	22.1	21.7	20.8	20.8	21.7	22.0
25 Latin American countries	14.7	15.2	16.6	18.0	19.2	20.1	19.9	19.6	18.7	17.0	16.4	15.4
10 Middle Eastern and North African countries	8.6	9.0	11.0	10.8	11.7	13.2	13.8	12.5	16.3	14.8	13.1	13.3
18 African countries	10.9	8.7	8.3	9.7	10.7	11.5	11.7	11.8	12.9	11.1	10.7	10.0
68 Developing countries	12.1	12.8	13.2	14.3	15.8	16.8	17.4	17.1	17.3	16.0	15.6	15.2
21 Advanced economies	29.4	30.0	30.3	31.0	27.4	25.0	22.9	21.7	20.6	19.3	18.2	16.1

Source:
See Table 8.2.

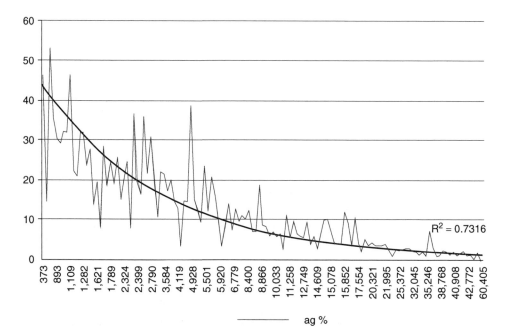

Figure 8.2 Agriculture as a percentage of GDP, 2011
Source: World Bank, *World Development Indicators Online, 2013* (130 countries, excluding countries with less than 1 million inhabitants (2011 PPP dollars)).

8.2   Capital accumulation and structural change

8.2.1   Capital accumulation and industrialisation

Physical capital and financial capital

The term 'capital' has two different meanings, one concrete and one financial. The word 'capital' in its concrete sense refers to the physical stock of machines, implements, buildings and devices used in the process of production. Economists usually define capital in this sense as produced means of production, with a lifetime of at least one year. The financial meaning of the term 'capital' refers to a hoarded amount of financial means and securities. In explaining economic growth, we are primarily interested in the growth of physical stocks of capital per person employed.

Savings and investment

Capital accumulation in both senses is only possible if people are voluntarily willing or are involuntarily forced to refrain from present consumption in order to free resources for investment in future production. This refraining from consumption is called *saving*.

In a subsistence economy, without a developed financial system of banks, financial institutions and money circulation, there is hardly any difference between saving and investing. If an agricultural household saves part of its harvest as seed, rather than consuming all of it, this represents saving and investment at the same time. A farmer who uses part of his labour to clear new land instead of producing food for consumption is both saving and investing. If a small industrial entrepreneur uses part of his profits to buy new machines and implements rather than consumer goods, his savings equal his investments. The value of his investments is his financial capital. The machines and implements are his physical capital. In early industrialisation processes in Europe much of the finance for investment came directly from within the industrial enterprises themselves.

In a highly developed economy the distance between consumers and producers, saving and investing has become much greater. One of the typical problems of developed economies (and of modern economic theory) is the match between the willingness to save and the willingness to invest. Financial intermediaries play an important role here. Savings are often deposited with financial institutions such as banks, pension funds and investment institutions. Through long and complex chains of financial institutions and financial markets, these savings are finally channelled to investors. Today well-functioning financial institutions and markets are considered to be of major importance for economic development (Hermes and Lensink, 1996; Thirlwall, 1999, Chapter 15; World Bank, 1990). The weakness of financial institutions was one of the causes of the disastrous economic crisis of 1997 in Asia (e.g. Hill, 2000a). It is also the root cause of the present economic crisis in the advanced economies since 2008.

What is the relationship between capital accumulation and industrialisation?

Capital goods are used in all sectors of the economy. For instance, the agricultural sector makes use of agricultural machinery and invests in irrigation systems (see Chapter 10). The service sector invests in buildings, computers and telecommunication equipment. The transport sector invests in aircraft, ships, railways and trucks (or ox carts). Nevertheless, in economic history, the increase in the amount of capital per worker was inextricably linked with industrialisation, structural change and the rise of manufacturing. It was the concentrated nature of factory production which offered and still offers the greatest opportunities for capital accumulation and increases in the scale of production.

The term 'industry' as used here refers not only to manufacturing, but also to the industrial sector in its broadest sense, including mining, construction and utilities (the supply of gas, electricity and water). Thus mining is extremely capital-intensive. But within industry, manufacturing is considered to be the most dynamic sector. The dramatic increase in labour productivity and income per capita in the Western capitalist economies since the mid eighteenth century is primarily the result of processes of capital accumulation and associated processes of technological change in manufacturing. Capital accumulation is a dynamic process, which not only consists of more capital goods but also of incremental and radical changes in production techniques.

Naturally, capital accumulation is not the only way to increase labour productivity. Labour productivity may also increase as a result of more efficient working methods, division of labour, specialisation in production, economies of scale, schooling or investment in improved health of workers and of course technological change. Still, capital accumulation has been one of the important means to increase labour productivity in the economy (see Maddison, 2001).[5]

Accumulation of industrial capital in open and closed models of the economy: early and late stages of development

Structural change involves changes in the structure of employment and output and transfers of resources from one sector to another. The resources are used to accumulate capital. To structure the discussion of industrialisation in the following sections, we make a rough distinction between (a) earlier and later stages of industrialisation; (b) open and closed models of economic development (Lewis, 1950, 1954, 1978b; Myint, 1975, 1980; Nicholls, 1964; Timmer, 1988).

Earlier and later stages of industrialisation

In order to invest in capital accumulation in the modern sector of the economy, savings need to be mobilised and transferred to the new sector. In this chapter, our main interest is in investment in manufacturing and in the infrastructure of roads, harbours, railways, telecommunications and energy supply.[6] Before the onset of industrialisation the great majority of the population found its livelihood in agriculture. The agricultural sector was the only domestic sector that could provide labour and savings, which could be used to start industrialisation. The construction of a modern industrial sector inevitably started with a transfer of productive resources from agriculture to industry.

---

[5] We abstract here from the complex issue of the distinction between growth of the capital stock and technological change.

[6] To a lesser extent we are also interested in investment in mining and construction.

At later stages of development the agricultural and the industrial sectors existed alongside each other. Strategic choices had to be made with respect to the priority given to either agriculture or industry in economic policy. Now, the question arises of the *appropriate balance between sectors* in the course of structural transformation.

Open and closed models of development and accumulation

The process of capital accumulation in the modern sector of developing countries can be studied either in the context of a closed or an open model of the economy. In a closed economy there are no economic ties with the outside world. There is no foreign trade. There are no international flows of profits, loans, or investments, and there is no international migration. In order to invest in the modern sector of a closed economy, all savings need to be earned and mobilised within the boundaries of the domestic economy. The most extreme example of a closed economy is a subsistence agriculture economy.

In a closed economy, the initial resources for industrialisation can only be forthcoming from the agricultural sector. Closed models of industrialisation, therefore, analyse the different mechanisms for transferring resources from one sector to another. These transfer mechanisms are studied within the framework of so-called *two-sector models* of economic development. These models focus on the interactions and resource flows between agricultural and industrial sectors in different stages of economic development. In closed economy models, an important issue is the *balance* between sectors of the economy. The output of one sector has to be absorbed by another sector. The inputs required by one sector have to be produced by the other sectors. Lack of balance may cause bottlenecks. Two-sector models will be discussed further in Chapter 9.

In open economy models, attention is paid to the relations with the international economy. Many of the interactions between agriculture and industry take place via the outside world. Agricultural exports can earn revenues and foreign exchange, which are potentially available for reinvestment in the industrial sector. Once the mining sector has developed, mineral export revenues can in turn provide resources for other sectors such as manufacturing. Theories that centre on primary agricultural and mining exports as the engines of growth and transformation are called *theories of primary export-led growth*. These theories will be discussed in section 8.5.

There are also financial flows from and to abroad. Capital accumulation and industrialisation may be speeded up by FDI, bank loans and aid flows from abroad. But, the pace of capital accumulation may also be retarded if resources drain away abroad (Baran, 1957).

An important difference between open and closed models is that there is less need to focus on the *balance between sectors* in open models. If the necessary inputs for a given sector are not produced domestically, they can be imported and can be paid for by the revenues from exported products.

Nevertheless, the open models of structural change also assume a transfer of resources from agriculture to industry during the initial stages of industrialisation. In this case, profits from agricultural exports are reinvested in industry. Government policy discriminates against agriculture by taxing exports and investing in and supporting other sectors. However, once the industrial sector has started developing, strategic decisions have to be faced in open models just as in closed models. Does policy continue to give priority to industry over agriculture or not?

The distinction between open and closed models can be used as an analytic approximation of reality, but also serves as an indication of the orientation of economic policy. Since the late nineteenth century there are no completely closed economies. But economies do vary substantially in their degree of openness. In terms of policy orientation, many developing countries have attempted to reduce their dependence on foreign trade and foreign finance through an inward-looking import substitution policy in the period 1950–80. Though they usually did try to attract foreign finance, investment and capital, the mental model underlying inward-looking policy making is a closed one, in which dependence on international trade and the outside world is seen as a threat. Other countries chose specialisation according to comparative advantage, openness to imports, openness to foreign investment and an outward-looking export orientation.

A stylised historical sequence of structural change in developing economies starts with the primacy of agriculture in a relatively closed economy. This is followed by a period dominated by primary agricultural or mining exports, which for developing countries roughly spans the period from 1830 to around 1929. The next phase is that of import-substituting industrialisation, which lasts from the 1930s to the mid 1980s. Since then the emphasis has shifted towards more outward-looking policies with an emphasis on labour-intensive manufactured exports from developing countries.

For an analysis of economic development in developing countries from the mid nineteenth century to 1929, an open model is most useful. Most developing countries started their modern economic development in the second half of the nineteenth century by exporting primary agricultural and mining products. Export revenues and foreign investment served to finance capital accumulation in infrastructure.

For an understanding of industrialisation strategies from 1930 to 1985 the closed model is more helpful. Export revenues had created an urban market for manufactured imports. Developing countries tried to reduce their dependence on international trade and primary exports and to replace manufactured products imported from Western countries by products manufactured at home (*import substitution*, see Chapter 9). This involved substantial protection of domestic manufacturing industries. Starting in the 1960s, East Asian countries such as South Korea, Hong Kong, Taiwan and Singapore pioneered the shift towards labour-intensive industrial exports from developing countries, following the earlier example of Japan, but they did continue to protect their domestic markets. Since the mid 1990s, the emphasis has shifted worldwide to more liberalisation and a more open export-oriented policy stance. But since 2000, the market-oriented Washington consensus has been under renewed attack following the disappointing economic developments in Latin America, Sub-Saharan Africa and the countries in transition from central planning (Stiglitz, 2002).

8.3   The debate about engines of growth

8.3.1   Introduction

Until recently, the orthodox view in development economics was that industrialisation was the only route to development. In recent years this view has been questioned (e.g. Timmer and de Vries, 2009). In the advanced economies, services are by far the most important sector. In developing countries such as India the software and IT sector has played an increasingly important role in growth. Also, we saw that many developing countries have very high shares of services, while manufacturing is levelling off. Within the service sector we find dynamic subsectors such as transport and trade, retailing, software, finance and business services. Other authors point to different kinds of structural change, such as the emergence of non-traditional exports (Iizuka and Gebreeyesus, 2012). As a result it is a legitimate question whether manufacturing is becoming less important as an engine of growth than in the past. The following sections summarise this debate.

8.3.2 Manufacturing as the engine of growth

There are powerful empirical and theoretical arguments in favour of industrialisation as the main engine of growth in economic development (see Szirmai, 2012; Szirmai *et al.*, 2013b). The arguments are summarised in Box 8.1.

BOX 8.1 : Arguments for manufacturing

- There is a **correlation** between industrialisation and economic development.
- Productivity is higher in the manufacturing sector than in the agricultural sector; this is referred to as the **structural change bonus**.
- The transfer of resources to a service sector with slow productivity growth provides a **structural change burden**.
- The industrial sector offers special opportunities for increases in the **scale of production**.
- The industrial sector offers special opportunities for **capital accumulation**.
- **Linkage and spillover effects** are stronger in manufacturing than in agriculture, mining or services.
- **Technological advance** is concentrated in the manufacturing sector; this sector offers special opportunities for embodied and disembodied technological progress
- As per capita incomes rise, the share of agricultural expenditures in total expenditures declines and the share of expenditures on manufactured goods increases; this is referred to as **Engel's law**.

Empirical correlations between industrialisation and economic development

The empirical argument points to the overall relationship between the degree of industrialisation and the level of economic development. There is not a single example of successful catch up since 1870 that has not involved industrialisation. The more successful developing countries are invariably those that have been able to industrialise.

Statistically, the relationship is less straightforward. Services account for an increasing portion of growth in developing economies (see Timmer and de Vries, 2009). In Figure 8.3, we have roughly graphed the share of manufacturing against the level of national income in 2011. At lower levels of income there is a positive relationship between share of manufacturing and income level. But this tends to taper off at middle-income levels, suggesting that industrialisation is more important for growth at lower levels of income per capita. Similar results have been found in other studies (e.g. Rodrik, 2009).

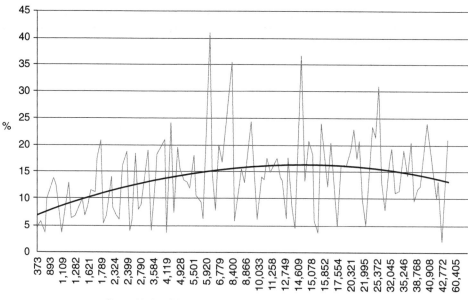

Figure 8.3 Manufacturing share and income per capita, 2011
Source: World Bank, *World Development Indicators Online* (130 countries, excluding countries with less than 1 million inhabitants).

Szirmai and Verspagen (2011) have regressed five-year average growth rates on shares of manufacturing at the beginning of these five-year periods in panel dataset from 1950 until 2005, controlling for a variety of country characteristics. On balance they find support for the manufacturing as engine of growth hypothesis, especially in combination with levels of human capital. But they also conclude that this relationship is becoming less pronounced over time (see also Fagerberg and Verspagen, 1999, 2002, 2007).

Structural change bonus

A second important argument in favour of industrialisation derives from the fact that labour productivity in agriculture is much lower than labour productivity in industry. A transfer of labour from low-productivity agriculture to high-productivity industry results in an immediate increase in overall productivity and income per capita. This transfer has been a major source of growth in developing countries. It is referred to as the structural change bonus (Timmer and Szirmai, 2000).

Structural change burden

In a classic article Baumol (1967) has argued that there are limits to productivity growth in many services, due to the inherently labour-intensive nature of these activities. As services are productivity resistant, structural change towards services will inevitably result in a slowdown of growth. Support for this reasoning is provided by the much slower rates of growth of the advanced service economies compared to developing countries and emerging countries such as Brazil, China, or India. However, parts of the modern service sector do turn out to be capable of rapid productivity improvements, for instance in IT services, financial services and transport, communication and logistics (for further elaboration see section 8.3.4).

Linkage effects

Another economic argument often put forward in favour of industrialisation is that the *forward and backward linkage* effects in the manufacturing sector are so much stronger than in agriculture and mining. Investment in one branch of manufacturing can have strong positive effects on other branches of the economy. Thus, industrialisation can contribute to the dynamism of the whole economy. This argument will be elaborated further in Chapter 9.

Opportunities for capital accumulation and technological change

Furthermore, it is argued that the manufacturing sector offers special opportunities for capital accumulation, economies of scale and technological progress. For instance in 1990, capital intensity in manufacturing in a sample of fifteen developing countries was 86 per cent higher than that of the economy as a whole, while capital intensity in agriculture was only 25 per cent of the total economy average (Szirmai, 2012a, Table 8).

In economic growth accounting studies, the contribution of growth of physical capital to growth of output in post-war advanced economies turns out to be less important than previously thought. Other factors such as growth of employment, growth of human capital and especially innovation and technological change are very important as well (Abramovitz, 1989b; Fagerberg and Godinho, 2005; Maddison, 1987). However, for developing countries, physical capital accumulation still seems to be of considerable importance, because they start with so much less capital per worker to begin with (Hofman, 1993; Nadiri, 1972; Pilat, 1994; Thirlwall, 1997).

In the past it was argued that productivity growth in manufacturing was much higher than in agriculture. This used to be the case, but this is no longer so obvious. In the advanced economies growth of labour productivity in agriculture in the post-war period has been higher than in industry – particularly due to biotechnological innovation (see Maddison, 1991: 150–1). A similar pattern has been found for sixteen developing countries in Asia and Latin America since 1973 (Szirmai, 2012a). However, with shrinking agricultural sectors, agricultural productivity growth does not contribute that much to aggregate growth in a country. Levels of labour productivity in industry and manufacturing are still much higher than in agriculture and growth rates of value added and output in these sectors are also much higher than agriculture.

Some brief remarks need to be made here about the difficulties in unscrambling capital accumulation and technological change (see also Chapter 4). From the perspective of a developing country, the use of more capital goods per worker in itself represents a kind of technological change. The mode of production changes dramatically, and the mastering of new – often imported – technologies – requires major innovative efforts on behalf of developing countries and their firms. In this sense, all capital accumulation represents technological change.

But one should distinguish between the increase in the pure volume of existing capital goods (more of the same) and the shift over time from technologically less sophisticated to technologically more advanced capital goods. This is called *embodied technological change*. Also, in the course of economic development, output per unit of input (total factor productivity) can increase due to various factors, among which are shifts from one economic sector to another, economies of scale and more efficient allocation of resources within sectors (see Chapter 3 on the proximate sources of growth). One of the most important factors which can cause increases in output per unit of input is so-called *disembodied technological change*. Disembodied technological change refers to general advances in science, technology and the state of knowledge, increased knowledge about products, markets, raw materials, organisation techniques, learning-by-doing effects and so forth. Cornwall (1977) has argued that manufacturing is indeed the sector where most disembodied and embodied technological change takes place. Lavopa and Szirmai (2012) document that R&D expenditures are indeed disproportionately concentrated in the manufacturing sector. This role of manufacturing as generator of technological change is one of the most powerful arguments in favour of the engine of growth hypothesis. In addition, there are important *technological spillover effects* from the manufacturing sector to other sectors, such as the service sector. Thus, advances in ICT technologies produced in the manufacturing sector fuel technological change in the service sector.

Engel's law

The lower the per capita income of a country, the larger the proportion of that income will be spent on basic agricultural foodstuffs. This is the famous Engel law (Engel, 1857) which approaches structural change from the demand side. As per capita incomes increase, the demand for agricultural products will decline and the demand for industrial products will tend to increase. Economic development creates a mass market for industrial products. If a country does not develop its domestic manufacturing industry, it will have to import all of its manufactured goods. In more recent times, however, a similar reasoning might be applied to services. As incomes increase, a larger proportion of these incomes is spent on – increasingly expensive – services.

8.3.3 Is the agricultural sector a stagnant or a dynamic sector?

In pre-industrial societies the majority of the population is active in the agricultural sector. In a closed economy, the resources required for developing a domestic manufacturing industry can only be found in the agricultural sector. In older development theories and strategies the agricultural sector is therefore mainly considered in negative terms as a reservoir of labour, food and savings (financial capital), which can and should be transferred to the industrial sector. The high prestige of industry coincided with a very dismal view of agriculture. The agricultural sector itself was regarded as traditional, stagnant, and characterised by low productivity and low potential. The dynamic sector was the industrial sector, which – for this very reason – should be developed as soon as possible. This justified squeezing and exploiting the agricultural sector.

Arthur Lewis's well-known model of 'economic development with unlimited supplies of labour' is an example of this view (Lewis, 1954, see Chapter 9 for a full presentation). This model assumes an extremely low marginal productivity in traditional agriculture. Therefore, labour can very simply be withdrawn from agriculture with little or no loss of food production. This labour can be employed more productively in industry and the construction of infrastructure. Lewis does acknowledge the fact that agriculture needs to grow along with the industrial sector in order to prevent economic development from grinding to a halt. If agricultural production stagnates, food prices will increase, and the internal terms of trade (the ratio of agricultural to industrial prices) will turn against the industrial sector.[7] Nevertheless, it cannot be denied that the Lewis model assumes a low agricultural productivity in the initial stages of industrialisation. His assumption is that labour productivity will automatically increase in agriculture when surplus labour is removed. Another example is provided by the famous study of agricultural involution in Java by the economic anthropologist Clifford Geertz (Geertz, 1963). According to Geertz's analysis, in hindsight very mistaken, Indonesian agriculture was a basket case, which should be written off. All energy should be focused on industrialisation.

A more dynamic and positive view of agriculture emphasises that a productive and flourishing agriculture is a precondition for successful industrialisation. Prior to industrialisation, productivity in the agricultural sector must increase sufficiently to produce a surplus over the subsistence needs of the agrarian population. Only when such a surplus is available can processes of transfer to the industrial sector be initiated. Therefore, several authors (development economists, economic historians and agronomists) argue that an increase in labour productivity in agriculture is a necessary condition for industrialisation (Boserup, 1981; Kuznets, 1965; Ranis, 1989; Rostow, 1960; Timmer, 1988).

why agric has to be product

In an open economy the agricultural sector contributes to economic development through its revenues from agricultural exports, which are available for reinvestment in the industrial sector. As in the closed model, a productive and dynamic agricultural sector produces a surplus over its subsistence needs, which can be utilised for development.

All this implies a more positive view of the role of the agricultural sector even in the early stages of industrialisation. Agriculture is a dynamic sector in its own right, with an important contribution to make to economic development. Prior to industrialisation there has to be an agrarian revolution.[8]

Is there any synthesis possible between these conflicting views – transfer of surpluses from a productive agricultural system or squeezing resources out of a low-productive agricultural sector? In a criticism of negative perspectives on agriculture, Reynolds (1975: 14) makes a helpful distinction between transfer of resources from a static agricultural system and transfer of resources from a dynamic agricultural system. In an economy where agricultural productivity prior to industrialisation is stagnant, there can still be surpluses of labour time, food and savings. These surpluses may be withdrawn from the agricultural sector as part of the industrialisation strategy. Forced transfer of surpluses, however, leads to the impoverishment of the rural population and possibly even to famines. Transfer in a more dynamic context implies that agricultural production and productivity can continue to increase as a result of agricultural investment, technological progress, positive incentives and intensification of production. Part of the increment in agricultural output and agricultural real incomes is available for transfer to industry. But sufficient portions of additional earnings are ploughed back into agriculture, to maintain its dynamic momentum.

In the history of European industrialisation, increases in agricultural productivity preceded industrialisation. In developing countries average agricultural output per worker in the 1960s was much lower than in Western countries between 1810 and 1860 (Bairoch, 1975).

---

[7] When food prices increase, wages in the industrial sector must increase in order to compensate for higher prices; thus, the share of profits in value added will tend to decline.

[8] Ester Boserup objects to the term 'agricultural revolution' and emphasises more gradual nature of long-run processes of productivity increase and intensification of production in the agricultural sector (Boserup, 1981).

Their experiences provide instances of transfer of resources out of relatively static agricultural sectors.[9] Both the stagnation of agricultural development in post-war Sub-Saharan Africa and the disappointing outcomes of industrialisation can be interpreted in this perspective (Lapperre, 2001; World Bank, 1989).

8.3.4　What about service-led growth?

There is considerable debate about the role of the service sector. In classical theories of structural change, the first stage was a shift from agriculture to industry, followed by a later shift from industry to services (Clark, 1940). As with agriculture, the image of the service sector was quite negative. This sector could only develop once the industrial sector had been able to supply the population with sufficient physical commodities. According to Veblen (1899), the service and financial sectors were parasites, which lived off the productive efforts of engineers and workers in industry and manufacturing. Marxists defined the service sector as inherently unproductive. Until recently, the national accounts of communist countries did not even measure the output of much of the service sector.[10] In neoclassical economics, Baumol (1967, 1986, 2000) argued that the productivity slowdown of the Western economies was caused by the rise of the service sector (Baumol's law). Haircuts, restaurants, medical services, musical performances and government services are inherently labour-intensive. There is no way of increasing the productivity of these activities through automation or the use of capital. Bloated government bureaucracies in post-war developing countries can be taken as a case in point. They absorb resources, but contribute little to development.

The more recent literature paints a much more positive picture of the service sector (Britton, 1998; Daniels, 1998; Dasgupta and Singh, 2006; De Vries, 2010; Eichengreen, 2009; Glassmeier and Howland, 1994; Marks, 2009; Riddle, 1986; Van Ark et al., 2003). This sector can also make valuable contributions to the process of industrialisation. It is an important intermediate input for an emerging manufacturing sector. As the Indian experience in software since the 1990s testifies, services can be an engine of regional and national growth. Services and manufacturing reinforce each other. At early stages of development, the emergence of communication, transport, trade and financial services is one of the prerequisites for industrialisation (Marks, 2009).

It is time to take a more disaggregated look at the role of services. Though Baumol's law may hold for haircuts and restaurants, government and public services, it does not hold for mobile telecommunication, software development, financial services, transport or distance learning. Recent research points to considerable technological dynamism in parts of the modern service sector, such as telecommunication, banking services, software development, transport, logistics, the explosive development of the internet and so forth (see Triplett, 2002; Van Ark et al., 2002, 2008). These services are increasingly traded internationally.

---

[9] The difference may be explained as follows. In a completely closed economy transfer from the agricultural sector is only possible when the agricultural sector produces a surplus exceeding subsistence needs in agriculture. This is more or less what happened in eighteenth-century England. In developing countries the foundations for industrialisation were laid in the late nineteenth century, in the context of an open model, with large amounts of foreign investment which subsequently attracted labour from the agricultural sector.

[10] The so-called material product system of national accounts (MPS) developed in the Soviet Union excluded most of service output in the calculation of national product. In most former communist countries the MPS has now been completely or partially replaced by the System of National Accounts (SNA).

Tourism may also offer major opportunities of employment creation and development in some developing countries, especially small Island economies where the prospects of industrial driven development are dim. Thus, the service sector is nowadays seen in a more dynamic light (see the collection of articles in Bryson and Daniels, 1998).

8.3.5　Conclusion

In summary, we conclude that different sectors and subsectors can serve as engines of growth, depending on different circumstances and conditions. On balance, the manufacturing sector definitely remains one of the key sectors that contributes in important ways to accelerated growth and catch-up. Industrialisation remains a promising strategy for developing countries and premature de-industrialisation in developing countries is a source of serious concern. In the remainder of this chapter and in Chapter 9, we will continue to focus on manufacturing.

8.4　Structural change in closed economies at early stages of development

8.4.1　The development of agriculture as a prerequisite for industrialisation at early stages of development

At early stages of development one can distinguish five important contributions of the agricultural sector to the process of economic development (Boserup, 1981; Johnston, 1970; Johnston and Mellor, 1961; Lewis, 1978b; Nicholls, 1964; Reynolds, 1975; Timmer, 1988): (1) agriculture as a source of food for a growing non-agricultural population; (2) agriculture as a source of inputs into manufacturing; (3) agriculture as a source of industrial labour; (4) agriculture as a source of domestic savings; (5) the agricultural sector as a market for industrial products.

Agriculture as a source of food
In early stages of development poor countries are characterised by a rapidly increasing demand for food. The rapidly growing population and rising per capita incomes determine the demand for food (Johnston and Mellor, 1961). Poor people tend to spend a large part of their additional income on food.[11] Since the industrial sector withdraws labour from the agricultural sector, the workers remaining in the agricultural sector must meet the growing demand.

This will not cause great problems if the agricultural sector is already quite productive before the onset of industrialisation. But if productivity is low and shows no improvement, urban food shortages will push food prices up. High food prices will exert an upward pressure on the costs of labour in the industrial sector, eroding the profitability of the sector.

Agriculture as a source of inputs
One of the routes to industrialisation starts with the processing of domestically available agricultural food, fibre and wood products. The food and beverages industries can process

---

[11] In economic terminology, the income elasticity of the demand for food is rather high (see n. 4 above).

primary food products. The textile and leather industries process fibres and leather. Wood and paper industries process primary wood products.

Agriculture as a source of labour

In early stages of development, labour has to be withdrawn from the agricultural sector to create an urban industrial labour force. Labour can also be withdrawn from agriculture for work on infrastructural projects. If productivity is increasing in agriculture, labour can be released much more easily than when productivity is stagnant.

Agriculture as a source of domestic savings

Until a modern sector has developed, there is no alternative source of domestic savings other than revenues from the sale of agricultural surpluses. The agricultural sector provides the necessary savings for investment in industry and infrastructure.

The agricultural sector as a market for industrial products

When a large proportion of the population is active within the agricultural sector, an increase in agricultural incomes as a result of productivity and output increases will create a broader domestic market for products of the new manufacturing industries. However, this function of the agricultural sector as a market conflicts with its function as provider of savings. The more people consume, the less they will be able to save. According to Nicholls (1964), the savings function is more important than the market function in the very early stages of industrialisation. The first manufacturing products can be sold in urban rather than rural markets. But urban markets are too small to sustain the expansion of domestic manufacturing, so that the market function will become more important over time.

8.4.2   ## Historical examples of relationships between agriculture and industry

England and Western Europe

From the eighteenth century onwards a productive agricultural sector provided a sound basis for industrialisation in Western Europe. In the eighteenth century,[12] English agriculture was the most productive in Europe. Farmers switched to more intensive forms of land use, annual harvests and crop rotation, instead of letting part of the land area lie fallow for one or more years. New high-quality food crops like turnips and potatoes were introduced. Farmers switched to intensive cattle breeding. Part of the farmland was used for the systematic production of fodder crops. Animal manure was used to maintain the fertility of the land.[13] Agriculture became commercialised. Until the 1930s, this highly efficient agricultural system was capable of feeding the expanding urban population. There was also a flow of labour from agriculture to the urban centres.

---

[12] This section is primarily based on Nicholls (1964: 16–26).

[13] Ester Boserup (1981b: 114–17) claims that there was no agricultural revolution in the eighteenth century. Rather, there was a gradual increase in output per hectare due to an increase in population density and a greater use of labour per unit of land. Still, Boserup agrees that British agriculture was the most productive agriculture in Europe.

Russia

Russia is an example of a country that started its industrialisation under relatively favourable initial conditions. Russian agriculture was potentially one of the most productive systems in the world. To this day, however, this potential has never been fully realised in Russia and the former Soviet republics.

Until 1861, a system of serfdom was maintained in Russia under which labour was tied to the land in an unproductive fashion. After the abolition of serfdom in 1861, large capitalist landowners benefited most from the land reforms. They made high profits, but output increased less than it would have done if smaller farmers had been allowed to work the land more intensively. Rural poverty increased rather than decreased. Large landowners invested part of their profits in infrastructure, railways and the industrial sector. The imposition of taxes forced smaller farmers to produce cash crops, so that Russia could export wheat.

The Russian pattern of rapid industrialisation and heavy-handed exploitation of the peasantry was continued in the communist Soviet Union. Despite resistance by the rural population, agriculture was collectivised. Coercion was used to force the agricultural sector to provide the growing urban population with cheap food, finally resulting in the great famine of 1932–3 in which up to 8.5 million people died of starvation or repression (Ellman, 2007).

From the perspective of industrialisation, the process of transferring resources from agriculture to industry was initially fairly successful – though it involved immense human sacrifices. Within a short time the Soviet Union succeeded in building an extensive industrial sector. But the overexploitation of the agrarian sector resulted in an agricultural sector performing far below potential, to this very day in the Russian Federation and former Soviet Republics such as the Ukraine. Also, the pattern of industrialisation did not prove to be sustainable after the collapse of the Soviet Union (Kuznetsov *et al.*, 2012; UNIDO, 2012).

8.4.3   Conclusion

The lesson we can derive from this section is that increases in output and productivity in the agricultural sector at early stages of development create favourable conditions for industrialisation and structural change. A dynamic agriculture, which produces surpluses above subsistence helps combat rural poverty. On the other hand, it also creates favourable conditions for the development of manufacturing. These experiences form an inspiration for modern agriculture-based development strategies such as the Ethiopian Agricultural Development Led Industrialisation (ADLI).

8.5   Open model: are primary exports an engine of growth and structural transformation?

8.5.1   Introduction

As long as we discuss the relationships between agriculture and industry in the context of a closed model, we assume that everything has to be produced within the confines of the domestic economy. The emergence of new sectors requires the transfer of resources from existing sectors. However, in an open model, developing countries have the option of exporting primary agricultural and mining products. The revenues from these exports may be reinvested in other sectors. For a proper understanding of the economic history of developing countries the open model is of major importance (Islam, 1989a). The modern economic development of these countries commenced with the export of cash crops and unprocessed mineral products in the nineteenth century.

8.5.2   Intermezzo: comparative advantage and the role of trade in development

The discussion about the role of primary exports in development should be seen in the context of theories about comparative advantage, the international division of labour and the role of trade in development. According to these theories, countries should specialise in lines of production in which they have a comparative advantage and import products in which other countries have a comparative advantage.

The arguments in favour of international free trade derive from classical economists like Adam Smith and David Ricardo and have been incorporated in modern economics through the works of Heckscher, Ohlin and Samuelson. The basic arguments have remained unchanged in spite of numerous elaborations and refinements. This section provides a very brief summary of the argument.

Let us assume that there are two countries, A and B, and two goods – for example, food and clothing. For simplicity's sake, we also assume that the production of these two goods only requires labour. This means that the costs of the goods can be expressed in labour hours.[14] When country A can produce food more cheaply than country B and country B can produce clothing more cheaply than country A, it is evident that both countries will benefit from the international trade in food and clothing. The classical economists, however, have shown that the two countries will also benefit from international trade, even when country A produces both products more cheaply than country B. According to the *law of comparative advantage* the two countries should specialise in producing those products in which they are most efficient in relative terms.

The following numerical example illustrates this principle (see Table 8.4). Using one day of labour, country A can produce either one unit of food or half a unit of clothing. If the price of the product is expressed in labour units, one unit of food in country A can be traded for half a unit of clothing in the absence of international trade. In country B, one labour day will produce one-third of a unit of food and one-fourth of a unit of clothing. In the absence of international trade, one unit of food can be traded for three-quarters of a unit of clothing.

In this example, country A is more efficient (cheaper) in absolute terms than country B in the production of both goods. However, in relative terms one gets less clothing per unit of food in country A (half a unit of clothing for one unit of food), than in country B (three-quarters of a unit of clothing for one unit of food). This means that country A is relatively more efficient at producing food and country B is relatively more efficient at producing clothing.

The simple example shows that in this case international trade will benefit both countries. If country A specialises in the production of food and exports part of it to country B, one day's work will produce one unit of food, which can be traded for three-quarters of a unit of clothing. This is more than the half a unit of clothing, which one can get in absence of international trade. If country B specialises in producing clothing and exports part of it to country A, it will be able

---

[14] This assumption is not essential. It is only used to explain the principle of free trade as briefly as possible.

Structural change and industrialisation

Table 8.4: Advantages of international trade

Labour days required for production of:	
	1 unit of
Country A	1
Country B	3
Terms of trade of food and clothing, without inter	
Country A	1
Country B	1
Terms of trade of food and clothing, with interna	
Country A	1
Country B	1

Source:
Samuelson and Nordhaus (1989: 903).

[Handwritten note overlapping table:]

Closed model : domestic economy
Open model : exporting agric + minerals
Primary exports should be based on
comparative advantage , division of labor
and role of trade .
law of comparative advantage : country
specialize on producing products in which
they're most efficient .
+ labor , − capital = labor-intense products
that are cheap .
+ capital , − labor = capital-intensive products
So, all benefit .
Dynamic version : long-run effect of
specialisation and trade .

to trade one unit of clothing for two units of food. Again, this is more than the one-and-one-third units of food it would get in absence of international trade. For both countries, therefore, specialisation and international trade is profitable. In addition, specialisation in production often gives rise to economies of scale, which make production even cheaper.

In the twentieth-century version of the theory of comparative advantage, the emphasis was on the proportions of the factors of production capital and labour (see e.g. Ethier, 1995; Kol and Mennes, 1990; Lin, 2010; Lin and Monga, 2010). Countries with surplus labour and a scarcity of capital will produce labour-intensive products relatively cheaply and will have a comparative advantage in such products. Countries with an abundance of capital and a shortage of labour will have a comparative advantage in capital-intensive products. This theory is also known as the Heckscher–Ohlin–Samuelson theory. The essence of the theory of comparative cost advantage is that international trade is beneficial to all parties involved: it increases total welfare. It is a plea for an international division of labour, international trade and liberalisation.

The theory of comparative advantage includes both static and dynamic arguments. The static version of the theory argues simply that countries will be better off if they specialise according to their comparative advantage. Thus, if developing countries have a comparative advantage in primary goods, they should export these goods and import manufactured goods.

The dynamic version of comparative advantage focuses on the long-run effects of specialisation and trade. There are potential dynamic advantages as well as dynamic disadvantages. The most powerful argument against following comparative advantage is that in the long run it reinforces existing patterns of production and specialisation and may act as an obstacle to structural change. If a developing country has a comparative advantage in a limited number of primary products, it may forever remain dependent on them. The possibility of importing industrial products relatively cheaply from abroad makes it difficult to build up a domestic industrial sector. Thus, a developing country may never industrialise.

Thus in a brilliant book Jeffrey Williamson (2011) compellingly argues that huge improvements in the terms of trade of primary exports of developing countries in the nineteenth century contributed to their early de-industrialisation and their inability to compete with manufactured exports from the European economies. In his view, the divergence in economic performance between the advanced and the developing countries in the nineteenth century is primarily explained by this pattern of comparative advantage that locked the developing periphery into ultimately less dynamic agricultural and mining activities.

A more positive version of dynamic comparative advantage suggests that primary exports can also serve as an engine of structural transformation. In early stages of development, the export of cash crops is an alternative to the direct processes of resource transfer from agriculture to industry in the closed model. In the first place, agricultural exports result in increases in income per capita. In the second place, the increased earnings of people involved in the export sector create a market for imported industrial consumer goods. In due time this market can be captured by import-substituting domestic industries. In the third place, agricultural exports generate savings, which can potentially be used for investment in industry and infrastructure. Finally, agricultural exports are a means of obtaining foreign exchange, which can be used to finance imports of the capital goods and intermediate inputs required for industrialisation. Like resource transfers in closed models, agricultural exports presume the availability of a surplus over subsistence needs in the agricultural sector, which can potentially be utilised for developmental purposes and structural transformation.

In the following sections we will discuss the role of primary exports in economic development in more detail.

8.5.3   Primary exports between 1870 and 1913: vent for surplus

In developing countries agricultural exports have played a crucial part in initiating changes in the economy (Lewis, 1969, 1970, 1978b; Maddison, 1989). By modern standards, the volume of international trade between poor and rich countries before the middle of the nineteenth century was limited. Prior to the emergence of roads and railways in the second half of the nineteenth century, the interior of developing countries and continents was isolated from the outside world. Geographic location was much more important than in the modern global economy. With the improvement of transport and communication and the growing demand for primary products in industrialised countries, there was an explosive growth of exports of cash crops from developing countries (cotton, oilseeds, cocoa, coffee, tea, bananas, rubber, pineapples, cotton fibres, copra and so on) between 1870 and 1913.[15]

Following Adam Smith, authors like Myint and Caves (Caves, 1965; Myint, 1959) use the term of *vent for surplus* to characterise agricultural exports during this period. In a traditional subsistence economy peasants produce food for their own needs. In general,

---

[15] Jeffrey Williamson (2011) argues that the international order in which poor peripheral countries export primary products and advanced economies export manufactures was established early in the nineteenth century rather than from 1870 onwards. But the period from 1870 onwards did have some special characteristics such as the acceleration of investment flows, migration flows and the breakdown of transport barriers due to technological advances.

outside the peak periods of sowing and harvesting, they have quite a good deal of spare time. Not all agricultural land is cultivated intensively. In the absence of market demand and storage facilities, there is little incentive to produce above subsistence. If new opportunities arise, peasants can easily use surplus time and land to cultivate new crops, without reducing their subsistence production of food crops. All over the tropics, smallholder peasants started growing cash crops on a large scale. Hence the term *vent for surplus*: unused factors of production were now employed for the first time.

Through agricultural exports money is introduced into traditional subsistence agriculture. In the beginning peasants produce food crops for their own needs and produce additional cash crops in their spare time. They have one leg in the subsistence economy and another in the money economy. The sale of their export crops provides them with money with which to buy imported manufactured goods. Later, some peasants specialise in production of export crops and others in food crops, which are sold to those specialising in non-food crops. Thus the money economy penetrates deeper into the traditional peasant economy (Myint, 1980, Chapter 2). Compulsion also played an important role in the expansion of peasant exports. Under colonial rule peasants were sometimes forced to grow cash crops, as under the *cultivation system* in the Netherlands Indies from 1830 to 1870. Or they had to grow cash crops in order meet their financial tax obligations. Another source of agricultural exports were large-scale plantations, owned by colonial expatriates. Unskilled labour was recruited from densely populated areas and set to work on these plantations.

Arthur Lewis has analysed the factors that explain why some countries benefited so much more from primary export opportunities than others (Lewis, 1970). The most important of these factors were the following: (1) establishment of internal law and order; (2) availability of surplus land; (3) access to surplus land; (4) availability of water; (5) government policy.

Internal pacification and the maintenance of law and order are among the most important prerequisites for expansion of trade and markets (see Chapter 11). Second in importance are the availability of sufficient water and land. Peasants will only start producing for export if there is still unused farmland or if they can easily increase the number of crops harvested per acre. Land tenure systems are also important. Latin American countries had abundant land. But systems of large landownership restricted the access to land for peasants. Large landowners could also have produced export products on their plantations, but absentee landlords did not always do so. Another factor affecting export growth was government policy. Governments determined who had access to land. Governments were responsible for the construction of infrastructure.

The most rapid expansion of exports was to be found in countries with abundant land and large-scale immigration, such as Malaysia, Brazil and Ceylon, or countries with sufficient land and surplus labour, such as Thailand (Manarungsan, 1989), Burma, Colombia, and Ghana. The slowest export growth could be observed in densely populated regions such as India and Java where land was scarce, or in countries where the government left monopolies in landownership unchallenged (Venezuela and the Philippines).

Lewis explicitly excludes differences in entrepreneurial talents and attitudes as an explanation of export performance. Wherever peasants in developing countries had opportunities to improve their economic situation permanently by producing for export, they were eager to take them. There is no shortage in the supply of entrepreneurship.

Why disappointing industrialisation?

On balance, the 1870–1913 period was a dynamic period for developing countries, with rapid increases in exports, investment, education and per capita incomes and the emergence of a modern sector of commercial agriculture and mining (Lewis, 1978a; Maddison, 1989). The conditions for investment in industry and infrastructure seemed to be quite favourable. Nevertheless, industrialisation made surprisingly little headway in this period, in spite of quite favourable initial conditions. Only a few countries such as Brazil, Ceylon, China, Colombia, Egypt, Mexico and India experienced some measure of industrialisation. How can this lack of structural transformation be explained?

According to Lewis, and more recently Williamson, the most important answer lies in the overwhelming profitability of agricultural exports. The incentive to embark on a difficult process of industrialisation was not very great when agricultural exports were such an easy alternative. Also, foreign trading houses had vested interests in imports and exports and resisted attempts at industrialisation. They were supported by agricultural oligarchies, whose power and influence were threatened by industrialisation. Lewis focuses on the period 1870–1913. Williams argues that a huge improvement of the terms of trade for primary products earlier in the nineteenth century had already killed off the prospects of industrialisation by 1870. Basically, both Lewis and Williamson argued that static comparative advantage locked developing countries into their specialisation in primary exports.

Finally, Lewis believes it takes at least one generation to grow a class of domestic industrial entrepreneurs in a country without a manufacturing tradition. Industrial entrepreneurship is less easily available than agricultural entrepreneurship. It requires more learning and longer experience.

More than Lewis, other authors emphasise the opposition of colonial authorities to industrialisation and the destructive impact of international competition on traditional handicraft industries in such countries as India (e.g. Batou, 1990). Instead of impeding industrialisation, governments could have protected domestic industries and could have invested more in infrastructure and education. Most colonial governments did too little in these areas. In independent Latin American countries industrialisation was hampered by the political influence of groups with interests in agriculture and foreign trade.

All in all, the contributions from agricultural exports to structural change and industrialisation were disappointing. Nevertheless, Lewis argues that important improvements were realised in this period in the fields of education, infrastructure and even industrialisation. Though more could have been done, his conclusion is that the foundations of later modern economic development in developing countries were laid during this period.

8.5.4 Can primary exports function as an engine of growth?

The vent for surplus theory extends our understanding of the process of economic development in a particular period in history. It is a typically classical economic theory focusing on the availability of unutilised factors of production, which may be employed in the process of economic development. Production of cash crops can be expanded, with no loss in food production. Vent for surplus theories are part of a wider category of development theories that emphasise the potentially positive contributions of primary mining and agricultural exports.

Due to increasing pressure of population, vent for surplus no longer represents a viable option for most developing countries. Land has become scarce and in most countries all available agricultural land has been taken into use. When the factors of production are fully employed, new exports can only be generated by either switching resources from one line of production to another or by increasing the productivity of resources, through investment, increased efficiency, or technological change.[16]

The potential benefits of primary exports are summarised in Box 8.2 (Gillis *et al.*, 1992: 421–3; Lord, 1989; Lundahl, 1985; Thoburn, 1977).

BOX 8.2 : Primary exports as an engine of growth

The potential benefits of primary exports include:

- Improved utilisation of existing factors of production:
  - Utilising hitherto unused production factors: **vent for surplus**.
  - More efficient use of available production factors: **static comparative advantage**.
- Dynamic comparative advantages:
  - Increased supply of production factors.
  - Inflow of investment.
  - Growth of market size.
  - Increasing returns to scale.
  - Exposure to international competition.
- Easing of foreign exchange constraints.
- Linkages:
  - Forward and backward linkages.
  - Consumption linkages.
  - Fiscal linkages.

Improved utilisation of existing factors of production

Exports result in improved utilisation of existing production factors. If there are surpluses of land or labour, as in the *vent for surplus model*, export demand provides a stimulus to employ the unused production factors. If production factors are already fully utilised, exports may result in a more efficient allocation of production factors as countries specialise in products in which they have a comparative advantage (*static comparative advantage*).

Dynamic comparative advantages

Entry into world export markets expands the size of the potential market. The increase in export opportunities for mining and agricultural products encourages an inflow of foreign capital, increases in domestic savings and immigration of skilled and unskilled labour. Thus the stock of production factors expands. Specialisation and larger markets allow countries to profit from increasing economies of scale in production. Competition on world markets contributes to increased productive efficiency. Finally, participation in world trade,

---

[16] In contrast to classical theories, neoclassical theories assume that all resources are fully employed and focus on the efficiency of the allocation of resources.

investment flows and competition on world markets promote the acquisition of new knowledge. This argument has primarily been used for manufacturing exports, but also holds for cash crops such as sugar or rubber and for mining.

Easing of foreign exchange constraints: primary exports as a source of foreign currency

The debate on the role of agricultural exports is based on an open model of the economy (Myint, 1975). In the early stages of economic development agricultural and mining exports and other primary exports are the most likely source of foreign exchange earnings. Foreign exchange is needed to finance imports of the capital goods and intermediate goods required for industrialisation.

In theory, an open economy could concentrate on manufacturing export production and neglect food production. It could meet the demand for food by exporting manufactures, mining products and cash crops, using part of the proceeds to import food (Myint, 1975). Even so, an increase in productivity in domestic food production would lead to considerable savings in scarce foreign exchange, which would otherwise have had to be used for food imports (Nicholls, 1964: 12).

In sum, primary exports are an import source of foreign exchange. This allows a country to ease possible bottlenecks in industrial production by importing productive capital goods and intermediate goods.

Linkages

Primary exports can have positive linkages with other sectors of the economy (Hirschman, 1977). One can distinguish three linkages:

(a) *Forward and backward linkages*. Primary exports can provide a positive stimulus to the establishment of industries that process primary agricultural and mining products (forward linkages). Examples of forward linkages are food processing, textiles, furniture and plywood industries, or oil refining. Backward linkages occur, for example, when agricultural exports call forth investment in railways, roads or harbours or when fishery exports stimulate the building of fishing boats or the production of fishing equipment.

(b) *Consumption linkages*. Incomes earned in export production may be spent in the domestic economy. This can provide a stimulus for other activities. This was the actual historical sequence in most developing countries. Primary export revenues created a domestic market for manufactured imports. Later these imports could be replaced by domestic industrial production in a process of import substitution (Hirschman, 1977, 1988).

(c) *Fiscal linkages*. Taxes on mining and agricultural exports are an important source of government revenue. These means can be employed to finance development in other areas such as infrastructure, industry, or education, as is presently occurring in the Gulf states.

Historical examples: Argentina, Australia, Canada and the USA

Examples of countries that have experienced major economic transformations fuelled by primary exports in the nineteenth century include the USA, Australia, Canada and the Scandinavian countries (Nicholls, 1964). The initial conditions in agriculture in sparsely populated countries such as Australia, Canada, the USA and Argentina were extremely favourable. At an early stage these countries were able to realise high labour productivity in agriculture, compensating for the scarcity of labour by employing much capital per worker (Baldwin, 1956). The agricultural sector produced large surpluses of food and other agricultural products, which could be exported. At a later stage, the export revenues were available to finance industrialisation in Australia, Canada and the USA, though less so in Argentina (Williamson, 2011). Immigration and foreign investment were incentives for rapid economic development.

Countries such as Australia, Canada, the USA and Norway provide interesting examples of successful primary export-led economic development. But such development does not follow automatically, as can be seen from the disappointing experience of developing countries such as Argentina and Brazil. In these countries inefficient institutions such as large landownership hampered the long-term development of the agricultural sector. Investments in industry were delayed and the very profitability of primary exports served as a disincentive for industrialisation, thereby retarding the economic development of many Latin American countries.

8.5.5   Export pessimism

In the 1930s, those developing countries that were most involved in the international economy through primary exports suffered most from the effects of the Great Depression. International trade collapsed and the barter terms of trade of primary exports (the ratio of export prices to import prices) deteriorated considerably. These traumatic historical experiences reinforced negative attitudes towards agriculture and stimulated the pursuit of import-substituting industrialisation. After The Second World War, several theories were formulated that stated that developing countries did not benefit from primary exports and international trade, contrary to the earlier experience of countries like the USA, Australia, and Canada. The key publications were those by Prebisch (1950) and Singer (1950), followed by a wide range of other authors (Amin, 1974; Bhagwati, 1958; Emmanuel, 1972; Lewis, 1969; Myrdal, 1957; Nurkse, 1962). Trade was no longer seen as an 'engine of growth'. The dynamic effects of comparative advantage in primary production were seen as negative. Export pessimists give several reasons why dependence on primary exports is bad for developing countries (Meier, 1989). These are summarised in Box 8.3.

BOX 8.3 : Export-pessimist arguments

- Stagnating world demand for primary products.
- Deteriorating terms of trade for developing country primary exports.
- Drain of mining profits to advanced economies.
- Instability of prices and export earnings due to fluctuations in international trade.
- Weak and ineffective linkages in primary production; the enclave export economy.
- Domestic food production constrained by production for export.
- Primary exports lead to overvalued exchange rates: the **Dutch disease** effects of primary exports.

Stagnating world demand

The growth of world demand for primary agricultural exports is sluggish. Demand for these exports will not keep up with the growth of income per capita in rich importing countries. As incomes rise, the share of food consumption in expenditure tends to decrease. With regard to non-food agricultural exports, technological advances result in the substitution of synthetic products for natural products like rubber or cotton. Furthermore, technological progress dramatically reduces the amount of raw materials used per unit of output (Hogendorn, 1996: 453).

Deteriorating terms of trade

In the long term, export pessimists believe that prices of primary exports fall relative to prices of imported industrial products. The prospects of a developing country, which is too dependent on primary exports, are unfavourable (Gillis *et al.*, 1992; Meier, 1968; Prebisch, 1950; Sarkar, 1986; Singer, 1950; Thoburn, 1977). There are several versions of the theory of deteriorating terms of trade:

(a) *Net barter terms of trade.* The first version of the theory of deteriorating terms of trade refers to changes in the ratio of the prices of exported and imported goods (P_x/P_m).[17] The prime explanation of the deteriorating terms of trade lies in the above-mentioned fact that the demand for agricultural products does not keep up with increases in income per capita in advanced countries, while the demand for manufactured goods tends to increase at higher levels of income.

   Also, primary export opportunities of developing countries are limited due to protectionist measures in rich, economically advanced countries (McBean, 1989). Domestic producers in the European Union and the USA are protected from competition for developing countries by a wide range of tariffs and subsidies. Both consumers in rich countries and producers in developing countries would benefit if agricultural protectionism were reduced.

(b) *Income terms of trade.* Usually, when the price of a product goes down, more of this product will be bought. When decreasing prices (P_x) are compensated for by an increase in the quantities sold (Q_x), total export revenues will increase. The so-called *income terms of trade* are defined as the changes in the ratio of revenues from exports and prices of imports $(\{P_x{}^*Q_x\}/P_m)$. Improving income terms of trade signify that total revenues from exports rise more than the prices of imports. Therefore a country can afford more imports, on the basis of its exports.

   However, when a country has a large share of the world market for a given product, an increase in its production may cause world prices to decrease so strongly that total export revenues decrease. Economists say this country is faced by an 'inelastic demand'. Consequently, this country can import less and less, while exporting more and more. Bhagwati (1958) calls this a process of 'immiserising growth'.

(c) *Factoral terms of trade.* A third version of the theory of terms of trade refers to the rewards for factors of production – capital and labour – in developing countries and the rewards in the advanced economies. The factoral terms of trade are defined as the ratio

---

[17] P_x and P_m are indexes of export and import prices.

of export prices (P_x) to import prices (P_m) multiplied by the productivity of the factors of production (Z_x). When increases in productivity are more than offset by declining barter terms of trade, we say there is a downward trend in the factoral terms of trade ($\{P_x/P_m\}*Z_x$). In principle, the productivity term can refer to capital productivity or labour productivity. In practice, the debate focuses on labour productivity. Our main interest is in the real value of labour incomes in a developing country, because this is what affects poverty and welfare. If productivity goes up and barter terms of trade remain the same, the real value of imported goods a worker could buy with his salary will go up.

Another way of looking at the factoral terms of trade is to ask who benefits from increased productivity in export producing sectors? Is it the producers of exports in the developing countries or the consumers of imports in the advanced countries? Under perfect competition and given demand, technological changes or efficiency gains that increase productivity will result in falling prices for consumers. However, in advanced industrial economies, powerful trade unions succeed in translating increased industrial productivity into higher wages, rather than lower prices. Monopolistic manufacturers pass on these increased wages in the form of higher prices charged to the consumers in poor developing countries. In developing countries, the immense surplus of labour keeps wages low. Fierce international competition depresses export prices. Thus, according to authors like Prebisch and Singer (Prebisch, 1950; Singer, 1950; see also Findlay, 1980) the benefits of increased productivity in export production are passed on to consumers in the rich countries in the form of lower prices. The real value of wages in the advanced countries will increase relative to wages in the export sector of developing countries. The institutional differences between rich and poor countries (trade unions, powerful monopolistic corporations, the oligopolistic structure of international trade) offer explanations for the deteriorating trend in the factoral terms of trade in developing countries and the improving terms of trade in rich countries. Rich countries benefit more from international trade than poor countries. International exchanges are unequal.

A special version of the theory of unequal exchange was formulated, once again, by Arthur Lewis (Lewis, 1969, 1978a). As long as productivity in the traditional subsistence agriculture sector is low, labour will be available at very low cost for export production. This keeps wages in the export sector down. Lewis' theory of the 'factoral terms of trade' predicts that the incomes of workers in the export sector of developing countries will lag behind labour incomes in the economically advanced countries. Competition on export markets translates low wages into low export prices. Therefore, prices of exports will also lag behind prices of imports. Only when labour productivity in food production increases will labour incomes in the export sector start to rise. Although this theory has its weaknesses (e.g. the role of demand in international trade is not mentioned at all), it leads to an interesting conclusion: improvement of export prices requires an increase in productivity in traditional food production. This is the argument for balance between sectors in another guise. Productivity in traditional agriculture has to be increased in order to reverse the declining trend in the factoral terms of trade.

Lewis also observes that developing countries concentrate on a rather limited range of primary export products. They export either products that only grow in tropical conditions or products where low wages compensate for the difference in productivity compared to economically more advanced countries.[18] The resulting overspecialisation in a few export products explains in part why developing countries are so vulnerable to export price instability. The same is true for dependence on one or two mining exports. This argument remains valid to the present day.

Drain of export profits abroad

A slightly different situation exists with respect to mining exports. In mining, productivity is high and minerals and energy sources are in high demand on world markets. Furthermore, the number of producers in mining is much smaller than in agriculture. Producers are sometimes able to form cartels to keep prices high. Thus, the factoral terms of trade for mining should be more positive than for agriculture.

However, the orthodox theory of international trade pays too little attention to the fact that mining and oil extraction were – and frequently still are – predominantly foreign owned. Foreign investors were the main beneficiaries of productivity increases and export earnings. A substantial part of these profits was and frequently still is repatriated abroad. Plantations producing export crops for foreign markets were also mainly controlled by foreign interests. Profits again tended to be repatriated abroad.

The wages in mines and plantations remained low due to the abundant supplies of labour. Thus domestic workers and the domestic economy profited little from these primary exports. Even if the factoral terms of trade for mineral exports go up, the domestic population does not profit from this in the form of higher wages. The abundance of low-wage labour also provides strong disincentives for providing education and training and upgrading the labour force.

Instability of prices and export earnings

When developing countries export a limited range of primary products, they are vulnerable to the effects of fluctuations in prices on the world market (e.g. Van der Ploeg and Poelhekke, 2007; Williamson, 2011). Prices of primary products are highly unstable. The resulting volatility of export revenues, prices and terms of trade is a threat to the overall development of a country.

Ineffective linkages

The forward and backward linkage effects of export agriculture and mining are limited (Gillis et al., 1992; Hirschman, 1958; Horesh and Joekes, 1985). Mines and plantations often form an enclave economy, isolated from the rest of the economy. The consumption linkages are weak, because incomes of workers in export production are so low. Profit incomes may be higher, but these are often remitted abroad. Fiscal linkages are disappointing, primarily because governments do not employ the revenues from export taxes very productively. Often they use them to finance current deficits on the government budget rather than for additional government investment. Export tax revenues allow politicians to postpone painful choices and decisions.

---

[18] Tobacco and cotton are examples of such products. If there had been no slavery in the USA, with its artificially low remuneration of labour, the South of the USA would not have been able to compete in these products.

Stagnating food production

Critics of agricultural exports often claim that the production of cash crops expands at the expense of the production of food crops. Land once used for food production is now used to grow cash crops. Traditional food producers are believed to lose their land to capitalist export farmers. As a result of export production, the local population will become more impoverished.

Boserup (1985) points to the fact that in Africa men concentrate on prestigious cash crops, whereas women are usually responsible for food production. As a result of expansion of export production, women have to use more distant plots of land of inferior quality to cultivate food. They have to travel long distances. Since women are forced to combine food production with housework, food production will suffer in the long run. However, according to Boserup, intensification of agricultural production and investment in agriculture offer possibilities to expand both food production and the production of cash crops, simultaneously. Of course, this requires greater attention to agriculture in government policy.

Overvalued exchange rates

The export of primary products, in particular mining and oil products, may lead to appreciation of the exchange rate. Higher exchange rates make manufactured exports more expensive and imports cheaper. Thus the prospects of manufacturing exports are diminished. This is often referred to as the *Dutch disease* effect, named after the economic impact of the discovery of enormous gas reserves in the Netherlands. A paper by Rodrik (2009) even suggests that undervaluation of the exchange rate is one of the keys to economic catch-up.

In summary, the export pessimists claim that participation in international trade contributes little to the economic development of poor countries. Incomes per capita do not increase. No savings are generated. The market for domestic industry is not enlarged. Under such conditions, 'trade gives poor countries an opportunity to stay poor'. Export pessimist theories gave a powerful theoretical underpinning to the import-substituting industrialisation policies characteristic of the period 1930–80, to be discussed in Chapter 9. They also contributed to the general policy climate after 1950 in which industry received preferential treatment and agriculture was neglected. Primary exports were taxed heavily, without the government providing any additional means for investment, R&D and infrastructure. Therefore, it is not surprising that the share of developing countries in world trade of primary products in that period decreased (McBean, 1989).

8.5.6   Debates about export pessimism and export optimism

As we shall show in Chapter 9, the results of import-substituting industrialisation strategies based on closed models were in many respects disappointing. Since the 1970s, this led to a renewed interest to the developmental potential of primary exports (Thoburn, 1977). Though not all the arguments of export pessimists have been refuted, the conclusions regarding primary exports have generally tended to be less negative.

The question of the trends in the terms of trade is an empirical one. It should be investigated systematically for different periods, regions and countries. The Prebisch–Singer thesis still has its defenders (see Gillis *et al.*, 1992; Sapsford, 1985, 1988; Sapsford and Balasubramanyam, 2003; Sapsford and Singer, 1998; Sarkar, 1986, 2001; Thirlwall, 1999; UNCTAD, 2002a). But most of the more recent literature concludes that there are no built-in laws and trends in the terms of trade (e.g. Bleaney and Greenaway, 1993;

Cuddington *et al.*, 2007; Grilli and Yang, 1988). In an exhaustive survey of the available empirical data, Spraos (1980) comes to the conclusion that authors such as Singer and Prebisch overestimated the deterioration of the terms of trade. New research by Jeffrey Williamson (2011) and his associates reveals that the terms of trade for primary products actually continued to increase between 1870 and 1890, declining dramatically afterwards. If one takes the whole period 1870–1950, there is actually no clear trend, though there is huge volatility. According to Spraos, no clear trends can be discerned for the period 1870–1980. Cuddington *et al.* (2007) find no clear terms of trade trends over very long periods, both before and after 1921. There is a clear downward break in 1921. Thoburn (1977) comes to the conclusion that there was a certain deterioration of the terms of trade until the eve of the Second World War. However, by 1950, the terms of trade were similar to those at the end of the nineteenth century. After 1945, developments in the terms of trade varied from country to country. Until the 1960s, the income terms of trade showed a marked improvement.

The estimation of the terms of trade involves a number of thorny problems (Cuddington *et al.*, 2007; Sarkar, 1986; Spraos, 1980; Williamson, 2011). First, if the quality of industrial products increases more rapidly than the quality of primary products, the deterioration of the net barter terms of trade of primary products might be overestimated. Second, shipping freights have declined substantially. As imports of primary goods in industrial countries are valued with cost, insurance and freight included (c.i.f.) and exports of industrial products are valued free on board (f.o.b.), the deterioration of the terms of trade might be overestimated. Third, it depends very much on which products are included or excluded in the calculation of the terms of trade. Terms of trade will be very different when developing country exports of oil products or industrial products are excluded. The composition of exports differs for each country and during each period of time. Among the most striking characteristics of the post-war period is the growth of the share of industrial products in total developing country exports (see Table 3.5, p. 117). Also, in the 1980s the advanced economies exported more primary products than developing countries.

Authors like Cuddington, Thoburn, Spraos, Myint and Lewis have concluded that in the long run there has been no systematic deterioration in the terms of trade of developing countries. Williamson adds that in most of the nineteenth century there was a huge improvement in the barter terms of trade for primary products.

A serious weakness of the modern proponents of the Singer–Prebisch thesis is their tendency to exclude oil, 'as a special case' (Sarkar, 1986: 365). There is nothing special about oil exports, other than that their prices rose tremendously in 1973 and 1979 and collapsed thereafter, only to rise again between 2001 and 2008. Another problem is their exclusive focus on net barter terms of trade. To evaluate the pros and cons of developing countries participating in international trade, the income terms of trade are at least as interesting. A third problem is that many developing countries are now important exporters of manufactured goods.

Table 8.5 and Table 8.6 present some rough calculations on the development of the *net barter terms of trade* and the *income terms of trade* since 1950. Figures from the IMF, *International Financial Statistics*, and the UNCTAD statistical database, *UNCTADstat*, have been used to reconstruct long-run movements in the terms of trade, referring to total export products (including agricultural products, mining products, oil products, and manufactures) versus total imports. It should be stressed that these tables do not immediately bear on the debates on the terms of trade of primary versus manufactured exports or on the terms

Table 8.5: Net barter terms of trade, selected countries, 1950–2011 (1980 =100)[a]

Country	1950	1955	1960	1970	1973	1980	1992	1997	2000	2011
Bangladesh						100	90	84	73	40
China						100	88	94	85	62
India	137	135	140	136	163	100	137	159	140	190
Indonesia						100	49	54	55	73
Iran										
Malaysia		121	92	81	71	100	153	156	140	141
Pakistan				114	135	100	81	92	77	40
Philippines	254	208	213	174	165	100	80	83	101	65
South Korea				134	125	100	117	107	88	55
Sri Lanka	366	364	281	168	132	100	110	120	115	83
Taiwan						100	132	133	134	84
Thailand		131	127	132	194	100	79	76	66	62
Turkey				160	175	100	106	102	92	81
Argentina						100	88	94	94	127
Brazil			122	136	130	100	111	155	135	184
Chile						100	45	46	41	88
Colombia			63	75	78	100	68	80	89	127
Mexico						100	32	32	33	35
Peru						100	48	52	41	65
Venezuela				18	30	100	45	46	65	168
Congo, Democratic Rep.						100	115	80	119	174
Côte d'Ivoire					100	100	80	58	49	78
Egypt						100	58	50	47	74
Ethiopia										
Ghana						100	45	54	48	88
Kenya		187	149	152	120	100	80	113	99	90
Morocco			91	92	81	100	102	105	111	156
Nigeria						100	36	36	55	117
South Africa	202	172	156	155	150	100	81	84	79	122
Tanzania		144	129	106		100	59	60	61	92
Zambia						100	57	64	45	87
Developing countries[b]			51	52	60	100	63	66	67	72
Africa	74	67	76	83	84	100	57	57	72	127
Asia[c]				103	104	100	66	67	68	65
Middle East[d]			25	20	22	100	51	51	74	141
Latin America and the Caribbean				69	102	100	61	68	67	93
Oil-exporting countries				12		100	47	48	67	141
Non-oil developing countries			115	121	124	100	79	81	78	
Advanced economies	108	108	118	123	121	100	113	116	112	110

Notes:

a Calculated as the ratio of indices of export and import unit values.

b 1980–2000, excl. South Africa.

c Excl. the Central Asian former Soviet Republics.

d 1980–2000, incl. Turkey.

e 1950–75: OPEC countries. In UNCTAD data from 1980 onwards nine non-OPEC countries are included.

Sources:

1950–1973, IMF, *International Financial Statistics Yearbook*, 1986, 1990, 1993, 1995, 1999, 2001.

1980–2011: UNCTAD: *UNCTADstat*, downloaded February 2013, supplemented by data from UNCTAD, *Handbook of Statistics*, 2012.

Table 8.6: Income terms of trade, selected countries, 1950–2011 (1980 =100)

Country	1950	1955	1960	1965	1970	1973	1980	1992	1997	2000	2011
Bangladesh							100	244	456	506	836
China							100	416	886	1184	5,500
India	48	56	56	60	78	112	100	257	530	661	2,640
Indonesia							100	126	198	242	369
Iran							100	222	182	313	749
Malaysia	30	29	35	37		54	100	301	597	797	1,292
Pakistan					54	104	100	248	268	269	252
Philippines	30	40	56	56	70	91	100	49	118	203	165
South Korea				3	16	46	100	430	829	1102	2,230
Sri Lanka	170	266	199	195	140	120	100	198	341	399	358
Taiwan							100	600	692	752	966
Thailand	18	21	25	39	46	77	100	376	532	679	1,311
Turkey					102	171	100	535	945	1050	2,561
Argentina							100	117	242	263	641
Brazil	28		27	33	53	76	100	229	397	430	1,082
Chile				60	133	60	100	130	228	245	769
Colombia	25	36	29		49	61	100	139	202	249	683
Mexico							100	148	336	517	769
Peru							100	63	116	121	382
Venezuela				35	39	34	100	63	93	141	269
Congo, Dem. Rep.							100	97	70	141	579
Côte d'Ivoire						72	100	90	103	88	117
Egypt							100	63	66	77	249
Ethiopia							100	43	139	120	347
Ghana							100	20	27	28	118
Kenya	26	38	51	102	130	138	100	128	213	192	301
Morocco	20	31	38	52	68	81	100	176	306	348	511
Nigeria							100	18	29	39	128
South Africa	23	32	24	47	59	80	100	90	131	134	229
Tanzania	56	86	127				100	67	79	106	344
Zambia							100	34	54	45	241
Developing countries	13		21	25	41	55	100	139	218	263	608
Africa	18	29	28	38	51		100	59	74	99	211
Asia				29	40	61	100	166	256	303	736
Middle East (incl. Turkey)			10	14	26	38	100	56	68	99	256
Latin America and the Caribbean	26		37	40	52	58	100	120	222	284	548
Oil-exporting countries			10	15			100	50	63	91	255
Non-oil developing countries	18		29	35	57	74	100	254	425	494	
Industrialised countries	12	18	28	41	67	85	100	185	264	314	429

Notes:

Index numbers of export values divided by index numbers of import unit values.

Sources:

See Table 8.5.

of trade of developing countries versus developed countries. Exports to all countries and imports from all countries are included, irrespective of their sectoral origin. The data do throw some light on the general question, whether participation in international trade is beneficial or harmful to developing countries.

The main conclusion about barter terms of trade to be derived from Table 8.5 is consistent with the literature discussed above: few laws, trends or general patterns can be discerned. The barter terms of trade for many developing countries in Table 8.5 show a downward tendency between the 1950s and 2000. However, this does not apply to all countries or all subperiods. Important exceptions include Brazil, China, India, Malaysia, Morocco and Taiwan, which experienced long-run improvements in their barter terms of trade. The aggregate figures for developing countries show huge gains between 1960 and 1980, declines between 1980 and 2000 and some improvement between 2000 and 2011. But if we zoom in on Africa and Latin America after 2000, many countries experience huge improvements in their barter terms of trade. In the long run the aggregate terms of trade for all developing countries show some net improvement since 1960.

The long-term income terms of trade in Table 8.6 show sharply increasing trends. Since 1980 there has not been a single country or region that has not experienced improvements, sometimes huge improvements. There was a sharp drop in the income terms of trade for Africa, the Middle East and the oil-exporting countries between 1980 and 1997. But by 2011 the income terms of trade were twice as high as in 1980 in Africa and more than seven times as high in Asia.

In the light of the most recent information, literature and insights, one must conclude that the Prebisch–Singer thesis of a built-in declining trend in the terms of trade of developing countries is dead. This does not mean, however, that the whole debate about primary exports is concluded. The consensus is still that an excessive reliance on a narrow range of primary exports is a recipe for long-run stagnation. The challenge remains to diversify from primary exports and achieve structural change, as has been argued throughout this chapter.

The main objection to the declining terms of trade hypothesis is not so much empirical, but rather that it has been used as an ideological justification for the continuation of inward-looking industrialisation policies that have proved to be ineffective and sometimes disastrous. The general conclusion that developing countries should not participate in international trade, because it is detrimental to their developmental prospects, is certainly not justified. We will return to this debate, when discussing export-oriented industrialisation in Chapter 9.

In the post-war period export pessimism had a major impact on development strategies. Priority was given to inward-looking industrialisation policies and primary exports were taxed and penalised. Both through policy interventions and autonomous influences, the share of developing countries in the world trade in primary exports decreased. Between 1961 and 1963 and 1982 and 1984 the share of developing countries in global primary exports fell from 63 to 48 per cent (McBean, 1989; see also Svedberg, 1993). Further declines were noted for Sub-Saharan Africa in the 1990s (Morrissey and Filatotchev, 2001). These declines are in part due to agricultural protectionism in the rich countries. However, they are also caused by the fact that developing countries themselves neglected their agricultural and mining sectors. If governments in developing countries had taxed export production less heavily and had invested more in infrastructure and improvement of production techniques in agriculture and mining, developing countries could have maintained the volume of their exports. For example, the share of farmers in Tanzanian export revenues fell from 70 per cent to 41 per cent, as a result of export taxes and payments to 'marketing boards' (McBean, 1989). Tanzanian cashew nut exports dropped from 145,000 tons (30 per cent of world production) in the early 1970s to 17,000 tons in the late 1980s, before recovering somewhat in the 1990s (World Bank, 1994). In Zambia, the volume of copper production declined by 60 per cent between 1973 and 1998 (Yamfwa, 2001: 65), due to sustained neglect. Zambia's share of the world copper market declined substantially.

The debate on structural adjustment in the 1980s ushered in a more positive evaluation of primary exports. This was also reflected in a reversal of previous exports trends after around 1995. Since then the share of developing countries in total primary exports has started to rise again. In 1995, the share of developing countries in total primary exports (including precious stones and gold) stood at 39 per cent. By 2011 this had increased to 51 per cent. A similar trend obtains for primary exports excluding fuels, precious stones and gold. Here the share stood at a modest 31 per cent in 1995, increasing to 40 per cent in 2011 (own calculations from UNCTADstat, 2014). It seems that liberalisation and structural adjustment in the 1980s and 1990s removed some of the obstacles to primary exports resulting in renewed growth of primary exports and increasing developing country shares in global trade. For instance, the acceleration of growth in many Sub-Saharan African countries since 2000 has clearly been fuelled by the growth of primary exports.

Just like the closed model of development, the open model of development requires choices between investment alternatives at later stages of development. If primary exports continue to be taxed too heavily in favour of investment in manufacturing, one risks stagnation of primary export growth, as was clearly evidenced by the trends between 1950 and 1990. The policy alternative is to reinvest at least part of export revenues in the primary sector. As long as a developing country succeeds in diversifying its export package and does not remain precariously dependent on one or two primary exports, it may still derive considerable benefit from continued agricultural and mining exports, even today.

More investment in the agricultural sector may also help countries avoid having to choose between food production and production for export. Food crops and export crops are often grown in rotation on one and the same piece of land. According to Boserup (1981), more intensive production techniques may expand both food production and the production of cash crops. But this does require investment in agricultural infrastructure (irrigation, water control) and changes in production techniques (Islam, 1989a). In addition, the option of importing part of food requirements using export revenues from cash crops is of course also still available.

Though we have argued that structural change is an important goal in the long run, the overwhelming priority given to domestic industrialisation over agricultural and mining exports has not always had positive results. Especially in Sub-Saharan Africa industrialisation did not get off the ground, while the primary export sector languished due to heavy charges, taxes and price regulations (Lensink, 1995; Szirmai and Lapperre, 2001; Yamfwa, 2001). The World Bank report *Sub-Saharan Africa: From Crisis to Sustainable Growth, A Long Term Perspective Study* (World Bank, 1989) stated that export revenues in Sub-Saharan Africa did not primarily decrease due to unfavourable developments in the terms of trade; they decreased due to a fall in the real volume of exports. The report and subsequent publications (World Bank, 1994; World Bank-WDR, 2000a; African Development Bank, 2000), therefore, argued in favour of renewed efforts to expand export production of both agricultural and mining products. These pleas seem to have been heeded.

In recent years a new strand of research has explored the potential of resource-based high-tech exports such as quality wines (Farinelli, 2012), flowers, vegetables, processed salmon, brand coffees or ethanol. Carlotta Perez (2008) has coined the phrase *resource-based industrialisation* to describe these opportunities. This type of industrialisation is based on processing of primary commodities, but offers exciting opportunities for diversification, innovation and technological upgrading.

8.5.7 Concluding remarks

On balance, the debate about the terms of trade has been concluded. There is no deterministic declining trend in the terms of trade and there is no reason why developing countries in the present global economy cannot profit from primary exports. But some important caveats remain. First, dependence on a too narrow range of primary exports is a risky strategy, exposing a country to potential volatility of prices and revenues, which is detrimental to growth. Second, it remains essential that in the long run developing countries achieve structural change and diversification of their production structure. Unless deliberate policies and strategies are developed to broaden the economic base and use export revenues for structural change, the very attractiveness of primary exports may act as an obstacle to structural change in the long run, as it did in the nineteenth century.

8.6 Closed model: interactions between agriculture and industry in later stages of development and structural change

In section 8.5, we focused on the relationships between primary exports and industrialisation in the context of an open model. After the negative experiences of primary exporting developing countries in the 1930s and the subsequent rise of export-pessimist theories, the policy orientation shifted towards more closed models. In Chapter 9, we will discuss the dominant post-war industrialisation strategy of import-substituting industrialisation. Here, we focus on the relationships between agriculture and industry in closed models of development. The key issue in the closed economy model is finding an appropriate balance between sectors in the course of structural transformation.

8.6.1 Introduction: import-substituting industrialisation in the closed model

In the initial stages of industrialisation a transfer of resources from agriculture to industry is justified. That the establishment of a new industrial sector should receive priority can also be defended. But once the process of industrialisation is underway, policy makers are inevitably confronted with difficult choices between investments in agriculture or industry. Should all resources continue to be channelled towards the industrial sector, or should the agricultural sector receive more priority? Post-war advocates of large-scale industrialisation and the 'Big Push', like Leibenstein, Higgins, and Hirschman (see Chapter 9), argued that industrialisation must be given top priority. This implied that the transfer of resources from agriculture to industry should be continued in later stages of development. Most developing countries have taken this advice and gave preference to industry over agriculture in the development strategies of the years between 1950 and 1980.

8.6.2   Transfer mechanisms

In the process of resource transfer from agriculture to the industry, government policy played an important role. Imposition of taxes was one of the ways to induce subsistence farmers to start producing for the market. They were forced to earn cash money in order to meet their tax obligations. Moreover, taxes skimmed off a considerable part of productivity increases and thus functioned as a kind of forced saving. Prices were kept low artificially by government intervention, for the benefit of the industrial sector. Often governments made use of 'marketing boards' that bought up the entire agricultural production at prices fixed below market rates. In several countries, including China, compulsory deliveries of rice and food grains were used to secure the supplies of food to the urban population. Deficit finance or increase of the money supply provided governments with funds to invest in the modern sector, while the resulting inflation functioned as a tax on agricultural incomes.

Government expenditure patterns were also biased in favour of industry. Industrial activities were subsidised, protected by tariffs, provided with cheap credit and underpriced inputs. Investment funds for agriculture were relatively scarce and credit facilities expensive and limited. Resource transfers sometimes also took place in the private sector, whenever large landowners reinvested their profits in the industrial sector or in infrastructure, while paying their agriculture labourers low wages.

8.6.3   Towards a balance between agriculture and industry

Since the 1960s, a more balanced approach to agriculture and industry has emerged as an alternative to post-war industrial growth strategies (Mellor, 1976). This approach was called the *balanced growth path* strategy (Myint, 1980, Chapter 8).[19] The basic idea of the balanced growth path is that the pace of economic development of a country depends on a balance between the rates of output growth in different sectors. When the growth of one sector lags behind the requirements of other sectors, these other sectors will be affected negatively as well. Thus, economic development in a closed economy is determined by the growth of the slowest-growing sector. If agriculture stagnates as a result of the too heavy burdens imposed upon it, this will also have adverse effects on industrial development. When industrialisation fails to get off the ground, this will act as a constraint for agriculture. Just as within industry, there are numerous linkages and complementarities between agricultural and industrial activities. In a closed model of the economy, successful economic development therefore implies that the growth of production in agriculture and industry should be kept in balance (Myint, 1980: 109–10).[20] In the course of the 1960s, countries such as India, Indonesia, and China changed course and started paying more attention to agriculture. In many other developing countries the neglect of the agricultural sector continued, despite some changes in official rhetoric.

In the following section, the various interactions between agriculture and industry in later stages of development will be discussed more systematically. We see many of the same

---

[19] In contrast to the crash industrialisation programmes, which were referred to as *balanced growth strategies*.

[20] Though Arthur Lewis (1954) is the intellectual father of the notion that production factors can be withdrawn from agriculture at little cost, he elsewhere emphasises the need for balance between agriculture and industry (e.g. Lewis, 1969). We have no satisfactory explanation for this seeming inconsistency in Lewis' thought. In the context of agricultural exports, Lewis also stresses the importance of productivity increases in food production.

relationships discussed in the section on structural change at early stages of development (section 8.4), but there is a great need to balance the needs of different sectors, rather than promoting one sector at the expense of another.

Contributions of the agricultural sector

1. *Food*. The industrial sector cannot continue to grow unless the production of food stays in step. If food production falls short, food prices will go up. This causes inflation. Inflation will start off a wage–price spiral, which has negative effects on profits and investment rates in the industrial sector. When food has to be imported to meet urban food requirements, this squanders scarce foreign exchange, which could have been used for investment. This occurred in India in the 1960s. In this country the attainment of economic objectives was impeded by recurring food shortages, which necessitated food imports (Bardhan, 1984; Cassen, 1978).

In the absence of positive incentives and technological change, farmers remaining in the countryside will not be willing to work harder to produce additional food for the urban population. They will only do so if they can sell their agricultural surpluses at reasonable prices and have the opportunity of buying industrial goods with the money thus earned.

This is one of the essential points of difference between so-called *classical two-sector models* (Fei and Ranis, 1964; Lewis, 1954) and *neoclassical two-sector models* (Jorgenson, 1961, 1967, 1969). The classical approach states that labour can be withdrawn from the agricultural sector 'free of charge' since this labour is being 'wasted' and has little or no opportunity costs. The neoclassical point of view argues that factors are fully employed. One can never withdraw factors of production from a given sector of the economy without some loss in output. This means that a transfer of resources from agriculture to industry involves costs. Among other things, these costs include the rewards needed to motivate those remaining in agriculture to increase their output.

Higher prices for agricultural products can contribute to technological progress and productivity increases in the agricultural sector. In the long term the resulting increase in food production will help stabilise food prices. The opposite is true when agricultural prices are kept low artificially. This causes food shortages and upward pressures on food prices. For political reasons (e.g. fear of political turmoil) governments start subsidising food for the urban population. In many countries these subsidies are an increasing burden on government budgets.

Of course, the neoclassical assumption that increasing prices would automatically result in increased supplies of food can also be criticised. Markets in developing countries do not function perfectly. There are all sorts of supply constraints such as lack of infrastructure, storage facilities or insufficient information (Helleiner, 1992a). Nevertheless, the neoclassical critique of the concept of costless development has served as a welcome counterbalance to the post-war neglect of agriculture.

2. *Employment*. In later stages of development, the agricultural sector no longer has to supply labour to the industrial sector as in the early stages. In the urban sector there is widespread unemployment and underemployment and an acute shortage of jobs. A new role for a dynamic agricultural sector is to provide additional employment opportunities. In the 1960s and 1970s, China, discouraged migration to the cities and tried to create more rural employment – both within agriculture and in other sectors of the rural economy (Rawski, 1979).

3. *Agriculture as a source of savings*. Other than in the very early stages of development, the industrial sector no longer depends exclusively on the agricultural sector for savings. Reinvestment of retained industrial profits and urban savings are important alternative [...] a dynamic agricultural sector can also be a source of [...] ment, provided that a sufficient part of the savings is [...] lture itself.

[...] *er goods and producer goods*. Newly established indus- [...] ernational markets. They first have to gain experience on [...] s where a large part of the labour force is still in the [...] urban market is limited. If industrialisation depends [...] he momentum of industrialisation will soon falter. An [...] comes may create a vast internal market for industrial [...] cultural machinery, implements, industrially produced [...] er stages of development this enlarged market provides [...] growth of the industrial sector.

[...] *trial sector*. There are important complementarities [...] gricultural products such as food, fruit, wood, cotton [...] he food processing industry, the plywood industry, the [...] , the textile industry or the rubber industry. The first [...] countries are often food processing, beverages and textiles.

The contributions of agriculture discussed here are rather similar to those in earlier stages of economic development. But there are a number of important differences. In early stages of development, supplies of labour and savings are of prime importance, while rural markets are less prominent. In later stages of development the agricultural sector becomes more important as a market for industrial products and as a supplier of inputs to industry. The agricultural sector also generates new employment for an increasing labour force. Finally, the linkages no longer run only from agriculture to industry. Agricultural development becomes ever-more dependent on industrial inputs (inorganic fertilisers, pesticides, herbicides, electrical energy, water pumps, irrigation equipment, industrially produced seeds, farming implements and agricultural machinery). The domestic manufacturing sector is a potential supplier of such inputs. It can make important contributions to agricultural development. In absence of inputs from the industrial sector productivity growth in the agricultural sector will eventually stagnate, and food prices will start increasing. This is an example of technical complementarities between the two sectors.

The industrial sector also provides the agricultural population with consumer goods. The possibility of acquiring industrially produced consumer goods is an important incentive for the rural population to increase its production (Myint, 1980).

8.6.4   The mix of negative and positive incentives in a balanced growth path

In the preceding section it was assumed that higher prices for agricultural products would automatically motivate farmers to increase production. But this is not always the case. Higher prices may lead to increased rural consumption, rather than investment in productive agricultural capacity. When governments do not provide new infrastructure, new inputs, agricultural R&D, agricultural credit and agricultural extension, agricultural production is unlikely to respond strongly to price increases (Bautista, 1989; Islam, 1989b). Price increases may also aggravate rural income inequality. Those who benefit most from higher prices are the large, market-oriented farmers. Peasants producing for their own consumption will not profit much. Farm labourers and other rural inhabitants who have to purchase their food on the market will be negatively affected by price increases.

In centrally planned economies, like pre-reform China, the government for a long time took on the task of providing capital goods, machinery, energy, irrigation and inputs. The farmers were compelled to provide the urban population with food. Proponents of a market-oriented approach to agriculture acknowledge the significance of infrastructural investment. However, they argue with some justification that farmers will only make optimal use of the available infrastructure, technology and institutions if price incentives are positive. Thus, newly developed technologies will diffuse only if price relations make it attractive for farmers to apply them (Islam, 1989b). Many countries have, therefore, chosen a mix of negative and positive incentives. Negative incentives include taxes and compulsory delivery of part of the output. These are combined with positive incentives such as public investment in infrastructure, investment in agricultural research, education and agricultural extension, provision of new inputs and the right to sell all production exceeding compulsory quotas at free market prices.

Japan in the late nineteenth century (Ohkawa and Rosovsky, 1964) and Taiwan and South Korea during the post-war period provide interesting examples of a policy of 'walking on two legs'. In such a policy, both industrial and agricultural development receive sufficient attention. Tax measures and other negative sanctions ensure that the agricultural labour force does not exclusively appropriate the benefits of agricultural development policy.

In Japan, Korea and Taiwan redistribution of land stimulated small and medium-size farmers to increase their investment. There was a lot of research on new seeds and new production techniques. Quite significant attention was paid to education and the adequate diffusion of new production techniques to the farmers. At the same time, tax measures skimmed off part of the agricultural surplus. Taiwan maintained the compulsory delivery of a portion of the harvest to the urban population. Part of the taxed surplus was invested in the industrial sector; another part, however, was channelled back into the agricultural sector in the form of expenditures for research, development, and irrigation.

After the liberalisation of Chinese agriculture in 1978, the terms of trade of agricultural products to industrial products improved very strongly. Agricultural output and productivity soared (Kalirajan and Wu, 1999). However, some observers feared that the increased revenues of farmers would be consumed and that infrastructural investments would be neglected in the long term (Griffin, 1987b). Since the early 1990s, agricultural growth has indeed slowed down and the urban–rural divide seems to be growing again under the impact of very rapid industrialisation.

In sum, agricultural development is hampered when the internal terms of trade become too unfavourable to the agricultural sector. In the long run this also affects industrial development adversely. However, if the terms of trade swing too much in favour of agriculture, the urban standard of living and wage levels will come under pressure. The strategy of balanced intersectoral growth, therefore, requires the search for a delicate dynamic equilibrium between the growth paths of the different sectors. Characteristic of such an approach is that one seeks to make optimal use of the complementarities between sectors and tries to realise parallel increases in output and productivity in both sectors. Intersectoral linkages are most effective, when industrial activities are decentralised, rather than concentrated in a few large urban centres (Ranis, 1989).

In addition to balanced terms of trade between agriculture and industry, policy should aim at a reasonable balance in the allocation of resources (credit, funds for R&D, subsidies on capital and inputs) to agriculture and industry, and a balance in the imposition of taxes and other burdens. Though balanced growth path strategies are no longer on the policy agenda, the notion of balance between sectors – agriculture and industry, but also services and industry and services and agriculture – is still extremely relevant today.

In the course of economic development and structural change, the industrial and service sectors gain in relative importance, whereas the agricultural sector becomes relatively less important. But on the path to economic development, it is very important to maintain and improve agricultural productivity and dynamism. A dynamic agricultural sector will also create new rural employment possibilities outside agriculture and is conducive to sustainable patterns of industrialisation (Ranis, 1989: 43).

8.7　Open model: labour-intensive manufactured exports

To complete the discussion of structural change, we now move to an open model where structural change takes place through labour-intensive manufactured exports. This development strategy is the one followed in East Asia by countries such as South Korea, Taiwan, Hong Kong, Singapore and later by Asian countries such as China, India, Indonesia, Malaysia, Thailand and Vietnam.

In contrast to the closed models where in principle a country produces in all sectors of the economy and focuses on the relationships between sectors, the export-oriented strategy chooses specialisation in specific lines of export production, according to comparative advantage. The open model of labour-intensive exports is typically associated with later stages of development. In almost all instances, the export-oriented phase is preceded by an earlier inward-looking import substitution phase. Interestingly, competing on international export markets should not be confused with complete liberalisation. In most countries – with the exception of Hong Kong – there is continued protection of production of manufactured goods for the domestic market, combined with incentives to compete internationally.

Over time in the most successful economies, there is a process of technological upgrading, moving from simple labour-intensive assembly activities to more and more complex and technologically sophisticated activities. Policy focuses not only on static comparative advantage, but anticipates future comparative advantages in a dynamic manner (see Amsden, 1989; Lin, 2010; Lin and Monga, 2010).

8.8　Concluding remarks

In this chapter, we have discussed three kinds of structural change, one based on primary exports in an open economy model, one based on a balanced growth path between sectors in a closed economy model and one based on labour-intensive manufactured exports in an open economy model. We made a distinction between earlier and later stages of development, highlighting how sectoral priorities shift over time. The discussion served to highlight the importance of the relationships between primary, secondary and tertiary sectors in the wider pattern of growth and structural change.

At later stages of development, the more open an economy, the more domestic imbalances it can afford. In an open economy countries will concentrate on those lines of production in which they have comparative advantages. The goods in which a country is relatively unproductive can be imported. For example, a country can export non-food cash crops or certain industrial products and import all of its food. Singapore is an example of such a food-importing economy. Other countries will export both food and labour-intensive manufactured products and import raw materials and capital goods, and so on. The smaller a country and the larger the share of foreign trade in national income, the more appropriate an open model of development will be. Densely populated countries with enormous internal markets like India and China can afford to produce a far wider range of products, but even here there is enormous scope for specialisation. Economic reforms in China since 1978 and India since 1990 have resulted in a radical opening up towards world trade. Industrialisation strategies will be discussed in much more detail in Chapter 9.

Questions for review

1. Why is industrialisation considered to be important for development?
2. Is manufacturing more important for growth than services?
3. Discuss four different kinds of sectoral classifications which are relevant for our understanding of structural change.
4. How does the pattern of structural change in developing countries since 1950 differ from earlier patterns of structural change in the presently advanced economies?
5. What are the contributions of agriculture to industrial development in earlier stages of economic development?
6. Why is an agricultural surplus often considered to be a precondition for industrialisation?
7. How do the relations between agriculture and industry differ between earlier and later stages of development?
8. Why is a balance between the agricultural sector and the industrial sector considered to be advantageous for economic development in later stages of development?
9. What are the main characteristics of the vent for surplus model of primary exports?
10. To what extent did primary exports contribute to the economic dynamism of developing countries between 1870 and 1913?
11. Give three definitions of the terms of trade and highlight the differences between them.
12. Discuss the Prebisch–Singer theory of declining terms of trade for primary products. To what extent is the Prebisch–Singer theory still relevant today?
13. Assess the various arguments of the export pessimists, who deny that primary exports can serve as an engine of growth.
14. What are the potential benefits of primary exports to economic development?
15. Why should agricultural stagnation affect the prospects of industrialisation negatively?

Further reading

Kuznets was one of the pioneers of the quantitative study of structural change in the context of modern economic growth. Among his many publications we mention: *Economic Growth and Structure* (1965), *Modern Economic Growth, Rate, Structure and Spread* (1966) and *Economic Growth of Nations: Total Output and Production Structure* (1971). Chenery and his associates have investigated patterns of structural change in developing countries. Interesting publications include Chenery, *Structural Change and Development Policy* (1979); Chenery, Robinson and Syrquin, *Industrialisation and Growth: A Comparative Study* (1986) and Chenery and Taylor, 'Development Patterns among Countries and over Time' (1968), in the *Review of Economics and Statistics*. Recently there has been renewed interest in structural change. Haraguchi and Rezonja have updated the Chenery analysis in their paper, 'Emerging Patterns of Structural Change in Manufacturing' (2013). In an influential publication, *Globalization, Structural Change and Productivity Growth*, McMillan and Rodrik (2011) have analysed growth-enhancing and growth-reducing patterns of structural change. Lin has made a nuanced argument for structural change that is in line with comparative advantages, not only with present comparative advantages but also with future latent advantages, thus adding a dynamic element to the discussion, see Lin, *New Structural Economics: A Framework for Rethinking Development* (2010) and Lin and Monga, *Growth Identification and Facilitation: The Role of the State in the Dynamics of Structural Change* (2010).

A classic reference for the contribution of the agricultural sector to economic development is Johnston and Mellor's article, 'The Role of Agriculture in Economic Development' (1961), in the American *Economic Review*. The same topic is addressed in an interesting collection of articles edited by Eicher and de Witt, *Agriculture in Development* (1964), as well as in a review article by Timmer on 'The Agricultural Transformation' (1988), in Volume I of Chenery and Srinivasan (eds.) *Handbook of Development Economics*. Also of interest is *The Primary Sector in Economic Development* (1985), edited by Lundahl. The balance between industry and agriculture is the topic of a collection of articles edited by Nurul Islam, *The Balance between Industry and Agriculture in Economic Development: Factors Influencing Change* (1989b).

For the increasingly relevant question concerning the role of the service sector in development, the reader can consult a three-volume compendium of articles edited by Bryson and Daniels entitled *Service Industries in the Global Economy* (1998).

For the debate about agricultural and mining exports some of the classic references include Caves' article on the vent of surplus '"Vent for Surplus" Models of Trade and Growth' (1965) and the studies by Nobel Prize winner Arthur Lewis, *Tropical Development 1880–1913* (1970) (an edited volume); *Growth and Fluctuations 1870–1913* (1978a) and the brilliant overview in *The Evolution of the International Economic Order* (1978b). The key publications representing the export-pessimist perspective on the declining terms of trade are Prebisch's *The Economic Development of Latin America and its Principal Problems* (1950) and Singer's article 'The Distribution of Gains between Investing and Borrowing Countries' (1950), in *The American Economic Review*. Important publications on the terms of trade include Bhagwati, 'Immiserizing Growth: A Geometrical Note' (1958), in the *Review of Economic Studies*; Grilli and Maw, 'Primary Commodity Prices, Manufactured Goods Prices, and the Terms of Trade of Developing

Countries: What the Long Run Shows' (1988); Sapsford, 'The Statistical Debate on the Net Barter Terms of Trade between Primary Commodities and Manufactures: A Comment and Some Statistical Evidence' (1985), in *The Economic Journal*, and 'The Debate over Trends in the Terms of Trade' (1988); Sapsford and Singer, 'The IMF, the World Bank and Commodity Prices: A Case of Shifting Sands?' (1998); Sapsford and Balasubramanyam, 'Globalization and the Terms of Trade: The Glass Ceiling Hypothesis' (2003); Sarkar, 'The Singer–Prebisch Hypothesis: A Statistical Evaluation' (1986), in the *Cambridge Journal of Economics*, and 'The Long-Term Behaviour of the North–South Terms of Trade: A Review of the Statistical Debate' (2001). An influential statistical publication by Cuddington, Ludema and Jayasriya, 'Prebisch–Singer Redux', in Lederman and Maloney's edited volume, *Natural Resources: Neither Curse nor Destiny* (2007), denies that there are any long-run trends in the terms of trade.

A delightful book by Jeffrey Williamson, *Trade and Poverty: When the Third World Fell Behind* (2011), argues that industrialisation made all the difference in the nineteenth century. The divergence between developing and advanced economies was based on the fact that the countries in the periphery continued to export primary products, while the countries of the core industrialised and specialised in manufactured exports. Industrialisation in the developing periphery was hindered by huge improvements in the terms of trade of primary products in the nineteenth century, which made specialisation in primary exports very profitable.

Two international organisations responsible for statistics on international trade are the International Monetary Fund (IMF, www.imf.org) and the United Nations Conference on Trade and Development (UNCTAD, www.unctad.org). Statistical sources include the *International Financial Statistics Yearbook* and *World Economic Outlook*, published annually by the IMF. IMF also posts statistical series on its website such as the *World Economic Outlook Database* (www.imf.org/external/pubs/ft/weo/2013/01/weodata/index.aspx). UNCTAD publishes the *UNCTAD Handbook of Statistics*, which provides time series of trade and international finance going back to 1950 (UNCTAD, 2012a) and the *World Investment Report* (UNCTAD, 2012b). A wealth of UNCTAD statistics is available on the UNCTAD database *UNCTADstat*, http://unctadstat.unctad.org/ReportFolders/reportFolders.aspx.

9

Industrial development

This chapter focuses on industrialisation experiences and industrialisation strategies in developing countries, in the period since 1945. The chapter opens with a discussion of the inward-looking industrialisation strategies of the post-war period in section 9.2. The common characteristic of such strategies was the pursuit of comprehensive industrialisation behind protective barriers.

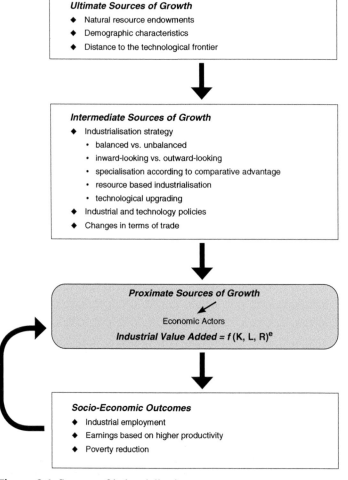

Figure 9.1 Sources of industrialisation

These strategies were characterised by large-scale investment, high degrees of protection and a key role for government interventions. The strategies were based on closed conceptions of the economy.

As time passed, the shortcomings of the post-war approaches became more apparent. Section 9.3 provides an overview of the various criticisms of the orthodox post-war policies. This paves the way for a discussion of alternative approaches in sections 9.4 and 9.5. These include the balanced growth path approach which focuses on the relationships between major sectors of the economy and unbalanced growth policies which aim at creating dynamic inbalances and provide more scope for the market and support for the small-scale and informal sector. The most important alternative is labour-intensive export-oriented industrialisation. In the discussion of export-oriented industrialisation, the role of MNEs and the emergence of global production chains receive special attention. The section also emphasises the key importance of innovation and technological upgrading. In section 9.6 attention is paid to criticisms of neoliberal market-oriented strategies and the re-emergence of industrial policy. Outcomes of industrialisation policies are discussed in section 9.7. The concluding section 9.8 lists some of the new challenges facing developing countries in their pursuit of industrialisation. Figure 9.1 summarises the position of industrialisation in the framework of proximate and ultimate causality.

9.1   Introduction

Major technological breakthroughs in textile production and the application of steam power in Great Britain in the second half of the eighteenth century made such a deep impression that in the nineteenth century the term 'industrial revolution' was coined to describe them.[1] The emergence of modern manufacturing would lead to dramatic changes in the structure of the world economy and to sustained increases in the growth of labour productivity and economic welfare. Great Britain became the technological leader in the world economy and the exemplar for other countries. The race for industrialisation had begun (Szirmai, 2012a).

Industrialisation can be seen as a single global process of structural change, in which individual countries follow different paths depending on their initial conditions and the timing of their entry into the race (Pollard, 1990). The first industrial followers were European countries such as Belgium, which faithfully copied the English pattern, Switzerland, which concentrated on technologically advanced products and France (Pollard, 1990; Von Tunzelmann, 1995). In the nineteenth century, the USA followed a different path towards industrialisation based on primary exports, abundance of land and natural resources and scarcity of labour. Scarcity of labour encouraged capital-intensive production techniques. Technology was taken over rapidly and creatively from the technological leader Great Britain and there was an inflow of skilled labour from Europe. Technological advance

---

[1] In some respects, the term 'industrial revolution' is misleading. It disregards the gradual nature of increases in productive capacity and the continuity with earlier developments in Northwest Europe, in particular in the Low Countries (Maddison, 1991). In other respects, it is an apt term. It captures the introduction of radically new production technologies which have fundamentally affected the nature of global production.

was labour-saving. Productivity growth in the USA was so rapid that the country would overtake Great Britain by the end of the nineteenth century. The USA has retained its technological leadership ever since.

Famous latecomers to the process of industrialisation were Germany, Russia and Japan. As argued compellingly by Alexander Gerschenkron (1962), latecomers can profit from the availability of modern technologies developed in the leading industrial economies, without bearing all the risks and costs involved in R&D. In modern terminology, they profit from international technology spillovers. Gerschenkron coined the term 'advantages of back-wardness'.[2] He reasoned that technological developments had tremendously increased the scale of industrial production. Therefore, late industrialisation would have an all-or-nothing character. If the conditions were right, once growth started in a late-developing country it would take the form of a leap or a growth spurt. The role of governments and large financial conglomerates in late industrialisation was more important than in early industrialisation. Governments and banks invested directly in industries and railways; they played a crucial role in the mobilisation of resources for investment and they were very active in education and technology acquisition.[3] Development-oriented governments set themselves the task of eliminating historical obstacles to industrialisation.

What about the developing countries? As described by Arthur Lewis (1978a, 1978b) and Jeffrey Williamson (2011), from the early nineteenth century onwards the world economy divided into industrial countries and agricultural countries (see Chapter 2). Colonies and non-colonised countries in the tropics remained predominantly agrarian, while the Western world industrialised.[4] Industrial growth in the West created an increasing demand for primary products from developing countries. Technological advances in transport, infra-structure and communication expanded the opportunities for trade. Thus, the so-called 'colonial division of labour' came into being. Developing countries exported primary agricultural and mining products to the advanced economies. Industrial economies exported their finished manufactured goods to the developing countries. Industrialisation became synonymous with wealth, economic development, technological leadership, political power and international dominance. The very concept of development came to be associated with industrialisation.

In developing countries, moves towards modern industrialisation were scarce and hesi-tant. Towards the end of the nineteenth century, one finds such beginnings in Latin American countries such as Brazil, Chile, Egypt and Mexico and large Asian countries such as India and China. But developing countries still remained predominantly dependent

---

[2] Earlier versions of this idea are to be found in the work of Veblen (1915) on Imperial Germany and the Dutch historian Romein (1937), who both tended to stress the disadvantages of technological leadership and its associated danger of lock-in to technological trajectories that were becoming obsolete.

[3] With the wave of mergers of the 1980s and 1990s, the role of government in the mobilisation of resources has became less important again. The resources of the mega-MNCs dwarf those of many national states and they are able to mobilise financial resources for gigantic investment projects without any public support.

[4] Economic historians such as Bairoch and Williamson even argue that developing countries *de-industrialised*. They claim that India and China accounted for 57 per cent of manufacturing value added around 1750 and had higher shares of manufacturing in GDP than the rest of the world (Bairoch, 1982; Williamson, 2011, Table 5.1). We find this de-industrialisation argument somewhat misleading. The manufacturing technology developed in Great Britain in the industrial revolution differed radically from the cottage industry technologies of the pre-industrial world. This new mode of production diffused primarily to the European countries and not to the peripheral developing countries.

on agriculture and mining. The groundswell of world industrialisation, which commenced in Great Britain, washed through Europe and the USA and reached Japan and Russia by the end of the nineteenth century, subsided after 1900 (Pollard, 1990; Szirmai *et al.*, 2013a). Only in 1945, after a pause of fifty years, would some developing countries rejoin the industrial race.

Between the two world wars of the twentieth century, the negative experiences of primary exporters reinforced the positive connotations of industrialisation. Exporters of primary products were severely hit by the crisis of the 1930s and the slowdown in world trade. A few countries such as Argentina, Brazil and South Africa profited from the crisis in Europe to build up their own manufacturing industries, providing early examples of successful import substitution. Manufacturing symbolised economic dynamism, agriculture backwardness and stagnation.

After The Second World War, leaders of newly independent countries in Asia and Africa had the highest expectations of industrialisation. These expectations were shared by foreign experts and advisors from the Western world, as well as by advisors from the communist countries, with their negative Marxist stereotypes of agriculture as a traditional and stagnant sector, representing an outmoded stage of development. Export-pessimist theories served as a further justification for a drive toward industrialisation. Priority was given to large-scale industrialisation strategies. Policy makers became almost obsessed with industrialisation.

This chapter provides an overview of industrialisation strategies and industrialisation experiences in developing countries. In spite of serious policy shortcomings and setbacks, we shall see that major advances have been made in many parts of the developing world, in particular in Asia. In the discussion of industrialisation strategies, we shall once more make use of the distinction between closed and open models of the economy, introduced in Chapter 8. We start with the inward-looking large-scale industrialisation strategies associated with the closed model. We then move on to discuss alternative strategies, the most important of which is export-oriented industrialisation, based on labour-intensive manufactures.

9.2   Large-scale industrialisation and balanced growth strategies, 1950–80

In the first decades after 1945, the emphasis was on a transfer of resources from agriculture to the industrial sector and the rapid accumulation of capital in manufacturing. In the following sections, we analyse the characteristics and theoretical foundations of post-war large-scale industrialisation strategies.

9.2.1   Economic development with unlimited supplies of labour

In a famous article 'Economic Development with Unlimited Supplies of Labour' (1954), Arthur Lewis analysed the process of capital accumulation in a closed two-sector model. We have already referred to this article in the context of the discussion of structural change and the relationships between agriculture and industry in Chapter 8. Here we focus on the implications of the model for the process of industrialisation and capital accumulation.

Lewis opens with the statement that the classical tradition in economics has much to teach us about the process of capital accumulation. Following in the footsteps of classical economists, it was Marx who studied the process of capital accumulation in Europe and who focused attention on the dynamic role of the entrepreneurial bourgeoisie in this process.

According to Marx, capitalists exploited workers and appropriated the surplus value of their production in the form of profits. These profits were then reinvested in capital accumulation, resulting in an enormous growth of productive capacity. Surplus value consisted of the value of production of workers minus a subsistence wage just sufficient for bare survival. Given the abundance of labour on the labour market, competition ensured that wages were never far above subsistence level.[5] According to Lewis, there was a similar surplus of labour in densely populated developing countries. The abundant supply of labour would keep wages at a very low level and would contribute to high profits and a rapid rate of capital accumulation.

The sources of unlimited supplies of labour

In densely populated developing countries, the majority of the population was initially employed in the agricultural sector, where labour productivity was very low. Since too many people worked too little land, Lewis argued that marginal productivity was close to zero.[6] Nevertheless, in rural communities traditional forms of solidarity ensured that all members of society would receive sufficient food to survive at the subsistence level. Further, there was also a reserve army of low-paid, low-productivity workers in the informal sector of urban society: household servants, security guards, shoeshine boys, traders, casual workers, handymen, street vendors and so forth.

As soon as the modern capitalist sector of plantations, mines, cities, and manufacturing industries offered wages that slightly exceeded subsistence levels in the traditional sector, there was an enormous flow of cheap labour to the modern sector. Thus, Lewis writes that from the mid nineteenth century to the 1930s some 50 million people migrated from densely populated regions in China, India, and Indonesia to find employment in mines and plantations in the modern sector of the economies of developing countries (Lewis, 1978a, 1978b; see also Hatton and Williamson, 2005).

Effects of labour outflow on agricultural production and productivity

The outflow of workers from the agricultural sector does not necessarily result in a decline in food production. After all, the marginal productivity of the departing workers is assumed to be close to zero. In other words, they do not really contribute to agricultural production. When they leave, the average productivity of those left behind will go up and the level of production will remain unchanged. Thus there is actually sufficient surplus food to feed the industrial workers in the cities, while enough is left to fulfil the subsistence needs of the rural population.

[5] By now, we know that Marx was wrong. Wages did rise under capitalism. In the long run the working classes shared in the increase in prosperity.

[6] Marginal productivity is the extra contribution to production made by the last worker (or hour) added to the production process. If marginal productivity is 0, the last person employed makes no further contribution to production.

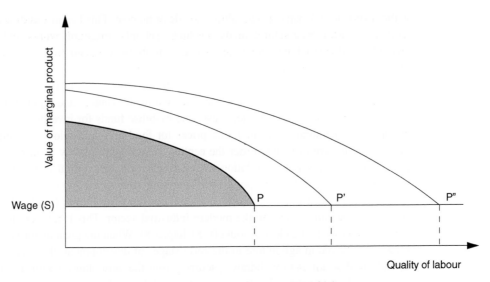

Figure 9.2 Economic development with unlimited supplies of labour

Effects of labour inflow into the industrial sector

In the modern industrial sector unlimited supplies of labour cause wages to remain at a low level. Thus huge profits can be made. The income distribution changes in favour of owners of capital. If the profits are reinvested in new capital goods, a rapid accumulation of capital leads to growth of industrial production. A crucial condition of the Lewis model is that high profits are indeed reinvested by a class of private capitalist entrepreneurs or by public managers of state owned firms. Capital accumulation will falter if profits are frittered away on luxury consumption by extravagant elites, wasted on wages of non-productive government bureaucrats, used for military purposes or industrial prestige projects, or spent on beautiful temples, churches, palaces, or monuments.

The process of economic development according to Lewis is summarised in Figure 9.2. At a fixed wage (*S*), slightly above subsistence level in traditional agriculture, an unlimited supply of labour is forthcoming.[7] In the initial situation capitalist entrepreneurs will expand production by adding workers to a given amount of industrial capital goods, until the revenue from the last additional worker (marginal revenue) is equal to the wage level (*S*). In Figure 9.2, entrepreneurs will increase production till the equilibrium point *P* is reached. Profits – the shaded part in Figure 9.2 – are reinvested in capital goods so that revenues per worker go up. In the new situation entrepreneurs will increase production to *P'*. This process repeats itself until the unlimited supplies of labour are exhausted and wage levels start to rise. In the phase of unlimited supplies of labour, capital accumulation and growth in the modern industrial sector can be very rapid.

There is a second mechanism in the Lewis model, which can be used to accumulate capital. When there is an unlimited supply of labour and a shortage of capital, labour can be

---

[7] Lewis emphasises the voluntary nature of migration. Other authors argue that coercion also played an important role (see Chapter 2).

withdrawn from subsistence agriculture at little or no cost. This labour can directly be set to work to create infrastructure: roads, viaducts, schools, irrigation works and so on. An example is Maoist China, which succeeded in mobilising labour from the rural sector in off-season periods for large infrastructural projects (Rawski, 1979). In the context of 'community development', India tried to mobilise labour during off-season periods for community projects such as building schools and health centres and digging wells.

According to Lewis, governments can also mobilise funds for investment in industry by taxing the agricultural sector or fixing prices for food products below their market value. Finally, the government may order the central bank to print money finance its investment expenditures. The resulting inflation works as a tax on agricultural incomes, because the purchasing power of the rural population decreases when prices go up.

The joint element in all these options is the transfer of resources (food, labour, savings) from the agricultural sector to the modern industrial sector. This is inherent in the logic of structural change in the closed model (see Chapter 8). When the great majority of the labour force is employed in agriculture in the early stages of development, the only way to create an industrial sector is to withdraw resources from the agricultural sector and use them to invest in industrialisation. The key assumptions of the model are that these resources can be transferred at very low cost and that subsistence levels of consumption in traditional agriculture determine wage levels in industry. If agricultural productivity and agricultural incomes were higher, workers would not be prepared to work at the lowest of wages in mines or factories.

9.2.2 Capital–output ratio

An often-quoted passage from Lewis' 1954 article is the following:

> *The central problem in the theory of economic development is to understand the process by which a community which was previously saving 4 or 5 per cent or less of its national income, converts itself into an economy where voluntary saving is running at about 12 to 15 per cent of national income or more.* (Lewis, 1954: 155)

The figures for the required savings rate of 12–15 per cent of national income are based on a simple growth model, which relates economic growth to annual investment in the capital stock, assuming a fixed ratio between the capital stock and output (the so-called Harrod–Domar production function). This model assumes that labour cannot be substituted for capital and that capital is the scarce factor of production. As labour is available in abundance in developing countries, the only thing that matters is the rate of investment in the capital stock. The fixed ratio between capital and output is called the *capital–output ratio*. Empirical observation indicates that capital–output ratios are usually somewhere between three to one and four to one. A ratio of four to one means that a net investment of $100 (after depreciation) is required to realise a $25 increase in annual output.[8]

The example in Table 9.1 shows that with a capital–output ratio of three to one and an annual average population growth of 2 per cent – not unusual for developing countries – a savings and investment rate of 6 per cent of net national income is just enough to keep per

---

[8] One can distinguish between the average capital–output ratio and the incremental or marginal capital–output ratio. Here we assume that incremental capital–output ratio and average capital–output ratio are equal.

Table 9.1: Capital–output ratios

	Country A	Country B
National income	1,000	1,000
Savings/investment	60	120
Savings ratio	0.06	0.12
Capital–output ratio	3	3
Increase in output	20	40
Increase in national income	2%	4%
Population growth	2%	2%
Growth of per capita income	0%	2%

capita income unchanged. If investment drops to 5 per cent or less, income per capita will decline. If a country aims at a target growth of income per capita of 2 per cent per year,[9] at least 12 per cent of national income needs to be saved and invested. If the capital–output ratio is more than three, the percentage of savings has to be over 12 per cent.

9.2.3 Shortage of capital as the key bottleneck in economic development

The pioneering article by Lewis set the tone for the post-war debate on the role of capital in development. Labour in developing countries was believed to be abundant and almost costless (see also Fei and Ranis, 1964). Capital was the scarce factor and therefore the main bottleneck in the process of development. The key policy issue was how to mobilise sufficient resources to accelerate the rate of capital accumulation in manufacturing. In post-war development plans, policy makers made rough estimates of the total amount of savings required to attain target rates of growth, using aggregate capital–output ratios, as illustrated in Table 9.1.

In an economy without much of a modern sector, the agricultural sector is the only possible source of such savings. Therefore, in a closed model the ultimate objective of development policy is to squeeze resources out of the agricultural sector and use them to create a modern industrial sector. Exploitation of the agricultural sector is inherent in the closed model of development.

9.2.4 Does economic development result in increasing income inequality?

The mobilisation of savings for capital accumulation may also have consequences for income inequality. In the closed model of the accumulation process, income inequality increases at the expense of the workers in subsistence agriculture and the industrial workers with fixed low wages. The beneficiaries are the entrepreneurs and capitalists in the modern sector, whose incomes derive primarily from profits. The assumption is that people who are

[9] An increase of income per capita by 2 per cent per year means that income per capita will double in thirty-five years. A rule of thumb is that a country will double its income per capita in a period roughly equal to 70 divided by the annual average growth rate in percentages.

trying to survive at subsistence level can hardly afford to save. It is the rich who save out of their profit incomes.[10] The increasing income inequality implies a redistribution of income from poor people, who consume most of their incomes, to rich classes, who are better able to save, thus leading to higher aggregate savings rates.

The increase in savings is not automatic. An ability to save does not necessarily imply an actual willingness to save, which depends on attitudes, culture and the quality of financial institutions. According to Lewis, a prerequisite for an increase in savings is the emergence of a capitalist class of entrepreneurs with a culturally sanctioned drive to save and to invest the savings productively (Lewis, 1954: 159). Lewis also notes that governments may perform this function of saving and investing. The socialist government may substitute for the capitalist entrepreneur.

The Lewis model offers a possible explanation for the frequently observed phenomenon of increasing income inequality in the course of economic development. Thus the present huge increases in inequality in rapidly growing economies such as China, India, Malaysia or Vietnam are perfectly consistent with the model.[11] Inequality only starts to decline once labour becomes scarce and wages start increasing at later stages of development.

A similar sequence is sketched in a famous article by Kuznets (1955), which claims that industrialisation and urbanisation initially lead to increases in income inequality, followed by a decline in inequality at later stages of development. Incomes in cities are higher than in the countryside, while the income inequality within urban communities tends to be greater than in rural communities. This implies that a transfer of population to the urban–industrial sector in the early stages of industrialisation automatically results in greater aggregate income inequality. At a later stage of economic development the income distribution becomes more equal as a result of demographic factors, increasing scarcity of labour, democratisation and the rise of trade unions and political lobby groups in the modern sector of the economy. The Kuznets hypothesis, often called the *inverted U-curve hypothesis,* has found support in international comparative research. Many studies find that the income distribution is more equal in rich countries than in middle-income countries and more unequal in middle-income countries than low-income countries (Bacha, 1979; Deininger and Squire, 1996; Paukert, 1973; World Bank, 1986).

Whether we may also conclude from such cross-country studies that the U-curve also holds for individual countries over time is contested. Critics argue that the U-curve is driven more by cross-country and regional differences than by historical country time series (Bacha, 1979; Deininger and Squire, 1998; Ferreira, 1999; Gillis *et al.*, 1992; Palma, 2011; Rubinson, 1976; Thorbecke and Charumilind, 2002). The relationship between income per capita and inequality tends to differ from country to country. In most advanced economies income inequality has actually been increasing rather than declining since the 1980s under the influence of globalisation and the pressure on wages levels due to

---

[10] The standard assumption in economic models is that workers consume all their income and capitalists save all of their profits. In this case, a redistribution of income to the profit-earning classes will increase aggregate savings (see, for instance, Kaldor, 1956; Sen, 1960; Thirlwall, 1999, Chapter 14)

[11] In these countries rapid growth results in simultaneous dramatic declines in poverty (for China and India see UNIDO, 2013) and large increases in income inequality. Opponents of the Kuznets curve often misguidedly pointed to the rapid declines of poverty in Asia. But declines in absolute poverty can coexist with increases in inequality.

competition from low-wage developing countries. Thus the optimistic expectation that income equality will decline at higher levels of income per capita is in question. However, it does seem obvious that rapid growth and structural change in low-income countries continue to be associated with large increases in inequality, as in the case of China, India, Indonesia or Malaysia since the 1990s. The statistical critics of the Kuznets curve do not give sufficient prominence to these developments.

The proposition that an increase in inequality is a necessary condition for increased saving, economic development and industrialisation has been strongly criticised (Ahluwalia, 1976; Stiglitz, 1996). The crucial assumption is that the poor do not save and that the rich have a high propensity to save and to invest their savings productively within the domestic economic. However, if profits are deposited in Swiss banks or are frittered away in luxury consumption by extravagant and unproductive elites, then inequality will contribute nothing to economic development but create more misery for the poor. In such cases redistribution may even be a necessary condition for increased savings and more productive investments. Several studies indicate that countries with a more equal initial distribution of income grow more rapidly, than countries starting with high inequality (Alesina and Rodrik, 1994; Persson and Tabellini, 1994). It has often been noted that the Asian countries that experienced successful industrialisation – e.g. China, Japan, South Korea and Taiwan – were characterised by rather equal initial distributions of income and large-scale redistribution of land in early stages of development. But in recent years, inequality has been increasing in these countries as well.

9.2.5   The two-gap model of foreign finance: the role of financial flows from abroad

In an open economy, financial flows from abroad are alternative sources of savings. The difference between aggregate savings requirements indicated in national plans and the savings that can actually be mobilised in the domestic economy is the so-called *savings gap*. The savings gap is an indication of the required inflow of foreign capital. This inflow can be supplied either by FDI, portfolio investment and loans from private banks, remittances or by official financial flows, including development aid.

Developing economies not only require foreign finance to supplement domestic savings, they also have an acute shortage of foreign exchange. The capital goods needed to expand manufacturing output are produced in the advanced economies. Foreign exchange is needed to finance the imports of industrial capital goods and imports of semi-finished goods and raw materials that are used as industrial inputs. Foreign exchange can be earned by exports. Typically, however, exports in post-war developing economies are less than imports. The difference between the value of exports and the value of imports is the *trade gap* or foreign exchange gap. This is a second indication of the amount of foreign finance required for growth.

In so-called *two-gap models* (Bruton, 1969; Chenery and Adelman, 1966; Chenery and MacEwan, 1966; Chenery and Strout, 1966), the need for foreign finance is determined by the larger of the two gaps. Two-gap models also provide an important rationale for development aid (see Chapter 14). Given target growth rates, the amount of development aid needed to supplement private capital flows can be calculated.

In the long run, two-gap analysis assumes that the need for foreign finance will become less. If the investment programmes are successful, income per capita will go up and domestic savings will increase. Further, as the economy develops, it will be able to substitute some domestically produced capital goods for imported capital goods and it will start expanding its exports. Thus, the foreign exchange gap will also decrease. In recent years, developments in the balance of payments have been in line with such theoretical predictions. Several of the successful emerging economies are now running surpluses on their balance of payments (see Table 3.6, p. 119) and have even become major investors in other economies.

Actually, two-gap models make reference to a third gap, a *technology gap*. To make productive use of imported capital goods, a developing economy may also need a complementary supply of technical assistance. The capital–output ratio is the inverse of the productivity of capital. As the technological capabilities of a country improve, through investment in human capital, the founding of R&D institutes, learning by doing and technical training, capital productivity will increase and the capital–output ratio will go down. Other things being equal, the amount of investment required for a given growth rate will then tend to diminish. A supply of technical assistance can contribute to increased technological capabilities and a reduction in the technology gap.

9.2.6 Big is beautiful: large-scale investment, government planning and import substitution

Three closely related elements have been prominent in post-Second World War industrialisation strategies: a preference for large-scale investment, extensive government planning and intervention and inward-looking import substitution policies.[12] With regard to scale, it was believed that there was a critical minimum size for the required investment effort. Industrial production is inherently a large-scale phenomenon. Piecemeal industrialisation was destined to fail. If a country was to industrialise successfully, a wide range of industrial activities should be undertaken simultaneously, so that all activities would reinforce each other. This was referred to as *balanced growth*. Central planning and regulation by the government was seen as necessary to mobilise sufficient resources for investment and to coordinate all the simultaneous investments in different industrial sectors. Finally, the newly established industries had to be protected against competition from powerful international competitors until they were strong enough to survive. To achieve this, governments erected a panoply of protective policy instruments and supportive selective industrial policies. The focus of policy was inward-oriented. The aim was to substitute imported manufactured goods on the domestic market by locally produced goods.

Arguments in favour of large-scale industrialisation

Advocates of industrialisation were convinced that there was a critical minimum size for the investment effort required for successful industrialisation. Several arguments were put forward in favour of large-scale industrialisation.

Rostow (1960) and his followers were of the opinion that sustained economic development could only be realised if investment was increased dramatically within a short period of time (see also Chapter 3). In the 'take-off' phase, an enormous investment boost would set the flywheel of sustained economic development in motion. According to Rostow, historical evidence from the growth experiences of Western countries supported the Lewis

---

[12] In *The Economics of the Developing Countries* (1980), Myint has provided an admirable summary of the debate on large-scale industrialisation strategies and balanced growth. The following sections are based on Myint's discussion of these issues.

hypothesis that investment should increase from less than 5 per cent to more than 12 per cent of net national income in a few decades.

The neo-Malthusian trap, discussed in Chapter 5, also leads to the conclusion that large-scale efforts are required for development (Leibenstein, 1954; Nelson, 1956). This model (see Figure 5.3 in Chapter 5) is based on the notion of a race between population growth and income per capita growth. When the critical minimum level of investment is not reached, an increase in income per capita results in population growth in excess of income growth. As a consequence, income per capita will be forced down until a low-level equilibrium is reached around subsistence level. Only a big investment push can move a country beyond the point where income per capita growth exceeds the growth of the population. Thus a 'Big Push' is required for sustained growth.

Important arguments in favour of large-scale industrialisation policies are the so-called *complementarity arguments* (Higgins, 1968; Myint, 1980, Chapter 7). The key idea here is that different economic activities will stimulate each other if they are undertaken simultaneously. Government planning and regulation ensures that the various activities are coordinated so that their mutual positive effects are strongest. The emphasis on complementarities in large-scale industrialisation is the main characteristic of *balanced growth* theory (Nurkse, 1953).

In his discussion of *balanced growth,* Myint distinguishes between three types of complementarities: complementarities in demand; complementarities between infrastructure and industry; and complementarities in industrial production.

1. *Complementarities in demand.* In the oldest version of the balanced growth strategy, Rosenstein-Rodan (1943) argued for the simultaneous setting up of a large number of factories for consumer goods. A single factory in an otherwise traditional economy will never be able to survive, as there is no market for its products. If many factories start operations at the same time, the wages paid to the workers will create sufficient purchasing power. Thus, there will be sufficient demand for the output of all factories together, while a single factory would go bankrupt.
2. *Complementarities with infrastructure.* For industrial production it is essential that there is an uninterrupted supply of raw materials, semi-finished goods, energy and water, and an uninterrupted outflow of the goods produced. Without an adequate infrastructure for transport, communications, and energy supply no industry can function properly. Therefore, investment in industry has its complement in investment in infrastructure and social overhead capital. Infrastructural investment is inevitably large scale in nature. Half a dam will not produce any hydroelectric energy; an uncompleted railway line or highway will not solve any transport problems. Industrialisation, therefore, requires simultaneous investment in a wide range of consumer goods industries and large-scale investments in infrastructure.
3. *Complementarities in production.* Consumers are not the only buyers of industrial output. Industries also supply intermediate inputs to each other. For instance, a car manufacturer needs machines, steel, tyres, spare parts, screws and semi-finished products. Industrial enterprises are dependent on each other via technical input–output relations, the so-called *vertical linkages*. When capital goods industries, intermediate industries and consumer goods industries are set up simultaneously, in the context of a national plan, expansion of output by one industry creates additional demand for inputs

from other industries (*backward linkages*). Its output can be used as input by other industries (*forward linkages*). All industries will benefit from one another's demand and the availability of one another's inputs.

The 'Big Push' development strategy

The most comprehensive development strategy within the framework of the balanced growth approach is the 'Big Push' strategy (Higgins, 1968; Rosenstein-Rodan, 1957). The 'Big Push' strategy is a comprehensive industrialisation plan in which large-scale investments in infrastructure, the capital goods sector, the intermediate sector and various consumer goods industries take place simultaneously. All positive 'external effects' can be realised in the form of technical complementarities in the production process, demand complementarities on markets for consumer goods and complementarities between infrastructure and industrial production.

Arguments in favour of planning and intervention

After the Second World War there was widespread distrust of the capitalist market economy. Leaders of developing countries associated capitalism with the imperialism and colonialism, from which their countries had suffered so painfully. They found inspiration in the experiences of the Soviet Union, which seemed to have succeeded in achieving accelerated industrialisation in the twentieth century through central planning. Non-communist developing countries like India also drew up Soviet-style Five-Year Plans and assigned a key role to the government in industrialisation policies.

The basic rationale for planning was that the anarchistic market – where each entrepreneur pursued his private interests and goals – would be unable to coordinate all activities effectively within the framework of large-scale industrialisation. Private entrepreneurs cannot be expected to coordinate their activities with those of others. They are only interested in their own profits, costs and benefits. Whether an investment has positive external effects on the profitability of other industrial activities plays no role in the calculations of a private investor. Thus many investment opportunities would remain underexploited in a market economy. For example, investment in infrastructure is of great importance to economic development as a whole, but not very profitable in itself.

Moreover, it was believed that an active entrepreneurial class had not yet emerged in developing countries – in part due to the stifling effects of colonialism. Governments had to compensate for the lack of private entrepreneurship. Finally, it was thought that the scale of required investment efforts had become so large that only the government would be able to mobilise sufficient resources for investment.

The conclusion was that the government needed to play a central role in industrialisation, partly by investing itself through parastatal enterprises and partly by coordinating activities of private entrepreneurs through extensive planning, licensing and regulation. A wide range of industrial policy instruments, often of a highly selective nature, were applied to support and stimulate industrial activities.

Following the example of the Soviet Union, many developing countries drew up Five-Year Plans. In countries such as China and India, input–output tables were used as a planning tool to set integrated production targets for all sectors of industry, based on their technical interrelationships. The degree of state intervention was highest in the communist economies such as China, Vietnam and Cuba. But, government intervention was also pervasive in developing countries all over the world, in non-communist India, in Latin America, the Middle East and in Sub-Saharan Africa.

In large-scale industrialisation plans, special attention was devoted to the promotion of the capital goods sector and heavy industry. In the history of industrialisation much of technological change in the past centuries has been generated by firms in the capital goods industry, which supply the machinery for industrial production (e.g. Rosenberg, 1982). Development of a domestic capital goods sector was seen as crucial for the supply of capital goods to other sectors and as a source of technological change. Heavy industries such as steel, basic chemicals and cement were seen as key industries, which would provide the intermediate inputs for other industries.

In a different guise, scale has received a new lease of life in the work of Paul Krugman on agglomeration economies (Krugman, 1991). Krugman added a spatial dimension to the discussion and argued that it was the large-scale agglomeration of different economic activities in urban centres which provided the foundations for productivity increases and export competitiveness. Agglomeration was required to achieve increasing returns and to benefit from externalities. Many developing countries suffered from the lack of such large-scale agglomerations and were therefore not competitive enough.

Import-substituting industrialisation and the arguments in favour of protection

The third characteristic element of post-war industrialisation strategies was import substitution. After the Second World War, there was a strong reaction against the colonial division of labour in international trade, in which developing countries exported primary (unprocessed) agricultural and mining products and imported all manufactured products from the Western countries. By simultaneously investing in infrastructure, capital goods industries, intermediate industries and a whole range of consumer goods industries, it was hoped that developing countries would become more self-reliant. Well-known examples of large countries that have pursued such industrialisation policies include Argentina, Brazil, China, India, Mexico, South Africa and Turkey (Bardhan, 1984; Gereffi, 1990; Kiely, 1998; Maddison et al., 1992; Weiss, 2002). The underlying goal was to reduce a country's dependence on manufactured imports and international trade.

In order to realise this goal, domestic industries were given as much protection as possible. Imports were restricted by the imposition of high import tariffs, quota and import licensing systems. The effect of these measures is that imports are restricted, domestic prices go up and newly established domestic industries have a chance to survive. Protection also makes it interesting for foreign MNCs to invest in a country, because they may thus penetrate or even capture a protected domestic market. Protection through tariffs on final products affects the prices of industrial outputs (*nominal protection*). But protection can also aim at making inputs cheaper, either through subsidies to producers or by maintaining overvalued exchange rates. The *effective rate of protection* which takes into account both input and output prices is usually much higher than the nominal rate of protection.[13] Import-substituting industries are also supported by subsidies on investment, preferential access to investment funds, provision of cheap energy, raw materials and other inputs at below market prices, access to cheap credit,

---

[13] The effective rate of protection ERP is calculated as $ERP = \frac{P_w t_o - C_w t_i}{P_w - C_w}$, where P_w is the world price of a final good, t_o the tariff on imports of a final good, C_w the world price of inputs needed to produce the final good and t_i the tariff on imported inputs.

various tax benefits and absorption of losses by the central government. Overvalued exchange rates also make imported capital goods and intermediate inputs cheaper. This complex of policy measures is called *import-substituting industrialisation* (ISI). It discriminates in favour of import-substituting industries, discourages imports and discriminates against exporters of industrial and primary goods through taxation and overvalued exchange rates.

Two stages of import substitution can be distinguished: *primary import substitution* and *secondary import substitution*. Primary import substitution focuses on replacing imported consumer goods by domestically produced consumer goods. Secondary import substitution aims at deepening the industrial structure by substituting imported intermediates and capital goods by domestically produced intermediates and capital goods. The first phase is easier than the second (Furtado, 1976).

Arguments in favour of protection

The chief justification for protection is the *infant industry* argument. Newly established enterprises in developing countries are unable to compete with their powerful and experienced international rivals, whether on international or domestic markets. To prevent the newly established firms and industries from collapsing under international competition, they need to gain experience on protected domestic markets. Through learning by doing and realisation of economies of scale these enterprises will gradually become more efficient and productive until they become internationally competitive and can dispense with protection (Bruton, 1998; Chang, 2002, 2003; Cimoli *et al.*, 2009). Purposes of protection are summarised in Box 9.1.

There is an important element of validity in the *infant industry* argument. In developing countries import substitution is an essential initial phase in the process of industrialisation. Almost without exception, developing countries that have been successful in developing a substantial industrial sector started out with import substitution. Two well-known examples are Taiwan and South Korea, which started with import substitution policies in the 1950s before moving on to manufactured exports.[14]

BOX 9.1 : Aims of industrial protection

- Providing newly established firms with time to expand the scale of their production and achieve **economies of scale**.
- Providing newly established firms with time to become more efficient and productive through **learning by doing**.
- Allowing for the realisation of **external economies and complementarities**.
- Promoting **diversification** of the economy, and making a country less dependent on the – presumed – deterioration of the terms of trade of primary exports.
- Reducing a country's **dependence on imports**.

---

[14] The present rules of the WTO prohibit industrial protection. This may make it difficult for newcomers to embark on industrialisation.

In the late nineteenth century, the revenues from primary agricultural and mining exports created a small urban market for industrial consumer goods. These goods were imported from abroad. Once these markets had been established they could be captured by developing a domestic import-substituting industry and protecting it from foreign competition. The Latin American experiences in the 1930s in particular have been quite significant in this respect. When international trade collapsed as a result of the international economic crisis, countries like Brazil and Argentina managed to develop an impressive domestic manufacturing industry. Other historical examples of successful import substitution include the USA in the early nineteenth century and Germany in the second half of the nineteenth century (Chang, 2002).

9.3 Criticisms of orthodox industrialisation strategies

The orthodox industrialisation strategies described above had a number of characteristics in common: large scale, emphasis on capital as the scarce factor in development, priority of industry over agriculture, faith in government planning and regulation and protection of the domestic market.

All these characteristics were rooted in a coherent industrialisation ideology and strategy. In the meantime, however, the initial enthusiasm for unbridled industrialisation has been tempered (Pack, 1988). In some countries industrialisation never got off the ground. In other countries isolated industrial enclaves developed, claiming disproportionate shares of available resources without contributing much to employment or national welfare. Many countries in Africa, Latin America and Eastern Europe suffered from de-industrialisation after their economies were liberalised from the 1980s onwards. Below, the various assumptions underlying the orthodox industrialisation strategies of the post-Second World War period are subjected to critical scrutiny.

9.3.1 Shortcomings of the Lewis model

One of the key assumptions in the Lewis model is that there is disguised unemployment in traditional subsistence agriculture. Therefore, labour can be withdrawn from this sector without any loss of food production. This leads to the optimistic notion of 'costless development', where developing countries can freely utilise their surplus labour for industrialisation.

The notion of costless development turns out to be problematic. Even if a traditional agricultural worker has a low marginal product, this does not mean that he or she does not contribute anything to agricultural output.[15] Agricultural tasks are shared among all workers.[16] Total food output will decrease when somebody moves to the city, unless the people remaining in agriculture start working harder. They will only do this if they can sell their surplus production at reasonable prices on the market and can use the additional income to acquire new industrial products. When there are no economic incentives, peasants will only produce as much as they need for their own subsistence. They have no reason to produce a surplus to feed the urban population. Agricultural production will stagnate. One

---

[15] In a later article Lewis actually acknowledges this (Lewis, 1983b). Still, he maintains that workers remaining in agriculture can maintain previous levels of production.

[16] We abstract here from the division of labour between men and women in agriculture (see Chapter 10).

can never transfer resources from one activity to another without incurring *opportunity costs* in the form of some loss of output. One has to weigh the costs and benefits of a transfer of resources from one sector to another.

A second important assumption in Lewis' original model is that wages in the modern sector are determined by the standard of living in rural areas. This is not always the case. In wage determination, political considerations and bargaining with powerful urban trade unions play an important role. As a result urban wages in the formal manufacturing sector of many countries following an inward-looking industrialisation strategy are relatively high. Small labour elites have emerged, consisting of comparatively well-paid employees in protected industries and government organisations. This elite profits from cheap and subsidised food supplies. Political survival dictates that governments in developing countries do not challenge these privileges. In Africa and Latin America, the combination of high wages and subsidies on investment in capital has resulted in a pattern of investment that typically uses too much capital and too little labour. Due to the capital-intensive nature of production, the modern sector has proved to be unable to absorb the inflow of labour from the rural sector.[17] Substantial urban unemployment has arisen, and many migrants try to survive in the informal sector of the urban economy (see section 9.4.3). This is one of the key differences between East Asia, which succeeded in effectively exploiting cheap labour in labour-intensive manufacturing, and Latin America and Africa, where this did not happen to a similar degree.

9.3.2 Is capital really so important?

Post-war industrialisation strategies emphasised the shortage of savings and investments. Raising the rate of capital accumulation would automatically result in increases in production. Applying fixed capital–output ratios, the levels of investment, saving and foreign finance required to achieve target growth rates could be calculated.

However, the real state of affairs is more complicated. Not all investments are equally effective or efficient. When an Indian steel plant operates at one-third of its capacity, the capital–output ratio will be much higher than when it operates at full capacity. When a Tanzanian airport is built without adequate roads leading to it, its contribution to the economy may be marginal. When workers and managers lack the skills, training and education to operate new machinery and technology, capital productivity will be low. The returns to investment in large-scale prestige projects are often very low. When linkages with the rest of the economy are weak or non-existent, investments will not have very positive effects on growth.

During the post-war period, savings and investment rates have increased in all countries, in accordance with the prescriptions of orthodox industrialisation policies. But the effects on growth have been mixed. The *capacity to absorb investment* differs widely from country to country (Abramovitz, 1989b; Myint, 1980). Countries differ in the efficiency of their governments, degrees of corruption, political stability, macro-economic and monetary stability, the capabilities and skills of the labour force and the managers. The levels of schooling of the labour force and the length of experience with industrialisation are of particular importance (Pack, 1988). Some countries in Southeast Asia have shown a great capacity to absorb

---

[17] It would not be correct to say that there would be no urban unemployment if more labour-intensive techniques were employed. Technological change has made industrial production generally more capital-intensive. However, an inappropriate choice of techniques certainly worsens employment prospects.

investments. In other countries, especially on the African continent, investment efforts have had much less positive effects. Critics argue that industrialisation is not primarily constrained by insufficient savings, but by lack of sufficient productive investment opportunities. Also, as argued in Chapter 4 on technology, capital accumulation without a dynamic process of innovation and technological upgrading will not result in successful development.

9.3.3   How important is the scale of investment?

Several authors have criticised the emphasis on the large scale of investment in orthodox industrialisation policies (e.g. Krueger, 1992; Little, Scitovsky and Scott, 1970; Myint, 1980). Industrialisation is rarely a question of all or nothing. It is more important to select the most appropriate and profitable investments, than to invest in all sectors simultaneously. Myint (1980) has deftly summarised the criticisms of various versions of balanced growth strategies.   ▷ combination

Complementarity in demand. When total demand increases due to the simultaneous setting up of several factories and the payments of wages to their employees, this does not necessarily mean that the sales of a single factory will increase as well. If a new factory does not produce more efficiently than traditional crafts industries, it will never be able to sell its products.

Infrastructure. There is some validity in the argument that infrastructural investment is inherently large scale. But again, it is not a question of all or nothing. There is always some infrastructure present. One can choose between improving a dirt track and constructing a four-lane highway, between small hydroelectric projects or large dams. There are many examples of infrastructure projects, which have not led to more industrial activities.

'Big Push'. The advocates of the 'Big Push' strategy avoided the choice between more and less efficient investments by arguing that everything should be done simultaneously: investing in consumer goods industries, capital goods industries and infrastructure. As a result, this strategy denied the scarcity of resources and the need to choose between alternative options on the basis of their costs and benefits. The greater the scale, the greater the risk of expensive mistakes and inefficient investments. Moreover, the emphasis on government planning in 'Big Push' strategies placed totally unrealistic demands on the administrative capabilities of weak governments and bureaucracies (e.g. Altenburg, 2013).

The shortcomings of ISI are summarised in Box 9.2 and discussed below (see, for example, Kirkpatrick, 1987; Pack, 1988; Thirlwall, 1999).

BOX 9.2 : Shortcomings of import substitution industrialisation

- Prolonged protection promotes survival of **inefficient firms**.
- The goal **of reduced import dependence** is seldom realised.
- The size of the domestic market is too restricted to achieve sufficient economies of scale.
- Import substitution may create **domestic monopolies**.
- Tariffs and quota result in **domestic distortions and higher prices for consumers** for fewer goods and services.
- The government's regulatory role creates opportunities and incentives for **pervasive rent seeking and corruption**.

Ideally, protection of domestic industries should be restricted to the early stages of production. Infant industries should be protected only when they are in their infancy. Once an industry has learned to produce efficiently and has started reaping economies of scale, protection should be discontinued. Countries which follow the path of protection too long get saddled with deeply inefficient, wasteful and non-competitive industries. When inputs and outputs of such industries are valued at international prices, their net contribution to national income may even be negative. Examples of such inefficient industries, which are unable to survive in a competitive environment are found in Latin America, South Asia and in particular in Sub-Saharan Africa (Szirmai and Lapperre, 2001; Yamfwa, 2001).

One of the objectives of import substitution is to reduce dependence on foreign imports. This objective is seldom realised. Usually, one type of dependence is simply exchanged for another. The dependence on imported consumer goods decreases. The dependence on imports of raw materials, semi-manufactured goods, capital goods and technological know-how tends to increase (e.g. Athukorala, 1998a). When developing countries try to build up their capital goods industries, they become more dependent on imports of technology.

A third objection to import substitution is that the size of the domestic market is restricted. In dualistic economies incomes per capita outside the modern sector are too low to create sufficient demand. In smaller countries in particular, import substitution will soon reach its limits, but even in large countries such as Brazil the limited size of the market causes serious problems.

A fourth objection is that import substitution may give rise to domestic monopolies, which may lead to even higher prices and more restricted supply. These domestic monopolies have a vested interest in maintaining protection indefinitely and will exert maximum political pressure to resist change. The possibility of establishing monopolies is one of the reasons why protective barriers attract FDI.

A fifth objection is that the controls involved in import substitution offer opportunities for corruption and collusion between powerful firms seeking rents and government officials. Market distortions result in officials having to make discretionary decisions about allocation of import licences or scarce foreign exchange, which makes them obvious targets for corruption. This is one of the key arguments of the political economy approach to rent seeking behaviour (Lal and Myint, 1996).

9.3.4   Urban industrial bias and the neglect of agriculture

Since the 1960s, there has been a growing tide of criticism of development strategies that favoured industry over agriculture and cities over the countryside, at all cost. The so-called *urban industrial bias* in policy had numerous adverse effects both on urban and rural areas, and on the economy as a whole. Instead of reducing the dualism between modern and traditional sectors, which the developing countries had inherited from the colonial era, orthodox industrial strategies have often reinforced it (Bos, 1984; Ranis, 1989). Major characteristics and shortcomings of the urban industrial bias in policy are summarised in Box 9.3.

In a great many developing countries in Africa, Latin America and Asia, protectionist policies and discrimination in favour of industry resulted in excessively large-scale and highly inefficient industrialisation, often dominated by state owned firms. Vast resources were wasted on unprofitable prestige projects. As protected industries could obtain their capital goods too cheaply, production was too capital-intensive and created insufficient

---

BOX 9.3 : **Urban industrial bias**

Characteristics:

- Preferential treatment and protection of manufacturing by means of:
  - o Tariffs, quotas, licensing arrangements.
  - o Provision of cheap inputs and raw materials.
  - o Overvalued exchange rates.
  - o Cheap credit.
  - o Preferential allocation of investment resources.

Consequences:

- High wages and capital-intensive choice of technology.
- High degrees of inefficiency, resulting in:
  - o Low quality of products and production processes.
  - o Low capacity utilisation.
  - o High costs of production.
  - o Negative contributions to national product when inputs and outputs are valued at world prices (in extreme cases).
  - o Lack of competitiveness.
- Lack of technological learning.
- Continued dependence on imported intermediate inputs, capital goods and technology.
- Production of luxury consumer goods instead of production for basic needs.
- Neglect of the agrarian sector and reinforcement of dualism.

---

employment. Scant attention was paid to the vast numbers of workers in small-scale industry and the informal sector. A small elite of industrial workers came into being. Industrial workers secured their positions through trade unions and political parties and were paid better wages than the rural population and most workers in the informal sector. Inefficient factories suffered from idle capacity, due to inadequate maintenance, lack of inputs, lack of sales or absence of the work force. At international prices their contribution to national income could even be negative (i.e. the value of their inputs at international prices was higher than the value of their outputs). Though the aim of industrialisation was to make developing countries less dependent on the advanced economies, in practice the industrial sector remained dependent on imported intermediates, capital goods and technology.

Agriculture and the rural sector were neglected. Most attention was directed to the formal urban sector. The prices paid to farmers were kept low artificially by means of a variety of price controls, compulsory deliveries and marketing boards. Overvalued exchange rates hampered agricultural exports. Moreover, revenues from agricultural and primary exports were heavily taxed in order to finance government expenditures. Credit facilities for the rural population were underdeveloped. Farmers could only obtain loans by borrowing from informal moneylenders at exorbitant interest rates. Government subsidies for agricultural investment were scarce. The bulk of public facilities – schools, health centres and so forth – was located in the cities.

All these factors had adverse effects on the agricultural sector and resulted in stagnating agricultural production and productivity. Due to the systematic neglect of agriculture, many Sub-Saharan African countries that had been self-supporting in food became dependent on imports of foodstuffs. The same was true in Asia for India and Bangladesh and in Latin America for the former food exporters Argentina and Chile.

In an interesting analysis of the Chinese industrial experience, Lin, Cai and Li (2000, 2003) show how the various elements of orthodox industrial strategy hang together. A capital-intensive heavy industry-oriented development strategy requires vast amounts of capital, which cannot be raised in a market economy. Distorted macro-policies are required to make heavy industry projects profitable (which they are not at market rates). These policies include low interest rates, overvalued exchange rates to cheapen imports, a policy of low input prices for energy, raw materials and transportation, and low nominal wage rates for workers.[18] The assumption was that low prices would create profits large enough to repay loans and to reinvest. Private enterprises soon had to be nationalised, because private entrepreneurs would not reinvest on the intended scale. This explains the similarities in industrial practice between communist China and non-communist India. The result is a trinity of a distorted macro-policy environment, a planned allocation mechanism and a puppet-like micro-management system, where managers follow government directives.

9.4　Alternative industrialisation strategies

Since the 1960s a variety of alternatives to the orthodox industrialisation strategies emerged in the theoretical debates and in policy practice. These alternatives include: (a) the balanced growth path strategy; (b) the strategy of unbalanced growth; (c) the promotion of SMEs; (d) labour-intensive export strategies; (e) technological upgrading and learning; (f) resource-based industrialisation; (g) structural adjustment, liberalisation and privatisation. The first three strategies are discussed in this section. A separate section (section 9.5) is devoted to export-oriented industrialisation strategies. Under this heading we discuss labour-intensive exports, technological upgrading and learning and resource-based industrialisation ((d), (e) and (f)). In section 9.6 we pay attention to the wave of liberalisation in the 1980s and 1990s, followed by renewed criticism of excessive reliance on market solutions.

9.4.1　Balanced growth path

In Chapter 8, we mentioned the emergence of the theory of a balanced growth path in the 1960s. The novelty of this approach is that it focused on the need for balance between evolving broad sectors of the economy, emphasising the need for an end to the discrimination against the agricultural sector. A healthy and dynamic agricultural sector was now seen as contributing to the success of industrialisation. One of the early examples of a balanced growth path policy was that of Taiwan in the 1950s. The balanced growth path reflected a major shift in policy stance. Important countries such as Indonesia, India and China started

agriculture contributes to industrialization.

---

[18] Socialist China was more successful in keeping wages low than other developing economies.

paying more attention to agriculture and following a policy of 'walking on two legs'. These policies have been remarkably successful. Unfortunately in Africa, neglect of agriculture continued far longer.

An interesting variant of the balanced growth path approach is found in rural industrialisation strategies, which try to capitalise on the links between agriculture and rural industry. This policy option will be discussed at more length in Chapter 10. It is worth noting that the balanced growth path theory is still very much a closed economy approach. It analyses the relationships and balances between broad sectors of the economy, from the perspective that balanced investments should be made across all sectors of the economy. Trade relations with the outside world remain outside the picture. In the past, the balanced growth path referred almost exclusively to the relationships between industry and agriculture. In the light of modern developments, we should also include balanced relationships between services and industry in our analysis.

9.4.2 Unbalanced growth

The function of dynamic imbalances

The 'Big Push' approach is a typical example of a development strategy that tries to identify prime movers or crucial bottlenecks in the process of development. When the scarce or missing factor – whether capital, education or technology – is made available, development is assumed to follow almost automatically. In *The Strategy of Economic Development*, a book first published in 1958, but still relevant today, Albert Hirschman argues that this approach is flawed (Hirschman, 1988). It is impossible to draw up a list of the necessary and sufficient conditions for growth and development.[19] First, there are alternatives to each prerequisite or factor. Second, the presence of a set of prerequisites does not necessarily result in growth.

Hirschman argues that attitudes and value systems favourable to entrepreneurship and economic initiative are of crucial importance in the process of development. But such attitudes should not be seen as a new set of static prerequisites for development, which has to be in place before things start moving. Wherever economic opportunities arise, entrepreneurship will sooner or later emerge. There will always be entrepreurial individuals coming forward – members of ethnic minorities or of indigenous populations – who will start exploiting new opportunities. However, where economic opportunities and incentives are lacking in a traditional society, entrepreneurship and initiative will remain dormant.

The main challenge in devising a development strategy is not the search for missing factors (savings, capital, education, entrepreneurship, natural resources) or the elimination of obstacles (risk aversion, land tenure systems) but rather the identification of pressures and inducement mechanisms that call forth hidden resources and entrepreneurial abilities. In principle, there is no savings bottleneck. In early stages of economic development sufficient savings can easily be mobilised. More important is the development of the capabilities to invest savings productively.

The essence of the theory of *unbalanced growth* is that investments should be made in strategic key sectors of the economy. These investments cause dynamic tensions, shortages

---

[19] For example, the growth experience of Japan challenged the notion that a resource poor nation cannot industrialise and that national resources are a prerequisite for industrialisation.

and imbalances, which call forth entrepreneurship and investment in other sectors. As the modern sector of the economy becomes larger and more dynamic, there will be ever-greater opportunities for new investment. This will elicit new entrepreneurship. Thus, growth sets virtuous circles in motion.

Backward and forward linkages

Like the advocates of balanced growth, Hirschman assumes the existence of various *complementarities* between economic activities. First, there are purely technical complementarities. When a factory produces reinforced concrete, it needs steel. More indirect complementarities occur in the construction of office buildings. Empty office buildings create a demand for office furniture. Further, there are complementarities associated with economies of scale in production. When the production of good A increases, the costs will usually decrease. Sector B, which uses product A as an input, will benefit from these lower costs. Another sequence is when the production of good A increases the demand for inputs of good C. This may allow economies of scale to be realised in the production of C. Thus C can also be produced at lower cost.

Hirschman's main thesis is that it is neither possible nor desirable to plan all these activities ahead. If we look at an economy at two different points in time, T_1 and T_2, it seems in retrospect that all activities were related in a process of balanced growth. However in reality the path from T_1 to T_2 is a dynamic one. Shortages and imbalances at a given point in time elicit new activities and investments at a later point in time, which create new shortages and imbalances. A shortage of steel for the production of reinforced concrete or cars will create profitable investment opportunities in the steel sector. As the number of factories increases, the need for an adequate infrastructure becomes more pressing, and so on. Development policy should create such dynamic imbalances. It is the movement from imbalance to imbalance which calls forth a stream of entrepreneurship and new investment.

Hirschman distinguishes two different kinds of linkages between economic activities: *forward linkages* and *backward linkages*. Backward linkages occur when an economic activity requires inputs that can be supplied by other domestic enterprises. Often, inputs are initially imported. Later local enterprises may emerge which can produce the imported inputs more efficiently in the domestic economy.

Forward linkages occur when the easy availability of a product, which serves as an input into another production process, calls forth investment in this other line of production. For example, the establishment of a basic iron and steel industry may lead to the emergence of fabricated metals industries. The availability of agricultural products may stimulate the rise of food processing industries. The availability of wood supplies in Indonesia enabled the rise of a large plywood industry and a furniture industry.

Hirschman also makes a distinction between the *strength* and the *importance* of a linkage. Sometimes a linkage is very strong, but not very important because the new activity has a low value added. For example, there is a strong linkage between the production of car parts and the assembly of these parts. But the value added of assembly is modest and contributes little to national income.

The relation between physical infrastructure and industrial production is an example of an important but weak forward linkage. The availability of infrastructure is permissive. It allows for other economic activities, but does not compel them. There are many examples of infrastructural investment that have not resulted in greatly increased industrial activity.

Conversely, investments in industry do have a compelling effect on infrastructure through backward linkages. It is absolutely essential for a factory to have uninterrupted supplies of energy and means of transport. Owners and managers will exert all possible pressure on the government to realise improved infrastructure in energy and transport. Such pressures can be observed in the industrialisation experiences of Thailand and Indonesia.

An often-mentioned objection to primary export-led development strategies is that the linkages involved are so weak. Investments in mines, oil wells and plantations have only very limited linkages with the rest of the economy. They result in dualist economies, with small modern enclaves oriented towards the international economy and a traditional sector isolated from the modern sector. One of the advantages of industrialisation is that the linkages involving industrial sectors are so much stronger than those of other sectors (see Lavopa and Szirmai, 2012). The notion of *resource-based industrialisation* – to be discussed in section 9.5.4 – can be seen as a response to the problem of weak linkages in the primary sector.

In a country with no manufacturing, industrialisation can only start in consumer goods industries delivering to final demand. In early stages of industrialisation, one will therefore find two kinds of industries: industries transforming domestic or imported primary products into consumer goods, or industries transforming imported semi-manufactured goods into final consumer goods (Hirschman, 1988, Chapter 6). The early industrialising European countries had no choice but to take the first road. In developing countries that followed this route, textiles, leather products, clothing, food processing, beverages and construction materials were of significance.

However, present-day developing countries also have the option of assembling or providing the final touches to almost finished intermediate products imported from abroad. This option is increasingly preferred. Foreign investors make use of surplus labour and low wages to transfer assembly activities to developing countries. Hirschman calls this option 'enclave-import industries' since it initially adds little value to the imported inputs and is completely dependent on imports. In the first stage, the linkages with the domestic economy are as weak as those of primary exports. However, in the course of industrialisation one may gradually work one's way back from these so-called 'final industries' to intermediate industries, basic industries and even capital goods industries. When sufficient consumer goods are being produced domestically, there is a growing market for domestic producers of intermediate goods and capital goods and the strength of linkages will increase.

The notion of linkages offers opportunities to investigate the dynamic effects of investments, through the use of input–output tables. Such studies help us identify the key sectors in the economy, with the strongest and most important linkages. These are the sectors which should receive priority in an unbalanced growth strategy.

While Hirschman emphasises the importance of the physical flows of inputs and outputs from sector to sector, modern authors focus on the importance of diffusion of technology and technology spillovers from sector to sector. Some sectors such as the capital goods industry or the electronic goods industry are seen as dynamic movers. Technological changes in these sectors diffuse to other sectors, either through new types of machinery or through transfers of knowledge (Fagerberg, 1994; James, 1991; Pack, 1994; Rosenberg, 1963a, 1963b; Stewart, 1977; Verspagen, 1997). This view is an important complement to the older notion of linkages and has received considerable emphasis in the modern literature on technological change and growth (see Chapter 4).

Shift to the market

The theory of unbalanced growth attributes a different and less central role to government in the process of capital accumulation. It marks the beginning of a shift towards markets in development theory. There is less emphasis on the shortage of capital and more emphasis on entrepreneurship and private initiative. Once dynamic imbalances have been set in motion through investment in the key sectors, it is left to the market to call forth investment in other sectors. The government's role is to stimulate and maintain dynamic imbalances and to identify key sectors for investment.

Despite the differences between balanced and unbalanced growth strategies, there are also some interesting similarities. In both strategies complementarities and linkages between industrial activities are seen as important. Unbalanced growth also assumes that the success of industrialisation depends on large-scale efforts, a wide range of industrial activities and acceleration of the investment process. The most important similarity lies in the high priority given to industrialisation. Both balanced and unbalanced growth policies tend to ignore the importance of the agricultural sector and the interactions between agriculture and industry.

9.4.3   Medium and small-scale enterprises and the urban informal sector

The notion of scale in 'Big-Push' industrialisation strategies has two different connotations. The first refers to the comprehensiveness of the investment programme. One should invest in all sectors simultaneously. The second refers simply to a preference for large-scale plants, employing thousands of workers per plant.

However, the formal large-scale manufacturing sector in many of today's developing countries is unable to provide the flow of labour from agriculture with sufficient paid employment. With the notable exception of East Asia, in most developing countries industrialisation so far has contributed only modestly to solving the problems of unemployment.[20]

One of the alternatives to large-scale crash industrialisation programmes was the promotion and support of smaller enterprises and the search for more appropriate small-scale technologies, which were better adapted to conditions in developing countries (Stewart, 1972, 1974, 1977). As time passed it was discovered that smaller enterprises were often more efficient than the largest ones. They tended to choose more labour-intensive methods of production, more in tune with the abundance of labour in developing countries. Several authors emphasised that medium and small-sized manufacturing firms were a major source of dynamism in both advanced economies and developing economies. In the history of the Western economies, small skill-intensive workshops, machine tool workshops and capital goods firms have played an important role, alongside larger firms (Rosenberg, 1963a, 1963b). In the advanced economies small technologically dynamic firms have become more and more important in recent decades (Audretsch, 2007). Especially in developing countries, small firms could play an important role in developing domestic technological capabilities (Romijn, 1999; Voeten et al., 2011). Taiwan provides the prime example of

---

[20] This is not to denigrate the employment contributions of investment in manufacturing. Manufacturing has a rather high employment multiplier creating on average one job outside manufacturing for every job within manufacturing. It also stimulates growth of employment in other sectors of the economy through external effects such as technology and knowledge spillovers (for reviews see Lavopa and Szirmai, 2012 and Szirmai et al., 2013a).

successful industrialisation based on relatively small firms (Kiely, 1998). Other authors have emphasised the complementarities between large establishments and small-scale subcontractors (e.g. Thee, 1997).

Within small-scale manufacturing, one finds both formal and informal enterprises. Alongside formal employment in industrial establishments, commercial services and government, an *urban informal sector* has emerged, where large numbers of people try to make a living in low-productivity activities. The distinction between small-scale and informal activities is not always easy to make (Breman, 1980; Gaillard and Beernink, 2001). But, it is clear that vast numbers of workers work in the small-scale and informal manufacturing sector. For instance, in Indonesia, in 1986, of the 5.2 million workers in manufacturing, 3.5 million were working in establishments with less than twenty persons engaged (Szirmai, 1994).

Migration to the cities

The expansion of employment in the public sector has not been sufficient to compensate for the slow growth of employment in the formal industrial and commercial sector. Still people continue to migrate to the cities in huge numbers, in spite of insufficient employment opportunities, swelling the ranks of the informally employed and the urban poor. Why is this so?

In his well-known model of labour migration, Todaro (1969) argues that the attractiveness of a job in the modern sector is so great that people will migrate to the city, even though the chances of finding a job in the modern sector are slight. They are willing stay unemployed for years in the hope of finally finding a better-paid position in the modern sector. In the meantime they can depend on traditional forms of solidarity (based on family, ethnic, or regional ties), which continue to exist in the city.

In one of his later publications Arthur Lewis recognises the growing levels of urban unemployment. The prime explanation for this is the large gap between formal urban income levels and rural income levels. Further, increasing levels of education create unrealistically high expectations. Education is associated with chances of an urban career. Finally, government expenditures on health, education, welfare and development are disproportionately concentrated in urban areas (Lewis, 1983b; de Soto, 2000).

The widespread feeling that rural life holds little future for young people also plays a role in migration. When young people come into contact with modern life styles through mass communication media, the traditional constraints and hierarchies of rural societies become hard to bear. Also, in many countries the economic prospects in rural areas are so poor that people prefer the risks of urban existence to the certainties of rural squalor.

The informal sector

In a society with no formal systems of social security, people cannot afford to be *openly* unemployed. A large *informal sector* has come into being in which people try to make some kind of a living. The informal sector acts as an employment buffer in the urban economy, providing some minimum of employment for the enormous supply of labour coming from both the countryside and from within the cities themselves. Non-agricultural informal activities have also developed in rural areas.

The informal sector includes a wide range of activities. Here one finds soft drink vendors, tiny food stalls, small traders, street hawkers, household servants, prostitutes, messenger boys, rickshaw drivers, shoeshine boys, casual workers, car attendants, postcard sellers, repair shops, small garages, photocopy shops, collectors of scrap metals and so forth. This sector also includes small industrial enterprises such as clothing producers, hand-weaving enterprises, potteries, breweries, shoemakers, furniture makers and saw mills, to name but a few.

It is hard to give an unambiguous definition of the rich variety of activities in the informal sector. Frequently mentioned characteristics include: labour-intensive technology, low levels of productivity, preponderance of family labour, irregular working hours, restricted use of capital, lack of legal protection and regulation, little formal schooling, absence of book-keeping procedures, few barriers to entry, personal relations with clients, a small and usually poor clientele, lack of access to credit and lack of government support (Breman, 1980; Gaillard and Beernink, 2001; de Soto, 2000; Van Dijk, 1980). One of the most important defining characteristics is that firms are non-registered and therefore have no formal ownership rights, legal status, or protection.

The term *informal sector* was first introduced by Hart (1973) and it soon penetrated into official terminology. Initially, the informal sector was defined in a purely negative sense: everything that did not belong to the 'modern sector'. This undifferentiated view of the informal sector as a 'buffer' for surplus labour was criticised at an early stage by Breman (1980). He points to the heterogeneity of the 'informal sector' and to the links between activities in the rural sector, the modern sector and the informal sector. Activities in the informal sector are dependent on and subordinated to those in the modern sector. The distinction between formal and informal is not clear-cut. Formal activities can easily become informalised when competition becomes fierce, while earnings in some informal activities can be much higher than in the formal sector (Gaillard and Beernink, 2001). The inflow into the informal sector does not only come from the countryside but also from the growing urban population. Entry is not as free as is often assumed. Different ethnic or social groups succeed in monopolising certain economic activities.

The attention paid to the informal sector in government policy is inversely related to its size and importance. While large companies have access to subsidised credit and are supported by the government, small firms cannot borrow any money from formal financial institutions. As they are non-registered, they cannot offer capital, housing, or fixed structures as collateral. They are dependent on informal sources of credit, where exorbitant rates of interest are charged due to the high risks of default. The informal sector is also deprived in terms of schooling opportunities, access to information and technology and government support. Sometimes entrepreneurs in the informal sector are actively hindered by the government (Tybout, 2000).

It has frequently been suggested that the informal sector could fulfil a dynamic function in the wider economy and that policy ought to give it more priority. Government should help provide cheaper credit, management know-how, upgrading of skills, market information and supply of raw materials. Discriminatory regulations should be repealed (ILO, 1972). The rapid emergence of micro-credit can also be seen as a response to the financing needs of the informal sector (Wahiduddin and Osmani, 2013).

In his book *The Mystery of Capital: Why Capitalism Triumphs in the West and Fails Everywhere Else*, Hernando de Soto (2000) has once more emphasised the developmental potential of the informal sector. De Soto celebrates the entrepreneurial dynamics of the informal sector and argues that in spite of poverty informal entrepreneurs have accumulated substantial assets in the form of non-registered housing, business premises and so forth. For instance, in Haiti, one of the poorest countries in the world, his estimate of the value of untitled urban and rural assets – mainly housing – comes to no less than 5.2 billion US dollars. However, the systematic exclusion of people in the informal sector from formal property rights makes it impossible to capitalise on existing assets for expansion of production. In the words of de Soto, the informal sector is a 'vibrant but undercapitalised' sector. De Soto provides impressive examples of the obstacles facing informal firms. For instance, in an experiment in Lima it took 289 workdays to register a one-person garment workshop. The cost of registration was no less than thirty-one times the monthly minimum wage. De Soto argues passionately for legal reform. When legal systems are reformed so as to protect property rights in the informal sector, its entrepreneurial potential will be unleashed.

There is much to be said for these suggestions. But one should beware of wishful thinking. The great majority of entrepreneurs in the informal sector are so-called survival or necessity entrepreneurs, struggling for bare survival (Rooks et al., 2011; Stam and van Stel, 2011). From morning till night they try to scratch together a living. There is little economic dynamism or economic potential involved. Lewis' assumption of a marginal productivity not far from zero seems to apply for many informal sector workers. However, there is a small subset of dynamic entrepreneurs in the informal sector which has potential for growth. Given better access to cheap credit, technical and managerial support and training, these 'constrained gazelles' could act as a dynamic force in development. They could create employment and contribute to pro-poor innovation (Grimm et al., 2011, 2012; Sonne, 2011; Szirmai et al., 2013c). They might be able to provide increasing numbers of workers with gainful and productive employment. So more attention for the developmental potential of the informal sector could be worthwhile.

From the perspective of industrial policy, there is a wide range of options to encourage both formal and informal small-scale enterprises. The most important policy priority is to reduce the discrimination between large-scale and small-scale activities. Small enterprises should be provided with better access to credit and banking facilities, business support services, subsidies, inputs such as water and energy, technical expertise, technology and education. Cooperation between firms in the acquisition of inputs and the marketing of products on a larger scale can be encouraged through cooperatives and cluster policies. The obstacles facing informal sector activities such as corruption, explicit harassment and lack of legal protection should be reduced. Very small firms alone will never transform a developing country into an industrialised economy. But they definitely have a role to play.

9.5   Export-oriented industrialisation

9.5.1   The shift from import substitution to export orientation

All the strategies discussed so far focus on the expansion of industrial production within the confines of a domestic economy. The underlying model is a closed economy model. The shift towards a more open model of the economy involves relinquishing the objective of producing a full range of consumer, intermediate and capital goods within the domestic economy. Instead a country should specialise in those lines of production in which it has a comparative advantage and in which it is internationally competitive. These products can be exported to world markets. Other products can be imported. This strategy is called *export-oriented industrialisation*. It is the most prominent alternative to the orthodox post-war model of *import-substituting industrialisation*.

Given the abundance of labour, developing countries have a comparative advantage in labour-intensive manufactures. In terms of industrialisation, the most successful countries were invariably countries that turned outwards and followed export-oriented industrialisation policies at a relatively early stage. The shift from import substitution to export orientation was pioneered by East Asian economies such as South Korea and Taiwan around 1960. In the 1980s, so-called second-tier NICs such as Thailand, Malaysia, Indonesia and the Philippines followed suit. In the 1990s, giants such as India and China turned outwards. Nowadays almost all countries profess to follow export-oriented policies, though with varying degrees of success. Least success has been achieved in Sub-Saharan Africa (Helleiner, 2002; Morrissey and Filatotchev, 2001; Page, 2013). But even here policy has become more outward-looking.

Table 9.2 provides evidence both of the rapid growth of manufacturing exports from developing countries and the variety of country experiences in different periods. In the period 1960–73, most countries have rapid export growth from very low initial levels. In the period 1973–81, high growth rates are found both in Asia and Latin America, but not in Africa. Since 1981, the highest growth rates are found in East Asia. Since that year, the growth rates of manufactured exports in developing countries exceed the average growth rate of world manufactured exports, pointing to a global shift towards developing countries.

Export shares in GDP are one of the indicators of outward orientation. The value of manufactured exports expressed as a percentage of GDP is found in Table 9.3. It shows a steady increase in almost all the countries in our sample between 1960 and 2000. After 2000 the share drops in ten countries but continues to increase, sometimes rapidly, in all the other countries. With the exception of India, Asian countries have the strongest outward orientation. With the exception of Mexico, Latin America has far lower export intensities.[21]

In a schematic view of historical developments, one can interpret the rise of import-substituting industrialisation as a response to traumatic experiences with primary exports and open economy models in the period between the two world wars. In turn, the rise of labour-intensive exports can be seen as a response to the shortcomings and disappointments of large-scale import-substituting industrialisation and the closed economy models of the post-war period.

An export-oriented policy makes it more attractive for firms to focus on the international market. In order to achieve this, overvalued exchange rates have to be devalued to make exports cheaper for foreign customers. Protection of the domestic market should be reduced and imports liberalised so that entrepreneurs have more incentives to look abroad. Reduced protection may also raise the efficiency of firms oriented towards the domestic market, as they are forced to compete with foreign competitors. Finally, exporting

---

[21] In interpreting the percentages, one should realise that exports refer to the total value of exports, while GDP refers to value added.

Table 9.2: Growth of manufactured exports, 1960–2010 (constant 1995 \$)[a]

Country	1960–73	1973–81	1981–96	1996–2000	2000–10
Bangladesh		7.4[b]	14.2	14.9c	10.8[d]
China			14.4	20.4	18.4
India		5.0	11.1	5.9[c]	9.8
Indonesia		7.4	28.4	7.0	2.0
Iran	−4.4[e]				8.0[f]
Malaysia	2.3	14.1	23.3	12.9	1.7
Pakistan		−0.3	12.0	0.0	5.6
Philippines	15.2	16.8	14.8	14.9	1.3
South Korea	58.4	15.8	11.8	17.4	9.6
Sri Lanka	20.4	17.3	16.6	5.8[g]	0.1
Thailand	26.5	17.6	20.2	13.7	5.2
Turkey				8.5	9.0
Argentina		14.2	4.0	7.9	6.1
Brazil	22.1	19.4	7.6	7.9	1.8
Chile	−5.3	28.4	14.5	11.1	2.9
Colombia	25.1	2.1	8.6	9.1	0.5
Mexico	15.8	−2.7	27.7	15.4	3.3
Peru	−1.1	34.0	2.9	15.8	3.5
Venezuela		3.3[b]	15.5	−4.7[g]	−0.3[h]
Congo, Dem. Rep.	30.8	−18.2			
Côte d'Ivoire	26.8	11.1	−0.1	28.2	6.5
Egypt	9.5	−12.8	11.2	8.0[g]	19.3
Ethiopia					10.1
Ghana	19.0	−5.8	14.1[i]		14.2[j]
Kenya	6.3	2.2	11.4	−7.7	10.9
Morocco	8.6	10.9	10.2	13.0	4.5
Nigeria	−0.6	−17.2	16.7	−35.7	
South Africa	6.4	−1.4	11.2	3.6	−0.2
Tanzania				21.5[k]	18.1
Zambia		10.5	13.1[l]		7.1
Sub-Saharan Africa			9.9	6.0	1.5[m]
Latin America & Caribbean	14.0[n]	5.3	11.6	11.1	4.6
East Asia & Pacific			13.7	16.2	8.8
South Asia		5.8	11.4	4.3	8.3
Developing countries			10.7	10.9	5.7
World		8.2	6.1	7.5	4.3[o]

Note:

[a] Manufactured exports in current prices, deflated by the price index for total exports; [b] 1974–81; [c] 1996–9; [d] 2000–7; [e] 1965–73; [f] 2000–6; [g] 1994–9; [f] 1994–81; [g] 1974–81; [h] Based on series in current values; [i] 1981–98; [j] We used the deflator for Kenya; [k] 1997–9; [l] 1981–95; [m] 2000–9; [n] 1963–73; [o] 2000–10 in 2000 constant dollars.

Sources:

World Bank, *World Development Indicators*, CD-ROM, 2002; except 2000–10, and Iran and Ethiopia all years from World Bank, *World Development Indicators Online*, downloaded February 2013.

Table 9.3: Manufactured exports as percentage of GDP, 1960–2010 (at current prices)

Country	1960	1970	1980	1990	2000	2010
Bangladesh		1.6*	2.8	4.3	12.3	16.1*
China		1.9	4.8*	12.5	18.3	24.9
India	2.2*	1.7	2.7	3.9	6.1*	8.3
Indonesia	0.3	0.1	0.6	8.0	22.6	8.4
Iran	0.9*	0.9			2.0	3.5*
Malaysia	8.5	2.6	9.7	36.0	84.2	54.1
Pakistan	2.3*	2.6	5.3	11.0	10.3	9.0
Philippines	0.6*	1.2	3.7	6.9	45.0	22.1
South Korea	0.2	7.2	24.6	23.1	29.3	40.9
Sri Lanka	0.3	0.2	4.9	12.8	22.1*	11.5
Taiwan			43.0*	39.1	45.9	
Thailand	0.3	0.5	5.1	17.1	42.4	46.1
Turkey	0.1	0.3	1.1	5.8	8.5	12.3
Argentina	0.4	0.8	2.4	2.5	3.0	6.1
Brazil	0.3	0.9	3.2	3.5	5.0	3.5
Chile	0.7	0.6	1.6	3.0	3.9	4.2
Colombia	0.3	0.8	2.3	4.2	4.2	3.1
Mexico	0.7	1.3	1.1	6.7	23.9	21.9
Peru	0.6	0.2	3.2	2.3	2.7	3.2
Venezuela	0.3	0.3	0.5	3.9	2.6	0.7
Congo, Dem. Rep.	0.8*	1.1	0.9			
Côte d'Ivoire	0.3	1.9	1.5	4.3*	5.4	7.3
Egypt	1.6	2.7	1.5	3.4	0.0*	5.2
Ethiopia					0.6	0.8
Ghana	0.1	0.1	0.3	1.5*	4.9	5.1
Kenya	1.9*	2.4	2.1	3.5	2.8	5.6
Morocco	1.3	1.2	3.1	8.6	12.9	13.0
Nigeria	0.3	0.1	0.1	0.3*	0.1	2.5
South Africa	6.0	6.4	5.8	4.6	12.2*	10.4
Tanzania		2.5*	1.4	0.6*	0.9	4.5
Zambia	0.1*	0.1	5.3	1.2*	2.9	2.8

Note:

* Other year than specified.

Source:

World Bank, *World Development Indicators Online*, downloaded February 2013. Supplemented with data from World Bank, *World Tables 1976* and various issues and World Bank, *World Development Indicators*, CD-ROM, 2002.

industries can be supported in a variety of ways, including preferential access to credit, tax holidays, export zones, pay back of import tariffs on imported inputs and export subsidies. Increased export orientation can also be achieved without complete import liberalisation as long as the policy incentives for export production are at least as strong as those for domestic production.

The prime models of successful export orientation are South Korea and Taiwan and the city-states of Singapore and Hong Kong. The policies these countries have followed differ substantially, ranging from strong interventionism in South Korea to complete *laissez-faire* in Hong Kong, but the common element has been the strong outward orientation (Hobday, 1995; Kiely, 1998; World Bank, 1993). These countries shifted to export orientation at an early stage. Initially, their export success was based on labour-intensive manufactures, based on abundant supplies of cheap unskilled labour. Later these economies upgraded their work force and production capabilities, moving into much more sophisticated lines of production such as automobiles, shipbuilding, or electronics. Acquisition of technological know-how and design capabilities was a crucial ingredient of this upgrading process.

In a well-known extension of the Lewis model, Fei and Ranis have analysed the experience of Korea and Taiwan (Fei and Ranis, 1964, 1976; Ranis, 1988; see also Cooper, 2001). They identify two crucial turning points. The first is the shift to export substitution. Traditional primary exports are replaced by labour-intensive manufactured exports. This greatly accelerates the absorption of surplus labour. The second is the 'commercialisation point', where cheap unskilled labour starts to become scarce and the economy is forced to start upgrading at the risk of losing its momentum.

In practice, export orientation seldom means that the economy is completely liberalised or that all forms of protection and regulation are abolished (Amsden, 1989; Kiely, 1998; Verbruggen, 1985; Wade, 1990). South Korea, for instance, has maintained substantial degrees of protection and has pursued active industrial and technology policies, supporting specific firms and conglomerates (*Chaebols*) in their export drive (Chang, 2002; Hobday, 1995). More important is the balance between incentives for production for domestic markets and incentives for exports and the transparency of the regulatory measures. If industries producing for the domestic market are protected or subsidised, export-oriented industries should be subsidised to a similar extent (Helleiner, 1995). Furthermore, support should not be given unconditionally. The efficiency and market conformity of protected industries should be monitored. Protection and support of inefficient and loss making activities will be eventually discontinued. In most – though not all – cases, outward orientation implies increased openness to foreign direct investment by TNCs (UNCTAD, 2000). In the past, Korea and Taiwan have tended to restrict FDI, as Japan had done before them (World Bank, 1993). But this strategy is less and less viable today. TNCs are of increasing importance in export-oriented industrialisation, especially in the second-tier NICs (Athukorala and Rajapatirana, 2000).

Industrialisation in developing countries has almost invariably started with import substitution. A new manufacturing industry must gain experience on a protected domestic market before venturing abroad on to the world market. In his major study of competitive advantage, Porter (1990) emphasises the importance of a strong home base for firms as a foundation for entering export markets. But, as discussed in section 9.3.3, too prolonged protection results in an inefficient allocation of factors of production and technical inefficiency (Little, Scitovsky and Scott, 1970; Pack, 1988). The most successful industrialisers among the developing countries switched from import-substituting industrialisation to export-oriented industrialisation in the 1960s (Verbruggen, 1985). Making use of abundant supplies of cheap labour, they concentrated on labour-intensive exports. Export-oriented activities were supported by a variety of policy measures, including subsidies, tax reduction schemes, access to cheap inputs and foreign exchange and export processing zones to attract FDI. In those branches of production in which they were competitive due to low labour costs, they successfully managed to penetrate international markets. In contrast, Latin American countries such as Mexico and Brazil, which had experienced fifty years of rapid growth based among others on import-substituting industrialisation, ran out of steam and stagnated after 1980, having failed to turn outward in time (Furtado, 1976; Maddison, 1989). When import liberalisation was imposed by international organisations in the wake of the 1982 debt crisis, Latin American firms were insufficiently prepared for a more competitive environment and had difficulty in competing in export markets. Since 1980, many Latin American countries have experienced premature de-industrialisation (Tregenna, 2009, 2013). Though Latin American economies have turned outwards since 1980, with the exception of Mexico, their export intensities are still lower than those of many of the Asian economies.

There is an interesting debate about the relationship between growth of manufacturing exports and prior import substitution. Do firms producing for the domestic market simply switch to exports in response to changing incentives after completing their learning curve, or are the exporters new firms? On the basis of statistical research, Athukorala concludes that for Sri Lanka, manufacturing exports emerged *de novo* in response to the creation of new incentives after 1977 (Athukorala, 1998b). The experiences of Sri Lanka are similar to those of Taiwan, Malaysia, Bangladesh and Chile. For Turkey, Colombia, Mexico and Tanzania, Helleiner draws the opposite conclusion (Helleiner, 1995). His position is that even when the exporting firms and import-substituting firms are not the same ones, import substitution does represent a necessary learning stage in the development of a national manufacturing sector.

The main advantage of an export-oriented industrialisation strategy is that economic development is no longer constrained by the limited size of the domestic market. Export-oriented countries also tend to make better use of their abundant labour resources, resulting in more equitable paths of development. The linkages between industry and the rest of the economy tend to be stronger than in import substitution. The tendency towards dualism tends to be weaker. It turns out that the internal balance between agriculture and industry – initially associated with a closed model – is positively correlated with an open, outward-oriented industrial development (Ranis, 1989).

In East and Southeast Asia, the availability of cheap and relatively well-educated labour has attracted massive flows of FDI. Competition on world markets has contributed to improved efficiency, improved product quality and the acquisition of modern technology.

Of course, export-oriented policies can also be criticised. They have sometimes attracted so-called 'footloose industries', which temporarily profit from absurdly low wages, tax holidays and unrestricted profit repatriation. These industries – such as textiles and shoe-making – move on when cheaper labour is available elsewhere, without making a lasting contribution to economic development. Critics have also pointed to exploitative labour relations, lack of domestic sourcing, environmental damage and political repression. Following Cline (1982), a criticism of industrialisation strategies is whether the world market is large enough to allow other economies to follow the example of the Asian industrialising countries (Kiely, 1998). But since Cline wrote his influential paper, several countries have broken through as industrial exporters, including China, which has now become 'the workplace of the world' and second-tier NICs, such as Bangladesh, Indonesia, Malaysia, Thailand, Sri Lanka, the Philippines, Turkey and Vietnam. But the number of industrialised developing countries is still limited and it is a valid question whether all latecomers can follow the same route. By and large only some twelve to fourteen major developing countries – admittedly including very large ones – have succeeded on the export markets and have profited from large inflows of FDI. Presently, a renewed form of the Cline criticism asks whether new countries can start industrialising in the face of the huge competitive pressure of China (Naudé and Szirmai, 2012).

On the whole, however, in terms of economic dynamics, the record of export orientation has been exceptionally positive. Countries with a strong export orientation have subsequently experienced substantially higher growth rates of industrial production than countries that stuck with import substitution (Krueger, 1978, 1984, 1992; Krueger *et al.*, 1989; Pack, 1988; Westphal, 2002; World Bank-WDR, 1993). Countries that switched to export orientation at an early stage, such as South Korea, Taiwan, Singapore, Hong Kong and to a lesser extent Thailand and Malaysia, experienced rapid economic growth. Countries that pursued import substitution policies too long, such as Brazil, Mexico, Argentina and India, experienced relative stagnation (Maddison, 1989). Countries that opened up their economies and turned outwards after the 1980s and 1990s, such as Indonesia, India, the Philippines and China, have experienced accelerated growth.

The choice between import substitution and export orientation depends to some extent on the size of a country. In very large countries such as India and China the case for balanced growth and import substitution is more compelling, provided one maintains a sufficient degree of competition on the vast domestic market. For the small economies of Singapore, Hong Kong, the Philippines, or Taiwan a strong export orientation seems inevitable. But even in the huge economies of China and India the choice for a more outward-looking orientation in the 1990s, has led to an acceleration of economic growth (UNIDO, 2012).

9.5.2   Technological upgrading and learning

For countries with large reserves of cheap labour, labour-intensive manufacturing is a vital stage in industrialisation. But in the longer run it is not a sustainable development strategy. Labour-intensive manufacturing depends on continued low wages and this conflicts with the longer-term goal of development: increased wages and welfare. As wages start increasing, a labour-intensive producer will become vulnerable to competition from new low-wage competitors. The only way forward is through technological upgrading and sustained productivity growth. This is where the East Asian economies have had their most remarkable achievements.

The route towards technological upgrading has differed from country to country (Hobday, 2013). South Korea relied upon huge conglomerates, supported by the government, which could cross-subsidise new developments. Taiwan relied on medium- and small-sized firms. Japan, Korea and Taiwan restricted the role of MNCs; Singapore and the South East Asian economies encouraged them. South Korea, Taiwan and Singapore followed highly selective industrial policies; Hong Kong practised complete *laissez-faire*.

But the common element was that the South East Asian economies invested heavily in education, and stimulated learning and innovation, in a stable macro-economic environment. Through a variety of mechanisms, the Southeast Asian economies rapidly learned about and mastered international technologies. They subsequently started adapting them and at later stages shifted to innovation at the frontiers of knowledge (Kim and Nelson, 2000). East Asian firms started in the 1960s and 1970s with *original equipment manufacturing* (OEM), a mode of subcontracting under which domestic firms produce products to specifications and designs supplied by MNCs, that sell these products under their own brand names. After a period of deliberate learning through reverse engineering, the domestic firms shifted in the 1980s to *own design manufacturing* (ODM), where the domestic firm contributes to design and innovation, while the TNC remains responsible for branding and distribution. The final stage is the shift to *own brand manufacturing* (OBM) in the 1990s, where the domestic firm takes control of distribution and develops its own brand names (Hobday, 2013). Well-known brand names include ACER, Samsung, Hyunday and L-G. A similar process of upgrading is presently taking place in China.

Technological upgrading contributed to very rapid catch-up. For instance, within a mere sixty years South Korea transformed itself from a very poor country with a GDP per capita equal to that of Ghana into an innovative high-income economy. The same is true for Taiwan and Singapore. However, if upgrading is less successful, industrialising economies may be caught in what is now called *the middle-income trap*. In such countries, economic success has resulted in wage increases which make them less and less competitive in labour-intensive manufactured exports. But technological upgrading has been too limited to allow countries to compete in high-tech segments, resulting in stagnation at middle-income levels. A possible escape from the middle-income trap is to specialise in sectors characterised by very rapid rates of technological change, where incumbent firms from advanced countries do not have an advantage because existing technologies become obsolete very quickly (Lee, 2013). Such a strategy requires a high level of technological capabilities, well-designed and implemented innovation policies and effective national systems of innovation.

9.5.3 Global value chains, FDI and the role of MNCs in development

One of the important issues in late industrialisation is the role of FDI. Though there were important differences from country to country, on the whole the import-substituting model was rather hostile to private enterprise and FDI. FDI was strongly regulated and foreign firms could often only enter domestic markets as partners in joint ventures with domestic firms and parastatals.

In some of the first export-oriented Asian NICS, such as Korea, Hong Kong and Taiwan, and earlier Japan, it was the domestic entrepreneurs who started to export. But, elsewhere the move towards export orientation was associated with increasing openness to foreign investment and transnational companies. In recent decades, the increases in developing country manufactured exports have been driven to a very considerable extent by FDI and transnational companies (Narula and Lall, 2006; UNCTAD, 2000, 2002a). Transnational companies were a major force in the global relocation of manufacturing activities to developing countries.

Rapid technological change has resulted in sharply falling transportation and communication costs and increased globalisation of production. In the second half of the 1980s, world merchandise trade grew twice as fast as world output, in the 1990s it grew three times as fast (Kumar, 1998).[22] One sees the emergence of global production and value chains dominated by TNCs, which locate different parts of production all across the world (Baldwin, 2011; Gereffi, 1990, 1999; Gereffi and Korzeniewicz, 1994; Kaplinsky and Farooki, 2010; Morrissey and Filatotchev, 2001). Thus research, design and development take place in one country, different components and semi-finished products are sourced from a variety of countries, final assembly takes place in yet another country, after which the products are marketed and distributed in a great many countries.

In distributed production, an increasing portion of international trade takes place between subsidiaries of transnational companies. Competition between firms is increasingly based on design, research and innovation, with production being outsourced. Competition between countries is no longer primarily in terms of competitive advantage for certain goods, but rather in terms of comparative advantages in given activities and segments of global value chains.

The emergence of global value chains is claimed to represent a new technological paradigm (Freeman and Perez, 1988; Gereffi, 1994). In the past, the location decisions of TNCs could be explained by the *product life cycle theory* (Vernon, 1966). According to this theory, the production of new products and services is located in the advanced economies. As a product and its associated production technology become mature, markets become saturated and cost competition increases, and production will be shifted to developing countries with an abundance of cheap labour. These countries will start exporting.

With the emergence of the global production chain, the nature of comparative advantage shifts. Rather than only having a comparative advantage in certain products, countries compete for productive activities in certain stages of the global production chain, such as final assembly, software development, R&D, production of components and so forth. Even traditional sectors such as textiles and clothing are subject to rapid technological change (Abernathy *et al.*, 1999; Cooper, 2001). Therefore, there are no safe niches for developing countries. The competitive challenge is intensifying, and developing innovation capabilities becomes more important than ever.

The slicing up of the value chain has important implications for industrialisation and industrial policy in late industrialising countries. Instead of having to build capabilities in a wide range of basic, intermediate and final manufactured goods, a country can enter the global value chains with highly specialised activities (Baldwin, 2011). The downside of global value chains is that it is not always easy to move up the global value chain to higher-value added goods and technologically more sophisticated products.

The rise of global production chains goes hand in hand with a substantial increase in global FDI flows, from an average of 65 billion 1995 US dollars per year between 1970 and 1974, to 1,477 billion between 2005 and 2008. The share of FDI going to developing countries has been increasing, from 21 per cent in 1970–4 to 45 per cent in 2009–11 (UNCTADstat, 2013).[23] In 1998 there were no less than 60,000 TNCs with 500,000 affiliates and a total turnover of 11 trillion dollars (UNCTAD, 2000). But the largest 100 TNCs account for the lion's share of total foreign investment.

---

[22] Between 2000 and 2011 merchandise trade was still growing more rapidly than world output, but the ratio is now much lower (1.3/1) than that in earlier decades due to the negative effects of the global financial crisis on world trade (UNCTADstat, 2013).

[23] UNCTAD data in current dollars, deflated by the US GDP deflator from World Bank, *World Development Indicators Online*, downloaded May 2013. After a peak of 1,649 billion 1995 US dollars in 2008, FDI dropped to an annual 1,206 billion between 2009 and 2011 under the influence of the global financial crisis.

Most of the FDI in developing countries went to a few countries. In the period 2009–11, six countries absorbed 55 per cent of all FDI to developing countries: China, including Hong Kong (29 per cent, of which 11 per cent to Hong Kong), Brazil (8 per cent), Singapore (8 per cent), India (5 per cent), Mexico (3 per cent) and Indonesia (2 per cent), But, as indicated in Table 9.4, the inflow of FDI was also significant elsewhere. In recent years, there has been a notable increase of flows of foreign investment and aid from China to Sub-Saharan Africa (Bräutigam, 2009).

Table 9.4 documents the importance of FDI in developing countries. Between 1970 and 2011, the share of FDI in GDP and in Gross Fixed Capital Formation (GFCF) has increased dramatically. In 2011, FDI accounted for 1.8 per cent of GDP in China and 1.6 per cent in India. In smaller countries the shares were often much higher. In Malaysia, the share was 4.3 per cent, in Chile 7.4 per cent and in Zambia 10.3 per cent. In China, the share of FDI in GDP and investment peaked between 1998 and 2000, after which domestic investment became more important (UNIDO, 2012).

From the perspective of developing countries, transnational companies have both potential advantages and disadvantages. Advantages include: increased competition, acquisition of technology and know-how, stimulus to local entrepreneurship and domestic supply and access to global markets, sales channels and brand names. Potential disadvantages are: decreased domestic competition when too many domestic firms are taken over by transnationals, reduced linkages when transnationals source their activities from abroad, absence of technology spillovers when transnational companies guard their technological knowledge too closely and the stifling of domestic entrepreneurship. In a highly critical analysis of excessive reliance on foreign investment, Amsden has contrasted the technologically dynamic performance of private owned enterprises in successful emerging economies in Asia with the less dynamic performance of foreign owned enterprises in Latin America (Amsden, 2009, 2013).

If we try to synthesise the insights from the optimistic and the critical literature, we may conclude that the net impact of TNCs on developing countries depends on how international transfers of capital, technology and skills build on and in turn affect the development of local markets, skills and capabilities (Dunning, 1993). The outcomes are determined by the interactions between TNC strategies and developing country policies, and the characteristics and capabilities of larger and smaller domestic firms. The extent to which a developing country can profit from the activities of TNCs depends to a considerable extent on domestic capabilities, such as skills and discipline of the work force, the quality of management, production capabilities, technological effort, macro-economic stability, domestic supply and infrastructure, the development of linkages with domestic subcontractors and the policies and bargaining capacities of governments (Fu *et al.*, 2011). The stronger the absorptive capacities and innovative capabilities of domestic firms and the domestic economy, the more positive the impacts of TNCs are likely to be.

9.5.4   Resource-based industrialisation as an alternative export strategy for resource rich economies

In much of the preceding discussion resource abundance has been seen as a disadvantage for industrialisation. Countries with a comparative advantage in oil, gas, mineral resources, or opportunities for agricultural exports have found it difficult to industrialise. This is due to 'Dutch disease' effects, the appreciation of the currency which makes it difficult to export manufactured goods, the high volatility of primary export earnings, weak linkages of

Table 9.4:   FDI as a percentage of GDP and total fixed capital formation, selected countries, 1960–2011[a]

Country	FDI as % of GDP						FDI as % of GFCF				
	1960	1970	1980	1990	2000	2011	1971–5	1981–5	1991–5	1998–2000	2005–10
Bangladesh	–	–	0.1	0.0	1.3	1.0	0.2	0.1	0.1	5.0	4.6
China	–	–	0.0	0.9	3.4	1.8		0.7	8.6	11.4	5.8
India	–	0.1	0.0	0.1	0.8	1.6	0.3	0.1	0.6	2.6	6.4
Indonesia	0.2	0.9	0.2	1.0	−3.0	2.2	0.3	0.1	0.6	2.3	6.6
Iran	0.0	0.3	0.1	−0.4	0.2	0.9	2.7	0.0	−0.2	0.3	3.5
Malaysia	–	2.6	3.7	5.7	4.0	4.3	14.0	11.6	19.8	17.2	15.6
Pakistan	–	0.2	0.2	0.6	0.4	0.6	0.5	1.0	3.7	3.9	13.7
Philippines	0.4	0.0	0.3	1.1	2.8	0.6	1.6	1.6	6.3	10.0	7.4
South Korea	–	0.7	0.0	0.3	1.7	0.4	5.3	0.4	0.6	6.0	2.4
Sri Lanka	–	0.0	1.0	0.5	1.0	0.5	0.1	3.4	4.9	4.3	5.7
Taiwan	–	1.1	0.4	0.8	1.5	−0.4	2.6	1.2	2.3	3.5	5.5
Thailand	0.1	0.6	0.6	3.0	2.8	2.8	3.2	2.7	4.7	22.2	13.5
Turkey	–	0.2	0.0	0.3	0.4	2.0	1.1	0.4	1.6	1.7	11.8
Argentina	–	0.3	0.9	1.3	3.7	1.6	1.0	2.4	8.6	27.3	10.4
Brazil	0.9	1.1	1.0	0.2	5.1	2.8	6.0	4.8	2.1	27.2	12.0
Chile	0.7	0.1	0.7	2.0	6.5	7.4	−0.1	5.1	10.7	37.0	34.1
Colombia	0.1	0.4	0.3	0.9	2.4	4.0	1.2	3.1	4.8	12.8	19.5
Mexico	−0.3	0.7	0.9	0.9	2.8	1.7	3.1	4.8	7.2	13.0	11.4
Peru	0.9	−0.2	0.2	0.1	1.5	4.6	2.5	0.6	9.1	12.4	20.4
Venezuela	−1.4	−0.2	0.1	1.7	4.0	1.7		−0.7	6.1	16.9	1.7
Congo, Dem. Rep.	–	0.2	1.1	−0.2	1.4	10.6	1.4	−2.1	0.7	31.8	50.7
Côte d'Ivoire	–	2.0	0.9	0.4	2.2	1.4	6.9	2.8	9.7	24.3	20.3
Egypt	–	0.0	2.7	2.0	1.3	−0.2	0.1	11.2	7.8	6.9	31.2
Ethiopia	–	0.2	0.0	0.1	1.7	1.1[b]	4.2		0.7	9.4	6.5
Ghana	0.3	1.9	0.3	0.1	2.1	8.4	10.0	6.0	6.1	11.0	21.5
Kenya	–	0.6	0.9	0.5	0.9	1.0	2.8	1.9	1.0	2.1	3.7
Morocco	–	0.5	0.4	0.6	1.1	2.5	1.3	1.4	5.3	7.4	9.4
Nigeria	1.3	1.8	−0.8	2.9	2.8	3.8	6.0	0.9	36.9	42.4	45.7
South Africa	–	1.9	0.0	−0.1	0.7	1.4	4.6	0.9	0.6	4.8	8.2
Tanzania	–	0.2	0.1	0.0	2.7	4.6	0.7	0.4	1.0	18.4	16.6
Zambia	–	0.5	1.6	5.4	3.8	10.3	3.6	3.9	31.3	29.5	34.0

Notes:

[a] FDI is defined as net inflows of investment to acquire a lasting management interest. It includes equity capital, reinvested earnings and short- and long-term capital flows.

[b] 2010. For 2011 there are large discrepancies between UNCTAD and the *World Development Indicators*.

Sources:

UNCTAD, *UNCTADstat*, downloaded March 2013, except FDI as % of GDP 1960 and 1965 and Indonesia, 1960–2000: FDI from IMF, *International Financial Yearbook, 1988* and *1995*; GDP at current market prices from World Bank, *World Development Indicators*, 2002.

primary sectors and limited potential for technological advance and spillovers. In addition, abundance of natural resources increases the opportunities for corruption and rent seeking behaviour. This negative view of natural resources is well captured in the term *natural resource curse* (Sachs and Rodriguez, 1999; Sachs and Warner, 1997, 2001; Van der Ploeg and Poelhekke, 2007).

In the discussion of primary export-led growth in Chapter 8 we have already noted that resource abundance does not always have to be a disadvantage. Resource rich economies such as the USA, Australia, Canada, New Zealand and Norway have achieved high levels of development. In Africa, Botswana stands out as a country which has used its main resource – diamonds – rather well (Acemoglu *et al.*, 2003b). In Asia, Indonesia was successful in using the proceeds of oil exports for the development of manufacturing (Hill, 2000b).

In recent years authors such as Perez have argued that in Latin America a resource-based development strategy can be an alternative for the labour-intensive industrialisation strategies characteristic of East Asia (Farinelli, 2012; Perez, 2008, 2010). The basic idea is to broaden the base of primary production by developing technologically sophisticated industrial activities for the processing of primary products. The purpose is to create high-value niches which are differentiated from traditional commodity markets. Examples that come to mind are the processing of aluminium, petrochemicals, beer, salmon processing in Chile, ethanol and brand coffee production in Brazil, high-quality wine production in Chile and Argentina and the pulp, paper and plywood industries in Indonesia and Brazil. The proponents of this strategy argue that it strengthens the linkages of primary production and offers opportunities for innovation and technological advance. This is a promising and interesting strategy, but some scepticism about its ability to create sufficient manufacturing employment opportunities is warranted.

9.6 Criticisms of market-oriented policies and the re-emergence of industrial policy

One of the main criticisms of orthodox inward-looking industrialisation strategies was the failure of state-led industrialisation, characterised by very high degrees of government control, regulation and intervention in domestic and foreign markets (Lal, 2000). While the apparatus of government in developing countries was still weakly developed, the burdens of planning and intervention were much higher than ever before in the history of the advanced economies. Regulation and planning created distorted economies characterised by massive inefficiencies.

Hand in hand with the liberalisation of international trade and the shift towards an export orientation, there was a strong move towards the market and towards a more limited role of the state in industrial development from the 1980s onwards. In the influential World Bank study *The East Asian Miracle: Economic Growth and Public Policy* (1993), the conclusion was drawn that the success of the Asian tigers was primarily due to liberalisation, deregulation, outward orientation and market-friendly policies, in combination with prudent macro-economic policies. This is referred to as the *Washington consensus*: a policy package oriented to macro-economic stability, privatisation of state owned enterprises, elimination of government intervention in markets, cuts in government expenditures, increased openness to FDI, reduction of tariffs and quotas (Williamson, 1990). The emergence of the Washington consensus reflected a worldwide change in the policy climate and was backed by powerful financial institutions such as the IMF and the World Bank. Aid was only provided to countries that were willing to implement market oriented reforms (*conditionality*). All across the developing world, countries engaged in market reforms, under both pressure from the major international financial institutions, but also under the influence of a changed intellectual climate. As a result any kind of selective industrial policies to promote industrialisation by targeting specific sectors, technologies, firms or investment projects came to be seen as unacceptable (Cimoli *et al.*, 2009; Peres, 2013). The preference was for so-called 'functional' policies that do not 'pick winners' but promote the 'competitiveness' of the entire manufacturing sector, or even the entire supply side of the economy through educational investment, tax measures, R&D credits or deregulation (Naudé and Szirmai, 2012).

In the wake of *The East Asian Miracle* study, a vehement and in our view still unresolved debate has erupted over the pros and cons of liberalisation versus interventionism (see further Chapter 13). The opening shot in the debate was fired by Amsden, in her study of Korean industrialisation (Amsden, 1989; see also Westphal *et al.*, 1985). Amsden argued that South Korea had followed highly interventionist economic and technology policies, targeting sectors for investment, subsidising exports, promoting the rise of large industrial conglomerates (the *Chaebols*) and stimulating technology acquisition and technological learning. In her view, South Korea followed successful interventionist policies focusing on pursuing dynamic comparative advantage by deliberating 'getting prices wrong' in the short run and working towards a gradual upgrading of technological and economic performance.

The authors of *The East Asian Miracle* study admitted that governments in East Asia had intervened systematically and extensively. But they argued that the interventions had basically been market-following or market-friendly. Policy makers withdrew support from sectors and firms that did not meet export targets or were in decline. Generic interventions were more successful than selective interventions, which frequently backfired on a very large scale. They claimed that governments 'cannot pick winners'. They also warned that East Asian policies could not be copied in African developing countries, because the state was insufficiently isolated from pressure groups and clients. It was unable to pursue similar independent and effective policies.

The authors criticising the neoliberal market orientation (Amsden, 1989; Chang, 2002; Helleiner, 1992a; Kiely, 1998; Lall, 1990, 1996, 1998, 2000; Rodrik, 1995, 1999, 2006; Wade, 1990; Westphal, 2002) countered with a number of arguments. In the first place, they argued that the neoliberals simply misrepresented how extensive both policy intervention and protection had been in Japan and all the Asian NICS except Hong Kong. Re-reading *The East Asian Miracle*, this argument is quite persuasive. In the second place, they argued that in a global economy characterised by accelerating technological change, industrial and technology policies were required to acquire and maintain competitiveness. Government policy should target promising sectors, which drive industrialisation and give opportunities for learning, such as the electronics sector or heavy industries such as steel (Amsden, 1989; Fagerberg, 2000). They should actively promote the acquisition of technological capabilities and technological learning (Lall, 1996). Promising industrial activities should still be able to profit from infant industry protection of some kind, at least for limited periods.

The critics of liberalisation were further strengthened by the disappointing results of structural adjustment and liberalisation in the 1980s and 1990s. In Latin America and

Sub-Saharan Africa economic growth stagnated and a process of de-industrialisation set in. In the countries of the former Soviet Union, sudden liberalisation – the 'Big Bang' propagated among others by Jeffrey Sachs – resulted in an economic meltdown. Many former Soviet republics, including the Russian Federation rapidly lost their manufacturing industries and suffered from a lasting decline in industrial capabilities (Kuznetsov *et al.*, 2012). This contrasted dramatically with the success of incremental reform in China after 1978, where the state continued to play an important role in the economy, while achieving spectacular export success in manufacturing (Qian, 2003). In Southeast Asia the sudden eruption of the Asian crisis of 1997 raised doubts about the wisdom of unrestricted financial liberalisation. The Asian crisis was basically caused by the increased volatility of international capital flows in an open economy.

In 2002, Ha-Joon Chang raised the intensity of the debate to new levels with his book *Kicking Away the Ladder: Development Strategy in Historical Perspective* (Chang, 2002). Chang argued that every successful process of industrialisation has involved a phase of heavy interventionism and protectionism, both in the now advanced economies and in the successful emerging economies. However, the current liberal international economic order makes it near-impossible for developing countries to embark on successful industrialisation as they do not have the policy space to protect and support their new industrial activities and infant industries (see also Westphal, 2002). Though not all countries have the same capacity for effective interventions as the East Asian economies, the present policy climate limits their policy options. It limits their possibilities of protecting and nurturing promising sectors and activities.

Further theoretical underpinnings for more interventionist industrial policies are provided in a brilliant article by Hausmann and Rodrik, 'Economic Development as Self-Discovery' (2003). According to Hausmann and Rodrik, structural change is initiated by innovative firms that discover what a country is good at producing. Once they have discovered a productive niche, their example will be followed by a multitude of followers and imitators. All the risk is born by the first innovators, while much of the benefits are reaped by the imitating firms. As result, there will be underinvestment in new activities and structural change will be delayed. The role of industrial policy, then, is to nurture new investment, providing rents to the innovators in the form of trade protection, temporary monopolies, subsidised credits and tax benefits. The authors do add an important warning that rents can backfire. Governments have to complement their supportive policies with other policies that subsequently rationalise industries and discipline firms that end up with high costs. Industrial policy does not only involve carrots, but also sticks.

An intermediate position in the debate is taken by former World Bank vice-president Justin Yifu Lin. In a set of interesting publications (Lin, 2010; Lin and Monga, 2010; Lin *et al.*, 2003) he argues that the success of China and other developing countries in Asia is due to *comparative advantage-following policies*. Prior to 1978, China followed distorted industrial policies, defying its comparative advantage in light industries and labour-intensive production. Its subsequent success was based on its capitalising on its supplies of surplus labour. This is close to classical liberal formulations of comparative advantage. However, Lin introduces a dynamic twist. A country's policy makers not only need to follow their static comparative advantages but also their *latent* future comparative advantages. Empirically, latent comparative advantage can be identified by comparing the productive structure of a country with the structures of countries with similar factor endowments but higher levels of income per capita. The role of industrial policy is to allow a country to move towards its latent comparative advantage, either through the public support of private or state owned domestic firms or through policies for attracting multinational firms if the domestic capabilities embarking on the new activities are not sufficiently developed.

The proponents of industrial policy have made a powerful and convincing case against the shortcomings of excessive reliance on free markets. They have shown that intervention and targeted industrial and technology policies have indeed contributed to the success of export-led growth in several East Asian countries and can do the same in other countries today. As we write, a profound rethinking of international policies towards protectionism and industrial policy is under way. Industrial policy is re-emerging from oblivion, in both the advanced economies and the developing world.

But a number of caveats is in order. First of all, liberalisation has clearly also had positive effects. In China, liberalisation, deregulation and opening up to foreign investment have resulted in one of the most powerful growth spurts in economic history (Maddison, 2007). Though the state is still prominent in the Chinese economy, the role of state owned enterprises has decreased over time and the role of private and foreign owned enterprises has increased. In India, liberalisation since 1991 has ended decades of relatively slow growth and has made the whole economy more dynamic (Mani, 2011).[24] In Indonesia, liberalisation of trade and progressive deregulation has resulted in very rapid industrial growth between 1980 and 1997 (Hill, 2000b). In Sri Lanka, neoliberal policies have been remarkably successful in promoting industrial exports (Athukorala and Rajapatirana, 2000). In the second place, the re-emergence of industrial policy does not in any way imply a return to the inward-looking policies of the orthodox strategy. No one is arguing for this. The focus is on strategic integration into world trade (Westphal, 2002).

In the third place, there is a real danger that if many countries start competing with others through subsidisation and protection of their domestic firms and industries, this might well result in a disastrous breakdown of international free trade. The proponents of renewed protectionism seem to be insufficiently aware of this danger.

In the fourth place, the interventionists seem to be forgetting the negative lessons of the period 1950–80, including the risks of rent seeking and corruption associated with discretionary decisions about industrial policies. Altenburg (2013) has pointed out that, whatever the theoretical case for industrial policies, they may not be feasible in the context of the neopatrimonial state in many countries in Sub-Saharan Africa. In Sub-Saharan Africa, one can only conclude that extensive state intervention in the process of industrialisation has been such an abysmal failure that for the time being interventionism should be put on hold. Though liberalisation in the 1990s indeed resulted in a marked decline of the industrial sector in many African countries (Szirmai and Lapperre, 2001; Yamfwa et al., 2002), this has more to do with the shortcomings of the pre-1980 policies which resulted in completely non-viable industrial establishments, than with liberalisation itself. Also, until state and administrative capabilities are greatly improved we consider a limited role for discretionary industrial policies to be the preferable option for Sub-Saharan Africa.

---

[24] Whether or not liberalisation is taking place in China and India is itself subject to academic debate.

Finally, the recent emphasis on innovation, learning and entrepreneurship marks a move away from top-down planning and regulation towards flexibility and experimentation. This requires the development of new types of relationships between entrepreneurs and the state (Ács and Naudé, 2013).

9.7   Outcomes of industrialisation strategies

Since 1945, developing countries have increased their savings and investment rates. In many cases the recommendations of Lewis and Rostow to invest at least 12–15 per cent of net national income were met or exceeded (see Table 3.2 in Chapter 3). A substantial part of all this investment went to manufacturing. But the results of industrialisation policies varied substantially from country to country and region to region. On balance, however, a rapid process of industrialisation has taken place in the developing world.

Table 9.5 serves to illustrate the diversity of country experiences in different periods. It is interesting to note that growth rates of manufacturing value added were highest during the period of the orthodox industrialisation model. After 1980, industrial growth in the developing world slowed down. Nevertheless, growth in Asia continued to be very rapid. In Latin America there was a dramatic slowdown in growth during the lost decade of the 1980s, in the wake of the debt crisis of 1982. There was some recovery after 1990, but growth remained sluggish. There was no return to the high growth rates of the post-war period. In Africa, the 1990s were the decade of slowest growth, averaging 1.6 per cent per year. After 2000, there was a very substantial recovery, with average growth rates of almost 5 per cent, albeit starting from very low levels.

Some country experiences stand out. In China, output has been growing at double-digit figures since 1990, with the highest rate of growth recorded in the period 2000–10. India has also experienced a growth acceleration. In Africa, growth rates in recent years are very high in two countries, Ethiopia and Tanzania. This is interesting given that Tanzania is a country that faithfully follows the market precepts of the Washington consensus, while the state plays a very important role in Ethiopian economic development. This shows how carefully one needs to be in drawing general conclusions. South Africa, the economic giant of Africa, is characterised by sluggish performance. In Latin America, weakest performance is recorded for oil-rich Venezuela.

Table 9.6 presents aggregate data for developing countries, classified on the basis of their income per capita in 1987.[25] Between 1960 and 1980 there was rapid growth in both industry (including mining, manufacturing, construction and utilities) and in manufacturing proper. Between 1960 and 1970, growth was most rapid in the upper-middle-income countries. Between 1970 and 1980, highest growth was found in the LMICs. China registered exceptionally high growth throughout the whole period covered in the table.[26]

---

[25] If one classifies developing countries on the basis of their present income levels, the phenomenal growth in some developing countries becomes invisible, because they have since become middle-income or even high-income countries. China is presently in the upper-middle income category. Taiwan and Korea in the high-income category.

[26] Official Chinese growth rates tend to be overestimated, but growth is undoubtedly very rapid (Szirmai et al., 2005, 2007). Table 9.5 presents downward-adjusted growth rates for China, which are lower than the official growth rates. These have also been inserted into Table 9.6.

Table 9.5: Growth of manufacturing GDP, 1950–2010 (average annual growth rate, %)

Country	1950–60	1960–70	1970–80	1980–90	1990–2000	2000–10
Bangladesh		5.7	1.7	2.4	6.9	7.5
China[a]	24.0	5.4	7.9	8.1	10.7	11.2
India	6.0	5.2	4.0	7.6	6.2	8.0
Indonesia		4.6	14.7	10.1	6.8	4.4
Iran[a,g]		10.9	9.2	6.0	6.0	10.0
Malaysia		12.3	11.6	9.8	9.9	3.5
Pakistan	17.3	9.9	5.4	8.2	3.8	7.3
Philippines		5.8	6.1	0.9	2.6	3.7
South Korea[b]	13.2	16.8	16.2	11.9	8.1	6.3
Sri Lanka		6.2	2.0	6.2	8.0	4.0
Taiwan[d,g]		17.2	13.3	7.2	5.1	4.0
Thailand		11.6	10.1	9.9	7.3	5.5
Turkey		10.9	5.6	7.3	4.3	4.1
Argentina	1.2	4.7	1.6	−2.1	2.7	4.4
Brazil	9.1	6.9	9.0	−0.2	1.4	2.5
Chile	8.1	5.3	1.1	2.5	4.5	1.9
Colombia	6.5	5.7	6.0	2.9	−1.9	3.7
Mexico	7.2	7.5	6.3	2.1	4.4	0.7
Peru	7.2	5.8	3.6	−1.7	3.5	5.7
Venezuela	11.0	10.1	5.4	0.9	1.1	0.8
Congo, Dem. Rep.[g]		12.5	−0.9	0.05	−10.0	4.6
Côte d'Ivoire		11.6	15.3	1.6	4.6	−0.9
Egypt		2.5	5.8	6.2	6.3	4.8
Ethiopia[c,e,f]				3.0	10.7	7.2
Ghana[d]		9.6	−1.6	0.9	−2.8	
Kenya[d]		5.5	11.7	4.8	1.2	3.8
Morocco		4.6	5.6	4.3	2.6	3.0
Nigeria		11.9	7.8	2.0	1.6	
South Africa		8.4	5.2	1.3	1.3	2.3
Tanzania[d]		11.0	5.3	−1.4	1.1	8.4
Zambia[d]		15.8	3.3	2.9	−7.3	4.2
Average Asia		9.4	8.3	7.4	6.6	6.1
Average Latin America		6.6	4.7	0.6	2.2	2.8
Average Africa		8.7	5.4	2.7	1.6	4.8
Average all countries		8.7	6.6	4.1	3.6	4.7

Notes:
[a] China, 1950–8, 1958–70; [b] Figures 1950–60 for other period than specified. [c] Ethiopia 1981–90, incl. Eritrea; 1992–2010, excl. Eritrea; [d] Figures for 1960–70 for other years than specified; [e] Figures 1980–90 for shorter period than specified. [f] 1990–2000 for shorter period than specified; [g] 2000–10 for shorter period than specified.

Sources:
World Bank, *World Development Indicators Online*, downloaded 2012. Supplemented by incidental data from *World Development Indicators*, 2002; Groningen Growth and Development Centre, *10 sector database*; IMF, *International Financial Statistics Dataset*; United Nations, *Statistics online*, downloaded 2012; UNIDO, *Indstat3, CD-ROM 2006*. For details see Szirmai, www.dynamicsofdevelopment.com, Table 9.5.

Table 9.6: Aggregate growth in industry and manufacturing, 1960–2010[a]

Growth of production in industry	1960–70[b]	1970–80	1980–90	1990–2000	1996–00	2000–10
Low-income economies	6.6	6.9	7.3	9.9	6.8	10.2
Excl. China & India	6.6	6.8	4.7	4.7	0.9	5.1
India	5.4	4.0	7.1	5.7	4.8	7.8
China	11.2	9.1	9.5	13.6	9.3	11.4
Middle-income economies	7.4[e]	6.3	2.7	1.5	3.2	3.7
Lower-middle-income economies	6.2	7.8	2.2	3.1	3.0	3.6
Upper-middle-income economies	9.1	4.1	3.4	−0.1	3.4	3.9
High-income economies	4.7	2.5	2.4	1.2	2.2	0.2

Growth of production in manufacturing	1960–70[b]	1970–80	1980–90	1990–00	1996–00	2000–10
Low-income economies	5.5	7.4	8.8	10.5	7.1	9.8
Excl. China & India	6.3	7.2	8.7	5.9	1.9	5.3
India	4.7	4.0	7.6	6.2	3.8	8.0
China	5.4	9.4	9.4	13.2	9.3	10.8
Middle-income economies	7.3	6.9	2.8	3.5	4.2	4.0
Lower-middle-income economies	6.5	7.7	1.9	3.5	3.2	3.4
Upper-middle-income economies	8.4	5.4	4.4	3.5	5.4	4.9
High-income economies	4.9	1.8	0.9	1.0	0.8[c]	0.9

Share in GDP[d]	Industry			Manufacturing		
	1960	2000	2010	1960	2000	2010
Low-income economies	32.5	41.0	41.1	23.3	26.1	24.5
Excl. China & India	15.3	33.4	36.9	8.1	16.8	16.8
India	17.9	24.4	25.3	12.8	14.4	13.6
China	44.9	50.9	46.7	32.6	34.5	29.6
Middle-income economies	29.6	30.0	31.8	19.2	19.5	16.4
Lower-middle-income economies	27.5	27.7	30.0	20.1	18.8	16.1
Upper-middle-income economies	32.7	32.9	34.2	16.8	20.5	16.9
High-income economies	39.9	27.4	22.2	30.1	17.9	16.4

Notes:

[a] Industry includes mining, manufacturing, construction and public utilities. Countries are classified on the basis of their GDP per capita in 1987. Many countries have since changed their classification. China is presently in the UMIC category, India in the LMIC category.

[b] The source for the period 1960–70 presents the median of growth rates, except for the high-income economies.

[c] 1999 instead of 2000.

[d] Where country shares were not available for the selected years, we used data of adjacent years.

[e] China manufacturing, 1958–70.

Sources:

Weighted growth rates 1960–70: *World Development Report, 1984*; 1970–2000: World Bank-WDI (2002), *World Development Indicators,* CD-ROM; Chinese manufacturing 1950–70: GGDC website. Shares: World Bank-WDI (2002). All data 2000–10 plus China and India manufacturing 1970–2000 from World Bank, *World Development Indicators Online,* downloaded March 2013.

In the manufacturing sector the increase in production was not restricted to consumer goods only. The share of intermediate goods and capital goods also increased over time (UNIDO, 1995).

After 1980, the pace of industrial growth in MICs slowed down dramatically. It was influenced by the weak performance of Latin American industrial economies after the debt crisis of 1982. Between 1980 and 1990, the annual growth rate in MICs was only 2.7 per cent for industry and 2.8 per cent for manufacturing. On the other hand, growth in low-income countries accelerated after 1980. Especially China showed rapid growth, followed by India. Excluding the Asian giants India and China, growth in the low-income economies was lower, especially between 1996 and 2000, due to the effects of the Asian crisis of 1997.

Between 1960 and 2000, the shares of industry and manufacturing in total GDP increased in all income categories, with the exception of the LMICs. After 2000, the shares of manufacturing start to decline, sometimes quite substantially. Even in China the share of manufacturing has started to decline, though it was still very high in 2010.

Table 9.7 indicates that the structure of world manufacturing is rapidly changing. Including China, the share of developing countries in world manufacturing GDP has increased from 13.7 per cent in 1980 to no less than 42 per cent in 2010, a veritable revolution. In 2010, China alone accounted for 17.6 per cent of global manufacturing value added. The share of West Asia almost tripled between 1980 and 2010. The share of South and Southeast Asia excluding China increased dramatically after 1960, reaching 11.2 per cent in 2010 (in current prices). The share of Latin America has not changed much since 1980. On the African continent, the share in total manufacturing production has remained stuck at around 1 per cent since 1960, though with an interesting jump to 1.4 per cent in 2008.

Data on global export shares are provided in Table 9.8. The main conclusion one can derive from this table is that the nineteenth-century division of labour, in which developing countries only exported unprocessed agricultural and mining products and imported manufactured goods, no longer exists. An increasing part of developing countries' exports consists of manufactures. The share of manufactured goods in total commodity exports has increased in all developing countries (see Table 3.4 in Chapter 3). In some countries, especially in Asia, manufactured goods are by far the most important exports. Most of these manufactures are sold on the markets of the advanced countries. Worldwide the share of developing countries in total world manufactured exports has increased from 6 per cent in 1963 to a staggering 38 per cent in 2010. Most of this increase comes from Asia, which accounts for 32 per cent of global manufactured exports (see Table 9.8). China is the largest manufacturing exporter with 14.8 per cent, followed by four small economies – Hong Kong, Singapore, South Korea and Taiwan – which together account for 11.9 per cent.[27] In comparison, the role of India is negligible.

Although the aggregate figures thus point to the success of industrialisation in developing countries, progress in manufacturing has been concentrated in a relatively small number of these countries. These include Argentina, Brazil, China, Hong Kong, India, Mexico, Singapore, South Korea, Taiwan and Turkey (Lall, 1998; UNCTAD, 2000; UNIDO, 2002). The lion's share of manufactured exports comes from only a few countries, including

---

[27] Since 1997 Hong Kong has been reunited with China, but is still registered as a separate economy in international statistics.

Table 9.7: Share of developing countries in world manufacturing value added, 1960–2010 (%)[a]

Year	Africa	West Asia and Europe[b]	South and East Asia, excl. China	China	Latin America	Developing countries
Excl. China (constant 1990 $)[c]						
1960[c]	0.8	0.7	1.8		4.9	7.9
1970[c]	0.8	1.3	2.4		6.0	10.5
1980	0.9	1.7	3.7		6.9	13.2
1990[g]	0.9	2.0	6.2		5.5	14.6
2000	1.0	2.2	9.4		5.5	18.0
2004	1.1	2.4	10.8		5.3	19.6
Incl. China (constant 1990 $)						
1980	0.9	1.7	3.6	1.4	6.8	14.4
1990[g]	0.9	1.9	6.0	2.6	5.4	16.8
2000	0.9	2.1	8.8	6.6	5.2	23.6
2004	1.0	2.2	10.0	8.5	4.9	26.6
Incl. China (current $)						
1980[d]	0.9	1.6	2.4	1.7	7.1	13.7
1990	0.9	1.8	3.5	2.6	5.6	14.4
2000	0.9	1.2	8.4	6.7	6.6	23.8
2002	0.9	1.2	8.9	8.2	5.6	24.8
2005	0.8	1.6	9.7	10.0	5.9	30.4
2007[e]	0.9	1.7	9.4	12.9	7.0	31.9
2008[f]	1.4	4.7	10.1	15.0	6.7	37.9
2009	1.4	4.2	10.6	17.9	6.8	41.1
2010	1.4	4.3	11.2	17.6	7.4	42.1

Notes:

[a] At exchange rates.

[b] Incl. European developing countries.

[c] Extrapolated using the ratio of the shares of 1960 and 1970 to 1980, at 1980 constant prices.

[d] China 1980 calculated using the China Southeast Asia ratio for 1990.

[e] The developing country statistics for 2007 exclude South Korea and Singapore which are no longer developing countries. We have reincluded them, so as to have consistency in the historical time series. Korea and Singapore account for around 2.5 per cent of world value added. The data for 2006 and 2007 no longer distinguish West Asia from South and Southeast Asia. Europe is added as a special category. Using ratios from the previous years, we have estimated figures for West Asia including Europe and South and Southeast Asia.

[f] 2008–10 from UNIDO (2013). Country classifications have changed. Africa now includes South Africa (+ 0.5%), West Asia now includes several former Asian Soviet Republics. East Asia includes former developing countries which are now advanced economies such as Taiwan, Korea, Singapore and Hong Kong. Excluding these would reduce the share of developing countries in world manufacturing by some 3–3.5 per cent.

[g] Figures after 1990 have 1995 as base year. We apply the indexes of shares in real output at 1995 prices to the 1990 figures at 1990 prices.

Sources:

Constant figures:

1960: Gosh (1984: 351); 1970: UNIDO (1990); 1980: UNIDO (1999); 1990–2004: UNIDO (2005), *International Yearbook of Industrial Statistics, 2005*.

Current figures: 1980–2010: UNIDO, *International Yearbook of Industrial Statistics*, several editions, as follows: 1999–2005: UNIDO (2005); 2006–7: UNIDO (2010); 2008–10: UNIDO (2013).

Table 9.8: Share of developing countries in world manufactured exports, 1963–2010

	1963	1973	1983	1993	2000	2010
Asia[a]	2.6	3.9	7.0	14.8	20.4	31.7
China[b]			1.2	2.7	4.6	14.8
India	0.7	0.4	0.4	0.6	0.7	1.4
Hong Kong, Singapore, S. Korea, Taiwan[c]	1.6	2.9	5.6	12.4	12.8	11.9
Latin America	0.8	1.6	1.7	2.7	4.2	3.8
Brazil	0.0	0.3	0.7	0.8	0.7	0.7
Argentina	0.1	0.2	0.1	0.2	0.2	0.2
Mexico	0.2	0.3	0.2	1.4	2.9	2.3
Africa, incl. South Africa	1.3	1.2	0.7	0.9	0.8	1.0
South Africa[c]	0.6	0.6	0.3	0.4	0.3	0.4
Middle East	0.1	0.3	1.2	0.6	0.9	1.3
Developing economies[d,e]	5.9	8.8	14.5	20.5	26.3	38.1
Developed economies[e]	75.3	79.0	69.5	75.3	71.9	58.7

Notes:

[a] Excluding advanced Asian economies Japan, Australia and New Zealand.

[b] 1984 instead of 1983.

[c] Since 1998, figures refer to South Africa only and no longer to the Southern African Customs Union.

[d] Developing economies, excl. former Soviet Asian Replublics and economies in transition.

[e] High-income economies Hong Kong, Taiwan, South Korea and Singapore are included for reasons of consistency with older data. Excluding these countries from developing Asia and developing economies total in 2010 of course results in much lower shares: 19.8 per cent for Asia and 26.2 per cent for developing economies.

[f] Prior to 1989, the Soviet Union and Eastern European countries were not included in the advanced economies. The percentages therefore do not add up to 100 per cent.

[g] From 2000 onwards the Russian Federation is included in the advanced economy category. Excluding the Russian Federation, the share of the advanced economies would be equal to 58 per cent in 2010.

Sources:

1963–193:

WTO, *International Trade Statistics, 2000*: 31.

WTO, *Annual Report 1997*, Volume 2: 22.

WDI, CD-ROM, 2002.

2000–10:

World Bank, *World Development Indicators Online*, downloaded February 2012.

Taiwan from UN, *Comtrade database*, downloaded 2012.

China, Hong Kong, Singapore,[28] Korea, Taiwan, Brazil, India, Mexico, and in more recent years Bangladesh, Indonesia, Malaysia, the Philippines and Thailand.

In the course of the 1980s, the Latin American industrial economies experienced great difficulties, due to the debt crisis, the legacy of inward-looking policies and exposure to

[28] Mainly re-exports.

international markets. At present, resource-based activities and services play an important role in many Latin American countries. In India, the industrial sector suffered from considerable inefficiency and low capacity utilisation. The liberalisation of the economy in the 1990s bought improvement of performance and acceleration of growth, but manufacturing is much less important than in China. The share of software and IT services has rapidly expanded.

In 1997, East Asia was severely affected by the Asian crisis, which led to a sudden interruption of economic growth in South Korea, Thailand, Indonesia, the Philippines and other South East Asian economies. The large economies of China and India were least affected. Some countries such as South Korea and Malaysia recovered very rapidly, reaching pre-crisis levels of output in a few years. Other countries such as Indonesia and the Philippines took longer to recover and were put on to slower growth paths (Hill, 2000). In Indonesia the role of manufacturing became less prominent in the post-crisis period (Aswicahyono *et al.*, 2013).

With the exception of South Africa and Mauritius, industrialisation in Sub-Saharan Africa never really got off the ground in spite of the high priority accorded to industrialisation by policy makers in the post-independence period (Page, 2013; Szirmai and Lapperre, 2001). Sub-Saharan Africa's share in world manufacturing is small, its share in world exports as well as FDI is negligible and technology gaps are increasing (Helleiner, 1995; Morrissey and Filatotchev, 2001; Wangwe, 1995). Unlike Asia, Africa has never been prepared to exploit its huge reservoir of cheap labour for labour-intensive manufacturing. The present growth spurt since 2010 may present new opportunities. Manufacturing is starting to relocate away from China as wage levels go up. Africa now has at least two generations of experience with manufacturing. After decades of investment in human capital, educational levels are much higher than in the 1960s. Finally there are new inflows of foreign investment, not only into resource-based activities, but also into infrastructure and manufacturing (e.g. Portelli, 2006).

9.8　Conclusions, new challenges and new paradigms

In conclusion, developing countries have made substantial progress in industrialisation since 1950. Many developing countries have experienced rapid structural change and the share of developing countries in world manufacturing output and exports has increased dramatically.

In recent years, the role of manufacturing as the prime engine of economic development has been questioned. It is clear that other sectors such as agriculture or services also have an important role to play in growth and development. Nevertheless, the countries that have been most successful in catch-up since 1950 are the countries which have achieved most success in industrialisation and industrial exports. Manufacturing remains one of the key sectors that deserve the attention of policy makers and academics.

So far, the benefits of industrialisation have been concentrated in a relatively small number of developing countries. Developing countries that want to embark on late industrialisation in the twenty-first century face new challenges, several of which have been touched upon in this chapter (see also Naudé and Szirmai, 2013). These challenges include the rise of global value chains and distributed production, which call for new kinds of industrial strategies, the need to respond to the competition of cheap manufactured exports from the giant economy of China, the difficulty of reversing the trend of premature de-industrialisation in Africa and Latin America, restrictions to policy space in a liberal international order and the danger of being caught in a middle-income trap. Also, manufacturing is one of the important contributors to global pollution and global climate change (see Chapter 5). One of the urgent challenges for future industrialisation is to develop more sustainable methods of industrial production, in terms of energy use, emissions and recycling. Finally, we have argued, both in this chapter and in Chapter 4, that innovation and technological change are becoming ever-more important in industrial development. In the absence of innovation, newcomers may become trapped at the low end of global value chains. Innovation and technological advance requires policies aimed at improving technological capabilities, learning and experimentation. This involves new and flexible modes of interaction between firms, entrepreneurs and policy makers.

In this chapter, we have discussed some of the policy failures of older industrialisation strategies, as well as some of the shortcomings of the neoliberal market-oriented strategies of the last quarter of the twentieth century. In thinking about industrialisation, one should try to derive lessons from the more recent experiences, without forgetting the lessons of past failures. One should also be aware of the new challenges facing countries that are trying to industrialise in the present century.

Questions for review

1. Does economic development necessarily imply industrialisation? Provide theoretical and empirical justifications for your answer.
2. Discuss the main characteristics of Arthur Lewis' model of economic development with unlimited supplies of labour. What are the most important criticisms levelled against the Lewis model?
3. What are the main arguments in favour of protection?
4. Provide an overview of the theoretical arguments for large-scale industrialisation in developing countries.
5. Analyse the relationships between large-scale, import substitution and government planning in post-war industrialisation strategies.
6. Summarise the most important criticisms of post-war industrialisation strategies.
7. What is the difference between unbalanced and balanced industrialisation strategies?
8. What is the development potential of the small-scale and informal sector? How should it be supported?
9. What is the difference between the strength and the importance of linkages?
10. Why is there less emphasis on the scale of the investment effort in export-oriented industrialisation than in import substituting industrialisation strategies?
11. To what extent have industrialisation strategies in developing countries been successful in the post-war period?
12. Is import substitution a necessary phase in industrialisation, before a country can engage in exports?

13. Discuss the differences between the balanced growth strategy and the balanced growth path strategy.
14. What are the implications of the increased importance of global value chains for industrialisation strategy?
15. Why is FDI important for growth of manufacturing in developing countries? What are the potential disadvantages of FDI?
16. Discuss and evaluate the main criticisms of the neoliberal market approach.
17. What are the new challenges facing developing countries trying to industrialise in the twenty-first century?

Further reading

One of the key early references for industrialisation in developing countries is Arthur Lewis' article 'Economic Development with Unlimited Supplies of Labour' (1954). Two-sector models are further elaborated by Fei and Ranis in *Development of the Labor Surplus Economy: Theory and Policy* (1964). The notion of balanced growth was introduced by Rosenstein-Rodan in 'Problems of Industrialisation of East and South-East Europe' (1943) and 'Notes on the Theory of the "Big Push"' (1957). Other seminal publications on balanced growth and large-scale industrialisation are Nurkse, *Problems of Capital Formation in Underdeveloped Countries* (1953), Nelson, 'A Theory of the Low-Level Equilibrium Trap in Underdeveloped Economies' (1956) and Leibenstein, *Economic Backwardness and Economic Growth: Studies in the Theory of Economic Development* (1957).

The concept of unbalanced growth is analysed in Hirschman, *The Strategy of Economic Development* (1958), which is still very stimulating to read today. Further readings on the small-scale and informal sector include Hart, 'Informal Income Opportunities and Urban Employment in Ghana' (1973), Little, Scitovsky and Scott, *Industry and Trade in Some Developing Countries* (1970) and Hernando de Soto's provocative *The Mystery of Capital: Why Capitalism Triumphs in the West and Fails Everywhere Else* (2000).

The modern debate on industrialisation in developing countries hinges on the interpretation of the success of East Asian industrialisation. Amsden has emphasised the importance of interventionist policies in her pathbreaking book *Asia's Next Giant: South Korea and Late Industrialization* (1989). The interventionist interpretation is also found in Wade, *Governing the Market: Economic Theory and the Role of Government in East Asian Industrialization* (1990). In a long series of publications, Lall has emphasised the importance of policies aimed at promoting technological learning and capability building. Here we only mention *Learning from the Asian Tigers: Studies in Technology and Industrial Policy* (1996) and 'Technological Change and Industrialization in the Asian NIEs: Achievements and Challenges' (2000). The liberal interpretation of East Asian success is argued in a study by the World Bank, entitled *The East Asian Miracle: Economic Growth and Public Policy* (1993). Other references in this debate include: Westphal, Kim and Dahlman, 'Reflections on The Republic of Korea's Acquisition of Technological Capability' (1985), Rodrik, 'Getting Interventions Right: How South Korea and Taiwan Grew Rich' (1995) and *Making Openness Work: The New Global Economy and the Developing Countries* (1999) and the thoughtful review article by Westphal, 'Technology Strategies for Economic Development in a Fast Changing Global Economy' (2002). A modern criticism of neoliberal theory and practice is offered by Chang in *Kicking Away the Ladder: Development Strategy in Historical Perspective* (2002). A theoretical justification for industrial policy is provided by Hausmann and Rodrik in their pathbreaking article, 'Economic Development as Self-Discovery' (2003). Another influential publication is Lin, *New Structural Economics: A Framework for Rethinking Development* (2010), emphasising the role of industrial policy in realising latent comparative advantage. Two edited volumes summarise the current state of the debate on industrial policy, Cimoli, Dosi and Stiglitz, *The Political Economy of Capabilities Accumulation: The Past and Future of Policies for Industrial Development* (2009) and Szirmai, Naudé and Alcorta, *Pathways to Industrialization in the 21st Century: New Challenges and Emerging Paradigms* (2013a).

Two interesting publications on the emergence of global value chains are Gereffi, 'Capitalism, Development and Global Commodity Chains' (1994) and Gereffi and Korzeniewicz (eds.), *Commodity Chains and Global Capitalism* (1994). Two recent papers about global value chains are Baldwin, *Trade and Industrialization after Globalization's 2nd Unbundling: How Building and Joining a Supply Chain are Different and Why it Matters* (2011), and Kaplinsky and Farooki, *What Are the Implications for Global Value Chains When the Market Shifts from the North to the South?* (2010).

For FDI, relevant publications include the classic article by Vernon, 'International Investment and International Trade in the Product Cycle' (1966), Dunning, 'Trade, Location of Economic Activity and the Multinational Enterprise: A Search for an Eclectic Approach' (1988) and Dunning's book *The Globalization of Business* (1993). More recent discussions of the impact of FDI in developing countries are found in the UNCTAD report, *The Competitiveness Challenge: Transnational Corporations and Industrial Restructuring in Developing Countries* (2000), the 2002 edition of UNIDO's, *Industrial Development Report, 2002/3: Competing through Innovation and Learning* and a volume of papers edited by Narula and Lall on *Understanding FDI-Assisted Economic Development* (2006).

A concise and well-written overview of the modern debates on industrialisation is provided by Kiely, *Industrialisation and Development: A Comparative Analysis* (1998). Broad overviews are also provided by John Weiss, *Industrialisation and Globalisation: Theory and Evidence from Developing Countries* (2002) and *The Economics of Industrial Development* (2011).

UNIDO publishes a variety of industrial statistics, including the *Handbook of Industrial Statistics* and its successor the *International Yearbook of Industrial Statistics*. The *UNIDO Industrial Statistics Database* is available in CD-Rom format. UNIDO also publishes the *Industrial Development Report* on an annual basis. The homepage of UNIDO is www.unido.org/. Statistics on FDI are presented in the IMF *International Financial Yearbook* and the UNCTAD *World Investment Reports*. UNCTAD statistics are also freely available on the UNCTAD website *UNCTADstat*, http://unctadstat.unctad.org/ReportFolders/reportFolders.aspx. Detailed time series for industrial sectors are found on the website of the Groningen Growth and Development Centre: www.rug.nl/research/ggdc/databases.

10 Agricultural development and rural development

The role of agriculture in development and the relationships between the agricultural and the industrial sector were discussed in Chapter 8. In the first half of this chapter, the focus shifts to the agricultural sector itself. Other sectors are only mentioned in as far as they contribute to agricultural development. In sections 10.1 and 10.2, we analyse long-term trends in agricultural production and identify some of the factors influencing these trends. Theories of agricultural development are also discussed here. Special attention will be paid to the old and new debates on the 'green revolution' and the role of biotechnology. Section 10.3 addresses issues of food consumption and undernourishment. It turns out that food supply is only one side of the equation. Access to food is just as important.

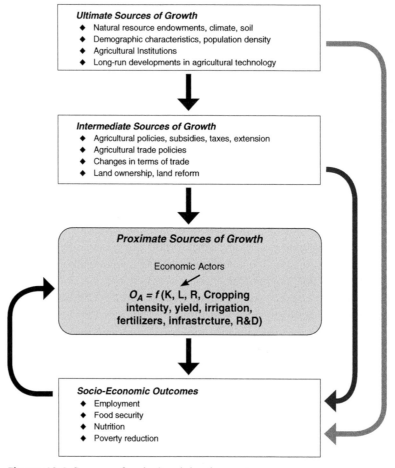

Figure 10.1 Sources of agricultural development

Using the framework of proximate, intermediate and ultimate causality agricultural development is represented in simplified form in Figure 10.1. At the proximate level, agricultural output O_A is determined by expansion of land (R), labour and human capital (L), physical capital (K), cropping intensity, yields per harvest, irrigation, fertiliser use, infrastructure and R&D.

In the second half of this chapter the focus shifts from agriculture to rural development. The concept of rural development is introduced in Section 10.4. Though rural society is characterised by the significance of agricultural activities, rural development is broader than agricultural development. First, various non-agricultural economic activities take place in rural areas. Second, rural development refers to the transformation of rural society as a whole, rather than only to the economic aspects of rural life. Section 10.5 discusses land reform, agricultural collectivisation and agricultural decollectivisation. In section 10.6, we examine policies for rural development.

10.1   Is there enough food to feed the world population?

From the eighteenth century to the present day a debate has been raging between Malthusians and anti-Malthusians (Alexandratos and Bruinsma, 2012; Smil, 2000). Malthusians fear that food production will not be able to keep up with population growth, that soils are becoming eroded and degraded as a consequence of new agricultural practices, that biodiversity is declining at an alarming rate (Hogg, 2000), that forests are disappearing and that the world climate is changing for the worse. Technological optimists argue that advances in technology will compensate for diminishing returns, that food production will outpace population and that negative environmental impacts can be mitigated through technological advance. Prominent modern Malthusians include Lester Brown and his co-workers at the Worldwatch Institute (Brown, 1996; Worldwatch Institute, 2001) and researchers at the World Resources Institute (2000). An extreme protagonist of the techno-optimistic perspective is Julian Simon (1996). The debate took a new turn with the publication in 2001 of a delightfully controversial book by Bjørn Lomborg, which trashed many of the basic empirical assumptions of the Malthusians (Lomborg, 2001). But one should realise that the debate is conducted on a variety of levels: assessment of empirical trends, evaluation of the seriousness of trends, assessment of risks involved, assessments of the advantages and costs of policy interventions, differences between global and local trends and so forth. In general, the conclusion of most macro-studies is that food production will be able to keep up with population growth in the next half-century (Alexandratos and Bruinsma, 2012; Bruinsma, 2003; Mitchell *et al.*, 1997). But climate change and global warming are posing new challenges, especially to agricultural production in developing countries.

To set the stage for the discussion of agricultural development, Table 10.1 presents data on the world growth of total agricultural production and food production from 1934 to 2011. The data derive from the FAO Production Yearbooks and the FAO statistical database FAOSTAT.[1] The table distinguishes between food production and total agricultural production, and between production and production per capita.

---

[1] FAOSTAT, *Agriculture Data, Agricultural Production Indices*, FAO, http://apps.fao.org/page/.

Table 10.1 illustrates some interesting trends:

- Despite very rapid growth of world population, global per capita production of food has increased. It is 1.6 times as high as in 1934–9. This is contrary to gloomy Malthusian predictions, which state that the production of food will lag behind the growth of population.
- Since 1979–81, the rate of growth of agricultural production, whether in absolute terms or per capita, has been much more rapid in developing countries than in economically more developed countries. The same applies to food production. Taking 1979–81 as 100, the index of per capita food production in 2011 stood at 177. In the advanced economies it stood at 103.
- The case of per capita food production in the densely populated large countries such as China, India and Indonesia is noteworthy. Countries such as Indonesia and India, which were dependent on food imports in the 1960s, have now become all but self-sufficient in food. As will be explained in section 10.2.2, population growth may provide incentives for technological change and intensification of agricultural production so that total production increases faster than population.
- The only regions where the increase in food production has not kept up with population growth were the countries of Eastern Europe and the former Soviet Union. After the sudden dissolution of the Soviet Union in 1991 and the abrupt but incomplete transition to the market, agriculture in the transition countries suffered. In 2000, food production per capita stood at only 77 per cent of its 1980 level. The potential for agricultural growth in this region remains great, but has not been realised in the past century.
- In Africa, the race between population growth and growth of production was a stalemate. Food output per capita in 2011 is about the same as it was in 1934, although since 1995, there has been some modest improvement in per capita food production.

The continued growth of total world food production per capita contrasts with concerns that the per capita supply of cereals is on the decline (Bruinsma, 2003; Lomborg, 2001). In the past, cereal production accounted for some 90 per cent of human food (World Bank, 1992). In fact Figure 10.2 shows that global cereal production per capita has stabilised since around 1985. In developing countries there is still a modest increase. The discrepancy between the substantial increase in total food production and the relative stagnation of cereal production indicates that there is some substitution between cereals and other types of food, such as meat or fowl.

In developed countries cereal production declined after 1986, among other things as a consequence of a partial winding down of agricultural protection schemes and the fact that average caloric needs are more than being met. Nevertheless, by 2011 per capita production was back at the level of 1986. The large productivity gap between developed and developing countries also indicates that there is still ample scope for further productivity improvement in the developing world.

It has often been claimed that expansion of the production of export crops and non-food crops will be at the expense of food production. Dixon (1990), for example, states that the most fertile and best-irrigated lands are often used for growing cash crops and export crops. Moreover, these crops are said to use disproportionate shares of modern inputs, investment and subsidies. In particular, when export crops are not food crops[2] and when export crops

---

[2] Rice, for example, is grown both as a food crop and as a cash crop.

Table 10.1: Indices of agricultural production, 1934–2011 (1979–81 =100)

	World total[a]		Developed countries total[b]		North America		Western Europe		Eastern Europe		(Former) USSR[c]		Eastern Europe and (Former) USSR[d]		Developing countries total[e]	
	T	PC	T	PC	T	PC	T	PC	T	PC	T	PC	T	PC	T	PC
Total agricultural production																
1934–9	40	82	–	–	40	74	47	63	–	–	–	–	41	55	–	–
1948–52	46	80	–	–	54	84	48	60	–	–	–	–	41	58	–	–
1961	63	90	68	81	65	79	69	76	66	76	75	91	72	83	57	89
1965	70	93	74	84	72	83	75	80	71	79	77	89	75	84	65	92
1970	79	96	83	90	75	83	86	89	79	85	95	104	90	94	76	95
1975	89	97	91	95	88	93	90	91	93	97	98	102	96	100	86	96
1979–81	100	100	100	100	100	100	100	100	100	100	100	100	100	100	100	100
1985	114	105	108	104	108	103	107	106	106	103	109	105	108	104	122	110
1990	128	107	112	104	110	99	108	105	104	100	123	113	117	106	144	117
1995	139	108	104	94	118	102	104	98	89	85	79	72	76	76	174	130
2000	159	115	111	99	134	109	108	101	83	80	75	68	72	72	207	142
2005	180	123	115	100	141	109	106	96	–	–	–	–	83	83	245	157
2011	209	133	121	103	147	108	109	98	–	–	–	–	76	76	299	177
Food production																
1934–9	39	79	–	–	36	63	47	63	–	–	–	–	41	55	–	–
1948–52	45	77	–	–	50	76	47	60	–	–	–	–	41	58	–	–
1961	62	89	67	80	63	77	69	76	66	76	75	92	72	84	57	88
1965	69	92	72	82	70	82	75	80	70	79	77	88	74	83	64	91
1970	79	95	82	89	74	82	86	89	78	85	96	105	90	94	75	94
1975	89	97	91	95	89	93	90	91	93	97	98	102	96	99	86	95
1979–81	100	100	100	100	100	100	100	100	100	100	100	100	100	100	100	100
1985	114	105	108	104	109	104	107	106	105	103	110	105	108	104	121	110
1990	128	107	112	104	110	99	108	105	105	101	125	115	118	107	144	118
1995	140	109	105	95	118	102	104	98	90	86	81	73	78	77	177	132
2000	160	116	112	100	136	110	109	101	84	81	77	70	74	74	212	146
2005	182	124	116	101	141	109	106	97	–	–	–	–	85	85	250	161
2011	212	135	124	105	150	110	109	98	–	–	–	–	78	78	306	181

Table 10.1: (*cont.*)

	Africa[f]		Latin America		Near East		Far East[g]		India		Indonesia		China	
	T	PC	T	PC	T	PC	T	PC	T	PC	T	PC	T	PC
Total agricultural production														
1934-9	38	110	33	102	33	84	39	94	–	–	–	–	–	–
1948-52	49	105	40	90	37	81	41	79	–	–	–	–	–	–
1961	67	110	56	91	55	92	56	87	67	102	53	85	47	70
1965	76	114	65	93	63	95	64	88	66	93	57	83	63	87
1970	89	116	74	94	73	96	74	92	80	101	70	90	72	86
1975	95	110	83	94	87	100	85	93	90	101	80	90	83	90
1979-81	100	100	100	100	100	100	100	100	100	100	100	100	100	100
1985	113	98	114	103	117	101	127	113	122	109	127	114	136	126
1990	133	100	125	103	137	103	153	123	145	116	158	129	173	149
1995	151	100	146	110	156	104	192	140	167	122	196	148	233	188
2000	179	105	168	117	178	106	232	156	187	125	198	140	292	226
2005	220	114	199	130	193	102	272	173	207	127	249	165	350	263
2011	248	110	236	143	219	100	340	203	271	153	315	196	431	315
Food production														
1934-9	40	114	31	93	32	81	38	90	–	–	–	–	–	–
1948-52	50	108	39	86	36	79	40	78	–	–	–	–	–	–
1961	66	110	53	85	55	91	57	87	67	102	52	83	48	71
1965	75	112	61	88	61	91	63	87	66	93	56	82	63	87
1970	87	115	73	93	71	93	74	91	80	101	70	89	71	86
1975	95	109	83	93	86	98	85	93	90	101	80	90	83	90
1979-81	100	100	100	100	100	100	100	100	100	100	100	100	100	100
1985	114	98	115	104	117	102	126	113	123	110	128	115	133	124
1990	134	101	127	104	139	105	153	123	146	117	160	131	173	148
1995	154	101	152	115	159	106	194	142	168	122	200	151	235	191
2000	183	107	175	122	182	109	237	159	190	126	201	142	298	231
2005	226	117	208	136	199	105	277	175	207	127	252	168	358	269
2011	256	114	247	150	228	105	346	206	268	151	321	200	441	322

Notes:

T = Total net production; PC = Net production per capita. To maintain the consistency of long-run series, we used population weights to reconstruct the older categories where necessary.

[a] World total until 1961, excl. China.

[b] North America, Australia, New Zealand, Israel, Japan, South Africa and Europe, excl. (Former) USSR.

[c] Former USSR includes Central Asian developing countries.

[d] FAO weighted averages for this category not available after 1991. We have calculated our own averages using population weights. This category includes Eastern Europe, the Russian Federation, Central Asia, Armenia, Azerbaijan and Georgia.

[e] Excl. republics of the Former Soviet Union and excl. South Africa.

[f] Africa, excl. South Africa. Pre-1961 data exclude Egypt, Sudan and Libya. These countries are included in post-1961 series.

[g] The data for the Far East include South Asian, East Asian and Southeast Asian developing countries. East Asia exclude Japan. The data for 1934–52 exclude what were the Central Asian republics of the Former Soviet Union.

Sources:

1934–53: FAO, *Production Yearbook*, various issues.

1961–2000: FAO, FAOSTAT, *Agriculture Data, Agricultural Production Indices*, accessed July 2003, http://apps.fao.org/page/form?collection=Crops. Primary&Domain=PIN&servlet=1&language=EN&hostname=apps.fao.org&version=default; 2000–11: All countries and regions and World total, North America, Western Europe, India, Indonesia and China 1961–2011 from FAOSTAT accessed June/July 2013, http://faostat.fao.org/site/291/default.aspx.

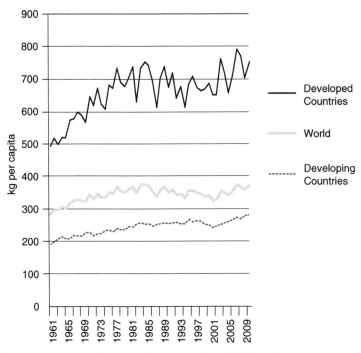

Figure 10.2 Cereals production per capita, 1961–2011
Source: Cereals from FAOSTAT, *Agricultural Production Indices*, accessed July 2013, http://faostat.
fao.org/site/612/DesktopDefault.aspx?PageID=612#ancor. Population data from UN, *World
Population Projections. The 2012 Revision*, http://esa.un.org/unpd/wpp/Excel-Data/population.htm.

and domestic food crops compete for scarce land and labour, expansion of cash crops may
lead to a decreasing food production (Gakou, 1987). An example of this is provided by
groundnut production in the East African Sahel (Devereux, 1993). But, this is not necessarily the case (see e.g. Braun and Kennedy, 1994; Ravallion, 1997). In a dynamic agricultural
system both food production and non-food production can increase simultaneously. In a less
dynamic agricultural system both food production and export production will stagnate
(Paarlberg, 2008). Even if domestic food production does stagnate, however, export revenues from cash crops may be used to import more food than could have been produced
locally.

From a technical point of view there is no reason to assume that food production cannot
continue to grow faster than the population. There are sufficient opportunities to increase
food supply, while the growth of food demand is expected to slow down to 1 per cent per
year until 2050, compared with a growth of 2.2 per cent in the four decades prior to 2005.
The slower growth of demand is caused by a slowdown in population growth and the
attainment of sufficiently high levels of per capita food consumption by significant parts of
the world population (Alexandratos, 1995; Alexandratos and Bruinsma, 2012; Bruinsma,
2003; FAO, 2012a). However, as will be shown in section 10.3, an increase in the average
per capita food production or food availability does not necessarily mean that each person
will get more food or that the absolute numbers of undernourished people will decline. Thus
increasing food prices may be one of the challenges of the coming years.

A warning is also in order with regard to the reliability of the data in Table 10.1. In her book *Development Economics on Trial: the Anthropological Case for a Prosecution* (1986) the anthropologist Polly Hill severely criticised standardised methods of data collection such as those applied by the FAO, on the basis of her field experience in West Africa and South India, and elaborates on the shortcomings of the basic data.

In West Africa and South India farmers questioned by surveyors seldom know how much land they actually cultivate and how much food and other agricultural products they produce. Farmers often work several scattered plots of land, some of which lie fallow for long periods of time. The amounts produced are hard to assess since many crops are interplanted. Some root crops like cassava are not harvested at once, but are rather dug up when food is actually needed. It is also hard to obtain reliable information on the amount and value of products used for household consumption, that is, products not traded on the market.

Usually only the male head of the household is questioned in agricultural surveys. In West Africa, in particular, food production is the preserve of female members of the household. The male head knows little about this subject. Furthermore, farmers are not used to aggregating income flows over longer periods of time, like a month or a year. Finally, the surveyors are usually underpaid, poorly trained and marginally supervised. Hill comes to the conclusion that the margin of error involved in such data is so wide that qualitative statements should be preferred over misleading quantitative data. Her criticisms are supported by an excellent study by Wiggins (2000), which claims that systematic analysis of case studies provides a less negative picture of agricultural growth in Sub-Saharan Africa than FAO data. All the indices for this region are dominated by giant Nigeria, a country notorious for the low quality of its agricultural statistics.

These criticisms should be taken seriously. Anyone working with FAO and other international statistics knows how deeply results can be influenced by changes in definitions, coverage and the quality of data collection. Nevertheless, this author completely disagrees with Polly Hill's conclusion. Qualitative verbal statements about trends are quantitative statements in disguise. They are too often based on a limited number of case studies and examples. They are even more difficult to check or verify than statistical time series, the sources and methods of which can be documented with considerable precision. Statistical series should never be regarded as conclusive statements about reality, but rather as working hypotheses, which are to be used until replaced by better estimates. They represent the latest state of our knowledge. Therefore, we should indicate as precisely as possible how these series have been constructed, and should distrust all statistical series where such information is lacking. Furthermore, the striving for aggregation and identification of global trends offers an important counterbalance to the possible biases involved in formulating general statements on the basis of observations at the micro-level in local settings.[3] Finally, data collection methods are continuously being revised and improved (e.g. FAO, 2012a) for instance, using techniques of aerial scanning.

---

[3] Lomborg (2001) provides numerous telling examples of generalisations based on highly specialised cases. For instance, a UNEP study of land degradation trends in Africa is based on a single case study in South Africa, dating from 1989. See also Waggoner and Ausubel (2001).

10.2   What are the sources of growth of agricultural production?

Expansion of agricultural production can be realised in three different ways (Alexandratos and Bruinsma, 2012; Van der Meer, 1983).[4] These are summarised in Box 10.1.

BOX 10.1   Three ways to expand agricultural production

1. **Expansion** of cultivated area.
2. **Intensification** of land use by shortening the period of fallowing or by harvesting more than one crop per year on the same piece of land (multicropping). Intensification will cause average returns per hectare to increase.
3. **Increase** in the returns per harvest per hectare:
    (a) When labour is scarce, returns per harvest may be increased by using mechanised equipment. Generally, investment in mechanisation is labour-saving.
    (b) When land is scarce, returns per harvest may be increased by making land-substituting investments, like investment in irrigation, organic and chemical fertilisers, and the development of high-productivity seeds. In general, land-substituting investments are land-saving and labour-intensive.

In the following sections these means of increasing production will be discussed in further detail.

10.2.1   How much land is still left for cultivation?

Table 10.2 presents information on the expansion of the cultivated area since 1961. This table shows that between 1961 and 2011 the cultivated area increased worldwide by 13.3 per cent. The largest percentage-wise expansion can be observed in South America (110.5 per cent), followed by Africa (52.9 per cent) and Australia and Oceania (46.7 per cent). Since 1990, however, the global expansion of cultivated area has slowed down. Substantial increases in developing regions such as Africa and South America are balanced by reductions in North America, Europe and the countries of the former USSR.

The opportunities for further expansion of the cultivated area are still far from exhausted. Taking Revelle's (1975) estimates of land potentially available for cultivation, updated using changes in cultivated area from FAOSTAT, currently, 36.9 per cent of all potential agricultural land in the world outside the humid tropics is being cultivated.[5] Including potential agricultural land area in humid tropical areas, the figure is 33.9 per cent. Especially in South America, by Africa and Oceania only a limited part of all potential agricultural land

---

[4] The format of this section has originally been inspired by articles by C. van der Meer, 'Voedselvoorziening en Agrarische Ontwikkeling' [Food Supply and Agricultural Development] (1983) and P. van der Eng, 'Food Supply and Agricultural Development' (1992).

[5] The estimates of potential land in 2011 based on updated figures from Revel are consistent with estimates from Fischer et al. (2011).

Table 10.2: Cultivated area, potential agricultural land, pastures, woodlands, 1961–2011 (million ha)[a]

	Cultivated area[b]				Pastures and meadows				Forests and woodlands				Potential cultivated land[c]		Cultivated area as % of potential area	
													excl. humid areas I	incl. Humid areas II	I	II
	1961	1990	2000	2011	1961	1990	2000	2011	1961	1990	2000	2011	2011	2011	2011	2011
Africa	168.9	203.6	221.9	258.3	888.3	900.4	902.1	911.4	735.0	749.2	708.6	671.0	619.2	658.4	29.4	28.2
Asia[d]	437.8	507.6	511.5	517.4	624.8	780.4	856.2	823.3	591.2	560.2	554.2	578.2	480.2	558.1	51.9	48.1
Oceania (incl. Australia)	34.3	52.2	50.6	50.3	444.5	430.5	422.4	373.1	200.8	198.7	198.4	190.3	146.1	146.1	25.6	25.6
Europe[d]	151.5	138.7	131.4	123.6	89.4	82.5	77.1	72.8	142.5	155.9	163.4	170.1	188.4	188.4	39.6	39.6
North and Central America	265.0	273.1	265.4	247.2	364.2	343.3	340.9	348.7	840.7	702.5	699.1	698.4	471.5	481.5	34.4	33.9
South America[e]	68.7	109.8	119.4	144.6	372.2	442.3	456.4	463.0	950.9	946.5	904.3	860.8	370.0	624.5	28.1	18.8
(Former) USSR	239.8	228.9	207.0	204.6	302.0	327.3	360.2	361.6	913.0	849.4	850.9	851.7	377.8	377.8	35.1	35.1
World[f]	1370.6	1520.8	1514.4	1553.0	3089.7	3312.0	3419.8	3358.6	4374.2	4168.4	4085.2	4027.5	2653.2	3034.7	36.9	33.9

Notes:

[a] Total land area, excl. surface waters, comprises: 1. Cultivated area; 2. Permanent meadows and pastures; 3. Forestry and woodlands, incl. cleared woodland that has been reforested; 4. Other land, incl. roads, cities and wastelands.

[b] Cultivated area comprises 'arable land' (land planted with temporary crops, agricultural land lying fallow, land temporarily used for mowing and pasture, and land used for horticultural crops, incl. cultivation under glass), and 'land under permanent crops' (coffee, cocoa, rubber, fruit trees, nuts).

[c] Potential land for agricultural use, either including or excluding humid tropical land area. 'Humid tropical areas' refer in particular to tropical rain forests. Besides woodlands, potential land for agricultural use also includes meadows and pastures.

[d] Excl. (Former) USSR.

[e] Excl. Caribbean.

[f] Incl. Caribbean.

Sources: FAO, *FAOSTAT, Land use Database*, downloaded July, 2013. http://faostat.fao.org/site/377/default.aspx#anco, except: Forests and woodlands 1961 from FAO, *FAOSTAT, Agriculture Data, land use*, updated August 2002, http://apps.fao.org/page/collections, downloaded 2003. Potential agricultural land from Revelle (1975, Table 4), updated using changes in cultivated area 1975–2011 from FAOSTAT.

is presently being cultivated. There is still ample opportunity to increase agricultural production by taking more land into cultivation.

The potential amount of land for agricultural use is determined by such factors as climate, soil conditions and the availability of water (Revelle, 1975). Land has to be frost-free for at least one complete crop cycle. Soil conditions must meet certain standards, like permeability to water and retention of water and nutrients. The land should not be too acidic or too alkaline, neither too steep nor too rocky. On the basis of climatic and soil conditions, potential farm land globally amounts to approximately 3 billion hectares. However, water is not equally available in the different parts of the world. Only 30 per cent of the land that is potentially suitable for irrigated agriculture can be actually irrigated. Water resources are becoming increasingly stressed. Furthermore, the quality of much agricultural land not yet taken into use is so poor that huge investments are necessary before it can be cultivated. In some regions, land degradation and salinisation has reduced land quality.

Of course, expansion of the cultivated area competes with other potential forms of land use, such as forestry and woodlands, pastures for food animals, production of biofuels and land used for urban development, construction, roads and recreation. Particularly in humid tropical areas potential farmland consists to an important extent of land covered by tropical rain forests. Expansion of agricultural land results in deforestation.

The disappearance of tropical rain forests has two potentially negative effects. Tropical rain forests are the main repositories of biodiversity and forest coverage serves as storage capacity for CO_2. Deforestation may lead to decrease in biodiversity, which can pose an evolutionary threat. Decrease in CO_2 storage capacity can contribute to the greenhouse effect and global warming.

According to Boserup (1981, quoted in Barrow, 1995), 75 per cent of the cereals that have fed growing populations in developing countries between the 1930s and the 1960s came from expansion of the cultivated area. Despite the increasing costs of further land reclamation, even in recent years a considerable part of the growth of production in developing countries can be attributed to the expansion of the cultivated land area. Between 1960 and 2000, 23 per cent of the growth of total crop production was achieved through expansion of land. According to the projections for the next thirty-five years, on average 21 per cent of growth in developing countries will be realised through continued expansion of the cultivated area. Especially in Latin America land expansion will continue to be important (see Table 10.7, p. 416).

Competition between agricultural land and forest land

As explained above, the expansion of the cultivated area is an important way of increasing agricultural production in many developing countries (Dixon, 1990). Even in densely populated India, 20 per cent of production growth of cereal products in the 1970s was attributable to the expansion of agricultural land. In some parts of South America and Africa at least 80 per cent of production growth was due to the expansion of agricultural land.

Expansion of the cultivated area encroaches on land available for pasture, for dwellings, roads and urbanisation and in particular on the forest and woodland area. Though potential agricultural land has not been exhausted, alternative uses, in particular forestry, impose constraints on the unlimited expansion of cultivated area. There is a competition between agricultural and forest land.

Table 10.3 provides a first rough indication of the long-term decline of forest and woodland area on a global scale. Unfortunately, the data for 1990 and 2011 are not strictly comparable. The sources and definitions of forest cover have changed since 1994 and the later data exclude woodlands. Therefore, this table cannot provide more than a rough approximation. More consistent data for the period 1990–2011 will be presented in Table 10.3. Both statistical and other evidence points to a serious reduction in forest cover. Of Africa's 160 million hectares of tropical rain forest an annual 1.3 million hectares were being converted to agricultural land in the 1980s. The situation in the Amazon region was even more extreme: here 180,000 square kilometres of tropical rain forests were cut down every year (Leite and Furley, 1985, quoted in Dixon, 1990).

Of the four main causes of deforestation – logging, collection of fuel wood, forest fires and expansion of agricultural land – expansion of agricultural land is by far the most important. Given the vital function of the remaining tropical rain forests in preserving biodiversity and a global ecological equilibrium, it is obvious that there are drawbacks to the continued expansion of the agricultural land area at the expense of forested area.

Globally, the world has lost around 20 per cent of original forest cover since the dawn of agriculture (Goudie, 1993; Lomborg, 2001). Deforestation has a long history. For instance, Europe felled most of its forest cover after the Middle Ages to build the wooden ships that circled the globe, to provide charcoal for iron and steel production and to make way for agriculture. Table 10.3 presents estimates of the rate of deforestation between 1980 and 2011. The data since 1990 derive from the newest assessments of the FAO, using methods such as remote sensing (FAO, 2010).

In the 1990s, there was a net annual loss of natural forest – mainly the conversion of tropical forest to agricultural land – of 16 million hectares in total. Between 2000 and 2010 the net loss was 13 million hectares (FAO, 2010). Apart from deforestation, an increasingly important source of loss of natural forest is conversion to forest plantations. Plantations now account for some 7 per cent of global forest cover (FAO, 2010, Figure 7).

The figures in Table 10.3 refer to total forest cover change, which is the net result of changes in natural forests and plantations. Between 1990 and 2000 there was a net loss of total forest cover of 8.3 million hectares per year, amounting to an annual deforestation rate of 0.2 per cent. Almost all the deforestation took place in tropical areas. In Europe, Russia and North America there was hardly any change. After 2000 there was a slowdown in the rate of net deforestation to 0.13 per cent per year. The annual loss between 2000 and 2010 was 5.2 million hectares. In North America and Europe there was even a slight amount of reforestation.

The highest rates of deforestation are found in South America and Africa, where most of the world's tropical rainforests are located. In Europe (including the forest-rich Russian Federation) and North America, there is some evidence of slight reforestation. In some tropical countries there is very rapid deforestation. Among the most extreme cases are Cameroun, Nigeria, Indonesia and the Philippines, where rain forests have been disappearing at an alarming rate. Thailand and Brazil had extremely high rates of deforestation in the 1980s, but much lower rates after 1990. In the last two decades the deforestation rate in Brazil has still been 0.5 per cent per year, and Brazil alone accounts for around 30 per cent of the world's rain forests.

Apart from the empirical problems involved, estimates of the pace of deforestation depend on the definitions used (see Jepma, 1993). The FAO and the WRI define deforestation as the complete disappearance of closed or open forests and the use of the land for

Table 10.3: Deforestation, 1980–2011 (regional aggregates and selected developing countries)

Country/Area	Land area (1,000 ha) 2011	Total forest area (1,000 ha) 1980[a]	1990	2000	2011	Annual deforestation % 1980–90	1990–2000	2000–10
Africa	2,964,767	787,751.6	749,238	708,564	670,999	−0.5	−0.6	−0.5
Cameroon	47,271	26,349.7	24,316	22,116	19,696	−0.8	−0.9	−1.0
Congo, Dem. Rep.	226,705	163,605.8	160,363	157,249	153,824	−0.2	−0.2	−0.2
Nigeria	91,077	22,659.9	17,234	13,137	8,631	−2.7	−2.7	−3.7
Asia	3,093,539	619,438.6	560,209	570,164	594,205	−1.0	0.2	0.4
China	932,749		157,141	177,001	209,624		1.2	1.6
India	297,319		63,939	65,390	68,579		0.2	0.5
Indonesia	181,157	128,459.6	118,545	99,409	93,747	−0.8	−1.7	−0.5
Malaysia	32,855	25,247.2	22,376	21,591	20,369	−1.2	−0.4	−0.5
Philippines	29,817	7,641.9	6,570	7,117	7,720	−1.5	0.8	0.7
Thailand	51,089	25,181.3	19,549	19,004	18,987	−2.5	−0.3	0.0
Europe, incl. Russia	2,207,228		1,005,372	998,239	1,005,771		−0.1	0.1
Russian Federation[b]	1,637,687		809,014	809,269	809,150		0.004	−0.002
North America	1,865,166		606,474	610,333	614,543		0.1	0.1
Central America[c]	245,227	110,544.8	96,008	88,731	83,897	−1.4	−0.8	−0.5
South America[c]	1,756,239	1,089,758.7	946,454	904,322	860,770	−1.4	−0.5	−0.5
Bolivia	108,330	64,064.8	62,795	60,091	56,888	−0.2	−0.4	−0.5
Brazil	845,942	689,336.6	574,839	545,943	517,328	−1.8	−0.5	−0.5
Colombia	110,950	74,212.5	62,519	61,509	60,398	−1.7	−0.2	−0.2
Oceania	848,655		198,744	198,381	190,312		−0.02	−0.4
World	13,003,420		4,168,400	4,085,169	4,027,468		−0.2	−0.1

Notes:

[a] Forest area 1980 rough estimate applying 1980–90 annual growth rates from World Resources Institute (1990) to 1990 FAO forest area data;

[b] Russian Federation from 1992 onwards;

[c] Deforestation rates 1980s for Latin America, excl. Caribbean.

Source:

1990–2011: FAOSTAT, land use database, downloaded July 2013. 1980s: http://faostat.fao.org/site/377/DesktopDefault.aspx?PageID=377#ancor.

1980s: World Resources Institute (1990, Table 19.1: 292–3); these data refer to the early 1980s. Forest area is defined as area with crown cover of at least 20 per cent in developed countries, and at least 10 per cent in developing countries. Developing country forest area includes plantations.

other purposes (see Table 10.3).[6] Biologists, ecologists and environmentalists employ a broader definition of deforestation, which also includes serious degradation of the quality of forests and woodlands due to forestry, environmental damage and agriculture. Thus, for the 1980s, the estimates of rates of deforestation in tropical rain forests vary from an annual 0.4

---

[6] Closed forest is forest where tree crowns cover at least 20 per cent of the land area. In open forests the tree crowns cover 5–20 per cent of the land. The recent FAO data take crown cover of 20 per cent in developed countries and 10 per cent in developing countries as a cut-off point for forest cover.

per cent (FAO, 1988) to an annual 1.8 per cent (Myers, 1989). There are also great differences in the estimates of the remaining land areas covered by tropical rain forests.

An important source of disagreement is the estimate of original forest cover. The higher the estimate of original forest cover, the higher the rates of deforestation. In an interesting article based on historical research in West Africa, Leach and Fairhead (2000) have argued that original forest cover has been severely overestimated. Estimates of 'original forest cover' have simply and unrealistically assumed that the whole zone capable of supporting forests was fully forested. Also, through lack of better data, population growth rates have been taken as proxies for the rates of deforestation. The authors conclude that for Benin, Côte d'Ivoire, Ghana, Liberia, Sierra Leone and Togo, deforestation since 1900 may be one-third of that suggested by official estimates.

Firm conclusions are difficult to draw. It would seem that earlier estimates of the rate of deforestation in the range of 0.8 per cent per year are too pessimistic. The present estimate of global deforestation is 0.13 per cent per year. But, though the present estimates of worldwide deforestation are lower than earlier ones, the rate of deforestation in tropical countries gives no cause for complacency. One should realise that continuation of a deforestation rate of 0.5 per cent per year in the tropical forest cover of Africa and South America means that total tropical forest cover will be reduced by more than 9 per cent in 20 years' time.

Competition between biofuels and food production

In Table 10.1 we saw that the indexes for food production and total agricultural production were very similar. Food production was increasing slightly more rapidly than total agricultural production. This suggests that food and non-food production can increase in tandem. In recent years, there has been concern that the use of crops for biofuel – supposedly a renewable and sustainable source of energy – is starting to compete with food production. Examples of this are the use of sugar for the production of ethanol in Brazil or the use of maize for the production of biofuels. Alexandratos and Bruinsma (2012) note that in 2005 3.2 per cent of cereals, 4.8 per cent of vegetable oils, 15.1 per cent of sugar and 0.4 per cent of cassava were used for the production of biofuels. In conservative estimates these percentages are expected to increase to 6.7 per cent for cereals, 27.4 per cent for sugar, 12.6 per cent for vegetable oils and 2.3 per cent for cassava in 2030. Along with other factors, such as increasing meat consumption, the expansion of biofuels has contributed to dramatic increases in food prices. In 2007–8 there was a major hike in food prices and food prices have remained high ever since (FAO, 2013).

Land degradation

The extent to which potential agricultural land can be cultivated is affected negatively by processes of soil degradation and desertification (Barrow, 1995, Chapter 6; World Bank-WDR, 2008, Chapter 8). Soil degradation refers to the decline of soil fertility, erosion and the loss of soil organic matter. Causes of soil degradation include pollution, use of inappropriate agricultural machinery, overuse of fertiliser and deforestation (Barrow, 1995). Irrigation can also lead to soil degradation through salinisation. One assessment (Harrison, 1992, quoted in Barrow, 1995) suggests that between 1945 and 1990 12.2 million square kilometres of agricultural land suffered serious loss of productivity due to soil degradation.

Soil degradation can be among the unintended consequences of intensification of cultivation and attempts to increase yields through fertilisation and irrigation in high-potential agricultural areas. Excessive and inappropriate use of agrochemicals lead to polluted waterways. Wasteful irrigation results in unsustainable pumping of ground water.

Extensive agriculture in less-favoured areas can result in nutrient depletion, soil erosion and even desertification. Desertification is a rather ill-defined catch phrase referring to dryland and semi-arid land degradation in less-favoured agricultural areas. As the end result is 'desert-like' it is called desertification, but Barrow warns that one should not think of deserts spreading outwards. Desertification is the result of combined effects of climatic conditions and human actions, which reduce the carrying capacity of soils. Human causes of desertification include increasing population density in combination with unchanged agricultural technologies, overgrazing, deforestation and fuel wood collection. Desertification is on the increase, but the estimates vary considerably. UNEP, 1993 (quoted in Barrow, 1995) estimates that some 7–9 per cent of the world land surface may have become desertified. However, other observers suggest that desertification may have been overestimated by a factor of 3.

According to estimates based on a world soil degradation map discussed in Lomborg (2001: 104 ff.), 17 per cent of all land is degraded to some extent. But only 0.07 per cent is severely degraded. Of agricultural land some 38 per cent is affected, 20 per cent moderately, 6 per cent strongly. Lomborg estimates that degradation has resulted in a total cumulative loss of agricultural production of 5 per cent in forty-five years. This amounts to 0.1 per cent per year. Compared with the annual productivity increase of 1–2 per cent per year, he concludes that the effect of land degradation on growth of production is limited.[7] However, in certain regions such as Sub-Saharan Africa, soil degradation can be a serious problem. Here such degradation results in productivity losses of up to 1 per cent per year (Bojo, 1996; World Bank-WDR, 2008). In extensively cultivated areas of Kenya, Ethiopia and Uganda the losses are even higher.

As will be emphasised in the following sections, land degradation is not necessarily irreversible. A switch to environmentally appropriate agricultural technologies, soil conservation policies and integrated soil and water management techniques can reclaim degraded soils, though sometimes at considerable cost.

10.2.2 Intensification of land use

Prior to the nineteenth century, the growth of agricultural production was to a large extent determined by two factors: the expansion of the land area used for agriculture and the intensification of land use (see Boserup, 1965, 1981, 1990). When population increased and further expansion of the cultivated area was not possible in a given region, increasing population density resulted in more intensive techniques of land use.

In a series of pioneering publications, Ester Boserup criticised the Malthusian notion that the natural environment sets unrelenting limits to the growth of food production. Increasing population density induces changes in agricultural technology, which primarily imply a more intensive use of 'natural' resources.

Boserup distinguishes six major vegetable food supply systems, which can be ranked according to length of fallowing (Boserup, 1981: 19). These are presented in Table 10.4.

---

[7] Similar conclusions are drawn by Ruttan (2002).

Table 10.4: Systems of supply for vegetable food

System	Description	Frequency of cropping (in %)[a]
Gathering	Wild plants, roots, fruits, and nuts are gathered	0
Forest-fallow	One or two crops followed by 15–25 years' fallow	0–10
Bush-fallow[b]	Two or more crops followed by 8–10 years' fallow	10–40
Short-fallow	One or two crops followed by one or two years' fallow	40–80
Annual cropping	One crop each year with only a few months' fallow	80–100
Multicropping	Two or more crops in the same fields each year without any fallow	200–300

Notes:

[a] Frequency of cropping is average annual harvested area as percentage of cultivated plus fallow area.

[b] Bush-fallow is often deceptively referred to as 'shifting cultivation'. In fact, it is a form of sedentary agriculture, where agriculturalists with fixed dwellings alternatively work different plots of land (Hill, 1986).

Source:

Boserup (1981, Table 3.2: 19).

Box 10.2 summarises the different functions of letting land lie fallow.

BOX 10.2   Functions of fallowing

- Prevention of soil fertility exhaustion. During the period of fallow the soil recovers its fertility. Trees and bushes grow back.
- Prevention of hillside erosion, by forest fallowing.
- Controlling weed growth: bushes and trees limit the growth of weeds and grasses.
- Limiting the spread of plant diseases and pests.

As population density increases, the period the land can be left fallow becomes shorter. The functions of fallowing increasingly have to be replaced by human operations. The production process becomes more and more labour-intensive. Soil fertility is maintained by the application of animal manure and vegetable matter. Parasites or affected plants are removed by hand. Weeds are removed or ploughed under. Seeds are transplanted by hand (e.g. in rice cultivation). Ever more water is required. Water has to be transported to the fields. Also, surplus water has to be drained away. For water control and prevention of erosion, land has to be terraced and levelled, canals and irrigation works dug and maintained. All this makes for increasing inputs of labour per hectare.

Since the nineteenth century, many of these functions can also be fulfilled by industrial inputs: herbicides, pesticides, chemical fertilisers, agricultural machinery, pumps and so forth. Before the nineteenth century, intensification of land use was the most viable alternative to fallowing in Western countries. In many developing countries this is still the case. The transition from extensive to more intensive forms of cultivation involves an increasing demand for labour in agricultural production. This demand is fulfilled by increasing the number of workers per hectare or by working more hours per person per year. Rawski, for example, calculated that in the Chinese agricultural sector the number of days worked per person increased from 119 per year to 250 per year between 1949 and 1978 (Rawski, 1979). In the process of intensification, returns per hectare increase sharply as fallowing is reduced and cropping intensity increases. However, since the hours worked per person tend to increase, returns per hour worked may well decline (Boserup, 1965).

Boserup also points to the correlation between livestock breeding and population density. Meat and dairy production are inefficient ways of producing calories. Many of the calories consumed by cattle and poultry are lost in the transformation into meat and dairy products. As the population continues to grow and space becomes scarce, the number of cattle per head of the population tends to decrease.

A low population density allows wild game and cattle to thrive in its natural habitat. When land is cultivated more intensively, this becomes more difficult. But land lying fallow can be used systematically as pasture for cattle. The manure from cattle contributes to the fertility of the soil. And cattle can be used as draft animals to work the soil more intensively. When there are annual harvests, farmers have to switch to intensive livestock breeding – part of the land being used for the production of fodder crops, such as maize. Fodder may also be produced industrially or it can be imported from regions with lower population densities. As land is cultivated more intensively, the share of animal food in the diet has tended to decline in pre-modern times.

Boserup (1981: 23) combines intensification of animal husbandry and intensification of agriculture in a typology consisting of seven systems of food supply, ranked according to increasing population density (see Box 10.3).

BOX 10.3 : Typology of systems of food supply

1. Hunting-gathering systems.
2. (Nomadic) pastoralism.
3. Forest-fallow.
4. Bush-fallow.
5. Short-fallow with domestic animals.
6. Annual harvesting with intensive animal husbandry.
7. Multicropping with little animal food.

This classification by density primarily applies to societies at lower technological levels. After the onset of industrialisation from the eighteenth century onwards, the correlations between population density and systems of food supply became weaker. At higher technological levels, a society has the option of producing fodder industrially or transporting it over long distances. Presently, the demand for animal food is increasing in densely populated countries such as Indonesia or China, as people strive to enrich their diets.

The transition from the first two systems of food supply to sedentary systems of cultivation first took place some 10,000 years ago. It is one of the fundamental technological transitions in the history of mankind (see Diamond, 1998; Goudsblom, 1992). In the agricultural history of pre-industrial Europe, England was the technological leader. Between the ninth and the fourteenth century the three-course rotation system was introduced. For two consecutive years, different cereal crops would be grown on one piece of land. In the third year, the land would lie fallow. Fallow land was used in common to let domestic cattle graze, the droppings of the cattle serving as manure. The cattle provided animal traction for tillage. In the eighteenth century there was a transition to annual harvesting. This is sometimes referred to as the 'agricultural revolution', but this term disregards the gradual nature of the process of intensification. The system of annual harvesting was characterised by crop rotation, the introduction of new root crops such as the potato, reserving part of the land for production of cattle fodder and a systematic use of manure.

In the course of the nineteenth century a second agricultural revolution took place, which resulted in farmers applying industrially produced chemical inputs and agricultural machinery. For the first time, the inputs came from outside the agricultural sector. Further, there was greater specialisation in agricultural production, and foodstuffs were often imported from abroad. This second 'agricultural revolution' falls outside the scope of the process of intensification analysed by Boserup.

In the course of the intensification process the demand for labour increased in the agricultural sector. The transition to annual harvests also involved a reinforcement of individual rights to land (of ownership or use), and increased investment in agriculture (Hayami and Ruttan, 1985: 46). Previously, fallow land had been in common use for cattle grazing. Intensification, however, demanded a more precise delimitation of ownership rights (cf. North and Thomas, 1973). The so-called 'enclosure' movement, which took place in England from the second half of the seventeenth century onwards involved fierce social conflicts between villagers who were losing their rights to graze cattle on the commons and (large) landowners who were trying to gain exclusive rights of ownership. Frequently, the acquired ownership titles were used for sheep raising. Currently similar processes are taking place in Africa and Asia, where communal rights to land are gradually and slowly being transformed into individual ownership titles. In the modern debates on land reform, defining and establishing individual ownership titles to land is seen as the key route to enhanced competitiveness and productivity of smallholder agriculture (World Bank-WDR, 2008).

From Boserup's analysis various lessons can be derived that may deepen our understanding of agricultural issues in developing countries. These are summarised in Box 10.4.

BOX 10.4 Lessons from the Boserupian analysis

- Intensification of agriculture requires hard work on the part of farmers.
- Much of our 'natural' environment is not natural.
- Intensification of agriculture requires greater inputs of labour.
- The concept of 'disguised unemployment' needs to be re-evaluated.
- Production per hectare may increase sharply as a result of intensification.
- New inputs can contribute to further intensification.
- Food aid can provide disincentives to production in developing countries.
- Low population density may be a disadvantage for agricultural development since a minimum degree of density is required to support infrastructural investment.

Intensification requires hard work

As long as sufficient land is available for more extensive agriculture, this will be the preferred option. Farmers will only switch to more intensive methods of agricultural production when extensive methods become unsustainable due to increased population density. The sufficient availability of land may, for example, provide an explanation for disappointing results of irrigation projects in Northeast Thailand. Farmers preferred to migrate to other areas, rather than participate in intensive irrigated agriculture (Dixon, 1990; Van der Meer, 1981; Wiggins, 2000).

How natural is the natural environment?

The natural environment is the result of centuries of interaction between people and their environments. The characteristics of the natural environment change under the influence of human interventions and actions. These may result in deforestation or reforestation, erosion or land reclamation, the creation of polders below sea level, desertification or irrigation. This approach puts the whole notion of fixed Malthusian limits to production in a different perspective.

Intensification and labour input

Higher labour input can take the form of more persons employed, longer hours worked, or both. Intensification also requires increasing investment in infrastructure and water control, which demands further inputs of labour.

Disguised unemployment?

The previous point implies a criticism of the notion of 'disguised unemployment' in agriculture. During peak periods in the agricultural cycle, such as sowing or harvesting, there is often an acute shortage of labour, rather than a surplus. This is particularly true for densely populated areas where multicropping and other forms of intensive agriculture are practised. (The assumption of low productivity per hour worked still seems to be justified.)

Intensification as a source of agricultural growth

The shift from extensive to intensive systems of agriculture is an important source of agricultural growth.

New inputs can result in further intensification

Nowadays, inputs from outside the agricultural sector, such as new seeds, chemical fertilisers, pesticides or herbicides are available. These inputs, together with investments in water control and agricultural infrastructure, contribute to further intensification of agriculture.

Food aid can provide disincentives for production

Subsidised food imports or food aid from economically advanced regions such as the European Union or the USA have negative effects on the development of agricultural production and productivity in developing countries. They form a powerful disincentive for agricultural development and allow developing countries to postpone the difficult and backbreaking process of agricultural intensification (Boserup, 1983).

Disadvantages of low population density

Without infrastructural investment, e.g. in water control or land preparation, it is hard to intensify agriculture. If there is rapid population growth in countries with low initial population densities, farmers may continue to use extensive methods of agriculture, in spite of diminishing supplies of land. Fallow periods are too short to allow the land to regenerate. The continuation of extensive agricultural practices may thus result in serious land degradation. A vicious circle arises in which the increase in agricultural production lags behind population growth. Circumstances like this seem to apply in several countries in Sub-Saharan Africa.

Cropping intensity

Intensification of agriculture manifests itself in increasing cropping intensities. Table 10.5 presents empirical data on cropping intensity by region.

A cropping intensity of one means that there is one harvest per year on any given plot of land. Table 10.5 illustrates the huge differences in cropping intensity between irrigated and non-irrigated land. Irrigation allows for far higher cropping intensities. Cropping intensity in Asia is much higher than in Sub-Saharan Africa and Latin America, for both irrigated and non-irrigated areas. Highest cropping intensities are found in East (and Southeast) Asia, and in particular in China. Over time, cropping intensities have been increasing in all regions. FAO projections up until 2030 indicate that there is still ample scope for further intensification, especially in irrigated areas. But the latest projections till 2050 indicate that after 2030 the opportunities for further intensification are diminishing for the developing world.

10.2.3 Increasing yields per harvest

The third and most important source of agricultural growth lies in increased yields per harvested crop. Increased returns can be generated through labour-saving mechanisation, which reduces crop losses through efficiency gains or allows for closer planting. But the most import sources of yield improvement are increased irrigation, the use of chemical and organic fertilisers, the use of chemical and other scientific methods of pest control and the development of new seeds with higher productivity. We will discuss increases in yields in more detail in the sections on the green revolution (section 10.2.5) and biotechnology (section 10.2.6). Here, we focus on the contributions of irrigation.

Irrigation

Irrigation contributes both to increased frequency of cropping (see Table 10.5) and to increased returns per crop. In some areas, irrigation allows crops to grow in areas, where there is insufficient rainfall for rain-fed crop production. In other areas, irrigation makes it possible to have more than one harvest per year, for example in rice production. Irrigation also contributes to higher yields. Without a well-regulated water supply new varieties with higher returns per harvest cannot flourish.

Table 10.6 provides information on irrigation intensity. The table shows that there is a steady growth of irrigation intensity in all regions.[8] The table also illustrates the large

---

[8] In China the percentage of land irrigated declined between 1980 and 2000 because cultivated area grew more rapidly than irrigated area. This trend was reversed after 2000.

Table 10.5: Cropping intensity, developing countries, 1974–2050[a]

	Non-irrigated					Irrigated					Total		
	1974–6	1982–4	1997–9	2030	2050	1974–6	1982–4	1997–9	2030	2050	1997–9	2030	2050
Sub-Saharan Africa	0.51	0.54	0.67	0.75		1.03	0.84	0.86	1.02		0.68	0.76	
Near East/North Africa	0.56	0.62	0.72	0.78		0.82	0.98	1.02	1.12		0.81	0.90	
Latin America and Caribbean	0.59	0.59	0.60	0.68		0.92	1.02	0.86	1.00		0.63	0.71	
Far East total			1.13	1.16				1.38	1.52		1.21	1.30	
South Asia			1.03	1.09				1.24	1.37		1.11	1.21	
India			1.06	1.06				1.29	1.40		1.14	1.21	
East Asia			1.20	1.22				1.54	1.69		1.30	1.39	
China			1.40	1.58				1.65	1.83		1.54	1.67	
Far East, excl. China	1.02	1.00	1.01	1.03		1.18	1.29	1.24	1.36		1.06	1.16	
Total developing countries, excl. China			0.76	0.81				1.14	1.27		0.83	0.90	
Total developing countries, excl. China and India			0.70	0.77	0.81			1.05	1.19	1.25	0.75	0.83	
Total developing countries	0.71	0.71	0.83	0.87	0.87	1.07	1.18	1.27	1.41	1.41	0.93	0.99	0.98

Note:

[a] Ratio of the annually harvested area to total arable land area in use.

Sources:

1974–6: FAO (1981), Annex Table 9 (90 developing countries, excl. China); 1982–4: Alexandratos (1988: 130) (93 developing countries, excl. China); 1997–2030: Bruinsma (2003: 145), table 4.8, incl. projections for 2030; 2050: Alexandratos and Bruinsma (2012, Table 4.9).

Table 10.6: Irrigated area, developing countries, 1961–2011

	Irrigated area (1,000 ha)					Irrigated area (%)[a]				
	1961	1980	1990	2000	2011	1961	1980	1990	2000	2011
Sub-Saharan Africa	2,007	3,207	4,093	5,162	5,406	1.5	2.1	2.5	2.9	2.6
South Africa	808	1,128	1,200	1,498	1,601	6.6	8.9	9.2	10.6	12.9
Latin America and Caribbean	8,242	13,651	16,686	19,033	22,479	8.0	9.6	11.1	11.8	12.0
North Africa/West Asia[b]	9,210	12,232	17,616	20,264	21,502	12.5	15.0	20.9	23.2	24.5
South Asia	44,615	65,492	79,306	95,511	106,605	20.9	29.2	34.6	41.3	46.0
India	25,945	40,835	49,500	60,432	66,750	16.1	24.3	29.2	35.2	39.3
East Asia[c]	46,361	50,898	52,639	56,625	68,713	42.0	48.0	38.3	41.1	52.4
China	45,206	48,850	50,157	54,201	66,384	43.0	48.7	38.2	41.0	52.6
Southeast Asia	8,049	11,603	14,886	18,945	22,661	11.8	14.8	16.4	20.1	20.6
Far East total	99,025	127,993	146,831	171,081	197,979	25.3	31.3	32.1	36.9	41.8
Developing countries total	118,484	157,083	185,226	215,540	247,366	16.8	20.0	21.6	24.2	25.8

Notes:

[a] Total area equipped for irrigation as percentage of cultivated area.

[b] West Asia, excl. Armenia, Azerbaijan, Georgia and Israel.

[c] East Asia, excl. Japan.

Source:

FAOSTAT *Agriculture Data, land use*, downloaded July 2013, http://faostat.fao.org/site/377/DesktopDefault.aspx? PageID=377#ancor.

differences between low irrigation intensities in Africa and Latin America, and high irrigation intensities in Asia. In East Asia irrigation intensity reached 52.4 per cent in 2011, in Sub-Saharan Africa it stood at 2.6 per cent. In 2011, 25.8 per cent of all agricultural land in developing countries was irrigated. But the contribution of irrigated land to agricultural growth is far greater than indicated by its share of land.

There are great differences in the quality of irrigation systems, which are not reflected in the FAO statistics. Irrigation systems vary from simple traditional techniques to large-scale modern systems (Van der Eng, 1993, Chapter 3). Also the area actually irrigated can be substantially lower than the area equipped for irrigation. The potential to expand irrigation has not yet been exhausted.

Unequal availability of water does set a limit to continued expansion of irrigation. Many of the locations most suited to irrigation, like river deltas, are already irrigated. (Alexandratos, 1988; Alexandratos and Bruinsma, 2012; Dixon, 1990). Further expansion is technically possible, but it is not always economically profitable to do so. Also there is increasing scarcity of water, especially in irrigated areas. Many farmers in developing countries will remain dependent on rain-fed agriculture. Also, part of the existing irrigated area is lost due to salinisation, when too much ground water is withdrawn, waterlogging and inadequate maintenance of irrigation facilities (Ruttan, 2002).

In 2005–7 around 53 per cent of land with irrigation potential in developing countries (estimated at 413 million hectares) is irrigated in some form or other (Alexandratos and Bruinsma, 2012, Figure 4.7). Irrigated area in developing countries is projected to increase by some 20 million hectares until 2050, which means that the rate of expansion of irrigated area is slowing down compared to the past thirty years.

One of the pressing concerns of recent years is whether there is enough water supply on a global scale. Fresh water in use for irrigation may compete with other uses such as drinking, hygiene or sanitation. Countries with the least rainfall are also the countries in greatest need of irrigation. Countries where irrigation withdraws more than 20 per cent of water resources are considered to be in danger of water scarcity (Ruttan, 2002). In 2005–7 the Near East/North Africa was already using 52 per cent of its water resources, South Asia was using 40 per cent. In other regions the pressure on water resources was much lower (Alexandratos and Bruinsma, 2012, Table 4.11). One of the ways to defer the advent of water scarcity is to increase irrigation efficiency, which is presently still at around 50 per cent worldwide.

10.2.4   Models of agricultural development

In their authoritative study *Agricultural Development: An International Perspective* (1971, 1985), Hayami and Ruttan distinguish five models of agricultural development: the resource exploitation model; the conservation model; the urban industrial impact model; the diffusion model; and the high-payoff input model. Three of these models – the resource exploitation model; the conservation model and the high-payoff input model – are directly related to the three ways of expanding agricultural output discussed in the previous section: expansion of land, crop intensification and increased yields per harvest. But the models place more emphasis on the mechanisms operating in agricultural growth and development. They also clarify the distinction between the increase in returns per harvested crop and more traditional ways of expanding production.

The resource exploitation model

The resource exploitation model corresponds to the process of expanding the cultivated agricultural area as described in section 10.2.1. During most of agricultural history, expansion of the cultivated area was the prime method to expand total production. In *frontier societies* like the USA, the frontier of the cultivated area expanded westwards at the expense of Indian hunter-gatherers and nomadic pastoralists. Hayami and Ruttan also include the vent for surplus model – discussed in Chapter 8 – under the heading 'resource exploitation'. According to the vent for surplus model, farmers reacted to the increasing demand for primary products after the middle of the nineteenth century by taking hitherto uncultivated land into use. As explained above, this route to growth of production has not yet been exhausted, but in different parts of the world the limits to further expansion of cultivated area are becoming visible.

The conservation model

In the transition to annual crops in eighteenth-century England, animal manure and organic wastes came to play an important role in maintaining soil fertility. The inputs into the agricultural system were all supplied from within the agricultural sector.

On the basis of this agricultural system in England, German agronomists in particular developed the concept of soil exhaustion. In the conservation model the development of agricultural production involves a struggle to maintain the fertility of the soils. Whatever is taken out of the soil has to be put back in later on. If one continues to add other production factors to limited amounts of land without soil conservation, agriculture will sooner or later run into diminishing returns.

This is a rather static perspective in which nature sets limits to agricultural production. However, Boserup's theory indicates that soil fertility and conservation can also be seen in a more dynamic perspective. By more intensive cultivation of the land, increasing returns per hectare may be realised without any loss of soil fertility. Nevertheless, Hayami and Ruttan include Boserup's theory in the conservation model, because the inputs into agriculture are forthcoming from within the agricultural sector itself in a self-sustaining system. The provision of agricultural inputs by the industrial sector dates from after the 'second agricultural revolution' in the nineteenth century.

The urban industrial impact model

The urban industrial impact model in its modern form was formulated by Theodor W. Schultz (1953). Schultz argued that productivity, agricultural incomes and growth of production are highest close to urban centres. This is because product markets and markets for factors of production function better in the vicinity of areas with rapid urban and industrial development. This leads to a more efficient allocation of production factors in agriculture.

Hayami and Ruttan consider the empirical evidence for this relationship to be inconclusive and its relevance for poorer developing countries rather limited.[9] A possible policy implication for developing countries would be to spread urbanisation and industry as much as possible over an entire country. This would be preferable to the growth of mega-cities. Decentralisation of urbanisation and rural industrialisation would intensify the linkages between agriculture and industry, which are positive for agricultural growth.

Irrespective of whether the distance to urban centres is really important, the degree to which agricultural markets contribute to efficient allocation is of obvious significance to agricultural development (Ellis, 1988: 75). With respect to West Africa, Hill argues that in some regions rural markets actually function quite well. One should not confuse production for the market with urbanisation (Hill, 1986). Lal and Myint (1996) speak of institutional underdevelopment, when lack of transport infrastructure, lack of information and inadequate channels of distribution isolate farmers from wider markets and stifle incentives to increase productivity. The Chinese agricultural reforms after 1978 provide a prime example of how improved functioning of agricultural markets contributed to very rapid growth of output and productivity between 1978 and 1985 (Huang, 1998).[10]

Presently, connecting isolated smallholder producers to national and global markets is seen as one of the most important routes towards agricultural progress (World Bank-WDR,

---

[9] However, see Wiggins (2000), who argues on the basis of case studies that proximity to large urban centres provides market access and contributes to agricultural development.

[10] After 1985, agricultural growth slowed down to a respectable 3.8 per cent per year, down from 7.4 per cent in the earlier period. New debates arose between proponents of further market reforms and proponents of reimposition of central planning.

2008). Global value chains offer opportunities for the production and sale of high-value agricultural crops (coffee, vegetables, fruit, flowers). Connecting smallholder producers to national markets provides incentives for higher productivity. Connecting smallholders to markets requires both infrastructural investment and a variety of institutional reforms, such as land reform, well-defined rights to land and better organisation of producers to achieve economies of scale in sales and marketing.

The diffusion model

There are huge differences in agricultural technology and productivity between countries, but also within countries, regions, and even between different farmers in the same village. The diffusion model takes such differences as its point of departure. International and national diffusion of the most advanced technologies can help narrow the gap between 'best practice' and the average farmer. *Inter alia*, the possibilities of transfer to developing countries of agricultural technologies developed in Western countries feature in the model.

The policy implications of this model include a strong emphasis on the construction of systems of agricultural extension and education. In many economically advanced countries (e.g. the Netherlands and the USA) there are highly developed networks of agricultural education and extension, which allow for very rapid diffusion of new agricultural technologies. Using the terminology of Chapter 4, these countries have very effective agricultural innovation systems. In many developing countries substantial efforts have been made to build up systems of agricultural extension, and there is widespread agreement on the fact that such extension is one of the important building blocks of successful agricultural development.

Nevertheless, the diffusion model can also be criticised. An important assumption of the model is that the reason why farmers do not adopt new production technologies is that they are ignorant or ill informed. This assumption is by no means justified. Farmers in developing countries are often better informed about local economic, ecological and social conditions than the extension workers sent out to educate them. According to Schultz (1964, 1968), farmers work quite efficiently and rationally, given the difficult conditions of their existence. They are poor but efficient.

Often, new seeds and agricultural techniques that perform well in laboratories, or model farms turn out to be less successful in the field. They are insufficiently adapted to local conditions. This is especially the case when technologies and seeds developed in the West are transferred to developing countries. Farmers are justified in treating innovations with a healthy degree of suspicion.

With the introduction of new varieties, numerous 'secondary functions' of existing varieties – provision of hay, fodder, building materials, fuel and so forth – are often forgotten. Also, traditional agricultural practices tend to minimise risk, which is of great importance to the survival of small farmers. In recent years, it is argued that agricultural innovation should try to build on existing local practices.

High-payoff input model

The high-payoff input model finds its inspiration in the work of Theodor Schultz (1964). As mentioned above, Schultz maintained that traditional farmers act rationally. Given the conditions in which they have to operate, they allocate their resources optimally. Within the constraints of a traditional economy there are not many opportunities to realise increases in output and productivity.

Schultz therefore argued for new inputs coming from outside the agricultural sector to be made available to farmers with government support and subsidies. In this approach, the emphasis was on stimulating technological progress which was adapted to local circumstances, the development of high-yielding varieties of maize, wheat and rice with high returns per harvest, and the search for the optimal conditions under which the new varieties would flourish. These conditions included the application of chemical fertilisers, chemical pesticides, irrigation and water control.

Schultz and his numerous followers argued in favour of investment in the following areas:

1. *Agricultural research centres* producing new, well-adapted, technical knowledge.
2. *Industrial activities oriented towards agriculture*. The industrial sector should develop and produce new agricultural inputs and supply them to farmers.
3. *Agricultural education and extension activities*, which help farmers to apply the technologies and use the new inputs.

The high-payoff input model incorporates the preceding three models – conservation, urban industrial impact and diffusion. The new inputs contribute to maintaining soil fertility when land use is intensified. Well-functioning factor and product markets are a prerequisite for the adequate utilisation of new inputs and technologies. Where small peasants have insufficient access to new inputs due to market imperfections, cheap agricultural credit should be made available. Attention should also be paid to transport infrastructure and the development of market systems through which agricultural surpluses can be traded. Schooling and agricultural extension are explicitly included in the high-payoff input approach, as in the diffusion model. However, in the high-payoff input model there is much more emphasis on adapting new technologies to local conditions. The name of the model, finally, refers to the positive relationship between investments in agricultural research, schooling and extension and the high returns of the new inputs. According to Schultz, the returns to agricultural investment in research, development and extension are even higher than returns to investment in industry.

Theory of induced technological development

According to Hayami and Ruttan, even Schultz's high-payoff input model has its limitations. Insufficient attention is paid to the direction of technological development and the process of institutional change. Technological development does not happen in a vacuum. Its course is influenced among other things by the relative scarcity of factors of production. If the market prices of production factors reflect their relative scarcity, farmers will prefer technologies that economise on the most scarce production factors. If agricultural research institutions are responsive to farmers' needs and preferences and there are effective interactions between farmers, research institutions and industrial producers of agricultural inputs, farmers' preferences for certain types of technological development will be translated into research programmes and in production plans of suppliers of agricultural inputs. The responsiveness of R&D institutions to local farmers' needs is an institutional characteristic.

The innovation systems literature has criticised the linear perspective of science-based technological progress, emphasising the importance of user involvement. The recent literature on institutional change emphasises the importance of bringing farmers' voices into decision making on agricultural R&D (World Bank-WDR, 2008). Thus the process of institutional development in the field of research, development and agricultural extension is also an important determinant of the nature and appropriateness of technological development.

Where research institutions are responsive to producers' needs, a relative scarcity of labour will induce labour-saving technological development. This has been the path followed in the USA and also in England since the late nineteenth century. Where labour is plentiful and land is scarce, technological development in a responsive research environment will be directed in a land-saving direction. Examples of the land-saving path of technological development include the Netherlands, Denmark, late nineteenth-century Japan, and Taiwan between 1900 and 1940.

Land-saving technology includes:

1. *Biological technology*, in particular selective breeding of plants, development of new varieties. In past decades, genetic modification techniques have been added to the arsenal of biotechnology.
2. *Chemical technology*, including organic and inorganic fertilisers that add nutrients for plant growth to the soil, and pesticides and herbicides.
3. Development of *land and water control*.

Hayami and Ruttan point to the fact that the process of induced technological change is not a gradual process – even under the best of conditions – but rather a succession of dynamic disequilibria. It is comparable to the process of 'unbalanced growth' analysed by Hirschman and discussed in Chapter 9. Changes in relative scarcity and changes in technology can also induce changes in agricultural institutions, such as large landownership, communal ownership, tenure relationships, market characteristics, credit institutions and the organisation of research and extension.

The theory of induced technological development links up economic analysis with the analysis of institutions. Nevertheless, Hogg (2000) has criticised this theory from an evolutionary perspective. The theory states that if institutions are open and flexible the scarcity of different factors of production will influence the direction of research. Hogg argues that this neglects the historical context of path dependence. Once a research system evolves in a certain direction, it gets locked into this path and change will be difficult. Hogg argues that there are environmentally more sustainable alternatives to the present emphasis on yield improvement through biotechnological change which are not sufficiently explored because of lock-in.

10.2.5   The green revolution: increase in yields per harvest

The high-payoff input model is closely related to the third way of increasing agricultural production mentioned in section 9.2: increasing returns per harvested crop.[11] This model is often also called the 'green revolution'. The green revolution refers to breakthroughs in research into new varieties of maize, wheat and rice which – together with a set of complementary inputs – have resulted in dramatic increases in the yields per harvest. When new varieties shorten the crop cycle from sowing to harvesting, the green revolution also allows more crops per year and thus contributes to further intensification of agriculture and

[11] Diffusion of technology, more intensive production and more efficient allocation can also take place within more traditional agricultural systems. These 'models' are not necessarily associated with recent technological breakthroughs in agriculture.

BOX 10.5 : **Characteristics of the green revolution**

- Development of new plant varieties with high yields that have been adjusted to local conditions.
- Use of industrially manufactured fertilisers, pesticides, and herbicides.
- Land-saving innovations.
- Increased volume of – relatively cheap – investments in agricultural research; a positive attitude towards science-based agriculture.
- Organisation of an effective system of agricultural extension.
- Investments in irrigation and water control.
- Development of delivery systems for new seeds and inputs.
- Development of credit institutions and facilities, which enable farmers to purchase the new inputs.
- Complementarities between the different inputs: research, new seeds, industrial inputs, irrigation, education and extension, delivery and credit facilities.

increase of output per unit of land. The characteristics of the green revolution are summarised in Box 10.5.

The complementarities between all these so-called 'non-conventional inputs' form one of the most basic characteristics of the green revolution. When some elements of the package are lacking, the potential increases in yields will not be realised.

The green revolution is associated with two well-known institutes for agricultural research: the International Rice Research Institute (IRRI) founded in 1960 in Los Baños in the Philippines and the International Maize and Wheat Improvement Centre (Centro Internacional de Mejoramiento de Maíz y Trigo, CIMMYT) in Mexico. In the 1950s, the CIMMYT developed high-productive varieties of maize and wheat. The new Mexican wheat varieties were highly sensitive to fertiliser use, not very sensitive to sunlight, more resistant to diseases and with shorter stems. The success of wheat research promoted research into rice varieties. In the 1960s, new varieties of rice were developed at the IRRI. The work at these institutes was initially financed by the Rockefeller Foundation. Since 1971 it has been financed and supervised by the CGIAR (Consultative Group on International Agricultural Research, see Colman and Nixson, 1986: 217; Oasa, 1987). In 2008–9 the CGIAR underwent major reforms. The consultative group was transformed into an independent international organisation, the Consortium of International Agricultural Research Centers, retaining the old name (see www.cgiar.org). Today the CGIAR supervises the work of an international network of fifteen agricultural research institutes.

The initial technological breakthroughs led to dramatically increased yields per crop. The dwarf wheat varieties introduced in India in 1965 had yields of 4,450 kilogrammes per hectare on experimental plots, compared to yields of 1,200 kilogrammes per hectare for older varieties. Outside experimental stations yields of 3,200 kilogrammes per hectare were also quite impressive (Dixon, 1990). Also the rapid maturing of dwarf varieties allowed for more harvests per year. The enthusiasm about these breakthroughs was translated into political rhetoric by the term 'green revolution'. This term suggests that technological breakthroughs might lessen the need for fundamental social reorganisation and prevent the rise of revolutionary movements.

In rice production there were green revolutions long before the 1950s and 1960s: in medieval China, in Japan between 1881 and 1920, Taiwan between 1900 and 1940 and Korea in the 1920s. The early varieties developed by IRRI were based on genetic materials drawn from China, Taiwan, Japan and Indonesia. Semi-dwarf wheat originated in Japan in the 1800s (Parayil, 1992). In their famous article 'The Role of Agriculture in Economic Development' Johnston and Mellor (1961) analysed the rapid increase in agricultural production and productivity in Japanese agriculture between 1881 and 1920. According to their estimates, production increased by 77 per cent, while the area of land used for agriculture was expanded by only 21 per cent. The yields per hectare increased by 46 per cent, per capita food production by 20 per cent. The Japanese example shows how technological developments of a mainly biological nature can lead to substantial increases in yields per hectare and per head of the population in a densely populated area (Van der Meer and Yamada, 1990: 73 ff.). Nevertheless, the sudden increases in productivity achieved in the research institutes in the 1950s and 1960s had the character of a technological breakthrough.

In India new wheat seeds were introduced in 1965, of which the yields per hectare were far in excess of the yields of traditional varieties. New rice varieties were introduced in the Philippines in 1966 and spread rapidly to different Asian countries. By 1970 the new strains were being cultivated over an area of 10 million hectares. Within a few years Pakistan ceased to be dependent on food imports from the USA and India became self-sufficient in food.

The success of the green revolution in the 1960s and the euphoria that followed gave rise to a wave of criticism. Part of this concerned technical matters. Outside the experimental fields and laboratory conditions yields of newly developed varieties were often disappointing. The seeds performed poorly under less than optimum conditions (Glaeser, 1987; Griffin, 1976; Pearse, 1977). The new varieties were susceptible to diseases, pests and weather conditions. They were not sufficiently adjusted to local conditions. Chambers (1983) argued that often valuable local knowledge and insights were lost due to international research programmes and their recommendations. Dixon gives an interesting example of the rejection by farmers of a new, fast-growing variety of sorghum in Ethiopia. The new variety grew faster but had fewer stems and leaves than existing varieties. Stems and leaves were traditionally used as roofing material and fodder. Agricultural researchers had neglected the secondary functions of sorghum (Dixon, 1990: 97). Furthermore, critics pointed to the dangers of the loss in genetic diversity due to the introduction of several standardised varieties (*genetic erosion*). Diversity acts as an insurance policy against natural calamities, climatic influences and plant diseases. The new production techniques were claimed to have various environmental hazards (Barrow, 1995). Topsoils were eroded due to intensive use. The use of nitrogenous fertilisers resulted in eutrophication of freshwater streams and lakes. Pesticides created health problems and pests were increasingly becoming resistant. Applications of fertiliser ran into diminishing returns (Glaeser, 1987; Oasa, 1987; Ramani and Thutupalli, 2013). Finally, it was claimed that the nutritional value of new varieties, particularly of rice, was lower than that of traditional varieties and food crops.

Technical problems and criticisms gave rise to the search for technical solutions: developing disease-resistant plants, better adjustment to local conditions, setting up gene banks, biological pest control, integrated pest management, improved nitrogen absorption of new varieties and so forth. In response to criticisms, new agricultural research institutes were founded, focusing on specific crops, climatic conditions or problems. According to Oasa (1987) there was a shift from the search for new breakthroughs to a second generation of research of a more incremental nature.

In the newer approaches there is more emphasis on the ecological consequences of new technologies and new approaches such as the *farming systems approach* try to integrate ecological, social and technological factors. Attempts are made to adapt existing traditional technologies and practices to present-day requirements. Since 1972 there is a specialised research institute for crops in the semi-arid tropics (ICRISAT) in Hyderabad, India. In 1976, ICARDA (the International Centre for Agricultural Research in the Dry Areas) was founded in Beirut. Since 1974, the International Board for Plant Genetic Resources (IBPGR) has focused on genetic diversity. For various crops and kinds of livestock there are specialised research institutes located in different parts of the world.[12] In the international research effort there are also attempts to focus on technologies which are useful and feasible for smaller resource poor-farmers.

The *2008 World Development Report* on *Agriculture for Development* even calls for a shift to a broader concept of agricultural innovation which combines the focus on productivity increases with a more comprehensive farm management approach. This approach also pays attention to reversing soil degradation through better farming practices, increasing the efficiency of water use in the light of water scarcity and reducing the use of pesticides, herbicides and fertilisers.

The most fundamental criticisms of the green revolution are of a political-economy nature (Glaeser, 1987; Griffin, 1976, 1981; Pearse, 1977; Pinstrup-Anderson, 1982; Pinstrup-Anderson and Hazell, 1985). These criticisms state that the introduction of the green revolution leads to increased rural inequality, increased landlessness and to impoverishment of the rural masses. The criticisms include the elements outlined in Box 10.6.

BOX 10.6 : Political economy criticisms of the green revolution

- **Large farmers have better access to new inputs than small peasants**. The green revolution therefore makes for more inequality. First, large farmers have financial reserves, which they can use to purchase expensive new inputs. Second, they have relationships and contacts with government officials and agricultural extension institutions. They have easier access to cheap loans, information and water supplies (Bol, 1983; Cassen, 1978).
- **The position of small peasants is threatened by the increasing cost of inputs**. Thus, the green revolution increases rural inequality and landlessness. Sometimes poor peasants are not dispossessed of land, but are forced to lease out their lands to rich farmers and work on these lands as farm labourers.

---

[12] These institutes include the International Potato Centre in Peru, the International Livestock Centre for Africa in Ethiopia and the West African Rice Development Association in Monrovia, Liberia.

- When **prices fall due to increases in total production**, small peasants who were unable to apply the new technologies will be worse off. This is also conducive to inequality.
- Due to their economic power, **large landowners pay too little for their production factors of land and capital**. For example, they have access to subsidised credit so they will use too capital-intensive methods. Large farmers tend to employ less farm labour and try to get out from under traditional sharecropping arrangements. All these factors together make for increasing landlessness, concentration of landownership and rural unemployment (for example, in India, see Singh, 1982).
- Farmers in developing countries become more and more dependent on a few **agricultural MNCs**, which have a monopoly on the provision of new seed varieties.
- Production for export may have negative effects on **women's allocation of time and energy**. The best plots of land are reserved for cash crops, which are often cultivated by males. Food production is shifted to land of marginal quality, often located far from the household dwelling.
- The green revolution involves **increasing production for the market and exports**. According to the critics, it is conceivable that an increase in production per hectare goes hand in hand with decreased availability of food in a given region, especially when the landless labourers have insufficient means to buy food. Thus, the green revolution may lead to impoverishment and malnutrition.

These criticisms provide some valuable insights. Introduction of technological changes, with no regard for power relationships, class structures and institutions, may result in reinforced dualism and increasing inequality. However, in some cases the initially even-handed critical analysis of the green revolution by authors like Griffin was replaced by outright ideological rejection in the 1970s and 1980s. The green revolution came to be seen as an international conspiracy of capitalist agribusiness at the expense of human values and food requirements in developing countries.

In reply to the often one-sided criticisms of the green revolution, numerous counter-arguments have been put forward (see, for example Ellis, 1988; Evenson and Gollin, 2003; Hayami and Ruttan, 1985; Hazell, 2010; Paarlberg, 2010; Pinstrup-Anderson, 1985).

First, the argument of critics is often fragmentary, based on case studies rather than aggregates. There is a tendency, especially among anthropologists, to idealise traditional agricultural systems. Second, technological change is an absolute must when population is increasing rapidly. If technology does not change and population increases rapidly, marginal returns to agricultural efforts will decrease. This inevitably results in a decrease in food availability per head of the population. The green revolution has in fact averted famine in India and China (Ruttan, 2004). In China, new rice technologies helped lift 200 million people out of poverty (Huang and Rozelle, 1996).

Critics like Griffin remarked that there were no significant differences in production trends before and after the introduction of new varieties. Therefore, they concluded that the outcomes of the new technologies were rather disappointing. Hayami and Ruttan (1985), however, note that this argument contains serious logical flaws. One should not compare the situation before and after the introduction of new varieties, since population density is changing over time. What one should compare is the productivity trend with a growing population *without* technological change and the productivity trend with population growth *with* technological change. In absence of new technologies, per capita production and production per hectare would have been much lower than is presently the case.

It is true that larger farmers usually introduce new varieties sooner than small peasants. After some years, however, there is usually a diffusion of the new technologies to other categories of farmers. Small farmers and peasants also start to adopt the new varieties and apply the new technologies. There is nothing intrinsically capital-intensive about the green revolution (Hayami and Ruttan, 1985; Ruttan, 2004). It can be applied just as well on small as on large farms. In Asia, the use of small seeds has effectively spread to smallholder farmers, increasing their productivity and earnings (World Bank-WDR, 2008).

Finally, growth of agricultural production due to new technologies has resulted in lower prices for food. Between 1965 and 2000, grain prices declined by 40 per cent (Juma, 2011). As production for own consumption becomes less important, an increasing part of the rural population of developing countries is dependent on the purchase of foodstuffs on the market. The poor thus benefit from lower food prices, in both urban and in rural areas.

In hindsight, one may conclude that increases in productivity and technological change in agriculture associated with the green revolution have been essential to feeding a growing world population. Nowadays, this is no longer disputed, even by critics of the green revolution. The green revolution has so far bypassed Sub-Saharan Africa, resulting in stagnating agricultural production on this continent (see Table 10.1, p. 402). There is great need for technological advances adapted to semi-arid agriculture, which may contribute to African agricultural growth, as happened previously in Asia and Latin America. More R&D in this field is urgently needed. Moreover, older research focused primarily on maize, wheat and rice and was not adapted to African agro-economic conditions and African food crops (tuberous crops like cassavas, sweet potatoes, potatoes, yams, taro, and tree crops like sago palm, plantain and breadfruit). Research into these crops is still underdeveloped.

In the introduction of technological innovations, an increase in rural inequality in some stages of the process of agricultural development is probably inevitable, as wealthy and less risk averse farmers will tend to adopt new highly productive technologies at an earlier stage than poor, risk vulnerable small farmers and peasants. In the light of the political economic criticisms discussed above, however, more attention should be paid to the institutional and political aspects of technological change. Institutions should be designed to promote technological developments which are more in line with factor proportions. When labour is abundant, labour-intensive technological improvements should be sought. Small farmers should get easier access to credit facilities. Subsidised credit to wealthy farmers should be abolished. Land reforms could help improve the position of peasants and landless rural workers.

10.2.6   The green revolution continued: biotechnology and genetically modified crops

The original technological breakthroughs of the green revolution were based on selective plant breeding. However, since the 1960s, the pace of biotechnological change has accelerated dramatically. Advances in gene splicing, tissue culture and genetic manipulation have created new possibilities to develop new strains of plants more rapidly and to equip them with desired features. Along with the emergence of new opportunities, the fears of unintended social and technological consequences of genetic manipulation have also been magnified. The debates on the green revolution are being refought with a new intensity since the end of the twentieth century.

Gene splicing allows for the industrial production of seeds with desirable characteristics. Due to patenting by seed producers, farmers in developing countries cannot replant part of their harvest. They have to buy seeds every year. This makes farmers in developing countries more and more dependent on the large profit-oriented agricultural MNCs.[13]

Genetic manipulation not only allows for a more rapid development of new strains, it even allows for transgenic modification of plants, by adding genes from other plants or even animals. (e.g. genes from frogs added to tomatoes). In agriculture, genetically modified foods have advanced at a rapid rate since 1995 in that genetically modified crops were only released for production in the mid 1990s, by 2000 they accounted for 54 per cent of soybean production, 72 per cent of cotton production and 33 per cent of corn production in the USA (Paarlberg, 2001). The USA has followed a permissive approach to genetically modified crops, arguing that genetic modification does not differ essentially from traditional selective breeding. Europe and Japan, on the other hand, have taken a precautionary stance. They argue that as long as the risks of genetically modified crops are unknown, one should be careful in introducing them. Developing countries are caught in the middle of this transatlantic trade debate. As potential exporters to European countries and potential recipients of European aid, they have been reluctant to introduce genetically modified crops.

Here, we provide a brief summary of the relevant issues in the modern debates on biotechnology. The critics of biotechnological advances emphasise the following points, many of which echo the debates about the green revolution (see Bruinsma, 2003, Chapter 11; Hogg, 2000; Ramani and Thutupalli, 2013; Ruttan, 2002):

- *Loss of genetic diversity.* The increased reliance on a few standardised strains of food crops, creates large evolutionary risks. Genetic diversity peaked in the nineteenth century and has since declined. There is increasing risk of catastrophic losses due to epidemics, against which variety would provide a defence.
- *Increasing danger of soil degradation, erosion and waterlogging.* As a result of the high input strategies and intensification strategies, ever-more fertilisers, more pesticides and more water are required.
- *Increased dependence of farmers in poor countries on monopolistic seed producers in the advanced countries.* Patenting of gene sequences has made farmers more dependent on the large biotechnology firms.[14] The strengthening of IPR protection may have speeded up innovation, but it reduces the spread of innovation in agriculture.
- *Threats to biosafety from genetic manipulation.* There are risks of gene leakage with unintended consequences, such as for instance the spread of pest resistance to weeds, creating super weeds, harmful competition with desirable species, unwanted resistance of pests to pesticides and the creation of new strains of viral pathogens.

---

[13] It is a myth that new seeds cannot reproduce (Paarlberg, 2010). The obstacles to replanting lie in patenting.

[14] While the research leading to the 'green revolution' was predominantly publicly funded, modern biotechnological research is dominated by a small number of private companies (Byerlee and Fischer, 2002; Ramani and Thutupalli, 2013)

- *Threats to consumer health through the spread of new allergens.*
- *Neglect of research on environmentally friendly alternatives to specialisation and high-input agriculture.* Both Hogg (2000) and Bruinsma (2003, Chapter 11) argue that Low External Input and Sustainable Agriculture (LEISA) alternatives, such as biodynamic farming, integrated pest management and polycultures can be surprisingly productive and show substantial productivity gains. But the bulk of ongoing research continues to go into high-input avenues of research.

The proponents of modern biotechnological research argue that the risks of genetically modified seeds and the differences between modern biotechnology and traditional breeding practices have been greatly exaggerated. So far the risks have not materialised (Paarlberg, 2008). Genetically modified plants have a number of important potential advantages for farmers in developing countries:

- *Increased yields.* Biotechnological research can contribute to the continued increase in yields per harvest, which are necessary to sustain food supply in excess of population.
- *Lower fertiliser needs.* Genetically modified varieties have lower fertiliser needs, as they are more efficient in absorbing nutrients. Reduced fertiliser use is environmentally advantageous and contradicts one of the important criticisms of biotechnology.
- *Pest resistance.* Genetic modification can produce pest-resistant varieties, which require far less pesticides, resulting in less pollution and health risks. Reduction of crop losses due to pests and plant diseases will be an important avenue for production increases once biological limits of further yield increases are approached.
- *Disease resistance.* Disease-resistant varieties such as new strains of sweet potatoes can substantially reduce the cost of labour and the cost of chemical inputs.
- *Efficiency.* Genetic modification is more efficient than traditional breeding techniques because it can focus on specialised traits.

Gale Johnson (2002) argues that opposition to genetically modified crops on the part of Europe and NGOs is harmful to developing countries, and forms a threat towards their prospects of improved productivity and nutrition. In an impassioned and convincing polemic, Paarlberg (2008) even accuses the European Union, environmental NGOs and the UN system of creating major barriers to biotechnical research on genetically modified new seeds for Africa, thus actively contributing to continued agricultural productivity stagnation and continued poverty.

While the green revolution spread very rapidly, the spread of genetically modified crops in developing countries has run in to obstacles, after an initially rapid take-off. Many developing countries have been hesitant to introduce genetically modified organisms (GMOs) because of active opposition from many developed countries, in particular in Europe. In Sub-Saharan Africa, imports of genetically modified crops are rejected, even in conditions of famine. African leaders have internalised rich-country doubts about GMOs. According to Paarlberg (2008), the negative attitudes of the public in advanced economies towards biotechnological research have contributed to a decline of agricultural R&D expenditures, both worldwide and in particular in Africa.

In a more positive vein, both the *2008 World Development Report* and a recent book by Calestous Juma on agricultural innovation in Africa (Juma, 2011) document promising examples of R&D-driven advances in Africa (e.g. Cassava projects in Nigeria and Ghana,

Table 10.7: Sources of growth of crop production, 1961–2050

	Production growth attributable to (%)					
	Expansion of arable land		Increases in cropping intensity		Increases in yield per harvest	
	1961–99	1997/99–2050	1961–99	1997/99–2050	1961–99	1997/99–2050
All developing countries,	23	21	8	6	70	73
excl. China	23	24	13	13	64	63
excl. China and India	29	28	16	16	55	56
Sub-Saharan Africa	31	20	31	6	38	74
Near East/North Africa	17	0	22	20	62	80
Latin America and Caribbean	40	40	7	7	53	53
South Asia	6	6	12	2	82	92
East Asia	14	10	9	10	77	80
World	14	10	9	10	77	80

Source:
Alexandratos and Bruinsma (2012, Table 4.4).

maize production in Malawi). They call for greater efforts in this direction. Our expectation is that once the dust of the debate has settled, the further spread of new varieties in developing countries will pick up again. The need for technological advances is great and the potential of new technologies for food security and poverty reduction is large.

10.2.7 Summary and prospects

Table 10.7 summarises the effects of expansion of the agricultural area and increases in yields per unit of land since 1961. The increase in yields per hectare incorporate the effects of increased cropping frequency and higher yields per crop.

Between 1961 and 1999, no less than 23 per cent of the increase in total crop production in developing countries can be explained by the expansion of the cultivated area.[15] In the same period, increases in cropping intensity account for 8 per cent of agricultural growth, with increases in yields accounting for the lion's share of 70 per cent. The FAO projections up till 2050 suggest that expansion of the area continues to be an important source of agricultural growth (21 per cent), with cropping intensity (6 per cent) and yield increases (73 per cent) accounting for the remainder. Yield increases are thus by far the most important sources of agricultural growth. This highlights the continued importance of biotechnological R&D. Without this, agricultural development will grind to a halt.

[15] Similar figures are found for the period 1961–88 by Gillin and Krane (1989). With respect to cereals the contribution of area expansion is much lower than for total food production: 8 per cent between 1986 and 1990, see World Bank (1992).

For the land-abundant region of Latin America, the projected contributions of area expansion are much higher than the developing country average (40 per cent). As Latin America and Africa harbour most of the world's tropical rain forests, increases in agricultural production through expansion of cultivated area in these regions may conflict with the preservation of tropical forests and woodlands. On the other hand, intensification of production and increasing yields per harvest may also threaten the environment, since intensification involves the use of increasing amounts of chemical fertilisers, pesticides and herbicides, which pollute the soil and ground water (Barrow, 1995: 194 ff.; World Bank, 1992: 134). According to the World Bank, the greatest challenge for agricultural policy is to increase production and at the same time to protect the natural environment. When population increases to an estimated 9.3 billion people in 2050, FAO projects an increase in the demand for agricultural products of 62 per cent (an increase of 1.1 per cent per year, a much slower increase than in the past decades (Alexandratos and Bruinsma, 2012, Table 4.4)). This is a difficult task in the light of the various constraints to expansion of the area, intensification of production and yield increase discussed above. But, given sufficient investment in agricultural R&D in developing countries and advanced economies, it is not an impossible task. Agricultural production is in fact projected to increase in line with demand by 1.1 per cent per year.

Summarising, we observe that agricultural production increased in the long run due to expansion of the cultivated area, increases in cropping frequency and improved yields per crop. In the history of agriculture, the most important factors were expansion of the cultivated area, and increases in cropping frequency and intensification of land use by applying more labour per unit of land. In many developing regions these avenues of production expansion have not yet been exhausted. But as the limits to labour intensification are being reached (e.g. in Asian countries like Indonesia and China), the emphasis will increasingly shift to the increase of yields per crop by means of biotechnological innovation. Technological innovation in turn may lead to further intensification of production, for example in glasshouse production of vegetables and intensive cattle and poultry breeding. There is no reason why technological change in future years should not continue to allow food production to expand more rapidly than population.

10.3   Food consumption and nutrition

In section 10.1, we showed that world food production exceeds the growth of world population. With the exception of Sub-Saharan Africa where per capita food production is the same as in 1961, this also holds for food production in developing countries. However, this does not mean that the appalling problems of undernourishment and starvation in developing countries are in any way close to a solution.

In his famous study, *Poverty and Famines* (1981), Amartya Sen argues that the occurrence of starvation and malnutrition does not only depend on food production and food availability, but also people's actual *entitlements* to food. These entitlements may be based on one's own labour (a family producing for its own needs), on land ownership (the owner of land is entitled to part of the harvest), on purchasing power (money that has been earned is used to purchase food) and on public social protection measures (e.g. food rationing, food aid, food distribution, social security). Analysing two notorious famines (the Bengal famine, 1942–4, and the famine in Ethiopia, 1972–4), Sen shows that they were not primarily due to insufficient production of food per head of population. In both famines, a slight shortfall in production led to widespread speculation, food hoarding and skyrocketing of prices. Food distribution systems failed in moving food surpluses to deficit areas. Consumers lacked the financial means to buy food at its inflated prices. If governments had imported limited amounts of food and taken the responsibility for its distribution, prices could have been brought under control and famines could have been averted. Since independence in 1947, India has pursued such policies. Unlike what has happened in China between 1958 and 1960, there have been no large-scale famines in India in the post-war period (Sen, 1982). A relatively open society and timely identification of food shortages are the prerequisites for success of a policy aimed at preventing famines. Sen's exposition illustrates the importance of prices. Poor people may profit greatly from price decreases due to production growth (see section 10.2.5).

One should distinguish between *malnutrition* and *starvation* (van de Meer, 1983). Malnutrition refers to a situation where, during longer periods of time, the diet is insufficient for people to lead a healthy and productive life. Starvation is a situation in which people die due to an acute shortage of food. *Malnutrition* typically occurs in rural areas prior to the harvesting season. In sparsely populated areas, with no scarcity of land, undernourishment results from shortfalls in production in terms of quantity or quality. In densely populated areas, social inequality and unequal access to the means of production play a more important role. Even when the volume of food production is sufficient, the poor and landless may have too little purchasing power to realise their entitlements to food. Thus, sometimes undernourishment can increase even while production is growing. *Famines* are mainly caused by crop failures, natural disasters, wars, civil wars and social disruption. Again, it is not always the absolute shortage of food at an aggregate level that causes famine. Rather, famines are associated with situations in which people in given areas are unable to effectuate their entitlements to food.

In the twentieth century great famines occurred primarily in China, the USSR, India and North Korea (Arnold, 1988). In 1920–1 a famine in China led to 0.5 million casualties. In 1943 the Chinese province of Honan was struck by a famine resulting in 2–3 million casualties. The latest great Chinese famine took place from 1958 to 1961. The estimates of the number of casualties during this period vary from 30 million (Banister, 1984) to 45 million (Dikötter, 2010). Between 1942 and 1944 a famine killed 3 million people in Bengal, part of former British India. In 1921 a famine claimed 1–3 million lives in the Soviet Union. Between 1932 and 1934 5 million persons died due to famines that resulted from Stalin's forced agricultural collectivisation. A famine hit Bangladesh in 1974; here, the number of deaths was estimated to be between 300,000 and 1 million. The Ethiopian famine in 1984–5 led to over 1 million casualties.

In sparsely populated areas, famines are also caused by shortcomings in infrastructure. When there are local shortages of food due to crop failures, poor infrastructure and malfunctioning distribution systems will hamper the transport of food from surplus areas or other countries. In densely populated areas infrastructure is usually better. These areas can import food whenever there are shortages. In such conditions, famines are primarily caused by social disruption, government policy failures, civil wars, rebellions and international wars. Countries where social disruption resulted in famine include Burundi, Cambodia, Bangladesh, Biafra, Ethiopia, Rwanda, Somalia and the Sudan.

The degree of openness of a society is also of the greatest importance for the prevention of famine. In China, massive famines could occur between 1958 and 1961 without any knowledge of them reaching the outside world and the international community. In India, on

Table 10.8: Average availability of calories, 1964–2030[a]

| | Kilocalories per person per day | | | | | as % of average requirements | | | | |
	1964/66	1979/81	2000/02	2012	2030	1964/66	1979/81	2000/02	2012	2030
Sub-Saharan Africa	2,058	2,021	2,280	2,380	2,530	96.2	94.5	105.6	109.3	116.2
Latin America and Caribbean	2,393	2,674	2,860	2,960	3,090	105.0	117.3	123.0	125.3	130.8
Near East/North Africa[b]	2,290	2,804	3,125	3,180	3,130	104.0	127.3	137.3	137.1	135.0
South Asia	2,017	2,024	2,310	2,420	2,590	93.7	94.1	104.7	107.3	114.8
East Asia[c]	1,957	2,216	2,655	2,905	3,130	86.1	97.5	114.0	122.5	132.0
Developing countries	2,054	2,236	2,580	2,720	2,860	92.0	102.0	113.3	117.5	123.6
Developed countries	2,947	3,223	3,410	3,370	3,430	118.5	129.6	135.7	134.3	136.7
World	2,358	2,497	2,740	2,840	2,960	108.8	115.2	123.8	126.3	131.7

Notes:

a The average dietary caloric energy requirement differs from country to country. It depends on average height, age and sex distribution of the population, climatic conditions and average requirement of physical effort. The harder the effort, the more calories required. The average caloric requirement in this table is the number of calories required for normal productive functioning in society. For 1964–81, we calculated the caloric supply as a percentage of 1990–2 requirements.

b Near East/North Africa from 1990 onwards: unweighted averages of the figures for North Africa and West Asia.

c East Asia from 1990 onwards: unweighted averages of the figures for East Asia and Southeast Asia.

Sources:

1964–91 from Bruinsma (2003, Table 2.1); 1979–81 and projection 2030 from Alexandratos and Bruinsma (2012); 1990–2012 kcal per day and ADER from FAO, *Food Security Indicators* (2013b).

the other hand, imminent famines rapidly led to mobilisation of national and international relief actions (Sen, 1982). Due to improved medical facilities, better infrastructure, better communication facilities and international relief organisations, the number of deaths due to famines since 1950 has declined in comparison with the first half of the twentieth century. The exception is the hermetically closed society of North Korea, where reportedly millions of people died of famine between 1994 and 1998 (Natsios, 1999).

Table 10.8 and Table 10.9 present trends in availability of food and undernourishment in developing countries. Average food availability is calculated as the sum of domestic food production (in calories) plus food imports and minus food exports, divided by total population.

Table 10.8 shows that the average amount of calories available per person in developing countries increased from 92 per cent of average dietary energy requirements (ADER) in 1964 to 118 per cent of average requirements in 2012.[16] In absolute numbers, average kilocalories (kcal) available per person increased worldwide from 2,358 in 1964 to 2,840 in

[16] ADER is a normative energy requirement based on a moderately active level of physical activity (1.85 times BMR) for the fiftieth percentile of the BMR distribution. If food were distributed in line with actual requirements of people, the ADER would be the level of caloric intake which would eliminate undernourishment

2012. In developing countries they increased from 2,054 to 2,720. Especially in East Asia and the Near East/North Africa, the availability of food calories improved considerably. The slowest progress is registered in Sub-Saharan Africa and South Asia, but even there caloric availability has improved substantially.

It should be stressed that these figures are averages. When one considers separate countries, in 29 out of 172 developing countries the adequacy of food supply has even declined since 1990 (FAO, 2013b). There are currently 62 developing countries with less than 2,200 kcal per person per day. On the other hand, there are 75 developing countries with more than 2,600 kcal per head of the population in 2010–12. It is important that many of the improvements took place in six large countries with more than 150 million inhabitants (Bangladesh, Brazil, China, India, Indonesia, Nigeria and Pakistan). Of the largest developing countries, India showed the slowest progress, increasing from 2,260 kcal in 1990 to 2,380 kcal in 2012.

Sufficient availability of food does not guarantee that there is no undernourishment. On the contrary. Access to food is very unequally distributed, not only among regions within a country, but also among households, and even among the members of a single household (men versus women, adults versus children). As explained above, not all individuals are equally capable of effectuating their entitlements to food. Availability of calories does not equal consumption, not even at aggregate levels (Alexandratos, 1988: 57). If the variation in nutrition is large enough, sufficient average availability in a country can coexist with widespread undernourishment. Within households young children in particular are likely to be exposed to undernourishment. Further, part of the available food is lost due to problems of transport or storage. Thus, a sufficient average availability of food does not necessarily preclude widespread undernourishment and hunger.

Table 10.9 contains data on numbers and percentages of undernourished people in developing countries. A person is considered to be undernourished when caloric intake is less than the minimum dietary energy requirement (MDER). FAO defines undernourishment in relation to the basal metabolism rate (BMR), the energy requirement of a person who is fasting and inactive in a warm environment. BMR varies according to age, body height and climate. The average BMR for a country depends on the age and sex structure of the population. The MDER depends on the BMR and the physical activity level (PAL). The MDER used as threshold for the prevalence of undernourishment is 1.55 BMR (see Alexandratos and Bruinsma, 2012: 27; FAO, 2012a).[17] This is sufficient for light physical activity As in the case of health, there is a clear-cut relation between nutritional status and economic productivity. Undernourished people are less productive and are less able to earn a decent living. Improving nutritional intake therefore contributes in a wider fashion to poverty reduction and economic performance. It is an investment in human capital.

Table 10.9 shows that remarkable progress has been made in combating undernourishment. In the forty-three years between 1969 and 2012, the percentage of undernourished

(see Naiken, 1998). If undernourishment persists in spite of a sufficient supply of calories, this is due to maldistribution.

[17] The prevalence of undernourishment is a concept comparable to the poverty head count, the number of persons below the poverty line. An MDER with moderate physical activity sufficient for a healthy and active life is 1.75 BMR. As with poverty lines, if one uses higher MDERs the numbers of undernourished people are higher.

Table 10.9: Undernourishment, developing countries, 1979–2030[a]

	Number of undernourished persons (million)				Undernourished persons as % of the population				
	1979–81	1995–7	2010–12	2030	1969–71	1979–81	1995–7	2010–12	2030
Sub-Saharan Africa	125	186	234	180	35.0	36.5	30.8	26.8	14.5
Latin America and Caribbean	46	63	49	28	19.0	12.9	13.0	8.3	4.1
Asia[b]	727	633	536	305		31.6	19.4	13.8	
Near East/North Africa	22	17	25	29	24.0	9.1	11.6	12.1	4.7
South Asia	331	323	304	211	34.0	37.3	23.8	17.6	10.5
India	262	227	217			38.0	23.1	17.5	
East and Southeast Asia	396	310	232	94		28.0	37.3	22.4	
East Asia	308	202	167		44.0	29.0	15.3	11.5	4.2
China	304	193	158			30.4	15.4	11.5	
Southeast Asia	88	108	65			24.9	22.0	10.9	
Developing countries	1,512	909	852	543	36.0	28.0	19.7	14.9	7.9
Developed countries		22	17				1.9	1.4	
World		931	868				16.1	12.5	

Notes:

[a] An undernourished person is a person consuming fewer calories than the MDER. The MDER depends on the BMR and the Physical Activity Level (PAL). The MDER used as threshold for undernourishment is 1.55 BMR. This is sufficient for light physical activity (see Alexandratos and Bruinsma, 2012: 27; FAO, 2012b).

[b] Asia, excl. West and Central Asia.

Sources:

1969–71: from Alexandratos (1995: 50); 1979–81 from FAO (2002: 9 and Table 1: 31); 1995–2012 from FAO (2013). Projections 2030 from Alexandratos and Bruinsma (2012).

persons in developing countries more than halved, declining from 36 per cent in 1969 to 14.9 per cent in 2012.[18] The absolute number of undernourished persons declined from 1.5 billion in 1979 to 868 million in 2010–12.

The declines have been especially marked in East, Southeast and South Asia. Highest rates of undernourishment are found in Sub-Saharan Africa (26.8 per cent in 2012). Here, the numbers of undernourished persons have swelled substantially, due to rapid population growth, while the percentages are declining modestly.

In spite of progress, the numbers of undernourished people are still unacceptably high. In 2012, there were in total 868 million undernourished persons. The greatest numbers of

[18] The definitions and coverage of undernourishment for 1979–81 are not consistent with those for the figures after 1979.

undernourished people are found in South Asia (304 million), followed by East Asia (232 million) and Sub-Saharan Africa (234 million). In Asia the absolute numbers are affected by population size. Yet, on this continent, the proportions of undernourished persons are declining rapidly. In Sub-Saharan Africa the number of undernourished people has increased rapidly and the proportions remain high, in spite of some marginal improvement. Present projections of the FAO (Alexandratos and Bruinsma, 2012) suggest that undernourishment will indeed continue to decline.

The second target of the MDGs and the 1996 World Food Summit was to halve the proportion of people suffering from hunger in 1990 by 2015 (FAO, 1996). The proportion of undernourished persons in the developing world in 1990 was 23.2 per cent. Thus in spite of substantial progress, the 2015 target of 11.6 per cent is not likely to be fully achieved by 2015. But if the FAO projections for 2030 can be accepted, the targets for 2015 could be achieved around the year 2018 (see also FAO, 2012a).

10.3.1   Concluding remarks on agricultural policy

The above data illustrate the urgency of further improvements in the world food situation. Since the 1970s the climate of opinion with respect to the potential contributions of agriculture to development has gradually become more positive. Policy makers have become conscious of the 'urban industrial bias'.[19] The examples of India, China and Indonesia since the 1960s illustrate that it pays for developing economies to give more attention to agriculture. In these densely populated countries it proved possible to realise substantial increases in agricultural production per hectare and per head by combining new inputs, infrastructural investment, institutional changes and better incentives. But the *2008 World Development Report* still notes that investment in agricultural growth is lagging, in particular in agriculture-based economies where a large proportion of the labour force is still employed in agriculture. Budgets for agricultural research and development have been shrinking (Paarlberg, 2008).

On the production side, price policies and subsidies should provide positive incentives for farmers to increase their production and productivity. In addition, policy should focus on maintenance and improvement of agricultural infrastructure with respect to water control, land development, storage and distribution and transport. Large increases in investments in agricultural research, development and extension remain essential. As large numbers of the rural poor are smallholder producers, improving the productivity of smallholder agriculture should be an important focus of agricultural policy. One of the routes towards productivity increase for smallholders is to connect them to national and international markets.

After a long period of declining food prices, prices have started increasing since 2000. Especially in 2007–8 there was a huge hike in prices, and prices have remained high ever since (FAO, 2013c). This is due to a variety of factors including the increased competition of biofuels, the increased consumption of meat and fowl, and increased energy prices which affect the prices of agricultural inputs. Depending on the source of price increases, higher prices can result in higher incomes for agricultural producers if they are not captured by middlemen. In the medium term this should provide positive incentives for

---

[19] In fact, countering the urban industrial bias was one of the policy planks of the Washington consensus.

increased production. But the short run effects on food consumption by poor non-producing consumers will certainly be negative. Price increases have slowed down the improvement of undernutrition since 2007, but have not reversed the underlying positive trends.

In the international arena, economically advanced countries should provide less protection to their agricultural sector and reduce subsidies on agricultural exports to developing countries. Such exports are dumped on developing country markets at prices far below world market prices, sometimes in the form of food aid. They provide strong disincentives to agricultural producers in developing countries and have negative effects on agricultural development. Some progress has been made toward reducing protectionism in the USA and the European Union, but levels of protection are still unacceptably high, especially in the European Union.

On the consumption side, entitlements to food should be extended. This can be done among others by improving access to land or by stimulating off-farm employment in the rural sector for those who can no longer find employment in agriculture. This subject will be taken up again in the following sections on rural development. In times of temporary food shortages, national governments and the international community should intervene in the market to prevent prices from soaring, disequilibria from getting out of hand and famines breaking out. But the disincentive effects of international food aid should be avoided. It is better to provide cash incentives with which the poor can buy food from surplus areas in developing countries than to provide food aid in kind. In the long run subsidised food for the urban population should be phased out.

10.4 Rural development versus agricultural development

Rural development is a broader concept than agricultural development in two senses. First, rural development refers not only to economic changes but also to transformations and changes in wider rural societies. A multidisciplinary approach is therefore called for. It is especially interesting to combine economic studies of agricultural development with anthropological and sociological studies of processes of socio-economic change in rural areas. Second, rural development indicates that economic activities in rural areas are not limited to agriculture. Though agriculture is the defining characteristic of rural areas, rural populations have always been involved in other economic activities such as trade, handicraft production and services. More recently public services and rural manufacturing industries have also been established in rural areas. Non-agricultural activities are becoming more and more important. The interrelationships between these various activities are studied in the context of rural development. Without claiming to be comprehensive, the following sections provide an introduction to some interesting aspects of changes in rural communities.

The study of rural development is interesting for quite a few reasons. The most important of these are first the sheer demographic size of the rural sector and second the fact that poverty is disproportionately concentrated in rural areas.

In spite of ongoing urbanisation and structural change, the majority of the population in developing countries still lives in rural areas and agriculture still accounts for a substantial part of total employment. Table 10.10 shows that in 2011 53.5 per cent of the total

Table 10.10: Shares of rural population, agricultural labour force and agricultural production, 1950–2010

	Rural population (1,000)				Share of rural Population (%)				Share of agricultural labour force (%)				Share of agriculture in GDP (%)			
	1950	1970	1990	2010[a]	1950	1970	1990	2011	1960	1980	2000	2010	1960	1965	1990	2010
Bangladesh	36,272	61,803	84,403	107,216	95.8	92.4	80.2	71.6	86.0	72.6	62.1	48.1	57.5	52.8	30.3	18.6
China	485,765	672,878	842,379	681,049	87.5	82.6	72.6	49.4	83.2	68.7	50.0	36.7	22.3	37.9	27.1	10.1
India	308,484	444,427	650,556	845,839	82.7	80.2	74.5	68.7	74.3	69.5	66.7	51.1	42.6	40.9	29.0	18.0
Indonesia	65,557	98,156	127,965	120,119	87.6	82.9	69.4	49.3	74.8	57.8	45.3	38.3	51.5	56.0	19.4	15.3
Iran	12,617	16,850	23,962	22,978				30.9			23.9	21.2		27.5	19.1	10.2
Malaysia	4,866	7,260	9,142	7,951	79.6	66.5	50.2	27.2	63.3	37.2	18.4	13.3	34.3	28.8	15.2	10.4
Pakistan	30,965	44,646	77,647	111,304	82.5	75.1	69.4	63.8	60.8	52.7	48.4	44.7	46.2	40.2	26.0	21.2
Philippines	13,405	23,760	31,683	47,891	72.9	67.0	51.2	51.2	63.6	51.8	37.1	33.2	26.9	27.2	21.9	12.3
South Korea	15,109	18,644	11,242	8,223	78.6	59.3	26.2	16.8	61.3	34.0	10.6	6.6	36.4	39.4	8.9	2.6
Sri Lanka	6,978	10,105	14,355	17,722	85.6	78.1	78.7	84.9	56.6	51.9	38.0	32.7	31.7	28.2	26.3	12.8
Thailand	17,211	29,204	40,279	45,807	89.5	86.7	81.3	65.9	83.7	70.8	48.8	38.2	36.4	31.9	12.5	12.4
Turkey	15,977	21,905	22,084	21,471	78.7	61.6	38.8	28.5	78.7	60.3	36.0	23.7	55.9	47.5	18.1	9.6
Argentina	5,945	5,065	4,249	3,092	34.7	21.6	13.5	7.5	20.6	13.0	11.2		17.0	12.9	8.1	10.0
Brazil	34,457	42,362	39,026	30,537	63.5	43.5	25.2	15.4	52.1	36.7	22.4	17.0	20.6	18.7	8.1	5.3
Chile	2,529	2,373	2,206	1,892	41.6	24.8	16.7	10.8	30.5	16.3	14.4	10.6	9.4	8.7	8.7	3.4
Colombia	8,076	9,637	10,533	11,564	57.9	43.4	31.1	24.7	50.2	40.5	22.2	17.9	34.0	29.3	16.7	7.1
Mexico	15,980	21,255	24,096	25,151	57.3	41.0	27.5	21.9	55.1	36.3	18.0	13.1	16.0	13.7	7.8	3.9
Peru	4,503	5,617	6,744	6,714	64.5	42.6	31.1	22.7	52.3	40.3	34.5	0.0	20.8	18.0	8.5	6.8
Venezuela	2,684	3,006	3,094	1,938	53.2	28.4	16.0	6.5	33.4	14.6	10.6	8.7	4.8	5.3	5.5	5.8
Congo, Dem. Rep.	9,857	14,126	26,306	43,718	80.9	69.7	72.1	65.7	79.3	71.6	67.8		20.1	31.0	46.2	
Côte d'Ivoire	2,368	3,891	7,593	9,759	86.8	72.6	60.2	48.7	83.9	64.8	59.9		47.9	39.6	32.5	23.9
Egypt	14,645	20,760	32,129	45,935	68.1	57.8	56.4	56.5	58.1	57.1	29.6	28.2	30.0	28.6	19.4	14.0
Ethiopia															54.3	46.7
Ghana	4,212	6,167	9,403	11,899	85.5	71.0	66.5	48.1	63.3	61.5	59.7	57.2	45.2	49.9	45.1	29.6
Kenya	5,737	10,094	19,520	30,963	94.4	89.7	76.1	76.0	87.9	82.2	70.3	61.1	38.2	35.3	29.5	25.1

Morocco	6,609	10,032	12,789	13,843	73.8	65.4	51.6	43.0	65.7	56.0	44.4	40.2		23.5	18.3	15.4
Nigeria	33,993	44,334	63,134	80,795	89.9	80.0	65.0	50.4	73.2	54.0	43.8	44.6	63.9	54.9	32.7	32.4
South Africa	7,905	11,744	17,647	19,278	56.9	52.2	51.2	38.0	37.5	17.3	15.6	4.9	11.2	9.2	4.6	2.6
Tanzania	7,383	12,536	20,667	33,057	96.2	93.3	78.3	73.3	92.6	85.8	82.1	76.5	57.0	46.0	46.0	28.1
Zambia	2,071	2,883	4,763	8,020	91.1	69.8	60.6	60.8	84.6	76.1	71.6	72.2	11.0	15.6	20.6	20.4
Africa[b]	196,891	281,580	431,904	621,583	85.3	76.9	68.2	60.4	79.7	68.9				21.4	17.2	11.7
Latin America & Caribbean	98,104	122,975	131,411	124,836	58.1	42.4	28.9	20.9	49.0	34.2	18.0	14.8		16.2	8.8	5.5
Asia	1,120,034	1,600,157	2,139,502	2,304,550	82.6	76.6	67.7	56.4	78.2	68.6	0.0	0.0	32.7	37.5	20.2	11.4
East Asia											49.6	36.7				
South Asia											59.2	50.8				
Developing countries	1,417,393	2,007,919	2,707,714	3,058,663	82.2	74.9	65.0	53.5	76.1	65.6	48.5	37.5		27.6	15.9	10.4

Notes:

[a] Most recent year for which data are available between 2004 and 2010.

[b] Incl. South Africa.

Sources:

Rural population from United Nations Population Division (2012b).

Rural population as a percentage of total population, 1950–90 from United Nations Population Division (2003), and United Nations Population Division (2002b). 2011 from United Nations Population Division (2012b).

Share of agricultural labour force in total labour force 1980–2010 from World Bank, *World Development Indicators*, downloaded July 2013, supplemented by WDI CD-ROM, 1999; WDI CD-ROM, 2002; Bangladesh 2000 and regional totals 1960–80: ILO, *LABORSTA*, downloaded, July 2003; Colombia and Peru from *LABORSTA*, 2013, downloaded July 2013.

Share of agriculture in GDP: World Bank, *World Development Indicators, 2002*, supplemented by World Bank, *World Development Report*, various issues.

From 1980 onwards updated with new data from *World Development Indicators Online*, downloaded July 2013.

population of developing countries lived in rural areas; 37.5 per cent of total employment in developing countries was in agriculture. Agricultural employment shares were highest in South Asia and Sub-Saharan Africa. Much lower shares were found in Latin America. The shares of the rural population were invariably higher than the shares of agricultural employment, indicating the importance of non-agricultural activities in rural areas. The absolute numbers of inhabitants of rural areas were increasing rapidly. They numbered over 3 billion persons, against 1.4 billion in 1950. Only in exceptional cases does the absolute number of rural inhabitants show a decline (e.g. Argentina, Brazil, South Korea, Turkey).

Apart from the demographic importance of the rural sector, the study of rural development is also very important because rural urban income differentials are increasing and a very substantial part of global poverty is concentrated in rural areas. Three out of every four poor people in developing countries live in rural areas (De Janvry et al., 2002; World Bank-WDR, 2008). Both rural development and agricultural productivity growth have been very important in reducing poverty and will continue to be important in the coming decades. Increasing the productivity of smallholder agriculture, while simultaneously expanding off-farm rural employment, is a key tool for poverty reduction (Atamanov, 2011; Haggblade et al., 2007; World Bank-WDR, 2008).

Table 10.10 also shows that the share of agricultural production in national income is much lower than the share of agriculture in the total labour force. There are two explanations for this. First, labour productivity in the agricultural sector is lower than in other sectors. Second, many persons who are registered as employed in agriculture are also active in other sectors of the economy.

Especially in Asian and African countries, the rural population share is much higher than the agricultural labour force share.[20] Again this is due to the fact that so many rural people primarily depend on some kind of off-farm employment for their livelihood.[21] For example, the UN organisation UNDP has estimated that as early as the 1980s 25 per cent of primary employment in rural areas consisted of non-agricultural activities (UNDP, 1988). Presently, non-farm work accounts for between one-third and one-half of rural incomes in the developing world (Haggblade et al., 2007).

10.4.1   Changes in rural societies

In the course of economic and social development, societies in which agriculture predominates change into societies in which industry and services become more important. While in the past most people used to live in rural conditions, more and more people came to live in an urban environment. The share of agriculture in national output and employment tended to decline.

The shifts from the countryside to the city and from agricultural to other economic activities are not the only transformations. Rural societies themselves undergo change. Rural areas are increasingly less isolated from the outside world due to improved transport, trade, mobility, communications and the emergence of new media. As the market economy expands, the importance of commercial production for both local and national markets

---

[20] With the strange exception of Turkey, 2000.

[21] In addition, demographic factors, such as the number of dependents per member of the labour force, may also play a role.

increases at the expense of non-market production for own consumption needs. In many rural areas, mobility increases as a result of migration and migrant labour. Traditional redistributive arrangements and institutions within village communities come under pressure due to commercial production for the market. Social relationships within households, between villagers, and between social groups and classes undergo change. Traditional diffuse patterns of rights and obligations between powerful patrons and their rural clients become more businesslike with the expansion of the market economy. The division of labour between men and women within households changes when new opportunities and challenges emerge (Doss, 2001).

Both increasing population density and commercialisation of agriculture put great pressure on *traditional farming systems, traditional communal rights to the use of land* and *other land* tenure arrangements. When extensive agricultural practices are maintained unchanged, increasing population density results in erosion and impoverishment of the soils. Agricultural investment in soil conservation, productivity increases and technological advance require clearer definitions of land property and land tenure rights (AFD, 2008; Deininger and Feder, 2001; World Bank-WDI, 2008). Processes of social differentiation take place, resulting in more unequal distribution of the access to land and rising landlessness. Within agriculture, the importance of agricultural wage labour is increasing, while non-agricultural activities such as rural manufacturing, trade and services gain in importance. The central authority of the national state penetrates ever-deeper into rural communities through regulation and taxation.

Thus, rural development refers to the whole complex of economic, social and cultural changes taking place in rural societies. Long (1977: 4) defines rural development as 'the processes by which rural populations of the Third World are drawn into the wider national and international economy and with the accompanying social transformations and local-level responses'.

10.4.2   Three perspectives on rural development

In the social sciences, one can distinguish three important theoretical approaches to rural development (De Janvry *et al.*, 2002; Druijven, 1990; Long, 1977):

1. The *modernisation* approach, which emphasises cultural obstacles to development.
2. The *incorporation* approach, which stresses the changes that take place in traditional rural communities under the influence of penetration of (capitalist) market relations.
3. The *transactionalist* approach, which concentrates on the ways in which individuals in various circumstances respond to the challenges and changes with which they are faced.

Modernisation theories

Modernisation theory was the predominant approach in the 1950s and 1960s (see also Chapter 3). Modernisation theories interpret rural development as a transformation process from a traditional to a modern community, under the influence of economic and technical developments (Moore, 1963). Driving forces for change are: technological development, commercialisation of agriculture, the rise of cash crops and agricultural wage labour, industrialisation and urbanisation.

From this theoretical perspective, modernisation implies a process of differentiation and specialisation. Diffuse, multifunctional, personal social relationships are replaced by specialised, one-stranded, anonymous social relationships. Extended families make way for nuclear families. The family loses many of its functions with regard to education and socialisation to specialised educational institutions. Consumption and production, which were integrated in the extended household, are gradually separated. Families' activities become more focused on emotional gratification. A social hierarchy based on ascription (class, family of origin, social background) changes into a hierarchy based on achievement criteria. Specialised political and religious institutions are established. The need arises for new mechanisms of integration within the context of national societies, such as political parties, unions, bureaucracies and so forth. When integration does not keep up with differentiation, social strains and tensions are the result.

Though modernisation theory contains useful insights, the prime weakness of this view is the implicit unilinear path running from a traditional pole to a modern pole, which is assumed to be the same for all societies. This unilinear perspective does not do sufficient justice to the diversity of circumstances and developmental paths in societies, lumped together under the heading 'traditional'. It also underemphasises the amount of individual ingenuity, creativity and entrepreneurship to be found in a great variety of cultural contexts. Further, there are also numerous examples of modern economic developments that contribute to the preservation of traditional cultural and social arrangements, rather than to their disruption (see Kuper, 1984). Some modernisation theorists such as Eisenstadt (1970) try to distinguish different traditional settings and different paths of modernisation, but the bipolarity of traditional versus modern continues to be the framework of analysis.

At present it is hard to find unequivocal supporters of unabashed modernisation theory. Nevertheless, the question whether there are 'cultural barriers' to development, which derives from modernisation theory, remains of interest. In a series of publications in the 1960s, the anthropologist Foster (1965, 1975) defended the thesis that the concept of *limited goods* functions as a cultural barrier to economic and social change in traditional societies. The external reality is seen as something that human beings are unable to control. People find it hard to imagine that total welfare could increase as the result of individual efforts. The total amount of goods and welfare is seen as limited. This implies a zero-sum game in which the success of one person is a threat to the welfare of other individuals. According to Foster, there is little solidarity within such traditional village communities. Cooperation is riddled with mutual mistrust, because it may result in claims to authority by some of the participants. Economic success gives rise to jealousy. It sets off redistributive mechanisms such as the obligation to organise social festivities or to support relatives. Thus, the idea that the total amount of goods is limited makes for conservatism and forms a barrier to entrepreneurship.

The main problem with this theory is a tendency towards overgeneralisation. It is conceivable that, under certain conditions of uncertainty or risk, the notion of a limited store of goods crystallises into a powerful cultural element, which inhibits change. But, as Long points out, there are also many instances where traditional cultural elements are quite compatible with modern economic behaviour. Economists like Myint (1980) and Higgins (1968) and anthropologists such as Geertz (1963) have pointed out that entrepreneurship emerges all over the world, whenever there are new opportunities for trade due to improvements in transport, communication and infrastructure.

Incorporation theories

Incorporation theories are much more historical in nature than modernisation theories. They study the effects of the penetration of a capitalist market economy in various non-capitalist agrarian societies in different historical periods (see Dixon, 1990; Druijven, 1990; Frank, 1969; Long, 1977). The term *'incorporation'* refers to the ways in which non-capitalist or pre-capitalist societies become involved in international market relationships.

Dixon (1990: 39 ff.) presents an interesting overview of different processes of incorporation. Incorporation took place through the establishment of plantation economies by colonists using native or imported slave and contract labour to cultivate export crops. In countries such as South Africa, Kenya, Zimbabwe and Algeria, settlement colonies (see Chapter 2) were created, where white settlers appropriated the most fertile lands. The indigenous population was resettled on 'native' reserves, which were overcrowded and had infertile lands. The dispossessed native population served as a labour reserve for settler farming activities.

The example of export production on plantations was frequently followed by smallholder peasants who also started to cultivate export crops. Opinions differ as to whether or not this occurred voluntarily. According to incorporation theory, colonial tax levies in cash in effect forced smallholders to cultivate cash crops. Also, the colonial authorities often imposed obligations on peasants to supply labour to plantations or to deliver a quota of export crops in kind (e.g. sugar). More positive incentives were provided by the availability of new consumer goods and new agricultural inputs, which could only be acquired by means of money.

In post-war Africa, mines and new industries attracted a flow of migrant labour. Able-bodied young males travelled long distances to find work in these new sectors, leaving women, children and the elderly to cope with food production in the rural areas.

The incorporation theories, mainly of a neo-Marxist bent, emphasise the negative aspects of the penetration of the market economy in pre-capitalist societies. Survival strategies, which offered protection against crop failures and other risks in traditional societies, are disrupted. Aspects of traditional societies that are incompatible with the market economy are undermined. Behavioural patterns, which can be made subservient to the market economy, are preserved. For example, land scarcity in Latin American *minifundia* simply forces peasants to offer their labour cheaply to large landowners. Incorporation theory focuses on the chains of dependence and exploitation which extend far outside the village community. After colonies gained their independence, foreign-owned plantations were often nationalised – but dependence remained. Dependency theories argued that a few multinational agribusinesses had a monopoly on the processing, distribution and marketing of agricultural export crops and the supply of new seeds, fertilisers, machinery and other inputs. Incorporation theories therefore call for state intervention and land reform to achieve more equitable types of rural development.

Like modernisation theories, incorporation theories suffer from a tendency to overgeneralisation. The emphasis on the disruptive effects of the market economy goes hand in hand with an idealisation of harmonious pre-capitalist relationships. In reality, production for the market often provides small farmers with an escape from traditional constraints and power relationships. Also, insufficient justice is done to examples of successful agricultural development in different periods and countries. For example, during the late colonial period cocoa exports had very positive effects on the economic development of Ghana. More generally, primary exports from tropical countries provided a stimulus to economic development in the late nineteenth century (see Chapter 8). Rice production in Indonesia provides an example of very successful agricultural development, despite the gloomy predictions of the 1960s (see Geertz, 1963; McCulloch and Timmer, 2008). In recent years, several Asian countries have become self-sufficient in fertilisers. In present-day debates connecting farmers in developing countries to markets, in particular for high-value agricultural products, is seen as a recipe for growth and poverty reduction.

Transactionalist and decision making theories

Long criticises both modernisation theories and incorporation theories for their tendency to depict rural populations as helpless victims, whether of traditional cultural obstacles or of external exploitation (Long, 1977; see also Druijven, 1990). He calls for an analysis of the differential responses to change shown by individuals and social categories within a population. As a third perspective on rural development, he distinguishes the *transactionalist approach,* which analyses the active strategies of the poorest, the less poor and the rich. In this approach, special attention is paid to entrepreneurship and the manipulation of networks of clients and middlemen. This approach provides a more active picture of the rural population.

Anthropological studies of entrepreneurship in 'traditional' societies, such as Hill's study of Ghanaian cocoa farmers (Hill, 1986), also give a much more dynamic image of rural communities and a more realistic assessment of potential resources of entrepreneurship and creativity. Simultaneously, more insight is gained into inequality and diversity within rural communities. Some individuals follow more effective strategies than others. There are both winners and losers.

The emphasis in transactionalist approaches is on survival strategies, in which farmers are flexible with regard to the use of their labour and can seek alternative sources of employment outside the agricultural sector, in trade, services and crafts production. Ceremonial obligations, which were primarily interpreted as redistributive mechanisms by modernisation theorists, are reinterpreted here as investments in social relations and networks. These social investments are made in order to achieve certain goals in the future. The transactionalist approach in anthropology (see among others Barth, 1966; Boissevain, 1974) provides a valuable bridge to modern micro-economic models of decision making in rural households (e.g. Moschini and Hennessy, 2001; Ray, 2000) and anthropological and sociological studies of resilience of rural households, rural livelihoods and rural household strategies (e.g. Ellis, 1998). Households have to choose between a variety of options including cultivating their own land, working as hired agricultural labourers, engaging in rural non-farm activities or migrating to cities or even other countries (Atamanov, 2011). However, in our view analysis of micro-decisions and strategies is most interesting when they are studied against the backdrop of wider changes, challenges and trends taking place at the macro-level.

10.4.3   The peasant economy and peasant households

In the discussion of rural development peasants play an important role. The study of peasant economies allows for a combination of transactionalist analysis of household behaviour and macro-analysis of major changes in rural societies.

The Chayanov model

As early as the 1920s the Russian agronomist Chayanov drew attention to interesting differences between the economic behaviour of large, commercial farmers producing for the market and small peasants producing mainly for their own consumption (Chayanov, 1966; see also Kitching, 1982). In his publications Chayanov defended Russian peasants against the communist reproach that they were capitalist farmers (*kulaks*). He did so by stressing the differences between capitalist farms and peasant agriculture. On such grounds, Chayanov rejected the collectivisation of agriculture.

A profit-maximising commercial farmer will expand employment up to the point where the additional financial returns to the last agricultural worker equal the wage rate. The wage rate is in part determined by wages being paid outside the agricultural sector. Russian peasants at the start of this century, however, did not produce for the market, but for their own subsistence. They used their own and their family's labour power, rather than wage labour. There were hardly any opportunities for full-time paid employment outside agriculture, so no implicit wage could be determined.

According to Chayanov, under such circumstances financial returns and wages have little meaning for a peasant household. The peasant does not weigh financial returns against the financial cost of labour. Rather, he looks at the amounts of food needed to feed the family and the amounts of backbreaking physical labour required to produce this food. Since labour of the peasant and his family does not 'cost' any money, he will continue to work until he can provide sufficiently in the subsistence of his household. Equilibrium is reached when the disutility of additional drudgery equals the utility of additional family consumption. At this point, the peasant will stop increasing his labour input. The labour input per hectare depends on family size and in particular on the number of dependents in the household (children and the elderly). The more mouths to be fed, the more work will be done. Labour input per hectare is also determined by the availability of land and the possibilities of part-time paid employment outside agriculture.

Other things being equal, the Chayanov model implies that a small self-supporting peasant will use more labour per unit of land and will realise a greater production per unit of land than a commercial farmer producing for the market. He will not stop working when the value of his output is less than his implicit wage. He will continue to work till he has produced enough to feed his family. Of course, other things are hardly ever equal, in particular with respect to the amount of capital and the kind of technology employed. Nevertheless, it is a common finding that yields per hectare on small and medium-sized farms are generally higher than on large farms. This does not hold for very small farms, with too little land to farm efficiently.

In a well-known study, incorporating data on a large number of countries, Berry and Cline (1979) found that both financial returns per hectare and real production per hectare are inversely related to the land area available to a farmer. The authors concluded (1979: 29) that redistribution of land from larger to smaller farmers would lead to an increase of total agricultural output and employment. Redistribution would reduce underutilisation of labour on tiny plots of land. Also there would be an increased demand for the labour services of the landless rural workers. Land reform will be discussed in more detail in section 10.5. Subsequent research has tended to confirm the Berry and Cline 'inverse relationship' (e.g. Akram-Lodhi, 2001; Kimhi, 2006; Rios and Shively, 2005), but there is an ongoing debate about the policy implications. Not all authors agree with the conclusions of Berry and Cline with regard to redistribution of land.

Characteristics of peasant economies

Inspired in part by Chayanov's work, a group of authors associated with the *Journal of Peasant Studies* has tried to identify general characteristics of the peasant economy, which call for a specific theoretical analysis (Shanin, 1971, 1973, 1974; see also Wolf, 1966).

Peasants are small farmers, producing primarily for their own consumption with the use of family labour. The peasant family is both a unit of production and of consumption. There is a relatively low level of occupational specialisation, although there is a division of labour between age groups and sexes. Peasants work with little capital. Ownership of land is not individualised. Households have rights of access to communal land on the basis of their membership in a village community. Access to communal land is allocated by the village authorities (Scott, 1976). A portion of agricultural surpluses is reserved for ceremonial obligations like feasts, religious rituals, payment of bride money, burials and so forth. Credit is hard to obtain, markets are underdeveloped and risks are high for households living close to subsistence levels. Security, therefore, is valued higher than innovativeness.

Peasants live in relatively closed village communities. Nevertheless, there are at least two kinds of links with the outside world. In the first place, there is always some contact with the world outside the village through kinship ties and rural market places. Second, there are always relationships with powerful outsiders who appropriate part of the agricultural surpluses, whether in kind, money, or labour. These outsiders can be feudal or prebendal landlords, colonial administrators, large landowners or modern tax collectors and bureaucrats. Peasant societies are to be found both in pre-industrial Europe and in present-day developing countries.

According to Wolf (1966), 'peasant economies' stand midway between isolated tribal communities of primitive agriculturalists, hunters and gatherers and fully integrated market economies. Many studies of changes in rural societies focus on the transformations of peasant economies. How do peasant economies respond when confronted with the rise of centralised state power and the penetration of market relationships (Ellis, 1988; Moore, 1967; Popkin, 1979; Scott, 1976; Wolf, 1966)?

Ellis (1988: 3) estimates – without any mention of sources – that over a billion people belong to peasant households, most of these in developing countries. On the basis of a survey of the literature, he distinguishes the following characteristics of the *peasant society*:

- Peasant society represents a *transition* from relatively dispersed, isolated and self-sufficient communities of farmers or pastoralists to fully integrated market economies.
- Although relatively isolated, peasant society is part of a *larger economic and political system*. Peasants are exposed in some degree to market influences. They stand in relations of subordination to powerful political outsiders (Wolf, 1966).
- *Internal differentiation.* Within peasant communities there are numerous differences in social and economic status. In particular, there are important differences between men and women.
- Peasants obtain their *livelihood from the land*, mainly by the cultivation of crops. This distinguishes them from landless labourers, pastoralists or nomads.
- A peasant household is both a unit of production and a unit of consumption. Households are, at least to some extent, *self-sufficient*. The degree of self-sufficiency varies strongly.

Production for their own consumption does not preclude part of the harvest being traded on the market.

- The primary source of labour is *family labour*. This characteristic distinguishes peasant households from capitalist farms employing wage labour. But this does not rule out the use of some hired labour in peak periods.
- In some way or other peasants have *access to land* to provide for their livelihood. This distinguishes them from landless agricultural workers and industrial labourers. Land is allocated on the basis of non-market criteria. Allocation depends on the social status of the household within the village community.
- Peasants are *partially integrated into markets for products and factors of production*. They stand with one leg in the non-market village economy and one leg in a market economy. The markets on which peasants are active are imperfectly functioning markets. This has to do with poor infrastructure (transport, communications), insufficient information, and power relationships that constrain peasants' freedom of choice. This implies that the supply of agricultural products responds only weakly to changes in price levels. In this context Lal and Myint (1996) use the term *institutional underdevelopment*.[22]
- Partial integration into markets implies that *non-market criteria of reciprocity* still play an important part in transactions between peasant households.

According to Ellis, partial integration into imperfectly functioning markets is the principal characteristic of peasant economies. It distinguishes peasants from commercially oriented family farmers who trade their entire product and purchase all their inputs on the market. On the other hand, access to the production factor land distinguishes peasants from landless agricultural labourers. In rural societies, peasants function alongside the commercial family farmers, who are more closely integrated into markets, and labourers working for wages on plantations or lands of large landowners. Also, as mentioned, agriculture is not the only source of livelihood in rural areas, though this is somewhat underemphasised in literature on peasants.

Diversity of conditions

In generalisations about rural development, there is – in spite of all qualifications and denials – a tendency to think in terms of a traditional–modern polarity. On the one side, one distinguishes the traditional self-supporting pre-capitalist agricultural society, with communal rights to land and redistributive institutions within villages. On the other side, one distinguishes a modern money and market economy in which farmers produce commercially for the market.[23] This schematic conception is present both in modernisation theories, which stress the institutional and cultural obstacles to change, and in the radical and Marxist literatures on peasant societies, which analyse the penetration of the money economy into traditional peasant societies and the associated processes of disruption.

In her book *Development Economics on Trial: The Anthropological Case for a Prosecution* (1986), Polly Hill launches a ferocious and delightful attack on universal developmental generalisations such as the transition from self-sufficiency to production for the market,

---

[22] They argue for expansion of agricultural exports, since this tends to diminish institutional underdevelopment.

[23] Our brief summary of trends of change in rural societies could also be easily misunderstood as a sketch of the transition from 'traditional' to 'modern'.

the penetration of the money economy, increasing inequality, migration from rural to urban areas, the transition from communal land rights to private ownership of land, Boserupian intensification of land use, or the thesis of Theodor Schultz that traditional peasants are efficient. Such generalisations do insufficient justice to the rich diversity of agricultural circumstances in developing countries and the dynamic entrepreneurship, which can often be found among members of so-called traditional societies. Often the generalisations are not only wrong. They may even be harmful when they lead to inadequate policy recommendations, which do not take the variations in local conditions into account.

Development economists and agricultural economists generalise because this is how they have been trained. They were nurtured on 'universal generalisations' and 'development schemes'. In as much as they do any empirical research at all, Hill argues they base themselves on deplorably unreliable statistics (see section 10.1) and make little attempts to become intimately familiar with the rural societies about which they are writing.

For example, Hill demonstrates that in some regions farmers have already been involved in market production for many centuries. In both West Africa and in South India money has played an important role in economic transactions far back in history. Rural marketplaces in the Sudan date back to the fourteenth century. The subsistence economy is a myth. So-called 'traditional' rural societies in the past have always known numerous non-agricultural activities – in trade, services and handicraft production. Extensive and intensive agricultural activities can coexist side by side in one and the same region.[24] In West Africa, rural markets developed earlier than urban-oriented markets. It is incorrect to state that the market economy penetrated rural areas from urban centres. Migration from one rural area to another is at least as important as rural–urban migration. Some rural societies have communal rights to land. In others there has long been private ownership of land, and land has long been freely saleable. These two types of land use can coexist.

In rural societies one finds a great variety of farmers: farmers who have rights to cultivate communal land owned by the village, clan, or tribe; agricultural labourers who receive wages to work on land that is owned by others; predominantly self-sufficient family farmers who rent or own their land; commercial family farms producing for the market; large commercial farms and plantations using hired wage labour. The distinctions between these categories are rather vague and indistinct. Self-sufficient farmers or their relatives, for example, often also work as hired workers on land owned by others. Both rich and poor farmers participate in non-agricultural activities, like trade and crafts. Rich farmers do so because non-agricultural activities are so profitable, poor farmers because they cannot survive on agriculture alone. The richest farmers enjoy the greatest trading advantages. Further, there are great differences in the amounts of land available to different farmers, and there is a great variety of land tenure institutions: individual ownership, rights of use, sharecropping arrangements, lease relations and so forth.

Hill argues that the use of the term *peasant economy* as a blanket term for all these different types of agricultural activities is inappropriate and misleading. It denies significant intravillage inequalities in power, wealth, income and status. It disregards the differences

---

[24] In her polemic sharpness, Hill does not always do justice to her opponents. For example, as early as 1965 Boserup explicitly pointed out that different intensities of land use can coexist in the same region, due to differences in soil quality and natural circumstances (Boserup, 1965: 57 ff.).

between cattle-raising societies and crop-raising societies, between irrigated agriculture and rain-fed agriculture, and differences in natural circumstances and climatic conditions.

Next, the focus on peasant economies also neglects the differentiation between males and females within village communities and households in Africa, Asia and Latin America. For example, in much of Africa there are generally two separate economic spheres for males and females. Women are responsible for subsistence food production to feed the household. On the side, they often engage in trade. Men are responsible for the raising of high-prestige cash crops and cattle breeding. Women tend to have less secure access to land, less access to inputs, finance and new technologies (Boserup, 1970; Doss, 2001).

Hill prefers terms such as 'country people', 'farmers', 'cultivators' to 'peasant'. The connotations of the term 'peasant' are derogatory. It does not do justice to the inventiveness, creativity and entrepreneurial spirit, which Hill observed in her empirical research among country people. In this respect, Hill comes very close to the positions of development economists such as Schultz, Lewis and Myint whom she elsewhere criticises so fiercely.

Hill's polemic is refreshing. It encourages readers to take into account the variety of local conditions in rural communities. Generalisations should relate to specific agrarian systems, e.g. dry-grain farming in densely populated regions. However, Hill has a tendency to misrepresent the positions she is attacking and to exaggerate the differences of opinion. Like Hill, Schultz – one of Hill's black sheep – pointed to entrepreneurial qualities and creativity among farmers. Boserup (1970) was one of the first authors to analyse the role of women within rural communities. Marxist studies also emphasise rural inequalities.

Finally, there is a risk that Hill's love for anthropological detail may end up in no more than ethnographic description and a rejection of all attempts to generalise and to formulate hypotheses on rural development. In our opinion, Ellis' synthesis of the characteristics of peasant societies, described earlier, meets most of Hill's objections. The characteristics of peasant societies are no longer defined in absolute terms but leave scope for variation. For example, the transition from self-sufficiency to production for the market is seen as a continuum. The use of family labour does not exclude the hiring of wage labour, nor family members themselves working as paid labourers on other farms. The existence of off-farm employment is acknowledged, as are the differences between households. Finally, Ellis admits that the peasant household is only one of many types of rural households, albeit an important one. Provided they are applied carefully, the characteristics of the peasant economy may contribute to a better understanding of processes of rural change.

10.4.4 Rationality, risk and survival strategies in peasant societies

Increases in agricultural production and productivity are prerequisites for improvements in living conditions in rural areas. Production may be raised through expansion of the amounts of production factors (land, labour, agricultural equipment), more efficient use of existing means of production, or introduction of new techniques of production. A crucial question is to what degree peasant societies are willing and able to increase efficiency and introduce new technologies. Ever since Boeke (1955) pointed to the 'limited needs' in Indonesian society, there is a tradition that stresses the cultural obstacles to increases in efficiency, to entrepreneurship, and to innovation. We have come across this view in the discussion of the diffusion model and modernisation theories.

In his pioneering work *Transforming Traditional Agriculture*, Theodor Schultz (1964), later awarded the Nobel Prize in economics, objected to this point of view. On the basis of fieldwork conducted by other researchers, he concluded that, given their circumstances, 'traditional farmers' use their production factors efficiently. According to the neoclassical economic theory, 'efficient' means that the marginal returns to the factors of production equal their marginal costs. The implication is that there are no cultural barriers to efficiency. Traditional farmers know exactly what they are doing and use their available factors of production in a rational fashion. They have a profound knowledge of the possibilities of traditional agriculture. Within the constraints of traditional economy, society and technology there are few opportunities to increase efficiency and productivity. Productivity is very low, but they are doing the best they can. Peasants live close to subsistence. They are unable to make large investments in new agricultural technologies (seeds, fertilisers, pesticides, irrigation and so on). In Schultz's words, farmers are 'poor but efficient'. The absence of rural credit markets and technology support keeps them trapped in poverty.

Schultz sees an important role for government in stimulating the development of new, highly productive technologies and making them available to farmers in traditional agriculture. There is sufficient entrepreneurship among farmers to ensure that new technologies will be adopted if they are likely to pay off. But economic incentives for the use of new technologies have to be created and negative incentives such as inadequate access to credit or too low prices for agricultural products should be eliminated (Schultz, 1978).

Schultz's view has been severely criticised by anthropologists such as Adams (1986) and Hill. Schultz bases himself on a limited number of ethnographical studies, which are not very representative; what is more, he does not always interpret them correctly. Adams' most serious objection is that Schultz pays no attention to the cultural context in rural societies, to values and attitudes, and to social stratification. Peasants may act rationally, but their efficiency depends on their culturally determined perceptions of reality and their informedness about technology, credit and the price movements of products and inputs. Character traits and motivation are also of great importance. In daily practice, there are great differences in performance and efficiency between different farmers in the same village. According to Adams, Schultz also pays too little attention to the significance of production for own needs – analysed by Chayanov – and the significance of risk in poor rural societies.

Cultural factors are stressed in James C. Scott's study *The Moral Economy of the Peasant: Rebellion and Subsistence in South East Asia* (1976). Scott belongs to the so-called *substantivist* tradition in anthropology (Polanyi, 1957), which stresses reciprocity in exchange, relationships and the differences between traditional multifunctional relationships and modern impersonal single-stranded relationships in a capitalist economy, in which rational calculation of costs and benefits prevails.

Unlike modernisation theorists, Scott places little emphasis on obstacles to modernisation. He stresses the positive survival functions of traditional institutions in Southeast Asia. Peasants live at the margin of subsistence. Crop failures and price fluctuations are an immediate threat to their bare survival. In their choice of production techniques, the essential criterion is safety and minimisation of risk rather than maximum output. This is why they cultivate different crops on scattered strips of land. They prefer to cultivate food crops rather than cash crops, the returns from which may fluctuate with market conditions.

The social institutions of rural communities were traditionally oriented to stability and the assurance of a minimum standard of living to the inhabitants (De Janvry et al., 2001). There were communal lands, which were periodically redistributed among the cultivators. The village community also allocated taxes and levies imposed by royal rulers, governments, or landlords. There were obligations for villagers to support each other with labour, when this was needed (work sharing). Norms of reciprocity were very important. There were redistributive social obligations for the richer villagers. They were expected to be charitable, sponsor ceremonial celebrations and festivities, donate to shrines and help indigent kin.[25] Decision making within village communities was aimed at reaching consensus.

Subsistence insurance was not confined to the village. Tenancy and sharecropping relations between peasants and powerful landlords also had survival aspects. Traditionally the rent consisted of a fixed share of the harvest. This meant lower rents when harvests were bad and higher rents when they were good. Furthermore, in times of need rich patrons had certain obligations to provide food to their starving tenants or to forgo the collection of rent. In exchange, peasants had obligations to their patrons, such as showing respect, providing corvée (unpaid) labour and political support.

Scott writes that a *moral economy* and a *subsistence ethic* had developed in Southeast Asia, in which survival was a central element. This subsistence ethic provided guidelines for individual actions. Though there was considerable inequality within the village and between villagers and external elites, there was also a moral claim to a guaranteed minimum income. According to Scott, this 'moral' survival economy was undermined by two tendencies: political centralisation and penetration of the market economy. Political centralisation involved the imposition of fixed taxes on land, which did not vary with harvest returns. The risk of output fluctuations was shifted onto the peasants. Commercialisation introduced the uncertainties of fluctuating market prices. Local crafts and services, which provided alternative sources of income in bad times, were disrupted due to increased competition from without. Where possible, influential groups tried to reduce common use of communal land and introduced individualised ownership. Finally, traditional paternalistic relationships between patrons and peasants became more impersonal and contractual. Guarantees for survival were undermined. Risks were shifted to the peasants. According to Scott, it was not the increase in inequality in itself, but rather the weakening of traditional guarantees for survival, which provided an explanation for the large-scale peasant uprisings in Southeast Asia during the first part of the twentieth century. (For a more general formulation of this perspective, see Barrington Moore, 1966.) Peasants revolt when their traditional moral expectations of support by fellow-villagers and patrons in times of need are violated.

Scott's view has been fiercely criticised by Samuel Popkin in his study *The Rational Peasant: the Political Economy of Rural Society in Vietnam* (1979). Popkin accuses authors like Scott, Wolf and other substantivists of idealising traditional peasant societies and

---

[25] Scott does not idealise the traditional village community to the extent that his critics suggest. He believes the redistributive obligations are enforced through expressions of envy, gossip and social control. Dependence on community support entails loss of status.

traditional power structures. For them, capitalist penetration was the main culprit, disrupting traditionally harmonious relationships and survival arrangements.

Popkin, on the contrary, argues that 'traditional' peasants in Vietnam – just as individuals elsewhere – are constantly engaged in the rational pursuit of their interests. They try to increase their welfare through short-term and long-term investments, including investments in social relations and social networks. Popkin's political economy approach is an example of the so-called *formalist* tradition in anthropology. This tradition insists that peasant societies can be analysed with the same analytic tools as social relations in Western societies. Popkin's work can be seen as one possible elaboration of the transactionalist approach introduced above.

Within villages there are continuous conflicts and feelings of mutual distrust. As in every social setting, some villages try to profit from communal arrangements as 'free riders', without making any contribution of their own. Traditional savings institutions are constantly threatened by the suspicion that some may benefit more than others. Also every village community has its outsiders who are denied access to communal land. In sum, the moral economy approach seriously underestimates the extent of inequality, exploitation, competition and conflict within village communities.

Popkin interprets the often paternalistic relationships between patrons and clients not as a result of cultural or moral factors, but rather as relations of dependence. In these relations, landlords have succeeded in monopolising all external relations of peasants – with regard to credit, purchase of inputs, marketing of surpluses, processing of agricultural products. The guarantees they offer peasants in times of need serve to maintain their dependence. The penetration of market relations offers peasants a chance to escape the monopoly power of local landlords. Often rich farmers and landlords try to block peasants' access to markets, fearing the peasants' increasing independence.

Popkin agrees that risk avoidance is a predominant feature of peasant society. However, he interprets it more as an individual survival strategy. Peasants are risk averse. But this does not necessarily mean that they will never invest or make a gamble. If the potential loss is small, and there is a chance of a big outcome, peasants are quite willing to gamble. Penetration of the money economy and the centralised state, therefore, is not always perceived as a threat. Sometimes it offers new opportunities and escape from traditional relations of subordination.

Popkin's criticism is supported by empirical research by Haggis *et al.* (1986) into peasant revolts in Asia. These authors conclude that peasant revolts did not start as a reaction to the disappearance of the moral economy. It was not necessarily the poorest peasants who revolted. Often richer farmers, who felt their opportunities were being restricted, played an important role. Much political turmoil was not directed towards the restoration of traditional 'moral' relations; class struggle and nationalist elements also played a role. Haggis *et al.* (1986) also come to the conclusion that Scott gives a too rosy view of the 'moral economy' of traditional relations of dependence and subordination.

By stressing the calculating aspects of peasant behaviour, Popkin narrows the gap between the thought of economists and anthropologists. Starting from pure neoclassical principles of utility maximisation, the economist Lipton arrived at an analysis of risk aversion very similar to that of Popkin (Lipton, 1966). In many developing countries, the large variability of rainfall makes it impossible to predict the volume of production. Many peasants live close to subsistence levels. A crop failure may force them to borrow money for food and result in loss of land or even starvation. New inputs and technologies demand large investments, while returns vary from year to year. Though these investments might result in higher average returns, they may cause severe indebtedness in years of bad harvests. Therefore, the calculating behaviour of peasants is determined by a risk averse *survival algorithm*. Traditional varieties with low but stable yields are preferred over newer varieties involving more uncertainty. Peasants also prefer to pay interest in kind rather than in money. Even if this costs them more, they are insured against sudden falls in the price of grains. Finally, Lipton points to the inequality relations, due to which peasants have less access to water, seeds, fertiliser, herbicides and pesticides, which are all required to achieve higher yields. All in all there is no contradiction between highly risk averse behaviour and an extremely rational consideration of costs and benefits. This is also referred to as the RAUI hypothesis: risk aversion causes under investment (see Wharton, 1970).

The lesson that can be derived from risk aversion analysis is that policy measures that reduce peasants' risks, such as access to cheap credit or buffer food stocks, will increase their willingness to innovate. However, in successive publications Roumasset warns against easy generalisations about risk aversion. Under suboptimal conditions, the recommended use of fertilisers may be objectively inefficient. The decision not to adopt new technologies is often based on considerations of efficiency, rather than risk aversion (David and Roumasset, 2000; Roumasset, 1976, 2002).

We feel that the more individualistic approach to peasant institutions and behaviour is rather convincing. If one considers changes in agriculture since the end of the nineteenth century, it seems obvious that peasants all over the world have responded dynamically, innovatively and rationally whenever they were offered new opportunities. Still, it would not be wise to neglect cultural constraints altogether, as most economists tend to do. Behaviour, which is a rational response to challenges in a given situation, tends to crystallise and harden into cultural patterns, patterns of behaviour, and institutions. These in turn influence future responses and choices. Individual behaviour is also determined by internalised norms, which are culturally transmitted. One should also not forget that cultural norms and institutions within societies are often maintained by means of powerful social sanctions. The very perception of the alternatives between which one has to choose is partly determined by culture and institutions (North, 1993). Also, the options and alternatives themselves are institutionally determined. If market institutions have not developed, peasants will not be unable to respond to modern economic incentives. The cultural and the individualistic approaches are not so opposed as would seem to be the case on first sight.

10.5   Land reform

10.5.1   Varieties of land reform

When referring to land reform, redistribution of land from larger to smaller landowners is the first thing that comes to mind. However, land reform comes in many forms, depending on the kind of land-tenure relationships in a country (see Box 10.7).

BOX 10.7 : Varieties of land reform

Differences in initial conditions

Sub-Saharan Africa
- Common rights to land cultivation.
- Land is not tradable.

Latin America
- Large landownership with land cultivated by hired labour.
- *Minifundia* cultivated by small peasants.

Asia
- Less inequality in access to land and size of farms.
- More sharecropping and tenant farmers.

Varieties of land reform
- Redistribution of landownership to smallholders.
- Registration of individual titles to land.
- Strengthening private ownership rights to land.
- Transforming communal rights to land into individual rights to land.
- Improvements in legal status of sharecroppers and tenant farmers/enhancing security of tenure.
- Decrease in land rents or payments in kind.
- Consolidation of plots.
- Bringing new land into cultivation.
- Collectivisation of agriculture/nationalisation of land.
- Decollectivisation of agriculture.

In addition to land redistribution, land reforms can include: cadastral reforms in which land rights are more clearly defined, improvements in the legal status of sharecroppers, bringing new land into cultivation, improved contractual arrangements, collectivisation and decollectivisation. Some types of land reform such as titling are aimed at counteracting environmentally unfriendly practices by poor farmers, by providing incentives to invest in maintaining soil quality (Fearnside 2001). Communal access to land under conditions of increasing population density can result in what is called the 'tragedy of the commons' (Hardin, 1968): land degradation through overuse or overgrazing.

Redistribution of land

Access to land is one of the central themes in the study of rural development. In many developing countries landownership and access to land is distributed very unequally. Inequality tends to increase in the course of time and the number of landless people in rural areas is on the rise (Griffin, 1981; Singh, 1982 for Southeast Asia; Ghai and Radwan, 1985 for African countries). A more equal distribution of land could contribute to a decrease in rural poverty since improved access to land would enable the poor to support themselves (De Janvry et al., 2002; Kanbur and Lustig, 1999).

Moreover, redistribution of land may also contribute to increased productivity and efficiency (De Janvry et al., 2001). In section 10.4.3 we noted that smaller farmers generally cultivate their fields more efficiently than larger farmers and realise higher yields per hectare. A survey article by Binswanger and associates concludes 'Most of the work on the relationship between farm size and productivity strongly suggests that farms that rely mostly on family labour have higher productivity levels than large farms operated primarily with hired labour' (Binswanger et al., 1995: 2664). Unlike manufacturing, the agricultural sector has relatively few economies of scale. Therefore, large-scale agriculture is not inherently more productive than small-scale agriculture. Besides, large absentee landowners do not always employ their production factors very efficiently. They often live in urban areas and are not personally involved in agricultural production. They are characterised by highly consumptive life styles. Frequently, ownership of land is no more than a safe investment. Also, it is harder to monitor the productive efforts of agricultural labourers, who are not working on their own account. Peasants employ more labour per hectare than large landowners, have higher cropping frequencies, and higher yields per crop. Improved access to land can also allow landless households to utilise family labour that cannot be put to use otherwise through the market (De Janvry et al., 2001).

Many Latin American countries are characterised by an extremely unequal distribution of landownership (see Dorner, 1972; Furtado, 1976; Maddison, 1992), which has its origin in the pattern of Spanish and Portuguese colonisation in the sixteenth century. On the one hand, there are vast estates owned by large landowners (*latifundia*). On the other hand, there are tiny plots of land owned by peasants (*minifundia*). These are too small to provide a decent living for peasant households. Therefore, peasants are forced to offer their labour to the large landowners. The large landowners have their land cultivated or their cattle grazed by agricultural labourers. Sometimes the agricultural labourers are even allocated small plots of land to cultivate for their own use in exchange for their labour services.

On the large estates cultivation of land is extensive, and relatively capital-intensive. The available reserves of labour are underutilised. Output per unit of land is not very high. At the same time, the smallest farms are so tiny, that their productivity is also low. Under such circumstances, *redistribution* of landownership creating more small and medium-sized farm holdings of viable size could contribute to an improvement in the living standards of the poor and increased production per unit of land.

In sum, many researchers believe that redistribution of land and other land reforms may not only contribute to a more equitable distribution of income, but also to reduction of poverty, and to increases in productivity and agricultural development (Alexandratos, 1988; Binswanger et al., 1995; De Janvry et al., 2001; Dorner, 1972). In countries where access to land has been distributed more equally – such as China, Japan, Korea and Taiwan – agricultural development has been more successful than in countries where there is a wide gap between large landowners with modern farm management and small peasants who cannot afford new inputs.

There is no complete consensus that the effects of redistribution of land are positive under all circumstances. Myint (1980) argues, for instance, that larger, modern-oriented farmers are often the bearers of agricultural innovation. He believes that one has to accept the associated inequalities. In a series of publications based on research in the Philippines, Roumasset fiercely criticises the general assumption that land reform will necessarily increase efficiency and productivity (Roumasset, 1995; David and Roumasset, 2000). Increasing landlessness can also be a consequence of productivity improvements in agriculture, which call for a shift of surplus labour to other sectors of the economy. Papers by Place (2009) and Barrett *et al.* (2010) indicate that the empirical evidence is mixed. Even if most authors agree with the stylised fact of the inverse relation between land size and land productivity, it does not necessarily follow that redistribution of land will automatically increase productivity.

Dorner (1972) and Hayami and Ruttan (1985) warn against inflated expectations. It is true that, other things being equal, peasants can realise higher yields per hectare by cultivating the land more intensively than large farmers. But like the 'vent for surplus' effects (see Chapter 8), the effects of land redistribution are once and for all. If new inputs and the means to purchase and use them are not made available to the peasants, agricultural development will stagnate after land reform. As was already noted, larger farmers are more likely to employ new techniques than peasants. For land redistribution to succeed, the total institutional structure has to be adjusted, so that small peasants and farmers can gain access to credit, schooling, agricultural extension, new inputs and water without being faced with unacceptable risks. We now know that redistribution of land to smaller farmers without substantial complementary investment in technology support, financial institutions and cooperation in marketing and logistics will not have the desired effects (Atamanov, 2011; World Bank-WDR, 2008).

Establishing individual rights to land

An important type of land reform is the strengthening of individual property rights to land. The main benefits deriving from well-defined and secure individual rights to land are the following (Deininger and Feder, 2001; World Bank-WDR, 2008):

1. *Greater incentives for long-term investment in increased productivity and environmental sustainability.* If producers have strong titles to land they will be more willing to make large investments in irrigation, machinery, land improvement and conservation, which they would not make if their titles to land were uncertain. Titles to land can be ownership titles, but strengthening the contractual rights of tenants to cultivate land has similar effects.
2. Individual rights to land allow for the emergence of land markets, which allows for the *transfer of land to the most productive users.* This assumes the existence of well-functioning land markets that allocate land to productive uses, rather than imperfect and speculative land markets which strengthen the position of speculative elites.
3. When land is *transferable*, it can be used as collateral in formal credit markets, thus improving the access of small farmers to credit. This contributes to the development of rural financial markets and also to the ability of farmers to invest in improved productivity.

Establishing individual titles to land may also have some important costs and drawbacks. The first of these is simply that there are large costs involved in land registration, land demarcation and the resolution of conflicts of land. Next, and even more important, communal land ownership may function as a social safety net. Individualisation of land ownership may deprive traditional communities of their sources of livelihood and mutual support (see the discussion of the *moral economy* in section 10.4.3). Finally, if rural markets are highly imperfect, markets for land will not result in reallocation of land to the most productive uses. It can result in land grabbing by members of powerful elites or foreign investors.

Selected experiences

In several Sub-Saharan African countries there is a tradition of common rights to land use.[26] Land is not for sale. Rights to cultivate land are in principle allocated to members of the community by chiefs of clans, village elders and so forth. Such land tenure relations date back to the time when population density was low, land was abundant and agriculture was extensive. When cultivation becomes more intensive and land becomes scarce, common rights to land form a disincentive for individual investment in maintenance or improvement of soil fertility. The value of land goes up, and conflicts break out over land rights (Van Hekken and Thoden van Velzen, 1972). There is a pressure for institutional change. Gradually more individualised property rights to land begin to emerge (Boserup, 1965; Deininger and Feder, 2001; Feeny, 1982, 1987; North, 1990; North and Thomas, 1973). It is interesting to note, though, that traditional practices of land allocation continued to function long after the formal legal relationships have changed (e.g. Firmin-Sellers and Sellers, 1999).

During the colonial period, the authorities tried to introduce *cadastral land reform*, that is, registration of individual ownership titles and consolidation of scattered plots of land. In addition, new land was brought into cultivation. Private property of land was to the advantage of colonists and plantation owners, who successfully laid claim to the most fertile lands in countries such as Kenya, Zambia, Zimbabwe and South Africa. It also gave rise to *apartheid*-type labour relations, where Africans lost their access to land and were forced to supply labour to the settler plantations. In present times, the establishment of markets for land also results in speculative land grabbing by elites, especially when land markets are very imperfect.

In the post-colonial period, the significance of foreign owned plantations declined. Many plantations were *expropriated*. Expropriated land was taken into collective use or was allocated to individual cultivators. Where possible, new land was brought under cultivation, as in the pre-war period. Allocation of newly cultivated and expropriated lands among African farmers sometimes led to an increase in rural inequality, rather than its decline (Ghai and Radwan, 1985). An example is the 'million acre scheme' in Kenya, which primarily benefited large farmers.

Mexico is the best-known example of a Latin American country where radical land reforms have taken place and large estates have been expropriated. The 1915 Land Reform Act gave rise to a type of communal landownership by the village community, the *ejido*. The *ejido* gave villagers rights to cultivate land, while pastures and woodlands remained in common use. In Mexico, the inequality of access to land is now less marked than in other

---

[26] Hill (1986), however, points out that in parts of West Africa some land is freely traded. Where white settlers have practised agriculture, as in Zimbabwe, Kenya or South Africa there are also large agricultural estates.

large Latin American countries. In addition to the *ejidos*, however, there is also private landownership. Lands of the highest quality are usually owned by individuals. Other countries in Latin America where land reforms have been implemented are Bolivia, Cuba, Chile (under President Allende), El Salvador and Nicaragua.

In many South and Southeast Asian countries, colonial practices and administrative centralisation long ago resulted in a diminishing importance of traditional communal rights to land. Except in communist countries, most land is in private hands. Despite inequality of land ownership, actual access to land is less unequal than in Latin America. Much land is rented out in some form to peasants who cultivate the land on their own account. The peasants pay rent in money or in kind, as a share of the crop. Under such circumstances land reforms are especially concerned with improvements in the *legal status of tenant farmers* and the reduction of the rent or the crop share owed to the landowner. When the position of tenant farmers is legally precarious or when a large portion of every increase in production automatically goes to the landowner, tenant farmers will have no incentive to invest in increased productivity and technological innovation.[27]

In Asia, the most radical land reforms were implemented in China after the revolution of 1949. In the process of land reform an estimated 900,000 farmers – justly or unjustly classified as large farmers or *kulaks* – lost their lives. Initially, expropriated land was reallocated to individual farmers. But in the 1950s agricultural cooperatives were established. In 1958 the agricultural sector was completely collectivised, and large communes were established, sometimes including over a million people. After 1978, a reverse process operated, with communes being gradually dismantled and family units being reinstated.

During the past twenty years, great emphasis has been put on the expansion of credit facilities for small farmers and increasing their access to new inputs, with good reason. Nevertheless, time and again larger farmers succeed in getting a disproportional part of the available credits and resources, due to their good political contacts, their social standing and power, their higher creditworthiness and their better education (Bol, 1983). The risks involved in granting credit to small peasants are so high that financial institutions mainly focus on larger, creditworthy farmers. In the end the net effect of many credit programmes is the granting of subsidised credit to the wealthier farmers, which makes for capital-intensive agriculture rather than the opposite. Following the success of the Grameen bank in Bangladesh, many developing countries in recent years have attempted to set up micro-credit schemes, where grass roots' mechanisms of social control ensure repayment of loans (Bornstein, 1996).

Although many developing countries in Africa, Asia and Latin America profess to pursue a policy of equalising access to land, not much redistribution has occurred in practice. Almost everywhere, the close political ties between large landowners, representatives of the government, and dominant political movements prevent the realisation of land reform. This holds for countries such as India (Cassen, 1978; Frankel, 1978), the Philippines, Brazil, Argentina, Kenya and Zambia. Attempts at gradual reform through legislation are effectively sabotaged.

---

[27] In the post-war literature tenant relations were considered to be less efficient than cultivation of the land by its owner. However, in particular in areas where markets for producers and production factors are quite underdeveloped, lease proportions may divide risks among the tenant farmer and his/her landlord (see Hayami and Ruttan, 1985: 391 ff.; De Janvry *et al.*, 2001).

There are instances of sweeping redistribution of land: China in 1949 (Hsu, 1982), Taiwan and Korea after the Second World War (Griffin, 1976), Mexico after the Mexican revolution and Japan in the Meiji reforms after 1867 and again during the initial years of the Second World War. Such radical land reforms all took place in exceptional periods in history, when the whole social fabric was in turmoil. In revolutionary countries, the new regimes implemented land reforms with the use of widespread coercion and physical violence. In other cases, societies had been seriously disrupted as a result of wars, occupations, or external threats, all circumstances in which the resistance of powerful landed elites could be overcome. Yet, one should realise the high cost of these changes, in terms of human life and human suffering.

Since the 1970s, large-scale state-led expropriative land distribution and other radical approaches to land reform have been off the agenda (De Janvry et al., 2001). The exception is Zimbabwe, where violent expropriation of large land holdings of white farmers by the Mugabe regime has lead to economic collapse and widespread food shortages. But according to a recent collection of studies in De Janvry et al. (2001), more gradual approaches to land reform are very much back on the agenda for the twenty-first century. The authors argue for an incremental and eclectic approach. Individual ownership titles are not a universal panacea and effects to introduce individual titling do not always succeed (Firmin-Sellers and Sellers, 1999). Access to land can also be improved through improved rental contracts, tenure reform and a reliance on a variety of informal tenure arrangements. Instead of a sharp dichotomy between communal and individual landownership, Deininger and Binswanger (2001) argue for increased effectiveness of individual property rights under existing arrangements. With regard to redistribution of land, countries such as Brazil, Colombia and South Africa are now trying to implement a gradualistic model of 'negotiated land reform'.

It is now widely accepted that land reform policies should be comprehensive. It is not enough that access to land be changed. There is need for a wide range of complementary policies with regard to infrastructure, transport, training and availability of finance and inputs and improved functioning of land and product markets.

Collectivisation and decollectivisation

Both collectivisation and decollectivisation are very important varieties of land reform. We stated above that there are few economies of scale in agriculture. This does not mean there are none. Some crops such as sugar and bananas have economies of scale in processing and distribution. These products have to be processed or shipped within hours of harvesting to avoid deterioration. Therefore plantation production of such products continues to be of importance (Binswanger et al., 1995). Certain activities and investments exceed the financial capacity of smaller individual farmers. These may include the construction of irrigation systems or the purchase of capital goods such as tractors and farm machinery. Finally, there may be very important economies of scale with respect to the marketing of output and the purchase of inputs.

Such arguments provide the theoretical justification for the formation of agricultural cooperatives. When many small farmers cooperate, they will be able to purchase inputs more cheaply and sell their products at better prices. They can profit from common investment in agricultural machinery, land improvement and water control.

In centrally planned economies like the Soviet Union, China and Vietnam the foundation of cooperatives was merely a step on the way to complete collectivisation of agriculture. In the Soviet Union and Romania, the authorities believed in the creation of a collectivised industrial agricultural system, in which economies of scale could be achieved through massive infusions of capital goods and large-scale production. Like other post-war industrialisation strategies and development theories, Marxist theory was pervaded with negative evaluations of 'backward' agriculture and a glorification of the industrial sector. In China one of the considerations for collectivisation was the fact that extremely large-scale infrastructural works and irrigation systems were required, which could only be realised by a massive mobilisation of labour. Consequently, communes were established which at their apex included more than 1 million people per commune (Hsu, 1982). With regard to the infrastructural aspects, some degree of success of this policy cannot be denied.

However attractive collectivisation of agriculture may be in theory, the problems of worker motivation and efficient allocation turned out to be insuperable in practice. In the Chinese communes the links between efforts and rewards were completely severed. Other than fear and political mobilisation, there was no incentive to work. The work points, which were the basis of rewards, were allocated according to political criteria. The forced introduction of communes during the Great Leap Forward in 1958–60 resulted in wide-spread famine in which, according to some estimates, between 30 and 47 million people died of hunger (Ashton *et al.*, 1984; Dikötter, 2010).

After 1960, Chinese agriculture was gradually decentralised. The introduction of a '*household responsibility system*' in 1978 led to a period of explosive growth of agricultural output until the mid-1980s. Total output grew by no less 7.4 per cent per year (Huang, 1998). Under the responsibility system Chinese farmers were allowed to sell the surpluses that remained after fulfilment of obligatory delivery quotas, at market prices. This provided them with strong incentives to increase their production. In addition, state procurement prices were increased. Further market reforms were introduced in 1985 and 1991. As yet land remains in public ownership, but individual farmers acquired the right to cultivate well-defined plots of land for periods of up to fifteen years. However, the lack of clear-cut private titles to land discouraged farmer investment after 1985 and growth in agriculture started to slow down, albeit to a still respectable rate of around 3.8 per cent per year.

The absence of a clear relationship between effort and reward is the main problem in all large-scale collectivised agriculture. It is one of the main diseconomies of scale. In former socialist countries in Eastern Europe, for example, the small plots of land that were privately cultivated had vastly higher productivity than collectivised agriculture. In agriculture, the family farm, whether or not supplemented by hired labour, has generally proved to be the most efficient form of organisation, in comparison with both large-scale collectivised agriculture and with large landownership (Deininger and Binswanger, 2001: 412). There is, however, still a valid case for voluntary cooperation and cooperatives in developing countries. In agrarian development projects, attempts are currently being made to build on existing traditional informal forms of cooperation, such as credit cooperatives and grain banks. Also, in settings of low population density individual cultivation can be combined with a variety of communal tenure arrangements.

After 1989, decollectivisation of agriculture also took place in Eastern Europe and many former Soviet Republics. Here the experiences were less positive than in China and East Asia (see Table 10.1, p. 385). There was a large decline in agricultural production per capita. In part, this was due to a long period of uncertainty about land ownership. In many countries, such as for instance Uzbekistan, decollectivisation was half-hearted and hesitant (Pomfret, 2000). In Kyrgystan, the lack of supporting institutions resulted in stagnating agricultural output after decollectivisation (Atamanov, 2011). In the Soviet Union, the experience of almost three-quarters of a century of collective agriculture left farmers badly prepared for privatisation. As mentioned before, all forms of land reform and changes in patterns of land tenure, including decollectivisation, require complementary policies. When these are not forthcoming, the results of reform will be disappointing.

10.6   Policies for rural development

Rural development requires two-pronged policies. The first set of policies focuses on promoting the dynamism of the agricultural sector. The second aims at expanding non-agrarian productive activities in rural areas. Given that agriculture will not be able to absorb the increase in rural population, diversifying into non-agricultural activities is of great importance. Presently non-agricultural activities account for 30–50 per cent of incomes in rural areas (Eicher and Staatz, 1984; World Bank-WDR, 2008, Chapter 9).

With regard to the agricultural sector, one of the routes to increase productivity is through connecting smallholder farmers to wider markets. Given the large number of smallholder farmers, the *2008 World Development Report* argues that increasing their productivity is especially important from the perspective of poverty reduction. Smallholders can engage in food production for markets, but can also participate in the production of high-value non-traditional exports such as flowers, vegetables, fruit juices, coffee, tea, alcoholic beverages and so forth (Iizuka and Gebreeyesus, 2012). Along with smallholders, larger plantations employing wage labour also play an important role in such non-traditional exports.

Agricultural productivity increases require complementary investments in infrastructure, financial institutions, technology support and cooperative efforts in marketing and logistics. Without such efforts, it will not be possible to connect smaller farmers to markets.

The second set of policies is aimed at non-agricultural activities in rural communities (see for example, Atamanov, 2011; Dixon, 1990; Druijven, 1983, 1990; Haggblade et al., 2007; Hogg, 1984; Teszler, 1984). Households almost invariably combine agricultural and non-agricultural sources of income and individual workers often have more than one job. One can distinguish between *off-farm employment* and *non-farm employment*. Off-farm employment refers to all activities of members of farming households outside their own household, including paid work within the agricultural sector. Non-farm employment refers to employment outside the agricultural sector, whether as side employment or as primary activity.

The most important non-farm activity is retail trade and a variety of private and public services. Participation in retail trade predominantly takes the form of self-employment, while services are mostly wage employment. Rural manufacturing accounts for some 20–25 per cent of non-farm employment (World Bank-WDR, 2008, Figure 9.6).

Over time, the nature of non-farm activities has been changing. Traditional methods of craft production change under the influence of new technical possibilities. For example, tailors can use pedal sewing machines or even electrically driven ones. The range of goods supplied in the informal sector undergoes change. For instance, waste products like old tyres are reworked into sandals (Teszler, 1984). Existing traditional craft activities are replaced by rural industries (Voeten *et al.*, 2011). New lines of activity are emerging, such as maintenance of motorcycles, solar panels, bicycles and cars, and putting-out arrangements, where some stages of industrial production – e.g. sewing of clothing or shoemaking – are performed in homes. New sources of employment include, among others, public works road construction, construction of communal facilities, irrigation and other infrastructural works. These often offer temporary employment outside agricultural peak periods. In services there are numerous activities in the informal sector. Furthermore, jobs are also being created in healthcare, education, administration and agricultural extension. Finally, employment in rural industry is growing. In part, this has to do with traditional production in small brickyards, carpentries, furniture making or potteries. But there are also small-scale rural factories. These factories are often established in smaller cities, but provide employment for the rural population. One of the well-known success stories is the rapid emergence and growth of township and village enterprises (TVEs) in China in the 1990s (Szirmai *et al.*, 2001). Nevertheless, the bulk of industrial production in China remains concentrated in urbanised coastal regions and urban–rural gaps are again on the increase.

Where agriculture does not provide sufficient employment and income, members of rural households have a number of options. They can seek employment in the rural non-farm economy, they can migrate – temporarily or permanently – to urban centres or they can seek employment in other countries. The rapid migration to urban centres imposes huge burdens and challenges with regard to housing, infrastructure, sanitation and living conditions. Policies oriented towards promoting and upgrading rural non-farm employment can simultaneously revitalise rural areas and slow down migration flows. There are all sorts of positive linkages – both supply linkages and demand linkages – between agricultural and non-agricultural activities which also provide new incentives for agricultural growth. Rural policies need to address bottlenecks such as poor education, access to credit, access to energy (Mirza and Szirmai, 2010), transport infrastructure and weak governance structures.

Questions for review

1. To what extent has the Malthusian prediction that food production cannot keep up with population growth been validated in the course of the past sixty years?
2. To what extent does an increase in food production in a country imply that the consumption of food is also increasing and that undernourishment and malnutrition are on the decrease?
3. Discuss the three ways in which agricultural output can be increased. What were the most common routes to growth of output in the past? What is the most applicable route in the present?
4. Discuss Ester Boserup's theory of the impact of increasing population density on changes in agricultural technology. What lessons can be derived from Boserup's analysis?
5. What are the implications of Schultz's proposition that small farmers in developing countries are 'poor but efficient'?
6. Discuss the five models of agricultural development of Hayami and Ruttan.

7. Why do farmers farming smaller plots often have higher productivity per hectare than large landowners?
8. What are the defining characteristics of the 'green revolution'? Provide a summary of the debate on the advantages and disadvantages of the green revolution.
9. What is the difference between rural development and agricultural development?
10. Discuss the differences between the three approaches to rural development: the modernisation approach, the incorporation approach and the transactionalist approach.
11. Why are the results of redistribution of land frequently disappointing?
12. What are the characteristics of a peasant economy? Summarise the debate on the advantages and disadvantages of the use of the concept of peasant economy.
13. Why do small farmers in developing countries generally prefer to minimise risks rather than maximise output? What kind of strategies do they pursue in order to minimise risks?
14. What are the positive and negative effects on individualisation of land titles on agricultural growth and rural development?
15. What are the risks and potential advantages of genetic manipulation as a source of agricultural growth in developing countries?

Further reading

An indispensible overview of theories and issues in agricultural development is provided by Hayami and Ruttan in *Agricultural Development: An International Perspective* (1985). Other influential publications include Eicher and Staatz (eds.), *Agricultural Development in the Third World* (1984), Mellor, *The Economics of Agricultural Development* (1966) and Schultz, *Transforming Traditional Agriculture* (1964). The process of agricultural intensification is analysed by Ester Boserup in two brilliant books: *The Conditions of Agricultural Growth* (1965) and *Population and Technology* (1981). Boserup was also one of the first authors to analyse the role of women in agriculture in *Women's Role in Economic Development* (1970). In a trendsetting book, *Poverty and Famines* (1981), Amartya Sen shows that producing enough food is not always sufficient to avert famines. This book develops the entitlements approach.

Two useful textbooks on rural development are Dixon, *Rural Development in the Third World* (1990) and Ellis, *Peasant Economics: Farm Households and Agrarian Development* (1988). Key publications on rural development include Chambers, *Rural Development: Putting the Last First* (1983), Lipton, 'The Theory of the Optimizing Peasant' (1966), Popkin, *The Rational Peasant: The Political Economy of Rural Society in Vietnam* (1979) and Scott, *The Moral Economy of the Peasant: Rebellion and Subsistence in South East Asia* (1976). In an article in Volume 2 of the *Handbook of Agricultural Economics*, 'Rural Development and Rural Policy', De Janvry, Sadoulet and Murgai (2002) review the past and present debates on rural development An interesting collection of papers on rural development is found in Haggblade, Hazell and Reardon (eds.), *Transforming the Rural Nonfarm Economy* (2007). Hill's *Development Economics on Trial: The Anthropological Case for a Prosecution* (1986), is a lively polemic against economists' tendencies to generalise about agricultural growth and rural development on the basis of insufficient evidence. Hill also provides a trenchant criticism of statistics on agricultural growth.

Three books published by the FAO provide a wealth of statistical data as well as comprehensive discussions of theories of agricultural development, policy options, prospects and environmental issues. They are: Alexandratos, *World Agriculture towards 2000* (1988), Alexandratos (ed.), *World Agriculture: Towards 2010* (1995) and Bruinsma (ed.), *World Agriculture towards 2015/2030: An FAO Perspective* (2003). Alexandratos and Bruinsma have now updated their earlier work in the excellent publication *World agriculture towards 2030/2050: The 2012 revision* (2012). Other publications on trends in agriculture and food production include Brown, *Tough Choices: Facing the Challenge of Food Scarcity* (1996), Mitchell *et al.*, *The World Food Outlook* (1997), Smil, *Feeding the World: The Challenge for the Twenty-First Century* (2000) and an article by Ruttan in the *Journal of Economic Perspectives*: 'Productivity Growth in World Agriculture: Sources and Constraints' (2002). Recent estimates and projections are published in *The State of Food Security in the World 2012* (FAO, 2012a). For a criticism of doomsday prophecies and Malthusian pessimism, students are advised to read Lomborg, *The Skeptical Environmentalist: Measuring the Real State of the World* (2001). This book was the starting point of a fierce polemic.

Griffin has written an early critical analysis of the green revolution in *The Political Economy of Agrarian Change* (1976). Other interesting books about the 'green revolution', technological change and biotechnology include: Glaeser (ed.), *The Green Revolution Revisited: Critique and Alternatives* (1987), Pinstrup-Anderson, *Agricultural Research and Technology in Economic Development* (1982), Pinstrup-Anderson and Hazell, 'The Impact of the Green Revolution and Prospects for the Future' (1985), Hogg, *Technological Change in Agriculture: Locking in to Genetic Uniformity* (2000) and Paarlberg, *The Politics of Precaution: Genetically Modified Crops in Developing Countries* (2001). Two recent interesting polemical books by Paarlberg are *Starved for Science: How Biotechnology is Being Kept out of Africa* (2008) and *Food Politics: What Everyone Needs to Know* (2010).

For land reform one can consult the article by Binswanger, Deininger and Feder, 'Power, Distortions, Revolt and Reform in Agricultural Land Relations', in the *Handbook of Development Economics* (1995), an article by Deininger and Binswanger, 'Evolution of the World Bank's Land Policy' (2001) and Deininger and Feder's excellent article, 'Land Institutions and Land Markets', in Volume 1A of the *Handbook of Agricultural Economics* (2001). The five volumes of this *Handbook*, published between 2001 and 2010, are an indispensible source for people interested in agricultural growth and rural development.

The FAO publishes a wide range of statistics on agriculture, fisheries, forestry and the environment. These include the FAO, *Production Yearbooks,* the FAO annual reports on *The State of Food and Agriculture* (1989, 1990, 1991, 1993), *The Sixth World Food Survey* (1996), the annual *Global Forest Resources Assessment 2000: Main Report* (2001) and successive editions of *The State of Food Insecurity in the World* (e.g. FAO, 2012a). Most reports and statistics can be accessed via the FAO website: www.fao.org/ and the FAO statistical database FAOSTAT: http://faostat.fao.org/.

11

State formation and political aspects of development

This chapter focuses on the processes of state formation and political development in developing countries. Until recently most economists have ignored the relationships between state formation and economic development. Nevertheless, political and economic developments are closely interconnected. It is of little use to discuss the economic development of Afghanistan without taking the conflicts with the Taliban into consideration. Also, it is not much use to analyse the economic development of African countries if one does not realise that many countries on the African continent are in a state of open or latent civil strife or international conflict. At the moment of writing (2014), this applies for instance to countries such as Congo, Central African Republic, Egypt, Libya, Mali, Nigeria, Somalia, South Sudan, Uganda and Zimbabwe.

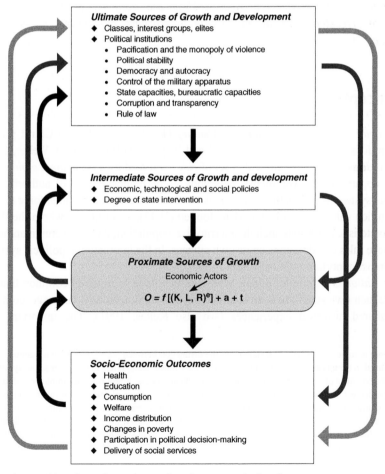

Figure 11.1 State formation and socio-economic development

The political aspects of development will be discussed from two perspectives with which the reader will by now be familiar. In the first place, the interactions between state formation and economic development will be analysed. These interactions are summarised in Figure 11.1. In this context, an interesting paradox comes to the fore. The tasks and demands nowadays facing the government apparatus in developing countries are heavier and more comprehensive than ever before in economic history. At the same time, in many countries the apparatus of government is less well equipped to fulfil these tasks.

In the second place, the characteristics of state formation and political development will be discussed as important independent aspects of development in their own right. In Chapter 1 we argued that 'development' is much more than economic change alone. Themes such as national independence, effectiveness of government policy, political democratisation and political participation are all included in a broader conception of development.

In this chapter the following themes and topics will be discussed: concepts of state and nation (section 11.1); classical perspectives on the relationships between the state and the economy (section 11.2); state formation as a prerequisite for economic development: European patterns of development (section 11.3); specific characteristics and problems of state formation in developing countries (section 11.4); the role of the state in economic development and industrialisation (section 11.5); interactions between political and economic developments (section 11.6); and the predatory state as an obstacle to economic development in Sub-Saharan Africa (section 11.7).

11.1   Concepts

In *Social Change in the Twentieth Century* (1977: 11–15) Daniel Chirot provides useful definitions of concepts such as 'state' and 'nation'. Following Max Weber, Chirot defines the *state* as a social system with a set of *rules* enforced by a *permanent administrative body* (the apparatus of government). This body is the highest source of authority in the wider social system. It claims the right to make collective decisions and to enforce them. A similar definition can be found in Van den Hoogen (1992), according to whom the distinguishing characteristics of a state include a territory, a population, and a sovereign authority that can impose rules and decisions on its own citizens. In the international political system *states* are the most important political actors.[1]

A *nation* is a group of people who feel they have so much in common that they should have their own state. The joint element may be religion, culture, language, common descent, or shared historical experiences (see also Kellas, 1991). The important thing is the

[1] There is some conceptual confusion about the distinction between 'state' and 'state apparatus'. The term 'state' as used in the text above (e.g. the Dutch state or the Chinese state) refers to the wider social system or society, the common rules of which are established in the political process. These rules are implemented and enforced by a permanent administrative body (the 'state apparatus'). However, elsewhere, for instance in the Marxist literature, 'state' is also used to refer to the 'apparatus of government' (which includes the civil service, the army, the police and such political institutions as the political executive, the head of state, the judiciary, parliament and other representative organs). When we discuss processes of state formation in this chapter, we are referring to the wider concept of state. When we discuss the role of the state in the process of economic development, we are referring to the apparatus of government.

subjective feeling that people share common descent or history, from which they derive their claim to statehood. Van den Berghe (1981) defines a nation as a politically conscious ethnic group.

The term *society* may have many different meanings. In the context of state formation and nation building the term 'society' refers to the population that is controlled by a state apparatus or the population that forms a nation or both. A *country* refers to a well-defined geographical territory, which is effectively controlled by a state apparatus. Effective control is the usual criterion for international diplomatic recognition of a country.

The term *nation-state* refers to the overlap of the population that is controlled by a state, and the population with shared feelings of belonging. This overlap is by no means self-evident. Nationalism – the idea that each nation should have its own independent state – is a relatively recent phenomenon, dating – in its modern form – from the nineteenth century. Prior to the nineteenth century most people used to identify more with village, region, or kin, than with larger territorial political units. In many developing countries today they still do so. Before the nineteenth century, European politics were mainly dominated by royal and noble elites. Kinship relationships within these elites played an important role in politics.

We do not mean to say that there were no nationalist sentiments or movements prior to the nineteenth century. Examples which immediately come to mind are the French popular resistance to British domination in the fifteenth century, inspired by Joan of Arc, the Dutch revolt against Spanish rule in the sixteenth and seventeenth century, and French nationalism following the French Revolution in the eighteenth century. Still, important defining characteristics of modern nationalism were lacking, such as the use of modern means of communication and organisation to mobilise large numbers of people into mass movements and the underpinning of mass movements by nationalist ideologies.

There are nations without their own state, like the Jews before the establishment of the state of Israel, the Kurds and the Palestinians. There are also movements that seek to unite larger groups with an appeal to their common identity, such as Pan-Slavism or Pan-Arabism. There are also *multinational states* in which several national groups with a distinctive 'we-feeling' coexist within a territory controlled by a single state apparatus. Well-known examples are the Habsburg monarchy until 1918, the Ottoman empire until 1918, the former Yugoslavia, the former Soviet Union and present-day India.

Finally, there are also examples of *multi-ethnic states*. These states comprise various ethnic groups that are characterised by ethnic 'we-feelings', but do not claim their own separate states (see Van den Berghe, 1981: 61). The Frisians in the Netherlands, or the Welsh in Great Britain are an example of such a group. Often countries like the USA and Brazil are also called multi-ethnic states. Most Western societies have become more multi-ethnic since the Second World War, as a result of massive immigration.

All these concepts represent sliding scales rather than absolutes. Within multi-ethnic states nationalist sentiments may develop, which may give rise to separatist movements. On the other hand, in processes of state formation separate groups may also develop common national identities. Although the term 'nation' sometimes has biological undertones of common descent or kinship, national awareness often develops as a result of shared historical experiences and political efforts. In *The Embarrassment of Riches*, Simon Schama (1988) has impressively shown how Dutch national feelings were cultivated in the seventeenth century, resulting in the emergence of a Dutch national identity. The struggle for independence contributed to the emergence of national awareness in many former colonies.

Chirot makes a distinction between *core* societies and societies, which is of relevance for an understanding of state formation processes in developing countries.[2] In countries in the core of world society, state, nation, society and geographical boundaries tend to coincide. Examples of highly integrated nation-states are Denmark, France, Japan, the Netherlands, Sweden and the USA. The main characteristic of such nation-states is a relatively high degree of political autonomy in national decision making,[3] strong cultural integration and associated feelings of cultural self-confidence, at times bordering on complacency and feelings of superiority. Such 'strong states' are also characterised by effective government institutions (Thomas, 1987). From an economic point of view, core states are generally rich, highly industrialised and have a diversified economy.

On the periphery of world society, states and nations coincide to a far lesser extent. Many states are multi-ethnic or multinational. Country borders cut across ethnic boundaries. People are more likely to relate to tribe, village, or region than to a far-off national state or national government. Separatist movements, religious conflict, civil wars and external interference constantly threaten the unity of the national state. The capacity of the state apparatus to make and implement collective decisions and rules is weakly developed. There is greater dependence on external influences than in core countries. Internally, there is a large degree of cultural heterogeneity. Externally, countries are confronted with the cultural challenges of the West and penetration by Western cultural influences and also challenges of newly emerging powers such as China. Van den Hoogen points out that attempts to establish a strong, central authority in developing countries may actually become a source of conflict, violence and repression (Van den Hoogen, 1992). There is resistance not only to authoritarian government but also to the very notion of nation building itself. In economic terms, peripheral states are poorer, less industrialised, and less diversified in their economic structure.

In recent decades, we have become more aware of the fragility of nation-states, even in core states of the world economy. In almost all Western countries, the unity of the nation-state has become less self-evident. Movements for regional autonomy and separatist movements have gained in strength and importance. Examples include Scotland, Wales, the Basque Provinces and Catalonia in Spain, Corsica and Brittany in France, Flanders and the Walloon provinces in Belgium, Northern Italy, Southern Tyrol, and Quebec. In the USA, Australia, and Western Europe cultural integration has weakened and identification with the dominant national culture has declined among members of so-called ethnic minorities. This holds both for peoples who have been living in a country for ages, like Indians and Spanish Americans, Australian Aborigines and Afro-Americans, and more recent immigrants. In particular in Western Europe, cultural heterogeneity increased rapidly during the

---

[2] The terms 'core' and 'periphery' derive from theories of dependence in which conditions in developing countries are primarily explained by external influences (see section 3.5). The use of these terms, however, does not necessarily imply acceptance of these theories.

[3] Since national states are part of networks of international interdependence, autonomy in national decision making is always a matter of degree. For example, the national autonomy of European countries is constrained by supranational institutions such as the European Union. The latitude for national economic policies in small countries such as the Netherlands or Belgium is determined by developments in the international economy.

post-war period due to migration flows from former colonies and other regions. Not only does the nation-state become less self-evident due to increased internal cultural and ethnic diversity, the latitude for independent national policy also diminishes due to supranational economic and political influences in an increasingly interdependent world socio-economic system.

In several former communist states a destructive process of national disintegration unfolded after 1989. The Soviet Union, Czechoslovakia and Yugoslavia broke up into smaller states. Within these new political entities ethnic groups struggled for ascendancy or claimed their own autonomy. In Yugoslavia, this resulted in a bloody civil war in which various groups of Slavic descent (including Catholic Croats, Orthodox Serbs and Islamic Serbs) fought each other ferociously and applied ethnic cleansing in an attempt to create smaller ethnically homogeneous nation-states. Similar processes took place in Georgia, Tajikistan, Azerbaijan and Chechnya.

The demographer Keyfitz argues that the formation of smaller, ethnically homogeneous states is nothing but a continuation of the worldwide process of decolonisation and breakdown of empires (Keyfitz, 1991). The borders of the present existing states are accidental. Some nations like the Kurds, the Tamils and the Kashmiris had the bad luck that the process of state formation was consolidated before they were granted states of their own.

This is a dangerous notion. It ignores the fact that most regions in the world are ethnically mixed. The smaller the political entities claiming national independence, the sharper and more murderous the conflicts between the various 'nations' within the borders of the 'state'. The ultimate consequence of Keyfitz's perspective is the acceptance of ethnic cleansing by victors in ethnic struggles.

Presently, many developing countries are faced with separatist movements and potential challenges to their survival as an integrated national entity. These countries include China (Tibet and Xinjiang), India, Indonesia, Iraq, Mali, Myanmar, the Philippines, Nigeria and Ukraine. In the case of Sudan, South Sudan secceeded as an independent state in 2011. In the case of Sri Lanka, the Tamil independence movement was crushed in 2009.

Many of these developments are taking place as this text is being written and it is not clear what their outcomes will be. They illustrate once again the fruitlessness of simple dichotomies opposing highly developed and less developed political units and the tendency to think of development as a process of irreversible change from 'less developed' to 'more developed'.

11.2 Marxist and Weberian perspectives on the state

Classical Marxist and Weberian writings provide important insights into the process of state formation in developing countries and the role of the state in the overall process of development.

In the Marxist tradition, class relationships – the contradictions and conflicts between social groups and categories that have objective economic interests in common – are the central focus. Together with technological change (the forces of production), class relationships form the substructure of society. The dynamics of class relationships and class conflicts ultimately determine what happens in the superstructure of society: culture, religion, law and the state.[4] Reduced to its bare bones, this view implies that at a given moment in time the activities of the members of the state apparatus are completely determined by the interests of the ruling class. For instance, the state in a capitalist society is said to be no more than the executive committee of the ruling class of capitalists and the bourgeoisie. In a feudal society, the state represents the interests of the landed gentry and feudal landlords. After a socialist revolution, class contradictions would be abolished and the state would finally wither away (Marx, *The Communist Manifesto*, 1955).

This short summary does no justice to the discussions and polemics within the Marxist tradition concerning the interactions between the state and class relationships. Several neo-Marxist writings point in particular to the *relative autonomy* of the state apparatus. This implies that the state apparatus has a margin of freedom in relation to other social institutions. Political decisions and government actions have an independent measure of influence on the course of social and economic development (see, for example, Miliband, 1969; Poulantzas, 1974).

In addition, both neo-Marxists and non-Marxists argue that government officials may be regarded as a separate 'class' with its own interests. Government actions and policies are in part determined by this interest group (Bardhan, 1984; Dahrendorf, 1963; Skocpol, 1979). In his analysis of communist states, Djilas even used the term 'the new class' for the politicians and bureaucrats who function within the state apparatus. Their position in government was the basis for their social and material privileges (Djilas, 1957; Lane, 1971). Nevertheless, one may safely conclude that in the Marxist and neo-Marxist tradition the functioning of the state is ultimately primarily determined by the interests of dominant groups and classes in the economic sphere.

The Marxist perspective provides a useful counterbalance to the notion that the state is a neutral institution, standing above social parties, which produces rules and decisions more or less in a social vacuum, with the goal of improving social welfare.[5] The Marxist perspective is a source of inspiration for the empirical study of the social constraints within which governments must operate and the influence of classes, interest groups and pressure groups on government actions and policies (Alavi, 1979). The idea of the state as an arena for contending economic and social interest groups, including interest groups from within the state apparatus itself, has found wide acceptance. It is now also the prevailing perspective among non-Marxist political scientists and political economists. However, the simple Marxist class categories have been left behind. In their place we see, both within and outside the apparatus of government, a multitude of interest groups, lobbies and pressure groups, whose influence can be analysed (Buchanan and Tullock, 1962; Frey, 1978; Olson, 1965; Tullock, 1965).[6] One of the non-Marxist founders of this 'new political economy' was Joseph Schumpeter in his study *Capitalism, Socialism and Democracy* (1946). Recent authors focusing on elites include Acemoglu and Robinson (2012), Khan (2010) and North, Wallis and Weingast (2009).

---

[4] 'State' in this section refers to the 'state apparatus': government and political institutions (see n. 1 above).

[5] This notion of the state as a neutral arbiter is part of the intellectual tradition of post-war social democracy in Western Europe.

[6] A potential drawback of this interesting strand of literature is that everything is reduced to interest groups and their supposedly rational calculations. The constraining role of institutions tends to be underemphasised (Evans, 1995).

Another important source of inspiration for present-day studies of the state is the work of Max Weber (1922). Unlike Marx, Weber emphasised that political power is not a mere reflection of economic power. The political sphere has an autonomy of its own, in relation to the economic sphere.[7] There is no question of the state withering away. On the contrary, Weber predicted correctly that the state would become increasingly important within the context of a long-term process of bureaucratisation and rationalisation. The general tendency towards bureaucratisation would be reinforced in countries where socialist revolutions would take place.

Although Weber was very concerned about the social consequences of continued bureaucratisation and rationalisation, 'bureaucracy' itself does not have a negative connotation in his work. On the contrary, 'bureaucracy' represents a newer and vastly more efficient form of organisation, in which the activities of large numbers of people are coordinated in a network of specialised functions. In a bureaucracy decisions are made on the basis of formal rules and precedents, rather than on the basis of the fancies and favours of royal sovereigns or personal obligations and ties between patrons and clients. Job qualifications are defined as objectively as possible, and functions are ordered in a hierarchical structure. Recruitment for functions is based on objective meritocratic criteria such as competence, education and experience, irrespective of personal relationships and ties. In theory, personal connections, relationships of kin and social background play no role. There is a complete separation between the bureaucratic office and the personal sphere of the functionary. Finally, fulfilling a function in a bureaucracy is a full-time and fully paid professional activity. According to Weber, the bureaucratic form of organisation was more rational (i.e. non-arbitrary), than previous forms of organisation. In both the political and in the economic domain, bureaucracy was superior to other forms of organisation. It made for greater effectiveness and predictability. Bureaucratic organisation was not only a characteristic of the modern state apparatus, but also of large modern rationally organised capitalist enterprises. Bureaucratisation, thus, was an important aspect of successful economic and political development.

Again in contrast to Marx, Weber considered state formation as one of the important *prerequisites* for economic development. State formation in Europe involved centralisation of power and rule making, and the pacification of the territory within the borders of the national state in the making. Political centralisation implied the abolition of all sorts of local legislation, toll barriers, privileges, tariffs and rules that hampered the emergence of national markets and the growth of trade. Local currencies were abolished and replaced by national currencies. The right to impose taxes became the monopoly of national authorities. Pacification implied that incessant conflicts and wars between local rulers gradually made way for a central power that acquired a monopoly on the use violence. Only the army and the police had the legitimate right to apply violence, on behalf of the central authority.

It is clear that pacification within a larger territory is an essential prerequisite for an expansion of trade and markets, an increase in investment and for economic growth in general. Where there are wars, conflicts and sporadic violence, no one's property is safe. Few people will be prepared to take the risks involved in long-term investments. Trade can only flourish when the transport of goods is not obstructed and when people can be sure that

---

[7] In this respect, modern neo-Marxist authors were not only inspired by Marx, but also by his intellectual opponent, Weber.

their property rights will be respected. Entrepreneurship will only make its appearance if people have some guarantee that future benefits of risky investments in the present will accrue to those who have taken the risks.

Political centralisation, uniformity of regulation at the national level and the development of a well-functioning government bureaucracy increase the predictability which is a pre-requisite for rational calculations of costs and benefits in a market economy. Legal protection of individual ownership rights by central rules, sanctioned by the central apparatus of violence, contributes to entrepreneurship and investment in capital goods and technical innovation. In the long term, these lead to an increase in collective welfare (North and Thomas, 1973).

11.3   Processes of state formation in Europe

In *Über den Prozess der Zivilisation* (1969b) Norbert Elias – building on insights of Max Weber and historians like Bloch, Lefebvre and Pirenne – presents an analysis of century-long processes of centralisation and state formation in Europe and in particular in what is now known as France. In this chapter, these processes serve as a basis for comparison with more recent processes of state formation in developing countries.

The European states developed out of the highly decentralised feudal system that had emerged in Europe after the fall of the Roman empire. The linchpin of this system consisted of local feudal landlords. They lived off agricultural surpluses produced in their territory and provided their serfs and dependents with some form of military protection against the depredations of other lords, robber barons, and overseas raiders. The peasants farmed primarily for their own consumption and were obliged to transfer part of their agricultural surpluses to their feudal landlord and his household. Although there was some trade, the small feudal domains were largely self-sufficient. The lords in turn were in vassalage to superior liege lords and sovereigns whom they owed military support in times of war; lords would then mobilise their serfs to serve as foot soldiers. The feudal value system had mystical elements, which at a later stage could be called upon by monarchs to legitimise strong central authority in emergent national states (Wallerstein, 1974).

Feudal landlords continually strove to make their rights to land hereditary and to increase their autonomy from their liege lords. At the same time they tried to expand their own spheres of influence and to subject others to their authority. For many centuries, the European feudal systems fluctuated between centralisation and decentralisation. Sometimes local rulers would succeed in gaining military superiority and expanded the territory under their control in processes of centralisation. However, these processes of centralisation were precarious. Military expansion required funds and people which had to be withdrawn from the local economy. This perpetually threatened to undermine the economic foundations of political expansion (cf. Elvin, 1973 for China). The centralised rule over larger areas also involved considerable costs such as the support of a centralised administrative apparatus and the maintenance of systems of transport and communication. These costs could easily exceed the carrying capacity of the economic base.[8] A telling example of the difficulty of maintaining a central apparatus of government is the way in which early rulers like Charlemagne had to travel around the country with their courts. Agricultural surpluses were simply insufficient to support a large, permanent court in a central seat of government. The sovereign and his court were fed from the yields of the lands of the vassals, who received the honour of a royal visit. Similar patterns were found in many of the older African states and empires (Isichei, 1997).

Centralisation

From the twelfth century onwards the scales tipped in favour of centralisation. Certain royal dynasties gradually succeeded in establishing their authority over other feudal lords, subjecting more and more regions to their rule. For example, the Duchy of the Île de France eventually became the nucleus of the later kingdom of France; London would become the centre of a British kingdom and Madrid of a Spanish kingdom. The new national kingdoms that came into being were much smaller than the ancient empires of Rome or China. But, they were more strongly centralised and were administered more effectively (Wallerstein, 1974; see also Chapter 2).

In the process of centralisation relations, the balance of power between social classes underwent great changes. In a feudal society one can distinguish (1) the landed classes (the nobility and the clergy);[9] (2) the serfs who worked the land, transferred parts of their agricultural surpluses to the landlords and provided them with various labour services; (3) the sovereign and his court; and (4) the rising classes of traders, financiers, artisans and urban citizens.

Alliances between bourgeois groupings and the royal courts in particular have been of decisive importance in processes of centralisation. Financial support by merchant bankers and taxes on urban economic activities provided the sovereign with independent means and increased his power *vis-à-vis* the nobility. The possibility of funding standing mercenary armies made it less necessary to appeal to feudal loyalties for military manpower and support. This also worked in favour of centralising tendencies.

Between the twelfth and the seventeenth century centralising tendencies prevailed, and feudalism was converted into royal absolutist states which were the forerunners of modern national states. These processes of centralisation involved struggles for two important monopolies: the *monopoly of violence* and the *tax monopoly*. The military pacification of larger areas involved the establishment of a monopoly of violence. Only the military and the police had the right to exercise violence on behalf of central authorities. Attempts were made to curb the use of violence by individuals, groups, and local rulers (see, for example, Tilly, 1975: 27 ff.). As the power of the central authorities increased, they increasingly claimed the exclusive right to impose taxes on their subjects. Step by step the rights of taxation of local feudal rulers and urban authorities were gradually curtailed or were integrated into a national system. Sovereigns who succeeded in setting up effective central bureaucracy had a head start in the battle for the tax monopoly.

---

[8] The tension between productive capacity and the costs of political expansion in feudal society is also found in much greater empires. It has been well analysed by authors such as Kennedy (1989), Elvin (1973) and Immanuel Wallerstein (1974). Kennedy uses the term 'imperial overstretch'.

[9] Elias does not pay much attention to the role of the clergy in processes of state formation, nor to the protracted conflicts between 'secular' and 'religious' powers. The clergy based part of its social influence on its religious functions. But the clergy also lived off the revenues of its estates and as such can be seen as belonging to the landed classes.

Changes in the balance of power between classes

For complex reasons – including demographic fluctuations and the gradual emergence of an economy based on trade, crafts and manufacturing centring on towns – the influence of the feudal landed nobility started to wane from the late Middle Ages onwards. The fourteenth century in particular was a century of crisis in the feudal system, in part due to the scarcity of labour induced by the Black Death. At the same time, the influence of commercial middle classes was growing. By the time the power and influence of these two competing social categories was more or less in balance, the central sovereign could act as the supreme arbiter. His power and latitude increased dramatically.

Members of the feudal nobility were losing out in the economic sphere, but their social standing was still very high. They spent part of their time at the king's court, cultivating an exclusive and refined life style (Elias, 1979). The commercial bourgeoisie became more powerful economically, but its members were not yet taken seriously socially. The monarchy could play off these rival classes against each other.

In the sixteenth and seventeenth century centralisation trends culminated in royal absolutism. The seemingly unlimited power of the crown reached its peak in France under the Sun King, Louis XIV. Here the contending classes were most evenly balanced. All over Europe there were similar processes of centralisation and concentration of power. However, in countries where either the bourgeoisie (as in England or in the Low Countries) or the landed nobility (as in German states) had more influence, the position of the central monarch was correspondingly weaker (see Barrington Moore, 1967; Elias, 1969b: 229 ff.).

Once a central authority with an effective monopoly of violence and a tax monopoly had been established, a *process of democratisation of power* got under way, in which the absolute power of the crown was gradually circumscribed. Bourgeois groupings, which had to raise most of the taxes, played a significant role in this process. The sovereign increasingly came to be answerable to institutions in which taxpayers were represented. Democratisation was also furthered by the continuing social ascent of bourgeois groups and the continuing decline of the landed nobility. The sovereign was no longer able to play these two groups off against each other. At later stages other social classes, such as the emerging industrial working classes, also participated in the process of democratisation.[10]

The process of democratisation also involved a gradual separation of the private and public functions of the crown. Initially, there was not much difference between public funds and the private fortune of the sovereign. Later, however, a distinction developed between the sovereign's personal finances and the finances of the state, for which the sovereign was accountable to representative bodies.[11] The central administrative apparatus also became more independent from the central sovereign. From a loose collection of people with personal ties and obligations to the sovereign, it was transformed into a professional bureaucracy. Democratisation in the nineteenth century took the form of the rise of political mass movements. Ever larger groups participated in the political process and the struggle for universal suffrage began.

---

[10] North, Wallis and Weingast (2009) refer to this as the transition from *limited access orders* (LAOs) to more inclusive *open access orders* (OAOs).

[11] A similar differentiation developed in the economic sphere between the private property of the entrepreneur and the assets of the firm.

The rise of nationalism

From the mid-eighteenth century onwards *nationalist movements* and *ideologies* arose, emphasising the connection between a people (nation) and a state. This type of nationalism came in the place of earlier feelings of identification with region, village, or town. Nationalist sentiments also come to predominate among members of political elites, between whom there had previously been more feelings of supranational loyalty based on kinship, social class and personal relationships.

In the nineteenth century, nationalism was one of the driving forces in colonial expansion. In the twentieth century, modern nationalism – the idea that all peoples or nations are entitled to their own independent states – was to be an important force in the colonial struggles for independence from Western colonisers.

European processes of state formation have a number of specific characteristics, which distinguish them from processes of state formation in other parts of the world. First, centralisation did not emanate from one single centre, but from various focal points within Europe. Second, centralisation never led to the establishment of an all-embracing European empire. Parallel processes of centralisation resulted in a multitude of national states, competing with each other for technological advance, military supremacy and economic and political expansion. Third, the resulting European states were strong and effectively centralised, compared to larger but more loosely organised political entities such as, for instance, the Chinese empire. Finally, rising bourgeois groups, who were the bearers of a money and market economy, had a relatively independent position. They were never completely subordinated to a central political authority, as was the case in the great empires of the past. In the competition between states, political leaders actually depended in part on the support of their entrepreneurial classes. These classes supported the new strong states in their financial needs and their competition with other states. The states in turn supported their entrepreneurial groups in their urge for external economic expansion. Initially, the European expansion in the world was economic rather than political in nature.

In *Social Origins of Dictatorship and Democracy: Lord and Peasant in the Making of the World* (1967) Barrington Moore analyses differences in state formation processes in France, Germany and England, which are closely associated with differences in the balance of power between social classes and groups. In France, the French Revolution led to a dramatic overthrow of the *ancien régime* by a popular movement led by bourgeois groupings whose social ascent and emancipation had been blocked. In England, this process was more gradual and less violent. The bourgeoisie and the nobility intermixed. The nobility participated in the modern market economy and the bourgeois classes underwent the cultural influences of the upper classes. In Germany, the process of state formation was altogether different. In part as a result of the Thirty Years' War (1618–48), the degree of political centralisation had lagged behind and political unity was not achieved until 1870. The landed nobility retained much of its influence, and the middle classes were weakly developed. When Germany achieved political integration in the second half of the nineteenth century under Prussian leadership, and strove for rapid economic development, a kind of coalition was formed between the landed nobility (the *Junkers*) and the rising working classes. Partly bypassing the middle classes, there was a policy of radical economic modernisation and industrialisation 'from the top down'.

In Great Britain and France, the development of capitalism, industrialisation and the rise of middle classes in France and England were associated with the rise of parliamentary democracy. According to Barrington Moore the insecure position of the middle classes in Germany weakened democratic tendencies and contributed to the later rise of fascism.[12] There are interesting parallels between German and Japanese economic and political development. Both countries were latecomers to industrial development. In both cases modernisation was initiated from above by groups originating in old feudal elites. In both cases there was a reactive kind of nationalism in response to external challenges and the examples of established and economically successful nation-states.

Modernising authoritarian regimes in Latin America and Asia show interesting similarities with the German and Japanese patterns of development, not in the least with regard to the weak development of the middle classes. The wider relevance of Barrington Moore's study for developing countries is that it focuses our attention to the interplay between changes in the class structure, processes of state formation and economic development.

11.4   State formation in developing countries

In section 11.3 we paid attention to the notion, deriving from Max Weber, that state formation – characterised by pacification, centralisation and the development of a monopoly of violence, a tax monopoly and effective government institutions – is a prerequisite for economic development (see also Righart et al., 1991, Chapters 2 and 3).

In many developing countries since 1945 the state has not been completely consolidated and the national territory has not been fully pacified. In several Latin American, African and Asian countries the tax monopoly is underdeveloped, especially with respect to income taxes. The fiscal basis of the state is often weak (O'Connor, 1973). Wealthy citizens pay little or no income tax. Government revenues are highly dependent on taxes on land and agricultural production, tariffs on exports and imports and, in some cases, financial aid from abroad. A potential source of government revenue is monetary financing of expenditures. This form of financing is passed on to citizens in the form of inflation tax or *seigniorage* (see de Haan et al., 1993). According to Myrdal (1968), many newly independent states were 'soft states', by which he meant that governments did not have effective means to implement policy intentions and to impose binding obligations on their citizens so as to harness efforts and resources for development. Myrdal referred in particular to noncommunist states in South and Southeast Asia, though his analyses are also relevant for an understanding of state formation in Latin America and Africa.

In the following sections attention will be paid to the specific characteristics and problems of state formation processes in developing countries. Here it can already be stated that political instability, malfunctioning of government, war and civil strife are at least important as purely economic factors in explaining economic stagnation in developing countries. The

---

[12] In the recent literature on political development, the rich legacy of class analysis seems to have been sadly forgotten. In the work of authors such as Acemoglu and Robinson (2006, 2012) and North, Wallis and Weingast (2009) and North et al. (2013), the economic classes are absent. The focus has shifted to elites, elite relationships and the balance of power between elites and masses.

interactions between processes of state formation and economic development will be discussed in more detail in section 11.6.

11.4.1   The importance of external penetration in processes of state formation

In Western Europe the nation-state was the outcome of centuries-long processes of decentralisation and centralisation from within, with modern political national institutions gradually evolving out of local traditions. With the exception of a limited number of countries such as China, Ethiopia, Iran, Japan, Thailand and Turkey, this is not the way states were formed in developing countries.[13] Usually the impetus for modern state formation in developing countries was *colonial penetration* by a foreign ethnic group (Acemoglu and Robinson, 2012; Goldthorpe, 1979, Chapter 12; Sandbrook and Barker, 1985; Van Benthem van den Bergh, 1980). The current borders of many developing countries have been decisively influenced by colonialism (Davidson, 1992) and the institutions of the modern state have been imposed from outside.

Within their borders, the new states often contain a multiplicity of ethnic groups that hardly identify with the national institutions (Desmet *et al.*, 2012; Easterly and Levine, 1997; Nettle, 2000). Furthermore, ethnic tensions and divisions have been exacerbated by the classical divide-and-rule policies of colonial regimes. In some respects the ethnic and tribal divisions are even the product of modern influences (Davidson, 1992). Traditional ethnic ties were used by various colonial and post-colonial elites for purposes for modern political mass mobilisation.

The legitimacy of the new state institutions is often weak. The internal pacification of the territory has not yet been completed, the tax monopoly is poorly developed and the effectiveness of national state institutions is limited. Moreover, especially in Africa, the colonial intermezzo has been brief. In this respect, also, modern state institutions have had relatively little time to take root (Sandbrook and Barker, 1985).

The following examples illustrate the significance of external penetration in state formation. Before the colonial period India was a hotchpotch of principalities. In the fifteenth and sixteenth centuries there had been a powerful Muslim empire in the centre and north of India, the Mogul empire, which reached its peak under Akbar (1556–1605). This empire might have been the potential core of a future Indian nation-state. However, after the arrival of the English, it disintegrated into a multitude of smaller kingdoms and principalities. Initially, British influence was concentrated in Bengal. In the nineteenth century British India was centralised as a colonial empire. This empire included the territory of present-day India, Pakistan, Bangladesh and Burma (Myanmar). After decolonisation Burma became an independent state. Religious differences between Muslims and Hindus resulted in a bloody partition of the rest of British India into India and Pakistan. After a civil war combined with a war with India in 1971, Pakistan broke up into two parts, Bangladesh and present-day Pakistan.

---

[13] Van den Berghe (1981) rightly points out that European states did not develop out of stateless societies. Almost all European states developed out of the fragmentation or decentralisation of older political entities or empires, or the merging of existing, smaller political entities. That is why we have emphasised both processes of decentralisation and centralisation. Of course there are also European examples of states whose borders have been determined by external forces, such as the former Yugoslavia and the former Czechoslovakia.

The current unitary state of Indonesia came into existence in a similar way as a result of Dutch colonial centralising impulses in the nineteenth century. A multitude of 'native' principalities, which had been politically independent until then, were united under colonial rule in a process that involved numerous wars and uprisings (Ricklefs, 1981). The last of these wars was the Aceh war at the end of the nineteenth century. During and after the struggle for independence nationalist leaders took the colonial borders as their point of departure for post-colonial state formation. Even the annexation of Dutch New Guinea by Indonesia in 1963 was justified by President Sukarno with reference to the fact that New Guinea had been part of the Dutch colonial empire. It should therefore be part of the new state of Indonesia. The bloody occupation and annexation of East Timor in 1976 was also justified by the idea that the borders of the Indonesian state should coincide with the areas formerly ruled by Europeans (including in this case the Portuguese who ruled East Timor as a colony till 1975).[14]

In Indochina, the modern borders of states such as Vietnam, Laos and Cambodia were determined by the brief period of French rule from the mid nineteenth century onwards. Here, too, national boundaries and ethnic dividing lines do not always coincide. Nevertheless, it is important to note that in Asia, powerful and well-established states existed prior to Western colonisation. There was long experience with centralised political rule.

In Latin America the present-day states came into existence after the disintegration of the Spanish and Portuguese colonial empires during the first decades of the nineteenth century. The Spanish colonisers had extirpated all vestiges of the earlier Inca and Aztec empires. Brazil had never known any form of centralised rule prior to Western colonisation. Thus, in Latin America, there was little or no precolonial political heritage as a source for modern nation building.

The former viceroyalty of New Granada broke up into Colombia, Ecuador and Vene-zuela. The viceroyalty of Peru was divided into Peru, Chile and Bolivia. Attempts by Simón Bolívar, the leader of the struggle for independence, to form a Greater Colombian republic uniting New Granada and Peru, failed. In 1903 Panama broke away from Colombia, partly on the instigation of and with the support of the USA.

Mexico evolved out of the viceroyalty of New Spain, which had included Central America, the Spanish West Indies and for some time Venezuela. Here, too, attempts to maintain larger political units failed. The Central American states broke away from Mexico between 1820 and 1830. In a war between 1845 and 1848 Mexico lost half of its territory to the USA (Texas, New Mexico, California, Arizona, Nevada, and Utah). Argentina, Paraguay and Uruguay developed out of the viceroyalty of Rio de la Plata. Brazil gained its independence from Portugal in 1822. Dom Pedro, the son of the last Portuguese king, became the first emperor of independent Brazil.

In each Latin American country the political scene was initially dominated by descend-ants of white colonists and immigrants. For a very long time descendants of the original Indian population, imported slaves and contract labourers hardly participated in the political

---

[14] East Timor became independent in 2002. In Aceh, a separatist movement fought for independence from Indonesia between 1976 and 2005, when a peace deal was finally achieved in the wake of the 2004 Tsunami.

process. To this day they are underrepresented in politics.[15] Since independence the military have played an important role in politics in most countries. There has been widespread political instability. In the nineteenth and twentieth century, foreign powers frequently intervened in order to safeguard their economic and political interests. There have also been numerous internal wars and conflicts that led to adjustments of national borders. Nevertheless, it is clear that modern processes of state formation in Latin America commenced at an earlier stage than in Africa and Asia. Despite the considerable ethnic diversity in Latin America, most territorial borders of the countries in this region are not in question. From the mid 1980s onwards, several countries in Latin America have experienced a process of democratisation, with military regimes gradually giving place to civilian rule.

The consequences of external penetration for the process of state formation have been most extreme in Africa and the Middle East. In Africa, borders were determined both by military conquest and by diplomatic negotiations between the European powers, which started with the Berlin conference of 1884–5 (see Ake, 1996; Jackson and Rosberg, 1982: 6). In a brief period in the late nineteenth century the whole of Africa was colonised in the 'Scramble for Africa', a process completed by 1900. By 1914, only two countries in Africa remained independent: Abyssinia and Liberia. In the Middle East, the European powers entered the vacuum left after the collapse of the Ottoman empire, and established a multitude of colonies and protectorates. Both in Africa and in the Middle East, the present borders are often straight lines that ignore geographic circumstances or ethnic composition. These lines were drawn on maps with rulers by representatives of the great colonial powers. In their land hunger, military rivalry and mutual competition, the great powers divided up the land among themselves. In particular, countries with few colonies, like Germany and France, were eager to get a stake.

One of the presumed distinguishing characteristics of African history, in comparison with Asia, is the absence of a tradition of centralised states prior to European colonisation. This view is manifestly incorrect. Egypt and Ethiopia are very ancient states and the Maghreb in North-West Africa has a long history of centralised rule. In Sub-Saharan Africa there has been a rich diversity of ancient states, empires and confederations (Davidson, 1992; Isichei, 1997; Sandbrook and Barker, 1985; Schoenmakers, 1992). We mention only a few: the medieval realms in the savannas of Ghana and Mali; the Songhay empire centred on Timbuktu from the second half of the fifteenth century to the end of the sixteenth century; the ancient kingdoms of Nubia and Ethiopia; the seventeenth-century kingdom of Buganda in present-day Uganda; the Asante kingdom in Ghana, founded at the end of the seventeenth century; the nineteenth-century Lozi kingdom in present-day Zambia; the great kingdom of Benin from the twelfth to the nineteenth century; the Kaabu empire in the region of Guinea Bissau from the sixteenth to the nineteenth century; the Zulu empire in Southern Africa in the nineteenth century; and many more.

However, absence of the written word outside the Arabic–Islamic sphere of influence restricted the strength of most African states. Writing is a prerequisite for the emergence of permanent, centralised systems of book-keeping and administration, which are essential

---

[15] The elections of Hugo Chávez as president of Venezuela in 1999 and Luiz Inácio Lula da Silva (Lulu) as President of Brazil in 2002 formed a significant break with this tradition. In Bolivia, Evo Morales gave voice to indigenous Indian interests.

ingredients of strong states. Except for warfare, conquest and the taking of slaves, the impact of precolonial African states on everyday life in agricultural and nomadic societies was much more limited than that of modern state formations or precolonial states in other parts of the world. Even in the 'great states', most people lived in villages or scattered hamlets and usually central government impinged very little on their lives (Isichei, 1997). The territorial size of precolonial states was also usually rather small. Precolonial political formations might possibly have formed a basis for political centralisation from within. But they were unable to resist the colonial penetration from Europe, from the second half of the nineteenth century onwards.

Apart from kingdoms, empires and tribal confederations, many African peoples lived in decentralised tribal configurations with no central political leadership, so-called *acephalous* political units (Mair, 1967). Their loyalty was to village, lineage, region, or tribe rather than to remote and unfamiliar concepts such as empires or national states. Nomadic and acephalous societies were the main sources of slaves. They were preyed upon by the more centralised states, which gained an important part of their revenues from the sale of slaves to Western and Arabic slave traders (Hopkins, 1973; Klein, 1999).

In the colonial period, bureaucracies in Africa were tiny and were far removed from local communities. The borders of the colonies cut across a rich variety of traditional political institutions, confederations and tribal communities. In the process of decolonisation in the decades following the Second World War, these extremely heterogeneous societies were transformed into independent national states, with inexperienced bureaucracies and imported political institutions such as parliaments or judiciaries. Soon after independence, these states quickly degenerated into one-party states and personal regimes (see section 11.7).

Linguistically, external influences on the process of state formation have also been of importance. In the process of gradual political centralisation in Europe, the local dialect of the dominant centre usually developed into a national language over the centuries. However, in many former colonies there was no linguistic unity: a great variety of languages was spoken. For want of a national language, the language of the colonial rulers was used as a common means of communication. This situation continued after independence. After all, a choice for the language of one of the principal ethnic or cultural groups could easily spark off feelings of resentment among other ethnic groups. Thus, English became a national language in India, Pakistan, and former British colonies in Africa like Ghana, Nigeria and Zimbabwe. French became the national language of the former West African colonies of France, Portuguese in Angola and Mozambique. Portuguese is now the national language in Brazil, Spanish in the rest of Latin America.

In Indonesia, the nationalist movement deliberately chose Bahasa Indonesia – a variant of Malay, used as a trade language – as the national tongue as early as 1928. Both Dutch and Javanese, the language of the dominant ethnic group in Indonesia, were rejected as the national language. By now Dutch has almost disappeared in Indonesia, except among people of sixty-five years and older. As the internationally oriented language, it has been replaced by English. In this respect, Indonesia is a unique example of successful cultural decolonisation. In a somewhat similar fashion, Israel succeeded in establishing modern Hebrew as the national language for Jewish immigrants coming from all over the world.

It is interesting to note that in their fight against Western colonialism, independence movements took colonial borders as given. The pursuit of 'national' independence was strongly influenced by Western ideas about nationalism and national states. It was based on the assumption that the population of a colony was a nation (Van Benthem van den Bergh, 1980).

11.4.2   Internal political instability

In the former colonies, nationalist resistance against foreign rule created a sense of national solidarity. However, when the tangible oppressor disappeared with the departure of the colonial rulers, contradictions between different ethnic groups and 'nations' within the borders of the newly independent states usually intensified (Ake, 1996). This was, and still is, an important and continuing source of political instability. Central authorities often regard expressions of ethnic, tribal, religious, cultural and linguistic individuality as a threat to the political unity of the national state. These expressions, therefore, are suppressed, frequently by force. This may lead to an intensification of political conflicts and to the rise of new nationalist separatist movements. Political leaders may also resort to ethnic mobilisation as a source of political power.[16] Thus the very process of state formation itself can become a new source of political conflict and instability (Van den Hoogen, 1992).

The instability of new states is augmented by the contradiction between what O'Connor calls the 'accumulation function' and the 'legitimation function' of the state. According to O'Connor (1973), governments have to choose between conflicting objectives: the use of state power in support of capital accumulation and investment by entrepreneurial classes, on the one hand, and maintenance of social harmony and legitimacy by means of redistributive and welfare oriented government expenditures, on the other. In developing countries, this contradiction can result in a permanent fiscal crisis and political crisis. A related contradiction is found in states characterised by personal rule. Here, the ruler uses state resources to distribute favours to client groups at the expense of accumulation and growth (see further section 11.7).

The greater the role of the government in the economy, the deeper the tension between these two functions. The legitimation function of the state implies that the government should not take any measures that will lastingly alienate politically important groups of the population. Maintaining social harmony may, however, require policies that hamper economic growth, such as food and energy subsidies, creation of employment in the government sector and subsidies to urban industry. Such measures lead to an overextended public sector, large fiscal deficits and inflation. In the long term these factors have negative effects on economic growth (e.g. in Brazil and Mexico, see Maddison et al., 1992).

In her pioneering study, *States and Social Revolutions*, Theda Skocpol (1979) discerns a similar tension between the necessity of levying taxes for purposes of warfare, putting government finances on a sound basis and economic modernisation, on the one hand, and maintaining the support of crucial sections of the population, on the other. She explains the sudden and seemingly inexplicable fall of regimes in the French and Russian revolutions

---

[16] For instance in the Kenyan elections of 2002, which where accompanied by bloodshed and ethnic strife (Bedasso, 2013).

and the 1911 revolution in China by the fact that governments were forced to implement unpopular economic reforms in order to cope with external challenges. These reforms conflicted with the specific interests of those groups that had been the most loyal allies of the ruling regime up till then. Thus, at a crucial juncture, a regime would suddenly lose the support of these groups. It would become more vulnerable to political opposition of other groups and classes. The meltdown of communism in 1989 provides a vivid example of the operation of such mechanisms in more recent times.

11.4.3   External political interference as a destabilising factor

Not only is the political unification of many developing countries the result of colonisation, but also after decolonisation processes of state formation continue to be influenced by external intervention and interference. Radical authors have even coined the term 'neo-colonial relations of dependence'. External interference may be of an economic or a political nature. Economic interference may be the result of factors such as the operations of MNEs, foreign investors, or conditions imposed by international economic institutions such as the IMF, the World Bank, the WTO or the large trade blocs of the rich countries (OECD, European Union). Here, we focus on political and military interference. *Internal* political instability invites political interference from without. *External* interference augments internal political instability. Initially minor differences between ethnic or religious groups within a country may easily acquire geopolitical or regional dimensions.

The Cold War between East and West from 1945 to 1989 found its counterpart in conflicts between the 'clients' of the two blocs. These clients were often recruited on an ethnic basis in the pursuit of geopolitical objectives. Regional powers such as South Africa, Vietnam, India, Libya, Iraq, Iran and Syria also tried to widen their spheres of influence. Their interventions in internal political conflicts in other countries exacerbated ethnic conflicts. Simultaneously, political leaders of ethnic groups solicited external military and political support in their struggles for control over the new national institutions. External interference made internal conflicts bloodier, less manageable and longer.

The list of developing countries in which external interference since the Second World War played a role in processes of state formation or national disintegration is long. Box 11.1 provides examples of external interference during this period (Banks *et al.*, 1998; Marshall, 2013; Marshall and Cole, 2011; Marshall and Gurr, 2003; Sivard, 1991; and for Africa, see, for example, David, 1987; Gavshon, 1981).

BOX 11.1 ⋮ State formation and external political interference

- **The Korean War**. In Korea, the USA and several Western allies fought a full-scale war against the Chinese in 1950–2. This war eventually resulted in the division of the former Japanese colony of Korea into present-day North and South Korea.
- **Secessionist movements in Zaire**. In 1960, France, England and Belgium first supported the secessionist movement of Moise Tshombe in Katanga, an area rich in

minerals, while the USA and the Soviet Union supported the Democratic Republic under the first President Patrice Lumumba. Later the USA collaborated in the overthrow of the Lumumba regime, when it oriented itself more towards the Soviet Union. The USA supported a takeover by Mobutu. In 1977–8 there was another secessionist movement in Katanga, initiated by Angolan exiles. This uprising was suppressed by Mobutu with the help of Moroccan troops and French logistic support. A second invasion from Katanga in 1978 was suppressed with the assistance of French and Belgian troops and American logistic support.

- **Civil war in Democratic Republic of Congo, 1996–2013**. Zaire, renamed Democratic Republic of Congo (DRC) since 1997, has remained unstable ever since. Cold War intervention has been replaced by regional interventions by Rwanda, Zimbabwe, Uganda, Angola and Namibia, each supporting their own factions and ethnic groups in a bloody civil war. A peace agreement in 2003 led to partial withdrawal of foreign troops, but conflicts continued till 2013, in spite of UN attempts at pacification.
- **The Vietnamese War**. After the defeat of French Forces by the independence movement led by Ho Chi Minh, Americans and American-supported regimes fought the nationalist independence movements and communist revolutionary movements, supported by China and the Soviet Union, from 1945 to 1973. In 1973, Vietnam was reunified under communist rule.
- **Cambodia**. In Cambodia the Americans, the Chinese and the Vietnamese tried to exert their influence in changing coalitions during different periods during much of the post-war period.
- **The war between Somalia and Ethiopia over the Ogaden, 1977–8**. Until 1977 the Americans offered military support to Ethiopia and the Soviet Union to Somalia. After the Somalian invasion of the Ogaden in 1977, the Soviet Union and Cuba supported Ethiopia by means of military supplies, advisors, and Cuban soldiers. The USA ended their support to Ethiopia and in time started to support Somalia. Eventually, the invasion of the Ogaden was repulsed and millions of ethnic Somalis fled across the Somalian border. In Somalia politics degenerated into clan warfare, which persists to this very day. The national state has ceased to exist.
- **The struggle for the secession of Eritrea from Ethiopia, 1962–92**. Until 1974 Haile Selassie received large-scale US support. Since 1977, Eritrean resistance against the communist regime of Haile Mariam Mengistu was supported by the Islamic countries and indirectly by the USA. After the fall of the communist regime in Ethiopia, Eritrea seceded peacefully in 1992. But full-scale trench warfare between Ethiopia and Eritrea erupted between 1998 and 2000 and an uneasy peace has prevailed since.
- **The Angolan civil war after the fall of the Portuguese regime in 1974**. The MPLA government of Agostinho Neto and José Dos Santos received large-scale military support from the Soviet Union and Cuba. The opposition of Holden Roberto's FNLA and Jonas Savimbi's UNITA was supported by South Africa and the USA. For a while the FNLA was also supported by China. South African support even took the form of a military invasion. Large numbers of Cuban soldiers fought on the government side. A peace agreement was finally signed in 1994, but implementation of the peace accords was slow and was only realised after the death of Savimbi in 2002.

- **The secession of Biafra from Nigeria**. During the Nigerian Civil War (1967–70) about the secession of Biafra, the USA offered some military support, albeit covertly, to the secessionist movement, whereas the UK and the Soviet Union supported the regime in Lagos. The unity of Nigeria was maintained.
- **Nicaragua, Cuba, Chile, the Dominican Republic, Panama and Granada**. In these countries the USA tried to prevent the establishment of communist regimes by means of either open or covert military and political intervention. In the case of Nicaragua a complete army of Contras was organised and funded by the USA for the violent overthrow of the Sandinist regime.
- **Lebanon**. In Lebanon interference by Syria, Iran, the Palestinians and Israel caused the fragile balance between various ethnic and religious groups to be destroyed, resulting in a protracted and destructive civil war lasting from 1975 to 1991. New tensions emerged after the assassination of president Hariri in 2005, periodically resulting in open conflict. These tensions and conflicts pitted Hezbollah supported by Syria and Iran against Christian and other groups. In 2006, there was a war with Israel in which Israel briefly invaded Lebanon.
- **The conflict over mineral-rich Western Sahara**. Since 1973, the Polisario independence movement has struggled for independence from Morocco, with the support of Algeria. A peace treaty was concluded in 1991, but has not yet been implemented.
- **Mozambique**. After independence, the South Africans and the Rhodesians gave military support to the opposition movement RENAMO. Cuba and several Eastern European countries supported the government of Samora Machel. The civil war lasted from 1975 to 1992.
- **The Kurdish struggle for autonomy or independence in Turkey, Iran and Iraq**. In their mutual conflicts the Turkish, Iranian and Iraqi regimes constantly supported separatist movements in the other countries with a view to weakening their opponents. Internally, even the peaceful pursuit of Kurdish autonomy was suppressed, for it was regarded as a threat to national unity. Kurdish autonomy in Iraq was supported by the international community, to keep up the pressure on the Baghdad regime of Saddam Hussein. After the war in Iraq and the overthrow of the Baathist regime in 2003, the Iraqi Kurds achieved substantial autonomy within the Iraq state.
- **Military interventions in Afghanistan**. In Afghanistan, the Soviet Union intervened militarily in favour of a communist government. Islamic and Western countries supported various oppositional groups and factions, resulting in the withdrawal of Soviet troops in 1989. After a period of instability and warlordism, the Taliban established a fundamentalist Muslim regime with the support of Pakistan in 1995–6. This regime was overthrown by an American-led coalition in the Afghan war of 2001. After some years the Taliban regrouped, with tacit and sometimes open support from Pakistan. Increasing numbers of US soldiers with minor support of other allies fought against the Taliban, while training the government forces. Conflicts continue as American forces prepare to leave the country in 2014.
- **Chad**. In Chad factions supported by the French and the Libyans fought for control for thirty years, until an unstable peace was achieved in 1990.
- **The war between Iran and Iraq**. In the Iran–Iraq war of 1980–8, the Western countries initially supported the Iraqis in their war against the deeply anti-American

Muslim-fundamentalist regime of the Ayatollah Khomeini in Iran. Later in the Gulf War in 1991 an international coalition under the leadership of the USA violently put an end to the sudden Iraqi annexation of the oil-rich sheikdom of Kuwait. In the second Gulf War of 2003, Saddam Hussein was overthrown by the Americans and British, who occupied Iraq. By 2014 most US forces have been withdrawn, while civil conflict between a Shiite government supported by Iran and a Sunni opposition continues.

- **Sri Lanka**. Since the mid 1980s Tamil separatists in the North have fought for independence from the Sinhalese majority. Tamils from the Indian federal state of Tamil Nadu supported the struggle for independence of the Tamil minority, originating in India. The Indian government, however, later sided with the central Sri Lankan authorities and was even briefly involved in an unsuccessful attempt at peace enforcement in Sri Lanka. In 2009 government forces gained a decisive victory and crushed the separatist movement.
- **Kashmir**. In Kashmir, the claims of Pakistan and India and Muslims and Hindus clashed, both in the Pakistan-ruled and in the Indian-ruled part of Kashmir. India and Pakistan fought a short war in 1971, which resulted in the independence of Bangladesh. They were on the brink of a nuclear confrontation in 2002. The conflict contributes to internal violence and instability in both countries.
- **Syria**. Violent suppression of initially peaceful opposition by President Bashar al-Assad in 2011 resulted in the eruption of a destructive civil war. This involved a conflict between Sunni Muslims and the Syrian government supported by Alawites, Shiites and Christians. Turkey, Saudia Arabia and the Gulf states support the Sunni opposition. Al Quaeda fighters entered the country. Iran, Hezbollah fighters from Lebanon and Russia support the Assad regime.

This list – by no means complete – illustrates the importance of both East–West competition and regional interventions in exacerbating conflicts within and between new states in Asia, Africa and the Middle East and older states in Latin America. For the Cold War superpowers, their mutual rivalry was more important than the question whether the regimes or movements they supported were in any way worthy of their support.

Table 11.1 provides rough figures on internal and external conflicts in developing countries and the numbers of victims involved. Between 1945 and 2012, 31.9 million people were killed in internal and external conflict: 20.8 million in internal conflicts, and 11.1 million in external warfare. In some countries (including Algeria, Angola, Guinea Bissau, Indonesia, Cameroon, Kenya, Mozambique, Morocco, Tunisia and Vietnam) the majority of casualties occurred in the fight for independence against colonial rulers.

One of the most striking features of Table 11.1 is the large number of victims of internal conflicts in Sub-Saharan Africa (almost 10 million) in relation to absolute population size. Casualties were also high relative to population in the Middle East, mainly due to external wars. In absolute terms, the highest numbers of casualties of internal and external conflicts combined are found in East Asia (13.2 million). More than half of these casualties (7.2 million) were caused by international wars.[17] Finally, though Latin America is generally

---

[17] From the preceding discussion, it should by now be clear that it is difficult to make unambiguous distinctions between external warfare and internal conflicts (see Small and Singer, 1982).

Table 11.1: Wars and war casualties, 1945–2012

	Civil wars		International wars and conflicts	
	Number of years	Number of casualties	Number of years	Number of casualties
Latin America		*764,500*		*81,500*
Argentina	5	23,000	1	1,000
Bolivia	2	3,000		
Brazil	1	1,000		
Chile	4	28000		
Colombia	49	306,000		
Costa Rica	2	3,000		
Cuba	2	5,000	1	75,000
Dominican Republic	1	3000		
Ecuador			1	1,000
El Salvador	13	75,000		
Guatemala	31	151,000		
Haiti	3	2000		
Honduras	1	1,000	2	3,500
Jamaica	1	1,000		
Mexico	7	61,000		
Nicaragua	10	70,000		
Panama			1	1,000
Paraguay	1	1,500		
Peru	15	30,000		
Suriname	3	900		
Middle East		*677,000*		*864,400*
Cyprus	6	7,000		
Egypt	3	4,000	1	3,000
Iran	25	93,800	9	501,000
Iraq	40	192,500	13	255,400
Israel	47	21,500	1	4,000
Israel–Arab conflict			15	101,000
Jordan	1	10,000		
Lebanon	18	102,500		
Libya	1	25,000		
Oman	5	3,000		
Saudi Arabia	*4*	*700*		
Syria	2	105,000		
Turkey	33	53,000		
Yemen	20	59,000		

Table 11.1: *(cont.)*

	Civil wars		International wars and conflicts	
	Number of years	Number of casualties	Number of years	Number of casualties
West Asia		**15,000**		
Azerbaijan	8	15000		
South Asia		**2,301,700**		**2,121,700**
Afghanistan	24	1,000,000	9	89,200
Bhutan	2	**1,200**		
Bangladesh	17	25,000	1	1,000,000
India	63	1,100,000	7	32,500
Nepal	6	8,000		
Pakistan	34	57,500	1	**1000000**
Sri Lanka	24	110,000		
Far East		**7,209,500**		**5,945,500**
Cambodia	15	1,655,000	14	76,000
China	41	3,189,000	6	110,000
Indonesia	37	576,500	8	194,500
Laos	28	35,000		
Malaysia	12	28,500		
Myanmar	64	102,000		
Philippines	33	1,590,000		
South Korea	2	2,000		
Korea War			3	3,000,000
Taiwan	2	10,000		
Thailand	9	6,500		
Vietnam	1	15,000	29	2,565,000
Sub-Saharan Africa		**9,782,000**		**1,070,700**
Angola	30	1,003,500	16	51,000
Burundi totaal	13	218,000		
Cameroon	1	**750**	5	30,000
Central African Republic	8	3,500		
Chad	34	82,000		
Congo-Brazzaville	4	12,500		
Congo, Dem. Republic	32	2,621,000	6	4,700
Côte d'Ivoire	3	6,000		
Djibouti	3	1,000		
Eritrea			2	100000

Table 11.1: *(cont.)*

	Civil wars		International wars and conflicts	
	Number of years	Number of casualties	Number of years	Number of casualties
Ethiopia	8	12,000	17	750,000
Gambia	1	650		
Ghana	2	2,000		
Guinée	1	1,000		
Guinea Bissau	1	6,000	12	15,000
Kenya	5	4,300	9	20,000
Lesotho	1	1,000		
Liberia	11	46,000		
Madagascar			1	40,000
Mali	5	1,000		
Mauritania			1	1,000
Mozambique	11	1,000,000	10	30,000
Namibia			25	25,000
Niger	7	1,000		
Nigeria	30	2,104,300		
Rwanda	18	607,500		
Senegal	7	3,000		
Sierra Leone	20	25,000		
Somalia	24	100,000	1	1,000
South Africa	14	21,000		
South Sudan	3	3500		
Sudan	34	1,500,000		
Tanzania	1	2500		
Uganda	29	368,000	1	3,000
Zambia	1	1,000		
Zimbabwe	13	23,000		
North Africa		**78,000**		**1,007,000**
Algeria	14	62,000	9	1,001,000
Morocco	14	15,000	3	3,000
Tunisia	1	1,000	2	3,000
Total		*20,812,700*		*11,090,800*

Sources:
Marshall (2013), with adjustments by the author. Supplementary sources: Kidron and Smith (1983); Marshall (2003); Smith (1997); White (2003).

perceived to be a violent continent, the number of casualties here is relatively low. Most of them are due to internal conflict.

At the end of the 1980s, it was widely expected that the thaw in East–West relations and the end of the Cold War would contribute to a pacification of internal conflicts within and wars between developing countries. So far, this expectation has not yet materialised. In retrospect it turned out that the East–West conflict not only exacerbated conflicts and tensions, but also had some important stabilising functions. With the disappearance of the East–West opposition and the sudden collapse of the Soviet empire, regional conflicts and internal ethnic, cultural and religious tensions increased rather than decreased. This is manifest in the continued fighting in Angola in the early 1990s, in the failed attempt by Saddam Hussein of Iraq to annex Kuwait in 1991, in the ethnic conflicts preceding the first free elections in South Africa, in the continued civil war in Afghanistan, in the secessionist movements in India (in the Punjab), Sri Lanka (the Tamils) and Indonesia (Aceh), in civil wars in Liberia, Sierra Leone, Somalia, the Sudan and Congo and many of the former Soviet Asian republics, in wholesale ethnic slaughter in Rwanda and Burundi and the brutal Ethiopian–Eritrean War of 1998–2000.

In India, the differences between Muslims and Hindus have deepened since 1991 due to the rise of Hindu fundamentalist movements. In North Africa and the Middle East tensions between fundamentalist Muslim movements – which can be to some extent interpreted as a cultural response to Western penetration – and nationalist regimes have increased, for example in Algeria, Tunisia and Egypt. In Algeria, this degenerated into a bloody civil war, which lasted from 1991 until around 2002.

The resurgence of nationalist sentiments led to the disintegration of the Soviet Union, Yugoslavia and Czechoslovakia, and to intensified social tensions within almost all of the new smaller political entities in Europe and Asia. The smaller the new nation, the more hostile it seems to be to its minorities. The civil war in the former Yugoslavia between 1991 and 1995 is said to have claimed between 200,000–300,000 victims. Worldwide the total number of refugees who had left their countries increased from 2.5 million in 1970 (WHO, 2002b: 225) to 15.4 million at the end of 2012 (UNHCR, 2013).[18] In addition, some 28.8 million persons were internally displaced. In the same year no less than 6.5 million people were newly displaced within the borders of their country. In total some 45.2 million people were displaced at the end of 2012, due to persecution, conflict, violence and human rights violations.[19] This was the highest level since 1994 (UNHCR, 2013).

Over time an increasing number of conflicts across the globe appeared to have a religious dimension involving Islam. This includes secessionist movements in Xinjiang in China, Chechnya in Russia, Aceh in Indonesia, tensions between North and South Nigeria, civil war between Christians and Muslims in the Sudan and on the Moluccan Islands of Indonesia, civil wars in Bosnia and Algeria, tensions between India and Pakistan, the Afghanistan war of 2001 and the ongoing civil wars in Iraq and Syria.

On the other hand, there are also countries where the improvement in East–West relations allowed breakthroughs in long-standing ethnic and political conflicts. Examples include the pacification of conflicts in Cambodia, Angola, Rwanda and Mozambique, the election of a multiracial government in Namibia and the abolition of the *apartheid* regime in South Africa.

---

[18] Including 4.9 million Palestinian refugees registered with the UNRWA.

[19] Including internally displaced persons, cross-border refugees and asylum seekers and other displaced groups.

Researchers argue whether the number of violent conflicts in developing countries shows a long-run declining trend in the course of time (Kende, 1972; Marshall and Gurr, 2003; Starr and Most, 1985). Starr and Most come to the conclusion that no long-term increase or decrease can be discerned. Rather, there is a cyclical trend with a peak between 1965 and 1968. In the period covered by their research, the locus of conflicts has unmistakably shifted from Europe to developing countries, and the importance of internal conflicts has increased in comparison to classical wars between countries. According to more recent quantitative estimates of the magnitude of armed conflict by Marshall (2013) and Marshall and Cole (2011), there was a huge – eightfold – increase in civil conflicts (societal warfare) between 1945 and 1990, while the index of interstate war remained low and showed no long-run increase or decrease. After 1989 there was a dramatic decrease in civil conflict as well as some decrease in interwar conflict. However, Collier (2007) is right to note that conflicts are predominantly located in the poorest countries housing the bottom billion of global populations.

The index of the total magnitude of armed conflict peaked around 1985 and subsequently declined to around 40 per cent of its peak level by 2012. The conclusion is that there has been an unmistakable decline in the magnitude of global conflict since the end of the Cold War in 1991 (see also Lacina and Gleditsch, 2005; Lacina *et al.*, 2006).[20]

Thus, there are two diametrically opposed trends. On the one hand, the weakening of East–West tensions since 1989 has led to a strengthening of centrifugal forces and a strong resurgence of nationalism, cultural contradictions and separatist movements. The scope for outside intervention has increased rather than decreased, now that regional powers are less dependent on the international superpowers. On the other hand, the decline of East–West tensions has contributed elsewhere to processes of pacification. This is the case in regions and countries where superpowers had backed different countries, parties or factions in their attempts to expand their spheres of influence. It is too early to say what the net outcome of these trends will be. In any event, the examples discussed above provide an indication of the overwhelming importance of external political and military interference and its impact on state formation processes in developing countries.

11.4.4   The role of the military in politics

During the past sixty years, the military have played very prominent roles in the political processes of many developing countries, even when they were not formally in power (Clapham and Philip, 1985; Collier, 2007; Finer, 1988; Goldthorpe, 1979).[21] The prominence of the military was especially pronounced in the 1970s and 1980s. The importance of the military in the post-war period is illustrated by the figures on political regimes in developing countries in Table 11.2.

For 1982 and 1995, Table 11.2 distinguishes between one-party states, military regimes, personal rule by a sovereign or an absolute ruler, restricted parliamentarism and multi-party systems. The table is based on a survey for 1982 by Kidron and Smith (1983), updated with a variety of sources.

---

[20] The index of the magnitude of armed conflict not only refers to casualties, but also to the comprehensive effects on the states affected by the warfare, including numbers of combatants, size of affected area, dislocated population and extent of infrastructural damage.

[21] This section has been inspired by Goldthorpe's excellent chapter on the political characteristics of states in poor countries in Goldthorpe (1979).

In 1982, no less than thirty developing countries had a military regime; sixteen of these were in Africa, eight in Latin America. Twenty-six countries had a one-party system; fourteen of these were located in Africa. In eighteen countries there was a system of personal rule; nine of these were in the Middle East and six in Africa. One should note that military influence is not restricted to countries with a purely military regime. In one-party states and in systems of personal rule, the military usually also play an important role behind the scenes. Even in some of the countries with a parliamentary system, the military wield considerable influence, for instance in a country like Pakistan.

In a later survey for 1991, Kidron and Smith (1991) distinguish between military regimes, regimes dominated by the military and other regimes. A regime dominated by the military is a regime in which civilian institutions are formally restored, but in which real power still lies with the military. Although the subdivisions in the two sources are hard to compare, the number of purely military regimes has clearly decreased since 1982. In 1990 there were only eleven countries with a military regime, compared to thirty in 1982. However, another twenty-six countries had a regime that was indirectly dominated by the military.

The data for 1995 confirm the decline in purely military regimes. As in 1991, eleven countries have military regimes. These data do not indicate the number of military domin-ated regimes. But compared to 1982, the total number of authoritarian regimes has declined from 70 to around 30 in 1995.

Using a variety of sources, we have updated the table with data from Freedom House and the Polity IV project (Center for Systemic Peace, 2013). For these years we only distinguish three categories, authoritarian regimes, restricted parliamentary systems and multiparty democracies. The data in Table 11.2 need to be interpreted with utmost caution, due to a host of empirical problems with regard to the comparability of data from different sources. Nevertheless, they do tentatively suggest that military and authoritarian regimes in developing countries have become less prevalent since 1982 (see further section 11.4.6). On the other hand, the number of countries classified as full-fledged democracies with multiparty elections also seems to have declined since a peak level in 1995. Though elections have become widespread, in many countries the electoral process has been captured by the ruling party, for instance in Ethiopia and Mozambique (see Torvinen, 2013).

Explanations for the important role of the military in developing countries in the post-war period are of two kinds, having to do with: (1) characteristics of societies and political systems; and (2) characteristics of the military system itself.

The role of the military and characteristics of societies and political systems

In advanced industrial societies the complexity of economic and political institutions and structures functions as a constraint to military intervention in politics. The lower degree of institutional complexity in many developing countries and the weaker development of other national political institutions allow a greater involvement of the military in politics (Finer, 1988). The unstable nature of political systems and their inability to accommodate sectional interests peacefully creates a political climate in which military intervention becomes conceivable. However, as societies and economies become more complex and differentiated in the course of their development, government by the military becomes more and more difficult. The trend towards restoration of civilian governments in Latin America since the mid 1980s seems to fit this line of reasoning. Military regimes in countries such as Brazil and Argentina proved unable to pursue effective economic policies in an increasingly

Table 11.2: Political regime in developing countries[a]

	One-party state no.	Military regime no.	Personal rule no.	Total authoritarian rule no.	(%)	Restricted parliamentary system no.	(%)	Multiparty democracy no.	(%)	Non-classif. no.	Total[b] no.
1982											
Africa	14	16	6	36	78	3	7	5	11	2	46
Asia	8	4	2	14	67	3	14	4	19	0	21
Latin America	1	8	1	10	45	5	23	7	32	0	22
Middle East	3	2	9	14	88	1	6	1	6	0	16
Total	26	30	18	74	70	12	11	17	16	2	105
1995											
Africa	1	10	3	14	30	7	15	21	46	4	46
Asia	3	1	2	6	29	1	5	13	62	1	21
Latin America	1			1	5			21	95		22
Middle East	2		7	9	60	4	27	2	13		15
Total	7	11	12	30	29	12	12	57	55	5	104
2000											
Africa				14	30	11	24	21	46		46
Asia				8	38	2	10	11	52		21
Latin America				1	5	1	5	20	91		22
Middle East				9	60	5	33	1	7		15
Total				32	31	19	18	53	51		104
2012[b]											
Africa				10	21	22	46	16	33		48
Asia				6	29	7	33	8	38		21
Latin America				1	4	4	17	18	78		23
Middle East				10	67	4	27	1	7		15
Total				27	25	37	35	43	40		107

Sources:

1982: Kidron and Smith (1983); 1995: CIA, *World Fact Book* (1995); 2000: Freedom House (2000), with adjustments by the author; 2012: Polity IV (2013), with adjustments by the author, supplemented with data from Freedom House (2013).

Notes:

[a] Excl. countries with less than 1 million inhabitants, excl. Former Soviet republics in Asia, excl. developing countries in Europe.

[b] 2012: Polity IV categories, democracies, anocracies and authoritarian regimes readjusted to the categories multiparty democracy, restricted parliamentary system and authoritarian rule with help of Freedom House (2013).

complex economic environment. They ended up relinquishing their power to civilian regimes.

The role of the military and characteristics of military institutions

The second category of explanatory factors refers to characteristics of military institutions themselves. First, the military have control over the means of violence. Potentially this allows them to play a political role. Secondly, the military are a subsector of society which is, in certain respects, more 'modern' than other subsectors (Bienen, 1971; Finer, 1988; Janowitz, 1981; Shils, 1964). For example, in Latin America in the 1920s, military officers had higher levels of education than comparable groups in civilian society (Philip, 1985). The military have access to modern technologies, modern means of communication and transport. They have a modern bureaucratic, hierarchical and centralised organisation structure, a tradition of internal discipline and a strong corporate spirit.

The self-image of military officer classes is one of standing above the daily wear and tear of politics, political parties and interest groups. All over the developing world, the military see themselves as the ultimate safeguard of national interests. The military outlook involves elements of puritanism and contempt for the corruption, indecisiveness and decadence which they associate with civilian rule (Janowitz, 1981). Thus the military come to see themselves as a factor contributing to the modernisation of society and to economic development (Bienen, 1971). Such attitudes can be found, for example, among military elites in Argentina, Brazil, China, Chile, Indonesia, Myanmar, Pakistan, South Korea, Thailand and Turkey.

The takeover of power by the military often takes the form of a coup d'état against the civilian government. To justify their intervention in politics, the military can appeal to deep-seated popular feelings of resentment about widespread corruption and ineffectiveness in politics. In Latin America the alleged or real threat of left-wing revolutionary movements often served as a justification for military takeovers. A third motive for intervention is the protection of the autonomy of the army against interference by civilian politicians (Philip, 1985). Sometimes, the military reacted to cuts in military expenditures, sometimes to attempts to politicise the military forces, and sometimes to attempts to introduce political patronage by controlling the recruitment of officers. Finally, factions in civilian politics sometimes actively seek the support of the military in their rivalry with other factions and parties.

In Latin America the military have played an important role in politics since 1822. During the first years of political independence, *caudillos* competed for power, frequently leading informal armies. Later the officers' corps was professionalised through the establishment of military academies. Politicians hoped that professionalisation would contribute to a more neutral army. Compulsory military service was introduced for the recruitment of common soldiers. Officers originated from the class of landowners and formed an internally homogeneous and highly united group of professionals. Professionalisation helped differentiate military institutions from civilian institutions and society. According to Philip (1985), by 1920 the military were one of the best-organised forces in society. They were highly trained and felt isolated from and superior to civilians.

Between 1922 and 1932, there was a wave of military coups d'état in South America, partially as a result of the collapse of civilian governments during the Great Depression. Vargas came to power in Brazil, Perón in Argentina, Benavides in Peru, Terra in Uruguay.

Even in Chile, with its tradition of civilian government, Ibáñez became the military president from 1927 to 1932. Sometimes with interruptions, elsewhere continuously, military regimes ruled Latin America until the 1980s. The longest period of military rule was in Argentina, where regimes controlled by the military stayed in power from 1930 until the inauguration of Alphonsin as President in 1983. Some military regimes – like that of Perón – pursued populist policies with which they tried to win the support of the trade unions and the urban poor.

Military coups, however, do not lead to more stable governments. Once the legitimacy of civilian government has been eroded, the first military coup may give rise to a succession of coups. Many military governments are just as much affected by corruption as the civilian governments they replace. Again and again dissatisfied groups emerge, often from the lower military ranks, attempting to take over power by force.

Coups have played a prominent role in political processes since 1945. Luttwak (1979) presents an overview of the total number of military coups in developing countries from 1945 to 1977. All in all, he registers 271 attempted coups: 147 of these were successful, while 124 were unsuccessful. In Africa there were 98 attempted coups, of which 44 were successful. In Latin America 95 coup attempts took place, of which 57 were successful.

Another estimate by Finer (1988) for the period between 1962 and 1980 comes to a total of 152 coups. In 1980, there were 37 countries in which the government had come to power through a coup d'état; 25 per cent of all independent states had a military government. Military regimes ruled over 55 per cent of Latin America population and almost 66 per cent of the population of the Arab states in North Africa and the Middle East. Similar percentages obtain for Sub-Saharan Africa (Finer, 1988). Ghana tops the list with no less than 5 successful coups, 6 attempted coups and 13 political conspiracies between 1965 and 1985 (Fosu, 1992).

Table 11.3 presents estimates of the number of successful coups from 1945 till 2002. Unsuccessful coup attempts are not included here. Due to differences in definitions, the number of successful coups for the period until 1977 is higher than in Luttwak (198 versus 147).[22] In this table, too, political instability is highest in Africa and Latin America. The average number of coups per year shows a significant decline since 1977.

11.4.5 One-party states

Another interesting characteristic of political systems in developing countries after 1950 is the frequent emergence of one-party states. In 1982 there were twenty-six one-party states throughout the world, fourteen of which were in Africa (see Table 11.2). In a one-party state the ruling party professes to be the personification of national aspirations and tries to channel all political activity within the party. Thus, the party integrates opposition parties, trade unions, youth movements, women's movements, employers' associations and so on.

Communist countries such as China, Vietnam, Laos and Cuba are good examples of one-party states. In such political systems the military are subordinate to the primacy of politics, even when individual military persons fulfil important political functions. The party organisation penetrates all sections of the military organisation. The line between one-party systems

---

[22] For the period 1945–77, the numbers of coups in the Polity IV database are also comparable to Luttwak's figures.

Table 11.3: Successful coups in developing countries, 1945–2012

	1945–77	1978–90	1991–2000	2001–12	1945–2012
Africa	64	28	13	9	114
Asia	28	6	4	4	42
Latin America	76	14	1	1	92
Middle East	30	3	1	0	34
Total	198	51	19	14	282
Coups per year	6	3.9	1.9	1.2	4

Source:
1945–77: De Haan and Sierman (1993). Original sources: Luttwak (1979), Taylor and Hudson (1972), Taylor and Jodice (1983), Banks (various issues) and Steinberg (various issues); 1978–2012: Center for Systemic Peace, *Coups d états, 1946–2012.*

and multiparty democracies is not always easy to draw. For instance, India has had a well-functioning parliamentary system of government since independence. Nevertheless, the Congress Party stayed in power continuously from 1947 to the early 1990s. In Mexico, the Institutional Revolutionary Party (PRI) stayed in power from 1910 to 2000. Ethiopia and Mozambique have multiparty elections, but the outcome is not in doubt and the political scene is increasingly dominated by the ruling party, as in more explicit one-party states.

The rapid rise of one-party states in Africa after independence is quite striking. Initially, Western-style parliamentary institutions were introduced in most countries after the proclamation of independence. However, before long all power was taken over by a single party, usually under the leadership of a charismatic leader who had played an important role in the struggle for independence. Other parties were forbidden or were absorbed into the dominant party. It is interesting to note that the transition from parliamentary systems to one-party states was not restricted to countries that became independent in the immediate post-war period, but also in countries which gained their independence in the late 1970s, such as Angola, Mozambique and Zimbabwe.

Several of the possible explanations for the rise of one-party states in Africa are summarised in Box 11.2 (Ake, 1996; Coleman and Rosberg, 1964; Zolberg, 1966).

BOX 11.2   Explanations for the emergence of one-party rule in Africa

- The legacy of centralised, bureaucratic and authoritarian colonial rule.
- The tribal and ethnic heterogeneity of many of the new states. In absence of traditions of national identification, political party organisation often followed ethnic dividing lines. Political opposition was regarded as a threat to the unity of the state.
- Strong one-party states were considered indispensable for the realisation of national integration between regional and tribal groupings and the creation of bonds between new national political elites and an electorate with little sense of national identification.

- In the struggle for independence one movement usually emerged as the most powerful or influential. This movement would obtain an 'aura of legitimacy' for its contributions in the struggle for independence (Coleman and Rosberg, 1964: 658). As political movements were generally weakly developed, the first nationalist movements would acquire a decisive head start. At an early stage they were recognised as discussion partners by colonial rulers, in search of representatives of the population with whom they could negotiate (Zolberg, 1966).
- With respect to ideology, there were strong socialist and communist influences on the new political movements. There was a generalised distrust of Western economic and political institutions. This is hardly surprising since both markets and Western political institutions were associated with colonial oppression. Communist ideology in particular provided a powerful underpinning to the notion of a one-party state.
- In many countries, leaders genuinely felt that they needed to find alternatives to Western capitalist solutions and that they had to search for a new synthesis between traditional African political institutions and modern political institutions. Sometimes attempts were made to anchor the dominant political party in village meetings, urban district meetings, or other base-level groupings (youth groups, women's groups) who sent delegates to higher branches of the party. Worsley interprets the 'African socialism' of leaders like Julius Nyerere in Tanzania, Léopold Senghor in Senegal and Sékou Touré in Guinea as a variant of 'populist ideologies' of rural populations threatened by the penetration of industrial and financial capital (Worsley, 1967: 118 ff.).
- Internal instability and external political interference reinforced the tendency towards the establishment of one-party states.

One-party states do not provide for a peaceful transfer of power by means of elections. As a result, the initial idealism of nationalist movements often degenerated into monopolisation of power by one ethnic group or even absolute rule by a strong man (see section 11.7). The one-party state became increasingly dependent on military support, or was overthrown in a military coup. The state itself was increasingly at stake in conflicts between ethnic groups, struggling for control of the state apparatus.

11.4.6   Is there a resurgence of democracy in developing countries?

As indicated above, there has been a tendency towards restoration of civilian governments and a (re)introduction of multiparty systems since the 1980s. In most cases this trend was the result of the inability of one-party states and military regimes to cope adequately with the economic and political challenges facing them, combined with outside pressure from the Western World. In Latin America this trend is unmistakable, in Africa more uncertain.

The data in Table 11.2 suggest that there is indeed a certain long-run trend towards less autocratic modes of governance.[23] The percentage of authoritarian regimes in developing

---

[23] It is not clear whether the classification criteria of the data for 2000 and 1995 are identical to those of 1982, so any conclusions from this table can only be tentative. The 2000 data no longer allow us to distinguish military regimes, personal rule and one-party states. Another problem is the classification of countries as restricted parliamentary systems versus fully democratic systems. A fully democratic system not only allows for competitive elections, but also allows full freedom of speech and organisation for opposition parties.

countries declined from 70 per cent in 1982 to 25 per cent in 2012. The percentage of countries with multiparty elections increased from 16 in 1982 to 40 per cent in 2012. The reduced role of the military and the decline of one-party states raises the question whether there is a genuine resurgence of democracy in developing countries.

This debate was fuelled by the publication of Samuel Huntington's study *The Third Wave: Democratisation in the Late Twentieth Century* (Huntington, 1991). Huntington identified three waves of democratisation. The first wave lasted from the beginning of the nineteenth century until 1926. The second wave occurred during the period 1943–62. The third wave started in 1974 with the overthrow of dictatorship in Portugal and affected countries in Southern Europe, Latin America and East Asia. It continued in the 1990s, spreading to Eastern Europe, Central America and Sub-Saharan Africa (Ake, 1996; Bratton and van de Walle, 1997; Doorenspleet, 2000; Lijphart, 2000; Widner, 1994). The only region where democratisation has not taken further hold is the Middle East, where authoritarian regimes continued to dominate till the start of the Arab Spring in 2011. Though the Arab Spring resulted in elections in countries such as Libya, Tunisia and Egypt, it has not yet resulted in stable multiparty democracies. In Egypt the military have reimposed a military dictatorship. Libya is on its way to becoming a failed state. Syria has descended into civil war.

In the mid 1970s, dictatorships in Greece, Portugal and Spain collapsed. In Latin America, Brazil began *abertura* or 'opening' in 1974, and completed its transition to civilian rule by 1985. New civilian regimes emerged in Ecuador in 1979, Peru in 1980 (later temporarily reversed), Bolivia, in 1982, Uruguay in 1984 and Chile in 1989. 1989 was the year of the fall of the Berlin Wall and the dissolution of the Soviet bloc. In 1991, the Soviet Union fell apart into fifteen independent republics, most of which have transformed into nationalist dictatorships or at best restricted parliamentary systems.[24] In Sub-Saharan Africa, the wave of democratisation began with popular protests in Benin in 1989, eventually resulting in a new constitution and multiparty elections. After that, events evolved very rapidly. In the five years prior to 1989 only five Sub-Saharan African countries had had competitive multiparty elections: Botswana, Gambia, Mauritius, Senegal and Zimbabwe. Another four countries had competitive elections, which were however severely flawed by electoral malpractice: Liberia, Madagascar, South Africa and Sudan. This record changed dramatically after 1990 (Bratton and van de Walle, 1997). In five years, 38 out of 47 countries held competitive legislative elections. In many cases, these elections resulted in leadership turnover. By 1994 not a single *de jure* one-party state remained. Democratisation was fuelled by a combination of internal protests and increased international pressure by donor nations after the end of the Cold War.

Bratton and van de Walle (1997) provide an excellent institutional analysis of political changes in Sub-Saharan Africa. The authoritarian political regimes in Africa were so-called neo-patrimonial regimes with a strongly personalistic nature. These regimes will be discussed in more detail in section 11.7. They can be contrasted with authoritarian regimes of a more bureaucratic nature. Neo-patrimonial rulers use state revenues to maintain their personal power in such a manner that in due course the potential for economic development is undermined. This creates hardship, dissatisfaction and opposition among people excluded from political power. At the same time, as a result of economic stagnation, the rulers are no longer able to pay off all their clients, supporters and civil servants, creating dissatisfaction within the elites (Bates, 1994). Multiparty elections are organised as an ultimate measure to diffuse political protest.

---

[24] Note that these countries are not included in Table 11.2.

Bratton and van de Walle sound a cautionary note about the prospects of democracy in Sub-Saharan Africa. The new regimes are often disappointingly similar in their behaviour to the old ones. The institutional characteristics of neo-patrimonial regimes do not suddenly disappear once elections have been held. Though there are instances of new leaders coming to power through elections, the political actors are often the same ones as in the old system. There is institutional continuity and the appropriation of public resources to maintain power is deeply embedded in the political system. In their path-breaking study, *Violence and Social Orders: A Conceptual Framework for Interpreting Recorded Human History* (2009), North, Wallis and Weingast introduce the opposition between limited access orders (LAOs) and open access orders (OAOs). In LAOs, dominant elites restrict the access of larger segments of the population to economic and political activities, thereby creating rents for the elites. In inter-elite negotiations these rents are used to create dominant elite coalitions with a modicum of precarious stability. Elections taking place in LAOs are a sign of realignment of elite coalitions, but do not necessarily herald a transition to genuine OAOs. Under such conditions elite coalitions can break down and elections are accompanied by extensive violence, as in Kenya in 2002 and Zimbabwe in 2002 and 2008. Multiparty elections in developing countries are often anything but fair and free, corruption and electoral manipulation are widespread and the military continue to be an important force behind the scenes. Freedom of speech for opposition parties is under pressure and democratic elections can be followed by a return to authoritarian rule.

The dominant parties of the post-war period find it very hard to give up power. They have usually made use of their hold on the government bureaucracy and the means of mass communication to gain an advantage in the electoral process. In other countries, election results have been falsified and violence has been applied to intimidate opposition parties. Some of these trends are also visible in Table 11.2, where we see that the percentage of fully fledged multiparty democracies has even declined from 51 per cent in 1995 to 40 per cent in 2012.

11.4.7 Rapid expansion of the public sector since 1945

In all developing countries the size of the apparatus of government has increased substantially since independence. Much of the rapid growth of the share of services in employment (see Table 3.8, p. 122) is due to the expansion of government employment. This has much to do with the building up of a social infrastructure of education, agricultural extension and medical care and with the increasing role of the government in the economy in the post-war period.

The new educational systems produced an increased outflow of graduates, with firm expectations of a guaranteed job in the public sector. The fear of political turmoil was one of the motives for governments to continue to employ many of these graduates. A government job was also considered as a reward for political loyalty and political services. As the legitimacy of one-party rule and military regimes declined, public employment became an important source of political patronage. This aspect of government would become a serious impediment to the effective functioning of the public sector. Partly in response to this, structural adjustment programmes and cuts in government spending since the 1990s have put limits to the further expansion of the public sector in developing countries.

11.4.8   'Soft states' and the political economy of rent seeking

The debate on the 'soft state' was opened by Nobel Prize winner Gunnar Myrdal in his study *Asian Drama: An Inquiry into the Poverty of Nations* (1968), dealing with India in particular and Southeast Asian states in general. The term 'soft state' implies that the government does not have the effective instruments to translate policy intentions into actual policy and to impose binding obligations on its citizens. Among others, this is caused by a lack of legitimacy of political institutions and by the underdeveloped administrative capabilities of the state apparatus.

Powerful interest groups (large landowners, civil servants, trade unions, foreign enterprises, members of the high castes, parastatal enterprises) manage to emasculate any policy that runs counter to their interests. For example, in India the legislation on land reform was never really implemented, in part because at local levels the dominant Congress Party was controlled by landed interests. Further, the richer segments of the population in Latin America and Asia pay little or no income taxes, as there is no effective system of taxation. For its revenues, the government depends on taxes that are easily collected, like taxes on land, agricultural production, or exports and imports. The tax base is small and taxes are typically paid by the poor. Because of the underdeveloped income tax system, government is continuously threatened by a *fiscal crisis* (O'Connor, 1973). For their financial requirements, governments depend on deficit finance, monetary financing of governmental expenditures and sometimes an inflow of foreign aid. This makes for inflation and economic instability.

There are few feelings of loyalty to the government or the state among the masses of the population. Therefore, it is hard for governments to mobilise the efforts of large groups of people for infrastructural works, community development, or other collective goals. Myrdal had a distinct preference for stronger totalitarian states, like Maoist China, which seemed to be more capable of mobilising their citizens for developmental purposes. But, Myrdal had little regard for the potentially disastrous consequences of flawed policies in strong states. One should only recall the casualties of the 'Great Leap Forward' in China between 1958 and 1960 when tens of millions of people died due to forced industrialisation and collectivisation of the agricultural sector (see Ashton, Piazza and Zeitz, 1984; Bannister, 1984; Dikötter, 2010; Wu, 2013), or the horrors of the Cultural Revolution between 1966 and 1969 when the Chinese regime persecuted millions of its educated citizens and intellectuals (see Chang, 1991; Chang and Halliday, 2005; Leys, 1978).

An interesting characteristic of 'soft states' is the abundance of regulatory instruments in the economic sphere. Myrdal aptly describes how one set of regulations calls forth further controls. When a government starts restricting imports and controlling financial transactions with foreign countries – as a result of a shortage of foreign exchange – it is forced to develop a licensing system for the establishment of new enterprises, the expansion of existing ones, or access to credit. When government plans determine the prices of inputs and final products, governments are also forced to draft rules to ration and allocate inputs and outputs to enterprises. Subsidising of some economic enterprises implies that other enterprises do not receive any subsidy. This means that government officials have to spend part of their time impeding the activities of new enterprises in favour of enterprises that are already being subsidised.

Since it is difficult to devise detailed rules for every conceivable situation, the rules leave considerable latitude for discretionary decisions by officials. This can easily result in arbitrariness and corruption. Large domestic and foreign firms and interest groups will try to influence key decisions to their own advantage. Since public officials are often underpaid, they are vulnerable to bribery.

In many developing countries with mixed economies there was, until very recently a marked degree of animosity and distrust between the large collective sector and the private sector – e.g. in Peru, Argentina, Mexico and India. This led to further attempts at regulation of the economy in the name of public interest. At the same time, private enterprises did their best to evade public regulations, or to influence them to their advantage. In India, the large enterprises were most successful in safeguarding their interests under this regulatory regime – whether by corruption or by other means. One of the explicit objectives of pre-1991 government policy in India was to prevent the rise of monopolies in the private sector. Nevertheless, the concentration ratios in the private sector (i.e. the shares of the largest enterprises in total output) tended to increase. Often the largest enterprises obtained monopolies through their access to licences.

Corruption

The combination of extensive intervention in the economy, low levels of payment of civil servants, the absence of a tradition of impartial public service and the absence of checks and balances has made corruption endemic (Jain, 2001). In many developing countries corruption is the rule rather than the exception, both at the top of the political system and at lower levels of the bureaucracy and state apparatus. In turn, corruption reduces the effectiveness of the government. It further undermines civilian faith in government, legal security and the rule of law and promotes further corruption. From high to low people turn to patron–client relationships, in which people render each other services and favours, rather than appealing to formal legal rights or procedures. The predictability of government behaviour declines and bureaucracy is replaced by a 'personalist system' in which networks of personal relationships are the determining factor. One of the most extreme examples of a corrupt machinery of government was the system of *cronyism* in the Philippines under the regime of Ferdinand Marcos, where huge amounts of public funds and development aid disappeared into private pockets. Other well-known examples include Indonesia under the Suharto regime, Nigeria and Zaire (the Republic of Congo) under Mobutu Sese Seko. Zaire is an example of a state where the whole apparatus of government has been made subservient to the survival and enrichment of the ruling clique.

One of the key problems with pervasive corruption is its unpredictability. As long as corruption is predictable, it functions like an informal tax. But it may not be enough to bribe officials at the top of political hierarchies. One might encounter unorganised and anarchistic corruption at all levels of the political system. Where this is the case, corruption may actual kill off all productive activity (Collier and Hoeffler, 2005; Labelle, 2014; Mauro, 1995, 2000).

The modern literature on rent-seeking behaviour goes beyond the analysis of corruption to look at the very nature of economic policy formation (e.g. Jain, 2001). Corruption does not only refer to bribes. Rent-seeking behaviour refers to activities by interest groups and firms to acquire monopolistic profits through manipulation of the political system. This involves not only manipulating specific decisions in the favour of a firm or an interest group, but also influencing the direction of policy formation. Thus, urban interest groups impose tax burdens on rural farmers or exporters in Sub-Saharan Africa, loss making state owned firms are subsidised in China and macro-economic stabilisation policies are not implemented when they run counter to major interests in many Latin American countries.

11.5   The role of government in economic development

With regard to the economic role of the government in development, there is an interesting paradox of a *weak state* with *disproportionately heavy tasks*. In the economically advanced countries of today, the role of the state in economic development in the nineteenth century was relatively restricted. The main tasks of government were the maintenance of law and order, the defence of private property and external defence (the so-called 'night-watch state'). In comparison, the role of the state in the economic process in developing countries since 1950 has been much greater. The demands on the functioning of the state apparatus are much higher. At the same time, the apparatus of government is less well equipped to fulfil these heavier demands.

It is indisputable that the role of government in the economic process has increased, both in poor and in rich countries (Evans, 1995; Gerschenkron, 1962; Maddison, 1986; Myint, 1980; White, 1984). In *Economic Backwardness in Historical Perspective* (1962), Gerschenkron offers an interesting explanation for this phenomenon. As a result of technological development, the required scale of investment is becoming ever-larger. The time span between the moment of committing financial resources and the moment an investment starts to yield a return grows longer. Thus it becomes more difficult and risky for individual private enterprises to mobilise the necessary funds for investment. During the Industrial Revolution in eighteenth-century England self-financing by firms was the main source of investment. In nineteenth-century Germany, large banks and financial conglomerates (*das Finanzkapital*) together with the government were the institutions which mobilised the necessary funds for investment (see Tilly, 1986). In late nineteenth-century Russia the risks of huge investments in railways and industry had become so large that they were mainly borne by government in cooperation with foreign investors. In Japan the government also played a crucial role in initiating processes of capital accumulation in the industrial sector. Thus in late development the task of the government is not only to create a favourable environment for private economic activities (legal security, predictability, pacification) but also to help mobilise savings and to act as an investor itself, where private investment is insufficient. In recent years, the nature of international competition has changed further. Modern competition is increasingly based on innovation and technological advance. One of the tasks of modern governments is to create or nurture the conditions under which a country's enterprises can keep up in the modern technology race.[25]

In developing countries, there are some additional considerations. First, it was believed that there was a shortage of entrepreneurship in the private sector. Entrepreneurial classes were weakly developed. There were no groups in the domestic private sector which would generate sufficient investment. The state had to compensate for the shortage of

[25] In the modern global economy, the great multinational enterprises command resources which dwarf those of smaller national states. Their role in the mobilisation of capital has increased, relative to the period discussed so astutely by Gerschenkron (1962).

entrepreneurship by acting as an investor itself. Second, there were enormous backlogs with respect to infrastructure, education and healthcare. Improvements in these fields required additional government efforts. Third, there was a policy goal of accelerated development in order to narrow the gap between rich and poor countries. This also called for a more active role on the part of government. In the Latin American context, this role is sometimes referred to as *developmentalism* (Urquidi, 1993). Notions concerning external effects and complementarities, discussed in Chapter 9, play a central role in this approach.

There were also subjective considerations. On the basis of their historical experiences, newly independent countries associated capitalism, market mechanisms and international trade with colonialism and foreign oppression. There was a deep distrust of the free market and a search for alternative paths of development. In the post-war years the Soviet Union served as a model of a poor and backward country that had succeeded in industrialising rapidly by means of socialist planning. This model provided a further ideological justification for extensive state intervention in the economy.

Since the mid 1980s there have been major swings in our thinking about state intervention. After the debt crisis of 1982, structural adjustment programmes called for a more modest role of the state in economic development. But disappointment with the outcomes of market-based solutions in the 1990s resulted in renewed attention to the role of the state and public policy in economic development. These debates will be revisited in this chapter and in Chapter 13.

11.5.1   The role of the state in economic development: five examples

This section provides illustrations of the pervasive role of the state in economic development in a discussion of the developmental experiences of Japan, China, Brazil, South Korea and India.

Japan

The government played an extremely important role in the economic development of Japan after the Meiji restoration in 1868 (Maddison, 1969; Pilat, 1994). The feudal system based on landownership by samurai, daimyo and the shogun was abolished (the shogun alone owned about one-quarter of all land). The large landowners were compensated with government obligations and were stimulated to invest their financial resources in industry. Land was redistributed to the actual cultivators, on whom land taxes were imposed. The financial system was reformed, and compulsory education was introduced in 1872.

The government played a decisive role in the process of industrialisation with investments in the military industry, shipbuilding and heavy industry. The government share in total investment was high. A pattern developed in which the government took the initiative for large-scale investments in industry. Once these industries started to function, they were sold off to the private sector. Large-scale investments were also made in the Japanese colonies (Korea, Taiwan, Manchuria). The government stimulated the growth of modern, very large industrial conglomerates (*zaibatsu*) that maintained strong ties with the government. At an early stage, government policy started promoting industrial exports and giving firms with export success preferential treatment.

The Japanese government pursued an active policy of R&D. Foreign investments were impeded, but Japan managed to obtain technological know-how by systematically inviting foreign scientists and technical specialists and by organising study tours to Western countries.

Traditionally, the government paid a great deal of attention to schooling, education and technological development. Both agricultural growth and participation in international trade were promoted at an early stage. In agriculture, a lot of attention was paid to the linkages between agricultural and industrial development. During recent decades overprotection of agriculture, however, led to increasing inefficiencies in this sector (Van der Meer and Yamada, 1990).

In the Japanese model of industrialisation, it is not quite clear whether government set the course for private enterprise, or whether private enterprise determined the direction of public policy. Rather, there was an intensive interaction between public and private sector. The government actively pursued an industrialisation policy in which key industries with bright prospects were identified and supported. 'Sunset' industries were drastically cut back.

The Japanese industrial sector has a dual structure, with small labour-intensive, market-oriented firms acting as subcontractors for large, capital-intensive firms pursuing long-term strategic objectives. Until recently these large companies offered their employees *lifetime employment*. In such a dual structure many of the risks of economic fluctuations are shifted to the small labour-intensive enterprises operating on the market.

The rapid economic and industrial development of Japan is an example of industrialisation and modernisation imposed from above (Barrington Moore, 1967). Members of the feudal class of samurai took control of the state apparatus during the Meiji reforms and took the initiative in transforming and modernising the entire economy and society. In this process the commercial middle classes played a less important role than they did earlier in European history.

As Japan drew closer to the technological frontier, its catch-up processes slowed down. The system, which was so successful in assimilating and further developing international technology, was less suited to the requirements of innovation. Since the 1990s, the Japanese economy has been in a state of semi-stagnation. The system of intensive interaction of the state, large-scale industry interaction and the financial system is now being re-examined in the light of new challenges.

China

In China, the role of the government in industrialisation and economic development was even greater than in Japan (Maddison, 1998). In the years following the communist revolution of 1949, all industrial enterprises were brought under public ownership. Large-scale land reforms were implemented. The land of large landowners was nationalised without compensation and redistributed among the peasants. After that, the agricultural sector was collectivised step by step, starting with voluntary cooperatives in the early 1950s and ending with the establishment of immense communes, sometimes involving over a million people in 1958–60 (Hsu, 1982). Initially, economic policy followed the example of the Soviet Union. The emphasis was on the development of heavy industries. In the Marxist terminology, this branch was referred to as 'Sector I': the production of machines to produce machines.

National Five-Year Plans were introduced in which the physical production goals for all industries were laid down and industries were allocated predetermined amounts of inputs. These plans had been based on input–output models with fixed technical coefficients and a complete elimination of price mechanisms. Just like Japan, China succeeded in realising a high level of savings. All investment was done via the public sector. Lin, Cai and Li (2000, 2003) explain brilliantly how the choice for heavy industry and the key role of the state interact, in China and elsewhere. Heavy industries require investment with long gestation periods, imported capital goods and large lump-sum investments. In a predominantly agricultural economy, capital is scarce, market interest rates are high, foreign exchange is scarce and the economic surplus is small. In order to make large-scale industrial enterprises profitable, one needs distorted macro-economic policies (cheap energy prices, low interest rates, low wages, overvalued exchange rates), which require government intervention. Private entrepreneurs were not willing to invest in heavy industry where the market prospects of profitability were low, so nationalisation became more or less inevitable. This resulted in what Lin *et al.* call the 'holy trinity' of a distorted macro-policy environment, a planned allocation mechanism and a puppet-like micro-management system. This was found irrespective of ideology in other countries pursuing heavy industry-oriented development, such as India or Brazil.

A difference with Soviet Russian development is that China paid more attention to agriculture. To be sure, agriculture was allocated a relatively modest part of total investment compared to heavy industry (Kitching, 1982). Still, the rural population was successfully mobilised for large-scale infrastructural works like land reclamation, terracing, road construction and irrigation works (see Hsu, 1982; Rawski, 1979).

Although the land reforms initially provided the communist regime with a degree of legitimacy amongst the peasant population, the collectivisation of agriculture eventually turned out to be a great failure. Links between effort and reward were completely severed. Since 1978, a liberalisation of the agricultural sector has commenced, which has led to an explosive growth in agricultural production. Simultaneously, inefficiency in the industrial sector is on the increase.

It seems possible – albeit often at great human and economic cost[26] – to build up a basic industrial sector by means of central planning and collective mobilisation of savings. At later stages of industrial development, however, the planning system seems to be too inflexible to respond to differentiated and varying consumer needs.

Since the mid 1980s, market reforms have been gradually introduced in the industrial sector as well (Lin, Cai and Li, 2003; Lin and Yu, 2015; Qian, 2003; Sachs and Woo, 1997; Xu, 2011; Yue, 2015). This is not done by privatising existing large public enterprises, but rather by permitting the rise of new market-oriented enterprises, stimulating foreign investment and encouraging exports and opening up the economy. Compared to the pre-reform period, the new production structure is more in line with China's latent comparative advantage (Lin and Monga, 2010). The share of private enterprises, semi-private enterprises such as TVEs and foreign enterprises has increased dramatically. The past decades have seen very rapid growth of industrial production and explosive growth of exports (Szirmai and Ren, 2000; Szirmai *et al.*, 2001; Wang and Szirmai, 2008). The performance of the state owned enterprises is still lagging behind. Attempts have been made to shed redundant labour on a large scale, but the authorities fear to privatise this sector of the economy because of fear of the employment consequences. In contrast to the disappointments of 'Big

[26] Sometimes disastrous mistakes were made, like the attempt at forced industrialisation during the Great Leap Forward between 1958 and 1960.

Bang' liberalisation in the former Soviet Union, China has opted for a policy of gradual liberalisation, which appears to be remarkably successful. Compared to the period before 1980, the role of the state has been reduced substantially but it still remains pervasive. One of the characteristics of the Chinese reform process is its experimental and gradualistic nature. There is a considerable degree of regional experimentation, where new policies are tried out in one region before being rolled out in others. Also, there is a tendency to maintain existing forms of organisation while experimenting with new ones, e.g. the dual-track pricing system in agriculture, or the emergence of TVEs, while state owned enterprises continue to be supported.

Brazil

Brazil is a well-known example of a country that pursued a strong policy of import-substituting industrialisation (Furtado, 1976; Evans, 1995; Maddison *et al.*, 1992). Brazilian economic policy has sometimes been characterised as *state capitalism*.

Since the mid nineteenth century revenues from agricultural exports, in particular coffee, created a domestic market for industrial consumer goods. But political power was controlled by agricultural oligarchies to which industrialisation was of little interest. 1930 saw the beginning of a new phase of economic development when Getúlio Vargas came to power after a military coup d'état. During this period export prices of primary products fell, and the flow of imports from Europe dried up. The government chose to pursue a strong policy of import substitution which protected Brazilian industries against foreign competition. This was realised by means of exchange rate policy, rationing and the allocation of foreign currencies, import tariffs on consumer goods and subsidies on investment. As in Japan, private and public interests were entwined, with the government itself acting either as an investor or as a partner in joint ventures. A characteristic of Brazilian economic policy is its relative openness to foreign investment. Foreign investors often formed *joint ventures* with domestic private companies and public enterprises. Many of these joint ventures acquired monopolies on the protected domestic market.

A populist industrialisation strategy was pursued in which the political elites maintained ties with organised labour. Industrial workers got preferential treatment over the rural population. Workers were organised into a kind of corporative state unions, which served among others to control the production factor of labour.

There was some degree of planning of economic activity and a high degree of state participation in investment. There were large government investments in the mining sector. Macro-economic policy was highly expansionary. Growth was given precedence over macro-economic stability and controlling inflation.

Between 1929 and 1980 Brazil (together with Mexico) ranked among the fastest-growing economies in the world. Within a relatively brief period of time, Brazil had succeeded in establishing a diversified industrial sector (Aldrighi and Colistete, 2015). Because of the great income inequality the poor benefited little from the economic growth, but even critics of the Brazilian economic miracle must admit that the poor suffered more from the economic stagnation of the 1980s than from the unequally distributed growth of earlier decades.

After 1980 the shortcomings of Brazilian economic policy became manifest. Prolonged protection of domestic industry had resulted in great inefficiencies, inflexibilities and low levels of capacity utilisation. The industrial sector was too inward-looking and had not succeeded in penetrating foreign markets. Macro-economic instability increased, inflation reached astronomic levels and Brazil proved to be incapable of servicing its debt. The inflow of new capital dried up. After 1980, Brazil experienced a decade of stagnation.

In the 1990s, Brazil belatedly followed the world trend of deregulation, privatisation of the large public owned sector and further export promotion. It succeeded in stabilising its economy, and growth has gradually been picking up, especially after 2000. However, the downside liberalisation has been a decided loss of manufacturing capabilities.

South Korea

South Korea is another example of an economy where the state played a large role in the process of industrialisation and capital accumulation (Amsden, 1989, 2013; Chang, 2002; Evans, 1995; Kiely, 1998; Pilat, 1994). According to Amsden and Pilat, government policy has been of crucial importance in the process of accelerated growth that took place in South Korea since 1953. In many respects, the role of the government in Korea has been similar to that in Brazil and Japan. The government actively participated in planning industrial activities through subsidies, credit facilities, protectionist tariffs, price controls and public investment. The government taxed the middle classes, without offering much in the way of social services for broad groups in the population. This provided the government with abundant financial means for investment. It encouraged the establishment of very large industrial conglomerates (*Chaebols*).

Like Brazil, South Korea had a period of import substitution during which the domestic industry was protected against foreign competition. The difference with Brazil is that the Korean government started to support and subsidise export-oriented activities as early as the 1960s. Government policy stopped discriminating in favour of firms that produced for the domestic market. Another difference is the far greater degree of discipline involved in subsidising private companies. The government consistently refused to bail out large companies in financial difficulties. Weakly performing sectors of industry were forced to restructure. Subsidies and other kinds of government support were made dependent on performance criteria in terms of production growth, increase in productivity and penetration into export markets. Until recently, Korea had an authoritarian political regime. Though the political system was not free from corruption, an effective bureaucracy succeeded in isolating itself from undue influence of pressure groups and was thus able to enforce performance criteria on the firms in the private sector (Booth, 1999). One of the important characteristics of the bureaucracy was *embedded autonomy*, a term coined by Evans (1995). Embedded autonomy implies that the professional bureaucracy succeeded in isolating itself from political interference and rent seeking, while establishing creative ties and links with enterprises in the productive sector.

According to Amsden's interpretation the government succeeded in identifying potentially successful branches of activity and supported these by means of subsidies and price policies. The government pursued a policy of 'getting prices wrong' in order to stimulate investments which would be profitable in the long run. This meant that short-term prices deviated from free market prices. In the long term the policy was market-oriented, because only efficiently producing enterprises would receive continued support. Monopolistic price-fixing by large conglomerates was not allowed. The outward orientation of industrial policy meant that Korean products had to be competitive on international markets. Amsden points to a possible relationship between the authoritarian nature of the 'strong' Korean state and the success of its economic policy. However, she sees no reason why a 'strong' state could not be compatible with political democracy (Amsden, 1989: 18). Korea is often seen as a crucial example of successful industrial policies and state intervention in the economy. However, it is not clear to what extent its policies can be replicated in countries with weaker state capabilities (Hobday, 2013).

India

After the attainment of independence in 1947 India pursued economic development in accordance with a model referred to as *Indian socialism* (Bardhan, 1984; Cassen, 1978; Maddison, 1974). This model had some typical characteristics. On the one hand, it emphasised the development of traditional crafts, like spinning, weaving and small-scale industry in the tradition of Mahatma Gandhi. In this respect, policy tried to build on traditional Indian patterns of craft production. Homespun clothing even became the symbol of the Indian struggle for independence. On the other hand, Jawaharlal Nehru strove to establish heavy industry along lines of the Soviet planning model. Physical production objectives were laid down in a series of Five-Year Plans. Socialism was to be realised by means of huge government investments in heavy industry, as it was believed that the required volume of investment exceeded the capabilities of the private sector. Especially in the second Five-Year Plan from 1956 to 1961, heavy industries were given high priority. The private sector was allowed to continue its operations, but a rapidly expanding apparatus of government tried to control and regulate private economic activities. The role of foreign investment was restricted.

One of the explicit objectives of regulation was to prevent monopolisation and the domination of the Indian economy by large foreign investors and large domestic enterprises. Paradoxically, though, the largest companies profited most from government regulation. Through their contacts within the bureaucracy and through corruption, they often succeeded in establishing monopolies or acquiring licences. The degree of concentration in the economy increased substantially. Smaller companies were not able to make their way through the red tape and the intricacies of government bureaucracies. There were long-standing complaints from the private sector that private entrepreneurs were bound hand and foot by government regulations. Nevertheless, the pressure for change was not very strong, as the largest companies benefited from the niches and monopolies which were the inadvertent consequence of government regulation.

The Indian industrialisation model can also not be denied a certain measure of success. India succeeded in building up a diversified industrial infrastructure with a large share of capital goods and intermediate goods in total output. In addition, there were substantial investments in education and R&D. After the mid 1960s, more attention was also paid to agricultural development.

Just as in China, the establishment of basic industries like steel plants or power stations proved to be possible by means of central planning. In later stages of industrial development, however, the planning model in India turned out to be too inflexible. After the 1970s industrial development in India stagnated. Production was plagued by industrial unrest, logistic problems and insufficient utilisation of capacity. Protectionism was conducive to inefficiency.

The emphasis on the capital goods industry required high levels of production in other sectors of the economy in order to generate sufficient demand for capital goods. But, domestic purchasing-power was insufficient to create a growing market for consumer goods industries, in part due to low income levels in the agricultural sector. Indian industries were not sufficiently competitive for international markets. The protection of the traditional craft production also involved great waste, as these activities were not viable without protection. Furthermore, distrust of foreign investors reduced the inflow of foreign capital. In comparison with other Asian countries, growth of the Indian economy in the post-war period was sluggish.

According to Bardhan (1984), the economic problems were especially caused by the fact that government policy was insufficiently insulated from the influence of powerful interest groups, as the legitimacy of government acquired in the struggle for independence was gradually eroded. Political contradictions between agricultural interests, the interests of professionals within the civil service and the interests of industrial capital paralysed government policy. They channelled government spending into wasteful direct and indirect subsidies to keep the different interest groups satisfied. The mobilisation of investible financial resources – in itself fairly successful – led to government consumption rather than more government investment. Bardhan sees declining public investment as an important explanation for the slowdown in industrial growth in the 1960s and 1970s.

Another characteristic of Indian socialism was the strong emphasis on equality and land reform. The rhetoric of egalitarianism, however, had few consequences in practice. Through their hold on the Congress Party at local levels, powerful landed interests succeeded in frustrating the implementation of land reform measures. Despite a policy of preferential recruitment of untouchables and other underprivileged groups, the highly inegalitarian caste system remained extremely influential. In India there has been much talk about 'democratic planning' from the bottom up. In practice, however, there was little participation of the population in the process of economic planning.

Since the mid 1980s, India has also participated in the worldwide trend towards deregulation, strengthening of market incentives and a reduction of the role of the government in the economy. The tensions between the public and the private sector are increasingly regarded as one of the impediments to economic development and an increased inflow of foreign investment. Many observers attribute the relatively slow economic growth in India, compared to other Asian economies as Korea, Malaysia, Thailand, Indonesia and Taiwan, to the negative influences of a cumbersome and ineffective apparatus of government, with great discretionary powers and a considerable degree of corruption.[27] 1991 is seen as a turning point in the liberalisation process and the rate of growth and technological upgrading accelerated after that year (Mani, 2011). India opened up to foreign investment. The private sector became more important and the share of exports and imports in GDP increased. New sectors emerged, such as software and telecommunications. India became one of the world leaders in software, while the importance of manufacturing declined (Aggarwal and Kumar, 2015). Economic growth accelerated substantially, though not

[27] Bardhan (1984) gives a similar critical analysis of the role of the government in relative stagnation. However, his conclusions are different. He does not argue in favour of liberalisation. Rather, he pleads for a more efficient government and an increase in public investment. Bardhan still defends the leading role of government in late industrial development. In his opinion, India should model its behaviour on South Korea and should try to insulate government policy from manipulation by interest groups.

crece economía pero

reaching the rates of China. But rates of poverty and illiteracy remained unacceptably high (Ramani and Szirmai, 2014).

These five examples illustrate that the role of the government in processes of late industrialisation has been larger than previously in economic history – irrespective of political system or ideology. They also illustrate that overprotection of domestic production, inward orientation and the elimination of economic incentives for efficient production and allocation result in economic stagnation.

A consensus has emerged that the kind of state intervention which prevailed in the period 1950–80 is not sustainable. The elements of the new consensus are the following:

1. In comparison with the practice of the period 1950–90, a *reduction of the dominant role of the state in the economic process* in developing countries seems advisable. Regulation of the private sector, which gives rise to misallocation of scarce resources, should be diminished.

2. The *effectiveness of the apparatus of government should be increased*. The government should take on fewer economic tasks and execute a more limited range of tasks more effectively (World Bank-WDR, 1997). Where corruption impedes the normal execution of government functions, privatisation of these functions should be considered. The success and failure of government intervention does not only depend on economic arguments. It also depends on the quality and capabilities of the administrative system. The lower the quality and the weaker the capabilities, the stronger the case for deregulation. The higher the quality, the greater the opportunities for interventionist policies.

3. Following the example of East Asian states, developing country governments *should not protect inefficient enterprises indefinitely.* Government policies should be more in conformity with market success. They should stimulate those activities in the private sector which are successful on national or international markets.

4. Nevertheless, *the role of the state in the economic process* will be larger than previously in earlier periods of economic history. The state retains essential tasks with respect to investment in education, infrastructure, healthcare, environmental protection, promotion of agricultural R&D, organisation of agricultural education, promotion of industrial R&D – also for the benefit of small-scale industries – and promotion of structural change. In addition, the state has a role in mobilising investment and functioning as a negotiating partner for powerful foreign investors.

The debate on the exact scope and mode of government intervention continues (Cimoli *et al.*, 2009; Szirmai *et al.*, 2013). After the mid 1980s, developing countries all over the world have tended to reduce the role of government and have liberalised their economies. In countries, such as China, Chile, Ghana, India, Sri Lanka and Tanzania, this has had a positive impact on economic dynamics. Elsewhere, liberalisation, transition to the markets and structural adjustment have frequently had very disappointing results, whether in Africa, Latin America or in the former Soviet Union. Some authors blame this on shortcomings of the Washington consensus and an excessive belief in the blessings of the market. As discussed in Chapter 9, authors like Amsden, Chang, Westphal, Lall and Bardhan point to South Korea, Taiwan and China to illustrate the fact that governments can indeed act in a proactive manner and can promote efficient and dynamic economic behaviour. They argue that government policy can and should contribute to the creation of dynamic comparative advantage. Other authors argue for decentralisation of government (Bardhan, 2002). In recent years, we have witnessed a rediscovery and rehabilitation of the role of selective industrial policies in promoting economic growth and structural change, but there is a danger that the lessons of the post-war period are being forgotten.

11.6 Interactions between political and economic developments

In this section we will discuss four aspects of the relationships between economic and political developments in developing countries: the effects of political instability on economic growth; the effects of economic growth on political instability; the relationships between authoritarian rule, democracy and economic development; and the the role of good governance.

11.6.1 Political instability as a source of economic stagnation

In section 11.2 we pointed to the importance of internal pacification as a prerequisite for economic development. The absence of violence within a state is one of the principal aspects of political stability. Kuznets (1966: 451) stresses that a minimum degree of political stability is required for entrepreneurial individuals to be assured of a stable relation between their efforts and their rewards. Only then will they be prepared to invest in future production. Political instability, social unrest and abuse of civil rights hamper long-run capital accumulation. They result in capital flight and a brain drain, with the most skilled and best-educated members of the labour force emigrating in search of better economic opportunities (Alesina and Tabellini, 1989; Alesina *et al.*, 1996; De Haan and Sierman, 1993; Fosu, 1992). Political instability, whether in the form of political turmoil, ethnic tensions or unpredictable changes in regimes and governments, causes economic stagnation (Collier, 2007, Chapter 2). The 2011 World Development Report on *Conflict, Security and Development* (World Bank-WDR, 2011) writes that no conflict-ridden low-income economy has achieved a single one of the MDGs.

It is not hard to come up with examples of political conflicts and political instability resulting in economic stagnation: the famines in Ethiopia and Somalia in the aftermath of the Ethiopian–Somalian wars, the total collapse of the economy of Uganda under Idi Amin and the impoverishment of Zimbabwe under Robert Mugabe, or the economic stagnation in countries like Somalia and the DRC. In quantitative, comparative studies many researchers observe a negative relationship between indicators of political instability and economic growth. For example, McGowan and Johnson (1984) find a negative correlation between an index of political instability and growth of income per capita in thirty-nine countries in Sub-Saharan Africa. Fosu (1992) distinguishes between countries with relatively high political stability and countries with relatively low political stability in Sub-Saharan Africa. He comes to the conclusion that, other things being equal, annual economic growth is at least 1 per cent lower in the 'high political instability' countries. De Haan and Sierman (1993) also note a negative correlation between political instability (represented by the frequency of changes of government) and economic growth in Sub-Saharan Africa. Civil wars tend to reduce growth by 2.3 per cent per year (Collier, 2007). With respect to Asian countries, there is an indirect negative relationship between instability and growth via an investment variable. For Latin America, Grier (2002) finds strong support for the argument that political instability negatively affects the stock of physical capital. He argues that increases in uncertainty result in negative effects on investment and growth. Also, war and civil war destroys the capital stock.

There is also an interesting body of literature on the negative relationship between ethnic diversity, linguistic fragmentation and economic growth (Alesina and Ferrara, 2005; Desmet, Ortuño-Ortin and Wacziarg, 2012; Easterly, 2001a; Easterly and Levine, 1997; Nettle, 2000). Nettle (2000) finds evidence of an inverse relationship between linguistic heterogeneity (measured as the per cent of the national population who are native speakers of the most widespread language) and economic development. The absence of a shared language may obstruct economic development, among other things because it is an obstacle for widening the scale of markets and economic activities. But the causality is complex. Economic development itself leads to increases in communication and fosters the emergence of standardised national and even international languages (such as English in the present world economy). This was the case in European history.

Easterly and Levine (1997) argue that ethnic diversity in Africa has important indirect negative effects on growth and development. Ethnically polarised societies are more prone to competitive rent seeking by different groups, which will have more difficulty in agreeing on public goods and effective public policies. Easterly and Levine present cross-country regression analyses relating ethnic fractionalism to growth and a variety of other indicators. There are significant negative relationships between ethnic diversity and school attainment, quality of infrastructure, black market premiums, distorted foreign exchange markets and underdeveloped financial systems. The authors conclude that ethnic diversity encourages poor public policies, with significant indirect negative effects on growth.

Interestingly enough, Easterly and Levine find little or no direct relationships between ethnic diversity and political instability. Whether ethnic diversity results in political instability depends very much on the quality of institutional arrangements, which can or cannot mitigate the effects of ethnic conflict. Ethnic diversity has a much more adverse effect on policy and growth when legal and political institutions are weak (Easterly, 2001a). In a more recent paper, Desmet, Ortuño-Ortin and Wacziarg (2012) argue that the effect of ethnolinguistic cleavages depends on how they are measured. For the onset of conflict, coarse, deeped-rooted classifications matter most. But finer linguistic classifications contribute more to the understanding of growth performance. Greater heteregeneity results in coordination problems, slower growth and weaker provision of public goods. In another recent paper, Bluhm, de Crombrugghe and Szirmai (2013) find that the duration of economic crises – an important determinant of long-run stagnation – is far longer in countries which combine high degrees of ethnic fractionalisation with low scores on governance indictors such as constraints on the executive. It is not ethnic fractionalisation as such that matters, but the combination of weak governance with ethnic polarisation (see also Collier, 2007).

11.6.2   Economic development and political stability

Just as political stability is a prerequisite for economic development, economic development is one of the prerequisites for political stability. Only when there is economic growth, capital accumulation and an increase in productivity can an effective government administration be financed and can the government play a mediating role in conflicts between social groups and classes. If there is no growth, standards of living will stagnate or even decline, creating widespread dissatisfaction and a potential for political protest and opposition. In economic stagnation, the government is threatened by fiscal crisis and is forced to take sides in clashes of interest between social classes. This may manifest itself in increased repression of workers, unions, peasants and oppositional movements (Anglade and Fortin, 1985). It may also manifest itself in attempts at economic reform, which sometimes alienate the very groups on which a regime relies for support (Skocpol, 1979). The potential for instability is especially marked when periods of rapid growth and rising expectations are followed by slower growth or stagnation. In *The Bottom Billion: Why the Poorest Countries are Failing and What Can be Done about it* (2007), Collier writes about the *conflict trap*. Low initial levels of income and slow growth result in conflict, which results in further economic stagnation. Low-income countries are much more prone to conflict than richer countries.

Surprisingly, under certain circumstances even economic growth may also give rise to political instability (Terhal, 1992). Income inequality tends to increase during the early stages of industrialisation and development (Kuznets, 1955). As an explanation of the tendency towards increased inequality in early stages of industrialisation, Ahluwalia (1976) points to the emergence of a new production factor, capital, with an extremely high productivity. Ownership of and access to this new production factor has a skewed distribution. Thus, economic growth leads to increasing inequality between those groups who benefit from the increase in productivity associated with the new factors of production and the groups who do not. Thus growth and industrialisation can give rise to political tensions and conflicts, as for instance in Iran under the regime of the Shah until 1979. Rapidly increasing inequality may well result in escalating political conflict and lasting political instability. Terhal (1992) identifies the following two groups as crucial in processes of social conflict during growth processes:[28]

1. *The mobile but unsatisfied group*. This group includes people whose position has improved economically, but who remain unsatisfied.
2. *The stagnating immobile group*. This includes a considerable group of poor people whose economic position remains more or less stagnant.

The groups that experience economic improvement in absolute and relative terms may still be dissatisfied if their aspirations to achieve equal footing with older ruling elites are frustrated. The groups whose economic situation remains unchanged in absolute terms may accept increasing inequality for quite a long time. They hope that sooner or later they will enjoy the same social and economic improvements which they can see other groups are enjoying at present.[29] However, if such expectations remain unfulfilled for too long, a dramatic switch may take place in which acquiescence and hope are replaced by extreme frustration (Hirschman, 1973). When both these types of frustration and dissatisfaction occur simultaneously, a politically explosive situation can arise, especially when economic dividing lines coincide with ethnic or geographic divisions. This explosive combination of growth in combination with rapidly increasing inequality can be found in many developing countries, such as for instance China, India, Brazil and Indonesia.

---

[28] In total, Terhal identifies four groups: the disadvantaged and impoverished the stagnating immobile, the mobile satisfied and the mobile but unsatisfied.

[29] Hirschman (1973) calls this the 'tunnel effect'. He draws an analogy with car drivers in a traffic jam before a tunnel; if they see cars moving in the other lane, they hope and expect that cars in their own lane will also start moving sooner or later.

According to Terhal, political elites can try to mitigate social tensions by coopting the economically rising groups and improving their access to political power and social status. At the same time, a regime can increase its legitimacy amongst the poor masses which are not profiting much from economic growth by a process of political democratisation. Terhal quite rightly remarks, by the way, that the political tensions associated with economic growth will be even more pronounced in conditions of economic stagnation.

In conclusion, it can be stated that political instability may result from economic growth as well as from economic stagnation. In the literature on social conflict there is no consensus on the question whether political instability is greatest under circumstances of rapid growth, declines in the rate of growth or straightforward economic stagnation (see Szirmai, 1988, Chapter 9). Under present circumstances, we would argue that continued economic stagnation would seem to be the most important threat to political stability in many developing countries. In many countries, where the promise of growth and development has failed to materialise in the past decennia, there is a tremendous reservoir of frustration and disillusionment that can be tapped by extremist political and religious movements.

11.6.3 Is there a relationship between democracy and economic development?

With the exception of colonial Hong Kong, the Asian tigers Singapore, Korea and Taiwan had dictatorial regimes during their take-off and high-growth phases. These regimes had admittedly tolerated a number of civil, religious and especially economic freedoms but were restrictive and repressive with regard to political freedoms such as the right of association and assembly or freedom of speech. Since 1978, China has experienced impressive growth rates while maintaining an authoritarian political system. These experiences gave rise to a painful question: whether democracy is compatible with rapid economic development in late developing countries.

In 1959, the political scientist Seymour M. Lipset (1959) noted that average income per capita in democratic countries was much higher than in non-democratic countries. He concluded that causality ran from economic development to democracy. Richer countries can afford to be democratic. But the causality of this relationship remains contested.

In the debate on the contributions of democratic regimes to economic growth, two opposing perspectives can be identified (Acemoglu and Robinson, 2012; Barro, 1996; Butkiewicz and Yanikkaya, 2006; Helliwell, 1994; Knack and Keefer, 1995; Papaioannou and Siourounis, 2008; Scully, 1988; Sirowy and Inkeles, 1990; Tavares and Wacziarg, 2001). One perspective states that democratic regimes retard growth in developing countries. There is a tension between democratic institutions and the requirements of economic development in developing countries, especially in the case of late industrialisation. A policy aimed at capital accumulation and rapid economic growth cannot be too democratic since accumulation and a sober macro-economic policy require consumptive sacrifices a poor population can hardly be expected to make voluntarily. Long-term economic growth can only be achieved if the political system can be insulated from the short-term wishes of the people. Examples of countries with more or less autocratic regimes that have achieved high economic growth rates include Brazil, China, Indonesia, Malaysia, Taiwan, Thailand and South Korea. Bardhan (1984) blames slow economic growth in India on the political regime's incapacity to insulate itself sufficiently from the influences of interest groups. O'Donnell (1979) has argued that bureaucratic authoritarian regimes are most capable of meeting the challenges of late industrialisation. These challenges include, among other things, building up intermediate and capital goods industries, achieving political predictability and stability, and pursuing sober macro-economic policies. A different strand of (neo-liberal) argument states that democracies can impose a reduction in growth rates through distributive and distortive interventions and too great scope for political interest groups (Barro, 1996; Olson, 1982). In these perspectives, one should focus on economic development as a route to later democratisation, rather than the other way round. Democratisation is not the first priority.

Other authors defend the thesis that political democratisation, civilian freedoms and economic growth have reinforced each other in history. Political pluralism is a prerequisite for economic pluralism and the flowering of entrepreneurship – in developing countries as well as advanced economies. Scully (1988) states that between 1960 and 1980 open societies with political civilian and economic freedoms grew three times as fast as societies in which these freedoms were restricted. Acemoglu and Robinson (2012) argue that sustained growth is only possible in inclusive democratic societies. Authoritarian societies with extractive institutions can achieve periods of rapid growth but cannot sustain growth in the long run. Over the past 300 years it was the more inclusive societies which forged ahead. Papaioannou and Siourounis (2008) analyse the effects of transitions to democracy and conclude that after these transitions economic growth is 1 per cent higher than before.

Though there are examples of growth in non-democratic societies, there are also many examples of authoritarian regimes that continue to pursue ineffective or harmful economic policies, in part due to the absence of democratic checks, balances and controls. We will return to this theme in our discussion of predatory states in section 11.7. The more authoritarian a regime, the greater chance of a dictator stealing or squandering a country's wealth (Barro, 1996).[30] From this perspective, democratisation is seen as contributing to economic development. This assumption is embedded in present foreign policies of Western countries and international institutions, when they include political democratisation and improved observance of human rights as conditions for financial support and trade advantages.

Quantitative empirical research has not yet resulted in any consensus about these questions. Studies continue to contradict each other, depending on the definitions used, the time span covered, the sample of countries included and the research methods employed. The complexity of the debate is increased by the fact that protection of private property and a market economy (indicators of economic freedoms) may well coexist with the absence of any form of political democracy. In an early review article Sirowy and Inkeles (1990) conclude that there is no support for the hypothesis that political democracy as such leads to more rapid economic growth. There are just as many studies claiming that there is no significant relation between democracy and growth as studies claiming that there is a negative relationship between these two factors.

---

[30] In this respect it is useful to distinguish different types of autocratic regimes. Some autocratic regimes pursue effective development policies. Others function as predatory states, which destroy the very basis of economic development. Such essential distinctions are not easily captured in cross-country regression studies.

Helliwell (1994) has refined the argument by distinguishing direct and indirect effects of democracy on growth, in cross-country statistical studies. Helliwell starts by reaffirming the correlation between income per capita and measures of democracy. Democracy takes root and survives where levels of economic development are high. He interprets these results as suggesting that democracy has an intrinsic value that is increasingly sought after as populations become better off and better educated.

With regard to the effects of democracy on growth, the indirect effects are positive. The adoption of democracy has a positive effect on schooling and investment – the finding for schooling is confirmed in many studies – which in turn contribute to growth. The direct effect of democracy on growth is negative. More democratic societies have slower growth. The net result of negative direct and positive indirect effects is positive, but very small. The best conclusion to be derived from the results is that there is no significant relationship between democracy and growth. The same conclusion was reached by Sirowy and Inkeles in their review article. Tavares and Wacziarg (2001) also distinguish different channels. Democracy fosters growth by improving education and reducing inequality. But it has negative effects on the rates of capital accumulation. The net results are moderately negative. Butkiewicz and Yanikkaya (2006) distinguish between the rule of law and democratic institutions. On first sight it seems that the rule of law has a positive effect on growth, while the effects of democratisation are insignificant. But if identical samples and instrumental variable techniques are used, the authors find that democratic countries enjoy superior growth performance.

We believe that econometric analysis will not provide general answers to these questions, because it cannot cope sufficiently with the diversity of experiences in time and space. It is obvious that there are cases of long periods of growth under autocratic regimes, while it is just as obvious that other autocratic regimes – or the same regimes in different periods – have followed catastrophic economic policies.

This empirical debate, however interesting, does not do sufficient justice to the fact that democratisation and the observance of human rights are of major importance as intrinsic objectives of development, irrespective of their economic significance. On balance, the average net effects of democracy on growth seem to be modest, in some studies marginally positive, in others marginally negative. The optimistic implication one can derive from this is that democracy, intrinsically valuable, is available at little economic cost. It may not be realistic to expect that introducing democracy will always accelerate growth. But there is no empirical support for the proposition that continued growth is incompatible with democracy.

11.6.4 Good governance and economic development

A key political condition for economic development is good governance (Ndulu and O'Connell, 1999). Good governance has a wide range of connotations, including the effectiveness of government bureaucracies, prudent macro-economic policies, the transparency and predictability of public decision making, the existence of checks and balances to control the abuse of political power, the insulation of the bureaucracy from undue influences from pressure groups, the rule of law and the impartial and independent functioning of the judicial system.

As the example of Singapore shows, good governance in the economic sphere is conceivable without full democracy. The Singapore political system is not democratic and even has a pervasive system of censorship. Nevertheless, it has an efficient, modern and non-corrupt system of administration and a severe but open and independent administration of justice.

Recent years have shown a proliferation of databases of governance indicators (see Arndt, 2009). These include the World Bank's World Governance Indicators (WGI) and the Country Policy and Institutional Assessments (CPIAs). The latter are used as a tool for aid allocation by the World Bank (see Chapter 14). These databases are sometimes criticised for their implicit equation of good governance with market-friendly institutions (for a critical discussion, see Torvinen, 2013). A database which is much broader in scope than most governance databases is the institutional profiles database developed by the French development agency AFD (see de Crombrugghe *et al.*, 2010). Researchers invariably find strong correlations between indicators of good governance/good institutions and level of income per capita (Kaufmann *et al.*, 2002), but the direction of causality is hotly debated, as in the case of democracy and growth (see for a further discussion, Chapter 13).

One of the important dimensions of good governance is a low degree of corruption. Corruption can take many forms. The most obvious one is that of bribery. But corruption also includes nepotism, official theft, fraud, patronage and extortion (Jain, 2001; Johnston, 2001; Rose-Ackerman, 2007).

Some authors have argued that corruption is the inevitable grease for the wheels of commerce, in a world stifled by bad governance. From the point of view of the individual firm, this may well be true. But, Tanzi and Davoodi (2001) argue that this view is not correct from a collective perspective. There are no social benefits associated with corruption (Jain, 2001). Bribes are usually not paid by the most efficient individuals, but by rent-seeking individuals. There are strong negative correlations between indexes of corruption and levels and growth rates of GDP per capita across the world. Tanzi and Davoodi summarise an increasing volume of recent empirical research showing that corruption has negative influences on economic growth (*inter alia*, Asiedu and Freeman, 2009; Azfar and Lee, 2001; Booth, 1999; Easterly, 2001; Ehrlich and Lui, 1999; Javorcik and Wei, 2009; Mauro, 1995, 2000; Wei, 1997a, 1997b; World Bank-WDR, 1997). This research correlates indexes of corruption with indicators of economic performance. Corruption indexes are usually based on surveys of perceptions of the degree and cost of corruption among business people.[31]

The negative effects of corruption on growth include the following. Corruption acts as a tax on investment, and substantially reduces the rate of investment and therefore of growth. It reduces the rates of return to capital. The more unpredictable corruption is, the more negative the effects on investment and growth. If unpredictability becomes too great, this can choke off all private investment.

Corruption reduces the rates of return to capital for small firms more than for large firms. Large firms find it easier to circumvent regulations and to protect themselves from corrupt petty officials. Larger firms use their political power to realise economic rents. Their

---

[31] One of the widely used indexes is the Corruption Perceptions Index (CPI) of Transparency International, www.transparency.org/documents/cpi. Johnston (2001) provides a useful discussion of the strengths and weaknesses of various indicators of corruption. While acknowledging the usefulness of existing measures, he argues for a broader more institutional approach to corruption.

corruption is of a cost-reducing kind, allowing them to enjoy monopoly profits and scale economies. New start-ups and small firms are more vulnerable to corruption. For them, corruption acts as an additional cost-increasing tax on their activities. Thus, corruption will impede the entry of small-scale firms, which can make important contributions to innovation and employment growth.

A somewhat unexpected effect of corruption is that it is likely to increase the rate of investment in public infrastructure, while decreasing its quality and productivity. The often-noted paradox that developing countries prefer investment in new infrastructural projects rather than maintaining existing infrastructure becomes more understandable. Thus, corruption contributes to the decay of existing infrastructure.

Finally, corruption and rent seeking may have negative impacts on growth if they create incentives for highly talented individuals to engage in rent seeking and other unproductive activities (Baumol, 1990; Murphy, Shleifer and Vishny, 1992).

That corruption has negative influences on the rate of growth does not mean that corrupt societies cannot experience rapid growth. Much depends on the ways in which the proceeds of corruption are applied. In some societies such as the Philippines under Marcos, or Nigeria under Abacha, the fruits of corruption are siphoned off into totally unproductive channels such as golden shoes or Swiss banks. In other societies, the proceeds of corruption are reinvested in new economic activity, contributing indirectly to economic dynamics. Thus, both China and Indonesia are countries that have combined pervasive corruption with rapid economic growth. But the experience of Indonesia in the Asian crisis of 1997 illustrates that corruption can reach such levels that a regime becomes totally incapable of responding adequately to economic challenges.

Reducing the extent of corruption is a difficult task, as corruption is deeply embedded in the nature of political systems. But, as the historical record indicates, it is not impossible. There are a variety of measures that can contribute to reduced corruption. The most important of these include introducing checks and balances into the political system, guaranteeing the effectiveness and independence of the judicial system, increasing accountability of officials towards the community and the public, increasing the independence and professionalisation of the bureaucracy, continued national and international monitoring of the extent of corruption, international legislation penalising MNCs for participating in bribery and reducing the discretionary power of officials, replacing arbitrary rules by standardised ones.

In this section, we have briefly discussed the relationships between good governance and economic development. But it is important to emphasise that good governance is vitally important from the perspective of human rights. Protection of individuals against arbitrary actions of the state and its officials is one of the key elements of a wider perspective on development.

11.7   The predatory state as an obstacle to economic development in Sub-Saharan Africa

In previous sections, we saw that the role of the government in developing countries may be more important today than previously in history. Also, several issues have been raised with regard to the functioning of the apparatus of government and the political process in developing countries. This section takes a closer look at the position of a number of authors (Ake, 1996; Bratton and van de Walle, 1997; Jackson and Rosberg, 1986; Ndulu and O'Connell, 1999; Sandbrook, 1986; Sandbrook and Barker, 1985; van de Walle, 1994) who claim that in several Sub-Saharan African countries the state itself has become an obstacle to economic development. In this literature, African states are characterised as extreme examples of *predatory states. Predatory* states are states that extract wealth from the citizens at the expense of society. Through their actions they undercut the dynamics of development (Evans, 1995; Lal, 1984).[32]

According to Sandbrook, Jackson and Rosberg, many African states are characterised by a system of *personal rule*. Personal rule is the answer of the political leaders to the question how to rule predominantly rural populations, only marginally integrated into national markets and national societies, under conditions in which national political institutions have little legitimacy (see also Jackson and Rosberg, 1986). The various ethnic groups have little feelings of loyalty towards the central state apparatus. National borders cut across ethnic and cultural dividing lines. Often the effective control of the state over its territory only exists in name. Under such circumstances, it is hardly surprising that parliamentary institutions and multiparty systems never took root. The state adapted itself to the particularist norms of a multi-ethnic society.

In the colonial period, bureaucracies were very small and had limited tasks. The higher positions in the administration were all filled by European expatriates. Middle positions in the civil service, commerce, trade and industry were predominantly occupied by members of minorities: Lebanese, Syrians and Indians. After the achievement of independence, government bureaucracies were rapidly Africanised and simultaneously expanded, in spite of the initially inadequate supply of trained and experienced officials. Bureaucratic characteristics of the civil service were soon diluted and replaced by networks of personal relations, which authors such as Sandbrook, Jackson and Rosberg, Bratton and van de Walle (1997) and Erdmann and Engel (2006) refer to as *neopatrimonialism*[33] or *personal rule*. The administration was commercialised. Officials exploited their positions for financial returns. Political leaders used public funds for private purposes and for those of friends, family and clients. The political classes lived in relative luxury, financed among others by bribes from foreign companies in return for trading concessions. According to Rosberg and Jackson, Mobutu, lifetime head of the state of Zaire, used 150 million dollars from the central bank for private ends between January 1977 and March 1979. Between 1979 and 1983 under Shehu Shagari's democratically elected government of Nigeria 5–7 billion dollars were appropriated by government officials (Jackson and Rosberg, 1986: 23). According to Bates and Collier (1993), Kenneth Kaunda controlled 40,000 patronage positions in Lusaka alone. The characteristics of personal rule are summarised in Box 11.3.

---

[32] Evans contrasts predatory states with developmental states, which through their actions and policies contribute positively to capital accumulation and socio-economic dynamics.

[33] The term 'patrimonialism' derives from Max Weber (1922) and refers to a form of traditional authority in which one owes obedience to the person of the ruler rather than to rules, principles, or procedures. Tradition is the prime source of legitimacy and circumscribes the power of the ruler. The term 'patrimonial' refers to the fact that members of the administrative apparatus are recruited from among the ruler's family, kin or tribe. Another characteristic is the absence of a distinction between the personal and the public sphere. Neo-patrimonialism or personal rule is a political system in which patrimonial rulers have no constitutional or traditional legitimacy.

....

BOX 11.3 : **Characteristics of personal rule**
....

- **A strong man** (the ruler, often the lifetime President). The person of the ruler is identified with the nation. All strategic positions within the political system, the government bureaucracy, the police force and the military are occupied by individuals who are personally loyal to the ruler. These individuals are usually recruited from the ethnic group of the political ruler.
- **Patron–client relationships**. Patron–client relationships pervade the entire apparatus of government, from top to bottom. At all levels individuals maintain and strengthen their positions by granting personal favours to loyal clients in the form of jobs, use of government funds and opportunities for corruption and enrichment. In return for political favours, the private sector is expected to reciprocate.
- Armed forces that are **personally loyal to the political ruler**. Due to personal rule, newly established African states have lacked the capabilities to create the conditions for capital accumulation. The economic rationality of state actions is low. The government administration and the public enterprises (*parastatals*) are characterised by mismanagement, inefficiency and widespread corruption. An impersonal, predictable and bureaucratically rational functioning of the state apparatus becomes impossible.

Public means are squandered and entrepreneurial efficiency is discouraged. Easy profits can be made by political manipulation. Much human creativity and entrepreneurial talent is directed at manipulating the political system in order to obtain subsidies, licences and market monopolies. Rent seeking behaviour comes in the place of economic efficiency and the search for economically productive investment opportunities. Foreign companies make their investments dependent on government guaranteed monopolies.

Personal rule is usually an unstable form of political organisation. Mostly the ruler depends on a single ethnic group to maintain his power. This group profits from the control of the apparatus of government to the exclusion of other groups. Other groups are prone to resort to violent opposition. Coups d'état and military revolts are quite common. The strong men seek military and financial support from foreign powers. Their opponents do the same, soliciting support from competing foreign powers to the further detriment of political stability.

The state is in an almost permanent fiscal crisis. The need for revenues to maintain the system of patronage is high. Wealthy citizens succeed in evading income taxes. For their financial requirements, governments are forced to impose heavy taxes on peasants, primary production, exports and imports. The agricultural marketing boards – discussed in Chapter 10 – are also used for such purposes. In some countries (e.g. Uganda under Idi Amin, Zaire under Mobutu), the financial burdens imposed on the peasants were so heavy that they withdrew from the official market economy, started trading on parallel black markets, or even moved back to subsistence production. This eroded the tax base even further.

According to Sandbrook personal rule prevailed in most African countries in the early 1980s. The major exceptions were militant socialist states such as Angola or Tanzania, where socialist ideology provided a degree of legitimacy. Sandbrook stresses the fact that political systems in Africa, as elsewhere, also show considerable variation. There are relatively strong states – Botswana, Côte d'Ivoire, Cameroon, Kenya, Malawi and Senegal – and extremely weak states – Chad, Ghana, Nigeria, Somalia and Zaire.[34] Moreover, he emphasises quite rightly (especially in Sandbrook and Barker, 1985), that the roots of the economic crisis in Sub-Saharan Africa are manifold and not limited to politics. Factors contributing to economic problems include the unfavourable international economic environment, the scarcity of natural resources, poor soil conditions, sustained droughts and rapid population growth. These factors interact with state formation processes. Economic stagnation leads to greater malfunctioning of government institutions. Characteristics of the state apparatus may result in further economic stagnation, resulting in a downward spiral.

Given the characteristics of state and politics in Sub-Saharan Africa, Sandbrook argues in favour of a more limited role of the public sector in the economy. This would leave more scope for a healthy development of the private sector. The government should concentrate on a selected number of key issues only. Reducing the size of the public sector is not enough.[35] The effectiveness of the smaller government apparatus has to be increased if the state is to contribute to the conditions for successful capital accumulation. The institutions of neo-patrimonialism and personal rule show remarkable persistence. The challenges of a policy of sustainable political reform are just as great as those of economic reform.

In a recent paper Tilman Altenburg (2013) has raised the question whether industrial policy – for which there is an increasing need in Sub-Saharan Africa – can work under conditions of neo-patrimonial rule. In a study of seven countries (Ethiopia, Mozambique, Namibia, Nigeria, Egypt, Syria and Tunisia), he finds that industrial policies are indeed seriously affected by the pervasiveness of neo-patrimonialism in decision-making. Nevertheless, between 2000 and 2008, all seven economies attracted substantial and increasing amounts of private investment and achieved quite rapid growth rates. There were also interesting differences. Resource rich countries typically performed worse than the others. Tunisia and Ethiopia, in particular, showed that even under neo-patrimonial conditions ambitious projects of productive transformation can be pursued.

11.8   Concluding remarks

This chapter has emphasised the importance of state formation and nation building in the process of development. The emergence of stable and effective states with good governance is important both from the perspective of economic development and from the wider perspective of the quality of life of individuals within these states. In many parts of the developing world, the political problems of the establishment of internal peace take precedence over economic problems and issues.

With regard to the economic role of the state, the analysis points to an interesting paradox between the weaknesses of the state apparatus on the one hand, and the wide range of tasks

---

[34] Uganda, which was high on Sandbrook's list of weak states in the early 1980s, has since then made a remarkable political and economic recovery. Zimbabwe, on the other hand, has recently degenerated into total chaos under the personal rule of the aged dictator Mugabe.

[35] According to Sandbrook, the share of the government in the national income in Sub-Saharan Africa is not exceptionally large in comparison with other developing countries and with affluent countries. What is rather more crucial in this respect is the regulating nature of government activities.

imposed on it in many countries since 1950. Though the debate on the exact role and scope of the state in the economy is far from resolved, there has been a shift in development strategy towards a more limited economic role for the state and stronger interactions with the private sector. Finally, good governance is not limited to the economic tasks of governments but also refers to the establishment of the rule of law and the respect for basic human rights of a country's citizens.

Questions for review

1. Provide definitions of the concepts of state, nation, society and nation-state. Give examples of states which are not nation-states and nations which are not nation-states.
2. Discuss the differences between the Marxist and the Weberian perspectives on the role of the state in socio-economic development.
3. Why does Max Weber interpret the emergence of bureaucracy as a positive factor in economic development?
4. Analyse the mutual interrelationships between economic growth and political stability or instability.
5. Analyse the typical characteristics of state formation in developing countries. What are the most important differences between processes of state formation in developing countries and earlier processes of state formation in Western Europe?
6. Provide an analysis of the economic effects of corruption in developing countries.
7. Why have the military played such a prominent role in politics in many developing countries?
8. To what extent is the post-Cold War international order more or less peaceful than the international order during the Cold War?
9. Why is the role of the state in economic development in present-day developing countries greater than the role of the state in the development of Western countries in the eighteenth and nineteenth century? To what extent is the increased importance of the state a stimulus for or an obstacle to economic development?
10. What kind of relationships can be identified between democracy and economic development? To what extent is democratic rule compatible with rapid economic development?
11. What are the characteristics of neo-patrimonial rule and why do these characteristics form an obstacle to economic development in Africa?
12. What are the main sources of political instability in developing countries?
13. Under what conditions can economic growth result in increasing instability?

Further reading

For the broad comparative study of state formation a good point of departure is Barrington Moore's *Social Origins of Dictatorship and Democracy: Lord and Peasant in the Making of the Modern World* (1967). From the extensive literature on state formation in developing countries in Africa, we mention: Coleman and Rosberg (eds.), *Political Parties and National Integration in Tropical Africa* (1964), Davidson, *The Black Man's Burden: Africa and the Curse of the Nation-*

State (1992), Ake, *Democracy and Development in Africa* (1996) and Sandbrook and Barker, *The Politics of Africa's Economic Stagnation* (1985).

For an analysis of the neo-patrimonial state in Africa, two interesting references are Sandbrook's article, 'The State as an Obstacle to Development' (1986), and an interesting article by van de Walle, 'Neopatrimonialism and Democracy in Africa, with an illustration from Cameroun' (1994). A recent application of the concept of neopatrimonialism is provided in an article by Altenburg: 'Can Industrial Policy Work under Neopatrimonial Rule?' (2013).

Two references for the role of the military in politics are Finer's excellent study *The Man on Horseback* (1988) and a volume edited by Janowitz, *Civil–Military Regimes: Regional Perspectives* (1981). A key reference for coups d'état is Luttwak, *Coup d'Etat: A Practical Handbook* (1979 and other issues). There is a large econometric literature examining the consequences of ethnic and linguistic diversity in developing countries. Interesting samples of this literature are: Easterly, 'Can Institutions Resolve Ethnic Conflict?' (2001b), Easterly and Levine, 'Africa's Growth Tragedy: Policies and Ethnic Divisions (1997) and Nettle 'Linguistic Fragmentation and the Wealth of Nations: The Fishman–Pool Hypothesis Reexamined' (2000). An authoritative recent paper focusing on the importance of measurement is Desmet, Ortuño-Ortin and Wacziarg, 'The Political Economic of Linguistic Cleavages' (2012).

For trends in civil and international conflicts one can consult Small and Singer, *Resort to Arms: International and Civil Wars, 1816–1980* (1982), Starr and Most, 'Patterns of Conflict: Quantitative Analysis and the Comparative Lessons of Third World Wars' (1985), Marshall and Gurr, *Peace and Conflict, 2003: A Global Survey of Armed Conflicts, Self-Determination Movements and Democracy* (2003), Marshall and Cole, *Global Report 2011:Conflict Governance and State Fragility* (2011) and Lacina, Gleditsch and Russett, 'The Declining Risk of Deaths in Battle' (2006). Also of interest is the 2011 issue of the World Development Report, *Conflict, Security and Development*. There is a valuable overview of armed conflicts by Marshall on the internet: *Major Episodes of Political Violence, 1946–2012*, www.systemicpeace.org/warlist.htm#N4. Other important databases are the Uppsala Conflict Data Program (UCDP), www.pcr.uu.se/research/ucdp/datasets/ and the database of the Peace Research Institute Oslo (PRIO), www.prio.no. UCDP and PRIO jointly provide the UCDP/PRIO database on battle deaths, www.pcr.uu.se/research/ucdp/datasets/ucdp_prio_armed_conflict_dataset.

Other sources of information include Smith, *The State of War and Peace Atlas* (1997 and other issues), WHO, *World Report on Violence and Health* (2002b) and Sivard, *World Military and Social Expenditures* (1991 and other issues).

A volume edited by Jain on *The Political Economy of Corruption* (2001) and the *International Handbook on the Economics of Corruption* edited by Rose-Ackerman (2007) give good overviews of ongoing research on this topic. Frequently cited references include: two articles by Mauro, 'Corruption and Growth' (1995) and 'The Effects of Corruption on Growth, Investment and Government Expenditure' (2000). A *Corruption Perceptions Index (CPI)*, is published on the website of Transparency International: www.transparency.org/.

For the debates on the role of the state in economic development, the reader is referred to the Further reading at the end of Chapter 9. An important additional reference is Evans' study *Embedded Autonomy: States and Industrial Transformation* (1995).

An early publication on the relationship between democracy and development is an article by Lipset, published in the *American Political Science Review*, 'Some Social Prerequisites of

Democracy, Economic Development and Political Legitimacy' (1959). A more recent reference is Huntington, *The Third Wave: Democratisation in the Late Twentieth Century* (1991). Two review articles on the statistical debate on the relationship between democracy and development are Sirowy and Inkeles, 'The Effects of Democracy on Economic Growth and Inequality: A Review' (1990) and Helliwell, 'Empirical Linkages between Democracy and Economic Growth' (1994). More recent contributions to these debates are found in Butkiewicz and Yanikkaya, 'Institutional Quality and Economic Growth: Maintenance of the Rule of Law or Democratic Institutions, or Both?' (2006) and Papaioannou and Siourounis, 'Democratisation and Growth' (2008). For analysis of democratisation in Africa, see Bratton and van de Walle, *Democratic Experiments in Africa: Regime Transitions in Comparative Perspective* (1997). New perspectives on state formation and political development are provided in an inspiring book by North, Wallis and Weingast, *Violence and Social Orders: A Conceptual Framework for Interpreting Recorded Human History* (2009).

Useful sources of data on political regimes include the Polity IV database at the University of Maryland, www.systemicpeace.org/inscr/inscr.htm and Freedom House, *Democracy's Century: A Survey of Global Political Change in the Twentieth Century* (2000), www.freedomhouse.org/reports/century.html, the annual Freedom House Report, *Freedom in the World*, www.freedomhouse.org/reports#.UtAcd7Qfjdk and Banks *et al.*, *Political Handbook of the World: Governments and Intergovernmental Organizations* (1998 and other issues).

12

Cultural and institutional dimensions of development

In the discussion of the concept of development in Chapter 1, we emphasised that development is not limited to the economic sphere. It also involves a broad range of social changes. One important dimension of development is cultural change. We cannot study economic developments in isolation, but also have to take into account cultural aspects such as attitudes, religious precepts, life styles, identities and values. Culture as a dimension of development is extremely important. It is also a somewhat slippery concept, as almost anything can be classified under the heading of 'culture': culture as art, identity, religion, language, nationalism, attitudes, institutions, material artefacts and so forth. A second and related dimension is institutional change: changes in the rules governing the games of human interaction.

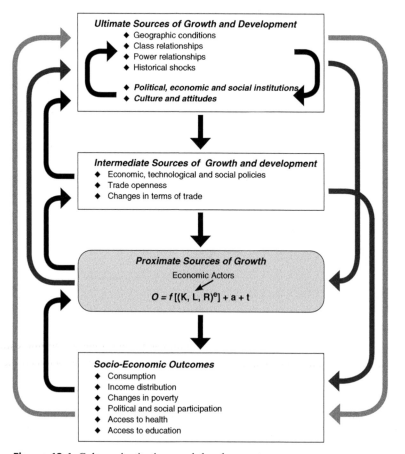

Figure 12.1 Culture, institutions and development

A full treatment of cultural and institutional change is not possible in the context of a single chapter. This chapter will have an exploratory and open character, focusing primarily on the interrelationships and interconnections between institutions, culture and economic development. In contrast to some of the literature, we do not see cultural and institutional explanations of development as mutually exclusive. Figure 12.1 classifies both culture and institutions among the more ultimate sources of development. They influence the formulation and implementation of economic, technological and social policies. They provide incentives and frameworks for the behaviour of economic actors.

The chapter addresses the following issues: the relationships between cultural change, institutional change and development, the role of religion in economic development, traditional versus modern culture and cultural obstacles to development. The last part of the chapter focuses on institutions and institutional change and their implications for economic development.

12.1 Introduction

12.1.1 Concepts: culture and institutions

We will not attempt a formal definition of culture. We do make a distinction between so-called 'high culture' (art, music and literature and so on) and the broader anthropological concept of 'culture', which refers to the complete life style of a society, which is transmitted through education and socialisation and which is passed on from generation to generation. It includes attitudes, expectations, knowledge, norms, values, habits, religion, ideology, notions of what is beautiful or ugly, traditions and standard solutions to the problems of social interaction. It is this anthropological concept that we will refer to in this chapter.

In this sense, culture primarily refers to the characteristic mental maps and values shared by members of a group or society. It excludes the material objects and artefacts that are produced by members of a culture (material culture). On the other hand, it also excludes the institutions which structure human behaviour. We agree with Huntington that a too broad conception of culture becomes scientifically useless, because it then explains everything and therefore nothing (cf. Huntington, 2000: xv).[1]

There is a tendency to think of cultures as homogeneous patterns. But one should keep in mind that there are contradictions and conflicts within every culture. There are cultural universals, which apply to all members of a social community, and cultural alternatives, which do not. There are cultural specialities, elements that are specific to certain sub-groups in a community. In every society, there are a variety of groups with their own subcultures. Some of these are dominant insider groups, others are outsiders. Elements of cultural patterns may even be in conflict with each other. One of the interesting cultural contradictions in advanced capitalist societies is the contradiction between the need for a

---

[1] We shall also steer clear of concepts such as post-modernism and deconstructionism, which abound in modern cultural studies, but which are so fuzzy that they do not serve to clarify any of the developmental issues we are discussing in this book.

disciplined work ethic, on the one hand, and a culture of hedonistic consumerism, on the other, as analysed by Daniel Bell in the 1960s in 'The Cultural Contradictions of Capitalism' (1971).

Following Douglass North, institutions are defined as 'the rules of the game in a society or, more formally, the humanly devised constraints that shape human interaction. In consequence they structure incentives in human exchange, whether political, social, or economic' (North, 1990: 3). In a similar vein, Gehlen (1958) defines institutions as a 'regulatory agency, channelling human actions in much the same way as instincts channel animal behaviour'. Institutions are not just any rules that shape human interactions; they refer to complexes of rules regulating the central problems of social life such as control of violence, political decision making, family relationships and economic production.[2] Family institutions regulate interactions between men, women and their children and issues of sex and procreation, military institutions regulate the use of violence, economic institutions, such as markets or planning systems, regulate how people provide for their livelihood. Political institutions regulate the access to positions of power and the ways in which collective decisions are arrived at.

As emphasised by earlier sociological literatures, institutional rules are deeply embedded in human consciousness through education and socialisation and are transferred from generation to generation. This is where culture and institutions meet. Culturally defined attitudes, cognitions and evaluations provide the foundations for political and economic institutions (cf. Licht *et al.*, 2007; Tabellini, 2008, 2010).[3] Institutions regulate specific spheres of human interaction, while culture captures a broader set of values, norms and cognitions that characterise societies.

12.1.2   How important is culture?

Can cultural differences explain differences in socio-economic dynamics, or does culture simply adapt to changes in the economic and the social sphere? One can contrast a *structuralist approach* and an *idealist approach* to culture. An example of the structuralist perspective is Marxist theory, which sees culture as determined by economic interests. When interests and power relationships change, cultural change will follow. The opposite view is the idealist perspective, which sees cultural traits as determining behaviour, economic activity and economic development. From this perspective, cultural differences explain differences in economic performance.

The debate between these polar positions is fruitless. One can analyse the social genesis of different cultural patterns and show how the structural patterns of relationships between individuals and groups crystallise into cultural patterns that influence their subsequent behaviour, (e.g. Elias, 1969b). But, once a cultural pattern has emerged and hardened, it will have a certain persistence of its own and will play an independent role in channelling and regulating behaviour for long periods of time. Of course, cultural elements can

---

[2] It is important to make a clear distinction between institutions (the rules) and organisations (actors influenced by rules and incentives).

[3] Institutional rules are not just expedient arrangements such as stopping before traffic lights, but involve internalised norms and compulsions.

gradually change under the influence of structural changes, such as the emergence of global markets, changes in the balance of power between interest groups, or the impact of mass media. But that does not warrant the conclusion that culture has no influence on development, as an independent variable. Our very perceptions of our interests and our identifications with interest groups are culturally influenced. So, even if one prefers the structuralist perspective on cultural change, as this author does, it is important and interesting to analyse cultural aspects of development. Culture does matter. In tracing the influence of religion and economic development, Platteau (2008) provides an interesting analysis of virtuous and vicious cycles of change where culture, institutions and economic developments interact in different ways in the long-run development of Western societies, on the one hand, and Islamic Arab societies, on the other.

On the other hand, one should not make the mistake of assuming that culture is immutable. It is subject to change when the social conditions change. One of the first development economists, J. H. Boeke (1947, 1961a), posited the notion of an *oriental culture* which was supposed to be inconsistent with modern rational market behaviour. Boeke's oriental culture included an emphasis on social rather than economic values, a short time span, a tendency to stop working when immediate needs were fulfilled (the hypothesis of the *backward-bending supply curve of labour*, which states that workers will work less if they receive higher wages). We now know that such a culture is a long-term adaptation of individuals to a real lack of economic opportunities for peasants in colonial and precolonial societies. When the opportunities improve, a rational and entrepreneurial spirit can emerge among peasants. They start to plant new cash crops for domestic and international markets and to employ new technologies. For instance, this occurred on a large scale at the end of the nineteenth century and effectively debunked the myth that peasants and farmers in developing countries had a culturally determined lack of entrepreneurial spirit.

But one should also realise that cultural change can be very slow. Attitudes and expectations that have evolved over centuries do not disappear overnight, apart from the fact that powerful groups in society may also have strong interests in maintaining traditional cultural elements. It is not easy to tinker with culture.

Once one concludes that culture matters for socio-economic development (Harrison and Huntington, 2000; Licht *et al.*, 2007; Platteau and Peccoud, 2011; Tabellini, 2010), the next question is how important cultural factors are for the explanation of socio-economic development. What weight do they have compared to other factors, such as technological change, economic cycles, natural resources, class dynamics, or power and dependence relationships in the international order? One of the ongoing debates is about the relative importance of institutions versus culture (Acemoglu and Robinson, 2012).

Structuralist authors such as Jeffrey Sachs and Jared Diamond argue that in the very long run geography, location, climate and natural resources determine economic success, rather than differences in culture (Diamond, 1998; Sachs, 2000). For instance, it is well known that almost all economically advanced nations lie in moderate climatic zones. But these ecological explanations cannot explain why in similar environmental conditions some societies develop, and others do not. Many authors have tried to explain lack of development or underdevelopment on the basis of the history of colonialism, exploitation, availability of resources, the terms of trade or the structure of the world economy. But, again these explanations fail to explain why some former colonies develop into advanced economies, while others stagnate. Cultural differences are at least part of the story, along with institutions.

12.1.3   How important are institutions?

There is an important strand of literature which argues that the key to understanding different paths of socio-economic development lies in the analysis of institutions. Thus in a long series of publications Acemoglu, Johnson and Robinson have argued that it is institutional characteristics that explain the divergence in long-run Western and non-Western economic performance (Acemoglu et al., 2001, 2002; Acemoglu and Robinson, 2006, 2012). They focus on protection of property against arbitrary expropriation and more inclusive institutions that provide positive incentives for large segments of the population. Among the institutions analysed are property rights, rights with regard to intellectual ownership, the rule of law, inheritance institutions (e.g. Kuran, 2011), the role of nuclear versus extended families, the rise of the corporation in medieval Europe (Greif, 2006b), restrictions on the power of the executive and democratic voting rights (see Chapter 11). As in the case of culture, one can distinguish more structuralist approaches in which institutions are seen as the outcomes of underlying power and class relationships and more idealistic approaches where the normal rules and regulations of institutions are seen as determining forces in their own right. There is also an ongoing debate about the relative importance of geographic factors versus institutional factors in explaining economic performance (e.g. Bhupatiraju and Verspagen, 2013; Rodrik et al., 2004). Finally, there is a polemical discussion of the relative importance of culture and institutions. Here, Acemoglu and Robinson (2012) take the extreme position that only institutions matter. Within one and the same culture, they argue, different institutional arrangements result in very different outcomes. In a similar fashion, Timur Kuran (2011) argues that it is not Islamic culture that is incompatible with economic development, but very specific Islamic legal institutions.

Our position is that cultural and institutional explanations of economic performance are not mutually exclusive and that both contribute to a better understanding of long-run economic performance. Institutions are buttressed by culture, which provides the – often unconscious – norms, values, expectations, roles and mental maps that help regulate behaviour.[4] So one of the ways in which culture affects economic development is through the shaping of institutions. But institutions are also shaped by power relationships and are important in themselves. It is not enough to have appropriate culturally determined attitudes or mental maps, such as a work ethic, if the institutions, policies and mode of governance of a society provide the wrong kind of incentives (Landes, 2000). Actual behaviour is influenced by a mix of culturally determined attitudes and structural and institutional constraints, which interact with each other in a process of change.[5]

---

[4] Weisner (2000) warns against a too rigid conception of cultural traits. They are not simply fixed patterns that determine institutions and behaviour. They are also tools for adaptation in the course of one's life.

[5] An interesting example of these interactions is provided by Patterson (2000) in his analysis of the emergence of fatherless households and parental abandonment in Afro-American communities, which are rooted in the legacies of slavery.

12.2   Culture and development

12.2.1   The Protestant Ethic and the rise of capitalism

A useful starting point for the discussion of the role of culture in development is Max Weber's classic article, 'Die Protestantische Ethik und der Geist des Kapitalismus', first published in 1905 (Weber, 1969). This article can be seen as a response to the Marxist disregard of culture as an independent force in development. Weber's core question was: why did capitalist economic development have a breakthrough in Northwest Europe, and not elsewhere in the world (see the discussion in Chapter 3)? What was the role of religion in this breakthrough?

Weber argued that many of the preconditions for capitalist growth could also be found in non-Western parts of the world and in other historical periods. The profit motive, the use of money, the emergence of markets, urbanisation, or individualism are not unique to the West. Innovation and technological advance have occurred in many societies. Mass manufacturing had already emerged in China in the twelfth century. But capitalism had not broken through. What was lacking in these societies, according to Weber, was the key notion of 'rentability'. Rentability refers to the systematic and rational planning for a sustainable flow of future profits. This notion of rentability was linked to religion.

Weber noted that all the countries where capitalism broke through in the sixteenth and seventeenth centuries were Protestant countries and more particularly Calvinist countries: the Netherlands, England, Scotland, the East Coast of the USA and Switzerland. The Protestant religion was what differentiated them decisively from other countries and societies. In Europe, Protestants were also strongly overrepresented among capitalists, traders and entrepreneurs. Therefore, Weber argued, Protestantism must have played an important role in the breakthrough of capitalism. This led Weber to a systematic comparison of the economic values (*Wirtschaftsethik*) embedded in the main world religions: Catholicism, Judaism, Islam, Hinduism, Buddhism and Confucianism (Weber, 1920a). Puritan Protestantism had a number of crucial elements, which differed from all other religions. These are listed in Box 12.1.

The Weber thesis gave rise to a fascinating ongoing polemic, which continues to this very day. Opponents of the Weber thesis argued that its empirical foundations were shaky (e.g. Tawney, 1947; Trevor-Roper, 1972). For instance, many entrepreneurs in the Protestant Low Countries turned out to be of Catholic origin and Catholic cities such as Antwerp were major centres of dynamic capitalist activities. The critics emphasised the role of migrants from Catholic to Protestant areas. In the sixteenth and seventeenth centuries, in the Low Countries, people fled to the Calvinist controlled areas to escape the turmoil of the Counter-Reformation. They became successful as entrepreneurs and many of them later adopted Protestantism as their religion. If this is correct, Protestantism does not explain the capitalist breakthrough, but rather capitalist entrepreneurs adopted a religion that was congenial to them.

Other critics have pointed to the entrepreneurial success of migrant groups with very different religious backgrounds: the Chinese in South East Asia and the Indians in East Africa. Religion was not the driving force for entrepreneurial success, but the marginal position of these migrant groups in their societies. The same holds for the prominent position of Jews in the history of West European capitalism.

BOX 12.1 : **Characteristics of the Protestant Ethic**

- The ideal of a **disciplined pursuit of one's profession in society** (*Innerweltliche Askese*) versus the ideal of ascetic withdrawal from society in convents, monasteries, or contemplation (*Ausserweltliche Askese*). In world religions such as Hinduism, Catholicism and Buddhism the religious ideals include withdrawal from the humdrum affairs of the world in order to focus on religious contemplation, by monks, mystics or sages. According to Weber, Protestantism was unique in the notion that one could follow one's religious calling in the daily world of work and profession.
- The **individual responsibility of the believer** versus the submission to hierarchy characteristic of, for instance, Catholicism. Among others, this manifested itself in the translation of the scriptures into the vernacular, so that everyone could read them. Protestantism provided a major impetus to literacy.
- The search for a **rational conduct of life and religious practice** versus submission to tradition and fate. The high value placed on rational conduct translated into the economic sphere, where the rational organisation of production and a rational approach to investment in search for sustained profit became the rule. Rationalisation also resulted in the emergence of bureaucracy as the dominant form of organisation.
- The belief in **predestination for eternal salvation or damnation**. The belief in predestination creates a tremendous psychic anxiety among individuals and an urgent search for signs of election. These signs include social and economic success in this world. This provides a strong unconscious motivation for economic effort, disciplined performance and a powerful work ethic.
- A high value placed on **sobriety and discipline**. Consumption and luxury were perceived as sinful and corrupt. The combination of the work ethic and sobriety had the unintended consequence of a high rate of savings and rapid capital accumulation.

Later observers pointed to the economic success of Japan and the East Asian economies in the twentieth century. These societies were predominantly Confucian in tradition. This was completely at odds with the Weber thesis about the importance of Protestantism, and the presumed negative economic impact of Confucian religious beliefs. These experiences have resulted in a whole new set of studies arguing that Confucian values are especially conducive to growth in the late twentieth century and that a *Confucian Ethic* was one of the explanations of modern economic success (Dore, 1987; Hofstede, 2001; Hofstede and Bond, 1988; Goodell, 1995–6; Pye, 2000; Senghaas, 1984).

Weber may well have overstated the uniqueness of Protestantism in relation to economic activity. But in spite of justified criticisms of the Weber thesis, the consequences of religious and cultural traits for economic performance have remained on the agenda ever since. One cannot but note that all economically successful societies are characterised by a powerful work ethic and entrepreneurial drive, by social discipline, sobriety and a high value placed on savings and future orientation. Probably, the role of Calvinism is not unique, but a puritan work ethic, future orientation and entrepreneurial and innovative attitudes seem to be important ingredients in individual and collective economic success all over the world.

The present entrepreneurial drive and economic success of devout Muslim entrepreneurs in Turkish Anatolia seems very similar to the Protestant Ethic.

12.2.2 Traditional versus modern cultures

Modernisation theory

Max Weber put forward a set of historical hypotheses about the cultural causes of the breakthrough of capitalism in the West. After the Second World War, modernisation theorists developed this theory into a theory of cultural obstacles to development, both generalising and simplifying the Weber thesis. Modernisation theorists posited a dichotomy between traditional and modern societies. The economic core of modernisation is industrialisation, which requires a measure of congruence between economic developments and their social and cultural environment. This was the position taken by Clark Kerr, in *Industrialism and Industrial Man: The Problems of Labour and Management in Economic Growth* (Kerr, Dunlop and Harbison, 1962). The dichotomy between traditional and modern societies involves changes in a number of cultural and institutional dimensions. Some of the most frequently mentioned dichotomies are listed in Box 12.2.

If industrialisation involves congruence between economic and social change, modernisation theories imply that industrialisation will not take off in societies with strong traditional cultures, collectivist orientations, fatalist attitudes, weak work ethics and social discipline, negative attitudes towards risk and entrepreneurship and inefficient institutions. The cultural obstacles to economic change and development will be too strong.

One of the most extreme formulations of the modernisation approach was that of David McClelland, in *The Achieving Society* (1961). McClelland emphasised the importance of entrepreneurship in economic development. Entrepreneurial attitudes are acquired through an educational process, which instils the need for achievement (N ach) in children. McClelland analysed the values emphasised in children's books to see which societies implanted the need for achievement in their younger generations. In modern societies, these books emphasised the value of hard work, openness to influences from the environment (against orientation towards tradition), control of one's own impulses and behaviour and control of one's natural environment.

Similar ideas are found in the study by Inkeles and Smith, *Becoming Modern: Individual Change in Six Developing Countries* (1974). Inkeles and Smith developed an index of modernity. Elements of modernity included: confidence in the possibilities of finding solutions to problems with the help of science and technology, a sense of efficacy and goal-orientedness; positive attitudes towards innovation and innovativeness; concern for planning and control of time and respect for subordinates.

The practical recipe derived from these studies is that one should try to change traditional cultures and mentalities through education, information, schooling and seminars. Among other things this involved the setting up of courses and workshops in entrepreneurship. This points to a rather simplistic belief in the short-term mutability of attitudes. It was not surprising that the results of such development strategies were disappointing. Attitudes are not easily changed by social tinkering. Strangely enough, Chinese communism manifested a not completely dissimilar attitude towards cultural change. The communist regime used massive political mobilisation and indoctrination as an instrument of thought change and modernisation of traditional mentalities.

Box 12.2 : **Modernisation theory: dichotomies between modern and traditional societies**

- **Achievement versus ascription.** In modern societies, social positions are assigned to individuals on the basis of achievement and meritocratic criteria. In traditional societies, social positions are assigned on the basis of birth, social origin and other ascriptive criteria.
- **Mobility versus hierarchy.** Modern societies are characterised by increased upward and downward social mobility in comparison with traditional static hierarchical societies.
- **Rational versus traditional behaviour.** Modern society is characterised by rational thinking about ends and means. In pre-modern societies traditionally defined patterns of behaviour predominate.
- **Future orientation versus fatalism.** In modern societies, people believe that their actions influence their future. They are willing to make long-term investments for a better future for themselves and their children. Traditional societies are characterised by fatalism and a short-term horizon.
- **Nuclear families versus extended families.** It is argued that extended families and kinship relationships act as a brake on economic development, because the strong pressure towards redistribution within the extended family impedes capital accumulation (Bauer and Yamey, 1957). Modernisation involves the breakdown of extended families and the emergence of nuclear families.
- **Political democratisation versus authoritarian rule.**
- **Increased role for civil society.** Modernisation implies increased roles for union, parties, political pressure groups and other associations of civil society.
- **Single-stranded versus multi-stranded social relationships.** Many transactions in modern markets and modern bureaucracies are anonymous and specialised (single-stranded). In traditional societies, relationships are more personal and involve many dimensions (a variety of economic and financial exchanges, relationships of kin and tribe, friendship, relationships of authority and dependence).
- **Universalistic versus particularistic relationships.** Modern societies define rules in formal and abstract ways, and try to apply them in social relationships irrespective of the persons in question. In traditional societies, the personal ties between participants in a social relationship are more important than the formal rules.
- **Affectivity versus affective neutrality in group relationships.**
- **Individualist orientation versus collectivist or communal orientation.** In traditional societies, social obligations are more important than in modern societies, where people feel free to pursue their individual interests.

Towards a more nuanced distinction between traditional and modern

In hindsight, modernisation theory now seems hopelessly dated, naive and ethnocentric. It was ethnocentric in the sense that modernisation was conceived of as 'becoming more like the West'. Every society was assumed to converge to the Western cultural pattern.

Modernisation theory disregarded the enormous variation in 'traditional societies' in different parts of the world. It assumed a one-dimensional movement along the axis from traditional to modern. The positive connotations of the modern pole of the axis tended to draw attention away from urgent social problems and shortcomings in the so-called advanced societies (Schech and Haggis, 2000; Sen, 1999).

As explained in Chapter 3, modernisation theory paid insufficient attention to differences in patterns of modes of economic development in different historical periods. In the eighteenth century a number of European countries pioneered industrialisation in a world economy without industry. Latecomers were in a very different position. They had to face established industrial giants. It is therefore not surprising that the economic and social development of Japan, Korea, Singapore, Hong Kong, Taiwan and China proceeded and proceeds along very different paths and patterns than those of Western Europe in the past.

Modernisation theory also had unrealistic expectations of the role of education in changing mentalities. Finally, the opposition between modern and traditional draws our attention away from the negative impacts of external penetration and colonisation. It tends to obscure the fact that many societies started to change in response to external challenges and threats.

Other strands of anthropological and sociological research argued for a more refined perspective on the opposition between traditional and modern cultures. Implicitly or explicitly most of these authors do accept that there are some cultural imperatives deriving from economic development and industrialisation. But the simple opposition between 'traditional' and 'modern' needs to be replaced by a more differentiated and empirically realistic approach.

In a classic study of entrepreneurship in two Indonesian cities, Clifford Geertz (1963) showed how various elements of presumably traditional societies and religions can contribute to modern economic development and innovative entrepreneurship. In the town of Modjokuto on Java, he showed how Bazaar-type trade networks were in a process of transition into modern firms. The key innovators were a group of traders of Reformist Islamic persuasion. They were deeply religious and far stricter in their religious observances than other inhabitants of the city. Geertz shows that in many ways they shared some of the characteristics of the Protestant Ethic: a strong work ethic, discipline and sobriety, and an orientation towards the world of work. This goes against the stereotypical view of Islam as a traditional value system that forms an obstacle to development. In Tabanan, on the Hindu Island of Bali, the role of modern entrepreneur was taken up by members of the traditional aristocracy who had been displaced by the colonial rulers and were struggling to maintain or regain their social pre-eminence through economic success. They used their social standing in a traditional agrarian society to mobilise people and resources for the construction of large-scale modern manufacturing enterprises. Geertz concludes that a wide range of cultures is capable of generating economic development if the favourable factors are used and the unfavourable factors are suppressed. Development policies should take these local differences into account and should try to capitalise on them. For Geertz, industrialisation and modern economic development does require changes in culture, but the sources of change can also be found in supposedly traditional cultures.

A second example of a more complex perspective on the opposition between traditional and modern is Kuper's discussion of the relationships between traditional African family institutions and the modern institution of migrant labour in Southern Africa (Kuper, 1984).

Traditional African economic institutions commonly distinguish between a so-called *sub-sistence mode* (which includes the cultivation of food crops, horticulture and gathering activities), and an *investment mode* (which is more future-oriented and includes cash crops, cattle and hunting). The division of labour between these activities depends on status, age, ethnic group and in particular gender. The women are responsible for food production and other activities in the labour-intensive subsistence mode. The males monopolise activities in the more capital-intensive investment sector. In traditional African cultures, women supply the labour for the labour-intensive sector. Males will invest the returns from the investment sector as bride wealth to acquire partners in polygamous relationships.

In the course of the twentieth century, migrant labour emerged as an important phenomenon, especially in areas where there was insufficient scope for animal husbandry and local cash crop production. Males went off to work in mines, plantations and the modern urban sector. From a comparison of Lesotho and Botswana, Kuper concludes that the 'modern' phenomenon of migrant labour served to buttress traditional family institutions and practices. In Lesotho, the proceeds of migrant labour were invested in bride wealth and the continuation of traditional or neo-traditional extended family relationships. In Botswana, where there was less migrant labour, the traditional extended family and traditional practices were in decline. Thus, in Lesotho traditional institutions do not impede modern developments and modernisation reinforces traditional family relationships.

A third example of the complexity of the relationship between traditional and modern culture and institutions refers to the economic implications of extended family institutions and kinship ties in China, the Middle East and Africa. It has been argued that the extended family acts as a major brake on entrepreneurship and economic development (e.g. Greif, 2006b; Levy and Shih, 1949; Platteau, 2009). It imposes redistributive obligations on its more successful members, which act as an obstacle to capital accumulation. It reduces the incentives for innovative behaviour and risk taking. Also, strong family ties may result in nepotism, clientelism and corruption.

While admitting the potential economic dysfunctions of extended family systems, the modern literature also points to positive functions of the extended family, especially in the Asian context. Perkins (2000) argues that the reliance on personal and kinship-type relationships in Asia has provided an alternative to the rule of law in the Western world. Personal relationships provide an element of security which is essential for commercial activities. Families and personal networks are collectively responsible for the enforcement of contracts. Networks and network obligations are more important than contracts. Family ties have played a very important role in the emergence of large business conglomerates and proved to be one of the means of mobilising large amounts of capital, both in East Asia and in Southeast Asian countries where Chinese minorities play such an important role in the economy. Perkins argues persuasively that this system served East and Southeast Asia well in the past thirty years. He also argues that the reliance on kinship relationships is now becoming an increasing liability for further economic development, as corruption spirals out of control and the expectation that the network will bail out the individual firm creates moral hazard. The Asian crisis of 1997 is a manifestation of these underlying problems, as is the stagnation of the once so dynamic Japanese economy between 1990 and 2000. In addition, it is interesting to note that Asian societies are presently experiencing an erosion of extended family relationships and the rise of nuclear families, as suggested by original modernisation theory.

12.2.3   Are there cultural obstacles to economic development?

Nowadays, there are few explicit adherents of modernisation theory in its simple and schematic form. However, if we drop the generalising and causal approach of modernisation theory, we can start re-examining the question whether certain elements of culture act as obstacles to economic growth and development in the modern globalised economic order, while other elements act as a stimulus. In the introduction to a World Bank-sponsored conference on culture, Salim (1994) notes that we live in an interdependent world within which each society must strive to keep pace with scientific and technological progress. It is a challenge to find a synergy between technological change and cultural values. Modernisation theory turns out to be less dead than we thought.[6]

The debate about cultural obstacles to development is fraught with difficulties. In the first place, it assumes that people across the world agree on the content and goals of development. In Chapter 1 we argued that development is inevitably a highly value-laden concept, but that one can indeed identify the contours of a development concept, including increased welfare, productivity, health, education and an extension of political and social freedoms. However, different societies may have different preferences and priorities. In the second place, the notion of cultural obstacles assumes that one can evaluate cultures against some universal yardstick, which goes against a deeply ingrained habit of cultural relativism which states that each culture can only be judged in terms of its own values.

In an impassioned and thought-provoking criticism of the platitudes of older and newer modernisation theorists, the anthropologist Richard Shweder (2000) argues that there are a great many valued social goals, which cannot be achieved at the same time (justice, autonomy, liberty, beneficence, care for the elderly and so forth). Every culture involves painful trade-offs between the valued things in life. Different cultures make different trade-offs. Cultural diversity is a fact of life. This is not a choice for the radical cultural relativism. All cultures contain indefensible practices which can be criticised. But, on the other hand, it should also be obvious that there is no one single way to lead a decent, rational and fulfilling life. Not everyone needs to become like a Western Protestant.

The position taken in this book is that one has to be very careful in evaluating cultures in terms of superior or inferior. Nevertheless, there are some inconsistencies in Shweder's stance. Criticising indefensible practices such as ethnic genocide, cronyism and corruption, torture or the stoning of unfaithful women, inevitably assumes some universal criterion of human dignity, which sets limits to cultural relativism. Also, from a perspective of socio-economic dynamics and progress, cultural patterns can be judged to the extent that they empirically contribute to such dynamics. If people in a society value economic dynamism highly, this may require certain kinds of cultural change. Though a variety of cultural arrangements may be compatible with economic development, this does not preclude the fact that some elements of a culture may act as obstacles to modern economic development. This is especially marked, if one looks at the dynamics of socio-economic development from a macro-perspective and notes the differences in dynamics in different

---

[6] Three interesting collections of articles (Serageldin and Taboroff, 1994; Harrison and Huntington, 2000; and Clague and Grossbard-Shechtman, 2001) were among the sources of inspiration for this chapter. Some of the articles in these collections revive the stark dichotomies of modernisation theory. Other contributions reflect the more differentiated perspective which informs the present chapter.

parts of the world. Selected examples of the possible impacts of culture on development are given below.

The caste system

In Hinduistic societies such as India, the caste system acts as an obstacle to the most efficient use of human capabilities and talents in the economic process (Lal, 1988; Maddison, 1974). The caste system defines a religiously legitimised hierarchy of social estates (*varnas*) which are restricted in their interactions with each other. At the top of the caste hierarchy are the Brahmins, specialising in religious and intellectual activities, followed by Kshatriyas (warriors and aristocrats), Vaisyas (merchants) and Sudras (workers). Right at the bottom are the untouchables, who perform the most menial tasks, such as leather working and sweeping. Within this wider framework of the *varnas*, there is a great variation of region-specific subcastes (*jatis*), or endogamous kinship and occupational groups. The interaction between groups and castes is restricted by rules and prohibitions of ritual pollution. The groups also differ in political influence, landholding and so forth (Adams, 2001).

A person's caste position is determined at birth (ascription). Each caste and subcaste specialises in given occupational, social and political activities which are proscribed for members of other castes. In the caste system, physical labour is a typically low-caste activity, with corresponding low status. Merchants and economic activities also stand relatively low on the social scale.

Though caste has now been rejected as an organising system in modern India, it still is deeply embedded in social life (Lal, 1988).[7] Lal himself denies that the caste system itself is the prime cause of slow economic growth in post-independence India. In his view, the slow rate of growth between 1950 and 1990 (sometimes called the Hindu rate of growth) is primarily due to inappropriate government policies. But while there may be many causes of slow growth, it is clear that discrimination by gender, caste, or ethnic group and the resulting inefficient allocation of labour are among the cultural and institutional obstacles to more rapid economic development.[8]

The low status of physical work and effort

In many cultures there are negative attitudes towards physical labour and effort. In African societies, the heaviest physical work in food production is usually left to the women, while men engage in activities with higher status. The negative stereotypes of physical effort have been further reinforced by agricultural extension workers and Western-oriented education, with its emphasis on cognitive and academic performance (Dumont, 1962).

---

[7] To some degree, elements of caste and estate are to be found in all societies, even societies that profess to be completely meritocratic.

[8] The example of the caste system epitomises the difficulty of the debate about culture versus institutions. On the one hand, the caste system represents very deeply entrenched cultural values. On the other, one could argue that it is a clear example of an institution regulating both economic and social interactions. The same ambiguity surfaces in the discussion of the influence of religion. In his well-known book on the influence of Islam on long-run economic stagnation in the Middle Eastern world since the sixteenth century Kuran (2011) focuses on the specific legal institutions of Islam rather than on Islamic culture as such. These institutions include inheritance law, the absence of a legal foundation for long-lived corporations, contract law and polygyny.

Along with the emergence of entrepreneurship, a work ethic involving the ability and willingness to work long, hard and in a disciplined fashion would seem to be one of the ingredients of successful economic performance.[9] The work ethic also makes it possible to subject an originally rural labour force to the disciplines and time-driven schedules of modern factories and organisations.

The work ethos was present in Japan, as well as among Chinese peasant populations. It is less frequently found on the African continent, where cultural attitudes to work tend to be different and where social obligations tend to absorb a large amount of time and energy. It has been suggested that the work ethic is a cultural adaptation to high population densities in Asian rice producing societies such as China and Japan. Intensive rice production requires enormous efforts on behalf of the peasants to produce sufficient food. On the contrary, Sub-Saharan Africa has always had low population density and was able to support its populations at relatively low levels of effort (Boserup, 1981).

An interesting example of differences in work ethic is provided by Malaysia. The indigenous Malay population tends to look down on physical labour, as something suitable for the Chinese coolie labourers who were imported in the nineteenth century to work in mines and plantations. The Malaysians of Chinese origin have not only developed more entrepreneurial attitudes, but also a strong work ethic. They have been extraordinarily successful in business, manufacturing and economic life, much more so than the indigenous population. The same holds for most economies in Southeast Asia.

Social obligations in African cultures

Many observers have remarked on the importance of social obligations in African cultures, where self-reliance and self-interest are subordinated to ethnicity and group loyalty (e.g. Dia, 1994; Nyang, 1994; Platteau, 2009; Rao, 2001). The value of economic behaviour is measured in terms of its effects on group reinforcement. The extended family is always present and imposes itself on its members in a variety of ways, including ceremonial obligations. Workers in modern African manufacturing enterprises are frequently absent from work for burials, marriage ceremonies and other festivities, which might last for days or even weeks. Excess income of individuals leads to more lavish consumption and a widening of the circle of those benefiting from income redistribution. Economic success is seen as deriving from luck, rather than risk taking and effort and imposes obligations to share.

From the perspective of individual entrepreneurship, the ability to save and accumulate capital and the successful operation of modern economic organisations, these social obligations may function as major obstacles to economic development and economic success. However, these social network obligations have important economic functions. Festivals and marriages are arenas where reputations are built, networks maintained and status achieved (Rao, 2001). They enhance relative positions in society and build social cohesion and capacity for collective action, which is important for people's survival. The high value attached to leisure reflects the importance of reinforcing social bonds. Rather than calling

---

[9] We do not claim that a work ethic is a 'cause' of development. For many centuries, an exploited Chinese peasantry has engaged in backbreaking labour in rice production without much evidence of economic dynamism. But a work ethic does seem to be a developmental resource, which can be tapped when a country starts industrialising.

for an emancipation from social obligations, Dia (1994) argues for the development of new management practices, which try to reconcile traditional practices with the requirements of economic efficiency and accumulation. Whether this is really feasible is the question: perhaps economic efficiency is really inconsistent with such heavy social obligations. But the Chinese example discussed in section 12.2.2 indicates that the use of kinship networks for capital accumulation is not impossible.

Gender discrimination

Inequality between the sexes and discrimination against women is embedded to different degrees in most world religions and cultures. Like caste systems, occupational discrimination by sex is a potential obstacle to the optimal use and allocation of human talents. In a great many societies, women have less access to paid jobs, health services and in particular education. In some – but not all – of the most orthodox Islamic societies, women are prohibited from engaging in education and paid work outside the house. In several of the preceding chapters we have shown that improved access to education and the labour market for women has positive impacts on spontaneous fertility decline and improved health of families and children. In addition, in many societies females have potentially important roles in trading and entrepreneurship, but are hampered by inadequate access to capital and support services.

Social capital, trust and civic culture

Many observers have remarked that trust is one of the cultural prerequisites for the functioning of modern impersonal market relationships and market exchanges. Trust is an element of culture which implies that in principle people expect that contracts should and will be fairly observed. If there is no trust, market transactions will simply break down. One has to believe that parties will fulfil their obligations; otherwise every rationally calculating individual has a short-term incentive to default on his own obligations. Thus, relations of trust complement the individual search for advantage via markets.

Where personalistic relations dominate, anonymous market relations will not function well, because the basis of trust is lacking. People turn to other mechanisms such as clientelism, nepotism, family ties, or corruption to pursue their interests. Trust is a nice example of how cultural elements emerge from experiences with previous interactions and feed back into future interactions. A culture of trust evolves from a history of experiences with successful exchanges, and solidifies into a system of expectations which structures further market relationships. It can also break down, when too many individuals exhibit free ridership and opportunistic behaviour. One of the characteristics of the culture of poverty is the complete absence of trust, weak participation in networks and associations and the belief that everybody is out to cheat each other, as documented in the classic study by Banfield (1958).

In an interesting study of the sources of differences in institutional performance in North and South Italian regions, the political scientist Robert Putnam pointed to the importance of civic culture (Putnam, 1993, 1994). Though this study focused on a European country it has wider implications for our understanding of the role of culture in development. In 1970, Italy introduced political decentralisation, creating twenty regional governments. Putnam found that, in spite of similar political structures, northern regions systematically scored higher on an index of institutional performance (based on indicators such as cabinet stability, timely presentation of budgets, statistical and information services, quality of legislation, day care centres, family clinics, housing and urban performance, bureaucratic responsiveness and so forth).

The most important explanatory factor for these differences turned out to be not, as expected, the level of socio-economic development, but socio-cultural factors such as civic engagement, active participation in public affairs, participation in voluntary associations, political equality, solidarity, trust and tolerance and political equality (measured by an index of civic community). To quote Putnam (1994: 56):

> Many theorists have associated the civic community with small, close-knit premodern societies, quite unlike our modern world – the civic community is the world we have lost. In its place arise large, modern agglomerations, technologically advanced but dehumanizing, which induce civic passivity and self-seeking individualism. Modernity, it is said, is the enemy of civility. Quite the contrary, our studies suggest. The least civic areas of Italy are precisely the traditional southern villages. Life in much of traditional Italy is marked by hierarchy and exploitation, not by share and share alike. The most civic regions of Italy . . . include some of the most modern towns and cities of the peninsula.

Putnam explains these differences by tracing historical developments since the twelfth century, contrasting the feudal monarchies in the South with the communal republics and city-states in the North. One of the most exciting results of the statistical analysis in this study is the strong correlation between indexes of civic traditions in the nineteenth century and those of the late twentieth century. Controlling for civic traditions, economic variables such as levels of economic development do not explain differences in modern institutional performance. Even more important, civic traditions seem to explain differences in levels of socio-economic development better than indicators of past socio-economic performance.

Putnam's conclusions are relevant for the study of development in general. Institutional reforms will not work without a civic foundation and these cultural foundations take very long to develop. Putnam explicitly refers to the disappointing outcomes of institutional reforms in the former Soviet Union as a case in point.

In the modern economic and sociological literature, trust and civic culture are seen as part of the social capital of a country along with related concepts such as national social capabilities and absorptive capacities (Akçomak and ter Weel, 2009; Woolcock, 1998). High levels of social capital are seen as contributing to economic development.[10]

The mysterious role of ethnic minorities in economic development

One of the famous puzzles of development is the important economic role of ethnic minorities. The Chinese have been extremely successful as entrepreneurs all across East and Southeast Asia, the Palestinians in the Arab world. Indians and Pakistanis dominate business activities in East Africa. In European history, Jews have played a prominent role in finance, business and also in culture and the intellectual pursuits. The interesting thing about

---

[10] The term 'social capital' is used at both the macro-level – as in this section – and at the micro-level. At the micro-level, social capital refers to 'the aggregate of the actual or potential resources which are linked to the possession of a durable network of more or less institutionalized relationships of mutual acquaintance or recognition' (Bourdieu, 1985: 248).

these successful minorities is that they often originated from rather traditional cultures and from societies that had long been economically stagnant. In spite of their economic success, or perhaps due to it, all these groups have usually been discriminated against. In the case of the Chinese in Asia and the Asians in Africa, the forefathers of the present inhabitants had been imported as contract labourers by the colonial authorities, but later received preferential treatment as middlemen in the context of divide-and-rule colonial policies.

Explanations for the extraordinary economic role of ethnic minorities are interesting from the point view of the role of culture. It is argued that migration frees migrants from the cultural and institutional constraints of their country of origin. Also, it is usually the most dynamic individuals and groups who are willing to migrate in the search of new opportunities and to escape the constraints of their own societies. Joseph Schumpeter, who saw the entrepreneur as the key driver of economic development, argued that entrepreneurs are typically marginal people (Schumpeter, 1976, first published in 1943). Their very marginality enables them to be innovative and entrepreneurial, terms which for Schumpeter were almost synonymous. In the case of migrants, they are not only freed from cultural constraints of their country of origin, they are also marginal in their newly chosen country of settlement.

Cultural differences between North and Latin America

Some authors points to cultural differences as contributing factors to the different paths followed by North America and Latin America (e.g. Harrison, 1985; Hartz, 1964; Hoetink, 1984). In the nineteenth century there were many similarities in conditions and levels of economic development between North America and Latin America. Both regions were thinly populated areas, with mass immigration from Europe.[11] Both areas were endowed with rich mineral resources. In both areas, independence was achieved at an early stage. Both areas had a history of slavery and contract labour. Both areas were predominantly agrarian, dependent on primary exports and imports of manufactures from Europe.

Nevertheless, economic development proceeded rapidly in North America, which had already overtaken Great Britain by 1890 as the technological leader, while Latin America stagnated and is presently still seen as part of the developing world. Hartz and Hoetink have emphasised the cultural differences as one of the factors contributing to the divergences of the two regions.

North America was characterised by an immigrant population of which a large portion originated in the Protestant countries of Northwest Europe with a strong work ethic, an emphasis on effort, discipline and the optimal utilisation of opportunities. Latin America was colonised by Catholic migrants from the Iberian Peninsula. Culturally, it had an aristocratic ethic, with an emphasis on honour, status, bravery and submission to fate. These cultural differences influenced the subsequent economic development of the Americas.

According to the historian Hartz the cultural differences can be linked to the cultural origins of the dominant colonists. The characteristic ethos of societies such as Australia, Canada, the USA and Latin America can only be understood if we connect this to the culture of their respective mother countries at the time of their founding. Latin America was

---

[11] Acemoglu et al. (2002) even argue that precolonial societies in Latin America were much richer than precolonial societies in Northern America (the so-called 'reversal of fortunes' discussion, see further section 12.3.4).

influenced by the hierarchical and corporative traditions of Iberian Europe, with a tradition of absolute leadership, Machiavellian power politics and a corporate state financed by taxes on land and agriculture. The USA was influenced by the Protestant culture of Northwest Europe and its entrepreneurial spirit.

Hartz argued that the transfer of cultural elements by migrants to new worlds resulted in magnification of the cultural traits of the society of origin. The checks and constraints operating in the region of origin were absent in the newly colonised areas. Therefore, it turns out to be vitally important that colonists imported a feudal-type culture from the Iberian Peninsula to Latin America, which did not exist in north Western Europe, from which the original colonisers of North America originated.

The Soviet legacy

All across the countries that made up the former Soviet Union, the legacy of seventy-five years of communism, preceded by a long period of royal absolutism under the tsars, has implanted and frozen anti-entrepreneurial attitudes, which persisted after the collapse of the communist regimes (Landes, 2000; Putnam, 1994). After 1989, it was hoped that the introduction of market reforms and political liberalisation would usher in a period of rapid growth. For a variety of reasons, including cultural ones, this hope has proved to be false. People remained oriented towards the state and dynamic private entrepreneurship was not readily available.

Asian values and the Confucian ethic

In the course of the twentieth century a number of East and Southeast Asian countries embarked on a remarkable process of development and catch-up. The pioneer was Japan, which commenced its catch-up process in the late nineteenth century. Japan was remarkably successful in acquiring and assimilating modern Western technology while maintaining vital elements of traditional Japanese culture and social relationships. Among other things, this resulted in totally new management practices such as quality circles and just-in-time (JIT) production, which spread from Japan to other parts of the world. Another new element was the close ties between the Ministry of Industry and Trade (MITI) and the large private conglomerates which were the pillars of Japanese industrialisation.

After the Second World War, the example of Japan was followed by South Korea, Taiwan, Singapore and Hong Kong, followed later by rapid growth and industrialisation in a second generation of countries such as Thailand, Malaysia, Indonesia, China and nowadays Vietnam. In one way or another, these countries have all been influenced by Chinese culture. Taiwan, Singapore and Hong Kong are Chinese societies. Chinese minorities play a vital role in the economic development of Thailand, Malaysia and Indonesia. Japan, Vietnam and Korea have been influenced by Chinese culture and the Confucian tradition for over a thousand years.

Some researchers have started to wonder whether the economic dynamism of the region cannot in some ways be explained by common cultural elements, more in particular by what they refer to as the *Confucian Ethic* (e.g. Dore, 1987; Hofstede, 2001; Hofstede and Bond, 1988). Important Confucian principles include the notion that the stability of society is based on unequal relations between people, characterised by respect and obedience and a sense of mutual obligations. The family is seen as the prototype of social and political organisation. The harmony of family-type relations is seen as vitally important. Individuals learn to subject their individuality to maintain harmonious social relations. The Confucian tradition also emphasises virtuous behaviour, benevolence and acquisition of skills, hard work and moderation.

On the basis of cross-cultural survey research, Hofstede (2001) has identified five basic dimensions of national culture which contribute to differences in social behaviour. These dimensions are: (1) *Power distance*, the extent to which less powerful members of organisations and institutions accept and expect that power is distributed unequally. (2) *Uncertainty avoidance*, the extent to which a culture programmes its members to feel uncomfortable or comfortable in unstructured situations. (3) *Individualism versus collectivism*, the degree to which individuals are supposed to look after themselves or remain integrated in groups, usually around the family (see also Ball, 2001). (4) *Masculinity versus femininity*, the distribution of emotional roles between the sexes. Masculine societies are societies where the values of men and women differ most. In typically masculine societies, males focus on masculine work goals such as money and careers, while females focus on caring, social goals and helping others. In more feminine societies the differences between male and female values were less marked. (5) *Long-term versus short-term orientation*, also referred to as the dimension of Confucian dynamism.

This fifth dimension was added to the first four on the basis of later survey research in China (Hofstede and Bond, 1988). The long-term orientation is characterised by values such as persistence (perseverance), ordering relationships by status and observing this order, thrift, having a sense of shame. The opposite pole of short-term orientation is characterised by values such as personal steadiness and stability, protecting 'face', respect for tradition and reciprocation of greetings, favours and gifts.

An interesting aspect of the Confucian dimension is that both the positive and the negative poles derive from the Confucian tradition. Hofstede recognises this explicitly when he writes: 'The correlation between certain Confucian values and economic growth over the past decades is a surprising, even a sensational finding' (Hofstede, 2001: 167).[12]

Since 1980, Hofstede's research has generated a vast amount of cross-cultural research on national value systems. This research has contributed to our knowledge and understanding of differences in national cultures and the ways in which they score on different dimensions. It has been less successful in demonstrating causal links between elements of culture and subsequent economic development. The argument is loose and impressionistic. Hofstede has more to say about measuring differences in cultural traits and dimensions than about the systematic relationship between these traits and economic development.

Based on more anecdotal evidence for Korea, Taiwan, Singapore and Hong Kong, Goodell (1995–6) identifies characteristics of the Asian values system, resulting in some paradoxical cultural combinations. In business life, eccentric individualism is combined with strong group bonding. On the one hand, there is cut-throat competition and a search for material advance through self-sacrifice. On the other, there is organisational efficiency based on ritual and a deep respect for traditional authority. Many observers emphasise the importance of personal relationships. In the classical bureaucratic paradigm officials and businessmen must deal with each other impersonally, through standardised procedures. But

---

[12] In an interesting criticism of the Confucian dimension, Fang (2003) argues that Chinese people would find it hard to distinguish the two poles of the dimension. For the Chinese, the values at the two ends of long-term orientation are not contrasting or opposing values, but rather closely interrelated with one another.

in Asian societies personal bonding is extremely important, as manifested by lavish partying and getting drunk together.

People develop privatised, personal networks. Capital does not flow through public channels, but through clan-like networks. Similar networks exist between government bureaucrats and private enterprises. There are strong outsider–insider perceptions: one has strong obligations to insiders, while it is permissible to defraud outsiders. Time and again observers point to the mistrust of formal law and a reliance on family networks (Perkins, 2000). Many observers point to the emphasis on hard work and high savings, and a strong achievement drive, which are also to be found in the Puritan ethic. The dynamic Asian societies seem to differ in these characteristics from developing countries that are less dynamic.

Much of this interesting literature remains highly speculative. It remains a puzzle why Chinese culture has coexisted with economic stagnation in China from the fourteenth century to 1950, suddenly becoming a dynamic force in development in the second half of the twentieth century (Pye, 2000).

One interesting hypothesis is that elements of East Asian culture have been especially conducive to growth in the specific conditions of late industrialisation and catch-up in a globalised economy. This is the position taken by the famous China scholar Dwight Perkins. He argues that the family- and network-based way of doing business has served Asia well for the past three decades, but that its limitations are now becoming more manifest since the Asian crisis of 1997 and the slowdown of economic dynamism in Japan (Perkins, 2000). There is an increasing need for strengthening the rule of law, reaching decisions more impartially, scaling down the conglomerates, reducing the vulnerability of banks and financial institutes, tackling rampant corruption and loosening the ties between government bureaucracies and private enterprise. An even stronger position is taken by Lucian Pye, who argues that Confucian values such as unlimited patience, insensitivity to monotony, controlled politeness and capacity for unlimited hard work are not the qualities which produce capitalism, but they are ideally suited for emulating capitalist and industrial practices in a process of catch-up (Pye, 2000).

The debate about Asian values and growth serves to illustrate the potentially important links between culture and economic development. It also illustrates the limitations of cultural explanations. The same cultural values operating in different circumstances and institutional and policy environments can have different results and outcomes. Both individualist and collective orientations can be compatible with growth and entrepreneurship (Ball, 2001). Cultures are complex and can have many different contradictory values[13] and in different periods different combinations of these values are selected.

12.3 Institutions as one of the key sources of development

One of the stylised facts emerging from the burgeoning research on the role of institutions in economic development is the strong correlation between institutional characteristics and levels of GDP per capita.[14] Thus De Crombrugghe and Farla (2012) find correlations

---

[13] For instance, traditional Confucianism scorned hard work and physical exertion.
[14] This section draws heavily upon a review paper by Bluhm and Szirmai (2012).

between the degree of formalisation of institutions and GDP per capita. Other researchers find correlations between GDP per capita and well-established property rights (Acemoglu *et al.*, 2001), constraints to the power of the executive, or democratic institutions (Lipset, 1959). However, correlations do not imply causality. The empirical and theoretical debate focuses on the direction of causality. Does economic development promote institutional reform or are efficient institutions a source of economic development? A second debate focuses on the existence of alternative paths of institutional and economic development, as opposed to a unilineal development towards modern institutions.

12.3.1   Rediscovery of institutions

The rediscovery of institutions in the modern literature on economic development can be traced to two sources (see Bluhm and Szirmai, 2012). On the one hand, it relates to theoretical innovations in the literatures of economic history and institutional economics spurred by the work of Douglass North (1990, 2005). On the other, disappointments with the results of the Washington consensus reforms of the 1990 – to be discussed in Chapter 13 – fuelled a renewed interest in institutional constraints and the quality of governance. The disappointments with the consensus provoked two very different sets of responses (see Rodrik, 2006). The first response was the rejection of market-oriented and neo-liberal policies, especially in the field of financial liberalisation (Chang, 2002; Cimoli *et al.*, 2009). These criticisms emphasised institutional constraints to the functioning of markets, non-standard solutions that allow for institutional diversity and a positive view of selective government interventions in the economy. The second type of response continued to press for market-oriented reforms, but concluded that the initial reform agenda did not go far enough. These authors stressed the importance of institutional reform and good governance as a condition for better-functioning markets and successful economic development.

12.3.2   Efficient institutions

In Chapter 3, we introduced the concept of efficient institutions. Economically efficient institutions are institutions that motivate self-interested individuals to act in ways that contribute to collective welfare and economic development (North, 1990; North and Thomas, 1973). Key economic institutions in the history of Western capitalist countries include clearly defined property rights, the rise of joint stock companies and corporations whose lifespan exceeds that of their founders, protection of intellectual property rights, book-keeping and financial accounting and interest. Well-defined property rights assigned the fruits of efforts to those who made investments in future returns. The rise of the joint stock company allowed individuals to cooperate in raising capital and limited the risks by isolating personal wealth from the specific assets invested in the company. Protection of intellectual property rights provided a spur to invention, innovation and technological change, by allowing the owners of such rights to charge fees for the use of their inventions. Book-keeping, financial accounting and interest were key institutional ingredients of the pursuit of sustainable profit through productive activity, with systematic reinvestment of part of the current profits. The notion of rentability contrasted with other types of search for profit such as piracy, rent seeking or maximisation of short-term speculative profits at the expense of long-run profitability. Medieval Catholicism (and traditional and modern Islam) prohibited the charging of interest on loans as an immoral activity (Lewis and Algaoud, 2001; Kuran, 2011).

This worked as a barrier to the rise of modern capital markets, capital accumulation and a rational attitude towards investment. Protestantism and Judaism had no such prohibitions.

What is economically efficient or inefficient varies in time and place. Institutions that are efficient at one stage of development may become inefficient at a later stage. North and Thomas (1973) have shown how feudal institutions were efficient in medieval Europe, given the prevailing conditions. They became inefficient when the conditions changed due to improvements in transport, technology and the emergence of extended markets. Lal (1988) has argued in a similar fashion that given the circumstances in pre-modern India, the Hindu caste system was relatively efficient for 2,000 years. Efficient financial institutions which served the Western countries well in the past have now become highly dysfunctional and contributed to the financial crisis in the advanced economies from 2008 onwards.

Much of the literature on efficient institutions suggests that in the modern world markets, individual property rights and family farms are economically superior to other types of economic institutions. But the characteristics of economic breakthroughs and processes of catch-up vary from historical period to period. Different conditions may require different economic institutions. It does seem clear that in a modern economy institutions that restrict the optimal use and allocation of human talents are economically less efficient (see section 12.2.3). But it is not by definition the case that market-based institutions always provide the optimal solutions. In his later work, North (1990, 1993, 2005) stressed that there is no guarantee that more efficient institutions will emerge and survive. Inefficient institutions can persist and institutional development is highly path dependent.

12.3.3   Colonial legacy: extractive or inclusive institutions

In an influential article, 'The Colonial Origins of Comparative Development: An Empirical Investigation', Acemoglu, Johnson and Robinson (2001) have argued that present levels of economic development are determined by the nature of the institutions implanted by colonisers in different parts of the world. In some regions, the colonists created highly extractive institutions, which favoured small colonial elites and excluded large segments of the population, for example in Belgian Congo. In other regions, such as North America, Australia, or New Zealand, the colonial settlers created inclusive institutions which tapped the potential of the mass of the population. Acemoglu et al. argue that key features of institutions set up during colonisation persist until today. Initial institutions thus had lasting effects on institutional development paths. Extractive institutions promoted extreme inequality and retarded economic growth. Inclusive institutions were more egalitarian, provided better protection against expropriation of property and contributed to long-run growth. According to these authors, the different institutional configurations were due to the different sizes of European settlements. These in turn were determined by settler mortality. Where settlers died in large numbers due to an unfavourable disease environment, as in Africa, Western settlement was limited and the institutional arrangements were extremely extractive. Where settler mortality was low, settlers settled permanently (colonies of settlement in the terminology of Fieldhouse, 1982, discussed in Chapter 2) and created more inclusive institutions. By using historical data on settler mortality as instrumental variables in regression analysis, Acemoglu et al. claim to have solved the problem of causality. Institutions are seen as the prime cause of development and underdevelopment.

This publication sparked a lively debate which continues to this day. Some criticisms focus on the data on settler mortality and the limited sample of countries. Other criticisms focus on the authors' tendency to neglect the almost complete eradication of the indigenous populations in regions with 'inclusive institutions' such as North America and Australia. In a recent contribution Easterly and Levine (2012) broaden the sample of countries by using the European share of population during colonisation as their key variable, rather than settler mortality. But they share the argument about the institutional legacies of colonialism. Yet other critics, in our view rightly, emphasise the importance of precolonial institutions (Michalopoulos and Papaioannou, 2012) and precolonial experiences with statehood (Putterman and Weil, 2010). Michalopoulos and Papaioannou show that in Africa differences in precolonial ethnic institutions are strongly correlated with differences in present incomes per capita.

12.3.4   Reversal of fortunes

In section 12.2 on the cultural explanations of economic performance, we discussed the divergence of economic performance between North and South America since the mid nineteenth century. The proponents of the so-called *reversal of fortunes hypothesis* go a step further, and argue that prior to colonisation South America was more prosperous than North America. Both Acemoglu, Johnson and Robinson (2002) and Engerman and Sokoloff (1997, 2002, 2005) argue that what needs to be explained is the *reversal of fortunes*. After the middle of the nineteenth century, the formerly poor North forged ahead due to industrialisation, while the formerly rich South America fell behind and failed to industrialise. The authors mentioned above agree that the explanation of this divergence is primarily institutional in nature: the more inclusive and egalitarian institutions in the North promoted development, while the extractive institutions and highly inegalitarian institutions of the South hindered economic development.[15] In their beautiful paper, 'Factor Endowments, Inequality and Paths of Development among New World Economies' (2002), Engerman and Sokoloff trace how institutional inequalities expressed themselves in six institutional spheres: suffrage and extension of the franchise, access to schooling, differing policies regarding access to land, regressive versus progressive tax regimes, patent regimes, and banking systems and access to finance.

But here the agreement ends. In the case of Engerman and Sokoloff, the more ultimate sources of growth and development are geography and economic factor proportions. Climate, soil quality and population size and density determine the factor proportions. The factor endowments of the Southern regions made them more suitable for growing and extracting sugarcane, minerals and other high-value commodities during the early colonial period. Sugarcane exhibited large economies of scale and was most efficiently processed in large plantations exploiting native and imported slave populations. In the North, the relatively large and homogeneous European population relied on small-scale wheat farming. The Northern factor endowments 'predisposed them towards paths of development with relatively equal distributions of wealth and human capital' (Engerman

---

[15] The same argument has been made by the dependency theorists of the 1970s (e.g. Frank, 1971, see Chapter 3), but this older literature is completely ignored by the modern institutionalist authors.

and Sokoloff, 2002: 56). Thus, causality runs from geography and associated economic factor proportions (large- or small-scale production) to institutions which influence subsequent economic developments. According to Acemoglu *et al.*, causality runs from political power relations to institutions which influence subsequent development. Settler mortality influences the pattern of colonial settlement and the share of people of European descent in the population. If European elites are small they tend to create extractive institutions, where there are large homogeneous settlements more inclusive institutions develop. After the industrial revolution, former colonies with more inclusive institutions were better placed to profit from the new mode of production.

12.3.5   Controlling violence: limited and open access orders

In an important and thought-provoking book, *Violence and Social Orders: A Conceptual Framework for Interpreting Recorded Human History* North, Wallis and Weingast have developed a very different framework for institutional analysis focusing on the central problem of human societies, namely the control of violence (North *et al.*, 2009, see also North *et al.*, 2013). Throughout most of human history violence has been controlled though coalitions of elites who control parts of the military, militia or other potentially violent groups. These elites limit access of the mass of population, the non-elites, to economic and political power. By limiting access, the elites can extract rents. These rents are used to negotiate – temporary – coalitions among elites controlling the means of violence, thus providing a measure of social stability. Such institutional orders are referred to as limited access orders (LAOs). The orders are fragile and can break down under the influence of external shocks, economic slowdowns or technological change, resulting in a descent into violence (cf. the modern literature on fragile states). It is the very fragility of order in limited access orders which provides the most important obstacle to sustained economic development. Once a coalition bargain has been negotiated it is very inflexible in responding to change, which reduces its ability to respond to crises, changes and challenges (for an elaboration of this view, see Bluhm *et al.*, 2012, 2013).

In a small number of societies there has been a transition to *open-access orders* (OAOs). Open access orders have active civil societies, broad access of large segments of the population to economic and political organisations, impersonal relationships, a strong rule of law, large numbers of long-lived organisations – one recognises the Weberian tradition of rationalisation, discussed in Chapter 3 – and a shared sense of equality. While limited access orders aim to create stability directly through distributing rents, open access orders create stability indirectly by institutionalising a peaceful process of rent creation through innovation and rent erosion through competition.

North *et al.* do not provide a theory of the transition from limited access orders to open access orders. They do however identify three so-called 'doorstep conditions' that are necessary conditions for the transition. These are: (1) the establishment of impartial rule of law for elites, (2) the emergence of public and private perpetually lived organisations, and (3) consolidated control of the military. The transition will occur when the doorstep conditions are in place and the elites in the limited access orders have incentives which motivate them to open up access, while providing them with some assurance that their interests will continue to be served in the new order. In the absence of a transition, the simple transfer of institutions such as elections or competitive market institutions from open access orders to developing countries may have unexpected and sometimes disappointing consequences (see North *et al.*, 2013).

12.4 ## Conclusion

In this chapter, we have provided a bird's eye view of various theories about the role of culture and institutions in the process of socio-economic development. Different strands of theory give different weights to ultimate sources of development. In particular, the institutional theorists tend to give priority to institutional explanations to the exclusion of other factors such as geography, culture, class, technological change or trade openness. In the words of Rodrik *et al.* (2004: 35): 'the quality of institutions trumps everything else'. In Chapter 3, we criticised monocausal theories of development. We would argue that both cultural and institutional theories provide valuable insights in socio-economic development, along with geographical theories and older theories emphasising the role of class dynamics and technological change.

Both cultural and institutional theories emphasise the importance of persistence of institutions and cultural elements. Thus, institutions created by colonisers have lasting influence on economic developments hundreds of years later and culturally defined attitudes have long-lasting effects. But we also need to understand how culture and institutions can change over time and how they are influenced by the other ultimate sources of development. Here, much is still unknown. The work of Greif (1993, 1994, 2006a, 2006b; Greif and Laitin, 2004) provides interesting clues to understanding institutional change. He shows how some institutional arrangements are self-reinforcing by creating the conditions for their own continuation, while other institutions set in motion changes such as economic development or demographic change that may undermine or change these very institutions.

In our view, one of the most promising theories of institutional change is still provided by the classic work of North and Thomas (1973).[16] In the *Rise of the Western World: A New Economic History*, institutional change is linked to the changing balance of power between economic classes and political power groups, in turn influenced by technological and demographic changes and the expansion of market relationships, to provide a historical analysis of why institutional changes took place in some regions and not in others. This allows for a link between the modern literature on institutional and cultural change and the classic and presently disregarded classic literature on class dynamics and class relationships in the tradition of Marx, Schumpeter and Weber.

Questions for review

1. Discuss theories about the role of religion in economic development. What are some of the main criticisms levelled against these theories?
2. What role do cultural factors play in explanations of the divergent developments in North America and Latin America? How important do you think cultural factors are in comparison with other determinants of economic development?
3. Discuss four of the often-mentioned differences between so-called traditional and so-called modern societies.

---

[16] Strangely enough this work is not even cited in North *et al.* (2009). The reason is probably that the 1973 publication focuses on economic efficiency, while the 2009 book focuses on the control of violence.

4. Provide an analysis of the extent to which traditional cultural elements form an obstacle to economic development.
5. Provide a brief summary of the reversal of fortunes hypothesis.
6. What are the key differences between the analysis of the colonial legacy by Engerman and Sokoloff, on the one hand, and Acemoglu, Johnson and Robinson, on the other?
7. Discuss the role of ethnic minorities in economic development.
8. Provide a critical discussion of the concept of efficient institutions. Give examples of efficient and inefficient institutions.
9. What are the arguments for and against the proposition that institutions trump all other factors in the explanation of development?
10. What are the differences between LAOs and OAOs? Why do LAOs have less potential for sustained economic growth? To what extent do you think the contrast between LAOs and OAOs is a useful distinction for the study of development?

Further reading

The following four collections of articles provide a good introduction to the topic of culture and development. They are: *Culture and Development: International Perspectives*, edited by Clague and Grossbard-Shechtman (2001), *Culture Matters: How Values Shape Human Progress* edited by Harrison and Huntington (2000), *Culture and Development in Africa*, edited by Serageldin and Taboroff (1994) and *Culture, Institutions and Development: New Insights into an Old Debate*, edited by Platteau and Peccoud (2011). Contributions from the perspective of economic anthropology include: Plattner (ed.), *Economic Anthropology* (1989), Wilk, *Economies and Cultures: Foundations of Economic Anthropology* (1996) and Evers and Schraders (eds.), *The Moral Economy of Trade: Ethnicity and Developing Markets* (1994).

For comparative empirical research on dimensions of culture, the work of Geert Hofstede is of importance. Here we mention Hofstede, *Culture's Consequences: Comparing Values, Behaviors, Institutions and Organizations Across Nations* (2001, first edition 1980) and *Cultures and Organisations: Software of the Mind* (1991), and an article in *Organization Dynamics* by Hofstede and Bond, 'The Confucius Connection: From Cultural Roots to Economic Growth' (1988).

The starting point for the debate on the role of religion in economic development is Max Weber's 1905 article, 'Die Protestantische Ethik under der Geist des Kapitalismus' (1969). It is still worth reading. Another classic study is Clifford Geertz's thoughtful analysis of the complexities of modernisation, in *Peddlers and Princes: Social Change and Economic Modernization in two Indonesian Towns* (1996). Two articles criticising simple contrasts between traditional and modern cultures are Kuper, 'African Culture and African Development' (1984) and Shweder 'Moral Maps, "First World" Conceits and the New Evangelists' (2000). The role of Islamic legal institutions is discussed in Kuran, *The Long Divergence: How Islamic Law Held Back the Middle East* (2011).

Banfield has analysed the absence of trust in traditional societies in another key book, *The Moral Basis of a Backward Society* (1958). The political scientist Putnam has highlighted the importance of an active civil society for socio-economic development in a comparative study of

Italian regions. This study has considerable relevance for the wider analysis of the role of culture in development. Publications about this topic include: Putnam (with Leonardi and Nanetti), *Making Democracy Work: Civic Traditions in Modern Italy* (1993) and Putnam, 'Democracy, Development and the Civic Community: Evidence from an Italian Experiment' (1994). From the large literature on social capital, we mention Bourdieu's paper on 'The Forms of Capital' (1985) and a paper by Woolcock, 'Social Capital and Economic Development: Toward a Theoretical Synthesis and Policy Framework' (1998). For an analysis of the economic functions of the caste system in India, we recommend Lal, *The Hindu Equilibrium*, Volume I: *Cultural Stability and Economic Stagnation: India, c. 1500 bc–ad 1980* (1988).

The cultural anthropologist Kottak has argued for cultural mapping of development projects, in 'Dimensions of Culture in Development' (1986) and 'When People Don't Come First: Some Sociological Lessons from Completed Projects' (1991). The cultural mapping approach has been criticised by Klitgaard in 'Taking Culture into Account: From "Let's" to "How"' (1994).

Key publications on the role of institutions in development include two articles by Acemoglu, Johnson and Robinson (2001, 2002): 'The Colonial Origins of Comparative Development: An Empirical Investigation' and 'Reversal of Fortune: Geography and Institutions in the Making of the Modern World Income Distribution'. Also worth reading is the volume by Acemoglu and Robinson, *Why Nations Fail? The Origins of Power, Prosperity and Poverty* (2012). In 'Factor Endowments, Inequality and Paths of Development among New World Economies' (2002), Engerman and Sokoloff analyse the influence of factor proportions on institutional development. The starting point of the modern institutionalist approach in economics is Douglass North's book *Institutions, Institutional Change and Economic Performance* (1990). In *Violence and Social Orders: A Conceptual Framework for Interpreting Recorded Human History*, North, Wallis and Weingast (2009) introduce the distinction between limited access orders and open access orders. A review of the recent literature on institutions is provided by Bluhm and Szirmai, *Institutions and Long-Run Growth Performance* (2012).

13

The international economic and political order since 1945

Chapter 2 introduced the concept of an international economic order. International economic orders are characterised by typical patterns of flows of goods and services, financial capital, people and knowledge. Other characteristics include the intensity of relationships between economies and the institutional structure of these relationships. In this chapter we discuss developments in the international order, and their significance for developing countries, since 1944. In addition to the economic aspects of the post-war international economic order, we deal extensively with political and institutional aspects such as the international balance of power, the role of international organisations such as the United Nations, the World Bank and the IMF and important international conventions and treaties. Figure 13.1 depicts the international order as one of the more ultimate sources of growth.

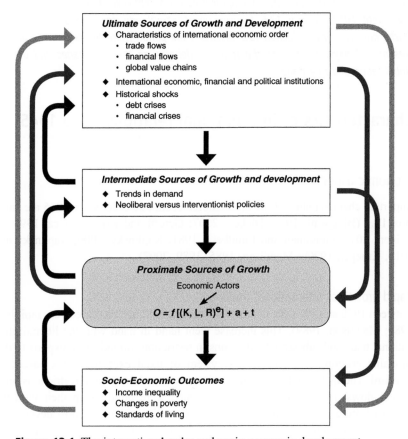

Figure 13.1 The international order and socio-economic development

This chapter identifies four stages in the development of international economic relationships since 1944. These stages are characterised by typical patterns of regional and global growth and by dominant policy orientations. Each period ends with a major system shock, which affects not only patterns of economic development but also theoretical and practical thinking about economic policies and development strategies. The periods are: the period of liberalisation of world trade (1944–73), the rise and eclipse of the policy goal of a New International Economic Order (NIEO) (1960–82), the period of debt crisis and structural adjustment (1982–97) and the period since 1997, which has been characterised by a revival of the intellectual debates on globalisation and liberalisation. The four major system shocks are the oil crisis of 1973, the debt crisis of 1982, the Asian crisis of 1997 and the financial crisis of 2008. The financial crisis of 2008 mainly affected the growth prospects of the advanced economies. It may herald a new phase in the development of the international economic order but in this book we discuss the period 1997 to the present as a single period.

The chapter is structured as follows. Important economic and political characteristics of the post-war international order are discussed in section 13.1. A chronological outline of the development of important international organisations and institutions is given in section 13.2. Section 13.3 describes the liberal economic order of the period 1944–73. Section 13.4 summarises the early criticisms of the liberal economic order and the debates on a new international order. Debt and its consequences are discussed in section 13.5. This section starts with a discussion of the 1982 debt crisis and contains empirical data on debt and international financial flows from 1982 until 2012. Section 13.6 focuses on structural adjustment and the emergence of the Washington consensus. Section 13.7 discusses the period from the Asian crisis of 1997 until the present and pays attention to the renewed debates on the advantages and disadvantages of globalisation and free trade.

13.1   Characteristics of international relations since 1945

13.1.1   Economic aspects

Important characteristics of the international economic order since 1945 are summarised in Box 13.1 (Bhagwati, 1988; Dicken, 2007; Gereffi and Korzeniewicz, 1994; Goldin and Reinert, 2012; Grassman and Lundberg, 1981; Kaplinsky, 2000; Kaplinsky and Farooki, 2010; Krueger, 1990b; Maddison, 1985, 1989, 2007).

Rapid growth of international trade
Between 1950 and 1973 the volume of international trade increased very rapidly (Bhagwati, 1988; Maddison, 1989). This increase went hand in hand with the liberalisation of international trade and substantial reductions in restrictions on industrial exports to the advanced capitalist economies. There was a system of fixed exchange rates based on the gold standard. The IMF acted as a lender of last resort and there were restrictions on speculative capital flows. In developing countries, which were building up their industrial sectors, industrial protectionism remained the rule. After the mid 1980s most developing countries were forced to reduce protectionism and open their economies to industrial imports. China in particular profited from new export opportunities.

BOX 13.1 : **Characteristics of the post-war economic order**

- Rapid growth of the volume of international trade.
- Breaking the mould of the colonial pattern of international trade: the emergence of industrial exports from developing countries.
- A modest share of developing countries in international trade until 2000, rapidly increasing share thereafter.
- Migration flows from poor to rich countries and from rural to urban areas.
- Financial flows from developed countries to developing countries from 1950 until 1982.
- Liberalisation of international trade.
- Liberalisation of capital flows; increase in the volume of capital flows.
- Emergence of global value chains and increased importance of intra-firm trade.
- Acceleration of growth of national income per capita in both rich and poor countries in the period 1950–73, followed by divergent growth trends.
- Increased financial instability, especially from the 1990s onwards.

With respect to agriculture, the advanced economies continued to follow highly protectionist policies. Expensive agrarian production by domestic farmers was protected against foreign competition; agricultural exports were massively subsidised. In recent years the level of agricultural protection has gradually been reduced, but it is still substantial. Since the mid 1970s, there has been some revival of industrial protectionism in the advanced economies, particularly through non-tariff restrictions on imports. However, there is no question of a return to the protectionism of the pre-war period.

The period of rapid growth of international trade and income per capita between 1950 and 1973 came to an end with the first oil crisis in 1973. After 1973, the growth of world trade slowed down (Table 13.1). A second dramatic hike in oil prices in 1979 contributed to the retardation of the growth of the world economy and world trade, along with the negative effects of the debt crisis of 1982. After 1985, the world export growth picked up again, accelerating towards the end of the 1990s, in spite of the negative effects of the Asian crisis of 1997. The financial crisis of 2008 resulted in a dramatic slowdown in export growth, but after 2010 it recovered. The average growth rate between 1973 and 2013 was 6.0 per cent per year, lower than in the golden age of 1950–73, but more rapid than in any previous period in history. Taking the post-war period as a whole, the growth of trade exceeded the growth of production, pointing to increasing interdependence in the world economy.

Breaking the mould of the colonial division of labour

The colonial pattern of international trade established between 1870 and 1913 involved a clear-cut international division of labour. Developing countries exclusively exported primary products and economically advanced countries exported manufactured products. In the post-war period, the share of industrial products in the total exports of developing countries increased strongly, as indicated in Tables 3.5 and 9.3

Table 13.1: Growth rate of world exports, 1720–2013 (%)

1720–1820	0.9
1820–70	4.2
1870–1913	3.4
1913–50	0.9
1950–73	7.9
1973–85	*4.2*
1985–96	*6.2*
1996–2000	*10.0*
2000–7	*6.8*
2007–10	*1.6*
2010–13	*5.7*
1973–2013	6.0

Sources: 1720–1820: Maddison (1982b: 254); 1820–70: Maddison (1995: 74); 1870–1973: Maddison (2001: 362); 1973–2013: IMF, *International Financial Statistics* (2014).

(pp. 117 and 360). Some developing countries, particularly in Asia, were successful in penetrating European and US markets for industrial products and became major industrial exporters (OECD, 1979, Chapter 9; Szirmai *et al.*, 2013a; UNCTAD, 2000; UNIDO, 2002, 2012). This involved a major restructuring of the pattern of international production and trade. On the other hand, this success in manufactured exports has been primarily restricted to some twelve large developing countries. In the poorest developing countries, in Sub-Saharan Africa and elsewhere, the share of primary exports in total exports still remains high.

A modest share of developing countries in international trade until 2000

In spite of the very rapid growth of exports, the share of developing countries in world trade has remained quite modest for most of the post-war period. The expansion of international trade until 1973 was mainly accounted for by the advanced industrial countries (Bhagwati, 1988; Thoburn, 1977). In 1970, the share of these countries in total world merchandise exports was no less than 76.4 per cent (UNCTAD, 2014). The share of the poorest countries in international trade was low and had declined even further between 1960 and 1977 (Lewis, 1978a; Streeten, 1984). After 1973, developing country shares in world merchandise exports started picking up, reaching 32 per cent of world exports in 2000. After 2000, things started to change rapidly. By 2012 developing countries accounted for 44.6 per cent of world exports, with the transition economies accounting for a further 4.6 per cent (UNCTAD, 2014).[1] The share of the advanced economies had declined to 50.8 per cent. The increase in developing country shares was mainly driven by the export performance of the East Asian countries (UNCTAD, 2003). The secular decline of the share of African developing countries continued. In 1950, the share of Sub-Saharan African countries in world commodity exports stood at 5.3 per cent. By 2012, it was no more than 2.3 per cent. Latin America's shares in world exports also almost halved between 1950 and 2012, from 11.6 to 6.1 per cent. It is interesting to note that the increase in the aggregate share of developing countries since the mid 1970s is in part due to increased trade among developing countries themselves.

Financial flows from rich to poor countries until 1982

In a reversal of earlier patterns between 1913 and 1950, there was a substantial net inflow of capital to developing countries, between 1950 and 1982 (see Chapter 3, Table 3.6). This meant that developing countries could afford to import more than they exported. Financial inflows can contribute to the expansion of the productive potential, especially if these resources are used for productive investments in infrastructure and capital goods, or imports of intermediate goods. However, the use of net capital inflows for consumptive purposes or defence expenditures is less conducive to future growth. The pattern of net capital inflows was temporarily interrupted after 1982 – as will be shown later in this chapter. In the years following the debt crisis of 1982, there was a net outflow of financial resources from poor to rich countries, especially from Latin America. In the 1990s net inflows resumed, until the outbreak of the Asian crisis of 1997. After 1997, several large Asian countries suffered from very large outflows of resources. But the interpretation of such outflows is not necessarily negative. It reflects the increasing export competitiveness of Asian countries, resulting in surpluses on the current account of the balance of payments.

In aggregate terms, there is an interesting shift from loans to FDI. In 1970, net inflows of loans into developing countries (net flows of debt) were three times as high as net inflows of FDI. Since the mid 1990s, however, net investment inflows were far more important than net flows of debt. Between 1993 and 2003 substantial negative transfers on debt – the balance of new loans, repayments and interest payments – were more than compensated for by large positive net transfers on FDI (see Table 13.3, p. 571). Since 2004, net transfers on debt have turned positive again.

Liberalisation of international trade and capital flows

The post-war economic order was characterised by a high degree of freedom in the trade of goods and services, and in movements of capital. In successive trade rounds, barriers to the free movement of goods and services were progressively reduced, with the notable exception of agriculture. Initially, less priority was given to full liberalisation of capital flows. In the 1990s, capital flows were also liberalised, leading to increased mobility of capital. Most of the financial flows are flows between the advanced economies, rather than

---

[1] All percentages in this section derive from the UNCTAD database UNCTADstat (UNCTAD, 2014).

between advanced economies and developing countries. The increased mobility of capital manifested itself in increases in long-term capital flows and FDI but also in more volatile short-term flows, including portfolio investment, short-term loans and currency speculation. According to Tobin (2000), the value of foreign exchange transactions per business day amounts to 1.5 trillion dollars. Nine-tenths of these transactions are reversed within a week, 40 per cent within a day.

Migration flows

Compared to goods, services and capital, there have been continued attempts to restrict the mobility of labour and people. In spite of these restrictions, there have been substantial increases in both international and internal immigration. As already discussed in Chapter 2 (section 2.4.6), the post-war international order is characterised by large migration flows from developing to advanced economies. Between 1950 and 2007, some 67.5 million persons migrated to the advanced economies. In addition, there were even larger migration flows from rural to urban areas. Between 1950 and 2011, urban populations in developing countries increased by some 1.6 billion people (United Nations Population Division, 2012b). If we assume that one-third of this increase is due to rural urban migration (cf. Lall et al., 2006), a staggering number of half a billion people have moved from rural to urban areas. In China alone some 130 million people had migrated to urban areas by 2006 (Yue, 2015). A third large migration flow is international migration from developing countries to developing countries (South–South migration). This flow is of comparable magnitude but even larger in size than migration flows from developing countries to advanced economies (World Bank, 2014).

Emergence of global production chains

The international order of 1870–1913 was characterised by increased trade in final goods and services. An interesting characteristic of the post-war economic order is the greatly increased importance of intra-firm trade and the emergence of distributed global value chains. The increasing volume of FDI is coordinated by large transnational companies. Some 77,000 TNCs dominate around 770,000 foreign affiliates (Dicken, 2003; UNCTAD, 2007). In the past, TNCs were primarily located in advanced economies. Recent decades, however, have witnessed the emergence of TNCs with their home base in emerging economies such as Brazil, China, India or South Korea (Carvalho, 2013).

Production processes have become fragmented, with different parts of the production process located in many different regions, including developing countries, depending on the availability of factors of production, national resources, investment climate and the proximity of markets (Dunning, 1988; Helleiner, 1989; Narula and Lall, 2006; Naudé and Szirmai, 2012). A substantial part of international trade takes place within the global production chains and within the transnational companies. Trade has changed from trade in goods to trade in tasks (Athukorala and Menon, 2010; Kaplinsky, 2011) The intensity of global interdependence has increased due to functional integration.

National income per capita trends in rich and poor countries

Between 1950 and 1973, national income and income per capita increased rapidly in both rich and in poor countries. Per capita income in the richer countries increased faster than in the poorer countries, so that international disparities increased. Between 1973 and 1982 the growth of per capita incomes decelerated, particularly in the economically advanced countries which pursued contractionary economic policies after the oil crisis of 1973. In Asia and Latin America, economic growth continued. In Sub-Saharan Africa, it stagnated. If oil-rich Nigeria is left out of consideration, average income per capita in Africa declined in this period (Toye, 1993).

After 1982, growth trends in different parts of the world diverged (see Table 3.2, p. 111). In the advanced economies there was a modest economic recovery, although the growth rates of per capita income remained lower than before 1973. Several large Asian economies experienced extremely rapid economic growth (World Bank, 1993). Latin America experienced economic stagnation in the aftermath of the debt crisis. In countries such as Argentina and Venezuela per capita incomes decreased on average by 2.5 per cent per year between 1980 and 1989. In Brazil real per capita income in 1989 was the same as in 1980 (Hofman, 1993). Sub-Saharan Africa experienced long-term stagnation since 1983 (World Bank, 1989, see also Chapter 3, Table 3.1). On average per capita income here decreased by 1.6 per cent per year (Elbadawi et al., 1992: 35). For Africa and Latin America the 1980s are often seen as a 'lost decade'.

In the 1990s, Asian growth continued to be very rapid, especially in China and the East and Southeast Asian NICs, but also in India. Growth in the USA and the European countries also recovered, though it did not reach the peak rates of the golden age. There was some recovery in Latin America, but it was shaky and interspersed with recurrent crises. Stagnation in Africa continued, though some African countries bottomed out in the mid-1990s. After the collapse of communism in 1989, many of the former Soviet Republics experienced deep economic stagnation with output and standards of living plummeting. Only a few of the former communist countries in 2000 had GDP levels exceeding those of a decade earlier, including Hungary, Poland, Slovakia and Slovenia. In 2000, Russia's GDP was two-thirds of that in 1989. In Moldova it was approximately one-third, in the Ukraine 43 per cent (Maddison, 2003; Stiglitz, 2002).

In 1997, the Asian growth path was rudely interrupted by the financial crisis of 1997. The crisis deeply affected Thailand, the Philippines, South Korea, Indonesia and Malaysia, which until then had been doing extremely well. Exchange rates collapsed, exposing weaknesses in the banking system and bankrupting many firms whose debts were denominated in dollars. There was massive capital flight and production contracted at alarming rates, calling into doubt the wisdom of liberalising capital markets and short-term capital flows (Stiglitz, 2002). The worst hit was Indonesia, where real output contracted by 13 per cent in one year (see Table 13.4, p. 592). Most of the countries recovered fairly quickly, with the notable exception of Indonesia, where political instability inhibited sustained recovery (Hill, 1999). The larger Asian countries such as India and China, with more closed capital accounts, were less affected by the crisis and continued their rapid growth.

From 2000 onwards, many African and Latin American countries embarked on a growth spurt, fuelled to an important extent by demand for primary exports from Asia. Asian countries continued to grow rapidly outperforming Western economies and providing an example of global catch-up. Since 2008, the advanced economies have experienced a double-dip recession in the wake of the financial crisis of 2008, while interestingly growth in the developing world was much less affected.

Growing financial instability

Since 1982, the international order has been characterised by increased vulnerability to major financial crises. In 1982, a debt crisis was triggered by the decision of Mexico to defer payment of its debt service. The debt crisis ushered in a decade of stagnation in Latin America and put the stability of the international financial system in question. Since 1994, there has been a series of major financial crises in developing countries, which have deeply affected their growth and development patterns. In 1994, Mexico had to turn to the IMF for massive balance of payments support, due to capital flight and the collapse of the peso. The Asian crisis erupted in 1997. In 1998, the financial crisis spread to Russia and Brazil, in 2000 to Turkey. In 2001 and 2002, a financial crisis all but destroyed the Argentine economy, while Brazil experienced further financial turmoil in 2001–2. In 2008, a banking crisis in the USA resulted in a major financial crisis and subsequent deep recession in the advanced economies (see Table 3.5, p. 117). In short, the international order seems to be characterised by increasing financial instability (Adelman, 2000; Citrin and Fischer, 2000; Eichengreen, 2004; Fischer, 2003; Griffith-Jones *et al.*, 2010; Soros, 2002; Stiglitz, 2000, 2002; Tobin, 2000).

13.1.2   Political aspects

Decolonisation

From a political point of view, decolonisation was one of the main characteristics of the period after 1945 (Emmer, 1992; Grimal, 1978; Morris-Jones and Fischer, 1980). Between 1945 and 1976, the Asian and African colonies of Great Britain, Belgium, the Netherlands, France, and Portugal achieved their independence. In the Middle East, decolonisation mainly took place in the inter-war period. Before 1919 regions like Syria, Lebanon, Iraq, Palestine, Kuwait and Jordan had been part of the Ottoman Empire. After the First World War, they were ruled as mandates in the name of the League of Nations by Great Britain and France (e.g. Lebanon, Syria). Between 1930 and 1947 these mandate territories were granted independence: Iraq in 1930, Syria and Lebanon in 1946, Jordan and Israel in 1947.

The decolonisation of Asia took place between 1947 and 1957. India and Pakistan became independent in 1947, Burma in 1948 and Malaysia in 1957. Ho Chi Minh proclaimed the independence of Vietnam in 1945, in the wake of the departure of the Japanese. France, however, was loath to relinquish its colonial authority to a communist-oriented nationalist movement. It waged war against the Viet Minh until it was decisively defeated at Dien Bien Phu in 1954. In 1954, Vietnam was partitioned into North and South Vietnam and the question of unification was deferred to the future. The French colonies of Laos and Cambodia also became independent in 1954. In South Vietnam, after 1954, an anti-communist government was strongly supported by the USA. The USA waged a full-scale but unsuccessful war to prevent a communist takeover of South Vietnam, but withdrew from Vietnam after the Paris peace agreements of 1973. In 1976, North and South Vietnam were reunited under a communist regime.

On the African continent, decolonisation commenced with the independence of Ghana in 1957. Between 1957 and 1980, all African colonies, with the exception of the South African mandate area of Namibia, became independent, sometimes after bloody conflicts. The Portuguese colonies were among the last to gain their independence. The independence of Mozambique, Guinea Bissau and Angola was not recognised until 1976. Namibia became independent in 1990.

Rhodesia (former Southern Rhodesia) is a special case. Here, white settlers unilaterally proclaimed their independence in 1965, in order to prevent power from passing to representatives of the black majority. In 1980, internal resistance and external pressure resulted in a transfer of power to a government under the leadership of Robert Mugabe and the declaration of the independence of the republic of Zimbabwe.

South Africa gained its *de facto* independence from Great Britain in 1931, but was ruled by representatives of the white minority till 1994. Racial oppression was formalised in the *apartheid* regime erected from the 1960s onwards. *Apartheid* was abolished in the early 1990s in a series of negotiations between President Botha and the African National Congress (ANC) and its charismatic president Nelson Mandela. After elections in April 1994, Mandela was inaugurated as the first black president of a multi-racial South Africa on 10 May 1994.

Many processes of decolonisation involved bitter struggles. These were often the consequence of the presence of large numbers of European settlers who fiercely resisted independence. Such was the case, for example, in Algeria, Mozambique, Angola, Rhodesia, Kenya and South Africa. A second reason for wars of decolonisation was when the former colonial powers were unable to transfer power to their preferred political successors. This was the case in Vietnam, Malacca and the Dutch East Indies (Emmer, 1992).

Some million people of European descent had settled in French Algeria. These settlers, initially together with the French government, opposed the independence movement FNL in a bloody war between 1954 and 1962. Over 800,000 Europeans had settled in the Portuguese colonies in Africa. They strove to maintain political ties with Portugal. In general, the decolonisation of the British colonies in Africa involved less bloodshed than that of the colonies of other countries. Among the British colonies, Kenya was the exception. Between 1952 and 1955 there was violent resistance to British rule on the part of the Mau-Mau movement, in the course of which the British interned 50,000 Kikuyus in detention camps (Grimal, 1978). British policy was aimed not so much at preventing the independence of Kenya, but rather at safeguarding the privileges of the European settlers.

In Vietnam, the French and later the Americans resisted the transfer of power to the communist-oriented nationalist movement Viet Minh. In Burma and Malacca the British government also resisted independence movements, for fear of the establishment of communist regimes. In Malacca independence was not granted until 1957, after the threat of communism had subsided. Sukarno proclaimed the independence of the Dutch East Indies on 17 August 1945, on the eve of the Japanese capitulation. The Dutch wars against Indonesian independence were partly inspired by the wish to restore pre-war colonial relations, but also in part by differences of opinion with regard to the political constitution of the future independent state (a federalist solution preferred by the Dutch versus the strong unified state claimed by the leaders of the independence movement). Indonesian military resistance and growing international pressure, especially by the USA, finally resulted in Dutch recognition of the independence of Indonesia in 1949.

According to Emmer (1992), decolonisation is generally the result of three factors: increasing resistance to foreign rule within the colonies, decreasing willingness to rule colonies in the home countries, and increasing international pressure. In the period immediately following the Second World War, not only the Soviet Union but also the USA actively supported the process of decolonisation. Later, however, fear of the emergence of communist regimes in the newly independent states came to play a significant role in US foreign policy. The USA shifted to a more colonial stance, as in the case of the Vietnam war. The delayed decolonisation of the Portuguese colonies in Africa was not only explained by the dictatorship of Salazar in Portugal, but also by US fears of an expansion of the communist sphere of influence in Africa.

Initially, in the years after the the Second World War it was assumed that colonial rule was one of the main sources of economic and social underdevelopment. It was widely hoped and expected that decolonisation would lead to rapid economic development (Franck and Munansangu, 1982; Meier, 1984). When this did not materialise quickly, some observers blamed this on neocolonial relations of economic dependence. Disappointing economic outcomes also led to a call for a new and more just international economic order.

In the 1980s, the climate of opinion changed. The quality of domestic economic policies in developing countries received more emphasis. This shift of opinion was influenced by the remarkable differences in economic performance between developing countries in different parts of the world.

Interdependence and the emergence of international institutions

Another important characteristic of international relationships in the post-war period is the great increase in the number of international intergovernmental organisations (IGOs) and international treaties. In 1939 there were 80 international organisations, in 1990 293 (Baehr, 1992). For 2013, the *Yearbook of International Organizations* lists more than 7,700 international intergovernmental organisations (UIA, 2013–14).

National states create international organisations to pursue common objectives and to improve international coordination. With the exception of the European Union, most of these organisations are not supranational. The participating states retain their sovereignty. The coordinating potential of international organisations is limited due to the absence of binding regulatory powers. Their effective functioning depends on the voluntary cooperation of sovereign states, in particular economically, politically and militarily powerful ones.

From an analytical point of view, an important characteristic of the international order is the combination of increasing interdependence of people, societies and states, on the one hand, and a poorly developed capability for international political coordination, on the other (Streeten, 1984). International trade has increased strongly. The economies of countries in the world economy have become highly interdependent. The disappearance of rain forests, the global warming due to the emission of CO_2 gases, damage to the ozone layer by CFCs, radiation risks associated with nuclear power stations and nuclear wastes, all indicate that the ecological consequences of economic activities have now become global. As a result of improved transport, international mobility is increasing strongly. As a result of improved communications, the dissemination of new ideas and technologies proceeds more rapidly and cultures are ever-more subject to influences from other cultures.

Given this increased interdependence, the capability of international institutions to fulfil a coordinating and regulating role has lagged behind. The creation of a patchwork of international organisations, international institutions and treaties may be regarded as a – very incomplete – first step in the direction of international coordination.

One can make a comparison with the formation of national states, as analysed in Chapter 11. In processes of state formation, political power is centralised by means of internal consolidation or external penetration. Centralisation results in a monopoly of the means of violence and, in due time, in some measure of democratisation of the control over the state apparatus. There is a process of standardisation, in which a national legal system replaces a diversity of local customs and regulations. Laws and regulations are enforced by the state through its monopoly of violence. The state finances its expenditures through its monopoly on taxation.

In a world order consisting of competing nation states there is no comparable process of international centralisation and pacification. Perhaps the *Pax Britannica* of the nineteenth century came closest to some kind of international centralisation. At that time, British economic, military, technical and cultural hegemony in the world resulted in a long period of relative international and national pacification.

The USA was the dominant power of the period after the Second World War, but has never achieved a degree of pacification similar to that of the *Pax Britannica*. First, until 1991 the Soviet Union was a major rival centre of power. The period 1945–91 was characterised by the rise and subsequent decline of the Soviet power bloc and the Soviet sphere of influence, by tensions between rich countries on the northern hemisphere and poor countries on the southern hemisphere, and by tensions between poor countries themselves. Only the direct conflicts between East and West were more or less pacified as a result of the threat of mutual nuclear destruction.

Secondly, decolonisation led to a proliferation of independent states in a non-pacified world. Wars mainly occurred in developing countries. Between 1945 and 1976 there have been no less than 104 wars. From 1945 until 2012, there have been more than 32 million casualties in wars and internal conflicts (see Chapter 11, Table 11.1). Prior to 1991, most of the international conflicts had an East–West dimension. The superpowers fought wars by proxy within and between developing countries.

Besides the East–West dimension, a factor of importance in post-war international political relations was the emergence and subsequent decline of the group of non-aligned developing countries as a coherent political force. The movement of non-aligned countries was founded at the Bandung conference of 1955. This movement received a new impetus when China joined it after its rift with the Soviet Union in 1960. After 1966, this movement organised itself in the international arena as the 'Group of 77'. The formation of this bloc was stimulated by the initial success of the cartel of Petroleum Exporting Countries (OPEC) in 1973. Since the 1970s, however, the bloc of developing countries has broken up again into a diversity of groups with differing interests. These include oil-exporting countries, oil-importing countries, NICs, or regional blocs like the ASEAN, the Organization of American States (OAS), the Latin American Free Trade Association (LAFTA) and the ACP countries associated with the European Union through the Lomé agreements. The political relevance of developing countries as a united bloc declined substantially in the 1980s and 1990s.

The joint position taken by China, Brazil and India in 2003 in the trade negations of the Doha trade round at Cancún marks a reversal of this trend. The economic rise and absolute size of the BRICS (Brazil, Russia, India, China and South Africa) is having its impact on the international order. The BRICS are now successfully claiming a more important voice in international organisations, a goal which has long eluded the developing countries. But, like the non-aligned bloc in the past, the BRICS are a very heterogeneous category (Naudé *et al.*, 2013; UNIDO, 2012).

After the disintegration of the Soviet Union in 1991, the USA emerged as the only remaining superpower. Quantitative estimates by Marshall and Gurr (2003), discussed in Chapter 11, suggest that the level of global armed conflict has indeed declined substantially from a peak level attained in 1985. Nevertheless, this has not resulted in a pacified international order. The wars in Iraq and Afghanistan revealed the limits of American military power and in the early years of the new millennium Russia and China have re-emerged as alternative centres of power in a multipolar world.

The nature of conflicts has changed. In addition to ethnic violence, civil wars and interstate wars, new forms of warfare involving non-state groups and terrorist actions have become more prominent, as witnessed by the dramatic terrorist attacks on the World Trade Centre in New York on September 11, 2001. These conflicts are sometimes referred to as 'asymmetric warfare', to indicate the immense difference between the means of violence at the disposal of states and the use of instruments of terror and suicide attacks against civilians by non-governmental networks.

Despite the lack of an international monopoly of violence, the post-war period has also seen several initiatives towards the creation of a supranational political and legal order. An important step in this direction was the setting up of the International Criminal Court (ICC) in The Hague, in July 2002. There were 139 signatories to the Rome Statute setting up the Court and by November 2013 122 countries had ratified the treaty. But such initiatives have been hard to sustain, precisely because there is no centralised monopoly of violence and there are no independent sources of finance for international institutions. The international legal order depends almost entirely on voluntary agreements between sovereign states. They may negotiate international treaties and agree to implement them with help of the organs of the national state. For example, a European agreement to reduce overfishing is implemented by national governments with respect to their own fishermen. In the case of the ICC, the most powerful nation, the USA, has refused to ratify the agreement and has claimed exemption from its clauses. Russia and China are also not parties to the treaty.

Apart from concluding international treaties and conventions, states may also found international organisations and institutions. In some cases they may voluntarily transfer some of their prerogatives to these institutions, for instance in the case of the European Union. Finally, states may voluntarily agree to submit their disputes to international arbitration. Such procedures can crystallise into international common law (Franck and Munansangu, 1982).

The development of an international legal order depends on the voluntary cooperation of national states. If the most powerful states are not willing to cooperate, international organisations will be paralysed. If one of the parties involved in a conflict is unwilling to bring this conflict before the International Court of Justice (ICJ) in The Hague, the Court is powerless. A further problem is the fact that international institutions do not have the independent means to implement their decisions. International organisations are also powerless against large-scale violations of human rights. Only if coalitions of powerful states are prepared to sanction violations of international norms and resolutions, and other powerful states do not oppose them actively, can some decisions of international bodies actually be enforced.

In recent years, further steps have been taken to create international legal institutions for the supranational adjudication of war crimes and crimes against humanity. Thus, the United Nations has set up international war crime tribunals for the Balkan Wars, the Rwandan Genocide and crimes committed in the Sierra Leone civil wars. In addition, the former dictator Pinochet of Chile has been accused of war crimes in a British court. With the legal cases against Pinochet in the UK, Slobodan Milošević, Ratko Mladić, Charles Taylor and Uhuru Kenyatta in The Hague, the immunity of heads of state and senior politicians is no longer self-evident. But prosecution can be obstructed if a country does not participate voluntarily, as currently is the case with Kenya.

13.2   International institutions and institutional change since 1945

13.2.1   A chronological overview

Many new international organisations were founded in the post-war period. In this context it is useful to distinguish between a cluster of specialised financial institutions dominated by the rich countries, and the United Nations and its numerous specialised daughter organisations, in which decisions are reached by majority vote and developing countries have much more influence on policy (Schrijver, 1985).

The UN family includes the FAO (Food and Agriculture Organisation), the ILO (International Labour Organisation), UNCTAD (United Nations Conference on Trade and Development), UNDP (United Nations Development Programme), UNESCO (for education, science and culture), UNICEF (the children's emergency fund), UNIDO (United Nations Industrial Development Organisation), UNEP (United Nations Environmental Programme), UNITAR (training), the WHO (World Health Organisation) and many more.[2] In theory, all specialised UN organisations fall within the compass of the responsibility of the UN Economic and Social Council (ECOSOC). They have to submit annual reports to the council. In practice, however, they are largely independent (Nerfin, 1985).

The financial institutions dominated by the rich countries include the institutions of General Agreement on Tariffs and Trade (GATT) and its successor the World Trade Organisation (WTO), the International Monetary Fund (IMF), the World Bank and its subsidiaries, the Asian Development Bank (ADB), the African Development Bank (AfDB), the Inter-American Development Bank (IDB), the International Development Association (IDA) and the International Finance Corporation (IFC), the OECD and the periodic meetings of the leaders of the seven largest industrialised countries (the G-7).[3] As specialised UN organisations, the IMF and the World Bank are accountable to the UN ECOSOC. But the number of votes in these organisations depends on financial contributions provided by member countries. This means that the policies of these organisations are determined by the rich countries. The founding of these organisations actually preceded the founding of the United Nations.

---

[2] Among others: the International Civil Aviation Organization, the Universal Postal Union, the International Telecommunication Union, the International Maritime Organisation, the World Meteorological Organisation, the World Organization for Intellectual Property.

[3] Since 1994, Russia has joined these meetings, which are now referred to as G-8 meetings.

The United Nations was founded in 1945 at a conference in San Francisco. Initially, its main objective was to safeguard international peace and security. It had fifty-one member states. Only four developing countries in Africa and Asia were represented. Between 1945 and 1965, sixty-five former colonies became independent and joined the United Nations as sovereign member states. More and more, the focus of UN attention shifted to problems of development. By 1992, 152 of the 180 UN member states were developing countries (United Nations, 1993a, 1993b). As of 2014, the United Nations has 193 member states. Box 13.2 summarises the principle organs of the United Nations.

BOX 13.2 : Principal organs of the United Nations

- **The General Assembly**. Each member state has one vote in the General Assembly.
- **The Security Council**. The Security Council has fifteen members. The victors of the Second World War (the USA, France, Great Britain, the Soviet Union and China) are permanent members with the power of veto. Ten other members are elected for two-year periods by the General Assembly.
- **The Economic and Social Council (ECOSOC)**. In principle, the ECOSOC coordinates the work of the numerous specialised UN organisations. The council has fifty-four members. These are elected for three-year periods by the General Assembly.

The rich countries have provided most of the funds for the work of the UN organisations. This provides them with considerable leverage. Still, on the basis of the 'one-country, one-vote' principle, developing countries have a great deal of influence within UN organisations, with respect to both policy making and staff recruitment. Through specialised organisations like UNCTAD and through the General Assembly, developing countries have been able to express their criticisms of the liberal international economic order.

Box 13.3 presents a chronological overview of international organisations, treaties, conventions, events and meetings defining the institutional characteristics of the international order since 1944. The subsequent sections will provide a more analytical discussion of the different phases of this order.

13.2.2　The evolution of the post-war international order

In the rest of this chapter we shall present an overview of different phases of the international order since 1944. We distinguish four main phases: (1) The period of liberalisation of international trade from 1944 until 1973; (2) The emergence and subsequent eclipse of a more interventionist new international order from 1960 till 1982, partly overlapping with the previous order; (3) The period of structural adjustment, market orientation and liberalisation from 1982 until the Asian crisis of 1997; this period is often referred to as the period of the Washington consensus (Williamson, 1990); (4) The period 1997–present. This period combines accelerated growth in many developing countries, on the one hand, with greatly increased financial instability and economic fluctuations, on the other. In this period, the debate between proponents and critics of the liberal international order intensifies.

Box 13.3 **Important international organisations, treaties and conferences, 1944–2015**

1944	Bretton Woods Conference:
	• IMF (International Monetary Fund).
	• IBRD (International Bank for Reconstruction and Development) (World Bank).
1945	Founding of the United Nations at the San Francisco conference:
	• General Assembly.
	• Security Council.
	• ECOSOC.
1947	General Agreement on Tariffs and Trade (GATT) signed in Geneva.
1947–8	Drawing up of the Havana Charter for the International Trade Organisation (ITO).
1948	Founding of the Organization of American States (OAS).
1949	Founding of the North Atlantic Treaty Organisation (NATO).
1949	Second round of GATT negotiations on tariff reductions (Annecy).
1951	Third round of GATT negotiations on tariff reductions (Torquay).
1955	Founding of the movement of non-aligned countries at Bandung.
1955	GATT gets permanent status.
1955	Founding of the Warsaw Pact.
1956	Fourth round of GATT negotiations on tariff reductions (Geneva).
1956	Founding of the International Finance Corporation (IFC), a subsidiary of the World Bank for the stimulation of private foreign investment in developing countries.
1957	Signing of the Treaty of Rome: founding of the European Economic Community (EEC) by six states: Belgium, the Federal Republic of Germany, France, Italy, Luxembourg and the Netherlands.
1960	Founding of the International Development Association (IDA), a subsidiary organisation of the World Bank; this organisation issues soft loans to developing countries.
1960–1	GATT: Dillon Round.
1961	Founding of the Organisation for Economic Cooperation and Development (OECD), with Western European countries, the USA, Canada and Japan as its members; South Korea and Mexico joined in the mid 1990s.
1961	UN proclaims the First Development Decade.
1963	Founding of the Organisation of African Unity (OAU).
1964	UNCTAD I (United Nations Conference on Trade and Development); first UNCTAD conference in Geneva, establishment of the group of 77 non-aligned countries within the UN. Raúl Prebisch, Secretary-General of the UN Economic Commission for Latin America (ECLAC), pleads for a new international economic order.
1964–7	GATT: Kennedy Round; with respect to GATT negotiation rounds up to and including the Kennedy Round, it was generally assumed that tariff reductions for

products from developing countries were lower than for other products: during the Kennedy Round the largest tariff reductions were negotiated for advanced technologies and capital-intensive products.

1965   Founding of the UNDP (United Nations Development Programme), which centred on technical assistance to developing countries and the financing of development projects.

1965   Addition of a new chapter, 'Trade and Development' to the GATT agreements; the requirement of reciprocity was abandoned for developing countries.

1968   Second UNCTAD conference in New Delhi.

1971   Collapse of the Bretton Woods fixed exchange rate system.

1971   Lima declaration of ministers of the G-77 on targets for industrial production – objective: by the year 2000 25 per cent of world industrial production should be produced in developing countries.

1971–6   GATT: gradual introduction of the Generalised System of Preferences (GSP) to facilitate the exports of industrial products from developing countries to the industrialised countries.

1972   Third UNCTAD conference in Santiago de Chile.

1973   First oil crisis.

1973   In a speech in Nairobi the President of the World Bank, Robert McNamara, calls attention to the basic needs of millions of people living in absolute poverty.

1973–9   GATT negotiations: Tokyo Round – tariffs reduced by 30 per cent.

1974   Sixth special meeting of the UN General Assembly; acceptance of a resolution on an NIEO; a 'Charter of the Economic Rights and Duties of States' is formulated.

1974   Multi-Fibre Arrangement (MFA): 'voluntary' quantitative import restrictions for textile exports from developing countries.

1975   Lomé Convention signed in February by the EEC and sixty-three ACP countries (former European colonies in Africa, the Caribbean and the Pacific); the agreement includes a series of non-reciprocal trade concessions by the EEC and the setting up of two funds for the stabilisation of export revenues of developing countries.

1975   UN resolution on 'Development and International Economic Cooperation'.

1976   UNCTAD IV in Nairobi.

1976   ILO world employment conference in Geneva calls for an emphasis on basic needs in development policy.

1979   UNCTAD V in Manila.

1979   Second oil crisis.

1979   World Bank introduces Structural Adjustment Loans (SALs).

1980   Treaty on an Integrated Programme for Commodities: the treaty has not yet been ratified by the required ninety states and therefore is still not being implemented.

1980   Publication of the Brandt report: *North–South: A Programme for Survival* (Brandt *et al.*, 1980): emphasis on mutual interests of rich countries and developing countries.

1980   Prime Minister Michael Manley of Jamaica refuses to meet IMF conditions for further financial support; first political conflict about 'conditionality'.

1981	World Bank introduces Sectoral Adjustment Loans (SECALs).
1982	Signing of a comprehensive treaty on maritime law, in Jamaica in December; among other things, this treaty deals with the common exploitation of natural resources on the seabed outside territorial waters, but it has not been signed by the USA, the UK and the Federal Republic of Germany and it has not been implemented.
1982	Mexico postpones payments of its debt service; start of the debt crisis: after 1982 the IMF and the World Bank increasingly emphasise 'structural adjustment policies' as a condition for obtaining new loans.
1983	Third ACP–EEC treaty signed in Lomé.
1985	Baker Plan introduced in Seoul: A Programme for Sustained Growth, which argues for renewed capital flows to developing countries; recognition of the fact that a solution of the debt crisis depends on resumption of economic growth.
1986–93	GATT: Uruguay Round on liberalisation of international trade, completed on 15 December 1993; agricultural products and services are included in the agreements for the first time; agreement on the creation of the World Trade Organization (WTO).
1986	IMF: Structural Fund Facility (SAF) to finance SAPs.
1987	IMF: Extended Structural Fund Facility (ESAF) to finance sectoral SAPs.
1989	Fall of the Berlin Wall.
1989	Fourth ACP–EEC agreement signed in Lomé.
1989	Brady Plan launched in March; first step towards voluntary debt reduction as a contribution to the resumption of economic growth.
1991	Disintegration of the Soviet Union.
1992	May 9: adoption of the text of the Framework Convention on Climate Change (FCCC) at UN Headquarters in New York.
1992	United National Conference on Environment and Development (UNCED) in Rio de Janeiro; resolutions are passed on pressing global environmental issues such as reduction of CO_2 emissions, CFCs and deforestation. The FCCC is opened to signature.
1993	Mexico, the USA and Canada agree on a North American Free Trade Association (NAFTA).
1993	Treaty of Maastricht: the EEC is transformed into the European Union (EU); agreement on the introduction of a common European currency by 1999.
1994	World Population Plan of Action adopted by the UN Conference on Population and Development in Cairo in September.
1994	15 April: Signing of the Agreement on Trade-Related Aspects of Intellectual Property Rights (TRIPS) at Marrakesh, Morocco; signature of the WTO agreements based on the Uruguay Round.
1995	Start of the WTO in Geneva; by 2013, 159 countries were members.
1995	Second Mexican debt crisis.
1996	The World Bank and the IMF launch the debt initiative for HIPCs, focusing on debt relief; the HIPC initiative further amended at the G-8 summit in June 1999; thirty-three countries became eligible for debt relief.

1997	Kyoto Protocol: on 11 December 1997 the Kyoto Protocol, for practical implementation of the FCCC, was adopted in Kyoto, Japan, focusing on reductions of emissions of CO_2; 1997–2001, further negotiations on Kyoto Protocol, resulting in an agreement which has been ratified by 191 countries as of June 2013; the Protocol entered into force in 2005 but it has not been ratified by the USA.
1997	The Asian crisis, sparked by devaluation of the Thai Baht.
1999	Anti-globalisation protests at the Seattle meeting of WTO.
2000	June: Lomé V convention between the EU and seventy-one ACP countries for the period 2000–7.
2000	The Cotonou Agreement between the EU and 79 ACP countries for the period 2000–20, entering into force in 2008, after expiry of ACP trade preferences in 2007.
2000	6–8 September: Millennium Summit in New York; Ratification of the UN Millennium Declaration and MDGs to be achieved by 2015.
2001	November: start of the Doha Round of trade liberalisation; this round is called the development round and is explicitly intended to improve the positions of developing countries in international trade and to address agricultural protection by the advanced economies; in spite of some progress, at a meeting in Cancún, Mexico, in September 2003, representatives of developing countries and advanced economies failed to reach agreement and the talks have stalled; a modest interim agreement on trade procedures was reached in December 2013.
2001	11 September: attack on the World Trade Center in New York.
2001	11 December: China joins the WTO after fifteen years of negotiations.
2002	18–22 March: UN International Conference on Financing for Development at Monterrey, Mexico; renewed commitment to the additional financing of development to the tune of 12 billion US dollars in the light of the Millennium Development Goals.
2002	1 July: Rome Statute on ICC in The Hague enters into force.
2005	2 March: Paris declaration on aid effectiveness: emphasis on country ownership, alignment, harmonisation, results and mutual accountability.
2008	4 September: Accra Agenda for Action: follow-up of Paris declaration on aid effectiveness, strengthening developing country ownership.
2008	Global financial crisis, originating in the USA.
2009	2009 UN Climate Change Conference in Copenhagen (COP15); the Copenhagen accord recognises climate change as one of the greatest challenges of the present, but no binding decisions are taken.
2010–12	Arab Spring: a series of protest movements across the Middle East and North Africa, starting in Tunisia on 18 December 2010.
2013	7 December: modest interim agreement in the Doha negotiations on trade facilitation signed in Bali.
2015	15 July: BRICS development bank launched as alternative to the World Bank.

Sources: Bhagwati (1988); Fey (1985); Hermes (1992); Johnson (1967); Meier (1984); Schrijver (1985); Raffer and Singer (2001); Riddell (2008); Sachs (2005); Singer (2001); Stiglitz (2002); Teunissen (1990).

For each phase, we discuss the international institutions and the issues and debates that characterise a given historical period. But institutions and issues outlast specific time periods, so we shall not always limit ourselves to a strict chronological time frame. Thus, the debt crisis of 1982 typically belongs to the period 1982–96, but debt issues continue to play a role in later years. The GATT typically belongs to the liberal period 1944–73, but GATT negotiations continued far beyond that period.

One of the recurrent themes in the succession of international conferences, resolutions and treaties in Box 13.3, as well as in the academic literature, is the debate between advocates of a liberal international order based on free trade and proponents of an international order based on some measure of national and international regulation. The financial institutions domin-ated by the affluent countries such as the World Bank, the GATT, the WTO, or the IMF tend to champion free trade and liberalisation and argue that free trade and an outward orientation will benefit developing countries as well as the advanced economies. UN organisations such as ILO, UNCTAD, UNESCO, UNICEF and UNIDO, dominated by developing countries, tend to argue that unrestricted free trade is a threat to poorer developing countries and call for a more just and more regulated international economic order which offers a better deal for developing countries. The debate is characterised by pendulum swings between more liberal and more interventionist stances. These swings will be discussed in the coming sections.

A second important theme in the discussion of the international order is that of *financial flows, debt crises and debt relief*. What role have debt crises played in post-war development, and how should we deal with debt and debt relief? A third theme concerns the role of foreign direct investment. In the earlier years, FDI inflows in developing countries were subject to many restrictions. In later years, the attitude towards FDI has become more positive. Almost all countries welcomed foreign investment, though there is an ongoing debate about the conditions under which FDI can make a positive contribution to development.

Since the Brundlandt report of 1982 (Brundtland *et al.*, 1987) *sustainability* has become one of the key themes in the international debates on global development. An important element in the evolution of the international order is a series of conferences and treaties on the environment, based on increasing fears of global warming due to greenhouse gas emissions. In 1992, the text of an FCCC was adopted at the United Nations and opened for signature. In December 1997, the Kyoto Protocol on greenhouse gas emissions was concluded in Kyoto, Japan. Between 1997 and 2001, there have been intensive negotiations on the implementation of measures to reduce greenhouse gas emissions in the context of the Protocol. As of 2013, the Kyoto Protocol has been ratified by 192 countries. The Protocol imposes caps on GHG emissions for advanced economies, but not for developing countries. The first phase of the Protocol ended in 2012. In 2012, the Protocol was amended to include a second period, 2013–20, but this has not yet entered into legal force and is not likely to do so. One of the contentious issues is whether or not developing countries, including in particular China, one of the most important polluters at present, should also curb their emissions. The impact of the Protocol on actual emissions has been limited.

13.3   The liberal international economic order, 1944–73

The foundations for the institutional structure of the post-war liberal international economic order were laid at a conference in Bretton Woods in 1944 (Burk, 1990). Forty-four countries were represented at this conference, among which were twenty-one developing countries. These only played a very minor role in the debates. At the conference, agreements were reached on a system of stable exchange rates, with the dollar as the base currency and with currencies convertible to gold at fixed rates. The IMF was set up to safeguard international financial stability. The IMF provided financial support to countries faced with sudden deficits in their balance of payments. The initial task of the new IBRD (World Bank) was to provide funding for economic reconstruction of war damage. The Bank started operations in 1946 and gradually shifted its focus of attention to developing countries after 1950. The Bank concentrated mainly on investment in infrastructure. By 1981 the total of outstanding loans was over 5 billion dollars (Meier, 1984). Voting power in institutions like the IMF and the World Bank depends on the amount of financial resources contributed by the member countries.

With the IMF and the World Bank, the GATT became the third pillar of the liberal international economic order. In the GATT treaty signed in Geneva in October 1947, 123 separate trade agreements between twenty-three advanced economies were combined into a single agreement (Fey, 1985). Important principles underlying this agreement are summarised in Box 13.4.

BOX 13.4 : GATT principles

- Governments should refrain from interference in international trade. They may only impose tariffs on imports.
- Quantitative restrictions and trade barriers are only permitted under specified conditions.
- Reciprocity: tariff reductions have to be reciprocal.
- Non-discrimination: trade advantages granted to one country have to be granted to all other countries. This is referred to as the 'most favoured nation' (MFN) clause.

GATT and WTO

The GATT agreement was meant to be a temporary arrangement in anticipation of the founding of an International Trade Organisation (ITO) with broader responsibilities. From November 1947 to March 1948 a charter for this organisation was negotiated in Havana. In these discussions, representatives of developing countries played a more prominent role than in the GATT negotiations. The draft version of the ITO charter, therefore, also included a chapter on 'Economic Development and Recovery', which paid attention to foreign direct investment and to the protection of infant industries. In another chapter, the subject of agreements to stabilise commodity prices was broached. The Havana conference ended in a conflict between developing countries and economically advanced countries. The ITO did not get off the ground. Therefore, in 1955 the GATT institutions, originally intended as temporary, received a semi-permanent status, which lasted until 1995.

Including the Uruguay Round concluded in December 1993, GATT negotiations took place in eight rounds. Between 1947 and 1979, the first seven rounds led to a reduction in the average import tariffs by no less than 92 per cent (Bhagwati, 1988). Until the Uruguay Round, agricultural products were excluded from the negotiations. Tariff reductions referred mainly to industrial products. The GATT agreements also included procedures to solve trade disputes between participating countries. The reduction of trade barriers mainly affected exports to the rich countries. Developing countries continued to protect their industrial sectors.

In part due to tariff reductions, trade between economically advanced countries increased twice as fast as their real output. The growth of trade was also spurred by the decreasing costs of transport and communication. Major exceptions to the liberalisation of international trade were agriculture and textiles. Until recently, US and European policy with respect to agricultural products has been highly protectionist. Attempts were also made to protect the textile industry in the rich countries against imports from low-wage countries by means of the so-called MFA of 1974, and its predecessors. In practice, developing countries were quite successful in evading these import restrictions in the 1980s. Exports of textiles and clothing from developing countries to the OECD countries increased annually by 13 and 20 per cent, respectively (Krueger, 1990b).

Until 1979, subsequent GATT negotiation rounds managed to reduce average import tariffs on manufactured goods to 5 per cent (Fey, 1985). The reduction of tariffs continued beyond 1979, but protectionist tendencies resurfaced along with the slowdown of economic growth in the rich countries after 1973, while agriculture and services continued to be excluded from the trade agreements. Tariff reductions were increasingly offset by the growth of non-tariff barriers (NTBs) to imports to rich countries. NTBs include 'voluntary agreements on the restriction of exports', appeals to 'anti-dumping clauses' of the GATT, and imposition of restrictive health, quality and environmental requirements. One of the GATT clauses referred to the right to take countermeasures in case of 'dumping' by another country. 'Dumping' is a very elastic concept. Between 1980 and 1985 the EEC countries, the USA and six other advanced economies appealed to anti-dumping provisions 1,155 times in order to restrict imports from other countries. There were another 425 appeals to anti-subsidy provisions (Bhagwati, 1988). Another exception to free trade is provided by situations in which there is the danger of 'serious injury to domestic producers'. In such cases, temporary relaxation of the GATT was possible. With this clause as a fall back, rich countries could blackmail developing countries into signing 'voluntary' agreements on export quotas. Another threat to the liberal international order was the rise of trade blocs with internal free trade and intensified protectionism at the outside borders (Krueger, 1993). Krueger (1990b, 1993) and later Stiglitz (2000, 2002) point to the paradoxical situation that during this period developing countries were under pressure from international financial institutions to liberalise their economies, while there was a simultaneous revival of protectionist tendencies in the rich countries that stood at the cradle of the post-war liberal economic order. However, according to Bhagwati (1988), there was no relapse into the protectionism of the inter-war period. The liberalisation of the 1950s and 1960s was not undone. Though further reductions of import tariffs were balanced by increases in other forms of protection, there was no fundamental break with a free trade regime. We agree with this assessment.

At the formal level, liberalisation of trade received a further impetus from the successful completion of the protracted negotiations of the eighth round of GATT negotiations – the Uruguay Round – in December 1993. These negotiations took place from 1986 to 1993. For the first time, agriculture was also included in the packet of tariff reductions, though progress remained slow. Agreement was reached on the phasing out of the multifibre agreements, which happened between 1993 and 2005. Trade in services was also liberalised.

The agreement contained provisions for the setting up of a permanent world trade organisation (WTO). The pressure on developing countries to open up their economies and abolish restrictions on trade and foreign investment increased. Among the provisions of the Uruguay Round was an important agreement on Trade-Related Intellectual Property Rights (TRIPS), which is generally seen as protecting the interests of the advanced economies and the large transnational corporations engaging in R&D (see Chapter 4). The WTO finally started operations on 1 January 1995. China joined the WTO in 2001 after protracted negotiations lasting fifteen years, achieving automatic MFN status under the terms of the WTO.

With some justification, developing countries claim that the WTO imposes import liberalisation on developing countries, making them vulnerable to competition from the advanced economies (and emerging economies such as China), prohibiting protection of promising infant industries and reducing the scope for industrial policy (Chang, 2002; Westphal, 2002). At the same time the advanced economies have continued to restrict trade in textiles, agricultural products and other products. They have also used environmental, health, labour and quality regulations to restrict imports. They do not always practice what they preach.

The Doha Round of trade negotiations, starting in 2001, was meant to repair some of the shortcomings of the Uruguay Round, for the first time giving priority to reduction of agricultural protection by the USA and the EU and targeting anti-dumping provisions and NTBs in the rich countries. At a meeting in Cancún, in 2003, the developing countries led by China, Brazil and India – three BRICS countries – refused to agree to the terms offered by the advanced economies, which were deemed inadequate in part because the advanced economies refused to abolish agricultural subsidies. The Doha negotiations have been stalled for years. A modest interim agreement was reached in 2013. In the absence of progress in multilateral trade negotiations, there was a proliferation of bilateral trade agreements between countries and between regional blocs. By 2011, there were some 400 bilateral trade agreements worldwide, often referred to as the 'Spaghetti bowl' (see Bhagwati, 1995).

The liberal order 1944–73: a summary

The economic order of 1944–73 was a period of unparalleled expansion of international trade. Interestingly, trade liberalisation did not preclude industrial policy and active state intervention in the domestic economy, both in advanced economies and in particular in many developing countries. It also did not preclude import substitution policies on the part of developing countries. The period came to an end with the first oil crisis of 1973 and the abandonment of the gold standard and the system of fixed exchange rates in that year. The oil crisis resulted in a slowdown in growth in the advanced economies and developing countries in Africa, but not in East Asia, and also not in the short run in Latin America. But the institutions of this liberal period such as the GATT and the WTO continued to evolve far beyond this period.

13.4   The New International Order, 1960–82

The principles underlying free trade have been discussed in Chapter 8. The basic arguments have remained unchanged since Adam Smith sang the virtues of free trade in the eighteenth century. Participation in international trade, specialisation and an international division of labour will increase the welfare of all parties, whether developing countries or advanced economies. There is strong theoretical and empirical support for the general argument that free trade is beneficial for growth and that those developing countries which have participated most in international trade have developed more rapidly than those which have not (Williamson, 2011).

Nevertheless, free trade has always had its critics. Despite the rapid growth of the world trade and per capita incomes in the 1950–73 period, there was increasing dissatisfaction with the liberal international economic order on the part of developing countries (see Brandt *et al.*, 1980; Johnson, 1967; Lewis, 1978b; Schrijver, 1985; Seers, 1979; Streeten, 1984). The essence of their criticisms was the argument, deriving from Friedrich List, that powerful countries with a highly developed economy benefit more from international free trade than poor countries trying to catch-up.[4] Developing countries had profited insufficiently from the growth of the world economy. Within developing countries, growth had largely bypassed the poorest classes of the population. The international order should be restructured in such a way that the masses of the population in poor developing countries could profit from international trade. Exports should provide developing countries with the financial resources needed for development. This would make them less dependent on development aid ('trade, not aid'). The main arguments of the critics of the liberal economic are summarised in Box 13.5.

BOX 13.5 : Criticisms of the liberal international order in the 1960s

- In the post-war period, neither decolonisation nor development aid resulted in sufficient economic growth in developing countries.
- Economic growth in developing countries did not result in much decrease in poverty due to the extremely unequal distribution of incomes.
- The share of the poorest developing countries in world exports decreased. Excluding oil-exporting countries, the share of the low-income countries in world trade decreased from 3.6 per cent in 1960 to 1.5 per cent in 1977.[5]
- Most prices of primary exports of developing countries showed downward trends, in both absolute terms and relative to prices of imported manufactured goods.
- Prices of primary exports of developing countries fluctuated strongly in the short run so that export revenues were very unstable.
- International income inequality increased, since per capita incomes in the rich countries increased faster than those in the poor countries.
- Large multinational enterprises contributed to a drain of resources. They tend to repatriate their profits abroad, they contribute little to the domestic economy and they reinforce the economic dependence of the developing countries on the advanced economies.

Sources: Bhagwati (1977); Corden (1979); Myint (1980); Streeten (1984: 474); Ul Haq (1976).

---

[4] The arguments of this period are very similar to the criticisms of the liberal international order being voiced today.

[5] As indicated in section 13.1.1, the share of the poorest countries in world trade has continued to decline since the 1970s (UNCTAD, 2003).

As an alternative to the liberal international economic order, a New International Economic Order (NIEO) was launched at the first meeting of the UN Conference on Trade and Development (UNCTAD) in 1964 in Geneva. The NIEO consisted of a comprehensive set of measures formulated by Raúl Prebisch, the Secretary-General of the Economic Commission for Latin America (ECLAC) and representatives of the newly formed bloc of 77 non-aligned countries. In this new economic order, the position of developing countries in the system of international trade was to be strengthened and their access to markets in developed countries would improve. The call for NIEO became stronger and stronger at subsequent UNCTAD conferences (see Box 13.2, p. 550). The pursuit of the NIEO received a substantial boost when a cartel of petroleum-exporting countries (OPEC) succeeded in raising oil prices dramatically in 1973 and subsequently in 1979.

In 1974, the UN General Assembly accepted a resolution on the NIEO. One of the important demands included in this resolution was more voting power for developing countries in the financial institutions dominated by the rich countries. Another aim was the stabilisation or even improvement of the terms of trade of primary exports, through the establishment of buffer funds and commodity agreements. Important elements of the NIEO proposals are summarised in Box 13.6. The commodity agreements have been worked out in the 1980 draft treaty for an integrated programme for commodities and a 1982 draft treaty on the exploitation of natural resources of the seabed. Neither of these treaties has ever been implemented.

13.4.1 Institutional responses to the New International Economic Order

The demand for more votes in the financial institutions was never met by the rich countries. But in several other important ways many international institutions did respond to the pressure for change. As early as 1955, it was already accepted that developing countries could continue to protect their domestic industries while trade barriers in the rich countries were being reduced. The justification for this exception was the 'infant industry' argument. In 1965, an extremely important chapter was added to the GATT agreements, in which the reciprocity requirement was dropped for developing countries. Developing countries did not have to reciprocate tariff reductions in rich countries. Between 1971 and 1976 a Generalised System of Preferences (GSP) was developed, in which industrial exports from developing countries were given a measure of preferential access to markets in rich countries. However, the effects of these measures on export growth in the poorest countries were disappointing.

The World Bank increasingly turned into a real development bank. It not only financed infrastructural projects but also increasingly supported agricultural, industrial and educational projects. In 1956, the International Finance Corporation (IFC) was established as a separate subsidiary, to promote private investment in developing countries. 1960 saw the founding of the International Development Association (IDA), which issued soft loans to developing countries on favourable conditions. Since 1973 the policy emphasis shifted, at least in theory, to poverty alleviation (Chenery *et al.*, 1974; Van Dam, 1989b). This change was heralded in a speech by the President of the World Bank, Robert McNamara, in October 1973. McNamara argued for policies to increase the productivity and the employment chances of the very poor. From the late 1960s till the late 1970s the share of infrastructural projects in World Bank lending decreased from 60 per cent to 33 per cent. By 1980, 50 per cent of all World Bank loans were being used to finance rural development, education, population projects, urbanisation, water supply and nutrition (Meier, 1984).

BOX 13.6 : **Elements of the New International Economic Order**

- **Commodity agreements for primary exports of developing countries**
  - (a) The creation of **buffer stocks** of important commodities. When world prices fall below critical levels, the commodities are bought up at guaranteed minimum prices. If prices go up again, the buffer stocks are sold on the market.
  - (b) The provision of **compensatory finance** in case of wildly fluctuating export revenues. If the export revenues of a country drop below given limits, the programme will compensate for the shortfalls. When revenues are high, payments are made to the compensatory fund.
  - (c) The provision of **financial resources** for the setting up of primary resource processing industries in developing countries, to reduce countries' dependence on primary exports.
  - (d) The **indexing of export prices** of developing countries to the prices of their imports, to avoid deterioration of the terms of trade.

  The overall objective of commodity agreements is to stabilise primary export prices and export revenues in the short term and to improve the terms of trade for developing countries in the long term:

- **Reducing protectionism on the part of the advanced industrial economies**
- **Preferential and non-reciprocal access to developed country markets for manufactured exports from developing countries**

  The developing countries retain the right to protect their domestic industries. The goal of these measures is to increase the share of developing countries in world manufacturing production and manufactured exports.

- **Producer cartels**

  Recognition of the right of developing countries to establish producer cartels in order to raise the prices of their primary export products. The model for such cartels was OPEC.

- **Nationalisation of foreign enterprises**

  Recognition of the right of developing countries to exploit their own natural resources such as oil and minerals. This includes the right to nationalise foreign enterprises.

- **Increased shares of developing countries in world transport**
- **Formulation of a code of conduct for multinational enterprises**

  A code of conduct should be formulated for multinational enterprises, including requirements such as the reinvestment of part of their profits, training of local employees, transfer of technology, respect for local rules and laws, cooperation with local entrepreneurs and subcontractors and domestic sourcing. The aim of the code is to increase the contributions of multinational enterprises to the domestic economy.

- **Increased financial resources for development**

  Increasing the volume of international financial resources available for development programmes of international organisations such as the World Bank and the IMF.

- **Debt relief for the poorest developing countries**
- **More voting rights for developing countries in the IMF and other IFIs**
- **Independent sources of funding for international organisations**

  Independent sources of funding for the United Nations and other international organisations would make them less dependent on financial contributions from the advanced economies. One of the proposals is to use the proceeds of the joint exploitation of the natural resources of the seabed for such funding.

- **Increasing South–South trade**

  Increasing trade flows between developing countries.

Since the 1970s, progress has been achieved in drawing up codes of conduct for multinational enterprises. Such codes specify the obligations of multinational enterprises, such as training local staff, reinvesting part of their profits, respecting domestic legislation, subcontracting, using local intermediate goods and entering into joint ventures with domestic investors. The codes also offer more certainty to foreign investors against arbitrary expropriation.

The tasks of the IMF were initially restricted to monetary stabilisation in case of balance of payments problems. Developing countries received no special attention. Later, the IMF also started focusing on the economic problems of developing countries. Separate facilities were created to assist developing countries with balance of payments problems and to compensate for shortfalls in export revenues. In the past thirty years, the bulk of IMF loans has gone to developing countries.

Among the institutional responses to the call for an NIEO, one should mention a series of agreements between the European Union and former European colonies in Africa, the Caribbean and the Pacific (the ACP countries). In the so-called Lomé agreements (Lomé I–IV), an attempt was made to provide a framework for policy dialogue between developing countries and rich European countries. Special funds were established to help stabilise export revenues from agricultural and mining exports of developing countries (STABEX and SYSMIN).[6] Exports from ACP countries were granted preferential access to European markets and the resources for financing development projects were expanded. Unfortunately, these measures have had little impact. The shares of the ACP countries on the European markets have declined, even in comparison to those of other developing countries excluded from the Lomé agreements (Fitzpatrick, 1983).

The pursuit of a NIEO reached its high point in the signing of an agreement on an integrated programme for commodities in 1980 and an agreement on the joint exploitation of the natural resources of the seabed in 1982. The integrated programme was meant to stabilise prices of primary exports at a high level through the creation of buffer stocks.

[6] To a fund for Stabilisation of Mining Exports. See section 13.3.2.

Neither this programme nor the treaty on the exploitation of the seabed has ever been implemented, due to resistance from the advanced economies. Finally, the NIEO disappeared from the international agenda, as a result of the debt crisis that broke out in 1982.

13.4.2   Criticisms of the New International Economic Order

In the late 1970s, there was a turning point in the debates on economic development. There was increasing criticism of the market-distorting impacts of government planning in developing countries and of attempts to regulate international trade in the context of the NIEO. First, there was criticism of the export-pessimist assumptions underlying the proposals. Some critics denied that there was a systematic deterioration of the terms of trade of exports from developing countries We concluded in Chapter 8 that no systematic patterns or trends can be discerned. The terms of trade vary from period to period, country to country and product to product. Thus in the past ten years the terms of trade for primary products have been improving. We may conclude that the Singer–Prebisch proposition of a systematic decline in the terms of trade of developing countries has been falsified (see Williamson, 2011).

With regard to price volatility, countries with a flexible production structure and a diversified export package are less affected by price movements than countries with inflexible production structures and dependence on a single export product (monocultures). According to Myint, export pessimists have made too much of the low income elasticity of the demand for primary products.[7] Western demand for some exotic agricultural products (e.g. mangoes, kiwi fruit, lichees) actually increases as incomes go up. Moreover, price elasticity (the relation between changes in quantities demanded of a product and changes in its price) may be more important for a developing country than aggregate income elasticity. The prices of primary exports turn out to be not more unstable than those of manufactured goods or capital goods. One should also not forget that many developing countries nowadays export manufactured products and services.

Even more important is the fact that export pessimism was used to prolong inward-looking and interventionist import substitution policies, which in retrospect have turned out to be very unsuccessful. The countries that turned outward at an early stage – many East Asian economies – performed much better than Latin American and African economies, which continued to follow inward-looking policies. The East Asian countries achieved export success without any changes in the international order.

Next, experience has shown that attempts to stabilise commodity prices above their market levels through commodity agreements or price cartels are hardly ever successful in the long run. If prices are higher than free market equilibrium prices, extra supply is elicited till the commodity fund is exhausted or prices collapse. This happened with oil. Attempts to stabilise the prices of commodities such as tin, cocoa, or coffee also failed dismally. The experiences with the Lomé agreements demonstrated that preferential access to advanced country markets does not guarantee successful export performance. Efficient low-cost industrial producers in Asian countries were able to compete on European markets, while producers in ACP countries with preferential access were not. Emphasising the right of developing countries to continue to protect their domestic industries indefinitely was seen

---

[7] A low income elasticity implies that the demand for primary products does not increase in proportion to the increase in average incomes per capita.

as prolonging the existence of non-viable industries in Latin America and Africa. Finally, the demise of the NIEO was also furthered by the increasing heterogeneity of developing countries. Attempts to legislate a comprehensive framework for the international order clashed with the diversity of interests and circumstances in developing countries (Van Dam, 1984). The bloc of developing countries did not speak with one voice. The shock of the debt crisis of 1982 marked the end the NIEO and the start of a second post-war period of liberalisation, privatisation and market orientation.

13.5   Debt and how to deal with it

One of the important dimensions of the international economic order consists of financial flows. The shock of the 1982 debt crisis drew renewed attention to the role of financial inflows in economic development and the dangers of excessive indebtedness. This section discusses debt, financial flows and debt reduction strategies from 1982 until the present. We shall see that the debt crisis which erupted in 1982 had huge negative consequences for economic development, in particular in Latin America in the 'lost decade' of the 1980s. However, over time indebtedness in the developing world has declined, in part due to successful efforts at debt reduction for the least developed economies. At present, excessive indebtedness is primarily a problem for the advanced economies suffering from the after-math of the 2008 financial crisis.

13.5.1   The 1982 debt crisis

In 1982, Mexico suspended the payment of its debt service due to insufficient foreign exchange. Other developing countries and countries in Eastern Europe also turned out to be unable to keep up payments on debt. Private banks responded by a sudden reduction in the supply of new credit to developing countries. Growth rates collapsed and the debt crisis was a fact (Hermes, 1992). There were two aspects to this crisis: a threat to the stability of the global financial system, and a threat to the economic development of poor countries. After 1982, all attention was focused on coping with the consequences of the debt crisis. The urgency of the crisis effectively ended the faltering debate on the new international economic order. The 1982 debt crisis acted as a major system shock that resulted in important changes in the nature of the international economic order.

13.5.2   Is there anything wrong with debt?

For most people, debt has negative connotations. In some stages of economic development, however, it is quite normal to incur debts. The accumulation of a stock of capital goods and the building up of industry and infrastructure in developing countries is facilitated by a substantial inflow of capital from abroad. This inflow may take the form of FDI, develop-ment aid, loans from governments, international financial institutions or private banks or remittances. Unlike FDI, loans result in increasing foreign indebtedness. As long as the borrowed funds are invested economically, debt causes few problems. Productive invest-ment of loans implies that the borrowed resources contribute more to the growth of national income than they cost in terms of interest payments. Interest payments can be financed from the increase in national income. According to Lewis (1978b), the absolute volume of debt is of no significance. As long as loans are invested economically, the more debt the better.

Lewis distinguishes four stages of the *debt cycle* (see also Hermes, 1992: 29; World Bank-WDR, 1985). During the first stage new borrowing exceeds debt service payments, so that interest payments, principal repayments and additional investment can all be financed from new loans.[8] The country imports more goods and services than it exports. During the second stage new borrowing exceeds repayments of outstanding loans, but it is less than total debt service. The volume of foreign debt is still increasing. In the third stage there is a surplus on the current account of the balance of payments and the volume of foreign debt starts to decrease. In the final stage of the debt cycle a country becomes a net creditor.

Debts only become a problem when loans are used unproductively (e.g. for consumptive purposes, for the financing of wasteful government bureaucracies, or for investments with dubious returns). Debts become even more of a problem when they only serve to finance debt service payments on previous debts. Then the volume of debt continues to increase, while no new financial resources become available for investment in future production. When all earnings from additional productive efforts are swallowed up by debt service payments, this creates a major disincentive for further economic development and can result in economic collapse.

During most of the post-war period many developing countries were at the first stage of the debt cycle. Table 3.6 and 13.3 in this book (pp. 119 and 571) point to a steady influx of capital to developing countries and sustained deficits on their trade balance of goods and services in particular until 1982. Until 1977, the relationship between foreign finance and development was a positive one. Around 1977, this situation changed for many Latin American and African countries. Economic growth faltered and a perverse situation arose. Developing countries had to go ever deeper into debt to finance debt service payments on outstanding debt, while their export revenues were shrinking and their economies were stagnating. They suffered from a situation of *debt overhang*.

13.5.3   What caused the 1982 debt crisis?

The debt crisis was the result of a complex of internal and external causes (Buiter and Srinivasan, 1987; Griffin, 1988; Hermes, 1992; Lensink, 1993a, Chapter 2; Maddison, 1985; Wood, 1985). After 1973, the growth of the world economy and world trade slowed down. Increased oil prices fuelled inflation. The Western countries responded to inflation by pursuing restrictive fiscal and monetary policies, at the expense of growth and employment. Developing countries were faced with declining export revenues, deteriorating terms of trade for their export products and, except for the oil-exporting countries, rising energy bills.

Nevertheless many developing countries, in particular in Latin America, responded differently to the slowdown than the Western countries. In anticipation of a recovery of world economic growth, they tried to stimulate their economies through expansionary Keynesian fiscal and monetary policies. Deficits on the current account of the balance of payments were increasingly financed by short-term loans from the private banking sector. Compared to the 1950s and 1960s, the share of FDI – which does not increase foreign indebtedness – in the capital flows to developing countries declined strongly. Initially this

---

[8] Debt service is the sum of repayments of principal and interest payments, in a given period.

was compensated for by loans from official financial institutions and governments (Lensink, 1993a). But the volume of finance supplied from these public sources fell far short of financial requirements. Private borrowing increased. By borrowing from private banks, developing countries were able to evade the increasingly strict conditions imposed by the World Bank and the IMF (Wood, 1985).

Private banks were eager to provide loans to developing countries. They had accumulated huge amounts of petrodollars, which were being 'recycled' into the banking system by the oil-exporting countries. Private banks even pursued aggressive marketing strategies to expand their credit to developing countries. Due to high inflation, real interest rates were low, sometimes even negative. The loans usually consisted of short-term credits with variable interest rates.

Until 1979, expansionary macro-economic policies in Latin America appeared to be quite successful. Latin American countries managed to keep up the momentum of economic growth, though at the price of high inflation. But the anticipated recovery of the world economy failed to materialise, especially in 1979 when oil prices again quadrupled and a new and even more serious depression followed (Maddison, 1985). Under the influence of the restrictive monetary policies of the Reagan administration, real interest rates suddenly soared. Since many loans were short term and interest rates variable, the debt service suddenly went up. More and more loans had to be contracted, just to meet debt service obligations.

As debt problems cumulated, the Latin American economic policies of the 1970s turned out to be less successful than initially assumed. There had been economic mismanagement on a vast scale. Many of the funds borrowed had been squandered on inefficient subsidies or non-profitable government projects.[9] In addition, financial resources were used to maintain systems of political patronage, clientelism and corruption. Due to huge government deficits and loose monetary policies, inflation increased sharply. High inflation disrupted domestic markets, discouraged the inflow of new FDI and stimulated capital flight. Unlike Southeast Asia, where outward-oriented policies had long been pursued, the protection of inefficient domestic industries in Latin America had been continued for far too long. Domestic economic structures had become rigid and attempts to penetrate export markets met with little success. Insufficient revenues from exports made it inevitable to finance debt service with new loans.

In the debates on the debt crisis, Latin American countries played a central role. It was their inability to meet their debt service payments that triggered the debt crisis. In Africa, private lending was of little importance. For foreign finance, African countries depended primarily on loans from foreign governments and international institutions. In absolute terms, the volume of debt was much smaller than in Latin American countries. Nevertheless, economic problems on the African continent had been mounting since 1975. A combination of poor economic policies – with respect to agriculture as well as industry and international trade – unfavourable natural circumstances and an unfriendly international economic climate resulted in a protracted period of economic stagnation and mounting debt.

---

[9] Contrary to what is generally assumed, a considerable part of the loans was used to keep up investment (Hermes, 1992). However, this says nothing about the efficiency of investments.

13.5.4 Trends in debt and financial flows in developing countries, 1982–2012

Debt indicators

Table 13.2 presents data on trends in debt burdens in twenty-five countries that have been classified as indebted in one or more years between 1982 and 2012. These include fourteen countries which were heavily indebted in 1982 (see note a), sixteen countries that were classified as 'severely indebted' in 2001 (see note b) in the World Bank publication *Global Development Finance: Striving for Stability in Development Finance* (2003a) and five countries that were classified as HIPCs after 1996 (see note c). The severely indebted countries (SICs) of 2001 were countries where the present value of total debt service was over 80 per cent of GNP and/or over 220 per cent of the value of exports.[10] *Debt service* comprises annual repayments of long-term and short-term debt (including IMF credit), interest on long-term debt, charges for IMF credit and interest on short-term debt.

Debt is a persistent problem. Of the sixteen countries severely indebted in 2001, eight countries were already classified as 'heavily indebted countries' (HICs) in 1982.[11] But, there are also dramatic changes in levels of indebtedness. In 1982, eight countries in the table – Argentina, Brazil, Ecuador, Nicaragua, Peru, Angola, Côte d'Ivoire and Sudan – were not yet classified as heavily indebted. In these countries the debt situation deteriorated between 1982 and 2001. But there are also seven countries that were considered heavily indebted in 1982 which were no longer classified as severely indebted in 2001. For almost all countries in the table, the debt situation substantially improved between 2001 and 2012.

Table 13.2 illustrates the important point that one need not worry about the volume of foreign debt as such. One should always consider debt in relation to other key variables such as national income or exports. Thus, South Korea and Brazil had foreign debt stocks of, respectively, 415 and 440 billion dollars in 2012. Nevertheless, they are no longer regarded as severely indebted. In dynamic economies such as South Korea, *debt service* does not cause great problems. Debts are only problematic when debt service obligations become an impediment to resumption of economic growth and development. In a situation of *debt overhang* there is little incentive to work at improving the economic situation, as all the fruits of growth accrue to foreign financial institutions.

The case of Mexico is also interesting. Mexico triggered the debt crisis in 1982. By 2001, it had accumulated a huge foreign debt of 158 billion dollars. Nevertheless, it was no longer listed as a severely indebted country, according to World Bank criteria. By 2012 its debt to GNI ratio had declined to 26.2 per cent and its debt service ratio to 18.3 per cent.

---

[10] The present value of debt service is the sum of all debt service due during the lifetime of a loan, discounted to current dollar values using the interest rates of the loans. Excluding Yugoslavia and Moldova, there were forty-five SICs in 2001. Table 13.2 includes the sixteen SICs with the largest absolute volume of debt in 2001. These countries accounted for 88 per cent of the total debt of the 45 SICs and 97 per cent of their total debt service. The data in the table are annual data, rather than discounted present values.

[11] The definitions for 1982 and 2001 are unfortunately not identical. The 'heavily indebted countries' (HICs) of 1982 also include countries classified as 'moderately indebted countries' (MICs) in 2001. In 1982, four criteria of indebtedness were used. The 1982 criteria refer to the value of debt service in a given year, rather than to the discounted value of debt service, as in 2001. From 1996 a new category of Heavily Indebted Poor Countries (HIPCs) was introduced. These were countries with a 1993 GNP per capita of less than $696 whose 1993 present value of debt to exports was higher than 200 per cent or whose present value of debt to GNP was higher than 80 per cent.

Table 13.2: Selected developing countries with heavy debt burdens, 1982–2012

	Total external debt (million current US$)				Total external debt (million current US$)				Debt as % of GNI				Debt service as % of exports			
	1982	1990	2001	2012	1982	1990	2001	2012	1982	1990	2001	2012	1982	1990	2001	2012
Indonesia[b]	25,133	69,872	135,704	254,899	3,856	9,946	15,530	36,605	27.9	64.0	97.2	29.9	16.1	33.3	23.6	17.2
Jordan[b]	2,752	8,333	7,480	18,632	294	628	669	987	55.9	219.0	84.6	60.7	15.5	20.4	10.7	7.3
Lebanon[b]	721	1,779	12,450	28,950	117	99	1,457	4,219		51.4	70.5	68.4		3.3	50.9	34.3
Pakistan[b]	11,704	20,663	32,020	61,867	877	1,902	2,958	4,743	38.5	52.9	55.4	26.1	28.7	23.0	25.8	17.1
South Korea[a]	37,330	34,968	110,109	415,060	6,348	8,274	26,040		50.6	13.8	26.1	36.5	25.1	10.8	13.8	
Syria[b]	6,184	17,259	21,305	4,736	500	1,189	266	765	36.9	144.4	113.5	6.7	21.6	21.8	3.4	2.3
Argentina[a,b]	43,634	62,233	136,709	121,013	4,876	6,158	24,254	12,969	55.1	46.0	52.5	26.0	63.6	37.0	66.3	13.8
Brazil[a,b]	93,932	119,964	226,362	440,478	19,215	8,172	54,322	45,483	35.2	26.5	46.9	19.9	89.6	22.2	75.4	16.1
Ecuador[a,b]	7,705	12,107	13,910	16,931	2,144	1,084	1,550	2,599	60.1	127.8	85.8	20.5	73.5	321.7	21.4	9.9
Mexico[a]	86,081	104,442	158,290	354,897	15,684	11,313	48,300	70,684	46.9	41.1	26.2	30.6	52.2	20.7	26.1	18.3
Nicaragua[a,b]	2,936	10,745	6,391	8,858	201	16	337	619	127.9	1087.6	302.9	86.7	51.4	4.0	26.2	13.4
Peru[a,b,c]	10,709	20,064	27,512	54,148	2,036	476	2,190	6,413	45.0	78.7	52.1	28.3	49.7	10.8	22.0	12.3
Uruguay[b]	2,647	4,415	9,706	14,762	513	987	1,489		29.6	49.3	52.9	30.5	39.2	40.8	36.3	
Angola[a,b]	447	8,594	9,600	22,171	11	326	1,865	4,243	7.6	104.6	122.1	21.6	0.5	8.1	26.5	6.2
Congo, Dem. Rep.[b,c]	5,078	10,259	11,392	5,651	222	348	18	279	38.6	119.6	238.8	35.2	13.4	13.5	1.7	2.9
Côte d'Ivoire[a,b,c,d]	8,961	17,251	11,582	9,871	1,540	1,262	618	1,343	127.5	187.3	118.4	41.7	55.9	35.4	13.5	9.6
Egypt[a]	27,332	33,016	29,234	40,000	1,714	3,073	1,932	3,233	114.8	78.6	29.4	15.6	24.8	22.5	8.9	7.1
Eritrea[d]			433	994			7	95			57.7	32.4			8.5	5.9
Nigeria[b]	11,972	33,439	31,119	10,077	2,087	3,336	2,562	303	24.6	130.7	81.4	4.2	25.7	22.6	12.0	0.2
Morocco[a]	12,090	24,458	16,962	33,816	1,721	1,793	2,628	3,681	79.9	98.5	51.0	36.3	58.0	21.5	17.8	10.6
Sudan[a,b,c]	7,169	14,762	15,348	21,840	296	50	56	402	81.0	119.2	137.5	38.8	32.2	8.7	2.3	10.9
Tanzania[a,c]	6,201	6,456	6,676	11,581	152	179	152	168	51.0	158.5	71.9	41.4	29.7	32.9	10.3	2.0

Zimbabwe[d]	1,872	3,279	3,605	7,713	208	471	168	726	22.5	38.5	55.9	81.9	14.4	23.4	7.1	16.7
Portugal[a]	13,589		498,430	2,443					61.0			32.9	29.0			
Romania[a]	10,003	1,140	131,889	2,910	18	2,607	22,133			3.0	30.4	21.5	12.6	0.3	18.8	33.6
40 HIPC countries	145,427	160,399			5,143	8,088			100.3	32.9					12.7	7.7
Developing countries	809,293	1,421,578	2,332,106	4,829,608	121,730	155,360	378,675	660,253	26.9	35.2	38.9	21.5	18.9	18.7	19.2	9.8

Notes:

[a] Classified as heavily indebted in 1982.
[b] Classified as severely indebted in 2001.
[c] Classified as HIPC from 1996 onwards.
[d] Classified as at risk in 2012.

Sources:

1982: World Bank, *World Development Indicators*, CD-ROM, 2002.
1990–2001: World Bank (2003a, 2003b).
2012: World Bank, *World Development Indicators*, downloaded February 2014.
1982: GNI and exports Angola calculated from 1985 figure, using growth rate from UNCTAD *Handbook of Statistics*, 2002.
1982: Debt–GNI ratio Tanzania and Portugal and Portugal debt as % of exports from World Bank, *World Debt Tables*, 1992–3.

In the last eight columns of Table 13.2, foreign debt is expressed as a percentage of Gross National Income, and annual debt service as a proportion of export earnings. The figures illustrate that debt servicing may absorb a considerable proportion of export earnings in developing countries. This was especially true for 1982. For Latin American countries debt service amounted to between 40 and 90 per cent of export earnings.

In terms of the debt service to exports ratio, Brazil topped the list in 2001 with 75 per cent, followed by Argentina (66 per cent) and Lebanon (51 per cent). Brazil's debt situation had worsened dramatically since 1990, when it seemed well on its way towards a more sustainable debt burden. The same held for Argentina, where the debt service–export ratio had almost doubled since 1990, in spite of Argentina's faithful adherence to IMF policy advice. The Argentine economy collapsed in 2001 and has temporarily defaulted on its debt obligations. But since then it has recovered from a very deep crisis.

The somewhat surprising conclusion to be derived from Table 13.2 is that by 2012 debt is no longer a serious problem for developing countries. Debt–GNI ratios for developing countries are at a modest average of 21.5 per cent. Only a few countries have ratios of higher than fifty per cent. The highest debt ratios are found in Jordan, Lebanon, Nicaragua and Zimbabwe. Debt–GNI ratios have declined substantially since 2001. A similar story emerges for debt service as a percentage of exports. For developing countries as a whole this stands at 9.8 per cent, down from 19.2 per cent in 2001. For forty heavily indebted countries the ratio declined from 12.7 per cent in 2001 to 7.7 per cent in 2012. This testifies to the success of debt reduction efforts and policies since 1996. Even countries with high debt–GNI ratios in 2012 have rather low debt service ratios, for instance countries such as Jordan, Lebanon, Nicaragua, Tanzania and Zimbabwe. Their low debt service export ratios either reflect some form of debt default or agreements with international financial institutions, deferring debt service payments to some future date. Another factor of importance is the restructuring of debt, with an increasing share of official loans with low interest rates. Finally, macro-economic policies have generally been more prudent since 1982.

Interestingly in terms of debt the world has been stood on its head. Debt is no longer a major problem for the developing world, but it has skyrocketed in the advanced economies due to bailouts of the banking system since 2008. In 2012 the UK had a debt–GDP ratio of 388 per cent, followed by France with more than 200 per cent and the USA with around 100 per cent.[12] On average the G-7 countries had a debt–GDP ratio of 127 per cent (World Bank, 2014).

Net financial flows, 1970–2012

For most of the post-war period, there was a net inflow of financial resources into developing countries, which increased the resources potentially available for investment in growth and development. However, in the mid 1980s a perverse situation arose in which there were net capital outflows from developing countries to rich countries. This switch is illustrated in Table 13.3. Table 13.3 presents an overview of aggregate financial flows to developing countries between 1970 and 2012.

---

[12] The figures are somewhat misleading because they also include private sector debt in countries with large financial service sectors. But even levels of public debt are very high.

Table 13.3: Debts, foreign investment and financial flows in developing countries, 1970–2012 ($ billion)[a]

	1970	1975	1980	1982	1987	1990	1996	1997	1999	1998	1999	2002	2005	2012
Long-term debts														
Total long-term debts	61	141	433	498	1,128	1,155	1,668	1,723	1,947	1,999	1,968	1,943	1,794	3,406
New loans	13	40	104	106	120	122	246	279	287	262	257	218	336	778
of which, private[b]	8	10	76	17	71	71	110	133	136	130	118	105	199	508
Total debt service	8	19	72	84	142	132	239	268	272	322	340	307	340	592
Repayments[c]	6	12	41	43	84	80	161	185	180	224	238	220	264	456
of which, private[b]	4	10	34	17		55	108	134	136	180	189	167	140	355
Interest payments	2	7	31	41	58	53	78	83	92	97	102	87	76	136
Net capital flows[d]	7	28	63	64	36	43	85	94	107	38	19	-1	72	322
Net transfers on debt[e]	4	21	32	22	-21	-10	7	11	15	-60	-83	-88	-4	186
Net inflows of FDI	2	5	5	11	15	24	128	169	174	179	161	143	293	612
Net portfolio investment	0	0	0	0	1	5	34	27	7	15	26	9	66	98
Profit remittances on FDI	1	3	19	15	13	18	47	55	57	60	75	66	177	486
Net transfers on FDI[f]	2	2	-14	-3	3	11	114	141	124	134	112	86	182	223
Grants[g]	2	7	13	11	17	28	28	27	28	29	30	33	71	100
Aggregate net transfers[h]	8	30	31	30	-2	29	149	178	168	104	59	31	249	510
Long- and short-term debts														
Total long- and short-term debt stocks[c]	70	165	580	669	1,369	1,422	2,126	2,189	2,395	2,427	2,363	2,384	2,338	4,830
Net flows on long- and short-term debt	6	33	96	78	44	58	114	102	57	14	-1	7	121	412
Net transfers on long- and short-term debt		26	50	20	-29	-10	15	-3	-52	-103	-124	-96	25	224
Aggregate net transfers, incl. short term	8	35	49	27	-9	29	157	164	100	61	18	24	278	548

Notes:

[a] This table contains data for 138 developing countries reporting to the World Bank from 1970 to 2002. The data for 1975, 1982, 2005 and 2012 refer to 124 developing countries reporting to the World Bank in 2012.

[b] Including publicly guaranteed loans from private creditors. For 2005–12, publicly guaranteed loans no longer classified as private loans.

[c] Including IMF credit, and short-term debt.

[d] Balance of new loans disbursed and principal repayments, also referred to as net flows on debt (discrepancies due to rounding errors).

[e] Net transfers on debt equal net capital flows minus interest payments (discrepancies due to rounding errors).

[f] Net transfers on FDI equal net inflows of FDI plus net portfolio investment minus profit remittances. This concept is based on own calculations.

[g] Grants equal the sum of grants, IDA grants and debt forgiveness grants. They exclude the value of technical cooperation grants.

[h] Aggregate net transfers equal net transfers on debt plus net transfers on FDI plus grants.

Sources:

1970, 1980, 1990–2002: World Bank, *Global Development Finance, 2003*; 1987: *World Debt Tables 1994–95, 1995*.

1975, 1982, 2005–12: World Bank, *International Debt Statistics*, http://databank.worldbank.org/data/views/variables/selection/selectvariables.aspx?source=international-debt-statistics#, downloaded March 2014.

Debts are subdivided into *long-term debts* with a maturity of more than one year and *short-term debts* with a maturity of less than one year. Table 13.3 provides comprehensive data, including short-term debts and IMF credits and profit remittances on FDI. The stock of total debt including short-term debt is much higher than that of long-term debt only, but the general trends for the two indicators are comparable. Table 13.3 also distinguishes between net capital flows on debt and net transfers on debt. *Net capital flows* (or net flows on debt) refer solely to the balance of new loans disbursed and principal repayments of old loans. Interest payments are left out of consideration. *Net transfers on debt* equal net capital flows minus interest payments on existing loans. The table also contains data on FDI, portfolio investment, grants and profit remittances out of foreign investment. Net transfers on FDI equal the sum of net FDI and net portfolio investment minus profit remittances on FDI. In spite of large profit remittances, net transfers on FDI are positive in all but one year – 1980 – between 1970 and 2012. Thus the fears that foreign investment may result in a net outflow of resources seem to be unfounded. The net balance of all flows is found in the lines referring to *aggregate net transfers*. Aggregate net transfers refer to the sum of net transfers on debt, net transfers on FDI and grants. Aggregate transfers can be calculated excluding or including short-term debt. The concept including short-term debt provides the best indication of net financial flows into or out of developing countries.

The total volume of long-term debts of the developing countries reporting to the World Bank increased from 61 billion dollars in 1970 to 561 billion dollars in 1982. By 2012 total long-term debt had increased further to 3.4 trillion dollars. Including short-term debts, the 2012 debt stock amounted to 4.8 trillion dollars. Of course, the nominal volume of debt also depends on the exchange rate. If the value of the dollar drops, as in 1985–7, 1990, 1995, or 2003, the nominal dollar value of debt contracted in other foreign currencies than the dollar will go up. If the currency of a country suddenly depreciates against the dollar, as in the Asian crisis, the value of a country's debt in national currency can soar, greatly increasing the burden of debt.

It is interesting to note the differences between net capital flows and net transfers on debt. In all but two years between 1970 and 2012, net capital flows were positive, while net transfers on debt were negative in twelve years out of forty-two. Thus, net capital flows remained positive during the entire period 1970–2012. The volume of new loans exceeded the sum of repayment of earlier loans and the outflow of capital to other countries. The net long-term capital inflow decreased from 68 billion dollars in 1982 to 36 billion dollars in 1987. After that it picked up again, increasing in nominal terms to 107 billion dollars by 1998. Hermes (1992) has calculated that, expressed in constant 1988 dollars, the real value of capital inflows between 1981 and 1989 halved. After 1998, net capital flows dried up in the wake of the Asian crisis, turning negative in 2001 and 2002. After 2002, net inflows rapidly resumed, reaching 322 billion dollars in 2012 (in real terms, ten times as high as in 1970).

The picture is different for net transfers on debt, which include the interest payments on debt. Net transfers on long-term debt turned negative after 1984. Instead of a net flow of resources from rich to poor countries, characteristic of the post-war economic order until the debt crisis of 1982, there was an outflow of resources from poor to rich countries in the second half of the 1980s. This net outflow reached its peak in 1988. Between 1992 and 1998 the net transfers on long-term debt became positive again. After the Asian crisis of 1997, there was once again a dramatic downturn. Suddenly, net transfers on debt took on vast negative proportions. If we include short-term debt flows, the picture becomes even more negative. Net transfers on total debt were continuously negative in all years between 1985 and 2004.

Increasing importance of FDI and grants

The picture of massive outflow of financial resources between 1987 and 2002 based on statistics of loans and interest payments is somewhat misleading. One of the striking trends emerging from Table 13.3 is the increasing importance of FDI. One of the advantages of FDI is that it is a non-debt-creating financial inflow.[13] Together with increases in grants, the increase in net transfers on FDI (net inflows of FDI plus net portfolio investment minus profit remittances) more than compensated for the decline in net capital flows. Long-term aggregate net transfers remained positive in all years between 1970 and 2012, with the exception of two years, 1987 and 1988. Even including volatile short-term debt, net aggregate transfers were positive in all years except the post-debt crisis period 1983–8. An example of such years with net outflows in Table 13.3 is 1987.

The havoc wrought by the Asian crisis of 1997 is clearly visible in the negative net transfers on total long-term and short-term debt from 1975 to 2002, but even in these years the net balance of aggregate transfers remains positive.

After 2005, all inflows start increasing rapidly. Our earlier conclusion in section 13.1.1 that the post-war economic order as a whole is characterised by important net inflows of financial resources to developing countries is borne out by the data in Table 13.3. But the table also serves to illustrate the amplitude and severity of the financial crises affecting developing countries.

Not all outflows in the table have negative connotations. Favourable economic developments in South Korea have created a basis for repayment of past debts and a lowering of debt–GDP ratios. Emerging economies such as China have started to provide loans to developing countries in Sub-Saharan Africa (Broich and Szirmai, 2014).

13.5.5   How to deal with debt?

One of the immediate consequences of the debt crisis of 1982 was a sudden drop in the flow of private loans to developing countries. When new loans were forthcoming, they served mainly to finance existing debt service. Finance for new investments or imports of indispensable intermediate inputs was scarce. Thus the debt crisis contributed to the stagnation of economic growth in many African and Latin American developing countries. The debt crisis also threatened the stability of the international banking system and consequently the entire international financial system. Many private banks, especially in the USA, had pursued reckless credit policies. Their existence was jeopardised when countries in Latin America and Eastern Europe suspended debt service payments following the Mexican example.

During the first years after 1982, therefore, international efforts were aimed mainly at preventing the imminent collapse of the financial system. Later, attention shifted to the consequences of the debt crisis for developing countries. The IMF played a prominent role

---

[13] From a nationalist perspective, one of the potential disadvantages is the increasing control of the domestic economy by foreign capital.

in the prevention of an international financial crisis. It imposed rigorous changes in domestic economic policy as conditions for balance of payments support, new loans and agreements on debt rescheduling. Since private capital flows had dried up, developing countries could no longer get around the 'conditionality' of official financial institutions. The World Bank had formerly operated independently of the IMF and had focused on long-term investment projects. Now it also made its loans conditional on acceptance of IMF policy recommendations. These recommendations are generally referred to as *structural adjustment policies*. Their short-term aim is to improve the balance of payments and reduce government deficits (*stabilisation*). The long-term objective is to achieve a more dynamic and flexible economic structure (*structural adjustment*).

In the short term, the goal was to cut back on developing country imports in order to reduce deficits in the balance of payments. This would decrease the need for external finance. Between 1982 and 1985 these policies have been fairly successful (Hermes, 1992). Deficits in the balance of payments were indeed reduced, not so much by growth of exports but by a decline in imports. Private banks that had overexposed themselves during the 1970s increased their reserves for non-repayable debts. By 1985, it was clear that a collapse of the international financial system had been averted. Between 1985 and 1990, debt service as a percentage of export revenues also started to go down (see Table 13.2).

The consequences of stabilisation policies were less positive for developing countries. The restrictions on imports of semi-finished goods and capital goods led to a slowdown in industrial production. In some Latin American countries and most countries in Sub-Saharan Africa per capita incomes fell sharply. Economic stagnation triggered a debate on how to mitigate or avoid the negative consequences of the debt crisis for developing countries through debt relief, which continues to this day.

In this debate, two conflicting points of view can be distinguished – that of debt forgiveness and that of moral hazard (e.g. Buiter and Srinivasan, 1987; Griffin, 1988; Neumayer, 2002; Raffer and Singer, 2001; Sanford, 2002; Stiglitz, 2002; Wood, 1985).

Debt relief versus moral hazard

Authors such as Griffin, Singer and Stiglitz argued that the debt crisis and economic stagnation were very much the result of external factors such as slower growth of the world economy, deteriorating terms of trade, protectionism by advanced countries and irresponsible policies of private banks and international institutions. Since the enormous debt service hinders all attempts to revive economic growth, debt relief or debt forgiveness is essential. Debt overhang reduces all incentives for economic development. Therefore debt relief should have the highest priority.

Buiter and Srinivasan (1987) have criticised this point of view. They represent the moral hazard point of view, which argues that debt forgiveness rewards bad economic policies and profligate behaviour (for an overview of the arguments see Neumayer, 2002). According to Buiter and Srinivasan, the main causes of economic stagnation and rising debt in Latin America were bad economic management and profligate economic policies. These countries had high budget deficits and pursued inefficient protectionist policies, which resulted in inflexible economic structures. Major debtors such as Brazil, Argentina and Mexico were much richer than the poor Asian countries, which pursued more prudent and effective macro-economic policies. Their financial problems were caused in part by capital flight. Debt relief would mean rewarding economic mismanagement and punishing countries that pursued more effective policies and paid their debts. In Latin American countries, structural adjustment policies were needed to restore the confidence of international financial institutions. Financial inflows would then resume and capital flight would be reversed.

Buiter and Srinivasan agreed that financial aid flows to very poor African countries should be increased. But they regarded debt restructuring in Latin America as a disguised subsidy to the American banking system. Moral hazard does not only refer to the policies of developing countries, but also to behaviour of private financial institutions. Interestingly a similar argument was used by critics of the international financial institutions (e.g. Stiglitz, 2000, 2002). The critics argued that debt problems had been in part caused by actions of irresponsible financial institutions in the rich countries, which should bear part of the costs of their own risky behaviour. Stiglitz argued with considerable force that bankruptcy laws in developing countries should be tightened. Inefficient firms and banks should be allowed to go bankrupt, so their assets could be bought up and recapitalised by new owners who could restart operations. International banks that had provided loans to inefficient or corrupt organisations in the conviction that they would be bailed out in any event by the international financial institutions should be forced to pay the price for their own decisions. Even the former vice-president of the IMF, Stanley Fischer, conceded this point. He argued that if private banks are in part responsible for financial crises, they should contribute to a recovery by providing new sources of finance (Citrin and Fischer, 2000).

Both parties in the debate acknowledge that resumption of economic growth in the poorest developing countries required renewed net transfers of resources. However, one point of view stressed outright cancellation or reduction of debts; the other emphasised the implementation of programmes of structural adjustment and improvements in domestic policies as a condition for new loans or the restructuring of earlier ones. As time passed, the notion of debt relief for the poorest developing countries gained ground. Private institutions have increasingly come to participate in these debt relief programmes, in line with the arguments concerning responsibility outlined above.

Grants versus loans

One of the elements in the debate about debt reduction is whether loans should be replaced by grants, as advocated by the Meltzer report (Meltzer, 2000). Grants provide development finance, without increasing the debt burdens of poor countries. Opponents of these proposals, however, have argued that the conversion of loans to grants involves a secret agenda for reduction of the total volume of aid (Sanford, 2002). If the total volume of aid remains unchanged, the shift to grants implies a reduction in the size of actual financial flows. They also argue that grants increase the danger of moral hazard. Finally, the provision of grants increasingly depends on evaluations of past performance, rather than on agreements about future policies. This increases the power and leverage of the international financial institutions. In spite of these objections, it seems that the role of grants has increased over time. Between 2005 and 2012, the average annual value of grants to developing countries amounted to 104 billion dollars per year (World Bank-WDI, 2014).

Debt relief

Three plans have been of major importance in the international responses to debt and the debt crisis:

1. The Baker Plan in 1985 (*A Programme for Sustained Growth*)
2. The Brady Plan for voluntary debt reduction in 1989
3. The Heavily Indebted Poor Countries Initiative of 1996 (the HIPC initiative)

The Baker Plan

This plan was put forward by the American Secretary of the Treasury, James Baker. It argued that revival of economic growth would only be possible if the net inflow of financial resources to developing countries resumed. The plan involved cooperation between the IMF, the World Bank and private banking institutions. Private institutions were encouraged to grant new loans. A precondition for the expansion of credit was the pursuit of adjustment policies. The aim was resumption of net capital inflows. At this stage, debt reduction was not yet on the cards. The Baker Plan has only been moderately successful. Most of the funds went to just three large countries: Brazil, Mexico and Argentina, and the renewed net inflow of capital was still modest.

As time went by, it was realised that direct debt reduction should also be considered. In the poor African countries the debt burden in the 1980s was so heavy that the problems could not be solved without outside help. A beginning was made with debt relief and cancellation of part of the debt stock. As official financial institutions had supplied almost all loans, policy in this area was not dependent on the cooperation of the private banking system. Similar policies were proposed with respect to severely indebted Eastern European countries such as Poland and Bulgaria. Further, private banks realised they were better off with repayment of a portion of outstanding debts than default on total debt. They started participating in plans and measures for voluntary debt reduction.

The Brady Plan

The Brady Plan of 1989 focused on voluntary debt reduction in a country-by-country approach. The IMF and the World Bank reserved financial resources for this purpose. Private banks were persuaded to write down the value of risky outstanding loans. The main argument for debt reduction was the so-called *debt overhang*. If a country has an excessive foreign debt, all benefits of domestic policy reforms accrue to foreign creditors. This undermines the political will to implement painful reform measures. Debt reduction will increase the capability to meet at least part of future debt service obligations. Another advantage is that more financial means are available for investment. The creditors themselves benefit more from partial repayment of debt in the future than from no repayment at all. Several techniques for the reduction of debt have been developed. They include buying back outstanding debts at reduced prices, selling debt on the second-hand market for debts, debt for equity swaps in which loans are exchanged for equity shares, cancelling debt in exchange for environmental protection (debt for nature swaps) and replacing short-term debt by long-term debt with lower interest rates. The willingness to implement structural adjustment packages negotiated with the IMF remained a precondition for all types of debt reduction deals.

Between 1985 and 1990, debt reduction totalled 25 billion dollars. In relation to the total volume of debt, this was merely a drop in the ocean – 2.4 per cent of the average long-term debt stock. Nevertheless, where economic growth resumed, debt service became less of a problem, in spite the high volume of debt. In the second half of the 1980s, capital flows to many developing countries resumed, as discussed above. By the early 1990s, the net total resources flows had turned positive again even in the case of Africa (see also Lensink, 1995).

The Heavily Indebted Poor Countries Initiative of 1996 (HIPC initiative)

During the second half of the 1990s, the debt situation of developing countries worsened again, and new initiatives were taken to reduce the debt burdens of the poorest developing countries, in addition to existing mechanisms for debt rescheduling and debt reduction. In 1996, the IMF and the World Bank adopted the Debt Relief under the Heavily Indebted Poor Countries (HIPC) Initiative (Neumayer, 2002). The main argument was that even with sound economic policies and the full use of all existing mechanisms for debt rescheduling, debt reduction and concessional finance, poor countries would not be able to reach sustainable levels of debt within a reasonable time period (Boote and Thugge, 1997). Later, the HIPC mechanism was supplemented by the Multilateral Debt Relief Initiative (MDRI) under which international financial institutions provided debt relief irrespective of contributions by other debtors.

Countries eligible for the HIPC initiative were the severely indebted countries with the lowest incomes per capita. The conditions for eligibility for debt relief included an unsustainable debt burden and a strong record of policy reform under IMF/World Bank-supported structural adjustment programmes. An interesting new condition for debt relief was the drafting of a poverty reduction strategy paper (PRSP): the resources that were freed through the reduction of debt service obligations should primarily be devoted to health, education, social services and poverty reduction. Some forty countries were potentially eligible, the great majority of them in Africa. The total cost of the initiative is estimated at US$ 74.3 billion in end-2012 present value terms (IMF, 2013).[14] Once the conditions have been met, debt is actually cancelled.

The initiative distinguished between an initial three-year first stage during which debts were rescheduled. If countries fulfilled the policy conditions during these three years, a second three-year stage of support began in which negative flows on debt were reduced. If the country met the policy conditions of the second stage, a completion point was reached after which the total stock of debt was reduced. Up to 80 per cent of the present value of the debt stock could be cancelled, depending on the country's circumstances. Debt sustainability was considered to be reached when a country was able to meet its current and future debt service obligations in full, without recourse to further rescheduling. A characteristic element of the HIPC programme was the shift from providing finance on the basis of agreements about future policies to the providing of finance on the basis of positive evaluations of past policies and achievements. At each stage, past performance was assessed before reaching a decision on debt reduction in the next stage. Thus, if the evaluation of past policies was positive at the completion point, debt relief was provided unconditionally. If the evaluation was not positive, debt relief would not be provided, at least in theory.

By September 2003, some twenty-seven countries had received some form of HIPC relief, twenty-three of them in Africa. Seven countries had reached their completion points, including Bolivia, Burkina Faso, Mali, Mauritania, Mozambique and Uganda. By end 2010,

---

[14] See also IMF, *Factsheet – Debt Relief under the Heavily Indebted Countries (HIPC) Initiative*, www.inmf.org/external/np/exr/facts/hipc.htm, March 24, 2014.

thirty-six countries of the potential forty countries had reached the decision point, and no less than thirty-two had reached their completion point (IDA/IMF, 2011).

The HIPC initiative has been very successful in reducing indebtedness. In the thirty-six countries mentioned above (thirty in Sub-Saharan Africa, six in Latin America), the IMF claims that the debt burden has been reduced by 90 per cent relative to pre-decision debt levels, from in total 140.8 billion dollars to 15.1 billion dollars (IDA/IMF, 2011, Figure 1). In addition, the HIPCs have been able to increase their average poverty-reducing expenditures from around 7 to around 11 per cent of GDP. Since, 2006, the HIPC initiative has been wound down, in part to avoid moral hazard. No new countries are eligible. The last three potentially eligible countries Bhutan, Laos and Nepal, have indicated that they do not want to participate in the initiative.

It should be noted that the remarkable acceleration of economic growth in Africa since the beginning of the twenty-first century coincides with the success in reducing debt overhang. But, as shown in Table 13.2, debt has not only been reduced in the HIPCs but in developing countries in general. Debt, one of the major obstacles to economic development in the developing world, no longer figures as such at present. Now it is the advanced economies that are suffering from excessive debt in the wake of the 2008 financial crisis.

13.6   Structural adjustment and the Washington consensus

13.6.1   The debt crisis and the rise of the Washington consensus

After 1982, all attention shifted to the debt crisis, which threatened world financial stability. The inflow of private financial capital to developing countries temporarily came to an end. Debt became one of the major issues in the international order. From the 1980s onwards, international financial institutions like the IMF and the World Bank increasingly started attaching conditions to the provision of new credit. Developing countries had to pursue 'structural adjustment policies' aimed at improving their balance of payments, reducing of the role of government, deregulating the economy, promoting market forces and stimulating exports. The 1980s were completely dominated by the debate on structural adjustment policy (see Lensink, 1995; Mosley *et al.*, 1995). The intellectual justification for this policy was provided by the economic success of several East Asian countries, where sober macro-economic policies had been followed and export orientation had been encouraged (World Bank, 1993).[15] Structural adjustment policies were consistent with the resurgence of liberal perspectives on both national and international economic policy. In 1990, John Williamson coined the phrase 'Washington consensus' to describe the policy prescriptions put forward by the powerful IFIs such as the World Bank and the IMF (Williamson, 1990).

The ideas of the Washington consensus were based on the negative experiences of state-led inward-looking development in Latin America and Africa and the success of export orientation in East Asia. This approach recommends the pursuit of macro-economic stability by controlling inflation and reducing fiscal deficits, the opening up of economies to the rest of the world through trade liberalisation and capital account liberalisation and the liberalisation of domestic

---

[15] The World Bank's interpretation of East Asian success disregarded the important role of interventionist government policies aimed at promoting growth and export success.

product and factor markets through structural adjustment programmes. The policy package includes import liberalisation, competitive exchange rates, tax reform, openness to FDI, privatisation, deregulation, protection of intellectual property rights and public expenditure priorities in education and health (Fischer, 2003; Gore, 2000; Rodrik, 2006; Williamson, 1990, 1993, 1997).

The discussion of structural adjustment actually predates the debt crisis (Lensink, 1995). As early as 1979 the World Bank introduced the financial instrument called Structural Adjustment Loans (SALs). At the time, the World Bank was deeply dissatisfied with its project-related financial flows. Too many funds were being allocated to large-scale capital-intensive projects of dubious effectiveness (Toye, 1993). Far from all projects were completed. After official completion, sometimes insufficient means were available to continue the projects. Developing countries were not so much in need of new project aid, but rather of additional resources for the completion, upkeep and maintenance of existing infrastructural projects. As prices did not reflect real scarcity relations due to distorted markets, it was almost impossible to formulate good projects and to weigh their costs and benefits. The sectoral adjustment loans were designed to make new, non-project-related funds available, and at the same time, to formulate conditions with respect to reinforcement of market mechanisms, strengthening economic incentives, improving macro-economic policies and liberalising the economy.

After the 1982 debt crisis, the pressures to implement structural adjustment policies increased. The roles of the World Bank and the IMF converged. Initially, the World Bank had focused on medium- and long-term project aid and the IMF on short-run financial support for countries with balance of payments difficulties. Now the World Bank moved from project to programme lending and the IMF created instruments for medium-term structural adjustment (Lensink, 1995). The World Bank and the IMF coordinated their actions and both set structural adjustment as a condition for the provision of new loans. First, a country had to turn to the IMF for a stand-by arrangement through which means were made available to finance deficits in the balance of payments. Only after IMF conditions had been met could a country apply for adjustment loans from the World Bank aimed at long-term restructuring of the economy. Between 1979 and 1991 ninety-nine developing countries received sectoral adjustment loans from the World Bank. The reforms developed into a coherent package which later came to be referred to as the Washington consensus, and which consisted of policies aimed at short-term stabilisation and long-term liberalisation and market reform (Williamson, 1990). The collapse of the Soviet Union in 1991 served to strengthen the Washington consensus, discrediting the alternative of state-led development strategies.

13.6.2   Neo-liberalism versus structuralism

The five main objectives of structural adjustment policy are summarised in Box 13.7. Structural adjustment policy stands in sharp contrast to the central ideas underlying development strategies from 1950 to 1980. In these strategies government was assigned a critical role in initiating development and industrialisation. The state acted as a large-scale investor itself and tried to coordinate private sector investment by means of planning. It provided protection to the industrial sector against cut-throat international competition, in order to give domestic industries time to mature.

The preference for government intervention was based on a *structuralist interpretation* of the economic conditions in poor countries (Colman and Nixson, 1986; Ocampo *et al.*, 2009; Sunkel, 1993; Sunkel and Zuleta, 1990; Urquidi, 1993; see also Chapter 3). Structuralist

BOX 13.7 **Objectives of structural adjustment policies**

1. Improvement of the external balance between imports and exports. This goal is pursued by reductions in expenditures, depreciation of overvalued exchange rates and shifts in expenditure to domestically produced goods and services.
2. Rationalisation of the public sector and cuts in government expenditures, in particular expenditures on loss-making public enterprises.
3. Structural adjustments in the production structure aimed at a more efficient allocation of production factors, greater flexibility and sustained growth.
4. Stable incentives for private enterprise, liberalisation of the economy and reinforcement of market mechanisms.
5. Opening up of the economy to international competition.

Source: Selowsky (1987).

theories assume that the conditions for a beneficial functioning of the market mechanism are absent in developing countries, because there are so many restrictions, bottlenecks and market imperfections. For instance, there is insufficient infrastructure, insufficient education for productive participation in the modern economy, lack of information and a lack of entrepreneurship. Underdeveloped financial markets cannot supply potential entrepreneurs with sufficient finance. The risks of traditional agriculture restrict the opportunities for innovation. Under such circumstances, a free market economy will not motivate people to engage in new productive activities that result in structural change. Rather, it will cause their situation to deteriorate. Structuralist policies aim at the supply side of the economy. But from the structuralist perspective, reinforcement of the supply side in developing countries requires government intervention to compensate for market imperfections (Mosley, 1991; Toye, 1993). Structuralist notions thus justify extensive government intervention in the economy.

Structural adjustment policy was a frontal neoliberal attack on post-war structuralist policies. Advocates of structural adjustment believed that many African and Latin American governments pursued policies which gave rise to increasing economic imbalances and market distortions. In some developing countries, the interventionist and rent seeking state itself had become an obstacle to economic dynamism. Although the debate on the role of the government is far from concluded, previous chapters have argued that such criticisms are not completely unfounded.

In the liberal explanations of economic stagnation in the 1980s, less importance was ascribed to external causes, such as decreasing export prices or the stagnation of the world economy. The emphasis was mainly on internal factors such as corruption, rent seeking and misguided domestic policies. It was emphasised that several Asian developing economies performed very well during the 1980s in spite of the same unfavourable external circumstances. It was argued that countries that converted from *inward-looking* to *outward-looking* development strategies at an early stage did much better economically than countries that continued to pursue inward-looking import substitution policies (see Chapter 9).

It is interesting to note that the advocates of structural adjustment policy also used a structuralist reasoning, in spite of their preference for free markets; hence the term 'structural' adjustment.

They agreed with the older structuralists that the supply side of the economy in developing countries did not function properly, due to bottlenecks, constraints and market imperfections. Economic institutions did not provide sufficient incentives for productive behaviour. Therefore, countries must explicitly pursue a structural policy aimed at increasing their productive capacities and the efficiency of the production structure. But in this case, government policies, parastatals, excessive regulation and intervention in the market were identified as the prime causes of structural inflexibility. The traditional structuralist argument was thus stood on its head (Toye, 1993). Liberalisation is the instrument for structural reform.

13.6.3   Stabilisation and structural adjustment

Although the term 'structural adjustment' is frequently used to refer to both *economic stabilisation policy* and *structural adjustment policy* in a more restricted sense, it is useful to distinguish clearly between these two kinds of policy (Hermes, 1992; Lensink, 1993a; Mosley, 1991).

Stabilisation policies

The aims of stabilisation policies are to restore the external balance on the balance of payments and to reduce inflation in the short term. Imports should be restricted and exports should be promoted. Financial means, which were employed to finance imports, thus become available for debt servicing. Stabilisation is realised by means of measures that influence the demand side of the economy. Demand is restricted by measures such as tax increases, reduction of government deficits and government expenditures, abolition of government subsidies, higher prices for government services, lower wages, tight monetary policies, increases in interest rates and, especially, depreciation of overvalued exchange rates. Depreciation makes imports more expensive and exports cheaper, contributing to a recovery of the external balance. Stabilisation measures are summarised in Box 13.8.

BOX 13.8 : Stabilisation measures

- Devaluation of overvalued exchange rates.
- Reduction of budget deficits; raising taxes; cutting expenditure, reforming the tax system.
- Restructuring foreign debts.
- Financing government debts on capital markets instead of through monetary financing.
- Increasing interest rates (financial liberalisation); increasing food prices; increasing prices of public services.
- Controlling wages.

Structural adjustment policy measures

In contrast with stabilisation methods, structural adjustment measures are measures directed towards long-run improvements in the supply side of the economy, so that production can increase and economic subjects can respond better to economic incentives. Structural adjustment packages usually include stabilisation measures, but their scope is much wider.

The long-run aim is to reduce the role of the state and liberalise the whole economy, so that prices actually reflect scarcity and promote more efficient economic behaviour. Discrimination against agriculture in favour of the industrial sector should be ended. Restrictions on trade and capital flows should be phased out. Protection of domestic industry by means of tariffs and quotas should be reduced. Domestic firms should be exposed more to foreign competition and should try to penetrate export markets. Exports should follow the lines of comparative advantage.

Of course, stabilisation programmes and structural adjustment programmes are complementary. The imbalances in the economy that result in financial crisis in the short term are partly due to the inadequacy of domestic supply with respect to domestic demand. This causes inflation and deficits on the current account of the balance of payments. In the long term, removal of structural impediments and increased flexibility of the production structure are the best way to prevent a financial crisis from recurring (Husain, 1993).

In negotiations with the IMF and the World Bank, a set of economic reform measures was drawn up for each specific country. The provision of new loans and development finance was made dependent on the wholehearted acceptance of the package of reforms. Ideally the concrete package differed from country to country, depending on the circumstances. But the IMF was increasingly accused of a one-size-fits-all approach to structural reform, imposing a uniform set of measures on all countries, with little regard for their differences and specific conditions (Stiglitz, 2002). A list of frequently used measures is reproduced in Box 13.9 (Doroodian, 1993; Greenaway and Morrissey, 1993; Mosley, 1991; Mosley, Harrigan and Toye, 1991; Lensink, 1995; Selowsky, 1987; Toye, 1993).

BOX 13.9 : Structural adjustment policy measures

Liberalisation of domestic markets
- Abolition of price controls and liberalisation of price policies; an end to the practice of indexing wages to inflation, abolition of minimum wage regulations.

Trade policy
- Depreciation of overvalued exchange rates. A cheaper currency makes imports more expensive and exports cheaper. Import-substituting domestic production becomes more profitable.
- Liberalisation of trade policy by abolishing import quotas; import tariff systems are made more transparent and tariffs themselves are reduced. When exchange rates are determined by market forces, growth of imports will lead to depreciation of the exchange rate. This in turn makes for recovery of the external balance. Liberalisation of imports also undermines the monopoly positions of traders who had profited from import licensing under a protectionist regime. Former domestic monopolists are exposed to the discipline of international competition.
- Striking a balance between incentives for import-substituting production and incentives for export production, so as to promote a stronger outward orientation.

The public sector, fiscal policy, government expenditures, public enterprises

- Reforms of the budgetary and fiscal system, aimed at better control of government expenditure and more effective collection of taxes.
- Reducing government expenditures and government deficits.
- Restructuring the priorities in government investment. More priority to investment in the agricultural sector.
- Increasing the government's capacity to formulate and execute government investment programmes; increasing the general efficiency of government.
- Increasing the output and efficiency of loss-making public enterprises (*parastatals*).
- Privatisation of public enterprises and public activities.
- Reducing subsidies for energy and food. Increasing taxes on consumer goods.

Capital market

- Liberalisation of domestic and foreign capital markets.
- Deregulation of interest rates. Higher interest rates elicit higher domestic savings. Higher interest costs lead to a more efficient use of capital in the production process.
- Creating new financial institutions; privatisation or restructuring of government controlled banks.

Agricultural policy

- Increasing agricultural prices in order to stimulate agricultural production.
- Abolishing or limiting the role of state marketing boards that used to have a monopoly on the trade in food and export products. Liberalisation of agricultural trade.
- Reducing subsidies for agricultural inputs.

Industrial policy

- Intensifying incentives for efficient production in the industrial sector, among other things by refusing to bail out unprofitable firms and investment projects.

Energy policy

- Increasing the domestic prices of energy to relieve the government budget; promoting the domestic supply and efficient use of energy.

13.6.4   The Cotonou agreements between the European Union and ACP countries

As a sign of the changing times, the Lomé agreements which had typically evolved as part of the new international order in the 1960s and 1970s, were no longer seen as compatible with the new rules of international trade embodied by the WTO. In 2000, the fourth Lomé agreement was replaced by the Cotonou agreements between the European Union and seventy-seven ACP countries, which were to enter into force in 2008, after a transition period. Under the Cotonou agreements, the preferential access of ACP countries to European markets is very gradually being phased out, in the context of a more general reduction of trade barriers. The condition for unlimited access to EU markets is that ACP countries abolish protection of their domestic markets. ACP countries have to sign economic partnership agreements (EPAs) which provide unrestricted access to European markets, but also involve gradual reductions in import tariffs in the ACP countries. STABEX and SYSMIN have been abolished.

The preferential access of the Lomé agreements was increasingly seen as conflicting with the WTO rules for international trade. At the time of writing many EPAs are still being negotiated. African policy makers and researchers worry about the negative consequences of complete abolition of protection of domestic markets for the prospects of growth and poverty reduction (Cissé and Fofana, 2013).

13.6.5 Foreign direct investment

One of the issues about which the climate of opinion has changed radically since the period of the NIEO is that of FDI. In the 1970s, MNCs and foreign investors were regarded with suspicion and hostility. Developing countries feared foreign domination of the economy and the drain on domestic resources through profit repatriation and transfer pricing. The right to nationalise foreign enterprises was included in the resolutions on the new international order. There was also a call for a code of conduct for multinationals.

Since the 1990s, developing countries have vied with each other to attract the most FDI, including formerly FDI-hostile economies such as China and India. In many countries, restrictions on FDI have been reduced, including local content requirements and obligations to engage in joint ventures. This has contributed to further increases in the inflow of FDI, especially in Asia, though the danger of footloose capital in low-wage sectors such as textiles and shoe making remains a serious problem.

The importance of FDI has fluctuated hugely over time. Its share in net capital flows to developing countries was quite high in the 1950s and 1960s. It reached a low point in 1980 and recovered after that. The debt crisis created renewed interest in FDI, as it can bring financial resources into a country without increasing the volume of debt. In 1980, net FDI was only 5.2 per cent of net total capital flows (including short-term loans). By 1987, FDI had increased to 25 per cent of net total capital flows. Since 1994, net FDI exceeds net total capital flows. It has replaced loans as the prime source of external financial resources for developing countries. Between 1999 and 2002 when loans once more suddenly dried up, FDI accounted for between 93 and 100 per cent of total inflows, but after 2002 the percentage declined as net inflows of loans recovered. By 2012 net inflows of FDI were 612 billion dollars, net portfolio investment was 98 billion dollars and net capital flows were 322 million dollars. Thus foreign investment in this year accounted for 63.3 per cent of the net inflow of foreign resources (see Table 13.3).

FDI comprises more than financial flows alone. It includes a complete package of finance, management experience, transfer of technology and skills, marketing expertise and access to world brand names and world markets (Blomström and Kokko, 1997; Dunning, 1988; Gillis et al., 1992; Helleiner, 1989; Lall, 2002; Narula, 2013; Narula and Lall, 2006; UNCTAD, 2000). A variety of new relationships with international firms has also developed over time such as joint ventures, licensing agreements, original equipment manufacturing (OEM), franchising, management contracts and subcontracting (see Chapter 9).

The right to nationalise multinational enterprises, emphasised in the NIEO proposals, increasingly clashed with the new goal of attracting more and more FDI. The very threat of nationalisation had adverse effects on the behaviour of multinationals. When the political future is uncertain, multinational enterprises will charge an 'uncertainty premium' and go for maximum short-term profits, which will be repatriated as soon as possible.

Multinationals will display a less 'predatory' behaviour if their long-term prospects in a country are more secure. Since the 1970s, progress has been achieved in drawing up codes of conduct for multinational enterprises. Such codes specify the obligations of multinationals – training local staff, reinvesting part of their profits, respecting domestic legislation, subcontracting, using local intermediate goods and entering into joint ventures with domestic investors. But the codes also offer more certainty to foreign investors.

This is not to say that FDI does not raise a number of major problems. Some multinationals raise much of their capital on domestic markets, while repatriating part of their profits. A sizeable minority of foreign investment projects costs more in terms of the opportunity cost of the resources used than the earnings generated (Helleiner, 1989). In some sectors such as textiles or electronic assembly, multinationals enter the economy in search of low-cost labour, but leave it just as quickly when wages increase. Whether or not multinationals provide technological spillovers to domestic firms is much debated (Coe and Helpman, 1995; Ito *et al.*, 2012; Wang *et al.*, 2013). The distribution of benefits between the multinational and the host country still depends in part on the bargaining power and absorptive capacity of the host country. Once a multinational has committed its resources and the host country has gained more experience, the latter's bargaining position can improve. But many national governments are in a weak position *vis-à-vis* giant foreign companies (Vernon, 1977). Clear delineation of the rights and obligations of multinational companies and governments continues to be an objective of negotiations within the UN Centre for Transnational Corporations (since 1993 part of UNCTAD).

The increased importance of FDI and multinational companies is part and parcel of the emergence of global production chains. According to Vernon's product life cycle theory (Perez and Soete, 1988; Vernon, 1966, 1974) new products and processes will be located in advanced economies. As mass markets are penetrated and the technologies become more mature, production is relocated to developing countries with an advantage in cheap labour, for instance in textiles, shoe making, or to countries with abundant resources, such as wood or rubber. However, in recent years, several developing countries have succeeded in upgrading their production processes, attracting investment not only in traditional industries such as textiles, but also in software, R&D and electronics. Global production chains are increasingly dispersed, offering new opportunities for some developing countries. Developing countries may attempt to 'unpackage' the total direct investment package in order to select those aspects that are most to their advantage (Kaplinsky, 2000, 2011; Naudé and Szirmai, 2012).

The eclectic theory of multinational investment (Dunning, 1988) gives three explanations for FDI. First there are unique firm-specific characteristics, which explain the foreign firms' advantages over domestic firms. These include intangible factors such as technologies and management skills, economies of scale, servicing networks and access to markets. A second set of factors refers to locational advantages, as determined by labour costs, transport costs, availability of natural resources, tariff protection, tax burdens and other government policies in the host country. The third set of factors, which Dunning calls 'internalisation advantages', is very interesting. A foreign firm has to choose between selling its firm-specific advantages to local firms or setting up lines of production itself. In a nutshell, Dunning argues that the uncertainties of markets lead foreign firms to prefer the internal hierarchy of the multinational organisation to market transactions between independent firms. The very attempt to internalise market uncertainties and imperfections again indicates that there is considerable leeway for bargaining.

An interesting phenomenon is the emergence of FDI from emerging economies and developing countries such Brazil, China, India, Russia and South Africa. The flows are still small compared to investment flows from the advanced economies but they are rapidly increasing in importance (see Broich and Szirmai, 2014 for China; Carvalho, 2013 for Brazil; Narula and Kodiyat, 2013 for India).

13.6.6   How effective have structural adjustment programmes been?

Since 1979, over 150 countries have received World Bank loans in the context of structural adjustment policies (Easterly, 2001b). While short-run stabilisation policies have been fairly effective, the long-run success of structural adjustment policies has been fiercely debated. Two central questions in this debate are: (1) How acceptable are the social consequences of adjustent policies? (2) To what degree does structural adjustment contribute to economic recovery and economic growth? Unfortunately, it is hard to provide unambiguous empirical answers to these questions. First, by no means all adjustment measures agreed upon are actually implemented; next, there are countries which do not receive adjustment loans but nevertheless implement their own adjustment policies (e.g. India, Indonesia in 1984). Third, circumstances and the initial conditions differ from country to country. Fourth, policy is only one of the many factors impinging on economic and social development.

Factors affecting the success of adjustment policies

In the older literature the following factors were identified as important for the success of adjustment policies (Edwards, 1990; Greenaway and Morrissey, 1993; Lensink, 1995; Mosley, 1991; Mosley, Harrigan and Toye, 1991):

1. *Implementation*. Is a government really prepared to implement painful measures? Isn't the drawing up of a structural adjustment programme just a feint to obtain new loans? On average only 60 per cent of all reform measures agreed upon were actually implemented (Mosley, 1991). In the nine countries studied by Mosley, Harrigan and Toye (1991), the implementation percentages varied from 25 to 90 per cent. Stabilisation measures are generally easier to implement than structural reform measures, which often meet with resistance from powerful interest groups whose 'rents' are threatened. In recent years, the emphasis has been shifting from conditionality to the provision of further development finance on the basis of evaluations of past performance (Meltzer, 2000).

2. *Credibility of government policy*. Is the government able to convince private entrepreneurs that it will continue to carry out adjustment policies in spite of their unpopularity? If credibility is lacking, positive responses from the private sector are very unlikely. Frequent changes in policy have negative effects on economic development.

3. *Sequencing of adjustment measures*. If policies are implemented in the wrong order, they may actually harm rather than aid the economy (Greenaway and Morrissey, 1993). This is illustrated by the following examples. Abolishing controls over capital flows before reforming domestic financial markets can result in capital flight. Without prior reduction of budget deficits, liberalisation of financial markets will lead to inflation. A sudden increase in interest rates may also increase government expenditures. Without prior macro-economic stabilisation, liberalisation of trade leads to a deterioration of the economic situation. Liberalisation of trade without depreciation of the currency leads to

increasing deficits on the balance of payments. Sooner or later these will force the government to intervene again.

In the literature the following sequence is suggested as most fruitful (Edwards, 1990; Greenaway and Morrissey, 1993; Lensink, 1995: 228 ff.; Toye, 1993; Tobin, 2000):

1. Reform policies start with *macro-economic stabilisation*, depreciation of exchange rates, tackling inflation and reducing government deficits. Almost all authors stress the importance of reducing budget deficits and depreciating the currency as the first step in any process of reform.
2. *Liberalisation of the domestic real economy*: liberalisation of prices and liberalisation of labour markets.
3. *Liberalisation of foreign trade*. Once the domestic economy has been liberalised, the stage has been set for liberalisation of foreign trade.
4. *Reform of domestic financial markets*. If financial markets are liberalised before step 2, financial resources may be wasted on unproductive activities. Most authors argue that financial liberalisation should come after trade liberalisation, to avoid resources being squandered on import substitution. According to some authors, efficient allocation of production factors only takes place if the financial system is already well developed. This argues for financial liberalisation preceding trade liberalisation. Thus the sequence of steps 3 and 4 is still disputed. In practice, trade liberalisation tends to precede financial liberalisation. It should be emphasised the liberalisation of financial markets requires increased regulation, oversight and transparency of the financial system, without which financial liberalisation contributes to corruption and risky investment behaviour.
5. The last stage involves *liberalisation of international capital flows*. If one does this before domestic financial markets have been liberalised, there will be capital flight because domestic interest rates are still too low due to interest and credit ceilings. Liberalisation of international flows comes in two steps: liberalisation of long-term investment flows and liberalisation of short-term capital flows and full exchange rate convertibility (Eichengreen, 2000). Liberal authors claim that full liberalisation of international capital markets is the ultimate goal for all countries. An increasing number of critics argue that the full liberalisation of short-term capital movements is extremely destructive for developing countries and for the global economy as a whole. For them, the debate is not about sequencing, but about pursuing the wrong objectives (see section 13.7.2).

Social consequences of adjustment policies

In their study, *Adjustment with a Human Face*, Cornia, Jolly and Stewart (1987) criticised the social consequences of adjustment programmes. Cutbacks in government expenditures were realised at the expense of education and healthcare expenditures. Abolition of subsidies and increased prices of food and energy subsidies hurt the poor. Thus structural adjustment policy did not only lead to further impoverishment, but also to insufficient investment in human capital, which endangers the opportunities for future economic growth. The authors pleaded for a more gradual implementation of structural adjustment policy and for compensatory finance to deal with the social consequences of expenditure cuts. The effect of cuts in expenditure on education and health are undeniable, as has been documented in Chapters 6 and 7 of this book.

As time passed, the call to address the consequences of retrenchment and budget cuts has increasingly been heeded by international organisations such as UNICEF, the Economic Commission for Africa and even the World Bank and the IMF. In the design of reform programmes the World Bank today pays attention to the consequences of policies for poverty. For instance, in order to qualify for debt relief under the HIPC initiative since 1996, countries have to draw up *Poverty Reduction Strategy Papers (PRSPs)* which specify how the reduced burden of debt service will result in increased social expenditure on poverty reduction. In 1999 the World Bank and the IMF abandoned the term ' adjustment lending' and started providing development finance on the basis of explicit country poverty reduction strategies (Riddell, 2008: 238 ff.). Bilateral donors followed this trend, which was reinforced by the adoption of the MDGs.

However, the key question is not really whether structural adjustment policies have negative social consequences. In the short term, it is obvious that they do. More important is the question whether or not adjustment policies lead to an improvement in economic dynamics in the long term (Gunning, 1988). If this is the case and long-term economic development contributes to poverty reduction, then short-term sacrifices might be justified. The worst case, however, is a situation in which adjustment policy takes its toll of the poor without the prospects of resumption of economic growth and development. This is what occurred in the Russian Federation and other former Soviet republics after their flawed transition from a centrally planned economy to a market economy after 1991 (Menshikov, 1993).

Have structural adjustment policies contributed to growth?

With respect to the economic effects of the structural adjustment policy, opinions in the literature varied from rather favourable (Husain, 1993; World Bank, 1989) to extremely critical (Cornia, Jolly and Stewart, 1987; Cornia, van der Hoeven and Mkandawire, 1992; Elbadawi, 1992; Elbadawi, Ghura and Uwugaren, 1992; Rodrik, 2006; Stiglitz, 2002; Van der Hoeven and Taylor, 2000). But before discussing the pros and cons of structural adjustment, it is important to note that countries may not have a choice whether or not to follow adjustment policies. Any country that is faced with external shocks and soaring deficits on its balance of payments will sooner or later be forced to implement or undergo some kind of economic adjustment, whether or not it formally negotiates with international financial institutions such as the IMF or the World Bank.[16] So the most interesting questions focus more on the kind of adjustment policies to be implemented rather than on whether or not adjustment policies should be followed.

In a large-scale evaluation study for the 1980s, Mosley, Harrigan and Toye (1991) concluded that countries that had implemented far-reaching structural adjustment policies were generally more successful in terms of economic growth and balance of payments. The effects on export performance were not all that clear (Greenaway and Morrissey, 1993). Of the ninety-nine structural adjustment programmes, forty-four were drawn up for extremely poor countries in Sub-Saharan Africa. The results in this region were definitely disappointing. Between 1982 and 2000 the trends of economic stagnation were not reversed. An early optimistic World Bank report on the success of structural adjustment policies in Africa

---

[16] Bertola and Ocampo (2012) argue that the macro-economic imbalances of Latin American countries were less pronounced than has commonly been portrayed, but that external deficits were indeed an increasing problem.

(World Bank, 1989b) was severely criticised (Mosley and Weeks, 1992). A later article by Mosley and his associates (Mosley *et al.*, 1995) concluded that there is no statistical support for the assertion that structural adjustment had promoted growth in Sub-Saharan Africa. Many countries suffered declines in investment rates.

In a review of studies on structural adjustment in Africa, Lensink (1995) concluded that there were modest positive effects on GDP growth, mixed results with respect to export growth and disappointing effects on savings and investments. But the methodological problems of ascertaining the impacts of structural adjustment remain great. In addition to economic policy, numerous other factors also play an important role in this region, such as constant political turmoil, ethnic conflicts, droughts and an unfavourable international economic climate. Easterly (2001c) found no systematic relationship between structural adjustment lending and growth for the period 1980–99. Many of the studies concluded that there are adverse effects of structural adjustment policies on investment levels. The explanation for this is that reductions in government expenditures of course also affect government investment. Contrary to what was anticipated, this was not compensated for in the short term by increases in private investment. In the long term, a decline in investment rates is incompatible with the goals of increasing productive capacity. Finally, during the period of structural adjustment, Sub-Saharan Africa suffered from substantial de-industrialisation (Szirmai, 2013).

For Latin America, the results of structural adjustment were also disappointing (Bertola and Ocampo, 2012; Dijkstra, 2000). Almost all Latin American countries had followed structural adjustment policies, but economic growth faltered for almost twenty years. While trade liberalisation contributed to static efficiency and export growth, Latin America experienced a decline in its technological capabilities and declines in many of the more advanced and high-tech branches of manufacturing, including capital goods sectors, which suffered from increased competition from imports. Many Latin American economies suffered from premature de-industrialisation and sluggish productivity growth in manufacturing (Cimoli and Katz, 2003; Katz, 2000, 2006; Tregenna, 2013).

Structural adjustment and infrastructural investment in Africa

Mosley (1991) presents a useful distinction between adjustment programmes in MICs and adjustment programmes in the poorest African countries with a stagnating economy. In MICs, structural reforms may help transform a too inward-looking economy into a more export-oriented economy. In this respect, structural adjustment policies in Turkey and the Philippines have been fairly successful. In countries like Chile, Mexico, pre-1997 Indonesia and at an earlier stage in South Korea, adjustment policies also met with positive outcomes.

In the poorest developing countries the inward-oriented strategy may not be the main problem. Rather the problem lies in the fact that the agricultural infrastructure, the transport system and the capital stock have been neglected. In Sub-Saharan Africa the cutbacks in government expenditure have been realised at the expense of essential investments in agricultural infrastructure, schooling and agricultural education. If prices of food and export crops are no longer controlled and state marketing boards are abolished, farmers will not necessarily respond by increasing their production. Farmers' ability to respond to market incentives is restricted by factors such as a sparse and scattered population, bad roads, poor transport and communication, insufficient agricultural schooling and education, insufficient agricultural research and poor possibilities for marketing (Helleiner, 1992a). Helleiner is convinced that investment in infrastructure is at least as important as higher prices. Both Mosley and Weeks (1992) and Helleiner (1992b) conclude that African countries that liberalised agricultural prices without simultaneously increasing government investment in infrastructure performed worse economically than other African countries.

When price liberalisation is combined with increased investment in the rural infrastructure and agricultural services, it may lead to remarkably positive results. An example of this was provided by Nigeria between 1986 and 1991 (Husain, 1993). During this period the value of food imports decreased from 2.5 million dollars to 300–400 million dollars per year due to increased agricultural self-sufficiency.

According to Mosley, structural adjustment in the poor countries of Sub-Saharan Africa does not require reduced government intervention. He and other authors of this school actually argue for an increased role for government and more investment in education, schooling and infrastructure. Provided governments can be made more efficient, government intervention is what is needed to combat market imperfections associated with poor infrastructure, an inadequate and dated capital stock and insufficient education to guarantee participation in economic life. The traditional structuralist arguments are still alive and kicking here. The argument for more infrastructural investment is quite convincing. What is less convincing is the faith in an increased role of government in the economic process in Africa (cf. Chapter 11). Also, during the period under review the share of Western aid going to infrastructure actually declined as attention shifted to capability building and good governance (Broich and Szirmai, 2014).

13.6.7 Summary

With the eruption of the Asian crisis in 1997, the debate on the international economic order took a new turn. As had happened before with the debt crisis of 1982, received wisdom came to be questioned. The advantages of continued globalisation came under fire. The modern empirical and statistical literature is increasingly sceptical about the beneficial effects of structural adjustment loans and structural adjustment policies in the period of the Washington consensus. The structural adjustment loans are seen as having been sufficient to save the global financial system from collapse in the 1980s, but insufficiently generous in scale to generate dynamic growth in Latin America. The consensus is that results of structural adjustment have been deeply disappointing in Latin America, Sub-Saharan Africa and the former Soviet Union. In an article reviewing the debates, Rodrik (2006: 974) concluded: 'it is fair to say that nobody really believes in the Washington consensus any more. The question now is not whether the Washington consensus is dead or alive; it is what will replace it.'

But in this changing context, the broader debates on liberalisation versus intervention continue. The proponents of liberal strategies argue that in spite of the disappointments of structural adjustment, the experiences with liberalisation and economic reform in a number of important developing countries are positive. They point to the cases of China and India where the dominant trend since 1987 in China and 1991 in India has indeed been one of liberalisation.

In a variety of developing countries a combination of increased fiscal discipline, economic liberalisation and export promotion have contributed positively to growth, development and poverty reduction. Examples include Botswana, Ghana, Mauritius, Tanzania and

Uganda in Africa (Acemoglu *et al.*, 2003; Dijkstra and van Donge, 2001; Easterly, 2001a; Portelli, 2006), Indonesia prior to 1997 and Sri Lanka in Asia and Chile in Latin America. It can also be argued that structural adjustment policies ended decades of discrimination against agriculture in Africa, Latin America and Asia, thereby removing one of the bottlenecks to growth discussed in section 9.3 of Chapter 9.

Another important strand in the literature argues that some of the failures of structural adjustment have been due to the fact that policy reforms have not really been implemented (Easterly, 2001a) or have not gone far enough. Part of the institutionalist literature discussed in Chapter 10 (e.g. Acemoglu and Robinson, 2006, 2012) argues that more fundamental institutional reform is required to unleash the forces of growth. In his review article, Rodrik (2006) refers to this school of thought as the 'augmented Washington consensus'.

13.7   1997–2014: financial instability, crises and accelerated growth

13.7.1   The post-1997 international economic order

The Asian crisis

In 1997, the Asian crisis erupted after the devaluation of the Thai Baht. One after another, the currencies of Asian countries went into free fall and short-term capital was withdrawn from these countries at an alarming rate. The collapse of the currencies increased the debt burdens of companies and banks, whose foreign liabilities were denominated in dollars or other international currencies. The fragility of the banking systems in countries such as Indonesia, Thailand and Korea, due to hidden non-performing loans, pervasive corruption and undercapitalisation, was exposed. The financial crisis quickly translated into a crisis in the real economy, which had been booming up until then. A number of Asian economies experienced unprecedented declines in real output, as documented in Table 13.4.

The Asian crisis acted as a major system shock and can be seen as the beginning of a new international order with the somewhat paradoxical combination of increased volatility and accelerated growth. On the one hand, the post-1997 economic order is characterised by increased volatility, with major financial crises erupting in different parts of the global economy: the Asian crisis of 1997, the severe crises affecting Argentina, Brazil and Russia around the turn of the century, the bursting of the dot.com bubble in the USA in 2000 and the global financial crisis of 2008, which primarily affected growth in the advanced economies. On the other hand, the economic order was characterised by rapid growth in many developing countries (see Table 3.2 in Chapter 3). In this period, the developing countries outperformed the advanced economies, resulting in major shifts in the international order.

The Asian crisis hit five countries most severely – Thailand, the Philippines, Malaysia, Korea and Indonesia – which up until that time had been seen as paragons of economic success. These countries were characterised by fiscal discipline, macro-economic balance, low inflation, modest deficits in government spending, export success, rapid growth of output and productivity and technological upgrading (Athukorala, 2001; Hill, 1999; Woo *et al.*, 2000). Admittedly countries like the Philippines, Indonesia and Thailand were

Table 13.4: Economic volatility and crises, 1995–2013 (GDP growth, selected countries)

	Indonesia	Malaysia	South Korea	Philippines	Thailand
1995	8.2	9.8	8.9	4.7	8.1
1996	7.8	10.0	7.2	5.9	5.7
1997	4.7	7.3	5.8	5.2	−2.8
1998	−13.1	−7.4	−5.7	−0.6	−7.7
1999	0.8	6.1	10.7	3.1	4.6
2000	4.9	8.9	8.8	4.4	4.5
2001	3.6	0.5	4.0	2.9	3.4

	Argentina	Brazil	Russia	Turkey
1998	4.4	0.0	−5.3	4.6
1999	−3.0	0.3	6.4	−3.4
2000	−0.5	3.9	10.0	6.8
2001	−4.3	1.4	5.1	−5.7
2002	−10.8	3.1	4.7	6.2
2003	7.9	1.2	7.3	5.3
2004	7.3	5.6	7.2	9.4
2005	8.4	3.0	6.4	8.4
2006	7.8	3.7	8.2	6.9
2007	8.0	5.8	8.5	4.7
2008	3.6	4.8	5.2	0.7
2009	−3.2	−0.3	−7.8	−4.8
2010	8.3	6.9	4.5	9.0

	USA	UK	Greece	Portugal	Spain	EU27
2006	2.7	2.8	5.5	1.4	4.1	3.5
2007	1.8	3.4	3.5	2.4	3.5	3.3
2008	−0.3	−0.8	−0.2	0.0	0.9	0.6
2009	−2.8	−5.2	−3.1	−2.9	−3.8	−4.5
2010	2.5	1.7	−4.9	1.9	−0.2	1.9
2011	1.8	1.1	−7.1	−1.3	0.1	1.7
2012	2.8	0.1	−6.4	−3.2	−1.6	−0.4
2013	1.9	1.3	−4.2	−2.3	−1.5	0.2

Note:

Percentage change relative to previous year.

Source:

Conference Board, *Total Economy Database*, January 2014.

plagued by extensive corruption, but so far this had not stood in the way of their growth dynamics.

Crises in Argentina, Brazil, Russia and Turkey

Financial instability spread across the global economy, with Russia and Brazil suffering major financial crises in 1998, Turkey in 1999 and 2001. Argentina suffered a huge crisis between 1999 and 2002, resulting in default on Argentinian debt. Growth in Brazil slowed down again in 2001.

The 2008 global financial crisis

In 2008, a major financial crisis erupted in the USA, where banks had recklessly speculated in shady derivatives, including housing loans to people who were unable to pay their mortgages when house prices declined (the subprime crisis). In a globalised financial world where financial institutions are highly interconnected, the crisis rapidly spread to banking institutions of the other advanced economies. Large banks and financial institutions started to collapse and, as in 1982, the stability of the global financial system was threatened. Governments decided to bail out the financial institutions, thereby incurring huge sovereign debts which affected their macro-economic stability. In Europe, the banking crisis was followed by a sovereign debt crisis where interest on debt skyrocketed and debt burdens of many countries became so high that national bankruptcy and the collapse of the Euro became a real possibility. In response, the governments in Europe embarked on a process of retrenchment, budget cuts and structural adjustment, which quickly resulted in a deep double-dip economic crisis in the real economy. Western countries, accustomed to preaching to the developing world about good governance, discovered that their financial institutions had become hugely dysfunctional. A system of institutionalised financial bonuses encouraged individuals to enrich themselves through reckless speculation (sometimes even outright fraud) at the expense of the survival of their organisations, their shareholders, their customers and the public at large. As we write, the financial crisis has abated, but as in 1982 the cost of excessive retrenchment has been high, especially in peripheral European countries such as Greece, Portugal and Spain.

Accelerated growth in the developing world

Since 1997, growth rates in Asia have been extremely high, while growth has accelerated in Sub-Saharan Africa. Growth also recovered in much of Latin America after the turbulent years at the turn of the century, though Latin American countries did not reach the rapid rates of growth they had experienced between 1950 and 1973. The developing world was less affected by the 2008 financial crisis than the advanced economies, in part, because developing countries were less connected to US financial markets. There was some slowdown in growth, but in countries such as India and China growth remained high and only a few countries experienced negative growth. Between 1997 and 2012, the population weighted growth of GDP per capita in our sample of thirty-one developing countries was 6.7 per cent compared to a growth rate of – 0.2 per cent in sixteen advanced economies (see Table 3.2, p. 111). Thus on balance, in spite of the Asian crisis and the global financial crisis, the period since 1997 until the time of writing – 2014 – has been a period of accelerated growth in much of the developing world.

Other characteristics of the post-1997 international economic order

Four other characteristics of the current international order are worth mentioning, namely the emergence of the BRICS, imbalances in international trade, the increasing importance of FDI originating in emerging economies and the increased presence of China in Africa.

Brazil, India, China, Russia and South Africa (the BRICS) are five emerging economies which through their sheer size are having an increasing impact on the international order (De Vries *et al.,* 2015; Naudé *et al.*, 2013, 2015; O'Neill, 2001; UNIDO, 2012). Though their levels of GDP per capita are far lower than those of the advanced economies,[17] their large populations, in particular in the case of India and China, make them economic giants. In 2010, the BRICS accounted for 26 per cent of World GDP and 13 per cent of world exports. They absorbed 13 per cent of global inward FDI (UNIDO, 2012). Though the BRICS are not a homogeneous category and have diverse interests, they nevertheless succeed in making the voice of emerging economies heard in international organisations and negotiations, as evidenced by the breakdown of the Cancún trade negotiations in 2003.

A second important phenomenon is that of a persisting negative balance on the current account of the world's largest economy, the USA, combined with large surpluses on the current account of China as an exporter of manufactured goods. This is accompanied by large capital flows from China to the USA to compensate for these trade imbalances. Other countries with a surplus on their current accounts are Indonesia, Malaysia, South Korea, Taiwan and Thailand. In the long run, these structural imbalances are not sustainable.

A third important phenomenon is the emergence of multinational companies located in emerging economies and increasing flows of FDI from emerging economies to both the advanced economies and the developing world. The share of emerging economies in global outward FDI increased from 7 per cent in 1990 to 15 per cent in 2010 (Carvalho, 2013; UNCTAD, 2011). South–South trade and South–South investment flows are becoming a reality.

An important manifestation of the increasing weight of emerging economies in the global economy is the entry of China into Africa (Bräutigam, 2009; Broich and Szirmai, 2014). During the past fifteen years, China has become the second most important trading partner of Africa, after the combined EU countries, while both its aid and its foreign investment have increased rapidly. In 2010, China provided more than 2.5 billion US dollars in aid to Africa. While this is still only a small fraction of Western aid, Broich and Szirmai argue that the presence of Chinese aid flows as an alternative is a game changer in negotiations between Western donors and African governments. Chinese aid is typically supplied with no strings attached (except non-recognition of Taiwan), compared to Western aid that comes with all sorts of conditions with regard to transparency and good governance. With regard to FDI, Chinese FDI inflows to Africa increased from 90 million dollars in 2000 to 5.5 billion dollars in 2008 (Broich and Szirmai, 2014).[18]

Together with the phenomenon of rapid growth in developing countries and sluggish growth in the advanced economies, the four trends discussed in this section – the rise of the BRICS, trade imbalances, FDI from emerging economies and the Chinese presence in

---

[17] In 2010, GDP per capita in the BRICS was one-sixth of that of the G-7 economies (UNIDO, 2012: 17).

[18] China is not the only emerging country investor in Africa. In fact, Malaysia and South Africa are even more important. But from a geopolitical perspective it is the Chinese presence that matters most.

Africa – are harbingers of important changes in the international order. But at the time of writing it is too soon to conclude how radical these changes will be.

The renewed debate on globalisation and liberalisation

After the Asian crisis, a renewed debate broke out on the advantages and disadvantages of liberalisation, free trade and globalisation. The debate on the international economic order received a further impetus from the global financial crisis of 2008, which called into doubt the self-regulating and self-correcting capabilities of free markets (Stiglitz, 2010). The need for far-reaching reform of national and international financial institutions became urgent.

Responses to the Asian crisis

The IMF response to the Asian crisis was severely criticised as contributing to a further worsening of the situation by imposing deeply contractionary policies on Asian countries that were not suffering from macro-economic imbalances prior to the crisis. The IMF was criticised for imposing standard conditions on countries irrespective of their actual circumstances. Of the Asian countries, Malaysia refused to follow IMF policies. It introduced restrictions on short-term capital movements to provide itself with a breathing space for a more expansionary response to the crisis (Athukorala, 2001; Stiglitz, 2002). With South Korea, Malaysia was the first country to resume growth after the crisis, though in fact all countries recovered quickly with the exception of Indonesia. Malaysia's recovery can be seen as an argument against IMF policies. But the rapid recovery of other countries has also been used as an argument in defence of these policies.

From the liberal side of the debate, publications such as the Meltzer report (Meltzer, 2000) called for a reduced role for the IMF and the World Bank. These institutions were seen as having outlived their usefulness. Much of their work could be taken over by private financial institutions. The Meltzer report proposed to replace loans by a smaller volume of outright grants, tied more strongly to prior economic performance and liberal economic reforms. In general, the neoliberal response has been to argue that the implementation of reform measures has been insufficient and that a second generation of more fundamental institutional reforms is required to make markets function as they should (Rodrik, 2006). These second-generation reforms, referred to as the 'augmented Washington consensus' included improvements in corporate governance, strengthening of property rights, promoting ease of doing business, anti-corruption measures, more flexible labour markets, financial codes and standards, independent central banks, social safety nets and targeted poverty reduction. The increasing popularity of the concept of good governance can be interpreted as an expression of this mode of reasoning.

On the other hand, there was a mounting wave of criticism of the Washington consensus and the liberal international order, sparked by the Asian crisis and increasing financial instability in the global economy (Adelman, 2000; Caballero, 2003; Eichengreen, 2000, Gore, 2000; Soros, 2000, 2002; Stiglitz, 2000, 2002; Tobin, 2000). One of the most influential critics was Nobel Prize winner in economics and former World Bank chief economist Joseph Stiglitz, who published an impassioned tract entitled *Globalisation and its Discontents* (2002). This book reflects the various strands of intellectual disenchantment with globalisation and the prevailing intellectual climate. It makes a powerful case for reform of international policies. Stiglitz argues that since the mid 1990s market fundamentalism has contributed to financial instability, crises and increased poverty in many developing countries in Latin America, Asia and the former Soviet Union and that the international financial institutions bear a major part of the blame. Key issues include the dangers of excessive liberalisation of international capital markets, the negative impacts of full trade liberalisation on the industrial prospects of poor developing countries, the perceived inflexibility and dogmatism of the IMF and the need to reduce the debt burdens of the poorest countries.

Fifteen years later, we see that the World Bank and the IMF have survived, but that at least some of the proposals mentioned above have been taken into account. In section 13.5.5 we have already discussed the success of debt reduction and the HIPC initiative and the renewed focus on poverty reduction. We also documented the increase in the volume of grants as part of financial flows. Unfortunately, the lessons of the success of the HIPC initiative have not been taken on board in dealing with the debt problems of poor peripheral European nations such as Portugal or Greece, where the contractionary policies imposed increased rather than reduced debt burdens. The fundamental debate between neoliberals and interventionists continues unabated.

Responses to the 2008 crisis

The official policy response to the 2008 global financial crisis was again primarily contractionary and orthodox, aimed at controlling deficits in the public sector and reducing indebtedness through massive budget cuts and retrenchment. But there was also an increasing groundswell of criticism of the neoliberal policy prescriptions in both the advanced economies and the developing world (Blanchard et al., 2012; Cimoli et al., 2009; Griffith-Jones et al., 2010; Krugman, 2009; Ocampo et al., 2009; Stiglitz, 2010).

Strands of criticism

Most of the critics believe that globalisation of international trade remains a key to development. There is no call for a return to the inward-looking policies of the early post-war period. However, the present architecture of the international order does not deliver on the promise of globalisation. On the contrary, it harms many developing regions. The criticisms can be summarised in the following points:[19]

1. *Complete capital account liberalisation is harmful to growth and stability in developing countries.* Full capital account convertibility and the free movement of short-term capital flows in and out of developing countries create a tremendous degree of financial instability. This manifests itself in a succession of financial crises, which harm developing countries as well as the advanced economies. The Asian crisis was preceded by a vast speculative inflow of hot money (short-term loans, portfolio investment, currency speculation), followed by sudden capital flight. Some form of regulation of international capital flows is urgently needed (Adelman and Yeldan, 2000; Caballero, 2003; Eichengreen, 2000; Tobin, 2000). Countries that continued to control capital flows such as China and India were not affected by the Asian crisis. Malaysia, which imposed capital

---

[19] The full list of criticisms and proposals for change is much longer. Many of them echo the debates on the new international order, such as more attention to poverty and inequality, debt relief, increases in financial resources for development and voting power for developing countries in the IFIs.

controls in spite of IMF pressure, recovered most rapidly from the crisis. Tobin (2000) has argued that a very modest tax of 0.1 or 0.2 per cent on short-term capital transactions will not affect long-term capital flows, but will seriously slow down short-term speculative flows. Malaysia was rather successful in devising effective capital controls – first restrictions on repatriation of short-term investments, later an exit tax for short-term capital flows – which left long-term foreign direct investment unaffected (Athukorala, 2001).

2. *Need for reform of the banking system in the advanced economies.* In the wake of the 2008 financial crisis, efforts were made to re-separate the investment functions of the financial system from the commercial function of providing banking services to customers.[20] Banks were required to increase their reserves and reduce their over-leveraged activities. Regulatory oversight of banking was increased in both the USA and in Europe. Tentative and incomplete steps were taken to tackle the kind of short-term bonuses which provide perverse incentives for bankers to indulge in destructive and risky behaviour.

3. *Across-the-board liberalisation of international trade favours the advanced economies more than the poor developing countries.* The new rules of the WTO prohibit protection and industrial and technology policies in developing countries, which might nurture promising industrial activities, protect them for a time from international competition and promote industrial upgrading. In his well-known book *Kicking Away the Ladder*, Ha-Joon Chang has argued that all past successful instances of economic development in both the advanced economies and the presently emerging economies have involved a phase during which infant industry activities were protected and selective industrial policies were applied to promote structural change (Chang, 2002). The present rules of the WTO reduce the policy space for newcomers among the developing countries and therefore make it more difficult for them to embark on growth and structural change.

4. *Strategic participation in international trade.* Most of the critics of globalisation do not call for a return to the inward-looking protectionist policies of the immediate post-war period. They are in favour of export promotion and strategic participation in world trade. The importance of fiscal discipline and control of inflation is recognised (e.g. Sunkel, 1993; Westphal, 2002). However, they argue with considerable force and credibility that the export success of the East Asian NICs was characterised by active policy interventions of governments – through export subsidies, support of domestic champions and through protection of domestic markets, which are now being denied to developing countries (Westphal, 2002). In a review article on the rise and fall of the Washington consensus, Gore (2000: 796) writes: 'The process of growth and structural change is best achieved through the "strategic integration" of the national economy into the international economy, rather than either de-linking from the rest of the world or rapid across-the board opening up of the economy to imports and external capital.' Strategic integration in world trade requires active industrial and technology policies by governments, including export subsidies and the use of instruments of protection. Also, the critics argue once again that the advanced economies do not practice what they

---

[20] In the USA the so-called Glass–Steagall Act which had separated these functions since 1933 had been repealed in 1999, exposing regular bank depositors to excessive risk from speculative investment activities.

preach. They continue to protect their agricultural systems and use dumping provisions of the WTO against manufactured exports from developing countries. Where the international system is becoming more liberal – as in the trade in services and in the protection of IPRs – it favours the advanced economic powers rather than the developing countries.

5. *Rejecting the one-size-fits-all approach and moving to country-specific policies and reforms targeting the most binding constraints to growth.* The international financial organisations have been far too rigid and dogmatic in their stabilisation policies and their imposition of rapid market reforms. The IMF does not take local conditions into account when responding to financial crises. Its procedures are secretive and lack transparency. It imposes a standard package of contractionary measures on all countries. In the former Soviet Union the rapid and imperfect transition from central planning to the market has led to the theft of state property by mafia-type oligarchs. Market reforms created a kind of monopolistic klepto-capitalism, which has resulted in years of economic stagnation and hardship (Menshikov, 1993). Russia compares unfavourably with China, which followed a more gradual path of reform.[21] Stiglitz argues that privatisation needs to be preceded by competition policies and institutional and legal changes which create a viable framework for market reforms. Stiglitz criticised the rapidity of market reforms in the countries of the former Soviet Union – the 'Big Bang' approach – calling for a more incremental approach.

In a series of influential publications, Hausmann, Rodrik, and Velasco have introduced the notion of binding constraints (Hausmann and Rodrik, 2003; Hausman *et al.*, 2005; Rodrik, 2006, 2008c). Rather than trying to apply a long standardised list of reforms, as in the augmented Washington consensus, one should try to identify the most urgent binding constraints holding down an economy in a specific period. Policy reforms should target these binding constraints, which can be lack of finance, weak returns to investment, lack of appropriability of returns to investment, dysfunctioning labour markets and so on. An interesting example is provided by El Salvador, which had faithfully implemented all the Washington consensus reforms, but without any positive results (Hausmann and Rodrik, 2003). The binding constraint here was that there was underinvestment in innovative entrepreneurship, as the results of successful entrepreneurs were immediately copied by other entrepreneurs, who had not borne any of the risks.

6. *Neo-Keynesian remedies.* Both Paul Krugman (2009) and Joseph Stiglitz (2002, 2010) have criticised the orthodox responses to successive crises which invariably focus on budget cuts, stabilisation and retrenchment. This goes against the Keynesian theories which prevailed when the IMF was set originally up, which called for expansionary finance in the context of a crisis (Stiglitz, 2002). In the Asian crisis, the IMF insistence on contractionary measures and liberalisation of capital accounts contributed to a worsening of the economic conditions. In the current crisis in the advanced economies

---

[21] Sachs and Woo (1997, 2000), however, point to the differences between the Soviet Union and China. China was a predominantly agricultural economy. In 1978, reform started in the agricultural sector and gradually spread to other sectors. The Soviet Union was an overindustrialised economy, where reform inevitably led to cut backs in industrial output, as inefficient activities were discontinued.

contractionary policies have been imposed in the USA and the European Union. In Europe, countries with budget deficits in excess of 3 per cent of GDP have been forced to slash their budgets, with negative effects on growth and employment. Huge budget cuts in the peripheral economies of Portugal, Greece and Spain have resulted in sustained negative GDP growth.

7. *Rediscovery of industrial policy.* Latin American neo-structuralist authors argue for a renewed emphasis on more selective industrial policies, as an instrument to promote structural change and economic development (Cimoli *et al.*, 2009; Ocampo *et al.*, 2009). This is consistent with the view of markets as non-self-correcting, as described above. Though not all arguments of the neo-structuralists have been accepted by mainstream policy makers, the climate with regard to industrial policy is now rapidly changing.

8. *Pursuing a dynamic comparative advantage.* In a series of publications former World Bank vice-president and chief economist Justin Yifu Lin takes a kind of middle position between the neoliberals and structuralists (Lin, Cai and Li, 2003, 2010; Lin and Monga, 2010). On the one hand, Lin argues that economic success depends on policies that follow a country's comparative advantage. He distinguishes between the successful comparative advantage-following policies that China has adopted since 1978 and the comparative advantage-defying policies that China followed between 1950 and 1978. This is more or less in line with liberal thinking on markets. But, on the other hand, policy should try to identify dynamic comparative advantages, the future comparative advantages of a country. Public policy interventions should actively focus on creating the conditions for realising future comparative advantage and structural change.

13.7.3   Concluding remarks

As was the case with earlier system shocks, the Asian crisis and the global financial crisis have forced policy makers, politicians and academics to start rethinking their policies and theories with regard to the international order. In this chapter, we have presented the different sides in this ongoing debate without attempting to arbitrate between them in any final sense. We do argue that future policy making should be informed by the various lessons that we can draw from the past, not only from the recent past but also from the earlier period 1950–82.

From the recent crisis-ridden period, we learn once again that national and international markets do not automatically correct themselves and that there is an important role for government policy to correct for imperfect information and other market imperfections. More expansionary fiscal and monetary policies could correct for insufficient demand and downward economic spirals. More active industrial policies could contribute to structural change and economic upgrading in developing countries. These policies should take the differences in initial conditions, institutions, binding constraints and – importantly – government capabilities into account. For the least developed countries a return to the non-reciprocity of the GATT years is well worth considering. Too rapid across-the-board abolition of import restrictions could harm the growth prospects of the poorest countries. Non-reciprocity would provide them with some opportunity to temporarily protect promising economic activities from competition from the advanced economies as well as emerging economies such as China.

On the other hand, there is also some danger that the lessons of the earlier post-war period are being forgotten. One of these lessons is that discretionary selective policies by corrupt, inefficient and venal governments can result in rent seeking behaviour, economic stagnation and non-sustainable development. Absence of competition and lack of penalties for bad performance tends to perpetuate inefficient, unproductive and non-innovative enterprises. In many instances and many countries, market reforms have indeed contributed to increased efficiency. Finally, if all countries start actively subsidising and supporting their domestic industries on an ever-increasing scale, at some stage international trade may start to suffer, to the detriment of both rich and poor countries. Export orientation and participation in international trade remain important for the growth prospects of developing countries.

Questions for review

1. What are the characteristics of the post-war international economic order?
2. What are the most important differences between the characteristics of globalisation in the period 1870–1913 and globalisation since the 1980s?
3. What are the new characteristics of the international economic order since 1997?
4. Discuss the characteristics and institutions of the liberal international order, devised at the Bretton Woods conference in 1944. What were the tasks assigned to the IMF and what were those assigned to the World Bank?
5. What were the main criticisms of the liberal international economic order on the part of the advocates of a NIEO in the 1960s and 1970s?
6. What were the most important policy proposals for a new international order?
7. What are the main criticisms of the Washington consensus of 1997? How do these criticisms compare with earlier criticisms of the liberal international order?
8. Discuss the neo-structuralist perspective on economic development and highlight the key differences with neoliberal perspectives.
9. What were the primary objectives of structural adjustment policies? Compare structural adjustment policy proposals with the characteristics of orthodox post-war development strategies.
10. How effective have structural adjustment policies been? Summarise the debate on the (positive or negative) consequences of structural adjustment policies in different parts of the developing world.
11. Discuss some of the important indicators of indebtedness.
12. Under what circumstances are debts a threat to the economic development of a country?
13. Is debt relief an appropriate response to excessive debt burdens in developing countries? What are the main arguments in favour of debt relief? What are the arguments against debt relief?
14. Discuss the main initiatives for reducing debt burdens of developing countries since 1982. How effective have these initiatives been, and what lessons can be derived from them?

15. Explain the reasoning underlying the 'augmented Washington consensus'.
16. Discuss the notion of binding constraints and its implications for policy.

Further reading

Characteristics of the post-war international order are documented in a series of important studies by Angus Maddison. Here we mention: *Two Crises: Latin America and Asia, 1929–1938 and 1973–1983* (1985), *The World Economy in the Twentieth Century* (1989) and *Monitoring the World Economy* (1995) and *Contours of the World Economy* (2007b). Another reference to the international order is a volume edited by Grassman and Lundberg, *The World Economic Order: Past and Present* (1981). Two useful publications about decolonisation are Grimal, *Decolonization: The British, French, Dutch and Belgian Empires, 1919–1963* (1978) and Morris-Jones and Fischer, *Decolonisation and After: The British and French Experience* (1980). Meier describes the emergence of the post-war international institutions in *Emerging from Poverty: The Economics that Really Matters* (1984). Goldin and Reinert, *Globalization for Development: Meeting New Challenges* (2012), provides a valuable book-length discussion of the dimensions of globalisation.

For the debates on the NIEO, the interested reader can consult Streeten, 'Approaches to a New International Economic Order' (1984), Corden, *The NIEO Proposals: A Cool Look* (1979) and Raffer and Singer, *The Economic North–South Divide: Six Decades of Unequal Development* (2001). The liberal policy recommendations which emerged in the wake of the debt crisis of 1982 are discussed in a number of often-cited publications by John Williamson: 'What Washington Means by Policy Reform' (1990), 'Democracy and the Washington Consensus' (1993) and 'The Washington Consensus Revisited' (1997).

An older article by Buiter and Srinivasan in *World Development* 'Rewarding the Profligate and Punishing the Prudent and Poor: Some Recent Proposals for Debt Relief' (1987), provides a good introduction to the debates about debt relief. Two other articles in *World Development* give the reader a taste of debates on this topic: Neumayer, 'Is Good Governance Rewarded? A Cross-National Analysis of Debt Forgiveness' (2002) and Sanford, 'World Bank: IDA Loans or IDA Grants?' (2002). The IMF publication, *Heavily Indebted Poor Countries (HIPC) Initiative – Statistical Update* (2013) provides statistical information on debt relief under the HIPC initiative. The IMF also publishes regular fact sheets on the HIPC initiative at www.imf.org/external/np/exr/facts/hipc.htm.

Lensink, *Structural Adjustment in Sub-Saharan Africa* (1995) provides an accessible introduction to the vast literature on structural adjustment. Overviews are also provided by Mosley, 'Structural Adjustment: A General Overview 1980–89' (1991) and Tarp, *Stabilization and Structural Adjustment: Macro-Economic Frameworks for Analysing the Crisis in Sub-Saharan Africa* (1993). The liberal perspective on structural adjustment is represented by Krueger, *Economic Policy Reform in Developing Countries* (1992) and Krueger and Duncan, *The Political Economy of Controls: Complexity* (1993). An influential publication criticising the negative social consequences of structural adjustment is Cornia, Jolly and Stewart (eds.), *Adjustment with a Human Face* (1987).

Two polar authors in the debates on globalisation and the architecture of the international financial system are Joseph Stiglitz and Stanley Fischer. Stiglitz has severely criticised the functioning of the IMF and the World Bank in his excellent book *Globalization and Its Discontents* (2002). Fischer takes a more positive view of their performance, though he also acknowledges the need for reforms. Of his publications, we mention: Citrin and Fischer, 'Strengthening the International Financial System: Key Issues' (2000) and Fischer's article in *the American Economic Review* 'Globalization and its Challenges' (2003). Important contributions to ongoing debates are Chang, *Kicking Away the Ladder: Development Strategy in Historical Perspective* (2002), which criticises trade liberalisation from the perspective of developing countries and Lin, *New Structural Economics: A Framework for Rethinking Development* (2010). An influential and well-written exposition of neo-structuralist theory is provided in Ocampo, Rada and Taylor, *Growth and Policy in Developing Countries: A Structuralist Approach* (2009). More recent publications on responses to the global financial crisis include a volume edited by Griffith-Jones, Ocampo and Stiglitz, *Time for a Visible Hand: Lessons from the 2008 World Financial Crisis* (2010); Stiglitz, *Free Fall: Free Markets and the Sinking of the Global Economy* (2010), Krugman, *The Return of Depression Economics and the Crisis of 2008* (2009) and a collection of short papers on the current crisis from varying perspectives edited by Blanchard, Romer, Spence and Stiglitz, *In the Wake of the Crisis: Leading Economists Reassess Economic Policy* (2012).

Statistics on debt and international financial flows are to be found in the publications and databases of the IMF, the World Bank, UNCTAD and the OECD. These include the annual IMF publications *International Financial Statistics Yearbook* and *World Economic Outlook,* and the World Bank publications *World Debt Tables* and *Global Development Finance: External Debt of Developing Countries*. Since 2014 these World Bank publications have been replaced by *International Debt Statistics* (2014). Important databases are World Bank, *International Debt Statistics*, http://databank.worldbank.org/Data/Views/VariableSelection/SelectVariables.aspx?source=International%20Debt%20Statistics; IMF, *International Financial Statistics*, http://elibrary-data.imf.org; UNCTAD, UNCTADstat, http://unctadstat.unctad.org/ReportFolders/reportFolders.aspx?sCS_referer=&sCS_ChosenLang=en. The OECD maintains a website on *International Development Statistics*, which contains a variety of datasets on debt, aid and financial flows to developing countries, www.oecd.org/dac/stats/idsonline.htm.

14

Foreign aid and development

In this concluding chapter, we discuss the role of foreign aid in development. The central question is whether aid works. To what extent and under which conditions can aid make a positive contribution to socio-economic development?[1]

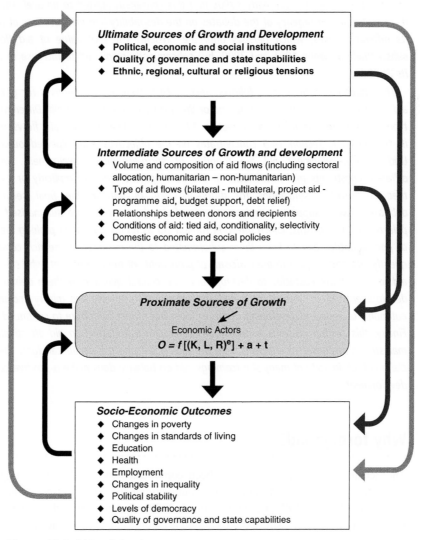

Figure 14.1 Aid and development

---

[1] In this chapter the terms 'development aid', 'development assistance' and 'foreign aid' are used interchangeably.

The decision to discuss foreign aid at the end of this book is a deliberate one. After all, socio-economic development is determined by a complex of factors, including proximate sources of growth, historical experiences, natural circumstances, demographic factors, power structures and processes of state formation, institutions, attitudes and aptitudes, international economic relations and economic policies. Foreign aid is just one of many factors. At best, its contribution can only be modest. The original theories of economic aid formulated in the 1950s and the 1960s by authors such as Chenery and Strout, Rostow and Rosenstein-Rodan, recognise this explicitly. They state that under certain conditions foreign aid may contribute to an acceleration of growth and development, but it cannot transform processes of stagnation into dynamic processes of development. In the heated debates between the supporters and opponents of foreign aid, this tends to be forgotten. Figure 14.1 depicts the role of aid amid other factors.

Until the 1990s, the desirability of development aid was not questioned in the political debate. It was not until the early 1990s that this consensus started to unravel. This manifested itself in a renewed urgency of the debates on the desirability and effectiveness of foreign aid in its different guises, which persists until the present. The real value of aid flows declined substantially between 1991 and 2000, but subsequently recovered to increase to almost twice its 2000 level by 2011.

This chapter is structured as follows. Section 14.1 examines the motives for granting foreign aid. Section 14.2 presents a brief outline of the history of development aid. Different sources and types of aid are distinguished in section 14.3. Quantitative data on aid flows are presented in section 14.4. Section 14.5 concentrates on the objectives and expected outcomes of aid. Underlying development aid are theories of socio-economic development, which identify different constraints and bottlenecks in the development process. Implicitly or explicitly these theories provide justifications for different kinds of aid. In the final section 14.6 the debates between supporters and opponents of development aid are summarised. Attention is paid to radical criticisms, which interpret foreign aid as an instrument to prolong the dependence of poor countries and to keep them subordinated to the interests of the rich countries. Subsequently, attention is paid to the criticisms of proponents of the free market, who see development aid as one of the obstacles to development. The central question in these debates is whether development aid, in spite of its stated aims of reducing poverty and misery and increasing the autonomy of people in developing countries, does not in fact contribute to continued dependence. Finally, this section presents a review of the empirical literature on aid effectiveness and the mainstream responses to criticisms from the radical left and the neoliberal right. The mainstream claim is that, in spite of many shortcomings, aid on balance does make a positive contribution to development.

14.1 Why foreign aid?

The debate on development aid has been complicated by a failure to distinguish clearly between the principles and moral motives underlying aid and the assessments of its effects and results (Riddell, 1987, Chapters 2 and 4, 2008). A statement to the effect that given the urgency of the poverty issue and the enormous income gap between rich and poor countries, governments have a moral obligation to provide aid, implicitly assumes that the effects of aid are positive. For if foreign aid was thought to have negative effects on development, the moral case for aid would automatically become invalid.

If the contributions of aid to development are disappointing, we have to ask whether this is due to inherent shortcomings of aid or whether this depends on the specific ways in which aid is provided. Since 2003, an important new literature has emerged focusing on how aid can be made more effective at micro-level on the basis of a systematic evaluation of its impacts (Banerjee and Duflo, 2011). Ultimately, our judgements concerning the desirability of aid also depend on our perspectives on the empirical reality of which aid is a constituent part. Here, we will first discuss the different motives underlying foreign aid. In section 14.6, we will discuss the empirical research on the effectiveness of aid.

The following kinds of motives for development aid can be distinguished: moral motives; references to mutual interests; commercial motives; and political and strategic motives (Alesina and Dollar, 2000; Claessens *et al.*, 2009; Dollar and Pritchett, 1998; Hoebink, 1988, 1990a, 1990b; Lumsdaine, 1993; Maizels and Nissanke, 1984; Riddell, 2008; Stern, 2002).

Moral motives

Moral motives for development aid include:

- *Humanitarian motives*. Given widespread poverty, malnutrition and unacceptable living conditions in many developing countries, there is a moral obligation to provide aid. These motives take some criterion of absolute human needs as their point of departure.
- *Egalitarian motives*. From an egalitarian point of view, the extreme inequalities between rich and poor countries, and rich and poor people, and the widening gaps between rich and poor in the world economy, are morally unacceptable. The rich have a moral duty to help the poor. Development aid is seen as an equalising transfer payment.
- *International solidarity*. It is not self-evident that criteria of need and egalitarian justice should be applied on a global scale. It can be argued that the main task of a state is to provide for the welfare of its own citizens, according to the criteria of justice within the society. The moral argument for development aid includes the proposition that moral obligations transcend the borders of national societies. In its most extreme version, this argument states that we are all members of a new global society.
- *Reparation of past wrongs*. In the past, rich Western countries have exploited poor countries and have harmed their chances of development through colonialism and external intervention. As the Western world is responsible for the underdevelopment of poor countries, Western countries have a moral obligation to repay past debts. From this perspective, development aid is a kind of compensation payment.

Mutual interests

Poor countries and rich countries are mutually interdependent in a global society. Economic and social development in poor countries is not only in the interest of the citizens of these countries. It is also in the interest of rich countries and their citizens (see

Brandt *et al.*, 1980, 1983). The mutual interest motive is expressed in different modalities, as follows:

- *Interdependence.* The world economy is increasingly an interdependent whole. Economic development and increasing incomes per capita in poor countries create new markets for exports from rich countries. Economic stagnation in the poor countries has negative effects on economic growth in the rich countries.
- *Global environmental problems.* Global environmental problems caused by pollution, depletion of resources, population growth and economic growth threaten the welfare and development prospects of both rich and poor countries. Protection of the global environment and sustainable development are common interests (e.g. the Brundtland report *Our Common Future*, 1987).
- *Global public goods.* The global public goods perspective is a further elaboration of the previous point. Development is increasingly linked to global challenges such as climate change, stagnation of world food production, global scarcity of water, growth of global population, declining biodiversity and increased financial instability. These issues require funding for global development (Van Lieshout *et al.*, 2010).
- *Avoiding international conflicts.* The enormous gaps in income levels in the world economy may lead to destructive conflicts between the rich countries in the North and the poor countries and their inhabitants in the South. Avoiding such conflicts by promoting economic development in poor countries is also in the interest of the rich countries.
- *Immigration.* A special version of the mutual interest motive is the prevention of massive immigration from developing countries to the economically advanced countries. This line of reasoning states that in the modern global economy extreme deprivation in the developing countries will spill over into the rich countries (World Bank, 2002a). If economic conditions in developing countries improve due to development aid and other efforts, migration flows to the rich countries, which are experienced as threatening, will come to an end.

Commercial motives

Development aid is seen as an instrument of export promotion. Development aid is used to support firms exporting to developing countries, and to help develop new export markets. It is hard to draw the boundary between commercial motives and mutual interests. Sometimes the only motive is blatant self-interest, with firms in rich countries lobbying for support and foreign aid functioning as a form of export credit in disguise. Sometimes there is a genuine conviction, that the promotion of economic development in a developing country is compatible with an expansion of exports to this country.

Foreign aid is frequently an instrument of foreign policy, aimed at cementing the political ties between donors and client countries or achieving strategic political goals (e.g. Alesina and Dollar, 2000; Browne, 2006; Easterly, 2006, 2008; Maizels and Nissanke, 1984; Radelet *et al.*, 2004; Schraeder *et al.*, 1998). Former European colonial powers tried to maintain or reinforce their political, economic and cultural ties with their former colonies through development aid. For the USA, preventing countries from falling within the communist sphere of influence was clearly an important motive for foreign aid during the Cold War. In the 1950s and 1960s, most of US foreign aid went to

South Korea, South Vietnam and Taiwan. In the 1970s, the lion's share of aid was provided to Egypt and Israel. Foreign aid was one of the main instruments of US foreign policy in the Middle East; 80 per cent of aid from the former Soviet Union was allocated to Cuba, Mongolia and Vietnam; most French development aid went to its former colonies in Africa. In the early period of Dutch development aid, a large proportion was reserved for (former) colonies. Japanese aid went to countries that voted along with Japan in the United Nations on issues such as whaling (Alesina and Dollar, 2000). In recent years huge amounts of US aid have gone to Afghanistan, Iraq and Pakistan for geostrategic reasons. Chinese aid is conditional on non-recognition of Taiwan as an independent state and the rapid increase in Chinese aid to Africa is driven in part by strategic motives such as access to natural resources (Bräutigam, 2009). For a public justification of their aid policies, governments tend to appeal primarily to moral motives. But in practice all the motives mentioned above play a role in maintaining broad political and social support of foreign aid policy.

In a lucid analysis of the ethical and moral arguments for foreign aid, Riddell (1987: 12–16) has identified seven propositions, which together constitute the argument that there is a moral obligation for governments to provide foreign aid to developing countries.[2] These are summarised in Box 14.1.

Each of these propositions can be challenged. The criticism of the moral motives for aid has been formulated by contract theorists such as Nozick, Bauer and Hayek, applying

---

BOX 14.1 : The case for foreign aid

1. On the basis of comparisons between domestic standards of living in rich countries and those in developing countries, potential donors accept that there are problems in developing countries, which provide a moral basis for action.
2. Direct intervention can help solve such problems.
3. External financial and/or technical assistance contributes to a development strategy aimed at solving these problems.
4. Aid flows from government to government contribute to the solution of problems.
5. There is a moral obligation to give aid to defined categories of countries, and – through the governments of these countries – to defined groups within these countries.
6. The moral obligation to provide aid to identified countries is so strong that the use of funds for foreign aid is justified in the light of other legitimate claims on a government's financial resources.
7. The resources furnished by means of foreign aid actually help promote development or have the potential of doing so in the future, based on the learning experiences of past mistakes.

Source: Riddell (1987).

---

[2] Riddell (2008) emphasises that private, non-governmental aid flows are increasingly important and that similar moral arguments can be made for private aid.

procedural theories of justice. From this perspective, all inequalities in outcomes and rewards obtained by individual effort and according to just procedures are justified. Redistribution of outcomes on the basis of needs or egalitarian criteria is rejected as unjust. Only when inequality is the result of unjust acquisition in the past may there be a basis for compensation in the present. However, here the debate shifts to the empirical domain. The critics of egalitarian and needs-based criteria are convinced that differences in economic development are empirically explained by differences in skills, talents, efforts, institutions and policies, and not by past exploitation.

A second line of criticism is that governments are only responsible for their own citizens and have no obligations to citizens of other countries. A third category of arguments, formulated in particular by Bauer, refers to the fact that aid is provided on a government-to-government basis. Even if one subscribes to the moral argument in favour of aid, which Bauer certainly does not, there may still be good reasons to be opposed to intergovernmental aid flows. In practice, according to Bauer, aid means that poor people in rich countries are taxed in order to subsidise rich people and members of political elites in poor countries. Once again, the discussion about principles of justice is mixed with a discussion about empirical realities. A fourth line of argument is that aid simply does not deliver what it promises. It does not contribute, or does not contribute much, to development. This issue will be discussed in section 14.6.

Without doing sufficient justice to the interesting debate on the moral foundations of development aid – well summarised by Riddell – we take the moral arguments for development aid as our point of departure. In the rest of the chapter our focus will be on the empirical discussions about the effects of aid on development. This means that less attention will be paid to other motives underlying foreign aid. These will only enter the discussion when they have negative effects on the realisation of the primary objectives of development aid: that is, contributing to an improvement in the living conditions and socio-economic dynamics in developing countries.

14.2   The emergence and evolution of foreign aid

In the period immediately after the Second World War, the first priority was the reconstruction of war damage in Europe. The USA provided support to Western European countries by means of the Marshall Plan, amounting to 2.5 per cent of GDP for a relatively short period of around four years (O'Connell and Soludo, 2001). The success of the Marshall Plan created a positive climate with regard to the role of international financial flows in economic development (Krueger *et. al.*, 1989, Chapter 1). The differences between the reparation of war damages in economically advanced areas and the transformation of economic structures in poor countries were hardly taken into consideration.

The official involvement of the USA in development aid dates back to January 1949, when President Harry S. Truman gave his inaugural address. In the fourth point of his address, Truman announced a new programme for making the benefits of scientific and industrial progress in the affluent countries available to developing countries. The emphasis was on technical assistance. This so-called Four Point programme was later enacted in legislation, although the budgeted resources remained much lower than those set aside for the Marshall Plan. In 1950, Congress allocated 34.5 million dollars to technical assistance. It was not until about 1960 that resource transfers to developing countries reached levels approximating those of the Marshall Plan.

The USA was not alone in starting foreign aid in 1950. In the same year the World Bank issued its first development loan to Colombia, and the United Nations Expanded Program of Technical Assistance (UNEPTA) was launched. Later, this programme would be replaced by the United Nations Development Programme (UNDP). In January 1950, Great Britain and the Commonwealth members Australia, Canada and New Zealand committed themselves to providing foreign aid by signing the Colombo Plan. Aid was especially intended for the countries that had been part of former British India. India, in particular, became a testing ground for foreign aid and theories of development. Other (ex-)colonial powers in Europe, such as France, Belgium and the Netherlands, also started to provide foreign aid. After some time, their example was followed by the countries defeated in the Second World War – Germany, Japan and Italy. In these countries, foreign aid commenced once their economies had recovered from the damage caused by the war.

By 1960, multilateral institutions like the World Bank, the International Finance Corporation (IFC) and the International Development Association (IDA) had become important sources of external financial flows to developing countries. Around 1960, the USA was responsible for more than half of all bilateral and multilateral development aid. Most of the rest was supplied by four former colonial European powers: France, England, Belgium and the Netherlands.

Prince (1976) and Riddell (2008) stress the continuity between the post-war development aid of European countries and the pre-war colonial policies, particularly in the field of technical assistance. In France and the UK, development aid was closely tied in with decolonisation and the objectives of decolonisation policy. An important goal of pre-war French colonial policies had been the assimilation of colonised peoples into French culture. In the postcolonial period French foreign aid flows concentrated on Francophone Africa. Elements of assimilation policy resurfaced in aid policies. There was a strong emphasis on the spread of French language and culture, on education by French experts and on maintaining the economic ties with France. Until 1993, the currencies of French West African countries were directly linked to the French Franc. According to research by Alesina and Dollar (2000), French aid was exceptional in the degree to which strategic political objectives dominated all other aid objectives.

The long-term objective of British colonial policies in the twentieth century was the association of former colonies in a Commonwealth of English-speaking countries. The system of colonial administration was based on *indirect rule*. In comparison with France, Great Britain intervened less into the internal political and social affairs of its colonies. Foreign aid was seen as a continuation of gradual preparations for independence in the context of the Commonwealth during the pre-war period. Therefore, aid flows were strongly centred on Commonwealth countries.

In the case of the Netherlands, there was a sudden rift with Indonesia in 1949 after the so-called police actions of 1947–9. The Netherlands attempted to restore its damaged international prestige by participating on a large scale in multilateral technical assistance, which was beginning at that time. The Netherlands had a reservoir of experience in the form of colonial training programmes, unemployed colonial civil servants and experts. It was successful in finding employment for its experts in multilateral aid programmes (Teszler, 1978; Van Soest, 1975). As small countries, the Netherlands and the Scandinavian countries used development aid as defining characteristics of their foreign policies.

The reasons for the USA to expand its bilateral aid in the 1950s and 1960s included, among other things, the fear of Chinese communist expansion in Asia and the influence of the Cuban revolution in Latin America. Because of the Cold War, large amounts of aid were provided to countries on the periphery of the communist bloc, such as Greece, Turkey, South Korea, Taiwan, South Vietnam and Laos. In 1960, President John Kennedy launched the *Alliance for Progress*, a programme for economic development and cooperation in Latin America. The same year saw the foundation of the Peace Corps, an initiative that would soon be copied by other countries.

In 1960, development aid from the OECD countries was institutionalised in the Development Assistance Committee (DAC). The DAC coordinated and recorded aid-related efforts by the OECD countries. More and more OECD countries started to provide foreign aid, while the US share in total aid flows gradually declined. In 1960 the share of the USA in total OECD foreign aid was 57.5 per cent. By 2012, this had dropped to 21.5 per cent. As a percentage of GNI US aid in 2012 was only 0.19 per cent, compared to a DAC average of 0.29 per cent. In absolute terms the USA was the largest donor in all years, except 2000 when Japan was briefly the largest donor (see Table 14.3, p. 618 and OECD, 2014). In 2012, three-quarters of total DAC–ODA was accounted for by eight countries, the USA, Japan, Germany, UK, France, the Netherlands, Canada and Sweden. Aid from Non-DAC countries was 5 per cent of aid from DAC countries. In the 1970s and early 1980s, poverty took the central stage, in line with the intellectual climate of the New International Order (see Chapter 13). Riddell (2008: 32) remarks that, to the present day, donors have successively swung between the extreme views that development aid is best deployed to assist poor people directly or that it is best deployed in accelerating and helping shape the process of wealth creation, contributing to poverty alleviation indirectly.

According to Van der Hoeven (2001: 110), the international economic climate of the 1980s forced many countries to adjust their economies in order to accommodate to external shocks. This led to a shift from project aid to programme aid in the form of structural adjustment programmes and conditionality. Aid was only provided if countries agreed to implement the adjustment programmes advocated by the IMF, the World Bank and the donor community. Conditionality was inspired by neoliberal theories of development, which focused on the importance of market reforms and the elimination of state-imposed distortions (see Chapter 13). The end of the Cold War at the end of the 1980s ushered in a new phase in development cooperation (Dijkstra and White, 2003; Doornbos, 2001). The strategic motives for aid became less important. The links between aid and policy reform and aid and good governance become more prominent. In the economic sphere, conditionality initially focused on macro-economic policy and structural adjustment. But aid also increasingly came to be linked with issues such as democratic reform, elections, human rights and the effective functioning of government bureaucracies and social service delivery. Alesina and Dollar (2000) showed that countries that introduced democratic reforms tended to receive substantial increases in aid.

In the 1990s, the donor community became increasingly disenchanted with the effectiveness of structural adjustment and conditionality (e.g. Meltzer, 2000). In 1999, the link between aid and structural adjustment was broken and the term 'structural adjustment loan' was formally abandoned by the World Bank (World Bank, 2005). The focus shifted to recipient-based strategies aimed at poverty eradication. There was a shift from *conditionality* to *selectivity*. Under conditionality, aid had been supplied to countries that had agreed to implement reforms in the future. But once aid had been made available, many reforms were not really implemented. Under selectivity, the allocation of aid and debt relief was increasingly guided by assessments of policy reforms that developing countries had already implemented in the past. Policy reforms were conceived of broadly, including democratic reforms, improvement in the effectiveness of government institutions, the protection of property rights and the rule of law and effective macro-economic policies. Criteria for the allocation of aid also came to include poverty reduction strategies (PRSs), in response to earlier criticisms that the international agencies had neglected poverty issues.

After a decade of aid fatigue in the 1990s, there was a major expansion of aid flows from the late 1990s onwards. The agreement on the MDGs served to reignite the support for aid. In the *End of Poverty: Economic Possibilities for Our Times* (2005), Jeffrey Sachs argued, without much theoretical underpinning, that poverty could be eliminated within a generation if sufficient flows of aid were made available for countries and individuals to escape poverty traps. Two important landmarks were the Monterrey conference of 2002, where the advanced economies pledged to increase aid, and the Paris declaration on aid effectiveness of 2005. In the Paris declaration a number of important reforms were agreed upon which continue to dominate the aid agenda until now (Bigsten and Tengstam, 2012).[3] These include (1) donor harmonisation; (2) developing country ownership – the notion that such countries should develop their own strategies to which aid could make a contribution: aid should be aligned to recipient priorities and policies; (3) the need for strong and effective partnerships between donors and recipients; (4) an emphasis on building of institutions and capabilities; and last but not least (5) result orientation – holding both donors and recipients accountable for the verifiable results of aid. As part of this process there was a shift from project aid to larger blocks of less-targeted aid such as budget support, debt relief or sector wide approaches (SWAps).

In his impressive overview of the evolution of the aid debate, *Does Foreign Aid Really Work?* Riddell (2008) argues, perhaps somewhat overoptimistically, that there is a shift from the notion of voluntaristic perspectives on aid to rights-based international obligations of advanced economies to provide aid in the light of human needs.

14.3   Development aid: sources and categories

Since 1977, the DAC of the OECD presents an annual survey of aid flows to developing countries in the *Geographical Distribution of Financial Flows to Developing Countries* (GDFF). This publication is now available in electronic format, with complete data for the whole period 1960–present (OECD, 2003a and online at OECD, http://stats.oecd.org/#). In this source official development assistance (ODA) is defined as financial flows to developing countries provided by official agencies, with the objective of promoting the economic

---

[3] These principles were further elaborated at subsequent international meetings in Accra in 2008 and in Busan, Korea, in 2011.

development and welfare of developing countries and with a grant element of at least 25 per cent.

The *sources* of development aid are summarised in Box 14.2.

BOX 14.2 : Sources of development aid

- **Aid provided by advanced economies in the OECD**. This aid is coordinated by the DAC. This includes both bilateral and multilateral ODA.
- **Aid provided by non-DAC countries**. Prominent among these are the Arab oil-producing countries. Aid flows from these countries increased in the 1970s when oil prices were raised. In the 1980s these flows declined again. Presently only three countries are specifically listed as non-DAC bilateral donors: Saudi Arabia, Kuwait and the United Arab Emirates. But there are also multilateral flows from the Arab countries. Other countries presently listed among this heading are Russia, Turkey, Taiwan and Israel.
- **Chinese aid**. Though not comparable in volume to DAC aid flows, Chinese aid has increased dramatically from around half a billion US dollars in 1999 to almost 3 billion by 2012 (Bräutigam, 2009; Broich and Szirmai, 2014). Chinese aid is not included in non-DAC aid flows.
- **Aid provided by voluntary development organisations (non-governmental organisations, NGOs)**. These flows are quite substantial and increasing over time. In the Netherlands voluntary organisations annually provide aid to the equivalent of 5–10 per cent of ODA (Kruyt and Koonings, 1988).[4] Globally, aid provided through NGOs in 2004 amounted to 23 billion dollars, of which 13 billion was raised from private contributions and 10 billion consisted of public contributions (Riddell, 2008).
- **Aid provided by private foundations**. This involves aid provided by large private foundations, the most well known of which is the Bill and Melinda Gates Foundation. According to its website, the Gates foundation has disbursed 28.3 billion US dollars since its creation in 1997 (www.gatesfoundation.org/). Since 2009 net private grants from foundations have been included in OECD statistics.

DAC statistics on development assistance primarily refer to aid provided by OECD member countries of the DAC and by non-DAC countries. Aid offered with other than developmental objectives (e.g. military assistance) is excluded. Aid flows include both outright grants (in money or kind) and soft loans with a grant element of at least 25 per cent. Loans without this grant element, like export credits, are not classified as part of ODA. They are referred to as other official flows (OOF). The concessionality of a loan – the softness or grant element – is the difference between the costs of a loan (depending on the maturity of the loan, the

---

[4] The distinction between official aid flows and voluntary aid flows is not always clear-cut. Some non-governmental aid organisations are entirely funded by voluntary donations of citizens. Other organisations are heavily subsidised by governments.

grace period before the first repayment and the annual interest) and the costs a borrower would have to pay at market rates. For practical purposes, the reference interest rate for commercial loans is set at 10 per cent. The grant element in development assistance differs from country to country, but it is quite high. In 2001 the average grant element was 82 per cent (OECD, 2003a). Aid is not always financial. Sometimes it consists of goods (food, machines, fertilisers) or services (technical experts, teachers). In such cases, the value of the goods and services is included in the statistics.

The OECD records both *bilateral aid*, which is provided directly on a country-to-country basis, and *multilateral aid* through international organisations. Important sources of multilateral aid are the World Bank; the IDA, a subsidiary organisation of the World Bank which issues soft loans for development objectives; the regional development banks (ADB, AfDB, IDB); the World Health Organisation (WHO); the International Fund for Agricultural Development (IFAD); and the European Development Fund (EDF). Multilaterally funded technical aid is offered by the United Nations Development Programme (UNDP) and the Food and Agriculture Organisation (FAO). There are also specific Arab-financed multilateral agencies such as the OPEC Fund for International Development (OFID). In 2012, multilateral aid was 30 per cent of total DAC–ODA and 26.4 per cent of total ODA including ODA from non-DAC countries (OECD, 2014).

In general, governments find it easier to put their stamp on aid policy in bilateral aid relations than via aid provided through multilateral agencies. Bilateral aid also offers more opportunities for support to domestic producers and exporters in the donor country. The distinction between bilateral and multilateral aid is not absolute, however. Much bilateral aid is coordinated on a recipient-country basis via international donor consortia. The European development fund is also a mixture of bilateral and multilateral aid.

The following five categories of aid can be distinguished (Cassen, 1986; Dijkstra and White, 2003; Riddell, 2008): project aid; programme aid; food aid; humanitarian and emergency aid; technical cooperation.

Project aid

Under the heading of project aid, support is provided for a consistent set of activities with a specified duration and a well-defined objective. Project aid makes available specific capital assets or packages of technical assistance. An important component of project aid consists of infrastructural works, such as roads, harbours, dams, irrigation projects, energy projects, or telecommunications projects. In addition, there are projects in both large-scale and small-scale industry, agriculture, integrated rural development, education, population, health, female emancipation and so forth.

Programme aid

In the case of programme aid, financial support is provided to governments in the form of financial grants or concessional loans in support of economic policy programmes. Programme aid may be provided for the benefit of the entire economy or for specific sectors (the so-called SWAps). In the latter case, the developing country receives financial resources to execute certain policies in one specific sector – education, agriculture, small-scale industry and so on. Programme aid comes in the form of balance of payments support, budget support, or debt relief. Programme aid leaves more to the discretion of the recipient than project aid. It is easier to disburse quickly, which makes it a more flexible instrument. It is usually linked to policy dialogue with the donors. It is clear that programme aid requires higher levels of government capabilities. Therefore, programme aid is typically provided to countries that have higher scores on governance indicators.

Food aid

Food aid is concerned with the provision of food in kind from the agricultural surpluses of the rich countries. This food is provided either free of charge or at low price. Apart from emergency aid in case of natural disasters and famines, food aid is also offered when the food production in a country fails to meet the demand for food. Food may also be provided to people in exchange for work on roads, infrastructure, or municipal facilities (*Food for Work*). In recent years, food aid has sometimes been provided in cash, allowing developing countries to buy food in their own or neighbouring countries to supply it to food-deficit regions.

Humanitarian and emergency aid

This category of aid is provided to cope with consequences of natural or man-made disasters: earthquakes, floods, tsunamis, droughts, famines, but also wars and civil conflicts. According to Riddell (2008), this type of aid has been increasing over time. Humanitarian aid increased from 1.5 per cent of total ODA in 1990 to 7.3 per cent in 2012.

Technical cooperation

Technical cooperation is defined as activities, the primary purpose of which is to augment the level of knowledge, skills and technical know-how in developing countries. It involves providing technical services of experts, volunteers and teachers and actions targeted at education, training and advice. The boundary between technical cooperation and project aid is not quite clear since elements of technical cooperation are included in almost all projects. However, project aid mainly finances physical capital goods which are supplied in kind or for which money is provided. Technical aid refers to 'experts', who contribute to engineering design and construction of capital projects, the transfer of knowledge, education and educational institution building, institutional development or technology transfer. Scholarships, short training programmes and education services of international educational institutions in donor countries are also considered part of technical cooperation.

In principal, programme aid could also be used to pay for services of technical experts or for investments in education. Most often, however, technical aid is provided in the form of payment of the salaries of experts posted in developing countries. If programme aid targets the educational sector, it will be supplied as budget support to ministries of education.

14.4   Quantitative data on aid flows

As an empirical background for the debates on aid, this section provides quantitative data on the magnitude, allocation and sources of aid flows, as well as data on the relative importance of aid for different countries.

Long-term trends in the magnitude and geographical distribution of aid flows

Table 14.1 presents data on the total volume of net ODA from OECD countries and non-DAC countries. Since 2009 these figures also include aid flows from private organisations. At constant 2000 dollars, the value of the total aid flows doubled between 1960 and 1990. As mentioned above, the share of the largest donor, the USA, decreased strongly during this period. The number of countries providing aid increased, as did the volume of aid per country. The 1970s were characterised primarily by a strong growth of aid flows from oil-exporting countries. Aid from the Soviet Union and former socialist countries in Eastern Europe had always been modest in volume and was discontinued after the collapse of the Soviet Union. Between 1990 and 2000 the volume of aid declined. In real terms, aid in 2000 was 19 per cent lower than in 1990. After 2000, the growth of aid resumed, reaching 86.7 billion dollars in 2012 (or 133 billion dollars in current values).

Most aid goes to low-income countries. Aid flows to least developed countries increased strongly between 1970 and 2012. The regional data show a dramatic threefold increase in the volume of aid to Sub-Saharan African countries between 1960 and 1990. Between 1990 and 2000 aid declined to the levels prevailing in the late 1970s. After 2000, aid to Africa grew to 2.3 times its 2000 level by 2012. Aid flows to Asia peaked in 1980, especially due to high aid levels in the Middle East. In the 1990s, they shrank to the levels of around 1960, but there were substantial increases after 2000. Aid to Latin America increased from 1.7 to 5.7 billion dollars between 1960 and 1990, staying more or less at the same level after 1990.

Since 1991, there have been increasing aid flows to several of the newly independent states of the former Soviet Union and to former communist countries in Eastern Europe. The aid flows to the Asian republics of the former Soviet Union are included in the totals for Asia in Table 14.1, Table 14.2 and Table 14.3. These flows amounted to 1.5 billion dollars in 2001. Aid flows to European countries in transition and more advanced developing countries are recorded separately as part of Other Official Flows. These flows are not included in the totals of Tables 14.1, 14.2 and 14.3, but amounted on average to 6.2 billion dollars a year in the 1990s (OECD, 2003a).

Table 14.2 presents further information on the distribution of aid over different regions. The table also includes population shares for the year 2011. Compared to their shares in total developing country population, two regions are clearly overrepresented in the aid flows: Sub-Saharan Africa, and North Africa and the Middle East. In recent years, the share of these regions in annual aid flows is two to three times as high as their share in population. For the Middle East, this is explained by the strategic importance of the region. Foreign political considerations determine the magnitude of aid flows to Israel, Jordan and Egypt. The overrepresentation of Sub-Saharan Africa has to do with the deep economic problems and the extent of poverty in this region. In proportion to its share in population, Asia is highly underrepresented in aid flows. Also striking are the overrepresentation of developing countries in Oceania and Europe.

Table 14.3 provides information about country contributions to total aid, bilateral as well as multilateral. In 2012, eight countries, the USA, Japan, Germany, UK, France, the Netherlands, Canada and Sweden provided three-quarters of all aid from the combined DAC countries. For all post-war years, the USA provided the largest share of aid, except in the year 2000, when it was temporarily eclipsed by Japan. Over time the number of donors has been increasing and the share of the USA has been declining from 59 to 20 per cent of

Table 14.1: Net receipts of development assistance by income level and region, 1960–2012[a] ($ billion, at constant 2000 prices and exchange rates)

	1960	1965	1970	1975	1980	1985	1990	1995	1997	2000	2005	2010	2012
All developing countries	29.7	39.1	35.3	50.5	56.3	59.5	62.1	51.6	46.5	50.3	83.8	89.0	86.7
Income category[b] [c]													
Low-income countries	12.7	21.0	17.5	23.2	25.3	27.9	29.8	27.1	22.6	24.4	21.4	32.4	31.1
Least developed countries	2.8	5.5	4.4	11.8	14.7	17.5	18.0	14.9	12.4	12.4	20.0	30.2	28.1
Lower-middle-income countries	7.5	7.7	7.0	15.3	14.3	14.3	16.3	11.3	11.4	11.7	37.8	21.5	20.3
Upper-middle-income countries	2.1	4.1	3.6	2.6	3.7	2.7	3.9	2.2	1.5	1.7	7.9	7.8	9.9
Unallocated	3.2	3.2	4.6	6.4	10.1	9.7	9.6	9.6	10.3	12.5	16.4	26.9	25.4
Region													
Total Africa	7.7	9.5	8.7	17.6	17.5	22.7	27.3	18.9	17.2	15.7	27.6	32.4	33.5
Sub-Saharan Africa	2.4	6.3	5.9	9.5	12.7	16.7	19.2	15.9	13.6	12.7	25.0	29.5	29.1
North Africa	5.4	3.0	2.6	8.0	4.6	5.3	7.7	2.6	2.8	2.2	2.1	1.8	3.1
Total Asia	16.2	19.6	17.2	21.8	22.9	21.6	19.5	16.2	13.6	16.1	36.0	24.8	22.1
Low-income countries in Asia	14.2	17.7	15.4	16.8	14.8	15.9	13.6	11.8	9.8	12.1	7.5	11.2	10.7
Middle East	2.1	1.7	2.4	6.2	9.0	7.3	5.1	2.5	2.4	2.3	19.7	6.4	5.9
Latin America	1.7	5.5	5.3	4.0	3.8	6.3	5.7	5.6	5.3	5.0	4.7	6.7	5.9
Oceania	0.2	0.9	1.4	1.7	1.7	1.7	1.5	1.6	1.5	0.8	0.9	1.4	1.4
Europe	2.9	2.3	0.9	0.4	2.0	0.8	1.5	2.0	1.7	3.7	3.1	4.0	5.2
Not specified by region	1.0	1.3	1.8	4.8	8.4	6.5	6.5	7.3	7.2	9.0	11.0	18.8	18.0
All developing countries (current US$)	4.0	6.2	6.9	17.8	33.5	32.3	57.9	59.8	48.7	50.3	108.7	131.7	133.0

Notes:

[a] New grants and loans minus repayment of outstanding loans for 152 developing countries. Net ODA receipts are total net ODA flows from DAC countries, multilateral organisations and non-DAC countries (excl. China). Since 2009 total ODA includes more than 2 billion dollars per year from private foundations such as the Gates Foundation. ODA excludes Other Official Flows (OOF) to European countries in transition and more advanced developing countries and territories. Between 1990 and 2012 net OOF was 14.2 billion dollars per year on average.

[b] 1960–2000: Countries have been classified on the basis of their 1998 GNI/per capita. Within the low-income category, 49 countries are classified as Least developed countries. 2005–12: Countries have been classified on the basis of their 2005 GNI per capita.

[c] Before 1997, not all aid is registered per income category. Even including the unallocated row the sum of subcategories is less than the total, especially for the earlier years.

Sources:

OECD *Geographical Distribution of Financial Flows to Aid Recipients, 1960–2001* (2003a).

2005–12: OECD, *International Development Statistics*, OECDstat, downloaded March 2014, http://stats.oecd.org/Index.aspx?datasetcode=TABLE2A#.

Table 14.2: Distribution of net official development assistance, by region (%)[a]

Region	Regional share in aid receipts						Population share (%)	Net ODA $ billion
	1960	1970	1980	1990	2000	2012	2011	2012
Sub-Saharan Africa	14.5	18.1	26.3	34.2	32.1	44.0	15.5	46.4
Asia (excl. Middle East),	45.9	44.3	27.9	25.1	33.0	23.3	65.4	24.6
of which								
Eastern Asia	20.2	23.0	9.0	13.3	19.0	6.0	33.8	6.3
South and Central Asia	25.7	21.3	18.9	11.8	14.0	17.3	31.5	18.3
North Africa and Middle East	24.3	15.0	30.7	25.2	11.9	13.5	5.9	14.2
Latin America	5.4	15.8	7.6	9.9	11.8	9.6	10.4	10.1
Europe	9.3	2.8	4.0	2.9	9.1	7.6	2.7	8.0
Oceania	0.6	4.1	3.5	2.6	2.0	2.0	0.2	2.1
Total, excl. Unspecified	100.0	100.0	100.0	100.0	100.0	100.0	100.0	105.4
Unspecified by region[b]	3.3	5.1	14.3	10.0	18.0	20.7		27.6

Notes:

[a] Net ODA from all donors (since 2009 including private donors).

[b] As % of total ODA including ODA unspecified by region.

Source:

OECD, *International Development Statistics*, OECDstat, http://stats.oecd.org/#, downloaded April 2014.

the total. There are now over 100 donors, which creates major coordination problems from both the perspective of recipients and from the perspective of donors (Riddell, 2008).

Net aid as a percentage of national income fell far short of the target of 0.7 per cent of GNI agreed upon in the 1960s and reaffirmed regularly at international meetings such as the 2002 Monterrey conference on financing for development. Only the Nordic countries and the Netherlands met these targets. For all DAC countries, the share of aid to GNP fell sharply from 0.33 per cent in 1990–1 to only 0.22 per cent in 2000, providing an indication of aid fatigue in this period. But it subsequently recovered to 0.29 per cent in 2012. The volatility of aid is especially marked for the USA, where aid as a percentage of national income declined from 0.23 per cent in 1985–6 to 0.11 per cent in 2001, before recovering to 0.19 per cent in 2012. In spite of its shrinking share in total aid, the USA remains the largest donor in absolute terms, making it a dominant force in shaping multilateral aid efforts. During much of the post-war period, the USA has targeted one-third of its bilateral assistance to Egypt and Israel. France has given overwhelmingly to former colonies. Japanese aid is highly correlated with UN voting patterns in line with Japanese preferences (Alesina and Dollar, 2000). The share of multilateral aid in total aid flows from the DAC countries showed a steady increase from 12.4 per cent in 1960 to 33 per cent in 2000, remaining at approximately 30 per cent in the years thereafter. The share of multilateral aid in total aid was slightly lower when non-DAC donors are included (26.4 per cent in 2012, see OECD, 2014).

Table 14.3: Country contributions to aid, 1960–2012 (at current prices and exchange rates)

	Country shares in total ODA						Net aid as % of GNI					
	1960	1970	1980	1990	2000	2012	1960	1970	1980	1990	2000	2012
USA	59.0	43.1	18.9	17.6	16.6	20.3	0.54	0.32	0.27	0.21	0.10	0.19
Germany	4.8	8.2	9.4	9.8	8.4	8.6	0.31	0.32	0.44	0.42	0.27	0.37
UK	8.7	6.6	4.9	4.1	7.5	9.2	0.56	0.39	0.35	0.27	0.32	0.56
France	17.6	10.1	7.6	11.1	6.8	8.0	1.35	0.52	0.44	0.60	0.30	0.45
Japan	2.2	6.3	8.9	14.0	22.5	7.0	0.24	0.23	0.32	0.31	0.28	0.17
Netherlands	0.8	2.7	4.3	3.9	5.2	3.7	0.31	0.62	0.97	0.92	0.84	0.71
Canada	1.4	4.6	2.8	3.8	2.9	3.7	0.16	0.41	0.43	0.44	0.25	0.32
Sweden	0.1	1.6	2.5	3.1	3.0	3.5	0.05	0.35	0.78	0.91	0.80	0.97
Spain		0.4	1.5	2.0	1.4	..	..	0.08	0.2	0.22	0.16
Norway	0.1	0.5	1.3	1.9	2.1	3.1	0.11	0.33	0.87	1.17	0.76	0.93
Other DAC	5.2	8.2	8.3	13.2	13.0	15.6						
DAC total	100.0	91.9	69.4	84.0	90.0	84.1	0.51	0.33	0.35	0.33	0.22	0.29
Non-DAC donors[b]	0.0	5.3	27.1	11.6	1.8	4.3						
Other donors[c]	0.0	2.9	3.4	4.4	8.2	11.6						
Total	100.0	100.0	100.0	100.0	100.0	100.0						

Notes:
[a] Ten largest donors based on average ranking in net ODA contribution 2008–12.
[b] Excl. China.
[c] The published figure for all donors is larger than the sum of DAC and non-DAC donors. Since 2009, aid from private donors is included in the total for all donors, but this does not account for all of the discrepancy.
Source:
OECD, *International Development Statistics*, OECDstat: http://stats.oecd.org/Index.aspx, downloaded 7 April 2014.

14.4.2   Development aid in proportion to total resource flows

It is important to realise that aid flows are part of the wider flow of financial resources to and from developing countries. These flows include other official flows, private flows (FDI, portfolio investment, bank loans) and a category which has been receiving increasing attention in recent years – remittances.[5] Table 14.4 contains information on the share of

---

[5] Total resource flows include concepts from the current account of the balance of payments, such as development aid and remittances, and concepts from the capital account, such as foreign investment and loans. But it excludes factor payments which are also part of the current account. Table 14.3 represents resource flows excluding remittances, Table 14.4 includes remittances.

Table 14.4: Net development aid as a percentage of the total net inflow of financial resources, by income and region, 1960–2012 (current US \$)[a]

	1960	1970	1975/6	1980	1985	1990	1996	2000	2001	2005	2012
All developing countries[b]	56.1	44.7	30.5	29.2	44.1	43.2	23.0	24.1	28.0	19.0	10.7
Income category[c]											
Low Income countries			71.3	70.2	55.7	56.9	26.0	30.4	38.0	96.8	65.5
Least developed countries[d]			80.4	75.0	89.3	86.4	84.1	74.0	68.9		
Other low-income countries							15.1	18.9	26.2		
Lower-middle-income countries					44.0	36.3	29.7	40.2	30.5	43.9	10.7
Upper-middle-income countries					15.0	13.5	2.2	1.7	2.4	2.5	1.8
Region[e]											
Total Africa				67.6	60.2	84.5	86.3	68.8	59.8	41.7	37.1
Sub-Saharan Africa			47.7	59.2	60.5	85.7	89.8	62.1	59.0	43.3	38.3
North Africa							63.8	92.0	53.3	24.0	21.5
Total Asia and the Pacific			47.6	41.7	37.4	25.8	17.0	21.1	25.0	16.7	4.8
Low-income countries in Asia & Pacific					36.0	31.0	16.4	20.9	28.3		
North Africa and the Middle East[f]			49.1	56.9	68.8	97.5	193.8	76.7	48.5	116.4	35.1
Latin America and Caribbean				6.8	16.4	23.3	7.7	5.5	7.5	6.5	2.8

Notes:

[a] Net total resource flows include ODA, other official flows and net private capital flows, including guaranteed export credits, FDI, portfolio investment and private bank loans. This concept excludes remittances.

[b] Not all ODA is specified by region or income category. For 1996–2001 on average 22 per cent of ODA is not specified by income category, 12 per cent is not specified by region. For the period 2002–12 this is even 26.5 per cent. The totals for developing countries include the unspecified figures.

[c] 1960–91: Countries have been classified by their 1991 GNP per capita. 1996–2001: countries have been classified by their 1998 income per capita. 2005–12: countries have been classified by their 2011 income per capita.

[d] In recent years the WDI no longer distinguishes the Least developed countries as a separate category.

[e] North Africa has been included in the total for Africa; the Middle East has been included in the total for Asia and the Pacific.

[f] Percentage above 100 indicates that net non-ODA flows are negative.

Sources:

ODA: 1960 from Krueger *et al.* (1989: 36); 1970 and 1985–91 from OECD (1993a); 1975–80 from OECD (1986); 1996–2001 from OECD, *Geographical Distribution of Financial Flows to Aid Recipients, 1960–2001*, International Development Statistics (IDS) CD-ROM, 2003.

Net resource flows (long-term) from World Bank (2003a). The World Bank regional categories have been readjusted to the GDFF categories, for regions and income groups.

2005–12: Net resource flows from World Bank, *International Debt Statistics*, http://databank.worldbank.org/data/views/variableselection/selectvariables.aspx?source=international-debt-statistics, downloaded April 2014; ODA from OECD, *International Development Statistics*, Statextracts, http://stats.oecd.org/Index.aspx?datasetcode=TABLE2A#, downloaded April 2014.

Table 14.5: Net official development assistance, remittances and net total resource flows, 1975–2012 (US $ million)

	1975	1980	1985	1990	1996	2000	2001	2005	2012
All developing countries									
ODA[a]	16112	28529	28735	51774	50154	41279	43199	92625	102195
Remittances	1,999	16,249	18,904	28,020	53,459	75,064	85,742	185,029	364,050
ODA as % of remittances	806.1	176.6	152.0	184.8	93.8	55.0	50.4	50.1	28.1
Net total resource flows, incl. remittances					247,155	208,105	213,927	756,239	1,605,329
ODA as % of adjusted net total resource flows					20.3	19.8	20.2	12.3	6.4
Remittances by regional destination[b]									
Total Africa	1,154	5,857	5,854	8,823	9,773	10,905	12,117	33,280	59,992
Sub-Saharan Africa	355	1,383	1,085	1,630	2,874	4,285	4,325	20,180	30,007
North Africa	799	4,474	4,768	7,193	6,899	6,620	7,791	13,100	29,985
Total Asia and the Pacific	634	8,465	10,441	13,484	30,111	43,813	48,998	102,670	242,801
North Africa and the Middle East	966	6,042	6,140	9,575	11,249	11,479	13,016	25,016	47,173
Latin America and Caribbean	211	1,927	2,610	5,713	13,574	20,346	24,627	49,078	61,257
ODA as % of adjusted net total resource flows by region[c]									
Total Africa					61	47	41	30	26
Sub-Saharan Africa					77	51	50	34	30
North Africa					28	24	19	11	9
Total Asia and the Pacific					14	14	15	12	4
North Africa and the Middle East					52	26	21	57	16
Latin America and Caribbean					7	4	6	4	2

Notes:

[a] Excl. not regionally allocated ODA. These figures are lower than the total ODA in Tables 14.1 and 14.4.

[b] Remittance data for developing countries recategorised into the same regional categories as those for ODA and NTRF.

[c] Adjusted net total resource flows equal net total resource flows from Table 14.5 plus remittances.

Sources:

ODA and NTRF, see sources cited in Table 14.4.

Remittances from World Bank, *Remittances Data*, updated October 2013, http://econ.worldbank.org/WBSITE/EXTERNAL/EXTDEC/EXTDECPROSPECTS/0,,
contentMDK:22759429~pagePK:64165401~piPK:64165026~theSitePK:476883,00.html#Remittances.

net development aid in total net financial flows to developing countries, Table 14.5 provides information about the relative importance of remittances.

Table 14.4 indicates clearly that in the long run the share of ODA in total resource flows has declined dramatically. This reflects not so much a reduction of aid flows but an increase in other financial flows. In 1960 ODA accounted for 56.1 per cent of net total resource flows. By 2012 this had dropped to 10.7 per cent. Between 1980 and 1986, the share of development aid recovered to reach 56 per cent of the net resource flow. This was primarily caused by the curtailment of private lending and FDI after the 1982 debt crisis. Subsequently, the trend reversed and the share of aid in net total resource flows declined again. This is not true, however, for the LDCs. Here the share of ODA fluctuates wildly, but remains high. In 2005 it even stood at 96.8 per cent, in 2012 at 65.5 per cent. Thus for poor countries aid flows remain very important. In the regional breakdown one sees that the role of ODA in Asia and Latin America is becoming negligible, while in Sub-Saharan African countries, less successful in attracting foreign investment, it still accounts for 37.1 per cent of all inflows. Dollar and Pritchett (1998: 8) conclude that private capital flows are heavily concentrated in a few developing countries and that these flows are very volatile. In a typical low-income country, foreign aid remains a very important source of external finance. Aid does matter here.

In Table 14.5, we compare the role of ODA with that of remittances. The pattern is very interesting. In 1975 the volume of ODA was eight times that of remittances. By 2012, the volume of remittances to developing countries had increased to 364 billion dollars, 3.6 times as high as total ODA. In absolute terms most remittances flowed to Asia. In the bottom panel of Table 14.5, we have added remittances to other resource flows and have calculated the share of ODA in the adjusted total of resource flows. Now even in the most aid-dependent region, Sub-Saharan Africa, ODA only accounts for 30 per cent of total resource flows.

14.4.3   Sectoral allocation of aid

Table 14.6 provides a snapshot of changes in the sectoral allocation of total aid flows since 1967. This table reflects the changing priorities in aid policy. The most striking insight deriving from the table is the decline in aid for the productive sector. In 1967, 36.6 per cent of all aid went to support activities in productive sectors. By 2012, this had dropped to 13.4 per cent. Most dramatic was the decline of support for industry, which accounted for 29.6 per cent of aid in 1967, but no more than 2.7 per cent in 2012. Aid policy makers seem to have lost interest in industry and manufacturing. Support for agriculture first increased from 7 per cent in 1967 to no less than 20.3 per cent in 1983 and then shrank to 6.4 per cent. In view of the importance of food security for poverty reduction, this is somewhat hard to understand.

As the attention to the productive sector declined, the share of resources devoted to social infrastructure increased (from 8.3 per cent in 1967 to 31.6 per cent in 2012). Especially marked is the increase in the share of expenditures for government and civil society. This reflects the increased importance of good governance, institutional quality and capability building in the development debate. Within the social infrastructure category, there is a large decline in the importance accorded to education, in spite of the fact that some of the most notable successes in development aid were recorded in the area of human capital formation. Expenditures for health, on the other hand, have become more important, increasing from

Table 14.6: Sectoral allocation of aid, 1967–2012 (%)[a]

	1967	1969	1971	1972	1975	1980	1983	1985	1990	1991	1995	2000	2005	2010	2012
I. Physical Infrastructure	**27.8**	**14.4**	**8.1**	**10.9**	**11.8**	**19.3**	**27.2**	**29.1**	**20.5**	**23.7**	**27.2**	**19.8**	**14.8**	**20.1**	**23.2**
1.1. Transport & Storage	11.1	6.6	2.4	4.2	2.5	9.2	8.6	9.6	7.0	8.6	9.6	9.0	5.9	8.4	9.2
1.2. Communications	3.2	3.9	1.3	1.4	1.8	1.9	1.7	1.1	2.4	1.5	1.4	1.0	0.4	0.3	0.4
1.3. Energy	13.5	3.9	3.0	2.3	5.4	6.6	12.9	13.1	7.4	9.7	9.9	3.9	3.7	6.9	7.8
I.4. Water Supply & Sanitation	0.0	0.0	1.3	2.9	2.1	1.5	3.9	5.3	3.7	3.8	6.3	5.9	4.8	4.6	5.8
II. Productive sector, incl. banking and business	**36.6**	**13.5**	**8.3**	**6.6**	**22.6**	**25.1**	**32.8**	**28.0**	**17.4**	**19.2**	**14.4**	**11.7**	**8.4**	**10.5**	**13.4**
II.1. Agriculture, Forestry, Fishing	7.0	4.5	3.5	2.7	8.6	11.5	20.3	18.2	9.9	8.8	8.9	5.8	3.7	5.5	6.4
II.2. Industry, Mining, Construction	29.6	9.0	4.8	3.9	6.2	5.5	6.4	7.2	4.3	5.1	1.6	2.1	1.8	1.3	2.7
II.3.a. Trade Policies & Regulations								0.1	0.6	0.1	0.2	0.1	0.4	0.8	0.7
II.3.b. Tourism								0.2	0.0	0.0	0.0	0.1	0.1	0.1	0.0
II.4. Banking & Financial Services								0.7	0.2	0.8	0.8	0.9	1.4	1.5	2.8
II.5. Business & Other Services					0.7	0.3	0.0	0.3	1.9	3.3	1.5	2.6	0.9	1.2	0.8
II.6. non-specified by sector[b]					7.2	7.8	6.1	1.2	0.5	1.2	1.3	0.1	0.0	0.0	0.0
III. Social Infrastructure & Services, excl. water	**8.3**	**6.0**	**26.6**	**28.5**	**20.6**	**23.2**	**18.3**	**18.7**	**20.9**	**19.1**	**24.8**	**27.9**	**29.0**	**34.0**	**31.6**
III.1. Education			23.5	23.8	11.1	13.9	8.5	8.5	9.3	9.0	10.5	7.9	6.4	8.0	7.2
III.2. Health			0.8	0.7	4.6	5.2	6.7	6.6	3.1	3.1	4.1	4.5	4.6	5.9	5.9
III.3. Population & Reproductive Health								0.1	0.9	0.7	1.7	2.2	3.3	5.9	5.2
III.5. Government & Civil Society			1.1	2.1	1.4	1.1	0.9	1.4	3.4	2.7	3.2	7.0	10.6	11.3	10.5
III.5.a. Government & Civil Society – general												1.9	9.0	9.0	8.5
III.5.b. Conflict, Peace & Security												0.3	1.5	2.3	2.0
III.6. Other Social Infrastructure & Services	8.3	6.0	1.3	1.9	3.5	3.1	2.3	2.1	4.3	3.8	5.3	6.3	4.1	3.0	2.7
IV. Multi-Sector/Cross-Cutting	**0.0**	**1.8**	**0.4**	**0.5**	**2.1**	**2.0**	**1.0**	**0.6**	**2.6**	**3.2**	**5.4**	**7.6**	**6.5**	**12.6**	**10.6**

V. Commodity Aid /General Programme Ass.	10.1	49.1	24.1	26.9	19.1	10.5	11.1	16.1	13.4	13.6	6.2	8.6	3.9	4.1	3.9
V.1. General Budget Support	0.0	0.0	0.0	0.0	0.0	0.0	0.0	0.0	1.0	1.9	2.7	2.9	2.7	3.0	2.7
V.2. Dev. Food Aid/Food Security Ass.	1.6	40.9	17.5	17.1	13.7	6.1	1.3	7.0	2.5	2.2	1.2	2.7	1.1	1.0	1.0
VI. Action Relating to Debt	6.5	4.8	9.5	4.5	4.1	5.7	0.7	1.3	17.3	9.1	6.2	5.7	21.2	2.9	1.8
VII. Humanitarian Aid	0.0	0.0	1.6	0.9	1.3	1.8	0.8	1.2	1.5	3.7	3.9	4.8	8.2	8.0	7.3
VIII. Unallocated / Unspecified[b]	10.8	10.5	21.4	21.2	18.4	12.4	8.1	4.9	6.4	8.3	12.0	13.8	8.1	7.7	8.2
Total	100.0	100.0	100.0	100.0	100.0	100.0	100.0	100.0	100.0	100.0	100.0	100.0	100.0	100.0	100.0

Notes:

[a] Sectors rearranged to emphasise differences between physical, social infrastructure and productive sectors. Water supply has been shifted from social infrastructure to physical infrastructure. Banking and financial services and business and other services have been shifted from social infrastructure to the productive sector. For early years, less breakdown is available. For annual data, see www.dynamicsofdevelopment.com.

[b] Between 1973 and 1996 there were large discrepancies between the sum of sectors and the total.

Source:

OECD, *International Development Statistics*, http://stats.oecd.org/, downloaded April 2014. Total ODA from all donors at current prices (US dollars). Donors include DAC countries, multilateral donors and non-DAC countries, excl. China.

0.8 to 5.9 per cent of total ODA. Finally, there is a striking increase in humanitarian and emergency aid from very low levels to 7.3 per cent in 2012.

14.4.4   Net development assistance as a percentage of GDP

In Table 14.7 the inflow of aid has been related to GDP. In 2012, the share of foreign aid in GDP was below 1 per cent of GDP in twenty-two of the thirty-one countries in the table; in another four countries it was between 1 and 1.5 per cent. In the large Latin American countries the role of foreign aid has always been marginal. In the Asian countries, the share of aid in GDP has tended to decline since the late 1970s, reflecting the increasing importance of private capital flows and FDI. Bangladesh is the only Asian country where the share of aid remains fairly high, at 1.8 per cent in 2012.

In contrast, the significance of foreign aid in most African countries included in the table is considerable. Between 1990 and 2000 several African countries had shares above 10 per cent of GDP. In 1992, the share for Zambia reached the astounding figure of 32.4 per cent, in 2000 it stood at 24.4. By 2012, however, it had declined to 4.7 per cent. Tanzania had a share of 29 per cent in 1992, though it declined thereafter to 10 per cent in 2012. Where aid–GDP ratios are so high, it is clear that a substantial part of all government expenditures and investments will be financed by foreign aid flows.

According to Lensink and White (2001), the early 1990s were a period of high aid inflows. In 1970, only eight developing countries had aid inflows above 20 per cent of GDP. By the first half of the 1990s, fourteen developing countries had aid ratios of 20–30 per cent (including Burundi, Mauritania, Tanzania and Malawi), eight countries had ratios of more than 30 per cent (including Zambia, Rwanda, Guyana, Nicaragua) and four countries had ratios of over 50 per cent (São Tomé, Mozambique, Somalia and Guinea-Bissau).[6] In recent years Mozambique and Ethiopia are well-known aid darlings. Country examples may be misleading, however. For all developing countries together, aid flows as a proportion of GDP were less than 1 per cent (van der Hoeven, 2001: 110).

14.4.5   Reduction of the real value of aid by tying

A part of bilateral foreign aid is 'tied' aid. The recipient of tied aid is obliged to spend it on the purchase of goods and services in the donor country. This means that development aid functions as an export credit for the donor country. Tying reduces the total value of aid, because the recipient is not free to use the financial resources provided to buy the cheapest and best goods and services available on international or domestic markets. Often the prices of imports from the donor country will be 20–30 per cent above world market prices. Moreover, it is very likely that the recipients of aid are forced to buy goods that are not optimally suited to their needs and local circumstances. Furthermore, a country may end up with many different and incompatible brands of the same product from different countries. Estimates of the percentage by which tying reduces the value of aid vary. Dollar and Pritchett (1998) suggest that tying reduces the value of aid by about 25 per cent. Riddell (2008) gives an estimate of 20 per cent on average (see also the discussion in Jepma, 1992).

---

[6] Lensink and White (2001) present data on aid as a percentage of GNP, rather than GDP, which gives somewhat higher percentages. The high-aid countries include several tiny island economies.

Table 14.7: Net development assistance as a percentage of GDP, selected developing countries, 1960–2012

	1960	1970	1980	1990	1992	1994	1998	2000	2004	2012
Bangladesh[a]		0.2	7.1	6.9	5.8	5.1	2.6	2.5	2.5	1.8
China			0.03	0.6	0.7	0.6	0.2	0.1	0.1	−0.002
India	1.9	1.3	1.2	0.4	0.8	0.7	0.4	0.3	0.1	0.1
Indonesia	0.9	4.8	1.2	1.5	1.4	0.9	1.3	1.0	0.1	0.0
Iran		0.2	0.0	0.1	*0.2*	0.2	0.2	0.1	0.1	0.0
Malaysia	0.5	0.6	0.5	1.1	0.3	0.1	0.3	0.0	0.2	0.0
Pakistan	6.8	4.2	5.0	2.8	2.1	3.1	1.7	1.0	1.5	0.9
Philippines	0.8	0.7	0.9	2.9	3.2	1.6	0.9	0.7	0.5	0.0
South Korea	6.4	3.1	0.2	0.02	−0.00	−0.03	−0.01			
Sri Lanka	6.0	2.1	9.6	9.1	6.6	5.1	2.7	1.7	2.5	0.8
Taiwan[a]	6.5	0.2	0.0	0.02	0.003	0.002				
Thailand	1.6	1.0	1.3	0.9	0.7	0.4	0.6	0.6	0.0	0.0
Turkey	1.7	1.0	1.4	0.9	0.2	0.2	0.0	0.2	0.1	0.4
Argentina[a]	0.16	0.03	0.03	0.12	0.12	0.06	0.03	0.02	0.06	0.04
Brazil	0.2	0.4	0.0	0.0	−0.1	0.0	0.0	0.0	0.0	0.1
Chile	0.3	0.8	0.0	0.3	0.3	0.3	0.1	0.1	0.1	0.0
Colombia	−0.3	2.2	0.3	0.2	0.5	0.1	0.2	0.2	0.4	0.2
Mexico	0.0	0.2	0.0	0.1	0.1	0.1	0.0	0.0	0.0	0.0
Peru	−0.5	0.8	1.0	1.5	1.1	0.7	0.9	0.7	0.7	0.2
Venezuela	−0.1	0.1	0.0	0.2	0.1	0.0	0.0	0.1	0.0	0.0
Congo, Dem. Rep.	2.4	0.0	3.0	9.6	3.3	4.2	2.0	4.1	29.5	16.6
Côte d'Ivoire	0.0	3.6	2.1	6.4	6.8	19.2	7.6	3.4	1.0	10.7
Egypt	4.3	2.2	6.1	14.0	8.9	5.2	2.3	1.4	2.0	0.7
Ethiopia				8.4	11.2	15.5	8.2	8.5	18.4	7.8
Ghana	0.2	2.7	4.3	9.5	9.6	10.0	9.4	12.0	16.0	4.4
Kenya	2.7	3.6	5.4	13.8	10.8	9.5	2.9	4.0	4.1	6.5
Morocco	2.9	2.2	6.2	4.8	3.4	2.3	1.3	1.2	1.4	1.5
Nigeria	0.8	0.9	0.1	0.8	0.9	1.0	0.6	0.4	0.7	0.7
South Africa						0.2	0.4	0.4	0.3	0.3
Tanzania[a]	1.7	4.0	13.2	27.3	29.0	21.4	10.7	10.4	13.8	10.0
Zambia	0.1	0.7	8.2	14.4	32.4	21.4	10.7	24.4	20.8	4.7
Average:										
Asia	3.3	1.6	2.2	2.1	1.7	1.4	0.9	0.7	0.7	0.4
Latin America	−0.03	0.7	0.2	0.3	0.3	0.2	0.2	0.2	0.2	0.1
Africa	1.7	2.2	5.4	11.2	11.7	9.4	4.8	6.2	8.9	5.6

Note:

[a] Taiwan, 1961 instead of 1960; Argentina, 1962 instead of 1960; Bangladesh, 1971 instead of 1970.

Sources:

ODA from OECD, *International Development Statistics*, OECDstat, http://stats.oecd.org/Index.aspx?datasetcode=TABLE2A#. Unless otherwise specified, GDP at current purchasing prices from World Bank, *World Development Indicators Online*, downloaded 2014. Indonesia, 1960: World Bank, *World Development Indicators* CD-ROM, 2002 converted with exchange rates from World Bank, *World Tables, 1980*. Tanzania, 1960 and 1970: *World Tables, 1980*; Tanzania, 1980: *World Tables, 1995*. Taiwan 1960–80: The Central Bank of Republic of China, www.cbc.gov.tw/EngHome/economic/statistics/Annual.htm; Taiwan, 1981–2012: GDP from DGBAS, National Statistics. Republic of China (Taiwan), *National Accounts*, http://eng.stat.gov.tw/ct.asp?xItem=25763&CtNode=5347&mp=5, downloaded April 2014; exchange rates from The Central Bank of Republic of China (Taiwan), www.cbc.gov.tw/content.asp?Cultem=1879.

Over time the percentage of tied bilateral aid seems to be declining. Thus the OECD–DAC figures suggest that by 2006, 90 per cent of bilateral aid was untied. But this excludes the important category of technical aid, which is frequently used to fund expensive expatriate consultants from the donor countries. Hancock (1991) estimated that there were some 80,000 highly paid expatriate experts working in Africa in the 1980s, more than in the colonial period. Worldwide, a total of 150,000 expatriates were employed. In addition, donors may influence the expenditure patterns of developing countries by providing aid for specific sectors in which their own industry or expertise is well represented, thus resulting in high flow-back percentages (Hoebink, 1988: 235, 330). Putting this all together, Riddell (2008) estimates that some 58 per cent of total aid flows remained tied in 2006, reducing the total value of aid by some 7 billion US dollars per year.

14.4.6 Conclusion: the volume of aid is not negligible

Although foreign aid flows represent a very modest percentage of the national income of the donor countries, the statistics presented above indicate that aid flows are not without importance in international economic relations. Foreign aid forms a substantial part of the resource flows to developing countries. In most large Latin American and Asian countries the role of foreign aid as a percentage of GDP is limited. Yet, especially in the poorest African countries the inflow of aid represents a considerable percentage of GDP. Aid is not a marginal phenomenon here. It represents one of the key facts of economic life. The debate on the quality and the effects of aid is not just an academic debate. It touches on the economic prospects of the poorest African countries.

14.5 Theories of development and objectives of aid

Discussions of foreign aid are implicitly or explicitly based on theories of socio-economic development, in which aid flows can fulfil certain functions (Bauer, 1981; Bos, 1990; Bruton, 1969; Cassen, 1986; Dijkstra and White, 2003; Krueger *et al.*, 1989; Hermes and Lensink, 2001b; Lensink, 1993a; Riddell, 1987, 2008). Together with normative considerations, these theories determine the specific goals and objectives one hopes to realise by means of development aid. Aid has a variety of objectives including: self-sustaining growth, poverty reduction, coping with humanitarian emergencies and disasters, environmental sustainability of economic development, improving the position of women and good governance and democratisation (Lensink and White, 2001; World Bank, 2002a). In keeping with the main focus of this book we focus primarily on the first two goals, though the other objectives will be discussed incidentally.

14.5.1 Aid as a source of investment, capital accumulation and growth

The foundations of theories of the role of foreign aid in development were laid in the 1950s and 1960s. As sketched in the chapter on industrialisation strategies (Chapter 9), the prevailing assumption was that developing countries were caught in vicious cycles of poverty. Due to low incomes per capita, savings were low. Due to low savings rates, investment was low, so that there were little prospects for future growth of national income and development of the industrial sector.

Capital was seen as the scarce factor in development. What was required was a large-scale investment programme in industry and infrastructure, which would help economies break out of their vicious circles (Millikan and Rostow, 1957; Rosenstein-Rodan, 1961; Rostow, 1971).

From this perspective, an influx of foreign capital and foreign aid could contribute to increased investment, without the necessity of a simultaneous decline in domestic consumption. Aid would come in two forms: finance for capital goods and industrial inputs; and technical aid to promote the transfer of complementary knowledge and skills. Starting from growth targets established in national plans, the required levels of savings and investments were calculated by means of fixed capital–output ratios (see Chapter 9). Given the domestic savings ratios, the need for foreign capital could be determined. Development aid would have to provide part of the required foreign capital flows. It was assumed that private capital markets would be unable to meet all the foreign finance requirements of developing countries. Distrust of markets dominated development strategies. This formed a justification for government intervention and financial aid flows from governments to governments. In Table 14.6, one can see that a substantial proportion of aid was indeed allocated to productive sectors in the 1960s.

14.5.2   The two-gap model of Chenery and Strout

The most complete formulation of the line of thinking described above is Chenery and Strout's (1966) *two-gap model* (see also Bruton, 1969; Chenery, 1979; Chenery and Adelman, 1966; Chenery and MacEwan, 1966). Transformation of the economic structure requires a large inflow of external financial resources in a short period of time. In poor developing countries private capital flows may be insufficient to provide for the need for foreign finance. Foreign aid can contribute to the acceleration of economic growth and structural transformation by relieving crucial bottlenecks in the process of development. This would increase the efficiency of the use of domestic economic resources.

Chenery and Strout distinguish two gaps: *the savings gap* and *the foreign exchange gap*. As mentioned above, economic growth requires large investments in industry and infrastructure. Domestic savings are insufficient to meet investment requirements. This is Chenery and Strout's first gap. The inflow of foreign financial resources, of which foreign aid is part, can compensate for the shortage of domestic savings. In this respect, the crucial assumption is that the inflow of aid will result in increased investment and does not result in a decline in domestic savings (see Bruton, 1969). If domestic savings do decline, the inflow of development aid will result in an increase in domestic consumption, but the investment and growth objectives will not be realised. In 1979, Chenery adjusted his model to allow for the possibility that part of the inflow of resources is consumed, so that the increase of total investment is less than the additional inflow of resources from abroad (Chenery, 1979).

Chenery and Strout's second gap refers to the shortage of foreign exchange. In a developing country where a new industrial sector and infrastructure is being built from scratch, most of the machines, capital goods, raw materials and intermediates have to be imported from abroad. This requires foreign exchange. Even when sufficient levels of domestic savings have been realised, exports from a developing country may yield insufficient foreign exchange to finance these imports. There is a balance of payments constraint. In this line of reasoning, foreign finance is necessary to finance the import of the required goods (and services and technical assistance) from economically advanced countries. The larger of the two gaps determines the aggregate need for foreign finance.

In the *two-gap model* there is a strong emphasis on the amounts of capital needed and the scale of investment required.[7] The question of the efficiency and effectiveness of investment is hardly raised. It should be stressed that the role of development aid in the total strategy is a fairly limited one. Foreign aid is part of total capital flows to developing countries. Under certain favourable conditions, it may contribute to an acceleration of growth and development by relieving specific bottlenecks. The idea was that both the large-scale investment push and development aid should be of relatively short duration (some ten–fifteen years). As incomes per capita go up, domestic savings will increase and the savings gap will shrink. As the industrial sector develops, it will start exporting manufactured goods, reducing the need for foreign exchange. Once sustained growth has been achieved, there would be no need for further aid flows. The private capital market would be able to meet the financial requirements of developing countries.

Gap analysis is now seen as somewhat dated. It is based on an unrealistic production function – the Harrod–Domar production function – with a one-sided focus on capital. A wider production function is required including capital, education, knowledge transfer, capacity building and the policy framework. and their interactions. Unsophisticated gap analysis pays insufficient attention to the absorptive capacity, and the institutions and policies of the receiving country.[8] According to gap models, the amounts of aid supplied to Zambia should have financed rapid growth that would have pushed income per capita to about 20,000 dollars. In reality income per capita stagnated at around 600 dollars (Easterly, 1997). Aid may substitute for domestic savings, rather than finance additional investment. In the past, aid has been provided to countries which have simultaneously restricted the inflow of private capital to the detriment of investment (Bauer, 1984). Tanzania is a prominent example of this phenomenon. Dijkstra and White (2003) argue that one should focus on the marginal impact of aid flows, rather than on the size of gaps.

Although the assumptions of the Chenery and Strout model have been strongly criticised, some kind of 'gap analysis' still underlies modern debates on the financial requirements of developing countries (Lensink, 1993a). When the World Bank called for a doubling of real aid flows to achieve the developmental targets of the MDGs by 2015, this implicitly assumed the existence of financial gaps (Sachs, 2005; World Bank, 2002a).[9]

14.5.3   Aid, growth and poverty reduction

One of the important objectives of development aid is the improvement of the living conditions of the poor in developing countries. Initially, theories of economic development assumed that economic growth would sooner or later automatically lead to a reduction of

---

[7] As explained in Chapter 9, Chenery and Strout also argue in favour of technical aid as a complement to aid for capital accumulation. The shortage of human capital could actually be seen as the third gap of the Chenery–Strout model.

[8] The early development economists were in fact quite aware of institutional constraints and the need for effective policies (see the discussion in Torvinen, 2013).

[9] The Millennium Development Goals 1990–2015 were adopted at a meeting of heads of state in 2000. Among other things they include the halving of the proportions people living on less than a dollar a day by 2015. The financial implications of the Millennium Development Goals were spelled out at the Monterrey conference on Financing for Development in March 2002 (World Bank, 2002a; UNDP, 2003).

poverty. It was seen as inevitable that income inequality would increase in the early stages of development. Economic growth and industrialisation require increased savings rates and increased savings rates imply shifts in income shares from poor classes who consume all their income to rich classes who are able to save and invest (e.g. Lewis, 1954; Sen, 1960). But as economic growth got under way and incomes per capita started increasing, the advantages of growth would *trickle down* to large sections of the population, as had happened in nineteenth-century Western Europe. Also, the income distribution tended to become more equal at later stages of development (Kuznets, 1955, see also Szirmai, 1988, Chapters 2 and 6).

In the 1960s and 1970s, the *trickle-down* theory was fiercely criticised. It was believed that even in countries that experienced rapid growth the poorer sections of the population profited little, due to increasing income inequality. Power structures and vested interests stood in the way of the benefits of growth trickling down automatically. The assumption that only the rich save, while the poor workers consume all their income, also came in for criticism. Poor people are eager to invest in increasing their productivity; the rich elites are sometimes characterised by wasteful consumptive life styles. A too high degree of inequality may become an obstacle to growth, because it inhibits the increase in productive capacity of the mass of the poor population and constrains the growth of domestic market demand. Redistribution of incomes and productive resources may contribute to growth.

On the basis of this theoretical analysis, a strategy of growth and redistribution was proposed in which production factors were to be reallocated to poor sections of the population (Chenery *et al.*, 1974; ILO, 1976). The key phrases were 'redistribution with growth' and 'basic needs strategy'. More credit for small peasants and better access to land would increase agricultural output and productivity. More credit and technological support for small enterprises in the informal sector would have favourable employment consequences. Better education and better systems of healthcare for the poor – investments in human capital – would result in increased labour productivity of the working population. Redistribution and growth were thus considered as complementary rather than conflicting objectives. Development aid should not only contribute to economic growth, it should explicitly aim at reducing poverty and inequality.

Since the early 1970s, policy statements on development aid concentrated increasingly on direct poverty reduction and on reaching target groups of the poor. In practice, only a limited part of funds targeted to the poor actually reached their destination. In Dutch aid policy, poverty reduction was the prime goal of aid policy between 1973 and 1977. Nevertheless, Hoebink (1988) estimates that only some 6–7 per cent of aid to Sri Lanka (a focus of Dutch aid) actually reached the designated poverty groups. In other countries these percentages were even lower.

The empirical foundations for this debate were rather weak. It was primarily an ideological debate, in which preoccupations existing within the rich countries were projected onto the developing countries (van Dam, 1978). It is now clear that growth remains the key to poverty reduction. Progress in poverty reduction, health, education and nutrition depends to an important, though not exclusive, extent on the acceleration of economic growth (Bluhm *et al.*, 2014; Dollar and Pritchett, 1998; Kraay, 2006; World Bank, 2002a).[10] When growth in Latin America stagnated in the 1980s or in Asia during the Asian crisis of 1997, the poorest segments of the population were the principal victims. Their situation was much worse than it had been in periods of growth and economic dynamism, despite the unequal distribution of the benefits of growth. When growth collapsed in the former Soviet Union, the impact of economic decline on the social indicators was catastrophic. As the cases of China, India and Indonesia forcefully illustrate, economic growth can lift millions of people out of poverty, in spite of rapidly increasing inequality. Economic growth remains one of the keys to poverty reduction.

This being said, it is undoubtedly true that the impact of growth on poverty would be much greater if the same rates of growth could be achieved with a more equitable distribution of income. There is a potential double dividend: redistribution not only directly provides more income for the poor, but it increases the poverty elasticity of growth (Bluhm et al., 2013, 2014; Bourguignon, 2003). In recent years Latin American countries like Brazil have shown that redistributive policies such as conditional cash transfers to the poor can indeed contribute to significant reductions in poverty. Next, the examples of East Asian growth in China, Taiwan and South Korea confirm the positive effects of a more equal initial distribution of incomes and productive resources on subsequent growth. There is also validity in the arguments for increasing the resources of the poor in developing countries. In the chapters on health, education and agricultural development, we argued that investments in human capital of the poorer segments of the population can increase productivity and contribute to growth. The same holds for investment in the human capital of women and reductions in gender inequality. What is being questioned here is the independent scope for aid policy in poverty reduction and the associated tendency to play down the benefits of growth. It is unlikely that any direct attack on poverty will be effective in the absence of adequate macro- and micro-economic policies.

The search for effective poverty alleviation policies in developing countries continues. In Asia, the micro-credit movement has succeeded in providing tailored finance to large numbers of poor households (Wahiduddin and Osmani, 2013). One of the most recent developments is that aid flows and debt relief are provided on the condition that a country formulates a poverty reduction strategy (PRS) as a part of its wider development strategies (see Chapter 13). Here, the emphasis shifts from the direct effects of aid flows on poverty to a wider policy dialogue.

14.5.4   Technical assistance, human capital theory and growth

In the 1950s and 1960s, there was a debate between the proponents of capital transfers and the proponents of technical assistance (Krueger et al., 1989). The supporters of capital transfers emphasised the required size of the investment effort. They focused on increasing the investment rate and increasing the availability of physical capital goods and intermediate inputs. Supporters of technical assistance pointed to the importance of the transfer of knowledge and technical know-how. They argued that output would increase through knowledge of new methods of production and more adequate and efficient use of existing means of production. Theoretically speaking, they emphasised the role of learning, technology transfer, technical efficiency and technological development in growth of output.

It seems obvious that capital transfers and technical assistance are complementary. It is useless to provide capital goods without training and schooling on how to use them

---

[10] Bruno, Ravallion and Squire (1998) estimate than on average a 1 per cent increase in income *per capita* in developing countries reduces poverty by 2 per cent.

effectively. It is also useless to increase levels of knowledge and proficiency when there are no physical means of production to which such knowledge can be applied (Pack and Paxson, 2001). Development projects, therefore, often included combinations of capital transfers and technical assistance.

In the course of time, technical assistance was reinterpreted in a broader sense as an *investment in human capital*. It was not limited to the transfer of existing Western technologies, by sending Western experts abroad. Rather it involved support for increases in levels of education in the broadest possible sense, so that the capabilities to absorb new technologies and insights would be increased (see Chapter 7). Specific training and transfer of know-how are of little value in the absence of prior investment in the general levels of schooling. Investment in human capital would also make it easier to adapt imported technologies to local circumstances in developing countries. In response to these insights, the World Bank and national aid agencies increased the priority of funding for the development of the educational systems in developing countries. In 1975, no less than 23.5 per cent of total aid flows was allocated to education, but later education fell out of favour in aid allocation and in 2012, its share was down to 7.2 per cent (Table 14.6).

Technical assistance is also provided in the form of doctors, nurses and family planning workers. Especially if this kind of technical assistance also involves the sustained training of domestic health personnel and other experts, it can also be considered as an another aspect of investment in human capital. As explained in Chapter 6, investments in the health of adults and children can contribute to economic dynamism and increased productivity. Health is also a form of human capital. In contrast to education, increasing amounts of aid have been allocated to health both by state donors and private foundations. It is one of the fields where aid has achieved notable successes.

The formulation of the theory of human capital has been influenced by *theories of agricultural development* inspired by the work of the Nobel Prize winner Theodor Schultz (1964, see also Chapter 10). Schultz emphasised the importance of so-called 'non-conventional' inputs into the agricultural sector. What he considered most important was not an increased supply of capital goods, but rather investment in agricultural education, extension and agricultural research. Following Schultz, it was realised that an expansion in agricultural research capacity in and for the benefit of developing countries could lead to breakthroughs in agricultural productivity (Hayami and Ruttan, 1985). In this context, it is important that agricultural technologies should be well adapted to local circumstances. According to Schultz, investment in human capital is a broad concept. It involves informing farmers about new techniques, training agricultural extension workers, setting up educational and research institutions which are closely linked to extension networks. Investment in human capital then shades into investment in *institution building*. Schultz and his followers have shown that such investments in human capital and institution building can have very high returns. Subsidies and contributions to agricultural R&D, diffusion of technology and institution building have been amongst the success stories of development aid.

In modern theories of innovation and growth, human capital and technological change are seen as core elements of both growth and catch-up (see Chapter 4). From the perspective of theories of aid, this involves support in improvement of technological capabilities. The notion of institution building discussed in the context of agriculture can be extended into the development of national systems of innovation (Lundvall, 1992; Lundvall *et al.*, 2009).

14.5.5   Policy dialogue and programme aid: policy reform and improvements in governance and institutions

Since the early 1980s, policy makers have realised that it does not make much sense to consider only the effects of a series of isolated development projects. Any positive impacts of development projects are nullified if bad macro-economic policies are being pursued, or if institutions at the micro-level are hostile to entrepreneurship, investment or growth of production and productivity. For example, it is not much use to provide capital to a country where inflation is running so high and expectations are so uncertain that entrepreneurs and financiers try to move all their resources out of the country. It is pointless to finance costly investments in irrigation if the prices of agricultural products are kept so low that there are no incentives for farmers to increase their production. If prices do not reflect scarcity relations, it also becomes impossible to make decent cost-benefit evaluations of projects.

As has been indicated in Chapter 13, many developing countries, in particular in Latin America and Africa, have pursued ineffective macro-economic policies. Excessive protection of domestic industries and overvalued exchange rates led to non-viable industries and an inability to compete on international markets. Preferential treatment of manufacturing and artificially low prices for agricultural products hampered the development of the agricultural sector. Too much government intervention, a poorly functioning administrative apparatus, huge deficits on government budgets, and loose monetary policies were conducive to macro-economic instability. As stressed by authors like Balassa (1978), Bhagwati (1985), Krueger (1978) and Sachs and Warner (1995), countries that started exporting early, pursued sober macro-economic policies and depreciated their exchange rates, performed much better economically than other countries.

Since the early 1980s, foreign aid, therefore, has increasingly been linked with a 'policy dialogue' aimed at improvement of macro-economic policy and institutional reform (OECD, 1985). In this context, there has been a shift from project aid to programme aid (Cassen, 1986). The dialogue element in programme aid is considered of great importance, as the success of policy reforms requires the active commitment and involvement of policy makers in developing countries. Financial support is provided to governments for the implementation of structural adjustment programmes aimed at macro-economic stabilisation and deregulation of the economy. In this period, restoration of market mechanisms and a reduced role for government is part of almost all reform programmes (Williamson, 1990).

Development aid may have three different functions within the context of policy dialogue. First, the traditional objectives of development projects are more likely to be realised if developing countries pursue better policies. Second, foreign aid and other financial flows are used to put pressure on policy makers in developing countries to engage in policy reform. This is referred to by the term *conditionality*. Third, programme aid may help mitigate the adverse effects of structural adjustment policies (Riddell, 1987). For instance, balance of payments support may allow firms to import the inputs they need, so that production will not needlessly stagnate. As shown in Chapter 13, the need for aid is probably the greatest in the poorest countries, where the absorptive capacity of the economy is the least developed.

Part of aid flows may be used for consumptive purposes or to maintain educational and health services, which would otherwise be subject to expenditure cuts. At the same time, some critics of policy dialogue argue that the availability of financial support diminishes the pressure to restore the health of government finances in developing countries (Knack, 2001). If the apparatus of government itself is an obstacle to development (see Chapter 11), providing more programme aid may not be of much help.

The intensification of policy dialogue does not mean that the debate on the role of governments and markets in economic development is concluded. On the contrary, the late 1990s saw a resurgence of the debates concerning the role of market liberalisation in development policy (see Chapter 13, sections 13.6 and 13.7).

One the one hand, the neoliberal critics of aid argue for ever-stronger links between policy reform and aid flows. Conditionality is seen as insufficient, because developing countries can make promises of reform on which they later renege once the aid funds have been disbursed. Reforms should be 'owned' by developing countries, rather than being imposed by donors from outside. In this context, there has been a shift in the aid debate from *conditionality* to *selectivity* (Dollar and Pritchett, 1998; Meltzer, 2000; Riddell, 2008). Under selectivity, aid and debt relief is provided to countries that have already implemented reforms in policies, institutions and governance. The content of reform is broadened beyond macro-economic policy to include more effective bureaucratic governance, the rule of law, transparency and the reduction of corruption and political reforms (see section 14.6.4).

On the other hand, there is a growing surge of criticism of the content of the proposed reforms, of which Nobel Prize winner Joseph Stiglitz is one of the most prominent exponents. Structural adjustment is seen to have failed. These critics believe that dogmatic imposition of free market reforms by the international institutions, especially with regard to the free movement of capital, threatens the growth and development prospects of developing countries. It is the international institutions themselves which are in need of reform (Rodrik, 2006; Stiglitz, 2002; van der Hoeven, 2001). We may safely conclude that the idea that aid will only contribute to development if a specific set of policies is implemented is now discredited.

14.5.6   Building institutions and capabilities

Going beyond policy reform, the past ten years have seen a renewed emphasis on the role of institutions and institutional reform in socio-economic development. Theoretically institutions are seen as one of the ultimate sources of growth and development (see Chapter 10 on culture and institutions). It is argued that aid will be most effective if it is provided to countries with strong institutions, good governance and well-developed bureaucratic capabilities (Collier and Dollar, 2002; Dollar and Burnside, 2000). Though the Dollar and Burnside study has been heavily criticised from an econometric perspective, the link between aid effectiveness and institutions is a very plausible idea. It is fairly obvious that the developing countries that are doing well are countries with stronger capabilities. But here the consensus ends. On the one hand, aid is increasingly tied to positive scores on evaluations of governance such as the *Country Policy and Institutional Assessments* of the World Bank or the *World Governance Indicators* (see Torvinen, 2013 for an excellent overview). On the other hand, Riddell has pointed to an interesting paradox: it may be the most fragile countries with the weakest institutions and capabilities that are most in need of aid, even though aid may not be especially effective in such a context. In Table 14.6, we indeed see that there is a huge increase in the amount of total aid flows allocated to government capability building, strengthening of civil society and maintenance of peace and security. In 2012, 10.5 per cent of a total of 133 billion aid dollars was allocated for these purposes (against 1.1 per cent in 1971).

14.6   Does aid work? Different perspectives on the effectiveness of development aid

14.6.1   Does aid contribute to socio-economic dynamism and poverty reduction?

The basic idea underlying development aid is that it contributes to building up the productive potential and the institutional structure of a country in order to promote the self-reliance of that country. This immediately brings us to the central dilemma of all aid relations: the tension between dependence and self-reliance. The debate on the pros and cons of development aid boils down to the following issue: does aid ultimately contribute to social welfare and economic dynamism in developing countries, or does it ultimately result in a permanent dependence of the aid recipient, which forms an obstacle to autonomous social and economic dynamics?

Basically, three positions can be distinguished in the debate on aid:[11]

1. The *orthodox view* that development aid on balance contributes to economic and social development and to the solution of socio-economic problems in developing countries.
2. The *radical left-wing view* that development aid promotes the penetration of capitalist market relationships in developing countries and consequently leads to the sustained dependence and underdevelopment of these countries.
3. The *neoliberal view* that development aid hinders economic growth and development, since it maintains inefficient government intervention and obstructs the unfolding of dynamic market relationships.

The orthodox or mainstream attitude is prevalent among governments in donor countries, governments in aid receiving countries, officials in national and international development organisations and development bureaucracies, aid workers, young idealist intellectuals and students, and – until very recently – the general public in the rich countries. Until recently there was a widespread consensus on the desirability of development aid. This consensus was partly maintained by intensive publicity campaigns funded from budgets for development aid. The political support for aid was not based on its proven effectiveness. Rather, it was based on the moral urge to do something about the problems of abject poverty, hunger, malnutrition, disease and inequality in world society.

In the orthodox approach, there are two central ideas. First, aid provides additional resources that would otherwise not have been available for development. Second, it contributes to the mobilisation of latent resources in developing countries. Within the mainstream, however, there is a great variety of opinions and points of view. Some people favour project aid, others programme aid. Some are supporters of poverty alleviation, others of investment in infrastructure. Some would like to provide aid without conditions, others prefer to increase conditionality and selectivity.

[11] See Riddell's excellent summary of the debate in *Foreign Aid Reconsidered* (1987).

Even within the mainstream there has been growing criticism of the ineffectiveness, inefficiency and waste in development aid (e.g. Cracknell, 2000; Dijkstra and White, 2003; Hoebink, 1988; Jepma, 1988; Lensink, 1993b; Meltzer, 2000). Some critics argue that under a smokescreen of idealistic motives, rich countries do nothing but pursue their national strategic interests. Other authors criticise the lack of coordination and coherence in aid policies. Often the mal-adaptedness of aid to local economic, social, and cultural circumstances is singled out for criticism. The organisational structure of development organisations and the relations between developmental bureaucracies are increasingly subjected to critical analysis (Meltzer, 2000; Quarles van Ufford et al., 1988; Raffer and Singer, 2001; Stiglitz, 2002).

Representatives of developing countries complain about the paternalist or even neocolonialist nature of foreign aid. They argue that aid should be made available to governments, organisations and individuals with no strings or demeaning conditions attached. Developing countries should determine their own priorities. Also, some of the conditions being imposed are seen as harmful for the development prospects of these countries.

On the other hand, for quite some time, the notion has been gaining ground that aid is only of use within the framework of an effective economic and social government policy. If the policy framework is not right, a string of separate projects can never be very successful. This line of reasoning leads to more and more conditions being attached to aid. This is referred to as 'conditionality', 'policy dialogue', or 'selectivity'. We already noted above that there has been a shift from project aid to programme aid, and that programme aid is increasingly provided on certain conditions. These conditions refer primarily, though not exclusively, to economic policy. The observation of human rights and democratic principles by governments may also be a condition for aid, but aid policy in this respect is very erratic.

A common characteristic of these mainstream approaches is that the desirability of aid as such is not questioned. The critics concentrate on the reform, reorganisation or change of specific aspects of aid policy. More fundamental are the criticisms by representatives of left-wing radical and right-wing neoliberal perspectives on development aid. From both perspectives, foreign aid is explicitly considered as an obstacle to development. The critics are not concerned with reforming aid but rather with abolishing it. Besides important differences, there are some interesting similarities between the radical and the liberal criticisms of foreign aid. Both point to the perpetuation of dependence as a central characteristic of aid relations. Thus, the debate on aid shows interesting parallels with the left- and right-wing criticisms of the Western European welfare states which surfaced in the 1980s.

The criticism from the left reached its peak in the 1970s in the context of a general radicalisation of the intellectual climate. The neo-liberal criticism became more strident during the 1980s and 1990s. It persists till the present in the repeated attacks on aid by authors such as Moyo (2009) or Easterly (2006). At present criticism by market liberals is the most fundamental challenge to the development establishment. But there is also a resurgence of radical criticisms of the neoliberal market ideologies prevailing since the late 1990s. The following sections present an overview of this debate. Section 14.6.2 discusses the arguments of the left-wing radical critics; section 14.6.3 pays attention to the criticism by neo-liberals. Section 14.6.4 focuses on criticisms of aid projects and programmes. Section 14.6.5 deals with responses from the mainstream to its radical and neoliberal critics. In this section attention is also paid to the results of empirical research into the effectiveness of foreign aid.[12]

Radical criticisms of development aid

The criticisms of development aid from the radical left (Griffin, 1970, 1987; Griffin and Enos, 1970; Griffin and Gurley, 1985; Hayter, 1971, 1981, 1989; Hayter and Watson, 1985; Lappé, Collins and McKinley, 1980; Mende, 1973; Zeylstra, 1975) were formulated mainly in the 1970s. These criticisms should be seen against the backdrop of the emergence of theories of underdevelopment and dependence discussed in Chapters 2 and 3. In these theories, poverty and social disintegration in developing countries are seen as the consequences of Western economic and political expansion. In contrast to the Western countries, the spread of capitalist market relations only leads to further impoverishment in developing countries. Tiny wealthy elites in business and government benefit from capitalist penetration. They ally themselves with foreign interests and help maintain the chains of exploitation in developing countries. From this perspective, foreign aid is one of the many ways in which developing countries are made subject to the Western capitalist sphere of influence. Foreign aid helps maintain repressive regimes that exploit their own people. Foreign aid primarily serves to promote the further penetration of capitalist market relations in developing countries, from which only the rich countries can benefit. It also maintains the dependence of the poor on the rich and of poor countries on rich countries.

The radical leftist criticism also contains a range of more specific objections to development aid and its workings in practice. Lappé et al. (1980) argue that aid does not reach the kind of people for whom it is officially intended. Official aid is provided by governments to governments. Aid flows channelled via powerful elites will never reach the powerless. Credit meant for poor peasants is provided to rich farmers. Most benefits of irrigation works go to large landowners. Funds for development end up in the bank accounts of politicians. Ultimately, aid results in a reinforcement of the positions of the more powerful at all levels of society. According to the radicals, only a drastic revolutionary change in the power structure could create a situation in which aid also has positive effects for the poor.

The thesis of Lappé et al. that development aid provided through governments and ruling elites hardly ever reaches the poor finds support in numerous less ideologically pronounced empirical studies. Bol (1983) has shown for Bangladesh and Hoebink (1988) for Tanzania and Sri Lanka how little aid actually reaches the poor, even when this is one of the main objectives of aid policy. In part this can be explained by the interests of Western donors, who use foreign aid as an instrument of export policy. It also has to do with the nature of power and inequality structures in developing countries. To implement a development project successfully one needs the cooperation of powerful and influential key figures at national, regional and local levels. But their interests are usually not served by improvements in the conditions of the poorest groups. This, by the way, also applies to other aspects of domestic policy in developing countries (Frankel, 1978; Myrdal, 1971).

In *Aid as Imperialism* Hayter (1971) argued that development aid in Latin America was one of the means to impose capitalist market relations on developing countries. She was one of the first to note that aid was provided on condition that Western policy prescriptions were followed. Countries that tried to pursue alternative policies focusing on the needs of the

---

[12] The classification of authors in schools is fraught with difficulties. Many of the empirically oriented studies contain conclusions which are in keeping either with the radical left-wing or the liberal right-wing criticisms. But an author is usually not classified as such unless he explicitly concludes that aid is an obstacle to development.

poor, like Cuba, Chile or Nicaragua, were cut off from aid, boycotted economically and attacked militarily.

For Mende (1973), the key to economic development lies in the domestic mobilisation of resources for investment. Only then can a truly autonomous and dynamic process of economic development start. Alienated ruling elites in developing countries, however, lack the capacity to start the process of internal mobilisation of people and financial resources. In order to maintain their positions, they depend on foreign aid and support from abroad. Mende concludes that development aid hardly ever has any positive effects. It merely helps maintain the *status quo*. Foreign aid thus weakens the capacity for domestic mobilisation of savings and self-reliant development.

Lappé *et al.* (1980) mention food aid as an example of aid that discourages domestic production. The provision of large quantities of cheap food to developing countries relieves affluent countries of their agricultural surpluses. However, this makes production of food in developing countries unprofitable. Thus, developing countries become permanently dependent on food imports. This criticism of food aid is echoed by numerous later studies (e.g. Boserup, 1983; Jackson and Rosberg, 1982).

Griffin (1970; see also Griffin and Enos, 1970) launched an explicit attack on orthodox theories of aid, in which expansion of the resources available for investment is a central element (see section 14.5). On the basis of a cross-section analysis, he concludes that there is a negative correlation between the inflow of development aid and the volume of domestic savings. His data also point to an absence of positive correlations between the magnitude of aid flows, on the one hand, and investment rates and economic growth, on the other.

Griffin (1987b) concludes that in twelve African countries foreign aid crowds out domestic savings. Development aid is spent by governments, partly for consumptive purposes, partly on defence expenditures, partially on wages. When aid is earmarked for investment, domestic means which come free are used for consumption (see the discussion of *fungibility* below). Even in those cases where investment does increase slightly as a result of aid flows, this has no positive consequences for economic growth. This is because donors have a distinct preference for large-scale capital-intensive prestige projects that are ill adapted to local circumstances. These projects have high capital–output ratios and contribute little to growth of output. Thus development aid encourages an inefficient use of resources in the economy. According to Griffin, recipients of large aid flows, such as Bangladesh, Ethiopia, Zaire, Haiti and the Sudan, grow more slowly than countries that receive less aid.

Like many other critics, Griffin observes that aid does not reach the poor in spite of all development rhetoric. Aid helps to maintain corrupt and repressive regimes. In their economic policies these regimes have tended to neglect agriculture, the sector in which most of the poor people have to eke out a living. Developing countries would benefit more from less aid and more independence, better access for their exports to the protected markets of rich countries and stronger governments, which would have better chances of mobilising domestic savings.

In recent years, there has been a resurgence of radical criticisms of the international order which argue that the whole structure of this order is weighted against the developing countries (e.g. Amsden, 2007; Chang, 2002, 2007; Hertz, 2001; Klein, 1999; Raffer and Singer, 2001, see also Chapter 13). According to these critics, the IMF, the World Bank and the WTO force developing countries to open up their economies to unrestricted competition from the advanced economies. They urge developing countries to liberalise their capital accounts, so that MNEs can take over control of their domestic economies. The TRIPS agreement for trade-related IPRs protects the property rights of firms from the advanced economies. Aid is seen as one of the tools used to blackmail developing countries into submission. At the same time the international organisations condone continued agricultural and industrial protectionism by the USA, Japan and the countries of the European Union. This issue of protectionism is a very valid point of criticism.

14.6.3   Neoliberal criticism of development aid

Just like radical leftist criticism of development aid, neoliberal criticism is part of a more comprehensive perspective on society, the economy and economic development. From this perspective, the main engine of growth and development consists of the efforts of creative and enterprising individuals on free markets. Intervention in the market discourages individual entrepreneurship and an efficient allocation of resources. Development aid is one of the guises of interventionism. Therefore, it is one of the obstacles to economic growth.

The neoliberal perspective on economic development goes back to the work of the economists Friedrich Hayek and Milton Friedman. In the 1980s it was specifically elaborated with regard to development aid. The main authors of this school are Bauer and Yamey (1981, 1986), Lal (1978, 1983, 2000) and Krauss (1983a, 1983b). In the 1990s, unlike in the 1970s, neoliberal criticism was the main challenge to foreign aid. This is partly due to the disintegration of the communist bloc and the loss of credibility of centralised planning as a development strategy (Fukuyama, 1992).

The most influential representative of this movement is Peter Bauer, who criticised the assumptions of foreign aid in a long series of publications (Bauer, 1976, 1981, 1984, 1988; Bauer and Yamey, 1981, 1986). Bauer's point of view is characterised by the following quotation: 'Aid promotes the delusion that a society can progress from indigence to prosperity without the intermediate stage of economic effort and achievement' (1981: 107). According to Bauer, all countries that experienced economic growth did so without foreign aid. They realised economic growth because they had the right skills, attitudes, motivations and institutions at their disposal. Foreign aid cannot help create such capabilities, but it can form an obstacle to their development. According to Bauer, the market is the bearer of economic growth. Development aid reinforces the positions of interventionist governments who have hostile attitudes towards the market.

Bauer presents a sharp, humorous, though not systematically empirically grounded, criticism of almost all aspects of development aid. His criticisms, which are representative of the entire range of neoliberal attacks on aid, can be summarised in the following five points.

Savings are not a bottleneck for economic development

Bauer argues that there is no shortage of savings in developing countries. Rather, there is an insufficient capacity to absorb investment. If there are sufficient opportunities for economically productive investment, domestic and foreign entrepreneurs and suppliers of capital will mobilise the resources needed. For example, if an investment in infrastructure contributes to increased productivity in the long run, the government can easily borrow money on the capital market and finance interest and repayments from future increases in tax receipts. Even under the most favourable circumstances, the positive impact of development aid is therefore restricted. It saves some of the costs of loans for investments, which would have been undertaken anyway in the absence of aid.

However, the fact that aid is 'free' increases the chances of waste and inefficient use of financial resources. In the modern economic terminology, aid is characterised by *moral hazard*. Aid stimulates investment in unprofitable projects, which do not contribute to the growth of the economic potential of a country, while increasing the indebtedness of a country (if aid is not provided as a grant, in which case the charges of waste of resources are even greater).

Together with the left-wing critics, Bauer is of the opinion that considerable portions of aid are used for consumptive purposes, the upkeep of patron–client relationships, payments of civil servant salaries, or investments in unrealistic prestige projects.

Development aid does not contribute to poverty alleviation

Official development assistance is provided to governments rather than to individuals. For governments in developing countries the interests of the poor seldom have high priority. For example, the European aid flows provided in compensation for shortfalls in agricultural export revenues did not end up in the hands of the farmers themselves. It was the governments that profited. According to Bauer, foreign aid means taxing the poor in rich countries for the benefit of the rich in poor countries. If foreign aid has to be provided at all, Bauer prefers to channel it through non-governmental organisations (NGOs). They are less dependent on the cooperation of governmental institutions in developing countries. There is a greater chance that some of the money reaches the people it is intended for. However, NGOs sometimes show the same failings as governmental aid organisations – waste, bureaucracy, dependence on powerful intermediaries and so forth (see, for example, Kruyt, 1988).

Foreign aid strengthens the position of regimes guilty of large-scale violations of human rights

Development is provided to regimes in total disregard of their respect for human rights and tolerance of political opposition. Thus the regimes of Papa Doc in Haiti, Mobutu in Zaire (now Democratic Republic of Congo) and Idi Amin in Uganda have been large-scale recipients of aid. Not infrequently the recipient governments are also hostile to the most entrepreneurial and economically successful ethnic groups in their country, which are discriminated against and are sometimes even deported *en masse*.[13] Examples that come to mind are the position of the Chinese in Indonesia, Malaysia and Thailand, and the position of Asian minorities in East Africa.

Foreign aid reinforces the position of governments pursuing anti-market policies harmful to economic development

Governments receiving aid have long pursued policies discriminating against the agrarian sector. They have protected inefficient and unviable industries by means of import substitution policies. They have intervened in markets through extensive regulation, licensing or support of poorly run parastatals. They have been hostile to private entrepreneurs and foreign investors. They pursued inadequate macro-economic policies characterised by huge government deficits, high inflation and overvalued exchange rates. And, finally, they have

---

[13] A well-known example is the deportation of 50,000 people of Indian descent from Uganda by dictator Idi Amin.

used aid as an instrument to safeguard their personal privileges and to secure their hold on power.

Development aid stimulates the politicisation of the whole society in developing countries

According to Bauer, this is the most fundamental objection to aid. Aid causes resources to be channelled to the government. Creative individuals are tempted to use all their talents to acquire subsidies and manipulate public resources, licences and regulations to their own benefit. This causes conflicts between ethnic groups that have access to the machinery of government and ethnic groups that do not. Thus aid can contribute to political instability. For instance, in *The Road to Hell: The Ravaging Effects of Foreign Aid and International Charity*, Michael Maren (1997) has documented how large-scale aid methodically under-mined civil society in Somalia in the 1980s, contributing ultimately to the total collapse of the Somali nation-state.

Economic entrepreneurship aimed at seeking new opportunities for productive activity in the private sector is discouraged. 'Rent seeking', the search for monopoly profits through governmental licenses and regulations, becomes the norm for entrepreneurial behaviour. Foreign aid can also weaken the state bureaucracies of recipient governments. It siphons scarce talent away from the civil service, as donor organisations pay so much more (Knack, 2001; Riddell, 2008).

A more recent version of the neoliberal attack on aid is provided by Dambisa Moyo in her book, *Dead Aid: Why Aid is Not working and How There is a Better Way for Africa* (2009). She sees aid as one of the factors contributing to sustained stagnation in Africa and argues passionately that Africa should wean itself off aid in order to achieve sustained growth. Though the empirical foundations of this book are decidedly flimsy, it does make an important point which cannot be disregarded. In the post-war period years, GDP per capita in many African countries was higher than that of most East Asian countries. In the past sixty years, Africa has received more than a trillion dollars in aid, while remaining mired in stagnation and poverty. In the same period, many of the formerly poor Asian economies have achieved experienced growth and catch-up without comparable infusions of aid. Van de Walle (2001) compares the volume aid to Africa with Marshall Aid, which accounted for some 2.5 per cent of GDP. By 1996, the average African country had received 12.3 per cent of its GDP in ODA, a historically unprecedented international transfer with questionable results. Clientelistic neo-patrimonial states are unable to absorb and allocate aid in an effective manner. Similar criticisms are voiced by Ayittey (2005), who argues that aid money ends up in the hands of vampire elites that destroy the prospects of economic progress.

It is interesting to see how many elements the criticisms from the left and from the right have in common. According to both schools of thought, aid never reaches the poor; aid crowds out domestic savings; aid helps maintain corrupt and repressive regimes; aid contributes to indebtedness and aid preserves the dependence of poor countries on rich countries. The crucial difference between the two perspectives, however, lies in their evaluation of the market. Left-wing critics regard aid as the handmaiden of exploitative capitalist market relationships in developing countries. Neoliberal critics believe profoundly in the beneficial workings of the market economy. Foreign aid is seen as an obstacle to the unfolding of the market mechanism.

The main weakness of both perspectives is that if one does not subscribe fully to *a priori* notions about the market – capitalist market relations frustrate development, all government intervention in markets is detrimental to development – the argumentation is not convincing. On the basis of impressionistic and selectively chosen examples, advocates of both perspectives come to very far-reaching general conclusions about aid which do not stand up to closer empirical analysis.

14.6.4 Criticism of development projects

A useful contribution to the debate is the fierce attack on the practice of development aid by the journalist Graham Hancock in *Lords of Poverty* (1991). This book contains a horrifying catalogue of the things that can go wrong in development projects. Some examples are listed in Box 14.3.

Hancock shows convincingly that these are not incidental mistakes. They occur with great regularity all over the world. His book also provides a wealth of concrete examples to illustrate that much financial aid is spent on salaries of expatriate experts living a life of relative luxury in developing countries, on imports of luxury consumer goods from Western countries, or is appropriated by members of the elites in developing countries. Hancock, too, stresses how little aid actually reaches the poor. Finally, he presents numerous examples of corrupt and totally inefficient regimes that have been supported liberally by means of development aid, including Mobutu in Zaire, Bokassa in the Central African Republic,

---

BOX 14.3 : **Examples of project shortcomings**

- Repeated shipments of food aid consisting of food stocks unfit for human or animal consumption.
- A shipment of polystyrene igloos to tropical regions in Africa.
- Shipments of electric blankets to tropical Africa under the terms of emergency aid.
- A supply of medicines for which the expiry dates had been exceeded by more than fifteen years.
- Large dams in river basins that caused the flooding of the dwellings of hundreds of thousands of people, displaced millions of people, severely damaged the environment, and silted up within a short period of time.
- Unsuccessful transmigration projects that caused deforestation and erosion without offering migrants much chances of making an acceptable living.
- Large shipments of trucks to Africa, of which 95 per cent were out of operation within a few months.
- Large-scale energy projects ill adapted to the local circumstances.
- Capital-intensive fishing projects in regions where cheap labour was easily available.
- Roads constructed without the necessary bridges across rivers.
- Experts whose expertise was based solely on the colour of their skin.
- The construction of a nuclear plant on a geological fault line in a earthquake prone area in the Philippines (George, 1988).
- Defence procurement in the donor country as a condition for aid.

Ferdinand Marcos in the Philippines and Papa Doc in Haiti. Often these regimes were also guilty of large-scale violations of human rights.

Like the other authors discussed above, Hancock comes to the conclusion that development aid mainly serves the interests of donor governments, Western businesses and members of development bureaucracies and governmental organisations in both rich countries and developing countries. Other studies provide further examples of what can go wrong in development projects. For instance, in Tanzania, donors poured a colossal 2 billion dollars into building roads over a period of twenty years. There was no improvement of the road network. Due to lack of maintenance, roads often deteriorated faster than they could be built (Dollar and Pritchett, 1998). On the basis of cross-country evidence, Knack (2001) concludes that in ethnically divided countries, aid is significantly correlated with increases in levels of corruption.

14.6.5   Empirical debates about aid effectiveness and proposals for reform

Since the 1980s, the international aid establishment has started paying more and more attention to the quality and effectiveness of aid flows in response to the growing stream of criticisms (Cracknell, 2000). The World Bank and national development organisations have commissioned thousands of evaluation studies and have set up research projects to examine the effectiveness of aid. In the 1980s, three authoritative studies in the mainstream tradition dealt extensively with all the criticisms of foreign aid and tried to formulate recommendations for its improved effectiveness. The studies were: Cassen, *Does Aid Work?* (1986), Riddell, *Foreign Aid Reconsidered* (1987) and Krueger *et al.*, *Aid and Development* (1989). In 2000, the Meltzer Commission in the USA formulated far-reaching recommendations for the reform of international organisations (Meltzer, 2000). Dollar and Pritchett published an interesting study for the World Bank, *Assessing Aid: What Works, What Doesn't and Why* (1998), which responded explicitly to earlier criticisms of aid effectiveness with detailed proposals for reform. These proposals have had a major impact on aid policies, resulting in more emphasis on the institutions, capabilities and policies of the recipient countries. In the past decade, the arsenal of evaluation studies has been enriched with the emergence of randomised controlled trials measuring the effects of development projects and policy interventions (Duflo *et al.*, 2007). In line with this literature, there has been a shift towards 'results-oriented' aid policies, where donors and recipients are held accountable for measurable results of aid. Aid effectiveness has been the major theme of international conferences since the Paris conference on aid effectiveness in 2005 (see section 15.3.6). In his book *Does Foreign Aid Really Work?* (2008), Riddell reviews the aid evaluation literature since the study of Cassen and his own earlier classic volume (Riddell, 1987).

Riddell rightly emphasises that in the past expectations concerning aid have been unrealistic. Development aid in itself cannot create economic growth, nor can it reverse patterns of economic stagnation. As one of the many factors impinging on development, foreign aid may – under favourable circumstances – contribute to some acceleration of economic development. At the micro-level, evaluation studies suggest that the majority of development projects do contribute positively to development. At the macro-economic level, the results of a spate of older and newer empirical studies are contradictory. There is no consensus about the hypothesis of a positive correlation between aid and economic growth. This is sometimes referred to as the *micro–macro paradox*: success at the micro-level, no clear evidence of success at the macro-level (Mosley, 1987). However, there is also little evidence for the opposite conclusion that aid is detrimental to economic development. The notion that development aid cannot be reformed or improved, is rejected outright.

The effectiveness of development projects

PROJECT EVALUATION   In his review of a large number of evaluation studies, Cassen (1986, 1988) concludes that about two-thirds of all development projects evaluated have been more or less successful in the light of the originally stated objectives.[14] Cost-benefit analyses often show returns of 10 per cent and higher. For instance, 80 per cent of all evaluated projects funded by the IDA proved to have returns of over 10 per cent.

The same picture emerges from evaluation studies performed in decades since the Cassen report, summarised in Riddell (2008). Most projects succeed in producing or delivering their intended outputs. Success rates recorded by the donors vary from 70 to 85 per cent. But Riddell (2008) qualifies these findings in two ways: first, the evaluators are usually the donors themselves, so there is a built in tendency to overestimate success. Next, most evaluations focus on the immediate outputs and do not look at the longer-term sustainability of the outcomes in a longer time frame. If we take both these biases into account, Riddell estimates that project success rates should be reduced by some 15–20 per cent. This would result in success rates of 50–65 per cent, which are still quite impressive. Riddell also emphasises that we know little about the contributions of projects to wider developmental objectives. In spite of the pro-poor rhetoric there is little evidence for direct impacts on the poor. A World Bank evaluation report (World Bank, 2005, cited in Riddell, 2008) argued that assessing projects from a country perspective provides a more realistic and complete picture than examinations of performance at microlevel. In this study, 53 per cent of the country assessments were positive and 33 per cent were negative.

In general, formal evaluations and cost-benefit analyses give a more positive picture of projects than qualitative assessments by eyewitnesses and participants (cf. Roth, 1993). It is hard to reach definitive conclusions. It almost seems as if the publications are coming from two completely different planets. It is even more confusing when critics such as Hancock freely quote from evaluations by international organisations when it suits their argument, but reach completely different conclusions than the organisations themselves. The moral outrage of critical observers like Hancock or George (1988) does not always contribute to the clarity of the argument. As Schumpeter wrote, the process of economic development is a process of creative destruction, with both 'winners' and 'losers'. When pros and cons are not dispassionately weighed, an extremely negative picture easily emerges.

On the other hand, cost-benefit analysis also has some serious limitations, especially in conditions in which the price mechanism does not function properly. The use of arbitrary 'shadow prices' offers ample opportunities to calculate oneself into economic success (see, for example, Bol, 1983, for a criticism of cost-benefit analysis of development projects). Riddell (1987) points out that the objectives of projects are often poorly defined, or even mutually contradictory. In such circumstances, it is hard to say whether a project is a success or a failure.

Often the long-run effects of projects are hard to determine. Some projects have unintended positive results and learning effects that were not foreseen in the project design. For

---

[14] In the fifteen years preceding 1987 the DAC recorded over 9,000 project evaluations (Riddell, 1987: 185).

instance, a project may not reach the very poor as intended, but can contribute to economic dynamics, technology transfer or learning in other ways.

FUNGIBILITY   One of the reasons why reliable evaluations of aid projects and programmes are so difficult is the so-called fungibility of money. According to the *fungibility thesis*, aid does not really finance the high-priority investments it ostensibly pays for. These would have been carried out anyway. Rather, development aid finances more marginal investments or consumption, using the funds released from the high-priority projects.

Cassen (1986) rejects the fungibility thesis. First, the number of investment projects in a developing country is not static. As investment increases, new investment opportunities continue to arise. Some worthwhile investment projects would not even exist in absence of aid. For instance, complicated irrigation or hydroelectric projects could not be realised without technical cooperation with foreign donors. In the second place, even if there is some replacement of investment, the notion that the recipient country has sufficient resources to finance all high-priority projects is evidently not correct. Many authors besides Cassen stress that national and international capital markets are far from perfect. The fact that there are very profitable investment projects does not mean that private finance will be automatically forthcoming. In the third place, there are complementarities between investments (see Chapter 9). Investment projects financed by foreign aid may make other investments in the private sector more profitable. Finally, it is no great problem if some part of financial aid is used for expansion of consumption in a very poor country, as long as a substantial part of the aid flow is available for additional investment.

In the more recent literature, fungibility is taken for granted (Burnside and Dollar, 1997, 2000; Dollar and Pritchett, 1998; World Bank, 2002a). There is simply no way of controlling what governments do with the resources that have been freed through aid. They may use these to increase the salaries of civil servants, reduce budget deficits, or lower taxes so that people can consume more. However they may also top up aid funds and actually spend more on a given line of activities than budgeted. This is referred to as the so-called *flypaper effect* (Pack and Pack, 1993). The interesting implication that Dollar and Pritchett derive from fungibility is that aid donors should pay more attention to the overall quality of policy in a country. If policy and governance are effective, then there is more reason to believe that funds will be used effectively, even if they are diverted from their original purposes.

REASONS FOR PROJECT FAILURE   Reasons for project failure include lack of coordination, conflicting objectives, imperfections in project design, expenditure deadlines, insufficient attention to maintenance and insufficient feedback and learning from past mistakes.

A common problem is the lack of coordination between donors and a lack of coordination capabilities in the recipient country. In some of the poorest developing countries, such as Burkina Faso or Tanzania, aid workers from different donor countries and international organisations stumble over each other. The projects from different countries are not integrated and heavy burdens are imposed on the scarce administrative capabilities of the receiving countries. A second reason for project failure is conflicting objectives. All authors agree that the pursuit of commercial objectives or foreign policy objectives has a negative effect on the chances of success of development projects. But environmental objectives and economic objectives may also conflict in a fashion fatal for the project. Many projects fail due to technical imperfections in the project design and the neglect of local circumstances (cf. Cochrane, 1979). Far too often projects make insufficient use of local expertise and knowledge.

Another cause of project failures is the pressure on donor organisations to spend their allocated budgets before the budgetary period runs out. This pressure to spend makes for built-in waste and inefficiency. It is a characteristic of all aid programmes that specify that certain sums have to be disbursed by certain dates.

One of the reasons for project failure mentioned in the Meltzer report (Meltzer, 2000) is that money is supplied to the providers of outputs and services, rather than to the users. If the funds were made available to the final users and paid to the suppliers on effective delivery of the service or product, this would improve the incentives for project success. In response to this criticism, many development projects nowadays involve conditional or unconditional cash transfers to poor households.

A major shortcoming is that development aid focuses too much on new projects and too little on the continuation and upkeep of existing projects. Thus, there is a systematic tendency to reserve insufficient funds for maintenance, spare parts, energy costs and the costs of local personnel. Donors expect the local costs of projects to be funded from the budgets of the aid recipients. But these budgets are inadequate for such purposes, especially when governments are forced to cut back on expenditure under the terms of structural adjustment programmes. Thus, newly built roads soon become impassable due to a lack of maintenance, and newly constructed energy facilities operate at a fraction of their capacity. At the recipients' end, the shortage of administrative capacity is identified as a problem, especially in combination with a preference for large-scale prestige projects.

Finally, critics point to lack of sufficient feedback and learning effects from past experience. Not enough lessons are learned from past mistakes (see also Burki and Ayres, 1986; Easterly, 2008; OECD, 1985). There is too little feedback from evaluation studies to new project design. There is insufficient exchange of information between different national and international organisations concerned with development aid. In more recent projects, the criticisms have been taken more to heart and there are indications that project success is increasing over time (Birdsall and Kharas, 2010).

EXAMPLES OF AID SUCCESS   To keep a balanced perspective on aid, it is important to emphasise that there have been important successes in aid as well as major failures. The mainstream literature identifies several areas in which development aid has been relatively successful. One of them is agricultural development. In many developing countries in Asia and Latin America, the growth of agricultural production exceeded the growth of population (see Chapter 10). This was realised in part due to investments in agricultural research, education, extension, irrigation and land improvement financed by development aid. Agricultural research financed from international aid flows made a major contribution to the advances of the green revolution and to the growth of agricultural production and productivity.

Positive results have also been achieved in the field of infrastructure – in spite of many disappointments. Infrastructural investment in roads, harbours, telecommunications systems, dams and energy supply are an essential component of all development strategies. These investments can seldom be financed via private capital markets.

Another area where aid has had a major positive impact is education. A substantial proportion of all World Bank loans goes to education and educational projects. The World

Bank is the world's largest external funder of education, having provided a cumulative 30 billion dollars for education projects over the years (World Bank, 2002a). The rapid expansion of the educational systems in developing countries since the Second World War (as described in Chapter 7) was facilitated by foreign aid flows. Despite many disappointments, it is clear that education in developing countries benefited from technical and educational assistance. In a country such as India, success has been achieved in building up an independent research infrastructure of high quality. Aid flows have also contributed to campaigns which have been instrumental in improving literacy.

A fourth area of relative success is that of family planning and healthcare policy (World Bank, 2005). Though population growth in many countries is still much too high, this does not mean that the resources invested in family planning have been wasted. With regard to health, the dramatic decreases in death rates discussed in Chapter 5 are in part the result of a multitude of projects which contributed to the transfer of medical technologies and the spread of new knowledge about disease and healthcare. The eradication of diseases such as river blindness in West Africa are cited as an instance of success. In Southern Africa, large-scale vaccination campaigns have virtually eliminated measles. Oral rehydration has reduced child mortality from diarrhoea. The provision of insecticide-treated bed nets provides protection again malaria. Substantial progress has been made in coping with HIV/AIDS. Banerjee and He (2008) provide lists of interventions demonstrated to be effective, that are available for upscaling if sufficient funds are made available. These interventions are in the areas of health, education, and agriculture (fertilisers).

Riddell examines the criticisms of food aid (Riddell, 1987: 228–36; Riddell, 2008). Besides many failures, there have also been examples of success. According to Riddell, these are not restricted to emergency aid, but also include other food aid programmes and projects. He recognises the danger of food aid acting as a disincentive to domestic food production. He concludes that the way in which food aid is provided may be more important than the question whether food aid should or should not be provided. One of the more recent innovations is to supply money rather than food in kind, so that food can be bought in the country or the region. Local purchase of food can result in savings of up to 46 per cent.

On the other hand, even the mainstream defenders of project aid also admit that there are many areas in which the results of project aid have been very disappointing. There has been a marked lack of success in integrated rural development programmes (Riddell, 2008; Ruttan, 1989a, 1989b), due to the difficulties of coordinating activities of various government organisations and departments. Special problems were encountered in the extension of small-scale pilot projects into general practice on a regional or national scale (Gupta *et al.*, 2006). There were also negative experiences with credit programmes aimed at small farmers. These projects often failed to appreciate the role of traditional credit institutions. The resources hardly ever reached the intended target groups. Another area of project failure is found in cattle breading projects. Technical assistance has far too often failed to contribute to sustainable capacity building, through its excessive reliance on expatriate experts. When domestic staff are hired, this may undermine the capacity of domestic bureaucracies and organisations by attracting the most talented staff through much higher international salary scales. Lack of coordination of a multitude of donors has resulted in duplication, ineffectiveness and waste of resources. Regionally, the success rate of projects has been the highest in

South and Southeast Asia. Project aid in Sub-Saharan Africa has been significantly less successful than in other areas of the world.

Macro-economic effects of development aid

At the macro-level, it is useful to consider foreign aid as part of the aggregate inflow of financial resources to developing countries, characterising the post-war international economic order (see Tables 3.6, 13.3 and 14.4, pp. 119, 571 and 619). This net inflow is one of the differences between the post-war period and the period between 1913 and 1950, when there were capital outflows from many colonies to the rich countries (Maddison, 1989). Potentially, a net resource inflow offers developing countries the opportunity of importing new means of production and adopting new technologies. In the post-war period the net inflow of financial resources, of which aid flows were a part, contributed to an economic climate that was favourable to growth and dynamism.

As regards the specific contribution of development aid, the macro-economic debate focuses on the relationships between the amounts of aid a country receives and its savings, investments and economic growth. Both the older and newer econometric studies in this field are deeply contradictory. Some studies conclude there are no significant effects of aid, some conclude that there are positive effects and some conclude that the effects are negative.

There are various reasons why it is extremely difficult to measure the impact of aid on economic development. First, aid is provided for a great many different purposes. These can include political and strategic purposes which have little to do with economic development. Some aid is provided to promote democracy or gender equality rather than economic development. Some aid is directly targeted at poverty reduction, health or educational access. A large chunk of aid flows is provided in response to disasters or humanitarian crises. Here it is obvious that the correlation with economic development will be negative. A tsunami will slow down economic development in a country and elicit increased aid flows. In general, countries that are poor will tend to receive more aid (see Table 14.1, p. 616), so one may not conclude that it is aid that results in slower growth. In econometric terms, aid is an endogenous variable.

Arndt, Jones and Tarp (2010) distinguish four generations of research on the aid–growth relationship. The first two generations were inspired by simple models of the growth process, the Harrod–Domar model and the Chenery and Strout two-gap model (see sections 14.5.1 and 14.5.2). The third generation of studies used more sophisticated techniques and panel datasets. It started to take the possible endogeneity of aid into account. In the third generation of studies, the discussion focused on the question whether or not the positive effects of aid are conditional on good policies and institutions (Burnside and Dollar, 1997, 2000). Since 2000, a fourth generation of studies uses even more advanced econometric techniques, is critical of previous methods used to deal with endogeneity and usually concludes that there no systematic relationship between aid and economic growth.

First- and second-generation research

Griffin (1970) and Griffin and Enos (1970) observe a negative relationship between aid and domestic savings, and aid and economic growth. Papanek (1972, 1973), found a positive relation, just as did Heller (1975). Rana and Dowling (1988, 1990) noted modest but positive effects of development aid. Mosley (1980) found no statistically significant relationships for all developing countries together. For the thirty poorest countries in his sample, however, there was a positive relation between aid and growth. In a later study Mosley

(1987) found no significant relations at all. This led him to posit the *micro–macro paradox*, namely that micro-studies usually report positive effects of aid while macro-studies tend not find any significant relationships. A negative relationship between aid and savings rates was reported by Gupta and Islam (1983). In a summary of the literature of the 1970s, Jepma (1997) concluded that foreign aid has crowded out private saving, has supported public consumption and has not had significant positive impacts on macro-economic policies and growth.

Third generation: the debate about selectivity

In the third-generation literature, using more sophisticated econometric techniques, some of the findings are more positive. Two groups of studies can be distinguished. The first group focuses on the interactions between aid and effective policies. The second group criticises the assumptions of the first group, and comes to more positive conclusions about the independent contributions of aid.

The first group of studies concludes that there is no significant overall relationship between aid flows and growth. However, if one includes an interaction term between aid and good governance in the regressions, the coefficient of aid becomes highly significant (Burnside and Dollar, 1997; Dollar and Burnside, 2000; Dollar and Pritchett, 1998). On the basis of these findings, the World Bank report by Dollar and Pritchett (1998) concludes that aid is very effective if it is provided to poor countries with effective macro-economic policies, effective institutions and good governance. In effective macro-economic policies, the study refers to low levels of inflation, modest government deficits, the introduction of market reforms and an outward orientation. Good governance also involves the effectiveness of government bureaucracies. The report advocates a reorientation of aid flows to poor developing countries with good governance. Donors should be willing to cut back financing to countries with persistently low-quality public sectors and policies. This report has been very influential for a number of reasons.

In the first place, it builds on the conclusions of an older generation of aid evaluations by Cassen, Riddell and Krueger, discussed above. These studies all concluded that the success of foreign aid depends to an important extent on the *development policies* pursued in the countries receiving aid. At the macro-level policies should aim at macro-economic stability, getting government finances under control, deregulation of the economy and a change from an inward orientation to more export-oriented development (see Chapter 13). At the micro-level, the goal should be the development of institutions and policies that provide positive incentives to the economic efforts of individuals. If there are no changes in policy, development projects – regardless of their individual merits – will not contribute much to a change in the underlying economic dynamics. If foreign aid contributes to a reorientation of policy, its impact should be judged to be positive, irrespective of the returns to specific development programmes. If, on the other hand, foreign aid only provides policy makers with the means to postpone painful measures of reform, its net effects will be negative.

In the second place, the 1998 World Bank report (Dollar and Pritchett, 1998) reaches similar conclusions as the 2000 Meltzer Commission on the future of international financial institutions. Together with many other authors, the Meltzer report (Meltzer, 2000) concluded that the older notion of conditionality, which linked aid and debt relief to agreement on policies of stabilisation and structural adjustment, had by and large failed. Promises of future reforms were insufficient, because developing countries that did not wholeheartedly support reform would renege on the implementation of reforms when the going got rough. Like the World Bank, Meltzer made a strong case for a shift from conditionality to selectivity. Rather than supply funds on the basis of agreement on structural adjustment policy, aid should be provided on the basis of past performance and past implementation of reform. This would guarantee that the developing country governments wholeheartedly supported the reforms, a policy which is referred to as 'ownership of reforms'. The Meltzer report also called for a substantial increase in development finance in the new context of selectivity. Grants should replace concessional loans to avoid increasing the indebtedness of developing countries. For countries that had met the criteria of good governance and policy reform, debts should be forgiven without further conditions. The call for additional aid flows was picked up at the 2002 Monterrey conference on Financing Development and the 2002 World Bank report on aid which called for a doubling of development finance to achieve the MDGs for 2015 (World Bank, 2002a).

Though not all recommendations of the World Bank and the Meltzer report have been adopted, they have had a major influence on aid policies in subsequent years. Many donor countries and donor agencies have shifted towards selectivity. For instance, the Dutch government reduced the number of countries receiving bilateral aid from more than 100 to some 17 countries.

The second group of studies comes to different conclusions, in two important respects. In the first place, they argue that the econometric evidence on which Burnside, Dollar and Pritchett base their conclusions is extremely shaky. Using the same dataset as Burnside and Dollar (2000), Dalgaard and Hansen (2001) and Easterly *et al.* (2004) show that if five deleted observations are reinserted into the sample of observations, or the time period is prolonged, the crucial coefficient for the interaction term between policy variables and aid flows becomes non-significant. Other econometric studies in the collection edited by Hermes and Lensink (2001b) all conclude that the interaction term is non-significant. They argue that the far-reaching policy conclusions with regard to selectivity drawn by the World Bank are not supported by the evidence.

A second important conclusion of this set of studies (Dalgaard and Hansen, 2001; Guillaumont and Chauvet, 2001; Hansen and Tarp, 2000a, 2000b, 2001; Lensink, 1993a, 1993b; Lensink and White, 2001) is that there is a significant positive relationship between aid and economic growth, after all. A third very important finding is that there tend to be *diminishing returns to aid*. The higher the share of aid in national income, the less effective additional aid becomes. Beyond a certain point, the impact of aid turns negative, because a country is unable to absorb more aid. However, according to the paper by Lensink and White, the turning point is very high, beyond 50 per cent of national income. Later papers support the notion of diminishing returns but find somewhat lower saturation points (e.g. Radelet *et al.*, 2004: 16–18 per cent of GDP; Clemens *et al.*, 2004: between 15 and 45 per cent).

The authors of the second set of studies do not deny the importance of policy reform. Good policies and improved governance do have significant effects on growth in developing countries. What they criticise is the empirical basis for the very strong conclusions about the interaction between aid and policy. Policy reform is important in its own right. However, if aid has an independent effect on growth irrespective of policy, the case for being very selective in the allocation of aid becomes weaker.

The empirical problems are compounded by theoretical ones. There is no full agreement on the content of policy reform. As we saw in Chapter 13, some aspects of market reforms in developing countries are increasingly being criticised. Market reforms need to be complemented by government policies and extreme liberalisation is not the answer to all problems. Countries at different levels of development require different reform packages (Dijkstra and White, 2003; Doornbos, 2001). Developing countries should be able to develop their own reform programmes, based on the specific conditions in each country. When all is said and done, however, the link between institutional quality and aid seems to be very plausible, in spite of the econometric uncertainties. It is obvious that aid will be less effective in countries with pervasive corruption and clientelistic institutions. It is also clear that aid will have more impact in countries with effective and accountable bureaucracies that are able to formulate and implement policies with high degrees of competence.

Fourth-generation studies

Many of the fourth-generation studies published since 2000 either conclude that no significant relations exist between aid and growth, or that the relationship is even negative. These papers also examine the relationships between aid and democracy or aid and governance.

In *Does Foreign Aid Help?*, Djankov et al. (2006) conclude that foreign aid has a negative impact on democracy as well as a negative impact on growth by reducing investment and increasing government consumption. In a subsequent article, 'The Curse of Aid', Djankov et al. (2008) conclude that the negative effects of abundant aid on democratic institutions are even more pronounced than the negative effects of abundant natural resources. Foreign aid provides a windfall of resources to recipient countries and may result in the same rent seeking behaviour as documented in the natural resource curse literature. Rajan and Subramanian (2008) analyse the relationship between aid and growth using a rich battery of instrumental variables to take the endogeneity of aid – aid tends to go to countries that are not doing well – into account. They try to focus on the relationships between aid and long-run growth. They find little evidence of either a positive or a negative relationship. In a later paper (Rajan and Subramanian, 2011), the authors focus on the effects of aid on manufacturing performance. They find that aid has a significant negative effect on manufacturing performance and competitiveness. The more aid a country receives, the slower its manufacturing growth relative to the growth of other sectors. The paper argues that negative effect of aid is due to *Dutch disease effects*. As a result of large inflows of aid, the exchange rate will tend to appreciate. This makes important exporting sectors such as manufacturing less competitive. Dutch disease effects are an important theme in modern literature. Two large review papers by Doucouliagos and Paldam (2008, 2009) perform a meta-analysis of about 100 studies on aid and growth. Like Rajan and Subramanian, they conclude that there is no significant relationship to be discerned. However, two very competent econometric papers by Arndt, Jones and Tarp (2010) and Mekasha and Tarp (2013) question the negative findings of the fourth-generation papers. The first paper re-does the analysis of Rajan and Subramanian but is more critical of the instrumental variables used. When unsatisfactory IVs are dropped and specifications are improved, a clear significant relation between aid and growth emerges. Arndt et al. (2010) conclude that the micro–macro paradox does not exist. There is a significant, though modest, positive effect of aid on growth. In a very recent paper Makasha and Tarp redo the meta-analysis of Doucouliagos and Paldam (2008) for the same set of studies, and provide econometric critiques of the methods of the earlier paper.

Re-estimation of the relationship shows a clear significant positive relation. An aid–GDP ratio of 10 per cent will result in 1 per cent more growth per year.

COUNTRY EXPERIENCES   An alternative way to assess the impacts of aid is to look at country experiences. Defenders of aid point to a number of countries where massive infusions of aid have contributed to socio-economic development. In the 1950s, South Korea and Taiwan profited from large inflows of aid, which contributed to their later growth. In the period 1966–97, Indonesia experienced rapid growth and reduction of poverty. It profited from large inflows of aid while engaging in an ongoing policy dialogue with international advisors. Other examples of positive impacts are provided by countries such as Lesoto, Botswana, Malawi and Bangladesh, which initially could not have survived as independent states without outside help. For recent years, the donor darlings Ethiopia and Mozambique were cited as examples where large-scale aid went hand in hand with very rapid economic growth. In Mozambique aid clearly contributed to the pacification and stabilisation of the country after the peace agreement of 1992. Countries such as Rwanda and Uganda are also cited as examples where policy and institutional reforms sparked an acceleration in economic growth and where aid flows contributed to the overall process of reform.

There are also many counterexamples of countries that received large amounts of aid, with little or no impact on development. These include countries such as Zambia, Tanzania, Kenya, Haiti, Congo, Somalia, Burkina Faso, or Suriname. Also, none of the examples of success is undisputed. For instance, some observers believe that in South Korea large-scale development aid in the 1950s and 1960s contributed to the build up of infrastructure and the educational system, which were prerequisites for later economic growth. Other observers argue that the economic development of South Korea did not take off till after 1960, when the USA curtailed financial aid. It was the prospect of the end of aid flows which forced South Korea to pursue more effective economic policies.

We conclude that neither the claims of the critics of aid, nor those of the unabashed supporters of aid, can be substantiated unequivocally. First, in most developing countries development aid is modest in proportion to national income and other financial flows. Other economic and non-economic factors are far more important. It is very difficult to isolate the independent effects of aid. Second, one of the reasons for providing aid is that some countries are in great economic difficulties. A lot of aid flows to the poorest African countries with the most intractable economic problems. Of course, one may not conclude from this that there is an inverse relationship between aid and economic stagnation. Rather, the magnitude of aid flows is influenced by the intractability of the economic problems.

We agree with Riddell (1987, 2008) who calls for a balanced approach to development aid, in which the effects of aid are analysed country by country and from period to period. Aid cannot set economic growth in motion. At best, it can help accelerate growth and assist directly or indirectly in some alleviation of poverty. Though the econometric evidence is contested, it is consistent with the analysis in this whole book that aid flows should be seen in relation to overall effectiveness of policies and institutions in different countries. In this respect, we find ourselves in sympathy with the shift towards the new more selective approach championed by the international institutions. However, selectivity calls for an undogmatic approach to what constitutes good policy and effective governance in the context of a given country.

14.6.6   Making aid work better

Since 2003, the work of authors such as Banerjee and Duflo of the Abdul Latif Jameel Poverty Action Lab at MIT has provided a new perspective in the aid debate In a series of influential publications (e.g. Banerjee, 2007; Banerjee and Duflo, 2009, 2011; Banerjee and He, 2008; Duflo *et al.*, 2007), they argue that we should stop debating whether or not aid is effective in general, but should start analysing how aid can be made to work better using the tools of scientific research. They show that large gains in the effectiveness of developmental interventions can be achieved if one adopts the experimental approaches of medical science. They develop randomised controlled trials (RCTs) where the effects of an intervention in treated groups are systematically compared with results in non-treated control groups. One famous example from this literature is that a very small expenditure on deworming school children has a far greater impact on school results through improved school attendance than much more expensive interventions such as reducing class size or investing in teacher training. In close interaction with practitioners, successive trials and experiments can result in real learning and greater success. Other experiments have to do with the impact of conditional cash transfers to poor families on school attendance in the PROGRESA programme in Mexico.

Banerjee and Duflo criticise the focus on grand questions such as whether good institutions are a precondition for aid effectiveness. Even in countries where the overall institutional setting is negative, there is scope for substantial improvement if one applies the right experimental approach.

The experimental approach to development economics has now taken off and there is a veritable explosion of papers based on randomised experiments (Banerjee and Duflo, 2009). We believe this approach is valuable and can contribute to greater effectiveness of aid and of development interventions and policies in general. However, sometimes, proponents of this approach overstate their case and seem to argue that this approach makes all other more macro-oriented approaches irrelevant. Angus Deaton (2010) and Dani Rodrik (2008b) have provided some useful counterarguments. In the first place, randomised experiments have a serious problem of external validity. What works in a specific experiment may not work elsewhere in other countries or under different conditions. The claim that only randomised experiments are scientific, while all other approaches are not, simply does not stand up to closer scrutiny. In the second place, there are important systemic effects at the macro-level which cannot be captured in micro-experiments focusing on differences between treated and not-treated populations. This refers to what happens when micro-experiments are scaled up to a national or regional level, but also to the larger puzzles of why South Korean development is more successful than that of Côte d'Ivoire. Rodrik (2008b) has argued that both modern macro-approaches and micro-approaches are now converging on a more experimental perspective. At macro-level we try to avoid applying the blueprints characteristic of earlier development strategies by looking at the specific binding constraints in a given setting. At the micro-level we try to learn from systematic experimentation. The plea for a more experimental approach is also echoed by Easterly (2006) in his book *The White Man's Burden: Why the West's Efforts to Aid the Rest Have Done So Much Ill and So Little Good*. Easterly contrasts the holistic planners who often do great harm with the searchers who have a more experimental mindset.

Development as a process of trial and error

In arriving at a considered judgement of the effectiveness of aid projects and interventions, one should not forget how often major investment projects are unsuccessful in Western countries and in the private sector. Major multinational electronics, telecommunication or automotive companies regularly write off hundreds of millions or even billions of dollars in risky investments in new technologies that have failed. Governments in Western Europe have invested billions of euros in failed attempts to shore up sunset industries such as shipbuilding, airlines, or steel production. Nevertheless, no one dreams of suggesting that firms discontinue investing in innovation or that governments discontinue investing in major infrastructural projects. It sometimes seems as if development aid is judged by different and stricter standards than the private sector or Western governments. This is unfair. In line with the previous paragraph, we should see socio-economic development and aid policy as a process of 'trial and error' in which 'learning by doing' is essential. In this process, failures and disappointments are inevitable. They are part and parcel of the learning process.

The Paris declaration on aid effectiveness

What the macro-evidence and the micro-evidence and the country examples make clear is that it is hard to draw general conclusions on the impacts of aid. Under some conditions, it has important positive impacts, under other conditions there are no impacts or even negative impacts. Aid interacts with so many other factors that it is hard to isolate its influence. Given the urgency of the problems in poor countries, it is perhaps more fruitful to think about how aid effectiveness can be improved. This was the theme of the previous paragraphs.

At the macro-level the question of how aid can be made to work better is also the theme of a whole series of high-profile international meetings, starting with the Paris conference of 2005 on aid effectiveness. The Paris meeting resulted in the Paris declaration on aid effectiveness. This declaration was further developed into an agenda for action at meetings in Accra in 2008 and Busan, South Korea, in 2011. The Paris declaration has five pillars: ownership, alignment of donors and recipients, donor coordination and harmonisation, results orientation and mutual accountability. The notion of *ownership* implies that aid be part and parcel of a national development and poverty reduction strategy developed by – i.e. owned by – the aid recipient. The recipient has the responsibility of developing its own strategy. Negotiations about aid take place in the context of that wider strategy. *Alignment of donors and recipients* implies that policies should not be imposed from outside, as in the past. Donors should try to align their aid efforts to the national strategies developed by the recipients. The third pillar of aid effectiveness is better *donor coordination and harmonisation*. A huge amount of waste is involved in a multitude of donors duplicating each other's activities and demanding the time and energy of harassed counterparts in developing countries. Through cooperation between donors, this waste could be dramatically reduced. Better coordination involves a shift from project- to programme-based approaches and a concentration on fewer partner countries per donor. Bigsten and Tengstam (2012) have estimated that better coordination and harmonisation and a shift towards more programme-based aid could save more than 2 billion dollars a year. Better coordination also involves a better allocation of aid to the countries most in need of aid from the perspective of poverty reduction. The fourth and fifth pillars, of *results orientation* and *mutual accountability*, are very much in line with the experimental approaches discussed above. It should be clear what the intended results of an intervention are and to what extent they are being achieved. Systematic evaluations of results should be built into the aid programmes at the outset. Both donors and recipients should be held accountable to their constituencies for the realisation of the results. As Bigsten and Tengstam have shown, even partial realisation of these objectives would lead to better results, but of course the political realisation of these high-sounding aims will not be easy.

14.6.7   Epilogue: an attempt at evaluation

Above, a small part of the extensive literature on the pros and cons of development aid has been discussed. The empirical results and theoretical analyses are so contradictory that it is illusory to expect to arrive at unambiguous conclusions. The final choices are inevitably value laden. Nevertheless, in order to avoid being too noncommittal, we have chosen to specify the reasoned conclusions we have derived from these important debates. They can be summarised in the following points:

1. *There are strong moral considerations to provide development aid.* These considerations gain in strength if aid on balance makes positive contributions to socio-economic development, the reduction of poverty and the solution of concrete problems in developing countries.

2. *The fact that large amounts of aid are wasted is in itself not an argument against aid.* Considering the urgency of developmental problems, a degree of waste is acceptable, as long as aid realises some part of its developmental objectives (see also point 5 below). Development is a risky process of trial and error, which inevitably involves mistakes. Of course, one should always try to increase the effectiveness of aid, and in particular the ability to learn from past mistakes.

3. *The fact that development aid also serves the interests of the donor countries is not an argument against aid*, provided that aid on balance contributes to the realisation of developmental objectives. However, when the strategic interests of the donor countries seriously conflict with the effectiveness of aid, aid programmes should be discontinued.

4. *The fact that aid does not immediately reach the poor is no reason to discontinue it* as long it contributes on balance to the economic dynamism of the recipient countries. An important theme in this whole book is that in the long run a dynamic economy is the main prerequisite for reducing poverty.

5. *Development aid should be discontinued if it can be shown to be an obstacle to development.* This may be the case when foreign aid is directly responsible for the continuation of regimes violating basic human rights or pursuing disastrous economic and social policies resulting in economic stagnation and widespread human suffering. Furthermore, especially in countries which pursue very inadequate economic policies and where government expenditures are overwhelmingly financed by aid flows, there is a clear relationship between foreign aid and policy failure. In such cases, reductions in the volume of aid or even discontinuation of the aid relationship should be considered.

6. *If the provision of goods as part of aid is a disincentive to the production of these goods in the developing countries themselves*, these kinds of aid should be discontinued. In this context, we refer mainly to food aid, in other than emergency situations.

7. *There are diminishing returns to aid.* Countries where net foreign aid flows exceed 10 per cent of GDP or 50 per cent of government revenue for years in succession are in danger

of becoming too dependent on aid. When human talents are exclusively oriented towards aid flows and their use, aid itself turns into a long-run obstacle to autonomous socio-economic development. Reduction of aid flows to below critical levels should be seriously considered, though the choice of the specific level beyond which aid becomes an obstacle remains open to debate.

8. *Countries engaging in effective development policies* should be able to rely on continued support for extended periods of time, even if the long-run goal is a reduction of aid flows. The volatility of aid flows should be reduced.

9. *It is very likely that more effective policies and institutions are associated with more positive impacts of aid.* This should be reflected in aid allocations. Nevertheless, aid should not be exclusively provided to countries with effective policies and institutions. The inhabitants of countries with ineffective policies and weak institutions are some-times the most in need of aid flows. In such cases, the mode of providing aid should take the conditions in the receiving countries into account.

10. Even when government-to-government aid flows are discontinued, *continuation of direct aid to poverty groups by NGOs can be defended.* Non-governmental agencies are usually more effective at channelling the aid to the groups for which it is intended, but this does certainly not mean they should be excluded from critical scrutiny.

11. *There is a strong humanitarian case for emergency aid in case of disasters, floods or famines.* Again, a condition is that a reasonable part of aid meets its objectives and reaches the target groups for which it is intended (see point 2 above). Also the avail-ability of aid should not undermine incentives for production (see point 5 above).

12. *On balance one may conclude that aid flows have been able to make positive contributions to development* in several countries and settings. It is more worthwhile to devote our energy to improving the effectiveness of aid than to argue about whether or not it should exist.

13. Nevertheless, the criticisms discussed in this chapter have shown that *aid relations between donor countries and developing countries leave much to be desired.* Part of development aid flows back to the rich donor countries. Much aid is of questionable effectiveness. Given these circumstances, improving the effectiveness of foreign aid has a higher priority than increasing the volume of aid flows.

14. *Development aid can never be a decisive factor in economic growth and development.* Economic development can only be achieved through the efforts and policies of indi-viduals and their governments. In the context of effective national and international policies, foreign aid may also make a positive contribution to development.

Questions for review

1. Discuss the different motives for providing foreign aid to developing countries.
2. How does the two-gap model of Chenery and Strout provide a theoretical justification for providing foreign aid to developing countries?
3. Discuss some of the shortcomings of gap analysis as a justification for aid.
4. Should aid be targeted directly at groups living in poverty?
5. How important is aid? Discuss the importance of foreign aid as a proportion of total financial flows to developing countries and as a percentage of GDP in different developing countries and regions.

6. Summarise the main characteristics of the radical left-wing and neoliberal criticisms of foreign aid. Discuss some of the similarities between the two sets of criticisms.
7. What are some of the potential disadvantages of food aid?
8. What is the connection between programme aid and good governance?
9. Discuss the fungibility thesis. What are the implications of fungibility for the evaluation of development projects? What are the implications for aid policies?
10. What are the main points of the orthodox argument in defence of foreign aid?
11. To what extent does the empirical literature conclude that there is a relationship between aid and growth?
12. Provide examples of aid success and aid failure. What are, in your opinion, the wider implications of such examples?
13. To what extent does the effectiveness of aid depend on development policies and development strategies in the countries receiving aid?
14. Discuss the differences between conditionality and selectivity.
15. What is meant by the term 'country ownership of aid'? Summarise and discuss the main elements for the Paris agenda for aid effectiveness.

Further reading

One of the most thoughtful books on aid is still Riddell, *Foreign Aid Reconsidered* (1987). It provides a balanced overview of the ethical, theoretical and empirical issues in the debate on aid and a fair treatment of different schools of thought. Riddell's more recent book, *Does Foreign Aid Really Work?* (2008) is much more than an update of the earlier book. It is an invaluable reflection on current issues and trends. A prominent liberal critic of aid is Bauer. Two of his books, *Dissent on Development* (1976) and *Equality, the Third World and Economic Delusion* (1981), have influenced the course of the debate on aid. Radical critics of aid include Hayter and Lappé. Here we mention: Hayter, *Aid as Imperialism* (1971), Hayter and Watson, *Aid: Rhetoric and Reality* (1985) and Lappé et al., *Aid as Obstacle: Twenty Questions about our Foreign Aid and the Hungry* (1980). Interesting examples of the shortcomings of aid projects and aid policies are provided in two journalistic books: Hancock, *Lords of Poverty* (1991) and Maren, *The Road to Hell: The Ravaging Effects of Foreign Aid and International Charity* (1997). Polar opposites in the latest round of debates are Sachs and Moyo. In the *End of Poverty: Economic Posibilities for our Time* (2005), Sachs calls for a major increase in aid flows to tackle poverty in the context of the MDGs. In *Dead Aid: Why Aid is Not Working and How There is a Better Way for Africa* (2009), Moyo argues that aid has harmed Africa. It has resulted in bad governance, and African countries should stop relying on aid. Other sharp criticisms of aid are found in Easterly, *The White Man's Burden: Why the West's Efforts to Aid the Rest Have Done So Much Ill and So Little Good* (2006).

Mainstream discussions of aid and its effectiveness are to be found in Krueger, Michalopoulos and Ruttan, *Aid and Development* (1989), an evaluation study by Cassen, *Does Aid Work?* (1986) and Riddell (2008) mentioned above. A volume edited by Dijkstra and White, *Programme Aid and Development: Beyond Conditionality* (2003), examines the effectiveness of aid in a series of country studies.

The macro-economic rationale for aid is set out in a classic article by Chenery and Strout in the *American Economic Review*: 'Foreign Assistance and Economic Development' (1966). Aid flows are linked to shortfalls in savings and foreign exchange. There is a large set of econometric studies assessing the impact of aid on growth and economic development, using cross-country panel datasets. An influential article is Burnside and Dollar, 'Aid, Policies and Growth' (2000), published in the *American Economic Review*. Burnside and Dollar argue that there is a positive relation between aid and growth, but only in countries with good governance. Two interesting policy reports argue in favour of linking aid to good governance in the recipient country. The first report is an influential World Bank report based on the econometric analysis by Burnside and Dollar quoted above: Dollar and Pritchett, *Assessing Aid: What Works, What Doesn't and Why* (1998). The second report is a report of a US commission chaired by Allan Meltzer on the future of international financial institutions, *Report of the International Financial Institutions Advisory Commission* (2000). Both reports suggest making the provision of aid conditional on liberalisation and policy reform. The conclusions of the Burnside–Dollar study have been criticised in other econometric work, for instance in 'Changing the Conditions for Development Aid: A New Paradigm?', a special issue of the *Journal of Development Studies* edited by Hermes and Lensink (2001a) and in an article in the *American Economic Review* on 'Aid, Policies and Growth' by Easterly, Levine and Roodman (2004).

Interesting selections from the recent empirical literature include: Alesina and Dollar, 'Who Gives Foreign Aid to Whom and Why? (2000); Hansen and Tarp, 'Aid Effectiveness Disputed' (2000a); Clemens, Radelet and Bhavnani, 'Counting Chickens when they Hatch: The Short Term Effect of Aid on Growth' (2004); and Radelet, Clemens and Bhavnani, *Aid and Growth: The Current Debate and Some New Evidence* (2004). Papers casting doubt on the contributions of aid are Djankov, Montalvo and Reynal-Querol, 'Does Foreign Aid Help?' (2006) and 'The Curse of Aid' (2008); Rajan and Subramanian, 'Aid and Growth: What Does the Cross-Country Evidence Really Show?' (2008) and 'Aid, Dutch Disease, and Manufacturing Growth' (2011); and Doucouliagos and Paldam, 'Aid Effectiveness on Growth: A Meta Study' (2008) and 'The Aid Effectiveness Literature: The Sad Results of 40 Years of Research' (2009). Two papers re-affirming the positive relationship between aid and growth and explicitly criticising the previous papers are Arndt, Jones and Tarp, 'Aid Growth and Development: Have We Come Full Circle?' (2010) and Mekasha and Tarp, 'Aid and Growth: What Meta-Analysis Reveals' (2013).

A series of influential books and papers by Abhijit Banerjee, Esther Duflo and other authors associated with the MIT poverty lab argue that randomised controlled trials can greatly improve the impact of aid and policy interventions on the lives of the poor. Examples of this burgeoning literature include Banerjee, *Making Aid Work* (2007) and Banerjee and Duflo, *Poor Economics: A Radical Rethinking of the Way to Fight Global Poverty* (2011) and three articles, Banerjee and Duflo, 'The Experimental Approach to Development Economics' (2009), in the *Annual Review of Economics*; Banerjee and He, 'Making Aid Work' (2008); and Duflo, Glennerster and Kremer (2007), 'Using Randomization in Development Economics Research: A Toolkit' (2007), in the *Handbook of Development Economics*. A spirited defense of macro-approaches and a call for convergence between micro- and macro-oriented approaches is provided by Rodrik in his paper *The New Development Economics: We Shall Experiment, but How Shall We Learn?* (2008b).

The primary source of empirical data on aid flows is the OECD website: *International Development Statistics (IDS) Online databases*, www.oecd.org/dac/stats/idsonline.htm. The data can also be accessed via the link: http://stats.oecd.org/.

REFERENCES

ABERNATHY, F.H. *et al.* (1999) *A Stitch in Time:Lean Retailing and the Transformation of Manufacturing. Lessons from the Apparel and Textile Industries*, New York: Oxford University Press.

ABERNETHY, D. (1969) *The Political Dilemma of Popular Education: An African Case*, Stanford University Press.

ABRAMOVITZ, M. (1989a) 'Resource and Output Trends in the United States since 1870', *American Economic Review*, **46** (2), pp. 5–23. Reprinted in: M. ABRAMOVITZ, *Thinking about Growth and Other Essays on Economic Growth and Welfare,* Cambridge University Press (first published in 1956).

(1989b) 'Thinking about Growth', in: M. ABRAMOVITZ, *Thinking about Growth and other Essays on Economic Growth and Welfare*, Cambridge University Press, pp. 3–79.

ABU-LUGHOD, J.L. (1989) *Before European Hegemony: The World System A.D. 1250–1350*, New York/Oxford: Oxford University Press.

ACEMOGLU, D. and D. AUTOR (2012) '"What Does Human Capital Do?" A Review of Goldin and Katz's The Race between Education and Technology', *Journal of Economic Literature*, **50** (2), pp. 426–63.

ACEMOGLU, D., S. JOHNSON and J.A. ROBINSON (2001) 'The Colonial Origins of Comparative Development: An Empirical Investigation', *American Economic Review*, **91**, pp. 1369–1401.

(2002) 'Reversal of Fortune: Geography and Institutions in the Making of the Modern World Income Distribution', *Quarterly Journal of Economics*, **117** (4), pp. 1231–94.

(2003a) 'Disease and Development in Historical Perspective', *Journal of the European Economic Association*, **1** (2–3), pp. 397–405.

(2003b) 'An African Success Story: Botswana', in D. RODRIK (ed.), *In Search of Prosperity. Analytic Narratives on Economic Growth*, Princeton University Press, pp. 80–119.

ACEMOGLU, D. and J.A. ROBINSON (2006) *Economic Origins of Dictatorship and Democracy*, Cambridge MA: MIT Press.

(2012) *Why Nations Fail? The Origins of Power, Prosperity and Poverty*, London: Profile Books.

ÁCS, Z. and W. NAUDÉ (2013) 'Entrepreneurship, Stages of Development and Industrialisation', in A. SZIRMAI, W. NAUDÉ and L. ALCORTA (eds.), *Pathways to Industrialisation in the 21st Century: New Challenges and Emerging Paradigms*, Oxford University Press, pp. 373–92.

ADAMS, J. (1986) 'Peasant Rationality: Individuals, Groups, Cultures', *World Development*, **14** (2), pp. 273–82.

(2001) 'Culture and Economic Development in South Asia', in: C. CLAGUE and SH. GROSSBARD-SHECHTMAN (eds.), *Culture and Development: International Perspectives*,

Special Issue of the Annals of the American Academy of Political and Social Science, **573**, January, pp. 152–73.

ADELMAN, I. (2000) 'Editor's Introduction', Special Issue on Architecture of Global Financial Systems, *World Development*, **28** (6), pp. 1053–60.

ADELMAN, I. and E. YELDAN (2000) 'The Minimal Conditions for A Financial Crisis: A Multi-Regional Intertemporal CGE Model of the Asian Crisis', *World Development*, **28** (6), pp. 1087–1100.

AFD (2008), Technical Committee on Land Tenure and Development, Land Governance and Security of Tenure in Developing Countries.

AFRICAN DEVELOPMENT BANK (2000) *African Development Report 2000*, New York: Oxford University Press.

AGGARWAL, A. and N. KUMAR (2015) 'Structural Change, Industrialization and Poverty Reduction: The Case of India', in: W. NAUDÉ, A. SZIRMAI and N. HARAGUCHI (eds.) *Structural Change and Industrial Development in the BRICS*, Oxford University Press, forthcoming.

AHLUWALIA, M.S. (1976) 'Inequality, Poverty and Development', *Journal of Development Economics*, **3** (4), pp. 307–42.

AKÇOMAK, I.S. and B. TER WEEL (2009) 'Social Capital, Innovation and Growth: Evidence from Europe', *European Economic Review*, **53** (5), pp. 544–67.

AKE, C. (1996) *Democracy and Development in Africa*, Washington, DC: Brookings Institution.

AKRAM-LODHI, A. H. (2001) *Vietnam's Agriculture: Is There an Inverse Relationship?* Working Paper, Institute of Social Studies.

ALAVI, H. (1979) 'The State in Post-Colonial Societies: Pakistan and Bangladesh', in: H. GOULYBORNE (ed.), *Politics and the State in the Third World*, London: Macmillan, pp. 38–70.

ALDRIGHI, A. and R. COLISTETE (2015), 'Industrial Growth and Structural Change: Brazil in a Long-Run Perspective ', in: W. NAUDÉ, A. SZIRMAI and N. HARAGUCHI (eds.), *Structural Change and Industrial Development in the BRICS*, Oxford University Press, forthcoming.

ALESINA, A. and D. DOLLAR (2000) 'Who Gives Foreign Aid to Whom and Why?', *Journal of Economic Growth*, **5** (1), pp. 33–63.

ALESINA A. and E. FERRARA (2005) 'Ethnic Diversity and Economic Performance', *Journal of Economic Literature*, **43**, pp. 762–800.

ALESINA, A., S. OZLER, N. ROUBINE and P. SWAGE (1996) 'Political Instability and Economic Growth', *Journal of Economic Growth*, **1** (2), pp. 189–211.

ALESINA, A. and D. RODRIK (1994) 'Distributive Politics and Economic Growth', *The Quarterly Journal of Economics*, **109** (2), pp. 465–89.

ALESINA, A. and G. TABELLINI (1989) 'External Debt, Capital Fight and Political Risk', *Journal of International Economics*, **XXVII**, pp. 199–220.

ALEXANDER, P., P. BOOMGAARD and B. WHITE (eds.) (1991) *In the Shadow of Agriculture: Non-farm Activities in the Javanese Economy, Past and Present*, Amsterdam: Royal Tropical Institute.

ALEXANDRATOS, N. (1988) *World Agriculture Towards 2000*, FAO, London: Belhaven.

(ed.) (1995) *World Agriculture: Towards 2010*, FAO, Chichester: John Wiley and Sons.

ALEXANDRATOS, N. and J. BRUINSMA (2012) *World Agriculture Towards 2030/2050: The 2012 Revision*, ESA Working Paper No. 12–03, Rome: FAO.

ALLEN, R.C. (2009) *The British Industrial Revolution in Global Perspective*, Cambridge University Press.

ALLEN, R.D.G. (1980) *An Introduction to National Accounts Statistics*, London: Macmillan.

ALTBACH, P.G. (1982) 'Servitude of the Mind? Education, Dependency and Neocolonialism', in: P.G. ALTBACH, R.F. ARNOVE and G.P. KELLY (eds.), *Comparative Education*, New York: Macmillan, pp. 469–84.

ALTBACH, P.G. and G.P. KELLY (1978) *Education and Colonialism*, New York/London: Longman.

ALTENBURG, T. (2013) 'Can Industrial Policy Work Under Neopatrimonial Rule', in A. SZIRMAI, W. NAUDÉ and L. ALCORTA (eds.) (2013), *Pathways to Industrialisation in the 21st Century: New Challenges and Emerging Paradigms*, Oxford University Press, pp. 345–72.

AMIN, S. (1974) *Accumulation on a World Scale*, New York: Monthly Review Press.

AMSDEN, A. (1989) *Asia's Next Giant: South Korea and Late Industrialization*, New York: Oxford University Press.

(2007) *Escape from Empire: The Developing World's Journey through Heaven and Hell*, Cambridge, Mass.: MIT Press.

(2009) 'Nationality of Firm Ownership in Developing Countries: Who Should "Crowd Out" Whom in Imperfect Markets?', in: M. CIMOLI, G. DOSI and J. STIGLITZ (eds.), *Industrial Policy and Development*, Cambridge University Press, pp. 409–23.

(2013) 'Firm Ownership and Entrepreneurship', in: A. SZIRMAI, W. NAUDÉ and M. GOEDHUYS (eds.), *Entrepreneurship, Innovation and Economic Development*, Oxford University Press, pp. 65–77.

ANDERSON, C.A. and M.J. BOWMAN (1976) 'Education and Economic Modernization in Historical Perspective', in: L. STONE (ed.), *Schooling and Societies. Studies in the History of Education*, Baltimore, MD: Johns Hopkins University Press, pp. 3–19.

ANGLADE, C. and C. FORTIN (1985) 'The State and Capital Accumulation in Latin America: A Conceptual and Historical Introduction', in: C. ANGLADE and C. FORTIN (eds.), *The State and Capital Accumulation in Latin America*, Vol. I, University of Pittsburgh Press.

ARNDT, C. (2009) *Governance Indicators*, Dissertation, Maastricht University.

ARNDT, C.H., S. JONES and F. TARP (2010) 'Aid Growth and Development: Have We Come Full Circle?', *Journal of Globalization and Development*, **1** (2), pp. 1–27.

ARNOLD, D. (1988) *Famine: Social Crisis and Historical Change*, Oxford: Basil Blackwell.

ASHTON, B., K. HILL, A. PIAZZA and R. ZEITZ (1984) 'Famine in China, 1958–61', *Population Development Review*, **10** (4), pp. 613–45.

ASIAN DEVELOPMENT BANK (2001) *Key Indicators 2001: Growth and Change in Asia and the Pacific*, http://www.adb.org/Documents/Books/Key_Indicators/2001/default.asp, ADB.

(2010) *Asian Development Outlook 2010: Macro-Economic Management beyond the Crisis*, Mandaluyong City, Philippines.

ASIEDU, E. and J. FREEMAN (2009) 'The Effect of Corruption on Investment Growth: Evidence from Firms in Latin America, Sub-Saharan Africa, and Transition Countries', *Review of Development Economics*, **13**, pp. 2002–14.

ASWICAHYONO H., H. HILL and D. NARJOKO (2013) 'Indonesian Industrialisation: A Latecomer Adjusting to Crises', in A. SZIRMAI, W. NAUDÉ and A. ALCORTA (eds.), *Pathways to Industrialization in the 21st Century: New Challenges and Emerging Paradigms*, Oxford University Press, pp.193–222.

ATAMANOV, A. (2011) *Rural Nonfarm Employment and International Migration as Alternatives to Agricultural Employment: The Case of Kyrgyzstan*, PhD thesis, Maastricht University.

ATHUKORALA, P. (1998a) *Trade Policy Issues in Asian Development*, London/New York: Routledge.

(1998b) 'Export Response to Liberalisation: The Sri Lankan Experience', *Hitotsubashi Journal of Economics*, **39** (1), pp. 49–65.

(2001) *Crisis and Recovery in Malaysia: The Role of Capital Controls*, Cheltenham: Edward Elgar.

ATHUKORALA, P. and S. RAJAPATIRANA (2000) 'Liberalization and Industrial Transformation: Lessons from the Sri Lankan Experience', *Economic Development and Cultural Change*, **48** (3), pp. 543–72.

ATHUKORALA, P. C. and J. MENON (2010) *Global Production Sharing Patterns and Determinants of Trade Flows in East Asia*, ADB Working Paper Series on Regional Integration No. 41, Asian Development Bank.

ATKINSON, A.B., TH. PIKETTY and E. SAEZ (2010) 'Top Incomes in the Long Run of History', in: A.B. ATKINSON and T. PIKETTY (eds.), *Top Incomes. A Global Perspective*, Oxford University Press.

AUBERT, J. E. (2005) *Promoting Innovation in Developing Countries: A Conceptual Framework*, World Bank Policy Research Working Paper 3554, April.

AUDRETSCH, D. B. (2007) *The Entrepreneurial Society*, Oxford University Press.

AYITTEY, G. B. N. (2005) *Africa Unchained: The Blueprint for Africa's Future*, Palgrave Macmillan.

AZARIADIS, C. and A. DRAZEN (1990) 'Threshold Externalities in Economic Development', *Quarterly Journal of Economics*, **105** (2), pp. 501–26.

AZFAR, O and Y. LEE (2001) 'The Causes and Consequences of Corruption', *The Annals of the American Academy of Political and Social Science*, **573** (1), pp. 42–56.

BACHA, E. L. (1979) 'The Kuznets Curve and Beyond. Growth and Changes in Inequality', in: E. MALINVAUD (ed.), *Economic Growth and Resources*, Vol. I, London: Macmillan.

BAEHR, P. R. (1992) 'De rol van internationale organisaties sinds 1945 [The role of internationalorganisations since 1945]', in: D.F.J. BOSSCHER, H. RENNER, R.B. SOETENDORP and R. WAGENAAR (eds.), *De wereld na 1945 [The World since 1945]*, Utrecht: Het Spectrum, Aula.

BAIROCH, P. (1975) *The Economic Development of the Third World since 1900*, Berkeley, CA: University of California Press.

(1980) 'Le bilan économique du colonialisme: mythes et réalités', in: L. BLUSSÉ, H.L. WESSELING, G.D. WINIUS (eds.), *History and Underdevelopment: Essays on Underdevelopment and European Expansion in Asia and Africa*, Centre for the History of European Expansion, Paris, Éditions de la maison de science de l'homme, pp. 29–41.

(1982) 'International Industrialization Levels from1750 to 1980', *Journal of European Economic History* **11** (Fall), pp. 269–333.

BAIROCH, P. and M. LEVY-LEBOYER (1981) *Disparities in Economic Development since the Industrial Revolution*, London: Macmillan.

BAKER, C. (1981) 'Economic Re-Organization and Slump in South and South East Asia', in: *Comparative Studies in Society and History*, **23** (3), pp. 325–49.

BALASSA, B. (1978) 'Exports and Economic Growth: Further Evidence', *Journal of Development Economics*, **5** (2), pp. 181–9.

BALDWIN, R.E. (1956) 'Patterns of Development in Newly Settled Regions', *Manchester School of Economic and Social Studies*, May.

(2011) *Trade and Industrialization after Globalization's 2nd Unbundling: How Building and Joining a Supply Chain are Different and Why it Matters*, Working Paper 17716, Cambridge, MA: NBER.

BALDWIN, R.E. and B.A. WEISBROD (1974) 'Disease and Labor Productivity', *Economic Development and Cultural Change*, **22** (3), pp. 414–35.

BALISACAN A. and H. HILL (eds.) (2003) *The Philippine Economy: Development, Policies, and Challenges*, Oxford University Press.

BALL, R. (2001) 'Individualism, Collectivism and Economic Development', in: C. CLAGUE, and SH. GROSSBARD-SHECHTMAN (eds.), *Culture and Development: International Perspectives, Special Issue of the Annals of the American Academy of Political and Social Science*, **573** (1), pp. 57–84.

BANERJEE, A.V. (2007) *Making Aid Work*, Cambridge, MA: MIT Press.

BANERJEE, A.V. and E. DUFLO (2009) 'The Experimental Approach to Development Economics', *Annual Review of Economics*, **1** (1), pp. 151–78.

BANERJEE, A.V. and E. DUFLO (2011) *Poor Economics: A Radical Rethinking of the Way to Fight Global Poverty*, New York, NY: Public Affairs.

BANERJEE A.V. and R. HE (2008) 'Making Aid Work', in W. EASTERLY (ed.), *Reinventing Foreign Aid*, Cambridge, MA: MIT Press.

BANFIELD, E.C. (1958) *The Moral Basis of a Backward Society*, New York: Free Press.

BANISTER, J. (1984) 'Analysis of Recent Data on the Population of China', *Population and Development Review*, **10** (1), pp. 241–71.

BANKS, A.S. (eds.) (various volumes) *Political Handbook of the World*, New York: McGraw Hill.

BANKS A.S, W. OVERSTREET, T.C. MULLER (eds.) (1998) *Political Handbook of the World: Governments and Intergovernmental Organizations*, London: McGrawHill.

BARAN, P. (1957) *The Political Economy of Growth*, New York: Monthly Review Press.

BARDHAN, P. (1984) *The Political Economy of Development in India*, New Delhi: Oxford University Press.

(1993) 'Economics of Development and the Development of Economics', *Journal of Economic Perspectives*, **7** (2), pp. 129–42.

(2002) 'Decentralization of Governance and Development', *Journal of Economic Perspectives*, **16** (4), pp. 185–205.

BARLOW, R. (1979) 'Health and Economic Development: A Theoretical and Empirical Review', *Human Capital and Development*, **1**, pp. 45–75.

BARRET, C.B., M.F. BELLEMARE and J.Y. HOU (2010) 'Reconsidering Conventional Explanations of the Inverse Productivity–Size Relationship', *World Development*, **38** (1), pp. 88–97.

BARRO, R. (1991) 'Economic Growth in a Cross Section of Countries', *Quarterly Journal of Economics*, **106** (2), pp. 407–43.

(1996) *Getting it Right: Markets and Choices in a Free Society*, Cambridge, MA: MIT Press.

BARRO, R. and J-W. LEE (1993) 'International Comparisons of Educational Attainment', *Journal of Monetary Economics*, **32**, pp. 363–94.

(2000) *International Data on Educational Attainment, Updates and Implications*, NBER Working Paper No. 7911.

(2010) *A New Data Set of Educational Attainment in the World, 1950–2010*, NBER Working Paper No. 15902, April.

(2011) *Barro–Lee Educational Attainment Dataset*, updated 2011.9, http://www.barrolee. com/.

BARRO, R. and X. SALA-I-MARTIN (1995) *Economic Growth*, New York: McGraw Hill.

BARROW, C.J. (1995) *Developing the Environment: Problems and Management*, London: Longman.

BARTH, F. (1966) *Models of Social Organisation*, London: Royal Anthropological Institute.

BASTA, S. *et al.* (1979) 'Iron Deficiency Anemia and Productivity of Adult Males in Indonesia', *American Journal of Clinical Nutrition*, **32** (4), pp. 916–25.

BATES, R.H. (1994) 'The Impulse to Reform in Africa', in: J.A. WIDNER (ed.), *Economic Change and Political Liberalisation in Sub-Saharan Africa*, Baltimore, MD and London: Johns Hopkins University Press, pp. 13–28.

BATES, R.H. and P. COLLIER (1993) 'The Politics and Economics of Policy Reform in Zambia', in: R.H. BATES and A.O. KRUEGER (eds.), *Political and Economic Interactions in Economic Policy Reform in Zambia*, Oxford: Basil Blackwell, pp. 391 ff.

BATOU, J. (1990) *Cent ans de résistance au sous-développement. L'industrialisation de l'Amérique latine et du Moyen-Orient face au défi européen, 1770–1870*, Genève: Droz.

BAUER, P.T. (1976) *Dissent on Development*, London: Weidenfeld & Nicolson.

(1981) *Equality, the Third World and Economic Delusion*, London: Weidenfeld & Nicolson.

(1984) *Reality and Rhetoric*, London, Weidenfeld & Nicolson.

(1988) 'Comment on R.A. Cassen, Aid Evaluation. Its Scope and Limits', in: C.J. JEPMA, *North–South Cooperation in Retrospect and Prospect*, London: Routledge, pp. 182–6.

BAUER, P. and B.S. YAMEY (1957) *The Economics of Underdeveloped Countries*, University of Chicago Press.

(1981) 'The Political Economy of Foreign Aid', *Lloyds Bank Review*, October, pp. 1–15.

(1986) *Development Forum*, **XIV** (3), United Nations: Geneva, April.

BAUMOL, W.J. (1967) 'Macro-Economics of Unbalanced Growth: The Anatomy of Urban Crises', *American Economic Review*, **57** (3), pp. 415–26.

(1986) 'Productivity Growth, Convergence and Welfare: What the Long Run Data Show', *American Economic Review*, **76** (5), pp. 1072–86.

(1990) 'Entrepreneurship, Productive, Unproductive and Destructive', *Journal of Political Economy*, **98** (5), pp. 893–921.

(2000) 'Services as Leaders and the leader of the services', in: J. GADREY and F. GALLOUJ (eds.), *Productivity, Innovation and Knowledge in Services*, Cheltenham: Edward Elgar.

BAUMOL, W.J., S.A.B. BLACKMAN and E.N. WOLFF (1989) *Productivity and American Leadership*, Cambridge, MA: MIT Press.

BAUTISTA, R.M. (1989) 'Domestic Terms of Trade and Agricultural Growth in Developing Countries', in: N. ISLAM (ed.), *The Balance between Industry and Agriculture in Economic Development: Factors Influencing Change*, Proceedings of the Eighth World Congress of the International Economic Association, Vol. 5, Basingstoke: Macmillan.

BEA, *National Income and Product Accounts*, http://www.bea.gov/national/nipaweb/ TableView.asp#Mid, downloaded 2008.

BECKER, C.M. and D.D. HEMLEY (1998) 'Demographic Change in the Former Soviet Union during the Transition Period', *World Development*, **26** (11), pp. 1957–97.

BECKER, G.S. (1960) 'An Economic Analysis of Fertility', in: NATIONAL BUREAU FOR ECONOMIC RESEARCH (ed.), *Demographic and Economic Change in Developed Countries*, Princeton University Press.

(1964) *Human Capital. A Theoretical and Empirical Analysis, with Special Reference to Education*, New York/London: Columbia University Press.

BECKERMAN, W. (1974) *In Defense of Economic Growth*, London: Jonathan Cape.

(1992) 'Economic Growth and the Environment: Whose Growth? Whose Environment?', *World Development*, **20** (4), pp. 481–96.

(1993) 'Is Economic Growth Still Desirable?', in: A. SZIRMAI, B. VAN ARK and D. PILAT (eds.), *Explaining Economic Growth: Essays in Honour of Angus Maddison*, Amsterdam: North-Holland, pp. 77–100.

BEDASSO, B. (2013) *Institutional Change in the Long Shadow of Elites: Essays on Institutions, Human Capital and Ethnicity in Developing Countries*, PhD thesis, Maastricht University.

BEHRMAN, J.R. (2010) 'Investment in Education – Inputs and Incentives', in: D. RODRIK and M.R. ROSENZWEIG (eds.), *Handbook of Development Economics*, Vol. 5, Amsterdam: Elsevier/North-Holland, Chapter 73, pp. 4883–975.

BEHRMAN, H. and T.N. SRINIVASAN (eds.) (1995a) *Handbook of Development Economics*, Vol. 3A, Amsterdam: North-Holland.

(1995b) *Handbook of Development Economics*, Vol. 3B, Amsterdam: North-Holland.

BEINE, M., F. DOCQUIER and H. RAPOPORT (2001) 'Brain Drain and Economic Growth: Theory and Evidence', *Journal of Development Economics*, **64** (1), pp. 275–89.

BELL, D. (1971) 'The Cultural Contradictions of Capitalism', in: D. BELL and I. KRISTOL (eds.), *Capitalism Today*, New York: Basic Books.

BENGTSSON, T. and C. GUNNARSSON (1994) 'Population, Development and Institutional Change: Summary and Analysis', in: K. LINDAHL-KIESSLING and H. LANDBERG, *Population, Economic Development and the Environment*, Oxford, New York: Oxford University Press, pp. 1–24.

BENHABIB, J. and M. SPIEGEL (1994) 'The Role of Human Capital in Economic Development: Evidence from Aggregate Cross-Country Data', *Journal of Monetary Economics*, **34** (2), pp. 143–79.

(2005) 'Human Capital and Technology Diffusion', in: P. AGHION and S. DURLAUF (eds.), *Handbook of Economic Growth*, Amsterdam: North-Holland, pp. 935–66.

BENTHEM VAN DEN BERGH, G. VAN (1980) *On the Dynamics of Development of Contemporary States: An Approach to Comparative Politics*, ISS Occasional Paper, The Hague, November.

BERG, I. (1970) *Education and Jobs: The Great Training Robbery*, New York: Praeger.

BERGHE, P.L. VAN DEN (1981) *The Ethnic Phenomenon*, New York/Oxford: Elsevier.

BERLAGE, L. and R. RENARD (1993) *Evaluatie van Ontwikkelingshulp in België en Nederland [Evaluation of Development Aid in Belgium and the Netherlands]*, Research Paper in Economic Development, No. 24, Centrum voor Economische Studieën, Leuven.

BERMAN, P.A. (1998) 'Rethinking Healthcare Systems: Private Healthcare Provision in India', *World Development*, **26** (8), pp. 1463–79.

BERRY, A., F. BOURGUIGNON and C. MORRISSON (1983) 'The Level of World Inequality: How Much Can One Say?', *The Review of Income and Wealth*, **29** (3), pp. 217–42.

BERRY, R. and W.R. CLINE (1979) *Agrarian Structure and Productivity in Developing Countries*, Baltimore, MD: Johns Hopkins University Press.

BERTOLA, L. and J.A. OCAMPO (2012) *The Economic Development of Latin America since Independence*, Oxford University Press.

BHAGWATI, J.N. (1958) 'Immiserizing Growth: A Geometrical Note', *Review of Economic Studies*, **25** (2), pp. 201–205.

(1977) *The New International Order: The North–South Debate*, Cambridge, MA: MIT Press.

(1985a) 'Foreign Trade Regimes,' in: J.N. BHAGWATI, *Dependence and Interdependence: Essays in Development Economics*, Vol. 2, ed. by G. GROSSMAN, Oxford: Basil Blackwell, pp. 123–38.

(1988) *Protectionism*, Cambridge, MA: MIT Press.

(1995) 'U.S. Trade Policy: The Infatuation with Free Trade Agreements', in: J.N. BHAGWATI and A.O. KRUEGER, *The Dangerous Drift to Preferential Trade Agreements*, Cambridge, MA: AEI Press.

BHAGWATI J. and K. HAMADA (1974) 'The Brain Drain: International Integration of Markets for Professionals and Unemployment. A Theoretical Analysis', *Journal of Development Economics*, **1** (1), pp. 19–42.

BHUPATIRAJU, S. and B. VERSPAGEN (2013) *Economic Development, Growth, Institutions and Geography*, UNU-MERIT Working Paper Series, 2013–056.

BIENEN, H. (1971) *The Military and Modernization*, Chicago: Aldine/Atherton.

BIGGS, T., M. SHAH, and P. SRIVASTAVA (1995) *Technological Capabilities and Learning in African Enterprises*, World Bank, Technical Paper No. 288, Africa Technical Department Series, Washington DC: World Bank.

BIGSTEN, A. and S. TENGSTAM (2012) *International Coordination and the Effectiveness of Aid*, ReCom, UNU-WIDER, Working Paper No. 2012/32.

BILS, M. and P. KLENOW (2000) 'Does Schooling Cause Growth?', *American Economic Review*, **90** (5), pp. 1160–83.

BINSWANGER, H.P., K. DEININGER, G. FEDER (1995) 'Power, Distortions, Revolt and Reform in Agricultural Land Relations', in: J. BEHRMAN and T.N. SRINIVASAN (eds.), *Handbook of Development Economics*, Vol. 3B, Amsterdam: North-Holland, pp. 2659–772.

BIRDSALL, N. (1988) 'Economic Approaches to Population Growth', in: H. CHENERY and T.N. SRINIVASAN (eds.), *Handbook of Development Economics*, Vol. I, Amsterdam: North-Holland, pp. 477–542.

(1994) 'Government, Population and Poverty: A Win-Win Tale', in: K. LINDAHL-KIESSLING and H. LANDBERG, *Population, Economic Development and the Environment*, Oxford/ New York: Oxford University Press, pp. 173–98.

BIRDSALL, N. and H. KHARAS (2010) *Quality of Official Development Assistance*, Washington, DC: Brookings/Center for Global Development.

BLANCHARD, O., D. ROMER, M. SPENCE and J. STIGLITZ (eds.) (2012) *In the Wake of the Crisis: Leading Economists Reassess Economic Policy*, Cambridge, MA: MIT Press.

(1972) *The Economics of Education*, Harmondsworth: Penguin.

(1976) 'The Empirical Status of Human Capital Theory: A Slightly Jaundiced Survey', *Journal of Economic Literature*, September, **XIV**, pp. 827–56.

(1979) 'Economics of Education in Developing Countries, Current Trends and New Priorities', *Third World Quarterly*, January, pp. 73–83.

(1985) 'Where Are We Now in the Economics of Education?', *Economics of Education Review*, **4** (1), pp. 17–28.

(1990) *The Economic Value of Higher Education*, NIAS, Ühlenbeck Lecture VIII, Wassenaar: NIAS.

BLAUG, M., R. LAYARD and M. WOODHALL (1969) *Causes of Graduate Unemployment in India*, London: Allen Lane.

BLEANEY, M. F. and D. GREENAWAY (1993) 'Long-Run Trends in the Relative Price of Primary Commodities and in the Terms of Trade of Developing Countries', *Oxford Economic Papers*, **45** (3), pp. 349–63.

BLOMSTRÖM, M. and A. KOKKO (1997) *How Foreign Investment Affects Host Countries*, Policy Research Working Paper No. 1745, World Bank.

BLUHM, R. and A. SZIRMAI, *Institutions and Long-Run Growth Performance*, UNU-MERIT Working Paper Series, 2012–033.

BLUHM R., D. DE CROMBRUGGHE and A. SZIRMAI (2012) *Explaining the Dynamics of Stagnation: An empirical examination of the North, Wallis and Weingast approach*, UNU-MERIT Working Paper Series, 2012–40.

(2013) *The Pace of Poverty Reduction – A Fractional Response Approach*, UNU-MERIT Working Paper Series, 2013-051, October.

(2013) *Do Weak Institutions Prolong Crises? On the Identification, Characteristics, and Duration of Declines during Economic Slumps*, Maastricht, UNU-MERIT Working Paper Series, 2013–069.

(2014) *Poor Trends: The Pace of Poverty Reduction after the Millennium Development Agenda*, UNU-MERIT Working Paper Series, 2014–006.

BOEKE, J.H. (1947) *Oriental Economics*, New York: Institute of Pacific Relations.

(1955) *Economie van Indonesië*, Haarlem: Tjeenk Willink.

(1961a) 'Dualistische Economie 1930', reprinted in J.H. BOEKE, *Indonesian Economics: The Concept of Dualism in Theory and Practice*, Den Haag: van Hoeve (first published in 1930).

(1961b) *Indonesian Economics: The Concept of Dualism in Theory and Practice*, The Hague: van Hoeve.

BOISSEVAIN, J. (1974) *Friends of Friends: Networks, Manipulators and Coalitions*, Oxford: Basil Blackwell.

BOJO, J. (1996) 'The Costs of Land Degradation in Sub-Saharan Africa', *Ecological Economics*, **16** (2), pp. 161–73.

BOL, D. (1983) *Economen en armoede: Moedwil en misverstand in de ontwikkelingshulp [Economists and Poverty: Bad Faith and Misunderstandings in Development Aid]*, Amsterdam: Van Gennep.

BONGAARTS, J. (1982) 'The Fertility-Inhibiting Effects of the Intermediate Fertility Variables', *Studies in Family Planning*, **13** (6/7), pp. 179–89.

(1997) 'The Role of Family Planning Programmes in Contemporary Fertility Transitions' in: G.W. JONES, R.M. DOUGLAS, J.C. CALDWELL and R.M. SOUZA (eds.), *The Continuing Demographic Transition*, Oxford: Clarendon Press, pp. 422–43.

BONGAARTS, J. and R.G. POTTER (1983) *Fertility, Biology and Behavior: An Analysis of the Proximate Determinants*, New York: Academic Press.

BONGENAAR, A. and A. SZIRMAI (2001) 'Development and Diffusion of Technology: The Case of TIRDO', in: A. SZIRMAI and P. LAPPERRE (eds.), *The Industrial Experience of Tanzania*, Basingstoke: Palgrave, pp. 171–93.

BOOTE, A.R. and K. THUGGE (1997) *Debt Relief for Low-Income Countries and the HIPC Initiative*, Working Paper of the International Monetary Fund, IMF, March.

BOOTH, A. (1999) 'Initial Conditions and Miraculous Growth: Why is South East Asia Different from Taiwan and South Korea?', *World Development*, **27** (2), pp. 301–21.

BORNSTEIN, D. (1996) *The Price of a Dream: The Story of the Grameen Bank and the Idea that is Helping the Poor Change their Lives*, New York: Simon & Schuster.

BOS, H.C. (1984) 'The Role of Industry and Industrial Policies in the Third Development Decade', in: P.K. GOSH (ed.), *Industrialization and Development*, Westport, CT: Greenwood Press.

BOS, H.C. (1990) 'Ontwikkelingseconomie [Development Economics]', *Economisch Statistische Berichten*, 5 December, pp. 1160–7.

BOSERUP, E. (1965) *The Conditions of Agricultural Growth*, London: Allen & Unwin.

(1970) *Women's Role in Economic Development*, New York: St. Martin's Press.

(1981) *Population and Technology*, Oxford: Basil Blackwell.

(1983) 'The Impact of Scarcity and Plenty on Development', *Journal of Interdisciplinary History*, **XIV** (2), pp. 383–407.

(1985) 'The Primary Sector in African Development', in: M. LUNDAHL (ed.), *The Primary Sector in Economic Development*, London: Croom Helm.

(1990) *Economic and Demographic Relationships in Development*, Essays Selected and Introduced by T. PAUL SCHULTZ, Baltimore, MD / London: Johns Hopkins University Press.

BOSWORTH, B. and S.M. COLLINS (2003) *The Empirics of Growth: An Update*, Brookings Papers on Economic Activity, **134** (2), pp. 113–206.

BOSWORTH, B., S.M. COLLINS and Y. CHEN (1995) *Accounting for Differences in Economic Growth, Paper for Conference on 'Structural Adjustment Policies in the 1990s: Experience and Prospects'*, Institute of Developing Economies, Tokyo, Japan October 5–6.

BOURDIEU P. (1985) 'The Forms of Capital', in: J.G. RICHARDSON (ed.), *Handbook of Theory and Research for the Sociology of Education*, New York: Greenwood Press, pp. 241–58.

BOURGUIGNON, F. (2003) 'The Growth Elasticity of Poverty Reduction: Explaining Heterogeneity across Countries and Time Periods', in: T.S. EICHER and S.J. TURNOVSKY (eds.), *Inequality and Growth: Theory and Policy Implications*, Cambridge, MA: MIT Press, pp. 3–26.

BOWLES, S. and H. GINTIS (1976) *Schooling in Capitalist America*, New York: Basic Books.

BOWMAN, M.J. and C.A. ANDERSON (1963) 'Concerning the Role of Education in Development', in: C. GEERTZ (ed.), *Old Societies and New States: The Quest for Modernity in Africa and Asia*, Glencoe, IL: Free Press.

(1973) 'Human Capital and Economic Modernisation in Historical Perspective', in: F.C. LANE (ed.), *Proceedings of the Fourth International Conference of Economic History*, Paris: Mouton (first published in 1968).

BRAINERD, E. (1998) 'Market Reform and Mortality in Transition Economies', *World Development*, **26** (11), pp. 2013–27.

BRANDT, W. *et al.* (1980) *North–South: A Programme for Survival*, London: Pan Books.

(1983) *Common Crisis: North–South Cooperation for World Recovery*, London: Pan Books.

BRATTON, M. and N. VAN DE WALLE (1997) *Democratic Experiments in Africa: Regime Transitions in Comparative Perspective*, Cambridge University Press.

BRAUDEL, F. (1978) 'Expansion of Europe and the Longue Durée', in: H.L. WESSELING (ed.), *Expansion and Reaction*, Leiden University Press.

BRAUN, J. VON and E. KENNEDY (eds.) (1994) *Agricultural Commercialisation, Economic Development and Nutrition*, Baltimore, MD: Johns Hopkins University Press.

BRÄUTIGAM, D. (2009) *The Dragon's Gift: The Real Story of China in Africa*, Oxford University Press.

BREMAN, J. (1980) *The Informal Sector in Research: Theory and Practice*, Rotterdam: CASP.

(1985) *Arbeidsmigratie en transformatie in koloniaal Azië [Labour Migration and Transformation in Colonial Asia]*, Series of Working Documents 7, Rotterdam: CASP.

(1986) 'Over hobbies en lobbies: de uitbesteding van de Nederlandse ont-wikkelingshulp [On Hobbies and Lobbies: Farming Out Dutch Development Aid]', *Internationale Spectator*, **XL** (6), June, pp. 353–63.

BRITTON, S. (1998) 'The Role of Services in Production', *Progress in Human Geography*, **14** (4), 1990, pp. 529–46 (reproduced in H.R. BRYSON and P.W. DANIELS (eds.), *Service Industries in the Global Economy, Volume II: Services, Globalization and Economic Development*, Cheltenham: Edward Elgar.

BROADBERRY, S.N. and B. GUPTA (2006) 'The Early Modern Great Divergence: Wages, Prices and Economic Development in Europe and Asia, 1500–1800', *Economic History Review*, **59**, pp. 2–31.

BROCK, W. and M.S. TAYLOR (2005) 'Economic Growth and the Environment: A Review of Theory and Empirics', in: S. DURLAUF and P. AGHION (eds.), *The Handbook of Economic Growth*, Amsterdam: North-Holland.

BROICH, T. and A. SZIRMAI (2014) *China's Embrace of Africa*, UNU-MERIT Working Paper Series, 2014-049.

BROWN, L.R. (1996) *Tough Choices. Facing the Challenge of Food Scarcity*, New York: Norton.

BROWN, L.R. and H.E. YOUNG (1990) 'Feeding the World in the Nineties', in: L.R. BROWN and L. STARKE (eds.), *State of the World 1990*, World Watch Institute Report, New York/London: Norton.

BROWNE, S. (2006) *Aid and Influence: Do Donors Help or Hinder?*, London: Earthscan.

BRUINSMA, J. (ed.) (2003) *World Agriculture Towards 2015/2030: An FAO Perspective*, Food and Agriculture Organization, Rome/London: Earthscan.

BRUNDTLAND, G.H. *et al.* (1987) *Our Common Future*, The World Commission on Environment and Development, Oxford University Press.

BRUNO, M., M. RAVALLION and L. SQUIRE (1998) 'Equity and Growth in Developing Countries: Old and New Perspectives on the Policy Issues', in: V. TANZI and K. CHU (eds.), *Income Distribution and High-Quality Growth*, Cambridge, MA: MIT Press.

BRUTON, H.J. (1969) 'The Two-Gap Approach to Aid and Development: Comment', *American Economic Review*, **59** (3), pp. 439–46.

(1998) 'A Reconsideration of Import Substitution', *Journal of Economic Literature*, **36** (2), pp. 903–36.

BRUYN, S. DE (1997) 'Explaining the Environmental Kuznets Curve: Structural Change and International Agreements in Reducing Sulfur Emissions', *Environment and Development Economics*, **2** (4), pp. 485–503.

BRYSON, H.R and P.W. DANIELS (eds.) (1998) *Service Industries in the Global Economy, Volume II: Services, Globalization and Economic Development*, Cheltenham: Edward Elgar.

BUCHANAN, J. and G. TULLOCK (1962) *The Calculus of Consent: Logical Foundations of Constitutional Democracy*, Ann Arbor, MI: Michigan University Press.

BUITER, W.H. and T.N. SRINIVASAN (1987) 'Rewarding the Profligate and Punishing the Prudent and Poor: Some Recent Proposals for Debt Relief', *World Development*, **15** (3), pp. 411–17.

BUNYARD, P. (1985) 'World Climate and Tropical Forest Destruction', *The Ecologist*, **15**, pp. 125–36.

BUREAU OF STATISTICS, TANZANIA (1995) *Selected Statistical Series, 1991–1994*, Dar es Salaam, Bureau of Statistics.

BURK, K. (1990) 'The International Environment', in: A. GRAHAM and A. SELDON, *Government and Economies in the Postwar World*, London: Routledge.

BURKI, S.J. and R. AYRES (1986) 'A Fresh look at Development Aid', *Finance and Development*, **23** (1), pp. 6–10.

BURNSIDE C. and D. DOLLAR (1997) *Aid, Policies and Growth*, Policy Research Working Paper, 1777, Washington: DC: World Bank.

BUTKIEWICZ, J.L. and H. YANIKKAYA (2006) 'Institutional Quality and Economic Growth: Maintenance of the Rule of Law or Democratic Institutions, or Both?', *Economic Modelling*, **23** (4), pp. 648–61.

BYERLEE, D. and K. FISCHER (2002) 'Accessing Modern Science: Policy and Institutional Options for Agricultural Biotechnology in Developing Countries', *World Development*, **30** (6), pp. 931–48.

CABALLERO, R.J. (2003) 'The Future of the IMF', *The American Economic Review*, **93** (2), pp. 31–38.

CALDWELL, J.C. (1976) 'Toward a Restatement of Demographic Transition Theory', *Population and Development Review*, **2** (2), pp. 321–66.

(1984) 'Introductory Remarks on Interactions between Health, Mortality and Development', in: UNITED NATIONS, *Mortality and Health Policy, Proceedings of the Expert Group on Mortality and Health Policy*, International Conference on Population, New York: United Nations, pp. 106–111.

(1986) 'Routes to Low Mortality in Poor Countries', *Population and Development Review*, **12** (2), pp. 171–221.

(1997) 'The Global Fertility Transition: The Need for a Unifying Theory', *Population and Development Review*, **23** (4), pp. 803–12.

CALDWELL J.C. and P. CALDWELL (1985) 'Cultural Forces Tending to Sustain High Fertility in Tropical Africa', *PHN Technical Note*, 85–16, Population, Health and Nutrition Department, Washington, DC: World Bank.

(1987) 'The Cultural Context of High Fertility in Sub-Sahara Africa', *Population and Development Review*, **13** (3), pp. 409–36.

(1997) 'What Do We Now Know about Fertility Transition?', in G.W. JONES, R.M. DOUGLAS, J.C. CALDWELL and R.M. SOUZA (eds.), *The Continuing Demographic Transition*, Oxford: Clarendon Press, pp. 15–25.

CANIËLS, M.C.J. (2000) *Regional Growth Differentials: The Impact of Locally Bounded Knowledge Spillovers*, Cheltenham: Edward Elgar.

CARNOY, M. (1974) *Education as Cultural Imperialism*, New York: David McKay.

CARVALHO, F. (2013) *What We Talk about when We Talk about Brazilian Multinationals*, PhD thesis, Maastricht University/UNU-MERIT.

CASSEN, R.A. (1986) *Does Aid Work?*, Oxford: Clarendon Press.

(1988) 'Aid Evaluation – Its Scope and Limits', in: C.J. JEPMA, (ed.), *North–South Cooperation in Retrospect and Prospect*, London: Routledge, pp. 167–81.

CASSEN, R.C. (1978) *India: Population, Economy, Society*, London: Macmillan.

CASTELLS, M. (2000) *The Information Age: Economy, Society and Culture, Vol. I: The Rise of the Network Society*, 2nd edn, Oxford: Blackwell.

CAVES, R.E. (1965) '"Vent for Surplus" Models of Trade and Growth', in: R.E. BALDWIN, *et al.* (eds.), *Trade, Growth and the Balance of Payments*, Chicago: Rand McNally.

CENTER FOR SYSTEMIC PEACE (2013) *Polity IV Project: Political Regime Characteristics and Transitions 1800–2012*, downloaded December 2013, http://www.systemicpeace.org/inscr/inscr.htm.

CENTRAL BANK OF REPUBLIC OF CHINA (2014) http://www.cbc.gov.tw/EngHome/economic/statistics/Annual.htm.

CHAMBERS, R. (1982) 'Health, Agriculture and Rural Poverty: Why Seasons Matter', *Journal of Development Studies*, **18** (2), pp. 217–38.

(1983) *Rural Development: Putting the Last First*, Harlow: Longman Scientific and Technical.

CHANG, H.-J. (2002) *Kicking away the Ladder: Development Strategy in Historical Perspective*, London: Anthem Press.

(2003) 'Kicking Away the Ladder: Infant Industry Promotion in Historical Perspective', *Oxford Development Studies*, **31** (1), pp. 21–32.

(2007) *Bad Samaritans: Rich Nations, Poor Policies, and the Threat to the Developing World*, London: Random House.

CHANG, J. (1991) *Wild Swans: Three Daughters of China*, New York: Doubleday.

CHANG, J. and J. HALLIDAY (2005) *Mao: The Unknown Story*, New York: Random House.

CHAYANOV, A.V. (1966) 'On the Theory of Non-Capitalist Economic Systems', in: D. THORNER, B. KERBLAY and R.F. SMITH, *The Theory of Peasant Economy*, Homewood, IL: Irwin, pp. 1–28.

CHEN, S.H. and M. RAVALLION (2001) 'How Did the World's Poorest Fare in the 1990s?', *Review of Income and Wealth*, **47** (3), pp. 283–300.

(2008) *The Developing World is Poorer Than We Thought, But No Less Successful in the Fight against Poverty*, World Bank, PRWP 4703, August.

(2010) 'The Developing World is Poorer Than We Thought, But No Less Successful in the Fight against Poverty', *The Quarterly Journal of Economics*, **125** (4), 1577–1625.

CHENERY, H.B. (1979) *Structural Change and Development Policy*, New York: Oxford University Press.

(1986) *Structural Transformation: A Program of Research*, Harvard Institute for International Development, Discussion Paper No. 232.

CHENERY, H.B. and I. ADELMAN (1966) 'Foreign Aid and Economic Development: The Case of Greece', *Review of Economics and Statistics*, February.

CHENERY, H.B., M.S. AHLUWALIA, C.L.G. BELL, J.H. DULOY and R. JOLLY (1974) *Redistribution with Growth*, New York/Oxford: Oxford University Press.

CHENERY, H.B. and A. MACEWAN (1966) 'Optimal Patterns of Growth and Aid: The Case of Pakistan', *Pakistan Development Review*, Summer.

CHENERY, H.B., S. ROBINSON and M. SYRQUIN (1986) *Industrialisation and Growth. A Comparative Study, World Bank*, Oxford University Press.

CHENERY, H.B. and T.N. SRINIVASAN (1988) 'Introduction': in: H. CHENERY and T.N. SRINIVASAN (eds.), *Handbook of Development Economics*, Vol. I, Amsterdam: North-Holland, pp. 1–8.

(eds.) (1989) *Handbook of Development Economics*, Vol. 2, Amsterdam: North-Holland.

CHENERY, H. and A.M. STROUT (1966) 'Foreign Assistance and Economic Development', *American Economic Review*, **LVI**, pp. 679–733.

CHENERY H.B., and L. TAYLOR (1968) 'Development Patterns among Countries and over Time', *Review of Economics and Statistics*, **50** (4), pp. 391–416.

CHIROT, D. (1977) *Social Change in the Twentieth Century*, New York: Harcourt, Brace, Jovanovich.

CIA, *World Factbook*, various issues, Online edition, www.cia.gov/cia/publications/factbook/index.html.

(2001) *World Factbook*, Washington, DC: CIA.

CIMOLI, M, G. DOSI and J.E. STIGLITZ (eds.) (2009) *The Political Economy of Capabilities Accumulation: The Past and Future of Policies for Industrial Development*, Oxford University Press.

CIMOLI, M. and J. KATZ (2003) 'Structural Reforms, Technological Gaps and Economic Development: A Latin American Perspective', *Industrial and Corporate Change*, **12** (2), pp. 387–411.

CIPOLLA, C.M. (1978) *An Economic History of World Population*, 7th edn, Harmondsworth: Penguin.

(1981) *Before the Industrial Revolution: European Society and Economy, 1000–1700*, 2nd edn, London: Methuen.

CISSE, F. and I. FOFANA (2013) *The Growth and Poverty Impact of the West African Free Trade Agreement with the European Union*, Paper presented at the International UNU-MERIT-CRES Conference *Africa's Quest for Sustained Growth: How to Accelerate the pace?* Dakar, Senegal, 25–26 November.

CITRIN, D., and S. FISCHER (2000) 'Strengthening the International Financial System: Key Issues', *World Development*, **28** (6), pp. 1133–42.

CLAESSENS, S., D. CASSIMON and B. VAN CAMPENHOUT (2009) 'Evidence on Changes in Aid Allocation Criteria', *World Bank Economic Review*, **23** (2), pp. 163–84.

CLAGUE, C. and S. GROSSBARD-SHECHTMAN (eds.) (2001) *Culture and Development: International Perspectives*, Special Issue of the Annals of the American Academy of Political and Social Science, **573**, pp. 8–15.

CLAPHAM, C. and G. PHILIP (eds.) (1985) *The Political Dilemma's of Military Regimes*, London: Croom Helm.

CLARK, C. (1940) *The Conditions of Economic Progress*, London: Macmillan.

CLARK, G. (2007) *A Farewell to Alms: A Brief History of the World*, Princeton/Oxford: Princeton University Press.

CLAY, E.J. and H. SINGER (1985) *Food Aid and Development Issues and Evidence*, World Food Programme, Rome, Occasional Papers, No. 3, September.

CLEMENS, M. A. (2011) 'Economics and Emigration: Trillion-Dollar Bills on the Sidewalk?, *Journal of Economic Perspectives* **25** (3), pp. 83–106.

CLEMENS M.A., S. RADELET, R.R. BHAVNANI (2004) 'Counting Chickens when they Hatch: The Short Term Effect of Aid on Growth', Center for Global Development Working Paper #44 November.

CLINE, W.R. (1982) 'Can the East Asian Model of Development be Generalized?', *World Development*, **10** (2), pp. 81–90.

COALE, A.J. and E.M. HOOVER (1958) *Population Growth and Economic Development in Low-Income Countries*, Princeton University Press.

COCHRANE, G. (1979) *The Cultural Appraisal of Development Projects*, New York: Praeger.

COE, D.T. and E. HELPMAN (1995) 'International R&D Spillovers', *European Economic Review*, **39**, 859–87.

COHEN, D. and M. SOTO (2007) 'Growth and Human Capital: Good Data, Good Results', *Journal of Economic Growth*, **12** (1), pp. 51–76.

COHEN W.M. and D. LEVINTHAL (1990) 'Absorptive Capacity: A New Perspective on Learning and Innovation', *Administrative Science Quarterly*, **35**, pp. 128–52.

COLCLOUGH C. and S. AL-SAMARRAI (2000) 'Achieving Schooling for All: Budgetary Expenditures on Education in Sub-Saharan Africa and South Asia', *World Development*, **28** (11), pp. 1927–44.

COLEMAN, J.S. and C.B. ROSBERG JR. (eds.) (1964) *Political Parties and National Integration in Tropical Africa*, Berkeley, CA: University of California Press.

COLLIER, P. (2007) *The Bottom Billion. Why the Poorest Countries are Failing and What Can be Done About It*, Oxford University Press.

COLLIER, P. and D. DOLLAR (2002) 'Aid Allocation and Poverty Reduction', *European Economic Review*, **45** (1), pp. 1–26.

COLLIER, P. and A. HOEFFLER (2005) 'The Economic Costs of Corruption in Infrastructure', in: TRANSPARANCY INTERNATIONAL, *Global Corruption Report 2005: Corruption in Construction and Post-Conflict Resolution*, Berlin.

COLMAN, D. and F. NIXSON (1985) *Economics of Change in Less Developed Countries*, 2nd edn, Oxford: Phillip Allen/Barnes and Noble.

CONFERENCE BOARD (2014) *Total Economy Database*, www.conference-board.org/data/economydatabase/, downloaded January 2014.

COOMBS, P. (1985) *The World Crisis in Education: The View from the 1980s*, New York/Oxford: Oxford University Press.

COOMBS, P. and M. AHMED (1974) *Attacking Rural Poverty: How Nonformal Education Can Help*, Baltimore, MD: Johns Hopkins University Press.

COOPER, C. (2001) 'The Role of Technological Factors in the Early Stages of Industrial Exports: A Note', in: A. SZIRMAI and P. LAPPERRE (eds.), *The Industrial Experience of Tanzania*, Basingstoke: Palgrave, pp. 114–32.

CORDEN, W. (1979) *The NIEO Proposals: A Cool Look*, London: Trade Policy Research Centre.

CORNIA, G.A. (1984) 'A Summary and Interpretation of the Evidence', *World Development*, **12** (3), pp. 381–91.

CORNIA, G.A, R. VAN DER HOEVEN and T. MKANDAWIRE (eds.) (1992) *Africa's Recovery in the 1990s: From Stagnation and Adjustment to Human Development*, New York: St. Martin's Press/UNICEF.

CORNIA, G.A., R. JOLLY and F. STEWART (eds.) (1987) *Adjustment with a Human Face*, Oxford: Clarendon.

CORNWALL, J. (1977) *Modern Capitalism: Its Growth and Transformation*, New York: St. Martin's Press.

CRACKNELL, B.E. (2000) *Evaluating Development Aid*, New Delhi/London: Sage.

CUDDINGTON, J.T., R. LUDEMA and S.A. JAYASRIYA (2007) 'Prebisch Singer Redux', in D. LEDERMAN and W.E. MALONEY (eds.), *Natural Resources: Neither Curse nor Destiny*, Stanford University Press, pp. 103–82.

CURLE, A. (1964) *World Campaign for Universal Literacy: Comment and Proposal*, Occasional Papers in Education and Development, Graduate School of Education, Harvard University.

CURTIN, P.D. (1969) *The Atlantic Slave Trade: A Census*, Madison, WI: University of Wisconsin Press.

CYHN, J. (2001) *Technology Transfer and International Production: The Development of the Electronics Industry in Korea*, Cheltenham: Edward Elgar.

DAHRENDORF, R. (1963) *Class and Class Conflict in Industrial Society*, London: Routledge.

DALGAARD, C. and H. HANSEN (2001) 'On Aid, Growth and Good Policies', *The Journal of Development Studies*, **37** (6), pp. 17–41.

DAM, F. VAN (1978) 'Mode in het ontwikkelingsvraagstuk [Trends in the Issue of Development]', *Economisch Statistische Berichten*, 17 May, pp. 496–500.

(1984) 'Honderd jaar ontwikkelingsvraagstuk [The Issue of Development: One Hundred Years]', *Economisch Statistische Berichten*, pp. 162–8.

(1989a) 'Het Ontwikkelingsvraagstuk op hoofdpunten bezien [Main Issues in Development]', *Economisch Statistische Berichten*, 31 May, pp. 529–33

(1989b) 'Zin en onzin over projecthulp [Sense and Nonsense in Project Aid]', *Internationale Spectator*, **XLIII** (6), pp. 372–3.

DANIELS, P.W. (1989) 'Some Perspectives on the Geography of Services', *Progress in Human Geography*, **13** (3), pp. 427–37, Reproduced in: BRYSON, H.R and P.W. DANIELS (eds.), *Service Industries in the Global Economy, Volume II: Services, Globalization and Economic Development*, Cheltenham:, Edward Elgar, 1998.

DARBY, H.C., and H. FULLART (1970) *The New Cambridge Modern History Atlas*, Cambridge University Press.

DASGUPTA, P., C. FOLKE and K-G. MÄLER (1994) 'The Environmental Resource Base and Human Welfare', in: K. LINDAHL-KIESSLING and H. LANDBERG, *Population, Economic Development and the Environment*, Oxford/New York: Oxford University Press, pp. 25–50.

DASGUPTA, S. and A. SINGH (2006) *Manufacturing, Services and Premature Deindustrialization in Developing Countries: A Kaldorian Analysis*, Working Papers RP2006/49, World Institute for Development Economic Research (UNU-WIDER).

DAVID C. and J. ROUMASSET (2000) *The Microeconomics of Agricultural Development in the Philippines*, Paper presented at the conference 'The Philippine Economy: On the Way to Sustained Growth?', ANU, November 2–3.

DAVID, P.A. (1975) *Technical Choice, Innovation and Growth*, Cambridge University Press.

DAVID, S.R. (1987) 'The Use of Proxy Forces by Major Powers in the Third World', in: S.G. NEUMAN and R.E. HARKAVY (eds.), *The Lessons of Recent Wars in the Third World*, Lexington, MA: D.C. Heath.

DAVIDSON, B. (1992) *The Black Man's Burden – Africa and the Curse of the Nation State*, London: James Currey.

DAVIS, K. (1951) *The Population of India and Pakistan*, Princeton University Press.

DEATON, A. (2010) 'Instruments, Randomization, and Learning about Development', *Journal of Economic Literature*, **48** (2), pp. 424–55.

DE CROMBRUGGHE, D. and K. FARLA (2012) *Preliminary Conclusions on Institutions and Economic Performance*, UNU-MERIT Working Paper Series, 2012–035.

DE CROMBRUGGHE, D., K. FARLA, N. MEISEL, C. DE NEUBOURG, J. OULD AOUDIA and A. SZIRMAI (2010) 'Institutional Profiles Database III, Presentation of the Institutional Profiles Database 2009 (IPD 2009)', AFD Working Paper No. 89, Paris: Agence Française de Développement.

DEININGER, K. and H. BINSWANGER (2001) 'Evolution of the World Bank's Land Policy', in: A. DE JANVRY, J-P. PLATTEAU, G. GORDILLO and E. SADOULET (eds.), *Access to Land, Rural Poverty and Public Action*, Oxford University Press, pp. 406–40.

DEININGER, K. and G. FEDER (2001) 'Land Institutions and Land Markets', in: B. L. GARDNER, and G. C. RAUSSER (eds.), *Handbook of Agricultural Economics, Vol. 1A: Agricultural Production*, Chapter 6, Amsterdam: Elsevier, pp. 288–331.

DEININGER, K. and L. SQUIRE (1996) 'A New Data Set Measuring Income Inequality', *World Bank Economic Review*, **10** (3), September, pp. 565–91.

(1998) 'New Ways of Looking at Old Issues', *Journal of Development Economics*, **57** (2), pp. 259–87.

DE JANVRY, A., J-P PLATTEAU, G. GORDILLO and E. SADOULET (2001) 'Access to Land and Land Policy Reforms', in A. DE JANVRY, J-P PLATTEAU, G. GORDILLO and E. SADOULET (eds.), *Access to Land, Rural Poverty and Public Action*, Oxford University Press.

DE JANVRY, A., E. SADOULET and R. MURGAI (2002) 'Rural Development and Rural Policy', in: B. L. GARDNER and G. C. RAUSSER (eds.), *Handbook of Agricultural Economics, Vol. 2: Agriculture and its External linkages*, Chapter 31, Amsterdam: Elsevier, pp. 1594–1658.

DE LA FUENTE, A. and R. DOMÉNECH (2006) 'Human Capital in Growth Regressions: How Much Difference Does Data Quality Make?', *Journal of the European Economic Association*, **4** (1), pp. 1–36.

DENISON, E.F. (1962) *The Sources of Economic Growth and the Alternatives Before Us*, New York: Committee for Economic Development.

(1967) *Why Growth Rates Differ*, Washington, DC: Brookings Institution.

DEOLALIKAR, A.B. (1988) 'Do Health and Nutrition Influence Labor Productivity in Agriculture? Econometric Estimates for South India', *Review of Economics and Statistics*, **70** (2).

DEPARTMENT OF EDUCATION, REPUBLIC OF SOUTH AFRICA (2009) *Trends in Education Macro Indicators*, Pretoria.

DESMET, K., I. ORTŪNO-ORTIN, R. WACZIARG (2012) 'The Political Economic of Linguistic Cleavages', *Journal of Development Economics*, **97**, pp. 322–38.

DE VRIES, G.J. (2010) *Firm Heterogeneity, Productivity, and Policy Reforms in Latin America*, PhD thesis, University of Groningen.

DE VRIES, G.J., A.A. ERUMBAN, M.P. TIMMER, I. VOSKOBOYNIKOV and H.X. WU (2015) 'Deconstructing the BRICs: Structural Transformation and Aggregate Productivity Growth', in: W. NAUDÉ, A. SZIRMAI and N. HARAGUCHI (eds.), *Structural Change and Industrial Development in the BRICS*, Oxford University Press, forthcoming.

DEVEREUX, S. (1993) *Theories of Famine*, New York: Harvester Wheatsheaf.

DGBAS (1994) Executive Yuan, *National Income of Taiwan Area of Republic of China*, Taipeh.

(2002a) Taiwan: Directorate-General of Budget, Accountings and Statistics, Executive Yuan, The Republic of China, database, http://www.dgbas.gov.tw/dgbas03/bs2/91chy/catalog.htm, accessed October.

(2002b) Republic of China (Taiwan), Directorate General of Budget Accounting and Statistics, *China Statistical Yearbook 2002*, Taipeh, http://www.stat.gov.tw/bs2/YearBook.htm.

(2003) Republic of China (Taiwan), Directorate General of Budget Accounting and Statistics, *China Statistical Yearbook 2003*, Taipeh, http://www.stat.gov.tw/bs2/2003YearBook.pdf.

(2009) Directorate General of Budget, Accounting and Statistics, Executive Yuan, Republic of China, *Statistical Yearbook of the Republic of China 2008*, http://eng.dgbas.gov.tw/public/data/dgbas03/bs2/yearbook_eng/Y094–5.pdf.

(2010) National Statistics of Taiwan, the Republic of China, National Accounts, http://eng.stat.gov.tw/ct.asp?xItem=25763&CtNode=5347&mp=5, downloaded October.

(2011) *Statistical Yearbook, 2011*.

(2012a), Directorate-General of Budget, Accountings and Statistics, Executive Yuan, The Republic of China, http://www.stat.gov.tw.

(2012b) Directorate-General of Budget, Accountings and Statistics, Executive Yuan, The Republic of China, http://www.dgbas.gov.tw/dgbas03/bs2/91chy/catalog.htm, downloaded 2012.

(2012c) *Monthly Bulletin of Statisticsi*, November.

(2014) National Statistics. Republic of China (Taiwan), National Accounts, http://eng.stat.gov.tw/ct.asp?xItem=25763&CtNode=5347&mp=5, downloaded April 2014

National Statistics of Taiwan, The Republic of China, http://www.stat.gov.tw/main.htm.

National Statistics of Taiwan, the Republic of China, http://www129.tpg.gov.tw/mbas/doc4/89/book/77.xls

DIA, M. (1994) 'Indigenous Management Practices: Lessons for Africa's Management in the 90s', in: I. SERAGELDIN and J. TABOROFF (eds.), *Culture and Development in Africa*, Washington: World Bank, pp. 165–91.

DIAMOND, J. (1998b) *Guns, Germs and Steel: The Fates of Human Societies*, New York: Norton.

DIAMOND, S. (1974) *In Search of the Primitive: A Critique of Civilization*, New York: Transaction Books.

DICKEN, P. (2003) *Global Shift: Reshaping the Global Map in the 21st Century*, 4th edn, London: Sage.

(2007) *Global Shift: Mapping the Changing Contours of the World Economy*, 5th edn, London: Sage.

DIJK, M. VAN (2003) 'South African Manufacturing Performance in a Comparative Perspective, 1970–99', *South African Journal of Economics*, **71** (1), pp. 119–42.

DIJK, M.P. VAN (1980) *De informele sector van Ouagadougou en Dakar: De ontwikkelingsmogelijkheden van kleine bedrijven in twee Westafrikaanse hoofdsteden [The Informal Sector of Ouagadougou and Dakar: The Development Opportunities of Small Enterprises in Two West African Capitals]*, Dissertation, Free University of Amsterdam.

DIJKSTRA, A.G. (2000) 'Trade Liberalization and Industrial Development in Latin America', *World Development*, **28** (9), pp. 1567–82.

DIJKSTRA, A.G. and J. K. VAN DONGE (2001) 'What Does the "Show Case" Show? Evidence of and Lessons from Adjustment in Uganda", *World Development*, **20** (5), pp. 841–63.

DIJKSTRA, A.G. and H. WHITE (eds.) (2003) *Programme Aid and Development. Beyond Conditionality*, London: Routledge.

DIKÖTTER, F. (2010) *Mao's Great Famine: The History of China's Most Devastating Catastrophe, 1958–62*, New York: Walker & Co.

DIXON, C. (1990) *Rural Development in the Third World*, London/New York: Routledge.

DJANKOV, S., J.G. MONTALVO and M. REYNAL-QUEROL (2006) 'Does Foreign Aid Help?', *Cato Journal*, **26** (1), pp. 1–28.

(2008) 'The Curse of Aid', *Journal of Economic Growth*, **13** (3), pp. 169–94.

DJILAS, M. (1957) *The New Class: An Analysis of the Communist System*, New York: Praeger.

DOCQUIER, F. and H. RAPOPORT (2012) 'Globalization, Brain Drain and Development', *Journal of Economic Literature*, **50** (3), pp. 681–730.

DOLLAR, D. and C. BURNSIDE (2000) 'Aid, Policies and Growth', *American Economic Review*, **90** (4), pp. 847–68.

DOLLAR, D. and L. PRITCHETT (1998) *Assessing Aid: What Works, What Doesn't and Why*, A World Bank Policy Research Report, New York: Oxford University Press.

DOORENSPLEET, R. (2000) 'Reassessing the Three Waves of Democratization', *World Politics*, **52** (3), pp. 384–406.

DOORNBOS, M. (2001) '"Good Governance": The Rise and Decline of a Policy Metaphor', *The Journal of Development Studies*, **37** (6), pp. 93–108.

DORE, R. (1976) *The Diploma Disease. Education, Qualification and Development*, London: Allen & Unwin.

(1987) *Taking Japan Seriously: A Confucian Perspective on Leading Economic Issues*, Stanford University Press.

DORNER, P. (1972) *Land Reform and Economic Development*, Harmondsworth: Penguin.

DOROODIAN, K. (1993) 'Macro-Economic Performance and Adjustment under Policies Commonly Supported by the International Monetary Fund', *Economic Development and Cultural Change*, **41** (4), pp. 349–864.

DOS SANTOS, T. (1970) 'The Structure of Dependence', *American Economic Review*, **60** (2), pp. 231–36.

DOSI, G. (1988) 'Technological Paradigms and Technological Trajectories', *Research Policy*, **11** (3), pp. 147–62.

DOSI, G., C. FREEMAN and R.R. NELSON (eds.) (1988) *Technical Change and Economic Theory*, London: Pinter.

DOSS, C.R. (2001) 'Designing Agricultural Technology for African Women Farmers: Lessons from 25 Years of Experience', *World Development*, **29** (12), pp. 2075–92.

DOUCOULIAGOS, H. and M. PALDAM (2008) 'Aid Effectiveness on Growth: A Meta Study', *European Journal of Political Economy,* **24** (1), pp. 1–24.

(2009) 'The Aid Effectiveness Literature: The Sad Results of 40 Years of Research', *Journal of Economic Surveys* **23** (3), pp. 433–61.

DUFLO, E., R. GLENNERSTER and M. KREMER (2007) 'Using Randomization in Development Economics Research: A Toolkit', in: T. P. SCHULTZ and J. STRAUSS (eds.), *Handbook of Development economics,* Vol. 4, Amsterdam: North-Holland/Elsevier Science Publishers, pp. 3895–962.

DRUIJVEN, P.C.J. (1983) *Rurale industrialisatie in de Volksrepubliek China [Rural Industrialisation in the Peoples' Republic of China],* Free University of Amsterdam, Geografisch en Planologisch Instituut, Bijdragen tot de Sociale Geografie en Planologie, No. 6, Amsterdam.

(1990) *Mandenvlechters en Mezcalstokers in Mexico [Basket Weavers and Mescal Distillers in Mexico],* Dissertation, Free University of Amsterdam.

DUIJSTERS, G. and J. HAGEDOORN (2000) 'International Technological Collaboration: Implications for Newly Industrialising Economies', in: L. KIM and R.R. NELSON (eds.), *Technology, Learning and Innovation. Experiences of Newly Industrializing Economies,* Cambridge University Press, pp. 193–215.

DUMONT, R. (1962) *L'Afrique Noire est Mal Partie,* Paris: Editions du Seuil.

DUNNING, J. (1988) 'Trade, Location of Economic Activity and the Multinational Enterprise: A Search for an Eclectic Approach', in: J. DUNNING, *Explaining International Production,* London: Unwin Hyman, pp. 13–40.

(1993) *The Globalization of Business,* London: Routledge.

(2003) *Re-Evaluating the Benefits of Foreign Direct Investment,* London: International Thomson Business Press.

DURAND, J.D. (1977) 'Historical Estimates of World Population: An Evaluation', in: *Population and Development Review,* **3** (3), pp. 253–95.

DURKHEIM, É. (1973) *Le Suicide,* Paris, Press Universitaires de France (first published 1897).

DYSON, T. (2011) 'The role of the Demographic Transition in the Process of Urbanization', *Population and Development Review,* **37** (Supplement), pp. 34–54.

EASTERLIN, R.A. (1972) 'Does Economic Growth Improve the Human Lot', in: P.A. DAVID and M.W. REDER (eds.), *Nations and Households in Economic Growth: Essays in Honor of Moses Abramovitz,* Stanford University Press.

(1978) 'The Economics and Sociology of Fertility: A Synthesis', in: C. TILLEY (ed.), *Historical Studies of Changing Fertility,* Princeton University Press.

(1981) 'Why Isn't the Whole World Developed?', *Journal of Economic History,* **41** (1), pp. 1–19.

EASTERLY, W. (1997) *The Ghost of the Financing Gap,* Policy Research Working Paper 1807, Washington, DC: World Bank, Development Research Group.

(1999) 'The Ghost of the Financing Gap: Testing the Growth Model Used in the International Financial Institutions', *Journal of Development Economics,* **60** (2), pp. 423–38.

(2000) *How did Highly Indebted Poor Countries Become Highly Indebted?, Reviewing Two Decades of Debt Relief,* Washington, DC., World Bank, mimeo.

(2001a) *The Elusive Quest for Growth,* Cambridge, MA: MIT Press.

(2001b) 'Can Institutions Resolve Ethnic Conflict?', *Economic Development and Cultural Change*, **49** (4), pp. 687–706.

(2001c) 'IMF and World Bank Structural Adjustment Programs and Poverty', World Bank, February, http://www.nber.org/~confer/2001/ccdf/easterly.pdf.

(2006) *The White Man's Burden: Why the West's Efforts to Aid the Rest Have Done So Much Ill and So Little Good*, Harmondsworth: Penguin.

(ed.) (2008) *Reinventing Foreign Aid*, Cambridge, MA: MIT Press.

EASTERLY, W. and R. LEVINE (1997) 'Africa's Growth Tragedy: Policies and Ethnic Divisions', *The Quarterly Journal of Economics*, **112** (4), pp. 1203–49.

(2012) *The European Origins of Economic Development*, NBER Working Paper Series, 18162, June.

EASTERLY, W., R. LEVINE and D. ROODMAN (2004) 'Aid Policies and Growth: Comment', *American Economic Review* **94** (3), pp. 774–80.

ECONOMIST (1996) 'The Mystery of Growth', *The Economist*, May 25, pp. 447 ff.

EDWARDS, S. (1990) 'The Sequencing of Economic Reform: Analytical Issues and Lessons from Latin America', *The World Economy*, **13** (1), pp. 1–14.

EGMOND, E. VAN (2000) *Technology Mapping for Technology Management*, PhD Thesis TU Delft.

EHRLICH, P. (1968) *The Population Bomb*, New York: Ballantine Books.

EHRLICH, I. and F.T. LUI (1999) 'Bureaucratic Corruption and Endogenous Growth', *Journal of Political Economy*, **107**, pp. 270–93.

EHRLICH, P.R. and A. H. EHRLICH (1990) *The Population Explosion*, New York: Simon & Schuster.

EICHENGREEN, B. (2000) 'Taming Capital Flows', *World Development*, **28** (6), pp. 1105–16.

(2004) 'The Challenge of Financial Instability', in: B. LOMBORG (ed.), *Global Crises, Global Solutions*, Cambridge University Press.

EICHENGREEN, B. (2009) *The Two Waves of Service Sector Growth*, NBER Working Paper Series, Working Paper 14968, Cambridge, MA: National Bureau of Economic Research.

EICHER, C.K., and J.M. STAATZ (eds.) (1984) *Agricultural Development in the Third World*, Baltimore/London: Johns Hopkins University Press.

EICHER, C.K. and L.W. DE WITT (eds.) (1964) *Agriculture in Development*, New York: McGraw Hill.

EISENSTADT, S.N. (1970) 'Social Change and Development', in: S.N. EISENSTADT (ed.), *Readings in Social Evolution and Development*, Oxford/London: Pergamon.

ELBADAWI, I.A. (1992) *Have World Bank-Supported Adjustment Programs Improved Economic Performance in Sub-Saharan Africa?*, World Bank, Policy Research Working Papers, WPS 1001, October.

ELBADAWI, I.A., DH. GHURA and G. UWUGAREN (1992) *Why Structural Adjustment Has Not Succeeded in Sub-Saharan Africa?*, World Bank, Policy Research Working Papers, WPS 1000, October.

ELIAS, N. (1969a) 'Zur Soziogenese des Begriffs "Civilisation" in Frankreich', in: N. ELIAS, *Über den Prozess der Zivilisation*, Erster Band, Bern/München: Franke Verlag, pp. 43–64.

(1969b) *Über den Prozess der Zivilisation*, Vol. II, 2nd edn, Bern: Franke Verlag.

(1970) 'Problemen van distantie en betrokkenheid' [Problems of Detachment and Involvement], in: N. ELIAS, *Sociologie en geschiedenis en andere essays*, Amsterdam: Van Gennep.

(1979) *Die höfische Gesellschaft*, 4th edn, Darmstadt/Neuwied: Luchterhand.

ELLIS, F. (1988) *Peasant Economics: Farm Households and Agrarian Development*, Cambridge University Press.

(1998) 'Household Strategies and Rural Livelihood Diversification', *The Journal of Development Studies*, **35** (1), pp. 1–35.

ELLMAN, M. (2007) 'Stalin and the Soviet Famine of 1932–33 Revisited', *Europe-Asia Studies*, **59** (4), pp. 663–93.

ELTIS, D. (1989) *Economic Growth and the Ending of the Transatlantic Slave Trade*, New York: Oxford University Press.

(2001) 'The Volume and Structure of the Transatlantic Slave Trade: a Reassessment', *William and Mary Quarterly*, **58**, pp. 17–46.

ELTIS, D., S.D. BEHREND, D. RICHARDSON and H.S. KLEIN (1998) *The Transatlantic Slave Trade, 1562–1867: A Database CD-Rom*, Cambridge University Press.

ELVIN, M. (1973) *The Pattern of Chinese Past*, London: Stanford University Press.

EMMANUEL, A. (1972) *Unequal Exchange: A Study of the Imperialism of Trade*, New York: Monthly Review Press.

EMMER, P.C. (1986) 'The Meek Hindu. The Recruitment of Indian Indentured Labourers for Service Overseas, 1870–1916', in: P.C. EMMER (ed.), *Colonialism and Migration. Indentured Labour before and after Slavery*, Dordrecht: Nijhoff, pp. 3–18.

(1992) 'De contractie van het Westen: de dekolonisatie na 1945 [Contraction of the West: Decolonisation after 1945]', in: D.F.J. BOSSCHER, H. RENNER, R.B. SOETENDORP and R. WAGENAAR (eds.), *De Wereld na 1945*, Utrecht: Het Spectrum, Aula.

EMMERIJ, L.J. (1984) 'Ontwikkelingssamenwerking op een kruispunt? Noodzaak tot omvorming van het Nederlandse beleid en Apparaat [Development Cooperation at Crossroads? The Need to Change Dutch Policy and Apparatus]', *Internationale Spectator*, **XXXVIII**, pp.121 ff.

ENG, P. VAN DER (1992) 'Food Supply and Agricultural Development', in: W.P.M.F. IVENS (ed.), *World Food Production Textbook* 1, Heerlen: Open University.

(1993) 'Agricultural Growth in Indonesia since 1880', Dissertation, Groningen.

(2008) *The Sources of Long-term Economic Growth in Indonesia, 1880–2007*, School of Management, Marketing and International Business, College of Business and Economics, ANU, 4 July, mimeo.

ENGEL, E. (1857) 'Die Produktions- und Consumptionsverhältnisse des Königreichs Sachsen', *Zeitschrift des Statistichen Bureaus des Königlich Sächsischen Ministeriums des Innern*, November.

ENGELEN, D. VAN, A. SZIRMAI and P.E. LAPPERRE (2001) 'Public Policy and the Industrial Development of Tanzania, 1961–1995', in: A. SZIRMAI and P. LAPPERRE (eds.), *The Industrial Experience of Tanzania*, Basingstoke: Palgrave, pp. 11–49.

ENGERMAN, S.L. (1986) 'Servants to Slaves to Servants: Contract Labour and European Expansion', in: P.C. EMMER (ed.), *Colonialism and Migration. Indentured Labour before and after Slavery*, Dordrecht: Nijhoff, pp. 263–94.

ENGERMAN, S.L and K.L. SOKOLOFF (1997) 'Factor Endownments, Institutions and Differential Growth Paths among New World Economies' in: S. HABER (ed.), *How Latin America Fell Behind*, Stanford University Press, pp. 260–96.

(2002) 'Factor Endowments, Inequality and Paths of Development among New World Economies', *Economia* **3** (1), pp. 41–109.

(2005) *Colonialism, Inequality and Long-Run Paths of Development*, NBER Working Paper 11057.

ERDMANN, G. and U. ENGEL (2006) *Neopatrimonialism Revisited: Beyond a Catch-All Concept*, Working Paper 16, Hamburg: German Institute of Global and Area Studies.

ETHIER, W.J. (1995) *Modern International Economics*, 3rd edn, New York/London: Norton.

ETTINGER, J. VAN, T.H. JANSEN and C.J. JEPMA (1989) *Climate, Environment and Development*, Paper for the International Steering Committee for the preparation of The Ministerial Conference on Atmospheric Pollution, November.

EVANS, P. (1995) *Embedded Autonomy. States and Industrial Transformation*, Princeton University Press.

EVENSON, R.E. and L.E. WESTPHAL (1995) 'Technological Change and Technology Strategy', in: H. BEHRMAN and T. N. SRINIVASAN (eds.), *Handbook of Development Economics*, Vol. IIIA, Amsterdam: North-Holland, pp. 2211–99.

EVENSON, R. and D. GOLLIN (2003) 'Assessing the Impact of the Green Revolution, 1960–2000', *Science*, **300** (5620), pp. 758–62.

EVERS, H.D. and H. SCHRADERS (eds.) (1994) *The Moral Economy of Trade. Ethnicity and Developing Markets*, London: Routledge.

EZZATI, M., B.H. SINGER and D.M. KAMMEN (2001) 'Towards an Integrated Framework for Development and Environmental Policy: The Dynamics of Environmental Kuznets Curves', *World Development*, **29** (8), pp. 1421–34.

FAGE, J.D. (1969) *A History of West Africa. An Introductory Survey*, 4th edn, Cambridge University Press.

(1977) 'Slavery and the Slave Trade in the Context of West African History', in: Z.A. KONCZACKI and J.M. KONCZACKI (eds.), *An Economic History of Tropical Africa, Vol. I: The Pre-Colonial Period*, London: Frank Cass, pp. 166–78

FAGERBERG, J. (1994) 'Technology and International Differences in Growth Rates', *Journal of Economic Literature*, **XXXII**, pp. 1147–75.

(2000) 'Technological Progress, Structural Change and Productivity Growth: A Comparative Study', *Structural Change and Economic Dynamics*, **11** (4), pp. 393–411.

FAGERBERG, J. and M.M. GODINHO (2005) 'Innovation and Catching Up', in: J. FAGERBERG, DC. MOWERY and R.R. NELSON (eds.) *The Oxford Handbook of Innovation*, Oxford University Press, pp. 514–42.

FAGERBERG, J., DC. MOWERY and R.R. NELSON (eds.) (2005) *The Oxford Handbook of Innovation*, Oxford University Press.

FAGERBERG, J. and B. VERSPAGEN (1999) 'Modern Capitalism in the 1970s and 1980s', in M. SETTERFIELD (ed.), *Growth, Employment and Inflation*, Basingstoke: Macmillan.

(2002). 'Technology-Gaps, Innovation-Diffusion and Transformation: an Evolutionary Interpretation', *Research Policy*, **31** (8–9), pp. 1291–1304.

(2007) 'Innovation, Growth and Economic Development: Have the Conditions for Catch-up Changed?', *International Journal of Technological Learning, Innovation and Development*, **1** (1), pp. 13–33.

FÄGERLIND, I. and L.J. SAHA (1989) *Education and National Development: A Comparative Perspective*, 2nd edn, Oxford: Pergamon.

FANG, T. (2003) 'A Critique of Hofstede's Fifth National Culture Dimension', *International Journal of Cross Cultural Management*, **3** (3), pp. 351–72.

FAO (1975) *State of Food and Agriculture*, 1975, Rome: FAO.

(1981) *Agriculture Towards 2000*, Rome: FAO.

(1988) *An Interim Report on the State of Forest Resources in the Developing Countries*, Rome: FAO.

(1989) *State of Food and Agriculture*, Rome: FAO.

(1990) *State of Food and Agriculture*, Rome: FAO.

(1991) *State of Food and Agriculture*, Rome: FAO.

(1993) *State of Food and Agriculture*, Rome: FAO.

(1996) *The Sixth World Food Survey*, Rome: FAO.

(2001) *Global Forest Resources Assessment 2000, Main Report*, FAO, http://www.fao.org/forestry/fo/fra/main/index.jsp?lang_id=1.

(2002) *State of Food Security in the World 2002*, FAO, FAO website: ftp://ftp.fao.org/docrep/fao/005/y7352e/y7352e01.pdf.

(2002) *The State of Food Insecurity in the World 2002*, Rome, www.fao.org/docrep/005/y7352e/y7352e00.htm.

(2003) *The State of the World's Forests*, Rome, www.fao.org/DOCREP/005/Y7581E/y7581e16.htm#TopOfPage.

(2008) *State of Food Security in the World 2008*, Rome FAO, FAO website: ftp://ftp.fao.org/docrep/fao/011/i0291e/i0291e00.pdf.

(2009) *State of Food Security in the World 2009*, Rome FAO, FAO website: ftp://ftp.fao.org/docrep/fao/012/i0876e/i0876e00.pdf.

(2010) *Global Forest Resources Assessment 2010, Main Report*, FAO forestry paper 163, Rome: FAO.

(2012a) *The State of Food Insecurity in the World 2012*, Rome: FAO.

(2012b) *The State of Food and Agriculture: Investing in Agriculture for a Better Future*, Rome: FAO.

(2013a) World Food Situation, www.fao.org/worldfoodsituation/foodpricesindex/en/, downloaded September 2013.

(2013b) *Food Security Indicators, Revision March 15 2013*, downloaded September 2013, www.fao.org/economic/ess/ess-fs/fs-data/en/.

(2013c) FAO Food Price Index, downloaded September 2013, www.fao.org/worldfoodsituation/foodpricesindex/en/.

Production Yearbook, Rome, various volumes.

FAOSTAT (2002) *Agriculture Data, Land Use*, FAO, updated August, http://apps.fao.org/page/collections.

(2003) *Agriculture Data, Agricultural Production Indices*, FAO, updated June, http://apps.fao.org/page/form?collection=Crops.Primary&Domain=PIN&servlet=1&language=EN&hostname=apps.fao.org&version=default.

(2013) *Agriculture Data, Agricultural Production Indices*, FAO, accessed July 2013, http://apps.fao.org/page/form?collection=Crops.Primary&Domain=PIN&servlet=1&language=EN&hostname=apps.fao.org&version=default.

(2013) *Landuse database*, downloaded July, 2013, FAO, http://faostat.fao.org/site/377/default.aspx#ancor.

FARINELLI, F. (2012) *Natural Resources, Innovation and Export Growth: The Wine Industry in Chile and Argentina*, PhD Thesis, Maastricht University.

FEARNSIDE, P. M. (2001) 'Land-Tenure Issues as Factors in Environmental Destruction in Brazilian Amazonia: The Case of Southern Pará', *World Development*, **29** (8), pp. 1361–2001.

FEENY, D. (1982) *The Political Economy of Productivity: Thai Agricultural Development 1880–1975*, Vancouver/London: University of British Columbia Press.

(1987) 'The Development of Property Rights in Land: A Comparative Study', in: R.H. BATES (ed.), *Toward a Political Economy of Development: A Rationalist Perspective*, Berkeley, CA: University of California Press.

FEI, J.C.H. and G. RANIS (1964) *Development of the Labor Surplus Economy: Theory and Policy*, Homewood, IL: Irwin.

(1976) 'A Model of Growth in the Open Dualistic Economy: The Case of Korea and Taiwan', *Journal of Development Studies*, **11** (2), pp. 32–63.

FERENCZI, I. and W.F. WILLCOX (1929) *International Migrations*, Vol. 1, New York: National Bureau of Economic Research.

FERREIRA, F.H.G. (1999) *Inequality and Economic Performance: A Brief Overview of Theories of Growth and Distribution*, World Bank Website on Inequality, Poverty and Socio-economic Performance: www.worldbank.org/poverty/inequal/index.htm, June.

FEY, J.N. (1985) 'GATT – Een vlucht naar voren? [GATT – An Escape Forwards?]', *Internationale Spectator*, **XXXIX**, (11), pp. 670–8.

FIELDHOUSE, D.K. (1973) *Economics and Empire, 1830–1914*, Ithaca, NY: Cornell University Press.

(1982) *The Colonial Empires: A Comparative Survey from the Eighteenth Century*, 2nd edn, London: Macmillan.

FIGUEIREDO, P. (2003) 'Does Technological Learning Pay Off? Inter Firm differences in Technological Capability Accumulation and Operational performance Improvement', *Research Policy*, **31**, pp. 73–94.

FINDLAY, R. (1980) 'The Terms of Trade and Equilibrium Growth in the World Economy', *American Economic Review*, **70** (3), pp. 291–9.

FINDLAY R. and K.H. O'ROURKE (2007) *Power and Plenty. Trade, War, and the World Economy in the Second Millennium*, Princeton/Oxford: Princeton University Press.

FINER, S.E. (1988) *The Man on Horseback*, 2nd enlarged edn, Boulder, CO: Westview Press.

FIRMIN-SELLERS, K. and P. SELLERS (1999) 'Expected Failures and Unexpected Successes of Land Titling in Africa', *World Development*, **27** (7), pp. 1115–38.

FISCHER, S. (2003) 'Globalization and its Challenges', Richard T. Ely Lecture, *American Economic Review*, **93** (2), May, pp. 1–30.

FITZPATRICK, J. (1983) *Trade and the Lomé Convention*, Lomé Briefing, No. 9.

FOGEL, R.W. (1986) 'Nutritition and the Decline in Mortality since 1700: Some Preliminary Findings', in S.L. ENGERMAN and R.E. GALLMAN (eds.), *Long Term Factors in American Economic Growth*, NBER/University of Chicago Press, pp. 439–555.

(1994) 'The Relevance of Malthus for the Study of Mortality Today: Long Run Influences on Health and Mortality, Labour Force Participation and Population Growth', in: L. LINDAHL-KIESSLING and H. LANDSBERG (eds.), *Population, Economic Development and the Environment*, Oxford/New York: Oxford University Press, pp. 231–84.

(1997) 'New Findings on Seculary Trends in Nutrition and Mortality: Some Implications for Population Theory', in: M.S. ROSENZWEIG and O. STARK (eds.), *Handbook of Population and Family Economics*, Vol 1.A, Amsterdam: Elsevier Science, pp. 433–81.

(2004). *The Escape from Hunger and Premature Death, 1700–2100*, Cambridge University Press.

FOSTER, G. (1965) 'Peasant Society and the Image of Limited Good', *American Antropologist*, **67** (2), pp. 293–315.

(1975) *Traditional Cultures and the Impact of Technological Change*, New York: Harper & Row.

FOSTER, P. (1965a) *Education and Social Change in Ghana*, London: Routledge & Kegan Paul.

(1965b) 'The Vocational School Fallacy in Development Planning', in: C.A. ANDERSON and M.J. BOWMAN (eds.), *Education and Economic Development*, Chicago: Aldine, pp. 142–6.

(1980) 'Education and Social Inequality in Sub-Saharan Africa', *Journal of Modern African Studies*, **18** (2), pp. 201–36.

FOSU, A.K. (1992) 'Political Instability and Economic Growth: Evidence from Sub-Saharan Africa', *Economic Development and Cultural Change*, **40** (4), pp. 829–41.

FRANCK, T.M. and M.M. MUNANSANGU (1982) *The New International Economic Order: International Law in the Making*, New York: United Nations Institute for Training and Research.

FRANK, A.G. (1969) *Capitalism and Underdevelopment in Latin America*, rev. edn, New York: Monthly Review Press.

(1971) *The Sociology of Underdevelopment and the Underdevelopment of Sociology*, London: Pluto Press.

(1998) *ReOrient: Global Economy in the Asian Age*, Berkeley, CA: University of California Press.

FRANKEL, F.R. (1978) *India's Political Economy*, 1947–1977, Princeton University Press.

FREDERIKSON, H. (1969) 'Feedbacks in Economic and Demographic Transition', *Science*, **166** (3907), pp. 819–912.

FREEDOM HOUSE (2000) *Democracy's Century: A Survey of Global Political Change in the Twentieth Century*, www.freedomhouse.org/reports/century.html.

(2013) *Freedom in the World 2013: Democratic Breakthroughs in the Balance*, www. freedomhouse.org/report/freedom-world/freedom-world-2013#.VAbxk2PIfdl.

FREEMAN, C. (1987) *Technology and Economic Performance: Lessons from Japan*, London: Pinter.

FREEMAN, C. and C. PEREZ (1988) 'Structural Crises of Adjustment, Business Cycles and Investment Behaviour', in: G. DOSI, C. FREEMAN, R. NELSON, G. SILVERBERG and L. SOETE (eds.), *Technical Change and Economic Theory*, London/New York: Pinter, pp. 38–65.

FREEMAN C. and L. SOETE (1997) *The Economics of Industrial Innovation*, 3rd edn, London/ Washington, DC: Pinter.

FREIRE, P. (1970) *Pedagogy of the Oppressed*, New York: Seabury Press.

FRENK, J., T. FREJKA, J.L. BOBADILLA, C. STERN, J. SEPULVEDA and M. JOSÉ (1989) 'The Epidemiologic Transition in Latin America', in: *International Population Conference*, New Delhi, Vol.1, Liège: IUSSP, pp. 419–32.

FREY, B.D. (1978) *Modern Political Economy*, Oxford: Martin Robertson.

FU, X., C. PIETROBELLI and L. SOETE (2011) 'The Role of Foreign Technology and Indigenous Innovation in the Emerging Economies: Technological Change and Catching-up', *World Development*, **39** (7), pp. 1204–13.

FUKUYAMA, F. (1992) *The End of History and the Last Man*, New York: Free Press.

FURTADO, C. (1976) *Economic Development of Latin America*, Cambridge University Press.

GAILLARD, H. and A. BEERNINK (2001) 'The Urban Informal Manufacturing Sector in Tanzania: Neglected Opportunities for Socioeconomic Development', in: A. SZIRMAI and P.E. LAPPERRE (eds.), *The Industrial Experience of Tanzania*, Basingstoke: Palgrave, pp. 318–40.

GAKOU, M.L. (1987) *The Crisis in African Agriculture*, London: Zed Books.

GALLUP, J. and J. SACHS (1998) 'Development and Poverty in a Global Age. Location, Geography and Economic Development', *Harvard International Review*, **21** (1), pp. 56–61.

GAULT, F. (2010) *Innovation Strategies for a Global Economy: Development, Implementation, Measurement and Management*, Cheltenham: Edward Elgar.

GAVSHON, A. (1981) *Crisis in Africa. Battleground of East and West*, Boulder, CO: Westview Press.

GEERTZ, C. (1963a) *Agricultural Involution: The Processes of Ecological Change in Indonesia*, Berkeley, CA: University of California Press.

(1996b) *Peddlars and Princes: Social Change and Economic Modernization in Two Indonesian Towns*, University of Chicago Press.

GEHLEN, A (1958) *Der Mensch: Seine Natur und Stellung in der Welt*, 6th edn, Bonn: Athenäum.

GEORGE, S. (1988) *A Fate Worse than Debt*, London/New York: Penguin.

GEREFFI, G. (1990) 'Paths of Industrialization: An Overview', in: G. GEREFFI and D. WYMAN (eds.), *Manufacturing Miracles*, Princeton University Press.

(1994) 'Capitalism, Development and Global Commodity Chains', in: L. SKLAIR (ed.), *Capitalism and Development*, London: Routledge.

(1999) 'International Trade and Industrial Upgrading in the Apparel Commodity Chain, *Journal of International Economics*, **48** (1), pp. 37–70.

GEREFFI, G. and M. KORZENIEWICZ (eds.) (1994) *Commodity Chains and Global Capitalism*, Westport, CT: Prager.

GERSCHENKRON, A. (1962) *Economic Backwardness in Historical Perspective*, Cambridge, MA: Harvard University Press.

GHAI, D. and S. RADWAN (eds.) (1985) *Agrarian Policies and Rural Poverty in Africa*, Geneva: ILO.

GIBSON, J. and D. MCKENZIE (2011) 'Eight Questions about Brain Drain', *Journal of Economic Perspectives* **25** (3), pp. 107–28.

GILLIN E.D and J. KRANE (1989) 'Where does the Increase in Crop Production Come From?', *FAO Quarterly Bulletin of Statistics*, **2** (4), pp. iii–iv.

GILLIS, M, D.H. PERKINS, M. ROEMER and D.R. SNODGRASS (1992) *Economics of Development*, 3rd edn, New York: Norton.

GIROD, B., A. WIEK, H. MIEG, and M. HULME (2009) 'The Evolution of the IPCC's Emission Scenarios', *Environmental Science Policy*, **12** (2), pp. 103–18.

GLAESER, B. (1987) 'Agriculture between the Green Revolution and Ecodevelopment: Which Way to Go?', in: B. GLAESER (ed.), *The Green Revolution Revisited. Critique and Alternatives*, London: Allen & Unwin, pp. 1–9.

GLAESER, E.L., R. LAPORTA, F. LOPEZ-DE-SILVANES and A. SHLEIFER, 'Do Institutions Cause Growth', *Journal of Economic Growth*, **9** (3) pp. 271–303.

GLASSMEIER, A. and M. HOWLAND (1994) 'Service-Led Rural Development: Definitions, Theories and Empirical Evidence', *International Regional science Review*, **16** (1/2), pp. 197–229. (Reproduced in: BRYSON, H.R and P.W. DANIELS (eds.), *Service Industries in the Global Economy, Volume II. Services, Globalization and Economic Development*, Cheltenham: Edward Elgar, 1998).

GLEWWE, P. (1996) 'The Relevance of Standard Estimates of Rates of Return to Schooling for Education Policy: A Critical Assessment', *Journal of Development Economics* **51**, pp. 267–90.

(2002) 'Schools and Skills in Developing Countries: Education Policies and Socioeconomic Outcomes', *Journal of Economic Literature*, **XL**, pp. 436–82.

GLEWWE, P. and E.A. MIGUEL (2008) 'The Impact of Child Health and Nutrition on Education in Less Developed Countries', in T. P. SCHULTZ and J. STRAUSS (eds.), *Handbook of Development Economics*, Vol. 4, Amsterdam: Elsevier.

GODO, Y. and Y. HAYAMI (2002) 'Catching Up in Education in the Economic Catch-up of Japan with the United States, 1890–1990', *Economic Development and Cultural Change*, **50** (4), pp. 961–78.

GOLDIN C. and L.F. KATZ (2008) *The Race between Education and Technology*, Cambridge, MA: Harvard University Press.

GOLDIN, I. and K. REINERT (2012) *Globalization for Development. Meeting New Challenges*, Oxford University Press.

GOLDSTONE, J.A. (2002) 'Efflorescences and Economic Growth in World History: Rethinking the Rise of the West and the British Industrial Revolution', *Journal of World History*, **13**, pp. 323–89.

GOLDTHORPE, J. (1979) *De derde wereld [The Third World]*, The Hague: Vuga, pp. 257–79.

GOODELL, G. (1995/6) 'Another Way to Skin a Cat: The Spirit of Capitalism and the Confucian Ethic', *The National Interest*, Winter, pp. 66–71.

GOODSTADT, L. (1982) 'China's One Child Family', *Population and Development Review*, **VIII**, pp. 37–50.

GORE, C.H. (2000) 'The Rise and Fall of the Washington Consensus as a Paradigm for Developing Countries', *World Development*, **28** (5), pp. 789–804.

GOSH, P.L. (1984) *Industrialization and Development*, Westport, CT: Greenwood Press.

GOUDIE, A. (1993) *The Human Impact on the Natural Environment*, Oxford: Basil Blackwell.

GOUDSBLOM, J. (1992) *Vuur en beschaving [Fire and Civilisation]*, Amsterdam: Meulenhof.

GRANSTRAND, O. (1995) 'Innovation and Intellectual Property Rights', in: J. FAGERBERG, DC. MOWERY and R.R. NELSON (eds.), *The Oxford Handbook of Innovation*, Oxford University Press, p. 266–90.

GRASSMAN, S. and E. LUNDBERG (eds.) (1981) *The World Economic Order: Past and Present*, London: Macmillan.

GREENAWAY, D. and O. MORRISSEY (1993) 'Structural Adjustment and Liberalisation in Developing Countries: What Lessons Have We Learned?', *Kyklos*, **46**, pp. 241–61.

GREIF A. (1993) 'Contract Enforceability and Economic Institutions in Early Trade: The Maghribi Traders' Coalition', *The American Economic Review* **83** (3), pp. 525–48.

(1994) 'On the Political Foundations of the Late Medieval Commercial Revolution: Genoa During the Twelfth and Thirteenth Centuries', *The Journal of Economic History*, **54** (2), pp. 271–87.

(2006a) *Institutions and the Path to the Modern Economy: Lessons from Medieval Trade*, Cambridge University Press.

(2006b) 'History Lessons: The Birth of Impersonal Exchange: The Community Responsibility System and Impartial Justice', *Journal of Economic Perspectives*, **20** (2), pp. 221–36.

GREIF, A. and D.D. LAITIN (2004) 'A Theory of Endogenous Institutional Change', *American Political Science Review*, **98** (4), pp. 633–52.

GRIER, R.M. (2002) 'On the Interaction of Human and Physical Capital in Latin America', *Economic Development and Cultural Change*, **50** (4), pp. 891–913.

GRIES, T.H. (2013) 'Global Asymmetries and their Implications for Climate and Industrial Policies', in: A. SZIRMAI, W. NAUDÉ and A. ALCORTA (eds.), *Pathways to Industrialization in the 21ˢᵗ Century: New Challenges and Emerging Paradigms*, Oxford University Press, pp. 293–323.

GRIFFIN, K. (1970) 'Foreign Capital, Domestic Savings and Economic Development', *Bulletin of the Oxford Institute of Economics and Statistics*, **32** (2), and 'Reply', **33** (2).

(1976) *The Political Economy of Agrarian Change*, London: Macmillan.

(1981) *Land Concentration and Rural Poverty*, 2nd edn, London: Macmillan.

(1987a) *World Hunger and the World Economy*, London: Macmillan.

(1987b) 'Doubts about Aid', in: K. GRIFFIN, *World Hunger and the World Economy*, London: Macmillan, pp. 235–54.

(1988) 'Toward a Cooperative Settlement of the Debt Problem', *Finance and Development*, June, pp. 12–14.

GRIFFIN, K. and J.L. ENOS (1970) 'Foreign Assistance: Objectives and Consequences', *Economic Development and Cultural Change*, **18** (3), pp. 313–27.

GRIFFIN, K. and J. GURLEY (1985) 'Radical Analyses of Imperialism, the Third World and the Transition to Socialism', *Journal of Economic Literature*, **XXIII** (3), pp. 1089–144.

GRIFFITH-JONES, S., J.A. OCAMPO and J.E. STIGLITZ (eds.) (2010) *Time for a Visible Hand: Lessons from the 2008 World Financial Crisis*, Oxford University Press.

GRILLI, E.R. and M.C. YANG (1988) 'Primary Commodity Prices, Manufactured Goods Prices, and the Terms of Trade of Developing Countries: What the Long Run Shows', *The World Bank Economic Review*, **2** (1), pp. 1–47.

GRIMAL, H. (1978) *Decolonization: The British, French, Dutch and Belgian Empires, 1919–1963*, London: Routledge & Kegan Paul.

GRIMM, M., P. KNORRINGA and J. LAY (2012) 'Constrained Gazelles: High Potentials in West Africa's Informal Economy', *World Development*, **40** (7), pp. 1352–68.

GRIMM, M., J. KRUGER and J. LAY (2011) 'Barriers to Entry and Returns to Capital in Informal Activities: Evidence from Sub-Saharan Africa', *Review of Income and Wealth*, **57**, pp. S27–S53.

GRONINGEN GROWTH AND DEVELOPMENT CENTRE (2002) Groningen Growth and Development Centre and The Conference Board, *Total Economy Database*, www.ggdc.net, accessed, 2002.

(2003) *ICOP Industry Database, Summary Tables* (http://www.eco.rug.nl/GGDC/icop.html), accessed June.

(2010) 10-sector database, www.ggdc.net/databases/10_sector.htm, downloaded November, 2010.

GUILLAUMONT, P. and L. CHAUVET (2001) 'Aid and Performance: A Reassessment', *The Journal of Development Studies*, **37** (6), pp. 66–92.

GUNNING, J.W. (1988) 'Structurele aanpassing en armoedebestrijding: de rol van de Wereldbank [Structural Adjustment and Poverty Prevention; The Role of the World Bank]', *Internationale Spectator*, December, pp. 751–5.

GUPTA, K.L. and M.A. ISLAM (1983) *Foreign Capital, Savings and Growth*, Boston, MA: Reidel.

GUPTA S., R. POWELL and Y. YANG (2006) *Macro-Economic Challenges of Scaling Up Aid to Africa: A Checklist for Practitioners*, Washington, DC: IMF.

HAAN, J. DE and C.L.J. SIERMAN (1993) 'Political Instability, Freedom and Economic Growth: Some Further Evidence', rev. version, Groningen, mimeo, September.

HAAN, J. DE, D. ZELHORST and O. ROUKENS (1993) 'Seignorage in Developing Countries', *Applied Financial Economics*, **3** (4), pp. 307–14.

HAAN, L.J. (1989) 'Over de kwaliteit van de ontwikkelingssamenwerking [On the Quality of Development Cooperation]', *Internationale Spectator*, **XLIII** (6), pp. 374–5.

HABIYAREMRE, A. (2009) *From Primary Commodity Dependence to Diversification and Growth. Absorptive Capacity and Technological Catch-Up in Botswana and Mauritius*, PhD thesis, Maastricht University/UNU-MERIT.

HAGGBLADE, S., P. HAZELL and T. REARDON (eds.) (2007) *Transforming the Rural Nonfarm Economy*, Baltimore, MD: Johns Hopkins University Press.

HAGEN, E.E. (1962) *On the Theory of Social Change: How Economic Growth Begins*, New York: Feffer & Simons.

HAGGIS, J., S. JARRET, D. TAYLOR and P. MAYER (1986) 'By the Skin of their Teeth: A Critical Examination of James Scott's The Moral Economy of the Peasant', *World Development*, **14** (12), pp. 1435–55.

HALLAK, J. (1990) *Investing in the Future: Setting Education Priorities in the Developing World*, UNESCO/International Institute for Education Planning, Paris/Oxford: UNDP.

HANCOCK, G. (1991) *Lords of Poverty*, London: Mandarin.

HANLEY, S.B. (1990) 'The Relationship of Education and Economic Growth: The Case of Japan', in G. TORTELLA (ed.), *Education and Economic Development Since the Industrial Revolution*, València: Generalitat Valenciana.

HANSEN, B. and G.A. MARZOUK (1965) *Development and Economic Policy in the UAR. (Egypt)*, Amsterdam: North-Holland.

HANSEN H. and F. TARP (2000a) 'Aid Effectiveness Disputed', *Journal of International Development*, **12** (3), pp. 275–398.

(2000b) 'The Effectiveness of Foreign Aid', in: F. TARP and P. HJERTHOLM (eds.), *Foreign Aid and Development*, London: Routledge.

(2001) 'Aid and Growth Regressions', *Journal of Development Economics* **64** (2): pp. 547–70.

HANUSHEK, E. and L. WÖßMANN (2007) *The Role of Education Quality in Economic Growth*, World Bank Policy Research Working Paper 4122, February.

(2008) 'The Role of Cognitive Skills in Economic Development', *Journal of Economic Literature*, **XLVI** (3), 607–68.

HAQUE, N.U. and S. KIM (1995) 'Human Capital Flight: Impact of Migration on Income and Growth', *International Monetary Fund Staff Papers*, **42** (3), pp. 577–607.

HARAGUCHI, N. and G. REZONJA (2013) 'Emerging Patterns of Structural Change in Manufacturing', in: A. SZIRMAI, W. NAUDÉ and L. ALCORTA (eds.), *Pathways to Industrialisation in the 21ˢᵗ Century*, Oxford University Press, pp. 102–28.

HARBISON. F. and C. MYERS (eds.) (1965) *Manpower and Education*, New York: McGraw Hill.

HARDIMAN, M. and J. MIDGLEY (1982) *The Social Dimension of Development. Social Policy and Planning in the Third World*, Chichester: Wiley.

HARDIN, G. (1968) 'The Tragedy of the Commons', *Science*, **162** (3859), pp. 1243–48.

HARKAVY, R.E. and S.G. NEUMAN (eds.) (1985) *The Lessons of Recent Wars in the Third World*, Vol. I, Lexington Books, pp. 33–52.

HARRISON, L.E. (1985) *Underdevelopment Is a State of Mind: The Latin American Case*, Boston, MA: Madison Books.

HARRISON, L.E. and S.P. HUNTINGTON (eds.) (2000) *Culture Matters: How Values Shape Human Progress*, New York: Basic Books.

HARRISON, P. (1992) *The Third Revolution: Population, Environment and a Sustainable World*, Harmondsworth: Penguin.

HART, K. (1973) 'Informal Income Opportunities and Urban Employment in Ghana', in: R. JOLLY, E. DE KADT and F. WILSON (eds.), *Third World Employment: Problems and Strategy*, Harmondsworth: Penguin.

HARTZ, L. (1964) *The Founding of New Societies*, New York: Harcourt Brace & World.

HATTON, T.J. and J.G. WILLIAMSON (2005) *Global Migration and the World Economy: Two Centuries of Policy and Performance*, Cambridge, MA/London: MIT Press.

HAUSMANN, R. and D. RODRIK (2003) 'Economic Development as Self-Discovery', *Journal of Development Economics*, **72** (2), pp. 603–33.

HAUSMANN, R., L. PRITCHETT and D. RODRIK (2005) 'Growth Accelerations', *Journal of Economic Growth*, **10**, pp. 303–29.

HAUSMANN, R., A. VELASCO and D. RODRIK (2008) 'Growth Diagnostics', in: J. STIGLITZ and N. SERRA, *The Washington Consensus Reconsidered: Towards a New Global Governance*, Oxford University Press.

HAYAMI, Y. and V.W. RUTTAN (1971) *Agricultural Development: An International Perspective*, Baltimore, MD: Johns Hopkins University Press.

(1985) *Agricultural Development: An International Perspective*, rev. edn, Baltimore, MD: Johns Hopkins University Press.

HAYTER, T. (1971) *Aid as Imperialism*, London: Penguin.

(1981) *The Creation of World Poverty: An Alternative View to the Brandt Report*, London: Pluto.

(1989) *Exploited Earth: British Aid and the Environment*, London: Earthscan Publications.

HAYTER, T. and C. WATSON (1985) *Aid: Rhetoric and Reality*, London: Pluto.

HAZELL, P. (2010) 'An Assessment of the Impact of Agricultural Research in South Asia since the Green Revolution', in: P.L. PINGALI and R.E. EVENSON (eds.), *Handbook of Agricultural Economics*, Vol. 4, Amsterdam: North-Holland, pp. 3470–530.

HEININK, A.L. and J.M.B. KOETSIER (1984) 'Onderwijs in de derde wereld: Hefboom voor ontwikkeling? [Education in the Third World: The Driving Force of Development?]', *INFO, Informatiebladen van het Instituut voor Onderwijskunde*, **15** (2), pp. 73–86.

HEKKEN, P.M. VAN and H.U.E. THODEN VAN VELZEN (1972) *Land Scarcity and Rural Inequality in Tanzania*, The Hague: Mouton.

HELLEINER, G.K. (1989) 'Transnational Corporations and Direct Foreign Investment', in: H. CHENERY and T.N. SRINIVASAN (eds.), *Handbook of Development Economics*, Vol. 2, Chapter 28, Amsterdam: North-Holland, pp. 1387–1439.

(1992a) 'Structural Adjustment and Long-Term Development in Sub-Saharan Africa', in: F. STEWART, S. LALL and S. WANGWE (eds.), *Alternative Development Strategies in Sub-Saharan Africa*, Basingstoke: Macmillan.

(1992b) 'The IMF, the World Bank and Africa's Adjustment and External Debt Problems: An Unofficial View', *World Development*, **20** (6), pp. 779–92.

(ed.) (1995) *Manufacturing for Export in the Developing World. Problems and Possibilities*, London: Routledge.

(ed.) (2002) *Non-Traditional Export Promotion in Africa. Experience and Issues*, Basingstoke: Palgrave.

HELLER, P.S. (1975) 'A Model of Public Fiscal Behavior in Developing Countries: Aid, Investment and Taxation', *American Economic Review*, **65** (3), pp. 429–45.

HELLIWELL, J.F. (1994) 'Empirical Linkages between Democracy and Economic Growth', *British Journal of Political Science*, **24** (2), pp. 225–48.

HERMES, C.L.M. (1992) *De internationale schuldencrisis [The International Debt Crisis]*, Groningen: Wolters-Noordhoff.

HERMES, N. and R. LENSINK (2001a) 'Changing the Conditions for Development Aid: A New Paradigm?', *Journal of Development Studies*, **37** (6), pp. 1–16.

HERMES, N. and R. LENSINK (eds.) (1996) *Financial Development and Economic Growth: Theory and Experiences from Developing Countries*, London: Routledge.

(2001b) *Changing the Conditions for Development Aid: A New Paradigm?* London: Frank Cass.

HERTZ, N. (2001) *The Silent Takeover: Global Capitalism and the Death of Democracy*, London: Heinemann.

HIGGINS, B. (1968) *Economic Development: Problems, Principles and Policies*, New York: Norton (first published in 1959).

HIGGINS, B. and J.D. HIGGINS (1979) *Economic Development of a Small Planet*, New York: Norton.

HILL, H. (1999) *The Indonesian Economy in Crisis: Causes Consequences and Lessons*, Singapore, Institute of South East Asian Studies.

(2000a) 'Indonesia: The Strange and Sudden Death of a Tiger Economy', *Oxford Development Studies*, **28** (2), pp. 117–39.

(2000b) *The Indonesian Economy since 1966: Southeast Asia's Emerging Giant*, Second Edition, Cambridge University Press.

HILL, P. (1986) *Development Economics on Trial: The Anthropological Case for a Prosecution*, Cambridge University Press.

HIRSCHMAN, A.O. (1967) *Development Projects Observed*, Washington, DC: Brookings Institution.

(1973) 'The Changing Tolerance for Income Inequality in the Course of Economic Development', *World Development*, **1** (12), pp. 29–36.

(1977) 'A Generalized Linkage Approach to Economic Development, with Special Reference to Staples', in: M. NASH (ed.), *Essays on Economic Development and Cultural Change in Honor of Bert F. Hoselitz*, Special Issue of *Economic Development and Cultural Change*, Supplement, **25**.

(1988) *The Strategy of Economic Development*, New Haven, CT: Yale University Press (first published 1958).

HOBDAY, M.G. (1995) *Innovation in East Asia: The Challenge to Japan*, Cheltenham: Edward Elgar.

(2013) 'Industrialization and Development: Lessons to be Learned from the Asian Experience', in A. SZIRMAI, W. NAUDÉ and L. ALCORTA (eds.), Pathways to Industrialization in the 21ˢᵗ Century, Oxford University Press, pp. 131–54.

HOBSBAWM, E. (1969) *Industry and Empire*, London: Penguin.

HOEBINK, P. (1988) *Geven en Nemen, De Nederlandse ontwikkelingshulp aan Tanzania en Sri Lanka [Giving or Taking: Dutch Development aid to Tanzania and Sri Lanka]*, Nijmegen: Stichting Derde Wereld Publikaties.

HOEBINK, P. (1990a) 'Tussen militair, dominee en koopman: hulpbeleid van westerse landen [Between Soldier, Clergyman and Merchant: Aid Policies in Western Countries]', *Internationale Spectator*, **XLIV**, pp. 126–39.

(1990b) 'De Nederlandse ontwikkelingshulp [Dutch Development Aid]', in: R. DOOM, *Derde wereld handboek: Deel I, Noord-Zuid en Zuid-Zuid in politiek perspectief*, Brussels/The Hague, pp. 197–218.

HOETINK, H. (1984) 'Culture vs. Progress? Notes on the Cultural Aspects of the US–Latin American Relations', in: C.A.D. VAN NIEUWENHUIJZE (ed.), *Development Regardless of Culture*, Leiden: Brill.

HOEVEN, R. VAN DER (2001) 'Assessing Aid and Global Governance', *Journal of Development Studies*, **37** (6), pp. 109–17.

HOEVEN, R. VAN DER and L. TAYLOR (2000) 'Introduction: Structural Adjustment, Labour Markets and Employment: Some Considerations for Sensible People', *The Journal of Development Studies, Special Section on Structural Adjustment and the Labour Market*, **36** (4), pp. 57–65.

HOFMAN, A. (1993) 'Economic Development in Latin America in the 20th Century', in: A. SZIRMAI, B. VAN ARK and D. PILAT (eds.), *Explaining Economic Growth: Essays in Honour of Angus Maddison*, Amsterdam: North-Holland, pp. 241–66.

(1998) *Latin American Development: A Causal Analysis in Historical Perspective*, Groningen University.

HOFSTEDE, G. (1991) *Cultures and Organisations: Software of the Mind*, London: McGraw Hill.

(2001) *Culture's Consequences: Comparing Values, Behaviors, Institutions and Organizations Across Nations*, 2nd edn, London: Sage, (1st edition 1980).

HOFSTEDE, G. and M.H. BOND (1988) 'The Confucius Connection: From Cultural Roots to Economic Growth', *Organization Dynamics*, **16** (4), pp. 5–21.

HOGENDORN, J.S. (1996) *Economic Development*, 3rd edn, New York: Harper Collins.

HOGG, D. (2000) *Technological Change in Agriculture: Locking in to Genetic Uniformity*, London: Macmillan.

HOGG, M.V. (1984) 'Industrialization and Rural Development: An Analysis of Basic Issues', in: P.K. GOSH (ed.), *Industrialization and Development*, Westport, CT: Greenwood Press, pp. 153–83.

HOOGEN, T.J. VAN DEN (1992) 'Security and Third World States: A Conceptual Analysis', *Development and Security*, No. 38, Centre for Development Studies, University of Groningen.

HOPKINS, A.G. (1973) *An Economic History of West Africa*, London: Longman.

HORESH, E. and S. JOEKES (1985) 'The Impact of Primary Exports on the Ghanaian Economy', in: M. LUNDAHL (ed.) (1985) *The Primary Sector in Economic Development*, London: Croom Helm.

HOSELITZ, B.F. (1960) *Sociological Aspects of Economic Growth*, New York: Free Press.

HSU, R.C. (1982) *Food for One Billion: China's Agriculture Since 1949*, Boulder, CO: Westview Press.

HUANG, Y. (1998) *Agricultural Reform in China*, Cambridge University Press.

HUANG, J. and S. ROZELLE (1996) 'Technological Change: Rediscovery of the Engine of Productivity Growth in China's Rural Economy', *Journal of Development Economics* **49** (2), pp. 337–69.

HUETING, P. and B. DE BOER BOSCH (1992) *Methodology for the Calculation of Sustainable National Income*, The Hague: Sdu Uitgeverij/CBS-publikaties.

HUGHES, T.P. (1983) *Networks of Power: Electrification in Western Society 1880–1930* Baltimore, MD: Johns Hopkins University Press.

HUNT, D. (1989) *Economic Theories of Development: An Analysis of Competing Paradigms*, New York: Harvester.

HUNTER, G. (1974) *Modernizing Peasant Societies*, London: Oxford University Press.

HUNTINGTON, S.P. (1991) *The Third Wave, Democratisation in the Late Twentieth Century*, Tulsa, OK: University of Oklahoma Press.

(2000) 'Cultures Count', in: L.E. HARRISON and S.P. HUNTINGTON (eds.), *Culture Matters: How Values Shape Human Progress*, New York: Basic Books, pp. xiii–xvi.

HUSAIN, I. (1993) *Structural Adjustment and the Long-Term Development of Sub-Saharan Africa*, Paper presented at the International Seminar of Structural Adjustment and Long-Term Development in Sub-Saharan Africa: Research and Policy Issues, DGIS, The Hague, 1–3 June.

IBGE, DIRETORIA DE PESQUISAS – *Departamento de Contas Nacionais*, various issues.

IDA/IMF (2003) *Heavily Indebted Poor Countries (HIPC) Initiative – Statistical Update*, International Development Association, IMF, IDA/R2003–0042/2, April 11.

(2011) Heavily Indebted Poor Countries (HIPC) Initiative and Multilateral Debt Relief Initiative (MDRI) – Status of Implementation and Proposals for the Future of the HIPC Initiative, November 8, 2011, https://www.imf.org/.../np/.../2011/110811.pdf.

IIZUKA, M. and M. GEBREEYESUS (2012) *A Systemic Perspective in Understanding the Successful Emergence of Non-Traditional Exports: Two Cases from Africa and Latin America*, UNU-MERIT Working Paper Series 052.

ILLICH, I. (1974) *Deschooling Society*, New York: Harper & Row.

ILO (1972) *Employment, Income and Equality: A Strategy for Increasing Productive Employment in Kenya*, Geneva.

(1976) *Employment Growth and Basic Needs: A One World Problem*, Geneva.

(2002) *Key Indicators of the Labour Market, 2001–2002*, Geneva.

(2003) LABORSTA, http://laborsta.ilo.org, July.

(2011) ILO: *Key Indicators of the Labour Market (KILM)* 6th edition, http://kilm.ilo.org/KILMnetBeta/default2.asp, downloaded November 2011.

(2013) LABORSTAT, http://laborsta.ilo.org.

IMF (1992) *International Financial Statistics Yearbook*, Washington, DC.

(1993) *Statistical Yearbook*, Washington, DC.

(1995) *International Financial Statistics*, Washington, DC., February.

(2001) *International Financial Statistics Yearbook 2001*, Washington DC.

International Financial Statistics Yearbook, Washington, DC., various issues.

(2003) *Factsheet – Debt Relief under the Heavily Indebted Poor Countries (HIPC) Initiative*, www.imf.org/external/np/exr/facts/hipc.htm, September.

(2013) *Heavily Indebted Poor Countries (HIPC) Initiative and Multilateral Debt Relief Initiative (MDRI)* – Statistical Update, December 19, 2013. www.imf.org/external/np/pp/eng/2013/121913.pdfIMF, *International Financial Yearbook*, various issues.

Various issues *International Financial Statistics Dataset*, www.imf.org/external/data.htm.

(2013) *Heavily Indebted Poor Countries (HIPC) Initiative And Multilateral Debt Relief Initiative (MDRI)* – *Statistical Update*, December 19.

(2014) *Factsheet – Debt Relief under the Heavily Indebted Poor Countries (HIPC) Initiative*, www.imf.org/external/np/exr/facts/hipc.htm, March 24.

INDIA, DEPARTMENT OF SCIENCE AND TECHNOLOGY (2006) *R&D Statistics*, New Delhi, Department of Science and Technology, Government of India.

INKELES, A. (1969) 'Making Men Modern: On the Causes and Consequences of Individual Change in Developing Countries', *American Journal of Sociology*, **75** (2), pp. 208–25.

INKELES, A. and D.H. SMITH (1974) *Becoming Modern: Individual Change in Six Developing Countries*, Cambridge, MA.: Harvard University Press.

IPCC, INTERGOVERNMENTAL PANEL ON CLIMATE CHANGE (2001) *Climate Change 2001: The Scientific Basis*, Contribution of Working Group I to the Third Assessment Report of the IPCC: Cambridge University Press.

(2007a) *Climate Change 2007 – The Physical Science Basis*, Contribution of Working Group I to the fourth Assessment Report of the Intergovernmental Panel on Climate Change, Cambridge University Press.

(2007b) 'Summary for Policymakers', in *Climate Change 2007 – The Physical Science Basis,* Contribution of Working Group I to the Fourth Assessment Report of the Intergovernmental Panel on Climate Change, Cambridge University Press.

(2007c) *Climate Change 2007 – Synthesis Report*, Contribution of Working Groups I, II and III to the Fourth Assessment Report of the Intergovernmental Panel on Climate Change, IPCC, Geneva, www.ipcc.ch/pdf/assessment-report/ar4/syr/ar4_syr.pdf.

ISIC (1990) *International Standard Industrial Classification of All Economic Activities. Third Revision*, Statistical Office of the United Nations, Statistical Papers, Series M. No 4, rev. 3, New York: United Nations.

ISICHEI, E. (1997) *A History of African Societies to 1870*, Cambridge University Press.

ISLAM, N. (1989a) 'Introduction to Part I, Relative Price Changes in Agriculture and Industry', in: N. ISLAM. (ed.), *The Balance between Industry and Agriculture in Economic Development, Factors Influencing Change*, Proceedings of the Eighth World Congress of the International Economic Association, Vol. 5, Basingstoke: Macmillan.

(ed.) (1989b) *The Balance between Industry and Agriculture in Economic Development, Factors Influencing Change*, Proceedings of the Eighth World Congress of the International Economic Association, Vol. 5, Basingstoke: Macmillan.

ISRAEL, J. (1995) *The Dutch Republic: Its Rise, Greatness and Fall, 1477–1806*, Oxford: Clarendon Press.

ITO, B., N. YASHIRO, Z. XU, X. CHEN and R. WAKASUGI (2012) 'How do Chinese Industries Benefit from FDI Spillovers?', *China Economic Review*, **23**, pp. 342–56.

JACKSON, R. and C. ROSBERG (1982) *Personal Rule in Black Africa*, Berkeley, CA: University of California Press.

(1986) 'Sovereignty and Underdevelopment: Juridical Statehood in the African Crisis', *The Journal of Modern African Studies*, **24** (1), pp. 1–31.

JACKSON, T. (1982) *Against the Grain: The Dilemma of Project Food Aid*, Oxford: Oxfam.

JAIN, A.K (ed.) (2001) *The Political Economy of Corruption*, London/New York: Routledge.

JAMES, D. (1991) 'Capital Goods Production and Technological Learning: The Case of Mexico', *Journal of Economics Issues*, **25** (4), pp. 977–91.

JAMES, J. (1999) 'Information Technology, Globalization and Marginalization', in: A.S. BHALLA (ed.), *Globalization, Growth and Marginalization*, Basingstoke: Macmillan.

(2002) *Technology, Globalization and Poverty*, Cheltenham: Edward Elgar.

JANOWITZ, M. (ed.) (1981) *Civil–Military Regimes: Regional Perspectives*, London: Sage.

JAVORCIK, B. S. and S. WEI (2009) 'Corruption and Cross-Border Investment in Emerging Markets: Firm-Level Evidence', *Journal of International Money and Finance*, **28** (4), pp. 605–24.

JAY, K. and C. MICHALOPOULOS (1989) 'Donor Policies, Donor Interests, and Aid Effectiveness', in: A.O. KRUEGER et al. (eds.), *Aid and Development*, Baltimore, MD: Johns Hopkins University Press, pp. 68–88.

JEPMA, C.J. (1984) 'Ontwikkelingssamenwerking op het nieuwe spoor [Development 'Cooperation on a New Track]', *Internationale Spectator*, **XXXVIII**, pp. 504 ff.

(1992) *EC-Wide Untying*, Development and Security, No. 37, Centre for Development Studies, Groningen, October.

(1993) *Deforestation in the Humid Tropics: A Socio-Economic Approach*, Stichting International Development Economics, Groningen, February.

(1997) *On the Effectiveness of Aid*, World Bank, unpublished.

(ed.) (1988) *North–South Cooperation in Retrospect and Prospect*, London: Routledge Kegan Paul.

JOHANSSON, S.R and K. MOSK (1987) 'Exposure, Resistance and Life Expectancy: Disease and Death during the Economic Development of Japan, 1900–1960', *Population Studies*, **XLI**, (2), pp. 207–36.

JOHNSON, D. GALE (2002) 'Biotechnology Issues for Developing Countries', *Economic Development and Cultural Change*, **51** (1), pp 1–2.

JOHNSON, H.G. (1967) *Economic Policies towards Less Developed Countries*, Washington, DC: Brookings.

JOHNSTON, B.F. (1970) 'Agriculture and Structural Transformation in Developing Countries: A Survey of Research', *Journal of Economic Literature*, **8** (2), pp. 369–404.

JOHNSTON, B.F. and P. KILBY (1975) *Agriculture and Structural Transformation: Economic Strategies in Late-Developing Countries*, New York: Oxford University Press.

JOHNSTON, B.F. and J.W. MELLOR (1961) 'The Role of Agriculture in Economic Development', *American Economic Review*, **51** (3), pp. 566–94.

JOHNSTON, M. (2001) 'Measuring Corruption: Numbers versus Knowledge versus Understanding', in: A.K. JAIN (ed.), *The Political Economy of Corruption*, London/New York: Routledge, pp. 157–79.

JONES, C.I. (1998) *Introduction to Economic Growth*, New York: Norton.

JONES, E.L. (1988) *Growth Recurring: Economic Change in World History*, Oxford: Clarendon Press .

JONES, G.W., R.M. DOUGLAS, J.C. CALDWELL and R.M. SOUZA (eds.) (1997) *The Continuing Demographic Transition*, Oxford: Clarendon Press.

JONES, P.W. (1988) *International Policies for Third World Education: UNESCO, Literacy and Development*, London/New York: UNESCO.

JORGENSON, D.W. (1961) 'The Development of a Dual Economy', *Economic Journal*, June, pp. 309–34.

(1967) 'Surplus Agricultural Labour and the Development of a Dual Economy', *Oxford Economic Papers*, **19** (2), pp. 288–312.

(1969) 'The Role of Agriculture in Economic Development: Classical versus Neoclassical Models of Growth', in: C. WHARTON (ed.), *Subsistence Agriculture and Economic Development*, Chicago, IL, Aldine.

(1995) *Productivity*, Vols. I & II, Cambridge, MA: MIT Press.

JUMA, C. (2011) *The New Harvest: Agricultural Innovation in Africa*, Oxford University Press.

JUNHONG, C.H. (2001) 'Prenatal Sex Determination and Sex-Selective Abortion in Rural Central China', *Population and Development Review*, **27** (2), pp. 259–81.

KADT, E. DE and M. LIPTON, (1988) *Agriculture–Health Linkages*, WHO Offset Publication No. 104, Geneva.

KAKWANI, N., S. KHANDKER and H.H. SON (2004) *Pro-Poor Growth: Concepts and Measurement with Country Case Studies*, UNDP, International Poverty Centre Working Paper No. 1, UNDP, August.

KALDOR, N. (1956) 'Alternative Theories of Distribution', *Review of Economic Studies*, **2** (2), pp. 83–100.

KALIRAJAN, H.P. and Y. WU (eds.) (1999) *Productivity and Growth in Chinese Agriculture*, Basingstoke: Macmillan.

KANBUR R. and N. LUSTIG (1999) *Why is Inequality Back on the Agenda?*, Annual Conference on Development Economics, Washington, DC: World Bank.

KAPLINKSKY, R. (2000) *Spreading the Gains from Globalisation: What Can Be Learned from Value Chain Analysis?* IDS Working Paper, No. 110.

(2011) *Commodities for Industrial Development: Making Linkages Work*, Development Policy, Statistics and Research Branch Working Paper 01/2011, UNIDO.

KAPLINSKY, R. and M. FAROOKI (2010) *What Are the Implications for Global Value Chains When the Market Shifts from the North to the South?*, Policy Research Working Paper 5205. Washington, DC: World Bank.

KATZ, J. (2000) 'Structural Change and Labor Productivity Growth in Latin American Manufacturing Industries 1970–1996', *World Development*, **28** (9), pp. 1583–96.

(2006) 'Structural Change and Domestic Technological Capabilities', *CEPAL Review*, **89**, pp. 55–68.

KAUFMANN, D., A. KRAAY, E. LORA and L. PRITCHETT (2002) 'Growth Without Governance', *Economia*, **3** (1), pp. 169–229.

KEATING, M. (1993) *Agenda for Change: A Plain Language Version of Agenda 21 and the Other Rio Agreements*, Geneva: Centre for Our Common Future.

KELLAS, J.G. (1991) *The Politics of Nationalism and Ethnicity*, London: Macmillan.

KELLEY, A.C. (1988) 'Economic Consequences of Population Change in the Third World', *Journal of Economic Literature*, **XXVI**, pp. 1685–728.

KELLY, A.C. and R.M. SCHMIDT (2007) 'Evolution of Recent Economic-Demographic Modeling: A Synthesis', in: A. MASON and M. YAMAGUCHI (eds.), *Population Change, Labor Markets and Sustainable Growth: Towards a New Economic Paradigm*, Amsterdam: Elsevier, pp. 5–38.

KENDE, I. (1972) *Local Wars in Asia, Africa and Latin America, 1945–1969*, Budapest: Center for Afro-Asian Research, Studies of Developing Countries, No. 60.

KENDRICK, J.W. (1961) *Productivity Trends in the United States*, New York, NBER/Princeton University Press.

KENNEDY, P. (1989) *The Rise and Fall of the Great Powers*, New York: Vintage.

KERR, C., J.T. DUNLOP and F.H. HARBISON (1962) *Industrialism and Industrial Man: The Problems of Labour and Management in Economic Growth*, London: Heinemann.

KEYFITZ, N. (1991) *The Demograpy of the Fission of Empires*, Groningen: Population Research Centre, November.

KEYZER, M.A. (1993) *Welfare Assessment of the Efficiency Wage Argument*, Development Economics Seminar Paper No. 93–3/13, Institute of Social Studies, November.

KHAN, M.H. (2010) *Political Settlements and the Governance of Growth-Enhancing Institutions*, London: SOAS, mimeo.

KIDRON, M. and D. SMITH (1983) *The War Atlas: Armed Conflict – Armed Peace*, London: Heinemann.

(1991) *The New State of War and Peace*, New York: Simon & Schuster.

KIELY, R. (1998) *Industrialisation and Development: A Comparative Analysis*, London: UCL Press.

KIM, L. and R.R. NELSON (eds.) (2000) *Technology, Learning and Innovation: Experiences of Newly Industrializing Economies*, Cambridge University Press.

KIMHI, A. (2006) 'Plot Size and Maize Productivity in Zambia: The Inverse Relationship Re-Examined', *Agricultural Economics*, **35** (1), 1–9.

KIRKPATRICK, C. (1987) 'Trade Policy and Industrialization in LDCs', in: N. GEMMELL (ed.), *Surveys in Development Economics*, Oxford: Basil Blackwell, pp. 56–89.

KIRSTEN, E., E.W. BUCHHOLTZ and W. KÖLLMAN (1956) *Raum und Bevölkerung in der Weltgeschichte*, Würzburg: Ploetz.

KITCHING, G. (1982) *Development and Underdevelopment in Historical Perspective*, London: Methuen.

KLEIN, H.S. (1999) *The Atlantic Slave Trade*, Cambridge University Press.

KLEIN, N. (1999) *No Logo: Taking Aim at the Brand Bullies*, New York: Picador.

KLINE, S.J. and N. ROSENBERG (1986) 'An Overview of Innovation', in T. LANDAU and N. ROSENBERG (eds.), *The Positive Sum Game*, Washington, DC: National Academy Press, pp. 275–305.

KLITGAARD, R. (1994) 'Taking Culture into Account: From "Let's" to "How"', in: I. SARAGELDIN and J. TABOROFF (eds.), *Culture and Development in Africa*, Washington, DC: World Bank, pp. 75–120.

KNACK, S. (2001) 'Aid Dependence and The Quality of Governance: A Cross-Country Empirical Analysis', *Southern Economic Journal*, **68** (2), pp. 310–29.

KNACK, S. and P. KEEFER (1995) 'Institutions and Economic Performance: Cross-Country Tests Using Alternative Institutional Indicators', *Economics and Politics*, **7** (3), pp. 207–27.

KOL, J. and L.B.M. MENNES (1990) 'Internationale handel – theorie en beleid [International Trade Theory and Policy]', *Economische en Statistische Berichten*, **21**, November, pp. 1088–93.

KOMENAN, A.G. (1987) *Improving the Efficiency of Education in Developing Countries*, Washington, DC: World Bank, Annex: World Education Indicators.

KOTTAK, C.P. (1986) 'Dimensions of Culture in Development', in: UNESCO, *The Cultural Dimension of Development*, The Hague: UNESCO.

(1991) 'When People Don't Come First: Some Sociological lessons from Completed Projects', in: M. CERNEA (ed.), *Putting People First: Sociological Variables in Rural Development*, 2nd edn, New York: Oxford University Press.

KRAAY, A. (2006) 'When is Growth Pro-Poor? Evidence from a Panel of Countries, *Journal of Development Economics*, **80** (1), 198–227.

KRAUSS, M. (1983a) *Development without Aid*, New York: McGraw Hill.

(1983b) *Transferring Incomes Versus Transferring Prosperity*, Report, New York: Manhattan Institute for Policy Research, January.

KRAVIS, I.B., A. HESTON and R. SUMMERS (1982) *World Product and Income*, Baltimore, MD: Johns Hopkins University Press.

KRIEGER, M. (1988) 'African Policy Linking Education and Development: Standard Criticisms and a New Departure', *International Review of Education*, **34** (3), pp. 293–311.

KRUEGER, A.O. (1978) *Foreign Trade Regimes and Economic Development: Liberalization Attempts and Consequences*, NBER, Cambridge, MA: Ballinger.

(1984) 'The Newly Industrializing Countries: Experience and Lessons', in: M. DUTTA (ed.), *Studies in United States–Asia Economic Relations*, Durham, NC: Acorn Press, pp. 253–74.

(1986) 'Aid in the Development Process', *World Bank Research Review*, **11** (1), pp. 57–78.

(1990a) *Perspectives on Trade and Development*, New York/London: Harvester Wheatsheaf.

(1990b) *Theory and Practice of Commercial Policy 1945–90*, Cambridge, MA: NBER, Working Paper, No. 3569, December.

(1992) *Economic Policy Reform in Developing Countries*, Cambridge, MA/Oxford: Blackwell.

(1993) *Free Trade Agremeents as Protectionist Devices: Rules of Origin*, Cambridge, MA: NBER.

KRUEGER, A.O. and R. DUNCAN (1993) *The Political Economy of Controls: Complexity*, NBER, Cambridge, MA: NBER.

KRUEGER, A.B. and M. LINDAHL (2001) 'Education for Growth: Why and for Whom?', *The Journal of Economic Literature*, **XXXIX** (4), pp. 1101–37.

KRUEGER, A.O., C. MICHALOPOULOS and V. RUTTAN (1989) *Aid and Development*, Baltimore, MD/London: Johns Hopkins University Press.

KRUGMAN, P. (1991) *Geography and Trade*, Cambridge, MA: MIT Press

(2009) *The Return of Depression Economics and the Crisis of 2008*, New York: Norton.

KRUYT, D. (1988) 'De Sociologie van ontwikkelingsbureaucratieën [The Sociology of Development Bureaucracies]', in: D. KRUYT and K. KOONINGS (eds.), *Ontwikkelingsvraagstukken: Theorie, beleid en methoden*, Muiderberg: Coutinho, pp. 57–73.

KRUYT, D. and K. KOONINGS (eds.) (1988) *Ontwikkelingsvraagstukken. Theorie, beleid en methoden [Development Issues. Theory, Policy, and Methods]*, Muiderberg: Coutinho.

KRUYT, D. and M. VELLINGA (1983) *Ontwikkelingshulp getest: Resultaten onder de loep [Development Aid Examined: A Closer Look at the Results]*, Muiderberg: Coutinho.

KUHN, R. (2010) 'Routes to Low Mortality in Poor Countries Revisited', *Population and Development Review*, **36** (4): 655–92.

KUMAR, N. 'Introduction', in: N. KUMAR (ed.) (1998), *Globalization, Foreign Direct Investment and Technology Transfers. Impacts and Prospects for Developing Countries*, London/New York: Routledge.

KUPER, A.J. (1984) 'African Culture and African Development', in: C.A.O. VAN NIEUWENHUIJZE (ed.), *Development Regardless of Culture*, Leiden: Brill.

KURAN, T. (2011) *The Long Divergence: How Islamic Law Held Back the Middle East*, Princeton University Press.

KUZNETS, S. (1955) 'Economic Growth and Income Inequality', *American Economic Review*, **XLV** (1), pp. 1–28.

(1965) *Economic Growth and Structure*, London: Heinemann.

(1966) *Modern Economic Growth: Rate, Structure and Spread*, New Haven, CT: Yale University Press.

(1971) *Economic Growth of Nations: Total Output and Production Structure*, Cambridge MA: Harvard University Press.

(1980) 'Recent Population Trends in Less Developed Countries and Implications for Internal Income Inequality', in: R. A. EASTERLIN (ed.), *Population and Economic Change in Developing Countries*, University of Chicago Press, pp. 471–515.

KUZNETSOV, B., A. YAKOVLEV and V. GIMPELSON (2012) *The Manufacturing Sector in Economic Development, Employment and Incomes: The Case of Russia*, Paper prepared for the UNIDO/UNU-MERIT Conference 'The Untold Story: Structural Change for Poverty Reducation. The Case of the BRICS', Vienna, 16–17 August.

LABELLE, H. (2014) 'Corruption' in: B. CURRIE-ALDER, R. KANBUR, D.M. MALONE and R. MEDHORA (eds.), *International Development: Ideas, Experience and Prospects*, Oxford University Press, pp. 239–55.

LACINA, B. and N.P. GLEDITSCH (2005) 'Monitoring Trends in Global Combat: A New Dataset of Battle Deaths', *European Journal of Population*, **21** (2–3), pp. 145–66.

LACINA, B., N.P. GLEDITSCH and B. RUSSETT (2006) 'The Declining Risk of Death in Battle', *International Studies Quarterly*, **50** (3), pp. 673–80.

LAL, D. (1978) *Poverty, Power and Prejudice: The North–South Confrontation*, London: Fabian Society.

(1983) *The Poverty of Development Economics*, London: Institute of Economic Affairs.

(1984) *The Political Economy of the Predatory State*, Washington, DC: World Bank, Development Research Papers, No. 105.

(1988) *The Hindu Equilibrium, Vol. I: Cultural Stability and Economic Stagnation: India, c. 1500 BC–AD, 1980*, Oxford University Press.

(2000) *The Poverty of Development Economics*. 2nd rev and Expanded US edn, Cambridge, MA/London: MIT Press.

LAL, D. and H. MYINT (1996) *The Political Economy of Poverty, Equity and Growth: A Comparative Study*, Oxford University Press.

LALL, S. (1987) *Learning to Industrialise: The Acquisition of Technological Capabilities in India*, London: Macmillan.

(1990) *Building Industrial Competitiveness in Developing Countries*, Paris: OECD.

(1992) 'Technological Capabilities and Industrialization', *World Development*, **20** (2), pp. 165–86.

(1994) 'Technological Capabilities and Industrialization', *World Development*, **22** (4), pp. 645–54.

(1996) *Learning from the Asian Tigers: Studies in Technology and Industrial Policy*, London: Macmillan.

(1998) 'Exports of Manufactures by Developing Countries. Emerging Patterns of Trade and Location', *Oxford Review of Economic Policy*, **14** (2), pp. 54–73.

(2000) 'Technological Change and Industrialization in the Asian NIEs: Achievements and Challenges', in: L. KIM and R.R. NELSON (eds.), *Technology, Learning and Innovation: Experiences of Newly Industrializing Economies*, Cambridge University Press, pp. 13–68.

(2002) 'Linking FDI and technology development for capacity building and strategic competitiveness', *Transnational Corporations*, **11** (3), pp. 39–88.

LALL S.V., H. SELOD and Z. SHALIZI (2006) *Rural–Urban Migration in Developing Countries: A Survey of Theoretical Predictions and Empirical Findings*, World Bank Policy Research Working Paper 3915, May.

LANDES, D. (1969) *The Unbound Prometheus: Technological Changes and Industrial Development in Western Europe from 1750 to the Present*, Cambridge University Press.

(1998) *The Wealth and Poverty of Nations: Why Some Are so Rich and Some so Poor*, New York/London: Norton.

(2000) 'Culture Makes Almost All the Difference', in: L.E. HARRISON and S.P. HUNTINGTON (eds.), *Culture Matters: How Values Shape Human Progress*, New York: Basic Books, pp. 2–13.

LANE, D. (1971) *The End of Inequality? Stratification under State Socialism*, Harmondsworth: Penguin.

LAPPÉ, F.M., J. COLLINS and D. KINLEY (1980) *Aid as Obstacle: Twenty Questions about our Foreign Aid and the Hungry*, San Francisco, CA: Institute for Food and Development Policy.

LAPPERRE, P.E. (1992) *Man, Technology, Society and Development*, Dissertation, Eindhoven University of Technology.

(2001) 'Industrialisation in Tanzania: Can Tanzania Learn from European History?', in: A. SZIRMAI and P.E. LAPPERRE (eds.), *The Industrial Experience of Tanzania*, Houndmills: Palgrave, pp. 283–300.

LAVOPA, A. and A. SZIRMAI (2012) *Industrialization, Employment and Poverty*, Report prepared for the International Finance Corporation, UNU-MERIT Working Paper #2012–81, December.

LAWN, J.E., J. ROHDE, S. RIFKIN, M. WERE, V.K. PAUL and M. CHOPRA (2008) 'Ama-Ata 30 Years On: Revolutionary. Relevant and Time to Revitalise', *The Lancet*, **30** (375), pp. 419–26.

LEACH, M. and J. FAIRHEAD (2000) 'Challenging Neo-Malthusian Deforestation Analyses in West Africa's Dynamic Forest Landscapes', *Population and Development Review*, **26** (1), pp. 17–43.

LEE, K. (2013) *Schumpeterian Analysis of Economic Catch-Up: Knowledge, Path Creation and the Middle Income Trap*, Cambridge University Press.

LEE, R.D. and A. MASON (2011) 'Generational Economics in a Changing World', *Population and Development Review*, **37**, Issue Supplement S1, pp. 159–82.

LEE, R.D. and D.S. REHER (2011a) 'Introduction: The Landscape of Demographic Transition and its Aftermath', *Population and Development Review*, **37**, Issue Supplement S1, pp. 1–7.

(eds.) (2011b) 'Demographic Transition and Its Consequences', *Population and Development Review*, **37**, Issue Supplement S1, pp. 1–275.

LEIBENSTEIN, H. (1954) *A Theory of Economic Demographic Development*, Princeton University Press.

(1957) *Economic Backwardness and Economic Growth: Studies in the Theory of Economic Development*, New York: Wiley.

LEISINGER, K.M. (1989) *Poverty, Sickness and Medicines: An Unholy Alliance? Development Policy, Health and the Role of the Pharmaceutical Industry in the Third World*, Geneva: Féderation International de l'Industrie du Medicament.

LEITE, L.L and P.A. FURLEY (1985) 'Land Development in the Brazilian Amazon', in: J. HEMMING (ed.), *Change in the Amazon Basin II*, Manchester University Press.

LENSINK, R. (1993a) *External Finance and Development*, Groningen: Wolters Noordhoff.

(1993b) 'Recipient Government Behavior and the Effectiveness of Development Aid', *De Economist*, **141** (4), pp. 543–62.

(1995) *Structural Adjustment in Sub-Saharan Africa*, London: Longman.

LENSINK, R. and H. WHITE (2001) 'Are there Negative Returns to Aid?' *The Journal of Development Studies*, **37** (6), pp. 42–65.

LERNER, D. (1958) *The Passing of Traditional Society: Modernizing the Middle East*, Glencoe, IL: Free Press.

LEVY, M. and SHIH, K. (1949) *The Rise of Modern Chinese Business Class: Two Introductory Essays*. New York: Institute of Pacific Relations.

LEWIS, W.A. (1950) *The Theory of Economic Growth*, London: Allen & Unwin.

(1954) 'Economic Development with Unlimited Supplies of Labour', *The Manchester School of Economic and Social Studies*, **22**, pp. 139–91.

(1969) *Aspects of Tropical Trade, 1883–1965*, Stockholm: Almquist & Wicksell.

(ed.) (1970) *Tropical Development 1880–1913*, London: Allen & Unwin.

(1978a) *Growth and Fluctuations 1870–1913*, London: Allen & Unwin.

(1978b) *The Evolution of the International Economic Order*, Princeton University Press.

(1983a) 'Reflections on Unlimited Labor', in: M. GERSOWITZ (ed.), *Selected Writings of Sir W.A. Lewis*, New York University Press, pp. 421–43 (original published 1967).

(1983b) 'Unemployment in Developing Countries', in: M. GERSOWITZ (ed.), *Selected Economic Writings of W. Arthur Lewis*, New York University Press, pp. 411–21.

LEWIS, M.K. and L.M. ALGAOUD (2001) *Islamic Banking*, Cheltenham: Edward Elgar.

LEYDESDORFF, L. and H. ETZKOWITZ (2000) 'The Dynamics of Innovation: From National Systems and Mode 2 to a Triple Helix of University–Industry–Government Relations', *Research Policy*, **29** (2), pp. 109–23.

LEYS, S. (1978) *Ombres Chinois*, Paris: Laffont.

LICHT, A.N., C.H. GOLDSCHMIDT and S.H. SCHWARTZ (2007) 'Culture Rules: The Foundations of the Rule of Law and Other Norms of Governance', *Journal of Comparative Economics*, **35**, pp. 659–88.

LIJPHART, A. (2000) *Democracy in the Twenty-First Century: Can We Be Optimistic?*', Uhlenbeck Lecture 18, Wassenaar: NIAS.

LIN, J.Y. (1995) 'The Needham Puzzle: Why the Industrial Revolution Did not Originate in China', *Economic Development and Cultural Change*, **43** (2), pp. 269–92.

(2010) *New Structural Economics. A Framework for Rethinking Development*, Washington, DC: World Bank, Policy Research Working Paper 5197.

LIN, J.Y., F. CAI and Z. LI (2000) *The Lessons of China's Transition to a Market Economy*, Paper for APSEM/ANU/World Bank Conference, 'Achieving High Growth, Experience of Transitional Economies in East Asia', Canberra, 6–7 September.

(2003) *The China Miracle: Development Strategy and Economic Reform*, rev. edn, Hong Kong: Chinese University Press.

LIN, J.Y. and C. MONGA, (2010) *Growth Identification and Facilitation: The Role of the State in the Dynamics of Structural Change*, Washington, DC: World Bank, Policy Research Working Paper 5313.

LIN, J.Y. and M. YU (2015) 'Industrial Structural Upgrading and Poverty Reduction in China', in: W. NAUDÉ, A. SZIRMAI and N. HARAGUCHI (eds.), *Structural Change and Industrial Development in the BRICS*, Oxford University Press, forthcoming.

LIND, A. and A. JOHNSTON (1986) *Adult Literacy in the Third World: A Review of Objectives and Strategies*, Education Division Documents, No. 32, Stockholm: SIDA.

LINDAHL-KIESSLING, K. and H. LANDBERG (eds.) (1994) *Population, Economic Development and the Environment*, Oxford/New York: Oxford University Press.

LIPSET, S.M. (1959) 'Some Social Prerequisites of Democracy, Economic Development and Political Legitimacy', *American Political Science Review*, **53** (1), pp. 69–105.

LIPTON, M. (1966) 'The Theory of the Optimizing Peasant', *Journal of Development Studies*, **IV**, pp. 327–51.

(1977) *Why Poor People Stay Poor: Urban Bias in World Development*, London: Temple Smith.

LITTLE, I.M.D., T. SCITOVSKY and M. SCOTT (1970) *Industry and Trade in Some Developing Countries*, New York: Oxford University Press.

LLOYD, C.B., C.E. KAUFMAN and P. HEWETT (2000) 'The Spread of Primary Schooling in Sub-Saharan Africa: Implications for Fertility Change', *Population and Development Review*, **26** (3), pp. 483–515.

LOMBORG, B. (2001) *The Skeptical Environmentalist: Measuring the Real State of the World*, Cambridge University Press.

(ed.) (2004) *Global Crises: Global Solutions*, Cambridge University Press.

(2007) *Cool it: The Skeptical Environmentalist's Guide to Global Warming*, New York: Random House.

(ed.) (2010) *Smart Solutions to Climate Change. Comparing Costs and Benefits*, Cambridge University Press.

LONG, N. (1977) *An Introduction to the Sociology of Rural Development*, London: Tavistock.

LORD, M.J. (1989) 'Primary Commodities as an Engine for Export Growth in Latin America', in: N. ISLAM. (ed.), *The Balance between Industry and Agriculture in Economic Development: Factors Influencing Change*, Proceedings of the Eighth World Congress of the International Economic Association, Vol. 5, Basingstoke: Macmillan.

LOVEJOY, P.E. (1982) 'The Volume of the Atlantic Slave Trade: A Synthesis', *Journal of African History*, **XXXIII**, pp. 473–501.

LUCAS, R.E. (1988) 'On the Mechanics of Economic Development', *Journal of Monetary Economics*, **22** (1), pp. 3–42.

LUMSDAINE, D.H. (1993) *Moral Vision in International Politics*, Princeton University Press.

LUNDAHL, M. (ed.) (1985) *The Primary Sector in Economic Development*, London: Croom Helm.

LUNDVALL, B.A. (ed.) (1992) *National Systems of Innovation: Towards a Theory of Innovation and Interactive Learning*, London: Pinter.

LUNDVALL, B.A, K.J. JOSEPH, CH. CAMINADE and J. VANG (2009) *Handbook of Innovation Systems and Developing Countries. Building Domestic Capabilities in a Global Setting*, Cheltenham: Edward Elgar.

LUTTWAK, E. (1979) *Coup d'Etat: A Practical Handbook*, London: Wildwood House.

LUTZ, W.A., S.K.C. GOUJON and W. SANDERSON (2007) 'Reconstruction of Population by Age, Sex and Level of Educational Attainment of 120 countries for 1970–2000', *Vienna Yearbook of Population Research*, **2007**, pp 193–235.

MCMILLAN, M.S. and D. RODRIK (2011) *Globalization, Structural Change and Productivity Growth*, NBER Working Paper Series 17143, June, www.nber.org/papers/w17143.

MADDISON, A. (1969) *Economic Growth in Japan and the USSR*, New York: Norton.

(1970) *Economic Progress and Policy in Developing Countries*, New York: Norton.

(1974) *Class Structure and Economic Growth in India and Pakistan*, London: Allen & Unwin.

(1982a) *Phases of Capitalist Development*, Oxford University Press.

(1982b) 'International Economic Orders Past and Present: The West and the Rest since 1500', in: *Syllabus Leergang Ontwikkelingsproblematiek*, Groningen, pp. 23–38.

(1983) 'A Comparison of Levels of GDP per Capita in Developed and Developing Countries, 1700–1980', *Journal of Economic History*, **XLIII** (1), pp. 27–41.

(1985) *Two Crises: Latin America and Asia, 1929–1938 and 1973–1983*, Paris: OECD.

(1986) 'Marx and Bismarck; Capitalism and Government, 1883–1953', in: H.J. WAGENER and J.W. DRUKKER (eds.), *The Economic Law of Motion of Modern Society: A Marx, Keynes, Schumpeter Centennial*, Cambridge University Press.

(1986) *Notes on Developing Country Performance*, mimeo, Groningen.

(1987) 'Growth and Slowdown in Advanced Capitalist Economies', *Journal of Economic Literature*, **XXV**, pp. 649–98.

(1988) 'Ultimate and Proximate Growth Causality: A Critique of Mancur Olson on the Rise and Decline of Nations', *Scandinavian Economic History Review*, **36** (2), pp. 25–9.

(1989) *The World Economy in the Twentieth Century*, Paris: OECD.

(1991) *Dynamic Forces in Capitalist Development*, Oxford University Press.

MADDISON, A. and associates (1992) *The Political Economy of Poverty, Equity and Growth: Brazil and Mexico*, New York: Oxford University Press.

(1995) *Monitoring the World Economy*, Paris: OECD Development Centre.

(1998) *Chinese Economic Performance in the Long Run*, Paris: OECD Development Centre.

(2007) *Chinese Economic Performance in the Long Run, 960–2030*, 2nd rev. edn, Paris: OECD Development Centre.

(2001) *The World Economy: A Millennial Perspective*, Development Centre Studies, Paris: OECD.

(2003) *The World Economy: Historical Statistics*, Development Centre Studies, Paris: OECD.

(2007) *Contours of the World Economy*, Oxford University Press.

(2009) *Statistics on World Population, GDP and GDP per Capita*, www.ggdc.net/Maddison/oriindex.htm.

MAIR, L. (1967) *Primitive Government*, Harmondsworth: Penguin.

MAIZELS, A. and M.K. NISSANKE (1984) 'Motivations for Aid to Developing Countries', *World Development*, **12** (9), pp. 879–900.

MALERBA, F. (2002) 'Sectoral Systems of Innovation and Production', *Research Policy* **31**, pp. 247–64.

(ed.) (2004) *Sectoral Systems of Innovation*, Cambridge University Press.

MANARUNGSAN, S. (1989) *Economic Development of Thailand, 1850–1950. Response to the Challenge of the World Economy*, Dissertation, University of Groningen.

MANI, S. (2011) 'Promoting Knowledge-Intensive Entrepreneurship in India', in: A. SZIRMAI, W. NAUDÉ and M. GOEDHUYS (eds.), *Entrepreneurship, Innovation and Economic Development*, Oxford University Press, pp. 194–227.

MANKIW, F., D. ROMER and D. WEIL (1992) 'A Contribution to the Empirics of Economic Growth', *Quarterly Journal of Economics*, **107** (2), pp. 407–38.

MAREN, M. (1997) *The Road to Hell: The Ravaging Effects of Foreign Aid and International Charity*, New York: Free Press.

MARKS, A.J. (2009) *Accounting for Services. The Economic Development of the Indonesian Service Sector, ca. 1900–2000*, PhD thesis, Utrecht University, Aksant.

MARSHALL, M.G. (2003) *Major Episodes of Political Violence, 1946–2002*, Centre for Systemic Peace, University of Maryland, http://members.aol.com/cspmgm/warlist.htm, updated May 25.

(2013) *Major Episodes of Political Violence, 1946–2012*, downloaded December, www.systemicpeace.org/warlist.htm#N4.

MARSHALL, M.G. and B.R. COLE (2011) *Global Report 2011: Conflict Governance and State Fragility*, Center for Systemic Peace.

MARSHALL, M.G. and T.R. GURR (2003) *Peace and Conflict, 2003: A Global Survey of Armed Conflicts, Self-Determination Movements and Democracy*, Centre for International Development and Conflict Resolution, University of Maryland.

MARX, K. (1955) *The Communist Manifesto*, New York: Appleton Century Cross (first published 1848).

MATHERS C.D., A.D. LOPEZ and C.L. MURRAY (2006) 'The Burden of Disease and Mortality by Condition: Data, Methods and Results for 2001', in: A.D. LOPEZ, C.D. MATHERS, M. EZZATI, C.J.L. MURRAY and D.T. JAMISON (eds.), *Global Burden of Disease and Risk Factors*, New York: Oxford University Press, pp. 45–240.

MAURICE, J. and A.M. PEARCE (eds.) (1987) *Tropical Disease Research: A Global Partnership*, Geneva: WHO.

MAURO, P. (1995) 'Corruption and Growth', *Quarterly Journal of Economics*, **110** (3), pp. 681–712.

(2000) 'The Effects of Corruption on Growth, Investment and Government Expenditure', in: A. J. HEIDENHEIMER and M. JOHNSTON (eds.), *Political Corruption*, New Brunswick, NJ: Transaction.

MAYER, D. (2001) 'The Long-Term Impact of Health on Economic Growth in Latin America', *World Development*, **29** (6), pp. 1025–33.

MCBEAN, A.I. (1989) 'Agricultural Exports of Developing Countries: Market Conditions and National Policies', in: N. ISLAM. (ed.), *The Balance between Industry and Agriculture in*

Economic Development: Factors Influencing Change, Proceedings of the Eighth World Congress of the International Economic Association, Vol. 5, Basingstoke: Macmillan.

MCCLELLAND, D. (1961) *The Achieving Society*, Princeton, NJ: Van Nostrand.

MCCULLOCH, N. and C.P. TIMMER (eds.) (2008) 'Rice Policy in Indonesia', Special Issue *Bulletin of Indonesian Economic Studies*, **44** (1).

MCEVEDY, C. and R. JONES (1978) *Atlas of World Population History*, Harmondsworth: Penguin.

MCGOWAN, P.J., (2003) 'African Military Coups d' État, 1956–2001: Frequency, Trends and Distribution' *Journal of Modern African Studies*, **41** (3), pp. 339–70.

MCGOWAN, P.J. and T. H. JOHNSON (1984) 'African Military Coups d'Etat and Under-Development: A Quantitative Historical Analysis', *Journal of Modern African Studies*, **22** (4), pp. 633–66.

MCKEOWN, T. (1976) *The Modern Rise of Population*, London: Arnold.

(1978) 'Fertility, Mortality and Causes of Death: An Examination of Issues Related to the Modern Rise of Population', *Population Studies*, **32** (3), pp. 535–42.

(1979) *The Role of Medicine*, Oxford: Basil Blackwell.

(1988) *The Origins of Human Disease*, Oxford: Basil Blackwell.

MCNEILL, W.H. (1976) *Plagues and Peoples*, Harmondsworth: Penguin.

(1989) 'European Expansion and Warfare since 1500', in: J.A. DE MOOR and H.L. WESSELING (eds.), *Imperialism and War*, London: Brill.

MCNICOLL, G. (1994) 'Institutional Analysis of Fertility', in: K. LINDAHL-KIESSLING and H. LANDBERG, *Population, Economic Development and the Environment*, Oxford/New York: Oxford University Press, pp. 199–230.

(2006) 'Policy Lessons of the East Asian Demographic Transition', *Population and Development Review*, **32** (1), pp. 1–25.

MCQUIRE, J.W. (2001) 'Social Policy and Mortality Decline in East Asia and Latin America', *World Development*, **29** (10), pp. 1673–97.

MEADOWS, D.H., D.L. MEADOWS, J. RANDERS and W.W. BEHRENS (1972) *Limits to Growth*, New York: Universe Books.

MEER, C.L.J. VAN DER (1981) *Rural Development in Northern Thailand*, Dissertation, Groningen.

(1983) 'Voedselvoorziening en Agrarische Ontwikkeling [Food Supply and Agricultural Development]', in: C.L.J. VAN DER MEER (ed.), *Landbouw en Ontwikkeling*, The Hague: VUGA, pp. 177–206.

MEER, C.L.J. VAN DER and S. YAMADA (1990) *Japanese Agriculture: An Economic Comparative Analysis*, London: Gower.

MEIER, G.M. (1968) *The International Economics of Development*, New York: Harper.

(1984) *Emerging from Poverty: The Economics that Really Matters*, New York: Oxford University Press.

(1989) 'The Old and New Export Pessimism: A Critical Survey', in: N. ISLAM (ed.), *The Balance between Industry and Agriculture in Economic Development: Factors Influencing Change*, Proceedings of the Eighth World Congress of the International Economic Association, Vol. 5, Basingstoke: Macmillan.

MEIER, G.M. and J.E. STIGLITZ (eds.) (2000) *Frontiers of Development Economics: The Future in Perspective*, Washington, DC: World Bank/New York: Oxford University Press.

MEKASHA, T.J. and F. TARP (2013) 'Aid and Growth: What Meta-Analysis Reveals', *Journal of Development Studies*, **49** (4), pp. 564–83.

MELLOR, J.W. (1966) *The Economics of Agricultural Development*, Ithaca, NY: Cornell University Press.

(1976) *The New Economics of Growth*, Ithaca, NY: Cornell University Press.

MELTZER, A. (2000) *Report of the International Financial Institutions Advisory Commission*, Washington DC, International Financial Institutions Advisory Committee, March.

MENDE, T. (1973) *From Aid to Recolonisation: Lessons of a Failure*, London: Harrap.

MENSHIKOV, S. (1993) 'The Socialist Experiment and Transition towards the Market', in: A. SZIRMAI, B. VAN ARK and D. PILAT (eds.), *Explaining Economic Growth. Essays in Honour of Angus Maddison*, Amsterdam: North-Holland, pp. 467–84.

MICHALOPOULOS, S. and E. PAPAIOANNOU (2012) *Pre-Colonial Ethnic Institutions and Contemporary African Development*, London Business School, NBER and CEPR, July 16.

MILANOVIC, B. (1999) *True World Income Distribution, 1988 and 1993: First Calculation Based on Household Surveys Alone*, Washington, DC: World Bank, Development Research Group, October.

(2005) *Worlds Apart: Measuring International and Global Inequality*, Princeton, NJ/ Oxford: Oxford University Press.

MILIBAND, R. (1969) *The State in Capitalist Society*, New York: Basic Books.

MILLIKAN, M.F. and W.E. ROSTOW (1957) *A Proposal: A Key to Effective Foreign Policy*, New York: Harper & Row.

MINCER, J. (1970) 'The Distribution of Labor Incomes: A Survey with Special Reference to the Human Capital Approach', *Journal of Economic Literature*, **8** (1), pp. 1–26.

(1974) *Schooling, Earnings and Experience*, New York: Columbia University Press.

MINISTRY OF EDUCATION, REPUBLIC OF CHINA (TAIWAN) (2013) *Education Statistics*, http:// english.moe.gov.tw/ct.asp?xItem=7444&ctNode=1184&mp=1, downloaded January.

MIRZA, B. and A. SZIRMAI (2010) *Towards a New Measure of the Energy Poverty: A Cross Community Analysis of Rural Pakistan*, UNU-MERIT Working Paper Series 2010–024.

MISHAN, E.J. (1967) *The Costs of Economic Growth*, New York: Praeger.

MITCH, D. (1990) 'Education and Economic Growth', in: G. TORTELLA, *Education and Economic Development Since the Industrial Revolution*, València: Generalitat Valenciana.

MITCHELL, B.R. (1982) *International Historical Statistics: The Americas and Australasia*, London: Macmillan.

MITCHELL, D.O., M.D. INGCO and R.C. DUNCAN (1997) *The World Food Outlook*, Cambridge University Press.

MOKYR, J. (1990) *The Lever of Riches: Technological Creativity and Economic Progress*, New York: Oxford University Press.

MOORE, B., JR. (1967) *Social Origins of Dictatorship and Democracy: Lord and Peasant in the Making of the Modern World*, Harmondsworth: Penguin.

MOORE, W.E. (1963) *Social Change*, Englewood Cliffs, NJ: Prentice Hall.

MORRIS-JONES, W.H. and G. FISCHER (1980) *Decolonisation and After: The British and French Experience*, London: Frank Cass.

MORRISSEY, O. and I. FILATOTCHEV (2001) 'Globalisation and Trade: The Implications for Exports from Marginalised Economies', in: O. MORRISSEY and I. FILATOTCHEV (eds.),

Globalisation and Trade: Implications for Exports from Marginalised Economies, London: Frank Cass, pp. 1–12.

MORRISSON C. and F. MURTIN (2009), *The Century of Education*, CEP Discussion Paper No. 934, LSE, June.

MOSCHINI, G. and D.A. HENNESSY (2001) 'Uncertainty, Risk Aversion and Risk Management for Agricultural Producers', in: B.L. GARDNER. and G.C. RAUSSER (eds.), *Handbook of Agricultural Economics, Vol. 1A; Agricultural Production*, Chapter 2, Amsterdam: North-Holland, pp. 87–153.

MOSLEY, P. (1980) 'Aid, Savings and Growth Revisited', *Oxford Bulletin of Economics and Statistics*, **42** (2), pp. 79–95.

(1987) *Overseas Aid: Its Defence and Reform*, Brighton: Wheatsheaf Books.

(1991) 'Structural Adjustment: A General Overview 1980–89', in: V.N. BALASUBRAMANYAM and S. LALL (eds.), *Current Issues in Development Economics*, London: Macmillan.

MOSLEY, P., J. HARRIGAN and J. TOYE (1991) *Aid and Power: The World Bank and Policy Based Lending, Vol. 1, Analysis and Policy Proposals, Vol. 2, Case Studies*, London: Routledge.

MOSLEY, P., T. SUBASAT and J. WEEKS (1995) 'Assessing Adjustment in Africa', *World Development*, **23** (9), pp. 1459–73.

MOSLEY, P. and J. WEEKS (1992) *Has Recovery Begun? Africa's Adjustment in the 1980s Revisited*, Department of Economics, School of Oriental and African Studies, Working Paper No. 29, November.

MOSLEY, W.H. (1983) 'Primary Care: Rhetoric and Reality', *Populi*, **10** (3), pp. 41–54.

(1984) 'Child Survival: Research and Policy', *Population and Development Review*, **10**, Supplement, pp. 3–23.

(1985a) 'Biological and Socio-Economic Determinants of Child Survival: A Proximate Determinants Framework Integrating Fertility and Mortality Variables', in: *Congrès International de la Population, Florence* 1985, Liège: Ordina Editions, pp. 189–208.

(1985b) 'Will Primary Healthcare Reduce Infant and Child Mortality? A Critique of Some Current Strategies, with Special Reference to Africa and Asia', in: J. VALLIN and A.D. LOPEZ (eds.), *Health Policy, Social Policy and Mortality Prospects*, Liège: Ordina Editions, pp. 103–38.

MOYO, D. (2009) *Dead Aid: Why Aid is Not Working and How There is a Better Way for Africa*, New York: Farrar, Strauss Giroux.

MURPHY, K., A. SHLEIFER and R. VISHNY (1991) 'The Allocation of Talent: Implications for Growth', *Quarterly Journal of Economics*, **106** (2), pp. 503–30.

MURRAY, C.J.L. and A. K. ACHARYA (1997) 'Understanding DALYs', *Journal of Health Economics*, **16** (6), pp. 703–30.

MURRAY, C.J.L. and A.D. LOPEZ (1996) *The Global Burden of Disease: A Comprehensive Assessment of Mortality and Disability from Diseases, Injuries and Risk Factors in 1990 and Projected to 2020*, Cambridge, MA: Harvard University Press.

MUSHKIN, S. (1962) 'Health as an Investment', *Journal of Political Economy*, **LXX** (5), pp. 129–57.

MYERS, N. (1989) *Deforestation Rates in Tropical Forests and their Climatic Implications*, London: Friends of the Earth.

MYERS, R.H. and M.R. PEATTIE (1984) *The Japanese Colonial Empire, 1895–1945*, Princeton University Press.

MYINT, H. (1959) 'The "Classical Theory" of International Trade and the Underdeveloped Countries', *Economic Journal*, **68** (270), pp. 317–37.

(1975) 'Agriculture and Economic Development in the Open Economy', in: L.G. REYNOLDS (ed.), *Agriculture in Development* Theory, New Haven, CT: Yale University Press.

(1980) *The Economics of the Developing Countries*, 5th edn, London: Hutchinson.

MYRDAL, G. (1957) *Economic Theory and Underdeveloped Regions*, London: Duckworth.

(1968) *Asian Drama: An Inquiry into the Poverty of Nations*, Harmondsworth: Penguin.

(1971) *The Challenge of World Poverty*, New York: Vintage Books.

NADIRI, M. (1972) 'International Studies of Factor Inputs and Total Factor Productivity. A Brief Survey', *Review of Income and Wealth*, **18** (2), pp. 129–54.

NAIK, J.P. (1975) *Equality, Quality and Quantity: The Elusive Triangle in Indian Education*, Bombay: Allied Publishers.

NAIKEN, L. (1998) 'On Certain Statistical Issues Arising from the Use of Energy Requirements in Estimating the Prevalence of Energy Inadequacy (Undernutrition)', *Journal of Indian, Social and, Agricultural Statistics*, **51** (2 & 3), pp. 113–28.

NARULA, R. (2013) *Exploring the Paradox of Competence-Creating Subsidiaries: Balancing Bandwidth and Dispersion in MNEs*, UNU-MERIT Working Paper Series 2013–046.

NARULA, R. and T.P. KODIYAT (2013) *The Growth of Outward FDI and the Competitiveness of the Underlying Economy: The Case of India`*, UNU-MERIT Working Paper Series 2013–042.

NARULA, R. and S. LALL (eds.) (2006) *Understanding FDI-Assisted Economic Development*, Oxford: Routledge.

NATIONAL STATISTICS OF TAIWAN, REPUBLIC OF CHINA (2001) *Social Indicators 2001*, www.stat.gov.tw/main.htm.

NATZIOS, A. (1999) *The Politics of Famine in North Korea*, Special Report, Washington, DC: United States Institute of Peace, www.usip.org.

NAUDÉ, W. (2007) *Geography and Development in Africa: Overview and Implications for Regional Cooperation,* UNU-WIDER, Discussion Paper. 2007/03.

(2010) 'Entrepreneurship is Not a Binding Constraint on Growth and Development in the Poorest Countries', *World Development*, **39** (1), pp. 33–44.

(2012) 'Climate Change and Industrial Policy', in: A. SZIRMAI, W. NAUDÉ and A. ALCORTA (eds.), *Pathways to Industrialization in the 21ˢᵗ Century: New Challenges and Emerging Paradigms*, Oxford University Press, 271–92.

NAUDÉ, W. and A. SZIRMAI (2012) *The Importance of Manufacturing in Economic Development: Past, Present and Future Perspectives*, UNU-MERIT, Working Paper Series, 2012–41.

(2013) *Industrial Policy for Development*, Policy Brief, No. 2, United Nations University.

NAUDÉ, W., A. SZIRMAI and N. HARAGUCHI (eds.) (2015) *Structural Change and Industrial Development in the BRICS*, Oxford University Press, forthcoming.

NAUDÉ, W., A. SZIRMAI and A. LAVOPA (2013). *Industrialization Lessons from BRICS: A Comparative Analysis*, IZA Discussion Papers 7543, Institute for the Study of Labor.

NBS (2000) *China Statistical Yearbook 2000*, National Bureau of Statistics, Beijing.

NDULU, B. and S.A. O'CONNELL (1999) 'Governance and Growth in Sub-Saharan Africa', *Journal of Economic Perspectives*, **13** (3), pp. 41–66.

NEEDHAM, J. *et al.* (1954) *Science and Civilisation in China*, Cambridge University Press.

NEHRU, V.E., A. SWANSON and A. DUBEY (1995) 'A New Database on Human Capital Stock in Developing and Industrial Countries: Sources, Methodology and Results', *Journal of Development Economics*, **46**, pp. 379–401.

NELSON, R. (1956) 'A Theory of the Low-Level Equilibrium Trap in Underdeveloped Economics', *American Economic Review, 46* (5), pp. 894–908.

(1981) 'Research on Productivity Growth and Productivity Differences: Dead Ends and New Departures', *Journal of Economic Literature*, **XIX**, pp. 1029–64, Reprinted in R. NELSON, *The Sources of Economic Growth*, Cambridge, MA: Harvard University Press, 1996.

(ed.) (1993) *National Innovation systems: A Comparative Analysis*, Oxford University Press.

(1996) *The Sources of Economic Growth*, Cambridge, MA: Harvard University Press.

NELSON, R.R. and E.S. PHELPS (1966) 'Investment in Humans, Technological Diffusion and Economic Growth', *American Economic Review*, **56** (2), 69–75.

NELSON, R.R. and S. WINTER (1982) *An Evolutionary Theory of Economic Change*, Cambridge, MA: Harvard University Press.

NERFIN, M. (1985) 'The Future of the United Nations System: Some Questions on the Occasion of an Anniversary', *Development Dialogue*, **1**, pp. 1–23.

NETHERLANDS DEVELOPMENT COOPERATION (1988) *Primary Healthcare: Evaluation of Dutch-Supported Activities in the Field of Extramural Healthcare since 1975*, The Hague: Ministry of Foreign Affairs, DGIS.

NETTLE, D. (2000) 'Linguistic Fragmentation and the Wealth of Nations: The Fishman–Pool Hypothesis Reexamined', *Economic Development and Cultural Change*, **48** (2), pp. 335–48.

NEUMAYER, E. (2002) 'Is Good Governance Rewarded? A Cross-National Analysis of Debt Forgiveness', *World Development*, **30** (6), pp. 913–30.

NICHOLAS, S. (1990) 'Literacy and the Industrial Revolution', in: G. TORTELLA (ed.), *Education and Economic Development since the Industrial Revolution*, València: Generalitat Valenciana.

NICHOLLS, W.H. (1964) 'The Place of Agriculture in Economic Development', in: C.K. EICHER and L.W. DE WITT (eds.), *Agriculture in Development*, New York: McGraw Hill, pp. 11–44.

NORDHAUS, W.D. (1969) *Invention, Growth and Welfare*, Cambridge MA: MIT Press.

(2007) 'A Review of the Stern Review on the Economics of Climate Change', *Journal of Economic Literature*, **45** (3), pp. 686–702.

NORREN, B. VAN and H.A.W. VAN VIANEN (1986) *The Malnutrition–Infections Syndrome and its Demographic Outcome in Developing Countries*, Programming Committee for Demographic Research, Publication No. 4, The Hague.

NORTH, DC. (1990) *Institutions, Institutional Change and Economic Performance*, Cambridge University Press.

(1993) 'The Ultimate Causes of Growth', in: A. SZIRMAI, B. VAN ARK and D. PILAT (eds.), *Explaining Economic Growth: Essays in Honour of Angus Maddison*, Amsterdam: North-Holland, pp. 65–75.

(2005) *Understanding the Process of Economic Change*, Princeton University Press.

NORTH, DC. and R.P. THOMAS (1973) *The Rise of the Western World: A New Economic History*, Cambridge University Press, pp. 65–76.

NORTH, DC., J. WALLIS and B. WEINGAST (2009) *Violence and Social Orders: A Conceptual Framework for Interpreting Recorded Human History*, New York: Cambridge University Press.

NORTH, DC., J.J. WALLIS, S.B. WEBB and B.R. WEINGAST (eds.) (2013) *In the Shadow of Violence. Politics, Economics, and the Problems of Development*, Cambridge University Press.

NUÑEZ, C. (1990) 'Literacy and Economic Growth in Spain, 1860–1977', in: G. TORTELLA (ed.), *Education and Economic Development Since the Industrial Revolution*, València: Generalitat Valenciana.

NURKSE, R. (1953) *Problems of Capital Formation in Underdeveloped Countries*, New York: Oxford University Press.

(1962) *Patterns of Trade and Development* (The 1959 Wicksell Lectures) Oxford: Basil Blackwell.

NYANG, S.S. (1994) 'The Cultural Consequences of Development in Africa', in: I. SERAGELDIN and J. TABOROFF (eds.), *Culture and Development in Africa*, Washington, DC: World Bank, pp. 429–46.

OASA, E.K. (1987) 'The Political Economy of International Agricultural Research: A Review of CGIAR's Response to Criticisms of the "Green Revolution"' in: B. GLAESER (ed.), *The Green Revolution Revisited. Critique and Alternatives*, London: Allen & Unwin, pp. 13–55.

OCAMPO, J.A., C. RADA and L. TAYLOR (2009) *Growth and Policy in Developing Countries. A Structuralist Approach*, New York: Columbia University Press.

O'CONNELL, S.E. and CH.C. SOLUDO (2001) 'Aid Intensity in Africa', *World Development*, **29** (9), pp. 1527–52.

O'CONNOR, J. (1973) *The Fiscal Crisis of the State*, New York: St. Martin's Press.

O'DONNELL, G. (1979) *Modernization and Bureaucratic-Authoritarianism in South American Politics*, Berkeley, CA: University of California Press.

OECD (1971) *National Accounts, 1950–1968*, microfiche edition.

(1979) *The Impact of the New Industrializing Countries*, Paris.

(1985) *Twenty Five Years of Development Cooperation: A Review*, Paris.

(1986) *Financing and External Debt of Developing Countries 1985*, Paris.

(1993a) *Financing and External Debt of Developing Countries 1992*, Paris.

(1993b) *Development Cooperation 1992*, Paris.

(1994) *Development Cooperation 1994*, Paris.

(1995) *Geographical Distribution of Financial Flows to Developing Countries 1989–1993*, Paris, and various earlier issues.

(1998a) *Science, Technology and Industry Outlook 1998*, Paris.

(1998b) *Development Cooperation 1997*, Paris.

(2000) *Development Cooperation 1999*, Paris.

(2002) *Main Economic Indicators*, database, www.oecd.org/EN/document/0, EN-document-7-nodirectorate-no-1–5194-7,00.html.

(2002) *Frascati Manual. Proposed Standard Practice for Surveys on Research and Experimental Design*, 6th edn, Paris.

(2003a) Development Assistance Committee, *Geographical Distribution of Financial Flows to Aid Recipients, 1960–2001*, CD-ROM, International Development Statistics (IDS).

(2003b) Development Assistance Committee, *Development Cooperation Report 2002, Statistical Annex*, CD-ROM, International Development Statistics (IDS).

(2003c) *CD-ROM, International Development Statistics (IDS)*.

(2005) *Oslo Manual. Guidelines for Collecting and Interpreting Innovation Data*, 3rd edn, Paris.

(2006) *International Migration Statistics Database*, http://titania.sourceoecd.org/vl=1127050/cl=18/nw=1/rpsv/ij/oecdstats/16081269/v225n1/s19/p1.

(2009) *International Migration Statistics Database, Database on Immigrants in OECD Countries: Immigrants by Citizenship and Age Vol 2009 release 01*, http://lysander.sourceoecd.org/vl=7305805/cl=49/nw=1/rpsv/ij/oecdstats/16081269/v225n1/s1/p1.

(2009) *Programme for International Student Assessment*, www.oecd.org/pisa/.

(VARIOUS VOLUMES) *National Accounts, Paris*.

(2014) *International Development Statistics*, OECD. Statextracts, http://stats.oecd.org/#.

OHKAWA, K. and H. ROSOVSKY (1964) 'The Role of Agriculture in Modern Japanese Economic Development', in: C. EICHER and L.W. DE WITT (eds.), *Agriculture in Development*, New York: McGraw Hill, pp. 45–68.

OLDEMAN, L.R., V.W.P VAN ENGELEN and J.H.M. PULLES (1990) 'The Extent of Human-Induced Soil Degradation', in: L.R. OLDEMAN, R.T.A. HAKKELING and W.G. SOMBROEK, *World Map of the Status of Human-Induced Soil Degradation: An Explanatory Note*, 2nd rev. edn, Wageningen: International Soil Reference Centre.

OLSON, M. (1965) *The Logic of Collective Action*, Cambridge, MA: Harvard University Press.

(1982) *The Rise and Decline of Nations*, New Haven, CT/London: Yale University Press.

OMRAN, A.R. (1971) 'The Epidemiologic Transition: A Theory of the Epidemiology of Population Change', *Millbank Memorial Fund Quarterly*, **49** (4), pp. 509–38.

O'NEILL, J. (2001) *Building Better Global Economic BRICs*, Global Economics Paper No. 66, Goldman Sachs & Co.

OOIJENS, J. and P. VAN KAMPEN (1989) *Analfabetisme en alfabetisering in Latijns Amerika en het Caribisch gebied [Illiteracy and Literacy Education in Latin America and the Caribbean]*, CESO, Verhandelingen, No. 46, December, The Hague.

OTSUKA, K., G. RANIS and G. SAXONHOUSE (1988) *Comparative Technology Choice in Development*, London: Macmillan.

PAARLBERG, R.L. (2001) *The Politics of Precaution: Genetically Modified Crops in Developing Countries*, Baltimore, MD: Johns Hopkins University Press.

(2008) *Starved for Science: How Biotechnology is Being Kept out of Africa*, Cambridge, MA: Harvard University Press.

(2010) Food Politics: What Everyone Needs to Know, New York: Oxford University Press, 2010.

PACK, H. (1987) *Productivity, Technology and Industrial Development*, New York: Oxford University Press.

(1988) 'Industrialization and Trade', in: H. CHENERY and T.N. SRINIVASAN, *Handbook of Development Economics*, Vol. I, Chapter 9, Amsterdam: North-Holland, pp. 334–80.

(1994) 'Endogenous Growth Theory: Intellectual Appeal and Empirical Shortcomings', *Journal of Economic Perspectives*, **8** (1), pp. 55–72.

PACK, H. and J.R. PACK (1993) 'Foreign Aid and the Question of Fungibility', *Review of Economics and Statistics*, **75** (2), pp. 258–65.

PACK, H. and C. PAXSON (2001) 'Is African Manufacturing Skill Constrained?', in: A. SZIRMAI and P. LAPPERRE (eds.), *The Industrial Experience of Tanzania*, Basingstoke: Palgrave, pp. 50–72.

PAGE, J. (2013) 'Should Africa Industrialise', in: A. SZIRMAI, W. NAUDÉ and L. ALCORTA (eds.) (2013), *Pathways to Industrialisation in the 21st Century: New Challenges and Emerging Paradigms*, Oxford University Press, pp. 244–67.

PALMA, J.G (2011) 'Homogeneous Middles vs. Heterogeneous Tails, and The End of the "Inverted-U": It's All about the Share of the Rich', *Development and Change* **42**, pp. 87–153.

PALMER, R.R and J. COLTON (1978) *A History of the Modern World*, 5th edn, New York: Knopf.

PAPAIOANNOU, E. and G. SIOUROUNIS (2008) 'Democratisation and Growth', *Economic Journal*, **118** (532), pp. 1520–51.

PAPANEK, G.F. (1983) 'Aid, Equity and Growth in South Asia', in: J. PARKINSON (ed.), *Poverty and Aid*, Oxford: Blackwell.

(1972) 'The Effect of Aid and Other Resource Transfers on Savings and Growth in Less Developed Countries', *The Economic Journal*, **82** (327), pp. 934–50.

(1973) 'Aid, Foreign Private Investment, Saving and Growth in Less Developed Countries', *The Journal of Political Economy*, **81** (1), pp. 120–30.

PARAYIL, G. (1992) 'The Green Revolution in India: A Case Study of Technological Change', *Technology and Culture*, **33** (4), pp. 737–56.

PATRINOS, H.A and G. PSACHAROPOULOS (2011) *Education. Past, Present and Future Challenges*, Policy Research Working Paper 5616, Washington, DC: World Bank, March.

PATTERSON, O. (2000) 'Taking Culture Seriously: A Framework and an Afro-American Illustration', in: L.E. HARRISON and S.P. HUNTINGTON (eds.), *Culture Matters: How Values Shape Human Progress*, New York: Basic Books, pp. 202–18.

PAUKERT, F. (1973) 'Income Distribution at Different Levels of Development: A Survey of the Evidence', *International Labour Review*, **108**, pp. 97–125.

PAVITT, K. (ed.) (1980) *Technical Innovation and British Economic Performance*, London: Macmillan.

PEACOCK, A. and D. DOSSER (1958) *The National Income of Tanganyika, 1952–54*, London: Her Majesty's Stationery Office.

PEARSE, A. (1977) 'Technology and Peasant Production: Reflections on a Global Study, *Development and Change*, **8** (2), pp. 125–59.

PENN WORLD TABLES, www.bized.ac.uk/dataserv/penndata/pennhome.htm.

PERES, W. (2013) 'Industrial Policies in Latin America', in: A. SZIRMAI, W. NAUDÉ and L. ALCORTA (eds.) (2013), *Pathways to Industrialisation in the 21st Century: New Challenges and Emerging Paradigms*, Oxford University Press, pp. 223–43.

PEREZ, C. (2008) *A Vision for Latin America: A Resource-Based Strategy for Technological Dynamism and Social Inclusion*, Globelics, Working Paper Series, No. 08-4, www.globelics.org/publication/a-vision-for-latin-america-a-resource-based-strategy-for-technological-dynamism-and-social-inclusion/.

(2010) 'Technological Dynamism and Social Inclusion in Latin America: A Resource-Based Production Development Strategy', *CEPAL Review*, **100**, pp. 121–41.

PEREZ, C. and L.L. SOETE (1988) 'Catching up in Technology: Entry Barriers and Windows of Opportunity', in: G. DOSI, C. FREEMAN, R.R. NELSON, G. SILVERBERG and L.L. SOETE (eds.), *Technical Change and Economic Theory*, London: Pinter, pp. 458–79.

PERKINS, D.H. (1969) *Agricultural Development in China 1368–1968*, Chicago IL: Aldine.

(2000) 'Law, Family Ties and the East Asian Way of Business', in: L.E. HARRISON and S.P. HUNTINGTON (eds.), *Culture Matters: How Values Shape Human Progress*, New York: Basic Books, pp. 232–43.

PERRATON, H.D. (2000) *Open and Distance Learning in the Developing World*, London: Routledge.

PERSSON, T. and G. TABELLINI (1994) 'Is Inequality Harmful for Growth? Theory and Evidence', *American Economic Review*, **84** (3), pp. 600–21.

PHILIP, G. (1985) 'Military Rule in South America: The Dilemmas of Authoritarianism', in: C. CLAPHAM and G. PHILIP (eds.), *The Political Dilemma's of Military Regimes*, London: Croom Helm.

PILAT, D. (1994) *The Economics of Rapid Growth: The Experience of Japan and Korea*, Aldershot: Edward Elgar.

PINSTRUP-ANDERSON, P. (1982) *Agricultural Research and Technology in Economic Development*, London/New York: Longman.

PINSTRUP-ANDERSON, P. and P.B.R. HAZELL (1985) 'The Impact of the Green Revolution and Prospects for the Future', *Food Review International*, **I** (1), pp. 1–25.

PLACE, F. (2009) 'Land Tenure and Agricultural Productivity in Africa: A Comparative Analysis of the Economics Literature and Recent Policy Strategies and Reforms', *World Development*, **37** (8), pp. 1326–36.

PLATTEAU, J.PH. (2008) 'Religion, Politics, and Development: Lessons from the Lands of Islam', *Journal of Economic Behavior & Organization*, **68** (2), pp. 329–51.

(2009) 'Institutional Obstacles to African Economic Development: State, Ethnicity and Custom', *Journal of Economic Behavior and Organization*, **71** (3), pp. 669–89.

PLATTEAU, J.PH. and R. PECCOUD (eds.) (2011) *Culture, Institutions, and Development: New Insights into an Old Debate*, London/New York: Routledge Studies in Development Economics.

PLATTNER, S. (ed.) (1989) *Economic Anthropology*, Stanford University Press.

POLITY IV (2013) *Political Regime Characteristics and Transitions, 1800–2013*, Center for Systemic Peace, www.systemicpeace.org/inscrdata.html, downloaded 2013.

POLLARD, S. (1990) *Typology of Industrialization Processes in the Nineteenth Century*, Chor: Harwood Academic Publishers.

POLYANI, K. (1957) *The Great Transformation*, Boston, MA: Beacon Press.

POMERANZ, K. (2000) *The Great Divergence*, Princeton University Press.

POMFRET, R. (2000) 'Agrarian Reform in Uzbekistan. Why the Chinese Model has Failed to Deliver?', *Economic Development and Cultural Change*, **48** (2), pp. 269–84.

POPKIN, B.M. (1978) 'Nutrition and Labor Productivity', *Social Science and Medicine*, **12C** (3/4), pp. 117–25.

POPKIN, S.L. (1979) *The Rational Peasant: The Political Economy of Rural Society in Vietnam*, Berkeley, CA: University of California Press.

PORTELLI, B. (2006) *Foreign Dierect Investment and Industrial Development. Backward Linkages and Knowledge Transfer in Tanzania*, PhD thesis, University of Oslo.

PORTER, M.E. (1990) *The Competitive Advantage of Nations*, New York: Free Press.

POULANTZAS, N. (1974) 'Internationalisation of Capitalist Relations and the Nation-State', *Economy and Society*, **3** (2), pp. 145–79.

PRAHALAD, P.K (2006) *The Fortune at the Bottom of the Pyramid*, Upper Saddle River, NJ: Prentice Hall.

PREBISCH, R. (1950) *The Economic Development of Latin America and its Principal Problems*, UN, Department of Economic Affairs, New York: United Nations.

PREKER, A., E. BOS, J. WANG, J. PEABODY and D.T. JAMISON (1999) *Measuring Country Performance on Health: Selected Indicators for 115 countries*, Washington, DC: World Bank.

PRESTON, S.H. (1975) 'The Changing Relation between Mortality and Level of Economic Development', *Population Studies*, **29** (2), pp. 231–48.

(1976) *Mortality Patterns in National Populations*, New York: Academic Press.

(1980) 'Causes and Consequences of Mortality Declines in Less Developed Countries in the 20th Century', in: R.A. EASTERLIN (ed.), *Population and Economic Change in Developing Countries*, University of Chicago Press, pp. 289–341.

PRINCE, G.H.A. (1976) 'Ontwikkelingssamenwerking; als voortzetting van koloniaal beleid [Development Cooperation as a Continuation of Colonial Policies]', *Internationale Spectator*, **XXX** (3), pp. 173–80.

PRINS, I.M. and A. SZIRMAI (1998) *A Reconstruction of GDP and Employment in Tanzanian Manufacturing, 1961–1995*, Report to the Tanzanian Bureau of Statistics, Eindhoven, January.

PRITCHETT, L. (1994) 'Derived Fertility and the Impact of Population Policies', *Population and Development Review*, **20** (3), pp. 1–55.

(2001) 'Where has All the Education Gone?', *World Bank Economic Review*, **15** (3), pp. 367–93.

(2006) 'Does Learning to Add Up Add Up? The Returns to Schooling in Aggregate Data', in: E.A. HANUSHEK and F. WELCH (eds.), *Handbook of the Economics of Education*, Amsterdam: North-Holland, pp. 635–95.

PSACHAROPOULOS, G. (1985) 'Returns to Education: A Further International Update and Implications', *Journal of Human Resources*, **20** (4), pp. 583–604.

(1989) 'Why Education Reforms Fail: A Comparative Analysis', *International Review of Education*, **35** (2), pp. 179–95.

(1993) *Returns to Investment in Education: A Global Update*, World Bank, Policy Research Working Papers in Education and Development, WPS 1067, Washington, DC: World Bank.

PSACHAROPOULOS, G. and A.M. ARRIAGADA (1986) 'The Educational Composition of the Labour Force', *International Labour Review*, **125** (5), pp. 561–74.

(1992) 'The Educational Composition of the Labor Force: An International Update', *Journal of Educational Planning and Administration*, **6** (2), pp. 141–59.

PSACHAROPOULOS G. and H.A. PATRINOS (2002) *Returns to Investment in Education: A Further Update*, World Bank Policy Research Working Paper, 2881, Washington, DC: World Bank, September.

PUTNAM, R.D., R. LEONARDI and R.Y. NANETTI (1993) *Making Democracy Work: Civic Traditions in Modern Italy*, Princeton University Press.

—— (1994) 'Democracy, Development and the Civic Community: Evidence from an Italian Experiment', in: I. SERAGELDIN and J. TABOROFF (eds.), *Culture and Development in Africa, Washington*, DC: World Bank, pp. 33–73.

PUTTERMAN, L. and D. WEIL (2010) 'Post-1500 Population Flows and the Long Run Determinants of Economic Growth and Inequality', *Quarterly Journal of Economics*, **125** (4), pp. 1627–82

PYE, L. (2000) 'Asian Values: From Dynamos to Dominoes', in: L.E. HARRISON and S. P. HUNTINGTON (eds.), *Culture Matters: How Values Shape Human Progress*, New York: Basic Books, pp. 244–54.

QIAN, Y. (2003) 'How Reform Worked in China', in: D. RODRIK (ed.), *In Search of Prosperity. Analytic Narratives on Economic Growth*, Princeton University Press, pp. 297–333.

QUARLES VAN UFFORD, P., D. KRUIJT and T. DOWNING (eds.) (1988) *The Hidden Crisis in Development: Development Bureaucracies*, Amsterdam: Free University Press.

RADELET, S., M. CLEMENS and R. BHAVNANI (2004) *Aid and Growth: The Current Debate and Some New Evidence*, London: Center for Global Development, February.

RAFFER, K. and H.W. SINGER (2001) *The Economic North–South Divide: Six Decades of Unequal Development*, Cheltenham: Edward Elgar.

RAJAN, R.G. and A. SUBRAMANIAN (2008) 'Aid and Growth: What Does the Cross-Country Evidence Really Show?', *The Review of Economics and Statistics*, **90** (4), pp. 643–65.

RAJAN, R.G. and A. SUBRAMANIAN (2011) 'Aid, Dutch Disease, and Manufacturing Growth', *Journal of Development Economics*, **94** (1), pp. 106–18.

RAMANI, S.V. (2009) MDG: 'What Why and Where with Respect to India', Presentation for the 7th Globelics conference, Dakar, 6–8 October.

RAMANI, S.V and A. THUTUPALLI (2013) *Emergence of Controversy in Technology Transitions: Green Revolution and Bt Cotton in India*, Paper prepared for the 11th Globelics International Conference, METU, Ankara, Turkey, 11–13 September.

RAMANI, S.V. and A. SZIRMAI (2014) 'Innovation in India: The Challenge of Combining Economic Growth with Inclusive Development', in: S.V. RAMANI (ed.), *Innovation in India: Economic Growth with Inclusive Development*, New Delhi: Cambridge University Press, pp. 1–33.

RANA, P.B. and J.M. DOWLING (1988) 'The Impact of Foreign Capital on Growth: Evidence from Asian Developing Countries', *The Developing Economies*, **XXVI** (1), pp. 3–11.

—— (1990) 'Foreign Capital and Asian Economic Growth', *Asian Development Review*, **8** (2), pp. 77–102.

RANIS, G. (1988) 'Analytics of Development', in: H. CHENERY and T.N. SRINIVASAN (eds.), *Handbook of Development Economics*, Vol. I, Amsterdam: North-Holland.

—— (1989) 'Macro-Policies, the Terms of Trade and the Spatial Dimension of Balanced Growth', in: N. ISLAM (ed.), *The Balance between Industry and Agriculture in Economic Development: Factors Influencing Change*, Proceedings of the Eighth World Congress of the International Economic Association, Vol. 5, Delhi: Macmillan.

RANIS, G., F. STEWART and A. RAMIREZ (2000) 'Economic Growth and Human Development', *World Development*, **28** (2), pp. 197–219.

RAO, V. (2001) 'Poverty and Public Celebrations in Rural India', in: C. CLAGUE and SH. GROSSBARD-SHECHTMAN (eds.), *Culture and Development: International Perspectives*,

Special Issue of the Annals of the American Academy of Political and Social Science, **573**, January, pp. 85–104.

RAUPACH, M.R, G. MARLAND, PH. CIAIS, C. LE QUÉRÉ, J.G. CANADELL, G. KLEPPER and CH. B. FIELD, (2007) *Global and Regional Drivers of Accelerating CO_2 Emissions: Proceedings National Academy of Sciences*, **104** (24), pp. 10288–93.

RAVALLION, M. (1997) 'Famines and Economics', *Journal of Economic Literature*, **XXXV**, pp. 1205–42.

(2001) 'Growth, Inequality and Poverty: Looking beyond Averages', *World Development*, **29** (11), pp. 1803–15.

RAWSKI, T.G. (1979) *Economic Growth and Employment in China*, Washington, DC: World Bank, New York/Oxford: Oxford University Press.

RAY, D. (2000) *Development Economics*, Princeton University Press.

REHER, D.S. (2011) 'Economic and Social Implications of the Demographic Transition', *Population and Development Review*, **37** (Supplement), pp. 11–33.

REVELLE, R. (1975) 'Will the Earth's Land and Water Resources Be Sufficient for Future Populations?', in: UN, *The Population Debate: Dimensions and Perspectives. Papers of the World Population Conference*, Bucharest, 1974, Vol. II, New York, pp. 3–14.

REYNOLDS, L.G. (1975) *Agriculture in Development Theory*, New Haven, CT: Yale University Press.

(1986) *Economic Growth in the Third World: An Introduction*, New Haven, CT: Yale University Press.

RICHARDSON, D. (1989) 'Slave Exports from West and West-Central Africa, 1700–1810: New Estimates of Volume and Distribution', *Journal of African History*, **30** (1), pp. 1–22.

RICKLEFS, M.C. (1981) *A History of Modern Indonesia*, London: Macmillan.

RIDDELL, R.C. (1987) *Foreign Aid Reconsidered*, Baltimore, MD/London: Johns Hopkins University Press/James Currey.

(1988) *Does Foreign Aid Really Work?*, Oxford University Press.

RIDDLE, D.I. (1986) *Service-Led Growth: The Role of the Service Sector in World Development*, New York: Praeger.

RIGHART, H. *et al.* (1991) *De trage revolutie: Over de wording van industriële samenlevingen [The Slow Revolution: On the Origin of Industrial Societies]*, Meppel en Amsterdam/Heerlen: Boom/Open Universiteit.

RIOS, A.R., and SHIVELY, G.E. (2005) *Farm Size and Nonparametric Efficiency Measurements for Coffee Farms in Vietnam*, Paper presented at the American Agricultural Economics Association Annual Meeting, Providence, RI.

RODRIK, D. (1995) 'Getting Interventions Right: How South Korea and Taiwan Grew Rich, *Economic Policy*, **20**, pp. 53–97.

(1999) *Making Openness Work: The New Global Economy and the Developing Countries*, Washington, DC: Overseas Development Council.

(2003a) 'Introduction', in: D. RODRIK (ed.), *In Search of Prosperity: Analytic Narratives on Economic Growth*, Princeton, NJ/Oxford: Princeton University Press, pp. 1–19.

(ed.) (2003b) *In Search of Prosperity: Analytic Narratives on Economic Growth*, Princeton, NJ/Oxford: Princeton University Press.

(2006) 'Goodbye Washington Consensus, Hello Washington Confusion? A Review of the World Bank's "Economic Growth in the 1990s: Learning from a Decade of Reform"', *Journal of Economic Literature*, **44** (4), pp. 973–87.

(2007) *One Economics, Many Recipes: Globalization, Institutions, and Economic Growth*, Princeton University Press.

(2008a) 'The Real Exchange Rate and Economic Growth', in *Brookings Papers on Economic Activity*, ed. D.W. ELMENDORF, N.G. MANKIW and L.H. SUMMERS, Washington, DC: Brookings Institution, pp. 365–412.

(2008b) *The New Development Economics: We Shall Experiment, but How Shall We Learn?*, Harvard Kennedy School, Faculty Research Working Papers Series, RWP08–055, October.

(2009) *Growth after the Crisis*, Centre for Economic Policy Research, Discussion Paper Series, No 7480, www.cepr.org/pubs/dps/DP7480.asp.

RODRIK, D., A. SUBRAMANIAN and F. TREBBI (2004) 'Institutions Rule: The Primacy of Institutions over Geography and Integration in Economic Development', *Journal of Economic Growth*, **9** (2), pp. 31–165.

ROMEIN, J. (1937) 'De dialectiek van de voorutgang: bijdrage tot het ontwikkelingsbegrip in de geschiedenis [The Dialectics of Progress. A Contribution to the Concept of Development in History]', in: J. ROMEIN, *Het onvoltooid verleden: cultuur-historische studies*, Amsterdam: Querido (first published 1935).

ROMER, P. (1986) 'Increasing Returns and Long-Run Growth', *Journal of Political Economy*, **94** (5), pp. 1002–37.

(1990) 'Endogenous Technological Change', *Journal of Political Economy*, **95** (5), pp. S71–102.

ROMIJN, H.A. (1997) 'Acquisition of Technological Capability in Development: A Quantitative Case Study of Pakistan's Capital Goods Sector', *World Development*, **25** (3), 359–77.

(1999) *Acquisition of Technological Capability in Small Firms in Developing Countries*, London/New York: Macmillan/St. Martin's Press.

ROOKS, G., A. SZIRMAI and A. SSERWANGA (2011) 'The Interplay of Human and Social Capital in Entrepreneurship in Developing Countries: The Case of Uganda', in: W. NAUDÉ (ed.), *Entrepreneurship and Development*, Basingstoke: Palgrave, pp. 609–36.

ROSE-ACKERMAN, S. (ed.) (2007) *International Handbook on the Economics of Corruption*, Cheltenham: Edward Elgar.

ROSENBERG, N. (1963a) 'Capital Goods, Technology, and Economic Growth', *Oxford Economic Papers*, pp. 217–27.

(1963b) 'Technological Change in the Machine Tool Industry, 1840–1910', *Journal of Economic History*, December, pp. 414–43.

(1982) *Inside the Black Box: Technology and Economics*, Cambridge University Press.

(1990) 'Science and Technology Policy for the Asian NICs: Lessons from Economic History', in: R.E. EVENSON and G. RANIS (eds.), *Science and Technology. Lessons for Development Policy*, Boulder, CO/San Francisco, CA: Westview Press, pp. 135–55.

ROSENSTEIN-RODAN, P. (1943) 'Problems of Industrialisation of East and South-East Europe', *Economic Journal*, June–September, pp. 201–11.

(1957) *Notes on the Theory of the 'Big Push'*, Cambridge, MA: MIT, CIS, March.

(1961) 'International Aid for Underdeveloped Countries', *Review of Economics and Statistics*, **43** (20), pp. 107–38.

ROSTOW, W.W. (1960) *The Stages of Economic Growth*, Cambridge University Press.

(ed.) (1965) *The Economics of Take-Off into Sustained Growth*, London: Macmillan.

(1971) *The Stages of Economic Growth*, 2nd edn, Cambridge University Press (first published 1960).

ROTH, D. (1993) 'Ontwikkelingshulp ter discussie: Kwaliteitsdecreet of kwaliteitsdebat? [Development Aid in Discussion: Quality Decree or Quality Debate]', *Internationale Spectator*, **47** (5), pp. 274–80.

ROUMASSET, J. (1976) *Rice and Risk: Decision-Making among Low-Income Farmers in Theory and Practice*, Amsterdam: North-Holland.

(1995) 'The Nature of the Agricultural Firm', *Journal of Economic Behaviour and Organization*, **26** (2), pp. 161–77.

(2002) *The Micro Economics of Agricultural Development in the Philippines*, Department of Economics, University of Hawaii, Working Paper 02–10, April.

RUBINSON, R. (1976) 'The World Economy and the Distribution of Income within States: A Cross National Study', *American Sociological Review*, **41** (4), August, pp. 638–59.

RUTTAN, V.W. (1989a) 'Improving the Quality of Life in Rural Areas', in: A.O. KRUEGER, C. MICHALOPOULOS and V. RUTTAN (eds.), *Aid and Development*, Baltimore, MD/London: Johns Hopkins University Press.

(1989b) 'Why Foreign Economic Assistance?', *Economic Development and Cultural Change*, **37** (2), pp. 411–24.

(2002) 'Productivity Growth in World Agriculture: Sources and Constraints', *Journal of Economic Perspectives*, **16** (4), pp. 161–84.

(2004) 'Controversy about Agricultural Technology. Lessons from the Green Revolution', *International Journal of Biotechnology*, **6** (1): 43–54.

SACHS, J. (2000) 'Notes on a New Sociology of Economic Development', in: L.E. HARRISON and S.P. HUNTINGTON (eds.), *Culture Matters: How Values Shape Human Progress*, New York: Basic Books, pp. 29–43.

(2005) *The End of Poverty: Economic Possibilities for Our Time*, New York: Penguin.

SACHS, J.D., J.W. MCARTHUR, G. SCHMIDT-TRAUB, M. KRUK, C. BAHADUR, M. FAYE and G. MCCORD (2004) 'Ending Africa's Poverty Trap', *Brookings Papers on Economic Activity*, **1**: 117–216.

SACHS, J.D. and R. RODRIGUEZ (1999) 'Why do Resource-Abundant Economies Growth More Slowly?', *Journal of Economic Growth*, **4**, pp. 227–303.

SACHS, J.D. and A. WARNER (1995) 'Economic Reform and the Process of Global Integration', *Brookings Papers on Economic Activity*, **1**, pp. 1–118.

(1997) *Natural Resources and Economic Growth*, rev. version, Center for International Development and Harvard Institute for International Development, Discussion Paper, Cambridge, MA: Harvard University.

(2001) 'Natural Resources and Economic Development: The Curse of Natural Resources', *European Economic Review*, **46** (4–6), pp. 827–38.

SACHS, J.D. and W.T. WOO (1997) 'Understanding China's Economic Performance', NBER Working Papers 5935, National Bureau of Economic Research.

(2000) 'Understanding China's Economic Performance', *Journal of Policy Reform*, **4** (1), pp. 1–50.

SALIM, S.A. (1994) 'Opening Remarks', in: I. SERAGELDIN and J. TABOROFF (eds.), *Culture and Development in Africa*, Washington, DC: World Bank, pp. 9–14.

SAMUELSON, P. and W.D. NORDHAUS (1989) *Economics*, 13th edn, New York: McGraw Hill.

SANDBERG, L.G. (1982) 'Ignorance, Poverty and Economic Backwardness in the Early Stages of European Industrialization: Variations on Alexander Gerschenkron's Grand Theme', *Journal of European Economic History*, **11** (3), pp. 675–98.

SANDBERG, L.G. (1990) 'Education and Economic Growth: Voices from Valencia', in: G. TORTELLA, (ed.), *Education and Economic Development Since the Industrial Revolution*, València: Generalitat Valenciana.

SANDBROOK, R. (1986) 'The State as an Obstacle to Development', *World Development*, **14** (3), pp. 309–22.

SANDBROOK, R. and J. BARKER (1985) *The Politics of Africa's Economic Stagnation*, Cambridge University Press.

SANFORD, J.E. (2002) 'World Bank: IDA Loans or IDA Grants', *World Development*, **30** (5), pp. 741–62.

SAPSFORD, D. (1985) 'The Statistical Debate on the Net Barter Terms of Trade between Primary Commodities and Manufactures: A Comment and Some Statistical Evidence', *The Economic Journal*, **95** (379), pp. 781–8.

(1988) 'The Debate over Trends in the Terms of Trade', in: D. GREENAWAY (ed.), *Economic Development and International Trade*, London: Macmillan, pp. 117–30.

SAPSFORD, D. and V.N. BALASUBRAMANYAM (2003) 'Globalization and the Terms of Trade: The Glass Ceiling Hypothesis', in: H. BLOCH (ed.), *Growth and Development in the Global Economy*, Cheltenham: Edward Elgar, pp. 157–69.

SAPSFORD, D. and H. SINGER (1998) 'The IMF, the World Bank and Commodity Prices: A Case of Shifting Sands?', *World Development*, **26** (9), pp. 1653–60.

SARKAR, P. (1986) 'The Singer-Prebisch Hypothesis: A Statistical Evaluation', *Cambridge Journal of Economics*, **10**, pp. 355–71.

(2001) 'The Long-Term Behaviour of the North–South Terms of Trade: A Review of the Statistical Debate', *Progress in Development Studies*, **1** (3), pp. 309–27.

SAVIOTTI, P.P. (1996) *Technological Evolution, Variety and the Economy*, Cheltenham: Edward Elgar.

SAVIOTTI, P.P. and A. PYKA (2009) 'Product Variety, Competition and Economic Growth', in: U. CANTNER, J.L. GAFFARD and L. NESTA (eds.), *Schumpeterian Perspectives on Innovation, Competition and Growth*, Heidelberg: Springer Berlin, pp. 71–95.

SCHAMA, S. (1988) *The Embarassment of Riches*, New York: Fontana Press.

SCHECH, S. and J. HAGGIS (2000) *Culture and Development: A Critical Introduction*, Oxford: Basil Blackwell.

SCHOENMAKERS, H. (1992) *Staatsvorming, Rurale Ontwikkeling en boeren in Guinée Bissau [State Formation, Rural Development and Peasants in Guinea Bissau]*, Dissertation, Catholic University Nijmegen.

SCHRAEDER, P., S. HOOK and B. TAYLOR (1998) 'Clarifying the Foreign Aid Puzzle: A Comparison of American, Japanese, French and Swedish Aid Flows', *World Politics*, **50** (2), pp. 294–320.

SCHRIJVER, N. (1985) 'De Verenigde Naties, de internationale economische organisaties en ontwikkelingssamenwerking [The United Nations, International Economic Organisations and Development Cooperation]', in: *Leergang Ontwikkelings-problematiek*, Groningen University.

SCHULTZ, T.P. (1997) 'Demand for Children in Low Income Countries', in: M. ROSENZWEIG and O. STARK (eds.), *Handbook of Population and Family Economics*, Amsterdam: North-Holland.

(2010) 'Population and Health Policies', in: D. RODRIK and M.R. ROSENZWEIG (eds.), *Handbook of Development Economics*, Vol. 5, Amsterdam: Elsevier, pp. 4785–881.

SCHULTZ, T.P. and A. TANSEL (1997) 'Wage and Labor Supply Effects of Illness in Côte d'Ivoire and Ghana', *Journal of Development Economics*, **53** (2), pp. 251–86.

SCHULTZ, T.W. (1953) *The Economic Organisation of Agriculture*, New York: McGraw Hill.

(1961) 'Investment in Human Capital', *American Economic Review*, **51**, pp. 17 ff.

(1964) *Transforming Traditional Agriculture*, New Haven, CT/London: Yale University Press.

(1968) *Economic Growth and Agriculture*, New York: McGrawHill.

(1971) *Investment in Human Capital: The Role of Education and Research*, New York: Free Press.

(1978) 'On Economics and Politics of Agriculture', in: T.W. SCHULTZ (ed.), *Distortions and Agricultural Incentives*, Bloomington, IN: Indiana University Press, pp. 1–23.

(1988) 'Education, Investment and Returns', in: H. CHENERY and T.N. SRINIVASAN (eds.), *Handbook of Development Economics*, Vol. I., Amsterdam: North-Holland, pp. 543–630.

SCHUMPETER, J.A. (1976) *Capitalism, Socialism and Democracy*, London: Allen & Unwin, (first published 1943).

(2000) *The Theory of Economic Development*, New Brunswick, NJ/London: Transaction Publishers (first published 1912 as *Theorie der Wirtschaftlichen Entwicklung*).

SCOTT, J.C. (1976) *The Moral Economy of the Peasant: Rebellion and Subsistence in South East Asia*, New Haven, CT: Yale University Press.

SCULLY, G.W. (1988) 'The Institutional Framework and Economic Development', *Journal of Political Economy*, **96** (3), pp. 652–62.

SEERS, D. (1979) 'The Meaning of Development', in: D. LEHMAN (ed.), *Development Theory: Four Critical Studies*, London: Frank Cass, pp. 9–30.

SELOWSKY, M. (1987) 'Adjustment in the 1980s: An Overview of the Issues', *Finance and Development*, June, pp. 11–13.

SEN, A.K. (1960) *Choice of Techniques*, Oxford: Basil Blackwell.

(1981) *Poverty and Famines*, Oxford: Clarendon Press.

(1982) 'How is India Doing?', *New York Review of Books*, December 16, pp. 41–5.

(1999) *Development as Freedom*, New York: Anchor Books.

SENGHAAS, D. (1984) 'Kultur und Entwicklung: Überlegungen zur aktuellen Entwicklungspolitischen Diskussion', *Zeitschrift für Kultur*, **4**, pp. 417–24.

SERAGELDIN, I. (1994) 'The Challenge of a Holistic Vision: Culture, Empowerment and the Development Paradigm', in: I. SERAGELDIN and J. TABOROFF (eds.), *Culture and Development in Africa*, Washington, DC: World Bank, pp. 15–32.

SERAGELDIN, I. and J. TABOROFF (eds.) (1994) *Culture and Development in Africa*, Washington, DC: World Bank.

SHANIN, T. (ed.) (1971) *Peasants and Peasant Societies*, Harmondsworth: Penguin.

(1973) 'The Nature and the Logic of the Peasant Economy, Part I: A Generalization', *Journal of Peasant Studies*, **1** (1), pp. 63–80.

(1974) 'The Nature and the Logic of the Peasant Economy, Part II: Diversity and Change, Part III: Policy and Intervention', *Journal of Peasant Studies*, **1** (2), pp. 186–206.

SHILS, E. (19164) 'The Military in the Political Development of New States', in: J. JOHNSON (ed.), *The Military and Society in Latin America*, Palo Alto, CA: Stanford University Press, pp. 7–67.

SHLEIFER, A. and R.W. VISHNY (1933) 'Corruption', *The Quarterly Journal of Economics*, **108** (3), pp. 599–617.

SHWEDER, R.A. (2000) 'Moral Maps, "First World" Conceits and the New Evangelists', in: L.E. HARRISON and S.P. HUNTINGTON (eds.), *Culture Matters: How Values Shape Human Progress*, New York: Basic Books, pp. 158–72.

SIMON, J. (1982) *The Ultimate Resource*, Princeton University Press.

  (1996) *The Ultimate Resource*, 2nd edn, Princeton University Press (first published in 1981).

SINGER, H.W. (1950) 'The Distribution of Gains between Investing and Borrowing Countries', *The American Economic Review*, **XLI**, pp. 473–86.

  (2001) *International Development Co-Operation: Selected Essays by H.W. Singer on Aid and the United Nations System*, ed., with contributions by D. JOHN SHAW, Houndmills: Palgrave.

SINGH, I. (1982) *The Landless Poor in South Asia*, Proceedings of the 18th Conference of the International Association of Agricultural Economists, Jakarta.

SIROWY, L. and A. INKELES (1990) 'The Effects of Democracy on Economic Growth and Inequality: A Review', *Studies in Comparative International Development*, **25**, (1), pp. 126–57.

SIVARD, R. (1991) *World Military and Social Expenditures*, Washington, DC: World Priorities.

SKOCPOL, T. (1979) *States and Social Revolutions*, Cambridge University Press.

SLICHER VAN BATH, B.H. (1989) *Indianen en Spanjaarden: Een ontmoeting tussen twee werelden, Latijns-Amerika, 1500–1800 [Indians and Spaniards: A Meeting between two Worlds, Latin America, 1500–1800]*, Amsterdam: Bakker.

SMALL, M. and J.D. SINGER (1982) *Resort to Arms: International and Civil Wars, 1816–1980*, Beverly Hills, CA: Sage.

SMIL, V. (2000) *Feeding the World: The Challenge for the Twenty-First Century*, Cambridge, MA: MIT Press.

SMITH, A. (1961) *An Inquiry into the Nature and Causes of the Wealth of Nations*, ed. E. CANNAN, London: Methuen (first published 1776).

SMITH, D. (1997) *The State of War and Peace Atlas*, International Peace Research Institute, Oslo/London: Penguin.

SNA (2009) *System of National Accounts 2008*, New York: EU/IMF/OECD/UN/World Bank.

SOEST, J. VAN (1975) *Het begin van de ontwikkelingshulp in de Verenigde Naties en in Nederland 1945–1952 [Early Development Aid in the United Nations and the Netherlands, 1945–1952]*, Nijmegen: University of Nijmegen.

SOLOW, R.M. (1956) 'A Contribution to the Theory of Economic Growth', *Quarterly Journal of Economics*, **70** (1), pp. 65–94.

  (1957) 'Technical Change and the Aggregate Production Function', *Review of Economics and Statistics*, **39** (3), pp. 312–20.

  (1991) 'New Directions in Growth Theory', in: B. GAHLEN, H. HESSE, H.J. RAMSER and G. BOMBACH (eds.), *Wachstumstheorie und Wachstumspolitik: Ein neuer Anlauf*, Tübingen: Mohr/Siebeck, pp. 3–17.

SOROS, G. (2000) *Open Society: Reforming Global Capitalism*, New York: Public Affairs.

  (2002) *On Globalisation*, Oxford: Public Affairs.

SOTO, H. DE (2000) *The Mystery of Capital: Why Capitalism Triumphs in the West and Fails Everywhere Else*, New York: Basic Books.

SPENCE, J.D. (1990) *The Search for Modern China*, New York/London: Norton.

SPENCE, M.A. (1973) 'Job Market Signaling', *Quarterly Journal of Economics*, **87** (3), pp. 355–74.

SPRAOS, J. (1980) 'The Statistical Debate on the Net Barter Terms of Trade between Primary Commodities and Manufactures', *The Economic Journal*, **90** (357), pp. 107–28.

SRETER, S. (1988) 'The Importance of Social Intervention in Britain's Mortality Decline c. 1850–1914: A Re-interpretation of the Role of Public Health', *Social History of Medicine*, **I** (I), pp. 1–38.

STAM, E and A. VAN STEL (2011) 'Types of Entrepreneurship and Economic Growth', in: A. SZIRMAI, W. NAUDÉ and M. GOEDHUYS (eds.), *Innovation, Entrepreneurship and Development*, Oxford University Press, pp. 78–95.

STARR, H. and B.A. MOST (1985) 'Patterns of Conflict: Quantitative Analysis and the Comparative Lessons of Third World Wars', in: R.E. HARKAVY and S.G. NEUMAN (eds.), *The Lessons of Recent Wars in the Third World*, Vol. I, Lexington Books, pp. 33–52.

STEINBERG, S.H. (various years) *The Statesman's Yearbook*, London: Macmillan, various volumes.

STERN, N. (2002) 'Making the Case for Aid', in: WORLD BANK, *A Case for Aid: Building a Consensus for Development Assistance*, Washington, DC: World Bank, pp. 15–24.

(2007) *The Economics of Climate Change: The Stern Review*, Cambridge University Press.

STEWART, F. (1972) 'Choice of Technique in Developing Countries', *Journal of Development Studies*. **9** (1), pp. 99–121.

(1974) 'Technology and Employment in Less Developed Countries', *World Development*, **2** (3), pp. 17–46.

(1977) *Technology and Underdevelopment*, Houndmills: Macmillan.

(ed.) (1987) *Macro-Policies for Appropriate Technology in Developing Countries*, Boulder, CO/London: Westview Press in cooperation with Appropriate Technology International, Washington, DC.

STIGLITZ, J. (1996) 'Some Lessons From The East Asian Miracle', *The World Bank Research Observer*, **11** (2): 151–77.

(1999) 'The World Bank at the Millennium', *Economic Journal*, **109** (459), pp. F577–F597.

(2000) 'Capital Market Liberalization, Economic Growth, and Instability', *World Development*, **28** (6), pp. 1075–86.

(2002) *Globalization and Its Discontents*, New York/London: Norton.

(2010) *Free Fall. Free Markets and the Sinking of the Global Economy*, London: Penguin.

STIGLITZ, J.E., A.K. SEN and J-P. FITOUSSI (2009) *Report by the Commission on the Measurement of Economic Performance and Social Progress*, www.stiglitz-sen-fitoussi.fr.

STRAUSS, J. and D. THOMAS (1998) 'Health, Nutrition and Economic Development', *Journal of Economic Literature*, **XXXVI** (2), pp. 766–817.

(2008) 'Health over the Life Course', in: T.P. SCHULTZ and J. STRAUSS (eds.) *Handbook of Development Economics* Vol. 4, Amsterdam: Elsevier.

STREETEN, P. (1972) *The Frontiers of Development Studies*, London: Macmillan.

(1984) 'Approaches to a New International Economic Order', in: C.K. WILBER (ed.), *The Political Economy of Development and Underdevelopment*, 3rd edn, New York: Random House, pp. 473–97.

SUMMERS, R. and A. HESTON (1991) 'The Penn World Table, Mark 5: An Expanded Set of International Comparisons, 1955–1988', in: *Quarterly Journal of Economics*, **106** (1), May, pp. 327–68.

SUNKEL, O. (1993) *Development from Within: Toward a Neostructuralist Approach for Latin America*, Boulder, CO: Lynne Reiner.

SUNKEL, O. and G. ZULETA, (1990) 'Neo-Structuralism versus Neo-Liberalism in the 1990s', *CEPAL Review*, **42**, pp. 36–51.

SVEDBERG, P. (1993) 'Trade Compression and Economic Decline in sub-Saharan Africa', in: M. BLOMSTRÖM and M. LUNDAHL (eds.), *Economic Crisis in Africa: Perspectives on Policy Responses*, London/New York: Routledge.

SYRQUIN, M. (1988) 'Patterns of Structural Change', in: H. CHENERY and T.N. SRINIVASAN (eds.), *Handbook of Development Economics*, Chapter 7, Amsterdam: North-Holland, pp. 205–73.

SZERESEWSKI, R. (1965) *Structural Changes in the Economy of Ghana, 1891–1911*, London: Weidenfeld & Nicolson.

SZIRMAI, A. (1988) *Inequality Observed: A Study of Attitudes towards Income Inequality*, Aldershot: Avebury.

(1993) 'Introduction', in: A. SZIRMAI, B. VAN ARK and D. PILAT (eds.), *Explaining Economic Growth: Essays in Honour of Angus Maddison*, Amsterdam: North-Holland, pp. 1–34.

(1994) 'Real Output and Labour Productivity in Indonesian Manufacturing, 1975–1990', *Bulletin of Indonesian Economic Studies*, **30** (2), pp. 49–90.

(2008) *Explaining Success and Failure in Development*, UNU–MERIT Working Paper 2008–013, Maastricht.

(2009) *Is Manufacturing Still the Main Engine of Growth in Developing Countries?*, UNU-MERIT, Working Paper 2009–10, Maastricht.

(2012a) 'Industrialisation as an Engine of Growth in Developing Countries, 1950–2005', *Structural Change and Economic Dynamics*, **23** (4), pp. 406–20.

(2012b) *Proximate, Intermediate and Ultimate Causality: Theories and Experiences of Growth and Development*, UNU-MERIT Working Paper Series 2012–32 (IPD WP09), May.

(2013) 'Explaining Success and Failure in Economic Development', in: D.S. PRASADA RAO and B. VAN ARK (eds.), *World Economic Performance: Past, Present and Future*, Cheltenham: Edward Elgar, pp. 227–67.

SZIRMAI, A., B. VAN ARK and D. PILAT (eds.) (1993) *Explaining Economic Growth: Essays in Honour of Angus Maddison*, Amsterdam: North-Holland.

SZIRMAI, A., M. BAI and R. REN (2001) *Labour Productivity Trends in Chinese Manufacturing, 1980–99*, ECIS Working Paper, 10 October.

SZIRMAI, A. and P.E. LAPPERRE (eds.) (2001) *The Industrial Experience of Tanzania*, Basingstoke: Palgrave.

SZIRMAI, A., W. NAUDÉ and L. ALCORTA (eds.) (2013a) *Pathways to Industrialisation in the 21st Century: New Challenges and Emerging Paradigms*, Oxford University Press.

(2013b) 'Introduction and Overview: The Past, Present and Future of Industrialisation', in: A. SZIRMAI, W. NAUDÉ and L. ALCORTA (eds.) (2013), *Pathways to Industrialisation in the 21st Century: New Challenges and Emerging Paradigms*, Oxford University Press, pp. 3–50.

SZIRMAI, A., M. GEBREEYESUS, F. GUADAGNO and B. VERSPAGEN (2013), *Promoting Productive Employment in Sub-Saharan Africa: A Review of the Literature*, UNU-MERIT Working Paper Series 2013–62.

SZIRMAI, A., W. NAUDÉ and M. GOEDHUYS (eds.) (2011) *Innovation, Entrepreneurship and Development*, Oxford University Press.

SZIRMAI, A., M. PRINS and W. SCHULTE (2001) 'Measuring Manufacturing Performance in Tanzania', in: A. SZIRMAI and P. LAPPERRE (eds.), *The Industrial Experience of Tanzania*, Basingstoke: Palgrave, pp. 73–113.

SZIRMAI, A. and R. REN (2000) 'Comparative Performance in Chinese Manufacturing, 1980–92', *China Economic Review*, **11** (1), pp. 16–53.

(2007) 'Measuring Labour Productivity in Chinese Manufacturing: Statistical Problems and Solutions', in B. PANT (ed.), *National Accounts of the People's Republic of China: Measurement Issues, Recent Developments and the Way Forward*, Manila: Asian Development Bank, pp. 58–113.

SZIRMAI, A., R. REN and M. BAI (2005), *Chinese Manufacturing Performance in Comparative Perspective, 1980–2002*, Yale Economic Growth Center, Discussion Paper No. 920, July.

SZIRMAI, A. and B. VERSPAGEN (2011) *Manufacturing and Economic Growth in Developing Countries, 1950–2005*, UNU-MERIT Working Paper Series 2011–069.

TABELLINI, G. (2008) 'Institutions and Culture', *Journal of the European Economic Association Papers and Proceedings*, **6** (2–3), pp. 255–94.

(2010) 'Culture and Institutions: Economic Development in the Regions of Europe', *Journal of the European Economic Association*, **8** (4), pp. 677–716.

TANZI, V. and H. DAVOODI (2001) 'Corruption, Growth and Public Finances', in: A.K. JAIN (ed.), *Political Economy of Corruption*, London: Routledge, pp. 89–110.

TARP, F. (1993) *Stabilization and Structural Adjustment: Macro-Economic Frameworks for Analysing the Crisis in Sub-Saharan Africa*, London: Routledge.

TARP, F. and P. HJERTHOLM (eds.) (2000) *Foreign Aid and Development*, London: Routledge.

TAVARES, J. and WACZIARG, R. (2001) 'How Democracy Affects Growth', *European Economic Review*, **45** (8), pp. 1341–78.

TAWNEY, R.H. (1947) *Religion and the Rise of Capitalism: A Historical Study*, New York: Penguin (first published 1926).

TAYLOR, C.L. and M.C. HUDSON (1972) *World Handbook of Political and Social Indicators*, New Haven, CT: Yale University Press.

TAYLOR, C.L. and D. JODICE (1983) *World Handbook of Political and Social Indicators*, New Haven, CT: Yale University Press.

TERHAL, P. (1992) 'Economic Growth and Political Insecurity: Towards a Multidisciplinary Approach', *Development and Security*, **36**, Centre for Development Studies, Groningen.

TESZLER, R.K. (1978) 'Nederlandse samenwerking met ontwikkelingslanden [Dutch Cooperation with Developing Countries]', in: E.H. V.D. BEUGEL *et al.*, *Nederlandse buitenlandse politiek: Heden en verleden [Dutch Foreign Policies: Past and Present]*, Baarn: In den Toorn.

(1984) 'Blotevoetenindustrie en plattelandsontwikkeling [Infant Industry and Rural Development]', *Internationale Spectator*, **XXXVIII** (12), pp. 702–12.

TEUNISSEN, P.J. (1990) *Een ambigue wereld: Compendium. Sociologie van de internationale betrekkingen [An Ambiguous World: Compendium. Sociology of International Relations]*, photocopy, Groningen.

THE CENTRAL BANK OF CHINA (TAIWAN), http://www.cbc.gov.tw/EngHome/economic/statistics/Annual.htm, accessed in December 2003.

THEE, K.W. (1997) 'The Development of the Motor Cycle Industry in Indonesia', in: M.E. PANGESTU and Y. SATO (eds.), *Waves of Change in Indonesia's Manufacturing Industry*, Tokyo: Institute of Developing Economies, pp. 95–135.

THIRLWALL, A.P. (1999) *Growth and Development with Special Reference to Developing Economies*, 6th edn, London: Macmillan.

(2003) *Growth and Development, with Special Reference to Developing Economies*, 7th edn, London: Palgrave.

THOBURN, J.T. (1977) *Primary Commodity Exports and Economic Development: Theory, Evidence and a Study of Malaysia*, London: Wiley.

THOMAS, C. (1987) *In Search of Security: The Third World in International Relations*, Boulder, CO: Lynne Rienner.

THOMPSON, E.P. (1963) *The Making of the English Working Class*, New York: Vintage.

THORBECKE, E. and C. CHARUMILIND (2002) 'Economic Inequality and Its Socioeconomic Impact', *World Development*, **30** (9), pp. 1477–95.

TILLY, R. (1986) 'Financing Industrial Enterprise in Great Brittain and Germany in the Nineteenth Century: Testing Grounds for Marxist and Schumpeterian Theories?', in: H.J. WAGENER and J.W. DRUKKER (eds.), *The Economic Law of Motion of Modern Society: A Marx, Keynes, Schumpeter Centennial*, Cambridge University Press.

(ed.) (1975) *The Formation of National States in Western Europe*, Princeton University Press.

TIMMER, C.P. (1988) 'The Agricultural Transformation', in: H.B. CHENERY and T.N. SRINIVASAN (eds.), *Handbook of Development Economics*, Vol. I, Chapter 8, Amsterdam: North-Holland, pp. 276–331.

(2000) *The Dynamics of Asian Manufacturing: A Comparative Perspective, 1963–1993*, Cheltenham: Edward Elgar.

TIMMER, M.P. and A. SZIRMAI (1997) *Australian Manufacturing Performance in Asian Perspective*, Eindhoven, mimeo.

(2000) 'Productivity in Asian Manufacturing: The Structural Bonus Hypothesis Examined', *Structural Change and Economic Dynamics*, **11**, pp. 371–92.

TIMMER, M. P. and G.J. DE VRIES (2009) 'Structural Change and Growth Accelerations in Asia and Latin America: A New Sectoral Dataset', *Cliometrica*, **3** (2), pp. 165–90.

TIMS, W. (1985) 'Commentaar: Organisatie en doeltreffendheid van de Nederlandse ontwikkelingssamenwerking [Comment: Organisation and effectiveness of Dutch Development Cooperation]', *Internationale Spectator*, **XXXIX** (12), pp. 759 ff.

(1989) 'Development Cooperation: A Dutch Preoccupation', *Internationale Spectator*, **XLIII** (11), pp. 714–17.

TOBIN, J. (2000) 'Financial Globalization', *World Development*, **28** (6), pp. 1101–04.

TODARO, M.P. (1969) 'A Model of Labor Migration and Urban Unemployment in Less Developed Countries', *American Economic Review*, **59** (1), pp. 138–48.

(1981) *Economic Development in the Third World*, 2nd edn, New York: Longman.

TOL R.S.J. (2009) 'The Economic Effects of Climate Change', *The Journal of Economic Perspectives*, **23** (2), pp. 29–51.

TORTELLA, G. (ed.) (1990) *Education and Economic Development Since the Industrial Revolution*, València: Generalitat Valenciana.

TORVINEN, L. (2013) *Assessing Governance Assessments: The Case of Mozambique. Governance Assessments in the Context of Aid Effectiveness Discourse*, PhD, Maastricht University, November.

TOYE, J. (1993) *Structural Adjustment: Context, Assumptions, Origin and Diversity*, Paper presented at the International Seminar of Structural Adjustment and Long-Term Development in Sub-Saharan Africa: Research and Policy Issues, The Hague: DGIS, 1–3 June.

TRANSPARENCY INTERNATIONAL, *Corruption Perceptions Index (CPI)*.

TREGENNA, F. (2009) 'Characterising Deindustrialisation: An Analysis of Changes in Manufacturing Employment and Output Internationally', *Cambridge Journal of Economics*, **33** (3), pp. 433–66.

(2013) 'Manufacturing Productivity, Deindustrialization, and Reindustrialization', in: A. SZIRMAI, W. NAUDÉ and A. ALCORTA (eds.), *Pathways to Industrialization in the 21st Century: New Challenges and Emerging Paradigms*, Oxford University Press, pp. 76–101.

TREVOR-ROPER, H. (1972) *Religion, The Reformation and Social Change, and Other Essays*, London: Macmillan.

TRIPLETT, J.E. (2002) ' "Baumol's Disease" has been Cured: IT and Multifactor Productivity in U.S. Services Industries', Paper, Som/TEG Conference: *The Empirical Implications of Technology Based Growth Theories*, Groningen, August, mimeo.

TULLOCK, G. (1965) *The Politics of Bureaucracy*, Washington, DC: Public Affairs Press.

TUNZELMANN, N. VON (1995) *Technology and Industrial Progress*, Cheltenham: Edward Elgar.

TUNZELMANN, N. VON and V. ACHA (2005) 'Innovation in "Low Tech" Industries', in J. FAGERBERG *et al.* (eds.), *The Oxford Handbook of Innovation*, Oxford University Press, pp. 407–32.

TYBOUT, J.R. (2000) 'Manufacturing Firms in Developing Countries: How Well Do They Do, and Why?', *Journal of Economic Literature*, **38** (1), pp. 11–44.

UIA (2013/14) *Yearbook of International Organizations*, Vol. V, 50th edn, Leiden/Boston, MA: Brill/Martinus Nijhoff.

UL HAQ, M. (1976) *The Poverty Curtain: Choices for the Third World*, New York: Columbia University Press.

UNAIDS (2002) *Report on the Global HIV/AIDS Epidemic*, Joint United Nations Programme on HIV/AIDS, New York, UN, www.unaids.org/Unaids/EN/Resources/Publications/.

(2011) *World AIDS Day Report 2011: How to Get to Zero. Faster, Smarter, Better*, UNAIDS.

(2012) *Together We Will End Aids*.

UNCTAD (2000) *The Competitiveness Challenge: Transnational Corporations and Industrial Restructuring in Developing Countries*, New York/Geneva: United Nations.

(2002a) *Least Developed Countries 2001 Report*, Geneva: United Nations.

(2002b) *Handbook of Statistics 2002*, New York/Geneva: United Nations.

(2003) *Back to Basics: Market Access Issues in the Doha Agenda*, United Nations, E.03. II.D.4, New York and Geneva, http://192.91.247.38/tab/pubs/itcdtabMisc9_en.pdf.

(2007) *The Universe of the Largest Transnational Corporations*, New York/Geneva: United Nations.

(2009) *World Investment Report*, New York/Geneva: United Nations (and various issues).

(2011), *World Investment Report 2011*, New York/Geneva: United Nations.

(2012a) *Handbook of Statistics 2012*, New York/Geneva: United Nations.

(2012b) *World Investment Report 2012*, New York/Geneva: United Nations.

(2014) *UNCTADSTATs*, http://unctad.org/en/Pages/Statistics.aspx.

UNDP (1988) *Development of Rural Small Industrial Enterprise: Lessons from Experience*, Joint Study by UNDP, Government of the Netherlands, Vienna: ILO/UNIDO.

(1991) *Human Development Report 1991*, New York/Oxford: Oxford University Press.

(2001) *Human Development Report 2001: Making New Technologies Work for Human Development*, New York/Oxford: Oxford University Press.

(2002) *Arab Human Development Report 2002. Creating Opportunities for Future Generations*, New York: Oxford University Press.

(2003) *Human Development Report 2003, Millenium Development Goals: A Compact among Nations to End Human Poverty*, New York: Oxford University Press.

(2005) *Human Development Report 2005*, New York: Oxford University Press.

(2007/8) *Human Development Report 2007/8*, New York: Oxford University Press.

UNEP (1993) *Ecoforum*, **17** (1/2), UNEP 17 May, p. 12.

UN/ESCAP (1985) *Mortality and Health Issues*, New York: UN.

(2002) 'Poverty and Social Equity', in: *Sustainable Social Development in a Period of Rapid Globalization*, United Nations, Economic and Social Commission for Asia and the Pacific, n.d., Chapter 11, pp. 21–65, downloaded from www.unescap.org/sdd/theme2002/ch2cd.htm, accessed 2002.

UNESCO (1983) *Trends and Projections of Enrolment, 1960–2000* (as accessed in 1982), UNESCO, Division of Statistics on Education, Office of Statistics, March, Paris.

(1997) *Statistical Yearbook 1997*, Paris: UNESCO.

(1999) *Statistical Yearbook 1999*, Paris: UNESCO.

Statistical Yearbook, Paris: UNESCO, various volumes.

(2000a) *Education for All: Year 2000 Assessment. Statististical Document*, Nîmes: UNESCO Institute for Statistics.

(2000b) *World Education Report 2000*, Paris: UNESCO.

(2001a) *Education Statistics, 2001*. Regional Report on Latin America, Paris: UNESCO.

(2001b) *Education Statistics, 2001*, Regional Report on Africa, Paris: UNESCO.

(2002a) *Educational Indicators: Technical Guidelines*, UNESCO Institute for Statistics, http://portal.unesco.org/uis/, 29–11–2002a.

(2002b and various years), *Institute of Statistics, Homepage: Global Statistics, Education, Statistical Tables*, updated 29–11–2002, UNESCO, Institute for Statistics, http://portal.unesco.org/uis/ev.php?URL_ID=2867&URL_DO=DO_TOPIC&URL_SECTION=201&reload=1043251662, UNESCO.

(2002c) *The 2002 Global Education for All Monitoring Report: Is the World on Track?*, Paris: UNESCO.

UNESCO INSTITUTE FOR STATISTICS (2011), http://stats.uis.unesco.org/unesco/ReportFolders/ReportFolders.aspx?IF_ActivePath=P,54&IF_Language=eng, January, downloaded September 2011.

(2012a), Homepage: http://stats.uis.unesco.org/unesco/tableviewer/document.aspx?ReportId=143.

(2012b) Global Education Digest 2012. *Opportunities Lost: The Impact of Grade Repetition and Early School Leaving*, Montreal.

UNHCR (1963) *Demographic Yearbook 1963*, New York: United Nations.

(2013) *Global Trends, 2012: Displacement. The New 21st Century Challenge*, New York: United Nations.

UNICEF (2012) *Levels and Trends in Child Mortality: Report 2012*, Estimates Developed by the UN Interagency Group for Child Mortality Estimation, www.unicef.org/videoaudio/PDFs/UNICEF_2012_child_mortality_for_web_0904.pdf.

UNICEF/WHO (2012) *Progress on Drinking Water and Sanitation, 2012 Update*, http://whqlibdoc.who.int/publications/2012/9789280646320_eng.pdf.

UNIDO (1985) *Industrial Development Review, Series Malaysia*, July.

(1986) *Industrial Development Review, Series Zaire*, July.

(1990) *Handbook of Industrial Statistics 1990*, Vienna.

(1995) *International Yearbook of Industrial Statistics 1995*, Vienna.

(1999a) *International Yearbook of Industrial Statistics 1999*, Vienna.

(1999b) *Handbook of Industrial Statistics 1990*, Vienna.

(2000) *Industrial Statistics, database*, www.unido.org/Regions.cfm?area=GLO.

(2002) *Industrial Development Report, 2002/3: Competing through Innovation and Learning*, Vienna.

(2003) *Industrial Statistics Database, 2003 at the 3-DIGIT LEVEL OF ISIC (Revision 2)*, CD-Rom, Vienna.

(2005) *International Yearbook of Industrial Statistics 2005*, and various editions, Vienna.

(2006) *Industrial Statistics Database, 2006 at the 3-DIGIT LEVEL OF ISIC (Revision 2)*, CD-Rom, Vienna.

(2012) *Structural Change, Poverty Reduction and Industrial Policy in the BRICS*, ed. A. SZIRMAI, W. NAUDÉ and N. HARAGUCHI, Vienna: UNIDO and UNU-MERIT, Chapter 3.2.

(2013) *International Yearbook of Industrial Statistics 2013*, Vienna.

UNITED NATIONS (1953 and 1963) *Demographic Yearbook*, New York: United Nations.

(1957), *Yearbook of National Accounts Statistics*, 1957, New York: United Nations.

(1962), *Yearbook of National Accounts Statistics*, 1962, New York: United Nations.

(1967), *Yearbook of National Accounts Statistics*, 1967, New York: United Nations.

(1984) *Mortality and Health Policy*, Proceedings of the Expert Group on Mortality and Health Policy, International Conference on Population, United Nations, Department of International Economic and Social Affairs, New York: United Nations.

(1985) *World Population Trends: Population and Development, Interrelations and Population Policies. 1983 Monitoring Report*, Vol. I, New York: United Nations.

(1986) *World Population Prospects: Estimates and Projections as Assessed in 1984*, New York: United Nations.

(1988a) *World Population: Trends and Policies, 1987*, Monitoring Report, New York: United Nations.

(1988b) *Mortality of Children under Age 5: World Estimates and Projections, 1950–2025*, Population Studies, No. 105, New York: United Nations.

(1989) *Prospects of World Urbanization*, New York: United Nations.

(1993a) *Stateman's Yearbook*, New York: United Nations.

(1993b) *World Population Prospects: The 1992 Revision*, New York: United Nations.

(1993c) *Monthly Bulletin of Statistics*, New York: United Nations, March.

(1994a) *Population, Environment and Development*, New York: United Nations.

(1994b) Department for Economic and Social Information and Policy Analysis, *Aids and the Demography of Africa*, New York: United Nations.

(2012a) Department of Economic and Social Affairs, *Coverage of Birth and Death Registration*, http://unstats.un.org/unsd/demographic/CRVS/CR_coverage.htm, August 2012: United Nations.

(2012b) *The Millenium Development Goals Report 2012*, New York: United Nations.

United Nations Statistics Online, http://data.un.org.

Comtrade Database, http://www.comtrade.org.

UNITED NATIONS POPULATION DIVISION (1993) *World Urbanization Prospects: The 1992 Revision*, New York: United Nations.

(1994) Department for Economic and Social Information and Policy Analysis, *World Population Plan of Action*, New York: United Nations.

(1999) *World Population Prospects: The 1998 Revision, Vol. I, Comprehensive Tables*, United Nations Publication, Sales No. E. 99. XIII.9, New York: United Nations.

(2001a) *World Population Prospects: The 2000 Revision*, Vols. I, II and III, New York: United Nations.

(2001b) *World Population Prospects: Population Data Base*, http://esa.un.org/unpp, New York: United Nations.

(2002a) *Long-Range World Population Projections: Based on the 1998 Revision. Dataset in Digital Form*, www.un.org./esa/population/publications/longrange/longrange.htm, New York: United Nations, September.

(2002b) *World Urbanization Prospects: The 2001 Revision*, www.un.org/esa/population/unpop.htm, New York: United Nations, March.

(2003) *World Population Prospects: The 2002 Revision*, New York: United Nations.

(2004) *World Population to 2300*, New York: United Nations.

(2005) *Population Challenges and Development Goals*, United Nations, Population Division, New York: United Nations.

(2007) *World Population Prospects: The 2006 Revision*, http://esa.un.org/unpp/p2k0data.asp, downloaded December 2007.

(2009) *World Urbanization Prospects: The 2009 Revision*, http://esa.un.org/unpd/wup/index.htm.

(2011a) *World Population Prospects: The 2010 Revision*, CD Rom edition, http://esa.un.org/unpd/wpp/Excel-Data/population.htm.

(2011b) United Nations Press Release on 2010 Revision of the World Population Projections. May.

(2012a) *World Population Projections: The 2012 Revision*, http://esa.un.org/unpd/wpp/Excel-Data/population.htm.

(2012b) *World Urbanization Prospects: The 2011 Revision*, October 2012, http://esa.un.org/unpd/wup/CD-ROM/Urban-Rural-Population.htm.

UNSO, UNITED NATIONS STATISTICAL OFFICE (1968) *A System of National Accounts*, Studies in Methods, Series F, No. 2, rev. 3, New York: United Nations.

UNU-WIDER, *World Income Inequality Database V2.0c May 2008*, downloaded January 2010, www.wider.unu.edu/research/Database/en_GB/wiid/.

URQUIDI, V. (1993) 'The Developmentalist View', in: A. SZIRMAI, B. VAN ARK and D. PILAT (eds.), *Explaining Economic Growth: Essays in Honour of Angus Maddison*, Amsterdam: North-Holland, pp. 447–65.

US DEPARTMENT OF COMMERCE, PATENT AND TRADE MARK OFFICE (1977) *Technology Assessment and Forecast*, 7th Report, Washington, DC, March.

US PATENT AND TRADEMARK OFFICE (2002) *Technology Assessment and Forecast Office, Special report, All Patents, January 1977–December 2001*, Washington DC.

(2004), *TAF Special Report, All Patents, All Types, January 1977–December 2004.*

(2006), *PTMT Special Report All Patents, January 1977–December 2006.*

(2009), *TAF Database, All Patents, All Types, 1/1/1977–31/12/2009.*

VALLIN, J. (1989) 'Conclusion: Théorie(s) de la baisse de la mortalité et situation Africaine', in: G. PISON, E. VAN DE WALLE and M. SALA-DIAKANDA, *Mortalité et Société en Afrique au Sud du Sahara, Travaux et Documents*, Cahier No. 124, Paris: Presses Universitaires de France, pp. 399–431.

VAN ARK, H.H., R. INKLAAR and R.H. MCGUCKIN (2002) *"Changing Gear", Productivity, ICT and Service Industries. Europe and the United States*, Paper for Som/TEG Conference: 'The Empirical Implications of Technology Based Growth Theories', Groningen, August, mimeo.

VAN ARK, H.H., R. INKLAAR and R.H. MCGUCKIN (2003) 'ICT and Productivity in Europe and the United States: Where Do the Differences Come From?', *Ifo Studien*, **3**, 295–318.

VAN ARK, H.H, M. O'MAHONY and M.P. TIMMER (2008) 'The Productivity Gap between Europe and the United States, Trends and Causes', *Journal of Economic Perspectives*, **22** (1), pp. 25–44.

VAN LIESHOUT, P., R. WENT and M. KREMER (2010) *Less Pretension, More Ambition: Development Policy in Times of Globalization*, Amsterdam University Press.

VAN DER PLOEG, F. and S. POELHEKKE (2007) *Volatility, Financial Development and the Natural Resource Curse*, Florence: European University Institute, mimeo.

VAN DE WALLE, N. (1994) 'Neopatrimonialism and Democracy in Africa, with an Illustration from Cameroun', in: J. WIDNER (ed.), *Economic Change and Political Liberalization in Sub-Saharan Africa*, Baltimore, MD: Johns Hopkins University Press.

(2001) *African Economies and the Politics of Permanent Crisis, 1979–1999*, Cambridge University Press.

VEBLEN, T. (1899) *The Theory of the Leisure Class*, New York: Macmillan.

(1915) *Imperial Germany and the Industrial Revolution*, New York: Macmillan.

VERBRUGGEN, H. (1985) *Gains from Export-Oriented Industrialization with Special Reference to South East Asia*, Dissertation, Amsterdam Free University.

VERNON, R. (1966) 'International Investment and International Trade in the Product Cycle', *Quarterly Journal of Economics*, **80** (2) pp. 190–207.

(1974) 'The Location of Economic Activity', in: J.H. DUNNING (ed.), *Economic Analysis and the Multinational Enterprise*, London: Allen & Unwin.

(1977) *Storm over Multinationals: The Real Issues*, Cambridge, MA: Harvard University Press.

VERSPAGEN, B. (1993) *Uneven Growth between Interdependent Economies: An Evolutionary View on Technology Gaps, Trade and Growth*, Aldershot: Avebury.

(2001) *Economic Growth and Technological Change: An Evolutionary Interpretation*, OECD, STI Working Papers, 1, Paris.

(2003) 'Intellectual Property Rights in the World Economy', in: O. GRANSTRAND (ed.), *Economics, Law and Intellectual Property. Seeking Strategies for Research and Teaching in a Developing Field*, Boston, MA: Kluwer Academic Publishers, pp. 489–518.

(1997). 'Measuring Intersectoral Technology Spillovers: Estimates from the European and US Patent Office Databases', *Economic Systems Research*, **9** (1), pp. 47–65.

VERTESY, D. (2011) *Interrupted Innovation: Emerging Economies in the Structure of the Global Aerospace Industry*, PhD thesis, Maastricht University.

VOETEN, J., J. DE HAAN and G. DE GROOT (2011) 'Can Small Firms Innovate? The Case of Clusters of Small Producers in Northern Vietnam', in: A. SZIRMAI, W. NAUDÉ and M. GOEDHUYS (eds.), *Entrepreneurship, Innovation and Economic Development*, Oxford University Press, pp. 96–121.

VRIES, G.J. (2010) *Productivity, Firm Heterogeneity and Policy Reforms in Latin America*, PhD thesis, Groningen University.

WADE, R. (1990) *Governing the Market: Economic Theory and the Role of Government in East Asian Industrialization*, Princeton University Press.

WAGENER, H.J. and J.W. DRUKKER (eds.) (1986) *The Economic Law of Motion of Modern Society: A Marx, Keynes, Schumpeter Centennial*, Cambridge University Press.

WAGGONER, P.E. and J.H. AUSUBEL (2001) 'How Much Will Feeding More and Wealthier People Encroach on Forests?', *Population and Development Review*, **27** (2), pp. 239–57.

WAHIDUDDIN, M. and S.R. OSMANI (2013) *The Theory and Practice of Microcredit*, Routledge Studies in Development Economics, London: Routledge.

WALLERSTEIN, I. (1974) *The Modern World System*, New York: Academic Press.

WALSH, J.A. (1990) 'Estimating the Burden of Illness in the Tropics', in: K.S. WARREN and A.F. MAHMOUD (eds.), *Tropical and Geographical Medicine*, New York: McGraw Hill, pp. 185–96.

WANG, L. and A. SZIRMAI (2008) 'Productivity Growth and Structural Change in Chinese Manufacturing, 1980–2002', *Industrial and Corporate Change*, **17** (4), pp. 841–74.

WANG, L., H. MEIJERS and A. SZIRMAI (2013) *Technological Spillovers and Industrial Growth in Chinese Regions*, UNU-MERIT Working Paper Series 2013–044.

WANGWE, S.M. (ed.) (1995) *Exporting Africa: Technology, Trade and Industrialisation in Sub-Saharan Africa*, UNU/INTECH, London/New York: Routledge & Kegan Paul.

WEBER, M. (1969) 'Die Protestantische Ethik und der Geist des Kapitalismus', in: *Die Protestantische Ethik*, ed. J. WINCKELMANN, Siebenstern, Munich (first published 1905).

WEBER, M. (1920a) *Gesammelte Aufsätze zur Religions-soziologie*, I, Tübingen: Mohr.

(1920b) 'Confuzianismus und Taoismus', in: M. WEBER, *Gesammelte Aufsätze zur Religions-soziologie*, I, Tübingen: Mohr.

(1922) *Wirtschaft und Gesellschaft*, Tübingen: Mohr.

WEI, S. (1997a) 'How Taxing is Corruption on International Investors?', NBER Working Paper 6030, Cambridge, MA: National Bureau of Economic Research.

(1997b) 'Why is Corruption So Much More Taxing than Tax?', NBER Working Paper 2048, Cambridge, MA: National Bureau of Economic Research.

WEISNER, T.S. (2000) 'Culture, Childhood and Progress in Sub-Saharan Africa', in: L.E. HARRISON and S.P. HUNTINGTON (eds.), *Culture Matters: How Values Shape Human Progress*, New York: Basic Books, pp. 141–57.

WEISS, J. (1988) *Industry in Developing Countries: Theory, Policy and Evidence*, London: Croom Helm.

—— (2002) *Industrialisation and Globalisation: Theory and Evidence from Developing Countries*, London: Routledge.

—— (2011) *The Economics of Industrial Development*, Milton Park: Routledge.

WESTPHAL, L.E. (2002) 'Technology Strategies for Economic Development in a Fast Changing Global Economy', *Economics of Innovation and New Technology*, **11** (4/5), pp. 275–320.

WESTPHAL, L.E., L. KIM and C.J. DAHLMAN (1985) 'Reflections on The Republic of Korea's Acquisition of Technological Capability', in: N. ROSENBERG and C. FRISCHTAK (eds.), *International Technology Transfer: Concepts Measures, and Comparisons*, New York: Praeger, pp. 167–221.

WHARTON, C.R. (ed.) (1970) *Subsistence Agriculture and Economic Development*, Chicago, IL: Aldine.

WHITE, G. (1984) 'Developmental States and Socialist Industrialisation in the Third World', *Journal of Development Studies*, **21** (1), pp. 97–120.

WHITE, M. (2003) *Tolls for the Major Wars and Atrocities of the Twentieth Century*, http://users.erols.com/mwhite28/warstats.htm, last update January.

WHO (1978) 'Primary Healthcare: Report of the International Conference on Primary Healthcare', *Health for All Series*, No. 1, Geneva: WHO.

—— (1981) *Global Strategy for Health for All by the Year 2000*, Geneva: WHO, ('Health for All' Series, No. 3), pp. 74–6.

—— (1987) *Evaluation of the Strategy for Health for All by the Year 2000*, Seventh Report on the World Health Situation, Vol. I, Global Review, Geneva: WHO.

—— (1993) *Implementation of the Global Strategy for Health for All by the Year 2000: Second Evaluation*, Eighth Report on the World Health Situation, Vol. 1. Global Review, Geneva: WHO.

—— (1996) *World Health Report 1996*, Geneva: WHO.

—— (1997) *World Health Report 1997*, Geneva: WHO.

—— (1998) *World Health Report 1998 Life in the 21st Century: A Vision for All*, Geneva: WHO.

—— (1999) *World Health Report 1999: Making a Difference*, Geneva, WHO.

—— (2000) *World Health Report 2000: Health Systems. Improving Performance*, Geneva, WHO.

—— (2001) *World Health Report 2001: Mental Health: New Understanding, New Hope*, Geneva: WHO.

—— (2002a) *World Mortality in 2000: Life Tables for 191 Countries*, Geneva: WHO.

—— (2002b) *World Report on Violence and Health*, Geneva: WHO.

—— (2004) *Water Sanitation and Hygiene. Links to Health. Facts and Figures*, www.who.int/water_sanitation_health/en/factsfigures04.pdf, updated March.

—— (2006) *Report of a WHO Technical Consultation on Birth Spacing*, Geneva: WHO.

—— (2008a) *The Global Burden of Disease, 2004 Update*, Geneva: WHO.

—— (2008b) *World Health Report 2008: Primary Healthcare. Now More than Ever.* Geneva: WHO.

—— (2010) *World Health Report 2010: Health Systems Financing. The Path to Universal Coverage*, Geneva: WHO.

(2011) *World Health Statistics 2011*, Geneva: WHO.

(2012a) *Global Health Observatory Data Repository/mortality and burden of disease/ cause specific mortality 2008*; http://apps.who.int/ghodata/?vid=10015, downloaded September.

(2012b) *Cholera Fact Sheet* No 107 July 2012, www.who.int/mediacentre/ factsheets/ fs107/en/index.html.

WIDNER, J.A. (ed.) (1994) *Economic Change and Political Liberalisation in Sub-Saharan Africa*, Baltimore, MD/London: Johns Hopkins University Press.

WIGGINS, S. (2000) 'Interpreting Changes from the 1970s to the 1990s in African Agriculture through Village Studies', *World Development*, **28** (4), pp. 631–62.

WIKIPEDIA (2003) *The Free Encyclopedia*, http://en.wikipedia.org/wiki/Coup_d'%e9tat, accessed in October.

WILK, R. (1996) *Economies and Cultures: Foundations of Economic Antropology*, Boulder, CO: Westview Press.

WILLIAMS, E. (1964) *Capitalism and Slavery*, 2nd edn, London: Deutsch.

WILLIAMSON, B. (1979) *Education, Social Structure and Development: A Comparative Analysis*, London: Macmillan.

WILLIAMSON, J. (1990) 'What Washington Means by Policy Reform', in: J. WILLIAMSON (ed.), *Latin American Adjustment: How much has Happened?*, Washington, DC: Institute for International Economics.

(1993) 'Democracy and the Washington Consensus', *World Development*, **21** (8), pp. 1329–36.

(1997) 'The Washington Consensus Revisited', in: L. EMMERIJ (ed.), *Economic and Social Development into the XXI century*, Washington, DC: Inter-American Development Bank/Baltimore, MD, John Hopkins University Press, pp. 48–61.

(2011) *Trade and Poverty: When the Third World Fell Behind*, Cambridge, MA: MIT Press.

WILLIS, R. (1973) 'A New Approach to the Economic Theory of Fertility', *Journal of Political Economy*, **81**, pp. S14–S64.

(1994) 'Economic Analysis of Fertility: Micro-Foundations and Aggregate Implications', in: K. LINDAHL-KIESSLING and H. LANDBERG (eds.), *Population, Economic Development and the Environment*, Oxford/New York: Oxford University Press, pp. 139–72.

WILSON, C. (2001) 'On the Scale of Global Demographic Convergence, 1950–2000', *Population and Development Review*, **27** (1), pp. 155–71.

WOLF, E.R. (1966) *Peasants*, Englewood Cliffs, NJ: Prentice Hall.

(1982) *Europe and the People without History*, Berkeley, CA: University of California Press.

WOLFF, E. and M. GITTLEMAN (1993) 'The Role of Education in Productivity Convergence: Does Higher Education Matter?', in: A. SZIRMAI, B. VAN ARK and D. PILAT (eds.), *Explaining Economic Growth: Essays in Honour of Angus Maddison*, Amsterdam: North-Holland, pp. 147–67.

WOLPIN, K. (1977) 'Education and Screening', *American Economic Review*, **67** (5), pp. 949–58.

WOO, W. TH, J.D. SACHS and K. SCHWAB (eds.) (2000) *The Asian Financial Crisis: Lessons for a Resilient Asia*, Cambridge, MA: MIT Press.

WOOD, R. (1985) 'The Aid Regime and International Debt: Crisis and Structural Adjustment', *Development and Change*, **16** (2), pp. 179–212.

WOOLCOCK, M. (1998) 'Social Capital and Economic Development: Toward a Theoretical Synthesis and Policy Framework', *Theory & Society*, **27**, pp. 151–208.

WORLD BANK (1994) *World Population Projections 1994–95*, Baltimore, MD: Johns Hopkins University Press.

(1986) *Poverty and Hunger: Issues and Options for Food Security in Developing Countries*, Washington, DC: World Bank.

(1989) *Sub-Saharan Africa: From Crisis to Sustainable Growth, A Long Term Perspective Study*, Washington, DC: World Bank.

(1990) *Trends in Developing Economies*, Washington, DC: World Bank.

(1992) *Trends in Developing Economies*, Washington, DC: World Bank.

(1993) *The East Asian Miracle. Economic Growth and Public Policy*, New York: Oxford University Press.

(1994) *Adjustment in Africa: Reforms, Results and the Road Ahead, A World Bank Policy Research Report*, New York: Oxford University Press.

(1995 and previous issues) *World Debt Tables 1994/95*, Washington, DC: World Bank.

(2002a) *A Case for Aid: Building a Consensus for Development Assistance*, Washington, DC: World Bank.

(2002b), *Constructing Knowledge Societies: New Challenges for Tertiary Education*, Washington, DC: World Bank.

(2003a) *Global Development Finance: Striving for Stability in Development Finance*, Washington, DC: World Bank. (Successor to the series *World Debt Tables*.)

(2003b) *Global Development Finance: Striving for Stability in Development Finance, Vol. 2: Summary and Country Tables,* Washington, DC: World Bank.

(2005) *Economic Growth in the 1990s: Learning from a Decade of Reform*, Washington, DC: World Bank.

Database, www.worldbank.org/data/countrydata/countrydata.html.

Global Poverty Monitoring Website, www.worldbank.org/research/povmonitor/index. htm.

(2013) *Remittances Data*, http://econ.worldbank.org/WBSITE/EXTERNAL/ EXTDEC/EXTDECPROSPECTS/0, contentMDK:22759429~pagePK:64165401~ piPK:64165026~theSitePK:476883,00.html#Remittances.

(2014a) *International Debt Statistics*, Washington, DC: World Bank.

(2014b) *Migration and Development Brief, April 11*, http://siteresources.worldbank.org/ INTPROSPECTS/Resources/334934–1288990760745/MigrationandDevelopmentBrief22. pdf.

WORLD BANK-WDI (1999) *World Development Indicators*, CD-Rom, Washington, DC: World Bank.

(2001) *World Development Indicators 2001*, 5th edition, Washington, DC: World Bank.

(2002) *World Development Indicators 2002*, CD-ROM, Washington DC: World Bank.

(2004) *World Development Indicators 2004*, CD-Rom, Washington, DC: World Bank.

World Development Indicators Online, http://databank.worldbank.org/ddp/home.do? Step=2&id=4&hActiveDimensionId=WDI_Series.

WORLD BANK-WDR (1984) *World Development Report, 1984: Population Change and Development*, Oxford/New York: Oxford University Press.

(1985) *World Development Report 1985*, New York/Oxford: Oxford University Press.

(1986a) *World Development Report 1986*, Oxford/New York: Oxford University Press.

(1986b) *World Development Report 1986, Part II,* Oxford/New York: Oxford University Press.

(1987) *World Development Report 1987*, Oxford/New York: Oxford University Press.

(1988) *World Development Report 1987: Public Finance in Development*, Oxford/New York: Oxford University Press.

(1989) *World Development Report 1989*, Oxford/New York: Oxford University Press.

(1990) *World Development Report 1990*, Oxford/New York: Oxford University Press.

(1992) *World Development Report 1992: Development and the Environment*, Oxford/New York: Oxford University Press.

(1993) *World Development Report 1993*, Oxford/New York: Oxford University Press.

(1994) *World Development Report 1994*, Oxford/New York: Oxford University Press.

(1995) *World Development Report 1995: Workers in an Integrating World*, Oxford/New York: Oxford University Press.

(1997) *World Development Report 1997. The State in a Changing World*, Oxford/New York: Oxford University Press.

(1999) *World Development Report 1989/99: Knowledge for Development*, Oxford/New York: Oxford University Press.

(2000) *World Development Report, 1999/2000: Entering the 21st Century*, Oxford/New York: Oxford University Press.

(2000) *World Development Report, 2000/2001: Attacking Poverty*, Oxford/New York: World Bank/Oxford University Press.

(2002) *World Development Report, 2002: Building Institutions for Markets*, Oxford/New York: World Bank/Oxford University Press.

(2003) *World Development Report 2003: Sustainable Development in a Dynamic World*, Oxford/New York: World Bank/Oxford University Press.

(2008) *World Development Report 2008: Agriculture for Development*, Oxford/New York: World Bank/Oxford University Press.

(2010) *World Development Report 2010: Development and Climate Change*, Washington, DC: World Bank.

(various issues) *World Development Report*, Oxford/New York: World Bank/Oxford University Press.

(2011) *World Development Report 2011, Conflict, Security and Development*, New York/Geneva: United Nations.

WORLD BANK-WT (1980) *World Tables 1980*, Baltimore, MD: Johns Hopkins University Press.

(1993) *World Tables 1983*, Baltimore, MD/London: Johns Hopkins University Press.

(1995) *World Tables 1985*, Baltimore, MD: Johns Hopkins University Press.

(1992) *World Tables 1992*, Baltimore, MD/London: Johns Hopkins University Press.

(1993) *World Tables 1993*, Baltimore, MD: Johns Hopkins University Press.

(1995) *World Tables 1995*, Baltimore, MD: Johns Hopkins University Press.

(various issues) *World Tables*, Baltimore, MD/London: John Hopkins University Press.

WORLD BANK AND UNDP (1989) *Africa's Adjustment and Growth in the 1980s*, Washington, DC/New York, World Bank/UNDP.

WORLD RESOURCES INSTITUTE (1990) *World Resources 1990–1991*, Oxford University Press.

(2000) *World Resources 2000–2001: People and Econosystems. The Fraying Web of Life*, New York: WRI in collaboration with UNEP, UNDP and the World Bank: Oxford University Press.

WORLDWATCH INSTITUTE (2001) *The State of the World 2001*, ed. L. BROWN, *et al.*, New York: Norton.

WORSLEY, P. (1957) *The Trumpet Shall Sound: A Study of 'Cargo Cults' in Melanesia*, London: McGibbon & Kee.

(1964) *The Third World*, London: Weidenfeld & Nicolson.

(1967) *The Third World*, 2nd edn, London: Weidenfeld & Nicholson.

WTO (1997) *Annual Report 1997*, Volume 2, Geneva: World Trade Organisation.

(2001) *International Trade Statistics 2001*, Geneva: World Trade Organisation, www.transparency.org/documents/cpi.

WU, H.J. (2013) 'Rethinking China's Path of Industrialization', in: A. SZIRMAI, W. NAUDÉ and L. ALCORTA (eds.), *Pathways to Industrialization in the 21st Century: New Challenges and Emerging Paradigms*, Oxford University Press, pp. 155–92.

XU C. (2011) 'The Fundamental Institutions of China's Reform and Development', *Journal of Economic Literature*, **49** (4), pp. 1076–1151.

YAMFWA, F.K. (2001) *Improving Manufacturing Performance: The Case of Zambia*, Dissertation, Eindhoven University of Technology, October.

YAMFWA, F.K., A. SZIRMAI and CH. LWAMBA (2002) *Zambian Manufacturing Performance in Comparative Perspective*, Eindhoven Centre for Innovation Studies Working Paper, 02–21, December (also published as Groningen Growth and Development Centre Working Paper, GD 53).

YOUNG, A. (1995) 'The Tyranny of Numbers: Confronting the Statistical Realities of the East Asian Growth Experience', *Quarterly Journal of Economics*, **110** (3), pp. 641–80.

YUE, X. (2015) 'Industrial Structural Change, Employment and Poverty Alleviation in China', in: W. NAUDÉ, A. SZIRMAI and N. HARAGUCHI (eds.), *Structural Change and Industrial Development in the BRICS*, Oxford University Press.

ZEYLSTRA, W.G. (1975) *Aid or Development: The Relevance of Development Aid to Problems of Developing Countries*, Leiden: A.W. Sijthoff.

ZOLBERG, A.R. (1966) *Creating Political Order: The Party States of West Africa*, Chicago, IL: Rand McNally.

AUTHOR INDEX

SUBJECT INDEX